D1364292

Paige Baltzan

University of Colorado

Business Driven Information Systems

EIGHTH EDITION

Mc Graw Hill

BUSINESS DRIVEN INFORMATION SYSTEMS, EIGHTH EDITION

Published by McGraw Hill LLC, 1325 Avenue of the Americas, New York, NY 10019. Copyright © 2023 by McGraw Hill LLC. All rights reserved. Printed in the United States of America. Previous editions © 2021, 2019, and 2016. No part of this publication may be reproduced or distributed in any form or by any means, or stored in a database or retrieval system, without the prior written consent of McGraw Hill LLC, including, but not limited to, in any network or other electronic storage or transmission, or broadcast for distance learning.

Some ancillaries, including electronic and print components, may not be available to customers outside the United States.

This book is printed on acid-free paper.

1 2 3 4 5 6 7 8 9 LWI 27 26 25 24 23 22

ISBN 978-1-264-13682-7 (bound edition)
MHID 1-264-13682-X (bound edition)
ISBN 978-1-264-74679-8 (loose-leaf edition)
MHID 1-264-74679-2 (loose-leaf edition)

Portfolio Manager: *Rebecca Olson*
Product Developer: *David Ploskonka*
Content Project Managers: *Harvey Yep, Rachael Hillebrand*
Buyer: *Susan K. Culbertson*
Design: *Aptara®, Inc.*
Content Licensing Specialist: *Sarah Flynn*
Cover Image: *George Hammerstein/Corbis/Glow Images*
Compositor: *Aptara®, Inc.*

All credits appearing on page or at the end of the book are considered to be an extension of the copyright page.

Library of Congress Cataloging-in-Publication Data

Names: Baltzan, Paige, author.
Title: Business driven information systems / Paige Baltzan.
Description: Eighth edition. | New York, NY : McGraw Hill Education, [2023] | Includes bibliographical references and index.
Identifiers: LCCN 2021051767 (print) | LCCN 2021051768 (ebook) | ISBN 9781264136827 (hardcover) | ISBN 9781264746798 (spiral bound) | ISBN 9781264750184 (ebook) | ISBN 9781264746705 (ebook other)
Subjects: LCSH: Information technology–Management. | Industrial management–Data processing.
Classification: LCC HD30.2 .B357 2023 (print) | LCC HD30.2 (ebook) | DDC 658.4/038–dc23/eng/20220107
LC record available at https://lccn.loc.gov/2021051767
LC ebook record available at https://lccn.loc.gov/2021051768

The Internet addresses listed in the text were accurate at the time of publication. The inclusion of a website does not indicate an endorsement by the authors or McGraw Hill LLC, and McGraw Hill LLC does not guarantee the accuracy of the information presented at these sites.

mheducation.com/highered

DEDICATION

To Hannah, Sophie, and Lou:
What do you always remember?
That I Love You! That I'm Proud of You!

Paige

BRIEF CONTENTS

CONTENTS

appendices

APPENDIX F
Business Intelligence and Data Mining F.1

Instructors: Student Success Starts with You

Tools to enhance your unique voice

Want to build your own course? No problem. Prefer to use an OLC-aligned, prebuilt course? Easy. Want to make changes throughout the semester? Sure. And you'll save time with Connect's auto-grading too.

65%
Less Time Grading

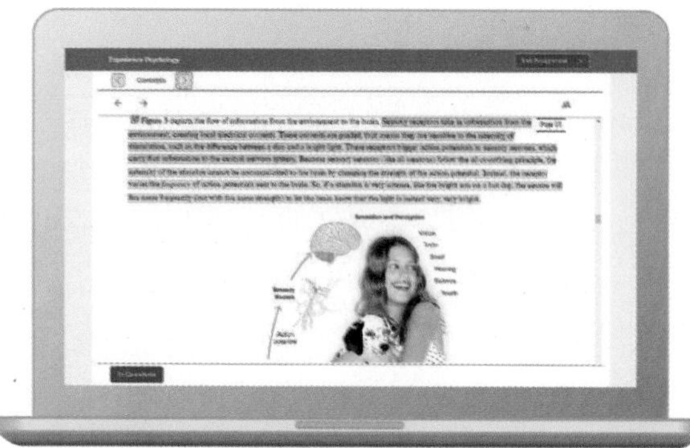

Laptop: McGraw Hill; Woman/dog: George Doyle/Getty Images

Study made personal

Incorporate adaptive study resources like SmartBook® 2.0 into your course and help your students be better prepared in less time. Learn more about the powerful personalized learning experience available in SmartBook 2.0 at **www.mheducation.com/highered/connect/smartbook**

Affordable solutions, added value

Make technology work for you with LMS integration for single sign-on access, mobile access to the digital textbook, and reports to quickly show you how each of your students is doing. And with our Inclusive Access program you can provide all these tools at a discount to your students. Ask your McGraw Hill representative for more information.

Padlock: Jobalou/Getty Images

Solutions for your challenges

A product isn't a solution. Real solutions are affordable, reliable, and come with training and ongoing support when you need it and how you want it. Visit **www.supportateverystep.com** for videos and resources both you and your students can use throughout the semester.

Checkmark: Jobalou/Getty Images

Students: Get Learning that Fits You

Effective tools for efficient studying

Connect is designed to help you be more productive with simple, flexible, intuitive tools that maximize your study time and meet your individual learning needs. Get learning that works for you with Connect.

Study anytime, anywhere

Download the free ReadAnywhere app and access your online eBook, SmartBook 2.0, or Adaptive Learning Assignments when it's convenient, even if you're offline. And since the app automatically syncs with your Connect account, all of your work is available every time you open it. Find out more at **www.mheducation.com/readanywhere**

"I really liked this app—it made it easy to study when you don't have your text-book in front of you."

- Jordan Cunningham,
Eastern Washington University

Calendar: owattaphotos/Getty Images

Everything you need in one place

Your Connect course has everything you need—whether reading on your digital eBook or completing assignments for class, Connect makes it easy to get your work done.

Learning for everyone

McGraw Hill works directly with Accessibility Services Departments and faculty to meet the learning needs of all students. Please contact your Accessibility Services Office and ask them to email accessibility@mheducation.com, or visit **www.mheducation.com/about/accessibility** for more information.

Top: Jenner Images/Getty Images, Left: Hero Images/Getty Images, Right: Hero Images/Getty Images

PREFACE

Business Driven Information Systems discusses various business initiatives first and how technology supports those initiatives second. The premise for this unique approach is that business initiatives should drive technology choices. Every discussion first addresses the business needs and then addresses the technology that supports those needs. This text provides the foundation that will enable students to achieve excellence in business, whether they major in operations management, manufacturing, sales, marketing, finance, human resources, accounting, or virtually any other business discipline. *Business Driven Information Systems* is designed to give students the ability to understand how information technology can be a point of strength for an organization.

Common business goals associated with information technology projects include reducing costs, improving productivity, improving customer satisfaction and loyalty, creating competitive advantages, streamlining supply chains, supporting global expansion, and so on. Achieving these results is not easy. Implementing a new accounting system or marketing plan is not likely to generate long-term growth or reduce costs across an entire organization. Businesses must undertake enterprisewide initiatives to achieve broad general business goals such as reducing costs. Information technology plays a critical role in deploying such initiatives by facilitating communication and increasing business intelligence. Any individual anticipating a successful career in business, whether it is in accounting, finance, human resources, or operations management, must understand the basics of information technology that can be found in this text.

We have found tremendous success teaching MIS courses by demonstrating the correlation between business and IT. Students who understand the tight correlation between business and IT understand the power of this course. Students learn 10 percent of what they read, 80 percent of what they personally experience, and 90 percent of what they teach others. The business driven approach brings the difficult and often intangible MIS concepts to the student's level and applies them using a hands-on approach to reinforce the concepts. Teaching MIS with a business driven focus helps:

- Add credibility to IT.
- Open students' eyes to IT opportunities.
- Attract majors.
- Engage students.

FORMAT, FEATURES, AND HIGHLIGHTS

Business Driven Information Systems is state of the art in its discussions, presents concepts in an easy-to-understand format, and allows students to be active participants in learning. The dynamic nature of information technology requires all students–more specifically, business students–to be aware of both current and emerging technologies. Students are facing complex subjects and need a clear, concise explanation to be able to understand and use the concepts throughout their careers. By engaging students with numerous case studies, exercises, projects, and questions that enforce concepts, *Business Driven Information Systems* creates a unique learning experience for both faculty and students.

- **Audience.** *Business Driven Information Systems* is designed for use in undergraduate or introductory MBA courses in management information systems, which are required in many business administration or management programs as part of the common body of knowledge for all business majors.
- **Logical Layout.** Students and faculty will find the text well-organized, with the topics flowing logically from one chapter to the next. The definition of each term is provided before it is covered in the chapter, and an extensive glossary is included at the back of the text. Each chapter offers a comprehensive opening case study, learning outcomes, closing case studies, key terms, and critical business thinking questions.

- **Thorough Explanations.** Complete coverage is provided for each topic that is introduced. Explanations are written so that students can understand the ideas presented and relate them to other concepts.
- **Solid Theoretical Base.** The text relies on current theory and practice of information systems as they relate to the business environment. Current academic and professional journals cited throughout the text are found in the Notes at the end of the book—a roadmap for additional, pertinent readings that can be the basis for learning beyond the scope of the chapters or plug-ins.
- **Material to Encourage Discussion.** All chapters contain a diverse selection of case studies and individual and group problem-solving activities as they relate to the use of information technology in business. Two comprehensive cases at the end of each chapter reinforce content. These cases encourage students to consider what concepts have been presented and then apply those concepts to a situation they might find in an organization. Different people in an organization can view the same facts from different points of view, and the cases will force students to consider some of those views.
- **Flexibility in Teaching and Learning.** Although most textbooks that are text-only leave faculty on their own when it comes to choosing cases, *Business Driven Information Systems* goes much further. Several options are provided to faculty with case selections from a variety of sources, including *CIO, Harvard Business Journal, Wired, Forbes,* and *Time,* to name just a few. Therefore, faculty can use the text alone, the text and a complete selection of cases, or anything in between.
- **Integrative Themes.** Several integrative themes recur throughout the text, which adds integration to the material. Among these themes are value-added techniques and methodologies, ethics and social responsibility, globalization, and competitive advantage. Such topics are essential to gaining a full understanding of the strategies that a business must recognize, formulate, and in turn implement. In addition to addressing these in the chapter material, many illustrations are provided for their relevance to business practice.

WALKTHROUGH

Learning Outcomes

Learning Outcomes. These outcomes focus on what students should learn and be able to answer upon completion of the chapter.

section 3.1 | **Web 1.0: Ebusiness**

LEARNING OUTCOMES

3.1 Compare disruptive and sustaining technologies and explain how the Internet and WWW caused business disruption.

3.2 Describe ebusiness and its associated advantages.

3.3 Compare the four ebusiness models.

3.4 Describe the five ebusiness tools for connecting and communicating.

Chapter Opening Case Study

Chapter Opening Case Study. To enhance student interest, each chapter begins with an opening case study that highlights an organization that has been time-tested and value-proven in the business world. This feature serves to fortify concepts with relevant examples of outstanding companies. Discussion of the case is threaded throughout the chapter.

opening case study

Andrey Suslov/Shutterstock

Data Analytics Careers: Top Skills for Your Future

Data analytics brings together theory and practice to identify and communicate data driven insights that allow managers, stakeholders, and other executives in an organization to make more informed decisions. Data is transforming and powering business everywhere—from smart homes and sustainable cities to online retail and green corporations. Business today is simple—it's data driven. Data in all forms and shapes provides insights into making strategic business decisions, including opening new markets, staffing hospitals and warehouses, and creating vaccines. Organizations in all industries increasingly rely on data to identify opportunities and solve business problems.

Any person competing in the business environment today must be able to capture, analyze, and decipher data to perform their jobs and advance their careers. We are living in the information age, a time when data is gold and offers the keys to the kingdom for running a successful business. Consider the following:

- Uber does not own a single car.
- Airbnb does not own a single hotel or rental property.
- Facebook does not create any content.
- Amazon does not make any products or own any inventory.
- Zappos does not make any shoes.

It is really simple: Data is driving and transforming business. As a result, shifting workforces have companies searching for data-savvy candidates who understand how to work with data to sleuth the patterns that provide insights into the business. Providing communication with visualizations that influence decision making is also key.

The data analyst hiring market is hot, and there are more than 2.5 million job openings for data-related roles. In fact, the U.S. Bureau of Labor Statistics has indicated 11.5 million data job openings will be created by 2026.

The explosion of data in all areas of business around the world has given rise to one of the most in-demand, booming fields today: analytics. The average salary for data analysts ranges between $85,000 and $138,000. Surprisingly, almost 50% of corporations report having issues finding qualified data analysts and data scientist professionals even with such high salaries.

Projects and Case Studies

Case Studies. This text is packed with 27 case studies illustrating how a variety of prominent organizations and businesses have successfully implemented many of this text's concepts. All cases are timely and promote critical thinking. Company profiles are especially appealing and relevant to your students, helping to stir classroom discussion and interest.

Apply Your Knowledge. At the end of each chapter, you will find several Apply Your Knowledge projects that challenge students to bring the skills they have learned from the chapter to real business problems. There are also 33 Apply Your Knowledge projects on the Connect site that accompanies this text. These projects ask students to use IT tools such as Excel and Access to solve business problems. These projects help to develop the application and problem-solving skills of your students through challenging and creative business-driven scenarios.

AYK APPLICATION PROJECTS

If you are looking for Excel projects to incorporate into your class, try any of the following after reading this chapter.

Project Number	Project Name	Project Type	Plug-In Focus Area	Project Level	Skill Set	Page Number
1	Financial Destiny	Excel	T2	Personal Budget	Introductory Formulas	AYK.3
2	Cash Flow	Excel	T2	Cash Flow	Introductory Formulas	AYK.3
3	Technology Budget	Excel	T1, T2	Hardware and Software	Introductory Formulas	AYK.3
4	Tracking Donations	Excel	T2	Employee Relationships	Introductory Formulas	AYK.3
5	Convert Currency	Excel	T2	Global Commerce	Introductory Formulas	AYK.4
6	Cost Comparison	Excel	T2	Total Cost of Ownership	Introductory Formulas	AYK.4
7	Time Management	Excel or Project	T12 Project Management	Introductory	Gantt Charts	AYK.5

End-of-Chapter Elements

Each chapter contains complete pedagogical support in the form of:

Key Terms. With page numbers referencing where they are discussed in the text.

KEY TERMS

Analytics 12
Big data 8
Business analytics 12
Business intelligence (BI) 11
Business process 34
Business strategy 25
Business unit 17
Buyer power 29
Data silo 17
Descriptive analytics 13
Diagnostic analytics 13
Digital value chain 35
Dynamic report 11
Entry barrier 31
Fact 5
Feedback 20
Management information systems (MIS) 21
MIS skills gap 25
Porter's Five Forces Model 29
Porter's three generic strategies 33
Predictive analytics 13
Prescriptive analytics 14

Two Closing Case Studies. Reinforcing important concepts with prominent examples from businesses and organizations. Discussion questions follow each case study.

CLOSING CASE ONE

The Fourth Industrial Revolution

The fourth industrial revolution is here and will exponentially change how we live, work, and interact. It is disrupting almost every industry globally and creating massive change at unprecedented speeds. Professor Klaus Schwab, founder and executive chair of the World Economic Forum's latest book, *The Fourth Industrial Revolution,* describes a world where physical, digital, and biological spheres merge. This revolution refers to how new technologies such as artificial intelligence, autonomous vehicles, voice recognition, and the Internet of Things are blending our digital and physical worlds. Expect to see changes in the ways individuals, businesses, and governments operate, ultimately leading to

Making Business Decisions. The best way to learn MIS is to apply it to scenarios and real-world business dilemmas. These projects require students to apply critical thinking skills and chapter concepts to analyze the problems and make recommended business decisions.

MAKING BUSINESS DECISIONS

1. **Working for the Best**
   Each year, *Fortune* magazine creates a list of the top 100 companies to work for. Find the most recent list. What types of data do you think *Fortune* analyzed to determine the company ranking? What issues could occur if the analysis of the data was inaccurate? What types of information can you gain by analyzing the list? Create five questions a student performing a job search could answer by analyzing this list.

2. **View from a Flat World**
   Bill Gates, founder of Microsoft, stated that 20 years ago, most people would rather have been a B student in New York City than a genius in China because the opportunities available to students in developed countries were limitless. Today, many argue that the opposite is now true due to technological advances making it easier to succeed as a genius in China than a B student in New York. As a group, discuss whether you agree or disagree with Gates's statement.

3. **Do You Trust Your Data?**
   Data is the new oil. Data drives fact-based decisions. As a manager you are going to rely on data to drive your business decisions. Can you imagine making a critical business decision on bad data? Have you ever stopped to ask yourself if you trust your data? What will happen if you make a business decision on incorrect, inaccurate, or low-quality data? Obviously, chances are high you will make the wrong decision, and that is the primary risk when using data to drive your decisions. Here are a few examples of organizations that fell into the trap of making important decisions on incorrect data.

About the Plug-Ins

Located in the Connect product that accompanies this text, the overall goal of the plug-ins is to provide an alternative for faculty who find themselves in the situation of having to purchase an extra book to support Microsoft Office. The plug-ins presented here offer integration with the core chapters and provide critical knowledge using essential business applications, such as Microsoft Excel, Microsoft Access, Dreamweaver, and Microsoft Project. Each plug-in uses hands-on tutorials for comprehension and mastery.

Plug-In	Description
T1. Personal Productivity Using IT	This plug-in covers a number of things to do to keep a personal computer running effectively and efficiently. The 12 topics covered in this plug-in are: ■ Creating strong passwords. ■ Performing good file management. ■ Implementing effective backup and recovery strategies. ■ Using zip files. ■ Writing professional emails. ■ Stopping spam. ■ Preventing phishing. ■ Detecting spyware. ■ Threads to instant messaging. ■ Increasing PC performance. ■ Using antivirus software. ■ Installing a personal firewall.

End-of-Plug-In Elements

Each plug-in contains complete pedagogical support in the form of:

Plug-In Summary. Revisits the plug-in highlights in summary format.

Making Business Decisions. Small scenario-driven projects that help students focus individually on decision making as they relate to the topical elements in the chapters.

T2. Basic Skills Using Excel	This plug-in introduces the basics of using Microsoft Excel, a spreadsheet program for data analysis, along with a few fancy features. The six topics covered in this plug-in are: ■ Workbooks and worksheets. ■ Working with cells and cell data. ■ Printing worksheets. ■ Formatting worksheets. ■ Formulas. ■ Working with charts and graphics.

T4. Decision Making Using Excel	This plug-in examines a few of the advanced business analysis tools used in Microsoft Excel that have the capability to identify patterns, trends, and rules, and create "what-if" models. The four topics covered in this plug-in are: ■ IF ■ Goal Seek ■ Solver ■ Scenario Manager

Support and Supplemental Material

All of the supplemental material supporting *Business Driven Information Systems* was developed by the author to ensure you receive accurate, high-quality, and in-depth content. Included is a complete set of materials that will assist students and faculty in accomplishing course objectives.

Test Bank. This computerized package allows instructors to custom design, save, and generate tests. The test program permits instructors to edit, add, or delete questions from the test banks; analyze test results; and organize a database of tests and students' results.

Instructor's Manual (IM). The IM, written by the author, includes suggestions for designing the course and presenting the material. Each chapter is supported by answers to end-of-chapter questions and problems and suggestions concerning the discussion topics and cases.

PowerPoint Presentations. A set of PowerPoint slides, created by the author, accompanies each chapter and features bulleted items that provide a lecture outline, plus key figures and tables from the text, and detailed teaching notes on each slide.

Image Library. Text figures and tables, as permission allows, are provided in a format by which they can be imported into PowerPoint for class lectures.

Project Files. The author has provided files for all projects that need further support, such as data files.

Assurance of Learning Ready

Many educational institutions today are focused on the notion of *assurance of learning,* an important element of some accreditation standards. *Business Driven Information Systems* is designed specifically to support your assurance of learning initiatives with a simple, yet powerful solution.

Each test bank question for *Business Driven Information Systems* maps to a specific chapter learning outcome/objective listed in the text. You can use our test bank software or *Connect MIS* to query easily for learning outcomes/objectives that directly relate to the learning objectives for your course. You can then use the reporting features to aggregate student results in similar fashion, making the collection and presentation of assurance of learning data simple and easy.

AACSB Statement

The McGraw Hill Companies is a proud corporate member of AACSB International. Understanding the importance and value of AACSB accreditation, *Business Driven Information Systems* recognizes the curricula guidelines detailed in the AACSB standards for business accreditation by connecting selected questions in the test bank to the six general knowledge and skill guidelines in the AACSB standards.

The statements contained in *Business Driven Information Systems* are provided only as a guide for the users of this textbook. The AACSB leaves content coverage and assessment within the purview of individual schools, the mission of the school, and the faculty. Although *Business Driven Information Systems* and the teaching package make no claim of any specific AACSB qualification or evaluation, within *Business Driven Information Systems* we have labeled selected questions according to the six general knowledge and skills areas.

McGraw Hill Customer Care Contact Information

At McGraw Hill, we understand that getting the most from new technology can be challenging. That's why our services don't stop after you purchase our products. You can email our product specialists 24 hours a day to get product training online. Or you can search our knowledge bank of Frequently Asked Questions on our support website. For Customer Support, call **800-331-5094** or visit **www.mhhe.com/support** where you can look for your question on our "Connect - Tips & FAQs" page, or you can email a question directly to customer support. One of our technical support analysts will be able to assist you in a timely fashion.

Apply Your Knowledge

Business Driven Information Systems contains 33 projects that focus on student application of core concepts and tools. These projects can be found on the Connect site.

Project Number	Project Name	Project Type	Plug-In	Focus Area	Project Level	Skill Set	Page Number
1	Financial Destiny	Excel	T2	Personal Budget	Introductory	Formulas	AYK.3
2	Cash Flow	Excel	T2	Cash Flow	Introductory	Formulas	AYK.3
3	Technology Budget	Excel	T1, T2	Hardware and Software	Introductory	Formulas	AYK.3
4	Tracking Donations	Excel	T2	Employee Relationships	Introductory	Formulas	AYK.3
5	Convert Currency	Excel	T2	Global Commerce	Introductory	Formulas	AYK.4
6	Cost Comparison	Excel	T2	Total Cost of Ownership	Introductory	Formulas	AYK.4
7	Time Management	Excel or Project	T12	Project Management	Introductory	Gantt Charts	AYK.5
8	Maximize Profit	Excel	T2, T4	Strategic Analysis	Intermediate	Formulas or Solver	AYK.5
9	Security Analysis	Excel	T3	Filtering Data	Intermediate	Conditional Formatting, Autofilter, Subtotal	AYK.6
10	Gathering Data	Excel	T3	Data Analysis	Intermediate	Conditional Formatting	AYK.6
11	Scanner System	Excel	T2	Strategic Analysis	Intermediate	Formulas	AYK.7
12	Competitive Pricing	Excel	T2	Profit Maximization	Intermediate	Formulas	AYK.7
13	Adequate Acquisitions	Excel	T2	Break-Even Analysis	Intermediate	Formulas	AYK.7
14	Customer Relations	Excel	T3	CRM	Intermediate	PivotTable	AYK.8
15	Assessing the Value of Information	Excel	T3	Data Analysis	Intermediate	PivotTable	AYK.8
16	Growth, Trends, and Forecasts	Excel	T2, T3	Data Forecasting	Advanced	Average, Trend, Growth	AYK.9
17	Shipping Costs	Excel	T4	SCM	Advanced	Solver	AYK.10
18	Formatting Grades	Excel	T3	Data Analysis	Advanced	If, LookUp	AYK.11

(continued)

Project Number	Project Name	Project Type	Plug-In	Focus Area	Project Level	Skill Set	Page Number
19	Moving Dilemma	Excel	T2, T3	SCM	Advanced	Absolute vs. Relative Values	AYK.11
20	Operational Efficiencies	Excel	T3	SCM	Advanced	PivotTable	AYK.12
21	Too Much Information	Excel	T3	CRM	Advanced	PivotTable	AYK.12
22	Turnover Rates	Excel	T3	Data Mining	Advanced	PivotTable	AYK.13
23	Vital Information	Excel	T3	Data Mining	Advanced	PivotTable	AYK.13
24	Breaking Even	Excel	T4	Business Analysis	Advanced	Goal Seek	AYK.14
25	Profit Scenario	Excel	T4	Sales Analysis	Advanced	Scenario Manager	AYK.14
26	Electronic Résumés	HTML	T9, T10, T11	Electronic Personal Marketing	Introductory	Structural Tags	AYK.14
27	Gathering Feedback	HTML	T9, T10, T11	Data Collection	Intermediate	Organization of Information	AYK.15
28	Daily Invoice	Access	T5, T6, T7, T8	Business Analysis	Introductory	Entities, Relationships, and Databases	AYK.15
29	Billing Data	Access	T5, T6, T7, T8	Business Intelligence	Introductory	Entities, Relationships, and Databases	AYK.17
30	Inventory Data	Access	T5, T6, T7, T8	SCM	Intermediate	Entities, Relationships, and Databases	AYK.18
31	Call Center	Access	T5, T6, T7, T8	CRM	Intermediate	Entities, Relationships, and Databases	AYK.19
32	Sales Pipeline	Access	T5, T6, T7, T8	Business Intelligence	Advanced	Entities, Relationships, and Databases	AYK.20
33	Online Classified Ads	Access	T5, T6, T7, T8	Ecommerce	Advanced	Entities, Relationships, and Databases	AYK.20

Mc Graw Hill **SIMnet®**

SIMNet Online is McGraw Hill's leading solution for learning Microsoft Office skills and beyond! SIMNet is our online training and assessment solution for Microsoft Office skills, computing concepts, Internet Explorer, and Windows content. With no downloads for installation and its contents completely online, SIMNet is accessible for today's students through multiple browsers and is easy to use for all. Its consistent user interface and functionality will help save you time and help you be more successful in your course.

Moreover, SIMNet offers you lifelong learning. Our codes never expire and the online program is designed with Self-Study and SIMSearch features to help you immediately learn isolated Microsoft Office skills on demand. It's more than a resource; it's a tool you can use throughout your entire time at your higher-education institution.

Finally, you will see powerful, measurable results with SIMNet Online. See results immediately in the student gradebook and generate custom training lessons after an exam to help you determine exactly which content areas you still need to study.

SIMNet Online is your solution for mastering Microsoft Office skills!

SIMnet: Keep IT SIMple!

To learn more, visit **https://www.mheducation.com/highered/simnet.html**

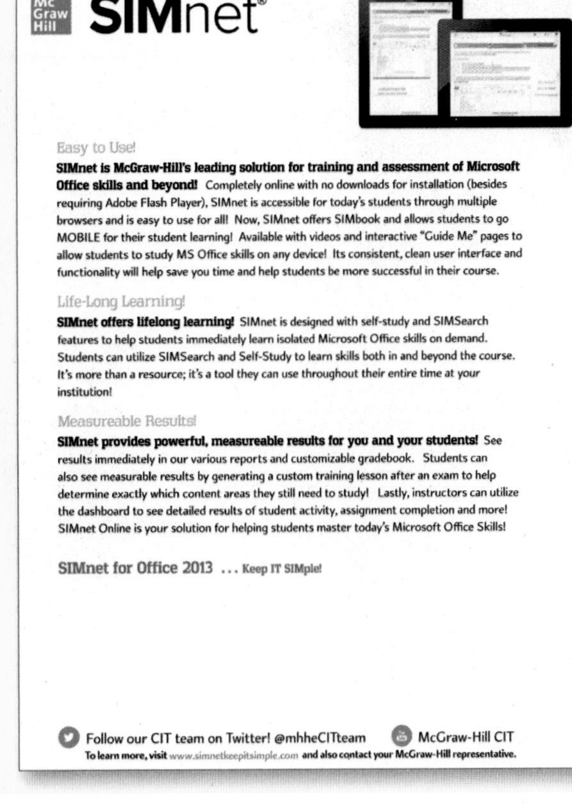

McGraw Hill create®

Craft your teaching resources to match the way you teach! With McGraw Hill Create, **www.mcgrawhillcreate.com,** you can easily rearrange chapters, combine material from other content sources, and quickly upload content you have written, such as your course syllabus or teaching notes. Find the content you need in Create by searching through thousands of leading McGraw Hill textbooks. Arrange your book to fit your teaching style. Create even allows you to personalize your book's appearance by selecting the cover and adding your name, school, and course information. Order a Create book and you'll receive a complimentary print review copy in 3–5 business days or a complimentary electronic review copy (eComp) via email in about one hour. Go to **www.mcgrawhillcreate.com** today and register. Experience how McGraw Hill Create empowers you to teach *your* students *your* way.

ACKNOWLEDGMENTS

Working on the eighth edition of *Business Driven Information Systems* has been an involved undertaking, and there are many people whom I want to heartily thank for their hard work, enthusiasm, and dedication. I offer my sincerest gratitude and deepest appreciation to the valuable reviewers whose feedback was instrumental in successfully compiling this text. I could not have done this without you!

Stephen Adams
Lakeland Community College

Adeyemi A. Adekoya
Virginia State University–Petersburg

Joni Adkins
Northwest Missouri State University

Chad Anderson
University of Nevada–Reno

Anne Arendt
Utah Valley University

Laura Atkins
James Madison University

William Ayen
University of Colorado

David Bahn
Metropolitan State University–St. Paul

Nick Ball
Brigham Young University–Provo

Patrick Bateman
Youngstown State University

Terry Begley
Creighton University

Craig Beytien
University of Colorado–Boulder

Sudip Bhattacharjee
University of Connecticut

Meral Binbasioglu
Hofstra University

Joseph Blankenship
Fairmont State College

Beverly Bohn
Park University

Brenda Bradford
Missouri Baptist University

Casey Cegielski
Auburn University–Auburn

Amita Chin
Virginia Commonwealth University

Steve Clements
Eastern Oregon University

Cynthia Corritore
Creighton University

Dan Creed
Normandale Community College

Don Danner
San Francisco State University

Sasha Dekleva
DePaul University

Robert Denker
Baruch College

Hongwei Du
California State University, East Bay

Kevin Duffy
Wright State University–Dayton

Annette Easton
San Diego State University

Barry Floyd
California Polytechnic State University

Valerie Frear
Daytona State College

Laura Frost
Walsh College

Don Gaber
University of Wisconsin–Eau Claire

Biswadip Ghosh
Metropolitan State College of Denver

Richard Glass
Bryant University

Lakshmi Goel
University of North Florida

Mark Goudreau
Johnson & Wales University

Katie Gray
The University of Texas at Austin

Gary Hackbarth
Northern Kentucky University

Shu Han
Yeshiva University

Peter Haried
University of Wisconsin–La Crosse

Rosie Hauck
Illinois State University

Jun He
University of Michigan–Dearborn

James Henson
California State University–Fresno

Terri Holly
Indian River State College

Scott Hunsinger
Appalachian State University

Ted Hurewitz
Rutgers University

Yan Jin
Elizabeth City State University

Brian Jones
Tennessee Technological University

Robert Judge
San Diego State University

B. Kahn
Suffolk University

Virginia Kleist
West Virginia University

Meagan Knoll
Grand Valley State University

Rick Kraas
Kalamazoo Valley Community College

Chetan Kumar
California State University–San Marcos

Guolin Lai
University of Louisiana–Lafayette

Jose Lepervanche
Florida State College–Jacksonville

Norman Lewis
Wayne State University

Mary Lind
North Carolina A&T State University

Steve Loy
Eastern Kentucky University

Joan Lumpkin
Wright State University–Dayton

Linda Lynam
University of Central Missouri

Nicole Lytle-Kosola
California State University–San Bernardino

Garth MacKenzie
University of Maryland University College

Michael Martel
Ohio University–Athens

Dana McCann
Central Michigan University

David McCue
University of Maryland

Lynn McKell
Brigham Young University

Patricia McQuaid
California Polytechnic State University

Michael Shawn Moore
Wayne State University

Fiona Nah
University of Nebraska–Lincoln

Eric Nathan
University of Houston Downtown

Bill Neumann
University of Arizona

Richard Newmark
University of Northern Colorado

Kathleen Noce
Pennsylvania State University–Erie

Gisele Olney
University of Nebraska–Omaha

Kevin Parker
Idaho State University–Pocatello

Neeraj Parolia
Towson University

Gang Peng
Youngstown State University

Julie Pettus
Missouri State University

Craig Piercy
University of Georgia

Clint Pires
Hamline University

Jennifer Pitts
Columbus State University

Carol Pollard
Appalachian State University

Lara Preiser-Houy
California State Polytechnic University–Pomona

John Quigley
East Tennessee State University

Muhammad Razi
Western Michigan University

Lisa Rich
Athens State University

Russell Robbins
University of Pittsburgh

Fred Rodammer
Michigan State University

Steve Ross
Western Washington University

Mark Schmidt
St. Cloud State University

Dana Schwieger
Southeast Missouri State University

Darrell Searcy
Palm Beach Community College

Jay Shah
Texas State University

Vijay Shah
West Virginia University–Parkersburg

Vivek Shah
Texas State University

Jollean Sinclaire
Arkansas State University

Changsoo Sohn
St. Cloud State University

Toni Somers
Wayne State University

Denise Sullivan
Westchester Community College

Yi Sun
California State University–San Marcos

Mike Tarn
Western Michigan University

Mark Thouin
The University of Texas at Dallas

Lise Urbaczewski
University of Michigan–Dearborn

Hong Wang
North Carolina A&T State University

Barbara Warner
University of South Florida

Connie Washburn
Georgia Perimeter College

Bruce White
Quinnipiac University

Raymond Whitney
University of Maryland University College

Rosemary Wild
California Polytechnic State University

Marie Wright
Western Connecticut State University

Yajiong Xue
East Carolina University

Ali Yayla
Binghamton University

Grace Zhang
Midwestern State University

Lin Zhao
Purdue University–Calumet

Jeanne Zucker
East Tennessee State University

ABOUT THE AUTHOR

Paige Baltzan

Paige Baltzan teaches in the Department of Business at the University of Colorado. She holds a BSBA specializing in accounting/MIS from Bowling Green State University and an MBA specializing in MIS from the University of Denver. She is a coauthor of several books, including *Business Driven Technology, Essentials of Business Driven Information Systems,* and *I-Series,* and is a contributor to *Management Information Systems for the Information Age.*

Business Driven MIS

module 1

MOST COMPANIES TODAY rely heavily on the use of management information systems (MIS) to run various aspects of their businesses. Whether companies need to order and ship goods, interact with customers, or conduct complex business analysis, management information systems are often the underlying infrastructure performing the activities. Management information systems allow companies to remain competitive in today's fast-paced world and especially when conducting business online. Organizations must adapt to technological advances and innovations to keep pace with today's rapidly changing environment. Their competitors certainly will!

No matter how exciting technology is, successful companies do not use it simply for its own sake. Companies should have a solid business reason for implementing technology. Using a technological solution just because it is available is not a good business strategy.

The purpose of Module 1 is to raise your awareness of the vast opportunities made possible by the tight correlation between business and technology. Business strategies and processes should always drive your technology choices. Awareness of emerging technologies, including artificial intelligence, machine learning, and data science, is leading us in new strategic directions.

Module 1: Business Driven MIS

Management Information Systems: Business Driven MIS

CHAPTER OUTLINE

SECTION 1.1
Business Driven MIS

- Competing in the Information Age
- Systems Thinking and Management Information Systems

SECTION 1.2
Business Strategy

- Identifying Competitive Advantages
- SWOT Analysis: Understanding Business Strategies
- The Five Forces Model—Evaluating Industry Attractiveness
- The Three Generic Strategies—Choosing a Business Focus
- Value Chain Analysis—Executing Business Strategies

What's in IT for me?

This chapter sets the stage for the [illegible]ook. It starts from ground zero by providing a clear description of what information is and how it fits into business operations, strategies, and systems. It provides an overview of how companies operate in competitive environments and why they must continually define and redefine their business strategies to create competitive advantages. Doing so allows them to survive and thrive. Information systems are key business enablers for successful operations in competitive environments.

You, as a business student, must understand the tight correlation between business and technology. You must first recognize information's role in daily business activities and then understand how information supports and helps implement global business strategies and competitive advantages. After reading this chapter, you should have a solid understanding of business driven information systems and their role in managerial decision making and problem solving.

Andrey Suslov/Shutterstock

opening case study

Data Analytics Careers: Top Skills for Your Future

Data analytics brings together theory and practice to identify and communicate data driven insights that allow managers, stakeholders, and other executives in an organization to make more informed decisions. Data is transforming and powering business everywhere—from smart homes and sustainable cities to online retail and green corporations. Business today is simple—it's data driven. Data in all forms and shapes provides insights into making strategic business decisions, including opening new markets, staffing hospitals and warehouses, and creating vaccines. Organizations in all industries increasingly rely on data to identify opportunities and solve business problems.

Any person competing in the business environment today must be able to capture, analyze, and decipher data to perform their jobs and advance their careers. We are living in the information age, a time when data is gold and offers the keys to the kingdom for running a successful business. Consider the following:

- Uber does not own a single car.
- Airbnb does not own a single hotel or rental property.
- Facebook does not create any content.
- Amazon does not make any products or own any inventory.
- Zappos does not make any shoes.

It is really simple: Data is driving and transforming business. As a result, shifting workforces have companies searching for data-savvy candidates who understand how to work with data to sleuth the patterns that provide insights into the business. Providing communication with visualizations that influence decision making is also key.

The data analyst hiring market is hot, and there are more than 2.5 million job openings for data-related roles. In fact, the U.S. Bureau of Labor Statistics has indicated 11.5 million data job openings will be created by 2026.

The explosion of data in all areas of business around the world has given rise to one of the most in-demand, booming fields today: analytics. The average salary for data analysts ranges between $85,000 and $138,000. Surprisingly, almost 50% of corporations report having issues finding qualified data analysts and data scientist professionals even with such high salaries.

If you believe the ability to analyze data will help your career path, then this course is perfect for you. Throughout this course, you will learn the following:

- Data analysis techniques
- Data transformation styles
- Data governance
- Data compliance
- Data warehousing
- Data driven business process automation
- Data ethics and privacy
- Data security

According to the McKinsey Global Institute, 30 percent of the hours worked globally could be automated by 2030, depending on the speed of adoptions, technical feasibility, the pace of technology development, and social and regulatory compliance. Of course, this is not always a bad thing as automation can also lead to an increase in new jobs. When the ATM was first introduced, it actually caused an increase in the number of bank tellers as banks competed to provide increased customer satisfaction with personal customer service. The invention of the personal computer destroyed 3.5 million jobs, including typewriter manufacturing, secretarial work, and bookkeeping. However, 19 million jobs were created, including computer manufacturing, computer scientists, and business computer specialists. Current estimates conclude that this new era could create 20 to 50 million new jobs globally.[1]

Jobs Eliminated Due to Technology Innovations

- **Drivers**
Autonomous vehicles or self-driving cars will replace bus drivers, taxi drivers, truck drivers, etc.

- **Farmers**
Automated farm equipment will be controlled remotely, and genetically engineered seeds and soil will speed crop development time.

- **Movie Stars**
One bad move by a movie star and a $300 million movie is destroyed. Green screens create sets and soon will create the actors.

- **Employees, Including Factory and Fast-Food Workers, Cashiers, Waitstaff, Bartenders, Stock Traders**
Robots will be taking over these functions, operating 24/7 with greater efficiency and effectiveness while requiring zero pay or health insurance benefits.

- **Military, Dispatchers, Firefighters, Police**
Robots and drones will take over these dangerous jobs

Jobs Created by Technology Innovation

- **Robot Manufacture and Service Technicians**
All of these new robotic devices will need to be maintained and fixed.

- **Big Data and Artificial Intelligence Scientists**
Data is being generated at an incredible speed, and proper analysis and interpretation of results will cause this field to grow.

- **Esports**
Epic games such as Fortnite are becoming legitimate sports.

- **Gene Designers**
Building artificial bodies and changing DNA will be a hot field in the future.

- **Cybersecurity and Privacy Data Brokers**
New technologies bring new problems, and cybersecurity is a hot topic today and will continue to grow.

section 1.1 | Business Driven MIS

LEARNING OUTCOMES

1.1 Describe the information age and the differences among data, information, business intelligence, and knowledge.

1.2 Explain systems thinking and how management information systems enable business communications.

COMPETING IN THE INFORMATION AGE

LO 1.1: Describe the information age and the differences among data, information, business intelligence, and knowledge.

Did you know that . . .

- The movie *Avatar* took more than 4 years to create and cost $450 million?
- Lady Gaga's real name is Stefani Joanne Angelina Germanotta?
- Customers pay $3.7 million for a 30-second advertising time slot during the Super Bowl?[2]

Today, by simply pushing a button, people can find out anything, from anywhere, at any time.

- ***Fact***: The confirmation or validation of an event or object. In the past, people primarily learned facts from books.
- ***Information age***: The present time, during which infinite quantities of facts are widely available to anyone who can use a computer.

The impact of information technology on the global business environment is equivalent to the printing press's impact on publishing and electricity's impact on productivity. College student start-ups were mostly unheard of before the information age. Now, it's not at all unusual to read about a business student starting a multimillion-dollar company from his or her dorm room. Think of Mark Zuckerberg, who started Facebook from his dorm, or Michael Dell (Dell Computers) and Bill Gates (Microsoft), who both founded their legendary companies as college students.

You may think only students well-versed in advanced technology can compete in the information age. This is simply not true. Many business leaders have created exceptional opportunities by coupling the power of the information age with traditional business methods. Here are just a few examples:

- Amazon's original business focus was to sell books.
- Netflix's original business focus was to rent videos via mailboxes.
- Zappos's original business focus was to sell shoes.

Amazon's founder, Jeff Bezos, at first saw an opportunity to change the way people purchase books. Using the power of the information age to tailor offerings to each customer and speed the payment process, he in effect opened millions of tiny virtual bookstores, each with a vastly larger selection and far cheaper product than traditional bookstores. The success of his original business model led him to expand Amazon to carry many other types of products. The founders of Netflix and Zappos have done the same thing for movies and shoes. All these entrepreneurs were business professionals, not technology experts. However, they understood enough about the information age to apply it to a particular business, creating innovative companies that now lead entire industries. Students who understand business along with the power associated with the information age will create their own opportunities, and perhaps even new industries.

- ***Internet of Things (IoT)***: A world where interconnected Internet-enabled devices or "things" have the ability to collect and share data without human intervention.
- ***Machine-to-machine (M2M)***: Refers to devices that connect directly to other devices. Just think of your smart watch directly connecting with your smart phone.

APPLY YOUR KNOWLEDGE

BUSINESS DRIVEN DISCUSSION

Data Bits

Have you ever wondered how your computer stores your data? The answer: Bits. A bit, which is short for *binary digit,* is the smallest unit of storage on a computer. Eight bits are equal to 1 byte. A byte is big enough to store a letter, number, space, or symbol. Each time you press a key, the computer translates the keystroke into a numerical code that takes up 1 byte of space. For example, the sentence "Your computer stores your data." uses 31 bytes of storage, with 8 bits per byte. When referring to disk storage on your computer, the hard drive manufacturers use the standard that a megabyte is 1,000,000 bytes. This means that when you buy a 250-gigabyte hard drive, you get a total of 250,000,000,000 bytes of available storage. The following is the bit table for hard disk storage.

- Binary Digit = 1 Bit
- 1 Byte = 8 Bits
- 1 Kilobyte = 1,000 Bytes
- 1 Megabyte = 1,000 Kilobytes
- 1 Gigabyte = 1,000 Megabytes
- 1 Terabyte = 1,000 Gigabytes
- 1 Petabyte = 1,000 Terabytes
- 1 Exabyte = 1,000 Petabytes
- 1 Zettabyte = 1,000 Exabytes
- 1 Yottabyte = 1,000 Zettabytes
- 1 Brontobyte = 1,000 Yottabytes
- 1 Geopbyte = 1,000 Brontobytes

Originally, computer hard drives had the capacity to store only 250 megabytes of data. The first Google server had only ten 4-megabyte hard drives. Today, personal computers can save and analyze gigabytes of data. This is one of the key drivers of the technologies radically changing our world and environment. It is estimated that by 2025, every second there will be 1.7 megabytes of new data created for every person in the world. That is an unimaginable amount of data.

It has been stated that future business leaders must be data literate to survive and thrive in the hyper-competitive business arena. In a group, answer the following questions:

- Do you agree or disagree that the ability to analyze data is critical to your future career?
- If you are a marketing major, how will understanding inventory data help your career?
- If you are a management major, how will analyzing employee data help your career?
- If you are a future business leader, how will analyzing competitor data help drive your business strategies?
- Overall, how will this course help prepare you for your future career?

You might be wearing a smart watch (IoT device) that is tracking each time your heart beats and every single calorie you burn during your day. Today, devices are connecting in ways not previously thought possible, and researchers predict that over 100 billion IoT devices will be communicating by 2025, creating petabytes of data. Just imagine the amount of data sent via Wi-Fi between these devices without any human intervention. This was not even possible a few decades ago because devices didn't have enough capacity to store the massive amounts of data, and Wi-Fi networks didn't exist.

IoT is transforming our world into a living information system as we control our intelligent lighting from our smart phone to a daily health check from our smart toilet. Of course, with all great technological advances come unexpected risks, and you have to be prepared to encounter various security issues with IoT. Just imagine if your devices were hacked by someone who now has the ability to shut off your water, take control of your car, or unlock the doors of your home from thousands of miles away. We are just beginning to understand the security issues associated with IoT and M2M, and you can be sure that sensitive data leakage from your IoT device is something you will most likely encounter in your life.

Students who understand business, along with the power associated with the information age, will create their own opportunities and perhaps even new industries. Realizing the value of obtaining real-time data from connected "things" will allow you to make more informed decisions, identify new opportunities, and analyze customer patterns to predict new behaviors. Learning how to collect, analyze, and communicate data is a critical skill for all business managers that want to lead by making data driven decisions. The core drivers of the information age include:

- Data
- Information
- Business intelligence
- Knowledge (see Figure 1.1)

FIGURE 1.1

The Differences among Data, Information, Business Intelligence, and Knowledge

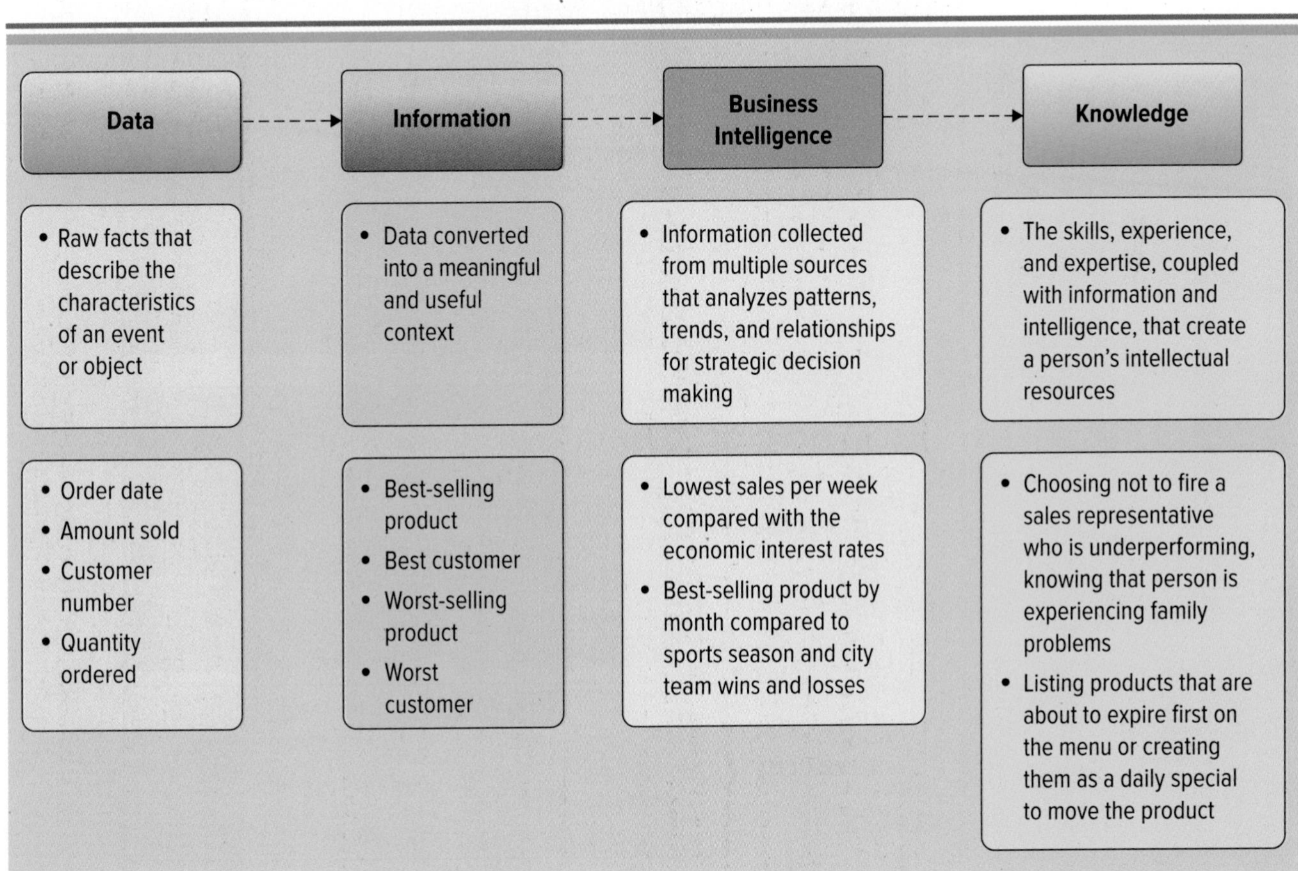

Data
Information
Business Intelligence
Knowledge
• Raw facts that describe the characteristics of an event or object
• Data converted into a meaningful and useful context
• Information collected from multiple sources that analyzes patterns, trends, and relationships for strategic decision making
• The skills, experience, and expertise, coupled with information and intelligence, that create a person's intellectual resources
• Order date
• Amount sold
• Customer number
• Quantity ordered
• Best-selling product
• Best customer
• Worst-selling product
• Worst customer
• Lowest sales per week compared with the economic interest rates
• Best-selling product by month compared to sports season and city team wins and losses
• Choosing not to fire a sales representative who is underperforming, knowing that person is experiencing family problems
• Listing products that are about to expire first on the menu or creating them as a daily special to move the product

Data

Today, data is your competitive advantage. It allows you to make evidenced-based decisions to help you run your operations and analyze past data to make future predictions. Before the information age, managers manually collected and analyzed data, a time-consuming and complicated task without which they would have little insight into how to run their business. Data driven decisions enable savvy companies to create business strategies that increase profits, reduce risk, and optimize business processes.

- ***Data***: Raw facts that describe the characteristics of an event or object.
- ***Big data***: A collection of large, complex datasets, which cannot be analyzed using traditional database methods and tools.

A simple way to think of big data is that it is too large to fit on a single computer. The move to big data combines business with science and research activities and includes petabytes of data, which is equivalent to 20 million four-drawer file cabinets filled with text files, or 13 years of HDTV content. The emergence of big data is a result of the last 50 years of technology evolution and its four common characteristics include large data volumes, with high velocity, wide variety, and veracity. A company can now analyze petabytes of data for patterns, trends, and anomalies, gaining insights into data in new and exciting ways. The four common characteristics of big data are detailed in Figures 1.2 and 1.3.

FIGURE 1.2

Four Common Characteristics of Big Data

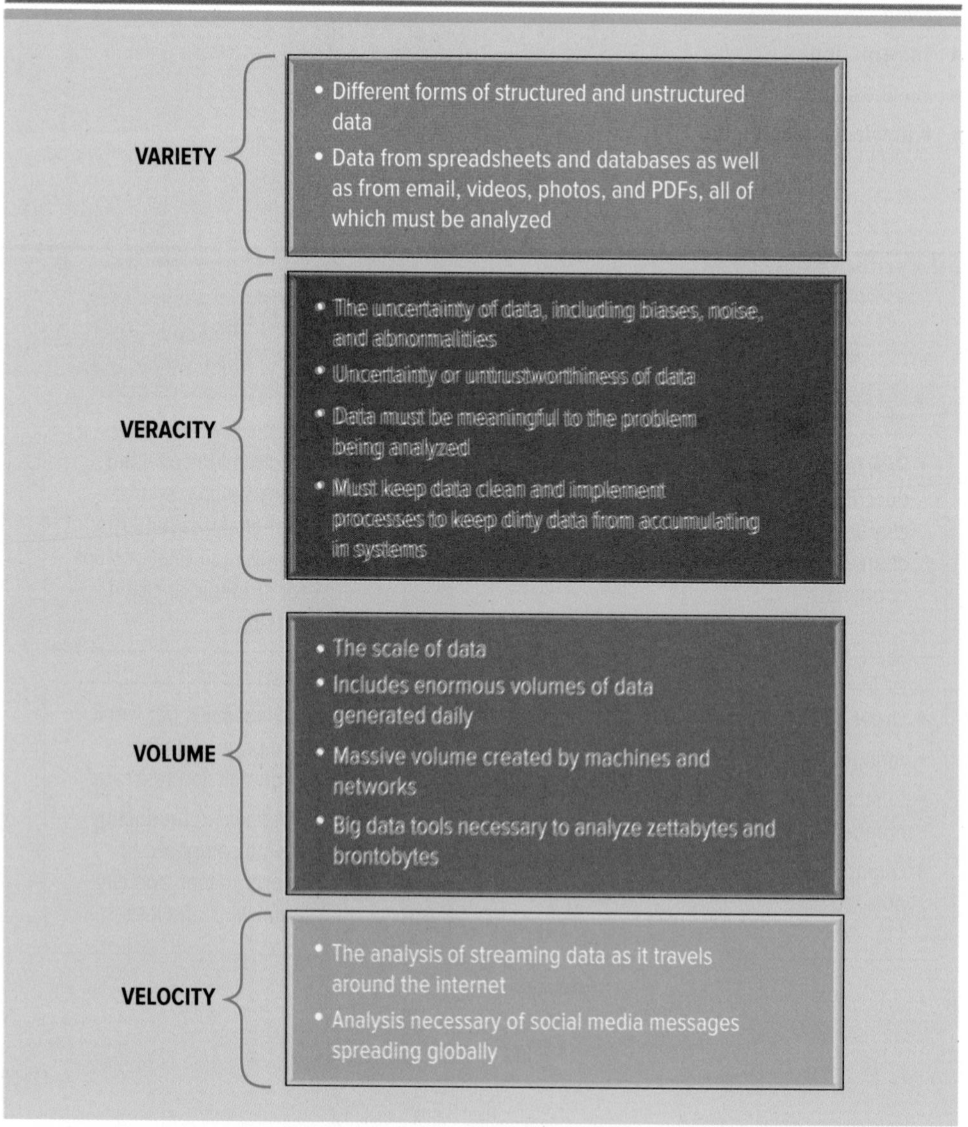

VARIETY
• Different forms of structured and unstructured data
• Data from spreadsheets and databases as well as from email, videos, photos, and PDFs, all of which must be analyzed
VERACITY
• The uncertainty of data, including biases, noise, and abnormalities
• Uncertainty or untrustworthiness of data
• Data must be meaningful to the problem being analyzed
• Must keep data clean and implement processes to keep dirty data from accumulating in systems
VOLUME
• The scale of data
• Includes enormous volumes of data generated daily
• Massive volume created by machines and networks
• Big data tools necessary to analyze zettabytes and brontobytes
VELOCITY
• The analysis of streaming data as it travels around the internet
• Analysis necessary of social media messages spreading globally

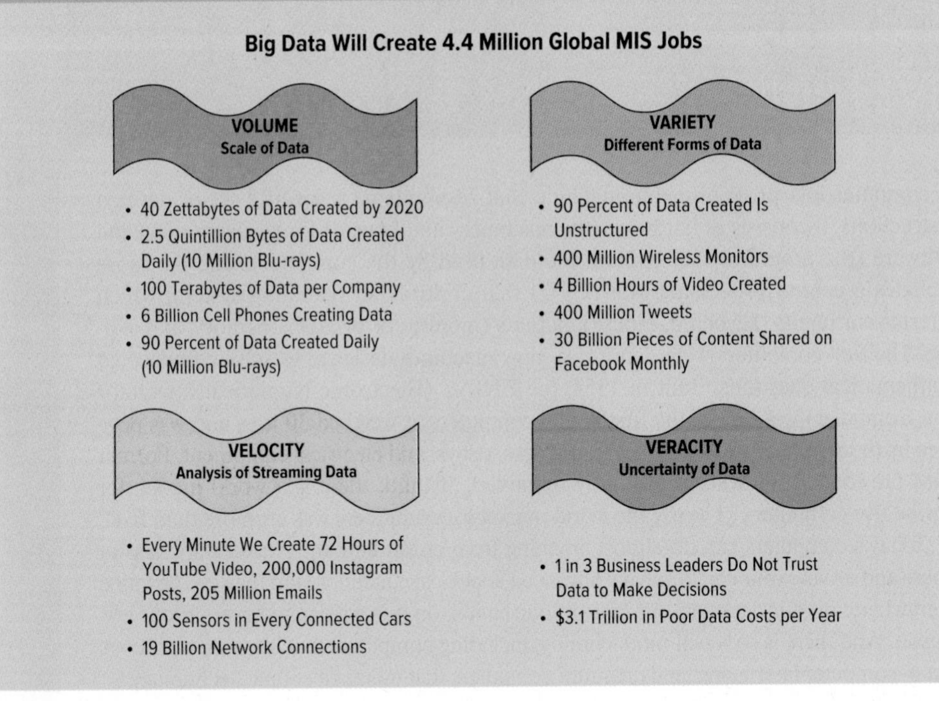
Big Data Will Create 4.4 Million Global MIS Jobs
VOLUME
Scale of Data
• 40 Zettabytes of Data Created by 2020
• 2.5 Quintillion Bytes of Data Created Daily (10 Million Blu-rays)
• 100 Terabytes of Data per Company
• 6 Billion Cell Phones Creating Data
• 90 Percent of Data Created Daily (10 Million Blu-rays)
VARIETY
Different Forms of Data
• 90 Percent of Data Created Is Unstructured
• 400 Million Wireless Monitors
• 4 Billion Hours of Video Created
• 400 Million Tweets
• 30 Billion Pieces of Content Shared on Facebook Monthly
VELOCITY
Analysis of Streaming Data
• Every Minute We Create 72 Hours of YouTube Video, 200,000 Instagram Posts, 205 Million Emails
• 100 Sensors in Every Connected Cars
• 19 Billion Network Connections
VERACITY
Uncertainty of Data
• 1 in 3 Business Leaders Do Not Trust Data to Make Decisions
• $3.1 Trillion in Poor Data Costs per Year

FIGURE 1.3

Big Data Will Create 4.4 Million Global MIS Jobs

Structured data has a defined length, type, and format and includes numbers, dates, or strings such as Customer Address. Structured data is typically stored in a traditional system such as a relational database or spreadsheet and accounts for about 20 percent of the data that surrounds us. The sources of structured data include:

- ***Machine-generated data***: Created by a machine without human intervention. Machine-generated structured data includes sensor data, point-of-sale data, and web log data.
- ***Human-generated data***: Data that humans, in interaction with computers, generate. Human-generated structured data includes input data, clickstream data, or gaming data.

Unstructured data is not defined, does not follow a specified format, and typically free-form text such as emails, Twitter tweets, and text messages. Unstructured data accounts for about 80 percent of the data that surrounds us. The sources of unstructured data include:

- ***Machine-generated unstructured data***: Such as satellite images, scientific atmosphere data, and radar data.
- ***Human-generated unstructured data***: Such as text messages, social media data, and emails (see Figure 1.4).

Figure 1.5 shows sales data for Tony's Wholesale Company, a fictitious business that supplies snacks to stores. The data highlight characteristics such as order date, customer, sales representative, product, quantity, and profit. The second line in Figure 1.5, for instance, shows that Roberta Cross sold 90 boxes of Ruffles to Walmart for $1,350, resulting in a profit of $450 (note that Profit = Sales − Costs).

- ***Snapshot***: A view of data at a particular moment in time.

FIGURE 1.4

Structured and Unstructured Data Examples

Structured Data	Unstructured Data
Sensor data	Satellite images
Web log data	Photographic data
Financial data	Video data
Clickstream data	Social media data
Point-of-sale data	Text message
Accounting data	Voice mail data

APPLY YOUR KNOWLEDGE

BUSINESS DRIVEN MIS

Computers Are Everywhere

A computer is a programmable machine that responds to a specific set of defined instructions. It consists of hardware (the machinery and housing for its electronics) and software (the programs that contain the data used by the computer). The hardware includes a central processing unit (CPU) that controls an operating system, which directs your inputs (keyboard, mouse), outputs (monitor or printer), memory, and storage. The first computers were enormous, slow machines designed to solve complicated mathematical questions. Built in 1954, the ENIAC (Electronic Numerical Integrator and Computer) was one of the first digital computers; it weighed 30 tons and was powered by thousands of vacuum tubes, capacitors, relays, and electrical equipment. Former IBM president Tom Watson famously remarked, "I think there is a world market for maybe five computers." Clearly the world market for computers was far more than five![3]

Today's computers can do almost anything from controlling the temperature in your house and driving your car, to solving advanced analytical equations, and they can be found everywhere: on our desks, in our laps, in our hands, on our wrists, and even in our eyeglasses. And there is so much more coming, including computers that learn on their own, brain–computer interfacing, and quantum computers that utilize fiber-optic technology.

Think of your life 5 years ago and list three IoT devices you use today that were not invented 5 years ago. What types of IoT devices will be introduced over the next 10 years? What types of data are your IoT devices collecting? As an organization leader, would you prefer structured data or unstructured data for your business analysis? Why?

These data are useful for understanding individual sales, but they do not give us much insight into how Tony's business is performing as a whole. Tony needs to answer questions that will help him manage his day-to-day operations, such as:

- Who are my best customers?
- Who are my least-profitable customers?
- What is my best-selling product?
- What is my slowest-selling product?
- Who is my strongest sales representative?
- Who is my weakest sales representative?

What Tony needs, in other words, is not data but *information.*

FIGURE 1.5

Tony's Snack Company Data

Order Date	Customer	Sales Representative	Product	Qty	Unit Price	Total Sales	Unit Cost	Total Cost	Profit
4-Jan	Walmart	PJ Helgoth	Doritos	41	$24	$ 984	$18	$738	$246
4-Jan	Walmart	Roberta Cross	Ruffles	90	$15	$1,350	$10	$900	$450
5-Jan	Safeway	Craig Schultz	Ruffles	27	$15	$ 405	$10	$270	$135
6-Jan	Walmart	Roberta Cross	Ruffles	67	$15	$1,005	$10	$670	$335
7-Jan	7-Eleven	Craig Schultz	Pringles	79	$12	$ 948	$ 6	$474	$474
7-Jan	Walmart	Roberta Cross	Ruffles	52	$15	$ 780	$10	$520	$260
8-Jan	Kroger	Craig Schultz	Ruffles	39	$15	$ 585	$10	$390	$195
9-Jan	Walmart	Craig Schultz	Ruffles	66	$15	$ 990	$10	$660	$330
10-Jan	Target	Craig Schultz	Ruffles	40	$15	$ 600	$10	$400	$200
11-Jan	Walmart	Craig Schultz	Ruffles	71	$15	$1,065	$10	$710	$355

Information

The simple difference between data and information is that computers or machines need data, and humans need information.

- ***Information***: Data converted into a meaningful and useful context.

Data is a raw building block that not been shaped, processed, or analyzed and frequently appears disorganized and unfriendly. Information gives meaning and context to analyzed data, making it insightful for humans by providing context and structure that is extremely valuable when making informed business decisions.

Having the right information at the right moment in time can be worth a fortune. Having the wrong information at the right moment or the right information at the wrong moment can be disastrous. The truth about information is that its value is only as good as the people who use it. People using the same information can make different decisions, depending on how they interpret or analyze the information. Thus, information has value only insofar as the people using it do as well. Changing variables allows managers to create hypothetical scenarios to study future possibilities.

- ***Variable***: A data characteristic that stands for a value that changes or varies over time.

Looking at Tony's data, the price and quantity ordered can vary. Tony may find it valuable to anticipate how sales or cost increases affect profitability. To estimate how a 20 percent increase in prices might improve profits, Tony simply changes the price variable for all orders, which automatically calculates the amount of new profits. To estimate how a 10 percent increase in costs hurts profits, Tony changes the cost variable for all orders, which automatically calculates the amount of lost profits. Manipulating variables is an important tool for any business.

- ***Report***: A document containing data organized in a table, matrix, or graphical format allowing users to easily comprehend and understand information. Reports can cover a wide range of subjects or a specific subject for a certain time period or event.
- ***Static report***: Created once, based on data that does not change. Static reports can include a sales report from last year or a salary report from 5 years ago.
- ***Dynamic report***: Changes automatically during creation. Dynamic reports can include updating daily stock market prices or calculating available inventory.

Tony can analyze his sales data and turn them into information to answer all the preceding questions and understand how his business is operating. Figures 1.6 and 1.7, for instance, show us that Walmart is Roberta Cross's best customer and that Ruffles is Tony's best product measured in terms of total sales. Armed with this information, Tony can identify and then address such issues as weak products and underperforming sales representatives.

Business Intelligence

Business intelligence (BI) is information collected from multiple sources such as suppliers, customers, competitors, partners, and industries that analyzes patterns, trends, and relationships for strategic decision making. BI manipulates multiple variables, and in some cases even hundreds of variables, including such items as interest rates, weather conditions, even gas prices. Tony could use BI to analyze internal data, such as company sales, along with external data about the environment, such as competitors, finances, weather, holidays, and even sporting events. Both internal and external variables affect snack sales, and analyzing these variables will help Tony determine ordering levels and sales forecasts. For instance, BI can predict inventory requirements for Tony's business for the week before the Super Bowl if, say, the home team is playing, the average temperature is above 80 degrees, and the stock market is performing well. This is BI at its finest, incorporating all types of internal and external variables to anticipate business performance.

Data-literate professionals are valued across all industries, in all corporate divisions, and at all seniority levels. As such, there are a wide range of jobs with impressive salaries that seek people who can analyze, organize, and interpret data.

- ***Data analyst***: Collects, queries, and consumes organizational data to uncover patterns and provide insights for strategic business decision making.

Order Date	Customer	Sales Representative	Product	Quantity	Unit Price	Total Sales	Unit Cost	Total Cost	Profit
26-Apr	Walmart	Roberta Cross	Fritos	86	$ 19	$ 1,634	$ 17	$ 1,462	$ 172
29-Aug	Walmart	Roberta Cross	Fritos	76	$ 19	$ 1,444	$ 17	$ 1,292	$ 152
7-Sep	Walmart	Roberta Cross	Fritos	20	$ 19	$ 380	$ 17	$ 340	$ 40
22-Nov	Walmart	Roberta Cross	Fritos	39	$ 19	$ 741	$ 17	$ 663	$ 78
30-Dec	Walmart	Roberta Cross	Fritos	68	$ 19	$ 1,292	$ 17	$ 1,156	$ 136
7-Jul	Walmart	Roberta Cross	Pringles	79	$ 18	$ 1,422	$ 8	$ 632	$ 790
6-Aug	Walmart	Roberta Cross	Pringles	21	$ 12	$ 252	$ 6	$ 126	$ 126
2-Oct	Walmart	Roberta Cross	Pringles	60	$ 18	$ 1,080	$ 8	$ 480	$ 600
15-Nov	Walmart	Roberta Cross	Pringles	32	$ 12	$ 384	$ 6	$ 192	$ 192
21-Dec	Walmart	Roberta Cross	Pringles	92	$ 12	$ 1,104	$ 6	$ 552	$ 552
28-Feb	Walmart	Roberta Cross	Ruffles	67	$ 15	$ 1,005	$ 10	$ 670	$ 335
6-Mar	Walmart	Roberta Cross	Ruffles	8	$ 15	$ 120	$ 10	$ 80	$ 40
16-Mar	Walmart	Roberta Cross	Ruffles	68	$ 15	$ 1,020	$ 10	$ 680	$ 340
23-Apr	Walmart	Roberta Cross	Ruffles	34	$ 15	$ 510	$ 10	$ 340	$ 170
4-Aug	Walmart	Roberta Cross	Ruffles	40	$ 15	$ 600	$ 10	$ 400	$ 200
18-Aug	Walmart	Roberta Cross	Ruffles	93	$ 15	$ 1,395	$ 10	$ 930	$ 465
5-Sep	Walmart	Roberta Cross	Ruffles	41	$ 15	$ 615	$ 10	$ 410	$ 205
12-Sep	Walmart	Roberta Cross	Ruffles	8	$ 15	$ 120	$ 10	$ 80	$ 40
28-Oct	Walmart	Roberta Cross	Ruffles	50	$ 15	$ 750	$ 10	$ 500	$ 250
21-Nov	Walmart	Roberta Cross	Ruffles	79	$ 15	$ 1,185	$ 10	$ 790	$ 395
29-Jan	Walmart	Roberta Cross	Sun Chips	5	$ 22	$ 110	$ 18	$ 90	$ 20
12-Apr	Walmart	Roberta Cross	Sun Chips	85	$ 22	$ 1,870	$ 18	$ 1,530	$ 340
16-Jun	Walmart	Roberta Cross	Sun Chips	55	$ 22	$ 1,210	$ 18	$ 990	$ 220
				1,206	**$383**	**$20,243**	**$273**	**$14,385**	**$5,858**

Sorting the data reveals the information that Roberta Cross's total sales to Walmart were $20,243, resulting in a profit of $5,858 (Profit $5,858 = Sales $20,243 − Costs $14,385).

FIGURE 1.6

Tony's Data Sorted by Customer "Walmart" and Sales Representative "Roberta Cross"

In essence, data analysts interpret and translate data into plain English or visualizations easily understood by all stakeholders. They take raw or unstructured data and come up with analyses that produce digestible results that executives and others can use to make decisions.

A data analyst focuses on using data to gain business insights, model future predictions, and create visualizations with storytelling narratives. As Figure 1.8 shows, a data analyst has three primary areas of expertise.

Without knowing all three areas, you are simply just a statistician or a software programmer. The key skill differentiating a data analyst is the business subject matter expertise. Data analysts are key in driving data driven decisions focusing on insights, predictions, and visualizations. Demand for data analysts is exponentially increasing in all industries and business areas. Key terms associated with data include:

- ***Analytics***: The science of fact-based decision making.
- ***Business analytics***: The scientific process of transforming data into insight for making better decisions.
- ***Data scientist***: Extracts knowledge from data by performing statistical analysis, data mining, and advanced analytics on big data to identify trends, market changes, and other relevant information.

Analytics is thought of as a broader category than business analytics, encompassing the use of analytical techniques in the sciences and engineering fields as well as business. In this text,

Tony's Business Information	Name	Total Profit
Who is Tony's best customer by total sales?	Walmart	$ 560,789
Who is Tony's least-valuable customer by total sales?	Walgreens	$ 45,673
Who is Tony's best customer by profit?	7-Eleven	$ 324,550
Who is Tony's least-valuable customer by profit?	King Soopers	$ 23,908
What is Tony's best-selling product by total sales?	Ruffles	$ 232,500
What is Tony's weakest-selling product by total sales?	Pringles	$ 54,890
What is Tony's best-selling product by profit?	Tostitos	$ 13,050
What is Tony's weakest-selling product by profit?	Pringles	$ 23,000
Who is Tony's best sales representative by profit?	R. Cross	$1,230,980
Who is Tony's weakest sales representative by profit?	Craig Schultz	$ 98,980
What is the best sales representative's best-selling product by total profit?	Ruffles	$ 98,780
Who is the best sales representative's best customer by total profit?	Walmart	$ 345,900
What is the best sales representative's weakest-selling product by total profit?	Sun Chips	$ 45,600
Who is the best sales representative's weakest customer by total profit?	Kroger	$ 56,050

FIGURE 1.7

Information Gained after Analyzing Tony's Data

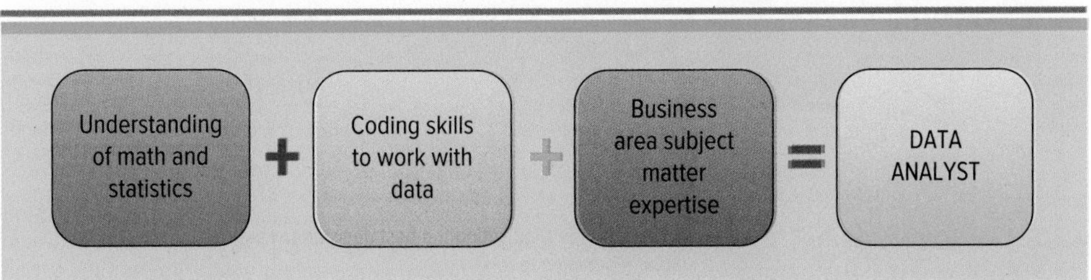

FIGURE 1.8

Three Key Skills for a Data Analyst

we will use the terms *analytics* and *business analytics* interchangeably. Analytics driven companies have the following characteristics:

- Use management information systems to perform rigorous analysis of a wide range of business functions from marketing to human resources.
- Senior executive teams recognize the importance of analytics and make their development and maintenance of it a primary focus.
- View fact-based decision making as a best practice and part of the company culture.
- Key organizational players have analytical skills.
- Use metrics as a key to monitoring and managing key business processes.
- Collect copious amounts of data from customers and suppliers.

Analytics is used for data driven or fact-based decision making, helping managers ensure they make successful decisions. A study conducted by MIT's Sloan School of Management and the University of Pennsylvania concluded that firms guided by data driven decision making have higher productivity and market value along with increased output and profitability. Analytics can range from simple reports to advanced optimization models (models that highlight the best course of actions). The four broad categories of analytics include:

- ***Descriptive analytics***: Describes past performance and history. These types of findings allow an organization to spot trends.
- ***Diagnostic analytics***: Examines data or content to answer the question, "Why did it happen?" This helps an organization determine the cause of a positive or negative outcome.
- ***Predictive analytics***: Extracts information from data to predict future trends and identify behavioral patterns. This allows an organization to take proactive action–such as reaching out to a customer who is unlikely to renew a contract.

FIGURE 1.9

Four Categories of Analytics

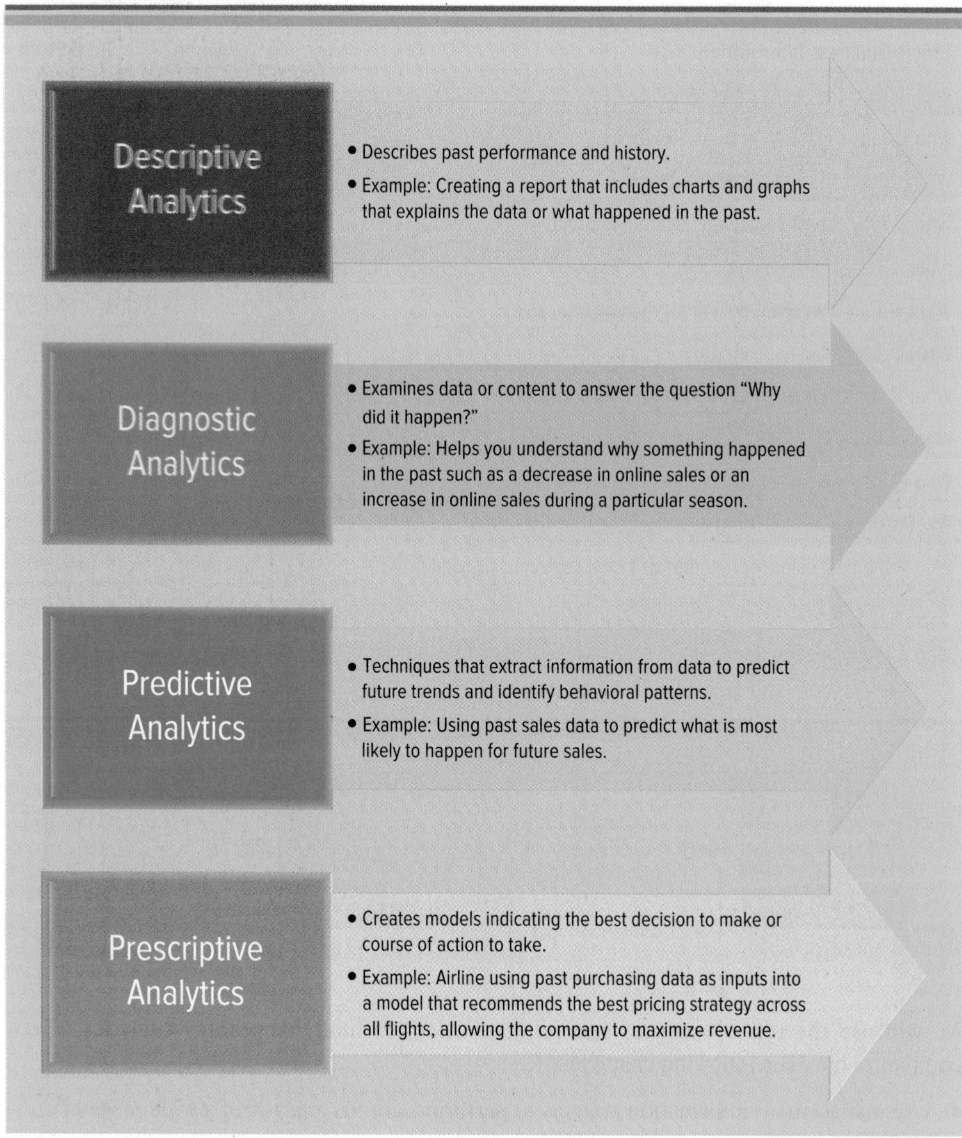

Descriptive Analytics
• Describes past performance and history.
• Example: Creating a report that includes charts and graphs that explains the data or what happened in the past.
Diagnostic Analytics
• Examines data or content to answer the question "Why did it happen?"
• Example: Helps you understand why something happened in the past such as a decrease in online sales or an increase in online sales during a particular season.
Predictive Analytics
• Techniques that extract information from data to predict future trends and identify behavioral patterns.
• Example: Using past sales data to predict what is most likely to happen for future sales.
Prescriptive Analytics
• Creates models indicating the best decision to make or course of action to take.
• Example: Airline using past purchasing data as inputs into a model that recommends the best pricing strategy across all flights, allowing the company to maximize revenue.

- ***Prescriptive analytics*:** Creates models indicating the best decision to make or course of action to take. While this type of analysis gives significant value to addressing potential problems or staying ahead of industry trends, it often requires using complex algorithms and advanced technology such as machine learning. Figure 1.9 displays the four broad categories of analytics.

Knowledge

Today's workers are commonly referred to as knowledge workers, and they use BI, along with personal experience, to make decisions based on both information and intuition, a valuable resource for any company.

- ***Knowledge*:** Includes the skills, experience, and expertise, coupled with information and intelligence, that create a person's intellectual resources.
- ***Knowledge worker*:** Individuals valued for their ability to interpret and analyze information.
- ***Knowledge assets*** (*intellectual capital*): The human, structural, and recorded resources available to the organization. Knowledge assets reside within the minds of members, customers, and colleagues and include physical structures and recorded media.
- ***Knowledge facilitators*:** Help harness the wealth of knowledge in the organization. Knowledge facilitators help acquire and catalog the knowledge assets in an organization.

BUSINESS DRIVEN ANALYTICS

Categorizing Analytics

The four techniques for business analytics include descriptive analytics, diagnostic analytics, predictive analytics, and prescriptive analytics. For each of the below examples, determine which analytical technique is being used.

Example	Descriptive Analytics	Diagnostic Analytics	Predictive Analytics	Prescriptive Analytics
Which candidate will win the election?				
What price for a product will maximize profit?				
How much money do I need to save each year to have enough money for retirement?				
How many products were sold last year?				
What is the best route for the delivery person to drop off packages to minimize the time needed to deliver all the packages?				
Why did the machine break down?				
How many Valentine's Day cards should Hallmark print to maximize expected profit?				
How will marketing affect the daily sales of a product?				
Why did seven people in marketing quit?				
How can a company minimize the cost of shipping products from plants to customers?				
Which team will win the Super Bowl?				
How can I schedule my workforce to minimize operating costs?				
What was the average purchase price for new customers last year?				
How will the placement of a product in a store determine product sales?				
How many customers do we have, and where are they located?				
Why did the stock price increase 45%?				

Imagine that Tony analyzes his data and finds his weakest sales representative for this period is Craig Schultz. If Tony considered only this information, he might conclude that firing Craig was a good business decision. However, because Tony has knowledge about how the company operates, he knows Craig has been out on medical leave for several weeks; hence, his sales numbers are low. Without this additional knowledge, Tony might have executed a bad business decision, delivered a negative message to the other employees, and sent his best sales representatives out to look for other jobs.

APPLY YOUR KNOWLEDGE

BUSINESS DRIVEN ETHICS AND SECURITY

Data Analysis Gone Wrong

Can you imagine receiving an add from Target informing you that your teenage daughter was pregnant? Yes, this actually happened a few years ago when Target sent an unsuspecting father discount coupons for cribs and baby clothes for his teenage daughter, who had not told anyone she was pregnant. This incident set off a flurry of outrage and privacy concerns against Target's data analysis practices.

Andrew Pole, statistician for Target, explained how big data helped analyze customers' purchases to determine pregnancy. Target analyzes its data using a unique ID linked to a customer's credit card, name, and purchases to look for patterns (for example: a woman buying prenatal vitamins) to then send them special deals and coupons for baby items. When Target's data analysis system analyzed customer purchase data based on 25 products that pregnant women frequently buy, it could assign a pregnancy prediction score to each shopper and estimate her due date so Target could send her relevant coupons for various stages of her pregnancy. After massive customer outrage against privacy concerns, Target began mixing customized coupons by offering a coffee maker with a crib or coupons for baby clothes with wine glasses, so someone reviewing the coupons could not determine anything about the customer.[4]

There is no doubt that some companies' data analysis practices feel more like stalking than strategic business moves. How would you feel if you received coupons indicating someone in your family or household was pregnant or sick? How does a company determine if its data analysis practices are crossing the line over data privacy? Do you agree it was a good idea for Target to mix coupons to help ensure customer privacy?

The key point in this scenario is that it is simply impossible to collect all the information about every situation, and yet without data, it can be easy to misunderstand the problem. Using data, information, business intelligence, *and* knowledge to make decisions and solve problems is the key to finding success in business. These core drivers of the information age are the building blocks of business systems. Figure 1.10 offers a few different examples of data through knowledge.

FIGURE 1.10

Transformation from Data to Knowledge

DATA: I have one item.

INFORMATION: The item I have is a product that has the most sales during the month of December.

BUSINESS INTELLIGENCE: The month of December this year is going to see interest rates rise by 10 percent and snow storms are expected to cause numerous problems throughout the East Coast.

KNOWLEDGE: Given the unexpected financial issues caused by the storms and the interest rate hike, we will offer a discount on purchases in November and December to ensure sales levels increase by 10 percent.

SYSTEMS THINKING AND MANAGEMENT INFORMATION SYSTEMS

LO 1.2: Explain systems thinking and how management information systems enable business communications.

A ***business unit*** is a segment of a company (such as accounting, production, marketing) representing a specific business function. The terms *department, functional area,* and *business unit* are used interchangeably, and corporations are typically organized by business unit such as:

- **Accounting:** Records, measures, and reports monetary transactions.
- **Finance:** Deals with strategic financial issues, including money, banking, credit, investments, and assets.
- **Human resources:** Maintains policies, plans, and procedures for the effective management of employees.
- **Marketing:** Supports sales by planning, pricing, and promoting goods or services.
- **Operations management:** Manages the process of converting or transforming resources into goods or services.
- **Sales:** Performs the function of selling goods or services.

A ***data silo*** occurs when one business unit is unable to freely communicate with other business units, making it difficult or impossible for organizations to work cross-functionally. Data silos exist because management does not believe there to be enough benefit from sharing data across business units and because data might not be useful to personnel in other business units.

Figure 1.11 provides an example of how an organization operates functionally, causing data silos as each department performs its own activities. Sales and marketing focus on moving

FIGURE 1.11

Departments Working Independently

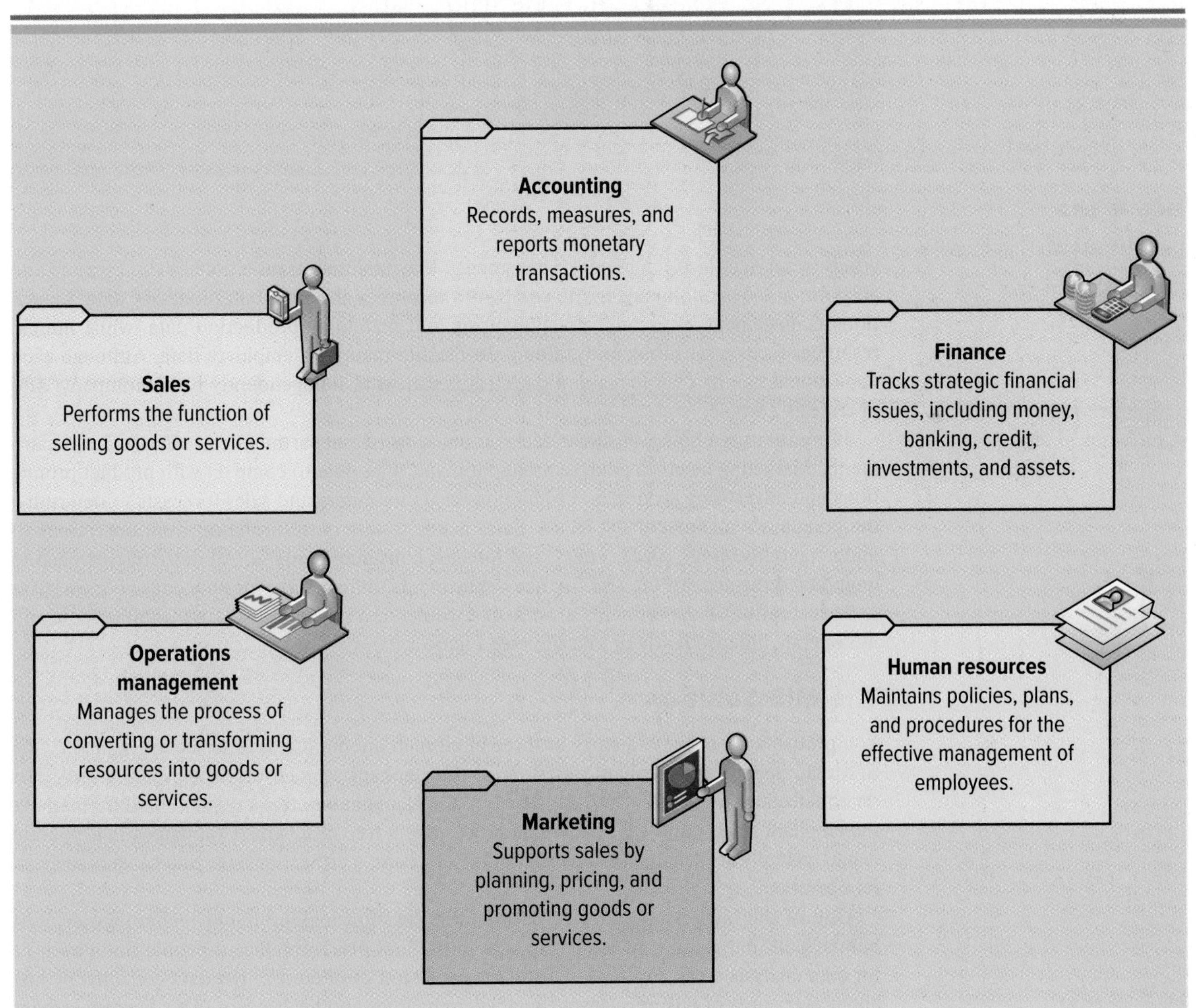

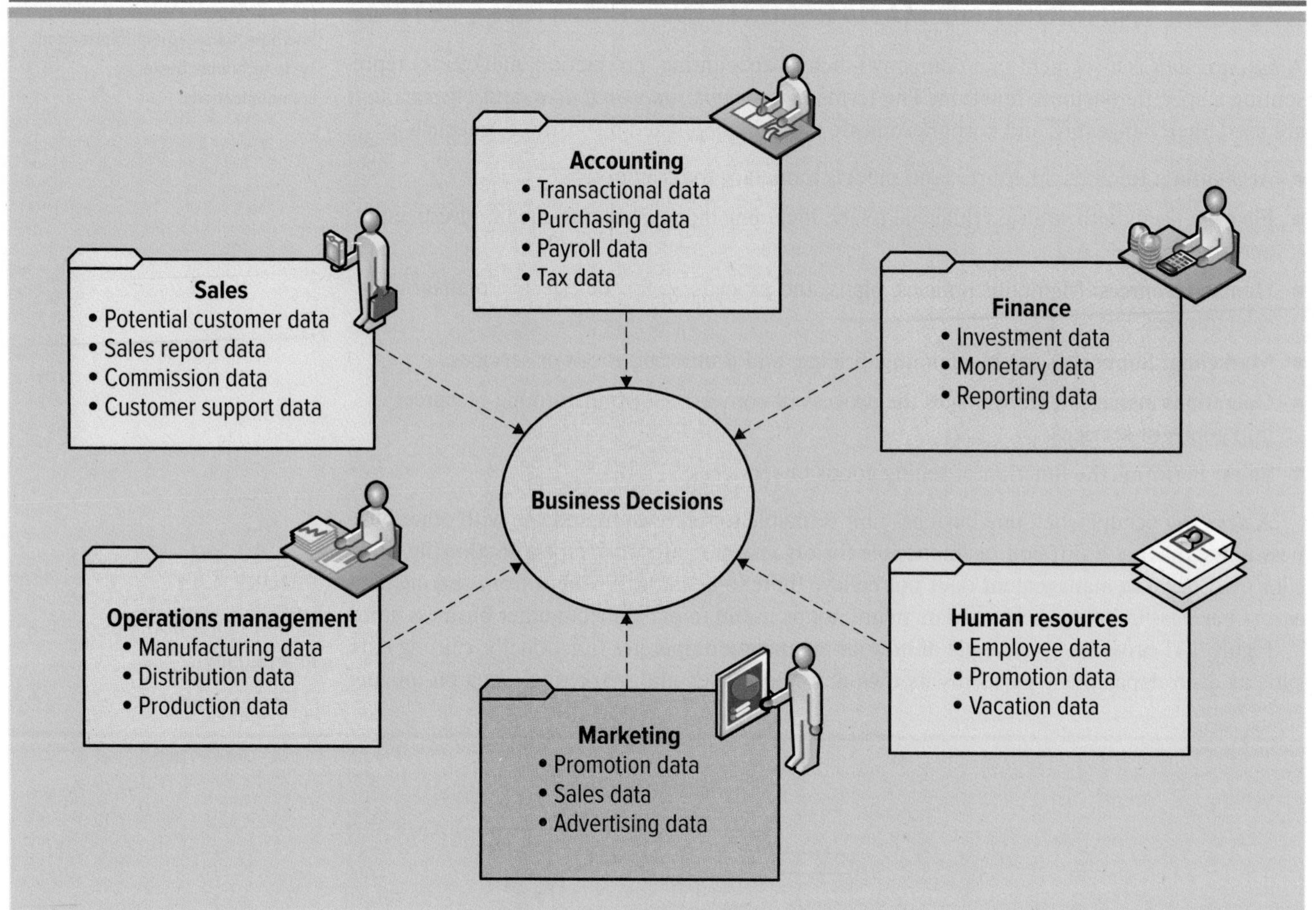

FIGURE 1.12

Departments Working Together

goods or services into the hands of consumers; they maintain transactional data. Finance and accounting focus on managing the company's resources and maintain monetary data. Operations management focuses on manufacturing and maintains production data, while human resources focuses on hiring and training people and maintains employee data. Although each department has its own focus and data, none can work independently if the company is to operate as a whole.

It is easy to see how a business decision made by one department can affect other departments. Marketing needs to analyze production and sales data to come up with product promotions and advertising strategies. Production needs to understand sales forecasts to determine the company's manufacturing needs. Sales needs to rely on information from operations to understand inventory, place orders, and forecast consumer demand. All departments need to understand the accounting and finance departments' information for budgeting. For the firm to be successful, all departments must work together as a single unit sharing common data and not operate independently or in a silo (see Figure 1.12).

The MIS Solution

You probably recall the old story of three blind men attempting to describe an elephant. The first man, feeling the elephant's girth, said the elephant seemed very much like a wall. The second, feeling the elephant's trunk, declared the elephant was like a snake. The third man felt the elephant's tusks and said the elephant was like a tree or a cane. Companies that operate departmentally are seeing only one part of the elephant, a critical mistake that hinders successful operation.

One of the biggest obstacles to data driven decision making is not technology or even human skills but gaining access to the data in the first place. Intelligent people find new uses for data analysis every day. Still, despite the explosion of interest in the data collected by just about every area of business–from financial companies and health care firms to management

Business Function	Data Analysis Business Improvement	Example
Customer Service	Identify and classify customers for marketing opportunities to retain customer loyalty	Harrah's, Capital One
Human Resources	Identify the best employee for specific tasks or jobs based on compensation levels	New England Patriots, Oakland A's
Operations Management	Detect quality problems early and address them immediately before problems arise	Intel, Boeing
Sales and Marketing	Identify the optimal price for a product or service that maximizes profit	Progressive, Marriott
Supply Chain	Evaluate the supply chain to reduce inventory and cut costs while simultaneously ensuring product availability	Dell, Walmart, Amazon

FIGURE 1.13

Data Democratization Example through an Organization

consultancies and the government—many organizations continue to relegate data analysis knowledge to a small number of employees. That is a huge mistake, and in the long run it can lead to business failure. Think of it this way: A company does not expect every employee to be a professional writer, yet all employees are expected to communicate via writing. So why does a company expect only professional data analysts to understand and analyze data when all employees need data to make data driven decisions to perform their jobs effectively?

- ***Data democratization***: The ability for data to be collected, analyzed, and accessible to all users (the average end user).

The goal of data democratization is to give all employees the ability to collect and analyze data without requiring outside help—for example, from a professional data analyst. This allows analytics to become a part of the organization's overall competitive strategy by pushing it down to decision makers at every organizational level. Arming employees with the best facts and evidence for making decisions, big and small, is a huge competitive advantage!

Eliminating data silos so the organization can leverage all of its data is the benefit of data democratization. When data is isolated in separate, fixed repositories (data silos), it is only available to a few people. Siloed data structures result in scenarios where a majority of an organization's data is simply unavailable for use by the organization. Data silos are wasteful and inefficient. Figure 1.13 displays different ways employees are using data to drive fact-based business decisions.

Systems Thinking

Successful companies operate cross-functionally, integrating the operations of all departments. Systems are the primary enabler of cross-functional operations.

- ***System***: A collection of parts that link to achieve a common purpose. A car is a good example of a system because removing a part, such as the steering wheel or accelerator, causes the entire system to stop working.

Before jumping into how systems work, it is important to have a solid understanding of the basic production process for goods and services.

- ***Goods***: Material items or products that customers will buy to satisfy a want or need. Clothing, groceries, cell phones, and cars are all examples of goods that people buy to fulfill their needs.
- ***Services***: Tasks people perform that customers will buy to satisfy a want or need. Waiting tables, teaching, and cutting hair are all examples of services that people pay for to fulfill their needs (see Figure 1.14).
- ***Production***: The process where a business takes raw materials and processes them or converts them into a finished product for its goods or services.

Just think about making a hamburger. First, you must gather all of the *inputs* or raw materials such as the bun, patty, lettuce, tomato, and ketchup. Second, you *process* the raw materials, so in this example you would need to cook the patty, wash and chop the lettuce and tomato,

FIGURE 1.14

Different Types of Goods and Services

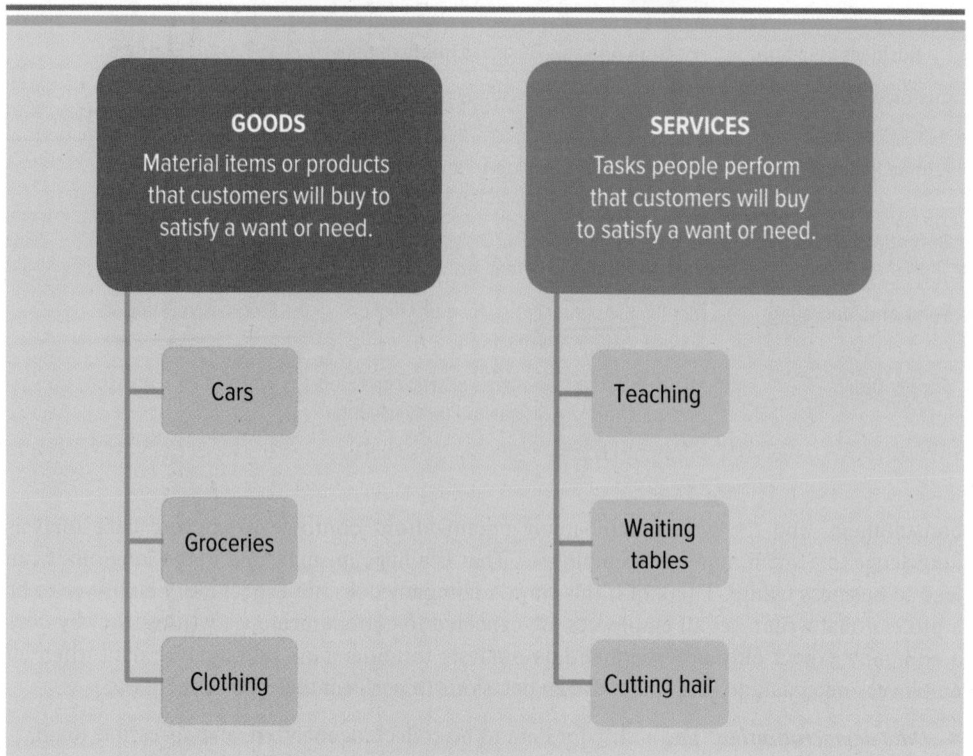

FIGURE 1.15

Input, Process, Output Example

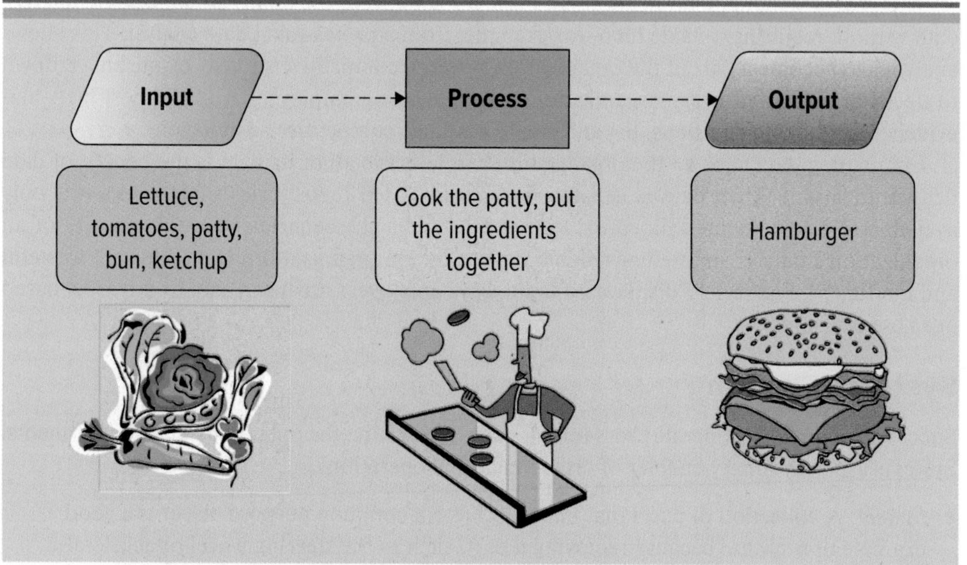

and place all the items in the bun. Finally, you would have your *output* or finished product–your hamburger! (See Figure 1.15.)

Productivity is the rate at which goods and services are produced based on total output given total inputs. Given our previous example, if a business could produce the same hamburger with less-expensive inputs or more hamburgers with the same inputs, it would see a rise in productivity and possibly an increase in profits. Ensuring the input, process, and output of goods and services work across all of the departments of a company is where systems add tremendous value to overall business productivity.

- ***Systems thinking***: A way of monitoring the entire system by viewing multiple inputs being processed or transformed to produce outputs while continuously gathering feedback on each part (see Figure 1.16).
- ***Feedback***: Information that returns to its original transmitter (input, transform, or output) and modifies the transmitter's actions.

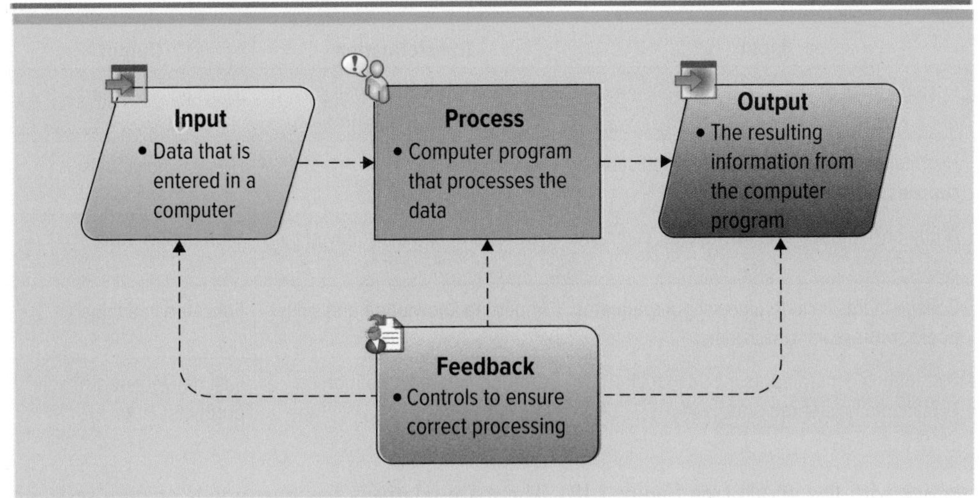

FIGURE 1.16

Overview of Systems Thinking

Feedback helps the system maintain stability. For example, a car's system continuously monitors the fuel level and turns on a warning light if the gas level is too low. Systems thinking provides an end-to-end view of how operations work together to create a product or service. Business students who understand systems thinking are valuable resources because they can implement solutions that consider the entire process, not just a single component.

Systems thinking is a possible solution to the unintended and dangerous side effects of centuries of focusing only on the individual parts of the system and not viewing the system as a whole. Whole-systems thinking invites us not to view different stakeholder perspectives in a competitive, win-lose frame of mind, and encourages us to explore win-win-win solutions that improve the overall health and sustainability of the system as a whole.

Systems thinking acknowledges that a whole is always more than the simple sum of its parts, paying attention to the diversity of elements, the quality of interactions and relationships, and the dynamic patterns of behavior that often lead to unpredictable and surprising innovations and adaptations.

- ***Management information systems (MIS)***: A business function, like accounting and human resources, which moves information about people, products, and processes across the company to facilitate decision making and problem solving.

MIS incorporates systems thinking to help companies operate cross-functionally. For example, to fulfill product orders, an MIS for sales moves a single customer order across all functional areas, including sales, order fulfillment, shipping, billing, and finally customer service. Although different functional areas handle different parts of the sale, thanks to MIS, to the customer the sale is one continuous process. If one part of the company is experiencing problems, however, then, like the car without a steering wheel, the entire system fails. If order fulfillment packages the wrong product, it will not matter that shipping, billing, and customer service did their jobs right because the customer will not be satisfied when he or she opens the package.

MIS can be an important enabler of business success and innovation. This is not to say that MIS *equals* business success and innovation or that MIS *represents* business success and innovation. MIS is a tool that is most valuable when it leverages the talents of people who know how to use and manage it effectively. To perform the MIS function effectively, almost all companies, particularly large and medium-sized ones, have an internal MIS department, often called information technology (IT), information systems (IS), or management information systems (MIS). For the purpose of this text, we will refer to it as MIS.

Figure 1.17 displays examples of inputs, transformation processes, and outputs. Although goods and services are listed separately in Figure 1.14, it is important to note that goods and services often occur jointly. For example, having the oil changed in a car is a service, but the oil that is delivered is a good. Similarly, house painting is a service, but the paint is a good. The goods-service combination is a continuum. It ranges from primarily goods with little service to primarily

FIGURE 1.17

Examples of Inputs, Transformation, and Outputs

Input	Transformation	Output
Restaurant inputs include hungry customers, good wait staff.	Well-prepared food, well served; agreeable environment	Satisfied customers
Hospital inputs include patients, medical supplies, doctors, nurses.	Health care	Healthy individuals
Automobile inputs include sheet steel, engine parts, tires.	Fabrication and assembly of cars	High-quality cars
College inputs include high school graduates, books, professors, classrooms.	Imparting knowledge and skills	Educated individuals
Distribution center inputs include stock-keeping units, storage bins, workers.	Storage and redistribution	Fast delivery of available products

service with few goods (see Figure 1.18). There are relatively few pure goods or pure services; therefore, organizations typically sell product packages, which are a combination of goods and services. This makes managing operations more interesting, as well as more challenging.

OM is critical to an organization because of its ability to increase value-added during the transformation process.

- ***Value-added***: The term used to describe the difference between the cost of inputs and the value of price of outputs.

In nonprofit organizations, the value of outputs (highway construction, police, and fire protection) is their value to society; the greater the value-added, the greater the effectiveness of the operations. In for-profit organizations, the value of outputs is measured by the prices that customers are willing to pay for those goods or services. Firms use the money generated by value-added for research and development, investment in new facilities and equipment, worker salaries, and profits. Consequently, the greater the value-added, the greater the amount of funds available for these important activities. The scope of OM ranges across the organization and includes many interrelated activities, such as forecasting, capacity planning, scheduling, managing inventories, assuring quality, motivating employees, deciding where to locate facilities, and more.

FIGURE 1.18

The Goods–Service Continuum: Most Products Are a Bundle of Goods and Services.

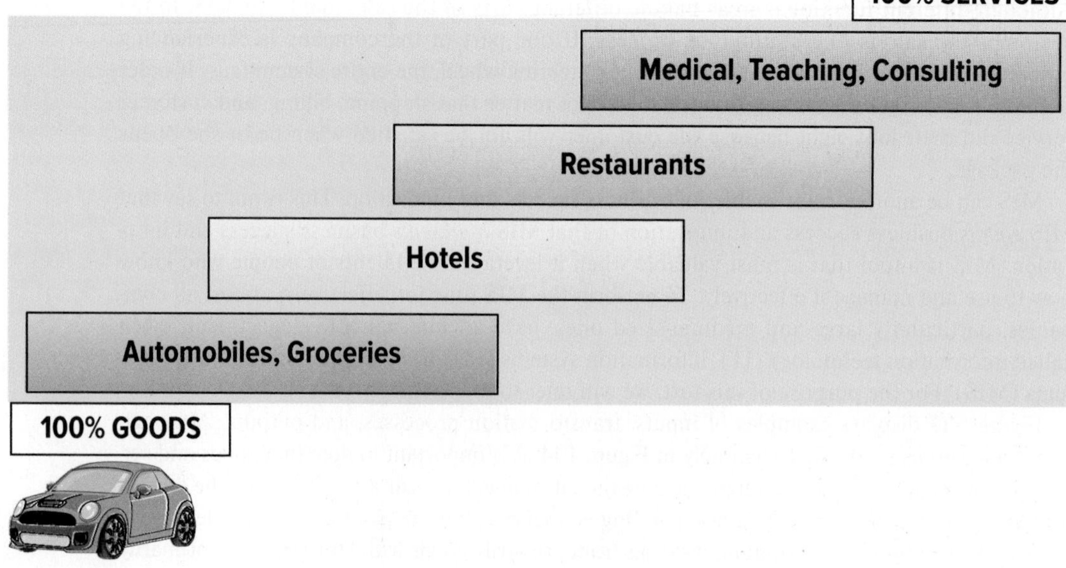

MIS Department Roles and Responsibilities

Management information systems is a relatively new functional area, having been around formally in most organizations only for about 40 years. Job titles, roles, and responsibilities often differ dramatically from organization to organization. Nonetheless, clear trends are developing toward elevating some MIS positions within an organization to the strategic level.

Most organizations maintain positions such as chief executive officer (CEO), chief financial officer (CFO), and chief operations officer (COO) at the strategic level. Lately, there are more MIS-related strategic positions, such as chief information officer (CIO), chief data officer (CDO), chief technology officer (CTO), chief security officer (CSO), chief privacy officer (CPO), and chief knowledge officer (CKO). See Figure 1.19.

The ***chief information officer (CIO)*** is responsible for (1) overseeing all uses of information technology and (2) ensuring the strategic alignment of MIS with business goals and objectives. The CIO often reports directly to the CEO. CIOs must possess a solid and detailed

FIGURE 1.19

The Roles and Responsibilities of MIS

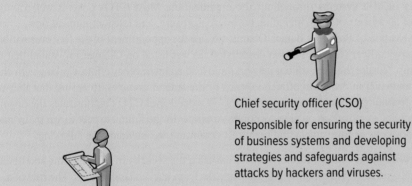

Chief security officer (CSO)
Responsible for ensuring the security of business systems and developing strategies and safeguards against attacks by hackers and viruses.

Chief knowledge officer (CKO)
Responsible for collecting, maintaining, and distributing company knowledge.

Chief technology officer (CTO)
Responsible for ensuring the speed, accuracy, availability, and reliability of the MIS.

MIS Department Roles and Responsibilities

Chief information officer (CIO)
Responsible for (1) overseeing all uses of MIS and (2) ensuring that MIS strategically aligns with business goals and objectives.

Chief privacy officer (CPO)
Responsible for ensuring the ethical and legal use of information within a company.

Chief data officer (CDO)
Responsible for determining the types of information the enterprise will capture, retain, analyze, and share.

understanding of every aspect of an organization coupled with tremendous insight into the capability of MIS. Broad functions of a CIO include:

- *Manager*–ensure the delivery of all MIS projects, on time and within budget.
- *Leader*–ensure the strategic vision of MIS is in line with the strategic vision of the organization.
- *Communicator*–advocate and communicate the MIS strategy by building and maintaining strong executive relationships.

The ***chief data officer (CDO)*** is responsible for determining the types of information the enterprise will capture, retain, analyze, and share. The difference between the CIO and CDO is that the CIO is responsible for the *information systems* through which data is stored and processed, while the CDO is responsible for the *data,* regardless of the information system.

The ***chief technology officer (CTO)*** is responsible for ensuring the throughput, speed, accuracy, availability, and reliability of an organization's information technology. CTOs are similar to CIOs, except that CIOs take on the additional responsibility for effectiveness of ensuring that MIS is aligned with the organization's strategic initiatives. CTOs have direct responsibility for ensuring the *efficiency* of MIS systems throughout the organization. Most CTOs possess well-rounded knowledge of all aspects of MIS, including hardware, software, and telecommunications.

With the election of President Barack Obama, we saw the appointment of the first-ever national chief technology officer (CTO). The job description, as was listed on Change.gov, stated that the first CTO must "ensure the safety of our networks and lead an interagency effort, working with chief technology and chief information officers of each of the federal agencies, to ensure that they use best-in-class technologies and share best practices." A federal-level CTO demonstrates the ongoing growth of technology positions outside corporate America. In the future, expect to see many more technology positions in government and nonprofit organizations, including the following:

- ***Chief security officer (CSO)***: Responsible for ensuring the security of MIS systems and developing strategies and MIS safeguards against attacks from hackers and viruses. The role of a CSO has been elevated in recent years because of the number of attacks from hackers and viruses. Most CSOs possess detailed knowledge of networks and telecommunications because hackers and viruses usually find their way into MIS systems through networked computers.
- ***Chief privacy officer (CPO)***: Responsible for ensuring the ethical and legal use of information within an organization. CPOs are the newest senior executive position in MIS. Recently, 150 of the *Fortune* 500 companies added the CPO position to their list of senior executives. Many CPOs are lawyers by training, enabling them to understand the often complex legal issues surrounding the use of information.
- ***Chief knowledge officer (CKO)***: Responsible for collecting, maintaining, and distributing the organization's knowledge. The CKO designs programs and systems that make it easy for people to reuse knowledge. These systems create repositories of organizational documents, methodologies, tools, and practices, and they establish methods for filtering the information. The CKO must continuously encourage employee contributions to keep the systems up-to-date. The CKO can contribute directly to the organization's bottom line by reducing the learning curve for new employees or employees taking on new roles.

All the above MIS positions and responsibilities are critical to an organization's success. While many organizations may not have a different individual for each of these positions, they must have leaders taking responsibility for all these areas of concern. The individuals responsible for enterprisewide MIS and MIS-related issues must provide guidance and support to the organization's employees. According to *Fast Company* magazine, a few executive levels you might see created over the next decade include:

- ***Chief automation officer***: Determines if a person or business process can be replaced by a robot or software. As we continue to automate jobs, a member of the core leadership team of the future will be put in charge of identifying opportunities for companies to become more competitive through automation.
- ***Chief intellectual property officer***: Manages and defends intellectual property, copyrights, and patents. The world of intellectual property law is vast and complicated as new innovations continually enter the market. Companies in the near future will need a core leadership team member who can not only wade through the dizzying sea of intellectual property laws

and patents to ensure their own compliance, but also remain vigilant to protect their own company against infringement.

- ***Chief sustainability officer***: Oversees the corporation's "environmental" programs, such as helping adapt to climate change and reducing carbon emissions.
- ***Chief user experience officer***: Creates the optimal relationship between user and technology. User experience used to be an afterthought for hardware and software designers. Now that bulky instruction manuals are largely (and thankfully) a thing of the past, technology companies need to ensure that their products are intuitive from the moment they are activated.

MIS skills gap is the difference between existing MIS workplace knowledge and the knowledge required to fulfill the business goals and strategies. Closing the MIS skills gap by aligning the current workforce with potential future business needs is a complicated proposition. Today, employers often struggle to locate and retain qualified MIS talent, especially individuals with application development, information security, and data analysis skills.

Common approaches to closing an MIS skills gap include social recruiting, off-site training, mentoring services, and partnerships with universities. In many instances, an MIS job will remain unfilled for an extended period of time when an employer needs to hire someone who has a very specific set of skills. In recruiting lingo, such candidates are referred to as purple squirrels. Because squirrels in the real world are not often purple, the implication is that finding the perfect job candidate with exactly the right qualifications, education, and salary expectations can be a daunting–if not impossible–task. This course is designed to help close the skills gap as we build data driven, fact driven future business leaders.

section 1.2 | Business Strategy

LEARNING OUTCOMES

1.3 Explain why competitive advantages are temporary.

1.4 Identify the four key areas of a SWOT analysis.

1.5 Describe Porter's Five Forces Model and explain each of the five forces.

1.6 Compare Porter's three generic strategies.

1.7 Demonstrate how a company can add value by using Porter's value chain analysis.

IDENTIFYING COMPETITIVE ADVANTAGES

LO 1.3: Explain why competitive advantages are temporary.

Running a company today is similar to leading an army: The top manager or leader ensures all participants are heading in the right direction and are completing their goals and objectives. Companies lacking leadership quickly implode when employees head in different directions, attempting to achieve conflicting goals. To combat these challenges, leaders communicate and execute business strategies (from the Greek word *stratus* for army and *ago* for leading).

- ***Business strategy***: A leadership plan that achieves a specific set of goals or objectives such as increasing sales, decreasing costs, entering new markets, or developing new products or services.
- ***Stakeholder***: A person or group that has an interest or concern in an organization. Stakeholders drive business strategies, and depending on the stakeholder's perspective, the business strategy can change. It is not uncommon to find stakeholders' business strategies have conflicting interests such as investors looking to increase profits by eliminating employee jobs. Figure 1.20 displays the different stakeholders found in an organization and their common business interests.

Good leaders also anticipate unexpected misfortunes, from strikes and economic recessions to natural disasters. Their business strategies build in buffers or slack, allowing the company the ability to ride out any storm and defend against competitive or environmental threats. Of course, updating business strategies is a continuous undertaking as internal and external

FIGURE 1.20

Stakeholders' Interests

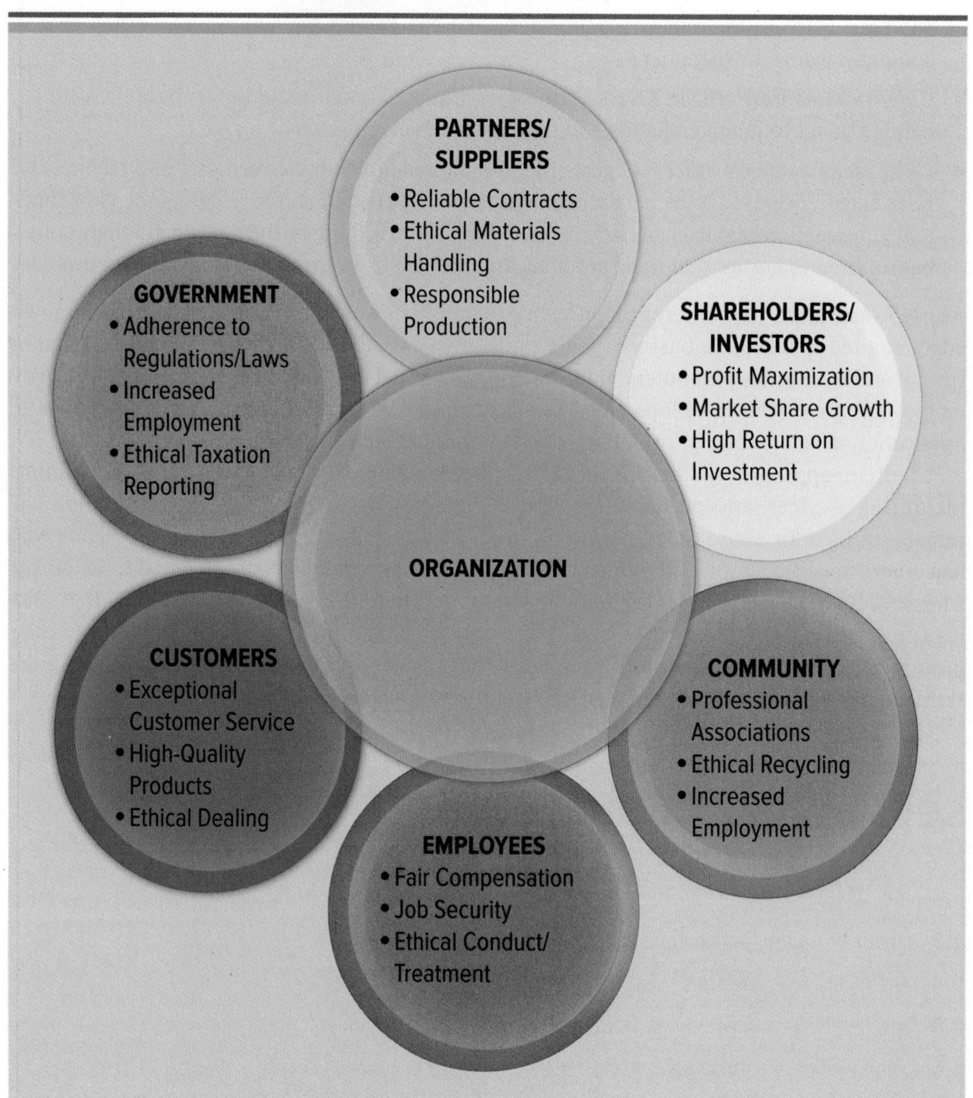

environments rapidly change. Business strategies that match core company competencies to opportunities result in competitive advantages, a key to success!

- ***Competitive advantage***: A feature of a product or service on which customers place a greater value than they do on similar offerings from competitors.

Competitive advantages provide the same product or service either at a lower price or with additional value that can fetch premium prices. Unfortunately, competitive advantages are typically temporary because competitors often quickly seek ways to duplicate them. In turn, organizations must develop a strategy based on a new competitive advantage. Ways that companies duplicate competitive advantages include acquiring the new technology, copying the business operations, and hiring away key employees. A historical example of the introduction of Apple's iPod along with iTunes offers a brilliant merger of technology, business, and entertainment.

- ***First-mover advantage***: Occurs when a company can significantly increase its market share by being first with a new competitive advantage.

FedEx created a first-mover advantage by developing its customer self-service software, which allows people to request parcel pickups, print mailing slips, and track parcels online. Other parcel delivery companies quickly began creating their own online services. Today, online customer self-service is a standard feature for all companies.

- ***Competitive intelligence***: The process of gathering information about the competitive environment, including competitors' plans, activities, and products, to improve a company's ability to succeed. It means understanding and learning as much as possible, as soon as possible, about what is occurring outside the company in order to remain competitive.

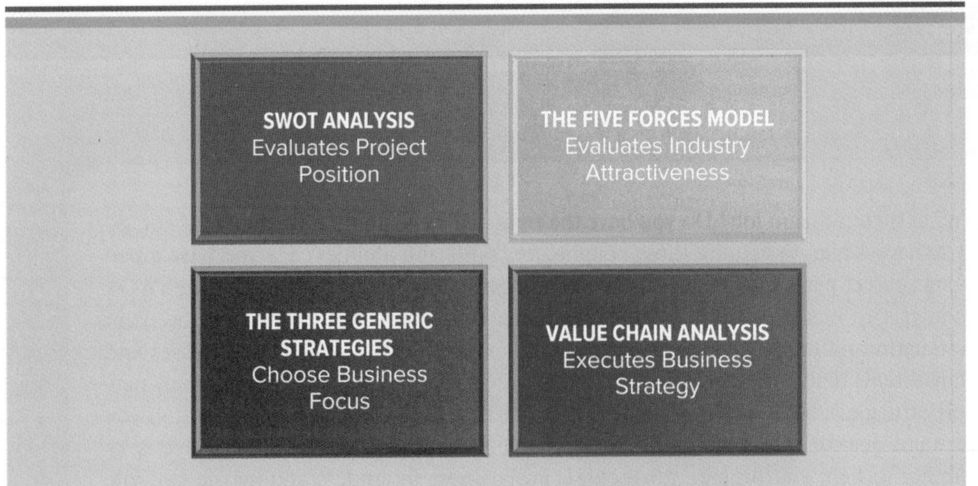

FIGURE 1.21

Business Tools for Analyzing Business Strategies

Frito-Lay, a premier provider of snack foods such as Cracker Jacks and Cheetos, does not send its sales representatives into grocery stores just to stock shelves. With IoT devices, they scan and record product offerings, inventory, and even the product locations of competitors. Frito-Lay uses this information to gain competitive intelligence on everything from how well-competing products are selling, to the strategic placement of its own products. Managers use four common tools to analyze competitive intelligence and develop competitive advantages, as displayed in Figure 1.21.

SWOT ANALYSIS: UNDERSTANDING BUSINESS STRATEGIES

LO 1.4: Identify the four key areas of a SWOT analysis.

Strengths and weaknesses originate inside an organization or internally. Opportunities and threats originate outside an organization or externally and cannot always be anticipated or controlled.

- ***SWOT analysis***: Evaluates an organization's strengths, **w**eaknesses, **o**pportunities, and **t**hreats to identify significant influences that work for or against business strategies (see Figure 1.22).
- **Potential internal strengths (helpful):** Identify all key strengths associated with the competitive advantage, including cost advantages, new and/or innovative services, special expertise and/or experience, proven market leader, improved marketing campaigns, and so on.
- **Potential internal weaknesses (harmful):** Identify all key areas that require improvement. Weaknesses focus on the absence of certain strengths, including absence of an Internet marketing plan, damaged reputation, problem areas for service, outdated technology, employee issues, and so on.

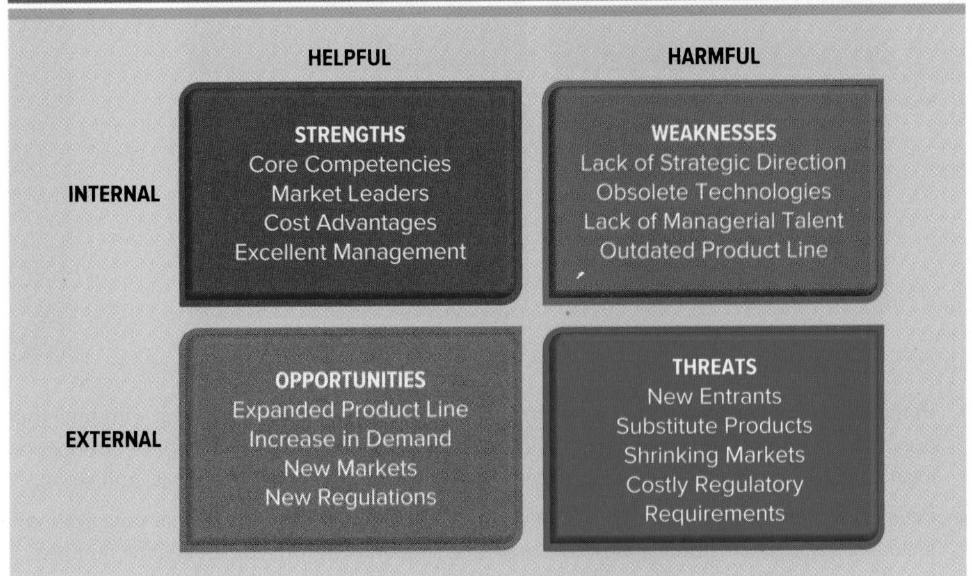

FIGURE 1.22

Sample SWOT Analysis

APPLY YOUR KNOWLEDGE

BUSINESS DRIVEN INNOVATION

SWOT Yourself

What is your dream job? Do you have the right skills and abilities to land it? If not, do you have a plan to acquire those sought-after skills and abilities? Do you have a personal career plan or strategy? Just like a business, you can perform a personal SWOT analysis to ensure your career plan will be successful. You want to know your strengths and recognize career opportunities while mitigating your weaknesses and any threats that can potentially derail your career plans. A key area where many people struggle is technology, and without the right technical skills, you might find you are not qualified for your dream job. One of the great benefits of this course is its ability to help you prepare for a career in business by understanding the key role technology plays in the different industries and functional areas. Regardless of your major, you will all use business driven information systems to complete the tasks and assignments associated with your career.[5]

Perform a personal SWOT analysis for your career plan, based on your current skills, talents, and knowledge. Be sure to focus on your personal career goals, including the functional business area in which you want to work and the potential industry you are targeting, such as health care, telecommunications, retail, or travel.

After completing your personal SWOT analysis, take a look at the table of contents in this text and determine whether this course will eliminate any of your weaknesses or create new strengths. Determine whether you can find new opportunities or mitigate threats based on the material we cover over the next several weeks. For example, Chapter 9 covers project management in detail–a key skill for any business professional who must run a team. Learning how to assign and track work status will be a key tool for any new business professional. Where would you place this great skill in your SWOT analysis? Did it help eliminate any of your weaknesses? When you have finished this exercise, compare your SWOT with your peers to see what kind of competition you will encounter when you enter the workforce.

PERSONAL CAREER SWOT ANALYSIS

- **Potential external opportunities (helpful):** Identify all significant trends, along with how the organization can benefit from each, including new markets, additional customer groups, legal changes, innovative technologies, population changes, competitor issues, and so on.
- **Potential external threats (harmful):** Identify all threats or risks detrimental to your organization, including new market entrants, substitute products, employee turnover, differentiating products, shrinking markets, adverse changes in regulations, economic shifts, and so on.[6]

THE FIVE FORCES MODEL—EVALUATING INDUSTRY ATTRACTIVENESS

LO 1.5: Describe Porter's Five Forces Model and explain each of the five forces.

Michael Porter, a university professor at Harvard Business School, identified the following pressures that can hurt potential sales:

- Knowledgeable customers can force down prices by pitting rivals against each other.
- Influential suppliers can drive down profits by charging higher prices for supplies.
- Competition can steal customers.
- New market entrants can steal potential investment capital.
- Substitute products can steal customers.

Formally defined, ***Porter's Five Forces Model*** analyzes the competitive forces within the environment in which a company operates to assess the potential for profitability in an industry. Its purpose is to combat these competitive forces by identifying opportunities, competitive advantages, and competitive intelligence. If the forces are strong, they increase competition; if the forces are weak, they decrease competition. This section details each of the forces and its associated MIS business strategy (see Figure 1.23).[7]

Buyer Power

Factors used to assess buyer power include number of customers, their sensitivity to price, size of orders, differences between competitors, and availability of substitute products. If buyer power is high, customers can force a company and its competitors to compete on price, which typically drives down prices.

- ***Buyer power***: The ability of buyers to affect the price they must pay for an item.
- ***Switching costs***: Costs that make customers reluctant to switch to another product or service.

Switching costs include financial as well as intangible values. The cost of switching doctors, for instance, includes the powerful intangible components of having to build relationships with the new doctor and nurses, as well as transferring all your medical history. With MIS, however, patients can store their medical records in the cloud or on a thumb drive, allowing easy transferability. Patients can also review websites for physician referrals, which takes some of the fear out of trying someone new.

- ***Loyalty program***: Rewards customers based on their spending.

FIGURE 1.23

Porter's Five Forces Model

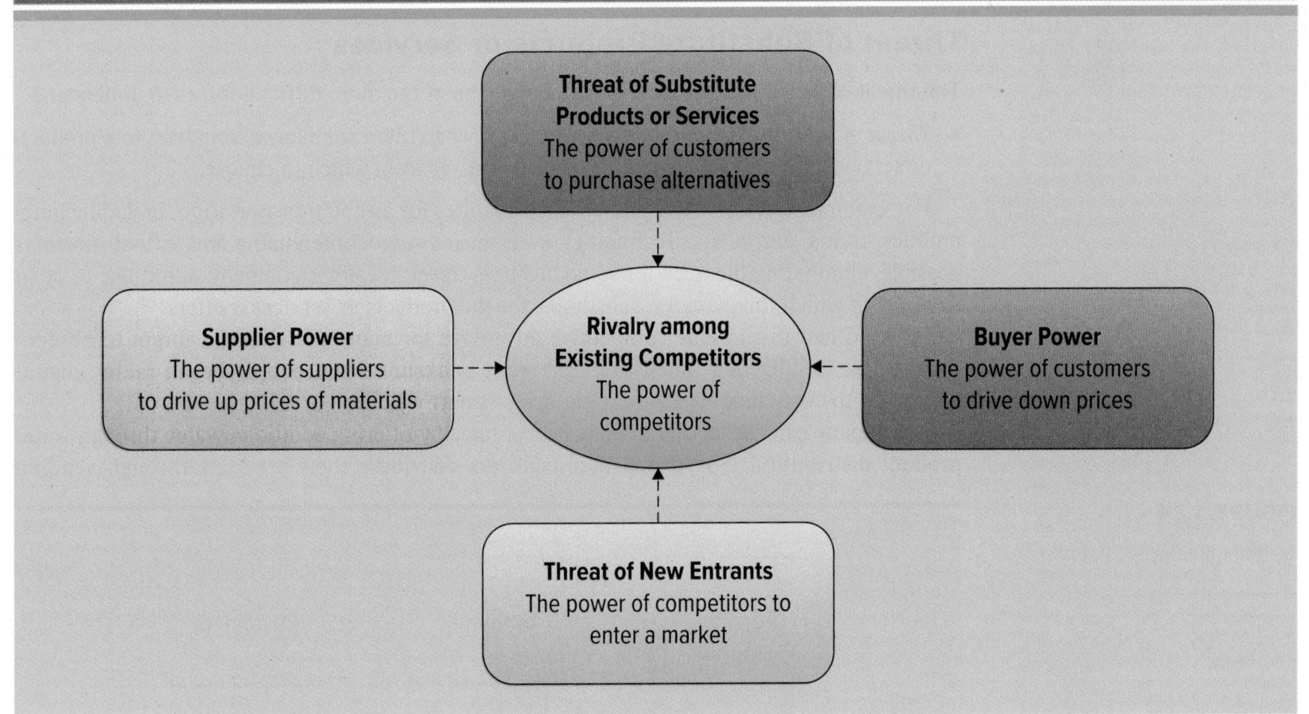

The airline industry is famous for its frequent-flyer programs, for instance. Because of the rewards travelers receive (free airline tickets, upgrades, or hotel stays), they are more likely to be loyal to or give most of their business to a single company. Keeping track of the activities and accounts of many thousands or millions of customers covered by loyalty programs is not practical without large-scale information systems, however. Loyalty programs are thus a good example of using MIS to reduce buyer power.[8]

Supplier Power

In a typical supply chain, a company will be both a supplier (to customers) and a customer (of other suppliers), as illustrated in Figure 1.24.

- ***Supply chain***: Consists of all parties involved, directly or indirectly, in obtaining raw materials or a product.
- ***Supplier power***: The suppliers' ability to influence the prices they charge for supplies (including materials, labor, and services).

Factors used to appraise supplier power include number of suppliers, size of suppliers, uniqueness of services, and availability of substitute products. If supplier power is high, the supplier can influence the industry by:

- Charging higher prices.
- Limiting quality or services.
- Shifting costs to industry participants.

Typically, when a supplier raises prices, the buyers will pass on the increase to their customers by raising prices on the end product. When supplier power is high, buyers lose revenue because they cannot pass on the raw material price increase to their customers. Some powerful suppliers, such as pharmaceutical companies, can exert a threat over an entire industry when substitutes are limited and the product is critical to the buyers. Patients who need to purchase cancer-fighting drugs have no power over price and must pay whatever the drug company asks because there are few available alternatives.

Using MIS to find alternative products is one way of decreasing supplier power. Cancer patients can now use the Internet to research alternative medications and practices, something that was next to impossible just a few decades ago. Buyers can also use MIS to form groups or collaborate with other buyers, increasing the size of the buyer group and reducing supplier power. For a hypothetical example, the collective group of 30,000 students from a university has far more power over price when purchasing laptops than a single student.

Threat of Substitute Products or Services

The threat of substitute products or services is one of the more difficult forces to understand.

- ***Threat of substitute products or services***: High when there are many alternatives to a product or service and low when there are few alternatives from which to choose.

For example, travelers have numerous substitutes for airline transportation, including automobiles, trains, and boats. Technology even makes videoconferencing and virtual meetings possible, eliminating the need for some business travel. Ideally, a company would like to be in a market in which there are few substitutes for the products or services it offers.

Polaroid had this unique competitive advantage for many years until it forgot to observe competitive intelligence. Then the firm went bankrupt when people began taking digital pictures with everything from smart phones to smart watches.

A company can reduce the threat of substitutes by offering additional value through wider product distribution. Soft-drink manufacturers distribute their products through vending

FIGURE 1.24

Traditional Supply Chain

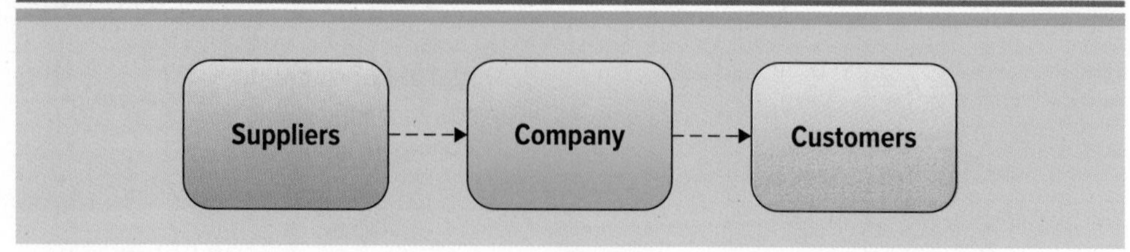

machines, gas stations, and convenience stores, increasing the availability of soft drinks relative to other beverages. Companies can also offer various add-on services, making the substitute product less of a threat. For example, iPhones include capabilities for games, applications, movies, and music, making other traditional technologies obsolete and less of a substitute.[9]

Threat of New Entrants

Another force includes the threat of new entrants, and companies create entry barriers to ensure they keep this threat low.

- ***Threat of new entrants***: High when it is easy for new competitors to enter a market and low when there are significant entry barriers to joining a market.
- ***Entry barrier***: A feature of a product or service that customers have come to expect; entering competitors must offer the same for survival.

For example, a new bank must offer its customers an array of MIS-enabled services, including ATMs, online bill paying, and online account monitoring. These are significant barriers to new firms entering the banking market. At one time, the first bank to offer such services gained a valuable first-mover advantage, but only temporarily, as other banking competitors developed their own MIS services.[10]

Rivalry among Existing Competitors

Competition is one of the main threats businesses must watch for and combat.

- ***Rivalry among existing competitors***: High when competition is fierce in a market, and low when competitors are more complacent.

Although competition is always more intense in some industries than in others, the overall trend is toward increased competition in almost every industry. The retail grocery industry is intensely competitive. Kroger, Safeway, and Albertsons in the United States compete in many ways, essentially trying to beat or match each other on price. Most supermarket chains have implemented loyalty programs to give customers special discounts while gathering valuable information about their purchasing habits. In the future, expect to see grocery stores using wireless technologies that track customer movements throughout the store to determine purchasing sequences.

- ***Product differentiation***: Occurs when a company develops unique differences in its products or services with the intent to influence demand.

Companies can use differentiation to reduce rivalry. For example, although many companies sell books and videos on the Internet, Amazon differentiates itself by using customer profiling. When a customer visits Amazon.com repeatedly, Amazon begins to offer products tailored to that particular customer based on his or her profile. In this way, Amazon has reduced its rivals' power by offering its customers a differentiated service.

To review, the Five Forces Model helps managers set business strategy by identifying the competitive structure and economic environment of an industry. If the forces are strong, they increase competition; if the forces are weak, they decrease it (see Figure 1.25).[11]

Analyzing the Airline Industry

Let us bring Porter's five forces together to look at the competitive forces shaping an industry and highlight business strategies to help it remain competitive. Assume a shipping company is

FIGURE 1.25

Strong and Weak Examples of Porter's Five Forces

	Weak Force: Decreases Competition or Few Competitors	Strong Force: Increases Competition or Lots of Competitors
Buyer Power	An international hotel chain purchasing milk	A single consumer purchasing milk
Supplier Power	A company that makes airline engines	A company that makes pencils
Threat of Substitute Products or Services	Cancer drugs from a pharmaceutical company	Coffee from McDonald's
Threat of New Entrants	A professional hockey team	A dog-walking business
Rivalry among Existing Competitors	Department of Motor Vehicles	A coffee shop

APPLY YOUR KNOWLEDGE

BUSINESS DRIVEN GLOBALIZATION

Global Data

One of the key requirements for solid data analysis is to always understand the data in its original form. Look at the following data and identify the errors. (Hint: Think globally.)

Customer	Date	Time	Amount
Hans Hultgren	01/15/2026	8:07	35,000
Remco Breokerman	01/16/2026	16:21	147,258
Dirk Laberman	02/04/2026	17:24	1,254,458
Lars Lager	02/09/2026	1:15	120
Patrick Romstaed	03/02/2026	14:14	3,357,458

FIGURE 1.26

Five Forces Model in the Airline Industry

	Strong (High) Force: Increases Competition or Lots of Competitors
Buyer Power	Many airlines for buyers to choose from, forcing competition based on price.
Supplier Power	Limited number of plane and engine manufacturers to choose from, along with unionized workers.
Threat of Substitute Products or Services	Many substitutes, including cars, trains, and buses. Even substitutes to travel, such as videoconferencing and virtual meetings.
Threat of New Entrants	Many new airlines entering the market all the time, including the latest sky taxis.
Rivalry among Existing Competitors	Intense competition–many rivals.

deciding whether to enter the commercial airline industry. If performed correctly, an analysis of the five forces should determine that this is a highly risky business strategy because all five forces are strong. It will thus be difficult to generate a profit.

- **Buyer power:** Buyer power is high because customers have many airlines to choose from and typically make purchases based on price, not carrier.
- **Supplier power:** Supplier power is high because there are limited plane and engine manufacturers to choose from, and unionized workforces (suppliers of labor) restrict airline profits.
- **Threat of substitute products or services:** The threat of substitute products is high from many transportation alternatives, including automobiles, trains, and boats, and from transportation substitutes such as videoconferencing and virtual meetings.
- **Threat of new entrants:** The threat of new entrants is high because new airlines are continually entering the market, including sky taxies offering low-cost, on-demand air taxi service.
- **Rivalry among existing competitors:** Rivalry in the airline industry is high, and websites such as Travelocity.com force them to compete on price (see Figure 1.26).[12]

LO 1.6: Compare Porter's three generic strategies.

THE THREE GENERIC STRATEGIES—CHOOSING A BUSINESS FOCUS

Once top management has determined the relative attractiveness of an industry and decided to enter it, the firm must formulate a strategy for doing so. If our sample company decided to join the airline industry, it could compete as a low-cost, no-frills airline or as a luxury airline

Cost Strategy

Low Cost | High Cost

Competitive Scope

Broad Market: Cost Leadership | Differentiation

Narrow Market: Focused Strategy

FIGURE 1.27

Porter's Three Generic Strategies

providing outstanding service and first-class comfort. Both options offer different ways of achieving competitive advantages in a crowded marketplace. The low-cost operator saves on expenses and passes the savings along to customers in the form of low prices. The luxury airline spends on high-end service and first-class comforts and passes the costs on to the customer in the form of high prices.

- ***Porter's three generic strategies***: Generic business strategies that are neither organization nor industry specific and can be applied to any business, product, or service.

These three generic business strategies for entering a new market are: (1) broad cost leadership, (2) broad differentiation, and (3) focused strategy. Broad strategies reach a large market segment, whereas focused strategies target a niche or unique market with either cost leadership or differentiation. Trying to be all things to all people is a recipe for disaster because doing so makes projecting a consistent image to the entire marketplace difficult. For this reason, Porter suggests adopting only one of the three generic strategies illustrated in Figure 1.27.[13]

Figure 1.28 applies the three strategies to real companies, demonstrating the relationships among strategies (cost leadership versus differentiation) and market segmentation (broad versus focused).

- **Broad market and low cost:** Walmart competes by offering a broad range of products at low prices. Its business strategy is to be the low-cost provider of goods for the cost-conscious consumer.
- **Broad market and high cost:** Neiman Marcus competes by offering a broad range of differentiated products at high prices. Its business strategy is to offer a variety of specialty and upscale products to affluent consumers.

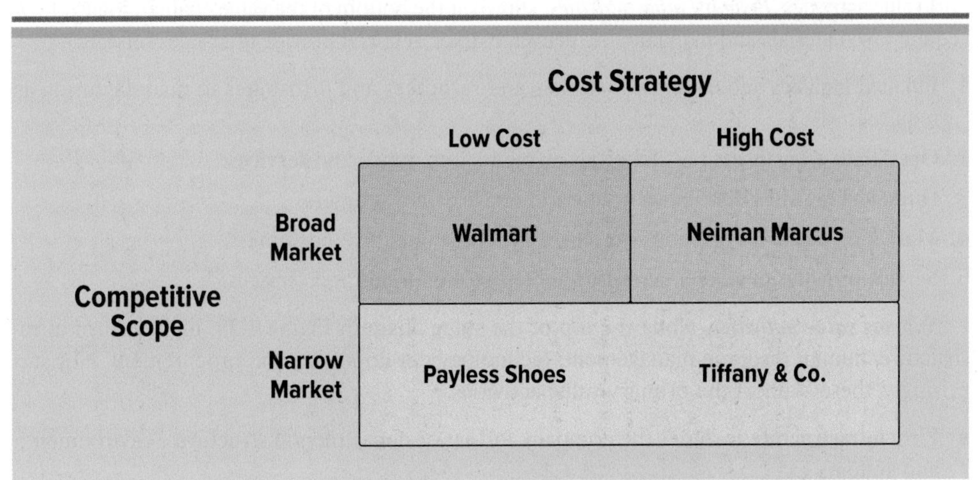

Cost Strategy
Low Cost
High Cost
Broad Market
Walmart
Neiman Marcus
Competitive Scope
Narrow Market
Payless Shoes
Tiffany & Co.

FIGURE 1.28

Examples of Porter's Three Generic Strategies

APPLY YOUR KNOWLEDGE

BUSINESS DRIVEN DEBATE

Is Technology Making Us Dumber or Smarter?

Choose a side and debate the following:

- **Side A:** Living in the information age has made us smarter because we have a huge wealth of knowledge at our fingertips whenever or wherever we need it.
- **Side B:** Living in the information age has caused people to become lazy and dumber because they are no longer building up their memory banks to solve problems; machines give them the answers they need to solve problems.

- **Narrow market and low cost:** Payless competes by offering a specific product, shoes, at low prices. Its business strategy is to be the low-cost provider of shoes. Payless competes with Walmart, which also sells low-cost shoes, by offering a far bigger selection of sizes and styles.
- **Narrow market and high cost:** Tiffany & Co. competes by offering a differentiated product, jewelry, at high prices. Its business strategy allows it to be a high-cost provider of premier designer jewelry to affluent consumers.

LO 1.7: Demonstrate how a company can add value by using Porter's value chain analysis.

VALUE CHAIN ANALYSIS—EXECUTING BUSINESS STRATEGIES

Firms make profits by applying a business process to raw inputs to turn them into a product or service that customers find valuable.

- ***Business process*:** A standardized set of activities that accomplish a specific task, such as processing a customer's order.

Once a firm identifies the industry it wants to enter and the generic strategy it will focus on, it must then choose the business processes required to create its products or services. Of course, the firm will want to ensure the processes add value and create competitive advantages. To identify these competitive advantages, Michael Porter created a value chain analysis.

- ***Value chain analysis*:** Views a firm as a series of business processes, each of which adds value to the product or service.

Value chain analysis is a useful tool for determining how to create the greatest possible value for customers (see Figure 1.29). The goal of value chain analysis is to identify processes in which the firm can add value for the customer and create a competitive advantage for itself, with a cost advantage or product differentiation.

The *value chain* groups a firm's activities into two categories, primary value activities and support value activities. ***Primary value activities,*** shown at the bottom of the value chain in Figure 1.29, acquire raw materials and manufacture, deliver, market, sell, and provide after-sales services.

1. **Inbound logistics** acquires raw materials and resources and distributes to manufacturing as required.
2. **Operations** transforms raw materials or inputs into goods and services.
3. **Outbound logistics** distributes goods and services to customers.
4. **Marketing and sales** promotes, prices, and sells products to customers.
5. **Service** provides customer support after the sale of goods and services.[14]

Support value activities, along the top of the value chain in Figure 1.29, include firm infrastructure, human resource management, technology development, and procurement. Not surprisingly, these support the primary value activities.

- **Firm infrastructure** includes the company format or departmental structures, environment, and systems.

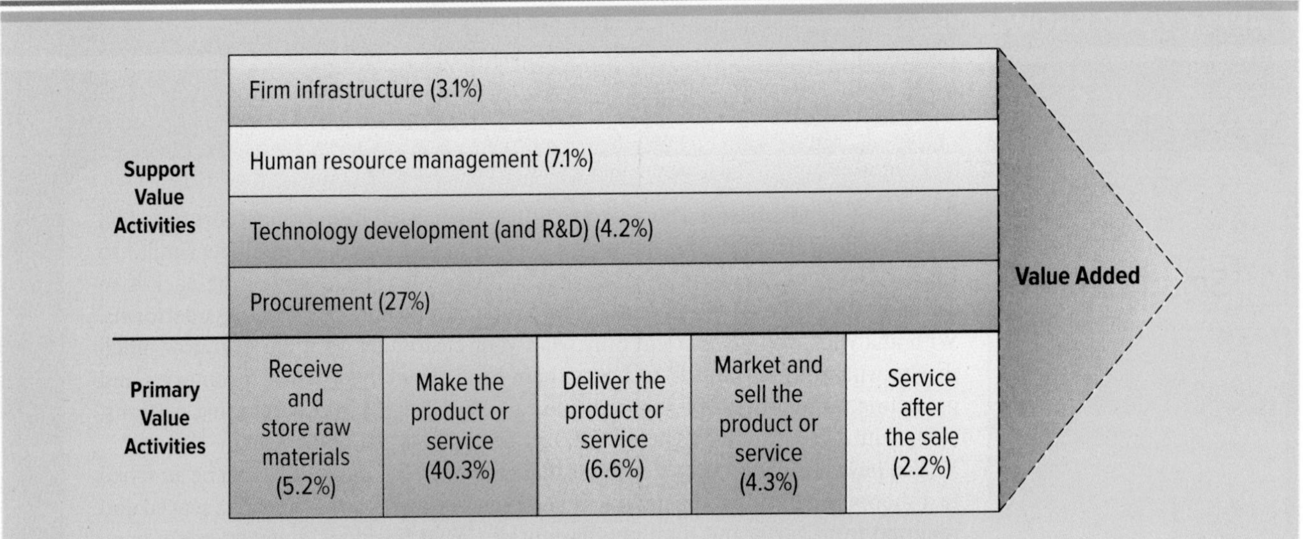

FIGURE 1.29

The Value Chain

- **Human resource management** provides employee training, hiring, and compensation.
- **Technology development** applies MIS to processes to add value.
- **Procurement** purchases inputs such as raw materials, resources, equipment, and supplies.

It is easy to understand how a typical manufacturing firm transforms raw materials such as wood pulp into paper. Adding value in this example might include using high-quality raw materials or offering next-day free shipping on any order. How, though, might a typical service firm transform raw inputs such as time, knowledge, and MIS into valuable customer service knowledge? A hotel might use MIS to track customer reservations and then inform front-desk employees when a loyal customer is checking in so the employee can call the guest by name and offer additional services, gift baskets, or upgraded rooms. Examining the firm as a value chain allows managers to identify the important business processes that add value for customers and then find MIS solutions that support them.

- ***Digital value chain***: Digitizes work across primary and supporting activities.

A digital value chain allows primary activities to connect digitally to help speed up the transition from sales to manufacturing. Advances in production equipment used in robotics and 3D printing speed up production to smart finished products (such as connected cars and IoT devices).

When performing a value chain analysis, a firm could survey customers about the extent to which they believe each activity adds value to the product or service. This step generates responses the firm can measure, shown as percentages in Figure 1.30, to describe how each activity adds (or reduces) value. Then the competitive advantage decision for the firm is whether to (1) target high value-adding activities to enhance their value further, (2) target low value-adding activities to increase their value, or (3) perform some combination of the two.

MIS adds value to both primary and support value activities. One example of a primary value activity MIS facilitates is the development of a marketing campaign management system that could target marketing campaigns more efficiently, thereby reducing marketing costs. The system would also help the firm pinpoint target market needs better, thereby increasing sales. One example of a support value activity MIS facilitates is the development of a human resources system that could more efficiently reward employees based on performance. The system could also identify employees who are at risk of quitting, allowing managers time to find additional challenges or opportunities that would help retain these employees and thus reduce turnover costs.

Value chain analysis is a highly useful tool that provides hard and fast numbers for evaluating the activities that add value to products and services. Managers can find additional value by analyzing and constructing the value chain in terms of Porter's Five Forces Model (see Figure 1.30). For example, if the goal is to decrease buyer power, a company can construct its value chain activity of "service after the sale" by offering high levels of customer service. This will increase customers' switching costs and reduce their power. Analyzing and constructing support value activities can help decrease the threat of new entrants. Analyzing and constructing primary value activities can help decrease the threat of substitute products or services.[15]

APPLY YOUR KNOWLEDGE

BUSINESS DRIVEN START-UP

Smart Carting

It is almost impossible for a company to differentiate itself from competitors based on products alone. Competitors are only a click away and can offer products similar to yours with better quality or cheaper prices. One way to stay ahead of the pack is to use sophisticated analysis to understand every area of how your business performs. With analytics, you discern not only what your customers want but also how much they're willing to pay and what keeps them loyal. Tracking existing inventories and predicting future inventory requirements can offer insights into purchasing patterns, along with significant cost savings that can be added to the bottom line.

You have decided to start a business that creates an IoT device that can be attached to a shopping cart or basket and tracks store navigation patterns, products placed and removed from carts, and total purchase price. What business strategies can a company such as Target gain from using your IoT device? What types of information can be gleaned by analyzing traffic patterns in the store? What business intelligence can be found by analyzing products placed and removed from carts? Do you think there will be a correlation between time and the amount of the total purchase? How can you use this information to help improve business operations? If you owned a store, would you consider purchasing this great new IoT device?

Revising Porter's three business strategies is critical. Firms must continually adapt to their competitive environments, which can cause business strategy to shift. In the remainder of this text, we discuss how managers can formulate business strategies using MIS to create competitive advantages. Figure 1.31 gives an overview of the remaining chapters, along with the relevant business strategy and associated MIS topics.

FIGURE 1.30

The Value Chain and Porter's Five Forces Model

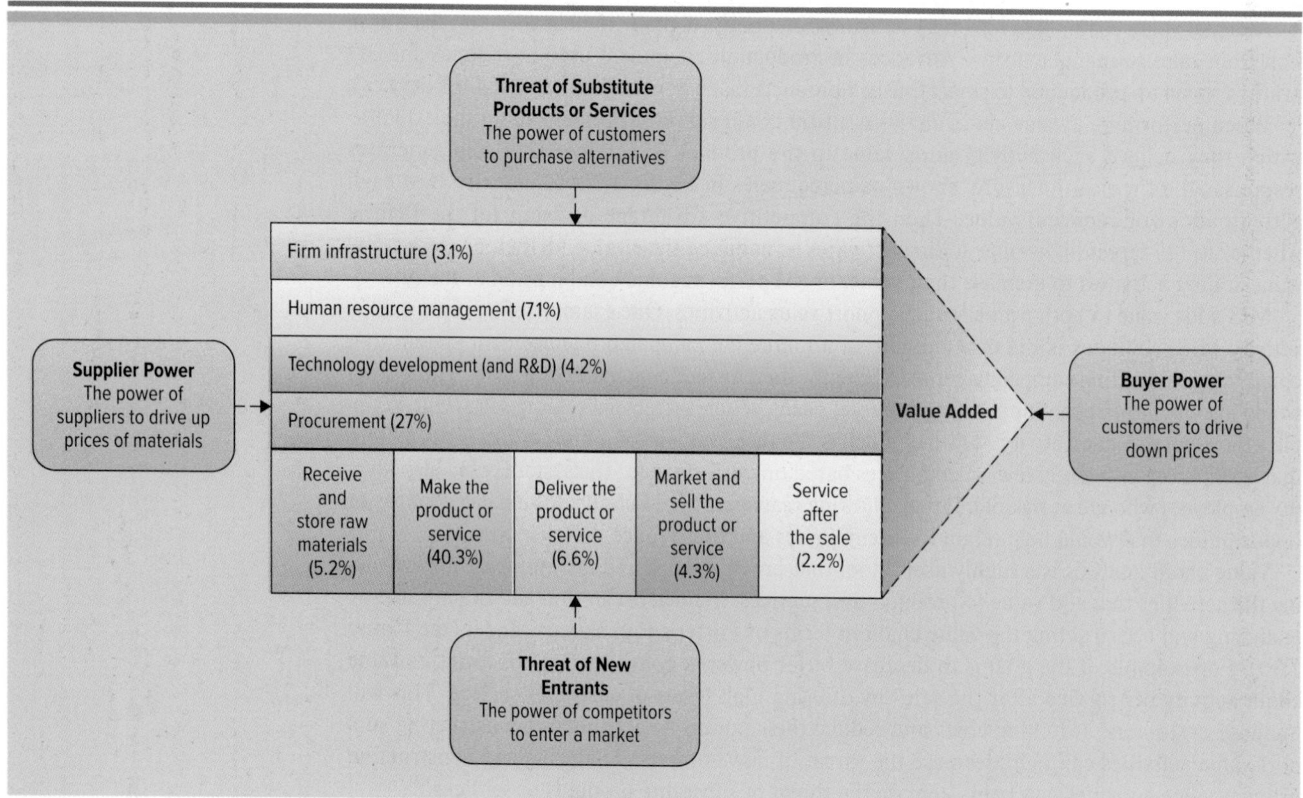

FIGURE 1.31

Overview of *Business Driven Information Systems*

MODULE 1: BUSINESS DRIVEN MIS

	Business Strategy	MIS Topics
Chapter 1: Management Information Systems	Understanding Business Driven MIS	Data Information Business Intelligence Knowledge Systems Thinking Porter's Business Strategies
Chapter 2: Decisions and Processes	Creating Value Driven Businesses	Transaction Processing Systems Decision Support Systems Executive Information Systems Artificial Intelligence Business Process Reengineering
Chapter 3: Ebusiness	Finding Electronic Business Value	eBusiness eBusiness Models Social Networking Knowledge Management Collaboration
Chapter 4: Ethics and Information Security	Identifying MIS Business Concerns	Information Security Policies Authentication and Authorization Prevention and Resistance Detection and Response

MODULE 2: TECHNICAL FOUNDATIONS OF MIS

	Business Strategy	MIS Topics
Chapter 5: Infrastructures	Deploying Organizational MIS	Grid Computing Cloud Computing Virtualization Sustainable MIS Infrastructures
Chapter 6: Data	Uncovering Business Intelligence	Database Data Management Systems Data Warehousing Data Mining
Chapter 7: Networks	Supporting Mobile Business	Business Networks Web 1.0, Web 2.0, Web 3.0 Mobile MIS Wireless MIS GPS, GIS, and LBS

MODULE 3: ENTERPRISE MIS

	Business Strategy	MIS Topics
Chapter 8: Enterprise Applications	Enhancing Business Communications	Customer Relationship Management Supply Chain Management Enterprise Resource Planning
Chapter 9: Systems Development and Project Management	Leading MIS Projects	MIS Development Methodologies Project Management Outsourcing

LEARNING OUTCOME REVIEW

Learning Outcome 1.1: Describe the information age and the differences among data, information, business intelligence, and knowledge.

We live in the information age, when infinite quantities of facts are widely available to anyone who can use a computer. The core drivers of the information age include data, information, business intelligence, and knowledge. Data are raw facts that describe the characteristics of an event or object. Information is data converted into a meaningful and useful context. Business intelligence (BI) is information collected from multiple sources such as suppliers, customers, competitors, partners, and industries that analyzes patterns, trends, and relationships for strategic decision making. Knowledge includes the skills, experience, and expertise, coupled with information and intelligence, that creates a person's intellectual resources. As you move from data to knowledge, you include more and more variables for analysis, resulting in better, more precise support for decision making and problem solving.

Learning Outcome 1.2: Explain systems thinking and how management information systems enable business communications.

A system is a collection of parts that link to achieve a common purpose. Systems thinking is a way of monitoring the entire system by viewing multiple inputs being processed or transformed to produce outputs while continuously gathering feedback on each part. Feedback is information that returns to its original transmitter (input, transform, or output) and modifies the transmitter's actions. Feedback helps the system maintain stability. Management information systems (MIS) is a business function, like accounting and human resources, which moves information about people, products, and processes across the company to facilitate decision making and problem solving. MIS incorporates systems thinking to help companies operate cross-functionally. For example, to fulfill product orders, an MIS for sales moves a single customer order across all functional areas, including sales, order fulfillment, shipping, billing, and finally customer service. Although different functional areas handle different parts of the sale, thanks to MIS, to the customer the sale is one continuous process.

Learning Outcome 1.3: Explain why competitive advantages are temporary.

A competitive advantage is a feature of a product or service on which customers place a greater value than they do on similar offerings from competitors. Competitive advantages provide the same product or service either at a lower price or with additional value that can fetch premium prices. Unfortunately, competitive advantages are typically temporary because competitors often quickly seek ways to duplicate them. In turn, organizations must develop a strategy based on a new competitive advantage. Ways that companies duplicate competitive advantages include acquiring the new technology, copying business processes, and hiring away employees.

Learning Outcome 1.4: Identify the four key areas of a SWOT analysis.

A SWOT analysis evaluates an organization's **s**trengths, **w**eaknesses, **o**pportunities, and **t**hreats to identify significant influences that work for or against business strategies. Strengths and weaknesses originate inside an organization, or internally. Opportunities and threats originate outside an organization, or externally, and cannot always be anticipated or controlled.

Learning Outcome 1.5: Describe Porter's Five Forces Model and explain each of the five forces.

Porter's Five Forces Model analyzes the competitive forces within the environment in which a company operates, to assess the potential for profitability in an industry.

- Buyer power is the ability of buyers to affect the price they must pay for an item.
- Supplier power is the suppliers' ability to influence the prices they charge for supplies (including materials, labor, and services).

- Threat of substitute products or services is high when there are many alternatives to a product or service, and low when there are few alternatives from which to choose.
- Threat of new entrants is high when it is easy for new competitors to enter a market, and low when there are significant entry barriers to entering a market.
- Rivalry among existing competitors is high when competition is fierce in a market, and low when competition is more complacent.

Learning Outcome 1.6: Compare Porter's three generic strategies.

Organizations typically follow one of Porter's three generic strategies when entering a new market: (1) broad cost leadership, (2) broad differentiation, and (3) focused strategy. Broad strategies reach a large market segment. Focused strategies target a niche market. Focused strategies concentrate on either cost leadership or differentiation.

Learning Outcome 1.7: Demonstrate how a company can add value by using Porter's value chain analysis.

To identify competitive advantages, Michael Porter created value chain analysis, which views a firm as a series of business processes, each of which adds value to the product or service. The goal of value chain analysis is to identify processes in which the firm can add value for the customer and create a competitive advantage for itself, with a cost advantage or product differentiation. The value chain groups a firm's activities into two categories—primary value activities and support value activities. Primary value activities acquire raw materials and manufacture, deliver, market, sell, and provide after-sales services. Support value activities, along the top of the value chain in the figure, include firm infrastructure, human resource management, technology development, and procurement. Not surprisingly, these support the primary value activities.

KEY TERMS

System 19
Systems thinking 20
Threat of new entrants 31
Threat of substitute products or services 30
Unstructured data 9
Value chain analysis 34
Value-added 22
Variable 11

REVIEW QUESTIONS

1. What is data and why is it important to a business?
2. How can a manager turn data into information?
3. What are the relationships among data, information, business intelligence, and knowledge?
4. Why is it important for a company to operate cross-functionally?
5. Why would a company want to have a CIO, CPO, and CSO?
6. Explain MIS and the role it plays in a company and global business.
7. Do you agree that MIS is essential for businesses operating in the information age? Why or why not?
8. Why is it important for a business major to understand MIS?
9. What type of career are you planning to pursue? How will your specific career use data, information, business intelligence, and knowledge?
10. Explain systems thinking and how it supports business operations.
11. What business strategies would you use if you were developing a competitive advantage for a company?
12. Explain Porter's Five Forces Model and the role it plays in decision making.
13. How could a company use loyalty programs to influence buyer power? How could a company use switching costs to lock in customers and suppliers?
14. What are Porter's three generic strategies, and why would a company want to follow only one?
15. How can a company use Porter's value chain analysis to measure customer satisfaction?

CLOSING CASE ONE

The Fourth Industrial Revolution

The fourth industrial revolution is here and will exponentially change how we live, work, and interact. It is disrupting almost every industry globally and creating massive change at unprecedented speeds. Professor Klaus Schwab, founder and executive chair of the World Economic Forum's latest book, *The Fourth Industrial Revolution,* describes a world where physical, digital, and biological spheres merge. This revolution refers to how new technologies such as artificial intelligence, autonomous vehicles, voice recognition, and the Internet of Things are blending our digital and physical worlds. Expect to see changes in the ways individuals, businesses, and governments operate, ultimately leading to transformations similar to what we witnessed in the first three industrial revolutions. Let's take a quick look at the first three industrial revolutions before we jump into the fourth.

- **The First Industrial Revolution (1760–1860):** Began in Britain with the invention of the steam engine, allowing businesses to fully harness the power of steam. This led to the creation of factories and dramatically improved manufacturing processes.

- **The Second Industrial Revolution (1860–1960):** Mass production in the steel, oil, and electricity industries drove the invention of the light bulb, telephone, and internal combustion engine.
- **The Third Industrial Revolution (1960–2006):** The beginning of the digital era saw the invention of the semiconductor chip, the Internet, and the personal computer. It is also referred to as the "Digital Revolution."
- **The Fourth Industrial Revolution (2006–present):** Represents the blending of the digital, physical, and biological worlds with rates of change that are at hypervelocities.

The fourth industrial revolution is expected to make the first three look like child's play, impacting every single discipline, industry, and economy. In this revolution, we will design and engineer the world around us by manipulating the very atoms and molecules that construct our reality. Atoms and molecules are the "digital" code of the real world, and we are just learning how to hack this code and change reality. Gene editing, nanotechnology, and synthetic biology will reprogram DNA, build human robots and space crafts, and even change the food we consume. The fourth industrial revolution offers a giant leap forward in productivity, generating numerous opportunities. Among the simplest is faster acceleration: Changes happen more quickly and organizations can do more things in less time. Just think, it took 75 years for 100 million users to adopt the telephone, 2 years to generate 100 million Instagram users, and one month to create 100 million Pokémon Go users. Clearly, the rate of technology adoption is occurring faster than ever before in history.

Obviously this era is filled with exciting opportunities as we cure diseases and monitor everything in real time, but it also creates a number of frightening scenarios if the revolution is not managed correctly. Just think of *The Matrix* or *The Terminator* movies! Therefore, it is critical to be proactive in shaping the technologies driving this massive disruption. This requires global cooperation and a shared view of how technology is reshaping our economic, social, cultural, and individual lives. Companies should begin by investing in their technical infrastructures and data analysis capabilities. All businesses should position themselves to be smart, connected organizations; otherwise, they will soon fall behind the competition.[16]

Questions

1. Explain how the fourth industrial revolution will impact your career.
2. Explain why it is important for business managers to understand that data analysis is the future for any industry or functional area.
3. Demonstrate how data can be transformed into information and business intelligence.
4. Propose a plan for how a start-up company can use data to make better business decisions and find success.

CLOSING CASE TWO

The Internet of Things

Over 20 years ago, a few professors at MIT began describing the Internet of Things (IoT), which is a world where interconnected Internet-enabled devices or "things" have the ability to collect and share data without human intervention. Another term for the Internet of Things is *machine-to-machine (M2M)*, which allows devices to connect directly to other devices. With advanced technologies, devices are connecting in ways not previously thought possible, and the current estimate indicates that over 50 billion IoT devices are communicating.

Imagine your toothbrush telling you to visit your dentist because it senses a cavity. How would you react if your refrigerator placed an order at your local grocery store because your milk and eggs had expired? Predictions indicate that over the next decade, almost every device you own—and almost every object imaginable—will be connected to the Internet as people share, store, and manage their lives online. Smoke detectors, alarms, refrigerators, stoves, and windows are just a few home devices already connected to the Internet, sharing information on how to make everything in your life more efficient, effective, safe, and healthy. The Internet of Things is reaching further into our daily lives by combining data from sensors in wearable devices and equipment with analytic programs to help improve the performance of individuals by gaining insights that were traditionally impossible to detect. A few examples of the incredible power of the IoT era include:

- **Smart yoga mats:** Smart yoga mats include sensors that provide feedback on yoga postures and calories burned, and can even provide users with guided practice in the comfort of their own home.
- **Smart thermostats:** IoTs share information in real time to help homeowners manage energy use more efficiently. The system will notify the homeowner if a door is left open, change the temperature in each room when it is occupied, and turn the thermostat up or down, depending on the weather and homeowner preferences.
- **Smart diapers:** Pixie Scientific created disposable diapers with sensors that monitor babies' urine for signs of infection, dehydration, or kidney problems before symptoms appear.
- **Smart trash cans:** The city of Allentown, Pennsylvania, connected community trash and recycling cans, allowing them to monitor fill rates, which are then used to recommend the most efficient routes for trash pickup services.
- **Smart tennis racket:** Babolat, a French tennis racket manufacturer, created the Play Pure Drive, a $400 smart tennis racket that has the capability to record data on every single shot a user takes, and then sends that data, along with an analysis, to the user's smart phone.
- **Smart frying pan:** Pantelligent is an innovative sensor-embedded frying pan that actually helps its users learn how to cook by measuring the temperature of the food and communicating with a smart phone when to add ingredients, change the heat, flip the food, cover it, and even tell users when the food is done.

The future of business will focus on big data as IoT devices create, capture, and share massive amounts of data. The business environment is currently collecting more data from IoT devices in one second than all of the data collected from the beginning of time until the year 2000. In fact, over 90 percent of the data in the world was created over the last 2 years. Every minute, over 204 million emails are sent and 200,000 photos are uploaded to Facebook. The terms *analytics, data analysis,* and *business intelligence* all refer to big data and the massive volumes of data being generated around the globe.

Understanding big data will be a critical skill for knowledge workers in every business, regardless of size, focus, or industry. Future managers will be responsible for analyzing data in ways that were not even possible a decade ago, allowing managers to predict customer behaviors, optimize and improve business processes, and analyze multiple variables for trends and patterns. The total amount of business data roughly doubles every 1.2 years. Big data has created an estimated 6 million new jobs and will assist companies in:

- Understanding consumer behaviors by combining purchasing data with social media data, weather data, competitor data, and economic data.
- Improving the delivery of products by combining delivery process information with current traffic data, vehicle maintenance data, and map data.
- Optimizing health care treatments by capturing diagnosis, tracking pharmaceuticals, and eventually predicting diseases.
- Preventing cyberattacks by analyzing credit card fraud, security system data, and police data.[17]

Questions

1. Explain the Internet of Things along with its potential impact on business. Also, list three IoT devices you are currently using in your own life.
2. Explain why it is important for business managers to understand that data collection rates from IoT devices are increasing exponentially.
3. Demonstrate how data from an IoT device can be transformed into information and business intelligence.
4. Propose a plan for how a start-up company can use IoT device data to make better business decisions.
5. Argue for or against the following statement: "The Internet of Things is just a passing fad and will be gone within a decade."

MAKING BUSINESS DECISIONS

1. Working for the Best

Each year, *Fortune* magazine creates a list of the top 100 companies to work for. Find the most recent list. What types of data do you think *Fortune* analyzed to determine the company ranking? What issues could occur if the analysis of the data was inaccurate? What types of information can you gain by analyzing the list? Create five questions a student performing a job search could answer by analyzing this list.

2. View from a Flat World

Bill Gates, founder of Microsoft, stated that 20 years ago, most people would rather have been a B student in New York City than a genius in China because the opportunities available to students in developed countries were limitless. Today, many argue that the opposite is now true due to technological advances making it easier to succeed as a genius in China than a B student in New York. As a group, discuss whether you agree or disagree with Gates's statement.

3. Do You Trust Your Data?

Data is the new oil. Data drives fact-based decisions. As a manager you are going to rely on data to drive your business decisions. Can you imagine making a critical business decision on bad data? Have you ever stopped to ask yourself if you trust your data? What will happen if you make a business decision on incorrect, inaccurate, or low-quality data? Obviously, chances are high you will make the wrong decision, and that is the primary risk when using data to drive your decisions. Here are a few examples of organizations that fell into the trap of making important decisions on incorrect data.

- Fidelity: A missing negative sign on a dividend report cost this financial company $2.6 billion.
- Harvard: Two professors reached an incorrect conclusion with an average formula that failed to pull all of the data.
- London Olympics: An accidental typo of 20,000 instead of 10,000 caused the sale of 10,000 additional tickets for the synchronized swimming event.
- MI5: The British intelligence agency accidentally bugged more than 1,000 wrong telephones based on a formatting error on a spreadsheet.
- TransAlta: This Canadian power company made a simple cut-and-paste error for buying power at the wrong price, which cost it $24 million.
- University of Toledo: A typo in a spreadsheet formula led to an overestimate of enrollment, overinflating revenue by $2.4 million.

There is a famous saying in the tech industry: "Garbage in is garbage out" (GIGO). I can be the greatest data analyst in my company, but if the data I am analyzing is wrong, then my analysis will be wrong. But many of us forget to ask about the quality of our data, and we respond too quickly and confidently. There is a common statistic stating that over 80 percent of spreadsheets have errors. Why are there so many errors in spreadsheets? It is simple. Spreadsheets are created by people and people make mistakes! It is important to remember that you should never assume that you have high-quality data. You should always do the upfront work to verify the quality of your data. This will require a great deal of work before you even begin your analysis, but it can pay off tremendously as you make decisions with greater confidence.

Bad data is costly. With data driving so many decisions in our lives, the cost of bad data truly impacts us all, whether or not we realize it. IBM estimates that bad data costs U.S. businesses over $3 trillion yearly. Most people who deal with data realize that bad data can be extremely costly, but this number is truly stunning. The majority of businesses analyze customer data, but there is little chance of the business succeeding if the data is wrong.

- Why do you believe data can be inaccurate?
- What can a business do to ensure data is correct?
- Explain how bad data will impact information, business intelligence, and knowledge.
- Have you ever made a decision based on bad data? If so, be sure to share it with your peers and explain how you could have verified the data quality.
- Argue for or against the following statement: "It is better to make a business decision with bad data than with no data."

4. Systems Thinking

Systems thinking argues that seeing the whole as greater than the sum of its parts can lead to unpredictable and surprising innovations and adaptations. Identify your course registration process. Determine the inputs, process, and outputs for the process. Identify the feedback. How can viewing the systems as a whole help you identify new ways to ensure course scheduling runs smoothly and effectively? Can you think of any new innovations in course registration that could help students? How is data transformed into information with course registration?

5. Manipulating Data to Find Your Version of the Truth

How can global warming be real when there is so much snow and cold weather? That's what some people wondered after a couple of massive snowstorms buried Washington, DC. Politicians across the capital made jokes and built igloos as they disputed the existence of climate change. Some concluded the planet simply could not be warming with all the snow on the ground. These comments frustrated Joseph Romm, a physicist and climate expert with the Center for American Progress. He spent weeks turning data into information and graphs to educate anyone who would listen about why this reasoning was incorrect. Climate change is all about analyzing data, turning the data into information to detect trends. You cannot observe climate change by looking out the window; you have to review decades of weather data with advanced tools to understand the trends.[18]

Increasingly we see politicians, economists, and newscasters boiling tough issues down to simplistic arguments over what the data mean, each interpreting and spinning the data to support their views and agendas. You need to understand the data and turn them into useful information, or you will not understand when someone is telling the truth and when you are being lied to.

Brainstorm two or three types of data economists use to measure the economy. How do they turn the data into information? What issues do they encounter when attempting to measure the economy? As a manager, what do you need to understand when reading or listening to economic and business reports?

6. Information Issues in the Information Age

We live in the information age, when the collection, storage, and use of data are hot topics. One example of inappropriate data handling occurred at a college where the monitoring of restrooms occurred every 15 seconds to observe the use of toilets, mirrors, and sinks. Students, faculty, and staff began complaining that the data collection was an invasion of their privacy and a violation of their rights.

Another example of inappropriate data handling occurred when a professor of accounting at a college lost a flash drive containing information for more than 1,800 students, including Social Security numbers, grades, and names. Social Security numbers were included because the data went back to before 1993, when the college used Social Security numbers to identify students.

What types of student data does your college collect? What could happen if your professor lost a thumb drive with all of your personal information? What types of issues could you encounter if someone stole your personal data? What can your college do to ensure this type of data storage violation does not occur?

7. Ten Best Things You Will Say to Your Grandchildren

Wired magazine recently posted the top 10 things you will say to your grandchildren. For each expression below, try to identify what it is referring to and why it will be considered outdated.[19]

1. Back in my day, we only needed 140 characters.
2. There used to be so much snow up here, you could strap a board to your feet and slide all the way down.
3. Televised contests gave cash prizes to whoever could store the most data in their head.
4. Well, the screens were bigger, but they only showed the movies at certain times of day.
5. We all had one, but nobody actually used it. Come to think of it, I bet my LinkedIn profile is still out there on the web somewhere.
6. Translation: "English used to be the dominant language. Crazy, huh?"
7. Our bodies were made of meat and supported by little sticks of calcium.
8. You used to keep files right on your computer, and you had to go back to that same computer to access them!
9. Is that the new iPhone 27G? Got multitasking yet?
10. I just can't get used to this darn vat-grown steak. Texture ain't right.

8. Sharing Data around the World

In the past few years, data collection rates have skyrocketed, and some estimate we have collected more data in the past 4 years than since the beginning of time. According to International Data Corporation, data collection amounts used to double every 4 years. With the massive growth of smart phones, tablets, and wearable technology devices, it seems as though data is being collected from everything, everywhere, all the time. It is estimated that data collection is doubling every 2 years, and soon it will double every six months. That is a lot of data! With the explosion of data collection, CTOs, CIOs, and CSOs are facing extremely difficult times as the threats to steal sensitive corporate data are also growing exponentially. Hackers and criminals have recently stolen sensitive data from retail giant Target and even the Federal Reserve Bank.

To operate, sensitive data has to flow outside an organization to partners, suppliers, communities, governments, and shareholders. List five types of sensitive data your school collects on students, faculty, and personnel. Review the list of stakeholders working at and with your school. Determine which types of sensitive data each has access to and whether you have any concerns about sharing this data. Do you have to worry about theft of your sensitive student data? How can you ensure your school does not have any data leakage problems?

9. Death of a Product

Porter's Five Forces Model is an essential framework for understanding industries and market forces. Choose one of the categories listed here and analyze what happened to the market using Porter's Five Forces:

- PDA and laptop computer.
- On-demand movies and Blu-ray player.

- Digital camera and Polaroid camera.
- GPS device and a road atlas.
- Digital books and printed books.
- High-definition TV and radio.

10. Upward Manage Your Boss

Business leaders need to be comfortable with data, MIS, and analytics for the following (primary) reasons:

- The sheer magnitude of the dollars spent on MIS and analytics must be managed to ensure business value.
- Research has consistently shown that when top managers are active in supporting these initiatives, they realize a number of benefits, such as gaining a competitive advantage, streamlining business processes, and even transforming entire industries.
- When business leaders are not involved in these initiatives, systems fail, revenue is lost, and entire companies can fail because of poorly managed systems.

How do companies get managers involved in MIS and analytics? One of the biggest positive factors is managers' personal experience with MIS and analytics, along with education, including university classes such as this one. Once managers understand the positive benefits of experience and education, they are more likely to lead their companies in achieving business success.

Your boss does not understand the value of data, MIS, and analytics. In fact, he does not even believe data is required to run a business. Create a 3-minute persuasive presentation demonstrating the relationship between data, MIS, and analytics. Be sure to explain how data is collected from MIS systems and how it is transformed into information and business intelligence, as well as how analytics can be applied to make better decisions. Be creative and have fun!

11. Competitive Analysis

To illustrate the use of the three generic strategies, consider the figure below. The matrix shown demonstrates the relationships among strategies (cost leadership versus differentiation) and market segmentation (broad versus focused).

Porter's Three Generic Strategies

(Hyundai): OvuOng/Shutterstock; (Audi): Emirhankaramuk/Shutterstock; (Kia): OtomobilShutterstock; (Hummer): Art Konovalov/Shutterstock

- Hyundai is following a broad cost leadership strategy. It offers low-cost vehicles in each particular model stratification that appeal to a large audience.
- Audi is pursuing a broad differentiation strategy with its Quattro models, available at several price points. Audi's differentiation is safety, and it prices its models higher than Hyundai's to reach a large, stratified audience.
- Kia has a more focused cost leadership strategy. Kia mainly offers low-cost vehicles in the lower levels of model stratification.
- Hummer offers the most focused differentiation strategy of any in the industry (including Mercedes-Benz).

Create a similar graph displaying each strategy for a product of your choice. The strategy must include an example of the product in each of the following markets: (1) cost leadership, broad market; (2) differentiation, broad market; (3) cost leadership, focused market; and (4) differentiation, focused market. Potential products include cereal, dog food, soft drinks, computers, shampoo, snack foods, jeans, sneakers, sandals, mountain bikes, TV shows, and movies.

12. Does Data Lie?

If you watched the Winter Olympics, you were probably excited to see your country and its amazing athletes compete. As you followed the Olympics day by day, you likely checked different websites to see how your country ranked. Depending on the website you visited, you probably got a very different answer to this seemingly easy question. On the NBC and ESPN networks, the United States ranked second, and on the official Sochie Olympic website, the United States ranked fourth. The simple question of who won the Winter Olympics changed significantly, depending on whom you asked.

In a group, take a look at the following two charts and brainstorm the reasons why each internationally recognized source has a different listing for the top five winners. What measurement is each chart using to determine the winner? Who do *you* believe is the winner? As a manager, what do you need to understand when reading or listening to business forecasts and reports?

Winter Olympics Medal Ranking According to NBC News

Rank	Country	Gold	Silver	Bronze	Total
1	Russian Fed.	13	11	9	33
2	United States	9	7	12	28
3	Norway	11	5	10	26
4	Canada	10	10	5	25
5	Netherlands	8	7	9	24

Winter Olympics Medal Ranking According to the Official Sochie Olympic Website

Rank	Country	Gold	Silver	Bronze	Total
1	Russian Fed.	13	11	9	33
2	Norway	11	5	10	26
3	Canada	10	10	5	25
4	United States	9	7	12	28
5	Netherlands	8	7	9	24

AYK APPLICATION PROJECTS

If you are looking for Excel projects to incorporate into your class, try any of the following after reading this chapter.

Project Number	Project Name	Project Type	Plug-In Focus Area	Project Level	Skill Set	Page Number
1	Financial Destiny	Excel	T2	Personal Budget	Introductory Formulas	AYK.3
2	Cash Flow	Excel	T2	Cash Flow	Introductory Formulas	AYK.3
3	Technology Budget	Excel	T1, T2	Hardware and Software	Introductory Formulas	AYK.3
4	Tracking Donations	Excel	T2	Employee Relationships	Introductory Formulas	AYK.3
5	Convert Currency	Excel	T2	Global Commerce	Introductory Formulas	AYK.4
6	Cost Comparison	Excel	T2	Total Cost of Ownership	Introductory Formulas	AYK.4
7	Time Management	Excel or Project	T12 Project Management	Introductory	Gantt Charts	AYK.5

Design Element: ©McGraw Hill Education

Decisions and Processes: Value Driven Business

2

CHAPTER

CHAPTER OUTLINE

SECTION 2.1
Decision Support Systems

- Making Organizational Business Decisions
- Measuring Organizational Business Decisions
- Using MIS to Make Business Decisions
- Using AI to Make Business Decisions

SECTION 2.2
Business Processes

- Managing Business Processes
- Using MIS to Improve Business Processes

What's in IT for me?

Working faster and smarter has become a necessity for everyone. A firm's value chain is directly affected by how well it designs and coordinates its business processes. Business processes offer competitive advantages if they enable a firm to lower operating costs, differentiate, or compete in a niche market. They can also be huge burdens if they are outdated, which impedes operations, efficiency, and effectiveness. Thus, the ability of management information systems, along with analytics, to improve business processes is a key advantage.

The goal of this chapter is to expand on Porter's Five Forces Model, three generic strategies, and value chain analysis to demonstrate how managers can learn the concepts and practices of business decision making to add value. It will also highlight how companies heading into the 21st century are taking advantage of advanced MIS capable of generating significant competitive advantages across the value chain.

After reading this chapter, you should have detailed knowledge of the types of information systems that exist to support decision making, automation, and business process reengineering, which in turn can improve organization efficiency and effectiveness and help an organization create and maintain competitive advantages.

opening case study

supparsorn/Shutterstock Andrey_Popov/Shutterstock Monty Rakusen/Getty Images

Attention People, We Are Tracking You Right Now, with Facial Recognition

Each time you unlock your phone do you wonder how it knows how to recognize your face? The technology behind this feature is facial recognition. Facial recognition is being used by law enforcement, criminal surveillance, airport screening, and employment and housing decisions.

Now imagine, you have been hired to investigate a convenience store robbery. You notice the thieves were looking at the camera while committing the crimes. You, as a criminal investigator, decide to use facial recognition to identify the suspects. Seems like a great idea to use the latest technology to help you bring justice to the store owner and the people hurt by the crimes.

Now imagine a city—say, Denver, Chicago, Paris, Madrid—that decides to ban criminal investigators from using any form of facial recognition. You ask yourself, "Why ban a technology that can help eliminate criminal behaviors? Everyone knows artificial intelligence technology can match faces with photos. So why are cities around the world banning facial recognition technologies?"

It is simple. Artificial intelligence technology has glitches and is invasive. The current implementation of these technologies involves significant racial bias. It also invades people's privacy, especially those in schools or public housing. The result of the glitches in this technology is a series of bans and restrictions by cities, states, and companies that could stifle one of the first and most significant results of superhuman AI.

The truth is, cameras are everywhere and people are constantly posting selfies and photos tagged with names. People have been unknowingly feeding AI billions of faces, along with identification of the images. Microsoft and Amazon have both denied police access to their face-matching systems. Many cities have also implemented technological bans on facial recognition and invasive cameras.

Did you realize that the police use facial recognition to compare potential suspects' mugshots to driver's licenses? Did you realize that when you had your driver's license photo taken that it could be used to incorrectly identify you as a suspect in a crime? Over 120 million Americans have photos taken that are used in a facial recognition network operated by law enforcement, without their consent.

Many believe the government should implement a national policy on the rights and wrongs of using AI. But many also believe "Big Brother" is watching, and think taking facial recognition photos without informed consent is unethical.[1]

section 2.1 | Decision Support Systems

LEARNING OUTCOMES

2.1 Explain the importance of decision making for managers at each of the three primary organization levels along with the associated decision characteristics.

2.2 Define critical success factors (CSFs) and key performance indicators (KPIs) and explain how managers use them to measure the success of MIS projects.

2.3 Classify the different operational support systems, managerial support systems, and strategic support systems and explain how managers can use these systems to make decisions and gain competitive advantages.

2.4 Describe artificial intelligence and identify its three main types.

MAKING ORGANIZATIONAL BUSINESS DECISIONS

LO 2.1: Explain the importance of decision making for managers at each of the three primary organization levels, along with the associated decision characteristics.

Porter's strategies outlined in Chapter 1 suggest entering markets with a competitive advantage in overall cost leadership, differentiation, or focus. To achieve these results, managers must be able to make decisions and forecast future business needs and requirements. The most important and most challenging question confronting managers today is how to lay the foundation for tomorrow's success while competing to win in today's business environment. A company will not have a future if it is not cultivating strategies for tomorrow, and as discussed in the opening case, the future of work is uncertain.

As we discussed in Chapter 1, decision making is one of the most important and challenging aspects of management. Decisions range from routine choices, such as how many items to order or how many people to hire, to unexpected ones, such as what to do if a key employee suddenly quits or needed materials do not arrive. Today, with massive volumes of information available, managers are challenged to make highly complex decisions—some involving far more information than the human brain can comprehend—in increasingly short time frames. Figure 2.1 displays the three primary challenges managers face when making decisions.

FIGURE 2.1

Managerial Decision-Making Challenges

MANAGERIAL DECISION-MAKING CHALLENGES

1. Managers need to analyze large amounts of information:
Innovations in communication and globalization have resulted in a dramatic increase in the variables and dimensions people need to consider when making a decision, solving a problem, or appraising an opportunity. Example: Analyze data from 500 hotels to determine when to discount rooms based on occupancy patterns.

2. Managers must make decisions quickly:
Time is of the essence and people simply do not have time to sift through all the information manually. Example: An important customer shows up at a hotel that is fully booked, and the reservation is missing.

3. Managers must apply sophisticated analysis techniques, such as Porter's strategies or forecasting, to make strategic decisions:
Due to the intensely competitive global business environment, companies must offer far more than just a great product to succeed. Example: Implement a loyalty program across 500 hotels.

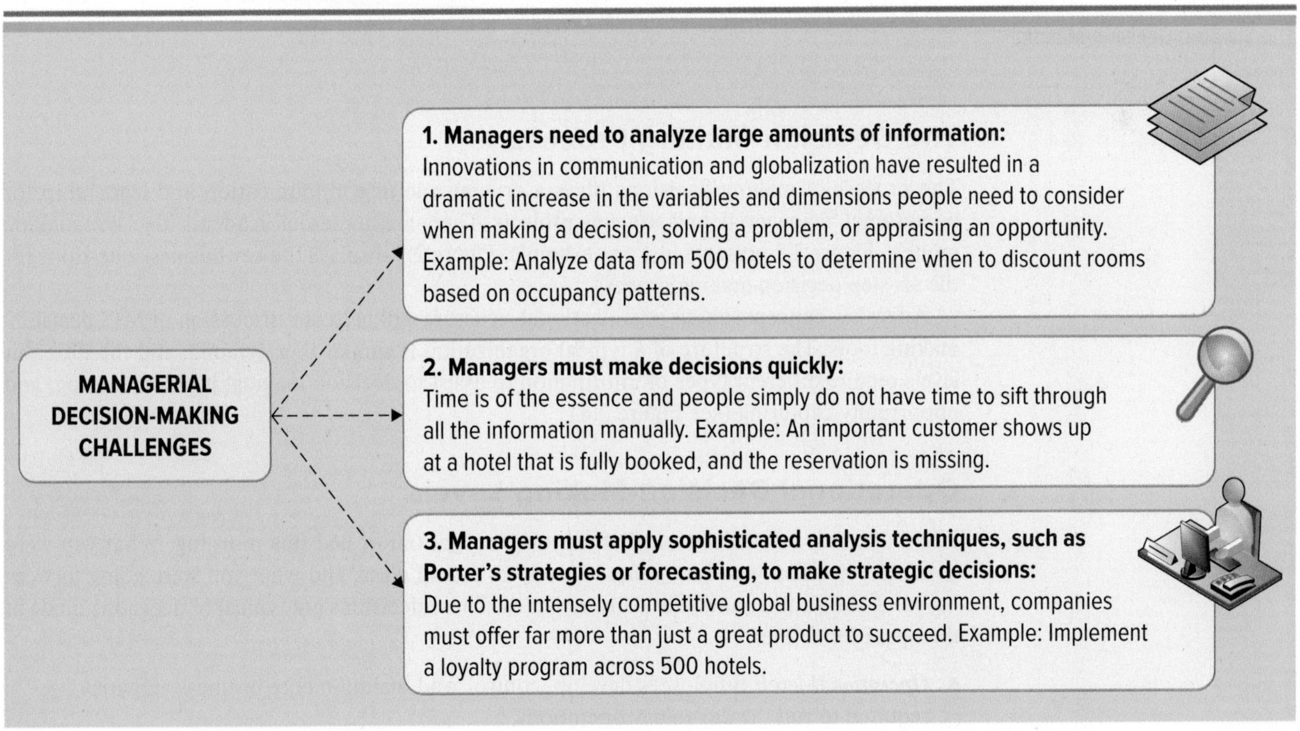

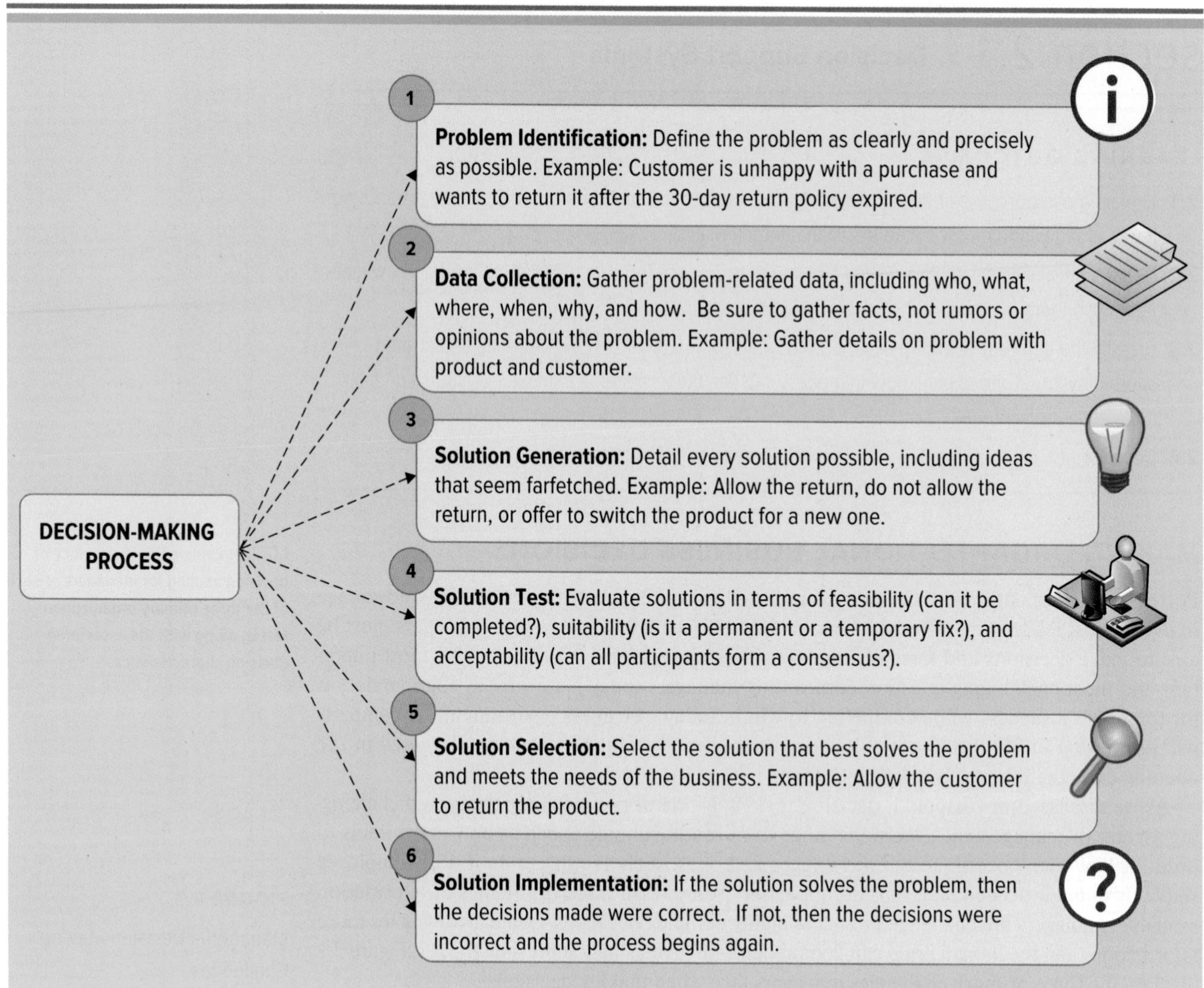

1
Problem Identification: Define the problem as clearly and precisely as possible. Example: Customer is unhappy with a purchase and wants to return it after the 30-day return policy expired.
2
Data Collection: Gather problem-related data, including who, what, where, when, why, and how. Be sure to gather facts, not rumors or opinions about the problem. Example: Gather details on problem with product and customer.
3
Solution Generation: Detail every solution possible, including ideas that seem farfetched. Example: Allow the return, do not allow the return, or offer to switch the product for a new one.
DECISION-MAKING PROCESS
4
Solution Test: Evaluate solutions in terms of feasibility (can it be completed?), suitability (is it a permanent or a temporary fix?), and acceptability (can all participants form a consensus?).
5
Solution Selection: Select the solution that best solves the problem and meets the needs of the business. Example: Allow the customer to return the product.
6
Solution Implementation: If the solution solves the problem, then the decisions made were correct. If not, then the decisions were incorrect and the process begins again.
?

FIGURE 2.2

The Six-Step Decision-Making Process

The Decision-Making Process

The process of making decisions plays a crucial role in communication and leadership for operational, managerial, and strategic projects. There are numerous academic decision-making models. Figure 2.2 presents just one example. Figure 2.3 displays the key business questions for the six-step decision-making process.

A few key concepts about organizational structure will help our discussion of MIS decision-making tools. The structure of a typical organization is similar to a pyramid, and the different levels require different types of information to assist in decision making, problem solving, and opportunity capturing (see Figure 2.4).

Operational Decision-Making Levels

I bet you made a few decisions before you even got out of bed this morning. What you were going to eat, when you were going to study or attend class, and what you were going to wear based on the weather and your daily activities. These decisions are typical of decisions made at the operational level.

- ***Operational level***: Employees develop, control, and maintain core business activities required to run the day-to-day operations.

PROBLEM IDENTIFICATION

- What are the key problems affecting the business?
- What are the customers saying about the service and the product?
- What are the root cause of any decline in revenue or production time?

DATA COLLECTION

- Why are certain processes falling short?
- What are the immediate steps the company can take to adjust the current processes to improve them?
- Who are you listening to? Are they actual or rumor complaints?
- What departments are struggling?

SOLUTION GENERATION

- What are some of the solutions you have for improvement?
- What are some of the solutions your management team has?
- How will you go about collecting all the best solutions?

SOLUTION TEST

- Are these solutions long-term or short-term solutions?
- What are some of the cost factors associated with the solutions?
- Does your team like the solution, or are they going to sabotage it because they are unhappy with the decision made?

SOLUTION SELECTION

- As the executive leader of the company, are you comfortable with the decision you made?
- How are you going to take a strong lead on this decision without alienating yourself from others?

SOLUTION IMPLEMENTATION

- Evaluate and track how the solution is working.
- Is it achieving the results that you wanted?
- If the results are poor, what steps do you need to take to adjust?
- As the leader for the company, how will you appropriately change the solution direction without upsetting the environment or flow of the employees and production?

FIGURE 2.3

Examples of Decisions in the Six-Step Decision-Making Process

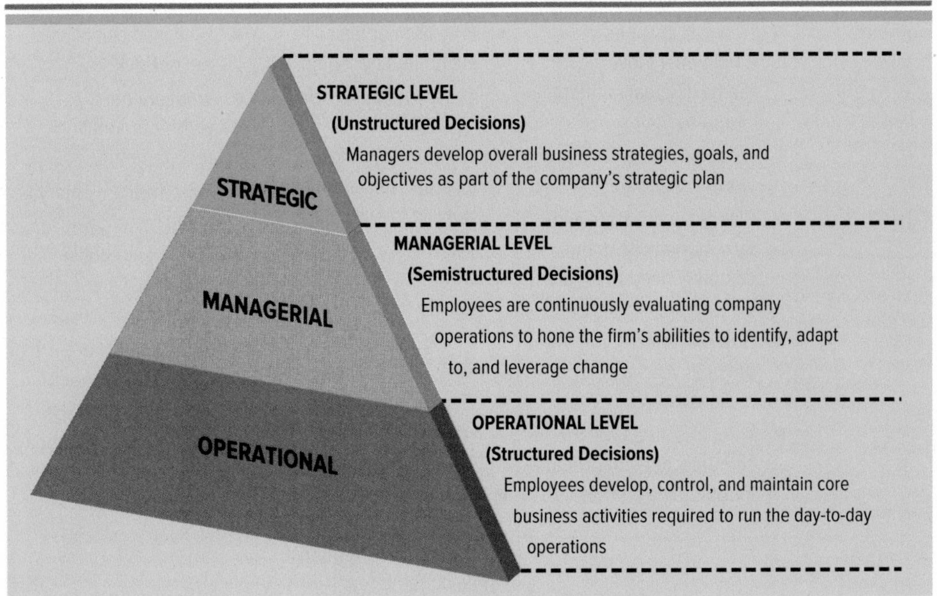

STRATEGIC LEVEL
(Unstructured Decisions)
Managers develop overall business strategies, goals, and objectives as part of the company's strategic plan
STRATEGIC
MANAGERIAL LEVEL
(Semistructured Decisions)
Employees are continuously evaluating company operations to hone the firm's abilities to identify, adapt to, and leverage change
MANAGERIAL
OPERATIONAL LEVEL
(Structured Decisions)
Employees develop, control, and maintain core business activities required to run the day-to-day operations
OPERATIONAL

FIGURE 2.4

Common Company Structure

The majority of employees can be found at the operational level performing important tasks that ensure the business's continuous operations. Operational level employees make operational decisions.

- ***Operational decisions***: Affect how the firm is run from day to day. They are the domain of operations managers, who are the closest to the customer.
- ***Structured decisions***: Arise when established processes offer potential solutions.

Operational decisions are considered structured decisions. Structured decisions are made frequently and are almost repetitive in nature; they affect short-term business strategies. Reordering inventory and creating the employee staffing and weekly production schedules are examples of routine structured decisions. Figure 2.5 highlights the essential elements required for operational decision making. All the elements in the figure should be familiar except metrics, which are discussed in detail below.

Managerial Decision-Making Levels

A company that has a competitive advantage needs to adjust and revise its strategy constantly to remain ahead of fast-following competitors. Managers make many decisions that help drive

FIGURE 2.5

Overview of Decision Making

	Strategic Level	Managerial Level	Operational Level
Employee Types	■ Senior management, presidents, leaders, executives	■ Middle management, managers, directors	■ Lower management, department managers, analysts, staff
Focus	■ External, industry, cross-company	■ Internal, cross-functional (sometimes external)	■ Internal, functional
Time Frame	■ Long term—yearly, multiyear	■ Short term, daily, monthly, yearly	■ Short term, day-to-day operations
Decision Types	■ Unstructured, nonrecurring, one time	■ Semistructured, ad hoc (unplanned) reporting	■ Structured, recurring, repetitive
MIS Types	■ Knowledge	■ Business intelligence	■ Information
Metrics	■ Critical success factors focusing on effectiveness	■ Key performance indicators focusing on efficiency, and critical success factors focusing on effectiveness	■ Key performance indicators focusing on efficiency
Examples	■ How will changes in employment levels over the next 3 years affect the company? ■ What industry trends are worth analyzing? ■ What new products and new markets does the company need to create competitive advantages? ■ How will a recession over the next year affect business? ■ What measures will the company need to prepare for due to new tax laws?	■ Who are our best customers by region, by sales representative, by product? ■ What are the sales forecasts for next month? How do they compare to actual sales for last year? ■ What was the difference between expected sales and actual sales for each month? ■ What was the impact of last month's marketing campaign on sales? ■ What types of ad hoc or unplanned reports might the company require next month?	■ How many employees are out sick? ■ What are next week's production requirements? ■ How much inventory is in the warehouse? ■ How many problems occurred when running payroll? ■ Which employees are on vacation next week? ■ How many products need to be made today?

the business forward. Choosing your course schedule for an entire semester over several months is equivalent to a decision at the managerial level.

- ***Managerial level***: Employees are continuously evaluating company operations to hone the firm's abilities to identify, adapt to, and leverage change.

Managerial decisions cover short- and medium-range plans, schedules, and budgets, along with policies, procedures, and business objectives for the firm. They also allocate resources and monitor the performance of organizational subunits, including departments, divisions, process teams, project teams, and other work groups.

- ***Managerial decisions***: These concern how the organization should achieve the goals and objectives set by its strategy. They are usually the responsibility of mid-level management.
- ***Semistructured decisions***: These occur in situations in which a few established processes help to evaluate potential solutions, but not enough to lead to a definite recommended decision.

Managerial decisions are considered semistructured decisions. For example, decisions about producing new products or changing employee benefits range from unstructured to semistructured. Figure 2.5 highlights the essential elements required for managerial decision making.

Strategic Decision-Making Levels

Not all decisions are easy and straightforward to make, as I am sure you know from having to decide on a college major. Choosing a major is a difficult decision, with long-lasting impacts on your life, and requires far more analysis than day-to-day decisions, such as what to wear to a job interview.

- ***Strategic level***: Managers develop overall business strategies, goals, and objectives as part of the company's strategic plan.

Focusing on the strategic level of a business includes monitoring the strategic performance of the organization and its overall direction in the political, economic, and competitive business environment.

- ***Strategic decisions***: Involve higher-level issues concerned with the overall direction of the organization. These decisions define the organization's overall goals and aspirations for the future.
- ***Unstructured decisions***: Occur in situations in which no procedures or rules exist to guide decision makers toward the correct choice.

Strategic decisions are highly unstructured decisions. They are infrequent, extremely important, and typically related to long-term business strategy. Examples include the decision to enter a new market or even a new industry over, say, the next 3 years. In these types of decisions, managers rely on many sources of information, along with personal knowledge, to find solutions. Figure 2.5 highlights the essential elements required for strategic decision making.

MEASURING ORGANIZATIONAL BUSINESS DECISIONS

LO 2.2: Define critical success factors (CSFs) and key performance indicators (KPIs) and explain how managers use them to measure the success of MIS projects.

Peter Drucker, a famous management writer, once said that if you cannot measure something, you cannot manage it. How do managers measure the progress of a complex business project? For example, the construction of a new subway station is a project, as is a movie theater chain's adoption of a software program to allow online ticketing.

- ***Project***: A temporary activity that a company undertakes to create a unique product, service, or result.
- ***Metrics***: Measurements that evaluate results to determine whether a project is meeting its goals.

Two core metrics are critical success factors and key performance indicators.

- ***Critical success factors (CSFs)***: The crucial steps companies perform to achieve their goals and objectives and implement their strategies (see Figure 2.6).
- ***Key performance indicators (KPIs)***: The quantifiable metrics a company uses to evaluate progress toward critical success factors. KPIs are far more specific than CSFs.

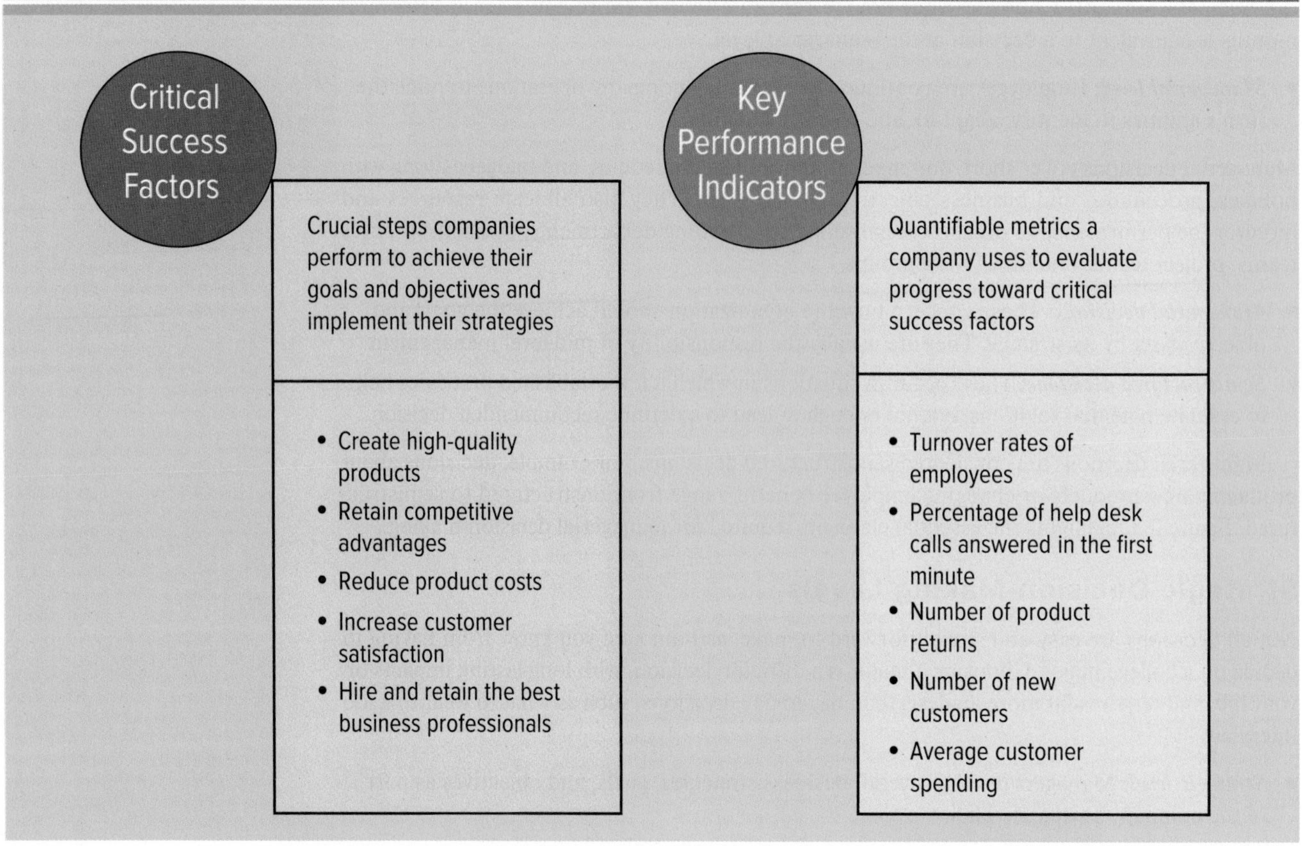

Critical Success Factors

Crucial steps companies perform to achieve their goals and objectives and implement their strategies

- Create high-quality products
- Retain competitive advantages
- Reduce product costs
- Increase customer satisfaction
- Hire and retain the best business professionals

Key Performance Indicators

Quantifiable metrics a company uses to evaluate progress toward critical success factors

- Turnover rates of employees
- Percentage of help desk calls answered in the first minute
- Number of product returns
- Number of new customers
- Average customer spending

FIGURE 2.6

CSF and KPI Metrics

The purpose of using KPIs is to focus attention on the tasks and processes that management has determined are most important for making progress toward declared goals and targets. KPIs differ per organization. For example, a KPI for a public company may be its stock price, while a KPI in government might be a low unemployment rate. KPIs will also differ for roles people play in the same organization. For example, a chief executive officer (CEO) might consider profitability as the most important KPI, while a sales team manager in the same company might consider successful service level agreement (SLA) delivery numbers as the most important KPI.

It is important to understand the relationship between critical success factors and key performance indicators. CSFs are elements crucial for a business strategy's success. KPIs measure the progress of CSFs with quantifiable measurements, and one CSF can have several KPIs. Of course, both categories will vary by company and industry. Imagine *improve graduation rates* as a CSF for a college. The KPIs to measure this CSF can include:

- Average grades by course and gender.
- Student dropout rates by gender and major.
- Average graduation rate by gender and major.
- Time spent in tutoring by gender and major.

The selection of appropriate KPIs depends, in part, on the organization's ability to actually measure the indicators. Typically, a management team will gather requirements and analyze correlations between metrics, but in the end, they must put the KPIs in practice and observe what behaviors the KPIs encourage. Each KPI should support the level above it so that all levels of the organization are working together toward the same strategic goals. KPIs can focus on external and internal measurements.

- ***Market share***: The proportion of the market that a firm captures.

A common external KPI is market share. It is calculated by dividing the firm's sales by the total market sales for the entire industry. Market share measures a firm's external performance relative to that of its competitors. For example, if a firm's total sales (revenues) are $2 million

APPLY YOUR KNOWLEDGE

BUSINESS DRIVEN DISCUSSION

What Level Are My Decisions?

For each of the following decisions, determine if it is operational, managerial, or strategic.

Decision	Operational Decision	Managerial Decision	Strategic Decision
How many employees are out sick?			
What are the sales forecasts for next month?			
What was the impact of last month's marketing campaign discount on the primary product?			
How will an increase in the interest rate over the next year affect sales?			
How will changes in health insurance laws impact the company over the next 5 years?			
How many paychecks were incorrect during the last payroll run?			
What was the difference between forecast sales and actual sales last month?			
How will new tax laws impact business?			
What are next week's production schedules?			

and sales for the entire industry are $10 million, the firm has captured 20 percent of the total market (2/10 = 20%), or a 20 percent market share.

- ***Return on investment (ROI)***: Indicates the earning power of a project.

A common internal KPI is ROI. It is measured by dividing the profitability of a project by the costs. This sounds easy, and for many departments where the projects are tangible and self-contained, it is; however, for projects that are intangible and cross departmental lines (such as MIS projects), ROI is challenging to measure. Imagine attempting to calculate the ROI of a fire extinguisher. If the fire extinguisher is never used, its ROI is low. If the fire extinguisher puts out a fire that could have destroyed the entire building, its ROI is astronomically high.

Although monitoring KPIs can help management identify deficiencies within an organization, it is up to management to decide how to correct them. Having too many KPIs can be problematic. It not only dilutes employee attention, it also makes it difficult for managers to prioritize indicators and make sure the key indicators get the attention they deserve. To that end, many successful companies limit KPI scope to small sets of indicators that evaluate the success of individuals in the organization.

Creating KPIs to measure the success of an MIS project offers similar challenges. Think about a firm's email system. How could managers track departmental costs and profits associated with company email? Measuring by volume does not account for profitability because 1 sales email could land a million-dollar deal, while 300 others might not generate any revenue. Nonrevenue-generating departments such as human resources and legal require email but will not be using it to generate profits. For this reason, many managers turn to higher-level metrics, such as efficiency and effectiveness, to measure MIS projects.

- ***Best practices***: The most successful solutions or problem-solving methods that have been developed by a specific organization or industry. Measuring MIS projects helps determine the best practices for an industry.

APPLY YOUR KNOWLEDGE

BUSINESS DRIVEN ANALYTICS

Personal CFSs and KPIs

Have you ever thought about how you will measure your college success? Will you focus on grades, clubs, sports, happiness, internships? There is an old saying that students remember only 10 percent of what they memorize. In other words, you might forget 90 percent of what you learned in college the day you graduate if you are challenged only with memorization. It also states that students remember 80 percent of what they apply to a problem or teach others. This is great news if you are focused on applying concepts to real-world problems and teaching your friends because you will remember 80 percent of what you learned in college.

Some students have great memories and can easily ace any multiple-choice exam, while other students are terrible test takers but can apply their knowledge to solve real-world problems. Some students are book smart but lack common sense, whereas other students have street smarts but lack communication skills. Bill Gates, Michael Dell, Mark Zuckerberg, and even Steve Jobs all dropped out of college to start their famous businesses. Clearly, they did not measure themselves by grades and degrees. Have you given much thought to how you will measure yourself?[2]

Break into groups of two or three and create a few CSFs and KPIs to measure your college success. Will you base them on grades or learning or fun? How will you gather the data to manage and measure these metrics? How frequently will you monitor your metrics to ensure you are successful? Here are a few to think about:

- Work enjoyment
- Professional connections
- Number of books you read
- Number of online courses you take
- Daily happiness index
- Trying something new
- Time spent with friends
- Calories burned during exercise

Efficiency and Effectiveness Metrics

Peter Drucker offers a helpful distinction between efficiency and effectiveness: Doing things right addresses efficiency–getting the most from each resource. Doing the right things addresses effectiveness–setting the right goals and objectives and ensuring they are accomplished.

- ***Efficiency MIS metrics***: Measures the performance of MIS itself, such as throughput, transaction speed, and system availability.
- ***Effectiveness MIS metrics***: Measures the impact MIS has on business processes and activities, including customer satisfaction and customer conversion rates.

Efficiency focuses on the extent to which a firm is using its resources in an optimal way, whereas effectiveness focuses on how well a firm is achieving its goals and objectives. Figure 2.7 describes a few of the common types of efficiency and effectiveness MIS metrics. KPIs that measure MIS projects include both efficiency and effectiveness metrics. Of course, these metrics are not as concrete as market share or ROI, but they do offer valuable insight into project performance.[3]

Large increases in productivity typically result from increases in effectiveness, which focus on CSFs. Efficiency MIS metrics are far easier to measure, however, so most managers tend to focus on them, often incorrectly, to measure the success of MIS projects. Consider measuring the success of automated teller machines (ATMs). Thinking in terms of MIS efficiency metrics,

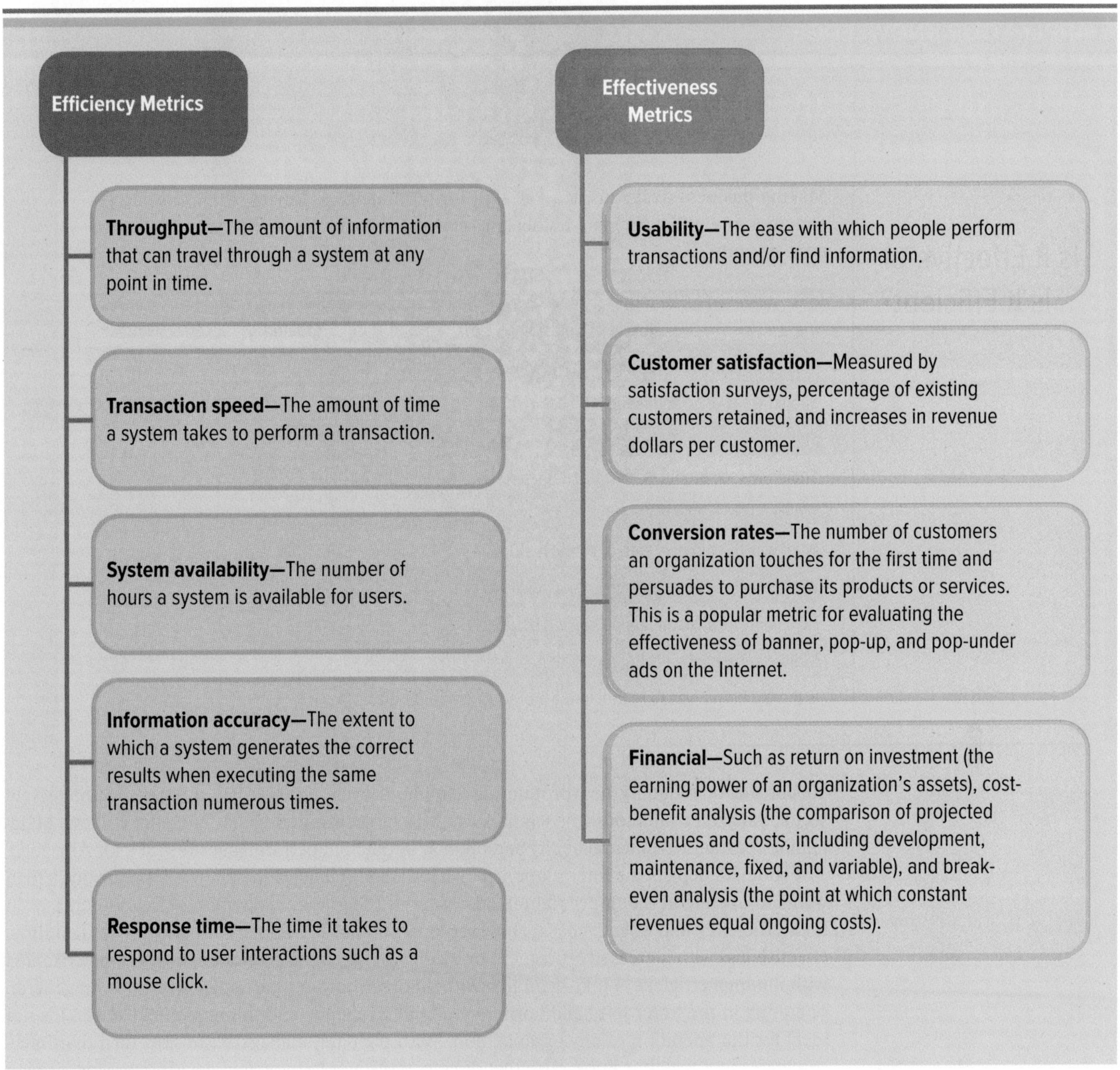

Efficiency Metrics

- **Throughput—**The amount of information that can travel through a system at any point in time.
- **Transaction speed—**The amount of time a system takes to perform a transaction.
- **System availability—**The number of hours a system is available for users.
- **Information accuracy—**The extent to which a system generates the correct results when executing the same transaction numerous times.
- **Response time—**The time it takes to respond to user interactions such as a mouse click.

Effectiveness Metrics

- **Usability—**The ease with which people perform transactions and/or find information.
- **Customer satisfaction—**Measured by satisfaction surveys, percentage of existing customers retained, and increases in revenue dollars per customer.
- **Conversion rates—**The number of customers an organization touches for the first time and persuades to purchase its products or services. This is a popular metric for evaluating the effectiveness of banner, pop-up, and pop-under ads on the Internet.
- **Financial—**Such as return on investment (the earning power of an organization's assets), cost-benefit analysis (the comparison of projected revenues and costs, including development, maintenance, fixed, and variable), and break-even analysis (the point at which constant revenues equal ongoing costs).

FIGURE 2.7

Common Types of Efficiency and Effectiveness Metrics

a manager would measure the number of daily transactions, the average amount per transaction, and the average speed per transaction to determine the success of the ATM. Although these offer solid metrics on how well the system is performing, they miss many of the intangible or value-added benefits associated with ATM effectiveness. Effectiveness MIS metrics might measure how many new customers joined the bank due to its ATM locations or the ATMs' ease of use. They can also measure increases in customer satisfaction due to reduced ATM fees or additional ATM services such as the sale of stamps and movie tickets, significant time savers and value-added features for customers. Being a great manager means using the added viewpoint offered by effectiveness MIS metrics to analyze all benefits associated with an MIS project.

The Interrelationship between Efficiency and Effectiveness

Efficiency and effectiveness are definitely related. However, success in one area does not necessarily imply success in the other. Efficiency MIS metrics focus on the technology itself. Although these efficiency MIS metrics are important to monitor, they do not always guarantee effectiveness. Effectiveness MIS metrics are determined according to an organization's goals, strategies, and objectives. Here, it becomes important to consider a company's CSFs, such as a broad cost leadership strategy (Walmart, for example), as well as KPIs such as increasing new customers by

APPLY YOUR KNOWLEDGE

BUSINESS DRIVEN DISCUSSION

Is It Effective or Is It Efficient?

Making business decisions is a key skill for all managers. Review the following list and, in a group, determine whether the question is focusing on efficiency, effectiveness, or both.

Business Decision	Efficiency	Effectiveness
What is the best route for dropping off products?		
Should we change suppliers?		
Should we reduce costs by buying lower-quality materials?		
Should we sell products to a younger market?		
Did we make our sales targets?		
What was the turnover rate of employees?		
What is the average customer spending?		
How many new customers purchased products?		
Did the amount of daily transactions increase?		
Is there a better way to restructure a store to increase sales?		

10 percent or reducing new-product development cycle times to six months. In the private sector, Amazon continuously benchmarks its MIS projects for efficiency and effectiveness. Maintaining constant website availability and optimal throughput performance are CSFs for Amazon.

Figure 2.8 depicts the interrelationships between efficiency and effectiveness. Ideally, a firm wants to operate in the upper right-hand corner of the graph, realizing significant increases in both efficiency and effectiveness. However, operating in the upper left-hand corner (minimal effectiveness with increased efficiency) or the lower right-hand corner (significant effectiveness with minimal efficiency) may be in line with an organization's particular strategies. In general, operating in the lower left-hand corner (minimal efficiency and minimal effectiveness) is not ideal for the operation of any organization. With big data, managers can now turn their measurements into real-time knowledge that directly translates to improved decision making, driving business efficiency and effectiveness.

FIGURE 2.8

The Interrelationships between Efficiency and Effectiveness

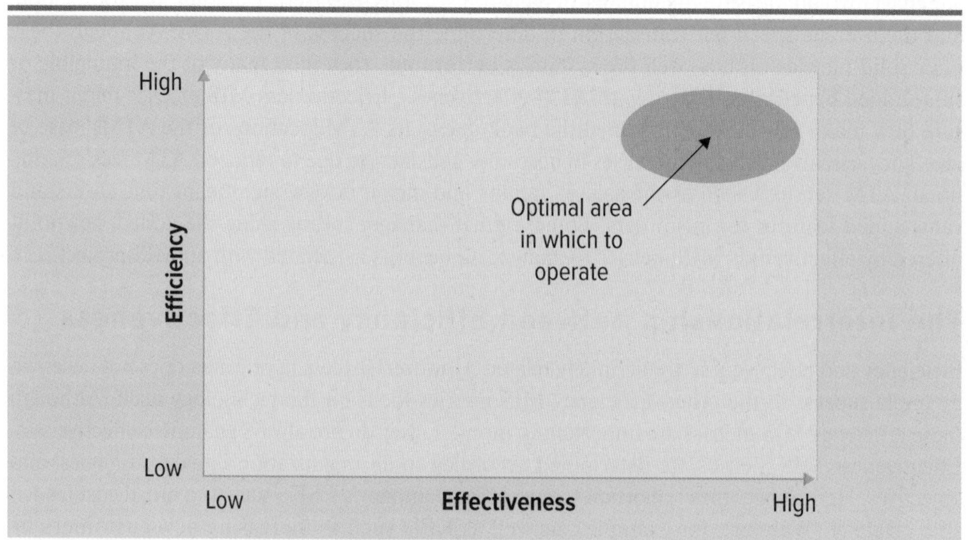

Regardless of what process is measured, how it is measured, and whether it is performed for the sake of efficiency or effectiveness, managers must set benchmarks and monitor benchmarking.

- ***Benchmarks***: Baseline values the system seeks to attain.
- ***Benchmarking***: A process of continuously measuring system results, comparing those results to optimal system performance (benchmark values), and identifying steps and procedures to improve system performance.

Benchmarks help assess how an MIS project performs over time. For instance, if a system held a benchmark for response time of 15 seconds, the manager would want to ensure response time continued to decrease until it reached that point. If response time suddenly increased to 1 minute, the manager would know the system was not functioning correctly and could start looking into potential problems. Continuously measuring MIS projects against benchmarks provides feedback so managers can control the system.

USING MIS TO MAKE BUSINESS DECISIONS

LO 2.3: Classify the different operational support systems, managerial support systems, and strategic support systems and explain how managers can use these systems to make decisions and gain competitive advantages.

Now that we've reviewed the essentials of decision making, we are ready to understand the powerful benefits associated with using MIS to support managers making decisions.

- ***Model***: A simplified representation or abstraction of reality.

Models help managers calculate risks, understand uncertainty, change variables, and manipulate time to make decisions. MIS support systems rely on models for computational and analytical routines that mathematically express relationships among variables. For example, a spreadsheet program, such as Microsoft Excel, might contain models that calculate market share or return on investment. MIS has the capability and functionality to express far more complex modeling relationships that provide information, business intelligence, and knowledge. Figure 2.9 highlights the three primary types of management information systems available to support decision making across the company levels.

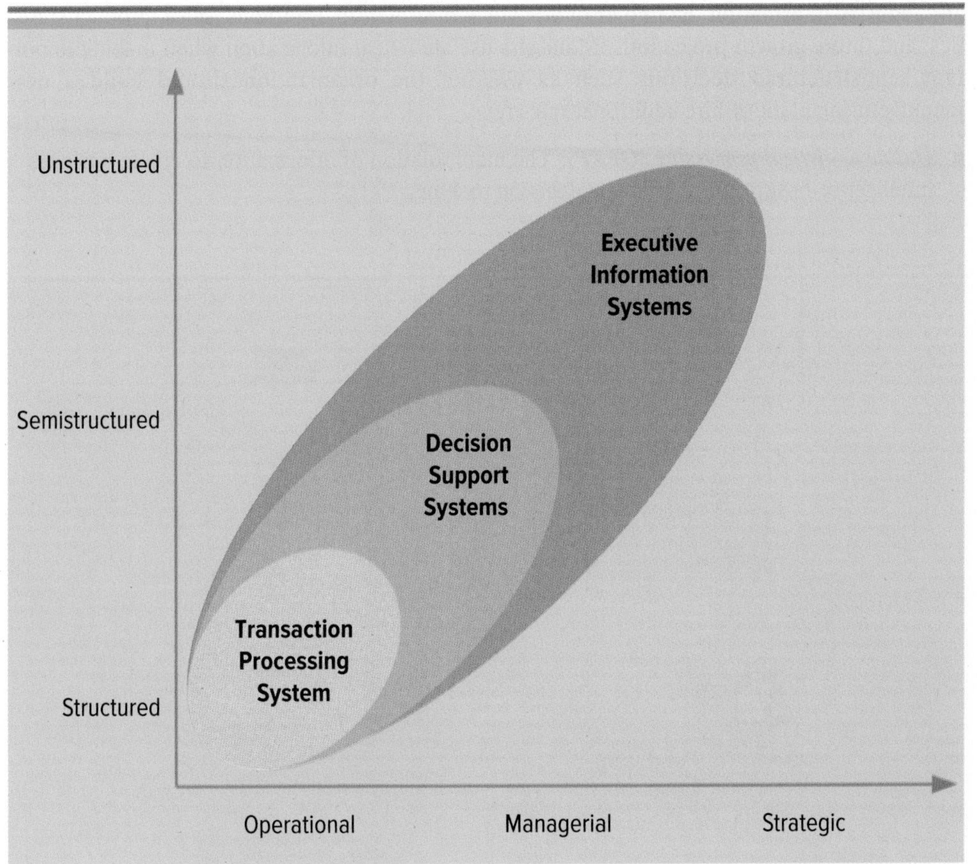

FIGURE 2.9

Primary Types of MIS Systems for Decision Making

Operational Support Systems

Transactional information encompasses all the information contained within a single business process or unit of work, and its primary purpose is to support the performance of daily operational or structured decisions. Transactional information is created, for example, when customers are purchasing stocks, making an airline reservation, or withdrawing cash from an ATM. Managers use transactional information when making structured decisions at the operational level, such as when analyzing daily sales reports to determine how much inventory to carry.

- ***Online transaction processing (OLTP)*:** The capture of transaction and event information using technology to (1) process the information according to defined business rules, (2) store the information, and (3) update existing information to reflect the new information. During OLTP, the organization must capture every detail of transactions and events.
- ***Transaction processing system (TPS)*:** The basic business system that serves the operational level (analysts) and assists in making structured decisions. The most common example of a TPS is an operational accounting system such as a payroll system or an order-entry system (such as a cash register at Target).
- ***Source documents*:** The original transaction record.

Using systems thinking, we can see that the inputs for a TPS are source documents. Source documents for a payroll system can include time sheets, wage rates, and employee benefit reports. Transformation includes common procedures such as create, read, update, and delete (commonly referred to as CRUD) employee records, along with calculating the payroll and summarizing benefits. The output includes cutting the paychecks and generating payroll reports. Figure 2.10 demonstrates the systems thinking view of a TPS.[4]

Managerial Support Systems

Analytical information encompasses all organizational information, and its primary purpose is to support the performance of managerial analysis or semistructured decisions. Analytical information includes transactional information along with other information such as market and industry information. Examples of analytical information are trends, sales, product statistics, and future growth projections. Managers use analytical information when making important semistructured decisions such as whether the organization should build a new manufacturing plant or hire additional sales reps.

- ***Online analytical processing (OLAP)*:** The manipulation of information to create business intelligence in support of strategic decision making.

FIGURE 2.10

Systems Thinking Example of a TPS

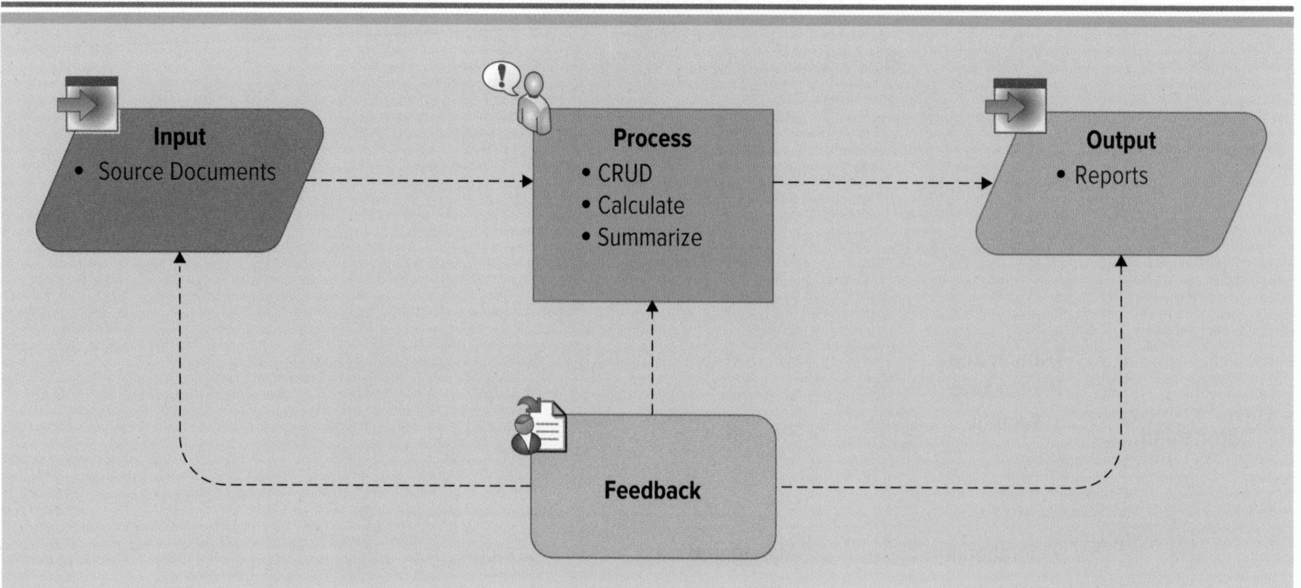

APPLY YOUR KNOWLEDGE

BUSINESS DRIVEN ETHICS AND SECURITY

Was Stephen Hawking Ever Wrong?

When you think of machine learning and artificial intelligence, do you think of scary movies like *The Terminator* or *The Matrix* in which computers take over the world? *Machine learning* is one of the scary terms in AI because it points to a future in which AI robots could be smarter than humans.

The great and brilliant Stephen Hawking was a major voice in the debate about how humanity can benefit from or be hindered by artificial intelligence. Hawking himself depended on AI to help him communicate from his wheelchair. Hawking made no secret of his fears that thinking machines could one day take charge. He went as far as predicting that future developments in AI could spell the end of the human race with superhuman AI, the point at which AI systems not only replicate human intelligence processes, but also keep expanding them, without our support.[5]

Do you agree or disagree with Stephen Hawking's view on AI's ability to take over the world? How can humans ensure this type of superhuman AI does not ever come into existence?

- ***Decision support systems (DSSs)***: Model information using OLAP, which provides assistance in evaluating and choosing among different courses of action.

DSSs enable high-level managers to examine and manipulate large amounts of detailed data from different internal and external sources. Analyzing complex relationships among thousands or even millions of data items to discover patterns, trends, and exception conditions is one of the key uses associated with a DSS. For example, doctors may enter symptoms into a decision support system so it can help diagnose and treat patients. Insurance companies also use a DSS to gauge the risk of providing insurance to drivers who have imperfect driving records. One company found that married women who are homeowners with one speeding ticket are rarely cited for speeding again. Armed with this business intelligence, the company achieved a cost advantage by lowering insurance rates to this specific group of customers.

Figure 2.11 shows the common systems view of a DSS. Figure 2.12 shows how TPSs supply transactional data to a DSS. The DSS then summarizes and aggregates the information from the different TPSs, which assist managers in making semistructured decisions.

FIGURE 2.11

Systems Thinking Example of a DSS

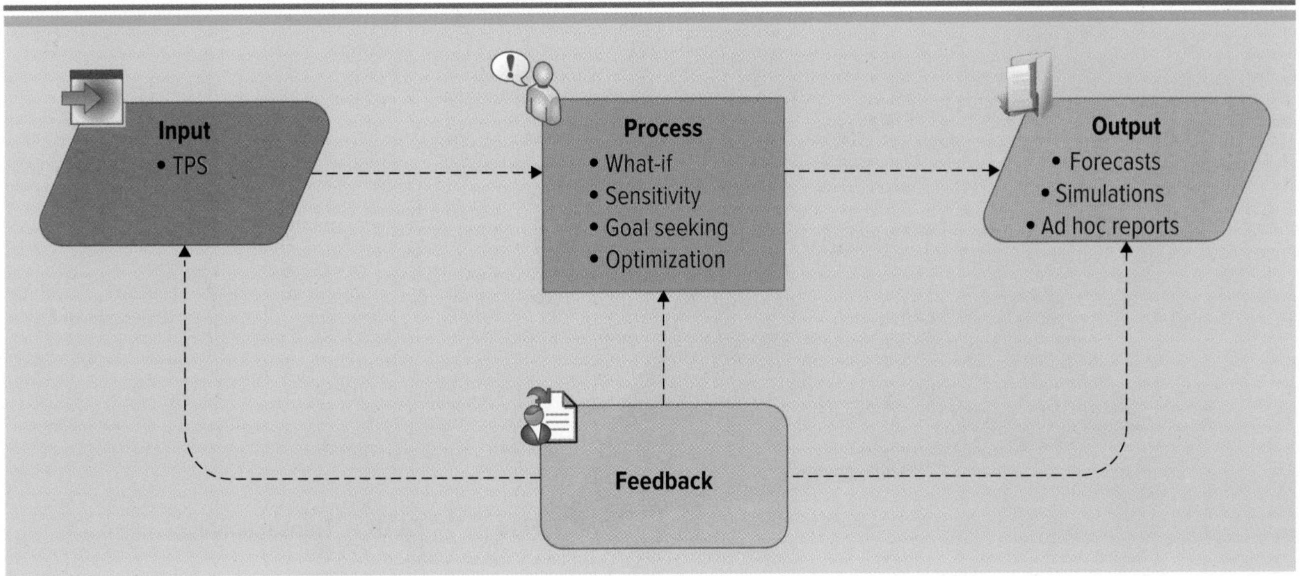

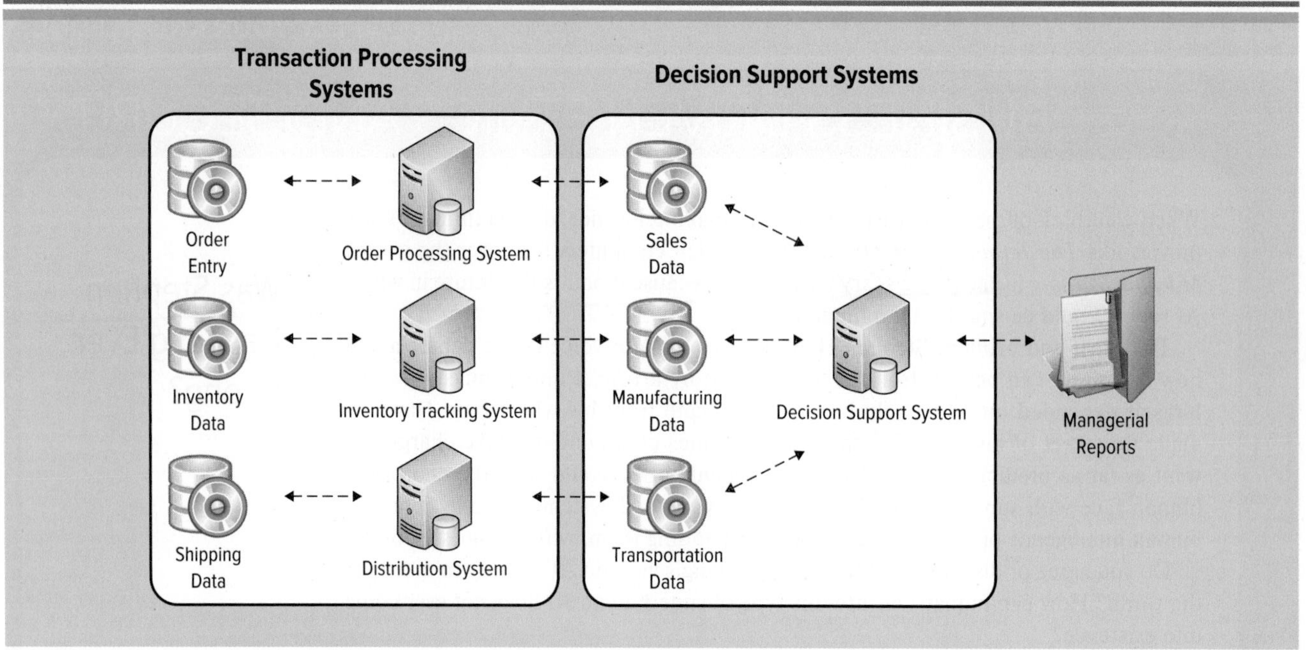

FIGURE 2.12

Interaction between TPS and DSS to Support Semistructured Decisions

Strategic Support Systems

Decision making at the strategic level requires both business intelligence and knowledge to support the uncertainty and complexity associated with business strategies.

- ***Executive information system (EIS)***: A specialized DSS that supports senior-level executives and unstructured, long-term, nonroutine decisions requiring judgment, evaluation, and insight.

These decisions do not have a right or wrong answer, only efficient and effective answers. Moving up through the organizational pyramid, managers deal less with the details (finer information) and more with meaningful aggregations of information (coarser information).

- ***Granularity***: Refers to the level of detail in the model or the decision-making process.

The greater the granularity, the deeper the level of detail or fineness of data (see Figure 2.13). A DSS differs from an EIS in that an EIS requires data from external sources to support

FIGURE 2.13

Information Levels throughout an Organization

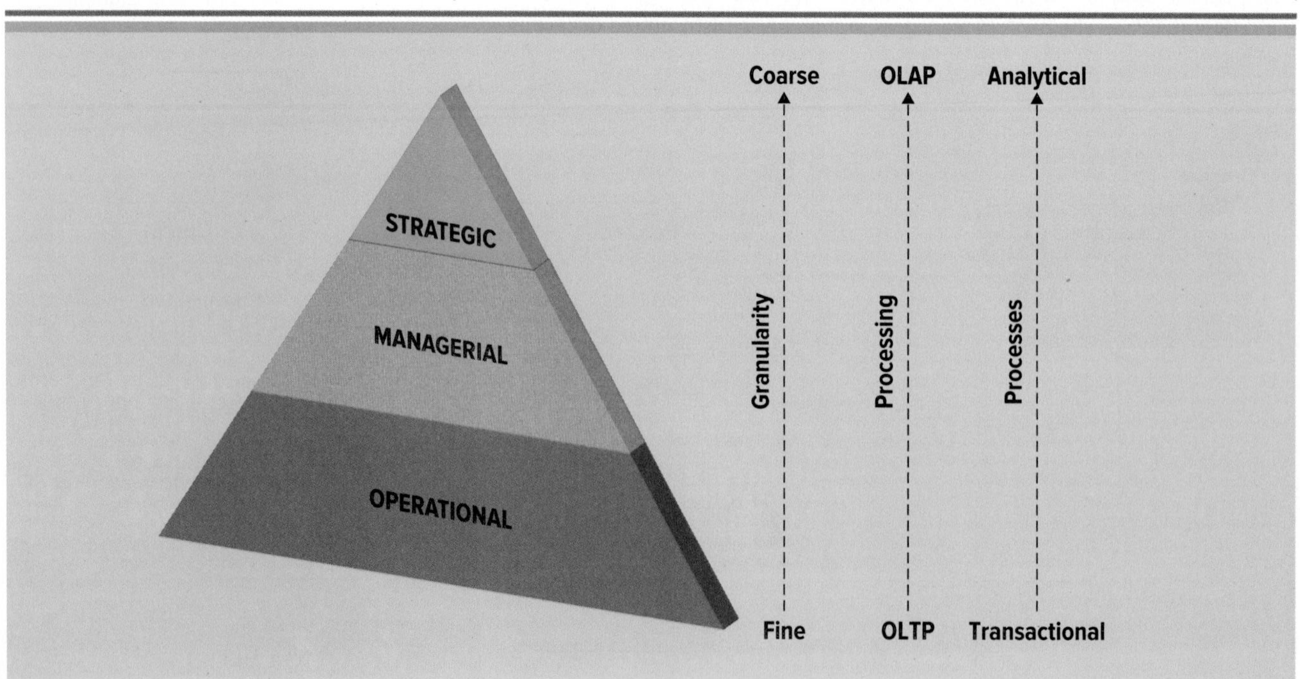

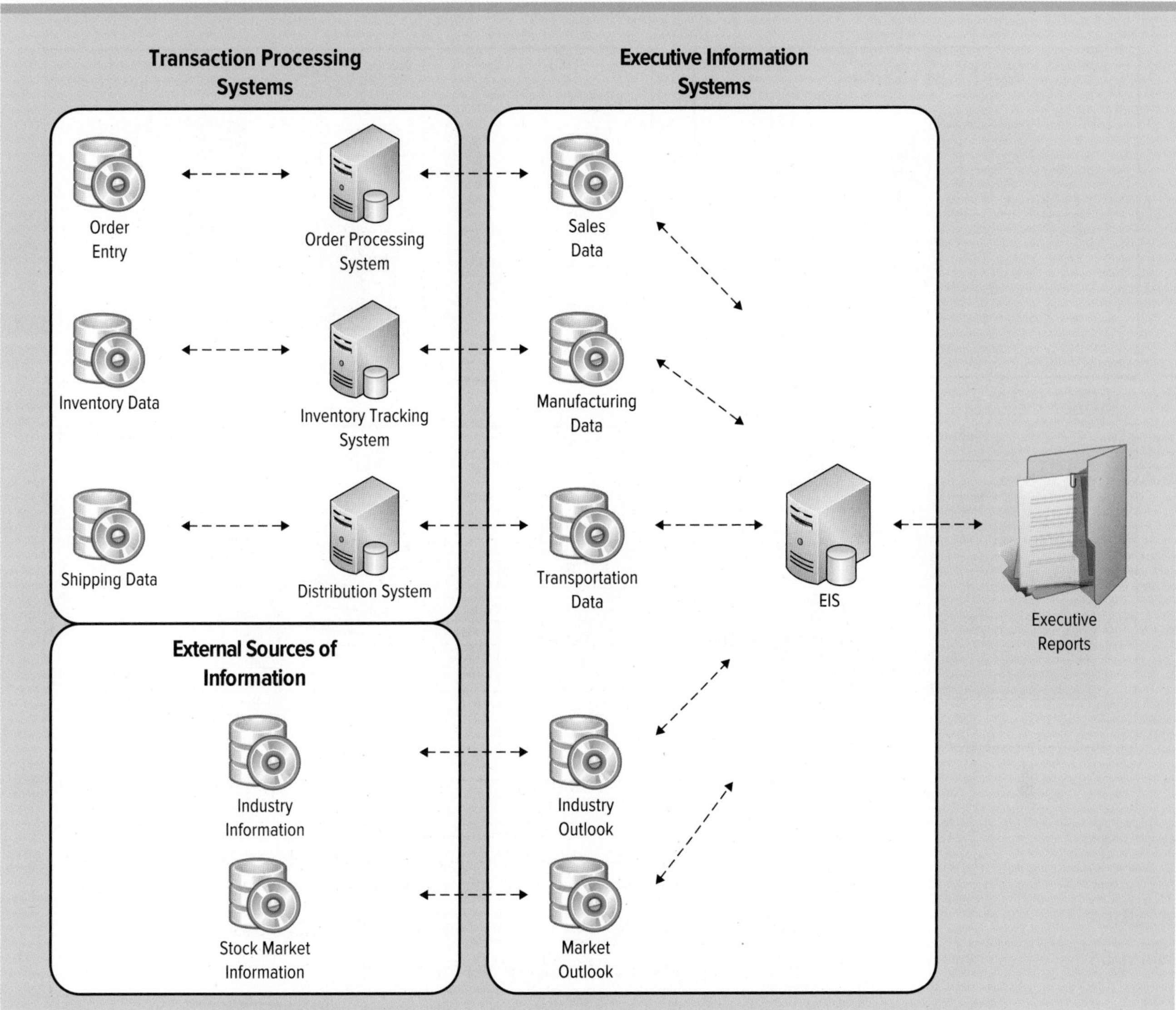

FIGURE 2.14

Interaction between a TPS and EIS

unstructured decisions (see Figure 2.14). This is not to say that DSSs never use data from external sources, but typically, DSS semistructured decisions rely on internal data only.

- ***Visualization***: Produces graphical displays of patterns and complex relationships in large amounts of data.
- ***Infographic*** (information graphic)**:** A representation of information in a graphical format designed to make the data easily understandable at a glance.

Executive information systems use visualization to deliver specific key information to top managers at a glance, with little or no interaction with the system. People use infographics to quickly communicate a message, to simplify the presentation of large amounts of data, to see data patterns and relationships, and to monitor changes in variables over time. Infographics abound in almost any public environment–traffic signs, subway maps, tag clouds, musical scores, and weather charts are just a few examples, among a huge number of possibilities. Common elements of an infographic include the following:

- ***Pie chart***: A type of graph in which a circle is divided into sectors that each represents a proportion of the whole.
- ***Bar chart***: A chart or graph that presents grouped data with rectangular bars with lengths proportional to the values that they represent.
- ***Histogram***: A graphical display of data using bars of different heights. It is similar to a bar chart, but a histogram groups numbers into ranges.

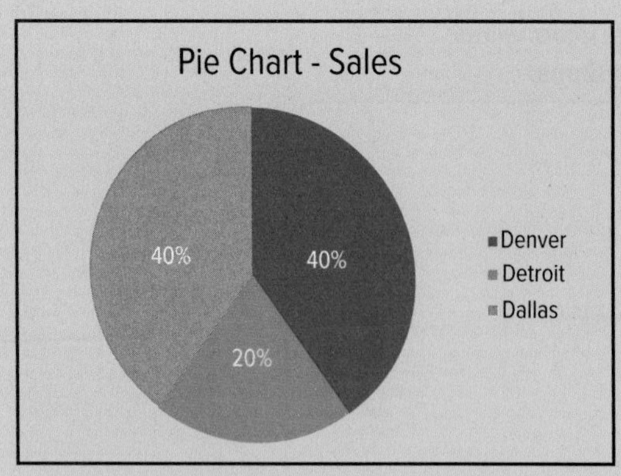

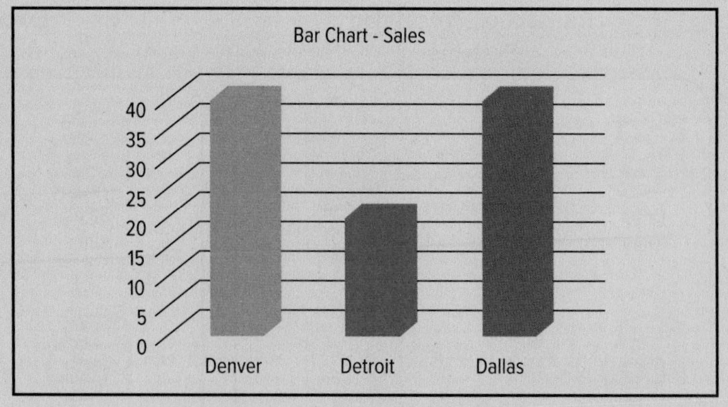

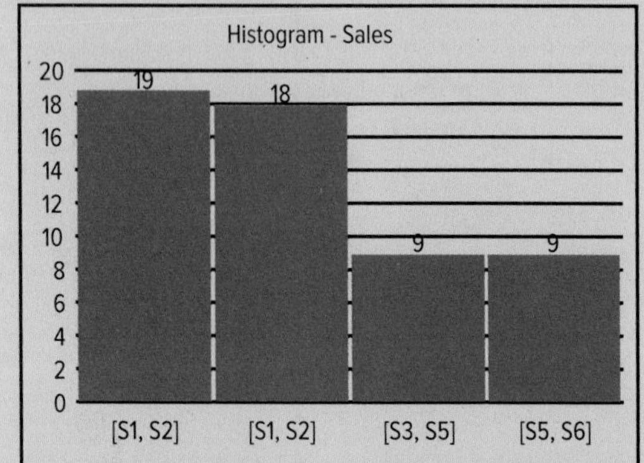

Sparklines for Sales

	Countries	1990	2008	2025	Line chart	Bar chart	Column chart
1	China	1,141	1,333	1,452			
2	India	849	1,140	1,398			
3	United States	250	304	352			
4	Indonesia	178	228	273			
5	Brazil	150	192	223			
6	Pakistan	108	166	226			
7	Bangladesh	116	160	198			
8	Nigeria	94	151	208			
9	Russia	149	143	137			
10	Japan	124	128	126			

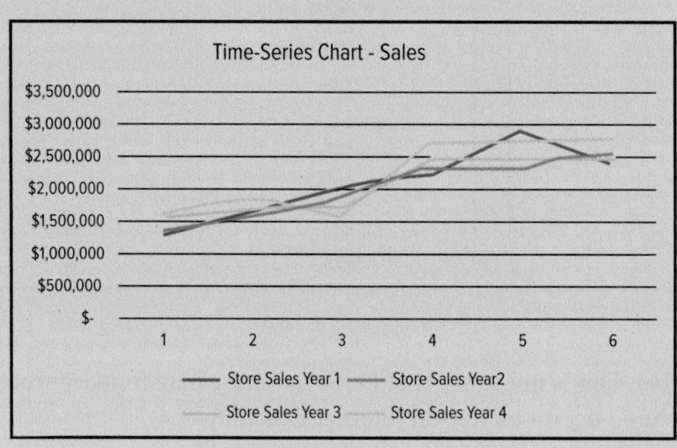

FIGURE 2.15

Visualization Chart Types

- ***Sparkline***: A small embedded line graph that illustrates a single trend. Sparklines are often used in reports, presentations, dashboards, and scoreboards. They do not include axes or labels; context comes from the related content.
- ***Time-series chart***: A graphical representation showing change of a variable over time. Time-series charts are used for data that changes continuously, such as stock prices. They allow for a clear visual representation of a change in one variable over a set amount of time (see Figure 2.15).

A common tool that supports visualization is a digital dashboard.

- ***Digital dashboard***: Tracks KPIs and CSFs by compiling information from multiple sources and tailoring it to meet user needs.

Following is a list of potential features included in a dashboard designed for a manufacturing team:

- A hot list of key performance indicators, refreshed every 15 minutes.
- A running line graph of planned versus actual production for the past 24 hours.
- A table showing actual versus forecasted product prices and inventories.
- A list of outstanding alerts and their resolution status.
- A graph of stock market prices.

BUSINESS DRIVEN START-UP

Jump into the Game

Have you ever considered starting your own business? You are not alone. It is the perfect time to create something new. Here is a list of fellow entrepreneurial thinkers who did jump in the game–while still in college.

- Bill Gates; Microsoft
- Steve Jobs; Apple
- Michael Dell; Dell Computers
- Mark Zuckerberg; Facebook
- Sergey Brin/Larry Page; Google
- Jerry Yang/David Filo; Yahoo
- Kevin Systeom; Instagram
- Evan Spiegel; Snapchat
- Steven Chen/Chad Hurley; YouTube

Did you believe that you have to wait until you graduate to jump into the game of business? You may need a license to drive a car, catch a fish, or hike in a National Park, but to jump into the game of business, you just need to try. In a group, think about a business you would enjoy starting–regardless of its success. What would make you jump out of bed every day excited to get to work and start building your dream business?

One thing to remember when making decisions is the old saying "Garbage in, garbage out." If the transactional data used in the support system is wrong, then the managerial analysis will be wrong, and the DSS will simply assist in making a wrong decision faster. Managers should also ask, "What is the DSS *not* telling me before I make my final decision?"

USING AI TO MAKE BUSINESS DECISIONS

LO 2.4: Describe artificial intelligence and identify its three main types.

Do you know how financial advisors try to predict stock price behavior by analyzing past information? Thanks to Neural Networks, computers can do the same thing faster and with a higher accuracy. Simply put, these are programs that take data you feed them, train themselves to recognize patterns, and attempt to predict the output for a new set of similar data.

- ***Artificial intelligence (AI)***: Simulates human thinking and behavior, such as the ability to reason and learn.

AI's ultimate goal is to build a system that can mimic human intelligence. *AI* is a hot buzzword, and if you are using Alexa or Siri, you are already using it. Entrepreneurs believe AI will soon be integrated with every product and service. To begin to understand AI, let's use a systems thinking approach so you can see how inputs are processed to new outputs (see Figure 2.16).

- ***Expert systems***: Computerized advisory programs that imitate the reasoning processes of experts in solving difficult problems.

FIGURE 2.16

Transforming Inputs to Outputs with AI

Input	Output
Email	Determine if the email is spam
Audio clip	Text transcript of the audio
English sentence	Chinese sentence

Typically, they include a knowledge base containing various accumulated experiences and a set of rules for applying the knowledge base to each particular situation. Expert systems are the most common form of AI in the business arena because they fill the gap when human experts are difficult to find or retain or are too expensive. The best-known systems play chess and assist in medical diagnosis.

You might have come across the word *algorithm* if you have been introduced to programming.

- ***Algorithms***: Mathematical formulas placed in software that perform an analysis on a dataset.

Algorithms use formulas to solve problems, such as driving cars or playing chess. Driving a car is a difficult task and takes hours and hours of training for humans, let alone computers. Playing chess has one goal–to win–and can take hundreds of hours to learn how to play. In artificial intelligence, an algorithm tells the machines how to figure out answers to different issues or questions.

- ***Genetic algorithm***: An artificial intelligence system that mimics the evolutionary, survival-of-the-fittest process to generate increasingly better solutions to a problem.

A genetic algorithm is essentially an optimizing system: It finds the combination of inputs that gives the best outputs. Genetic algorithms are best suited to decision-making environments in which thousands, or perhaps millions, of solutions are possible. Genetic algorithms can find and evaluate solutions with many more possibilities, faster, and more thoroughly than a human. Organizations face decision-making environments for all types of problems that require optimization techniques, such as the following:

- Business executives use genetic algorithms to help them decide which combination of projects a firm should invest in, taking complicated tax considerations into account.
- Investment companies use genetic algorithms to help in trading decisions.
- Telecommunication companies use genetic algorithms to determine the optimal configuration of fiber-optic cable in a network that may include as many as 100,000 connection points. The genetic algorithm evaluates millions of cable configurations and selects the one that uses the least amount of cable.

Figure 2.17 displays several examples of AI. This text covers three primary areas of artificial intelligence:

- Machine learning
- Neural networks
- Virtual reality

FIGURE 2.17

Examples of Artificial Intelligence

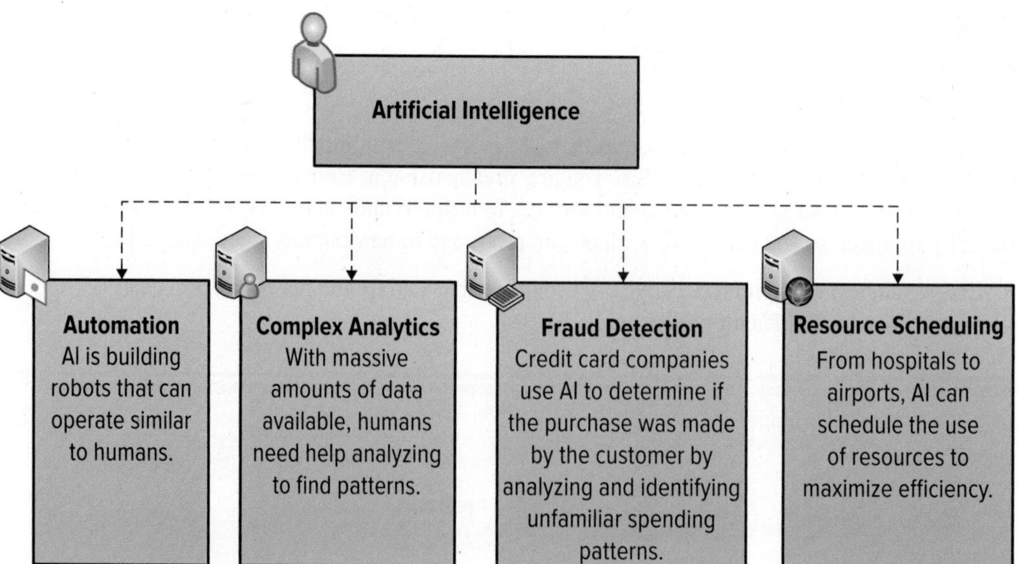

Artificial Intelligence
Automation
AI is building robots that can operate similar to humans.
Complex Analytics
With massive amounts of data available, humans need help analyzing to find patterns.
Fraud Detection
Credit card companies use AI to determine if the purchase was made by the customer by analyzing and identifying unfamiliar spending patterns.
Resource Scheduling
From hospitals to airports, AI can schedule the use of resources to maximize efficiency.

Machine Learning

If you read the news, you have probably heard about machine learning.

- ***Machine learning*:** A type of artificial intelligence that enables computers to understand concepts in the environment and to learn.

It is typically referenced when reporters are covering stories on amazing inventions. Just imagine stopping in front of a large office building downtown and not having to worry about parking? As you exit your vehicle, it automatically finds a parking space and self-parks. This is the future of autonomous vehicles and is a feature of machine learning. The words *AI* and *machine learning* are sometimes used interchangeably; however, it is important to note that machine learning is a *type* of AI. AI has far more capabilities than just machine learning. Figure 2.18 highlights three different forms of machine learning.[6]

Machine learning couples algorithms and data to discover patterns and trends that make predictions. It is based on the principle that systems can learn from data, identify patterns, and make decisions with minimal human interaction. With machine learning, machines are able to act without human programs detailing how to perform tasks. Machine learning has a vast and ever-expanding assortment of use cases, including:

- Amazon marketing personalization
- Google search optimization
- Customer churn prediction
- Financial credit score modeling
- Netflix recommendation engine
- Police facial recognition

FIGURE 2.18

Types of Machine Learning

Supervised Machine Learning

Training a model from input data and its correponding labels. Supervised machine learning is analogous to a student learning a subject by studying a set of questions and their corresponding answers. After mastering the mapping between questions and answers, the student can then provide answers to new (never-before-seen) questions on the same topic.

Unsupervised Machine Learning

Training a model to find patterns in a dataset, typically an unlabeled dataset. The most common use of unsupervised machine learning is to cluster data into groups of similar examples. For example, an unsupervised machine learning algorithm can cluster songs together based on various properties of the music. The resulting clusters can become an input to other machine learning algorithms (for example, to a music recommendation service). Clustering can be helpful in domains where true labels are hard to obtain. For example, in domains such as anti-abuse and fraud, clusters can help humans better understand the data.

Transfer Machine Learning

Transferring information from one machine learning task to another. For example, in multitask learning, a single model solves multiple tasks, such as a deep model that has different output nodes for different tasks. Transfer learning might involve transferring knowledge from the solution of a simpler task to a more complex one, or involve transferring knowledge from a task where there is more data to one where there is less data. Most machine learning systems solve a single task. Transfer learning is a baby step toward artificial intelligence in which a single program can solve multiple tasks.

Machine Learning Training The secret to building successful machine learning models is to ensure the training data has enough data to train the model. This is also the difficult part of building machine learning models.

- ***Data augmentation*:** Occurs when adding additional training examples by transforming existing examples.

For example, if your model includes images of only 10 people, there might not be enough differences to distinguish between males and females. Data augmentation can rotate, stretch, and reflect each image to produce many variants of the original images, providing enough examples for training. Once you have your training data, watch for two additional learning problems: overfitting and underfitting.

- ***Overfitting*:** Occurs when a machine learning model matches the training data so closely that the model fails to make correct predictions on new data. Essentially, the model knows the training data too well and is unable to make future predictions. Overfitting happens when a model learns the details in the training data to the extent that it negatively impacts the performance of the model on new data.
- ***Underfitting*:** Occurs when a machine learning model has poor predictive abilities because it did not learn the complexity in the training data. When underfitting occurs, the solution is to try different machine learning algorithms. Many problems can cause overfitting and underfitting, and finding the sweet spot between the two is a difficult task.

Machine Learning Bias One of the common complaints associated with machine learning is ***bias***, a disproportionate weight in favor of or against an idea or thing, usually in a way that is closed-minded, prejudicial, or unfair. Even if you don't actively think about gender, age, or looks, it is common to subconsciously select or reject people based on identity. A few forms of recognized bias include:

- ***Affinity bias*:** A tendency to connect with, hire, and promote those with similar interests, experiences, or backgrounds.
- ***Conformity bias*:** Acting similarly, or conforming to those around you, regardless of your own views.
- ***Confirmation bias*:** Actively looking for evidence that backs up preconceived ideas about someone.
- ***Name bias*:** The tendency to prefer certain types of names.[7]

Machine learning models, along with the training data, are created by humans and will do exactly what they are taught to do. Clearly, with humans building the algorithms and feeding the training data, there are problems with bias being introduced into the artificial intelligence models. Algorithms that are biased will end up doing things that reflect that bias. Bias can be detected and mitigated if you know what bias looks like and can identify its source. The four types of bias in machine learning include:

- ***Sample bias*:** A problem with using incorrect training data to train the machine. For example, you are training an autonomous vehicle to drive in all weather conditions, but your sample only has driving data on sunny days over 85 degrees. You have now introduced sample bias into your model. Training the algorithm to drive in rain, snow, sleet, hail, and other conditions would eliminate this source of sample bias.
- ***Prejudice bias*:** A result of training data that is influenced by cultural or other stereotypes. For example, you are training a machine vision algorithm, and you have men going to work and women taking care of children in your data images. The algorithm is likely to learn that men work and women stay at home. The primary issue with prejudice bias is that the training data decisions consciously or unconsciously reflected cultural and social stereotypes. The solution to reducing prejudice bias is to ensure the humans gathering the training data are aware of and sensitive to introducing their own societal prejudices or stereotypes into the training data.
- ***Measurement bias*:** Occurs when there is a problem with the data collected that skews the data in one direction. For example, if the same camera takes photos of all the

BUSINESS DRIVEN DEBATE

Where Are You Placing Your Data?

A robot named Ai-Da (after the 19th-century mathematician Ada Lovelace) is creating self-portraits by "looking" into a worm through her camera eyes. Ai-Da can draw people's portraits using her camera eye and a pencil in her hand with the help of algorithm programs that transform each coordinate. The hand of the artistic robot calculates a virtual route and interprets the coordinates to create the artwork.

We now live in a culture of selfies, and nobody thinks twice about posting them on Instagram, Facebook, or Snapchat. But have you ever thought about who is collecting all of that data and what they are doing with it? Do you realize that each time you post a selfie or photo you are giving your data to the technology giants, who are using it to predict your behavior.[9]

Do you agree or disagree that through technology you have been unknowingly outsourcing your own decisions?

training data and there is a problem with the camera's filter, then the images could be distorted. The algorithm would be trained on image data that is incorrect and does not represent reality. Measurement bias can be avoided by collecting additional data using different devices.

- ***Variance bias***: A mathematical property of an algorithm. This is the only bias not associated with the input of training data. Models with high variance can easily fit into training data and welcome complexity, but they are sensitive to noise. Models with low variance are more rigid and less sensitive to data variations and noise. Importantly, data scientists are trained to arrive at an appropriate balance between these two properties.[8]

Neural Networks

Neural networks are emulating human brains. You can give a neural network company data and train it to perform the task, generating reports, and it will use that training, new information, and its "work experience" to adapt and improve in much the same way a human worker learns.

- ***Neural network,*** also called artificial neural network: A category of AI that attempts to emulate the way the human brain works.

Unlike humans, these software robots work at a much faster rate and never sleep, both saving your business money and freeing up employees to work on more creative and exciting tasks. A key feature of neural networks is that they are self-learning and can adapt on-the-fly or learn as the input data changes.

Imagine you are deciding whether you should go for a hike in the mountains. You never hike if it is snowing or hotter than 95 degrees (Fahrenheit). These two factors are inputs into your decision model. Your preference to not go hiking in the snow is stronger than your preference to not go hiking when it is above 95 degrees outside. You look at both of these variables, and for any given instance you consider these two criteria in regard to whether you want to go hiking. If you decide to go, your decision has been satisfied (it is not snowing and not above 95 degrees). If you decide not to go, your decision was not satisfied (it is snowing or it is above 95 degrees). This is a simplistic analogy for how neural networks work. In reality, neural networks can analyze massive quantities of data to establish patterns and characteristics when the logic or rules are unknown. Neural networks' many features include:

- Learning and adjusting to new circumstances on their own.
- Lending themselves to massive parallel processing.
- Functioning without complete or well-structured information.

- Coping with huge volumes of information with many dependent variables.
- Analyzing nonlinear relationships in information. (They have been called fancy regression analysis systems.)[10]

Fuzzy logic is a mathematical method of handling imprecise or subjective information. The basic approach is to assign values between 0 and 1 to vague or ambiguous information. Zero represents information not included, whereas 1 represents inclusion or membership. For example, fuzzy logic is used in washing machines that determine by themselves how much water to use or how long to wash (they continue washing until the water is clean). In accounting and finance, fuzzy logic allows people to analyze information with subjective financial values (intangibles such as goodwill) that are very important considerations in economic analysis. Fuzzy logic and neural networks are often combined to express complicated and subjective concepts in a form that makes it possible to simplify the problem and apply rules that are executed with a level of certainty.

- ***Black box algorithms***: Decision-making process that cannot be easily understood or explained by the computer or researcher.

Google's Deep Dream, an AI program, uses neural networks to digest millions of images, identify visual patterns, and then create something new—a kind of aesthetic prediction. The growth of computer capacity that can train larger and more complex models will lead to the development of two forms of neural networks, including deep learning and reinforcement learning.

- ***Deep learning***: A process that employs specialized algorithms to model and study complex datasets; the method is also used to establish relationships among data and datasets.

To understand deep learning, imagine a toddler whose first word is *dog*. The toddler learns what is (and what is not) a dog by pointing to objects and saying the word *dog*. The parent might say, "Yes, that is a dog" or "No, that is not a dog." As the toddler continues to point to objects, he becomes more aware of the features that all dogs possess. What the toddler does, without knowing it, is to clarify a complex abstraction (the concept of dog) by building a hierarchy in which each level of abstraction is created with knowledge that was gained from the preceding layer of the hierarchy. Deep learning technology mimics the human brain; hence, this model is a form of neural network, consisting of neurons. Similar to the structure of the human brain, neurons in neural networks are also organized in layers. Deep learning trains each layer and then uses that learning in the next layer to learn more, until the learning reaches its full stage through cumulative learning in multiple layers. Deep learning models require thousands of data records for the models to become good at classification tasks, and millions of data records for them to perform at the level of a human.

- ***Reinforcement learning***: The training of machine learning models to make a sequence of decisions.

The model learns to achieve a goal in an uncertain, potentially complex environment—for example, a game-like situation. The model uses trial and error to find a solution to the problem. To train the model, the programmer uses either rewards or penalties for the actions it performs. The model's goal is to maximize the total reward.[11]

Virtual Reality

Virtual reality is a fast-growing area of artificial intelligence that had its origins in efforts to build more natural, realistic, multisensory human–computer interfaces.

- ***Virtual reality***: A computer-simulated environment that can be a simulation of the real world or an imaginary world.

Virtual reality enables telepresence by which users can be anywhere in the world and use virtual reality systems to work alone or together at a remote site. Typically, this involves using a virtual reality system to enhance the sight and touch of a human who is remotely manipulating equipment to accomplish a task. Examples range from virtual surgery, during which surgeon

BUSINESS DRIVEN INNOVATION

My Virtual Reality Check

Virtual reality is the use of computer technology to create a simulated environment. Unlike traditional user interfaces, VR places the user inside an experience. Instead of viewing a screen in front of them, users are immersed and able to interact with 3-D worlds. By simulating as many senses as possible, such as vision, hearing, touch, even smell, the computer is transformed into a gatekeeper to this artificial world. The only limits to near-real VR experiences are the availability of content and cheap computing power. Here are some of the leaders in virtual reality:

- Virtual reality can train soccer players by participating in a virtual reality match.
- Find your own virtual personal trainer at a simulated gym.
- Immerse yourself in the Minecraft metaverse.
- Six Flags is turning to virtual reality to enhance its rollercoaster experience.
- The U.S. military uses virtual reality therapy to treat post-traumatic stress disorder.
- Virtual reality can train surgeons for complex operations.
- Students can attend a virtual field trip.
- Prospective students can take virtual campus tours.
- Virtual reality can simulate public speaking—a common phobia for many.
- Amnesty International uses virtual reality to help people appreciate the ravages of the Syrian conflict.

In a group, create a new product or service using virtual reality. What are the advantages and disadvantages of virtual reality? What potential social problems do you foresee with virtual reality?

and patient may be on opposite sides of the globe, to the remote use of equipment in hazardous environments such as chemical plants and nuclear reactors.

- ***Augmented reality*:** The viewing of the physical world with computer-generated layers of information added to it.

Google Glass is a wearable computer with an optical head-mounted display (OHMD). Developed by Google, it adds an element of augmented reality to the user's world by displaying information in a smart phone–like hands-free format. Google Glass became officially available to the general public in May 2014. Before that, users were required to receive invitations before they could try Google Glass.

Virtual reality (VR) and augmented reality (AR) are two sides of the same coin. You could think of augmented reality as a form of virtual reality with one foot in the real world: augmented reality simulates artificial objects in the real environment; virtual reality creates an artificial environment to inhabit.

In augmented reality, the computer uses sensors and algorithms to determine the position and orientation of a camera. AR technology then renders the 3-D graphics as they would appear from the viewpoint of the camera, superimposing the computer-generated images over a user's view of the real world.

In virtual reality, the computer uses similar sensors and math. However, rather than locating a real camera within a physical environment, the position of the user's eyes are located within the simulated environment. If the user's head turns, the graphics react accordingly. Rather than compositing virtual objects and a real scene, VR technology creates a convincing, interactive world for the user.[12]

section 2.2 | Business Processes

LEARNING OUTCOMES

2.5 Explain the value of business processes for a company and differentiate between customer-facing and business-facing processes.

2.6 Demonstrate the value of business process modeling and compare As-Is and To-Be models.

2.7 Differentiate among automation, streamlining, and reengineering.

LO 2.5: Explain the value of business processes for a company and differentiate between customer-facing and business-facing processes.

MANAGING BUSINESS PROCESSES

Most companies pride themselves on providing breakthrough products and services for customers. But if customers do not receive what they want quickly, accurately, and hassle-free, even fantastic offerings will not prevent a company from annoying customers and ultimately eroding its own financial performance. To avoid this pitfall and protect its competitive advantage, a company must continually evaluate all the business processes in its value chain. Recall from Chapter 1 that a *business process* is a standardized set of activities that accomplish a specific task, such as processing a customer's order. Business processes transform a set of inputs into a set of outputs—goods or services—for another person or process by using people and tools. Understanding business processes helps a manager envision how the entire company operates.

Improving the efficiency and effectiveness of its business processes will improve the firm's value chain. The goal of this section is to expand on Porter's value chain analysis by detailing the powerful value-adding relationships between business strategies and core business processes. Figure 2.19 illustrates several common business processes.

The processes outlined in Figure 2.19 reflect functional thinking. Some processes, such as a programming process, may be contained wholly within a single department. However, most, such as ordering a product, are cross-functional or cross-departmental processes and span the entire organization. The order-to-delivery process focuses on the entire customer order process across functional departments (see Figure 2.20). Another example is product realization, which includes not only the way a product is developed but also the way it is marketed and serviced. Some other cross-functional business processes are taking a product from concept to market, acquiring customers, processing loans, providing postsales service, processing claims, and handling reservations.

The reality is that people now rely on technology and data to achieve everything. One way to create a dramatic improvement in value is to embrace digital transformation. Research shows that organizations embracing digital transformation are almost 20 percent more likely to innovate with cost-effectiveness that beats the competition.

- ***Customer-facing processes,*** also called front-office processes, result in a product or service received by an organization's external customer. They include fulfilling orders, communicating with customers, and sending out bills and marketing information.
- ***Business-facing processes,*** also called back-office processes, are invisible to the external customer but essential to the effective management of the business; they include goal setting, day-to-day planning, giving performance feedback and rewards, and allocating resources. Figure 2.21 displays the different categories of customer-facing and business-facing processes along with an example of each.[13]

A ***business process patent*** is a patent that protects a specific set of procedures for conducting a particular business activity. A firm can create a value chain map of the entire industry to extend critical success factors and business process views beyond its boundaries.

- ***Core processes***: Business processes, such as manufacturing goods, selling products, and providing service, that make up the primary activities in a value chain.
- ***Static process***: Uses a systematic approach in an attempt to improve business effectiveness and efficiency continuously. Managers constantly attempt to optimize static processes. Examples of static processes include running payroll, calculating taxes, and creating financial statements.

FIGURE 2.19

Sample Business Processes

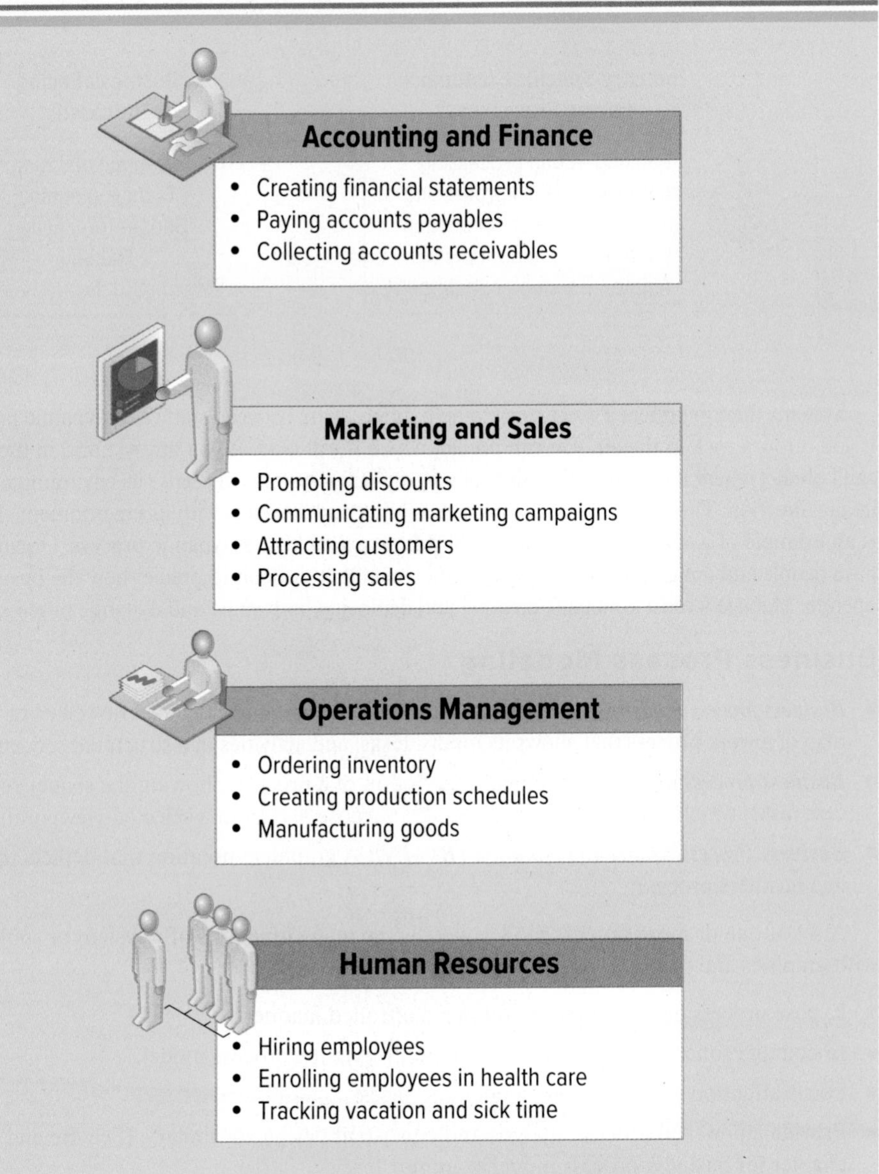

Accounting and Finance
• Creating financial statements
• Paying accounts payables
• Collecting accounts receivables
Marketing and Sales
• Promoting discounts
• Communicating marketing campaigns
• Attracting customers
• Processing sales
Operations Management
• Ordering inventory
• Creating production schedules
• Manufacturing goods
Human Resources
• Hiring employees
• Enrolling employees in health care
• Tracking vacation and sick time

- *Dynamic process*: Continuously changing; provides business solutions to ever-changing business operations. As the business and its strategies change, so do the dynamic processes. Examples of dynamic processes include managing layoffs of employees, changing order levels based on currency rates, and canceling business travel due to extreme weather.

FIGURE 2.20

Five Steps in the Order-to-Delivery Business Process

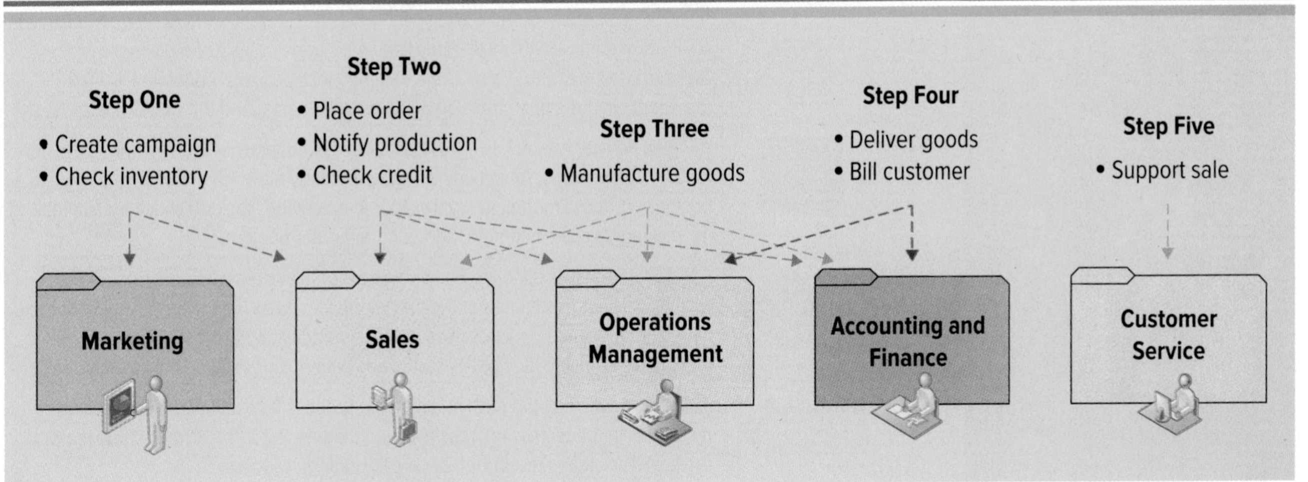

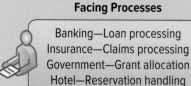

Customer-Facing Processes	Industry-Specific Customer-Facing Processes	Business-Facing Processes
Order processing Customer service Sales processing Customer billing Order shipping	Banking—Loan processing Insurance—Claims processing Government—Grant allocation Hotel—Reservation handling Airline—Baggage handling	Strategic planning Tactical planning Budget forecasting Training Raw materials purchasing

FIGURE 2.21

Customer-Facing, Industry-Specific, and Business-Facing Processes

Systems thinking offers a great story to help differentiate between static and dynamic processes. If you throw a rock in the air, you can predict where it will land. If you throw a bird in the air, you can't predict where it will land. The bird, a living, dynamic system, will sense its environment and fly in any direction. The bird gathers and processes input and interacts with its environment. The rock is an example of a static process, and the bird is an example of a dynamic process. Organizations have people and are characteristically dynamic, making it difficult to predict how the business will operate. Managers must anticipate creating and deploying both static and dynamic processes.

LO 2.6: Demonstrate the value of business process modeling and compare As-Is and To-Be models.

Business Process Modeling

- ***Business process modeling***, or ***mapping***: The activity of creating a detailed flowchart or process map of a work process that shows its inputs, tasks, and activities in a structured sequence.
- ***Business process model***: A graphical description of a process, showing the sequence of process tasks, which is developed for a specific purpose and from a selected viewpoint.
- ***Business Process Model and Notation (BPMN)***: A graphical notation that depicts the steps in a business process.

A set of one or more process models details the many functions of a system or subject area with graphics and text, and its purpose is to:

- Expose process detail gradually and in a controlled manner.
- Encourage conciseness and accuracy in describing the process model.
- Focus attention on the process model interfaces.
- Provide a powerful process analysis and consistent design vocabulary. (See the end of the chapter for business process model examples.)

BPMN provides businesses with a graphical view of the end-to-end flow of their business processes. Diagramming business processes allows for easy communication and understanding of how core business processes are helping or hindering the business. Figure 2.22 displays the

FIGURE 2.22

BPMN Notation

	Business Process Model and Notation (BPMN)
EVENT	A BPMN event is anything that happens during the course of a business process. An event is represented by a circle in a business process model. In Figure 2.23, the events include customer requests, time requests, and the end of the process.
ACTIVITY	A BPMN activity is a task in a business process. An activity is any work that is performed in a process. An activity is represented by a rounded-corner rectangle in a business process model. In Figure 2.23, the activities include checking availability, picking up the customers, and confirming the booking.
GATEWAY	A BPMN gateway is used to control the flow of a process. Gateways handle the forking, merging, and joining of paths within a process. Gateways are represented by a diamond shape in a business process model. In Figure 2.23, the gateways include determining availability status and accepting/declining the request.
FLOW	BPMN flows display the path in which the process flows. Flows are represented by arrows in a business process model. In Figure 2.23, the arrows show the path the customer takes through the taxi cab booking process.[15]

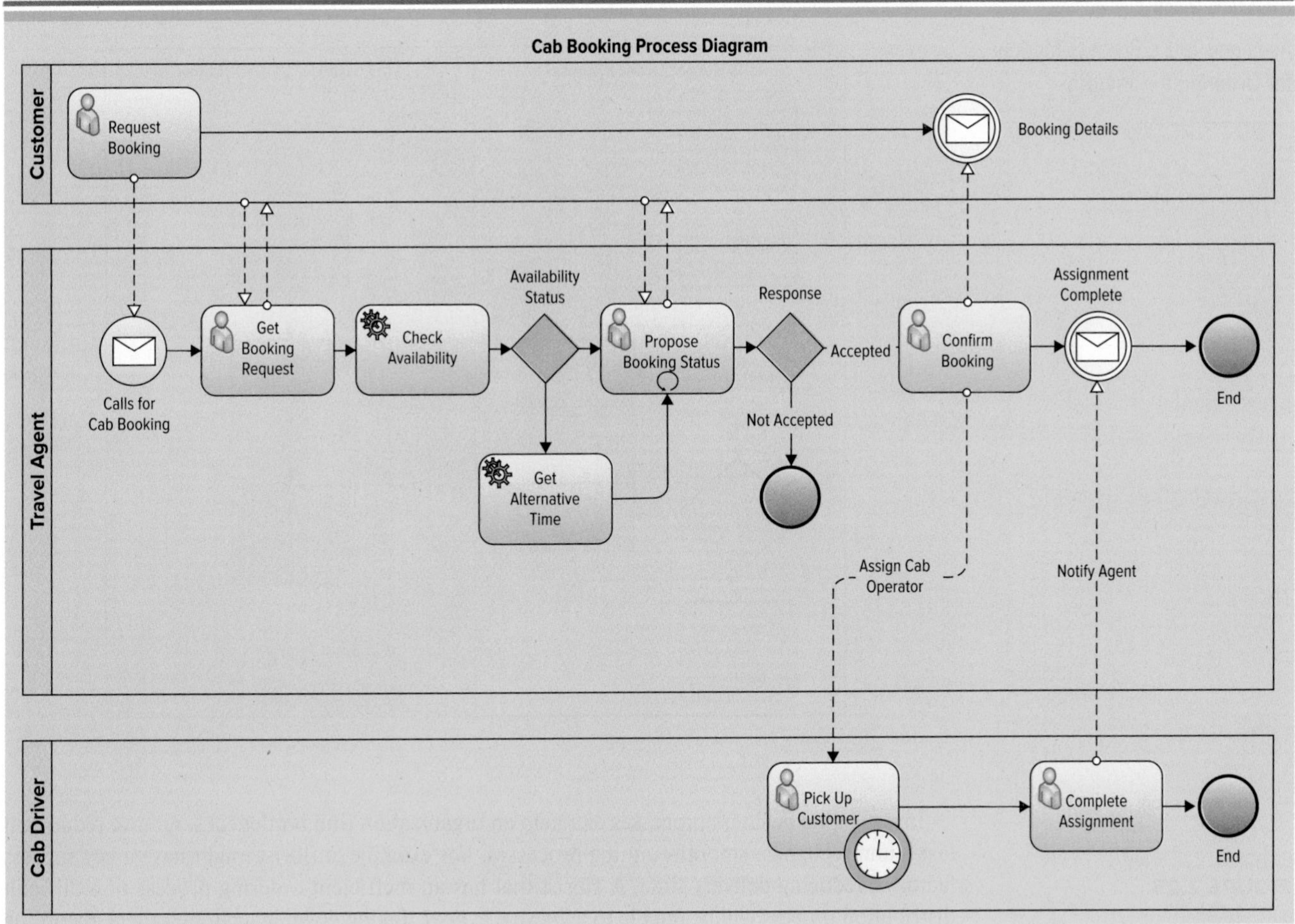

FIGURE 2.23

BPMN Sample Diagram for Hiring a Taxi Cab

standard notation from www.BPMN.org, and Figure 2.23 displays a sample BPMN diagram for hiring a taxi cab.[14]

Business process modeling usually begins with a functional process representation of the process problem, or an As-Is process model.

- ***As-Is process models***: Represent the current state of the operation that has been mapped, without any specific improvements or changes to existing processes.

The next step is to build a To-Be process model that displays how the process problem will be solved or implemented.

- ***To-Be process models***: Shows the results of applying change improvement opportunities to the current (As-Is) process model.

This approach ensures that the process is fully and clearly understood before the details of a process solution are decided on. The To-Be process model shows how "the what" is to be realized. Figure 2.24 displays the As-Is and To-Be process models for ordering a hamburger.

As-Is and To-Be process models are both integral in business process reengineering projects because these diagrams are very powerful in visualizing the activities, processes, and data flow of an organization. Figure 2.25 illustrates an As-Is process model of the order-to-delivery process, using swim lanes to represent the relevant departments.

- ***Swim lane***: Layout arranges the steps of a business process into a set of rows depicting the various elements.

You need to be careful not to become inundated in excessive detail when creating an As-Is process model. The primary goal is to simplify, eliminate, and improve the To-Be processes. Process improvement efforts focus on defining the most efficient and effective process identifying all of the illogical, missing, or irrelevant processes.

FIGURE 2.24

As-Is and To-Be Process Models for Ordering a Hamburger

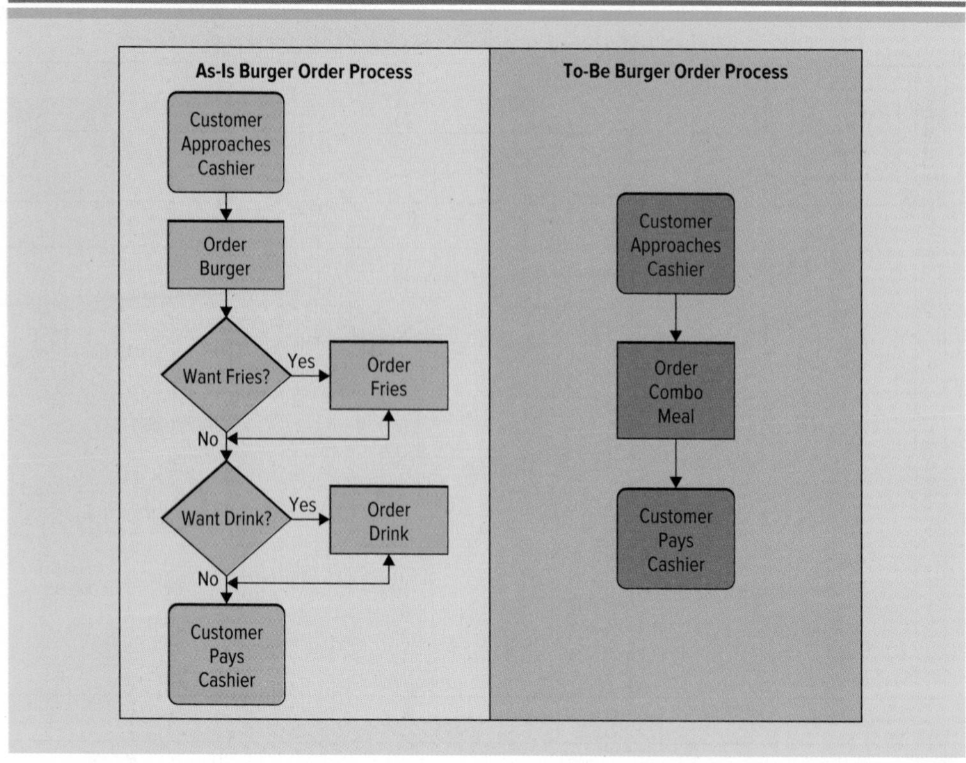

Investigating business processes can help an organization find bottlenecks, remove redundant tasks, and recognize smooth-running processes. For example, a florist might have a key success factor of reducing delivery time. A florist that has an inefficient ordering process or a difficult distribution process will be unable to achieve this goal. Taking down inaccurate orders, recording incorrect addresses, or experiencing shipping delays can cause errors in the delivery process. Improving order entry, production, or scheduling processes can improve the delivery process.

FIGURE 2.25

As-Is Process Model for Order Fulfillment

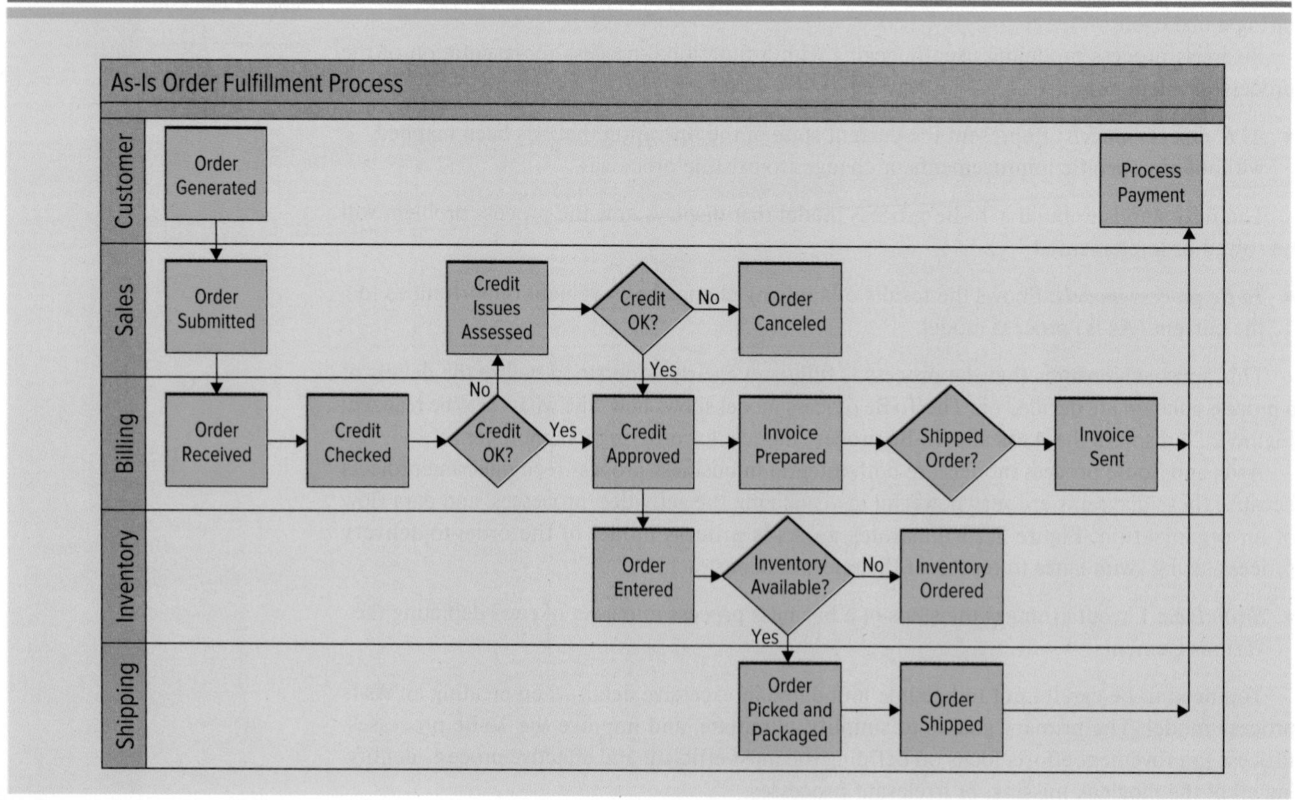

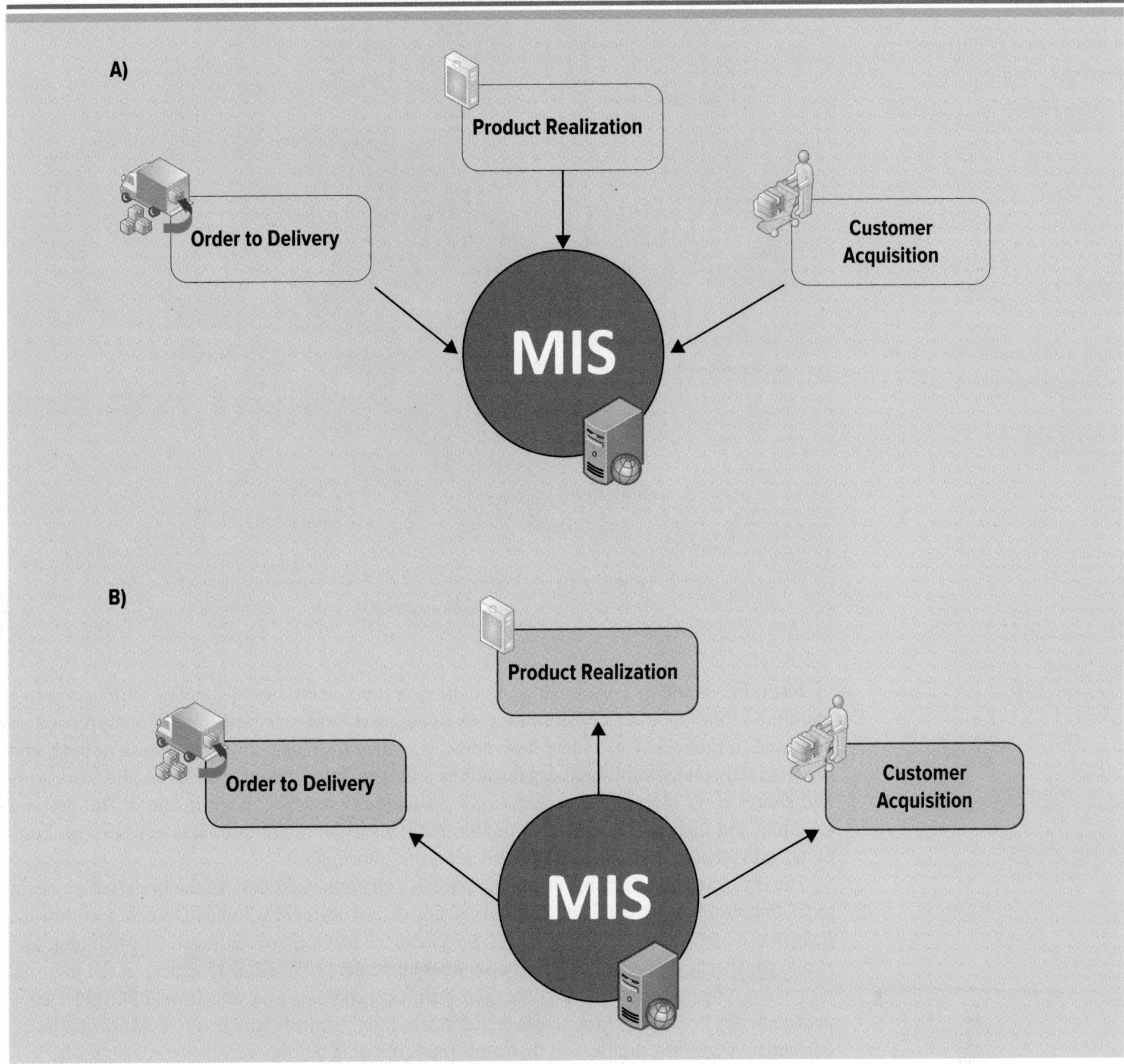

FIGURE 2.26

For Best Results, Business Processes Should Drive MIS Choices

Business processes should drive MIS choices and should be based on business strategies and goals (see Figure 2.26 A). Only after determining the most efficient and effective business process should an organization choose the MIS that supports that business process. Of course, this does not always happen, and managers may find themselves in the difficult position of changing a business process because the system cannot support the ideal solution (see Figure 2.26 B). Managers who make MIS choices and only then determine how their business processes should perform typically fail.

USING MIS TO IMPROVE BUSINESS PROCESSES

LO 2.7: Differentiate among automation, streamlining, and reengineering.

Understanding workflow, customers' expectations, and the competitive environment provides managers with the necessary ingredients to design and evaluate alternative business processes in order to maintain competitive advantages when internal or external circumstances change.

- ***Workflow***: Includes the tasks, activities, and responsibilities required to execute each step in a business process.
- ***Digitization***: The automation of existing manual and paper-based processes and workflows to a digital format.

FIGURE 2.27

Primary Types of Business Process Change

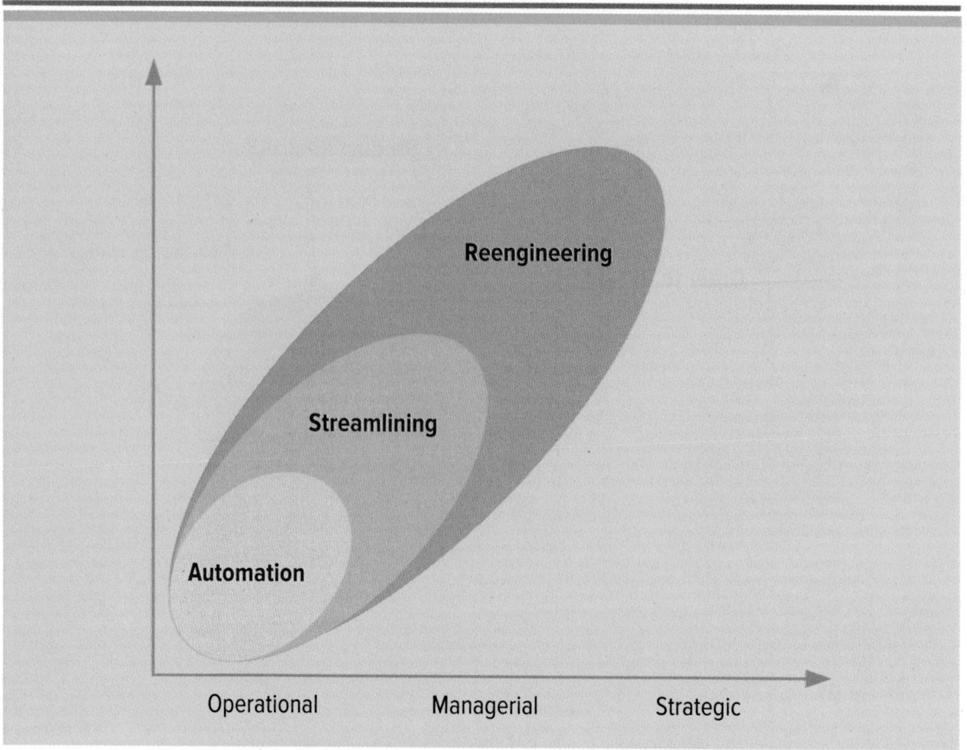

Just think of energy customers wanting to view their electricity bills online with access to a real-time report of their consumption. Or imagine a bank customer being preapproved or approved in minutes. Customers have come to expect to have immediate access to data, and unfortunately many traditional organizations still work with manual processes and workflows and simply can't meet these expectations. As a result, attackers born in the digital age can swoop in and disrupt the market through rapid delivery of digital products and services combined with advanced algorithms and full access to information.

The digitization of daily life is making phones and connected devices the preferred payment tools for consumers—preferences that are causing digital payment volume to blossom worldwide. Easy-to-use applications and websites, 24/7 customer service, special personal treatment, and global consistency are just a few of the services customers have come to expect in the information age. Companies that can digitize their business processes and workflows offer more competitive prices because of lower costs, better operational controls, and less risk. More and more, consumers want fast, simple, and digitized—that's opening up opportunities for businesses.

Alternative business processes should be effective (deliver the intended results) and efficient (consume the least amount of resources for the intended value). They should also be adaptable or flexible and support change as customers, market forces, and technology shift. Figure 2.27 shows the three primary types of business process change available to firms and the business areas in which they are most often effective.

Operational Business Processes—Automation

Improving business processes is critical to staying competitive in today's electronic marketplace. Organizations must improve their business processes because customers are demanding better products and services; if customers do not receive what they want from one supplier, often they can simply click a mouse to find many other choices.

- ***Operational business processes***: Static, routine, daily business processes such as inventory stocking, customer checkout, or daily opening and closing processes.
- ***Business process improvement***: Attempts to understand and measure the current process and make performance improvements accordingly. Figure 2.28 displays a typical business process improvement model.[16]
- ***Automation***: The process of computerizing manual tasks, making them more efficient and effective, and dramatically lowering operational costs.

BUSINESS DRIVEN GLOBALIZATION

Build-Robot, Save-Life

Robots are often associated with science fiction films and books and not always with business. Today, robots are performing surgery, disarming bombs, vacuuming kitchen floors, and packaging boxes in warehouses. Robots certainly can make life easier but are difficult to design and build. Most robots have three basic components: a brain, sensors (IoT), and mechanical devices that move the robot. The robot's brain collects the sensor information and tells the robot what to do. Programmers code the brains of simple robots to perform single tasks such as vacuuming or cleaning. Complex robots allow the robot to detect changes in its environment, such as light, sound, and temperature. Sensors can also measure the shape and size of spaces between objects, allowing the robot to adapt to its surroundings.

Think of all the problems people experience due to poverty around the world. In a group, create a robot capable of helping people combat the issues associated with poverty. How would your robot work? What problem would it solve? Present your robot to the class.

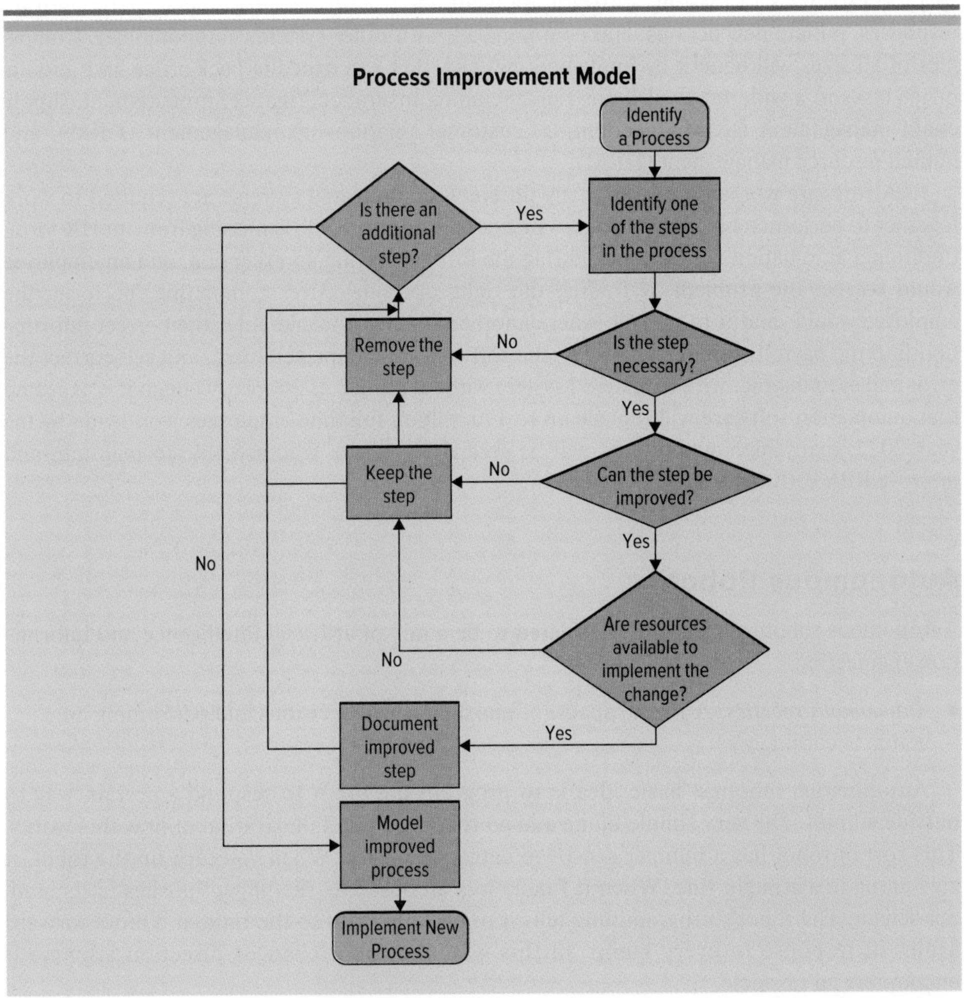

FIGURE 2.28

Business Process Improvement Model

Payroll offers an excellent example. Calculating and tracking payroll for 5,000 employees is a highly labor-intensive process requiring 30 full-time employees. Every two weeks, accounting employees must gather everyone's hours worked, cross-check with wage rates, and then calculate the amount due, minus taxes, and other withholding such as pension contributions and insurance premiums, to create the paychecks. They also track benefits, sick time, and vacation time. If the payroll process is automated, however, one employee can easily calculate payroll, track withholding and deductions, and create paychecks for 5,000 people in a few hours, since everything is performed by the system. Automation improves efficiency and effectiveness and reduces head count, lowering overall operational costs. Transaction processing systems (TPSs) are primarily used to automate business processes.

When tasked with improving a business process, be sure to take full advantage of the power of analytics to measure the process, IoT to provide real-time feedback for the process, and AI to re-imagine the process. AI includes robots, and the factories of tomorrow will be driven by autonomous robots. Just imagine how current business models can be transformed with AI to create new innovative business models for tomorrow.

Robotic Process Automation

- ***Robotic process automation (RPA)***: The use of software with artificial intelligence (AI) and machine learning capabilities to handle high-volume, repeatable tasks that previously required a human to perform.

Tasks such as running payroll and stocking and reordering inventory will be completely automated with the use of RPA. The difference between RPA and traditional MIS automation is RPA software's ability to be aware of and adapt to changing circumstances, exceptions, and new situations. Once RPA software has been trained to capture and interpret the actions of specific processes in existing software applications, it can then manipulate data, activate responses, initiate new actions, and communicate with other systems autonomously. Companies of all sizes will benefit by implementing RPA that can expedite back-office and middle-office tasks in a wide range of industries, including insurance, finance, procurement, supply chain management (SCM), accounting, customer relationship management (CRM), and human resource management (HRM).

RPA software works best when many different, complicated systems are required to work together to perform a business process. For example, if a zip code is missing from an HR form, traditional automation software would flag the form as having an exception, and an employee would correct the problem by finding the right zip code. After completing the form, the employee would send it to payroll, where another employee would enter the correct information into the payroll system. With RPA, the software can adapt, self-learn, and self-correct the error and even interact with the payroll system without human assistance. Though it is expected that automation software will replace up to 140 million full-time employees worldwide by the year 2025, many high-quality jobs will be created for those who are able to maintain and improve RPA software.[17]

Autonomous Robotics

Autonomous robotics is usually considered to be a mix of artificial intelligence and information engineering.

- ***Autonomous robotics***: A robot capable of making its own decisions and performing an action accordingly.

Autonomous robotics' basic idea is to program the robot to respond a certain way to outside stimuli. The very simple bump-and-go robot is a good illustration of how this works. This sort of robot has a bumper sensor to detect obstacles. When you turn on the robot, it zips along in a straight line. When it finally hits an obstacle, the impact pushes in its bumper sensor. The robot's programming tells it to back up, turn to the right and move forward again, in response to every bump. In this way, the robot changes direction anytime it encounters an obstacle.

Advanced robots use more elaborate versions of this same idea. Roboticists create new programs and sensor systems to make robots smarter and more perceptive. Today, robots can effectively navigate a variety of environments. Simpler mobile robots use infrared or ultrasound sensors to see obstacles. These sensors work the same way as animal echolocation: The robot sends out a sound signal or a beam of infrared light and detects the signal's reflection. The robot locates the distance to obstacles based on how long it takes the signal to bounce back. More advanced robots can analyze and adapt to unfamiliar environments, even to areas with rough terrain. These robots may associate certain terrain patterns with certain actions. A rover robot, for example, might construct a map of the land in front of it based on its visual sensors. If the map shows a very bumpy terrain pattern, the robot knows to travel another way. This sort of system is very useful for exploratory robots that operate on other planets. Three types of robotic vision include:

- ***Machine vision***: The ability of a computer to "see" by digitizing an image, processing the data it contains, and taking some kind of action. A machine vision system uses a video camera to capture data and send it to the robot controller. Machine vision is similar in complexity to voice recognition and can be used for handwriting recognition, signature identification, and currency inspection.
- ***Machine vision sensitivity***: The ability of a machine to see in dim light or to detect weak impulses at invisible wavelengths.
- ***Machine vision resolution***: The extent to which a machine can differentiate between objects. In general, the better the resolution, the more confined the field of vision. Sensitivity and resolution are interdependent. All other factors held constant, increasing the sensitivity reduces the resolution, and improving the resolution reduces the sensitivity.

Managerial Business Processes—Streamlining

Managerial business processes are semidynamic, semiroutine, monthly business processes such as resource allocation, sales strategy, or manufacturing process improvements.

- ***Streamlining***: Improves business process efficiencies by simplifying or eliminating unnecessary steps.
- ***Bottlenecks***: Occur when resources reach full capacity and cannot handle any additional demands; they limit throughput and impede operations. A computer working at its maximum capacity will be unable to handle increased demand and will become a bottleneck in the process. Streamlining removes bottlenecks, an important step if the efficiency and capacity of a business process are being increased. It also eliminates redundancy.
- ***Redundancy***: Occurs when a task or activity is unnecessarily repeated; for example, if both the sales department and the accounting department check customer credit.

Automating a business process that contains bottlenecks or redundancies will magnify or amplify these problems if they are not corrected first. Here's an example based on a common source of tension in an organization. Increasing orders is a standard KPI for most marketing/sales departments. To meet this KPI, the sales department tends to say yes to any customer request, such as for rush or custom orders. Reducing cycle time, the time required to process an order, is a common KPI for operations management. Rush and custom orders tend to create bottlenecks, causing operations to fall below their benchmarked cycle time. Removing these bottlenecks, however, can create master streamlined business processes that deliver both standard and custom orders reliably and profitably. The goal of streamlining is not only to automate but also to improve by monitoring, controlling, and changing the business process.

Strategic Business Processes—Reengineering

Strategic business processes are dynamic, nonroutine, long-term business processes such as financial planning, expansion strategies, and stakeholder interactions. The flat world is bringing more companies and more customers into the marketplace, greatly increasing competition.

APPLY YOUR KNOWLEDGE

BUSINESS DRIVEN MIS

Email Overload—Just Streamline It

The biggest problem with email is that it interferes with workflow. Many employees stop what they are working on and begin checking new email as soon as it arrives. If they do not have the time or capacity to answer it immediately, however, they leave it in the inbox, creating a bottleneck. This process continues all day, and eventually, the inbox is overflowing with hundreds of emails, most of which require a response or action. Employees begin dreading email and feel stressed because their workflow process is off track, and they do not know which tasks need to be completed and when.

To streamline workflow, you can designate certain times for email processing (at the top of the hour or for 30 minutes at three set times a day, for example). Turning off email notification also ensures you are not interrupted during your workflow. When you do begin to check your emails, review them one at a time from top to bottom and deal with each one immediately. Reply, put a note on your to-do list, forward the email, or delete it. Now you are working far more efficiently and effectively, and you are less stressed because your inbox is empty.

Choose a process in your life that is inefficient or ineffective and causing you stress. Using the principles of streamlining, remove the bottlenecks and reduce redundancies. Be sure to diagram the As-Is process and your newly created To-Be process and include artificial intelligence, machine learning, or robotics in your new process.

Wine wholesalers in the United States must now compete globally, for instance, because customers can just as easily order a bottle of wine from a winery in France as from them. Companies need breakthrough performance and business process changes just to stay in the game. As the rate of change increases, companies looking for rapid change and dramatic improvement are turning to business process reengineering.

- ***Business process reengineering (BPR)***: The analysis and redesign of workflow within and between enterprises.

Figure 2.29 highlights an analogy to process improvement by explaining the different means of traveling along the same route. A company could improve the way it travels by changing from foot to horse and then from horse to car. With a BPR mind-set, however, it would look beyond automating and streamlining to find a completely different approach. It would ignore the road and travel by air to get from point A to point B. Companies often

FIGURE 2.29

Different Ways to Travel the Same Route

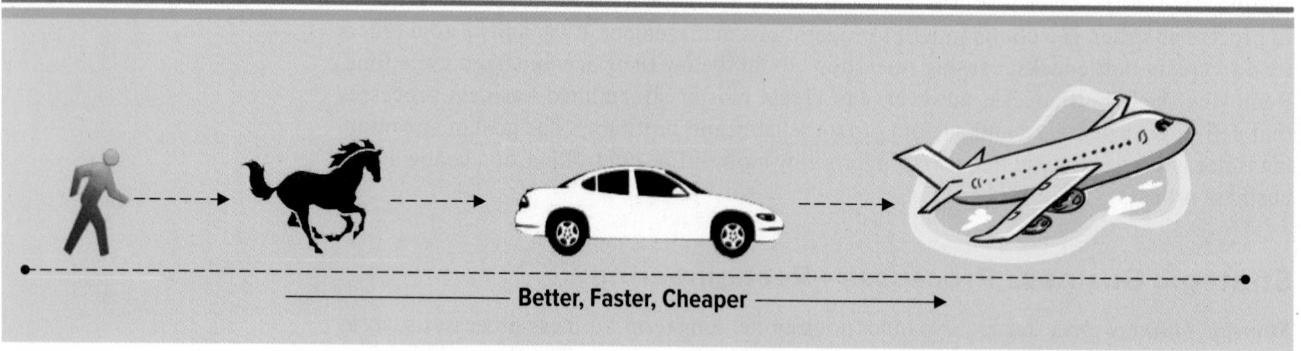

APPLY YOUR KNOWLEDGE

BUSINESS DRIVEN DEBATE

No Guts in Business

With IoT devices, automation, and digitization, it is now possible to watch business process changes in real time, rather than waiting for the end of the month, quarter, or year to receive a report. Your CEO has just come into your office and states the following: "Numbers have value only when they are put to work. Relying on statistical information rather than a gut feeling allows the data to lead you to be in the right place at the right time. To remain as emotionally free from the crazy of the here and now is one of the only ways to succeed. Moving forward, I want you to make decisions only on the data, not your gut." How do you respond to your CEO?

follow the same indirect path for doing business, not realizing there might be a different, faster, and more direct way.

An organization can reengineer its cross-departmental business processes or an individual department's business processes to help meet its CSFs and KPIs. When selecting a business process to reengineer, wise managers focus on those core processes that are critical to performance, rather than on marginal processes that have little impact. The effort to reengineer a business process as a strategic activity requires a different mind-set than that required in continuous business process improvement programs. Because companies have tended to overlook the powerful contribution that processes can make to strategy, they often undertake process improvement efforts by using their current processes as the starting point. Managers focusing on reengineering can instead use several criteria to identify opportunities:

- Is the process broken?
- Is it feasible that reengineering this process will succeed?
- Does it have a high impact on the agency's strategic direction?
- Does it significantly affect customer satisfaction?
- Is it antiquated?
- Does it fall far below best-in-class?
- Is it crucial for productivity improvement?
- Will savings from automation be clearly visible?
- Is the return on investment from implementation high and preferably immediate?

Systems Thinking and BPR

Systems thinking plays a big role in BPR. Automation and streamlining operate departmentally, whereas BPR occurs at the systems level or companywide level and the end-to-end view of a process.

Creating value for the customer is the leading reason for instituting BPR, and MIS often plays an important enabling role. Fundamentally new business processes enabled Progressive Insurance to slash its claims settlement time from 31 days to four hours, for instance. Typically, car insurance companies follow this standard claims resolution process: The customer gets into an accident, has the car towed, and finds a ride home. The customer then calls the insurance company to begin the claims process, which includes an evaluation of the damage, assignment of fault, and an estimate of the cost of repairs, which usually takes

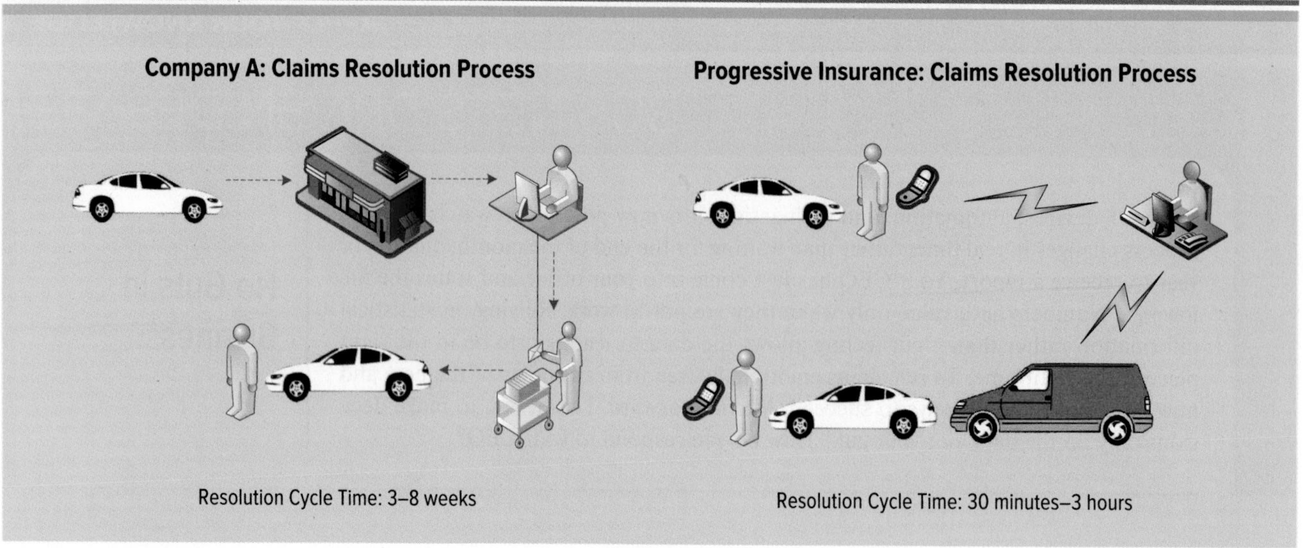

FIGURE 2.30

Auto Insurance Claims Processes

about a month (see Figure 2.30). Progressive Insurance's innovation was to offer a mobile claims process. When a customer has a car accident, he or she calls in the claim on the spot. The Progressive claims adjuster comes to the accident site, surveying the scene and taking digital photographs. The adjuster then offers the customer on-site payment, towing services, and a ride home. A true BPR effort does more for a company than simply improve a process by performing it better, faster, and cheaper. Progressive Insurance's BPR effort redefined best practices for an entire industry.[18] Figures 2.31 through 2.34 provide additional examples of business process modeling.

FIGURE 2.31

Online Sales Process Model

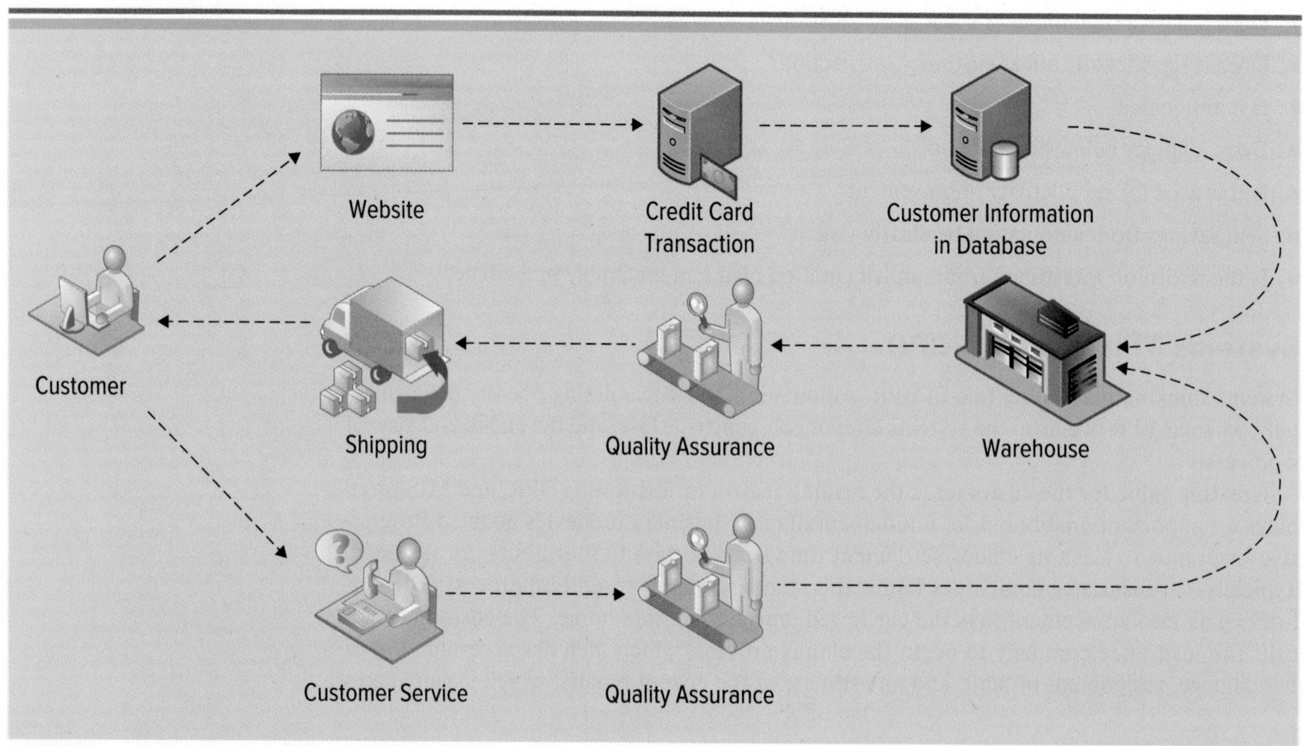

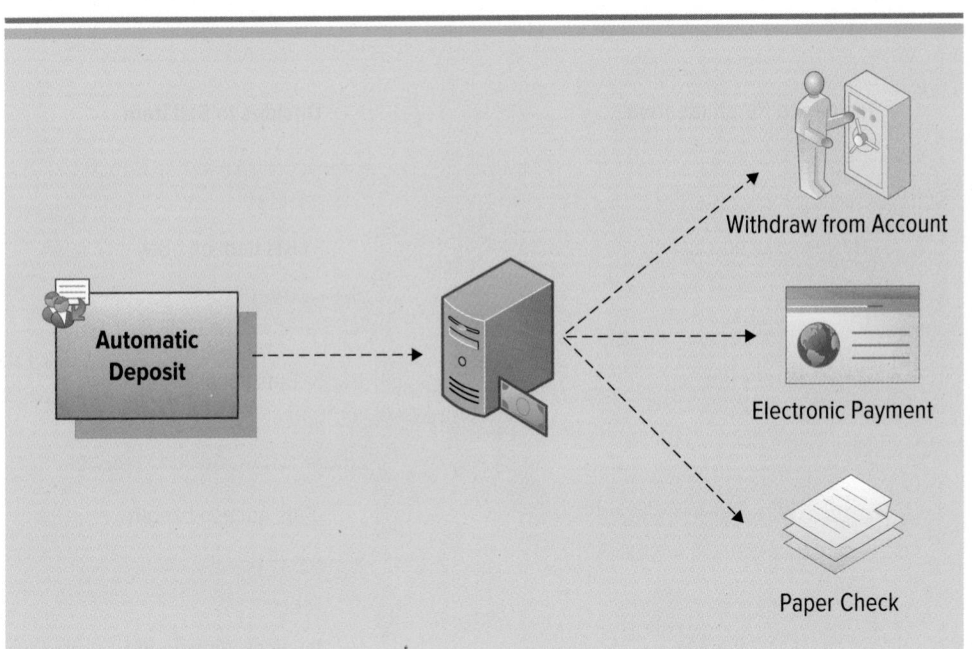

FIGURE 2.32

Online Banking Process Model

FIGURE 2.33

Order Fulfillment Process Model

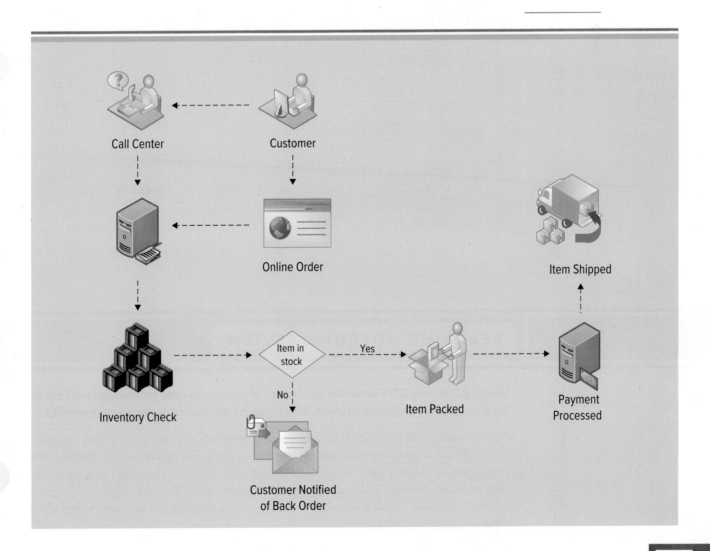

FIGURE 2.34

Purchasing an Item on eBay and Selling an Item on eBay Process Model

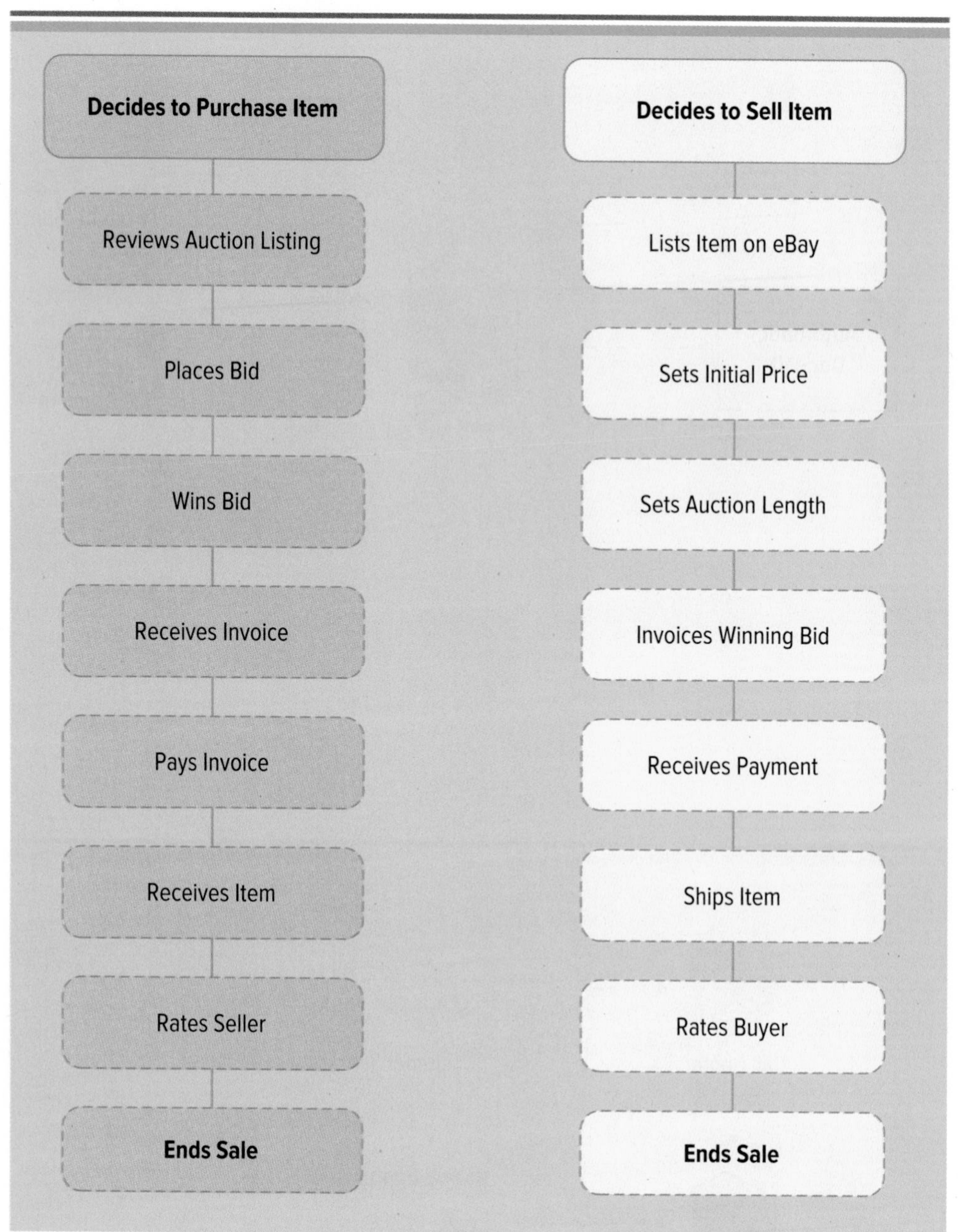

LEARNING OUTCOME REVIEW

Learning Outcome 2.1: Explain the importance of decision making for managers at each of the three primary organization levels, along with the associated decision characteristics.

Decision-making skills are essential for all business professionals, at every company level, who make decisions that run the business. At the operational level, employees develop, control, and maintain core business activities required to run the day-to-day operations. Operational decisions are considered structured decisions, which arise in situations in which established processes offer potential solutions. Structured decisions are made frequently and are almost repetitive in nature; they affect short-term business strategies.

At the managerial level, employees are continuously evaluating company operations to hone the firm's abilities to identify, adapt to, and leverage change. Managerial decisions cover short- and medium-range plans, schedules, and budgets, along with policies, procedures, and business objectives for the firm. These types of decisions are considered semistructured decisions; they occur in situations in which a few established processes help to evaluate potential solutions but not enough to lead to a definite recommended decision.

At the strategic level, managers develop overall business strategies, goals, and objectives as part of the company's strategic plan. They also monitor the strategic performance of the organization and its overall direction in the political, economic, and competitive business environments. Strategic decisions are highly unstructured decisions, occurring in situations in which no procedures or rules exist to guide decision makers toward the correct choice. They are infrequent, extremely important, and typically related to long-term business strategy.

Learning Outcome 2.2: Define critical success factors (CSFs) and key performance indicators (KPIs) and explain how managers use them to measure the success of MIS projects.

Metrics are measurements that evaluate results to determine whether a project is meeting its goals. Two core metrics are critical success factors and key performance indicators. CSFs are the crucial steps companies perform to achieve their goals and objectives and implement their strategies. They include creating high-quality products, retaining competitive advantages, and reducing product costs. KPIs are the quantifiable metrics a company uses to evaluate progress toward critical success factors. KPIs are far more specific than CSFs. Examples include turnover rates of employees, percentage of help-desk calls answered in the first minute, and number of products returned.

It is important to understand the relationship between critical success factors and key performance indicators. CSFs are elements crucial for a business strategy's success. KPIs measure the progress of CSFs with quantifiable measurements, and one CSF can have several KPIs. Of course, both categories will vary by company and industry. Imagine improved graduation rates as a CSF for a college.

Learning Outcome 2.3: Classify the different operational support systems, managerial support systems, and strategic support systems and explain how managers can use these systems to make decisions and gain competitive advantages.

Being able to sort, calculate, analyze, and slice-and-dice information is critical to an organization's success. Without knowing what is occurring throughout the organization, there is no way managers and executives can make solid decisions to support the business. The different operational, managerial, and strategic support systems include:

- **Operational:** A transaction processing system (TPS) is the basic business system that serves the operational level (analysts) in an organization. The most common example of a TPS is an operational accounting system such as a payroll system or an order-entry system.
- **Managerial:** A decision support system (DSS) models information to support managers and business professionals during the decision-making process.
- **Strategic:** An executive information system (EIS) is a specialized DSS that supports senior-level executives within the organization.

Learning Outcome 2.4: Describe artificial intelligence and identify its three main types.

Artificial intelligence (AI) simulates human thinking and behavior, such as the ability to reason and learn. The three most common categories of AI are:

- Machine learning—enables computers to both understand concepts in the environment and also to learn.
- Neural networks—attempts to emulate the way the human brain works.
- Virtual reality—a computer-simulated environment that can be a simulation of the real world or an imaginary one.

Learning Outcome 2.5: Explain the value of business processes for a company and differentiate between customer-facing and business-facing processes.

A business process is a standardized set of activities that accomplish a specific task, such as processing a customer's order. Business processes transform a set of inputs into a set of outputs (goods or services) for another person or process by using people and tools. Without processes, organizations would not be able to complete activities. Customer-facing processes result in a product or service that an organization's external customer receives. Business-facing processes are invisible to the external customer but essential to the effective management of the business.

Learning Outcome 2.6: Demonstrate the value of business process modeling and compare As-Is and To-Be models.

Business process modeling (or mapping) is the activity of creating a detailed flowchart or process map of a work process, showing its inputs, tasks, and activities in a structured sequence. A business process model is a graphical description of a process, showing the sequence of process tasks, which is developed for a specific purpose and from a selected viewpoint.

Business process modeling usually begins with a functional process representation of the process problem, or an As-Is process model. As-Is process models represent the current state of the operation that has been mapped, without any specific improvements or changes to existing processes. The next step is to build a To-Be process model that displays how the process problem will be solved or implemented. To-Be process models show the results of applying change improvement opportunities to the current (As-Is) process model. This approach ensures that the process is fully and clearly understood before the details of a process solution are decided on.

Learning Outcome 2.7: Differentiate among automation, streamlining, and reengineering.

Business process improvement attempts to understand and measure the current process and make performance improvements accordingly. Automation is the process of computerizing manual tasks, making them more efficient and effective, and dramatically lowering operational costs. Streamlining improves business process efficiencies by simplifying or eliminating unnecessary steps. Bottlenecks occur when resources reach full capacity and cannot handle any additional demands. These limit throughput and impede operations. Streamlining removes bottlenecks, an important step if the efficiency and capacity of a business process are being increased. Business process reengineering (BPR) is the analysis and redesign of workflow within and between enterprises and occurs at the systems level or companywide level and is the end-to-end view of a process.

KEY TERMS

Affinity bias 70
Algorithm 68
Analytical information 62
Artificial intelligence (AI) 67
As-Is process model 77
Augmented reality 73
Automation 80
Autonomous robotics 82
Bar chart 65
Benchmark 61
Benchmarking 61
Best practices 57
Bias 70
Black box algorithm 72
Bottleneck 83
Business-facing process 74
Business process improvement 80
Business process model 76
Business Process Model and Notation (BPMN) 76
Business process modeling (or mapping) 76
Business process patent 74
Business process reengineering (BPR) 84
Confirmation bias 70
Conformity bias 70
Core processes 74
Critical success factors (CSFs) 55
Customer-facing process 74
Data augmentation 70
Decision support system (DSS) 63
Deep learning 72
Digital dashboard 66
Digitization 79
Dynamic process 75
Effectiveness MIS metrics 58
Efficiency MIS metrics 58
Executive information system (EIS) 64

REVIEW QUESTIONS

1. Why must business professionals understand how MIS supports decision making and problem solving?
2. What is the relationship between critical success factors and key performance indicators? How can a manager use them to understand business operations?
3. What are the three levels of management found in a company? What types of decisions are made at each level?
4. Define transaction processing systems and describe the role they play in a business.
5. Define decision support systems and describe the role they play in a business.
6. Define expert systems and describe the role they play in a business.
7. What are the capabilities associated with digital dashboards?
8. What are the common DSS analysis techniques?
9. How does an electronic spreadsheet program, such as Excel, provide decision support capabilities?
10. What is artificial intelligence? What applications of AI offer the greatest business value?
11. What is a business process and what role does it play in an organization?
12. Why do managers need to understand business processes? Can you make a correlation between systems thinking and business processes?
13. Why would a manager need to review an As-Is and To-Be process model?
14. How can a manager use automation, streamlining, and business process reengineering to gain operational efficiency and effectiveness?
15. Explain the difference between customer-facing processes and business-facing processes. Which one is more important to an organization?
16. Explain how finding different ways to travel the same road relates to automation, streamlining, and business process reengineering.

CLOSING CASE ONE

Alexa: Can You Hear Me?

Voice-based artificial intelligent devices are not just jukeboxes with attitude; in fact, they just might be the primary way we interact with all future machines. August 31, 2012, was the date four Amazon engineers filed the patent for Alexa, an artificial intelligence system designed to engage with one of the world's biggest and most tangled datasets: human speech. The patent had a simple diagram and 11 words. "Please play 'Let It Be' by the Beatles." A small device replies "No problem, John," and the song begins playing. Millions of Alexa machines were sold when the device debuted in 2014.

Home-based AI systems are turning out to be big business as banks, universities, law firms, and others compete to create simple devices that people can talk to directly. What makes voice-based AI so appealing to consumers is its promise to conform to us, to respond to the way we speak and think—without requiring us to type on a keyboard or screen. That's also what makes it so technically difficult to build. We aren't at all orderly when we talk. Instead, we interrupt ourselves. We let thoughts dangle. We use words, nods, and grunts in odd ways, and we assume we are making sense even when we are not.

Thousands of Amazon staffers are working on this challenge, and the company currently lists over 1,100 Alexa job requests on its website. Machine learning techniques reexamined thousands of exchanges in which Alexa stumbled. With Alexa's usage surging, Amazon now has access to an expansive repository of human–computer speech interactions, giving it an edge in fine-tuning its voice technology. External data adds value, such as a massive database of song lyrics loaded into Alexa in 2016, helping ensure if you ask for the song with "drove my Chevy to the levee," you will be steered to Don McLean's "American Pie."

Of course, with all technology, there are bugs and glitches. You have likely heard of the frightening Alexa rogue laughter that was happening in people's homes during the night. Amazon stated Alexa's random laugh that was creeping out customers was the result of Alexa mistakenly hearing the phrase "Alexa, laugh." Amazon changed the phrase to "Alexa, can you laugh?" which is less likely to have false positives, and disabled the short utterance "Alexa, laugh." Amazon also reprogrammed Alexa's response from simply laughter to "Sure, I can laugh" followed by laughter.

This confirms the theory that Alexa was falsely triggered and not possessed. While it's promising the company issued a fix, that probably isn't enough to comfort users who allegedly heard Alexa laughing for no reason in the middle of the night.[19]

Questions

1. Define the three primary types of decision-making systems and how machine learning technology could help transform decision making.
2. Identify how machine learning can transform a traditional business process like checking out of a grocery store.
3. Explain the relationship between bias and machine learning for Alexa.
4. Argue for or against the following statement: Machine learning systems like Alexa invade user privacy.

CLOSING CASE TWO

Robots Took My Job

Have you ever seen the movie *The Terminator,* in which machines take over the world? Do you think that scenario could ever come true? Researching the Internet of Things makes you wonder if robots can gain self-consciousness, making the possibility of them taking over the Earth a reality. If these are your thoughts, you are not alone. Many prominent people in the field of science and technology are debating this hot topic.

"The primitive forms of artificial intelligence we already have, have proved very useful. But I think the development of full artificial intelligence could spell the end of the human race," the late British physicist Stephen Hawking told the BBC. "Once humans develop artificial intelligence, it would take off on its own and re-design itself at an ever-increasing rate." According to Hawking, the robots may take over the planet if artificial intelligence research is not done properly.

The debate on artificial intelligence has two sides: (1) in agreement with Hawking, stating artificial intelligence will overtake human intelligence; and (2) in disagreement with Hawking, stating that "true" AI—loosely defined as a machine that can pass itself off as a human being or think creatively—is at best decades away. The one truth about AI that is occurring today is that robots are taking over jobs in the workplace. Years ago, the horse was displaced by the automobile. In today's workplace, human labor is being displaced by robots. Oxford University researchers have estimated that 47 percent of U.S. jobs could be automated within the next two decades. But which ones will robots take first? According to Shelly Palmer, CEO of The Palmer Group, the following are the first five jobs robots are replacing, along with the last five jobs robots will replace. (See Figures 2.35 and 2.36.)[20]

FIGURE 2.35

The First Five Jobs Robots Will Replace

1. Middle Management
If your main job function is taking a number from one box in Excel and putting it in another box in Excel and writing a managerial report, then you are a prime target for a hostile takeover from a robot. Be ready.

2. Salespersons
Robots will dramatically reduce the cost of sales by removing the person from the sales process (request for proposal, quotation, order and fulfillment system), making the entire company far more profitable.

3. Report Writers, Journalists, Authors
Report writing is easy, and robots are being taught to read data, pattern match images or video, or analyze almost any kind of research materials, creating useful managerial reports. Text-to-speech systems are evolving quickly, and even commentators will be replaced by robots.

4. Accountants and Bookkeepers
Machine learning accountants and bookkeepers will operate infinitely better than humans and far cheaper. Robo-accounting is in its infancy, but it is awesome at dealing with accounts payable, accounts receivable, inventory control, auditing, and several other accounting functions.

5. Doctors
Robots make amazing doctors, diagnosticians, and surgeons. IBM's Watson is teaming up with a dozen U.S. hospitals to offer advice on the best treatments for a range of cancers and to help spot early stage skin cancers. And ultra-precise robo-surgeons are currently used for everything from knee replacement surgery to vision correction. This is great news because robotic doctors are going to become a necessity as the world population is expected to reach 11 billion in 2100. With that many people on Earth, even if everyone who ever wanted to be a doctor became one, we still would not have enough doctors.

FIGURE 2.36

The Last Five Jobs Robots Will Replace

1. Preschool and Elementary School Teacher
Children need to be taught by humans if we want our children to grow up to be human. A robot would be unable to teach a child to be human.

2. Professional Athlete
A robot playing a sport would simply take all of the fun out of the game. Professional athletes need to be human!

3. Politician
As long as fairness and equality are important topics, humans will be the only ones on the political scene.

4. Judge
Judging requires both objective and subjective assessments and simply cannot be replaced by a robot.

5. Mental Health Professional
It takes a great deal of human knowledge to understand mental health issues, and psychologists and psychiatrists will not be replaced by robots due to the delicate nature of humans.

Questions

1. Define the three primary types of decision-making systems and how robots in the workplace could affect each.
2. Describe the difference between transactional and analytical information, and determine how robots could improve the process for gathering and manipulating each type for a grocery store such as Safeway.
3. Illustrate the business process model used by a robot to perform an analysis on a patient with a cold.
4. Explain business process reengineering and how robots might dramatically change the current sales process.
5. Formulate different metrics that a personal trainer robot for a fitness club could provide a customer.
6. Argue for or against the following statement: Robots are better than humans in all business capacities.

MAKING BUSINESS DECISIONS

1. Modeling a Business Process

- Do you hate waiting in line at the grocery store?
- Do you hate being told you don't have the correct paperwork after waiting in line for three hours?
- Do you get annoyed when the pizza delivery person brings you the wrong order?

This is your chance to reengineer the process that drives you crazy. Choose a problem you are currently experiencing and reengineer the process to make it more efficient. Be sure to provide As-Is and To-Be process models.

2. Classroom Robots

What does a classroom look like in 2030? Can you imagine a beautiful steel robot flying around your classroom helping to answer questions and ensure you understand the material? A telepresence robot is a remote-controlled, wheeled device with a display to enable video chat and videoconferencing. Although telepresence robots aren't inexpensive, they are typically much more affordable than the travel costs or fees they might replace. They also enable much more interactivity than regular video chat. In a distance education class, for example, a telepresence robot can move around the room and interact face to face with individual students, just as an on-premises instructor might. Here are a few examples of telepresence robots:

- The doctor can see you now—virtually! iRobots are being used in hospitals where they make it possible for doctors to consult with patients, guide staff, and confer with other medical practitioners remotely. The robot travels around the hospital wearing a doctor's coat, and on its face is a screen on which the patients and staff can see the doctor and through which the doctor can see the patients and staff.
- Tired of Skype and long, boring conference calls? No more stagnant monitor in the meeting room. iRobots are being designed for a business environment to enhance telecommuting or teleconferencing. iRobots can sit at the table, write on the whiteboard, and engage in the conversation as if the person were actually at the meeting.
- Afraid your teenager is going to have a party while you are out for the evening or that Grandpa is eating all the sugary food that is bad for his diabetes? iRobots for in-home uses, such as mobile video chat, oversight of children or elderly people, and remote security monitoring, are already hitting the market.

Telepresence robots can enable remote tour guides, administrative assistants, home visitors, night security guards, and factory inspectors, among many other possibilities. In a group, discuss the pros and cons of telepresence robots. Can you think of any additional uses for a telepresence robot?

3. What Type of System Would You Use?

You have been hired as senior director for a large manufacturing company. Your first assignment is to decide which type of MIS can best support your decision-making needs. For all of the following, determine which type of system you would use to help solve the business problem or make a business decision. Be sure to label each as strategic, managerial, or operational.

	Operational Decision	Managerial Decision	Strategic Decision
You need to analyze daily sales transactions for each region			
You need to analyze staffing requirements for each plant.			
You need to determine which customers are at risk of defaulting on their bills.			
You need to analyze your competition, including prices, discounts, goods, and services.			
You need to analyze critical success factors and key performance indicators for status on operations.			
You need to produce a graphical display of patterns and complex relationships for large amounts of data.			

4. Is the Computer Smarter Than a Human?

In 2011, the IBM Watson computer defeated the two best contestants in the TV game show *Jeopardy!* What made the achievement so remarkable was that the computer had to read the question, understand what was being asked, search through 200 million pages of text, figure out what the best answer would be, and then hit a buzzer before the other contestants did. It accomplished all these steps in about 3 seconds. IBM predicts that Watson could be the ultimate researcher, helping professionals in various industries find the information they are looking for in a matter of seconds. What do you think about Watson's powerful services? Do you think you could one day have access to this powerful technology through your favorite search engine? How would having an IBM Watson help you in your college career?

5. Will They Stay or Will They Go?

Workplace turnover is a huge issue for business today. Each time an employee walks out the door, the business loses large amounts of capital, including training investments, business process knowledge, and organizational performance history. Anything a business can do to keep employees satisfied and motivated will help the company succeed. Human resource analytics software can analyze employee data to help determine which employees are at risk of leaving the company. The following variables describe the types of data being analyzed to forecast potential employee turnover. Review each variable and explain how it is helping to predict employee turnover. Do you agree this is the best way to determine employee turnover? What other variables would you recommend a business collect to determine employee turnover?

- Time required for next promotion
- Yearly bonus
- Time since last raise
- Employee performance
- Manager performance
- Attrition under employee's manager
- Time off taken

- Time off not taken
- Stock grants over time
- Location of employee
- Location of employee's team
- Location of employee's manager

6. **Reengineer Your Class**

It seems to be a problem at every college and soon becomes every student's nightmare: registering for classes. In an effort to increase efficiency, your college has hired you to analyze its current business processes and workflows for registering for classes. Analyze the current process and determine which steps are:

- Broken
- Redundant
- Antiquated

Be sure to define how you would reengineer the processes for efficiency and effectiveness. Feel free to create As-Is and To-Be diagrams and try to add machine learning into your To-Be course registration process flow.

7. **READY, SET, ALPHAGO!**

Have you ever played the game Go? Go is a board game for two players who strategically compete to surround more territory than their opponent. The game was invented in China more than 2,500 years ago and is believed to be the oldest board game continuously played to the present day.

Google's AI think tank DeepMind created AlphaGo, an AI system that defeated legendary player Lee Sedol, winner of 18 Go world titles and widely considered to be the greatest player of the past decade. During the games, AlphaGo played a handful of highly inventive winning moves, several of which—including move 37 in game two—were so surprising, they overturned hundreds of years of received wisdom and have since been examined extensively by players of all levels. In the course of winning, AlphaGo somehow taught the world completely new knowledge about perhaps the most studied and contemplated game in history.

Why do you think an AI system could not only beat the world champion but find new strategies to a 2,500-year-old game? If you could build an AI system to help you with a game, what would the system be, and how would you gather the training data? Can you think of any business uses for an AI system that could potentially gain insights into something that is 100 years old?

8. **Dashboard Design**

Digital dashboards offer an effective and efficient way to view enterprisewide information at near real time. According to Nucleus Research, there is a direct correlation between use of digital dashboards and a company's return on investment (ROI). Hence, all executives should be using or pushing the development of digital dashboards to monitor and analyze organizational operations.

Customer Tracking System	Enterprise Operations
Customers	Accounting
Marketing	Finance
Order entry	Logistics
Collections	Production
Sales	Distribution
Customer service	Manufacturing
Billing	Human resources
Credit limits	Sales
Transportation	Total profit

Design a digital dashboard for a customer tracking and enterprise operations system. Be sure to address at least four of the indicators by showing how you would measure them, such as red, yellow, green status; percentage complete status; and what metrics you would assign to ensure the status is measured accurately. Is each metric a CSF or KPI?

9. Driving Decisions

How do people make decisions? Almost daily, you can read about someone who makes a decision most people would find mind-boggling. Here are a few examples:

- A woman in Ohio was charged with child endangerment after police said she admitted to breast-feeding her child and talking on a cell phone while driving her other children to school.
- A woman in South Florida was caught driving while talking on a cell phone on her left shoulder and eating from a cup of soup in her left hand. The woman would take her right hand off the wheel to spoon soup, driving with no hands while she continued to talk on the phone.
- A man in California was cited for driving while carrying a swimming pool. He drove with one hand while he held his new swimming pool on the roof of his car with the other. His three children were leaning out of the car windows, not wearing seat belts, to help hold the pool.
- A woman in Baltimore was charged with diapering her child in the front seat of the car while driving at 65 miles per hour down the highway.

Find an example of a company that found itself in trouble because its employees made bad decisions. What could the company have done to protect itself from these types of employee blunders? Have you ever been in trouble due to a bad decision? What was it, and what could you have done to avoid the problem? Could an MIS system or AI have helped prevent your problem by enabling you to make a better decision?

10. Dashboard for Tracking Junk

Do you enjoy kidnapping your rivals' team mascots or toilet-papering their frat houses? If so, you might find your ideal career at College Hunks Hauling Junk. The company hires college students and recent grads to pick up junk and take it away. The founder, Nick Friedman, had a goal of capturing that friendly rivalry so often associated with college life and turning it into profits. When the company launched in 2005, the haulers from Virginia found their truck had been lathered in shaving cream and draped with a University of Maryland flag. The Virginia haulers retaliated, and soon after, dead fish were found on the seats of Maryland's truck. Friedman decided to use this energy as an incentive instead of condemning the unorthodox behavior. "We wanted to harness that competitive, prankster enthusiasm and channel it for good," he said.

Friedman made a bold move and decided that instead of tracking typical key performance indicators such as revenue, average job size, and customer loyalty, he would set up his dashboard to track the volume of junk collected and the amount donated or recycled. The winning team gains such things as bragging rights and banners, modest monetary prizes, and the right to eat first at the annual company meeting. Most employees check the dashboard daily to view their own and rivals' latest standings.

Why do you think competition is helping College Hunks Hauling Junk exceed its revenue goals? If you were to build a team competition dashboard for your school or your work, what types of metrics would you track? What types of motivators would you use to ensure your team is always in the green? What types of external information would you want tracked in your dashboard? Could an unethical person use the information from your dashboard to hurt your team or your organization? What can you do to mitigate these risks?

11. Building Robots

Humans are not permitted inside Staples' Denver distribution center. So, who is filling all the orders, you ask? Robots! This 100,000-square-foot space belongs to 150 orange robots that resemble overstuffed ottomans and race around with uncanny accuracy. They're making Staples employees more than twice as productive. The robots, or bots, are built by Kiva Systems, a company with a single critical success factor: Replace the labyrinth of conveyor belts and humans that most distributors rely on to pack items in the online mail-order business. Companies using Kiva bots include Walgreens, Zappos, The Gap, and Amazon.

Robots have captured people's attention for years. From the quirky droids in *Star Wars* to the powerful fighting machines in *Transformers,* they seem to fascinate everyone. Assume your professor has asked you to participate in the Robot Challenge, and you must design a robot that will enhance business operations. It must contain a digital dashboard and provide decision support capabilities for its owners. Be sure to describe your robot, its functions, how the digital dashboard works and supports users, and why customers would purchase your robot. Feel free to include a picture or diagram of how your robot works.

AYK APPLICATION PROJECTS

If you are looking for Excel projects to incorporate into your class, try any of the following after reading this chapter.

Project Number	Project Name	Project Type	Plug-In Focus Area	Project Focus	Project Skill Set	Page Number
1	Financial Destiny	Excel	T2	Personal Budget	Introductory Formulas	AYK.3
2	Cash Flow	Excel	T2	Cash Flow	Introductory Formulas	AYK.3
3	Technology Budget	Excel	T1, T2	Hardware and Software	Introductory Formulas	AYK.3
4	Tracking Donations	Excel	T2	Employee Relationships	Introductory Formulas	AYK.3
5	Convert Currency	Excel	T2	Global Commerce	Introductory Formulas	AYK.4
6	Cost Comparison	Excel	T2	Total Cost of Ownership	Introductory Formulas	AYK.4
7	Time Management	Excel or Project	T2 or T12	Project Management	Introductory Gantt Charts	AYK.5
8	Maximize Profit	Excel	T2, T4	Strategic Analysis	Intermediate Formulas or Solver	AYK.5
9	Security Analysis	Excel	T3	Filtering Data	Intermediate Conditional Formatting, Autofilter, Subtotal	AYK.6
10	Gathering Data	Excel	T3	Data Analysis	Intermediate Conditional Formatting, PivotTable	AYK.6
11	Scanner System	Excel	T2	Strategic Analysis	Intermediate	AYK.7
12	Competitive Pricing	Excel	T2	Profit Maximization	Intermediate	AYK.7
13	Adequate Acquisitions	Excel	T2	Break-Even Analysis	Intermediate	AYK.7

Design Element: © McGraw Hill Education

Ebusiness: Electronic Business Value

CHAPTER OUTLINE

SECTION 3.1
WEB 1.0: Ebusiness

- Distruptive Technology
- Web 1.0: The Catalyst for Ebusiness
- Analyzing Website Data
- The Four Ebusiness Models
- Ebusiness Tools for Connecting and Communicating

SECTION 3.2
Web 2.0: Business 2.0

- Web 2.0: Advantages of Business 2.0
- Business 2.0: All about Social
- Web 3.0: Defining the Next Generation of Online Business Opportunities

What's in IT for me?

Internet and communication technologies have revolutionized the way business operates, improving upon traditional methods and even introducing new opportunities and ventures that were simply not possible before. More than just giving organizations another means of conducting transactions, online business provides the ability to develop and maintain customer relationships, supplier relationships, and even employee relationships between and within enterprises.

As future managers and organizational knowledge workers, you need to understand the benefits ebusiness can offer an organization and your career, the challenges that accompany web technologies, and their impact on organizational communication and collaboration. You need to be aware of the social media strategies organizations can use to deploy ebusiness and the methods of measuring ebusiness success. This chapter will give you this knowledge and help prepare you for the social media driven economy of the future.

opening case study

gorodenkoff/Getty Images

Social Media: The New Weapon of Mass Destruction

Imagine trying to obtain information about what was happening around the world during the 1980s. You didn't have a cell phone, the Internet, Google, or even a computer. Imagine waiting to receive the morning paper, or listening to the news on the radio or TV to find out about current events. In the 1980s, information on current events typically came from only a few sources in different formats. The world was a different place.

Enter the era of disruptive technology. A *disruptive technology* is a new way of doing things that initially does not meet the needs of existing customers. Typically, it's a new technology that enters a market and then changes everything without anyone noticing. Just think of Netflix taking over Blockbuster Video or Amazon killing off numerous bookstores. But did you ever think of social media as a disruptive technology? Or worse, a weapon of mass destruction?

Facebook, Twitter, TikTok, Instagram, and Snapchat are all examples of social media platforms that were originally intended as a simple means of public collaboration and communication. Now they have become the nervous system of the electronic world and are driving how we conduct business. These platforms do everything from setting up dates and meetups to disseminating information on everything. Unfortunately, they've also become hostile spaces for battles over everything from political campaigns to marketing wars to school bullying.

Nobody could have predicted the millions of worldwide users that would flock to these addictive social applications. It is incredible how social media has so quickly developed and expanded in the last 20 years, impacting every aspect of our lives. A few examples of how social media platforms have affected society include:

- Fake news stories. Misinformation and disinformation appear in all platforms:
    - COVID-19 vaccine effectiveness and side effects
    - 5G networks cause cancer
- Hacking and the release of private communications:
    - Hacks of Jeff Bezos' cell phone
    - Facebook data hacks
- Disinformation, fabrication of events, statements, or outcomes:
    - Russian hacking efforts to influence American elections
- Misinformation and fear mongering used to affect target nations:
    - Terrorist groups such as ISIS recruiting members

- Cyberbullying:
  - Posting of revenge photos
  - Student harassment

Before social media, public political conversations occurred through traditional media, including newspapers, magazines, radio, and television. These media forms were expensive and heavily regulated, allowing only a few individuals or organizations to participate and control the messaging and dialogue provided to the public. Any opinions or thoughts not voiced in the media didn't have an outlet or any form of mass communication.

The Internet, and specifically the proliferation of social media, fundamentally altered this paradigm. Suddenly the national dialogue belonged to everyone and anyone from anywhere around the globe. In this new framework, social media has become an effective tool to fuel disruption. Anonymity and the difficulty of vetting content make it easy for propagandists to establish flash narratives and influence the dialogue. Regulating global boundaries is also next to impossible, and misinformation and disinformation abound with zero consequences for the creators.

It is now evident that an inherent danger lurks in social media. Bad actors use social media to promote their personal political agendas of hatred and bigotry, to further terrorism, amplify dangerous messages and misinformation, and steal consumer personal data and other valuable information. Simply stated, social media in the wrong hands is a weapon of mass destruction.[1]

section 3.1 | Web 1.0: Ebusiness

LEARNING OUTCOMES

3.1 Compare disruptive and sustaining technologies and explain how the Internet and WWW caused business disruption.

3.2 Describe ebusiness and its associated advantages.

3.3 Compare the four ebusiness models.

3.4 Describe the five ebusiness tools for connecting and communicating.

LO 3.1: Compare disruptive and sustaining technologies and explain how the Internet and WWW caused business disruption.

DISRUPTIVE TECHNOLOGY

Polaroid, founded in 1937, produced the first instant camera in the late 1940s. The Polaroid camera, whose pictures developed themselves, was one of the most exciting technological advances the photography industry had ever seen. The company eventually went public, becoming one of Wall Street's most prominent enterprises, with its stock trading above $60 per share in 1997. In 2002, the stock dropped to 8 cents, and the company declared bankruptcy.[2]

How could a company such as Polaroid, which had innovative technology and a captive customer base, go bankrupt? Perhaps company executives failed to use Porter's Five Forces Model to analyze the threat of substitute products or services. If they had, would they have noticed the two threats—one-hour film processing and digital cameras—that eventually stole Polaroid's market share? Would they have understood that their customers, people who want instant access to their pictures, would be the first to try these alternatives? Could the company have found a way to compete with one-hour film processing and the digital camera to save Polaroid?

Many organizations face the same dilemma as Polaroid: What's best for the current business might not be what's best for it in the long term. Some observers of our business environment have an ominous vision of the future—digital Darwinism.

- ***Digital Darwinism***: Implies that organizations that cannot adapt to the new demands placed on them for surviving in the information age are doomed to extinction.

Disruptive versus Sustaining Technology

As the opening case discussed, disruptive technologies refer to new technologies that enter a market and then change everything without anyone noticing.

- ***Disruptive technology***: A new way of doing things that initially does not meet the needs of existing customers. Disruptive technologies tend to open new markets and destroy old ones.

Disruptive technologies typically enter the low end of the marketplace and eventually evolve to displace high-end competitors and their reigning technologies. Sony is a perfect example. Sony started as a tiny company that built portable, battery-powered transistor radios. The sound quality was poor, but customers were willing to overlook that for the convenience of portability. With the experience and revenue stream from the portables, Sony improved its technology to produce cheap, low-end transistor amplifiers that were suitable for home use and invested those revenues in improving the technology further, which produced still-better radios.

- ***Sustaining technology***: Produces an improved product customers are eager to buy, such as a faster car or larger hard drive.

Sustaining technologies tend to provide us with better, faster, and cheaper products in established markets. Incumbent companies most often lead sustaining technology to market, but they virtually never lead in markets opened by disruptive technologies.[3]

The Innovator's Dilemma, a book by Clayton M. Christensen, discusses how established companies can take advantage of disruptive technologies without hindering existing relationships with customers, partners, and stakeholders. Xerox, IBM, Sears, and DEC all listened to existing customers, invested aggressively in technology, had their competitive antennae up, and still lost their market-dominant positions. They may have placed too much emphasis on satisfying customers' current needs and neglected new disruptive technology to meet customers' future needs, thus losing market share.[4]

A principle of Christensen's theory of disruption is that technology itself is not the disruptor. For example, Netflix created a new business model; streaming video made that business model possible. Technology enables the new business model to coalesce. Technology is the tool—not the end result.

The Internet and World Wide Web—The Ultimate Business Disruptors

The ***Internet*** is a massive network that connects computers all over the world and allows them to communicate with one another (see Figure 3.1). Computers connected via the Internet can send and receive information, including text, graphics, voice, video, and software. Originally, the Internet was essentially an emergency military communications system operated by the U.S. Department of Defense Advanced Research Project Agency (DARPA), which called the network ARPANET. No one foresaw the dramatic impact it would have on both business and personal communications. In time, all U.S. universities that had defense-related funding installed ARPANET computers, forming the first official Internet network. As users began to notice the value of electronic communications, the purpose of the network started shifting from a military pipeline to a communications tool for scientists. In 1971, Ray Tomlinson was the first person to send an email using the @ symbol to separate users and their network in the ARPANET system.[5]

Most of us have been using the Internet in our personal and professional lives for the past 30 years. During that time, the Internet has changed from a simple data-sharing device used only by government officials and scientists to a network used by people around the world. British scientist and computer programmer Tim Berners-Lee established the World Wide Web, a literal web of information that everyone could access. Berners-Lee was a computer scientist at CERN when in March 1989 he wrote a memo suggesting the creation of a network of hypertext-linked nodes to help his fellow researchers organize and share information about the experiments they were running. His original name for it was "Mesh," but a year later when writing the code for it, he changed it to the World Wide Web. The first website created is still online and can be found at http://info.cern.ch/hypertext/WWW/TheProject.html. Its purpose was to describe the WWW and tell people how to make their own web page.

Any time a series of computers are connected and enabled to communicate and exchange information, the Internet is being used and the WWW might not even be involved. For example, an office building might build a computer/information network that is only accessed via a private network and customized applications. To keep corporate data safe, the company might not even allow access to the WWW from company computers. The "Internet" here is referring to the connection and flow of information. When you use data on your mobile phone, or check

FIGURE 3.1

Overview of the Internet

How the Internet Works
1. Just as your home has a unique address, so does your computer. Instead of street names and zip codes, your computer has an Internet Protocol (IP) address.
2. Your computer connects to the Internet through your modem and an Internet service provider (ISP). When you turn on your browser, your computer sends a request to your ISP to open an Internet connection through your modem. The modem connects your computer to the Internet. Computers talk to each other through electronic signals that follow the same rules and language, called protocols.
3. When you visit a website, you are really connecting to another computer's IP address. The Domain Name Service (DNS) is a series of databases that keeps track of every computer name and IP address on the Internet. If the website you want is not located on the first DNS database that your computer visits, that database sends your request to the next database, until your website is found. When your computer finds the web page you want in the DNS database, the database retrieves the page's IP address and sends it back to your computer.
4. Your browser requests access to the web page, or IP address. This is accomplished through HTTP (hypertext transport protocol). The website's server, which is the computer that hosts the web page, checks to make sure the page you requested exists. If it does, the website's server allows your computer access and you will see the page you want on your screen. If it doesn't, you will get an "HTTP 404" message, which typically states "Page not found."

APPLY YOUR KNOWLEDGE

BUSINESS DRIVEN DISCUSSION

What Will Net Neutrality Cost Small Business?

Net neutrality is about ensuring that everyone has equal access to the Internet. Its founding principle is that all consumers should be able to use the Internet and be free to access its resources without any form of discrimination. However, a great debate has been raging for some time about this, with the battle lines clearly drawn.

On one side of the debate are the ISPs, such as Comcast, that are building the Internet infrastructure and want to charge customers relative to their use, namely, the amount of bandwidth they consume. The ISPs argue that more and more users accessing bandwidth-intense resources provided by the likes of YouTube and Netflix place huge demands on their networks. They want Internet access to move from a flat-rate pricing structure to a metered service.

On the other hand, content providers, such as Google, support the counterargument that if ISPs move toward metered schemes, this may limit the usage of many resources on the Internet, such as iTunes and Netflix. A metered service may also stifle the innovative opportunities that an open Internet provides.

The U.S. Court of Appeals for the District of Columbia Circuit struck down the Federal Communications Commission's net neutrality rules, which would have required Internet service providers to treat all web traffic equally. The ruling will allow ISPs to charge companies such as Netflix and Amazon fees for faster content delivery.[6]

Do you agree that the government should control the Internet? Should website owners be legally forced to receive or transmit information from competitors or other websites they find objectionable? Provide examples of when net neutrality might be good for a business and when net neutrality might be bad for a business. Overall, is net neutrality good or bad for business?

your email, or play a video game in real time with other gamers around the world, you are sending and receiving information through the Internet. In this process, your device actually becomes a part of the Internet.

The Internet and the World Wide Web (WWW) are not synonymous. The WWW is just one part of the Internet, and its primary use is to correlate and disseminate information. The Internet includes the WWW and other forms of communication systems such as email. The primary way a user navigates around the WWW is through a ***universal resource locator (URL),*** which contains the address of a file or resource on the web, such as www.apple.com or www.microsoft.com. Figure 3.2 lists the key terms associated with the WWW, and Figure 3.3 lists the reasons for the massive growth of the WWW.[7]

FIGURE 3.2

Overview of the WWW

Term	Definition	Example
Domain name hosting (web hosting)	A service that allows the owner of a domain name to maintain a simple website and provide email capacity	GoDaddy is a prime example of a domain name hosting company
Hypertext markup language (HTML)	Publishes hypertext on the WWW, which allows users to move from one document to another simply by clicking a hot spot or link	HTML uses tags such as <h1> and </h1> to structure text into headings, paragraphs, lists, hypertext links, and so on
Hypertext transport protocol (HTTP)	The Internet protocol that web browsers use to request and display web pages using universal resource locators (URLs)	To retrieve the file at the URL http://www.somehost.com/path/file.html
Web browser	Allows users to access the WWW	Internet Explorer, Mozilla's Firefox, Google Chrome
World Wide Web	Provides access to Internet information through documents, including text, graphics, and audio and video files that use a special formatting language called hypertext markup language	Tim Berners-Lee, a British computer scientist, is considered the inventor of the WWW on March 12, 1989

The microcomputer revolution made it possible for an average person to own a computer.
Advancements in networking hardware, software, and media made it possible for business computers to be connected to larger networks at a minimal cost.
Browser software such as Microsoft's Internet Explorer and Netscape Navigator gave computer users an easy-to-use graphical interface to find, download, and display web pages.
The speed, convenience, and low cost of email have made it an incredibly popular tool for business and personal communications.
Basic web pages are easy to create and extremely flexible.

FIGURE 3.3

Reasons for Growth of the World Wide Web

WEB 1.0: THE CATALYST FOR EBUSINESS

LO 3.2: Describe ebusiness and its associated advantages.

Ebusiness opened up a new marketplace for any company willing to move its business operations online.

- ***Paradigm shift***: Occurs when a new, radical form of business enters the market that reshapes the way companies and organizations behave.

Ebusiness created a paradigm shift, transforming entire industries and changing enterprise-wide business processes that fundamentally rewrote traditional business rules. Deciding not to make the shift to ebusiness proved fatal for many companies. As people began learning about the WWW and the Internet, they understood that it enabled a company to communicate with anyone, anywhere, at any time, creating a new way to participate in business. The competitive advantages for first movers proved to be enormous, thus spurring the beginning of the Web 1.0 Internet boom.

- ***Ebusiness***: Includes ecommerce, along with all activities related to internal and external business operations, such as servicing customer accounts, collaborating with partners, and exchanging real-time information. Ebusiness connects buyers, sellers, manufacturers, and suppliers, acting as a global marketplace. During Web 1.0, entrepreneurs began creating the first forms of ebusiness.
- ***Ecommerce***: The buying and selling of goods and services over the Internet. Ecommerce refers only to online transactions.
- ***Web 1.0 (or Business 1.0)***: A term to refer to the World Wide Web during its first few years of operation between 1991 and 2003.

As the Internet became accessible to the masses during the 1990s, organizations began to see the potential offered by the new ebusiness platform. The first books were sold online in 1992, and in 1994 Pizza Hut in Santa Cruz, California, enabled people to order a pizza delivery via the Internet.

The idea of online selling took off in 1995 when Jeff Bezos dispatched the first book sold by Amazon.com, then located in his Seattle garage. Around the same time, software programmer Pierre Omidyar was starting a simple website called AuctionWeb from his San Jose living room. The first product he posted for sale was a broken laser pointer. It sold for $14.83. Omidyar recognized the Internet's power to reach individual customers anywhere in the world when he checked whether the buyer understood that the pointer was broken. One year later, with two full-time employees, he launched eBay, an auction service linking customers who bid on items. The best part of ebusiness is it removed the entry barrier, so anyone can compete as long as they have a computer and a part-time person.

Both individuals and organizations have embraced ebusiness to enhance productivity, maximize convenience, and improve communications. Companies today need to deploy a comprehensive ebusiness strategy, and business students need to understand its advantages, outlined in Figure 3.4. Let's look at each.

Expanding Global Reach

Ebusinesses operate 24 hours a day, 7 days a week, 365 days per year (24/7/365). This availability directly reduces transaction costs because consumers no longer have to spend a lot of

APPLY YOUR KNOWLEDGE

BUSINESS DRIVEN ETHICS AND SECURITY

DuckDuckGo!

Have you ever been online and noticed an ad pop-up for something you searched for two weeks ago? Creepy, right? This is the power of Google ad networks. Can you imagine someone having access to all of your Google searches? What could they find out about you? Most of your intimate secrets are shared with your search engine, including medical, financial, and personal questions. Should this information be private?

On Google, your searches are tracked via your IP address and browser fingerprints, mined, and packaged into a data profile for advertisers to follow you around the Internet through banner ads. It is how Google makes money–selling search. Google is also tracking you on YouTube, Gmail, Chrome, Android, Gmaps, and all of its other services. Google analytics is installed on most websites, tracking you behind the scenes and allowing website owners to know who is visiting their sites, but also feeding that information back to Google.

DuckDuckGo is an alternative to Google for search and operates on the premise that it does not track your searches or allow advertising on your browsing habits. Every search on DuckDuckGo is like a new search, and the site does not even know who you are or track your IP. The site does not store any of your personal information or tie search history together that can later be tied back to you.[8]

In a group, visit the DuckDuckGo website. Do you believe Google has the right to track you, your search history, and your website browsing actions? How are marketing firms using your search and browsing history to cyberstalk you with banner ads?

FIGURE 3.4

Business Advantages of Operating Online

time researching purchases or traveling great distances to make them. The faster delivery cycle for online sales helps strengthen customer relationships, improving customer satisfaction and, ultimately, sales. Easy access to real-time information is a primary benefit of ebusiness.

- ***Information richness***: Refers to the depth and breadth of details contained in a piece of textual, graphic, audio, or video information. Buyers need information richness to make informed purchases.
- ***Information reach***: Measures the number of people a firm can communicate with all over the world. Sellers need information reach to market and differentiate themselves from the competition properly.

A firm's website can be the focal point of a cost-effective communications and marketing strategy. Promoting products online allows the company to target its customers precisely, whether they are local or around the globe. A physical location is restricted by size and limited to those customers who can get there, but an online store has a global marketplace with customers and information seekers already waiting virtually online.

Opening New Markets

Ebusiness is perfect for increasing niche-product sales. A proven marketing strategy is to personally reach each customer with specific sales information directed to the individual's tastes. In the past, reaching an individual customer with a specific marketing campaign was next to impossible. With the invention of the Internet, companies are now able to reach each customer, recommend purchases based on their past purchasing history, and offer entirely special one-time products, created exactly to the customer's preferences.

- ***Mass customization***: The ability of an organization to tailor its products or services to the customers' specifications. For example, customers can order M&M's in special colors or with customized sayings such as "Marry Me."
- ***Personalization***: Occurs when a company knows enough about a customer's likes and dislikes that it can fashion offers more likely to appeal to that person, say by tailoring its website to individuals or groups based on profile information, demographics, or prior transactions. Amazon uses personalization to create a unique portal for each of its customers.

Reducing Costs

One of the most exciting benefits of ebusiness is its low start-up costs. Today, anyone can start an ebusiness with just a website and a great product or service. Operational benefits of ebusiness include business processes that require less time and human effort or that can be eliminated. Compare the cost of sending out 100 direct mailings (paper, postage, labor) to the cost of a bulk email campaign. Think about the cost of renting a physical location and operating phone lines versus the cost of maintaining an online site. Switching to an ebusiness model can eliminate many traditional costs associated with communicating by substituting systems, such as Live Help, that let customers chat live with support or sales staff. Even a dog-walking operation or tutoring services can benefit from being an ebusiness. Chris Anderson, editor-in-chief of *Wired* magazine, describes niche-market ebusiness strategies as capturing the long tail.

- ***Long tail***: Refers to the tail of a typical sales curve (see Figure 3.5).

This strategy demonstrates how niche products can have viable and profitable business models when selling via ebusiness. In traditional sales models, a store is limited by shelf space when selecting products to sell. For this reason, store owners typically purchase products that will be wanted or needed by the masses, and the store is stocked with broad products because there isn't room on the shelf for niche products that only a few customers might purchase. Ebusinesses such as Amazon and Netflix eliminated the shelf-space dilemma and were able to offer infinite products, destroying traditional businesses such as Blockbuster and Borders Group.

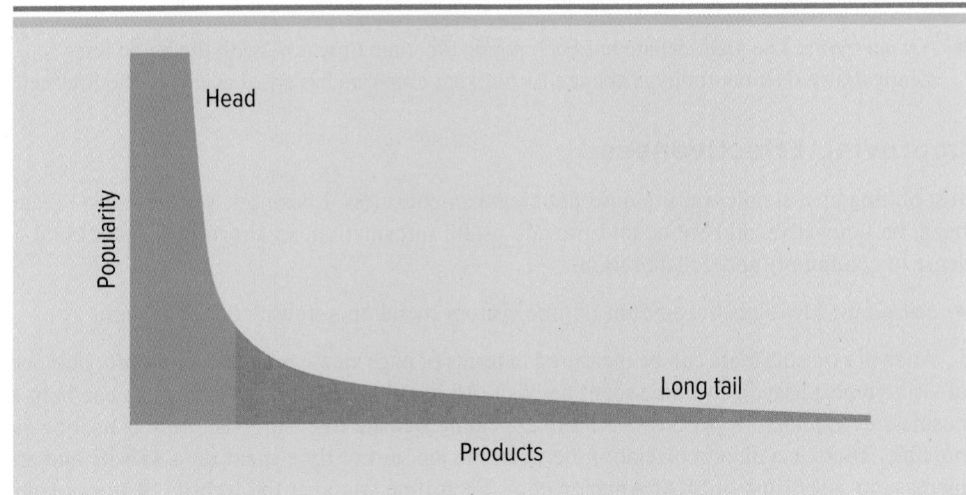

FIGURE 3.5
The Long Tail

FIGURE 3.6

Business Value of Disintermediation

The more intermediaries that are cut from the distribution chain, the lower the product price. When Dell decided to sell its PCs through Walmart, many were surprised because Dell's direct-to-customer sales model was the competitive advantage that had kept Dell the market leader for years.

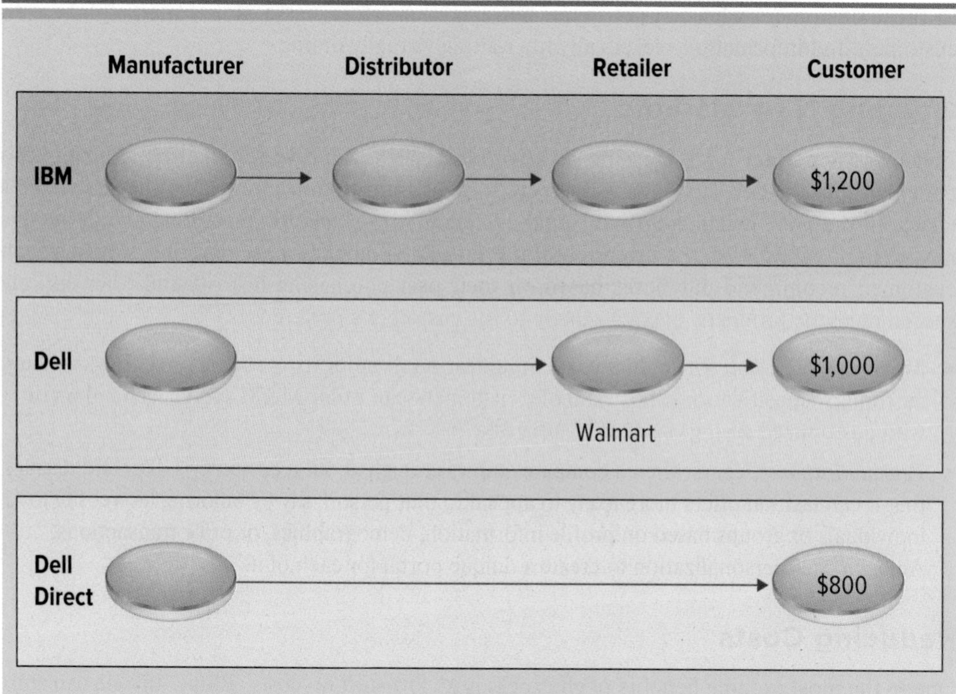

Amazon offers an excellent example of the long tail. Let's assume an average Barnes & Noble store maintains 3,000 books in its inventory, whereas Amazon, without physical shelf limitations, can maintain 1,000,000 books in its inventory and many more digitally. Looking at sales data, the majority of Barnes & Noble revenue comes from new releases, whereas older selections don't repay the cost of keeping them in stock. Thus, Barnes & Noble's sales tail ends at title 3,000. However, Amazon, with no physical limitations, can extend its tail beyond 1,000,000 (and with digital books perhaps 20,000,000). By extending its tail, Amazon increases sales, even if a title is purchased only a few times. Another great strategy for cost cutting created by the Internet is disintermediation.

- ***Disintermediation***: Occurs when a business sells directly to the customer online and cuts out the intermediary (see Figure 3.6).
- ***Intermediaries***: Agents, software, or businesses that provide a trading infrastructure to bring buyers and sellers together.

This business strategy lets the company shorten the order process and add value with reduced costs or a more responsive and efficient service. The disintermediation of the travel agent occurred as people began to book their own vacations online, often at a cheaper rate. At Amazon.com, anyone can publish and sell print-on-demand books, online music, and custom calendars, making the publisher obsolete.

- ***Net neutrality***: The great debate has been raging for some time now, with the battle lines clearly drawn. Net neutrality is about ensuring that everyone has equal access to the Internet.

Improving Effectiveness

Just putting up a simple website does not create an ebusiness. Ebusiness websites must create buzz, be innovative, add value, and provide useful information. In short, they must build a sense of community and collaboration.

- ***Stickiness***: Measures the amount of time visitors spend on a website or application.

Analytics on stickiness can be measured in terms of page views, minutes per month, number of visits (repeat usage), and time spent per visit. All of the information on stickiness can help a business determine how to create a more appealing website to ensure visitors stay as long as possible. There is a direct correlation between the amount of time spent on a website and an increase in sales. Just think of Amazon.com. Each time you visit the website, it tracks your

Term	Definition	Example
Affiliate program	Allows a business to generate commissions or referral fees when a customer visiting its website clicks a link to another merchant's website	If a customer to a company website clicks a banner ad to another vendor's website, the company will receive a referral fee or commission when the customer performs the desired action, typically making a purchase or completing a form.
Banner ad	A box running across a website that advertises the products and services of another business, usually another ebusiness	The banner generally contains a link to the advertiser's website. Advertisers can track how often customers click a banner ad resulting in a click-through to their website. Often the cost of the banner ad depends on the number of customers who click the banner ad. Web-based advertising services can track the number of times users click the banner, generating statistics that enable advertisers to judge whether the advertising fees are worth paying.
Freemium	A technique where a business offers a free basic product, giving the customer an option to use an advanced version for a premium cost	An idea that giving away free content will keep customers on the website and perhaps spend more for access to additional content. Many video games are available for free, and then the user must pay to gain additional products while playing the game.
Pop-up ad	A small web page containing an advertisement that appears outside of the current website loaded in the browser	A form of ad that users do not see until they close the current web browser screen.

FIGURE 3.7

Marketing Benefits from Ebusiness

spending and browsing habits and personalizes your visit, showing you products you might like based on past products you have purchased. The longer you stay on the website, the better it gets to know you as a customer, showing you products you didn't even know you wanted to purchase that miraculously end up in your shopping cart.

MIS measures of efficiency, such as the amount of traffic on a site, do not always tell the whole story of a website's stickiness. Large amounts of traffic do not necessarily indicate large sales volumes, for instance. Many websites with lots of traffic have minimal sales. The best way to measure ebusiness success is to use *effectiveness* MIS metrics, such as the revenue generated by web traffic, number of new customers acquired by web traffic, and reductions in customer service calls resulting from web traffic.

- ***Interactivity***: Measures advertising effectiveness by counting visitor interactions with the target ad, including time spent viewing the ad, number of pages viewed, and number of repeat visits to the advertisement. Interactivity measures are a giant step forward for advertisers, since traditional advertising methods–newspapers, magazines, radio, and television–provide few ways to track effectiveness.
- ***Heat map***: A two-dimensional representation of data in which values are represented by colors. A simple heat map provides an immediate visual summary of information. More elaborate heat maps allow the viewer to understand complex data. Figure 3.7 displays the ebusiness marketing initiatives allowing companies to expand their reach while measuring effectiveness.[9]

ANALYZING WEBSITE DATA

Viral marketing encourages users of a product or service supplied by an ebusiness to encourage friends to join. Viral marketing is a word-of-mouth type of advertising program.

- ***Viral marketing***: A technique that induces websites or users to pass on a marketing message to other websites or users, creating exponential growth in the message's visibility and effect.

Many small companies have small marketing budgets, and if you can't inform your customers about your product, you simply can't drive sales. With a limited marketing budget, small businesses have one potential solution–create a series of videos appropriate for YouTube audiences and hope they go viral. The Dollar Shave Club used viral marketing to launch its successful brand. Michael Dubin had a background in media, marketing, brand development, and improv! Using his years of improv training, he created Dollar Shave Club's first video spot that was shot in one day for $4,500 and within 48 hours of launching had over 24 million views and 12,000 orders.

Attracting customers via viral marketing is just the beginning of the sales cycle. Once the customer is attracted to a website, it is critical to understand how they interact with the website, how traffic flows, and if the interaction resulted in a purchase.

- ***Clickstream***: The exact path a visitor takes through a website including the pattern of a consumer's navigation. Clickstream data can include:
  - Length of stay on a page
  - Number of page views
  - How they arrived on the page
  - Where they went after leaving the page
  - Number of abandoned shopping carts

When a visitor reaches a website, a hit is generated, and his or her computer sends a request to the site's computer server to begin displaying pages. Each element of a request page is recorded by the website's server log file as a hit. Businesses want their websites to be sticky and keep their customer's attention. To interpret such data properly, managers try to benchmark against other companies. For instance, consumers seem to visit their preferred websites regularly, even checking back multiple times during a given session.

- ***Cookie***: A small file deposited on a hard drive by a website, containing information about customers and their browsing activities. Cookies allow websites to record the comings and goings of customers, usually without their knowledge or consent.
- ***Click-thru***: A count of the number of people who visit one site and click an advertisement that takes them to the site of the advertiser.

Click-thrus are commonly used to measure the success of an online advertising campaign for a particular website, as well as the effectiveness of email campaigns. Tracking effectiveness based on click-throughs guarantees exposure to target ads; however, it does not guarantee that the visitor liked the ad, spent any substantial time viewing the ad, or was satisfied with the information contained in the ad.

- ***Clickstream analytics***: The process of collecting, analyzing, and reporting aggregate data about which pages a website visitor visits–and in what order.

Clickstream analytics is considered to be most effective when used in conjunction with other, more traditional, market evaluation resources. Since extremely large volumes of data are gathered by clickstream analytics, many businesses rely on big data analytics and related tools to help interpret the data and generate reports for specific areas of interest. There are two levels of clickstream analytics, traffic analytics and ebusiness analytics.

- ***Website traffic analytics***: Uses clickstream data to determine the efficiency of the site for the users and operates at the server level.
- ***Website ebusiness analytics***: Uses clickstream data to determine the effectiveness of the site as a channel-to-market.

Website traffic analytics tracks data on how many pages are served to the user, how long it takes each page to load, how often the user hits the browser's back or stop button, and how much data is transmitted before the user moves on. Website ebusiness analytics tracks what pages the shopper lingers on, what the shopper puts in or takes out of a shopping cart, what items the shopper purchases, whether or not the shopper belongs to a loyalty program and uses a coupon code, and the shopper's preferred method of payment.

- ***Showrooming***: Occurs when a customer browses at a physical store and then decides to purchase the product online for a reduced cost.

An example would be a customer browsing books at Barnes & Noble and then purchasing the book on Amazon for a reduced price. This is one area where website analytics will help determine if the customer came from a physical store and decided to purchase on the web.

BUSINESS DRIVEN ANALYTICS

Website Analytics

Stars Inc. is a large clothing corporation that specializes in reselling clothes worn by celebrities. The company's four websites generate 75 percent of its sales. The remaining 25 percent of sales occur directly through the company's warehouse. You have recently been hired as the director of sales. The only information you can find about the success of the four websites is displayed in the table below.

You decide that maintaining four websites is expensive and adds little business value. You propose consolidating to one site. Create a report detailing the business value gained by consolidating to a single website, along with your recommendation for consolidation. Be sure to include your website profitability analysis. Assume that, at a minimum, 10 percent of hits result in a sale; at an average, 30 percent of hits result in a sale; and at a maximum, 60 percent of hits result in a sale.

Website	Classic	Contemporary	New Age	Traditional
Traffic analysis	5,000 hits/day	200 hits/day	10,000 hits/day	1,000 hits/day
Stickiness (average)	20 minutes	1 hour	20 minutes	50 minutes
Number of abandoned shopping carts	400/day	0/day	5,000/day	200/day
Number of unique visitors	2,000/day	100/day	8,000/day	200/day
Number of identified visitors	3,000/day	100/day	2,000/day	800/day
Average revenue per sale	$1,000	$1,000	$50	$1,300

THE FOUR EBUSINESS MODELS

LO 3.3: Compare the four ebusiness models.

A ***business model*** is a plan that details how a company creates, delivers, and generates revenues. Some models are quite simple: A company produces a good or service and sells it to customers. If the company is successful, sales exceed costs and the company generates a profit. Other models are less straightforward, and sometimes it's not immediately clear who makes money and how much. Radio and network television are broadcast free to anyone with a receiver, for instance; advertisers pay the costs of programming.

- ***Dot-com***: The original term for a company operating on the Internet. The majority of online business activities consist of the exchange of products and services either between businesses or between businesses and consumers.
- ***Ebusiness model***: A plan that details how a company creates, delivers, and generates revenues on the Internet. Ebusiness models fall into one of the four categories: (1) business-to-business, (2) business-to-consumer, (3) consumer-to-business, and (4) consumer-to-consumer (see Figure 3.8).

Business-to-Business (B2B)

Business-to-business (B2B) applies to businesses buying from and selling to each other over the Internet. Examples include medical billing service, software sales and licensing, and virtual assistant businesses. B2B relationships represent 80 percent of all online business and are more complex with greater security needs than the other types. B2B examples include Oracle and SAP.

Electronic marketplaces, or emarketplaces, are interactive business communities providing a central market where multiple buyers and sellers can engage in ebusiness activities. By tightening and automating the relationship between the two parties, they create structures for conducting commercial exchange, consolidating supply chains, and creating new sales channels.

Ebusiness Term	Definition
Business-to-business (B2B)	Applies to businesses buying from and selling to each other over the Internet.
Business-to-consumer (B2C)	Applies to any business that sells its products or services to consumers over the Internet.
Consumer-to-business (C2B)	Applies to any consumer that sells a product or service to a business over the Internet.
Consumer-to-consumer (C2C)	Applies to sites primarily offering goods and services to assist consumers interacting with each other over the Internet.

	Business	Consumer
Business	B2B	B2C
Consumer	C2B	C2C

FIGURE 3.8
Ebusiness Models

Business-to-Consumer (B2C)

Business-to-consumer (B2C) applies to any business that sells its products or services directly to consumers online. Carfax offers car buyers detailed histories of used vehicles for a fee. There are three ways to operate as a B2C: brick and mortar, click and mortar, and pure play (see Figure 3.9).

Consumer-to-Business (C2B)

Consumer-to-business (C2B) applies to any consumer who sells a product or service to a business on the Internet. One example is customers of *Priceline.com,* who set their own prices for items such as airline tickets or hotel rooms and wait for a seller to decide whether to supply them. The demand for C2B ebusiness will increase over the next few years due to customers' desire for greater convenience and lower prices.

Consumer-to-Consumer (C2C)

Consumer-to-consumer (C2C) applies to customers offering goods and services to each other on the Internet. A good example of a C2C is an auction in which buyers and sellers solicit consecutive bids from each other and prices are determined dynamically. Craigslist and eBay are

FIGURE 3.9
Forms of Business-to-Consumer Operations

Brick-and-Mortar Business
A business that operates in a physical store without an Internet presence.
Example: T.J. Maxx

Click-and-Mortar Business
A business that operates in a physical store and on the Internet.
Example: Barnes & Noble

Pure-Play (Virtual) Business
A business that operates on the Internet only without a physical store.
Example: Google

BUSINESS DRIVEN START-UP

Are You Ready for Your Next Gig?

The word *gig* comes from the music world; a gig is a paid appearance of limited duration. A gig economy is an environment in which temporary employment is common and organizations contract with independent workers for short-term engagements. Today's workforce is expected to change jobs at least seven times before retirement. The gig economy will make workers independent of one company, and job changing will be far easier than ever before.

Forces driving the gig economy include the proliferation of websites and mobile applications designed to help employers and people seeking part-time work find each other. Another important influence is a millennial generation workforce that values work–life balance. Today's workforce is increasingly mobile, and if a job is decoupled from location and work can be done from anywhere, gig workers are free to choose to work a series of jobs that are interesting and enjoyable, rather than making a long-term commitment to a single job that's not interesting or enjoyable, just for the sake of financial security.

From a business perspective, a gig economy can save a company money with lower investments in health insurance, office space, and training expenses. Businesses can also hire experts for individual projects, choosing from the best professionals available without having to maintain high-salaried workers.[10]

A study by Intuit predicted that by 2025, 50 percent of American workers would be independent contractors and members of the gig economy. What are the pros and cons to working in the gig economy? Do you believe you will be part of the gig economy? How can this course help you prepare for work in the gig economy?

two examples of successful C2C websites, linking like-minded buyers with sellers. Other types of online auctions include forward auctions, in which sellers market to many buyers and the highest bid wins, and reverse auctions, in which buyers select goods and services from the seller with the lowest bid.

Ebusiness Forms and Revenue-Generating Strategies

As more and more companies began jumping on the ebusiness bandwagon, new forms of ebusiness began to emerge (see Figure 3.10). Many of the new forms of ebusiness went to market without clear strategies on how they would generate revenue. Google is an excellent example of an ebusiness that did not figure out a way to generate profits until many years after its launch.[11]

FIGURE 3.10
Ebusiness Forms

Form	Description	Examples
Content providers	Generate revenues by providing digital content such as news, music, photos, or videos	Netflix, iTunes, CNN
Infomediaries	Provide specialized information on behalf of producers of goods and services and their potential customers	Bloomberg, Zillow
Online marketplaces	Bring together buyers and sellers of products and services	Amazon, eBay
Portals	Operate a central website for users to access specialized content and other services	Google
Service providers	Provide services such as photo sharing, video sharing, online backup, and storage	YouTube
Transaction brokers	Process online sales transactions	Etrade

Search Engines When a typical user types a keyword into a search engine, it returns results based on algorithms of what other people have searched for and then selected.

- ***Keyword***: A word used in a performing a search.
- ***Search engine***: A website software that finds other pages based on keyword matching similar to Google. It is a program that indexes documents, then attempts to match documents relevant to the users' search requests.
- ***Search engine ranking***: Evaluates variables that search engines use to determine where a URL appears on the list of search results.

Each time you visit a search engine, it returns two types of results:

- ***Organic search***: The unpaid entries in a search engine results page that were derived based on their contents' relevance to the keyword query. Organic search results most closely match the user's search query based on relevance.
- ***Paid search***: Links a company paid to have displayed based on your keywords. On a search results page, you can tell paid results from organic ones because search engines set apart the paid listings, putting them above or to the right of the organic results, or giving them a shaded background, border lines, or other visual clues such as the word *Ad*.

Search engine optimization (SEO) combines art with science to determine how to make URLs more attractive to search engines, resulting in higher search engine ranking. SEO is the process of choosing targeted keyword phrases related to a site, and ensuring that the site places well when those keyword phrases are part of a web search. The better the SEO, the higher the ranking for a website in the list of search engine results. SEO is critical because most people view only the first few pages of a search result. After that, a person is more inclined to begin a new search than review pages and pages of search results. Websites can generate revenue through:

- ***Pay-per-click***: Generates revenue each time a user clicks a link to a retailer's website.
- ***Pay-per-call***: Generates revenue each time a user clicks a link that takes the user directly to an online agent waiting for a call.
- ***Pay-per-conversion***: Generates revenue each time a website visitor is converted to a customer.

Keywords are chosen by the advertiser and are displayed on the results pages when the search keywords match the advertiser's keywords. The advertiser then pays a fee to Google for the search display. Ebusinesses must have a revenue model, or a model for making money.

- ***AdWords***: Keywords that advertisers choose to pay for and appear as sponsored links on the Google results pages.

Google's primary line of business is its search engine; however, the company does not generate revenue from people using its site to search the Internet. It generates revenue from the marketers and advertisers that pay to place their ads on the site. About 200 million times each day, people from all over the world access Google to perform searches. AdWords, a part of the Google site, allows advertisers to bid on common search terms. The advertisers simply enter the keywords they want to bid on and the maximum amounts they want to pay per click per day. Google then determines a price and a search ranking for those keywords based on how much other advertisers are willing to pay for the same terms. Pricing for keywords can range from 5 cents to $10 a click. Paid search is the ultimate in targeted advertising because consumers type in exactly what they want. A general search term such as *tropical vacation* costs less than a more specific term such as *Hawaiian vacation*. Whoever bids the most for a term appears in a sponsored advertisement link either at the top or along the side of the search-results page. Figure 3.11 lists the different benefits and challenges of various ebusiness revenue models.[12]

Ebusiness Fraud

As with any great technology, there is always someone using it for unethical purposes. When it comes to online advertising and AdWord strategies, there are people who purposely click on Google searches just to cost their competitors money.

- ***Affiliate programs***: Allow a business to generate commissions or referral fees when a customer visiting its website clicks a link to another merchant's website.

Ebusiness Revenue Model	Benefits	Challenges
Advertising fees	■ Well-targeted advertisements can be perceived as value-added content by trading participants. ■ Easy to implement.	■ Limited revenue potential. ■ Overdone or poorly targeted advertisements can be disturbing elements on the website.
Subscription fees	■ Create incentives to do transactions. ■ Price can be differentiated. ■ Possibility to build additional revenue from new user groups.	■ Fixed fee is a barrier to entry for participants.
Transaction fees	■ Can be directly tied to savings (both process and price savings). ■ Important revenue source when high level of liquidity (transaction volume) is reached.	■ If process savings are not completely visible, use of the system is discouraged (incentive to move transactions offline). ■ Transaction fees likely to decrease with time.

FIGURE 3.11

Ebusiness Revenue Models

- ***Click fraud***: The practice of artificially inflating traffic statistics for online advertisements. Some unethical individuals or click fraud scammers even use automated clicking programs called hitbots.
- ***Hitbots***: Create the illusion that a large number of potential customers are clicking the advertiser's links, when in fact there is no likelihood that any of the clicks will lead to profit for the advertiser.

Click-fraud scammers often take advantage of the affiliate programs by agreeing to provide exposure to an advertisement in order to receive a portion of the pay-per-click fees the advertiser is paying the affiliate. Instead of placing the ad on legitimate websites, the scammer might place the ad on websites created solely for the purpose of placing the ad. And a site like that, quite naturally, will not have any real, organic traffic. Once the ads are in place, the hitbots generate large volumes of fraudulent clicks, often in a very short time period, for which the scammer bills the owner of the affiliate program. This, of course, costs the company a tremendous amount of money.

EBUSINESS TOOLS FOR CONNECTING AND COMMUNICATING

LO 3.4: Describe the five ebusiness tools for connecting and communicating.

A ***cyborg anthropologist*** is an individual who studies the interaction between humans and technology, observing how technology can shape humans' lives. Cyborg anthropology as a discipline originated at the 1993 annual meeting of the American Anthropological Association. Cyborg anthropologists study the different online communication methods for businesses, including the technology tools highlighted in Figure 3.12 and covered below in detail.

Email

Email, short for *electronic mail,* is the exchange of digital messages over the Internet. No longer do business professionals have to wait for the mail to receive important documents; email single-handedly increased the speed of business by allowing the transfer of documents with the same speed as the telephone. Its chief business advantage is the ability to inform and communicate with many people simultaneously, immediately, and with ease. There are no time or place constraints, and users can check, send, and view emails whenever they require.

- ***Internet service provider (ISP)***: A company that provides access to the Internet for a monthly fee. Major ISPs in the United States include AOL, AT&T, Comcast, EarthLink, and NetZero, as well as thousands of local ISPs, including regional telephone companies.

FIGURE 3.12

Ebusiness Tools

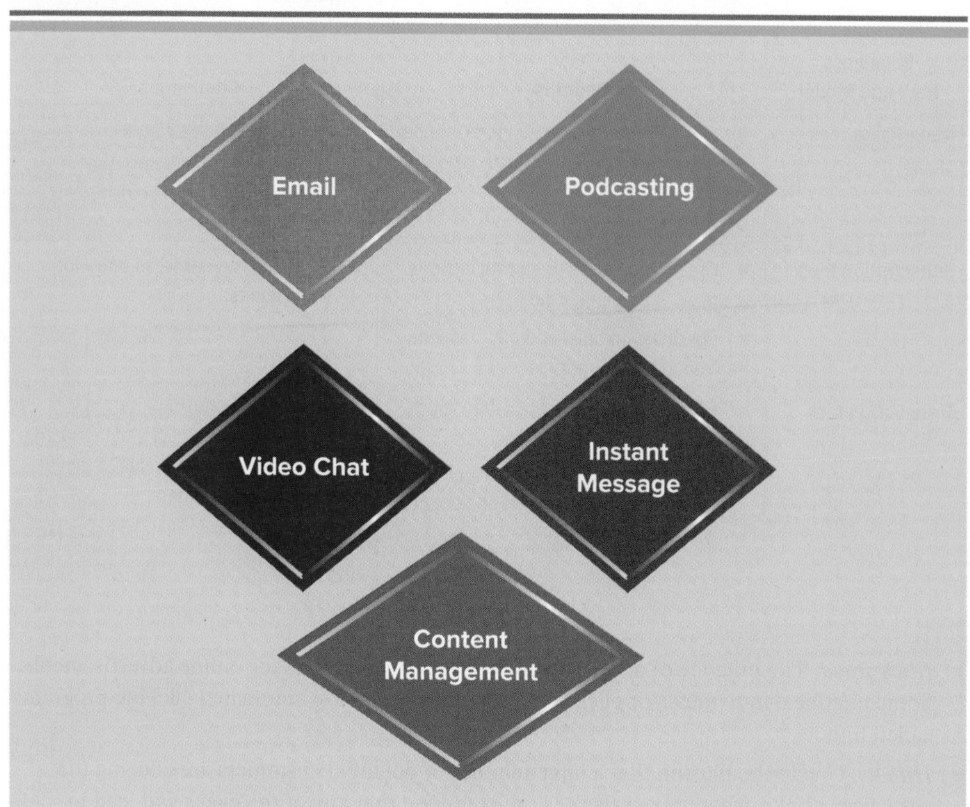

Instant Messaging

Real-time communication occurs when a system updates information at the same rate it receives it. Email was a great advancement over traditional communication methods such as the U.S. mail, but it did not operate in real time.

Instant messaging (IM, or IMing) is a service that enables instant or real-time communication between people. Businesses immediately saw what they could do:

- Answer simple questions quickly and easily.
- Resolve questions or problems immediately.
- Transmit messages as fast as naturally flowing conversation.
- Easily hold simultaneous IM sessions with multiple people.

Podcasting

Podcasting converts an audio broadcast to a digital music player. Podcasting is one of the fastest-growing digital formats available and offers a great tool for increasing your knowledge on any subject. Podcasting makes learning simple and convenient, which makes it particularly appealing to an on-the-go busy person.

Podcasts can increase marketing reach and build customer loyalty. A podcast is a more personal way to reach out to new potential customers. They get a better idea of your values and way of running the business. Your audience also has more flexibility on how they listen to the podcast. Companies use podcasts as marketing communication channels discussing everything from corporate strategies to detailed product overviews. The senior executive team can share weekly or monthly podcasts featuring important issues or expert briefings on new technical or marketing developments.

If you are looking to improve your business skills, open your Apple Podcast app or your Android Stitcher app and listen to the following best business podcasts on your commute to work.

- **HBR IdeaCast:** IdeaCast, hosted by Alison Beard and Curt Nickisch, both senior editors at *Harvard Business Review,* offers incredible insight from the greatest minds in the business community.

- **Rise:** Rachel Hollis has a particularly positive and motivating voice that extends into her podcast series. She also takes time to interview industry experts that give you insight into their own success and what you can take from their success.
- **Art of the Hustle:** This podcast's host is Jeff Rosenthal, co-founder of Summit. He invites guests onto his show to explore success stories, stories of failures, milestone events, and key advice to help any entrepreneur.
- **The Tim Ferriss Show:** It's difficult to talk about successful business podcasts without talking about The Tim Ferriss Show. Tim Ferriss approaches business with a creativity unlike that of any other, and it pays off. Tim is the bestselling author of *The 4-Hour Workweek.*

Video Chat

The COVID-19 pandemic caused every person on the planet to rethink how we communicate and connect without being in the same room together. Thanks to new technologies such as Zoom and Microsoft Teams, the pandemic allowed us to find creative new ways to virtually connect. ***Video chat*** is an online face-to-face, visual communication performed with other Internet users by using a webcam and dedicated software. It allows people at two or more locations to interact via a two-way video, and audio transmissions simultaneously, as well as share documents, data, computer displays, and whiteboards. Skype, Zoom, and Microsoft Teams are the leading video chat tools.

Content Management Systems

In the fourth century BC, Aristotle cataloged the natural world according to a systematic organization, and the ancient library at Alexandria was reportedly organized by subject, connecting like information with like. Today ***content management systems (CMSs)*** help companies manage the creation, storage, editing, and publication of their website content. CMSs are user-friendly; most include web-based publishing, search, navigation, and indexing to organize information; and they let users with little or no technical expertise make website changes.

A search is typically carried out by entering a keyword or phrase (query) into a text field and clicking a button or a hyperlink. Navigation facilitates movement from one web page to another. Content management systems play a crucial role in getting site visitors to view more than just the home page. If navigation choices are unclear, visitors may hit the Back button on their first (and final) visit to a website. One rule of thumb to remember is that each time a user has to click to find search information, there is a 50 percent chance the user will leave the website instead. A key principle of good website design, therefore, is to keep the number of clicks to a minimum.

- ***Taxonomy***: The scientific classification of organisms into groups based on similarities of structure or origin.

Taxonomies are also used for indexing the content on the website into categories and subcategories of topics. For example, car is a subtype of vehicle. Every car is a vehicle, but not every vehicle is a car; some vehicles are vans, buses, and trucks. Taxonomy terms are arranged so that narrower/more specific/"child" terms fall under broader/more generic/"parent" terms. Many companies hire information architects to create their website taxonomies. A well-planned taxonomy ensures search and navigation are easy and user-friendly. If the taxonomy is confusing, the site will soon fail.

section 3.2 | Web 2.0: Business 2.0

LEARNING OUTCOMES

3.5 Explain Web 2.0 and identify its four characteristics.

3.6 Explain how Business 2.0 is helping communities network and collaborate.

3.7 Describe Web 3.0 and the next generation of online business.

LO 3.5: Explain Web 2.0 and identify its four characteristics.

WEB 2.0: ADVANTAGES OF BUSINESS 2.0

In the mid-1990s, the stock market reached an all-time high as companies took advantage of ebusiness and Web 1.0, and many believed the Internet was the wave of the future. When new online businesses began failing to meet earning expectations, however, the bubble burst. Some then believed the ebusiness boom was over, but they could not have been more wrong.

- ***Web 2.0*** (or ***Business 2.0***): The next generation of Internet use–a more mature, distinctive communications platform characterized by new qualities such as collaboration and sharing, and being free.

Business 2.0 encourages user participation and the formation of communities that contribute to the content. In Business 2.0, technical skills are no longer required to use and publish information to the World Wide Web, eliminating entry barriers for online business.

Traditional companies tended to view technology as a tool required to perform a process or activity, and employees picked up information by walking through the office or hanging out around the water cooler. Business 2.0 technologies provide a virtual environment that, for many new employees, is just as vibrant and important as the physical environment. Just think of all the new companies launched using the direct-to-consumer models.

- ***Direct-to-consumer (DTC)***: Ebusiness model where companies build, market, sell, and ship their products themselves, without relying on traditional stores or intermediaries.

Companies like Nike, Timberland, REI, and Under Armour are finding success expanding their DTC channels. It's no wonder more brands plan to open their own retail shops and invest in their ebusiness websites. As more retailers aggressively pursue this strategy, the brands that can deliver the best experience–both to their customers and to their partners–are in a position to win.

Nike, one of the largest retailers in the world, is betting on the DTC sales channel and expects a revenue increase of 250 percent reaching $16 billion by 2022–a massive increase from the $6.6 billion this channel generated in 2015. Retailers everywhere are investing in DTC sales channels. Even in the automobile industry, where the traditional dealership model is long-established, forward-thinking companies like Tesla Motors are going the DTC route. There are three main drivers of the DTC sales channel.

- **Customer Experience:** Consumers are demanding a better experience. Customer experience is the new battlefield and customers want it seamless. When wholesale manufacturers sell through retail distributors, they have very little say on how the product is sold. They're at the mercy of the distributor to ensure that the customer leaves the store (or the website) happy and satisfied. By selling directly to consumers, companies can envision how the customer journey should take place and execute the tactics required to make that vision a reality. A huge competitive advantage for any company wishing to attract and retain loyal customers.
- **Data Collection:** Direct sales allow them to collect customer data. For many brands, the most compelling reason to sell directly to consumers is the potential to collect massive amounts of customer data. Clothes retailer Zara collects more information from its returns than from the products customers keep. A huge win for not only Zara but also the clothing manufacturers.
- **Reduced Costs:** DTC companies manufacture and ship their products directly to buyers without relying on traditional stores or other intermediaries. This allows DTC companies to sell their products at lower costs than traditional consumer brands, and to maintain end-to-end control over the making, marketing, and distribution of products. Selling DTC avoids the costs associated with retail markups and therefore allows the companies to offer some combination of better design, quality, and service at a lower price. DTC eliminates the use of intermediaries.[13]

For many brands, DTC is a new frontier. Although it does provide more control and eliminates costs, the onus is solely on the brand to maintain strong customer relationships and effectively leverage customer-validated insight to improve products and marketing campaigns. Figure 3.13 highlights the common characteristics of Web 2.0.

Content Sharing through Open Sourcing

Thousands of hardware devices and software applications created and sold by third-party vendors interoperate with computers, such as iPods, drawing software, and mice. There are many

APPLY YOUR KNOWLEDGE

BUSINESS DRIVEN GLOBALIZATION

Search Engines

Did you know that a single Google search takes more energy than it took to send *Apollo 11* to the moon? Google searches have gone from 500,000 searches per day in 1998 to 2.3 million searches per second. Search engines such as Google and Firefox collect, analyze, and return content on demand. Enter a search term into the search engine's prompt, and a three-stage process launches and completes within seconds. When you use a search engine, you rely on its ability to return the websites that provide you with updated, accurate content.

Did you know some countries ban websites or edit the content that can be displayed? Google Search is partially blocked in China, and requests from the mainland to Google Search, including Google.com and Google.cn, are automatically redirected to Google.com.hk, the company's Hong Kong servers. Depending on what you search for, the results may or may not be censored. Searching in Chinese for sensitive keywords–Dalai Lama, Falun Gong, Tiananmen Square incident, etc.–will likely turn up an error page. This is a result of keyword filtering by the Great Firewall, China's nationwide Internet censorship system. More benign searches may return results normally, but whether links are accessible depends on their individual standing with Chinese authorities.[14]

Although the Internet and WWW have connected the world, there are still problems with sharing information. Do you agree with a country's right to block websites or censor keywords for search results?

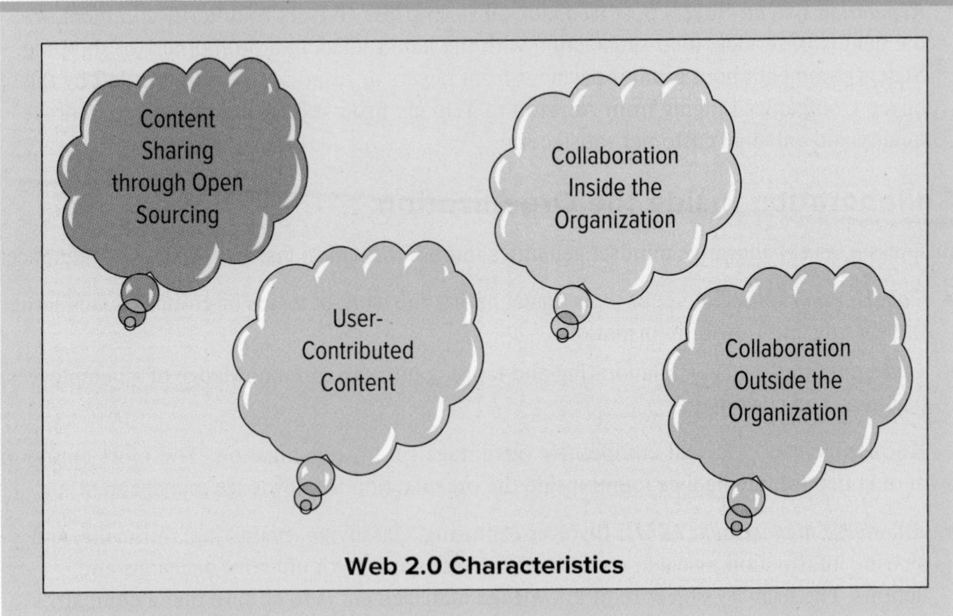

FIGURE 3.13

Four Characteristics of Web 2.0

different applications for sharing content freely. A few key terms to understand when analyzing open sharing applications include:

- ***Open system***: Consists of nonproprietary hardware and software based on publicly known standards that allow third parties to create add-on products to plug into or interoperate with the system.
- ***Source code***: Contains instructions written by a programmer specifying the actions to be performed by computer software.

- ***Open source***: Refers to any software whose source code is made available free (not on a fee or licensing basis as in ebusiness) for any third party to review and modify.
- ***Closed source***: Any proprietary software licensed under exclusive legal right of the copyright holder.

Business 2.0 is capitalizing on open source software. Just think of Gmail, Google Docs, and Google Sheets. Another example is Mozilla and its Firefox web browser and Thunderbird email software free. Mozilla believes the Internet is a public resource that must remain open and accessible to all. It continuously develops free products by bringing together thousands of dedicated volunteers from around the world. Mozilla's Firefox now holds over 20 percent of the browser market and is quickly becoming a threat to Microsoft's Internet Explorer. How do open source software companies generate revenues? Many people are still awaiting an answer to this very important question.

User-Contributed Content

Ebusiness was characterized by a few companies or users posting content for the masses. Business 2.0 is characterized by the masses posting content for the masses.

- ***User-contributed content*** (or ***user-generated content***): Created and updated by many users for many users.

Websites such as Flickr, Wikipedia, and YouTube, for example, move control of online media from the hands of leaders to the hands of users. Netflix and Amazon both use user-generated content to drive their recommendation tools, and websites such as Yelp use customer reviews to express opinions on products and services. Companies are embracing user-generated content to help with everything from marketing to product development and quality assurance.

- ***Native advertising***: An online marketing concept in which the advertiser attempts to gain attention by providing content in the context of the user's experience in terms of its content, format, style, or placement.
- ***Reputation system***: Buyers post feedback on sellers. eBay buyers voluntarily comment on the quality of service, their satisfaction with the item traded, and promptness of shipping. Sellers comment about prompt payment from buyers or respond to comments left by the buyer. Companies ranging from Amazon to Yelp are using reputation systems to improve quality and enhance customer satisfaction.

Collaboration Inside the Organization

Business 2.0's collaborative mindset generates more information faster from a wider audience.

- ***Collaboration system***: A set of tools that supports the work of teams or groups by facilitating the sharing and flow of information.
- ***Collective intelligence***: Collaborating and tapping into the core knowledge of all employees, partners, and customers.

Knowledge can be a real competitive advantage for an organization. The most common form of collective intelligence found inside the organization is knowledge management.

- ***Knowledge management (KM)***: Involves capturing, classifying, evaluating, retrieving, and sharing information assets in a way that provides context for effective decisions and actions. The primary objective of knowledge management is to be sure that a company's knowledge of facts, sources of information, and solutions are readily available to all employees whenever it is needed.
- ***Knowledge management system (KMS)***: Supports the capture, organization, and dissemination of knowledge (i.e., know-how) throughout an organization. KMS can distribute an organization's knowledge base by interconnecting people and digitally gathering their expertise.

KM has assumed greater urgency in American business over the past few years as millions of baby boomers prepare to retire. When they punch out for the last time, the knowledge they gleaned about their jobs, companies, and industries during their long careers will walk out with them–unless companies take measures to retain their insights.

Not all information is valuable. Individuals must determine what information qualifies as intellectual and knowledge-based assets. In general, intellectual and knowledge-based assets fall into one of two categories: explicit or tacit.

- ***Explicit knowledge***: Consists of anything that can be documented, archived, and codified, often with the help of MIS. Examples of explicit knowledge are assets such as patents, trademarks, business plans, marketing research, and customer lists.
- ***Tacit knowledge***: The knowledge contained in people's heads. The challenge inherent in tacit knowledge is figuring out how to recognize, generate, share, and manage knowledge that resides in people's heads. Although information technology in the form of email, instant messaging, and related technologies can help facilitate the dissemination of tacit knowledge, identifying it in the first place can be a major obstacle.

Collaboration Outside the Organization

For many years, organizations believed that good ideas came from the top. CEOs collaborated only with the heads of sales and marketing, the quality assurance expert, or the road warrior salesperson. The organization chart governed who should work with whom and how far up the chain of command a suggestion or idea would travel. Communication during this era was asynchronous.

- ***Asynchronous communication***: Communication, such as email, in which the message and the response do not occur at the same time. Traditional ebusiness communications were limited to face-to-face conversations and one-way technologies.
- ***Synchronous communication***: Communications that occur at the same time, such as IM or chat. With Business 2.0, asynchronous communication is being challenged with different forms of synchronous communication.

In business, continuous connections are now expected in today's collaborative world. There are numerous examples where the ideas coming from a group of diverse individuals are far more creative and energized than from an individual. Groupthink tends to lead to innovative ideas along nontraditional production paths. Synchronous communication outside the organization has led to two amazing business resources:

- ***Crowdsourcing***: Refers to the wisdom of the crowd. The idea that collective intelligence is greater than the sum of its individual parts has been around for a long time (see Figure 3.14). One of the most successful crowd-powered start-ups is Waze. It's an app that allows users to report traffic jams and automatically gives directions for the best route to take. Waze crowdsources information by measuring drivers' speeds to determine traffic jams and by asking users to report road closures.

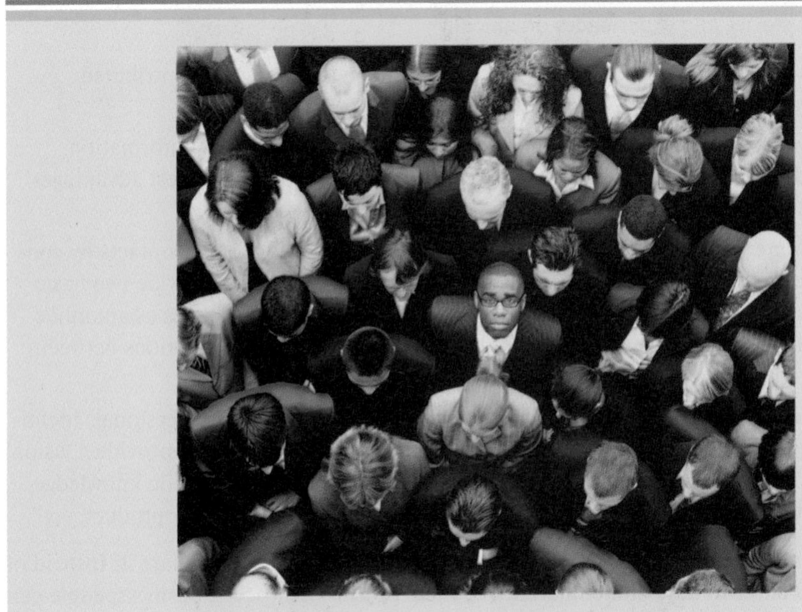

FIGURE 3.14

Crowdsourcing: The Crowd Is Smarter Than the Individual

Digital Vision/Getty Images

APPLY YOUR KNOWLEDGE

BUSINESS DRIVEN INNOVATION

Disrupt Yourself

The employment marketplace is highly competitive, and landing your dream job is typically on the top of a student's goals when graduating from college. Have you ever thought of how you can apply disruptive innovation to yourself to ensure you are the number one choice for the job? In a group, answer the following questions:

1. Can you target a need that is currently not being met or met well? Disruptors look for gaps where they can add value and disrupt a market.
2. What are your disruptive strengths? As you think about disrupting yourself, don't think just about what you do well–think about what you do well that most other people cannot do. Perhaps you have searchlight intelligence, the ability to see connections across different areas and find opportunities for new ventures.
3. How will you build the right skills to find your niche? You are the engine driving your future. If you want to move the world forward, you will need to be innovative, building skills in many different areas.
4. How will you deploy your personal disruption strategy? Disruptors do not follow a traditional career path. To be disruptive, you will need to strike out on new paths, rather than travel traditional paths.

- ***Crowdfunding*****:** Sources capital for a project by raising many small amounts from a large number of individuals, typically via the Internet. Kiva offers a great example of a crowdfunding application. Kiva allows individuals from all over the world to connect with microfinanciers to support their business ideas. With Business 2.0, people can be continuously connected, which is a driving force behind collaboration.

LO 3.6: Explain how Business 2.0 is helping communities network and collaborate.

BUSINESS 2.0: ALL ABOUT SOCIAL

Facebook. Twitter. LinkedIn. YouTube. Pinterest. In the connected world, marketing opportunities are abundant. Social media sites were traditionally designed to enable individuals to share their interests, and opinions have now morphed into vehicles to promote products and services. Many opportunities arise from choices to pay for ads in social media sites to hoping customers share stories and experiences organically.

- ***Social media*****:** Refers to websites that rely on user participation and user-contributed content, such as Facebook, YouTube, and LinkedIn.
- ***Social network*****:** An application that connects people by matching profile information. Providing individuals with the ability to network is, by far, one of the greatest advantages of Business 2.0.
- ***Social networking*****:** The practice of expanding your business and/or social contacts by constructing a personal network (see Figure 3.15). Social networking sites provide two basic functions. The first is the ability to create and maintain a profile that serves as an online identity within the environment. The second is the ability to create connections between other people within the network.
- ***Social networking analysis (SNA)*****:** Maps group contacts (personal and professional) identifying who knows each other and who works together. In a company, it can provide a vision of how employees work together. It can also identify key experts with specific knowledge, such as how to solve a complicated programming problem or launch a new product.

Business 2.0 simplifies access to information and improves the ability to share it. Instead of spending $1,000 and two days at a conference to meet professional peers, businesspeople can now use social networks such as LinkedIn to meet new contacts for recruiting, prospecting, and

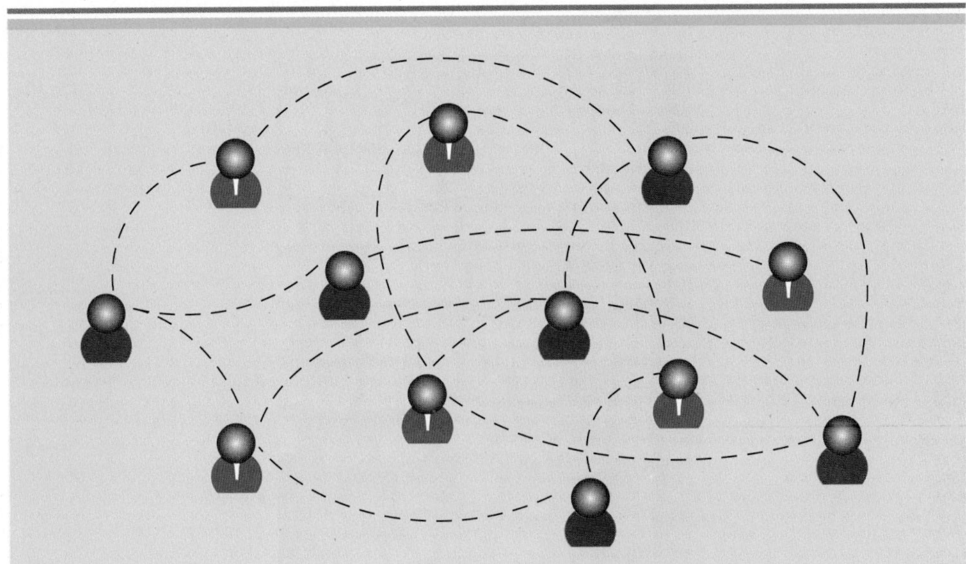

FIGURE 3.15

Social Network Example

Source: Google Images. http://www.google.com/images?

identifying experts on a topic. With executive members from all the *Fortune* 500 companies, LinkedIn has become one of the more useful recruiting tools on the web.

Social media can help a company with the following:

- Spread the word and create buzz about your products and services
- Advertise with campaigns designed to target your specific audience
- Create your own group or community to get feedback from customers
- Build referral sources and networking connections
- Engage more deeply with prospects and customers
- Enhance your credibility by contributing meaningful content to others' sites or posting positive recommendations or reviews

Social Tagging

Tags are specific keywords or phrases incorporated into website content for means of classification or taxonomy. An item can have one or more tags associated with it to allow for multiple browsable paths through the items, and tags can be changed with minimal effort (see Figure 3.16). If you have ever seen a word with a # before it on Facebook or Twitter, you have seen a hashtag.

A ***hashtag*** is a keyword or phrase used to identify a topic and is preceded by a hash or pound sign (#). For example, the hashtag #sandiegofire helped coordinate emergency responses to a fire. Hashtags provide an online audience to expand business exposure and directly engage with customers. Customers can type any search keyword into a social media site, with a hashtag before the word, and the search results will show all related posts. Hashtags can be used to reference promotions, observe market trends, and even provide links to helpful tips.

- ***Social tagging***: Describes the collaborative activity of marking shared online content with keywords or tags as a way to organize it for future navigation, filtering, or searching.

The entire user community is invited to tag, and thus essentially define, the content. Websites using social tagging allow users to upload images and tag them with appropriate keywords. After enough people have done so, the resulting tag collection will identify images correctly and without bias.

Using the collective power of a community to identify and classify content significantly lowers content categorization costs because there is no complicated nomenclature to learn.

- ***Folksonomy***: Similar to taxonomy except that crowdsourcing determines the tags or keyword-based classification system.

Users simply create and apply tags as they wish. For example, although cell phone manufacturers often refer to their products as mobile devices, the folksonomy could include *mobile phone, wireless*

FIGURE 3.16

Social Tagging Occurs When Many Individuals Categorize Content

Radius Images/Alamy Stock Photo

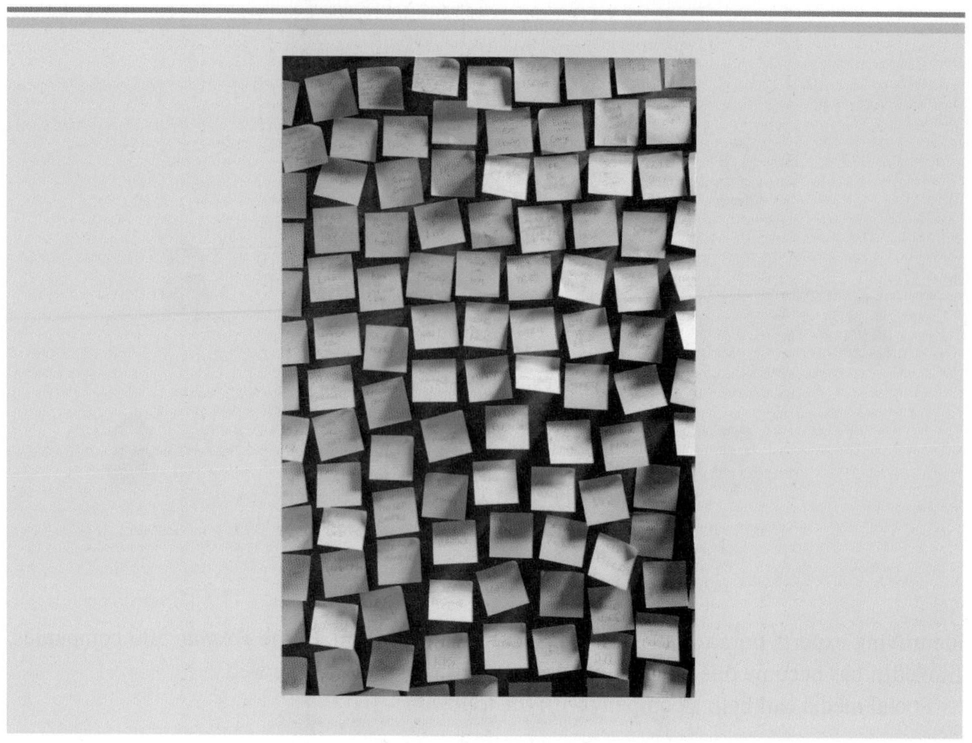

phone, smart phone, iPhone, and so on. All these keywords, if searched, should take a user to the same site. Folksonomies reveal what people truly call things (see Figure 3.17). They have been a point of discussion on the web because the whole reason for having a website is for your customers to find it. The majority of websites are found through search terms that match the content.[15]

Social Collaboration

Snackable content is content that is designed to be easy for readers to consume and to share. Snackable content captures website visitors' attention by offering small consumable pieces of information that can be quickly read and understood. Infographics, photos, and attention-grabbing headlines that ask questions or use humor play a critical part when attracting readers attention who are browsing and don't have the time or patience to consume long, text-heavy articles. Many people believe that snackable content is dumbing down the Internet, while others believe it fits the mobile delivery channel so many consumers use today. To make long-form

FIGURE 3.17

Folksonomy Example: The User-Generated Names for Cellular Phones

Chinnapong/Shutterstock

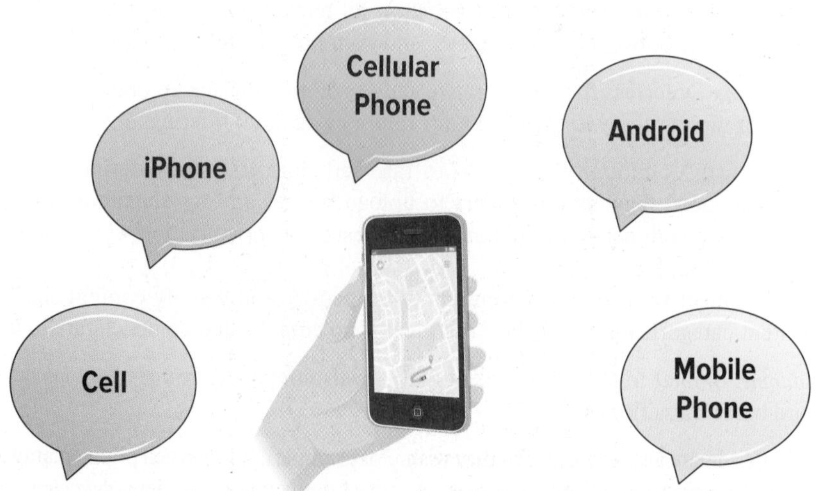

BUSINESS DRIVEN DEBATE

The Disruption Debate

Clayton Christensen's theory of disruptive innovation has been a powerful tool for predicting which industry entrants would succeed and which would fail. However, many believe the "disruptive" label has often been applied incorrectly, simply because a newcomer shakes up a market.

For example, Zipcar qualifies as a disruptive innovation as it launched a market for cars rented by the hour. However, Uber is not classified as disruptive because it neither offered a low-end service nor created a new market. Uber is basically a taxi service, and it is not considered a disruptive innovation. Do you agree or disagree with the assessment that Zipcar is a disruptive innovation and Uber is not?

articles more snackable, they can be broken down into smaller components. Responsive or adaptive website design can also help make content more snackable, as flexible website design makes content easier to view on smart phones and tablets.

Blogs

A ***blog***, or ***web log***, is an online journal that allows users to post their own comments, graphics, and video. Unlike traditional HTML web pages, blog websites let writers communicate–and readers respond–on a regular basis through a simple yet customizable interface that does not require any programming.

- ***Selfie***: A self-photograph placed on a social media website.

From a business perspective, blogs are no different from marketing channels such as video, print, audio, or presentations. They all deliver results of varying kinds. Many creative individuals use their blogs for marketing, sharing ideas, gathering feedback, press response, and image shaping. Starbucks has developed a blog called My Starbucks Idea, allowing customers to share ideas, tell Starbucks what they think of other people's ideas, and join discussions. Blogs are an ideal mechanism for many businesses since they can focus on topic areas more easily than traditional media, with no limits on page size, word count, or publication deadline.[16]

- ***Microblogging***: The practice of sending brief posts (140 to 200 characters) to a personal blog, either publicly or to a private group of subscribers who can read the posts as IMs or as text messages.

The main advantage of microblogging is that posts can be submitted by a variety of means, such as instant messaging, email, or the web. By far the most popular microblogging tool is Twitter, which allows users to send microblog entries called tweets to anyone who has registered to follow them. Senders can restrict delivery to people they want to follow them or, by default, allow open access.[17]

Wikis

Although blogs have largely drawn on the creative and personal goals of individual authors, wikis are based on open collaboration between anyone and everyone.

- ***Wiki*** (the word is Hawaiian for "quick"): A type of collaborative web page that allows users to add, remove, and change content, which can be easily organized and reorganized as required.

Wikipedia, the open encyclopedia that launched in 2001, has become one of the 10 most popular web destinations, reaching an estimated 217 million unique visitors a month.

A wiki user can generally alter the original content of any article, whereas the blog user can only add information in the form of comments. Large wikis, such as Wikipedia, protect the quality and accuracy of their information by assigning users roles such as reader, editor,

APPLY YOUR KNOWLEDGE

BUSINESS DRIVEN MIS

Social Media Marketing

One of the first things you need to determine when planning your social media marketing platform is what best suits your target market. Are you trying to reach consumers or businesses? Does a mass-market site (Facebook, Twitter, YouTube), a special interest site (such as Hello Fresh), or a professional networking site (LinkedIn) suit your offerings? Before launching a social media campaign, answer two very important questions: Where are my customers? and Where are my competitors?

How will you find out where your customers and competitors are? Once you find the answers to these two critical questions, you can then choose the social media site that best fits your needs. In a group, brainstorm different ways you can find your customers and competitors. Then list the target audience and potential social media marketing strategy for each of the following:

- LinkedIn
- Facebook
- Pinterest
- YouTube

---

administrator, patroller, policy maker, subject matter expert, content maintainer, software developer, and system operator. Access to some important or sensitive Wikipedia material is limited to users in these authorized roles.

- ***Metcalfe's law***: States that the value of a telecommunications network is proportional to the square of the number of connected users of the system.
- ***Network effect***: Describes how products in a network increase in value to users as the number of users increases.

The more users and content managers on a wiki, the greater the network effect because more users attract more contributors, whose work attracts more users, and so on. For example, Wikipedia becomes more valuable to users as the number of its contributors increases.

Wikis internal to firms can be vital tools for collecting and disseminating knowledge throughout an organization, across geographic distances, and between functional business areas. For example, what U.S. employees call a "sale" may be called "an order booked" in the United Kingdom, an "order scheduled" in Germany, and an "order produced" in France. The corporate wiki can answer any questions about a business process or definition. Companies are also using wikis for documentation, reporting, project management, online dictionaries, and discussion groups. Of course, the more employees who use the corporate wiki, the greater the network effect and value added for the company.

Whoever thought technology could help sell bananas? Dole Organic now places three-digit farm codes on each banana and creates a mashup using Google Earth and its banana database. Socially and environmentally conscious buyers can plug the numbers into Dole's website and look at a bio of the farm where the bananas were raised. The site tells the story of the farm and its surrounding community, lists its organic certifications, posts some photos, and offers a link to satellite images of the farm in Google Earth. Customers can personally monitor the production and treatment of their fruit from the tree to the grocer. The process assures customers that their bananas have been raised to proper organic standards on an environmentally friendly, holistically minded plantation.[18]

Social Trust

Have you ever shared an article or post you believed to be true at the time, but then later discovered it actually contained falsehoods or outdated information? Long before Facebook, Twitter, or even Google existed, the fact-checking website Snopes.com was running down the half-truths, misinformation, and outright lies that ricochet across the Internet. Today, Snopes.com remains a widely respected clearinghouse of all things factual and not. Being a critical consumer of the news means identifying and distinguishing real news from fake news.

- ***Misinformation*:** Refers to false information that is presented as fact without an intent to deceive. Misinformation about the COVID-19 vaccine or about 5G allegedly causing cancer are two examples of misinformation spread through the Internet.
- ***Disinformation*:** Refers to false information that is presented as fact, with an intent to deceive and mislead. This includes disinformation and outright fabrication about events, statements, or outcomes. The hackings and distribution of misinformation conducted by Russia to influence the American elections is an example.
- ***Fake news*:** Refers to false news stories created to be widely shared or distributed for the purpose of promoting or discrediting a public figure, political movement, or a company. Fake news campaigns are also created to generate revenue.

While both misinformation and disinformation can deceive audiences, the distinction is that disinformation is created to intentionally and maliciously deceive the audience. Both forms intend to spread the information to as many users as possible around the globe.

It's important for everyone to know how to spot misinformation and disinformation online to avoid spreading falsehoods and to be critical consumers of online news, particularly through social media. A few rules to follow when reviewing online information include:

- Where is the information coming from?
- Is the source clearly listed?
- Is the organization legitimate?
- Does the information seem too good to be true?
- Does it reflect your opinions, biases, and judgments?
- Is it extremely positive or extremely negative?
- Are the statistics out of date?

The best, baseline way to interrogate a source of information is to check:

- The author
- The organization
- The date it was published
- The evidence

WEB 3.0: DEFINING THE NEXT GENERATION OF ONLINE BUSINESS OPPORTUNITIES

LO 3.7: Describe Web 3.0 and the next generation of online business.

Although Web 1.0 refers to static text-based information websites and Web 2.0 is about user-contributed content, Web 3.0 is based on intelligent web applications using natural language processing, machine-based learning and reasoning, and intelligent applications. Web 3.0 is the next step in the evolution of the Internet and web applications. Business leaders who explore its opportunities will be the first to market with competitive advantages.

Web 3.0 offers a way for people to describe information so that computers can start to understand the relationships among concepts and topics. To demonstrate the power of Web 3.0, let's look at a few sample relationships: Adam Sandler is a comedian, Lady Gaga is a singer, and Hannah is friends with Sophie. These are all examples of descriptions that can be added to web pages, allowing computers to learn about relationships while displaying the information to humans. With this kind of information in place, interaction between people and machines will be far richer with Web 3.0.

Applying this type of advanced relationship knowledge to a company can create new opportunities. After all, businesses run on information. Whereas Web 2.0 brings people closer together with information by using machines, Web 3.0 brings *machines* closer together by using *information.* These new relationships unite people, machines, and information so a business can be smarter, quicker, more agile, and more successful.

Deep Web

The deep web is the portion of the web not indexed by search engines.

- ***Deep web*** (sometimes called the invisible web): The large part of the Internet that is inaccessible to conventional search engines.

Deep web content includes email messages, chat messages, private content on social media sites, electronic bank statements, electronic health records, and other content that is accessible over the Internet but is not crawled and indexed by search engines such as Google or Bing.

It is not known how large the deep web is, but many experts estimate that search engines crawl and index less than 1 percent of all the content that can be accessed over the Internet. This part of the Internet that is crawled and indexed by search engines is sometimes referred to as the surface web.

The reasons for not indexing deep web content are varied. It may be that the content is proprietary, in which case the content can only be accessed by approved visitors coming in through a virtual private network. Or the content may be commercial, in which case the content resides behind a member wall and can only be accessed by customers who have paid a fee. Or perhaps the content contains personal identifiable information, in which case the content is protected by compliance regulations and can only be accessed through a portal site by individuals who have been granted access privileges. When mashups have been generated on the fly and components lack a permanent uniform resource location, they also become part of the deep web.

Dark Web

The term *deep web* was coined by BrightPlanet in a 2001 white paper titled "The Deep Web: Surfacing Hidden Value" and is often confused in the media with the term *dark web*.

- ***Dark web*:** The portion of the Internet that is intentionally hidden from search engines, uses masked IP addresses, and is accessible only with a special web browser.

The key takeaway here is that the dark web is part of the deep web. Like deep web content, dark web content cannot be accessed by conventional search engines, but most often the reason dark web content remains inaccessible to search engines is because the content is illegal.

One goal of Web 3.0 is to tailor online searches and requests specifically to users' preferences and needs. For example, instead of making multiple searches, the user might type a complex sentence or two in a Web 3.0 browser, such as "I want to see a funny movie and then eat at a good Mexican restaurant. What are my options?" The Web 3.0 browser will analyze the request, search the web for all possible answers, organize the results, and present them to the user.

Semantic Web

- Tim Berners-Lee has described the ***semantic web*** as a component of Web 3.0 that describes things in a way that computers can understand.

The semantic web is not about links between web pages; rather it describes the relationships between *things* (such as A is a part of B and Y is a member of Z) and the properties of things (size, weight, age, price). If information about music, cars, concert tickets, and so on is stored in a way that describes the information and associated resource files, semantic web applications can collect information from many sources, combine it, and present it to users in a meaningful way. Although Web 3.0 is still a bit speculative, some topics and features are certain to be included in it, such as:[19]

- **Integration of legacy devices:** The ability to use current devices such as iPhones, laptops, and so on as credit cards, tickets, and reservations tools.
- **Intelligent applications:** The use of agents, machine learning, and semantic web concepts to complete intelligent tasks for users.
- **Open ID:** The provision of an online identity that can be easily carried to a variety of devices (cell phones, PCs) allowing for easy authentication across different websites.
- **Open technologies:** The design of websites and other software so they can be easily integrated and work together.
- **A worldwide database:** The ability for databases to be distributed and accessed from anywhere.

LEARNING OUTCOME REVIEW

Learning Outcome 3.1: Compare disruptive and sustaining technologies and explain how the Internet and WWW caused business disruption.

Disruptive technologies offer a new way of doing things that initially does not meet the needs of existing customers. Disruptive technologies redefine the competitive playing fields of their respective markets, open new markets and destroy old ones, and cut into the low end of the marketplace and eventually evolve to displace high-end competitors and their reigning technologies.

Sustaining technologies produce improved products customers are eager to buy, such as a faster car or larger hard drive. Sustaining technologies tend to provide us with better, faster, and cheaper products in established markets and virtually never lead in markets opened by new and disruptive technologies.

The Internet and the World Wide Web caused business disruption by allowing people to communicate and collaborate in ways that were not possible before the information age. The Internet and WWW completely disrupted the way businesses operate, employees communicate, and products are developed and sold.

Learning Outcome 3.2: Describe ebusiness and its associated advantages.

Web 1.0 is a term that refers to the World Wide Web during its first few years of operation, between 1991 and 2003. Ebusiness includes ecommerce along with all activities related to internal and external business operations such as servicing customer accounts, collaborating with partners, and exchanging real-time information. During Web 1.0, entrepreneurs began creating the first forms of ebusiness. Ebusiness advantages include expanding global reach, opening new markets, reducing costs, and improving operations and effectiveness.

Learning Outcome 3.3: Compare the four ebusiness models.

- Business-to-business (B2B) applies to businesses buying from and selling to each other over the Internet.
- Business-to-consumer (B2C) applies to any business that sells its products or services to consumers over the Internet.
- Consumer-to-business (C2B) applies to any consumer who sells a product or service to a business over the Internet.
- Consumer-to-consumer (C2C) applies to sites primarily offering goods and services to assist consumers interacting with each other over the Internet.

The primary difference between B2B and B2C are the customers; B2B customers are other businesses, whereas B2C markets to consumers. Overall, B2B relations are more complex and have higher security needs and are the dominant ebusiness force, representing 80 percent of all online business.

Learning Outcome 3.4: Describe the five ebusiness tools for connecting and communicating.

As firms began to move online, more MIS tools were created to support ebusiness processes and requirements. The ebusiness tools used to connect and communicate include email, instant messaging, podcasting, content management systems, and video chat.

Learning Outcome 3.5: Explain Web 2.0 and identify its four characteristics.

Web 2.0, or Business 2.0, is the next generation of Internet use—a more mature, distinctive communications platform characterized by new qualities such as collaboration, sharing, and being free. Web 2.0 encourages user participation and the formation of communities that contribute to the content. In

Web 2.0, technical skills are no longer required to use and publish information to the World Wide Web, eliminating entry barriers for online business. The four characteristics of Web 2.0 include:

- Content sharing through open sourcing.
- User-contributed content.
- Collaboration inside the organization.
- Collaboration outside the organization.

Learning Outcome 3.6: Explain how Business 2.0 is helping communities network and collaborate.

A social network is an application that connects people by matching profile information. Providing individuals with the ability to network is, by far, one of the greatest advantages of Business 2.0. Social networking is the practice of expanding your business and/or social contacts by constructing a personal network. Business 2.0 simplifies the way individuals communicate, network, find employment, and search for information.

Learning Outcome 3.7: Describe Web 3.0 and the next generation of online business.

Web 3.0 is based on intelligent web applications using natural language processing, machine-based learning and reasoning, and intelligent applications. Web 3.0 is the next step in the evolution of the Internet and web applications. Business leaders who explore its opportunities will be the first to market with competitive advantages.

Web 3.0 offers a way for people to describe information in ways that enable computers to understand the relationships among concepts and topics.

KEY TERMS

AdWords 114
Affiliate program 114
Asynchronous communication 121
Blog, or web log 125
Business model 111
Business-to-business (B2B) 111
Business-to-consumer (B2C) 112
Click fraud 115
Clickstream 110
Clickstream analytics 110
Click-thru 110
Closed source 120
Collaboration system 120
Collective intelligence 120
Consumer-to-business (C2B) 112
Consumer-to-consumer (C2C) 112
Content management system (CMS) 117
Cookie 110
Crowdfunding 122
Crowdsourcing 121
Cyborg anthropologist 115
Dark web 128
Deep web 128
Digital Darwinism 102
Direct-to-consumer (DTC) 118
Disinformation 127
Disintermediation 108
Disruptive technology 102
Dot-com 111
Ebusiness 105
Ebusiness model 111
Ecommerce 105
Explicit knowledge 121
Fake news 127
Folksonomy 123
Hashtag 123
Heat map 109
Hitbot 115
Information reach 106
Information richness 106
Instant messaging (sometimes called IM or IMing) 116
Interactivity 109
Intermediaries 108
Internet 103
Internet service provider (ISP) 115
Keyword 114
Knowledge management (KM) 120
Knowledge management system (KMS) 120
Long tail 107
Mass customization 107
Metcalfe's law 126
Microblogging 125
Misinformation 127
Native advertising 120
Net neutrality 104
Network effect 126
Open source 120
Open system 119
Organic search 114
Paid search 114
Paradigm shift 105
Personalization 107
Podcasting 116
Real-time communication 116
Reputation system 120
Search engine 114
Search engine optimization (SEO) 114
Search engine ranking 114
Selfie 125
Semantic web 128
Showrooming 110

Snackable content 124
Social media 122
Social network 122
Social networking 122
Social networking analysis (SNA) 122
Social tagging 123
Source code 119
Stickiness 108
Sustaining technology 102
Synchronous communication 121
Tacit knowledge 121
Tags 123
Taxonomy 117
Universal resource locator (URL) 104
User-contributed content (also referred to as user-generated content) 120
Video chat 117
Viral marketing 109
Web 1.0 (or Business 1.0) 105
Web 2.0 (or Business 2.0) 118
Website ebusiness analytics 110
Website traffic analytics 110
Wiki 125

REVIEW QUESTIONS

1. What is the difference between sustaining and disruptive technology?
2. Do you consider the Internet and World Wide Web forms of sustaining or disruptive technology?
3. How have the Internet and WWW created a global platform for business?
4. What is the difference between ebusiness and ecommerce?
5. What are the benefits associated with ebusiness?
6. What are the benefits associated with Business 2.0?
7. Explain business models and their role in a company. How did ebusiness change traditional business models?
8. How can a company use mass customization and personalization to decrease buyer power?
9. How does ebusiness differ from Business 2.0?
10. What are the differences among collective intelligence, knowledge management, and crowdsourcing?
11. Why is knowledge management critical to a business?
12. What is the difference between the deep web and the dark web?
13. Why would a company want to use viral marketing?
14. What is the difference between a blog and a wiki?
15. What is the semantic web?

CLOSING CASE ONE

Collaboration During Coronavirus

In late 2019, the world experienced a new type of infectious disease, the novel coronavirus COVID-19. COVID-19 causes respiratory problems, with symptoms ranging from a dry cough and fever to severe breathing difficulties that require hospitalization. As COVID-19 spread across the world, many nations were forced to shut down their economies and order citizens to stay at home and shelter in place. Suddenly and without notice, customers stopped eating out, riding public transportation, and traveling for work or leisure, and simply retreated into their homes. The economic impact of this virus will be felt for many years as small and large businesses struggle to operate in a world where customers are scarce.

One innovative young man refused to allow COVID-19 to keep him from collaborating with the world. Avi Schiffmann, a 17-year-old from Washington State, launched his own website (ncov2019.live) using data from the World Health Organization and the U.S. Centers for Disease Control and Prevention to report the movement of COVID-19. Since launching his website, Avi has received over 100 million visitors, quickly catapulting the young genius to technical stardom.

On his website, Avi scraped the data from several different sources and then displayed the numbers of current cases, new cases, and deaths in simple, easy-to-understand tables divided by continent, nation, and states. The website updates every minute and has quickly become a reputable phenomenon for people around the globe.

Avi was not the only one looking to help disseminate information during the crisis. Businesses, schools, and governments were all looking for a way to collaborate online. Thankfully, the demand for video and chat software was not new as online schools and work-from-home policies were already being implemented and supported worldwide. Individuals who had never worked from home suddenly found themselves needing to chat from anywhere, host meetings with participants around the globe, port classes from physical environments to online, and share files. Several technological companies helped solve the problem by offering their online collaboration tools for free, including Microsoft's Teams, Google GSuite, Zoom, and Slack.[20]

Questions

1. If you could build a data tracking website, what sources would you scrape from and how would you communicate its existence to your audience?
2. Why would a company offer its application for free during a crisis such as COVID-19?
3. Review Microsoft's Teams, Google GSuite, Zoom, and Slack. Which collaboration tool would you choose for each of the following situations?
   a. Online college with students all over the globe
   b. Online elementary school in a neighborhood
   c. Virtual meeting with participants all over the globe
   d. Daily call with family and friends
   e. Virtual happy hour with co-workers
   f. Online fitness class

CLOSING CASE TWO

Direct-to-Consumer: The Warby Parker Way

The direct-to-consumer (DTC) space is viciously competitive and yet extremely exciting to watch as hundreds of products from razors to mattresses are attempting to dominate this space. This market has come to fruition with the invention of the Internet and mass distribution of PCs and mobile devices. The appeal of the DTC movement goes like this: By selling directly to consumers online, you can avoid exorbitant retail markups and therefore afford to offer some combination of better design, quality, service, and lower prices because you've cut out the intermediary. By connecting directly with consumers online, you can also better control your messages to them and, in turn, gather data about their purchase behavior, thereby enabling you to build a smarter product engine. If you do this while developing an "authentic" brand—one that stands for something more than selling stuff—you can effectively steal the future out from under giant legacy corporations. There are now an estimated 400-plus DTC start-ups that have collectively raised some $3 billion in venture capital since 2012.

For most of its history, University of Pennsylvania's Wharton School of Business's reputation has been built on turning out the world's finest spreadsheet jockeys. But a few years ago, four students met at Wharton and started a company that would help ignite a start-up revolution: Warby Parker. The concept: selling eyeglasses directly to consumers online. Few thought the idea would work, but today Warby is valued at $1.75 billion, and its founding story has become a fairy tale at Wharton. Cofounders and co-CEOs Neil Blumenthal and Dave Gilboa give guest lectures at the business school—as does Jeff Raider, the third Warby cofounder, who went on to help hatch Harry's, a DTC razor brand. Professors, venture capitalists, and entrepreneurs are fueling an entire generation of Warby Parkers.

James McKean wants to revolutionize the manual toothbrush. It's January 2018. The 31-year-old MBA candidate at the University of Pennsylvania's Wharton School whirls his laptop around to show me the prototype designs. Bristle, as the product might be called, has a detachable head and a colorful pattern on the handle—such as faux woodgrain, flowers, or plaid. Customers would pay somewhere around $15 for their first purchase and then get replacement heads, at $3 or $4 a pop, through a subscription service.

There are a few reasons McKean likes this plan. A Bristle subscription would be more convenient than going to CVS when you need a new toothbrush: You'd order online, set your replacement-head frequency, and forget about it. Also, Bristle brushes are friendlier looking than, say, Oral-B's spaceshiplike aesthetic. Who knows what product will be launched next as over 400 start-ups begin tackling this market with products from toothbrushes to strollers?[21]

Questions

1. Why does DTC allow a company to offer products at a lower cost than traditional manufacturers?
2. What is the relationship between disintermediation and a DTC business model?
3. What types of clickstream analytics will a DTC business want to monitor on its website to ensure success?

MAKING BUSINESS DECISIONS

1. Anything but Online

Your best friend, Susan Stewart, has started a highly successful custom T-shirt business from your dorm room. Susan is an art major, and each week she creates a limited edition T-shirt focusing on the lyrics from up-and-coming indie bands. You, as an MIS major, see the advantages Susan could reap by porting her business to the Internet. Susan, as an art major, does not like technology and does not believe she needs it to grow her business. Do you agree or disagree that Susan needs to compete online? How can creating an ebusiness benefit Susan? What are the challenges Susan will face as she moves her business to the Internet? How could Susan use Web 2.0 to build loyalty among her followers?

2. The Future of Wikipedia

Wikipedia is a multilingual, web-based, free-content encyclopedia project written collaboratively by volunteers around the world. Since its creation in 2001, it has grown rapidly into one of the largest reference websites. Some people believe Wikipedia will eventually fail under an assault by marketers and self-promoting users. Eric Goldman, a professor at the Santa Clara University School of Law, argues that Wikipedia will see increasingly vigorous efforts to subvert its editorial process, including the use of automated marketing tools to alter Wikipedia entries to generate online traffic. The site's editors will burn out trying to maintain it, he projects, or Wikipedia will change its open-access architecture and its mission. Do you agree or disagree with Professor Goldman's argument? What can Wikipedia do to combat the challenges of information vandalism and copyright/plagiarism issues?

3. **The Toughest College Test You'll Ever Take**
If your professor asked you today to kick your social networking habits, do you think you could do it? Can you go without Facebook, cell phones, or the Internet for a week? For a day? A University of Minnesota professor challenged her public relations class to go five days without media or gadgets that didn't exist before 1984. Out of the 43 students in the class, just a handful made it even three days without new technology. Among those who didn't, one student said, "My mother thought I died." How long could you go without any social media? What types of issues might you encounter without constant connections to your friends? How has social media affected society? How has social media affected businesses?

4. **Five Ways Google Docs Speeds Up Collaboration**
Google Docs wants you to skip Microsoft Office and collaborate with your group in your browser for free, especially when you're not in the same physical space. Visit Google Docs and answer the following questions.

- What are five ways the new Google Docs can help your team accomplish work more efficiently, even when you're not in the same room together?
- Is Google Docs open source software? What revenue model is Google Docs following?
- Why would putting Google Docs and Microsoft Office on your résumé help differentiate your skills?
- What other applications does Google create that you are interested in learning to help collaborate and communicate with peers and co-workers?

5. **Working with Your Heart—Kiva**
Kiva's mission is to connect people through lending for the sake of alleviating poverty. Kiva is a microlending online nonprofit organization that enables individuals to lend directly to entrepreneurs throughout the world. If you want to participate in Kiva, you simply browse the website (www.kiva.org) and choose an entrepreneur that interests you, make a loan, then track your entrepreneur for the next 6 to 12 months while he or she builds the business and makes the funds to repay the loan. When the loan is up, you can relend the money to someone else who is in need.

Kiva is an excellent example of blending ethics and information technology. How is Kiva operating differently than traditional nonprofits? What are the risks associated with investing in Kiva? When you invest in Kiva, you run three primary risks: entrepreneur risk, local field partner risk, and country risk. Analyze each of these risks for potential unethical issues that might arise when donating to Kiva.

6. **Antisocial Networking**
Before the Internet, angry customers could write letters or make phone calls, but their individual power to find satisfaction or bring about change was relatively weak. Now, disgruntled consumers can create a website or upload a video bashing a product or service, and their efforts can be instantly seen by millions of people. Though many companies monitor the Internet and try to respond to such postings quickly, power has clearly shifted to the consumer. Create an argument for or against the following statement: "Social networking has given power to the consumer that benefits society and creates socially responsible corporations."

7. **Using Hashtags**

If you have ever seen a word with a # before it in Facebook or Twitter, you have seen a hashtag. A hashtag is a keyword or phrase used to identify a topic and is preceded by a hash or pound sign (#). Hashtags provide an online audience to expand business exposure and directly engage with customers. Customers can type any search keyword in a social media site with a hashtag before the word and the search results will show all related posts. Hashtags can be used to reference promotions, observe market trends, and even provide links to helpful tips.

When you understand hashtags, you can use them to find business ideas and research potential employers. Pick a company you would like to work for and see whether you can find any related hashtags, including what they are tweeting and posting. See whether you can find any information on partners and competitors. Which hashtags generate discussion or offer business insights? Check Twitter's and Facebook's trending topics to see whether there are any issues or insights on your career area.

8. **Is It Web 1.0 or Web 2.0?**

Deciding whether a given site is Web 1.0 or Web 2.0 is not as straightforward as it appears. Websites do not have version numbers, and many are dynamic enough to be in permanent beta testing. Facebook and MySpace are good Web 2.0 examples, primarily due to their social networking functions and their reliance on user-generated content. Some sites are easy to identify as Web 1.0 in their approach: Craigslist, for example, emulates an email list server and has no public user profiles or dynamic pages. Many other sites are hard to categorize.

Amazon.com launched in the mid-1990s and has gradually added features over time. The principal content (product descriptions) is not user-created, but much of the site's value is added by user reviews and ratings. Profiles of users do exist, but social features such as friend links, although present, are not widely adopted.

Review the following websites and categorize them as Web 1.0, Web 2.0, or both. Be sure to justify your answer with the characteristics that classify the website as 1.0, 2.0, or both. Why would certain types of businesses choose to remain Web 1.0 and not offer collaboration or open source capabilities?

- www.ebay.com; www.amazon.com; www.facebook.com; www.craigslist.com; www.paypal.com; www.twitter.com; www.irs.gov; www.google.com; www.youtube.com. www.wikipedia.com
- For the following, be sure to use your personal websites as references: your college's website; www.YourVisaCard.com; www.YourBank.com.

9. **Virtual Abandonment**

Approximately 35 percent of online shopping carts are abandoned prior to checkout. Abandoned shopping carts relate directly to lost revenues for a business. It is like customers walking out of the store, leaving their cart full of chosen items. Businesses need to focus on why the customers are virtually walking out of their stores. The problem typically lies in the checkout process and can be fixed by the following:

- Make sure the checkout button is easy to find.
- Make sure personal information is safe and the website's security is visible.
- Streamline the checkout process so the customer has to click as few buttons as possible.
- Do not ask shoppers to create an account prior to checkout. You can ask them to create an account after checkout.
- Ensure your return policy is visible.

Have you ever abandoned a virtual shopping cart? In a group, visit a website that you or your peers have recently abandoned and review the checkout process. Was it difficult, cumbersome, or lacking security? Then visit Amazon.com and review its checkout process and determine whether Amazon is meeting the preceding recommendations.

AYK APPLICATION PROJECTS

If you are looking for Excel projects to incorporate into your class, try any of the following after reading this chapter.

Project Number	Project Name	Project Type	Plug-In Focus Area	Project Focus	Project Skill Set	Page Number
1	Financial Destiny	Excel	T2	Personal Budget	Introductory Formulas	AYK.3
2	Cash Flow	Excel	T2	Cash Flow	Introductory Formulas	AYK.3
3	Technology Budget	Excel	T1, T2	Hardware and Software	Introductory Formulas	AYK.3
4	Tracking Donations	Excel	T2	Employee Relationships	Introductory Formulas	AYK.3
5	Convert Currency	Excel	T2	Global Commerce	Introductory Formulas	AYK.4
6	Cost Comparison	Excel	T2	Total Cost of Ownership	Introductory Formulas	AYK.4
7	Time Management	Excel or Project	T2 or T12	Project Management	Introductory Gantt Charts	AYK.5
8	Maximize Profit	Excel	T2, T4	Strategic Analysis	Intermediate Formulas or Solver	AYK.5
9	Security Analysis	Excel	T3	Filtering Data	Intermediate Conditional Formatting, Autofilter, Subtotal	AYK.6
10	Gathering Data	Excel	T3	Data Analysis	Intermediate Conditional Formatting, PivotTable	AYK.6
11	Scanner System	Excel	T2	Strategic Analysis	Intermediate	AYK.7
12	Competitive Pricing	Excel	T2	Profit Maximization	Intermediate	AYK.7
13	Adequate Acquisitions	Excel	T2	Break-Even Analysis	Intermediate	AYK.7
26	Electronic Résumés	HTML	T9, T10, T11	Electronic Personal Marketing	Introductory Structural Tags	AYK.14
27	Gathering Feedback	HTML	T9, T10, T11	Data Collection	Intermediate Organization of Information	AYK.15

Design Element: © McGraw Hill Education

Ethics and Information Security: MIS Business Concerns

4

CHAPTER

CHAPTER OUTLINE

SECTION 4.1
Ethics

- Information Ethics
- Developing Information Management Policies

SECTION 4.2
Information Security

- Protecting Intellectual Assets
- The First Line of Defense—People
- The Second Line of Defense—Technology

What's in IT for me?

This chapter concerns itself with protecting information from potential misuse. Organizations must ensure that they collect, capture, store, and use information in an ethical manner. This means any type of information they collect and use, including about customers, partners, and employees. Companies must ensure that personal information collected about someone remains private. This is not just a nice thing to do. The law requires it. Perhaps more important, information must be kept physically secure to prevent it from being accessed and disseminated, and possibly used by unauthorized sources.

You, the business student, must understand ethics and security because they are the top concerns that customers voice today. The way they are handled directly influences a customer's likelihood of embracing electronic technologies and conducting business over the web—and thus the company's bottom line. You can find evidence in recent news reports about how the stock price of organizations falls dramatically when information privacy and security breaches are made known. Further, organizations face potential litigation if they fail to meet their ethical, privacy, and security obligations in the handling of information.

opening case study

chrisdorney/Shutterstock Tanuha2001/Shutterstock Catwalker/Shutterstock

Clicking "I Agree"—The Death of Privacy in the Information Age

Have you ever received an ad for something just after having a private conversation over a cell phone with a friend? Have you ever received a text message requesting a contribution to a political campaign or charity after listening to a certain podcast? Have you ever received a coupon for a product that you recently searched? How did these companies access your personal information? Perhaps it was from a data breach or an unethical cookie tracking application.

One of the biggest issues facing the information age is the protection of privacy. Privacy allows you, the user, to set a boundary allowing only specific people to see the what, when, and where of your personal data. Privacy is an inside job, allowing you to determine who views your web browsing, shopping habits, movie and music preferences, and book selections. It should be your decision to determine when you are okay with someone using your personal data to gain financially.

One of the largest data hacks occurred at Facebook where the cell numbers, email addresses, names, and birthdates of 533 million global Facebook users in over 100 countries were hacked. Facebook stated the data was scraped from people's profiles by bad actors using its contact importer tool, a feature that utilizes people's contact lists to help them find friends on Facebook. Facebook has experienced numerous data breaches over the years (most famously, the Cambridge Analytica scandal—see Closing Case Two).

Information security is part of corporate responsibility, and new laws and governance are being created to ensure personal data is protected when it is outside its users' control. Information security is really about how personally identifiable data is protected when it is outside of the user's control. It includes technical hardware such as firewalls and passwords, and policies and procedures, to ensure that your personal data is not subject to unauthorized access. Unfortunately, not all companies take information security seriously, and most companies experience data breaches of some kind. That means, ultimately, the protection of one's personal data is in the hands of a third party and not in the user's control.

With all of the amazing technological advances associated with the information age, there are also pitfalls. The information age is still evolving, and the question remains as to how individuals will maintain, lose, or gain control over their personal data. Are governments and corporations doing enough to keep personal data safe? It is critical that anyone placing personal information on the Internet understands what types of data are being gathered, saved, and shared, so they can make informed decisions about how they post and share data. Unfortunately, most companies bury how they are using your data by having you willingly share it in their terms and services agreements. The real question is have you ever actually read the terms and services agreement before clicking "I agree"?[1]

section 4.1 | Ethics

LEARNING OUTCOMES

4.1 Explain the ethical issues in the use of information technology.

4.2 Identify the six epolicies organizations should implement to protect themselves.

INFORMATION ETHICS

LO 4.1: Explain the ethical issues in the use of information technology.

Ethics and security are two fundamental building blocks for all organizations. In recent years, enormous business scandals along with 9/11 have shed new light on the meaning of ethics and security. When the behavior of a few individuals can destroy billion-dollar organizations, the value of ethics and security should be evident. Technology poses new challenges for our ethics.

- ***Ethics***: The principles and standards that guide our behavior toward other people.

Ethical dilemmas in this area usually arise not as simple, clear-cut situations but as clashes among competing goals, responsibilities, and loyalties. Inevitably, there will be more than one socially acceptable or correct decision. The protection of customers' privacy is one of the largest and murkiest ethical issues facing organizations today (see Figure 4.1).

Trust among companies, customers, partners, and suppliers is the support structure of ebusiness. Privacy is one of its main ingredients. Consumers' concerns that their privacy will be violated because of their interactions on the web continue to be one of the primary barriers to the growth of ebusiness. Each time employees make a decision about a privacy issue, the outcome could sink the company. As it becomes easier for people to copy everything from words and data to music and video, the ethical issues surrounding copyright infringement and the violation of intellectual property rights are consuming the ebusiness world (see Figure 4.2).

Legal vs. Ethical ***Data scraping,*** also known as web scraping, is the process of extracting large amounts of data from a website and saving it to a spreadsheet or computer. It is one of the

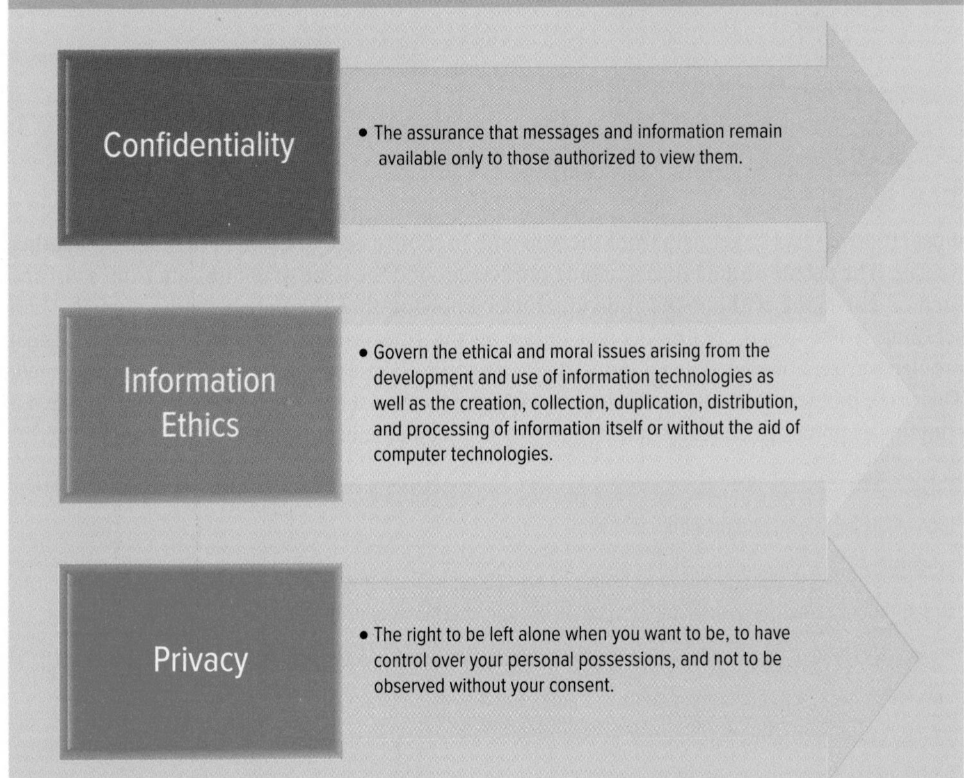

Confidentiality
• The assurance that messages and information remain available only to those authorized to view them.
Information Ethics
• Govern the ethical and moral issues arising from the development and use of information technologies as well as the creation, collection, duplication, distribution, and processing of information itself or without the aid of computer technologies.
Privacy
• The right to be left alone when you want to be, to have control over your personal possessions, and not to be observed without your consent.

FIGURE 4.1
Information Ethics Overview in the Information Age

FIGURE 4.2

Ethical Issues in the Information Age

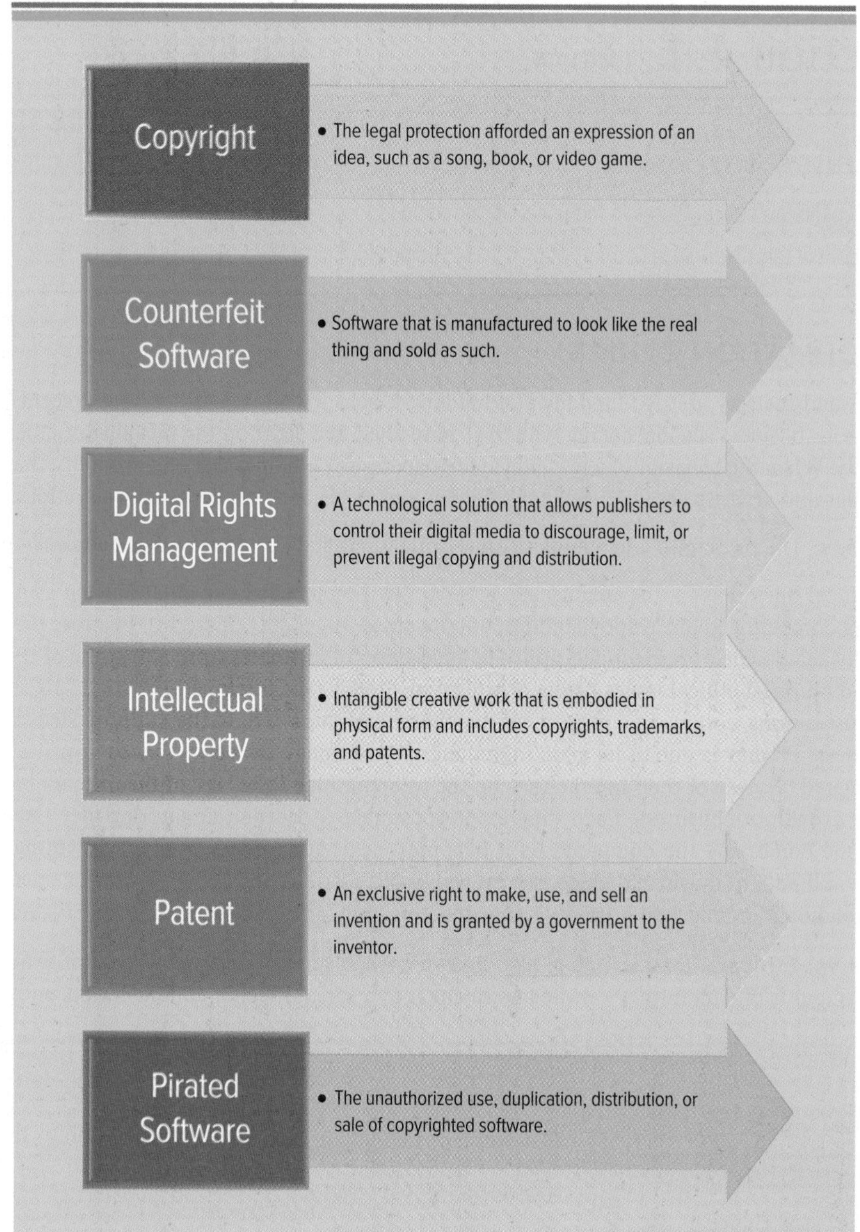

most efficient ways to get data from the web and, in some cases, to channel that data to another website. The debate around data scraping revolves around the issue of taking data from a website such as Facebook without the individual user knowing that the data is being copied. Data scraping is not illegal, as long as you follow all the rules associated with the website. Legal problems arise, however, when it comes to how people choose to use the data they have scraped. This is the problem for many technologies: analyzing the intersection of legal vs. ethical. Figure 4.3 contains examples of ethically questionable or unacceptable uses of information technology.[2]

FIGURE 4.3

Ethically Questionable or Unacceptable Information Technology Use

Individuals copy, use, and distribute software.
Employees search organizational databases for sensitive corporate and personal information.
Organizations collect, buy, and use information without checking the validity or accuracy of the information.
Individuals create and spread viruses that cause trouble for those using and maintaining IT systems.
Individuals hack into computer systems to steal proprietary information.
Employees destroy or steal proprietary organization information such as schematics, sketches, customer lists, and reports.

BUSINESS DRIVEN DISCUSSION

Information—Does It Have Ethics?

A high school principal decided it was a good idea to hold a confidential conversation about teachers, salaries, and student test scores on his cellular phone in a local Starbucks. Not realizing that one of the students' parents was sitting next to him, the principal accidentally divulged sensitive information about his employees and students. The irate parent soon notified the school board about the principal's inappropriate behavior, and a committee was formed to decide how to handle the situation.[4]

With the new wave of collaboration tools, electronic business, and the Internet, employees are finding themselves working outside the office and beyond traditional office hours. Advantages associated with remote workers include increased productivity, decreased expenses, and boosts in morale as employees are given greater flexibility to choose their work location and hours. Unfortunately, disadvantages associated with workers working remotely include new forms of ethical challenges and information security risks.

In a group, discuss the following statement: Information does not have any ethics. If you were elected to the committee to investigate the principal's inappropriate Starbucks phone conversation, what types of questions would you want answered? What type of punishment, if any, would you enforce on the principal? What types of policies would you implement across the school district to ensure that this scenario is never repeated? Be sure to highlight how workers working remotely affect business along with any potential ethical challenges and information security issues.

Rule 41 is the part of the United States Federal Rules of Criminal Procedure that covers the search and seizure of physical and digital evidence. Rule 41 originally granted a federal judge magistrate the authority to issue a warrant to search and seize a person or property located within that judge's district if the person or property is part of a criminal investigation or trial. In April 2016, the Judicial Conference of the United States proposed an amendment to Rule 41 that allows a federal judge magistrate to issue a warrant that allows an investigator to gain remote access to a digital device suspected in a crime, even if the device is located outside of the geographic jurisdiction of the judge issuing the warrant. An important goal of the amendment to Rule 41 is to prevent criminals from hiding the location of a computing device with anonymization technology in order to make detection and prosecution more difficult.[3]

Privacy advocates are concerned that the amendment will expand the government's authority to legally hack individuals and organizations and monitor any computer suspected of being part of a botnet. In addition to giving the government the authority to seize or copy the information on a digital device no matter where that device is located, the amendment also allows investigators who are investigating a crime that spans five or more judicial districts to go to one judge for warrants instead of having to request warrants from judges in each jurisdiction.

Unfortunately, few hard and fast rules exist for always determining what is ethical. Many people can either justify or condemn the actions in Figure 4.3. Knowing the law is important, but that knowledge will not always help because what is legal might not always be ethical and what might be ethical is not always legal.

Figure 4.4 shows the four quadrants in which ethical and legal behaviors intersect. The goal for most businesses is to make decisions within quadrant I that are both legal and ethical. There are times when a business will find itself in the position of making a decision in quadrant III, such as hiring child labor in foreign countries, or in quadrant II, such as when a business might pay a foreigner who is getting her immigration status approved because the company is in the process of hiring the person. A business should never find itself operating in quadrant IV. Ethics are critical to operating a successful business today.

FIGURE 4.4

Acting Ethically and Acting Legally Are Not Always the Same Thing

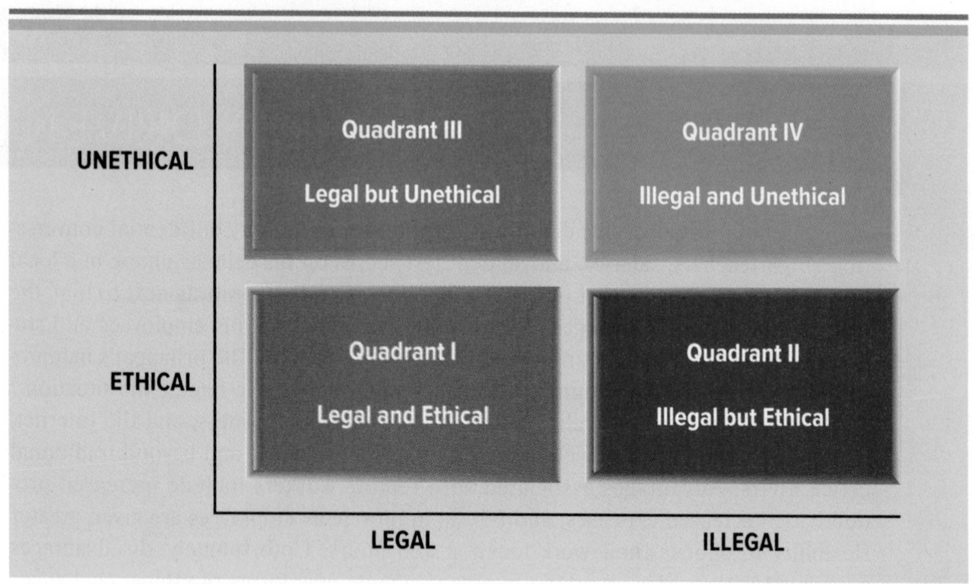

Information Does Not Have Ethics; People Do

Information itself has no ethics. It does not care how it is used. It will not stop itself from spamming customers, sharing itself if it is sensitive or personal, or revealing details to third parties. Information cannot delete or preserve itself. Therefore, it falls to those who own the information to develop ethical guidelines about how to manage it. The intersection of security, privacy, and accountability is essential to designing digital transactions/trust.

- ***Digital trust*:** The measure of consumer, partner, and employee confidence in an organization's ability to protect and secure data and the privacy of individuals.

Years ago, the ideas of digital trust, information management, governance, and compliance were relatively obscure. Today, these concepts are a must for virtually every company, both domestic and global, primarily due to the role digital information plays in corporate legal proceedings or litigation. Frequently, digital information serves as key evidence in legal proceedings, and it is far easier to search, organize, and filter than paper documents. Digital information is also extremely difficult to destroy, especially if it is on a corporate network or sent by email. In fact, the only reliable way to obliterate digital information reliably is to destroy the hard drives on which the file was stored.

- ***Ediscovery*** **(or *electronic discovery*):** Refers to the ability of a company to identify, search, gather, seize, or export digital information in responding to a litigation, audit, investigation, or information inquiry. As the importance of ediscovery grows, so does information governance and information compliance.
- ***Child Online Protection Act (COPA)*:** Passed to protect minors from accessing inappropriate material on the Internet. Figure 4.5 displays the ethical guidelines for information management.

LO 4.2: Identify the six epolicies organizations should implement to protect themselves.

DEVELOPING INFORMATION MANAGEMENT POLICIES

Treating sensitive corporate information as a valuable resource is good management. Building a corporate culture based on ethical principles that employees can understand and implement is responsible management. Organizations should develop written policies establishing employee guidelines, employee procedures, and organizational rules for information. These policies set employee expectations about the organization's practices and standards and protect the organization from misuse of computer systems and MIS resources. If an organization's employees use computers at work, the organization should, at a minimum, implement epolicies.

- ***Epolicies*:** Policies and procedures that address information management, along with the ethical use of computers and the Internet in the business environment.

BUSINESS DRIVEN ETHICS AND SECURITY

Would You Cash Another Person's Stimulus Check?

As the pandemic continues, customer reports of fake check scams are on the rise. Some thought they received a payment for a new job, others received an overpayment for something they sold online, and still others received prize money in the mail for a lottery or sweepstakes they had supposedly won.

Regardless of the situation, the scammer's goal is always the same: to convince you to deposit the fraudulent check and then send some of the money back.

There are a few things to look for to help you avoid a scam. If you spot any of these warning signs, don't deposit the check:

- A prospective buyer sends you a check for more than your asking price "by mistake" and wants the overage back.
- You receive your first check for a new work-from-home job, and the "employer" asks you to send some money back right away for supplies.
- You receive a check for sweepstakes winnings that can only be claimed by sending some money back to cover taxes.[5]

FIGURE 4.5

Ethical Guidelines for Information Management

Information Secrecy

The category of computer security that addresses the protection of data from unauthorized disclosure and confirmation of data source authenticity

Information Governance

A method or system of government for information management or control

Information Management

Examines the organizational resource of information and regulates its definitions, uses, value, and distribution, ensuring that it has the types of data/information required to function and grow effectively

Information Compliance

The act of conforming, acquiescing, or yielding information

Information Property

An ethical issue that focuses on who owns information about individuals and how information can be sold and exchanged

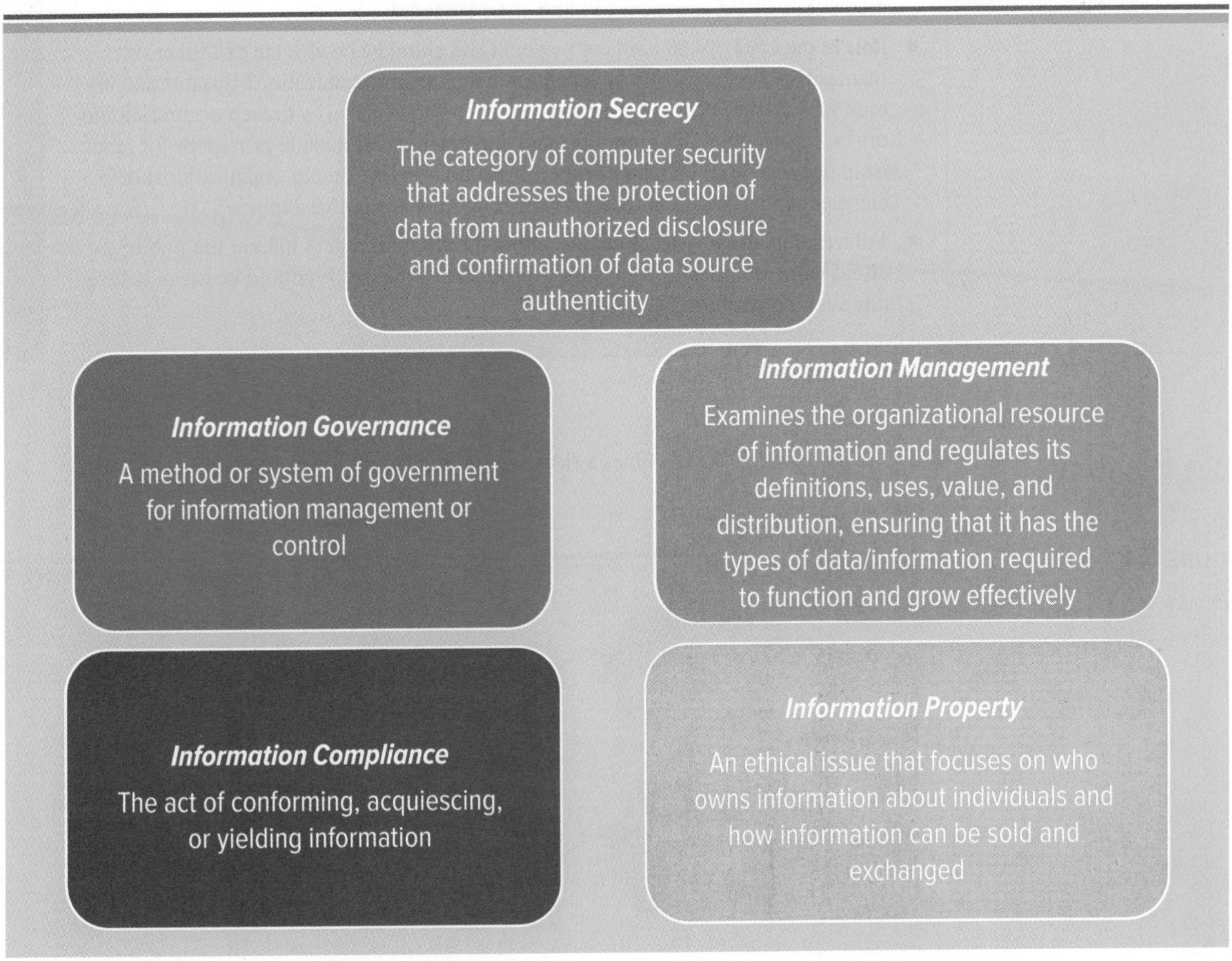

APPLY YOUR KNOWLEDGE

BUSINESS DRIVEN DEBATE

Is It Ethical? Is It Legal?

Below are a number of ethical dilemmas currently being discussed as we enter the era of big data and the fourth industrial revolution.

- **Automated security tools:** Is it ethical to release into the wild tools that can automate attacks on a broad array of systems?
- **Cybersecurity incident response:** How much time and energy should be spent investigating a breach? What is an appropriate level of incident detail to share with customers and other stakeholders? How thick is the line between satisfying organizational obligations and finding the complete truth behind an incident?
- **Encryption:** What should companies do in response to legal law enforcement requests for encrypted data? Should known vulnerabilities in systems be used to comply with requests that would otherwise be impossible? Should law enforcement agencies use such vulnerabilities themselves if they suspect a formal legal request will not bear fruit?
- **Research:** How should researchers balance the use of potentially aggressive penetration testing techniques against the legal rights of the owners of systems they are researching? Does that balance change in cases in which those system owners are not implementing reasonably strong security methods?
- **Sale restrictions:** What (if any) is the responsibility of cybersecurity professionals to try to prevent the sale of products they have developed to autocratic governments that would use them to harm their citizens?
- **Role of the CSO:** What kinds of personal risk should a chief security officer or manager-level security officer accept on behalf of an organization? It is not uncommon for CSOs to be fired or forced out when a cybersecurity breach occurs; should organizations offer CSOs employment agreements that include provisions for relief from personal legal liability or other protections? How should organizational deficiencies (underinvestment, bad practices, etc.) factor in this analysis?
- **Vulnerability disclosure:** When and how should researchers inform the public about vulnerabilities in widely used products? What steps should be taken before any such notification?[6]

Figure 4.6 displays the epolicies a firm should implement to set employee expectations.

FIGURE 4.6

Overview of Epolicies

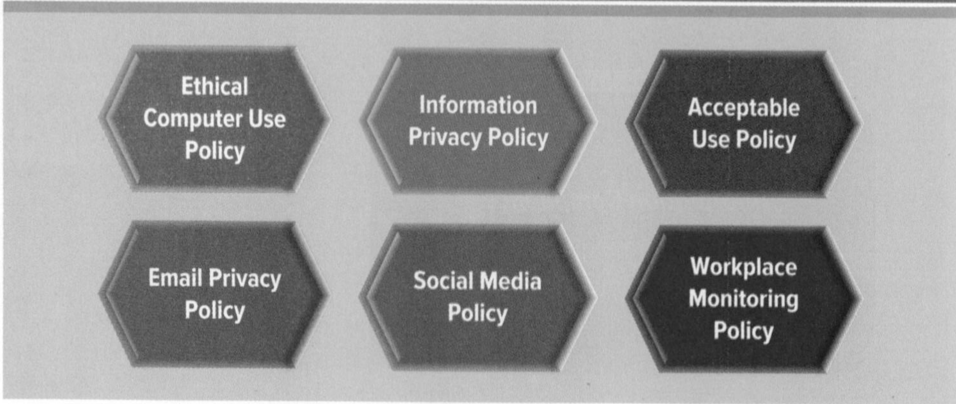

Ethical Computer Use Policy

One essential step in creating an ethical corporate culture is establishing an ethical computer use policy.

- ***Ethical computer use policy***: Contains general principles to guide computer user behavior. For example, it might explicitly state that users should refrain from playing computer games during working hours.

This policy ensures that the users know how to behave at work and the organization has a published standard to deal with infractions. For example, after appropriate warnings, the company may terminate an employee who spends significant amounts of time playing computer games at work. Cyberbullying and click-fraud are just a few examples of the many types of unethical computer use found today.

- ***Click-fraud***: The abuse of pay-per-click, pay-per-call, and pay-per-conversion revenue models by repeatedly clicking a link to increase charges or costs for the advertiser.
- ***Competitive click-fraud***: A computer crime in which a competitor or disgruntled employee increases a company's search advertising costs by repeatedly clicking the advertiser's link.
- ***Cyberbullying***: Includes threats, negative remarks, or defamatory comments transmitted through the Internet or posted on the website.
- ***Threat***: An act or object that poses a danger to assets.

Organizations can legitimately vary in how they expect employees to use computers, but in any approach to controlling such use, the overriding principle should be informed consent. The users should be *informed* of the rules and, by agreeing to use the system on that basis, *consent* to abide by them.

Managers should make a conscientious effort to ensure all users are aware of the policy through formal training and other means. If an organization were to have only one epolicy, it should be an ethical computer use policy because that is the starting point and the umbrella for any other policies the organization might establish. Part of an ethical computer use policy can include a BYOD policy.

- ***Bring your own device (BYOD)***: Policy allows employees to use their personal mobile devices and computers to access enterprise data and applications. BYOD policies offer four basic options, including:
  - Unlimited access for personal devices.
  - Access *only* to nonsensitive systems and data.
  - Access but with IT control over personal devices, apps, and stored data.
  - Access but preventing local storage of data on personal devices.

Information Privacy Policy

An organization that wants to protect its information should develop an information privacy policy.

- ***Information privacy policy***: Contains general principles regarding information privacy.
- ***Fair information practices (FIPs)***: A general term for a set of standards governing the collection and use of personal data and addressing issues of privacy and accuracy.

Europe is now covered by the world's strongest fair information practices.

- ***General Data Protection Regulation (GDPR)***: A legal framework that sets guidelines for the collection and processing of personal information of individuals within the European Union (EU).

GDPR came into effect across the EU on May 25, 2018, and was designed to update laws that protect the personal information of individuals. GDPR also gives individuals a lot more power to access the information that is held about them. Massive data breaches occur regularly, including at companies such as Sony, Equifax, LinkedIn, and Target. Data protection is about ensuring people can trust you to use their data fairly and responsibly.

- If you collect information about individuals for any reason other than your own personal, family, or household purposes, you need to comply.
- The United Kingdom (UK) data protection regime is set out in the Data Protection Act 2018, along with the GDPR (which forms part of UK law). It takes a flexible, risk-based approach that puts the onus on you to think about and justify how and why you use data.
- The Information Commissioner's Office regulates data protection in the UK. It offers advice and guidance, promotes good practice, carries out audits and advisory visits, considers complaints, monitors compliance, and takes enforcement action where appropriate.

Under GDPR, the "destruction, loss, alteration, unauthorized disclosure of, or access to" people's data has to be reported to a country's data protection regulator where it could have a detrimental impact on those whom it is about.[7] This can include, but isn't limited to, financial loss, confidentiality breaches, damage to reputation, and more. There are two key types of personal data in the UK, and they cover different categories of information.

- Personal data can be anything that allows a living person to be directly or indirectly identified. This may be a name, an address, or even an IP address. It includes automated personal data and can also encompass "pseudonymized" data if a person can be identified from it.
- Sensitive personal data includes "special categories" of information. These include trade union membership, religious beliefs, political opinions, racial information, and sexual orientation.

One of the biggest, and most talked about, elements of the GDPR has been the ability of regulators to fine businesses that don't comply with it. If an organization doesn't process an individual's data in the correct way, it can be fined. If it requires and doesn't have a data protection officer, it can be fined. If there's a security breach, it can be fined. In the first major example, the French data protection authority announced in 2019 that it had fined Google 50 million euros, or about $57 million, for not properly disclosing to users how data is collected across its services–including its search engine, Google Maps, and YouTube–to present personalized advertisements.[8]

Acceptable Use Policy

- ***Acceptable use policy (AUP)***: Requires a user to agree to follow it to be provided access to corporate email, information systems, and the Internet.
- ***Nonrepudiation***: A contractual stipulation to ensure that ebusiness participants do not deny (repudiate) their online actions.

A nonrepudiation clause is typically contained in an acceptable use policy. Many businesses and educational facilities require employees or students to sign an acceptable use policy before gaining network access. When signing up with an email provider, each customer is typically presented with an AUP, which states that the user agrees to adhere to certain stipulations. Users agree to the following in a typical acceptable use policy:

- Not using the service as part of violating any law.
- Not attempting to break the security of any computer network or user.
- Not posting commercial messages to groups without prior permission.
- Not performing any nonrepudiation.

Some organizations go so far as to create a unique information management policy focusing solely on Internet use.

- ***Internet use policy***: Contains general principles to guide the proper use of the Internet.

Due to the large amounts of computing resources that Internet users can expend, it is essential for such use to be legitimate. In addition, the Internet contains numerous materials that

BUSINESS DRIVEN GLOBALIZATION

Who Filed My Taxes?

One day, an unsuspecting accountant was sitting at her desk when she received an email from the CEO asking for all of the employees' tax information. Of course, the diligent worker quickly retrieved all of the information and returned the email with the attached information as requested. A few months later, the company began an investigation to find out why so many of its employees were experiencing tax fraud–someone was illegally filing their taxes and claiming the refunds. Only then did they discover the fraudulent email from the fake CEO that the diligent employee returned, feeding the criminal the exact information he or she was phishing for in the first place.

During tax season, your personal information may be emailed, shared, and saved more than usual. Criminals may find ways to access your information and use it to file a tax return in your name. In fact, the IRS estimates that at least $12.2 billion in identity theft tax refund fraud occurs yearly. In a group, discuss if you believe the woman in the above example should be held accountable for emailing the tax information. What can a company do to ensure this type of email theft does not happen? What can you do to protect your tax information?

some believe are offensive, making regulation in the workplace a requirement. Generally, an Internet use policy:

- Describes the Internet services available to users.
- Defines the organization's position on the purpose of Internet access and what restrictions, if any, are placed on that access.
- Describes user responsibility for citing sources, properly handling offensive material, and protecting the organization's good name.
- States the ramifications if the policy is violated.

The following are all examples of unacceptable Internet use.

- ***Cybervandalism***: The electronic defacing of an existing website.
- ***Typosquatting***: A problem that occurs when someone registers purposely misspelled variations of well-known domain names. These variants sometimes lure consumers who make typographical errors when entering a URL.
- ***Website name stealing***: The theft of a website's name that occurs when someone, posing as a site's administrator, changes the ownership of the domain name assigned to the website to another website owner.
- ***Internet censorship***: Government attempts to control Internet traffic, thus preventing some material from being viewed by a country's citizens.

Email Privacy Policy

Email is so pervasive in organizations that it requires its own specific policy. Most working professionals use email as their preferred means of corporate communications.

- ***Email privacy policy***: Details the extent to which email messages may be read by others.

Although email and instant messaging are common business communication tools, risks are associated with using them. For instance, a sent email is stored on at least three or four computers (see Figure 4.7). Simply deleting an email from one computer does not delete it from the others. Companies can mitigate many of the risks of using electronic messaging systems by implementing and adhering to an email privacy policy.

FIGURE 4.7

Email Is Stored on Multiple Computers

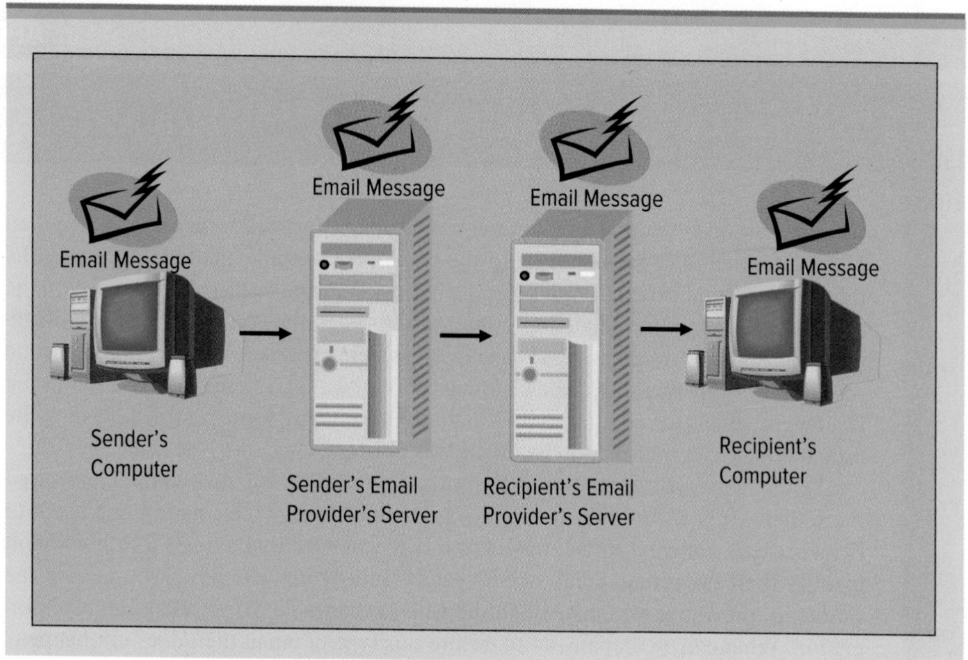

One major problem with email is the user's expectations of privacy. To a large extent, this expectation is based on the false assumption that email privacy protection exists somehow analogous to that of U.S. first-class mail. Generally, the organization that owns the email system can operate the system as openly or as privately as it wishes. Surveys indicate that the majority of large firms regularly read and analyze employees' email looking for confidential data leaks such as unannounced financial results or the sharing of trade secrets that result in the violation of an email privacy policy and eventual termination of the employee. That means that if the organization wants to read everyone's email, it can do so. Basically, using work email for anything other than work is not a good idea. A typical email privacy policy does the following:

- Defines legitimate email users and explains what happens to accounts after a person leaves the organization.
- Explains backup procedure so users will know that, at some point, even if a message is deleted from their computer, it is still stored by the company.
- Describes the legitimate grounds for reading email and the process required before such action is performed.
- Discourages sending junk email or spam to anyone who does not want to receive it.
- Prohibits attempting to mail bomb a site.
  - ***Mail bomb***: Sends a massive amount of email to a specific person or system that can cause that user's server to stop functioning.
- Informs users that the organization has no control over email once it has been transmitted outside the organization.

Spam is unsolicited email. It plagues employees at all levels within an organization, from receptionist to CEO, and clogs email systems and siphons MIS resources away from legitimate business projects.

- ***Anti-spam policy***: Simply states that email users will not send unsolicited emails (or spam).

It is difficult to write anti-spam policies, laws, or software because there is no such thing as a universal litmus test for spam. One person's spam is another person's newsletter. End users have to decide what spam is because it can vary widely not just from one company to the next, but also from one person to the next.

- ***Opt out***: A user can stop receiving emails by choosing to deny permission to incoming emails.
- ***Opt in***: A user can receive emails by choosing to allow permissions to incoming emails.

- ***Teergrubing***: An anti-spamming approach by which the receiving computer launches a return attack against the spammer, sending email messages back to the computer that originated the suspected spam.

Social Media Policy

Did you see the YouTube video showing two Domino's Pizza employees violating health codes while preparing food by passing gas on sandwiches? Millions of people did, and the company took notice when disgusted customers began posting negative comments all over Twitter. Because they did not have a Twitter account, corporate executives at Domino's did not know about the damaging tweets until it was too late. The use of social media can contribute many benefits to an organization, and implemented correctly, it can become a huge opportunity for employees to build brands. But there are also tremendous risks because a few employees representing an entire company can cause tremendous brand damage. Defining a set of guidelines implemented in a social media policy can help mitigate that risk. Companies can protect themselves by implementing a social media policy.

- ***Social media policy***: Outlining the corporate guidelines or principles governing employee online communications.

Having a single social media policy might not be enough to ensure that the company's online reputation is protected. Additional, more specific, social media policies a company might choose to implement include:

- Employee online communication policy detailing brand communication.
- Employee blog and personal blog policies.
- Employee social network and personal social network policies.
- Employee Twitter, corporate Twitter, and personal Twitter policies.
- Employee LinkedIn policy.
- Employee Facebook usage and brand usage policy.
- Corporate YouTube policy.

The former European Commissioner for Justice, Fundamental Rights, and Citizenship, Viviane Reding, announced the European Commission's proposal to create a sweeping individual privacy right named The Right to be Forgotten.

- ***The right to be forgotten***: allows individuals to request to have all content that violates their privacy removed.

The right to be forgotten addresses an urgent problem in the digital age: the great difficulty of escaping your past on the Internet now that every photo, status update, and tweet lives forever in the cloud. To comply with the European Court of Justice's decision, Google created a new online form by which individuals can ask search providers to remove links that violate their online privacy. In the first month, Google received more than 50,000 submissions from people asking the company to remove links. Many people in the United States believe that the right to be forgotten conflicts with the right to free speech. It is an interesting dilemma.

Organizations must protect their online reputations and continuously monitor blogs, message boards, social networking sites, and media sharing sites. However, monitoring the hundreds of social media sites can quickly become overwhelming. To combat these issues, a number of companies specialize in online social media monitoring. For example, the social media monitoring company might create a digital dashboard that allows executives to view at a glance the date published, source, title, and summary of every item tracked. The dashboard highlights not only what's being said but also the influence of the particular person, blog, or social media site.

- ***Social media monitoring***: The process of monitoring and responding to what is being said about a company, individual, product, or brand.
- ***Social media manager***: A person within the organization who is trusted to monitor, contribute, filter, and guide the social media presence of a company, individual, product, or brand.

APPLY YOUR KNOWLEDGE

BUSINESS DRIVEN MIS

Fake News

How do you find facts in a world of fake news? I am sure we have all read something and wondered, is this news real or fake? In today's online world, it is a breeze to create a fake newspaper online. Jestin Coler, founder of the fake newspaper "Denver Guardian," posted a story stating that an FBI agent involved in leaking Hillary Clinton's emails was found dead in an "apparent murder-suicide." Everything about the article and the newspaper was fictional: the town, the people, even the sheriff and FBI guy. The made-up tale went viral on Facebook and spread like wildfire.

In today's world, we have lost signs of credibility. Before the online era, you would need to shell out a lot of money to print a fake newspaper; online, however, there is little distinction between an article from *The Wall Street Journal* and a sham from the "Denver Guardian." It is easier than ever to be fooled.[9]

Do you believe it is unethical for a company to circulate fake news if it results in great sales? What can you do to ensure the information you are reading is accurate, trustworthy, and validated? What can happen to an organization that believes fake news?

Workplace MIS Monitoring Policy

Increasingly, employee monitoring is not a choice; it is a risk-management obligation. Michael Soden, former CEO of the Bank of Ireland, issued a mandate stating that company employees could not surf illicit websites with company equipment. Next, he hired Hewlett-Packard to run the MIS department, and illicit websites were discovered on Soden's own computer, forcing Soden to resign. Monitoring employees is one of the biggest challenges CIOs face when developing information management policies.[10]

Physical security is tangible protection, such as alarms, guards, fireproof doors, fences, and vaults. New technologies enable employers to monitor many aspects of their employees' jobs, especially on telephones, on computer terminals, through electronic and voice mail, and when employees are using the Internet. Such monitoring is virtually unregulated. Therefore, unless company policy specifically states otherwise (and even this is not ensured), your employer may listen, watch, and read most of your workplace communications.

- ***Workplace MIS monitoring***: Tracks people's activities by such measures as number of keystrokes, error rate, and number of transactions processed (see Figure 4.8 for an overview).

The best path for an organization planning to engage in employee monitoring is open communication, including an employee monitoring policy.

- ***Employee monitoring policy***: Stating explicitly how, when, and where the company monitors its employees.

Several common stipulations an organization can follow when creating an employee monitoring policy include:

- Be as specific as possible, stating when and what (email, IM, Internet, network activity, etc.) will be monitored.
- Expressly communicate that the company reserves the right to monitor all employees.
- State the consequences of violating the policy.
- Always enforce the policy the same for everyone.

BUSINESS DRIVEN DEBATE

Monitoring Employees

Every organization has the right to monitor its employees. Organizations usually inform their employees when workplace monitoring is occurring, especially regarding organizational assets such as networks, email, and Internet access. Employees traditionally offer their consent to be monitored and should not have any expectations of privacy when using organizational assets.

Do you agree or disagree that organizations have an obligation to notify employees about the extent of workplace monitoring, such as how long employees are using the Internet and which websites they are visiting? Do you agree or disagree that organizations have the right to read all employees' email sent or received on an organizational computer, including personal Gmail accounts?

Many employees use their company's high-speed Internet access to shop, browse, and surf the web. Most managers do not want their employees conducting personal business during working hours, and they implement a Big Brother approach to employee monitoring. Many management gurus advocate that organizations whose corporate cultures are based on trust are more successful than those whose corporate cultures are based on mistrust. Before an organization implements monitoring technology, it should ask itself, "What does this say about how we feel about our employees?" If the organization really does not trust its employees, then perhaps it should find new ones. If an organization does trust its employees, then it might want to treat them accordingly. An organization that follows its employees' every keystroke might be unwittingly undermining the relationships with its employees, and it might find the effects of employee monitoring are often worse than lost productivity from employee web surfing.

FIGURE 4.8

Internet Monitoring Technologies

Common Internet Monitoring Technologies	
Key logger, or key trapper, software	A program that records every keystroke and mouse click.
Hardware key logger	A hardware device that captures keystrokes on their journey from the keyboard to the motherboard.
Cookie	A small file deposited on a hard drive by a website containing information about customers and their web activities. Cookies allow websites to record the comings and goings of customers, usually without their knowledge or consent.
Adware	Software that generates ads that install themselves on a computer when a person downloads some other program from the Internet.
Spyware (sneakware or stealthware)	Software that comes hidden in free downloadable software and tracks online movements, mines the information stored on a computer, or uses a computer's CPU and storage for some task the user knows nothing about.
Web log	Consists of one line of information for every visitor to a website and is usually stored on a web server.
Clickstream	Records information about a customer during a web surfing session such as what websites were visited, how long the visit was, what ads were viewed, and what was purchased.

APPLY YOUR KNOWLEDGE

BUSINESS DRIVEN ANALYTICS

Office Bullying

A hostile work environment is detrimental to productivity and office morale alike, making the workplace where people spend 40-plus hours a week a living nightmare. However, a recent study may show that bullying and violence in the workplace can have effects well beyond one's mental state. According to new research, working in such an environment can increase one's risk of type 2 diabetes. The study was carried out by distributing questionnaires to 20,000 men and 27,000 women to determine the link between type 2 diabetes and workplace bullying, including everything from colleagues' unpleasant behavior to violent threats and even actions. The researchers discovered that those bullied at work are 46 percent more at risk for type 2 diabetes. Being bullied is regarded as severe social stress that may activate the stress response and lead to a range of downstream biological processes that may contribute to the risk of diabetes.[11]

Have you ever been a victim of cyberbullying? What can you do if you are cyberbullied at work? How can epolicies help prevent cyberbullying and provide managers with a path out if an employee is engaging in cyberbullying? How can you use analytics to track cyberbullying threats to an organization?

section 4.2 | Information Security

LEARNING OUTCOMES

4.3 Describe the relationships and differences between hackers and viruses.

4.4 Describe the relationship between information security policies and an information security plan.

4.5 Provide an example of each of the three primary information security areas: (1) authentication and authorization, (2) prevention and resistance, and (3) detection and response.

LO 4.3: Describe the relationships and differences between hackers and viruses.

PROTECTING INTELLECTUAL ASSETS

To reflect the crucial interdependence between MIS and business processes accurately, we should update the old business axiom "Time is money" to say "Uptime is money."

- ***Downtime***: Refers to a period of time when a system is unavailable.

Unplanned downtime can strike at any time for any number of reasons, from tornadoes to sink overflows to network failures to power outages (see Figure 4.9). Although natural disasters may appear to be the most devastating causes of MIS outages, they are hardly the most frequent or most expensive. Figure 4.10 demonstrates that the costs of downtime are associated not only with lost revenues but also with financial performance, damage to reputations, and even travel or legal expenses. A few questions managers should ask when determining the cost of downtime are:[12]

- How many transactions can the company afford to lose without significantly harming business?
- Does the company depend on one or more mission-critical applications to conduct business?
- How much revenue will the company lose for every hour a critical application is unavailable?

Sources of Unplanned Downtime		
Bomb threat	Frozen pipe	Smoke damage
Burst pipe	Hacker	Snowstorm
Chemical spill	Hail	Sprinkler malfunction
Construction	Hurricane	Static electricity
Corrupted data	Ice storm	Strike
Earthquake	Insects	Terrorism
Electrical short	Lightning	Theft
Epidemic	Network failure	Tornado
Equipment failure	Plane crash	Train derailment
Evacuation	Power outage	Vandalism
Explosion	Power surge	Vehicle crash
Fire	Rodents	Virus
Flood	Sabotage	Water damage (various)
Fraud	Shredded data	Wind

FIGURE 4.9

Sources of Unplanned Downtime

- What is the productivity cost associated with each hour of downtime?
- How will collaborative business processes with partners, suppliers, and customers be affected by an unexpected MIS outage?
- What is the total cost of lost productivity and lost revenue during unplanned downtime?

Financial Performance
Revenue recognition
Cash flow
Payment guarantees
Credit rating
Stock price

Revenue
Direct loss
Compensatory payments
Lost future revenue
Billing losses
Investment losses
Lost productivity

$
Know your cost of downtime per hour, per day, per week.

Damaged Reputation
Customers
Suppliers
Financial markets
Banks
Business partners

Other Expenses
Temporary employees
Equipment rentals
Overtime costs
Extra shipping charges
Travel expenses
Legal obligations

FIGURE 4.10

The Cost of Downtime

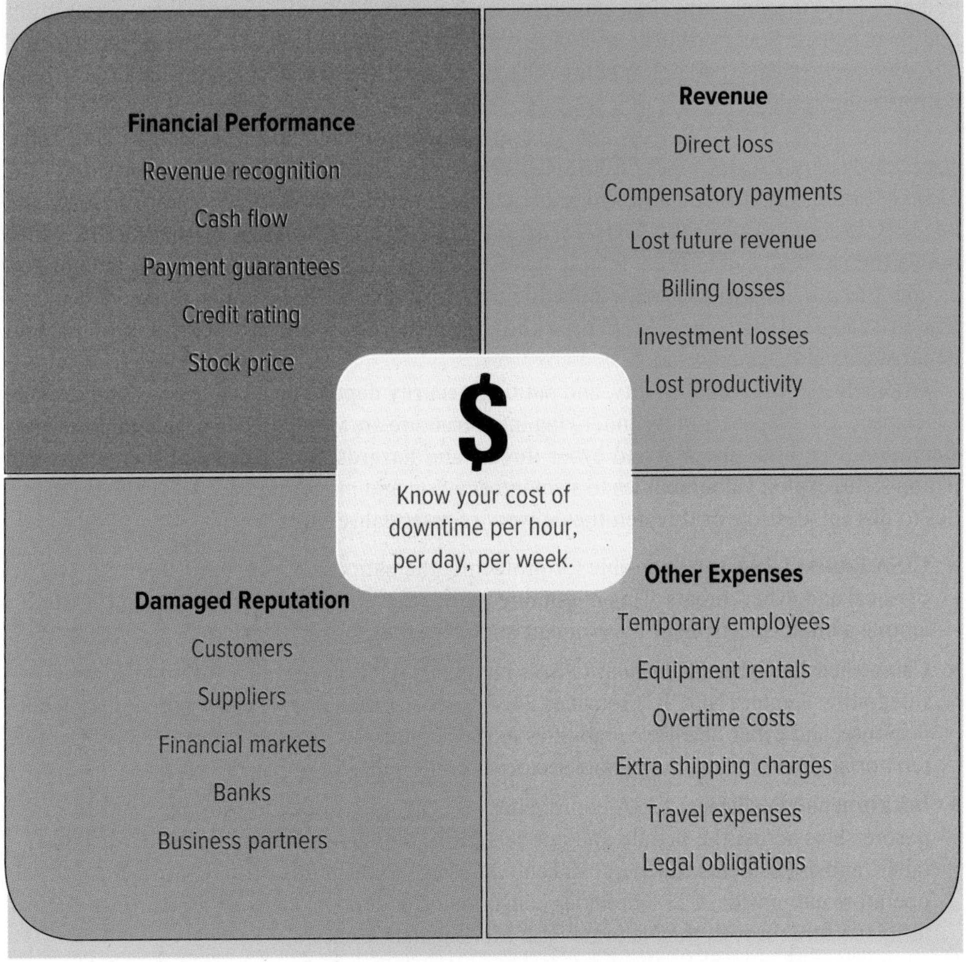

The reliability and resilience of MIS systems have never been more essential for success as businesses cope with the forces of globalization, 24/7 operations, government and trade regulations, global recession, and overextended MIS budgets and resources. Any unexpected downtime in today's business environment has the potential to cause both short- and long-term costs with far-reaching consequences.

- ***Cybersecurity***: Involves prevention, detection, and response to cyberattacks that can have wide-ranging effects on individuals, organizations, communities, and nations.
- ***Cyberattacks***: Malicious attempts to access or damage a computer system. Cyberattacks have the following attributes:
  - Use computers, mobile phones, gaming systems, and other devices.
  - Include identity theft.
  - Block your access or delete your personal documents and pictures.
  - Target children.
  - Cause problems with business services, transportation, and power.

Cyberattacks can lead to loss of money, theft of personal information, and damage to a person's reputation and safety.

- ***Information security***: A broad term encompassing the protection of information from accidental or intentional misuse by persons inside or outside an organization.

Information security is the primary tool an organization can use to combat the threats associated with downtime. Understanding how to secure information systems is critical to keeping downtime to a minimum and uptime to a maximum. Hackers and viruses are two of the hottest issues currently facing information security.

Equifax, one of the nation's largest credit monitoring companies, was the victim of a massive cybersecurity attack, one of the largest in history. Unauthorized data access occurred from mid-May 2017 through July 2017, impacting a whopping 146 million consumers. The victims had their names, Social Security numbers, birth dates, and addresses stolen—all the information required to steal a person's identity. The attack occurred via access to the data files from a website vulnerability.

On November 16, 2018, President Trump signed into law the Cybersecurity and Infrastructure Security Agency Act of 2018. This landmark legislation elevates the mission of the former National Protection and Programs Directorate within the Department of Homeland Security and establishes the ***Cybersecurity and Infrastructure Security Agency (CISA),*** which builds the national capacity to defend against cyberattacks and works with the federal government to provide cybersecurity tools, incident response services, and assessment capabilities to safeguard the ".gov" networks that support the essential operations of partner departments and agencies.

Our daily life, economic vitality, and national security depend on a stable, safe, and resilient cyberspace. Cyberspace and its underlying infrastructure are vulnerable to a wide range of risks stemming from both physical and cyber threats and hazards. Sophisticated cyber actors and nation-states exploit vulnerabilities to steal information and money and are developing capabilities to disrupt, destroy, or threaten the delivery of essential services.

- **CISA Duties:** CISA is responsible for protecting the nation's critical infrastructure from physical and cyber threats. This mission requires effective coordination and collaboration among a broad spectrum of government and private-sector organizations.
- **Comprehensive Cyber Protection:** CISA's National Cybersecurity and Communications Integration Center (NCCIC) provides 24/7 cyber situational awareness, analysis, incident response, and cyber defense capabilities to the federal government; state, local, tribal, and territorial governments; the private sector; and international partners.
- **Infrastructure Resilience:** CISA coordinates security and resilience efforts using trusted partnerships across the private and public sectors, and delivers training, technical assistance, and assessments to federal stakeholders, as well as to infrastructure owners and operators nationwide. CISA provides consolidated all-hazards risk analysis for U.S. critical infrastructure through the National Risk Management Center.

- **Emergency Communications:** CISA enhances public safety interoperable communications at all levels of government, providing training, coordination, tools, and guidance to help partners across the country develop their emergency communications capabilities. Working with stakeholders across the country, CISA conducts extensive, nationwide outreach to support and promote the ability of emergency response providers and relevant government officials to continue to communicate in the event of natural disasters, acts of terrorism, and other human-made disasters.
- **National Risk Management Center (NRMC):** The NRMC is a planning, analysis, and collaboration center that works in close coordination with the private sector and other key stakeholders to identify, analyze, prioritize, and manage the most strategic risks to the nation's critical infrastructure and functions.[13]

Hackers: A Dangerous Threat to Business

Smoking is not just bad for a person's health; it is apparently also bad for company security because hackers regularly use smoking entrances to gain building access. Once inside, they pose as employees from the MIS department and either ask for permission to use an employee's computer to access the corporate network or find a conference room where they simply plug in their own laptop.

- ***Hackers*:** Experts in technology who use their knowledge to break into computers and computer networks, either for profit or simply for the challenge. Figure 4.11 lists the various types of hackers.
- ***Drive-by hacking*:** A computer attack in which an attacker accesses a wireless computer network, intercepts data, uses network services, and/or sends attack instructions without entering the office or organization that owns the network.
- Russia has developed a reputation for using ***troll farms,*** which includes groups of hundreds of people whose job is to infiltrate message boards and comments sections in order to advance Russian national aims or seed discord and disharmony.

Ethical Hackers Not all hackers are bad. In fact, it can be a good business strategy to employ white-hat hackers to find the bugs and vulnerabilities in a corporation.

- ***Bug bounty program*:** A crowdsourcing initiative that rewards individuals for discovering and reporting software bugs.

Bug bounty programs are also called vulnerability rewards programs as they provide financial compensation as a reward for identifying software vulnerabilities that have the potential to be exploited. Typically, payment amounts are commensurate with the size of the organization, the difficulty in hacking the system, and the potential impact of the bug. Here are a few examples:

- Mozilla pays a $3,000 flat rate bounty for bugs.
- Facebook has paid as much as $20,000 for a single bug report.
- Google pays Chrome operating system bug reporters on average $700,000 per year.
- Microsoft paid UK researcher James Forshaw $100,000 for an attack vulnerability in Windows 8.1.
- Apple pays $200,000 for a flaw in the iOS secure boot firmware components.

FIGURE 4.11

Types of Hackers

Common Types of Hackers
■ ***Black-hat hackers*** break into other people's computer systems and may just look around or may steal and destroy information.
■ ***Crackers*** have criminal intent when hacking.
■ ***Cyberterrorists*** seek to cause harm to people or to destroy critical systems or information and use the Internet as a weapon of mass destruction.
■ ***Hactivists*** have philosophical and political reasons for breaking into systems and will often deface the website as a protest.
■ ***Script kiddies*** or ***script bunnies*** find hacking code on the Internet and click-and-point their way into systems to cause damage or spread viruses.
■ ***White-hat hackers*** work at the request of the system owners to find system vulnerabilities and plug the holes.

FIGURE 4.12

How Computer Viruses Spread

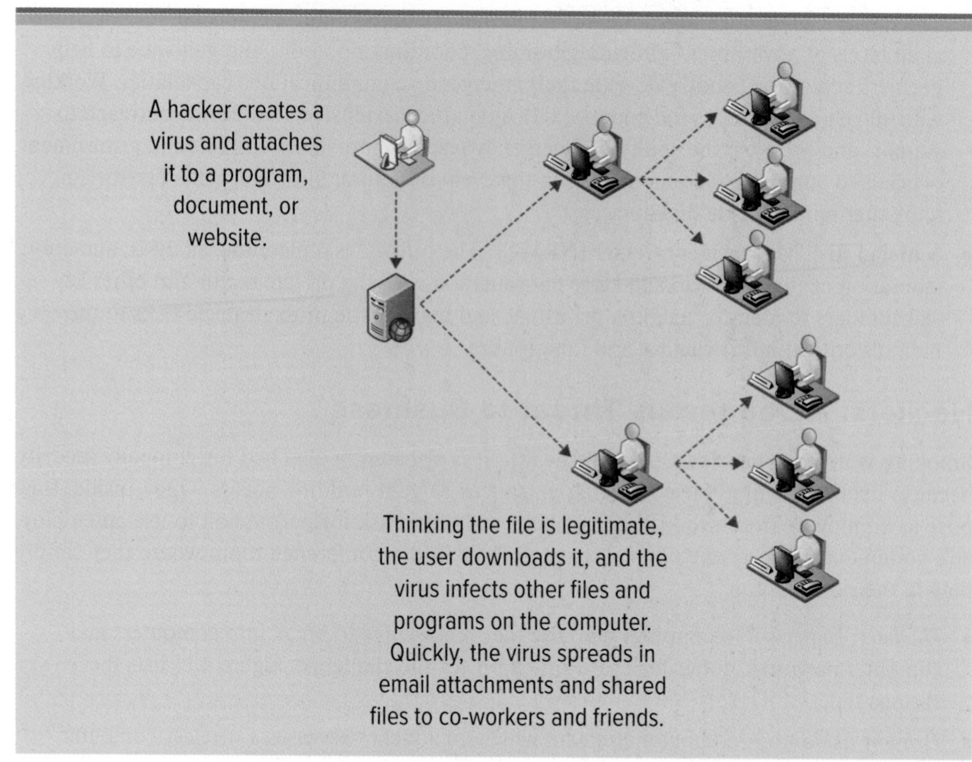

A hacker creates a virus and attaches it to a program, document, or website.
Thinking the file is legitimate, the user downloads it, and the virus infects other files and programs on the computer. Quickly, the virus spreads in email attachments and shared files to co-workers and friends.

While the use of white-hat ethical hackers to find bugs is effective, such programs can also be controversial. To limit potential risk, some organizations are offering *closed bug bounty programs* that require an invitation. Apple, for example, has limited bug bounty participation to a few dozen researchers. A new form of testing, penetration testing, also called pen testing or ethical hacking, is the practice of testing a computer system, network, or web application to find security vulnerabilities that an attacker could exploit. Penetration testing can be automated with software applications or performed manually. Either way, the process involves gathering information about the target before the test, identifying possible entry points, attempting to break in—either virtually or for real—and reporting back the findings.

Viruses: A Dangerous Threat to Business

One of the most common forms of computer vulnerabilities is a virus.

- ***Virus***: Software written with malicious intent to cause annoyance or damage. Some hackers create and leave viruses, causing massive computer damage. Figure 4.12 shows how a virus is spread.
- ***Malware***: Software that is intended to damage or disable computers and computer systems.
- ***Botnets***: Malware that causes a collection of connected devices to be controlled by a hacker. Botnets perform distributed denial-of-service attacks, steal data, send spam, and allow the hacker to access devices without the owner's knowledge.

A ***worm*** spreads itself not only from file to file but also from computer to computer. The primary difference between a virus and a worm is that a virus must attach to something, such as an executable file, to spread. Worms do not need to attach to anything to spread and can tunnel themselves into computers. Figure 4.13 provides an overview of the most common types of viruses. Two additional computer vulnerabilities include adware and spyware.

- ***Adware***: Software that, although purporting to serve some useful function and often fulfilling that function, also allows Internet advertisers to display advertisements without the consent of the computer user.
- ***Spyware***: A special class of adware that collects data about the user and transmits it over the Internet without the user's knowledge or permission. Spyware programs collect

Backdoor programs open a way into the network for future attacks.
Denial-of-service attack (DoS) floods a website with so many requests for service that it slows down or crashes.
Distributed denial-of-service attack (DDoS) targets multiple computers and floods a website with so many requests for service that it slows down or crashes. A common type is the Ping of Death, in which thousands of computers try to access a website at the same time, overloading it and shutting it down.
Polymorphic viruses and worms change their form as they propagate.
Trojan-horse virus hides inside other software, usually as an attachment or a downloadable file.

FIGURE 4.13

Common Forms of Viruses

specific data about the user, ranging from general demographics such as name, address, and browsing habits, to credit card numbers, Social Security numbers, and user names and passwords. Not all adware programs are spyware, and, used correctly, they can generate revenue for a company, allowing users to receive free products. Spyware is a clear threat to privacy.

Two forms of malicious software programs include ransomware and scareware.

- ***Ransomware***: A form of malicious software that infects your computer and asks for money.

Simplelocker is a new ransomware program that encrypts your personal files and demands payment for the files' decryption keys. Ransomware is malware for data kidnapping, an exploit in which the attacker encrypts the victim's data and demands payment for the decryption key. Ransomware spreads through email attachments, infected programs, and compromised websites. A ransomware malware program may also be called a cryptovirus, cryptotrojan, or cryptoworm. Attackers may use one of several different approaches to extort money from their victims:

- After a victim discovers he cannot open a file, he receives an email ransom note demanding a relatively small amount of money in exchange for a private key. The attacker warns that if the ransom is not paid by a certain date, the private key will be destroyed and the data will be lost forever.
- The victim is duped into believing he is the subject of a police inquiry. After being informed that unlicensed software or illegal web content has been found on his computer, the victim is given instructions for how to pay an electronic fine.
- The malware surreptitiously encrypts the victim's data but does nothing else. In this approach, the data kidnapper anticipates that the victim will look on the Internet for how to fix the problem and makes money by selling anti-ransomware software on legitimate websites.

To protect against data kidnapping, experts urge that users back up data on a regular basis. If an attack occurs, do not pay a ransom. Instead, wipe the disk drive clean and restore data from the backup.

- ***Scareware***: A type of malware designed to trick victims into giving up personal information to purchase or download useless and potentially dangerous software.

Scareware often takes advantage of vulnerabilities in a computer's browser to generate pop-ups that resemble system error messages. The warnings, which are designed to look authentic, typically alert the user that a large number of infected files have been found on the computing device. The user is then prompted to call a phone number or click on a hyperlink to get the infection cleaned up. If the end user calls the phone number, he is urged to share credit card information in order to make a purchase for bogus software or sent to a website to download a "cleanup" software application that actually contains malware and infects the computer. If the user falls for the scam, he will not only lose the money he paid for the useless software, he may also make his computer unusable. Figure 4.14 displays a few additional weapons hackers use for launching attacks.[14]

Organizational information is intellectual capital. Just as organizations protect their tangible assets–keeping their money in an insured bank or providing a safe working

Elevation of privilege is a process by which a user misleads a system into granting unauthorized rights, usually for the purpose of compromising or destroying the system. For example, an attacker might log on to a network by using a guest account and then exploit a weakness in the software that lets the attacker change the guest privileges to administrative privileges.
Hoaxes attack computer systems by transmitting a virus hoax with a real virus attached. By masking the attack in a seemingly legitimate message, unsuspecting users more readily distribute the message and send the attack on to their co-workers and friends, infecting many users along the way.
Malicious code includes a variety of threats such as viruses, worms, and Trojan horses.
Packet tampering consists of altering the contents of packets as they travel over the Internet or altering data on computer disks after penetrating a network. For example, an attacker might place a tap on a network line to intercept packets as they leave the computer. The attacker could eavesdrop or alter the information as it leaves the network.
A **sniffer** is a program or device that can monitor data traveling over a network. Sniffers can show all the data being transmitted over a network, including passwords and sensitive information. Sniffers tend to be a favorite weapon in the hacker's arsenal.
Spoofing consists of forging the return address on an email so that the message appears to come from someone other than the actual sender. This is not a virus but rather a way by which virus authors conceal their identities as they send out viruses.
Splogs (spam blogs) are fake blogs created solely to raise the search engine rank of affiliated websites. Even blogs that are legitimate are plagued by spam, with spammers taking advantage of the comment feature of most blogs to comment with links to spam sites.
Spyware is software that comes hidden in free downloadable software and tracks online movements, mines the information stored on a computer, or uses a computer's CPU and storage for some task the user knows nothing about.

FIGURE 4.14

Hacker Weapons

environment for employees—they must also protect their intellectual capital, everything from patents to transactional and analytical information. With security breaches and viruses on the rise and computer hackers everywhere, an organization must put in place strong security measures to survive.

LO 4.4: Describe the relationship between information security policies and an information security plan.

THE FIRST LINE OF DEFENSE—PEOPLE

Organizations today can mine valuable information such as the identity of the top 20 percent of their customers, who usually produce 80 percent of revenues. Most organizations view this type of information as intellectual capital and implement security measures to prevent it from walking out the door or falling into the wrong hands. At the same time, they must enable employees, customers, and partners to access needed information electronically. Organizations address security risks through two lines of defense: The first is people; the second is technology.

Surprisingly, the biggest problem is people because the majority of information security breaches result from people misusing organizational information.

- ***Insiders***: Legitimate users who purposely or accidentally misuse their access to the environment and cause some kind of business-affecting incident. For example, many individuals freely give up their passwords or write them on sticky notes next to their computers, leaving the door wide open for hackers.

A few forms of unethical scams used by hackers to gain information include:

- ***Social engineering***: Occurs when hackers use their social skills to trick people into revealing access credentials or other valuable information.
- ***Pretexting***: A form of social engineering in which one individual lies to obtain confidential data about another individual.
- ***Dumpster diving***: Occurs when a hacker looks through people's trash to obtain information.

With all the unethical behavior that is constantly bombarding an organization, it is best to create policies that prevent these types of scams.

- ***Information security policies***: Identify the rules required to maintain information security, such as requiring users to log off before leaving for lunch or meetings, never sharing passwords with anyone, and changing passwords every 30 days.
- ***Information security plan***: Details how an organization will implement the information security policies.

BUSINESS DRIVEN ETHICS AND SECURITY

Stop the Hacks

Year after year, the number of records stored online grows–and hackers are getting better and better at stealing them. The frequency of "mega-breaches," where the data of tens of millions of people is stolen, is rising. More than 7,000 data breaches have occurred in the past 10 years, with over 4 billion total records stolen. Stolen records may be circulated online by cybercriminals and used for fraud, while hackers can use their access to companies' systems to deploy ransomware or cause even more damage.

- Hackers breached the insurance giant Anthem in 2015, stealing at least 78 million people's personal information.
- JPMorgan Chase discovered a breach in 2014 that affected 83 million customers' personal information.
- Throughout early 2021, hackers have exploited flaws in Microsoft Exchange Server to attack tens of thousands of companies–and we likely won't know the full scope of the attacks for months.
- Russian hackers infiltrated the networks of dozens of U.S. agencies and major corporations in 2020 after compromising SolarWinds' Orion software.
- Yahoo disclosed in 2016 that it had previously suffered two breaches that could have affected personal information of all of its 3 billion users.
- Target was hacked in 2013, exposing 40 million credit and debit card accounts.
- Hackers breached Equifax in 2017, stealing highly sensitive information on 143 million customers.
- Marriott was hacked in 2018, with cybercriminals stealing over 500 million guests' personal information.
- A hacker breached Capital One, stealing information on over 100 million people, including their Social Security numbers and bank account numbers.
- A Facebook vulnerability made half a billion users' personal data up for grabs.
- The real estate insurance giant First American accidentally leaked 885 million records from 2017 to 2019, including people's Social Security numbers and driver's license photos, resulting in criminal charges against First American.[15]

The best way a company can safeguard itself from people is by implementing and communicating its information security plan. This becomes even more important with Web 2.0, as the use of mobile devices, remote workforce, and contractors continues growing. A few details managers should consider regarding information security policies include defining best practices for the following:[16]

- Applications allowed to be placed on the corporate network, especially various file sharing applications (e.g., Kazaa, now defunct), IM software, and entertainment or freeware created by unknown sources (e.g., iPhone applications).
- Corporate computer equipment used for personal reasons on personal networks.
- Password creation and maintenance, including minimum password length, characters to be included while choosing passwords, and frequency for password changes.
- Personal computer equipment allowed to connect to the corporate network.
- Virus protection, including how often the system should be scanned and how frequently the software should be updated. This could also include if downloading attachments is allowed and practices for safe downloading from trusted and untrustworthy sources.

LO 4.5: Provide an example of each of the three primary information security areas: (1) authentication and authorization, (2) prevention and resistance, and (3) detection and response.

THE SECOND LINE OF DEFENSE—TECHNOLOGY

Once an organization has protected its intellectual capital by arming its people with a detailed information security plan, it can begin to focus on deploying technology to help combat attackers.

- ***Destructive agents***: Malicious agents designed by spammers and other Internet attackers to farm email addresses off websites or deposit spyware on machines.

Figure 4.15 displays the three areas in which technology can aid in the defense against attacks.

People: Authentication and Authorization

Identity theft consists of forging someone's identity for the purpose of fraud. The fraud is often financial because thieves apply for and use credit cards or loans in the victim's name. Two means of stealing an identity are phishing and pharming. Let's take a look at phishing first.

- ***Phishing***: A technique to gain personal information for the purpose of identity theft, usually by means of fraudulent emails that look as though they came from legitimate businesses.

The messages appear to be genuine, with official-looking formats and logos, and typically ask for verification of important information such as passwords and account numbers, ostensibly for accounting or auditing purposes. Because the emails look authentic, up to one in five recipients responds with the information and subsequently becomes a victim of identity theft and other fraud. Figure 4.16 displays a phishing scam attempting to gain information for SkyLine Bank. You should never click emails asking you to verify your identity because companies will never contact you directly asking for your user name or password.[17]

Different forms of phishing include:

- ***Phishing expedition***: A masquerading attack that combines spam with spoofing. The perpetrator sends millions of spam emails that appear to be from a respectable company. The emails contain a link to a website that is designed to look exactly like the company's website. The victim is encouraged to enter his or her user name, password, and sometimes credit card information.
- ***Spear phishing***: A phishing expedition in which the emails are carefully designed to target a particular person or organization.
- ***Vishing (or voice phishing)***: A phone scam that attempts to defraud people by asking them to call a bogus telephone number to confirm their account information.

FIGURE 4.15

Three Areas of Information Security

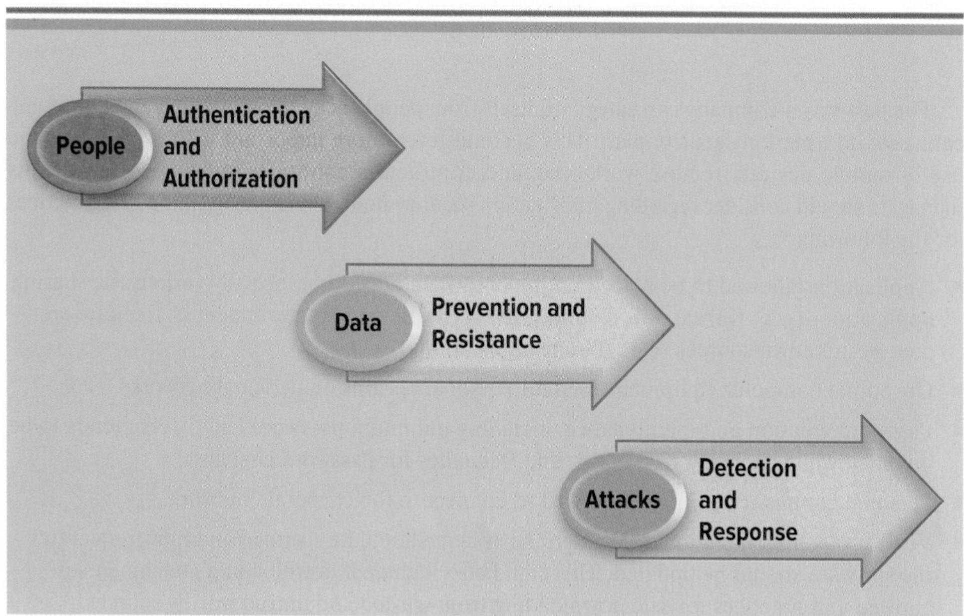

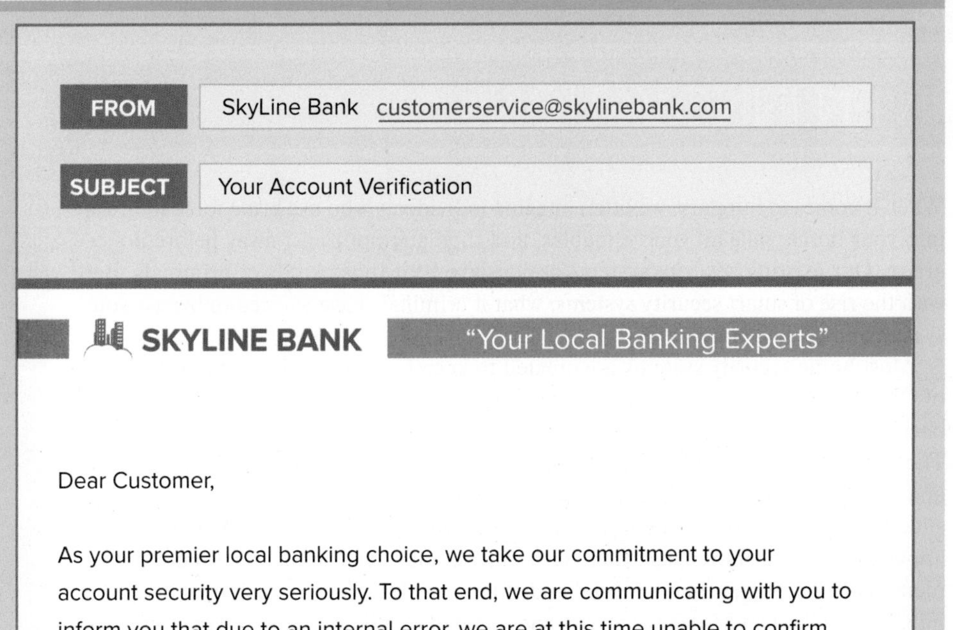
FROM SkyLine Bank customerservice@skylinebank.com

SUBJECT Your Account Verification

SKYLINE BANK "Your Local Banking Experts"

Dear Customer,

As your premier local banking choice, we take our commitment to your account security very seriously. To that end, we are communicating with you to inform you that due to an internal error, we are at this time unable to confirm your account data. It is of the utmost importance that you reply to this email in a timely fashion to avoid any interruption of service on your account.

To avoid suspension of your account, please click the link below to verify your account details. We apologize for this inconvenience.

Click Here

Thank you,
SkyLine Bank Corp.
Online Banking Division

FIGURE 4.16

SkyLine Bank Phishing Scam

The second form of stealing an identity is pharming.

- ***Pharming***: Reroutes requests for legitimate websites to false websites. For example, if you were to type in the URL to your bank, pharming could redirect to a fake site that collects your information.
- ***Zombie***: A program that secretly takes over another computer for the purpose of launching attacks on other computers. Zombie attacks are almost impossible to trace back to the attacker.
- ***Zombie farm***: A group of computers on which a hacker has planted zombie programs.
- ***Pharming attack***: A zombie farm, often by an organized crime association, to launch a massive phishing attack.

Sock puppet marketing is the use of a false identity to artificially stimulate demand for a product, brand, or service. A false identity on the Internet is known colloquially as a sock puppet or catfish, depending upon the level of detail attached to the false identity. Typically, a sock puppet has very little (if any) detail attached to it and may simply be a fictional name attached to a new Google or Yahoo! email account.

Sock puppet marketing is one example of ***astroturfing,*** the practice of artificially stimulating online conversation and positive reviews about a product, service, or brand. Sock puppets can be created quickly and are frequently used on social media websites that rely on customer reviews. For this reason, many websites only allow customer reviews from a verified customer. Sock puppet marketing is unethical and, in some cases, illegal. In the United States, the Federal Trade Commission has the legal authority to levy fines if a company engages in sock puppet marketing.

APPLY YOUR KNOWLEDGE

BUSINESS DRIVEN INNOVATION

Home Security Systems

When it comes to burglary, we often imagine individuals who use brute force to break into your home, take all your valuables, and then attempt to get away before police arrive. Our existing security systems are designed for those kinds of criminals. But with the rise of smart security systems, what if criminals have learned to bypass your system and disable your alarms?

Most home security systems are created to keep intruders out. Nest, a subsidiary of Google parent Alphabet, built its Secure system completely the other way around, choosing to focus just as much on making it simpler for its users to get into the home. The Secure hub can be disarmed by waving a key fob instead of typing a pass code, and those key fobs can be programmed to work within certain time frames, so a babysitter, for example, could access your home only while she is working. A smart phone application lets users manage their system from afar. Of course, the Secure hub is plenty capable of guarding a home, and if an intruder tries to break or unplug the hub, it will sound an 85-decibel alarm, and companion motion sensors can alert users when a door or window had been opened.[18]

In a group, evaluate home security systems and determine if the technology can be hacked. Do you feel safe using an IoT home security device? Why or why not?

Authentication and authorization technologies can prevent identity theft, phishing, and pharming scams. ***Authentication*** is a method for confirming users' identities. Once a system determines the authentication of a user, it can then determine the access privileges (or authorization) for that user. ***Authorization*** is the process of providing a user with permission, including access levels and abilities such as file access, hours of access, and amount of allocated storage space. Authentication and authorization techniques fall into three categories; the most secure procedures combine all three:

1. **Something the user knows, such as a user ID and password.** The first type of authentication, using something the user knows, is the most common way to identify individual users and typically consists of a unique user ID and password. However, this is actually one of the most *ineffective* ways for determining authentication because passwords are not secure. All it typically takes to crack one is enough time. More than 50 percent of help-desk calls are password related, which can cost an organization significant money, and a social engineer can coax a password from almost anybody.
2. **Something the user has, such as a smart card or token.** The second type of authentication, using something the user has, offers a much more effective way to identify individuals than a user ID and password. Tokens and smart cards are two of the primary forms of this type of authentication.
   - ***Tokens***: Small electronic devices that change user passwords automatically. The user enters his or her user ID and token-displayed password to gain access to the network.
   - ***Smart card***: A device about the size of a credit card containing embedded technologies that can store information and small amounts of software to perform some limited processing. Smart cards can act as identification instruments, a form of digital cash, or a data storage device with the ability to store an entire medical record.
3. **Something that is part of the user, such as a fingerprint or voice signature.** The third kind of authentication, something that is part of the user, is by far the best and most effective way to manage authentication.
   - ***Biometrics*** (narrowly defined): The identification of a user based on a physical characteristic, such as a fingerprint, iris, face, voice, or handwriting.

BUSINESS DRIVEN MIS

Netflix Is Stopping the Password Share

Netflix is going to start cracking down on one of the oldest traditions in subscription streaming: password sharing. Netflix is testing a new prompt when customers attempt to use a Netflix account that belongs to someone outside their household, and if you don't live with the owner of this account, you need your own account to keep watching. Users will then be directed to either verify the account with a text or email code, or start their own free 30-day trial. The feature is being tested only on TVs. Sharing passwords with people outside your household is already forbidden in Netflix's terms and conditions, but the streaming giant hasn't enforced the rule in the past. The company limits the number of devices on which you can simultaneously stream its content, which is dictated by your subscription tier.

Do you agree that Netflix should stop allowing users to share passwords? What are the financial impacts of making the decision to stop password sharing? What are the financial impacts of continuing to allow users to share passwords?

- ***Voiceprint***: A set of measurable characteristics of a human voice that uniquely identifies an individual. These characteristics, which are based on the physical configuration of a speaker's mouth and throat, can be expressed as a mathematical formula. Unfortunately, biometric authentication such as voiceprints can be costly and intrusive.

The goal of authentication is to make it difficult for an unauthorized person to gain access to a system because if one security level is broken, the attacker will still have to break through additional levels.

- ***Single-factor authentication***: The traditional security process, which requires a user name and password.
- ***Two-factor authentication***: Requires the user to provide two means of authentication, what the user knows (password) and what the user has (security token).
- ***Multifactor authentication***: Requires more than two means of authentication, such as what the user knows (password), what the user has (security token), and what the user is (biometric verification).

These measures are known as ***countermeasures***—actions, processes, devices, or systems that can prevent, or mitigate the effects of, threats to a computer, server, or network. In this context, a threat is a potential or actual adverse event that may be malicious or incidental and that can compromise the assets of an enterprise or the integrity of a computer or network. Countermeasures include:

- Using strong passwords and two-factor authentication (two methods of verification)
- Frequently deleting stored cookies and temporary files from web browsers
- Regularly scanning for viruses and other malware
- Regularly installing updates and patches for operating systems
- Refusing to click on links that appear within email messages
- Refraining from opening email messages and attachments from unknown senders
- Staying away from questionable websites
- Regularly backing up data on external media
- Watching for suspicious activity—when in doubt, don't click

Data: Prevention and Resistance

A ***privilege escalation*** is a network intrusion attack that takes advantage of programming errors or design flaws to grant the attacker elevated access to the network and its associated data and applications. There are two kinds of privilege escalation:

- ***Vertical privilege escalation***: Attackers grant themselves a higher access level such as administrator, allowing the attacker to perform illegal actions such as running unauthorized code or deleting data. For example, an attacker might log on to a network by using a guest account and then exploit a weakness in the software that lets the attacker change the guest privileges to administrative privileges.
- ***Horizontal privilege escalation***: Attackers grant themselves the same access levels they already have but assume the identity of another user. For example, someone gaining access to another person's online banking account would constitute horizontal privilege escalation.

Prevention and resistance technologies stop intruders from accessing and reading data by means of content filtering, encryption, and firewalls.

- ***Time bombs***: Computer viruses that wait for a specific date before executing their instructions.
- ***Content filtering***: Occurs when organizations use software that filters content, such as emails, to prevent the accidental or malicious transmission of unauthorized information.

Organizations can use content filtering technologies to filter email and prevent emails containing sensitive information from transmitting, whether the transmission was malicious or accidental. It can also filter emails to prevent any suspicious files from transmitting, such as potentially virus-infected files. Email content filtering can also filter for spam, a form of unsolicited email.

- ***Encryption***: Scrambles information into an alternative form that requires a key or password to decrypt.

If there were a security breach and the stolen information were encrypted, the thief would be unable to read it. Encryption can switch the order of characters, replace characters with other characters, insert or remove characters, or use a mathematical formula to convert the information into a code. Companies that transmit sensitive customer information over the Internet, such as credit card numbers, frequently use encryption.

- ***Decrypt***: To decrypt information is to decode it. It is the opposite of *encrypt.*
- ***Cryptography***: The science that studies encryption, which is the hiding of messages so only the sender and receiver can read them.

Personally identifiable information (PII) is any data that could potentially identify a specific individual. The two types of PII include sensitive PII and nonsensitive PII.

- ***Nonsensitive PII***: Information transmitted without encryption. This includes information collected from public records, phone books, corporate directories, websites, etc. Nonsensitive PII is information that does not harm an individual, such as an address.
- ***Sensitive PII***: Information transmitted with encryption and, when disclosed, results in a breach of an individual's privacy and can potentially cause the individual harm. Sensitive PII includes biometric information, financial information, medical information, and unique identifiers such as passport or Social Security numbers.

The ***HIPAA Security Rule*** ensures national standards for securing patient data that is stored or transferred electronically. The HIPAA Security Rule requires the placement of both physical and electronic safeguards on sensitive PII health information. The goal of the HIPAA Security Rule is to protect patient security while still allowing the health care industry to advance technologically. All organizations need to understand and govern PII by:

- Identifying all sources of created, received, maintained, or transmitted PII.
- Evaluating all external sources of PII.
- Identifying all human, natural, and environmental threats to PII.

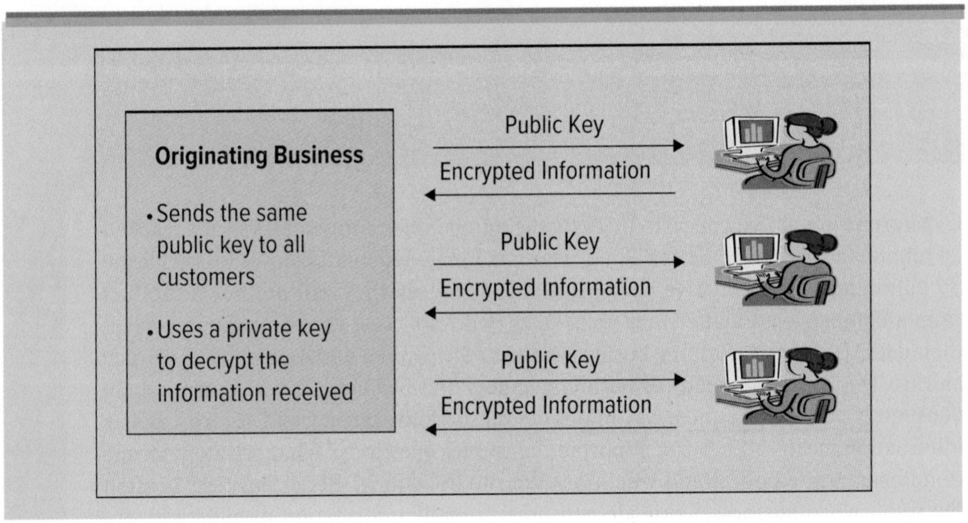

Originating Business

- Sends the same public key to all customers
- Uses a private key to decrypt the information received

Public Key →
← Encrypted Information

Public Key →
← Encrypted Information

Public Key →
← Encrypted Information

FIGURE 4.17

Public Key Encryption (PKE)

Some encryption technologies use multiple keys.

- ***Public key encryption (PKE)***: Uses two keys: a public key that everyone can have, and a private key for only the recipient (see Figure 4.17).

The organization provides the public key to all customers, whether end consumers or other businesses, who use that key to encrypt their information and send it via the Internet. When it arrives at its destination, the organization uses the private key to unscramble it.

Public keys are becoming popular to use for authentication techniques consisting of digital objects in which a trusted third party confirms correlation between the user and the public key.

- ***Certificate authority***: A trusted third party, such as VeriSign, that validates user identities by means of digital certificates.
- ***Digital certificate***: A data file that identifies individuals or organizations online and is comparable to a digital signature.

A ***firewall*** is hardware and/or software that guard a private network by analyzing incoming and outgoing information for the correct markings. If they are missing, the firewall prevents the information from entering the network. Firewalls can even detect computers communicating with the Internet without approval. As Figure 4.18 illustrates, organizations typically place a firewall between a server and the Internet. Think of a firewall as a gatekeeper that protects

FIGURE 4.18

Sample Firewall Architecture Connecting Systems Located in Chicago, New York, and Boston

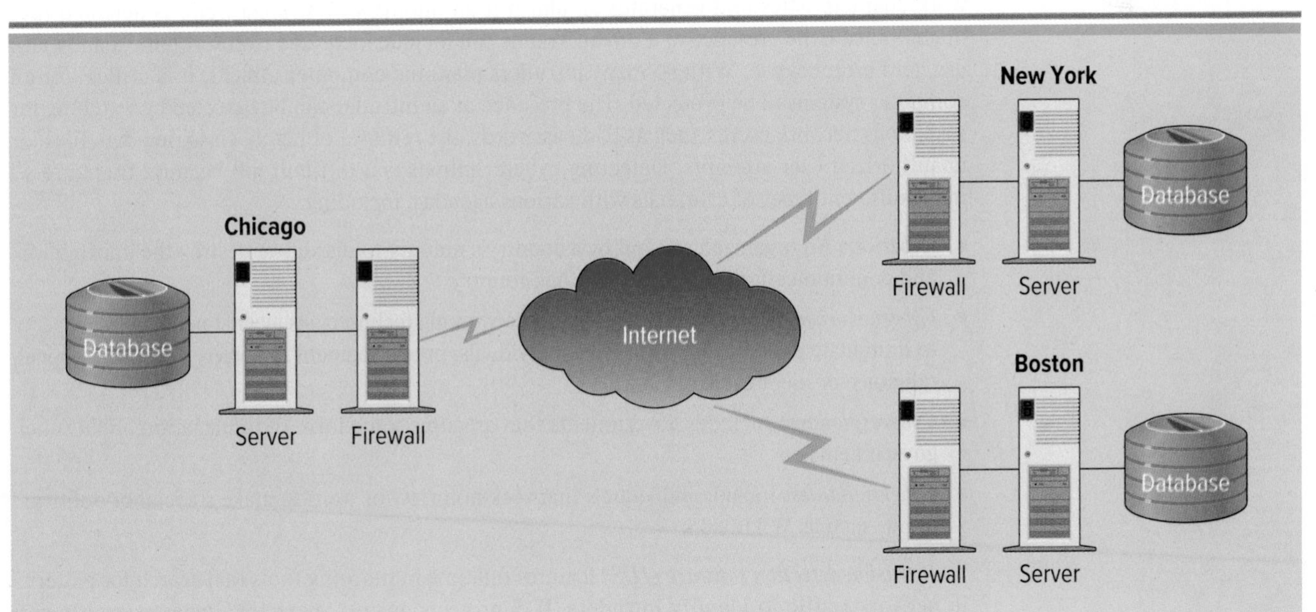

APPLY YOUR KNOWLEDGE

BUSINESS DRIVEN START-UP

Relationships of Trust

Cybercrime is a global concern. In 2020, the number of identity theft victims reached 24 million in the United States alone. The same year, account takeover losses hit the $6 billion mark. Seventy-five percent of customers say they will not buy a product from a company–no matter how great–if they do not trust the company to protect their data. Trust in performing business online relies on the understanding of privacy and trust information needs of both consumers and businesses in key areas where consumers perceive the most risk in online transactions: privacy and security. Better information means addressing important consumer questions: What private information does the site collect and what does the site do with it? Better business is often the result when businesses provide consumer-friendly information to build and sustain the confidence of their customers.

Given the nature of online cybercrime, what would it take a company to get you to purchase a product online? If the company you purchased a product from had a security breach, would you continue to buy products from the company? If you worked for a company that had an online security breach, what would you do to ensure customers are safe and continue buying from you?

computer networks from intrusion by providing a filter and safe transfer points for access to and from the Internet and other networks. It screens all network traffic for proper passwords or other security codes and allows only authorized transmissions in and out of the network.

Firewalls do not guarantee complete protection, and users should enlist additional security technologies such as antivirus software and antispyware software.

- ***Antivirus software***: Scans and searches hard drives to prevent, detect, and remove known viruses, adware, and spyware. Antivirus software must be frequently updated to protect against newly created viruses.

Attack: Detection and Response

Network behavior analysis gathers an organization's computer network traffic patterns to identify unusual or suspicious operations. Network behavior analysis software tracks critical network characteristics and generates an alarm if an anomaly or strange trend is detected that might indicate the presence of a threat. Trends can include increased traffic volume, bandwidth use, and protocol use. With so many intruders planning computer attacks, it is critical for all computer systems to be protected. The presence of an intruder can be detected by watching for suspicious network events such as bad passwords, the removal of highly classified data files, or unauthorized user attempts. Detecting cybercriminals is a difficult job because there are so many different types of criminals with various agendas, including:

- ***Cyberwar***: An organized attempt by a country's military to disrupt or destroy the information and communication systems of another country.
- ***Cyberterrorism***: The use of computer and networking technologies against persons or property to intimidate or coerce governments, individuals, or any segment of society to attain political, religious, or ideological goals.
- ***Cyberespionage***: Includes governments that are after some form of information about other governments.
- ***Cybervigilantes***: Include individuals that seek notoriety or want to make a social or political point, such as WikiLeaks.

Intrusion detection software (IDS) features full-time monitoring tools that search for patterns in network traffic to identify intruders. IDS protects against suspicious network traffic and attempts to access files and data. If a suspicious event or unauthorized traffic is identified, the IDS will generate an alarm and can even be customized to shut down a particularly sensitive part of a network. After identifying an attack, an MIS department can implement response tactics to mitigate the damage. Response tactics outline procedures such as how long a system under attack will remain plugged in and connected to the corporate network, when to shut down a compromised system, and how quickly a backup system will be up and running.

Guaranteeing the safety of organization information is achieved by implementing the two lines of defense: people and technology. To protect information through people, firms should develop information security policies and plans that provide employees with specific precautions they should take in creating, working with, and transmitting the organization's information assets. Technology-based lines of defense fall into three categories: authentication and authorization; prevention and resistance; and detection and response.

LEARNING OUTCOME REVIEW

Learning Outcome 4.1: Explain the ethical issues in the use of information technology.

Information ethics govern the ethical and moral issues arising from the development and use of information technologies, as well as the creation, collection, duplication, distribution, and processing of information itself (with or without the aid of computer technologies). Ethical dilemmas in this area usually arise not as simple, clear-cut situations but as clashes among competing goals, responsibilities, and loyalties. Inevitably, there will be more than one socially acceptable or correct decision. For this reason, acting ethically and legally are not always the same.

Learning Outcome 4.2: Identify the six epolicies organizations should implement to protect themselves.

1. An ethical computer use policy contains general principles to guide computer user behavior. For example, it might explicitly state that users should refrain from playing computer games during working hours.
2. An information privacy policy contains general principles regarding information privacy.
3. An acceptable use policy (AUP) is a policy that a user must agree to follow to be provided access to corporate email, information systems, and the Internet.
4. An email privacy policy details the extent to which email messages may be read by others.
5. A social media policy outlines the corporate guidelines or principles governing employee online communications.
6. An employee-monitoring policy states explicitly how, when, and where the company monitors its employees.

Learning Outcome 4.3: Describe the relationships and differences between hackers and viruses.

Hackers are experts in technology who use their knowledge to break into computers and computer networks, either for profit or just for the challenge. A virus is software written with malicious intent to cause annoyance or damage. Some hackers create and leave viruses, causing massive computer damage.

Learning Outcome 4.4: Describe the relationship between information security policies and an information security plan.

Information security policies identify the rules required to maintain information security, such as requiring users to log off before leaving for lunch or meetings, never sharing passwords with anyone, and changing passwords every 30 days. An information security plan details how an organization will implement the information security policies. The best way a company can safeguard itself from people is by implementing and communicating its information security plan.

Learning Outcome 4.5: Provide an example of each of the three primary information security areas: (1) authentication and authorization, (2) prevention and resistance, and (3) detection and response.

Authentication and authorization: Authentication is a method for confirming users' identities. Once a system determines the authentication of a user, it can then determine the access privileges (or authorization) for that user. Authorization is the process of providing a user with permission, including access levels and abilities such as file access, hours of access, and amount of allocated storage space.

Prevention and resistance: Content filtering occurs when organizations use software that filters content, such as emails, to prevent the accidental or malicious transmission of unauthorized information. Encryption scrambles information into an alternative form that requires a key or password to decrypt. In a security breach, a thief is then unable to read encrypted information. A firewall is hardware and/or software that guard a private network by analyzing incoming and outgoing information for the correct markings.

Detection and response: Intrusion detection software (IDS) features full-time monitoring tools that search for patterns in network traffic to identify intruders.

KEY TERMS

REVIEW QUESTIONS

1. What are ethics, and why are they important to a company?
2. What is the relationship between information management, governance, and compliance?
3. Why are epolicies important to a company?
4. What is the correlation between privacy and confidentiality?
5. What is the relationship between adware and spyware?
6. What are the positive and negative effects associated with monitoring employees?
7. What is the relationship between hackers and viruses?
8. Why is security a business issue, not just a technology issue?
9. What are the growing issues related to employee communication methods, and what can a company do to protect itself?
10. How can a company participating in ebusiness keep its information secure?
11. What technologies can a company use to safeguard information?
12. Why is ediscovery important to a company?
13. What are the reasons a company experiences downtime?
14. What are the costs associated with downtime?

CLOSING CASE ONE

Five Ways Hackers Can Get into Your Business

Hackers don't care what size your business is; they only care if they can get past your defenses and relieve you of your valuables. Hackers actually like small businesses because they tend to have more to steal than an individual person but fewer cyber defenses than a large company. The hard reality is that most small businesses stand at least a 50–50 chance of being targeted for attack by hackers. Did you know:

- Once every three minutes, the average company comes into contact with viruses and malware.
- One in every 291 email messages contains a virus.
- Three things hackers want most are customer data, intellectual property, and bank account information.
- The top five file names used in phishing scams are Details.zip, UPS_document.zip, DCIM.zip, Report.zip, and Scan.zip.
- The average annual cost of a cyberattack on a small or medium-sized business is $188,242.

Cyberthieves are always looking for new ways to gain access to your business data, business networks, and business applications. The best way to protect your business from cybertheft is to build a strong defense and be able to identify vulnerabilities and weak spots. The top five ways hackers will try to gain access to your businesses, according to John Brandon of *Inc.* magazine, are highlighted in Figure 4.19. (Please note there are far more than five ways. These are just the five most common.)

Questions

1. Define information ethics and information security, and explain whether they are important to help prevent hackers from gaining access to an organization.
2. Identify two epolicies that a business could implement to ensure the protection of sensitive corporate data from hackers.
3. Demonstrate how a business can use authentication and authorization technologies to prevent hackers from gaining access to organizational systems.
4. Analyze how a business can use prevention and resistance technologies to safeguard its employees from hackers and viruses.
5. Explain why hackers want to gain access to organizational data.
6. Evaluate additional ways hackers can gain access to organizational data.

FIGURE 4.19

Five Ways Hackers Gain Access to Your Business

WEAK PASSWORDS

- With a $300 graphics card, a hacker can run 420 billion simple, lowercase, eight-character password combinations a minute.
- Cyberattacks involve weak passwords 80 percent of the time; 55 percent of people use one password for all logins.
- Hackers cracked 6.4 million LinkedIn passwords and 1.5 million eHarmony passwords in separate attacks.

Your Best Defense:

- Use a unique password for each account.
- Aim for at least 20 characters and preferably gibberish, not real words.
- Insert special characters: @#$*&.
- Try a password manager such as LastPass or Dashlane.

MALWARE ATTACKS

- An infected website, USB drive, or application delivers software that can capture keystrokes, passwords, and data.
- An 8 percent increase in malware attacks against small businesses occurs yearly; the average loss from a targeted attack was $92,000.
- Victims of infected mobile developers' website attacks include Apple, Facebook, and Twitter.

Your Best Defense:

- Run robust malware-detection software such as Norton Toolbar.
- Keep existing software updated.
- Use an iPhone; Android phones are targeted more than any other mobile operating system.

PHISHING EMAILS

- Bogus but official-looking emails prompt you to enter your password or click links to infected websites.
- A 125 percent rise in social media phishing attacks has occurred since 2012.
- Phishers steal $1 billion from small businesses yearly.
- Many small businesses are targeted with phishing emails designed to look like Better Business Bureau warnings.

Your Best Defense:

- Keep existing software, operating systems, and browsers updated with the latest patches.
- Don't automatically click links in emails to external sites; retype the URL in your browser.

SOCIAL ENGINEERING

- Think 21st-century con artist tactics; e.g., hackers pretending to be you to reset your passwords.
- Twenty-nine percent of all security breaches involve some form of social engineering. Average loss is $25,000 to $100,000 per incident.
- In 2009, social engineers posed as Coca-Cola's CEO, persuading an executive to open an email with software that infiltrated the company's network.

Your Best Defense:

- Rethink what you reveal on social media—it's all fodder for social engineers.
- Develop policies for handling sensitive requests such as password resets over the phone.
- Have a security audit done.

RANSOMWARE

- Hackers hold your website hostage, often posting embarrassing content such as porn, until you pay a ransom.
- Five million dollars is extorted each year. The real cost is the data loss—paying the ransom doesn't mean you get your files back.
- Hackers locked the network at an Alabama ABC TV station, demanding a ransom to remove a red screen on every computer.

Your Best Defense:

- As with malware, do not click suspicious links or unknown websites.
- Regularly back up your data.
- Use software that specifically checks for new exploits.[19]

FIGURE 4.19
(continued)

CLOSING CASE TWO

Cambridge Analytica: Illegal Data Scraping

Cambridge Analytica is a data analysis firm that worked on Donald Trump's 2016 presidential campaign. In so doing, its related company, Strategic Communications Laboratories, scraped the data of over 50 million Facebook users without their knowledge. Data scraping, also known as web scraping, is the process of importing information from a website into a spreadsheet or local file saved on a computer. It is one of the most efficient ways to get data from the web, and in some cases, to channel that data to another website. The fact that Facebook allowed data from millions of its users to be captured and improperly used without their knowledge or consent to influence the presidential election caused a storm of problems for the social media giant. Cambridge Analytica used the information to target voters based upon their psychological profiles. Of course, all of this prompted concerns about what "psychographic targeting" really means. Britain's Channel 4 News released a series of undercover videos filmed over the course of a year that showed executives at Cambridge Analytica appearing to say they could extort politicians, send women to entrap them, and help proliferate propaganda to help their clients.

Mark Zuckerberg, Facebook's CEO, posted on his Facebook account an apology recognizing the mistakes made by his company and even offered new regulations to ensure this type of data theft did not occur again. Facebook suspended both Cambridge Analytica and Strategic Communications Laboratories accounts while it investigates whether both companies retained Facebook user data—a violation of Facebook's terms. Facebook says it knew about the breach but had received legally binding guarantees from the company that all of the data was deleted.

When Facebook users learned the social media giant had given their sensitive information to political-data firm Cambridge Analytica, Mozilla reacted fast: Within eight hours, the product team had built a browser extension called the Facebook Container. The plug-in, now the most popular browser extension Mozilla had ever built, prevents Facebook from trailing its users around the Internet. Firefox Monitor uses your email address to determine whether your personal information has been compromised by a data breach. The Firefox browser also blocks all cross-site third-party trackers, strengthening privacy without your having to do anything. Mozilla wants to make it simple for people to create walls around data that is important.[20]

Questions

1. How would you feel if your personal data was sold without your consent?
2. Do you believe data scraping from websites like Facebook should be illegal?
3. What can you do to protect the things you post to social media like Twitter, Instagram, or Facebook?
4. Do you believe businesses should be allowed to scrap data from social media websites?

MAKING BUSINESS DECISIONS

1. WikiBlunders—Thin Ice Reports

According to *PC World,* these false facts all appeared on Wikipedia:

- David Beckham was a Chinese goalkeeper in the 18th century.
- Paul Reiser (an actor) is dead. Sinbad (an actor) is dead.
- Sergey Brin is dating Jimmy Wales, and both are dead. (Brin founded Google, and Wales founded Wikipedia.)
- Tony Blair worships Hitler. (Blair is the former prime minister of the United Kingdom.)
- The Duchess of Cornwall's Christian name is Cow-miller.
- The University of Cincinnati's former president is a lady of the night.
- Conan O'Brien assaults sea turtles while canoeing.

We know that people use information technology to work with information. Knowing this, how could these types of errors occur? What could happen if you decided to use Wikipedia to collect business intelligence for a research paper? What could Wikipedia do to help prevent these types of errors?

2. Yes, I Started the Internet

Imagine that your favorite co-worker is Mary, a hard-working employee who excels at her job and continuously receives outstanding performance reviews. Suddenly, after two years of hard work, Mary is fired, and you are wondering what happened. What will you say when you find out that Mary lied on her résumé about having a master's degree? Will you feel that Mary got what she deserved, or should her outstanding job performance have helped management look past this issue? After all, she is excellent at her job.

Every student should know that if dishonesty is discovered, it is often grounds for termination and possibly legal action. Information integrity is a measure of the quality of information. According to Steven D. Levitt, co-author of *Freakonomics* and a renowned economics professor at the University of Chicago, more than 50 percent of people lie on their résumés. Given such repercussions as Mary's fate, you will want to think twice before ever lying on your résumé. The integrity of the information on your résumé is a direct representation of your personal integrity. How would you handle Mary's situation if you were her manager?

3. What Happens on YouTube Stays on YouTube FOREVER!

Are you looking for great career advice? Here it is: Never post anything on publicly accessible websites that you would not feel comfortable showing a recruiter or hiring manager. This includes inappropriate photos; negative comments about jobs, professors, or people; and images of you binge drinking at a holiday party. Future employers will Google you!

The bad news: You have to continue to keep your cyber profile squeaky clean for the rest of your life. Companies can and will fire you for inappropriate online postings. One interesting story occurred when two employees created a private, password-protected group on Facebook where they would complain about their jobs, post derogatory comments about their managers, and highlight new top-secret product information. The managers, being computer savvy, obtained the password and immediately fired the two individuals after reviewing the site. Now one of the individuals is suing the former managers for invasion of privacy.

Do you agree that if you post something online, it is open for the world to see? What do you consider is inappropriate material that you should never post to the web? What can you do to remove inappropriate material posted to the web by a friend who identifies you? How do efficiency and effectiveness enter into this scenario? Was social media the most efficient and effective way for the two employees to communicate? What is the potential argument each of these sides might use in order to win the lawsuit?

4. **Police Records Found in Old Copy Machine**

Copy machines all contain a hard drive that stores a copy of every document the machine has ever scanned, printed, copied, or faxed. If the hard drive is not erased or scrubbed when the copy machine is resold, all of that digital information is still maintained inside the machine. The Buffalo (New York) Police Sex Crimes Division recently sold several copy machines without scrubbing the hard drives. The hard drives yielded detailed domestic violence complaints and a list of wanted sex offenders. A machine from the Buffalo Police Narcotics Unit contained targets in a major drug raid, and a copier once used by a New York construction company stored 95 pages of pay stubs with names, addresses, and Social Security numbers.[21]

Who do you think should be held responsible for the information issues at the Buffalo Police Department? What types of ethical issues and information security issues are being violated? What types of epolicies could a company implement to ensure that these situations do not occur? What forms of information security could a company implement to ensure that these situations do not occur? How does this case support the primary reason that ediscovery is so important to litigation?

5. **Spying on Email**

Technology advances now allow individuals to monitor computers that they do not even have physical access to. New types of software can capture an individual's incoming and outgoing email and then immediately forward that email to another person. For example, if you are at work and your child is home from school and she receives an email from John at 3:00 p.m., at 3:01 p.m. you can receive a copy of that email sent to your email address. If she replies to John's email, within seconds you will receive a copy of what she sent to John. Describe two scenarios (other than those described here) for the use of this type of software: one in which the use would be ethical and one in which it would be unethical.

6. **Sources Are Not Friends**

The Canadian Broadcasting Company (CBC) has issued a social networking policy directing journalists to avoid adding sources or contacts as friends on social networking sites such as Facebook or LinkedIn. Basic rules state that reporters must never allow one source to view what another source says, and reporters must ensure that private conversations with sources remain private. Adding sources as friends can compromise a journalist's work by allowing friends to view other friends in the network. It may also not be in a journalist's best interest to become a friend in a source's network. The CBC also discourages posting any political preferences in personal profiles or comments on bulletin boards or Facebook walls.

This might seem like common sense, but for employees who do not spend countless hours on the Internet, using social networking sites can be confusing and overwhelming. Why is it critical for any new hire to research and review all policies, especially social media policies? Research three companies you would like to work for after graduation, and detail the types of social media policies that each company has or should implement.

7. **Identity Theft**

Identity theft has quickly become the most common, expensive, and pervasive crime in the United States. The identities of more than 15 million U.S. citizens are stolen each year, with financial losses exceeding $50 billion. This means that the identities of almost 10 percent of U.S. adults will be stolen this year, with losses of around $4,000 each, not to mention the 100 million U.S. citizens whose personal data will be compromised due to data breaches of corporate and government databases.

The growth of organized crime can be attributed to the massive amounts of data collection along with the increased cleverness of professional identity thieves. Starting with individually tailored phishing and vishing scams, increasingly successful corporate and government database hackings, and intricate networks of botnets that hijack millions of computers without a trace, we must wake up to this ever-increasing threat to all Americans.

You are responsible for protecting yourself from data theft. In a group, visit the Federal Trade Commission's Consumer Information Identity Theft website at http://www.consumer.ftc.gov/features/feature-0014-identity-theft and review what you can do today to protect your identity and how you can ensure that your personal information is safe.

8. Setting Boundaries

Even the most ethical people sometimes face difficult choices. Acting ethically means behaving in a principled fashion and treating other people with respect and dignity. It is simple to say, but not so simple to do because situations are complex or ambiguous. The important role of ethics in our lives has long been recognized. As far back as 44 BC, Cicero said that ethics are indispensable to anyone who wants to have a good career. Having said that, Cicero, along with some of the greatest minds over the centuries, struggled with what the rules of ethics should be.

Our ethics are rooted in our history, culture, and religion, and our sense of ethics may shift over time. The electronic age brings with it a new dimension in the ethics debate—the amount of personal information that we can collect and store, and the speed with which we can access and process that information.

In a group, discuss how you would react to the following situations:

a. A senior marketing manager informs you that one of her employees is looking for another job, and she wants you to give her access to look through the employee's email.

b. A vice president of sales informs you that he has made a deal to provide customer information to a strategic partner, and he wants you to copy all of the customer information to a thumb drive.

c. You are asked to monitor your employee's email to discover whether he is sexually harassing another employee.

d. You are asked to install a video surveillance system in your office to find out whether employees are taking office supplies home.

e. You are looking on the shared network drive and discover that your boss's entire hard drive has been copied to the network for everyone to view. What do you do?

f. You have been accidentally copied on an email from the CEO about who will be targeted in the next round of layoffs. What do you do?

9. Fired for Smoking on the Weekend

New technologies make it possible for employers to monitor many aspects of their employees' jobs, especially when it comes to telephones, computer terminals, and both electronic and voice mail, and when employees use the Internet. Such monitoring is virtually unregulated. Therefore, unless company policy specifically states otherwise (and even this is not ensured), your employer may listen, watch, and read most of your workplace communications.

Employers are taking monitoring activity a step further and monitoring employees, and employees' spouses, at home and on weekends. Yes, you read that correctly. Numerous employees have been fired for smoking cigarettes on the weekend in the privacy of their own home. As health care costs escalate, employers are increasingly seeking to regulate employee behavior—at home as well as in the workplace. Weyco, an insurance benefits administrator in Michigan, initiated a program requiring mandatory breath tests to detect for nicotine, and any employee testing positive would be sent home without pay for one month. If the employee failed the nicotine test a second time, that person would be fired—no matter how long the employee had been with the company.

Weyco's smoking prohibition does not stop with employees either. It extends to spouses, who must also pass monthly nicotine tests. A positive test means the employee must pay a monthly fee of $80 until the spouse takes a smoking cessation program and tests nicotine-free.

Do you agree that companies have the right to hold employees accountable for actions they perform on weekends in the privacy of their own homes? If you were the CEO of Weyco, what would be your argument supporting its smoking prohibition policies? Do you think Weyco's monitoring practices are ethical? Do you think Weyco's monitoring practices are legal?

10. Hacking the Ultimate Hack

Have you ever seen a LifeLock advertisement? If so, you know the Social Security number of LifeLock CEO Todd Davis because he posts it in all the ads, daring hackers to try and steal his identity. Davis has been a victim of identity theft at least 13 times. The first theft occurred when someone used his identity to secure a $500 loan from a check-cashing company. Davis discovered the crime only after the company called his wife's cell phone to recover the unpaid debt.

If you were starting an identity theft prevention company, do you think it would be a good idea to post your Social Security number in advertisements? Why or why not? What do you think happened that caused Davis's identity to be stolen? What types of information security measures should LifeLock implement to ensure that Davis's Social Security number is not stolen again? If you were LifeLock's CEO, what type of marketing campaign would you launch next?

11. How Much Would You Pay for Your Life?

Imagine getting a call from a hospital. "Hello, your mother's life support system was deactivated, and we are so sorry to inform you that your mother has passed away." If the machine were turned off because ransomware infected the system, would you expect the hospital to pay the ransom demand? Would the hacker release control over the device if the hospital could even afford to pay? This scenario is terrifying and possible.

Disruptive cyberattacks within the health care industry are occurring and should scare every patient. Imagine having an implanted heart monitor and relying on it to send data about heart rhythms to a remote center to analyze and monitor heart health. Every IoT device is at risk for attack from bad actors with malicious intent.

While no single solution can mitigate vulnerabilities, there are many companies working to defend against attacks on all levels, from nuisances to life-threatening. Security experts must get it right every single time. Hackers only have to get it right once. Cybersecurity solutions need to consider all types of risks to any IoT device. In a group, look at the IoT devices you are using and assess three situations in which cybercriminals could steal your information or use ransomware on your device.

AYK APPLICATION PROJECTS

If you are looking for Excel projects to incorporate into your class, try any of the following after reading this chapter.

Project Number	Project Name	Project Type	Plug-In Focus Area	Project Focus	Project Skill Set	Page Number
1	Financial Destiny	Excel	T2	Personal Budget	Introductory Formulas	AYK.3
2	Cash Flow	Excel	T2	Cash Flow	Introductory Formulas	AYK.3
3	Technology Budget	Excel	T1, T2	Hardware and Software	Introductory Formulas	AYK.3
4	Tracking Donations	Excel	T2	Employee Relationships	Introductory Formulas	AYK.3
5	Convert Currency	Excel	T2	Global Commerce	Introductory Formulas	AYK.4
6	Cost Comparison	Excel	T2	Total Cost of Ownership	Introductory Formulas	AYK.4
7	Time Management	Excel or Project	T2 or T12	Project Management	Introductory Gantt Charts	AYK.5
8	Maximize Profit	Excel	T2, T4	Strategic Analysis	Intermediate Formulas or Solver	AYK.5
9	Security Analysis	Excel	T3	Filtering Data	Intermediate Conditional Formatting, Autofilter, Subtotal	AYK.6
10	Gathering Data	Excel	T3	Data Analysis	Intermediate Conditional Formatting, PivotTable	AYK.6
11	Scanner System	Excel	T2	Strategic Analysis	Intermediate	AYK.7
12	Competitive Pricing	Excel	T2	Profit Maximization	Intermediate	AYK.7
13	Adequate Acquisitions	Excel	T2	Break-Even Analysis	Intermediate	AYK.7
26	Electronic Résumés	HTML	T9, T10, T11	Electronic Personal Marketing	Introductory Structural Tags	AYK.14
27	Gathering Feedback	HTML	T9, T10, T11	Data Collection	Intermediate Organization of Information	AYK.15

Design Element: © McGraw Hill Education

module 2

Technical Foundations of MIS

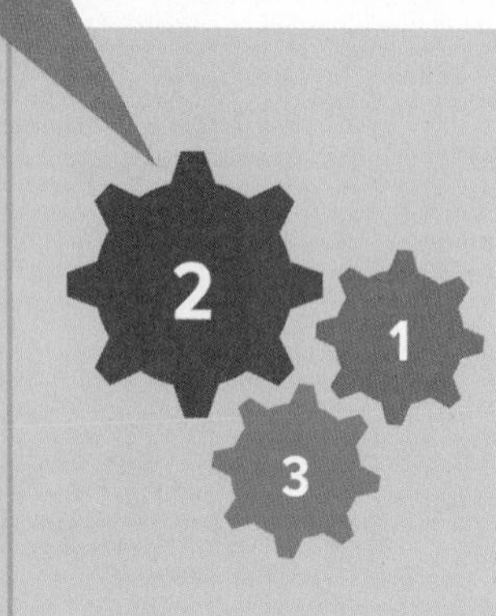

MODULE 1:
Business Driven MIS

MODULE 2:
Technical Foundations of MIS

MODULE 3:
Enterprise MIS

MODULE 2 CONCENTRATES on the technical foundations of MIS. The power of MIS comes from its ability to carry, house, and support information. And information is power to an organization. This module highlights this point and raises awareness of the significance of information to organizational success. Understanding how the MIS infrastructure supports business operations, how business professionals access and analyze information to make business decisions, and how wireless and mobile technologies can make information continuously and instantaneously available are important for strategically managing any company, large or small. Thus, these are the primary learning outcomes of Module 2.

The module begins by reviewing the role of MIS in supporting business growth, operations, and performance. We quickly turn to the need for MIS to be sustainable, given today's focus on being green, and then dive into databases, data warehousing, networking, and wireless technologies—all fundamental components of MIS infrastructures. A theme throughout the module is the need to leverage and yet safeguard the use of information as key to the survival of any company. Information must be protected from misuse and harm, especially with the continued use, development, and exploitation of the Internet and the web.

Module 2: Technical Foundations of MIS

Infrastructures: Sustainable Technologies

CHAPTER OUTLINE

What's in IT for me?

Why do you, as a business student, need to understand the underlying technology of any company? Most people think "that technical stuff" is something they will never personally encounter, and for that reason they do not need to know anything about MIS infrastructures. Well, those people will be challenged in the business world. When your database fails and you lose all of your sales history, you will personally feel the impact when you don't receive your bonus. When your computer crashes and you lose all of your confidential information, not to mention your emails, calendars, and messages, then you will understand why everyone needs to learn about MIS infrastructures. You never want to leave the critical task of backing up your data to your MIS department. You want to ensure personally that your information is not only backed up but also safeguarded and recoverable. For these reasons, business professionals in the 21st century need to acquire a base-level appreciation of what MIS can and cannot do for their company. Understanding how MIS supports growth, operations, profitability, and, most recently, sustainability is crucial, whether one is new to the workforce or a seasoned *Fortune* 500 employee. One of the primary goals of this chapter is to create a more level playing field between you as a business professional and the MIS specialists with whom you will work. After reading it, you should have many of the skills you need to assist in analyzing current and even some future MIS infrastructures; in recommending needed changes in processes; and in evaluating alternatives that support a company's growth, operations, and profits.

opening case study

commerceandculturestock/Moment/Getty Images

Ariel Skelley/Blend Images/Getty Images

SIBSA Digital Pvt. Ltd./Alamy Stock Photo

Envision 2030: 17 Goals to Transform the World for Persons with Disabilities

In 2015, the UN General assembly adopted the Agenda for Sustainable Development 2030. It included seventeen sustainable development goals (SDGs). The agenda focuses on creating sustainable development for all using a holistic approach.

The SDGs reference disabilities multiple times, emphasizing education, maintaining sustainable growth, and improving issues of inequality and accessibility. They also call for better data collection and monitoring of SDGs. The goals do apply to people with disabilities even though they do not directly use the term disability.

The new 2030 Agenda will apply to people with disabilities everywhere. The goals were first implemented in 2016. One of Envision 2030's goals is to make planning for disability be mainstream with focus on increasing awareness and promoting more dialogue between stakeholders, and creating web resources related to each SDG and disability. The 17 SDGs are summarized below in Figure 5.1.

FIGURE 5.1

United Nations 17 Sustainable Development Goals

GOAL 1: No Poverty: Eradicate extreme poverty everywhere.
GOAL 2: End Hunger: End hunger and ensure food access for all people.
GOAL 3: Health and Well-being: Lower the rate of global maternal mortality.
GOAL 4: Quality Education: Ensure all children have access to free, quality primary and secondary education.
GOAL 5: Gender Equality: End all forms of discrimination against all women and girls everywhere.
GOAL 6: Safe, Clean Water: Ensure availability and sustainable management of water and sanitation for all.
GOAL 7: Clean Energy: Ensure access to affordable, reliable, sustainable, and modern energy for all.
GOAL 8: Economic Growth: Promote sustained, inclusive, and sustainable economic growth, full and productive employment, and decent work for all.
GOAL 9: Industry Infrastructure: Build resilient infrastructures, promote inclusive and sustainable industrialization, ensuring affordable and equitable access for all.
GOAL 10: Reduced Inequality: Reduce inequality within and among countries.
GOAL 11: Sustainable Communities: Make cities and human settlements inclusive, safe, resilient, and sustainable.
GOAL 12: Sustainable Consumption and Production: Ensure sustainable consumption and production patterns.
GOAL 13: Climate Action: Take urgent action to combat climate change and its impacts.
GOAL 14: Conserve our oceans and marine life: Conserve and sustainably use the oceans, seas, and marine resources for sustainable development.
GOAL 15: Life on Land: Protect, restore, and promote the sustainable use of terrestrial ecosystems, sustainably manage forests, combat desertification, and halt and reverse land degradation and halt biodiversity loss.
GOAL 16: Peace, Justice, and Strong Institutions: Promote peaceful and inclusive societies for sustainable development, provide access to justice for all and build effective, accountable, and inclusive institutions at all levels.
GOAL 17: Achieve the Goals through Partnership: Strengthen the means of implementation and revitalize the Global Partnership for Sustainable Development.[1]

section 5.1 | MIS Infrastructures

LEARNING OUTCOMES

5.1 Explain MIS infrastructure and its three primary types.

5.2 Identify the three primary areas associated with an information MIS infrastructure.

5.3 Describe the characteristics of an agile MIS infrastructure.

LO 5.1: Explain MIS infrastructure and its three primary types.

THE BUSINESS BENEFITS OF A SOLID MIS INFRASTRUCTURE

Management information systems have played a significant role in business strategies, affected business decisions and processes, and even changed the way companies operate. What is the foundation supporting all of these systems that enables business growth, operations, and profits? What supports the volume and complexity of today's user and application requirements? What protects systems from failures and crashes?

- It is the ***MIS infrastructure,*** which includes the plans for how a firm will build, deploy, use, and share its data, processes, and MIS assets.

A solid MIS infrastructure can reduce costs, improve productivity, optimize business operations, generate growth, and increase profitability.

- ***Hardware***: Consists of the physical devices associated with a computer system.
- ***Software***: The set of instructions the hardware executes to carry out specific tasks.
- ***Network***: A communications system created by linking two or more devices and establishing a standard methodology in which they can communicate.
- ***Client***: A computer designed to request information from a server.
- ***Server***: A computer dedicated to providing information in response to requests.

As more companies need to share more information, the network takes on greater importance in the infrastructure. Most companies use a specific form of network infrastructure called a client and server network. A good way to understand this is when someone uses a web browser (the client) to access a website (a server that would respond with the web page being requested by the client). Anyone not familiar with the basics of hardware, software, or networks should review Appendix A, "Hardware and Software Basics," and Appendix B, "Networks and Telecommunications," for more information.

In the physical world, a detailed blueprint would show how public utilities, such as water, electricity, and gas, support the foundation of a building. MIS infrastructure is similar because it shows in detail how the hardware, software, and network connectivity support the firm's processes. Every company, regardless of size, relies on some form of MIS infrastructure, whether it is a few networked personal computers sharing an Excel file or a large multinational company with thousands of employees interconnected around the world.

An MIS infrastructure is dynamic and agile; it continually changes as business needs change. Each time a new form of Internet-enabled device, such as IoT devices, is created and made available to the public, a firm's MIS infrastructure must be revised to support the device. This moves beyond just innovations in hardware to include new types of software and network connectivity.

- ***Enterprise architect***: A person grounded in technology, fluent in business, and able to provide the important bridge between MIS and the business.

Firms employ enterprise architects to help manage change and dynamically update MIS infrastructure. Figure 5.2 displays the three primary areas on which enterprise architects focus when maintaining a firm's MIS infrastructure.

- **Supporting operations:** ***Information MIS infrastructure*** identifies where and how important information, such as customer records, is maintained and secured.

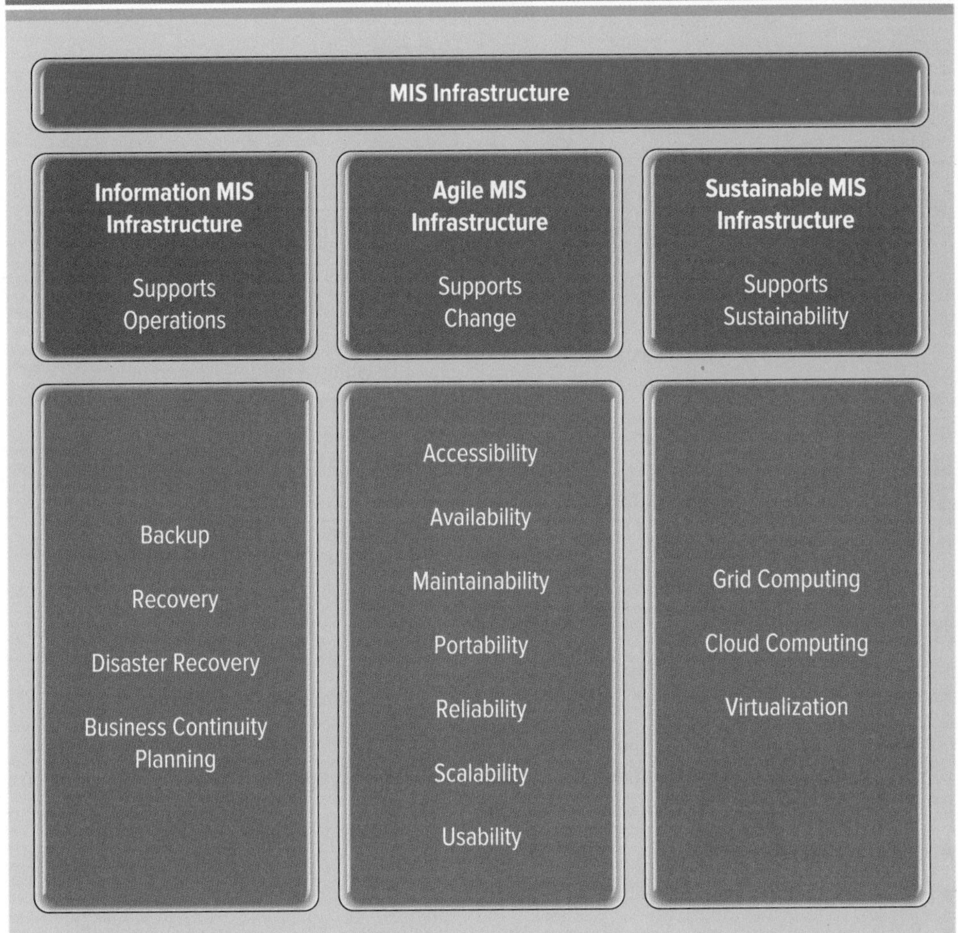

FIGURE 5.2

MIS Infrastructures

- **Supporting change:** ***Agile MIS infrastructure*** includes the hardware, software, and telecommunications equipment that, when combined, provides the underlying foundation to support the organization's goals.
- **Supporting the environment:** ***Sustainable MIS infrastructure*** identifies ways that a company can grow in terms of computing resources while simultaneously becoming less dependent on hardware and energy consumption.

SUPPORTING OPERATIONS: INFORMATION MIS INFRASTRUCTURE

LO 5.2: Identify the three primary areas associated with an information MIS infrastructure.

Imagine taking a quick trip to the printer on the other side of the room, and when you turn around, you find that your laptop has been stolen. How painful would you find this experience? What types of information would you lose? How much time would it take you to recover all of that information? A few things you might lose include music, movies, emails, photos, assignments, saved passwords, not to mention that all-important 40-page paper that took you more than a month to complete. If this sounds painful, then you want to pay particular attention to this section and learn how to eliminate this pain.

An information MIS infrastructure identifies where and how important information is maintained and secured. An information infrastructure supports day-to-day business operations and plans for emergencies such as power outages, floods, earthquakes, malicious attacks via the Internet, theft, and security breaches to name just a few. Managers must take every precaution to make sure their systems are operational and protected around the clock every day of the year. Losing a laptop or experiencing bad weather in one part of the country simply cannot take down systems required to operate core business processes. In the past, someone stealing company information would have to carry out boxes upon boxes of paper. Today, as data storage technologies grow in capabilities while shrinking in size, a person can simply walk out the front door of the building with the company's data files stored on a thumb drive or external hard drive. Today's managers must act responsibly to protect one of their most valued assets,

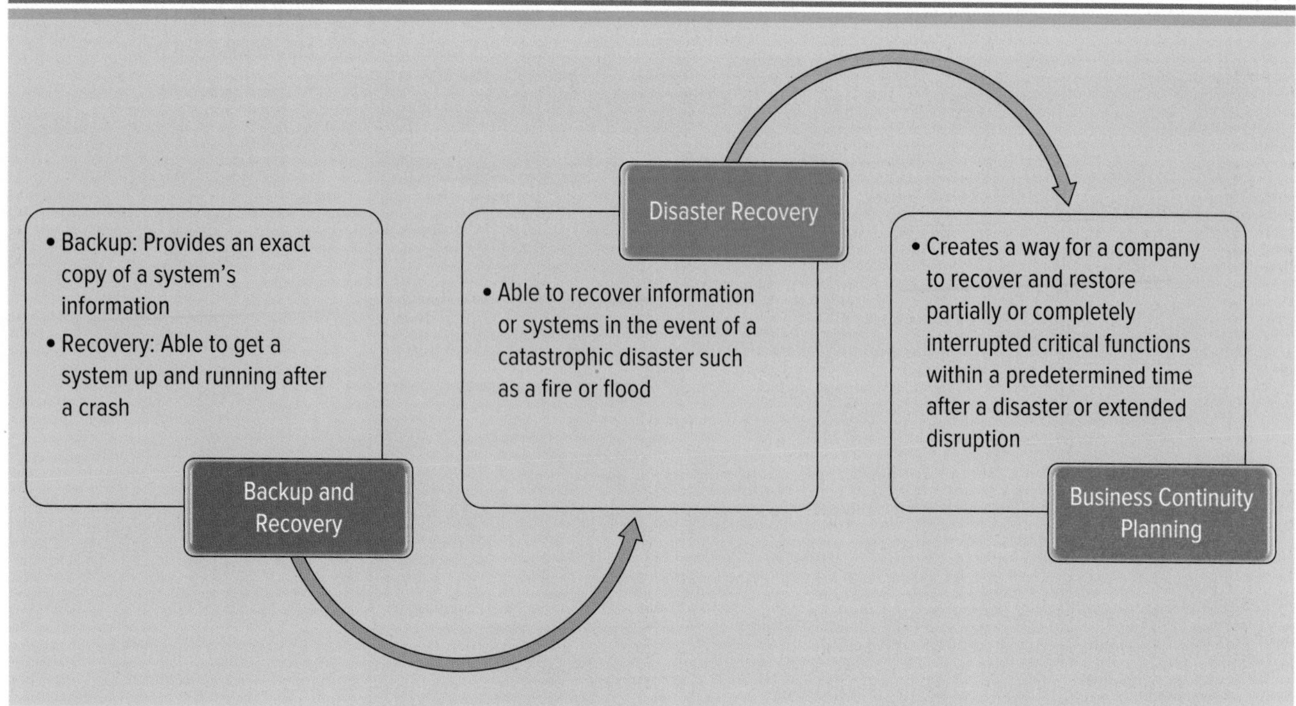

FIGURE 5.3

Areas of Support Provided by Information Infrastructure

information. To support continuous business operations, an information infrastructure provides three primary elements:

- Backup and recovery plan
- Disaster recovery plan
- Business continuity plan (see Figure 5.3)

Backup and Recovery Plan

Each year businesses lose time and money because of system crashes and failures. One way to minimize the damage of a system crash is to have a backup and recovery strategy in place.

- ***Backup***: An exact copy of a system's information.
- ***Recovery***: The ability to get a system up and running in the event of a system crash or failure that includes restoring the information backup.

Many types of backup and recovery media are available, including maintaining an identical replica or redundant copy of the storage server, external hard drives, thumb drives, and backup to the cloud. The primary differences between them are speed and cost.

Fault tolerance is the ability for a system to respond to unexpected failures or system crashes as the backup system immediately and automatically takes over with no loss of service. For example, fault tolerance enables a business to support continuous business operations if there is a power failure or flood. Fault tolerance is an expensive form of backup, and only mission-critical applications and operations use it.

- ***Failover,*** a specific type of fault tolerance, occurs when a redundant storage server offers an exact replica of the real-time data, and if the primary server crashes, the users are automatically directed to the secondary server or backup server. This is a high-speed and high-cost method of backup and recovery.
- ***Failback*** occurs when the primary machine recovers and resumes operations, taking over from the secondary server.

Using external hard drives, thumb drives, or the cloud to store your data offers a low-speed and low-cost backup method. It is a good business practice to back up data at least once a week using a low-cost method. This will alleviate the pain of having your laptop stolen or your system crash because you will still have access to your data, and it will only be a few days old.

APPLY YOUR KNOWLEDGE

BUSINESS DRIVEN START-UP

Turning Carbon Emissions into Power

LanzaTech, a Chicago-based company, discovered a way to make ethanol from the carbon waste emissions secreted by factories—the exhaust you can see billowing out of their smokestacks. Bacteria found in the gut of a rabbit can now help cars run in a more eco-friendly way. The method uses the rabbit-gut bacteria to ferment the waste gas from factories, which then generates ethanol. So gas fermentation to produce ethanol can not only help solve the land issue, according to LanzaTech, it also tackles another problem: pollution.

The process is similar to making beer, except that instead of converting sugar to ethanol, it converts pollution to ethanol. The process reduces waste gas emissions at the same time, preventing these from becoming pollution. The resulting ethanol can currently be mixed with gasoline for use in cars and eventually with airplane fuel.

LanzaTech estimates that if its bioreactors were in place at the world's largest steelworks—accounting for roughly 65 percent of all production—it would be the equivalent of taking 55 million cars off the road.[2]

How does LanzaTech help companies such as Virgin Atlantic and United Airlines create a backup plan for fossil fuels? What other industries besides automobile manufacturers and airlines can benefit from this type of technology?

Deciding how often to back up information and what media to use is a critical decision. Companies should choose a backup and recovery strategy in line with their goals and operational needs. If the company deals with large volumes of critical information, it will require daily, perhaps hourly, backups to storage servers. If it relies on small amounts of noncritical information, then it might require only weekly backups to external hard drives, thumb drives, or the cloud. A company that backs up on a weekly basis is taking the risk that, if a system crash occurs, it could lose a week's worth of work. If this risk is acceptable, a weekly backup strategy will work. If it is unacceptable, the company needs more frequent backup.

Disaster Recovery Plan

Disasters such as power outages, fires, floods, and hurricanes, and even malicious activities such as hackers and viruses, strike companies every day. Disasters can have the following effects on companies and their business operations.

- **Disrupting communications:** Most companies depend on voice and data communications for daily operational needs. Widespread communications outages, from either direct damage to the infrastructure or sudden spikes in usage related to an outside disaster, can be as devastating to some firms as shutting down the whole business.
- **Damaging physical infrastructures:** Fire and flood can directly damage buildings, equipment, and systems, making structures unsafe and systems unusable. Law enforcement officers and firefighters may prohibit business professionals from entering a building, thereby restricting access to retrieve documents or equipment.
- **Halting transportation:** Disasters such as floods and hurricanes can have a deep effect on transportation. Disruption to major highways, roads, bridges, railroads, and airports can prevent business professionals from reporting to work or going home, slow the delivery of supplies, and stop the shipment of products.
- **Blocking utilities:** Public utilities, such as the supply of electric power, water, and natural gas, can be interrupted for hours or days even in incidents that cause no direct damage to the physical infrastructure. Buildings are often uninhabitable and systems unable to function without public utilities.

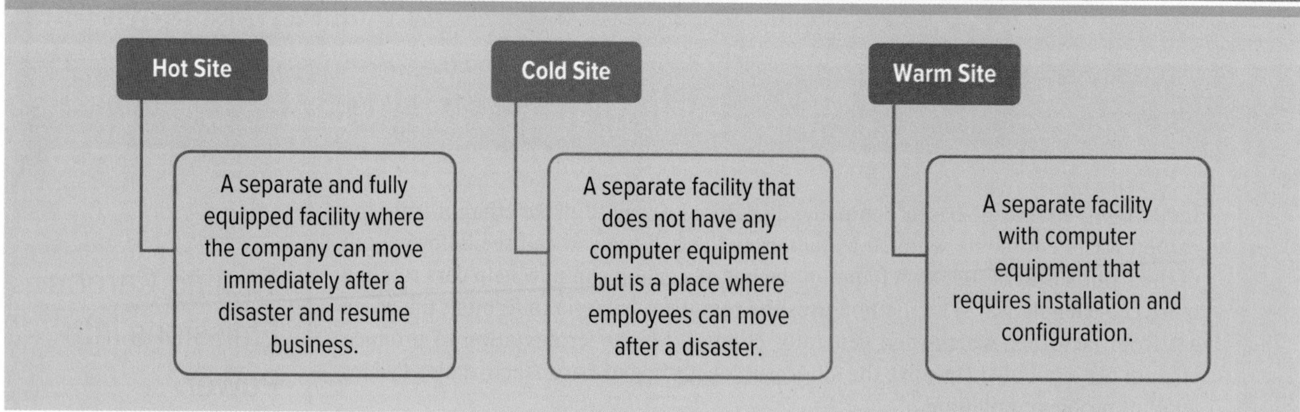

FIGURE 5.4

Sites to Support Disaster Recovery

These effects can devastate companies by causing them to cease operations for hours, days, or longer and risk losing customers whom they cannot then supply. Therefore, to combat these disasters, a company can create a disaster recovery plan.

- ***Disaster recovery plan*:** A detailed process for recovering information or a system in the event of a catastrophic disaster.

This plan includes such factors as which files and systems need to have backups and their corresponding frequency and methods along with the strategic location of the storage in a separate physical site that is geographically dispersed. A company might strategically maintain operations in New York and San Francisco, ensuring that a natural disaster would not have an impact on both locations. A disaster recovery plan also foresees the possibility that not only the computer equipment but also the building where employees work may be destroyed.

- ***Hot site*:** A separate and fully equipped facility where the company can move immediately after a disaster and resume business.
- ***Cold site*:** A separate facility that does not have any computer equipment but is a place where employees can move after a disaster.
- ***Warm site*:** A separate facility with computer equipment that requires installation and configuration. Figure 5.4 outlines these resources that support disaster recovery.

A disaster recovery plan usually has a disaster recovery cost curve to support it.

- ***Disaster recovery cost curve*:** Charts (1) the cost to the company of the unavailability of information and technology and (2) the cost to the company of recovering from a disaster over time.

Figure 5.5 displays a disaster recovery cost curve and shows that the best recovery plan in terms of cost and time is where the two lines intersect. Creating such a curve is no small task.

FIGURE 5.5

Disaster Recovery Cost Curve

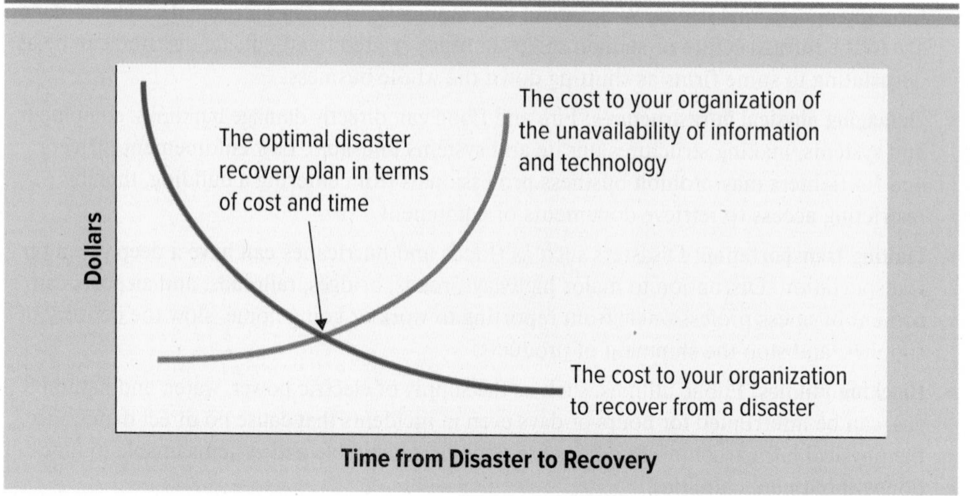

Disaster Recovery Strategies	
1. Activate backup and recovery facilities in secondary company data center; transfer production to that site.	Assumes the secondary data center has sufficient resources, e.g., storage capacity, server hardware to accommodate additional processing requirements.
2. Activate recovery resources in a cloud-based service; failover critical systems to that site and resume operations.	Ensure that your contract for this service has the ability to flex as your needs dictate; ensure that security of your data can be maintained.
3. Activate backup systems and data at a hot site; transfer operations to that site.	Be sure you know what resources you have available at the hot site, what the declaration rules and fees are, and what your options are if multiple declarations are occurring at the same time.
4. Replace damaged equipment with spare components.	As much as possible, have available spare systems,- circuit boards, and power supplies; backup disks with system software; and hard and soft copies of critical documentation.
5. Recover virtual machines at an alternate site; assumes VMs have been updated to be current with production VMs.	Create VM clones at an alternate site and keep them updated, and if needed, they can quickly become production VMs.
6. Activate alternate network routes and re-route data and voice traffic away from the failed network service.	Ensure that network infrastructures have diverse routing of local access channels, as well as diverse routing of high-capacity circuits.[3]

FIGURE 5.6

TechTarget's Disaster Recovery Strategies

Managers must consider the cost of losing information and technology within each department or functional area and across the whole company. During the first few hours of a disaster, those costs may be low, but they rise over time. With those costs in hand, a company must then determine the costs of recovery. Figure 5.6 displays TechTarget's disaster recovery strategies for business.

On April 18, 1906, San Francisco was rocked by an earthquake that destroyed large sections of the city and claimed the lives of more than 3,000 inhabitants. More than a century later, a rebuilt and more durable San Francisco serves as a central location for major MIS corporations, as well as a major world financial center. Managers of these corporations are well aware of the potential disasters that exist along the San Andreas Fault and actively update their business continuity plans anticipating such issues as earthquakes and floods. The Union Bank of California is located in the heart of downtown San Francisco and maintains a highly detailed and well-developed business continuity plan. The company employs hundreds of business professionals scattered around the world who coordinate plans for addressing the potential loss of a facility, business professionals, or critical systems so that the company can continue to operate if a disaster happens. Its disaster recovery plan includes hot sites where staff can walk in and start working exactly as if they were in their normal location. It would be a matter of minutes, not hours, for the Union Bank of California to be up and running again in the event of a disaster.[4]

Business Continuity Plan

Natural disasters and terrorist attacks are on the minds of business professionals who take safeguarding their information assets seriously.

- ***Emergency***: A sudden, unexpected event requiring immediate action due to potential threats to health and safety, the environment, or property.
- ***Emergency preparedness***: Ensures that a company is ready to respond to an emergency in an organized, timely, and effective manner.

Disaster recovery plans typically focus on systems and data, ignoring cross-functional and intraorganizational business processes that can be destroyed during an emergency. For this reason, many companies are turning to a more comprehensive and all-encompassing emergency preparedness plan known as business continuity planning.

FIGURE 5.7

TechTarget's Business Continuity Strategies

Business Continuity Strategies	
1. Evacuate existing building and relocate to a prearranged alternate work area.	Assumes the alternate site is ready for occupancy, or can be made ready quickly, based on recovery time objectives; ensure that transportation is available.
2. Work from home.	Ensure that staff have broadband and Internet access at home; ensure that there are sufficient network access points to accommodate the increase in usage.
3. Move selected staff to a hot site.	Assumes a hot site program is in place and that space is available at the site for staff.
4. Move alternate staff into leadership roles in the absence of key leaders; ensure that they have been cross-trained.	Succession planning is a key strategy in business continuity; it ensures that loss of a senior manager or someone with special expertise can be replaced with minimal disruption to the business.
5. Move staff into local or nearby hotels and set up temporary work space.	Make sure this kind of arrangement is set up with hotels in advance, especially in case of an incident that disrupts many other businesses in the same area.
6. Relocate staff to another company office.	Organizations with multiple offices that have access to the company network, as well as work space, can be leveraged to temporarily house employees.[5]

- ***Business continuity planning (BCP)***: Details how a company recovers and restores critical business operations and systems after a disaster or extended disruption.

BCP includes such factors as identifying critical systems, business processes, departments, and the maximum amount of time the business can continue to operate without functioning systems (see Figure 5.7). BCP contains disaster recovery plans along with many additional plans, including prioritizing business impact analysis, emergency notification plans, and technology recovery strategies.

Business Impact Analysis A ***business impact analysis*** identifies all critical business functions and the effect that a specific disaster may have on them. A business impact analysis is primarily used to ensure that a company has made the right decisions about the order of recovery priorities and strategies. For example, should the accounting department have its systems up and running before the sales and marketing departments? Will email be the first system for recovery to ensure that employees can communicate with each other and outside stakeholders such as customers, suppliers, and partners? The business impact analysis is a key part of BCP because it details the order in which functional areas should be restored, ensuring that the most critical are focused on first.

Emergency Notification Services A business continuity plan typically includes an ***emergency notification service,*** that is, an infrastructure built for notifying people in the event of an emergency. Radio stations' occasional tests of the national Emergency Alert System are an example of a very large-scale emergency notification system. A firm will implement an emergency notification service to warn employees of unexpected events and provide them with instructions about how to handle the situation. Emergency notification services can be deployed through the firm's own infrastructure, supplied by an outside service provider on company premises, or hosted remotely by an outside service provider. All three methods provide notification using a variety of methods such as email, voice notification to a cell phone, and text messaging. The notifications can be sent to all the devices selected, providing multiple means in which to get critical information to those who need it.

Technology Recovery Strategies Companies create massive amounts of data vital to their survival and continued operations. A ***technology failure*** occurs when the ability of a company to operate is impaired because of a hardware, software, or data outage. Technology failures can destroy large amounts of vital data, often causing ***incidents,*** unplanned interruptions of a service.

- ***Incident record***: Contains all of the details of an incident.

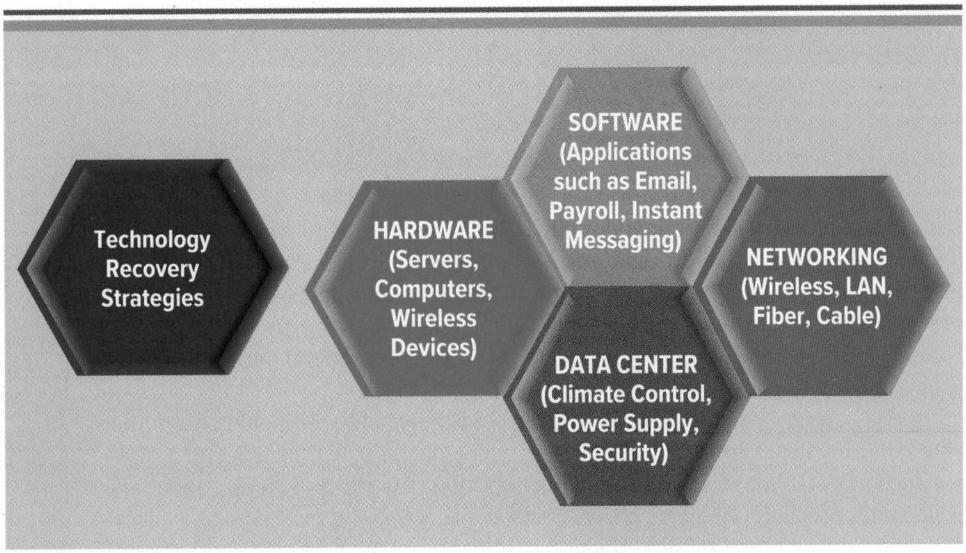

FIGURE 5.8

Key Areas of Technology Recovery Strategies

- ***Incident management***: The process responsible for managing how incidents are identified and corrected.
- ***Technology recovery strategies***: Focus specifically on prioritizing the order for restoring hardware, software, and data across the organization that best meets business recovery requirements.

A technology recovery strategy details the order of importance for recovering hardware, software, data centers, and networking (or connectivity). If one of these four vital components is not functioning, the entire system will be unavailable, shutting down cross-functional business processes such as order management and payroll. Figure 5.8 displays the key areas a company should focus on when developing technology recovery strategies.

SUPPORTING CHANGE: AGILE MIS INFRASTRUCTURE

LO 5.3: Describe the characteristics of an agile MIS infrastructure.

Agile MIS infrastructure includes the hardware, software, and telecommunications equipment that, when combined, provides the underlying foundation to support the organization's goals. If a company grows by 50 percent in a single year, its infrastructure and systems must be able to handle a 50 percent growth rate. If they cannot, they can severely hinder the company's ability not only to grow but also to function.

The future of a company depends on its ability to meet its partners, suppliers, and customers any time of the day in any geographic location. Imagine owning an ebusiness and everyone on the Internet is tweeting and collaborating about how great your business idea is and how successful your company is going to be. Suddenly, you have 5 million global customers interested in your website. Unfortunately, you did not anticipate this many customers so quickly, and the system crashes. Users typing in your URL find a blank message stating the website is unavailable and to try back soon. Or even worse, they can get to your website, but it takes three minutes to reload each time they click a button. The buzz soon dies about your business idea as some innovative web-savvy fast follower quickly copies your idea and creates a website that can handle the massive number of customers. The characteristics of agile MIS infrastructures can help ensure that your systems can meet and perform under any unexpected or unplanned changes. Figure 5.9 lists the seven abilities of an agile infrastructure.

Accessibility

Imagine the people at your college accessing the main student information system. Each person who accesses the system will have different needs and requirements; for example, a payroll employee will need to access vacation information and salary information, or a student will need to access course information and billing information.

- ***Accessibility***: Refers to the varying levels that define what a user can access, view, or perform when operating a system.

APPLY YOUR KNOWLEDGE

BUSINESS DRIVEN MIS

Disaster Recovery

Backup and recovery are essential for any computer system. How painful would it be if someone stole your laptop right now? How much critical information would you lose? How many hours would it take you to re-create your data? Perhaps that will motivate you to implement a backup procedure. How many of you have a disaster recovery plan? Disaster recovery is needed when your best friend dumps a latte on your computer or you accidentally wash your thumb drive.

Disaster recovery plans are crucial for any business, and you should ensure that your company has everything it needs to continue operations if there is ever a disaster, such as 9/11. You need to decide which disasters are worth worrying about and which ones probably will never occur. For example, if you live in Colorado, chances are good you don't have to worry about hurricanes, but avalanches are another story.

How often does a company need to back up its data? Where should the backup be stored? What types of disasters should companies in your state prepare for? Why is it important to test the backup? What could happen to a company if it failed to create a disaster recovery plan? Do you have a backup of your computer? If not, what could happen if your computer were stolen right now?

FIGURE 5.9

Agile MIS Infrastructure Characteristics

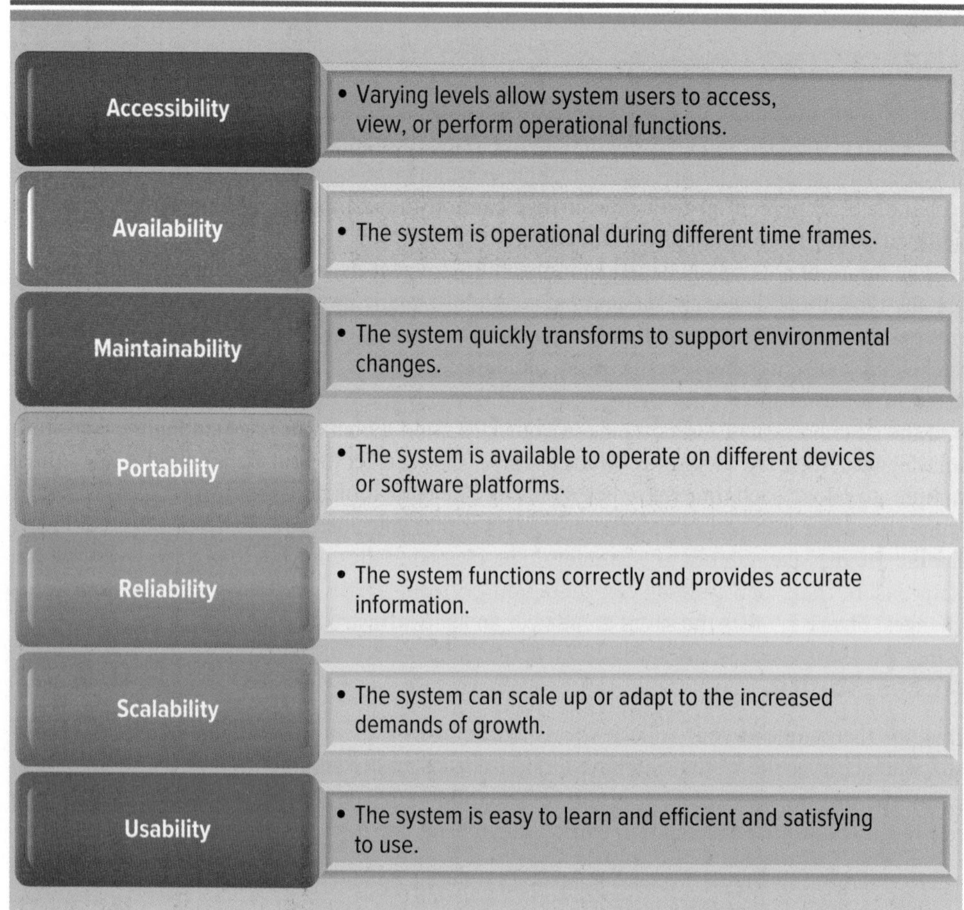

Accessibility
• Varying levels allow system users to access, view, or perform operational functions.
Availability
• The system is operational during different time frames.
Maintainability
• The system quickly transforms to support environmental changes.
Portability
• The system is available to operate on different devices or software platforms.
Reliability
• The system functions correctly and provides accurate information.
Scalability
• The system can scale up or adapt to the increased demands of growth.
Usability
• The system is easy to learn and efficient and satisfying to use.

Each system user is provided with an access level that details which parts of the system the user can and cannot access and what the user can do when in the system. For example, you would not want your students to be able to view payroll information or a professor's personal information; also, some users can only view information and are not allowed to create or delete information. Top-level MIS employees require ***administrator access,*** or unrestricted access to the entire system. Administrator access can perform functions such as resetting passwords, deleting accounts, and shutting down entire systems.

Tim Berners-Lee, W3C director and inventor of the World Wide Web, stated, "The power of the web is in its universality. Access by everyone regardless of disability is an essential aspect."

- ***Web accessibility*:** Means that people with disabilities can use the web.
- ***Web accessibility initiative (WAI)*:** Brings together people from industry, disability organizations, government, and research labs from around the world to develop guidelines and resources to help make the web accessible to people with disabilities, including auditory, cognitive, neurological, physical, speech, and visual disabilities.

The goal of WAI is to allow people to access the full potential of the web, enabling people with disabilities to participate equally. For example, Apple includes screen magnification and VoiceOver on its iPhone, iPad, and iPod, which allows the blind and visually impaired to use the devices.

Availability

In a 24/7/365 ebusiness environment, business professionals need to use their systems whenever they want from wherever they want.

- ***Availability*:** Refers to the time frames when the system is operational.
- ***Unavailable*:** When it is not operating and cannot be used.
- ***High availability*:** When a system is continuously operational at all times.

Availability is typically measured relative to "100 percent operational" or "never failing." A widely held but difficult-to-achieve standard of availability for a system is known as "five 9s" (99.999 percent) availability. Some companies have systems available around the clock to support ebusiness operations, global customers, and online suppliers.

Sometimes systems must be taken down for maintenance, upgrades, and fixes, which are completed during downtime. One challenge with availability is determining when to schedule system downtime if the system is expected to operate continuously. Performing maintenance during the evening might seem like a great idea, but evening in one city is morning somewhere else in the world, and business professionals scattered around the globe may not be able to perform specific job functions if the systems they need are unavailable. This is where companies deploy failover systems so they can take the primary system down for maintenance and activate the secondary system to ensure continuous operations.

Maintainability

Companies must watch today's needs, as well as tomorrow's, when designing and building systems that support agile infrastructures. Systems must be flexible enough to meet all types of company changes, environmental changes, and business changes.

- ***Maintainability (or flexibility)*:** Refers to how quickly a system can transform to support environmental changes.

Maintainability helps to measure how quickly and effectively a system can be changed or repaired after a failure. For example, when starting a small business, you might not consider that you will have global customers, a common mistake. When building your systems, you might not design them to handle multiple currencies and different languages, which might make sense if the company is not currently performing international business. Unfortunately, when the first international order arrives, which happens easily with ebusiness, the system will be unable to handle the request because it does not have the flexibility to be easily reconfigured for a new language or currency. When the company does start growing and operating overseas, the system will need to be redeveloped, which is not an easy or cheap task, to handle multiple currencies and different languages.

Building and deploying flexible systems allow easy updates, changes, and reconfigurations for unexpected business or environmental changes. Just think what might have happened if Facebook had to overhaul its entire system to handle multiple languages. Another social networking business could easily have stepped in and become the provider of choice. That certainly would not be efficient or effective for business operations.

Portability

Apple's iTunes is readily available to users of Mac computers and PC computers, smart phones, iPods, iPhones, iPads, and so on. It is also a portable application. Because Apple insists on compatibility across its products, both software and hardware, Apple can easily add to its product, device, and service offerings without sacrificing portability.

- ***Portability***: Refers to the ability of an application to operate on different devices or software platforms, such as different operating systems.

Many software developers are creating programs that are portable to all three devices–the iPhone, iPod, and iPad–which increases their target market and, they hope, their revenue.

Reliability

Inaccuracy can occur for many reasons, from the incorrect entry of information to the corruption of information during transmissions. Many argue that the information contained in Wikipedia is unreliable. Because the Wikipedia entries can be edited by any user, there are examples of rogue users inaccurately updating information.

- ***Reliability (or accuracy)***: Ensures that a system is functioning correctly and providing accurate information.

Many users skip over Google search findings that correlate to Wikipedia for this reason. Housing unreliable information on a website can put a company at risk of losing customers, placing inaccurate supplier orders, or even making unreliable business decisions.

- ***Vulnerability***: A system weakness, such as a password that is never changed or a system left on while an employee goes to lunch, that can be exploited by a threat. Reliable systems ensure that vulnerabilities are kept at a minimum to reduce risk.

Scalability

Estimating company growth is a challenging task, in part because growth can occur in a number of forms–the firm can acquire new customers, new product lines, or new markets.

- ***Scalability***: Describes how well a system can scale up, or adapt to the increased demands of growth.

If a company grows faster than anticipated, it might experience a variety of problems, from running out of storage space to taking more time to complete transactions. Anticipating expected and unexpected growth is key to building scalable systems that can support that development.

- ***Performance***: Measures how quickly a system performs a process or transaction.

Performance is a key component of scalability because systems that can't scale suffer from performance issues. Just imagine your college's content management system suddenly taking five minutes to return a page after a button is pushed. Now imagine if this occurs during your midterm exam and you miss the two-hour deadline because the system is so slow. Performance issues experienced by firms can have disastrous business impacts causing loss of customers, loss of suppliers, and even loss of help-desk employees. Most users will wait only a few seconds for a website to return a request before growing frustrated and either calling the support desk or giving up and moving on to another website.

- ***Capacity***: Represents the maximum throughput a system can deliver; for example, the capacity of a hard drive represents its size or volume.
- ***Capacity planning***: Determines future environmental infrastructure requirements to ensure high-quality system performance.

BUSINESS DRIVEN ANALYTICS

Ranking the Ab-"ilities"

Do you know how Google makes so much money? Unlike traditional businesses, Google does not make money from the users of its service. Google makes money by charging the companies that want to appear in the sponsored section of a search result. After performing a Google search, you will notice three sections on the resulting page. Along the top and side are the sponsored search results, and the middle lists the organic search results. Google's innovative marketing program, called AdWords, allows companies to bid on common search terms, and the highest bidder is posted first in the sponsored search results. Every time a user clicks a sponsored link, the company that owns the link has to pay Google. This is also called pay-per-click and can cost anywhere from a few cents to a few dollars for each click. A general search term such as "tropical vacation" costs less than a more specific search term such as "Hawaiian vacation." Whichever company bids the most for the search term appears at the top of the sponsored section. Clicking the links in the organic search results does not incur any charges for the company that owns the link.

Rank the agile infrastructure ab-"ilities" for Google from most important to least important in terms of supporting Google's MIS infrastructure and business operations. Then rank the agile infrastructure ab-"ilities" for Amazon from most important to least important in terms of supporting Amazon's MIS infrastructure and business operations. Finally, rank the agile infrastructure ab-"ilities" for your course content software such as Blackboard or Canvas. Be sure to provide the justification for your ranking.

If a company purchases connectivity software that is outdated or too slow to meet demand, its employees will waste a great deal of time waiting for systems to respond to user requests. It is cheaper for a company to design and implement agile infrastructure that envisions growth requirements than to update all the equipment after the system is already operational. If a company with 100 workers merges with another company and suddenly 400 people are using the system, performance time could suffer. Planning for increases in capacity can ensure that systems perform as expected. Waiting for a system to respond to requests is not productive.

Web 2.0 is a big driver for capacity planning to ensure that agile infrastructures can meet the business's operational needs. Delivering videos over the Internet requires enough bandwidth to satisfy millions of users during peak periods such as Friday and Saturday evenings. Video transmissions over the Internet cannot tolerate packet loss (blocks of data loss), and allowing one additional user to access the system could degrade the video quality for every user.

Usability

No matter how well an application is built, if users have a hard time knowing how to navigate or use the application, it simply will not sell.

- ***Usability***: The degree to which a system is efficient, easy to learn, and satisfying to use.

Providing hints, tips, shortcuts, and instructions for any system, regardless of its ease of use, is recommended. Apple understood the importance of usability when it designed the first iPod. One of the iPod's initial attractions was the usability of the click wheel. One simple and efficient button operates the iPod, making it usable for all ages. And to ensure ease of use, Apple also made the corresponding iTunes software intuitive and easy to use.

- ***Serviceability***: How quickly a third party can change a system to ensure it meets user needs and the terms of any contracts, including agreed-to levels of reliability, maintainability, or availability.

APPLY YOUR KNOWLEDGE

BUSINESS DRIVEN DEBATE

Who Can Fix My iPhone?

The proposed Right to Repair laws (known as the Fair Repair Act in some states) are designed to make it easier for people to repair their broken electronic equipment, such as cell phones, computers, appliances, cameras, and even tractors. The legislation would require manufacturers to release repair information to the public and sell spare parts to owners and independent repair shops. If passed, the laws would give consumers more options than just the manufacturer for repair.

One in 10 iPhones purchased in the United States is refurbished. Refurbished equipment is typically returned to a manufacturer or vendor for various reasons and repackaged and sold as used but certified new. Back Market, a Paris-based used electronics marketplace, has over 250 fix-it shops and uses machine learning to predict demand. Back Market earned over $100 million last year. Of course, big tech companies, including Apple and John Deere, are fighting the Right to Repair laws, making it harder for smart phone owners and farmers to fix their own products. Do you agree or disagree with the Right to Repair laws, given the ownership of the intellectual property of the devices?

When using a system from a third party, it is important to ensure the right level of serviceability for all users, including remote employees.

section 5.2 | Building Sustainable MIS Infrastructures

LEARNING OUTCOMES

5.4 Identify the environmental impacts associated with MIS.

5.5 Explain the three components of a sustainable MIS infrastructure along with their business benefits.

LO 5.4: Identify the environmental impacts associated with MIS.

MIS AND THE ENVIRONMENT

The general trend in MIS is toward smaller, faster, and cheaper devices. Gordon Moore, cofounder of Intel, the world's largest producer of computer chips or microprocessors, observed in 1965 that continued advances in technological innovation made it possible to reduce the size of a computer chip (the brains of a computer, or even a cell phone now) while doubling its capacity every 2 years. His prediction that this trend would continue has come to be known as Moore's law.

- ***Moore's law***: Refers to the computer chip performance per dollar doubling every 18 months.

Although Moore originally assumed a 2-year period, many sources today refer to the 18-month figure.

Moore's law is great for many companies because they can acquire large amounts of MIS equipment for cheaper and cheaper costs. As ebusinesses continue to grow, companies equip their employees with multiple forms of electronic devices ranging from laptops to smart phones to tablets. This is great for supporting a connected corporation, but significant unintended side effects include our dependence on fossil fuels and increased need for safe disposal of outdated computing equipment. Concern about these side effects has led many companies to turn to an ecological practice known as sustainable MIS.

- ***Sustainable, or green, MIS***: Describes the production, management, use, and disposal of technology in a way that minimizes damage to the environment.

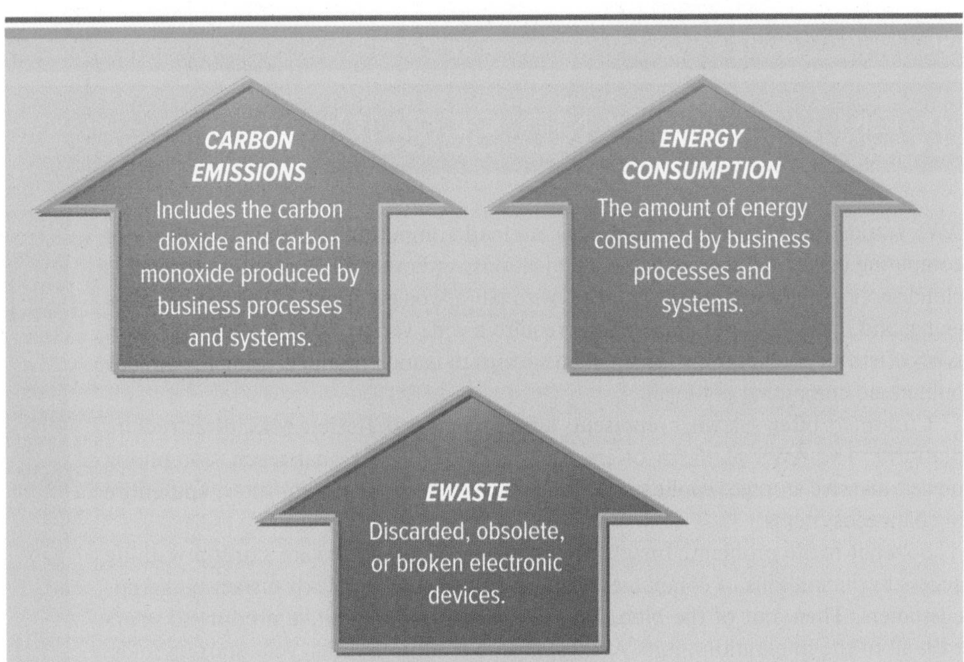

FIGURE 5.10

Three Pressures Driving Sustainable MIS Infrastructures

Sustainable MIS includes the following:

- ***Corporate social responsibility***: Companies' acknowledged responsibility to society.
- ***Clean computing***: Refers to the environmentally responsible use, manufacture, and disposal of technology products and computer equipment. Although sustainable MIS refers to the environmental impact of computing as a whole, clean computing is specifically focused on the production of environmental waste.
- ***Green personal computer (green PC)***: Built using environment-friendly materials and designed to save energy.

Building sustainable MIS infrastructures is a core initiative and critical success factor for socially responsible corporations. Figure 5.10 displays the three primary side effects of businesses' expanded use of technology.

Increased Electronic Waste

The fulfillment of Moore's law has made technological devices smaller, cheaper, and faster, allowing more people from all income levels to purchase computing equipment. This increased demand is causing numerous environmental issues.

- ***Ewaste***: Refers to discarded, obsolete, or broken electronic devices.

Ewaste includes CDs, DVDs, thumb drives, printer cartridges, cell phones, iPods, external hard drives, TVs, VCRs, DVD players, microwaves, and so on. Some say 1 human year is equivalent to 7 years of technological advancements. A personal computer has a life expectancy of only 3 to 5 years, and that of a cell phone is less than 2 years.

- ***Sustainable MIS disposal***: Refers to the safe disposal of MIS assets at the end of their life cycle.
- ***Upcycle***: Reuses or refurbishes ewaste and creates a new product.

It ensures that ewaste does not end up in landfills, causing environmental issues. A single computer contains more than 700 chemicals; some are toxic, such as mercury, lead, and cadmium. If a computer ends up in a landfill, the toxic substances it contains can leach into our land, water, and air. Recycling costs from $15 to $50 for a monitor or computer. Many companies, including public schools and universities, simply can't afford the recycling costs.[7]

Ewaste also occurs when unused equipment stored in attics, basements, and storage facilities never reaches a recycling center. Retrieving the silver, gold, and other valuable metals from these devices is more efficient and less environmentally harmful than removing it from its natural environment.

APPLY YOUR KNOWLEDGE

BUSINESS DRIVEN ETHICS AND SECURITY

The Problem with Amazon

AWS stands for Amazon Web Services, a cloud computing on-demand delivery of computing power, database storage, applications, and other MIS resources through a cloud services platform via the Internet with pay-as-you-go pricing. Developing, managing, and operating your applications require a wide variety of technology services. AWS offers an excellent way for small businesses to launch products using the already built cloud computing platform.

Customers often ask what represents a fully functional, flexible MIS infrastructure platform. The AWS platform offers customers security, global reach, computing power, massive storage, application services, content management tools, and entire big data ecosystems.

So what is the problem? Imagine launching your own software start-up wanting access to the millions of companies that use AWS and you quickly attract numerous customers. Then, out of the blue, Amazon creates a competitive product to yours with all of the integration on its AWS platform. Within months, your start-up folds. Google saw Yelp building a nice business around restaurant reviews and soon created its own listings and privileged them in searches, causing Yelp's stock to decrease by 60 percent.[6]

Starting a business now typically means using one of the big tech companies' MIS infrastructures, such as Amazon, Apple, or Google. All provide start-ups with instant access to vast markets, efficient ads, and cheap and reliable infrastructures. If you were launching a start-up, would you risk one of the tech giants becoming a fast follower and taking over your market? Do you believe it is ethical or unethical for the big tech giants to compete with customers using their MIS infrastructure service? Why or why not?

Currently, less than 20 percent of ewaste in the United States is recycled; however, even recycling does not guarantee that the equipment is disposed of safely. Although some recyclers process the material ethically, others ship it to countries such as China and India, where environmental enforcement is weak. This action poses its own global environmental problems.

Increased Energy Consumption

Huge increases in technology use have greatly amplified energy consumption. The energy consumed by a computer is estimated to produce as much as 10 percent of the amount of carbon dioxide produced by an automobile.

- ***Energy consumption***: The amount of energy consumed by business processes and systems.

Computer servers in the United States account for about 1 percent of the total energy needs of the country. Put in perspective, this is roughly equivalent to the energy consumption of Mississippi.

Computers consume energy even when they are not being used. For convenience and to allow for automatic updates and backup, the majority of computer equipment is never completely shut down. It draws energy 24 hours a day.

Increased Carbon Emissions

The major human-generated greenhouse gases, such as carbon emissions from energy use, are very likely responsible for the increases in climatic temperature over the past half a century. Additional temperature increases are projected over the next 100 years, with serious consequences for Earth's environment, if ***carbon emissions,*** including the carbon dioxide and carbon monoxide produced by business processes and systems, are not reduced.

APPLY YOUR KNOWLEDGE

BUSINESS DRIVEN ANALYTICS

Sustainable Analytics

Companies are facing rapidly changing expectations for improving and reporting sustainability performance and strengthening environmental sustainability initiatives. Applying analytics to sustainability data has many benefits. It helps companies detect opportunities for reducing cost and risk, even when those opportunities are hidden in the massive amounts of big data. It can also reveal which sustainability efforts are most likely to achieve their desired objectives. Applying analytics to sustainability data:

- Examines pressing issues such as climate change, water scarcity, and environmental justice.
- Explains how to develop a business case and global strategy for social responsibility.
- Includes both corporate and public policy perspectives on sustainability economics.
- Covers emerging regulations on sustainability disclosure and responsible investing.

Leading organizations are finding that efficient and effective management of sustainability information requires careful data stewardship and enterprise-strength solutions to support a variety of information needs, including forecasting, performance evaluations, and analysis. At the same time, these companies are discovering that their current applications and MIS infrastructures are often inadequate for gathering and analyzing sustainability data. What types of data would a sustainability analytics program track? Why would current MIS infrastructures have a difficult time supporting sustainability programs? What can a company do to ensure it is tracking, monitoring, and analyzing data from its sustainability programs?

In the United States, coal provides more than 30 percent of electrical power. When left on continuously, a single desktop computer and monitor can consume at least 100 watts of power per hour. To generate that much energy 24 hours a day for a year would require approximately 714 pounds of coal. When that coal is burned, it releases on average 5 pounds of sulfur dioxide, 5 pounds of nitrogen oxides, and 1,852 pounds (that is almost a ton) of carbon dioxide.[8]

SUPPORTING THE ENVIRONMENT: SUSTAINABLE MIS INFRASTRUCTURE

LO 5.5: Explain the three components of a sustainable MIS infrastructure along with their business benefits.

Combating ewaste, energy consumption, and carbon emissions requires a firm to focus on creating sustainable MIS infrastructures. A sustainable MIS infrastructure identifies ways that a company can grow in terms of computing resources while becoming less dependent on hardware and energy consumption. The components of a sustainable MIS infrastructure are displayed in Figure 5.11.

Grid Computing

When a light is turned on, the power grid delivers exactly what is needed, instantly. Computers and networks can now work that way using grid computing.

- ***Grid computing***: A collection of computers, often geographically dispersed, that are coordinated to solve a common problem.

APPLY YOUR KNOWLEDGE

BUSINESS DRIVEN DISCUSSION

How Big Is Your Carbon Footprint?

Inevitably, in going about our daily lives—commuting, sheltering our families, eating—each of us contributes to the greenhouse gas emissions that are causing climate change. Yet there are many things each of us as individuals can do to reduce our carbon emissions. The choices we make in our homes, our travel, the food we eat, and what we buy and throw away all influence our carbon footprint and can help ensure a stable climate for future generations.[9]

The Nature Conservancy's carbon footprint calculator measures your impact on our climate. Its carbon footprint calculator estimates how many tons of carbon dioxide and other greenhouse gases your choices create each year. Visit the Nature Conservancy's carbon footprint calculator to determine your carbon footprint and what you can do to reduce your emissions (http://www.nature.org/greenliving/carboncalculator/).

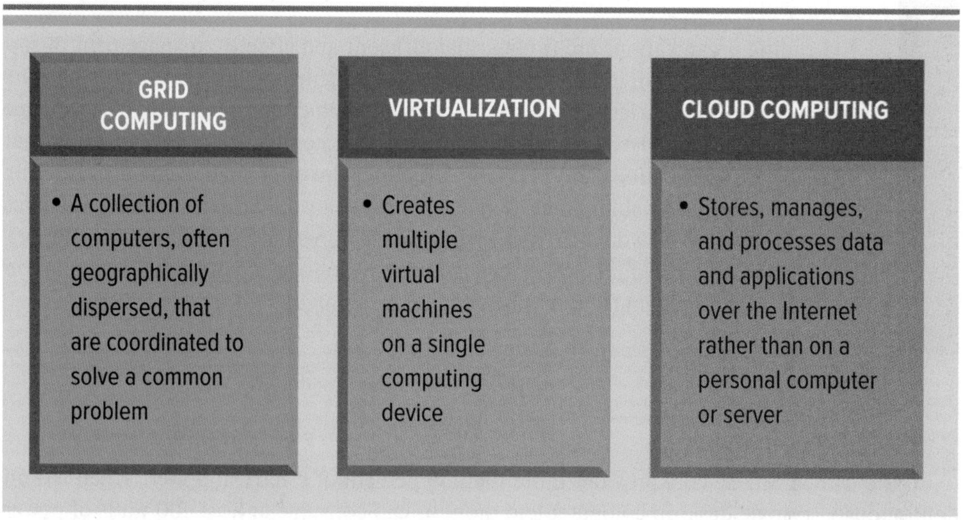

FIGURE 5.11

Sustainable MIS Infrastructure Components

GRID COMPUTING	VIRTUALIZATION	CLOUD COMPUTING
• A collection of computers, often geographically dispersed, that are coordinated to solve a common problem	• Creates multiple virtual machines on a single computing device	• Stores, manages, and processes data and applications over the Internet rather than on a personal computer or server

With grid computing, a problem is broken into pieces and distributed to many machines, allowing faster processing than could occur with a single system (see Figure 5.12). Computers typically use less than 25 percent of their processing power, leaving more than 75 percent available for other tasks. Innovatively, grid computing takes advantage of this unused processing power by linking thousands of individual computers around the world to create a virtual supercomputer that can process intensive tasks. Grid computing makes better use of MIS resources, allowing greater scalability because systems can easily grow to handle peaks and valleys in demand, become more cost efficient, and solve problems that would be impossible to tackle with a single computer (see Figures 5.13 and 5.14).[10]

The uses of grid computing are numerous, including the creative environment of animated movies. DreamWorks Animation used grid computing to complete many of its hit films, including *Antz, Shrek, Madagascar,* and *How to Train Your Dragon.* The third *Shrek* film required more than 20 million computer hours to make (compared to 5 million for the first *Shrek* and 10 million for the second). At peak production times, DreamWorks dedicated more than 4,000 computers to its *Shrek* grid, allowing it to complete scenes in days and hours instead of months. With the increased grid computing power, DreamWorks's animators were able to add more realistic movement to water, fire, and magic scenes. The 3D images were created on graphic

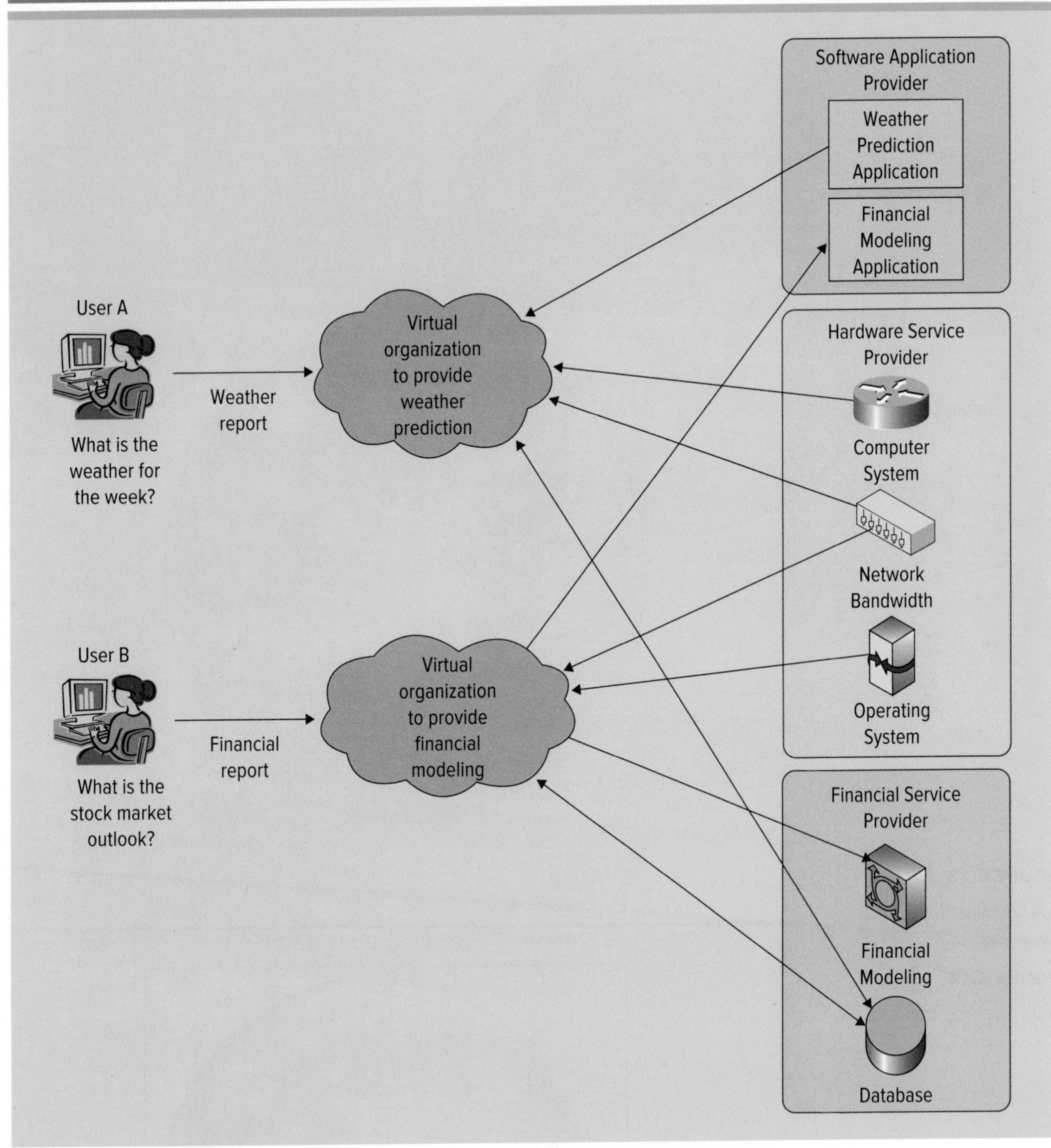

FIGURE 5.12

Virtual Organizations Using Grid Computing

workstations. These images were then divided into small sections and shared out across a cluster of server computers where details were added to each small section. The sections were then brought back together and edited to create the final version. With grid computing, a company can work faster or more efficiently, providing a potential competitive advantage and additional cost savings.[11]

Solving the Energy Issue with Smart Grids A ***smart grid*** delivers electricity using two-way digital technology. It is meant to solve the problem of the world's outdated electrical grid, making it more efficient and reliable by adding the ability to monitor, analyze, and control the transmission of power remotely. The current U.S. power grid is said to have outlived its life expectancy by as much as 30 years. Smart grids provide users with real-time usage monitoring,

Input/Output
Data
Storage
Processing
Applications
Operating System

FIGURE 5.13

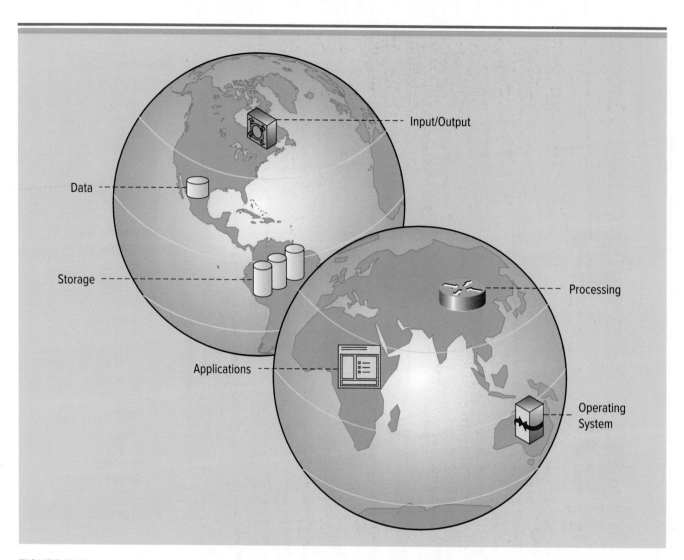

Grid Computer Network

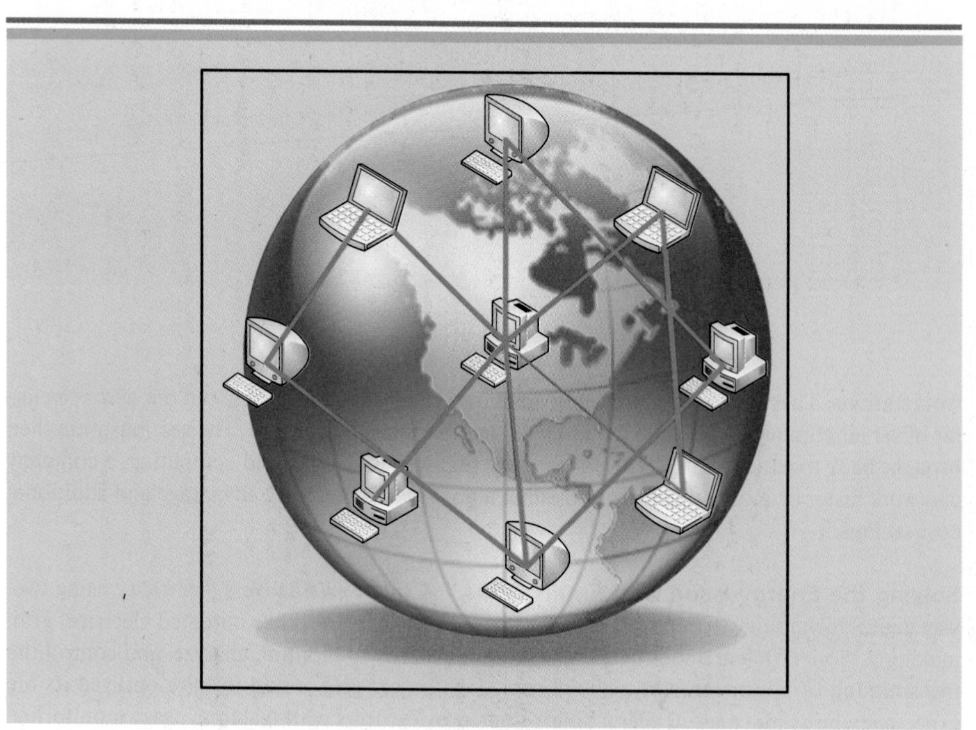

FIGURE 5.14

Grid Computing Example

allowing them to choose off-peak times for noncritical or less urgent applications or processes. Residents of Boulder, Colorado, can monitor their use of electricity and control appliances remotely due to the city's large-scale smart grid system. Xcel Energy has installed 21,000 smart grid meters since the $100 million program started several years ago. Energy use by early adopters is down as much as 45 percent.[12]

Virtualized Computing

Virtualized systems create a virtual (rather than actual) version of computing resources, such as an operating system, a server, a storage device, or network resources (see Figure 5.15). With big data, it is now possible to virtualize data so that it can be stored efficiently and cost-effectively. Improvements in network speed and network reliability have removed the physical limitations of being able to manage massive amounts of data at an acceptable pace. The decrease in the price of storage and computer memory allows companies to leverage data that would have been inconceivable to collect only 10 years ago.

Most computers and even servers typically run only one operating system, such as Windows or Mac OS, and only one application. When a company invests in a large system such as inventory management, it dedicates a single server to house the system. This ensures that the system has enough capacity to run during peak times and to scale to meet demand. Also, many systems have specific hardware requirements along with detailed software requirements, making it difficult to find two systems with the same requirements that could share the same machine. Through the use of virtualization, computers can run multiple operating systems along with multiple software applications–all at the same time.

- ***Virtualization***: Creates multiple virtual machines on a single computing device.

A good analogy is a computer printer. In the past, you had to purchase a fax machine, copy machine, answering machine, and computer printer separately. This was expensive, required enough energy to run four machines, and created additional amounts of ewaste. Today, you can buy a virtualized computer printer that functions as a fax machine, answering machine, and copy machine all on one physical machine, thereby reducing costs, power requirements, and

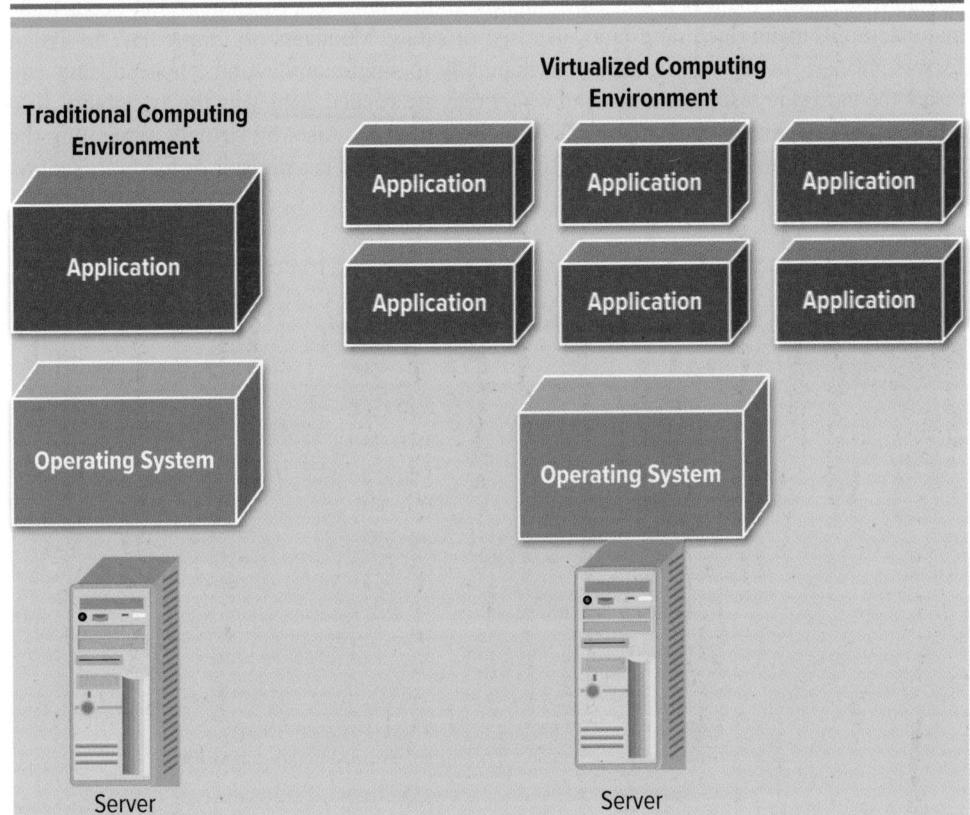

FIGURE 5.15

Virtualized System Example

ewaste. Virtualization is essentially a form of consolidation that can benefit sustainable MIS infrastructures in a variety of ways, for example:

- By increasing the availability of applications that can give a higher level of performance, depending on the hardware used.
- By increasing energy efficiency by requiring less hardware to run multiple systems or applications.
- By increasing hardware usability by running multiple operating systems on a single computer.

Originally, computers were designed to run a single application on a single operating system. This left most computers vastly underutilized. (As mentioned earlier, 75 percent of most computing power is available for other tasks.) Virtualization allows multiple virtual computers to exist on a single machine, which allows it to share its resources, such as memory and hard disk space, to run different applications and even different operating systems. Mac computers can run both the Apple operating system and the Windows PC operating system, with the use of virtualization software (see Figure 5.16). Unfortunately, virtualization, at least at the moment, is not available for a PC to run Mac software.

There are four basic categories of virtualization:

- ***Network virtualization***: Combines networks by splitting the available bandwidth into independent channels that can be assigned in real time to a specific device.
- ***Server virtualization***: Combines the physical resources, such as servers, processors, and operating systems, from the applications. (This is the most common form, and typically, when you hear the term *virtualization,* you can assume server virtualization.)
- ***Storage virtualization***: Combines multiple network storage devices so they appear to be a single storage device.
- ***System virtualization***: The ability to present the resources of a single computer as if it is a collection of separate computers ("virtual machines"), each with its own virtual CPUs, network interfaces, storage, and operating system.

Virtualization is also one of the easiest and quickest ways to achieve a sustainable MIS infrastructure because it reduces power consumption and requires less equipment that needs to be manufactured, maintained, and later disposed of safely. Managers no longer have to assign servers, storage, or network capacity permanently to single applications. Instead, they can assign the hardware resources when and where they are needed, achieving the availability, flexibility, and scalability a company needs to thrive and grow. Also, by virtually separating the operating system and applications from the hardware, if there is a disaster or hardware failure,

FIGURE 5.16

Virtualization Allows an Apple Macintosh Computer to Run OS X and Windows

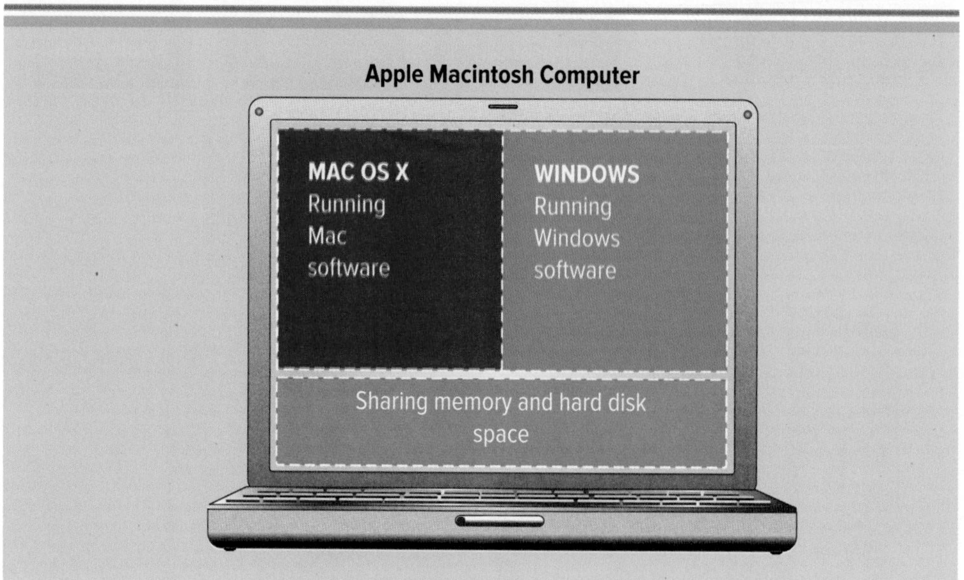

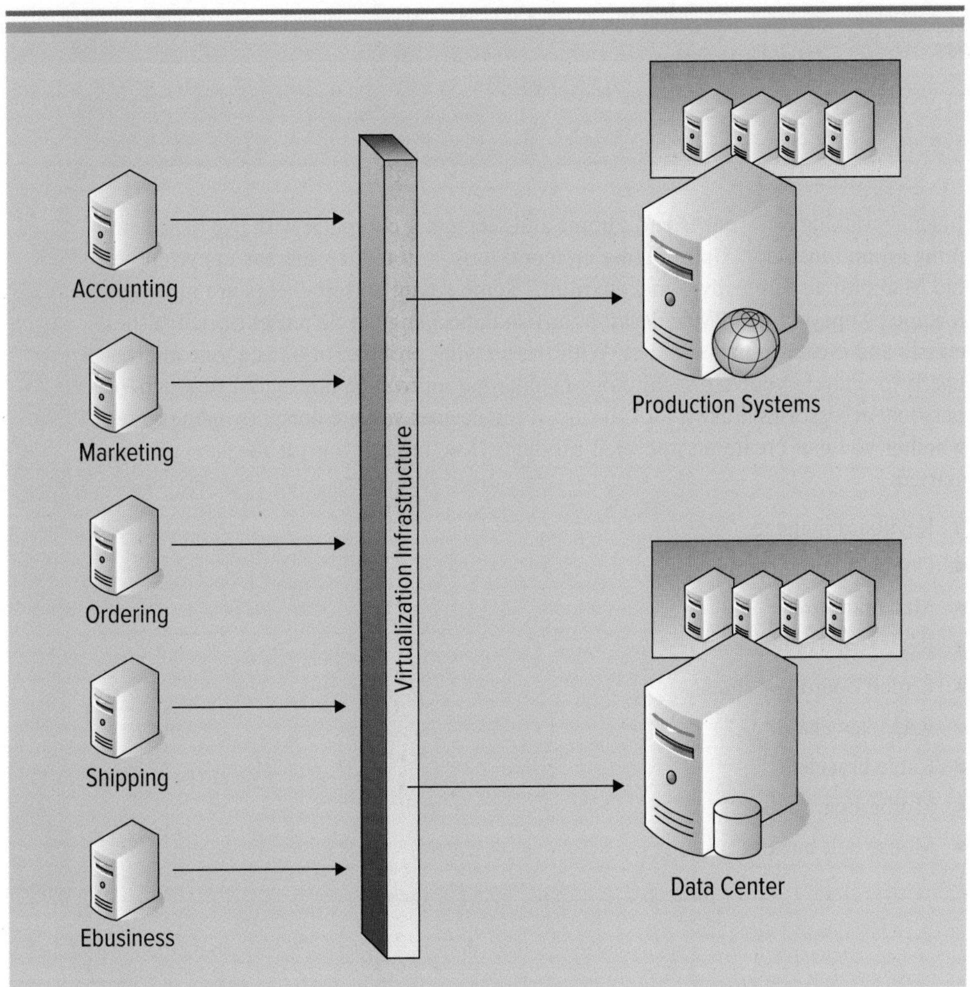

FIGURE 5.17

Virtualization Architecture

it is easy to port the virtual machine to a new physical machine, allowing a company to recovery quickly. One of the primary uses of virtualization is for performing backup, recovery, and disaster recovery. Using virtual servers or a virtualization service provider, such as Google, Microsoft, or Amazon, to host disaster recovery is more sustainable than a single company incurring the expense of having redundant physical systems. Also, these providers' data centers are built to withstand natural disasters and are typically located far away from big cities (see Figure 5.17).

Virtual machine technology was first implemented on mainframes in the 1960s to allow the expensive systems to be partitioned into separate domains and used more efficiently by more users and applications. As standard PC servers became more powerful in the past decade, virtualization has been brought to the desktop and notebook processors to provide the same benefits.

Virtual machines appear both to the user within the system and the world outside as separate computers, each with its own network identity, user authorization and authentication capabilities, operating system version and configuration, applications, and data. The hardware is consistent across all virtual machines. While the number or size of them may differ, devices are used that allow virtual machines to be portable, independent of the actual hardware type on the underlying systems. Figure 5.18 shows an overview of what a system virtualization framework looks like.

Virtual Data Centers A ***data center*** is a facility used to house management information systems and associated components, such as telecommunications and storage systems. Data centers, sometimes referred to as server farms, consume power and require cooling and floor space while working to support business growth without disrupting normal business operations and the quality of service. The amount of data a data center stores has grown exponentially

APPLY YOUR KNOWLEDGE

BUSINESS DRIVEN INNOVATION

Upcycle Your Old PCS

Imagine walking into your friend's home and seeing her computer with live fish swimming around inside it. Upon taking a second look, you realize she has upcycled her old Mac into an innovative "macquarium." Some young entrepreneurs are making a fortune by upcycling old Mac desktops as fish tanks. An upcycle reuses or refurbishes ewaste and creates a new product. With the growing problem of ewaste, one alternative is to upcycle your old technology by creating innovative household products or personal accessories. Take a look at one of the devices you are currently using to see whether you can create an upcycled product. Here are a few great ideas to get you started:

- Keyboard magnets
- Computer aquariums
- Mac mailboxes
- Keyboard calendars
- Circuit board key rings
- RAM key chains
- Cable bracelets
- Motherboard clocks
- Mouse belt buckles

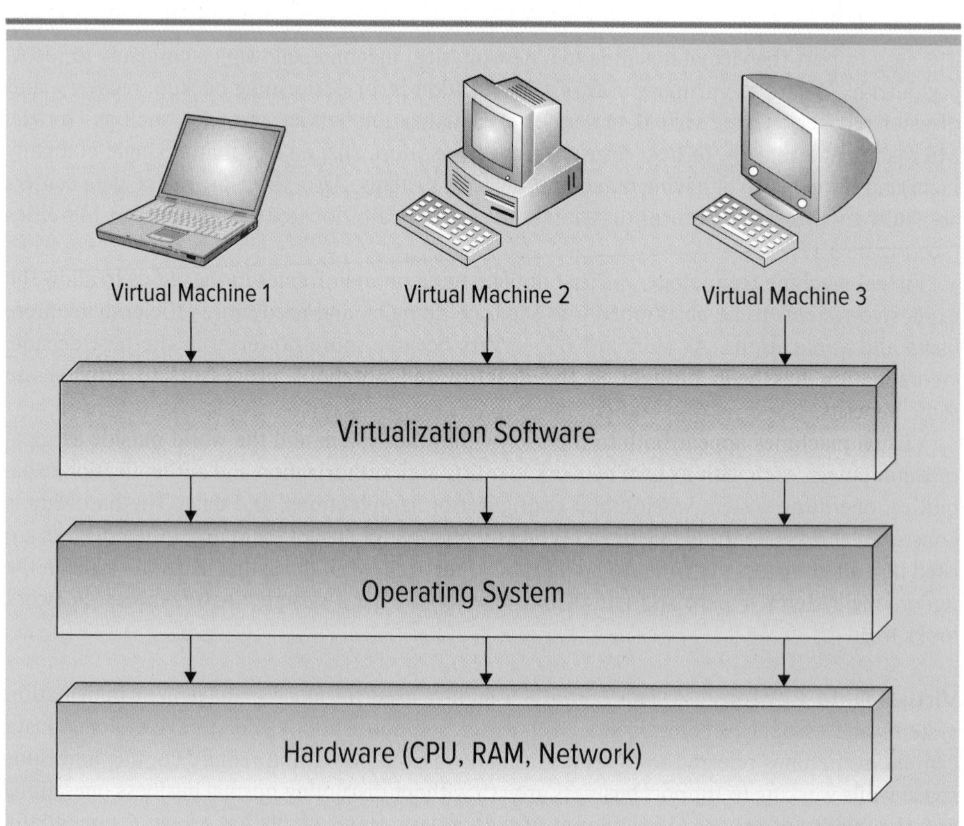

FIGURE 5.18
System Virtualization

FIGURE 5.19

Ways for Data Centers to Become Sustainable

over the years as our reliance on information increases. Backups, graphics, documents, presentations, photos, and audio and video files all contribute to the ever-expanding information footprint that requires storage. One of the most effective ways to limit the power consumption and cooling requirements of a data center is to consolidate parts of the physical infrastructure, particularly by reducing the number of physical servers through virtualization. For this reason, virtualization is having a profound impact on data centers as the sheer number of servers a company requires to operate decreases, thereby boosting growth and performance while reducing environmental impact, as shown in Figure 5.19.

Google, Microsoft, Amazon, and Yahoo! have all created data centers along the Columbia River in the northwestern United States. In this area, each company can benefit from affordable land, high-speed Internet access, plentiful water for cooling, and, even more important, inexpensive electricity. These factors are critical to today's large-scale data centers, whose sheer size and power needs far surpass those of the previous generation. The Microsoft data center in Quincy, Washington, is larger than 10 football fields and is powered entirely by hydroelectricity, power generated from flowing water rather than from burning coal or other fossil fuel.[13]

If we take a holistic and integrated approach to overall company growth, the benefits of integrating information MIS infrastructures, environmental MIS infrastructures, and sustainable MIS infrastructures become obvious. For example, a company could easily create a backup of its software and important information in one or more geographically dispersed locations using cloud computing. This would be far cheaper than building its own hot and cold sites in different areas of the country. In the case of a security breach, failover can be deployed as a virtual machine in one location of the cloud and be shut down as another virtual machine in a different location on the cloud comes online.

Cloud Computing

Imagine a cyclical business that specializes in Halloween decorations and how its sales trends and orders vary depending on the time of year. The majority of sales occur in September and October, and the remaining 10 months have relatively small sales and small system usage. The company does not want to invest in massive expensive servers that sit idle 10 months of the year just to meet its capacity spikes in September and October. The perfect solution for this company is cloud computing, which makes it easier to gain access to the computing power that was once reserved for large corporations. Small to medium-size companies no longer have to make big capital investments to access the same powerful systems that large companies run.

According to the National Institute of Standards and Technology, ***cloud computing*** stores, manages, and processes data and applications over the Internet rather than on a personal computer or server. Cloud computing offers new ways to store, access, process, and analyze information and connect people and resources from any location in the world an Internet connection is available. As shown in Figure 5.20, users connect to the cloud from their personal computers or portable devices by using a client, such as a web browser. To these individual users, the cloud appears as their personal application, device, or document. It is like storing all of your software and documents in the cloud, and all you need is a device to access the cloud. No more hard drives, software, or processing power—that is all located in the cloud, transparent to the users. Users are not physically bound to a single computer or network; they can access their programs

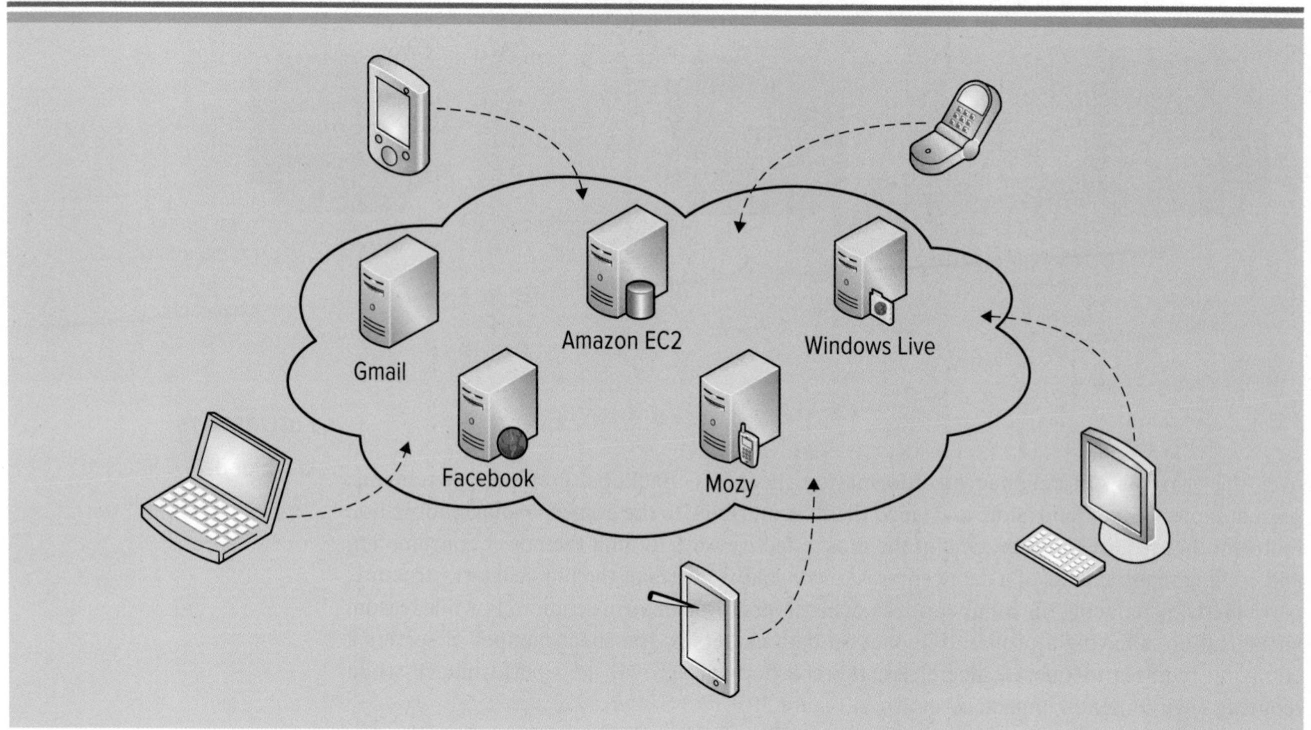

FIGURE 5.20

Cloud Computing Example

and documents from wherever they are, whenever they need to. Just think of having your hard drive located in the sky and being able to access your information and programs using any device from wherever you are. The best part is that even if your machine crashes, is lost, or is stolen, the information hosted in the cloud is safe and always available. (See Figure 5.21 for cloud providers and Figure 5.22 for cloud computing advantages.)

The subscription economy is driven by cloud computing. These are Internet-based business models like Amazon Prime, which charges a yearly subscription for free two-day shipping. It has more than 100 million subscribers. Or Netflix, the world's biggest streaming video service, which has 139 million subscribers. Or the music-streaming service Spotify, which has 200 million active users. Companies such as these charge only $9 or $10 a month, so their customers don't worry about the cost. And this business model provides a reliable stream of revenue.

- ***Single-tenancy***: In the cloud means each customer or tenant must purchase and maintain an individual system. With a single-tenancy cloud approach, the service provider would have to update its system in every company where the software was running.
- ***Multi-tenancy***: In the cloud means that a single instance of a system serves multiple customers. In the cloud, each customer is called a tenant, and multiple tenants can access the same system. Multi-tenancy helps reduce operational costs associated with implementing large systems because the costs are dispersed across many tenants. With a multi-tenancy cloud approach, the service provider only has one place to update its system.

FIGURE 5.21

Overview of Cloud Providers

Cloud Providers	
Amazon—Cloud Drive, Cloud Player, Amazon Prime	Amazon Kindle Fire is sold at a loss to push various types of media through Amazon Prime and Cloud Player, where users can stream videos and music.
Apple—iCloud, iWork, iBooks, iTunes	iCloud brings together iPhones, iPads, and Macs to synchronize data across Apple devices. iWork helps users collaborate.
Google—Google Apps, Google Drive, Gmail, Google Calendar	Google offers a number of cloud services, including Google apps, Gmail, and Google Drive to store data.
Microsoft—Office 365, OneDrive, OneNote, Exchange	OneDrive and Office 365 offer ways to collaborate and share data, photos, email, and documents.

APPLY YOUR KNOWLEDGE

BUSINESS DRIVEN GLOBALIZATION

Solving the Ewaste Problem

The United States disposes of more than 384 million units of ewaste yearly and currently recycles less than 20 percent, according to the Electronics TakeBack Coalition. The remaining 80 percent is burned or dumped in landfills, leaking toxic substances such as mercury, lead, cadmium, arsenic, and beryllium into the environment. Reports predict that ewaste will weigh as much as 200 Empire State Buildings by 2017. Solving the Ewaste Problem (StEP) Initiative is a group represented by the United Nations organizations, governments, and science organizations, and its mission is to ensure safe and responsible ewaste disposal. StEP predicts ewaste will grow by a third in the next 5 years, with the United States and China being the biggest contributors. Until recently, comprehensive data on global ewaste has been hard to collect because the definition of ewaste differs among countries. For example, the United States only includes consumer electronics such as TVs and computers, whereas Europe includes everything that has a battery or power cord in the ewaste category.[14]

The growth of ewaste is an opportunity for entrepreneurs. Research the web and find examples of schools around the country that are responsibly tackling the ewaste problem. In a group, create a plan for implementing an ewaste recycling program at your school.

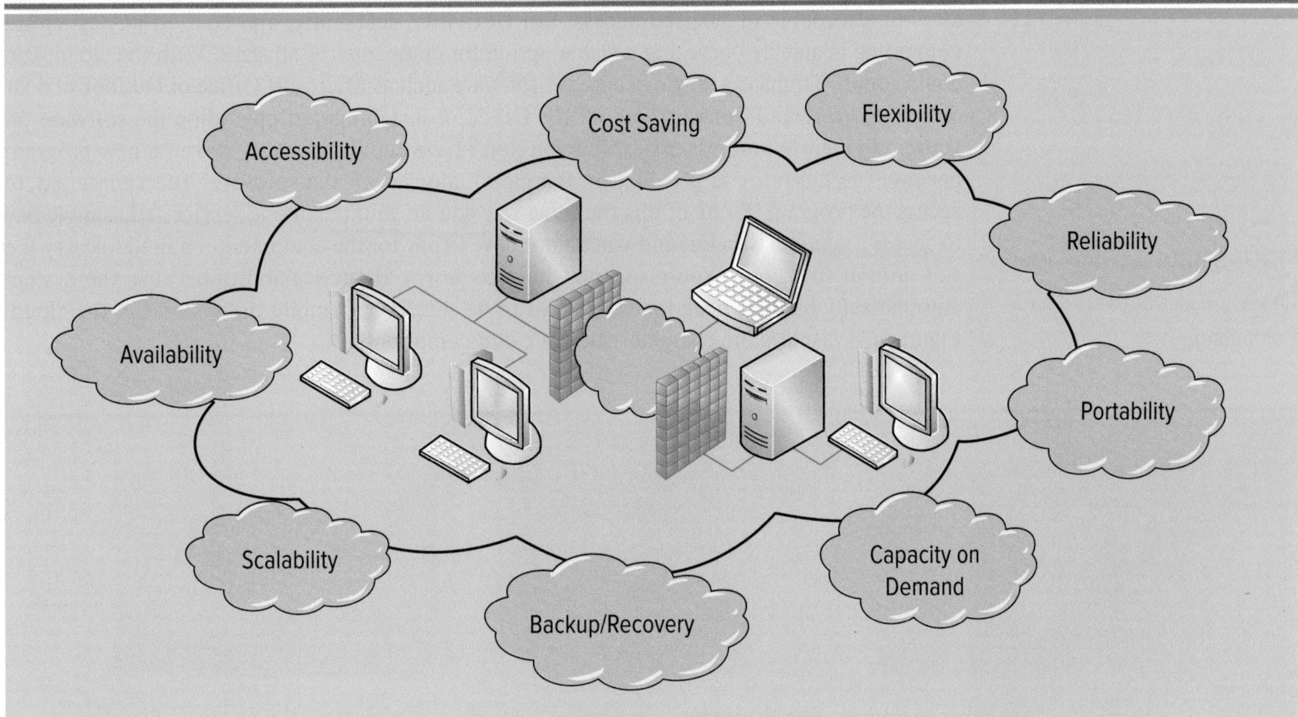

FIGURE 5.22
Cloud Computing Advantages

The cloud is a multi-tenant environment, which means that a single architecture hosts multiple customers' applications and data. A ***noisy neighbor*** refers to a multi-tenancy co-tenant that monopolizes bandwidth, servers, CPUs, and other resources that cause network performance issues. The noisy neighbor effect occurs when one tenant uses the majority of available resources and causes network performance issues for others on the shared infrastructure. Figure 5.23 displays the top business cloud applications.[15]

FIGURE 5.23

Top Cloud-Based Business Applications

CLOUD APPLICATIONS	
Box box.com	Box is like a file folder that all your gadgets and devices can access. You simply drag a file into Box, and you can instantly access it from anywhere.
Evernote evernote.com	Evernote makes organizing notes simple. It organizes online all the sticky notes, scribbled-on notepads, and random pictures that you would have cluttering up your desk. It can even recognize writing in images, so if you take a picture of a whiteboard full of notes, you can find that image by searching for one of the phrases in it.
Google Apps Google.com	Google Apps pretty much eliminates the need for many computer programs. You can create and save text documents, spreadsheets, slide shows, and more on Google Docs, and several people can work on one file simultaneously. Google Calendar makes creating and sharing calendars easy, and event reminders can be emailed to invitees. Gmail for Business gives companies personalized email accounts that are easy to set up and amend and that have the flexibility and storage space of Gmail.
MailChimp mailchimp.com	MailChimp is an email publishing platform that allows businesses of all sizes to design and send their email campaigns. Measuring the success of your email campaigns is really easy because the software integrates with Google Analytics for tracking purposes.
QuickBooks quickbooks.intuit.co.uk	QuickBooks is an online accounting service and can help with all accounting needs, including monitoring cash flow, creating reports, and setting budgets, and is accessible from anywhere in the world.
Skype skype.com	Skype turns your computer into a phone; you can call or chat (with or without video) to other Skype users for free.

The cloud offers a company higher availability, greater reliability, and improved accessibility—all with affordable high-speed access. For flexibility, scalability, and cost efficiency, cloud computing is quickly becoming a viable option for companies of all sizes. With the cloud, you could simply purchase a single license for software such as Microsoft Office or Outlook at a far discounted rate and not worry about the hassle of installing and upgrading the software on your computer. No more worries that you don't have enough memory to run a new program because the hardware is provided in the cloud, along with the software. You simply pay to access the program. Think of this the same way you do your telephone service. You simply pay to access a vendor's service, and you do not have to pay for the equipment required to carry the call around the globe. You also don't have to worry about scalability because the system automatically handles peak loads, which can be spread out among the systems in the cloud. Figure 5.24 displays the characteristics of cloud computing.

FIGURE 5.24

Characteristics of Cloud Computing

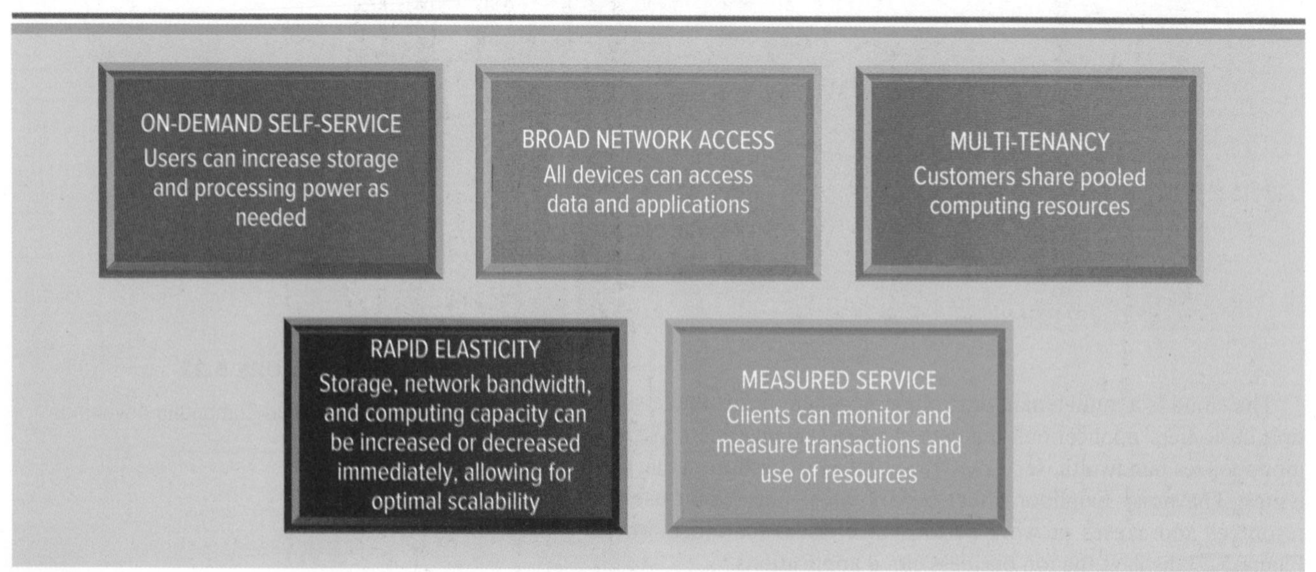

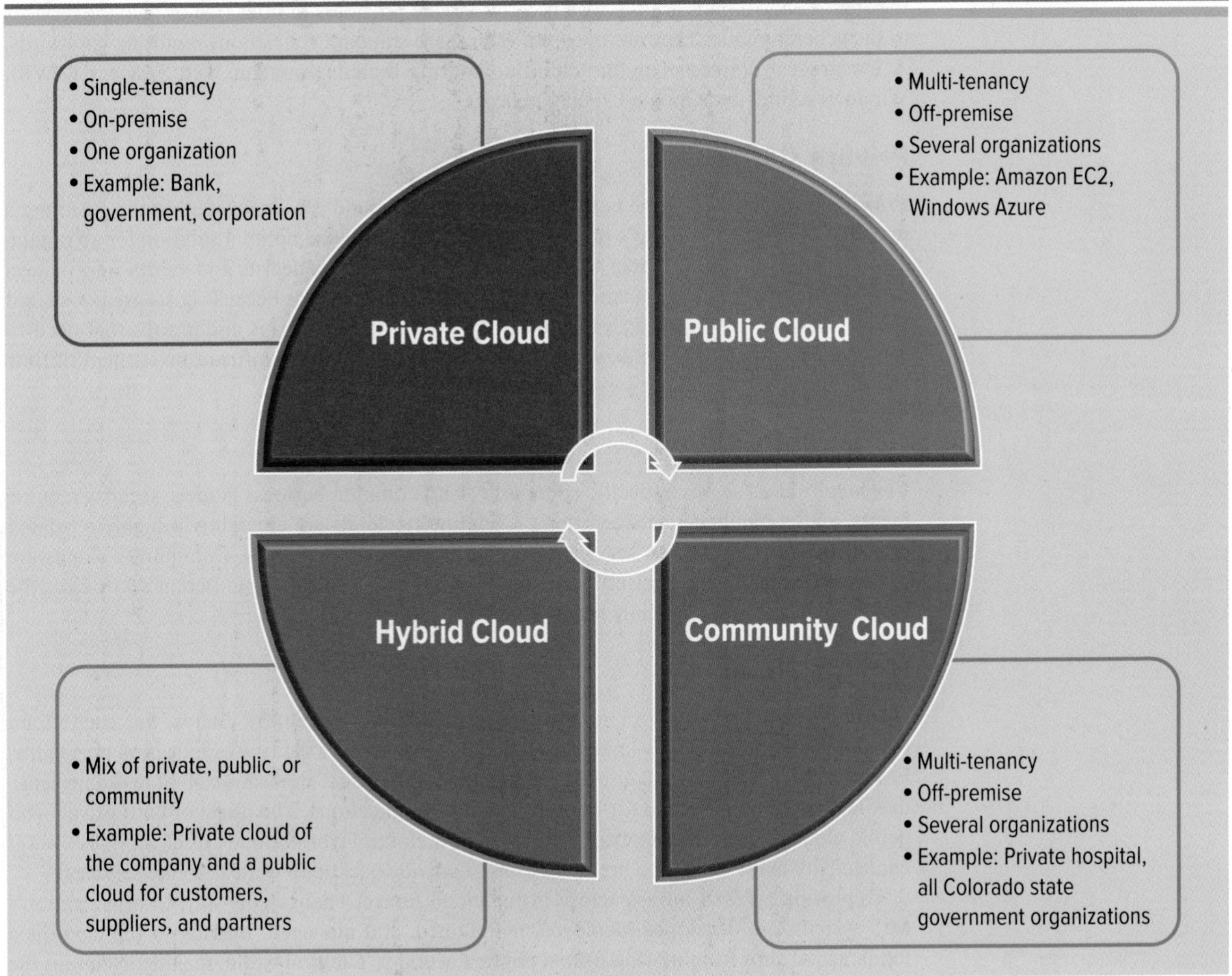

FIGURE 5.25

Cloud Computing Environments

Because additional cloud resources are always available, companies no longer have to purchase systems for infrequent computing tasks that need intense processing power, such as preparing tax returns during tax season or increased sales transactions during certain holiday seasons. If a company needs more processing power, it is always there in the cloud–and available on a cost-efficient basis. Heroku is the leading cloud platform for building and deploying social and mobile customer applications. Built on open standards, Heroku supports multiple open frameworks, languages, and databases.

With cloud computing, individuals or businesses pay only for the services they need, when they need them, and where, much as we use and pay for electricity. In the past, a company would have to pay millions of dollars for the hardware, software, and networking equipment required to implement a large system such as payroll or sales management. A cloud computing user can simply access the cloud and request a single license to a payroll application. The user does not have to incur any hardware, software, or networking expenses. As the business grows and the user requires more employees to have access to the system, the business simply purchases additional licenses. Rather than running software on a local computer or server, companies can now reach to the cloud to combine software applications, data storage, and considerable computing power. Regardless of which cloud model a business chooses, it can select from four different cloud computing environments–public, private, community, and hybrid (see Figure 5.25).

Public Cloud

Public cloud promotes massive, global, and industrywide applications offered to the general public. In a public cloud, customers are never required to provision, manage, upgrade, or replace hardware or software. Pricing is utility-style, and customers pay only for the resources they use. Public clouds are the type used by service providers to offer free or paid-for services to the general public. They are open but often have standard restrictions requiring passwords. A few great examples of public cloud computing include Amazon Web Services (AWS), Windows Azure, and Google Cloud Connect.

Private Cloud

Private cloud serves only one customer or organization and can be located on the customer's premises or off the customer's premises. A private cloud is the optimal solution for an organization such as the government that has high data security concerns and values information privacy. Private clouds are far more expensive than public clouds because costs are not shared across multiple customers. Private clouds are mostly used by firms and groups that need to keep data secure. The main downside is that they still require significant investment of time and money to set them up.

Community Cloud

Community cloud serves a specific community with common business models, security requirements, and compliance considerations. Community clouds are emerging in highly regulated industries such as financial services and pharmaceutical companies. Community clouds are private but spread over a variety of groups within one organization. Different sections of the cloud can be set up specifically for each department or group.

Hybrid Cloud

Hybrid cloud includes two or more private, public, or community clouds, but each cloud remains separate and is only linked by technology that enables data and application portability. For example, a company might use a private cloud for critical applications that maintain sensitive data and a public cloud for nonsensitive data applications. The usage of both private and public clouds together is an example of a hybrid cloud. Hybrid clouds offer services even if connectivity faults occur and are often used to provide backup to critical online services.

Deploying an MIS infrastructure in the cloud forever changes the way an organization's MIS systems are developed, deployed, maintained, and managed. Moving to the cloud is a fundamental shift from moving from a physical world to a logical world, making irrelevant the notion of which individual server applications or data reside on. As a result, organizations and MIS departments need to change the way they view systems and the new opportunities to find competitive advantages.

UTILITY COMPUTING

Utility computing offers a pay-per-use revenue model similar to a metered service such as gas or electricity. Many cloud computing service providers use utility computing cloud infrastructures, which are detailed in Figure 5.26.

Infrastructure as a Service (IaaS)

Infrastructure as a Service (IaaS) delivers hardware networking capabilities, including the use of servers, networking, and storage, over the cloud using a pay-per-use revenue model. With IaaS, the customer rents the hardware and provides its own custom applications or programs. IaaS customers save money by not having to spend a large amount of capital purchasing expensive servers, which is a great business advantage considering some servers cost more than $100,000. The service is typically paid for on a usage basis, much like a basic utility service such as electricity or gas. IaaS offers a cost-effective solution for companies that need their computing resources to grow and shrink as business demand changes. This is known as ***dynamic scaling,*** which means the MIS infrastructure can be automatically scaled up or down based on requirements.

Disaster Recovery as a Service (DRaaS) offers backup services that use cloud resources to protect applications and data from disruption caused by disaster. It gives an organization a total system backup that allows for business continuity in the event of system failure. DRaaS is typically part of a disaster recovery plan or business continuity plan.

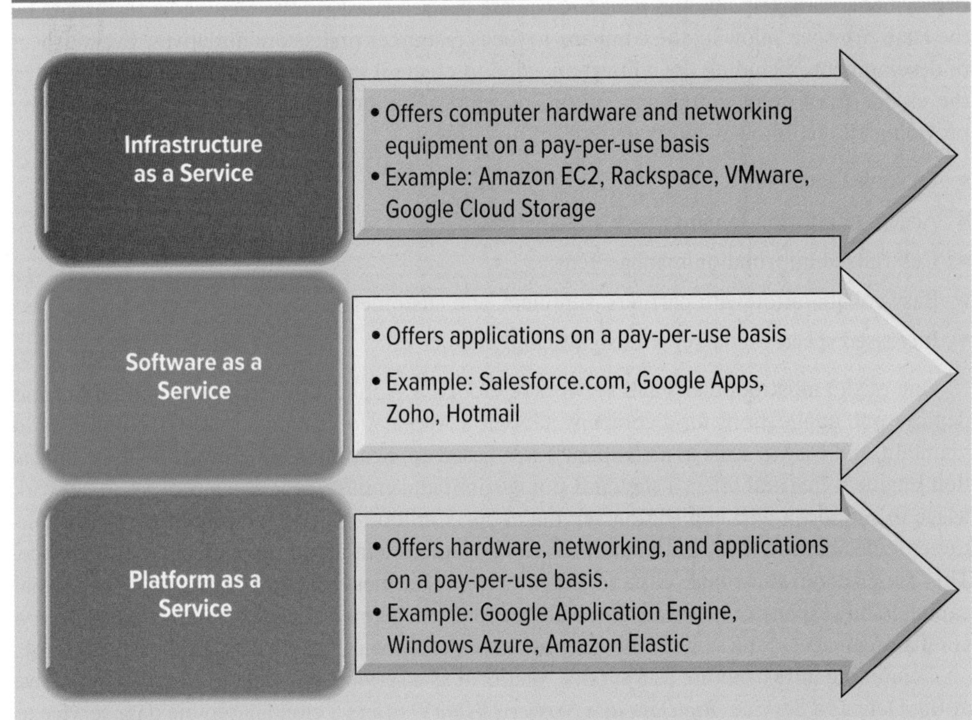

FIGURE 5.26

Cloud Service Delivery Models

Software as a Service (SaaS)

Software as a Service (SaaS) delivers applications over the cloud using a pay-per-use revenue model. Before its introduction, companies often spent huge amounts of money implementing and customizing specialized applications to satisfy their business requirements. Many of these applications were difficult to implement, expensive to maintain, and challenging to use. Usability was one of the biggest drivers for creating interest in and success for cloud computing service providers.

SaaS offers a number of advantages; the most obvious is tremendous cost savings. The software is priced on a per-use basis with no up-front costs, so companies get the immediate benefit of reducing capital expenditures. They also get the added benefits of scalability and flexibility to test new software on a rental basis.

Salesforce.com is one of the most popular SaaS providers. It built and delivered a sales automation application, suitable for the typical salesperson, which automates functions such as tracking sales leads and prospects and forecasting. Tapping the power of SaaS can provide access to a large-scale, secure infrastructure, along with any needed support, which is especially valuable for a start-up or small company with few financial resources. A few SaaS extensions include:

- ***Data as a Service (DaaS)***: Facilitates the accessibility of business-critical data in a timely, secure, and affordable manner. DaaS depends on the principle that specified, useful data can be supplied to users on demand, irrespective of any organizational or geographical separation between consumers and providers.
- ***Security as a Service (SaaS)***: Involves applications such as anti-virus software delivered over the Internet with constant virus definition updates that are not reliant on user compliance. Security as a Service is sometimes referred to as cloud security. Security as a Service provides top security expertise that is traditionally better than can be found in an organization. Security as a Service providers include Cisco, McAfee, and Symantec.

Platform as a Service (PaaS)

Platform as a Service (PaaS) supports the deployment of entire systems, including hardware, networking, and applications, using a pay-per-use revenue model. PaaS is a perfect solution for a business because it passes on to the service provider the headache and challenges of buying, managing, and maintaining web development software. With PaaS the development, deployment, management, and maintenance are based entirely in the cloud and performed by the PaaS provider, allowing the company to focus resources on its core initiatives. Every aspect of development, including the software needed to create it and the hardware to run it, lives in the cloud. PaaS helps companies minimize operational costs and increase productivity by providing all the following without up-front investment:

- Increased security.
- Access to information anywhere and anytime.
- Centralized information management.
- Easy collaboration with partners, suppliers, and customers.
- Increased speed to market with significantly less cost.

One of the most popular PaaS services is Google's Application Engine, which builds and deploys web applications for a company. Google's Application Engine is easy to build, easy to maintain, and easy to scale as a company's web-based application needs grow. Google's Application Engine is free and offers a standard storage limit and enough processing power and network usage to support a web application serving about 5 million page views a month. When a customer scales beyond these initial limits, it can pay a fee to increase capacity and performance. This can turn into some huge costs savings for a small business that does not have enough initial capital to buy expensive hardware and software for its web applications. Just think, a two-person company can access the same computing resources as Google. That makes good business sense.

Combining infrastructure as a service, platform as a service, and data as a service we arrive at Big Data as a Service. ***Big Data as a Service (BDaaS)*** offers a cloud-based big data service to help organizations analyze massive amounts of data to solve business dilemmas. BDaaS is a somewhat nebulous term often used to describe a wide variety of outsourcing of various big data functions to the cloud. This can range from the supply of data, to the supply of analytical tools with which to interrogate the data (often through a web dashboard or control panel), to carrying out the actual analysis and providing reports. Some BDaaS providers also include consulting and advisory services within their BDaaS packages.

LEARNING OUTCOME REVIEW

Learning Outcome 5.1: Explain MIS infrastructure and its three primary types.

The three primary areas where enterprise architects focus when maintaining a firm's MIS infrastructure are:

- Supporting operations: Information MIS infrastructure identifies where and how important information, such as customer records, is maintained and secured.
- Supporting change: Agile MIS infrastructure includes the hardware, software, and telecommunications equipment that, when combined, provides the underlying foundation to support the organization's goals.
- Supporting the environment: Sustainable MIS infrastructure identifies ways that a company can grow in terms of computing resources while becoming less dependent on hardware and energy consumption.

Learning Outcome 5.2: Identify the three primary areas associated with an information MIS infrastructure.

The three primary areas an information infrastructure provides to support continuous business operations are:

- Backup and recovery: A backup is an exact copy of a system's information. Recovery is the ability to get a system up and running in the event of a system crash or failure that includes restoring the information backup.

- Disaster recovery plan: This plan provides a detailed process for recovering information or a system in the event of a catastrophic disaster.
- Business continuity plan: This details how a company recovers and restores critical business operations and systems after a disaster or extended disruption.

Learning Outcome 5.3: Describe the characteristics of an agile MIS infrastructure.

- Accessibility refers to the varying levels that define what a user can access, view, or perform when operating a system.
- Availability refers to the time frames when the system is operational.
- Maintainability (or flexibility) refers to how quickly a system can transform to support environmental changes.
- Portability refers to the ability of an application to operate on different devices or software platforms, such as different operating systems.
- Reliability (or accuracy) ensures that a system is functioning correctly and providing accurate information.
- Scalability describes how well a system can scale up or adapt to the increased demands of growth.
- Usability is the degree to which a system is efficient, easy to learn, and satisfying to use.

Learning Outcome 5.4: Identify the environmental impacts associated with MIS.

Increased energy consumption, increased electronic waste, and increased carbon emissions are all associated with MIS. Ewaste refers to discarded, obsolete, or broken electronic devices. Sustainable MIS disposal refers to the safe disposal of MIS assets at the end of their life cycle.

Learning Outcome 5.5: Explain the three components of a sustainable MIS infrastructure along with their business benefits.

The components of a sustainable MIS infrastructure include:

- Grid computing: A collection of computers, often geographically dispersed, that are coordinated to solve a common problem.
- Cloud computing: The use of resources and applications hosted remotely on the Internet. The term comes (at least in part) from the image of a cloud to represent the Internet or some large networked environment.
- Virtualized computing: The creation of multiple virtual machines on a single computing device.

KEY TERMS

REVIEW QUESTIONS

1. How often should a business back up its data?
2. Why is it important to ensure that backups are working and can be restored?
3. What is the difference between a disaster recovery plan and a business continuity plan?
4. What are the three forms of MIS infrastructures and what do they support?
5. List the characteristics of an agile MIS infrastructure and explain why they are all critical for supporting change.
6. Explain what capacity planning is and how it can help a business prepare for growth.
7. Explain the difference between fault tolerance and failover.
8. Compare the differences between hot, cold, and warm sites.
9. What is Moore's law and how does it affect companies?
10. List the business benefits of using grid computing.
11. Identify the benefits and challenges of cloud computing.
12. What is a data center and why would a business develop one?
13. List and describe the three most popular cloud computing delivery models.
14. Why would a company want to use virtualization?
15. Explain why a business today would want to follow sustainable MIS practices.

CLOSING CASE ONE

Peloton: Fitness-as-a-Service

Peloton streams boutique-style cycling classes to high-tech, at-home exercise bikes. Peloton's goal is to replicate the type of boutique fitness classes like SoulCycle right in an individual's living room. The $2,000 Peloton bike offers a subscription-based, $39 monthly payment to receive on-demand access to over 8,000 classes, creating the Fitness as a Service business model. Fitness is a $31 billion industry, and trends indicate that people are spending more money on fitness each year but giving it less time; hence, the rise of the boutique fitness industry.

Peloton does not claim to be a stationary bike company, but rather a disruptive technology company. Every interaction a rider has with a Peloton bike is collected as data that feeds the experience. The company is paying attention to what songs riders like, what instructors they prefer, what type of workout they gravitate toward, and what rating they give individual classes. Peloton uses that data to compare rider profiles and suggest better, more targeted content. During live classes—in which instructors and riders alike can track participants' progress up and down the leaderboard—a community of virtual friends develops. Instructors in New York can acknowledge riders in Denver, Colorado, by name; encourage them to pedal a little faster; or congratulate them on taking their 100th ride.

The revenue model favors an active customer. If a Peloton customer rides 200 times per year, that will cost $2,690 (including the cost of the bike and the monthly subscription rate). A typical SoulCycle class costs $35. If a customer attends 200 classes a year, that is $7,000.

The company is launching a $4,000 treadmill, the second product for Peloton. The subscription fee will remain the same, and if you already pay for the bike, you don't have to pay again for the treadmill: The same fee applies for both products. With the creation and launch of new products, Peloton is fast on its way to being a disruptive technology company.[16]

Questions

1. List five types of data Peloton might be collecting from its customers as they ride on a bike or treadmill.
2. What types of business questions can Peloton answer from the data listed in question 1?
3. How can Peloton take advantage of Fitness as a Service beyond bikes and treadmills?
4. How does cloud computing work in Peloton's subscription model?

CLOSING CASE TWO

Moore's Law Is Dead

Moore's law is named after Intel cofounder Gordon Moore. He observed in 1965 that transistors were shrinking so fast that, every year, twice as many could fit onto a chip, and in 1975, he adjusted the pace to a doubling every 2 years. The chip industry has kept Moore's prediction alive, with Intel leading the charge. In the meantime, computing companies have found plenty to do with the continual supply of extra transistors.

Mobile apps, video games, spreadsheets, and accurate weather forecasts . . . that's just a sampling of the life-changing things made possible by the reliable, exponential growth in the power of computer chips over the past five decades. In a few years, however, technology companies may have to work harder to bring us advanced new-use cases for computers. Although this continual cramming of more silicon transistors onto chips has been the feedstock of exuberant innovation in computing, it now looks to be slowing to a halt. The last few years have shown a stagnation in chip development, and that is bad news for research programs reliant on supercomputers, such as efforts to understand climate change, develop new materials for batteries and superconductors, and improve drug design.

Intel recently pushed back its next transistor technology and has also decided to increase the time between future generations. In addition, a technology roadmap for Moore's law maintained by an industry group, including the world's largest chipmakers, is being scrapped. Intel has suggested silicon transistors can keep shrinking for only another 5 years. The world's top supercomputers aren't getting better at the rate they used to and are already feeling the effects of Moore's law's end times.

Mobile devices are powered by chips made by companies other than Intel, and they've generally been slightly behind in transistor technology. However, many useful things that mobile devices can do rest on the power of billion-dollar data centers, where the end of Moore's law would be a more immediate headache. Companies such as Google and Microsoft eagerly gobble up every new generation of the most advanced chips, packed more densely with transistors. Alternative ways to get more computing power include working harder to improve the design of chips and making chips specialized to accelerate particular crucial algorithms.

The coming plateau in transistor density will stir more interest in redrawing the basic architecture of computers among supercomputer and data-center designers. Getting rid of certain design features dating from the 1940s could unlock huge efficiency gains. Yet taking advantage of those would require rethinking the design of many types of software, and would require programmers to change their habits.[17]

Questions

1. Do you agree or disagree that Moore's law is coming to an end?
2. What will happen to the business environment if Moore's law does die?
3. What can companies do to remain competitive when hardware advances are not driving the companies forward?

MAKING BUSINESS DECISIONS

1. I Don't Have a Temperature, but I'm Positive I Have a Virus

Think how horrible it would be to finish your term paper at 4 a.m. and find out your computer has a virus, and that you just lost your entire document. Or perhaps you submit your final paper, which is worth 50 percent of your grade, and head off to Colorado for winter break. You return to find that you failed the course, and you frantically check your email to find out what happened. A message from your professor informs you that your document was corrupt and couldn't be opened and that you had 24 hours to resend the file, which you missed because you were skiing down the slopes.

Have you ever experienced having a file corrupted? If so, what could you have done to recover from this situation? Do you think your instructor ever receives corrupted files? How did the file become corrupted? Do you think your instructor would be suspicious if you submitted a corrupted file?

2. Sustainable Departments

Energy prices and global warming are discussed daily in the news as the environmental impact of ewaste is just beginning to be recognized. Sustainability and corporate social responsibility need to be taken seriously by all managers because everyone should take an active role in helping to preserve the environment. List the different departments in a business and the types of environmental issues they typically encounter. Which department do you think creates the most ewaste? Which department uses the greatest amount of electricity or has the largest carbon footprint? What can each department do to help combat its environmental issues? Why do all managers and, for that matter, all employees need to be aware of environmental issues and ways they can create sustainable MIS infrastructures?

3. Facebook's Energy Use

Cheap electricity is great for keeping business costs down, but it often means relying on coal for power. Facebook recently commissioned a new computing facility in Oregon and is using power from PacifiCorp, a utility that gets the majority of its energy from coal-fired power stations, which are major contributors of greenhouse gas emissions. As more and more people subscribe to Facebook, its energy needs are increasing almost exponentially.

Do you agree that Facebook made a wise business decision in selecting a utility provider that uses coal-fired power stations? What alternative sources of energy could Facebook have used to power its computing facility? Do you think Facebook's core customers care about the environment? What types of business challenges might Facebook encounter if it continues using coal-fired power stations?

4. **Creating Your BCP**

Business disruption costs money. In the event of a disaster or emergency, you will not only lose revenue, you will also incur additional expenses. If you are expecting your insurance to cover your losses, be careful: There are many losses your insurance will not cover, such as lost sales, lost business intelligence, and lost customers. To mitigate the risks of a catastrophe, you will want to create a detailed business continuity plan. A business continuity plan (BCP) is not only a good idea but also one of the least expensive plans a company can develop. A BCP should detail how employees will contact each other and continue to keep operations functioning in the event of a disaster or emergency, such as a fire or flood. Regrettably, many companies never take the time to develop such a plan until it is too late.

Research the web for sample BCPs for a small business or start-up. In a group, create a BCP for a start-up of your choice. Be sure to think of such things as data storage, data access, transaction processing, employee safety, and customer communications.

5. **Ewaste and the Environment**

By some estimates, there may be as many as 1 billion surplus or obsolete computers and monitors in the world. Consider California, where 6,000 computers become surplus every day. If not disposed of properly, this enormous ewaste stream, which can contain more than 1,000 toxic substances, is harmful to human beings and the environment. Beryllium is found in computer motherboards, chromium in floppy disks, lead in batteries and computer monitors, and mercury in alkaline batteries. One of the most toxic chemicals known is cadmium, found in many old laptops and computer chips.

In poorer countries, where the United States and Europe export some of their ewaste, the full impact of the environmental damage is quickly being realized. These areas have little use for obsolete electronic equipment, so local recyclers resell some parts and burn the rest in illegal dumps, often near residential areas, releasing toxic and carcinogenic substances into the air, land, and water.[18]

Have you ever contributed to ewaste? What can you do to ensure that you are safely disposing of electronic equipment, including batteries? What can governments do to encourage companies to dispose of ewaste safely? What can be done to protect poorer countries from receiving ewaste? Create a list of the ways you can safely dispose of cell phones, computers, printers, ink cartridges, and batteries. What could you do to inform citizens of the issues associated with ewaste and educate them on safe disposal practices?

6. **Volkswagen Emissions Scandal**

It's been dubbed the "diesel dupe." The U.S. Environmental Protection Agency (EPA) found that many VW cars being sold in America had a "defeat device"—or software—in diesel engines that could detect when they were being tested and change the car's performance accordingly to improve results. The German car giant has since admitted cheating emissions tests in the United States. Full details of how the scheme worked are sketchy, although the EPA has said that the engines had computer software that could sense test scenarios by monitoring speed, engine operation, air pressure, and even the position of the steering wheel.

When the cars were operating under controlled laboratory conditions—which typically involve putting them on a stationary test system—the device appears to have put the vehicle into a sort of safety mode in which the engine ran below normal power and performance. Once on the road, the engines switched out of this test mode. The result? The engines emitted nitrogen oxide pollutants up to 40 times above what is allowed in the United States.

Why is it important that all vehicles adhere to the EPA testing limits? What environmental impacts could occur from Volkswagen's false emission tests? How could the EPA create metrics for testing to ensure cars are operating as expected? How should the EPA handle the Volkswagen scandal?

7. **Laptop? Notebook? Netbook? Tablet?**

Thanks to Moore's law, computing devices are getting smaller, cheaper, and faster every year, allowing innovative companies to create new devices that are smaller and more powerful than current devices. Just look at desktop, laptop, notebook, and tablet computers. These are all different devices allowing users to connect and compute around the globe. Moore's law has been accurate about computing power roughly doubling every 18 months. Do you agree or disagree that Moore's law will continue to apply for the next 20 years? Why or why not?

8. Ranking MIS Characteristics

In a group, review the list of MIS infrastructure characteristics that support growth and rank them in order of their impact on a company's success, using 1 to indicate the biggest impact and 7 the least.

MIS Infrastructure Characteristics	Business Impact
Accessibility	
Availability	
Maintainability	
Portability	
Reliability	
Scalability	
Usability	

9. Recycle Your Cell Phone

For all those excited to get a new iPhone with its numerous applications and cool games, what will you do with your old cell phone? You can help the environment and recycle your phone, PDA, charger, and batteries. Recycling cell phones helps save energy and keep reusable materials out of landfills. Cell phones are made of plastic, copper, and precious metals, which require energy to extract and manufacture. If you decide to recycle your cell phone, be sure to terminate the service, delete any contacts or stored information, and take out the SIM card.

If your old cell phone is still working, you might also want to consider donating it to charity. Many programs will accept working cell phones, which they donate to people in need, such as survivors of domestic violence, because old cell phones can still dial 911 even after the service is disconnected. To find local agencies where you can donate your cell phone, visit ncadv.org. Cell phones are only a small percentage of the total computer equipment organizations replace each year. What happens to all of those old laptops, notebooks, servers, and monitors? What is the environmental impact of throwing a computer system into a landfill? What can companies do to recycle their computer equipment? What can the government do to help motivate companies and individuals to recycle?

10. Excuses, Excuses, Excuses

Here are a few examples of the strangest and most unusual excuses employees have used for missing work.

- I have a sunburn.
- I'm not sure why, but I woke up in Canada.
- I was caught selling an alligator.
- I was locked in the trunk of an abandoned car.
- I have a note from my mom that I could not go to work yesterday.
- I'm just not into it today.
- I was riding my motorcycle and I accidentally hit a nun.
- Some person threw poison ivy at me and now I have a rash on my face.
- I need to stay home as I am convinced I can catch my spouse having an affair.
- I was chasing a seagull and fell down and had to go to the hospital.
- I have a migraine from eating too many jalapeño peppers.

This chapter focuses on MIS infrastructures, the main building blocks that function together to control the entire organization's systems. If your systems cannot operate, your organization cannot work, similar to how your health controls your ability to work. Attempting to do business with an organization when its systems have crashed, its Internet access is down, or the wireless network is malfunctioning can be very frustrating. When these types of issues occur, companies do not want to broadcast that they are experiencing technical difficulties because of hackers, an unpaid utility bill, or squirrels that got into the data center and ate through all of the wires (yes, that has really happened).

How many times have you called a company and had the customer service representative state that the system is down or is really slow today? How many times have you missed submitting an assignment because your Internet service was down? Why is it important for an organization's systems to be available 24 hours a day, 7 days a week, and 365 days a year? Why would a company hide the real reason its systems are malfunctioning? What could happen if customers were informed that the systems were down due to hackers? How can an organization safeguard its systems?

11. Ewaste Not, Want Not

On Earth Day every year, many people, including corporate citizens, devote themselves to recycling and reducing, along with identifying items they can repurpose. Companies such as Dell and Microsoft, two producers of materials that eventually become ewaste, have joined forces with an electronics recycling program run by Goodwill Industries International. Goodwill reports that the program has diverted about 96 million pounds in electronics from landfills.[19]

Assisting in a similar effort are office supply stores Office Depot and Staples, which offer their own sorting and recycling services for used electronics. Apple has even jumped on this bandwagon, allowing customers to turn in their old products to retail locations when they buy something new.

There are so many opportunities to reduce ewaste. Make a list of how the popular technology manufacturers are already trying to reduce ewaste. Would starting a company that helped people locate used computers or other technologies for reuse be a worthwhile venture? Why or why not? Create a list of new alternatives any company could adopt to reuse, recycle, and reduce ewaste.

12. One Laptop Per Child

The One Laptop Per Child (OLPC) project intends to create a $100 laptop for distribution to the world's poorest children. The machine, called the OLPC or XO laptop, has a rubberized keyboard and an ultra-bright screen readable in daylight. When flipped, it converts to an electronic book reader. To keep the cost as low as possible (at $175, it is currently a bit more than the target), the computer has a host of free software and other tools to support learning opportunities. A special type of networking allows machines within 100 feet or so to communicate with each other and relays a single Internet connection for them to use (where the Internet is available). The XO is targeted at communities where power generation is unreliable or nonexistent; it gets its power via a hand crank, pull cord, or foot pedal.[20]

Do you agree that the One Laptop Per Child project will help educate children around the world? How does the XO computer provide learning opportunities for children in poor regions of the world? What issues could these children encounter if they have an XO laptop? How will cloud computing play an important role in the XO laptop, especially in terms of keeping costs low and data safe? What do you think the typical environment will be like where the XO laptop will be used? What issues will users of the XO laptop encounter that are not common in the United States? What can the creators of the XO laptop do to ensure its functionality even in the most extreme environments?

13. Virtualizing Your Cell Phone

Virtualization is a challenging concept to understand. The formal definition is that it creates multiple virtual machines on a single computing device. OK, let's try that again in English. Imagine you have three cell phones, one for the company you work for, one for a company you are starting on the side, and one for personal calls. For the most part, the phones are idle, and they seldom ever ring at the same time. Because the phones are idle the majority of the time, you notice it is a waste of time and resources to support idle time, especially when you are paying for cell service on each phone. So, you decide to use virtualization to help your situation.

Essentially, this would put three virtual cell phones on one device. The individual services and applications for each phone would be independently stored on the one device. From the device's perspective, it sees three virtual phones. This saves time and money in expenses and maintenance.[21]

Virtualization is a hot topic these days because more and more businesses are focusing on social responsibility and attempting to find ways to reduce their carbon footprints. Create an analogy similar to the cell phone that demonstrates virtualization. What are the potential environmental impacts associated with virtualization? What are the business advantages of virtualization? What are the business risks associated with virtualization?

14. Data Centers on the High Seas

Google is considering constructing a floating data center 3 to 7 miles offshore that could be both powered and cooled by the ocean. It would consist of containers stacked with servers, data storage systems, and networking equipment on barges or other platforms and could be located close to users wherever it is not feasible, cost-effective, or efficient to build on land. Bringing the data closer to the user allows the data to arrive quicker. And because the ocean is a rent-free space, data centers can be as large as 100,000 square feet without real estate fees. The ocean can provide two critical factors that support a sustainable MIS infrastructure: water for cooling and power.[22]

What are the advantages and disadvantages of housing data centers in the ocean? Do you foresee any issues for these data centers with natural disasters? What types of security issues would Google encounter with a floating data center? Do you agree it is good business sense to house a data center on a barge in the ocean? Why or why not?

AYK APPLICATION PROJECTS

If you are looking for Excel projects to incorporate into your class, try any of the following after reading this chapter.

Project Number	Project Name	Project Type	Plug-In	Focus Area	Project Level	Skill Set	Page Number
8	Maximize Profits	Excel	T2, T4	Strategic Analysis	Intermediate	Formulas or Solver	AYK.5
9	Security Analysis	Excel	T3	Filtering Data	Intermediate	Conditional Formatting, Autofilter, Subtotal	AYK.6
10	Gathering Data	Excel	T3	Data Analysis	Intermediate	Conditional Formatting	AYK.6
11	Scanner System	Excel	T2	Strategic Analysis	Intermediate	Formulas	AYK.7
12	Competitive Pricing	Excel	T2	Profit Maximization	Intermediate	Formulas	AYK.7
13	Adequate Acquisitions	Excel	T2	Break Even Analysis	Intermediate	Formulas	AYK.7
15	Assessing the Value of Information	Excel	T3	Data Analysis	Intermediate	PivotTable	AYK.8
16	Growth, Trends, and Forecasts	Excel	T2, T3	Data Forecasting	Advanced	Average, Trend, Growth	AYK.9
18	Formatting Grades	Excel	T3	Data Analysis	Advanced	If, LookUp	AYK.11
22	Turnover Rates	Excel	T3	Data Mining	Advanced	PivotTable	AYK.13
24	Breaking Even	Excel	T4	Business Analysis	Advanced	Goal Seek	AYK.14
25	Profit Scenario	Excel	T4	Sales Analysis	Advanced	Scenario Manager	AYK.14

Design Element: © McGraw Hill Education

Data: Business Intelligence

CHAPTER OUTLINE

SECTION 6.1

Data, Information, and Databases

- Data Quality
- Storing Data Using a Relational Database Management System
- Using a Relational Database for Business Advantages

SECTION 6.2

Data Warehouse and Blockchain

- Business Intelligence
- Data Warehouse
- Blockchain: Distributed Computing

What's in IT for me?

This chapter introduces the concepts of information and data and their relative importance to business professionals and firms. It distinguishes between data stored in transactional databases and powerful business intelligence gleaned from data warehouses. Students who understand how to access, manipulate, summarize, sort, and analyze data to support decision making find success. Information has power, and understanding that power will help you compete in the global marketplace. This chapter will provide you with an overview of database fundamentals and the characteristics associated with high-quality data. It will also explain how the various bits of data stored across multiple, operational databases can be transformed in a centralized repository of summarized information in a data warehouse, which can be used for discovering business intelligence.

You, as a business student, need to understand the differences between transactional data and summarized information, as well as the different types of questions you could use a transactional database versus a data warehouse to answer. You should be aware of the complexity of storing data in databases and the level of effort required to transform operational data into meaningful, summarized information. You also need to realize the power of information and the competitive advantage a data warehouse brings an organization in terms of facilitating business intelligence. Armed with the power of information, business students will make smart, informed, and data-supported managerial decisions.

opening case study

Elnur/Shutterstock

Welcome to the Field of Data Science

Storing large amounts of data is nothing new—in fact, businesses and governments have been storing huge amounts of data for decades. What is new is the capability to do something meaningful with the data, quickly and cost effectively. The field of data science is one of the hottest and fastest-growing fields, promising exciting and challenging careers. Surprisingly, the field of data science is only about 20 years old. The modern conception of data science as an independent discipline was first attributed to William S. Cleveland in 2001 and has evolved to encompass methods of recording, storing, and analyzing data to effectively extract useful information. Let's take a quick look at a few of the major milestones that led to the creation of this field to understand how it grew and where it is headed.

The Modern History of Data Science

- 2001: William S. Cleveland called for the new field and term *data science*. It became more widely used in the next few years.
- 2002: *Data Science Journal* launches.
- 2002: Torch machine learning library is created.
- 2003: Columbia University launches the *Journal of Data Science*.
- 2004: MapReduce algorithm is created.
- 2006: The Netflix prize is established.
- 2007: Machine learning library Scikit-learn is created.
- 2008: The data scientist role emerged due to DJ Patil and Jeff Hammerbacher. Data scientists collect large amounts of data, transform it into a more usable format, and solve business-related problems using data-driven techniques and tools.
- 2009: ImageNet, a large data collection used for computer vision research, spawns the AI boom.
- 2010: The Kaggle machine learning competition launches.
- 2010: *The Economist* declares a new kind of professional: the data scientist.
- 2011: Jeff Dean and Andrew Ng build a neural net that sees cats, which marks the start of the Google Brain project.
- 2012: Geoffrey Hinton unleashes deep neural networks.
- 2012: Snowflake launches a cloud computing–based data warehousing company.
- 2015: Google open sources TensorFlow, its AI engine.
- 2016: PyTorch is released.
- 2016: AlphaGo defeats the human Go champion.
- 2017: Amazon Web Services SageMaker launches.
- 2018: The BERT language model is created by Jacob Devlin and his colleagues from Google.

While the list of data science tools above is definitely not exhaustive, it is a broad overview of the techniques and skills you should be familiar with to jump into the data science field.[1]

section 6.1 | Data, Information, and Databases

LEARNING OUTCOMES

6.1 Explain the four primary traits that determine the value of data.

6.2 Describe a database, a database management system, and the relational database model.

6.3 Identify the business advantages of a relational database.

DATA QUALITY

LO 6.1: Explain the four primary traits that determine the value of data.

Information is powerful. It can tell an organization how its current operations are performing and help it estimate and strategize about how future operations might perform. The ability to understand, digest, analyze, and filter data is key to growth and success for any professional in any industry. Remember that new perspectives and opportunities can open up when you have the right data, which you can turn into information and ultimately business intelligence.

Data is everywhere in an organization. Managers in sales, marketing, human resources, and management need data to run their departments and make daily decisions. When addressing a significant business issue, employees must be able to obtain and analyze all the relevant data so they can make the best decision possible. Data comes at different levels, formats, and granularities.

- ***Data granularity***: Refers to the extent of detail within the data (fine and detailed or coarse and abstract).

Employees must be able to correlate the different levels, formats, and granularities of data when making decisions. For example, a company might be collecting data from various suppliers to make needed decisions, only to find that the data is in different levels, formats, and granularities. One supplier might send detailed data in a spreadsheet, whereas another supplier might send summary data in a Word document, and still another might send a collection of data from emails. Employees will need to compare these differing types of data for what they commonly reveal to make strategic decisions. Figure 6.1 displays the various levels, formats, and granularities of organizational data.

FIGURE 6.1

Levels, Formats, and Granularities of Organizational Data

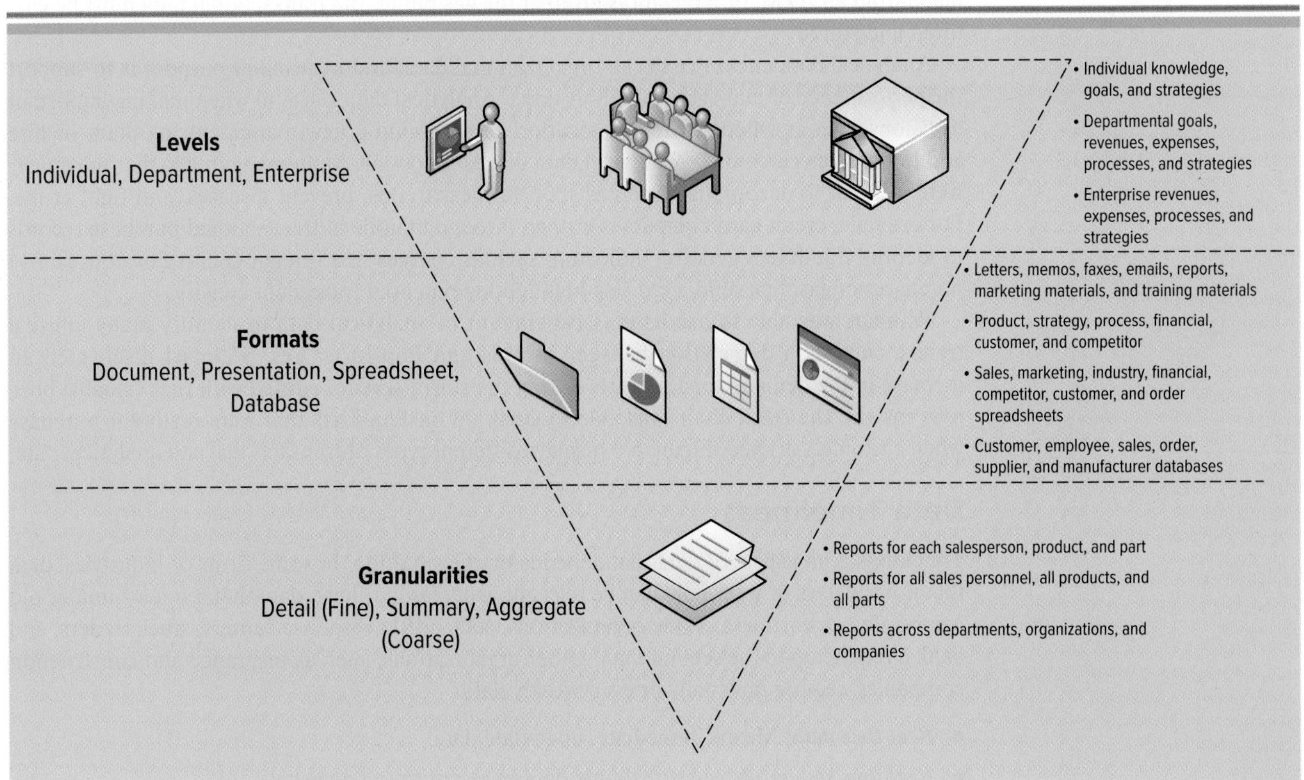

FIGURE 6.2

The Four Primary Traits of the Value of Data

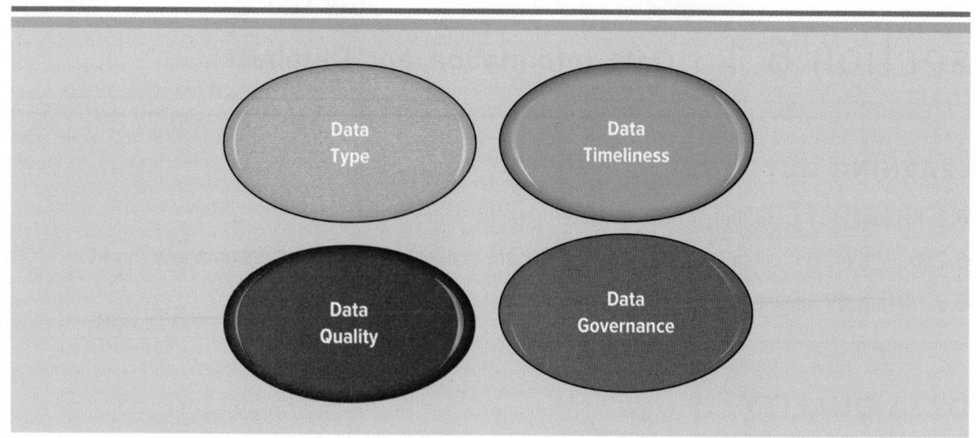

Successfully collecting, compiling, sorting, and finally analyzing data from multiple levels, in varied formats, and exhibiting different granularities can provide tremendous insight into how an organization is performing. Exciting and unexpected results can include potential new markets, new ways of reaching customers, and even new methods of doing business. After understanding the different levels, formats, and granularities of data, managers next want to look at the four primary traits that help determine the value of data (see Figure 6.2).

Data Type: Transactional and Analytical

The two primary types of data are transactional and analytical. Transactional data encompasses all of the data contained within a single business process or unit of work, and its primary purpose is to support daily operational tasks. Organizations need to capture and store transactional data to perform operational tasks and repetitive decisions such as analyzing daily sales reports and production schedules to determine how much inventory to carry. Consider Walmart, which handles more than 2 million customer transactions every hour, and Facebook, which keeps track of 800 million active users (along with their photos, friends, and web links). In addition, every time a cash register rings up a sale, a deposit or withdrawal is made from an ATM, or a receipt is given at the gas pump, the transactional data must be captured and stored.

Analytical data encompasses all organizational data, and its primary purpose is to support the performance of managerial analysis tasks. Analytical data is useful when making important decisions such as whether the organization should build a new manufacturing plant or hire additional sales personnel. Analytical data makes it possible to do many things that previously were difficult to accomplish, such as spot business trends, prevent diseases, and fight crime. For example, credit card companies crunch through billions of transactional purchase records to identify fraudulent activity. Indicators such as charges in a foreign country or consecutive purchases of gasoline send a red flag highlighting potential fraudulent activity.

Walmart was able to use its massive amount of analytical data to identify many unusual trends, such as a correlation between storms and Pop-Tarts. Yes, Walmart discovered an increase in the demand for Pop-Tarts during the storm season. Armed with that valuable business insight, the retail chain was able to stock up on Pop-Tarts that were ready for purchase when customers arrived. Figure 6.3 displays different types of transactional and analytical data.

Data Timeliness

Timeliness is an aspect of data that depends on the situation. In some firms or industries, data that is a few days or weeks old can be relevant, whereas in others, data that is a few minutes old can be almost worthless. Some organizations, such as 911 response centers, stock traders, and banks, require up-to-the-second data. Other organizations, such as insurance and construction companies, require only daily or even weekly data.

- ***Real-time data***: Means immediate, up-to-date data.
- ***Real-time system***: Provides real-time data in response to requests.

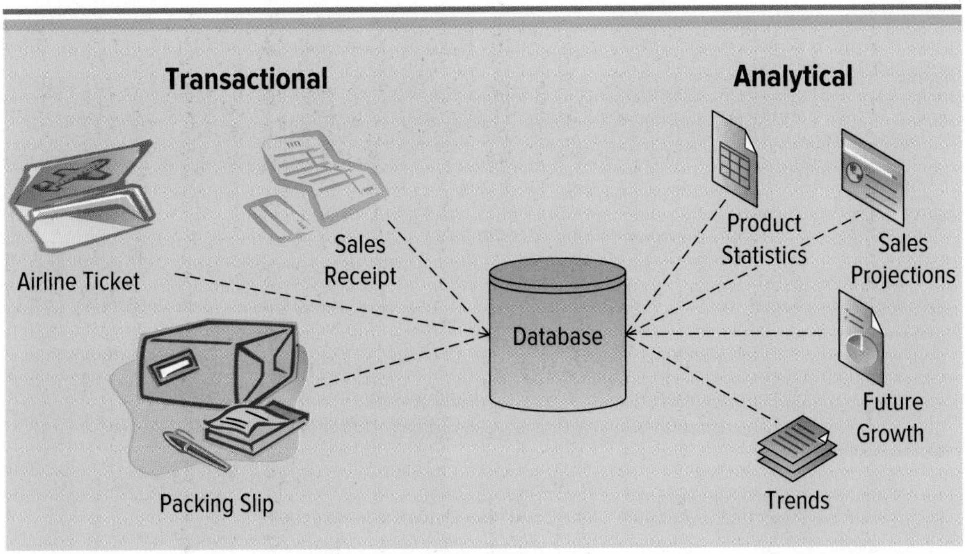

FIGURE 6.3

Transactional versus Analytical Data

Transactional

Analytical

Airline Ticket

Sales Receipt

Packing Slip

Database

Product Statistics

Sales Projections

Future Growth

Trends

Many organizations use real-time systems to uncover key corporate transactional data. The growing demand for real-time data stems from organizations' need to make faster and more effective decisions, keep smaller inventories, operate more efficiently, and track performance more carefully. Data also needs to be timely in the sense that it meets employees' needs but no more. If employees can absorb data only on an hourly or daily basis, there is no need to gather real-time data in smaller increments.

Most people request real-time data without understanding one of the biggest pitfalls associated with real-time data—continual change. Imagine the following scenario: Three managers meet at the end of the day to discuss a business problem. Each manager has gathered data at different times during the day to create a picture of the situation. Each manager's picture may be different because of the time differences. Their views on the business problem may not match because the data they are basing their analysis on is continually changing. This approach may not speed up decision making, and it may actually slow it down. Business decision makers must evaluate the timeliness of the data for every decision. Organizations do not want to find themselves using real-time data to make a bad decision faster.

Data Quality

Business decisions are only as good as the quality of the data used to make them.

- ***Data inconsistency***: Occurs when the same data element has different values. Take, for example, the amount of work that needs to occur to update a customer who had changed her last name due to marriage. Changing this data in only a few organizational systems will lead to data inconsistencies, causing customer 123456 to be associated with two last names.
- ***Data integrity issues***: Occur when a system produces incorrect, inconsistent, or duplicate data. Data integrity issues can cause managers to consider the system reports invalid and make decisions based on other sources.

To ensure that your systems do not suffer from data integrity issues, review Figure 6.4 for the five characteristics common to high-quality data: accuracy, completeness, consistency, timeliness, and uniqueness. Figure 6.5 provides an example of several problems associated with using low-quality data, including:

1. *Completeness*. The customer's first name is missing.
2. Another issue with *completeness*. The street address contains only a number and not a street name.
3. *Consistency*. There may be a duplication of data since there is a slight difference between the two customers in the spelling of the last name. Similar street addresses and phone numbers make this likely.

FIGURE 6.4

Five Common Characteristics of High-Quality Data

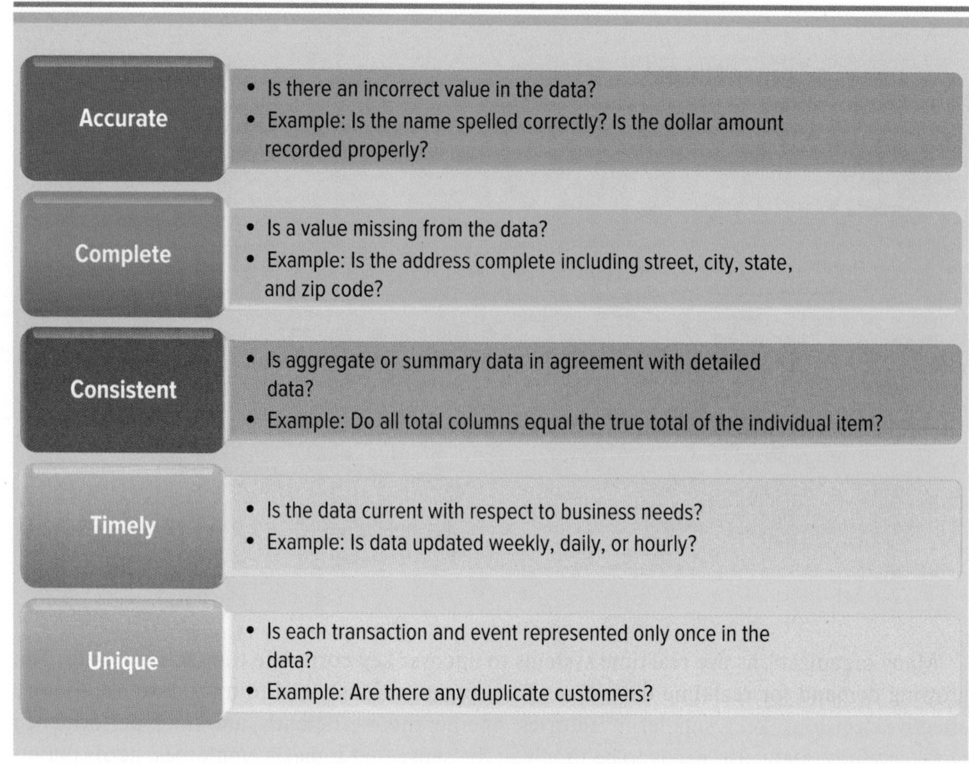

Accurate
• Is there an incorrect value in the data?
• Example: Is the name spelled correctly? Is the dollar amount recorded properly?
Complete
• Is a value missing from the data?
• Example: Is the address complete including street, city, state, and zip code?
Consistent
• Is aggregate or summary data in agreement with detailed data?
• Example: Do all total columns equal the true total of the individual item?
Timely
• Is the data current with respect to business needs?
• Example: Is data updated weekly, daily, or hourly?
Unique
• Is each transaction and event represented only once in the data?
• Example: Are there any duplicate customers?

4. *Accuracy*. This may be inaccurate data because the customer's phone and fax numbers are the same. Some customers might have the same number for phone and fax, but the fact that the customer also has this number in the email address field is suspicious.
5. Another issue with *accuracy*. There is inaccurate data because a phone number is located in the email address field.
6. Another issue with *completeness*. The data is incomplete because there is not a valid area code for the phone and fax numbers.

Knowing how low-quality data issues typically occur can help a company correct them. Addressing these errors will significantly improve the quality of company data and the value to be extracted from it. The four primary reasons for low-quality data are:

1. Online customers intentionally enter inaccurate data to protect their privacy.
2. Different systems have different data entry standards and formats.

FIGURE 6.5

Example of Low-Quality Data

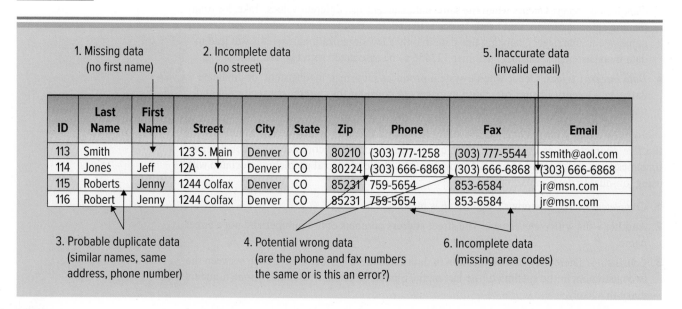

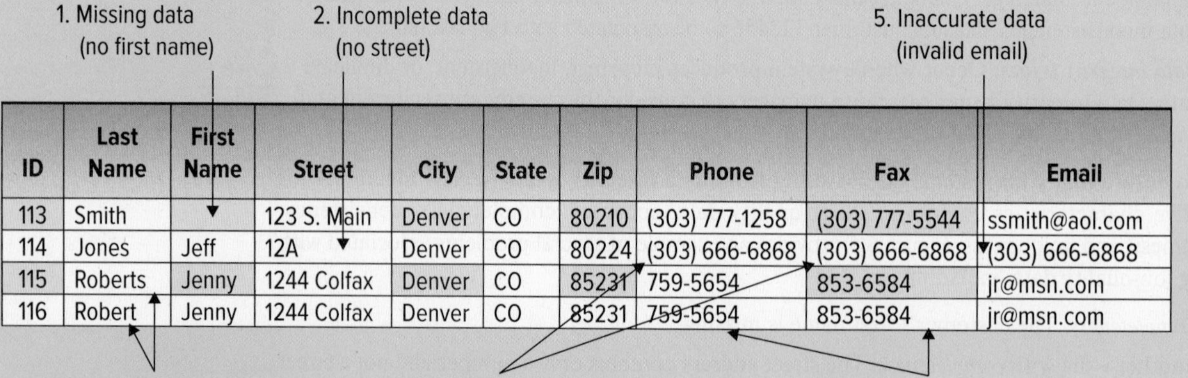

ID	Last Name	First Name	Street	City	State	Zip	Phone	Fax	Email
113	Smith		123 S. Main	Denver	CO	80210	(303) 777-1258	(303) 777-5544	ssmith@aol.com
114	Jones	Jeff	12A	Denver	CO	80224	(303) 666-6868	(303) 666-6868	(303) 666-6868
115	Roberts	Jenny	1244 Colfax	Denver	CO	85231	759-5654	853-6584	jr@msn.com
116	Robert	Jenny	1244 Colfax	Denver	CO	85231	759-5654	853-6584	jr@msn.com

BUSINESS DRIVEN MIS

Determining Data Quality Issues

Real People magazine is geared toward working individuals and provides articles and advice on everything from car maintenance to family planning. The magazine is currently experiencing problems with its distribution list. More than 30 percent of the magazines mailed are returned because of incorrect address data, and each month, the magazine receives numerous calls from angry customers complaining that they have not yet received their copies. Below is a sample of *Real People*'s customer data. Create a report detailing all the issues with the data, potential causes of the data issues, and solutions the company can follow to correct the situation.

ID	First Name	Middle Initial	Last Name	Street	City	State	Zip Code
433	M	J	Jones	13 Denver	Denver	CO	87654
434	Margaret	J	Jones	13 First Ave.	Denver	CO	87654
434	Brian	F	Hoover	Lake Ave.	Columbus	OH	87654
435	Nick	H	Schweitzer	65 Apple Lane	San Francisco	OH	65664
436	Richard	A		567 55th St.	New York	CA	98763
437	Alana	B	Smith	121 Tenny Dr.	Buffalo	NY	142234
438	Trevor	D	Darrian	90 Fresrdestil	Dallas	TX	74532

3. Data-entry personnel enter abbreviated data to save time or erroneous data by accident.
4. Third-party and external data contains inconsistencies, inaccuracies, and errors.

Understanding the Costs of Using Low-Quality Data Using the wrong data can lead managers to make erroneous decisions. Erroneous decisions in turn can cost time, money, reputations, and even jobs. Some of the serious business consequences that occur due to using low-quality data to make decisions are:

- Inability to track customers accurately.
- Difficulty identifying the organization's most valuable customers.
- Inability to identify selling opportunities.
- Lost revenue opportunities from marketing to nonexistent customers.
- The cost of sending undeliverable mail.
- Difficulty tracking revenue because of inaccurate invoices.
- Inability to build strong relationships with customers.

Understanding the Benefits of Using High-Quality Data High-quality data can significantly improve the chances of making a good decision and directly increase an organization's bottom line.

- ***Data steward*****:** Responsible for ensuring the policies and procedures are implemented across the organization and acts as a liaison between the MIS department and the business.
- ***Data stewardship*****:** The management and oversight of an organization's data assets to help provide business users with high-quality data that is easily accessible in a consistent manner.

One company discovered that even with its large number of golf courses, Phoenix, Arizona, is not a good place to sell golf clubs. An analysis revealed that typical golfers in Phoenix are tourists who usually bring their clubs with them. The analysis further revealed that two of the best places to sell golf clubs in the United States are Rochester, New York, and Detroit, Michigan. Equipped with this valuable information, the company was able to strategically place its stores and launch its marketing campaigns.

High-quality data does not automatically guarantee that every decision made is going to be a good one, because people ultimately make decisions and no one is perfect. However, such data ensures that the basis of the decisions is accurate. The success of the organization depends on appreciating and leveraging the true value of timely and high-quality data.

Data Governance

Data is a vital resource, and users need to be educated on what they can and cannot do with it. To ensure that a firm manages its data correctly, it will need special policies and procedures establishing rules on how the data is organized, updated, maintained, and accessed. The purpose of data is to provide guidance that helps our leaders make smart policy decisions. The data themselves are not the policy. The data exist to help us know whether reopening or locking down or whatever is working. Every firm, large and small, should create a policy concerning data governance.

- ***Data governance***: Refers to the overall management of the availability, usability, integrity, and security of company data.
- ***Master data management (MDM)***: The practice of gathering data and ensuring it is uniform, accurate, consistent, and complete, including such entities as customers, suppliers, products, sales, employees, and other critical entities that are commonly integrated across organizational systems. MDM is commonly included in data governance.

A company that supports a data governance program has a defined policy that specifies who is accountable for various portions or aspects of the data, including its accuracy, accessibility, consistency, timeliness, and completeness. The policy should clearly define the processes concerning how to store, archive, back up, and secure the data. In addition, the company should create a set of procedures identifying accessibility levels for employees. Then, the firm should deploy controls and procedures that enforce government regulations and compliance with mandates such as Sarbanes-Oxley.

It is important to note the difference between data governance and data stewardship. Data governance focuses on enterprisewide policies and procedures, while data stewardship focuses on the strategic implementation of the policies and procedures.

Data validation includes the tests and evaluations used to determine compliance with data governance polices to ensure the correctness of data. Data validation helps to ensure that every data value is correct and accurate. In Excel, you can use data validation to control the type of data or the values that users enter into a cell. For example, you may want to restrict data entry to a certain range of dates, limit choices by using a list, or make sure that only positive whole numbers are entered.

LO 6.2: Describe a database, a database management system, and the relational database model.

STORING DATA USING A RELATIONAL DATABASE MANAGEMENT SYSTEM

The core component of any system, regardless of size, is a database and a database management system.

- ***Database***: Maintains data about various types of objects (inventory), events (transactions), people (employees), and places (warehouses).
- ***Database management system (DBMS)***: Creates, reads, updates, and deletes data in a database while controlling access and security.

Managers send requests to the DBMS, and the DBMS performs the actual manipulation of the data in the database. Companies store their data in databases, and managers access these systems to answer operational questions such as how many customers purchased Product A in

BUSINESS DRIVEN DEBATE

Data Cleansing Debate

Having perfect data is simply not a reality. The cost to cleanse data is high, and most organizations have to make a decision on how clean they want the data before they make business decisions. For each of the following, decide if you would be comfortable or uncomfortable using the data to make the decisions.

1. Marketing: You have sent out a quick electronic survey to potential and current customers about an exciting new product. The survey is optional and does not track who is completing the survey. You have the results: 100 percent complete survey data. However, you do not know who completed the surveys and believe the data to be about 50 percent accurate. Would you use the results to launch a new product or want to reissue the survey requiring authentication of each participant?
2. Human resources: You have sent out a quick electronic survey to all 500 of your employees to determine job satisfaction. Only 30 percent of the employees completed the survey with 100 percent completion; 20 percent completed the survey with 50 percent completion; and 50 percent chose not to complete the survey. Would you feel comfortable using the results as an accurate predictor of job satisfaction?
3. Salary comparisons: One of your employees has collected data from four external sources on average salaries for each job posting in your company. The employee recently quit and did not document where the data was collected from. Do you feel comfortable using the data to analyze your salaries?

December or what the average sales were by region. Two primary tools available for retrieving data from a DBMS include:

- ***Structured query language (SQL)***: Asks users to write lines of code to answer questions against a database.
- ***Query-by-example (QBE) tool***: Helps users graphically design the answer to a question against a database.

Managers typically interact with QBE tools, and MIS professionals have the skills required to code SQL. Figure 6.6 displays the relationship between a database, a DBMS, and a user. Some of the more popular examples of DBMS include MySQL, Microsoft Access, and SQL Server.

Figure 6.7 displays a few additional terms you need to be familiar with when learning about databases.

FIGURE 6.6

Relationship of Database, DBMS, and User

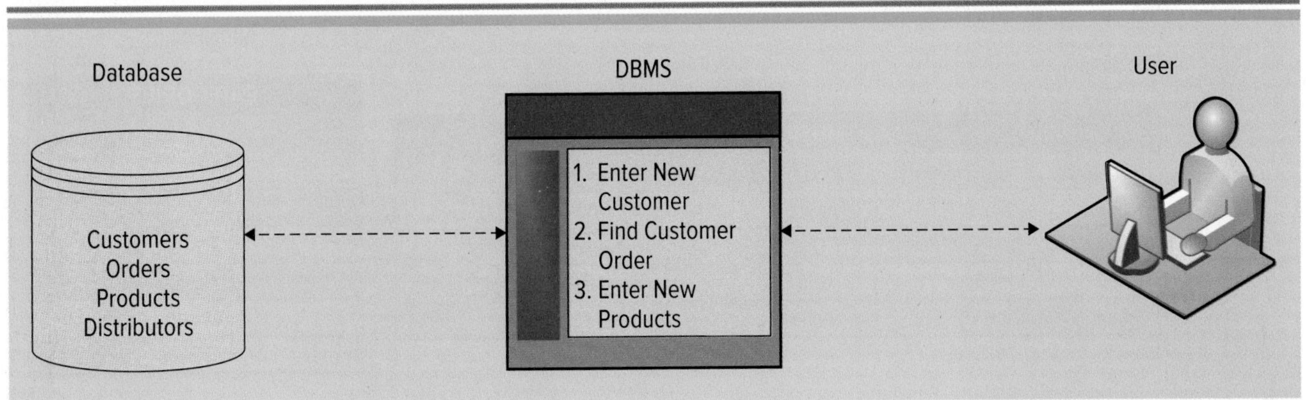

FIGURE 6.7

Common Database Terms

Term	Example
Data element (or data field): The smallest or basic unit of data.	Data elements can include a customer's name, address, email, discount rate, preferred shipping method, product name, quantity ordered, and so on.
Data models: Logical data structures that detail the relationships among data elements by using graphics or pictures.	Each data element is given a description, such as Customer Name; metadata is provided for the type of data (text, numeric, alphanumeric, date, image, binary value) and descriptions of potential predefined values such as a certain area code; and finally the relationship is defined.
Metadata: Provides details about data.	For example, metadata for an image could include its size, resolution, and date created. Metadata about a text document could contain document length, data created, author's name, and summary.
Data dictionary: Compiles all of the metadata about the data elements in the data model.	Looking at a data model, along with reviewing the data dictionary, provides tremendous insight into the database's functions, purpose, and business rules.

Storing Data Elements in Entities and Attributes

For flexibility in supporting business operations, managers need to query or search for the answers to business questions such as which artist sold the most albums during a certain month.

- ***Relational database model:*** Stores data in the form of logically related two-dimensional tables.
- ***Relational database management system:*** Allows users to create, read, update, and delete data in a relational database. The relationships in the relational database model help managers extract this data. Figure 6.8 illustrates the primary concepts of the relational database model: entities, attributes, keys, and relationships.

FIGURE 6.8

Primary Concepts of the Relational Database Model

Entities

Foreign keys

Primary keys

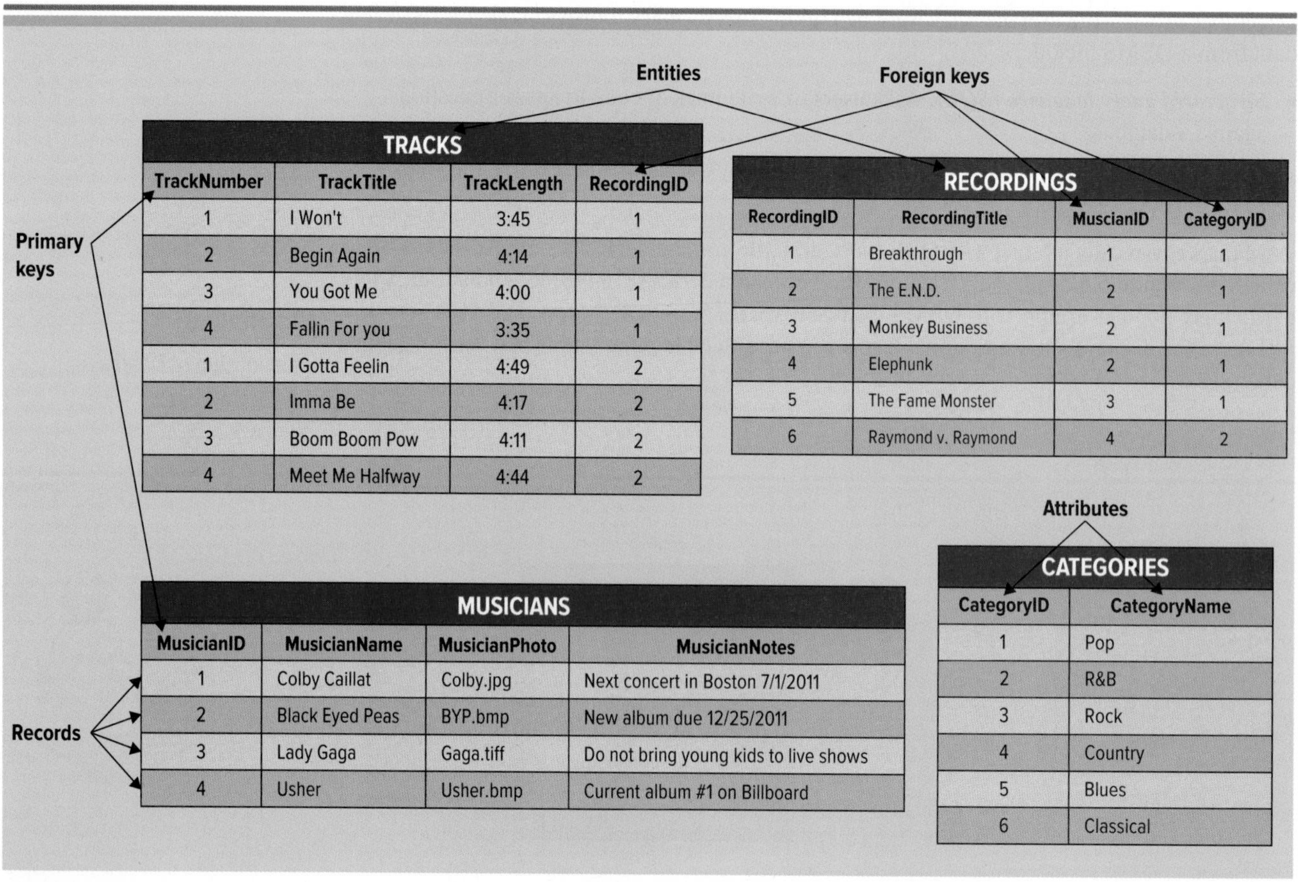

TRACKS

TrackNumber	TrackTitle	TrackLength	RecordingID
1	I Won't	3:45	1
2	Begin Again	4:14	1
3	You Got Me	4:00	1
4	Fallin For you	3:35	1
1	I Gotta Feelin	4:49	2
2	Imma Be	4:17	2
3	Boom Boom Pow	4:11	2
4	Meet Me Halfway	4:44	2

RECORDINGS

RecordingID	RecordingTitle	MuscianID	CategoryID
1	Breakthrough	1	1
2	The E.N.D.	2	1
3	Monkey Business	2	1
4	Elephunk	2	1
5	The Fame Monster	3	1
6	Raymond v. Raymond	4	2

Attributes

CATEGORIES

CategoryID	CategoryName
1	Pop
2	R&B
3	Rock
4	Country
5	Blues
6	Classical

Records

MUSICIANS

MusicianID	MusicianName	MusicianPhoto	MusicianNotes
1	Colby Caillat	Colby.jpg	Next concert in Boston 7/1/2011
2	Black Eyed Peas	BYP.bmp	New album due 12/25/2011
3	Lady Gaga	Gaga.tiff	Do not bring young kids to live shows
4	Usher	Usher.bmp	Current album #1 on Billboard

BUSINESS DRIVEN ANALYTICS

Lies, Lies, and More Lies: How to Lie with Statistics

It is great that we can now collect massive amounts of rich, granular data for businesses of all shapes and sizes. However, understanding what to do with these massive amounts of data can be difficult and costly, and even with the right tools, it can be overwhelming. Analyze the following common big data analysis errors and rank them depending on the error that would cause the most damage for problems with inaccurate analysis to least damage to a data analysis.

- **Analysis Paralysis:** Impossible to make a decision with the overwhelming amount of data collection.
- **Lack of a Data Steward:** Without a data steward, the rules to how data is collected are lacking and you find duplicates, columns being used incorrectly, and inaccurate input. Always have a role (or committee) responsible for data hygiene along with the mandate to keep it clean.
- **Data Silos:** Data is the new oil. As a result, countless companies are collecting and storing as much of it as they can and letting it sit idle because they do not have a need or direction for analysis. Don't just let your data sit in a silo. It has the power to improve operations, inform your product road map, and solve long-standing obstacles–but only if you actually use it.
- **Lack of Analytics:** Businesses are finding they do not have the talent or expertise to properly analyze the massive amounts of data they are collecting. For example, predictive maintenance tools such as sensors collect massive amounts of data that sometimes do not get analyzed. A good practice for big data is to hire someone who is dedicated to taking action–not just sharing insights from data, but also driving organizational change.
- **Thinking You Control Your Data:** No business or individual has full control over their data. The way things work now, data is copied every time a new person or application wants to work with it. This results in thousands of copies of data, which makes it impossible to truly have control over anything. You might have the best security in the world, but that's only protecting one copy out of thousands.

- ***Entity*** (also referred to as a table): Stores data about a person, place, thing, transaction, or event. The entities, or tables, of interest in Figure 6.8 are *TRACKS, RECORDINGS, MUSICIANS,* and *CATEGORIES*. Notice that each entity is stored in a different two-dimensional table (with rows and columns).
- ***Attributes*** (also called columns or fields): The data elements associated with an entity. In Figure 6.8, the attributes for the entity *TRACKS* are *TrackNumber, TrackTitle, TrackLength,* and *RecordingID*. Attributes for the entity *MUSICIANS* are *MusicianID, MusicianName, MusicianPhoto,* and *MusicianNotes*.
- ***Record***: A collection of related data elements (in the *MUSICIANS* table, these include "3, Lady Gaga, Gaga.tiff, Do not bring young kids to live shows"). Each record in an entity occupies one row in its respective table.

Creating Relationships through Keys

To manage and organize various entities within the relational database model, you use primary keys and foreign keys to create logical relationships. Let's jump into an analysis of a primary key.

- ***Primary key:*** A field (or group of fields) that uniquely identifies a given record in a table. In the table *RECORDINGS,* the primary key is the field *RecordingID* that uniquely identifies each record in the table.

Primary keys are a critical piece of a relational database because they provide a way of distinguishing each record in a table; for instance, imagine you need to find data on a customer named Steve Smith. Simply searching the customer name would not be an ideal way to find the data because there might be 20 customers with the name Steve Smith. This is the reason the relational database model uses primary keys to identify each record uniquely. Using Steve Smith's unique ID allows a manager to search the database to identify all data associated with this customer. You have a primary key on your university ID (student number), driver's license (State ID), Social Security card (SS#). Without a way to uniquely identify an individual (individual record), it would be impossible to track your data. Every item in a database must be uniquely identified. Product IDs, Sales IDs, Store IDs, Employee IDs, Customer IDs–these entities all have a unique primary key to identify their data (attributes).

Now that you understand primary keys, let's look at the second form of keys in a database: foreign keys.

- ***Foreign key:*** A primary key of one table that appears as an attribute in another table and acts to provide a logical relationship between the two tables.

A foreign key would be similar to your student ID appearing in a particular class. The class has a unique primary key to identify the course. In the course, you have a professor and many students. The professor ID (primary key) identifying the professor would appear in the course to ensure you know who is teaching the class. Each unique Student ID (primary key) would appear in the course to ensure you can identify each student enrolled in the course. When a primary key from one table appears in another table, it is called a foreign key and forms the relationship to allow you to understand how the data relates.

For instance, Black Eyed Peas in Figure 6.8 is one of the musicians appearing in the *MUSICIANS* table. Its primary key, *MusicianID,* is "2." Notice that *MusicianID* also appears as an attribute in the *RECORDINGS* table. By matching these attributes, you create a relationship between the *MUSICIANS* and *RECORDINGS* tables that states the Black Eyed Peas *(MusicianID 2)* have several recordings, including *The E.N.D., Monkey Business,* and *Elephunk*. In essence, *MusicianID* in the *RECORDINGS* table creates a logical relationship (who was the musician that made the recording) to the *MUSICIANS* table. Creating the logical relationship between the tables allows managers to search the data and turn it into useful information.

Coca-Cola Relational Database Example

Figure 6.9 illustrates the primary concepts of the relational database model for a sample order of soda from Coca-Cola. Figure 6.9 offers an excellent example of how data is stored in a database. For example, the order number is stored in the ORDER table, and each line item is stored in the ORDER LINE table. Entities include CUSTOMER, ORDER, ORDER LINE, PRODUCT, and DISTRIBUTOR. Attributes for CUSTOMER include Customer ID, Customer Name, Contact Name, and Phone. Attributes for PRODUCT include Product ID, Product Description, and Price. The columns in the table contain the attributes.

Consider Hawkins Shipping, one of the distributors appearing in the DISTRIBUTOR table. Its primary key, Distributor ID, is DEN8001. Distributor ID also appears as an attribute in the ORDER table. This establishes that Hawkins Shipping (Distributor ID DEN8001) was responsible for delivering orders 34561 and 34562 to the appropriate customer(s). Therefore, Distributor ID in the ORDER table creates a logical relationship (who shipped what order) between ORDER and DISTRIBUTOR.

LO 6.3: Identify the business advantages of a relational database.

USING A RELATIONAL DATABASE FOR BUSINESS ADVANTAGES

Many business managers are familiar with Excel and other spreadsheet programs they can use to store business data. Although spreadsheets are excellent for supporting some data analysis, they offer limited functionality in terms of security, accessibility, and flexibility and can rarely scale to support business growth. From a business perspective, relational

FIGURE 6.9

Potential Relational Database for Coca-Cola Bottling Company of Egypt

Order Number: 34562

Coca-Cola Bottling Company of Egypt
Sample Sales Order

Customer: Dave's Sub Shop	Date: 8/6/2028

Quantity	Product	Price	Amount
100	Vanilla Coke	$0.55	$55

Distributor Fee $12.95

Order Total $67.95

CUSTOMER

Customer ID	*Customer Name*	*Contact Name*	*Phone*
23	Dave's Sub Shop	David Logan	(555)333-4545
43	Pizza Palace	Debbie Fernandez	(555)345-5432
765	T's Fun Zone	Tom Repicci	(555)565-6655

ORDER

Order ID	*Order Date*	*Customer ID*	*Distributor ID*	*Distributor Fee*	*Total Due*
34561	7/4/2028	23	DEN8001	$22.00	$145.75
34562	8/6/2028	23	DEN8001	$12.95	$67.95
34563	6/5/2028	765	NY9001	$29.50	$249.50

ORDER LINE

Order ID	*Line Item*	*Product ID*	*Quantity*
34561	1	12345AA	75
34561	2	12346BB	50
34561	3	12347CC	100
34562	1	12349EE	100
34563	1	12345AA	100
34563	2	12346BB	100
34563	3	12347CC	50
34563	4	12348DD	50
34563	5	12349EE	100

DISTRIBUTOR

Distributor ID	*Distributor Name*
DEN8001	Hawkins Shipping
CHI3001	ABC Trucking
NY9001	Van Distributors

PRODUCT

Product ID	*Product Description*	*Price*
12345AA	Coca-Cola	$0.55
12346BB	Diet Coke	$0.55
12347CC	Sprite	$0.55
12348DD	Diet Sprite	$0.55
12349EE	Vanilla Coke	$0.55

APPLY YOUR KNOWLEDGE

BUSINESS DRIVEN ETHICS AND SECURITY

Unethical Data Mining

Mining large amounts of data can create a number of benefits for business, society, and governments, but it can also create a number of ethical questions surrounding an invasion of privacy or misuse of data. Facebook recently came under fire for its data mining practices because it followed 700,000 accounts to determine whether posts with highly emotional content are more contagious.

The study concluded that highly emotional texts are contagious, just as emotions are contagious with real people. Highly emotional positive posts received multiple positive replies, whereas highly emotional negative posts received multiple negative replies. Although the study seems rather innocent, many Facebook users were outraged; they felt the study was an invasion of privacy because the 700,000 accounts had no idea Facebook was mining their posts.

As a Facebook user, you willingly consent that Facebook owns every bit and byte of data you post, and once you press Post, Facebook can do whatever it wants with your data. Do you agree or disagree that Facebook has the right to do whatever it wants with the data its 1.5 billion users post on its site?

databases offer many advantages over using a text document or a spreadsheet, as displayed in Figure 6.10.

Increased Flexibility

Databases tend to mirror business structures, and a database needs to handle changes quickly and easily, just as any business needs to be able to do. Equally important, databases need to provide flexibility in allowing each user to access the data in whatever way best suits his or her needs. The distinction between logical and physical views is important in understanding flexible database user views.

- ***Physical view of data***: Deals with the physical storage of data on a storage device.
- ***Logical view of data***: Focuses on how individual users logically access data to meet their own particular business needs.

In the database illustration from Figure 6.8, for example, one user could perform a query to determine which recordings had a track length of four minutes or more. At the same time,

FIGURE 6.10

Business Advantages of a Relational Database

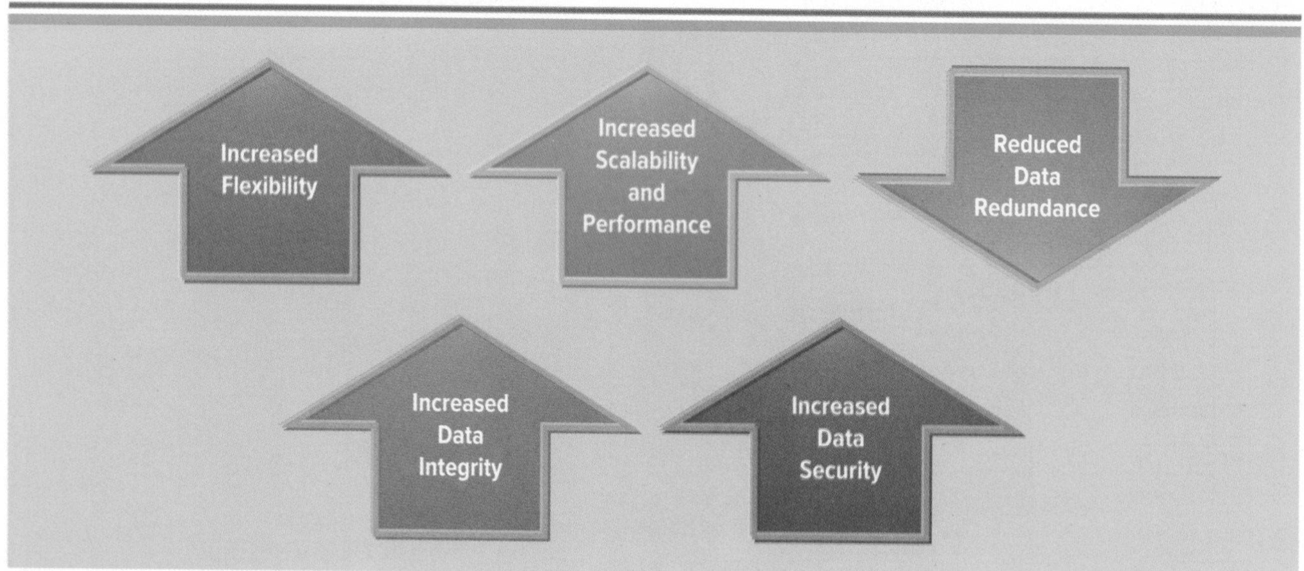

another user could perform an analysis to determine the distribution of recordings as they relate to the different categories. For example, are there more R&B recordings than rock, or are they evenly distributed? This example demonstrates that although a database has only one physical view, it can easily support multiple logical views that provide for flexibility.

Consider another example: a mail-order business. One user might want a report presented in alphabetical format, in which case the last name should appear before the first name. Another user, working with a catalog mailing system, would want customer names appearing as first name and then last name. Both are easily achievable but different logical views of the same physical data.

Increased Scalability and Performance

The database has to be scalable to handle the massive volumes of data and the large numbers of users expected for the launch of the website. In addition, the database needs to perform quickly under heavy use.

- ***Data latency***: The time it takes for data to be stored or retrieved.

Some organizations must be able to support hundreds or thousands of users including employees, partners, customers, and suppliers, who all want to access and share the same data with minimal data latency. Databases today scale to exceptional levels, allowing all types of users and programs to perform data-processing and data-searching tasks.

Reduced Data Redundancy

Redundant data can cause storage issues along with data integrity issues, making it difficult to determine which values are the most current or most accurate.

- ***Data redundancy***: The duplication of data, or the storage of the same data in multiple places.

Employees become confused and frustrated when faced with incorrect data, causing disruptions to business processes and procedures. One primary goal of a database is to eliminate data redundancy by recording each piece of data in only one place in the database. This saves disk space, makes performing data updates easier, and improves data quality.

Increased Data Integrity (Quality)

Data streaming into a database must be validated and checked to ensure it is accurate beyond just being entered into the system.

- ***Business rule***: Defines how a company performs certain aspects of its business, and typically results in either a yes/no or true/false answer. Stating that merchandise returns are allowed within 10 days of purchase is an example of a business rule.
- ***Data integrity***: A measure of the quality of data.
- ***Integrity constraints***: Rules that help ensure the quality of data.

The database design needs to consider integrity constraints. The database and the DBMS ensure that users can never violate these constraints. Figure 6.11 displays the two types of integrity constraints: (1) relational and (2) business critical.

FIGURE 6.11

Relational and Business Critical Integrity Constraints

Term	Example
Relational integrity constraints: Rules that enforce basic and fundamental information-based constraints.	For example, a relational integrity constraint would not allow someone to create an order for a nonexistent customer, provide a markup percentage that was negative, or order zero pounds of raw materials from a supplier.
Business-critical integrity constraints: Enforce business rules vital to an organization's success and often require more insight and knowledge than relational integrity constraints.	Consider a supplier of fresh produce to large grocery chains such as Kroger. The supplier might implement a business-critical integrity constraint stating that no product returns are accepted after 15 days past delivery. That would make sense because of the chance of spoilage of the produce. Business-critical integrity constraints tend to mirror the very rules by which an organization achieves success.

APPLY YOUR KNOWLEDGE

BUSINESS DRIVEN GLOBALIZATION

Integrity Information Inc.

Congratulations! You have just been hired as a consultant for Integrity Information Inc., a start-up business intelligence consulting company. Your first job is to help work with the sales department in securing a new client, The Warehouse. The Warehouse has been operating in the United States for more than a decade, and its primary business is to sell wholesale low-cost products. The Warehouse is interested in hiring Integrity Information Inc. to clean up the data stored in its U.S. database. To determine how good your work is, the client would like your analysis of the following spreadsheet. The Warehouse is also interested in expanding globally and wants to purchase several independent wholesale stores located in Australia, Thailand, China, Japan, and the United Kingdom. Before the company moves forward with the venture, it wants to understand what types of data issues it might encounter as it begins to transfer data from each global entity to the data warehouse. Please create a list detailing the potential issues The Warehouse can anticipate encountering as it consolidates the global databases into a single data warehouse.[2]

CUST ID	First Name	Last Name	Address	City	State	Zip	Phone	Last Order Date
233620	Christopher	Lee	12421 W Olympic Blvd	Los Angeles	CA	75080-1100	(972)680-7848	4/18/2028
233621	Bruce	Brandwen	268 W 44th St	New York	PA	10036-3906	(212)471-6077	5/3/2028
233622	Glr	Johnson	4100 E Dry Creek Rd	Littleton	CO	80122-3729	(303)712-5461	5/6/2028
233623	Dave	Owens	466 Commerce Rd	Staunton	VA	24401-4432	(540)851-0362	3/19/2028
233624	John	Coulbourn	124 Action St	Maynard	MA	1754	(978)987-0100	4/24/2028
233629	Dan	Gagliardo	2875 Union Rd	Cheektowaga	NY	14227-1461	(716)558-8191	5/4/2028
23362	Damanceee	Allen	1633 Broadway	New York	NY	10019-6708	(212)708-1576	
233630	Michael	Peretz	235 E 45th St	New York	NY	10017-3305	(212)210-1340	4/30/2028
233631	Jody	Veeder	440 Science Dr	Madison	WI	53711-1064	(608)238-9690 X227	3/27/2028
233632	Michael	Kehrer	3015 SSE Loop 323	Tyler	TX	75701	(903)579-3229	4/28/2028
233633	Erin	Yoon	3500 Carillon Pt	Kirkland	WA	98033-7354	(425)897-7221	3/25/2028
233634	Madeline	Shefferly	4100 E Dry Creek Rd	Littleton	CO	80122-3729	(303)486-3949	3/33/2028
233635	Steven	Conduit	1332 Enterprise Dr	West Chester	PA	19380-5970	(610)692-5900	4/27/2028
233636	Joseph	Kovach	1332 Enterprise Dr	West Chester	PA	19380-5970	(610)692-5900	4/28/2028
233637	Richard	Jordan	1700 N	Philadelphia	PA	19131-4728	(215)581-6770	3/19/2028
233638	Scott	Mikolajczyk	1655 Crofton Blvd	Crofton	MD	21114-1387	(410)729-8155	4/28/2028
233639	Susan	Shragg	1875 Century Park E	Los Angeles	CA	90067-2501	(310)785-0511	4/29/2028
233640	Rob	Ponto	29777 Telegraph Rd	Southfield	MI	48034-1303	(810)204-4724	5/5/2028
233642	Lauren	Butler	1211 Avenue Of The Americas	New York	NY	10036-8701	(212)852-7494	4/22/2028
233643	Christopher	Lee	12421 W Olympic Blvd	Los Angeles	CA	90064-1022	(310)689-2577	3/25/2028
233644	Michelle	Decker	6922 Hollywood Blvd	Hollywood	CA	90028-6117	(323)817-4655	5/8/2028
233647	Natalia	Galeano	1211 Avenue Of The Americas	New York	NY	10036-8701	(646)728-6911	4/23/2028
233648	Bobbie	Orchard	4201 Congress St	Charlotte	NC	28209-4617	(704)557-2444	5/11/2028
233650	Ben	Konfino	1111 Stewart Ave	Bethpage	NY	11714-3533	(516)803-1406	3/19/2028
233651	Lenee	Santana	1050 Techwood Dr NW	Atlanta	GA	30318-KKRR	(404)885-2000	3/22/2028
233652	Lauren	Monks	7700 Wisconsin Ave	Bethesda	MD	20814-3578	(301)771-4772	3/19/2005
233653	Mark	Woolley	10950 Washington Blvd	Culver City	CA	90232-4026	(310)202-2900	4/20/2028

The specification and enforcement of integrity constraints produce higher-quality data that will provide better support for business decisions. Organizations that establish specific procedures for developing integrity constraints typically see an increase in accuracy that then increases the use of organizational data by business professionals.

Increased Data Security

Managers must protect data, like any asset, from unauthorized users or misuse. As systems become increasingly complex and highly available over the Internet on many devices, security becomes an even bigger issue. Databases offer many security features, including passwords to provide authentication, access levels to determine who can access the data, and access controls to determine what type of access they have to the data.

For example, customer service representatives might need read-only access to customer order data so they can answer customer order inquiries; they might not have or need the authority to change or delete order data. Managers might require access to employee files, but they should have access only to their own employees' files, not the employee files for the entire company. Various security features of databases can ensure that individuals have only certain types of access to certain types of data.

- ***Identity management***: A broad administrative area that deals with identifying individuals in a system (such as a country, a network, or an enterprise) and controlling their access to resources within that system by associating user rights and restrictions with the established identity.

Security risks are increasing as more and more databases and DBMSs are moving to data centers run in the cloud. The biggest risks when using cloud computing are ensuring the security and privacy of the data in the database. Implementing data governance policies and procedures that outline the data management requirements can ensure safe and secure cloud computing.

section 6.2 Data Warehouse and Blockchain

LEARNING OUTCOMES

6.4 Identify the advantages of using business intelligence to support managerial decision making.

6.5 Describe the roles and purposes of data warehouses and data marts in an organization.

6.6 Explain blockchain and its advantages over a centralized relational database.

BUSINESS INTELLIGENCE

LO 6.4: Identify the advantages of using business intelligence to support managerial decision making.

Many organizations today find it next to impossible to understand their own strengths and weaknesses, let alone their biggest competitors', because the enormous volume of organizational data is inaccessible to all but the MIS department.

- ***Data point***: An individual item on a graph or a chart.

Organizational data includes far more than simple structured data elements in a database; the set of data also includes unstructured data such as voice mail, customer phone calls, text messages, and video clips, along with numerous new forms of data, such as tweets from Twitter.

An early reference to business intelligence occurs in Sun Tzu's book titled *The Art of War*. Sun Tzu claims that to succeed in war, one should have full knowledge of one's own strengths and weaknesses and full knowledge of the enemy's strengths and weaknesses. Lack of either one might result in defeat. A certain school of thought draws parallels between the challenges in business and those of war, specifically:

- Collecting data.
- Discerning patterns and meaning in the data.
- Responding to the resultant data.

FIGURE 6.12

Data Analysis Cycle

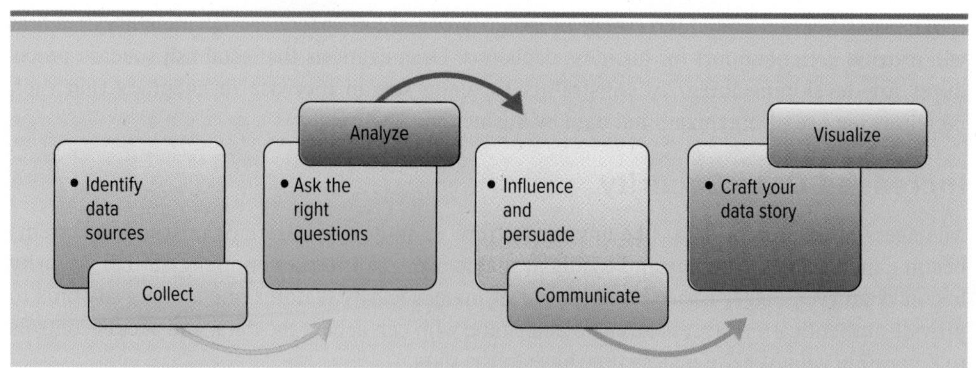

Before the start of the information age in the late 20th century, businesses sometimes collected data from nonautomated sources. Businesses then lacked the computing resources to properly analyze the data and often made commercial decisions based primarily on intuition.

As businesses started automating more and more systems, more and more data became available, especially given IoT and M2M. However, collection remained a challenge due to a lack of infrastructure for data exchange or to incompatibilities between systems. Reports sometimes took months to generate. Such reports allowed informed long-term strategic decision making. However, short-term tactical decision making continued to rely on intuition. In modern businesses, increasing standards, automation, and technologies have led to vast amounts of available data. Business intelligence has now become the art of sifting through large amounts of data, extracting information, and turning that information into actionable knowledge (see Figure 6.12).

The Problem: Data Rich, Information Poor

An ideal business scenario would be as follows: As a business manager on his way to meet with a client reviews historical customer data, he realizes that the client's ordering volume has substantially decreased. As he drills down into the data, he notices the client had a support issue with a particular product. He quickly calls the support team to find out all of the data and learns that a replacement for the defective part can be shipped in 24 hours. In addition, he learns that the client has visited the website and requested information on a new product line. Armed with all this information, the business manager is prepared for a productive meeting with his client. He now understands the client's needs and issues, and he can address new sales opportunities with confidence.

For many companies, the above example is simply a pipe dream. Attempting to gather all of the client data would actually take hours or even days to compile. With so much data available, it is surprisingly hard for managers to get data, such as inventory levels, past order history, or shipping details. Managers send their data requests to the MIS department, where a dedicated person compiles the various reports. In some situations, responses can take days, by which time the data may be outdated and opportunities lost. Many organizations find themselves in the position of being data rich and information poor. Even in today's electronic world, managers struggle with the challenge of turning their business data into business intelligence.

The Solution: Data Aggregation

Employee decisions are numerous and include providing service information, offering new products, and supporting frustrated customers.

- ***Dataset***: An organized collection of data.
- ***Comparative analysis***: Compares two or more datasets to identify patterns and trends.

Employees can base their decisions on datasets, experience, or knowledge and, preferably, a combination of all three. Business intelligence can provide managers with the ability to make better decisions. A few examples of how different industries use business intelligence include:

- **Airlines:** Analyze popular vacation locations with current flight listings.
- **Banking:** Understand customer credit card usage and nonpayment rates.

APPLY YOUR KNOWLEDGE

BUSINESS DRIVEN INNOVATION

Big Data to the Rescue

As hardware storage space increases, the ability to save huge amounts of data is created. Big data is here, and there are so many business benefits, it is impossible to list them all. Here are three common benefits:

1. **Answer Questions Quickly and Completely:** In the past, answering simple questions such as who are my best and worst customers could take weeks or months. With big data, answering questions becomes a relatively straightforward process and takes only days, hours, or minutes.
2. **Trust in Your Data:** Making decisions on bad data means bad decisions. Big data can gather huge amounts of data from a large number of sources, reducing the risk of siloed data. Having a complete view of all data from each functional area helps to validate the accuracy of the data.
3. **Empower Employees:** In the past, limited datasets meant businesses could ask and answer only a few questions. Now, with big data analytics, businesses can not only answer more questions quickly, but also more questions about the questions themselves.

In a group, brainstorm three additional benefits a business and its employees can gain from big data.

- **Health care:** Compare the demographics of patients with critical illnesses.
- **Insurance:** Predict claim amounts and medical coverage costs.
- **Law enforcement:** Track crime patterns, locations, and criminal behavior.
- **Marketing:** Analyze customer demographics.
- **Retail:** Predict sales, inventory levels, and distribution.
- **Technology:** Predict hardware failures.

Figure 6.13 displays how organizations using BI can find the cause to many issues and problems simply by asking "Why?" The process starts by analyzing a report such as sales amounts by quarter. Managers will drill down into the report looking for why sales are up or why sales are down. Once they understand why a certain location or product is experiencing an increase in sales, they can share the information in an effort to raise enterprisewide sales. Or once they

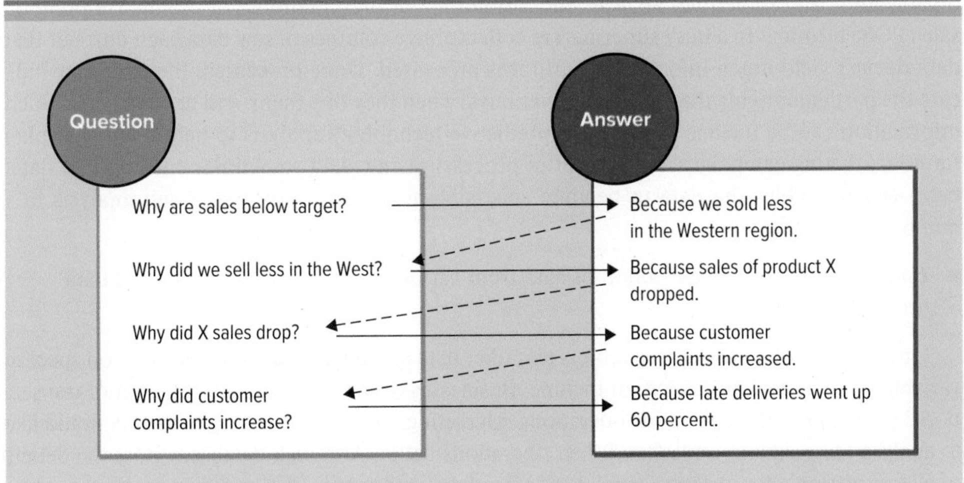

FIGURE 6.13
How BI Can Answer Tough Customer Questions

understand the cause for a decrease in sales, they can take effective action to resolve the issue. BI can help managers with competitive monitoring.

- ***Competitive monitoring***: Occurs when a company keeps tabs on its competitor's activities on the web using software that automatically tracks all competitor website activities such as discounts and new products.

Here are a few examples of how managers can use BI to answer tough business questions:

- Where has the business been? Historical perspective offers important variables for determining trends and patterns.
- Where is the business now? Looking at the current business situation allows managers to take effective action to solve issues before they grow out of control.
- Where is the business going? Setting strategic direction is critical for planning and creating solid business strategies.

Ask a simple question–such as who is my best customer or what is my worst-selling product–and you might get as many answers as you have employees. Databases, data warehouses, and data marts can provide a single source of "trusted" data that can answer questions about customers, products, suppliers, production, finances, fraud, and even employees.

In the early days of computing, it usually took a specialist with a strong background in technology to mine data for information because it was necessary for that person to understand how databases and data warehouses worked. Today, business intelligence tools often require very little, if any, support from the MIS department. Business managers can customize dashboards to display the data they want to see and run custom reports on the fly. The changes in how data can be mined and visualized allow business executives who have no technology background to be able to work with analytics tools and make data-driven decisions.

Data-driven decision management is usually undertaken as a way to gain a competitive advantage. A study from the MIT Center for Digital Business found that organizations driven most by data-based decision making had 4 percent higher productivity rates and 6 percent higher profits. However, integrating massive amounts of data from different areas of the business and combining it to derive actionable data in real time can be easier said than done. Errors can creep into data analytics processes at any stage of the endeavor, and serious issues can result when they do.

LO 6.5: Describe the roles and purposes of data warehouses and data marts in an organization.

DATA WAREHOUSE

- ***Source data***: Identifies the primary location where data is collected. Source data can include invoices, spreadsheets, time sheets, transactions, and electronic sources such as other databases.
- ***Raw data***: Data that has not been processed for use. Raw data that has undergone processing is sometimes referred to as cooked data.

Although raw data has the potential to become "information," it requires selective extraction, organization, and sometimes analysis and formatting for presentation. For example, a point-of-sale (POS) terminal in a busy supermarket collects huge volumes of raw data each day, but that data doesn't yield much information until it is processed. Once processed, the data may indicate the particular items that each customer buys, when they buy them, and at what price. Such information can be further subjected to predictive technology analysis to help the owner plan future marketing campaigns. As a result of processing, raw data sometimes ends up in a database, which enables the data to become accessible for further processing and analysis in a number of different ways.

- ***Data aggregation***: The collection of data from various sources for the purpose of data processing.

One example of a data aggregation is to gather data about particular groups based on specific variables such as age, profession, or income. Businesses collect a tremendous amount of transactional data as part of their routine operations. Marketing, sales, and other departments would like to analyze these data to understand their operations better. Although databases store the details of all transactions (for instance, the sale of a product) and events (hiring a new employee), data

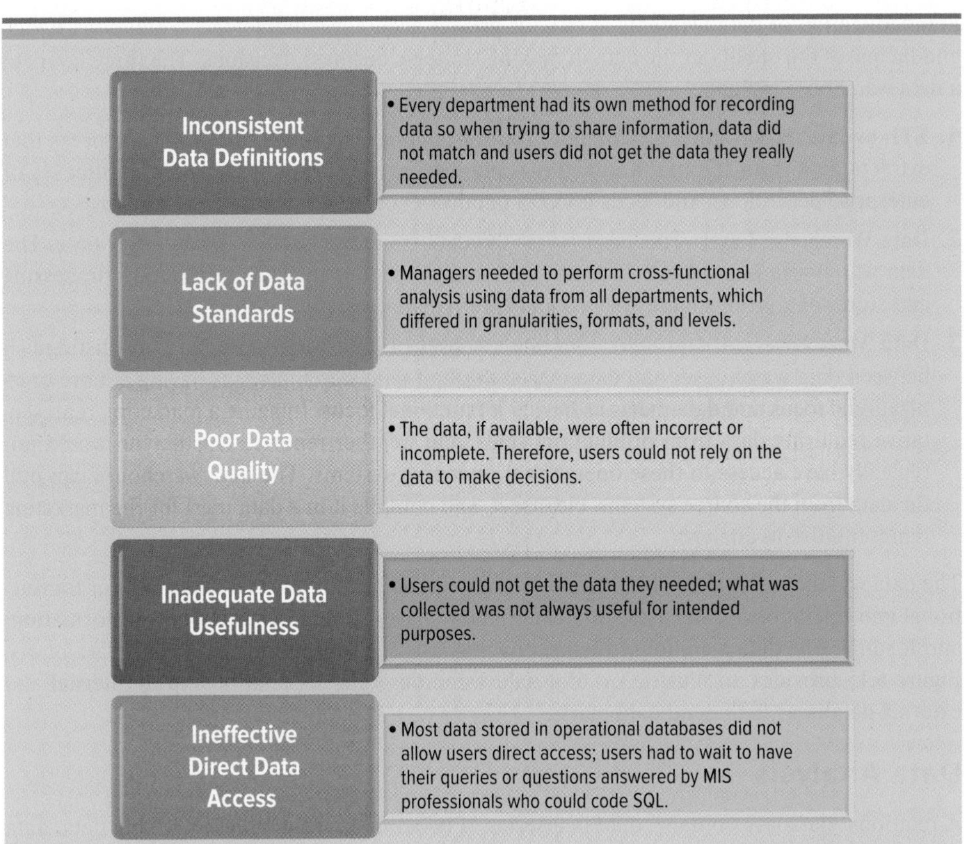

Inconsistent Data Definitions
• Every department had its own method for recording data so when trying to share information, data did not match and users did not get the data they really needed.
Lack of Data Standards
• Managers needed to perform cross-functional analysis using data from all departments, which differed in granularities, formats, and levels.
Poor Data Quality
• The data, if available, were often incorrect or incomplete. Therefore, users could not rely on the data to make decisions.
Inadequate Data Usefulness
• Users could not get the data they needed; what was collected was not always useful for intended purposes.
Ineffective Direct Data Access
• Most data stored in operational databases did not allow users direct access; users had to wait to have their queries or questions answered by MIS professionals who could code SQL.

FIGURE 6.14

Reasons Business Analysis Is Difficult from Operational Databases

warehouses store that same data but in an aggregated form more suited to supporting decision-making tasks. Aggregation, in this instance, can include totals, counts, averages, and the like.

Relational databases are excellent for supporting the business rules and processes required to run the different functional areas of the business—marketing, accounting, finance—that all tend to have their own databases. The only issue facing companies is how do we integrate the data among all of the functional systems to gain a holistic view of the business? Operational databases are specifically designed to run each department; however, looking across departments we find many problems as highlighted in Figure 6.14.

Many large businesses find themselves with data scattered across multiple systems with different file types (such as spreadsheets, databases, and even word processing files), making it almost impossible for anyone to use the data from multiple sources. Completing reporting requests across operational systems could take days or weeks using antiquated reporting tools that were ineffective for running a business. From this idea, the data warehouse was born as a place where relevant data could be stored and accessed for making strategic queries and reports.

- ***Data warehouse***: A logical collection of data—gathered from many different operational databases—that supports business analysis activities and decision-making tasks.

The primary purpose of a data warehouse is to combine data, more specifically, strategic data, throughout an organization into a single repository in such a way that the people who need that data can make decisions and undertake business analysis. A key idea within data warehousing is to collect data from multiple systems in a common location that uses a universal querying tool. This allows operational databases to run where they are most efficient for the business, while providing a common location using a familiar format for the strategic or enterprisewide reporting data.

Data warehouses go even a step further by standardizing data. Gender, for instance, can be referred to in many ways (Male, Female, M/F, 1/0), but it should be standardized on a data warehouse with one common way of referring to each data element that stores gender (M/F).

Standardization of data elements allows for greater accuracy, completeness, and consistency and increases the quality of the data in making strategic business decisions. The three layers to a data warehouse include:

1. **ETL or Integration Layer:** ***Extraction, transformation, and loading (ETL)*** is a process that extracts data from internal and external databases, transforms it using a common set of enterprise definitions, and loads it into a data warehouse.
2. **Data Warehouse Layer:** This layer stores the data from every source system over time. The data warehouse is designed for query and analysis rather than for transaction processing and stores data from source systems and external systems.
3. **Data Mart Layer:** A ***data mart*** contains a subset of data warehouse data. To distinguish between data warehouses and data marts, think of data warehouses as having a more organizational focus and data marts as having a functional focus. Imagine a marketing representative requiring data from production, sales, and weather reports. This person would not typically have access to these operational or source systems. The data warehouse can pull the data from the source systems, cleanse it, and compile it in a data mart for the marketing representative to analyze.

The data warehouse modeled in Figure 6.15 compiles data from internal databases (or transactional and operational databases) and external databases through extraction, transformation, and loading. The data warehouse then sends portions (or subsets) of the data to data marts. Figure 6.15 provides an illustration of a data warehouse and its relationship to internal and external databases, ETL, and data marts.

Data Analysis

A relational database contains data in a series of two-dimensional tables. With big data, data is multidimensional, meaning it contains layers of columns and rows. A dimension is a

FIGURE 6.15

Data Warehouse Model

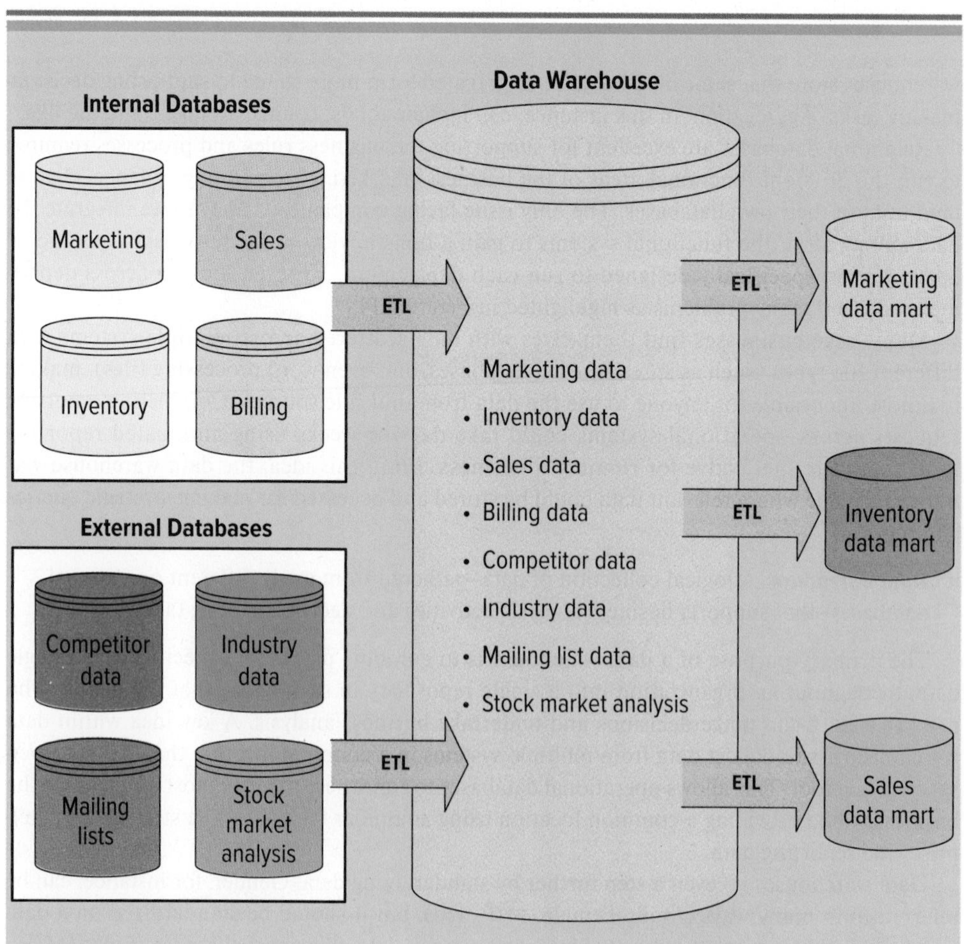

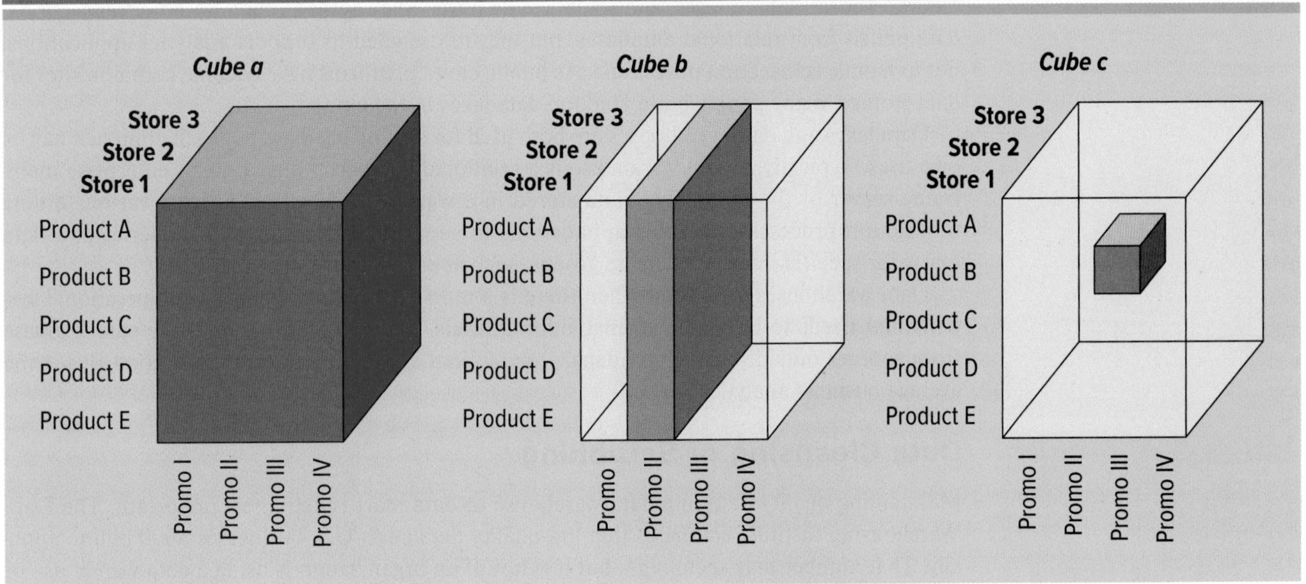

FIGURE 6.16

A Cube of Data for Performing a Multidimensional Analysis on Three Stores for Five Products and Four Promotions

particular attribute of data. Each layer in big data represents data according to an additional dimension.

- ***Data cube***: The common term for the representation of multidimensional data.

Figure 6.16 displays a cube (Cube a) that represents store data (the layers), product data (the rows), and promotion data (the columns).

Once a cube of data is created, users can begin to slice and dice the cube to drill down into the data. The second cube (Cube b) in Figure 6.16 displays a slice representing promotion II data for all products at all stores. The third cube (Cube c) in Figure 6.16 displays only data for promotion III, product B, at store 2. By using multidimensional analysis, users can analyze data in a number of different ways and with any number of different dimensions. For example, users might want to add dimensions of data to a current analysis including product category, region, and even forecasts for actual weather. The true value of big data is its ability to provide multidimensional analysis that allows users to gain insights into their data.

Big data is ideal for off-loading some of the querying against a database. For example, querying a database to obtain an average of sales for product B at store 2 while promotion III is under way might create a considerable processing burden for a database, essentially slowing down the time it takes another person to enter a new sale into the same database. If an organization performs numerous queries against a database (or multiple databases), aggregating that data into big data databases could be beneficial.

Data Lake

While a traditional data warehouse stores data in files or folders, a data lake uses a flat architecture to store data.

- ***Data lake***: A storage repository that holds a vast amount of raw data in its original format until the business needs it.

Each data element in a data lake is assigned a unique identifier and tagged with a set of extended metadata tags. When a business question arises, the data lake can be queried for all of the relevant data, providing a smaller dataset that can then be analyzed to help answer the question.

The term *data lake* is often associated with Hadoop storage. In such a scenario, an organization's data is first loaded into the Hadoop platform, and then business analytics and data mining tools are applied to the data where it resides on Hadoop's cluster of computers. A Hadoop data lake is a data management platform comprising one or more Hadoop clusters. It is used principally to process and store nonrelational data, such as log files, Internet clickstream records, sensor data, images, and social media posts. Such systems can also hold transactional data pulled from relational databases, but they're designed to support analytics applications, not to handle transaction processing. As public cloud platforms have become common sites for data storage, many people build Hadoop data lakes in the cloud.

Data lakes and data warehouses are both used for storing big data, but each approach has its own uses. Typically, a data warehouse is a relational database housed on an enterprise mainframe server or the cloud. The data stored in a warehouse is extracted from various online transaction processing (OLTP) applications to support business analytics queries and data marts for specific internal business groups, such as sales or inventory teams.

Data warehouses are useful when there is a massive amount of data from operational systems that needs to be readily available for analysis. Because the data in a lake can originate from sources outside of the company's operational systems, lakes are not a good fit for the average business analytics user.

Data Cleansing or Scrubbing

Maintaining quality data in a data warehouse or data mart is extremely important. The Data Warehousing Institute estimates that low-quality data costs U.S. businesses $600 billion annually. That number may seem high, but it is not. If an organization is using a data warehouse or data mart to allocate dollars across advertising strategies, low-quality data will definitely have a negative impact on its ability to make the right decision.

- ***Dirty data***: Erroneous or flawed data.

The complete removal of dirty data from a source is impractical or virtually impossible. According to Gartner Inc., dirty data is a business problem, not an MIS problem. Over the next 2 years, more than 25 percent of critical data in *Fortune* 1000 companies will continue to be flawed; that is, the data will be inaccurate, incomplete, or duplicated (see Figure 6.17).

- ***Data cleansing or scrubbing***: A process that weeds out and fixes or discards inconsistent, incorrect, or incomplete data.

Obviously, maintaining quality data in a data warehouse or data mart is extremely important. To increase the quality of organizational data and thus the effectiveness of decision making, businesses must formulate a strategy to keep data clean.

FIGURE 6.17

Dirty Data Problems

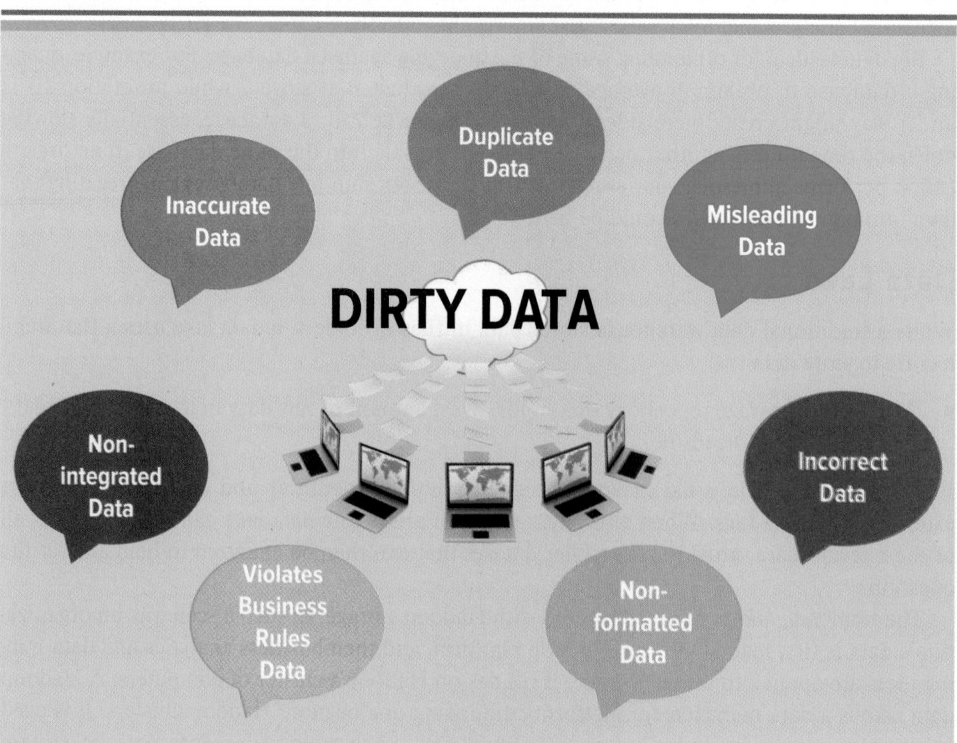

APPLY YOUR KNOWLEDGE

BUSINESS DRIVEN DISCUSSION

Data Warehouse or Data Lake?

A data lake is a vast pool of raw data, the purpose for which is not yet defined. A data warehouse is a repository for structured, filtered data that has already been processed for a specific purpose. Here are a few primary differences between data lakes and data warehouses.

- **Data Storage**: During the development of a data warehouse, a considerable amount of time is spent analyzing data sources, understanding business processes, and profiling data. The result is a highly structured data model designed for reporting. Data lakes retain all data—not just data that is in use today but data that may be used and even data that may never be used just because one day it might have value.
- **Data Types:** Data warehouses generally consist of data that is extracted from transactional or source systems and consist of quantitative metrics and the attributes that describe them. Data lakes save all data in raw form, regardless of source and structure.
- **Data Users:** The data warehouse supports operational and managerial users generating reports for KPIs and CSFs. These users' favorite tool is the spreadsheet, and they create new reports that are often distributed throughout the organization. The data warehouse is their go-to source for data, but they often go beyond functional boundaries. The data lake supports all of these users equally well. The data scientists can go to the lake and work with the very large and varied datasets they need, while other users make use of more structured views of the data provided for their use.
- **Data Change:** One of the chief complaints about data warehouses is how long it takes to change them. Considerable time is spent up front during development getting the warehouse's structure right. A good warehouse design can adapt to change, but because of the complexity of the data loading process and the work done to make analysis and reporting easy, these changes will necessarily consume some developer resources and take some time. In the data lake, on the other hand, since all data is stored in its raw form and is always accessible to someone who needs to use it, users are empowered to go beyond the structure of the warehouse to explore data in novel ways and answer their questions at their pace.

In a group, identify business examples of when you would choose to use a data warehouse and when you would choose to use a data lake.

Specialized software tools exist that use sophisticated procedures to analyze, standardize, correct, match, and consolidate data warehouse data. This step is vitally important because data warehouses often contain data from several databases, some of which can be external to the organization. In a data warehouse, data cleansing occurs first during the ETL process and again once the data is in the data warehouse. Ideally, scrubbed data is accurate and consistent.

Looking at customer data highlights why data cleansing is necessary. Customer data exists in several operational systems. In each system, all the details could change—from the customer ID to contact data—depending on the business process the user is performing (see Figure 6.18).

FIGURE 6.18

Contact Data in Operational Systems

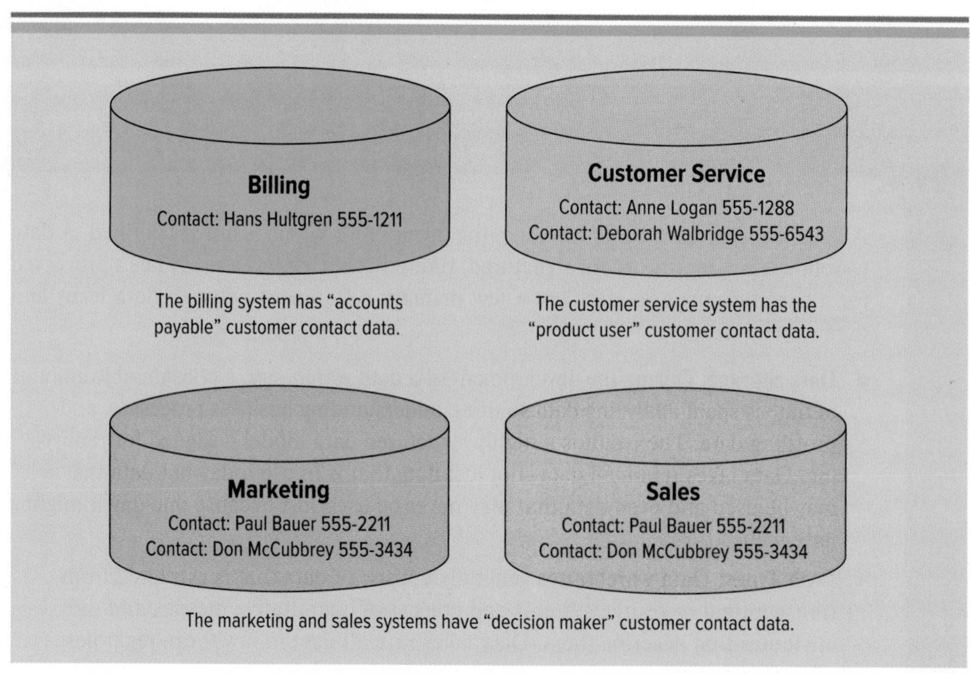

FIGURE 6.19

Standardizing a Customer Name in Operational Systems

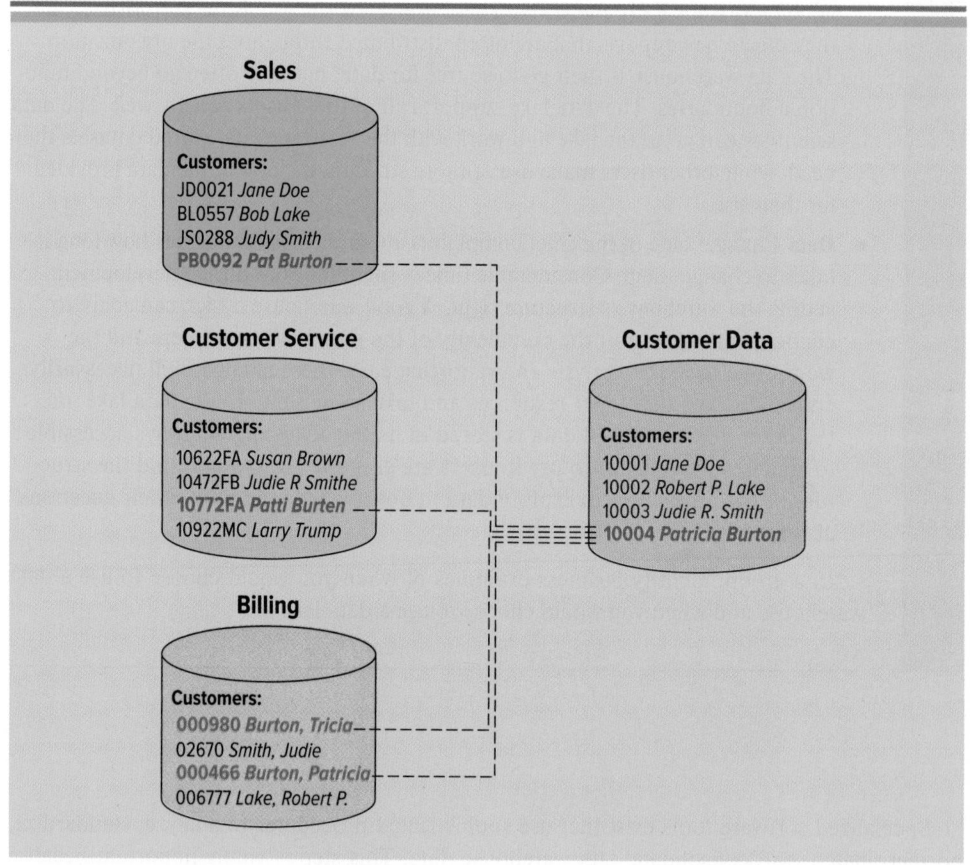

Figure 6.19 displays a customer name entered differently in multiple operational systems. Data cleansing allows an organization to fix these types of inconsistencies in the data warehouse. Figure 6.20 displays the typical events that occur during data cleansing.

Achieving perfect data is almost impossible. The more complete and accurate a company wants its data to be, the more it costs (see Figure 6.21). Companies may also trade accuracy for completeness. Accurate data is correct, whereas complete data has no blanks. A birth date of 2/31/25 is an

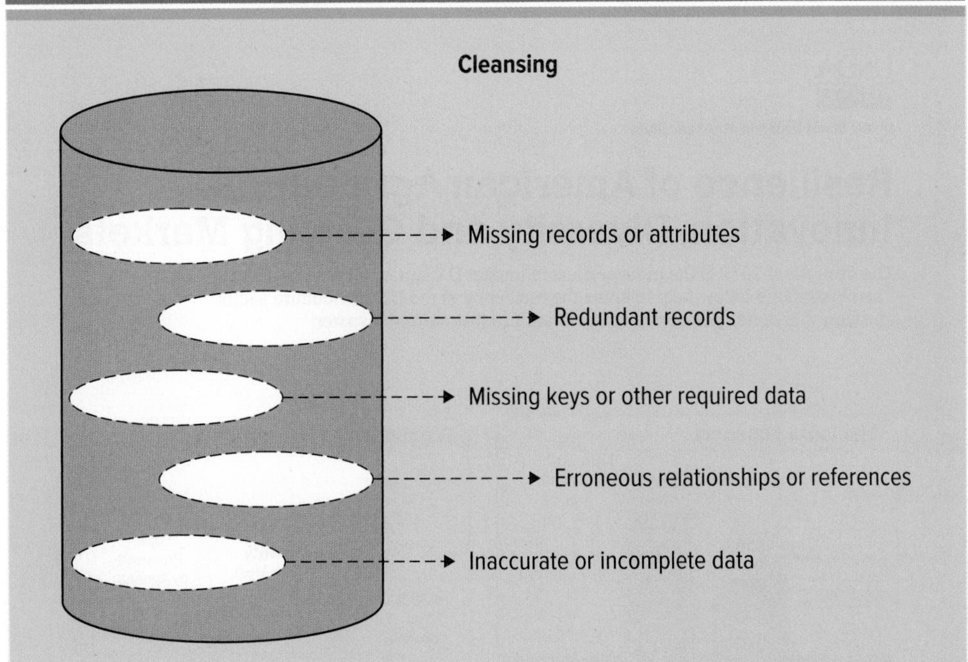

FIGURE 6.20

Data Cleansing Activities

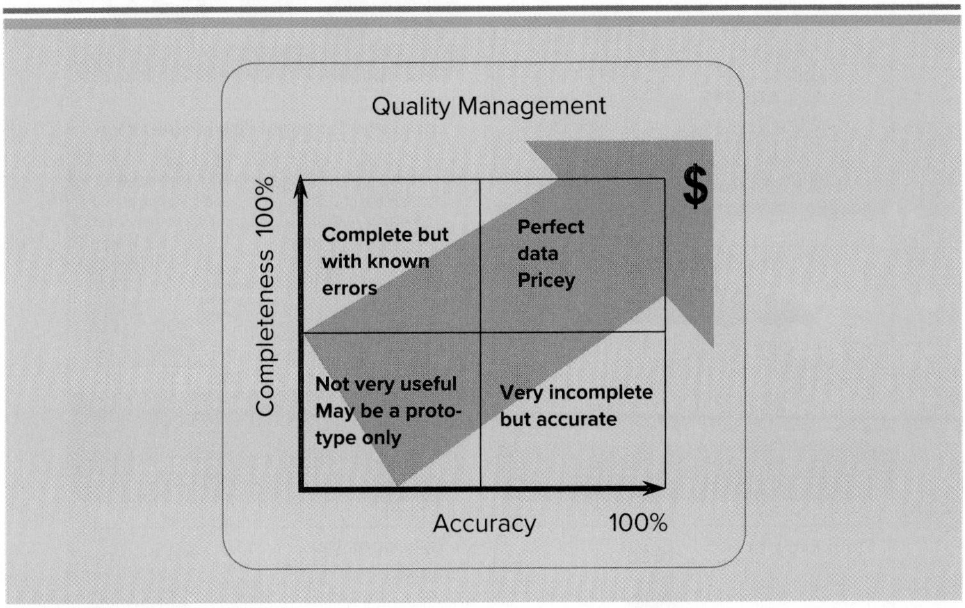

Quality Management

Completeness 100%

Complete but with known errors

Perfect data Pricey

$

Not very useful May be a proto-type only

Very incomplete but accurate

Accuracy 100%

FIGURE 6.21

The Cost of Accurate and Complete Data

example of complete but inaccurate data (February 31 does not exist). An address containing Denver, Colorado, without a zip code is an example of accurate data that is incomplete.

- ***Data quality audits*:** Determines the accuracy and completeness of its data.

Many firms complete data quality audits to ensure they are making decisions based on high-quality data. Their goal is to determine a percentage of accuracy and completeness high enough to make good decisions at a reasonable cost, such as 85 percent accurate and 65 percent complete.

Data Visualization

Traditional bar graphs and pie charts are boring and at best confusing and at worst misleading. As databases and graphics collide more and more, people are creating infographics, which display data graphically so it can be easily understood.

- ***Infographics (information graphics)*:** Present the results of data analysis, displaying the patterns, relationships, and trends in a graphical format.

FIGURE 6.22

Infographic News Example

Source: U.S. Department of Agriculture

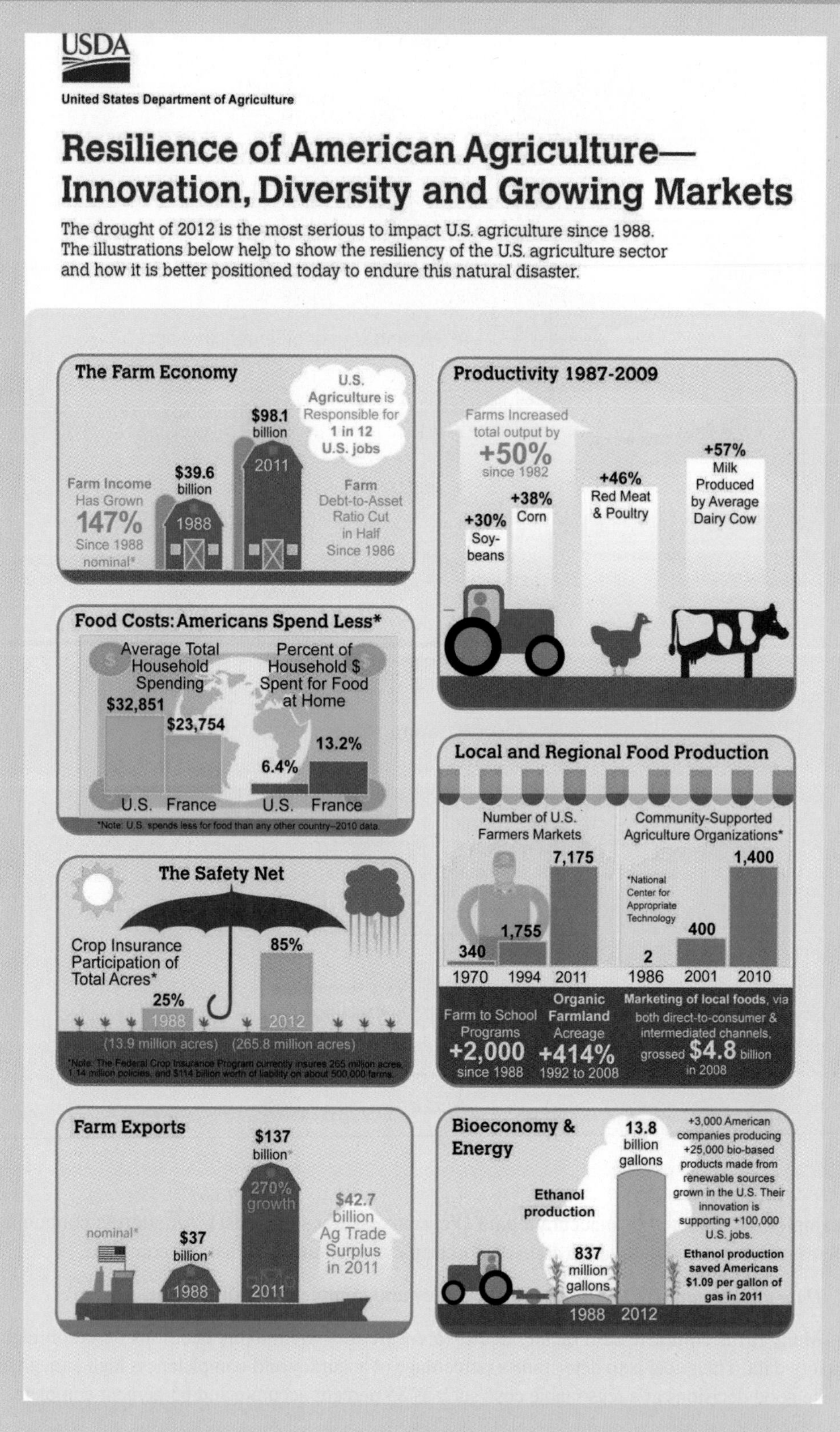

Infographics are exciting and quickly convey a story users can understand without having to analyze numbers, tables, and boring charts (see Figures 6.22, 6.23 and 6.24).

Great data visualizations provide insights into something new about the underlying patterns and relationships. Just think of the periodic table of elements and imagine if you had to look at an Excel spreadsheet showing each element and the associated attributes in a table format. This would be not only difficult to understand but easy to misinterpret. By placing the

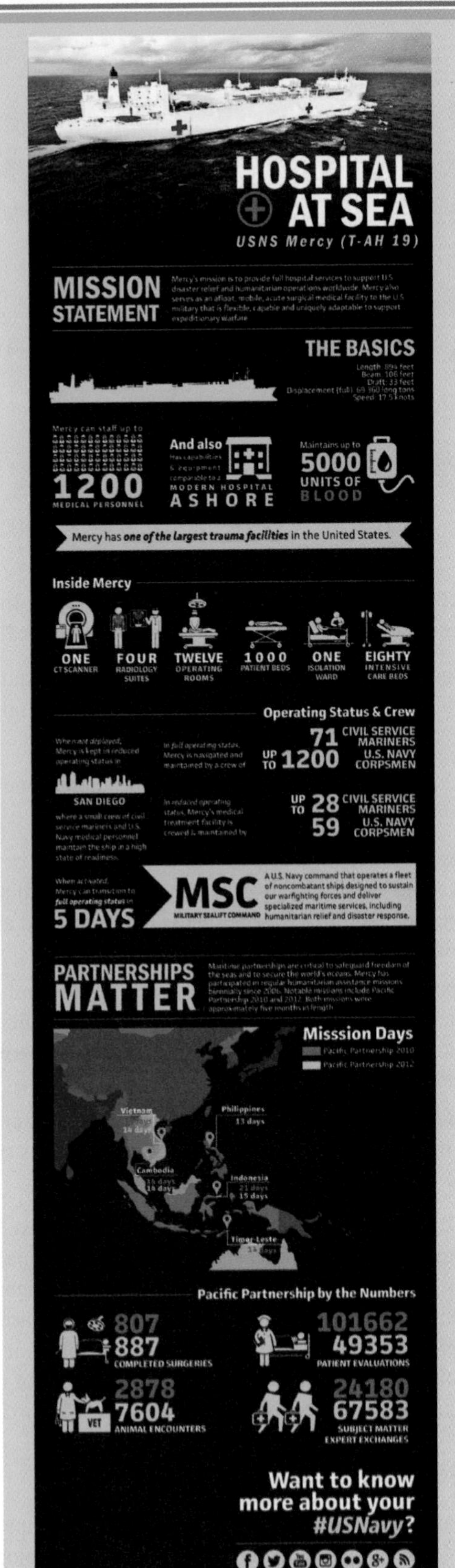

FIGURE 6.23

Infographic Example

Source: U.S. Navy

elements in the visual periodic table, you quickly grasp how the elements relate and the associated hierarchy.

- ***Data artist***: A business analytics specialist who uses visual tools to help people understand complex data.

FIGURE 6.24

Infographic Health Example

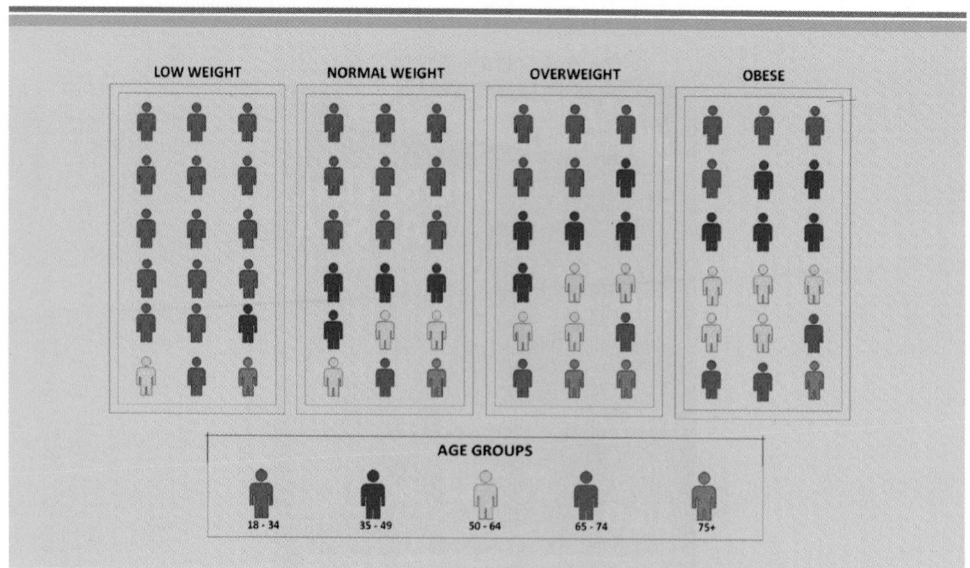

Data artists are experts at creating a story from the information. Infographics perform the same function for business data as the periodic table does for chemical elements.

- ***Analysis paralysis*:** Occurs when the user goes into an emotional state of overanalyzing (or overthinking) a situation so that a decision or action is never taken, in effect paralyzing the outcome.

In the time of big data, analysis paralysis is a growing problem. One solution is to use data visualizations to help people make decisions faster.

- ***Data visualization*:** Describes technologies that allow users to see or visualize data to transform information into a business perspective. Data visualization is a powerful way to simplify complex datasets by placing data in a format that is easily grasped and understood far quicker than the raw data alone.
- ***Data visualization tools*:** These tools move beyond Excel graphs and charts into sophisticated analysis techniques such as controls, instruments, maps, time-series graphs, and more. Data visualization tools can help uncover correlations and trends in data that would otherwise go unrecognized.
- ***Business intelligence dashboards*:** Track corporate metrics such as critical success factors and key performance indicators and include advanced capabilities such as interactive controls, allowing users to manipulate data for analysis.

Business intelligence dashboards, whether basic or comprehensive, deliver results quickly. As they become easier to use, more employees can perform their own analyses without inundating MIS staff with questions and requests for reports. Business intelligence dashboards enable employees to move beyond reporting to using information to increase business performance directly. With them, employees can react to information as soon as it becomes available and make decisions, solve problems, and change strategies daily instead of monthly. Business intelligence dashboards offer the analytical capabilities illustrated in Figure 6.25.

LO 6.6: Explain blockchain and its advantages over a centralized relational database.

BLOCKCHAIN: DISTRIBUTED COMPUTING

Blockchain is being talked about in almost every industry as a disruptive technology that will come into widespread use, changing society. It has been stated that blockchain will disrupt the global business environment in the same way the Internet did in the mid-1990s. Blockchain's disruptive potential and its applications constitute a revolution that will affect the operation of industries as diverse as finance, news media, medical, legal, and supply chain. Before we dive into the details of blockchain, let's take a quick look at how distributed computing works.

- ***Distributed computing*:** Processes and manages algorithms across many machines in a computing environment.

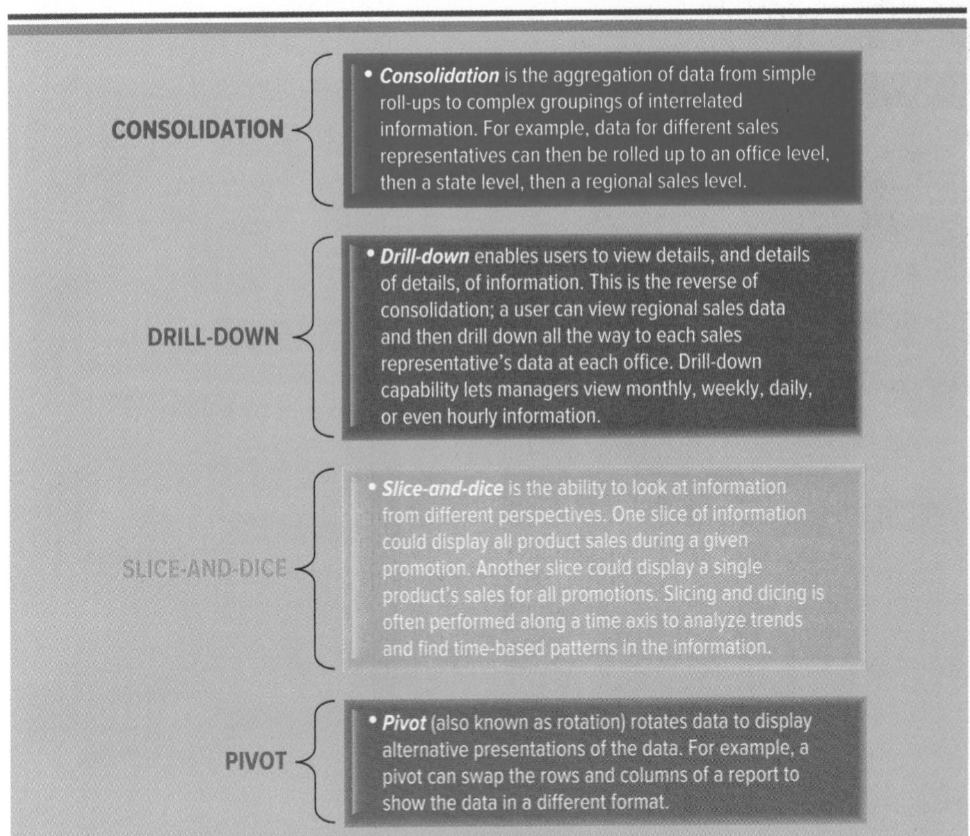

CONSOLIDATION
• Consolidation is the aggregation of data from simple roll-ups to complex groupings of interrelated information. For example, data for different sales representatives can then be rolled up to an office level, then a state level, then a regional sales level.
DRILL-DOWN
• Drill-down enables users to view details, and details of details, of information. This is the reverse of consolidation; a user can view regional sales data and then drill down all the way to each sales representative's data at each office. Drill-down capability lets managers view monthly, weekly, daily, or even hourly information.
SLICE-AND-DICE
• Slice-and-dice is the ability to look at information from different perspectives. One slice of information could display all product sales during a given promotion. Another slice could display a single product's sales for all promotions. Slicing and dicing is often performed along a time axis to analyze trends and find time-based patterns in the information.
PIVOT
• Pivot (also known as rotation) rotates data to display alternative presentations of the data. For example, a pivot can swap the rows and columns of a report to show the data in a different format.

FIGURE 6.25
Business Intelligence Dashboards' Analytical Capabilities

A key component of big data and blockchain technologies is a distributed computing environment that shares resources ranging from memory to networks to storage. With distributed computing, individual computers are networked together across geographical areas and work together to execute a workload or computing processes as if they were one single computing environment. For example, you can distribute a set of programs on the same physical server and use a message service to allow them to communicate and pass data. You can also have a distributed computing environment in which many different systems or servers, each with its own computing memory, work together to solve a common problem. Figure 6.26 displays a typical distributed environment.

Blockchain may become the norm of data records sooner than we think. Wide acceptance of blockchain and smart contract platforms is expected. A peer-to-peer immutable database that can safely store and transfer digital assets is a truly disruptive idea that can change the world. Industries that will be served using blockchains include:

- **Banking:** Blockchain-based solutions are going to be the next big thing in finance. Banking systems based on blockchain are more secure and cost-effective.
- **Counterfeit and Fraud Detection:** If an irregularity is detected somewhere along the supply chain, a blockchain system can lead you all the way to its point of origin. This makes it easier for businesses to carry out investigations and execute the necessary actions; for example, in the food sector, where tracking the origination, batch data, and other important details is crucial for quality assurance and safety.
- **Payments:** Blockchain will be the future of payment solutions, with direct, fast, and secure payment methods without transaction costs.
- **Health Care:** Blockchain will help to secure patient data sharing between platforms, fostering better collaboration between health data providers, which will result in higher possibilities of accurate diagnoses.
- **Legal and Smart Contracts:** Time-consuming contractual transactions can bottleneck the growth of a business, especially for enterprises that process a torrent of communications on a consistent basis. With smart contracts, agreements can be automatically validated,

FIGURE 6.26
Distributed Computing Environment

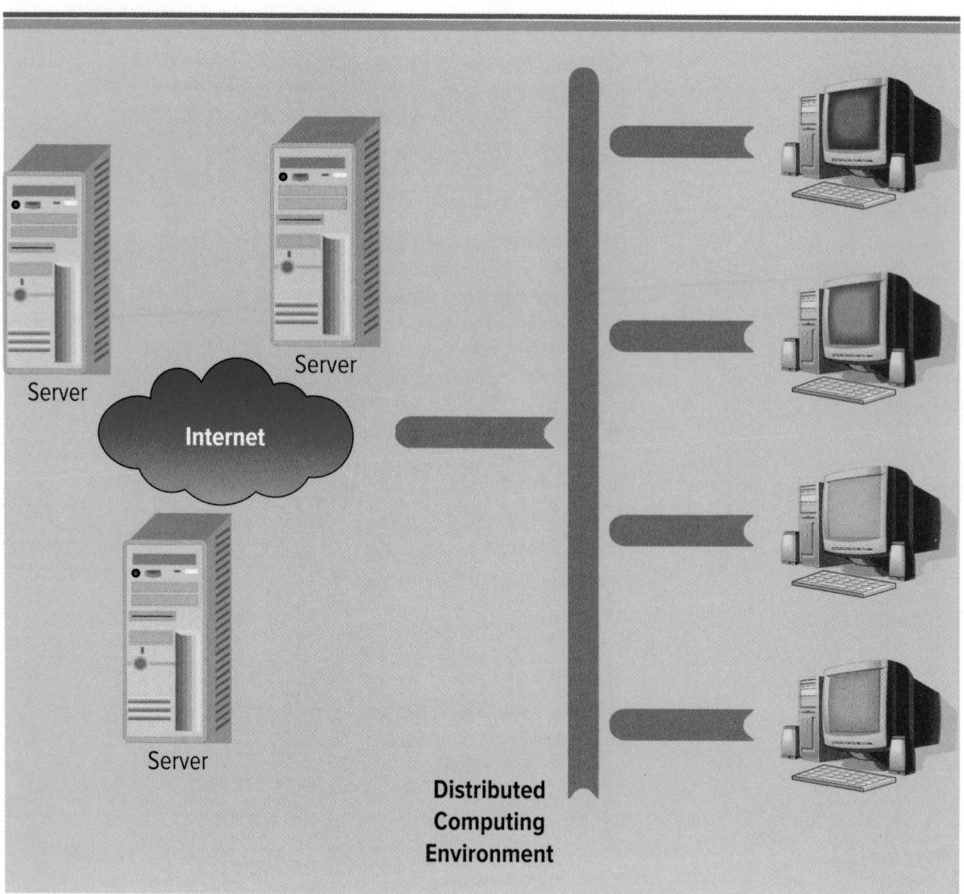

signed, and enforced through a blockchain construct. This eliminates the need for mediators and therefore saves the company time and money.

- **Supply Chain:** The key benefits of blockchain for logistics networks is that it establishes a shared, secure record of data across the network. For supply chain management, blockchain technology offers the benefits of traceability and cost-effectiveness. Put simply, a blockchain can be used to track the movement of goods, their origin, quantity, and so forth. This brings about a new level of transparency to B2B ecosystems–simplifying processes such as ownership transfer, production process assurance, and payments.
- **Voting:** Just like in supply chain management, the promise of blockchains in voting all boils down to trust. Currently, opportunities that pertain to government elections are being pursued. One example is the initiative of the government of Moscow to test the effectiveness of blockchains in local elections. Doing so will significantly diminish the likelihood of electoral fraud, which is a huge issue despite the prevalence of electronic voting systems.

How Blockchains Work

Whenever you need to build a decentralized system that stores unalterable data records, blockchain is the answer.

- ***Ledger*:** Records classified and summarized transactional data.
- ***Blockchain*:** A type of distributed ledger, consisting of blocks of data that maintain a permanent and tamper-proof record of transactional data.

Distributed ledgers allow many different parties around the world to access and verify the same data. Blockchains are a form of distributed computing in which a decentralized database is managed by computers belonging to a network. Each of the computers in the distributed network maintains a copy of the ledger to prevent a single point of failure, and all copies are updated and validated simultaneously. Because data is shared and continually reconciled by thousands or even millions of computers, it is almost impossible to corrupt a blockchain.

BUSINESS DRIVEN DEBATE

Do Cryptocurrencies Damage the Environment?

Cryptocurrencies have become a major culprit for energy consumption, with the world's Bitcoin network using as much power as the whole of Ireland in 2018. Bill Gates is an outspoken advocate fighting against climate change. Gates believes that Bitcoin is causing environmental damage by using more electricity to conduct a transaction than any other method. Others believe that digital wallets containing cryptocurrencies will replace traditional banking methods. Do you believe cryptocurrencies will disappear as more and more people understand the environmental issues associated with these types of transactions, or will the digital wallet replace traditional banking methods?

Let's look at an example of how blockchains help financial transactions. Traditional methods of payment require trust in a third party to execute transactions (e.g., Visa, PayPal, banks). The third party keeps its own private ledger storing the transactions and balances of each account. For example, if Hannah wants to pay Sophie $150, the trusted third-party service would debit Hannah's account and credit Sophie's, and both participants trust that the third party is going to do the right thing.

A blockchain is just a chain of blocks, and each new block incorporates by reference the block before it. Each block can contain transactional data that transfers digital assets between the blocks or parties. A valid blockchain cannot contain conflicting transactions. Invalid blockchains are simply ignored by all participants. When participants see a payment of $150 from Hannah to Sophie, they can easily check that there is not a prior transaction in the blockchain of that same $150 from Hannah to Sophie.

This alone does not solve the problem, as there can be more than one valid blockchain. There could be one containing Hannah's payment to Sophie and one containing Hannah's payment to Louey. For the system to be useful, we need some way to ensure that we do not consider either payment confirmed until we know which blockchain will "win."

- ***Proof-of-work***: A requirement to define an expensive computer calculation, also called mining, that needs to be performed in order to create a new group of trustless transactions (blocks) on the distributed ledger or blockchain.

Proof-of-work has two primary goals:

1. To verify the legitimacy of a transaction, or avoid the so-called double-spending.
2. To create new digital currencies by rewarding miners for performing the previous task.

Without proof-of-work, anyone could edit a transaction, recalculate all the hash values, and make a new blockchain with its own valid set of hash-linked transactions. Proof-of-work ensures the participants in the blockchain are confident that a particular block will forever remain part of the winning blockchain. This is accomplished by attaching billions of expensive computations to a blockchain and rewarding miners for extending the longest blockchain. Here is an example of what happens in a blockchain transaction.

- Transactions are bundled together into what we call a block.
- Miners verify that transactions within each block are legitimate.
- To do so, miners should solve a mathematical puzzle known as a proof-of-work problem.
- A reward (such as Bitcoins) is given to the first miner who solves each block's problem.
- Verified transactions are stored in the public blockchain.

Figure 6.27 provides an example of a centralized ledger, such as Dropbox, in which one central copy is stored and all participants access the centralized copy, as well as a decentralized blockchain in which a distributed ledger is accessed by all nodes on the network.

APPLY YOUR KNOWLEDGE

BUSINESS DRIVEN STARTUP

Bitcoin: I Lost My Password and $200 Million

Bitcoin owners are getting rich because the cryptocurrency has soared. But what happens when you lose your password and there isn't a help desk to call because there is no central authority? It is estimated that of the existing 18 million Bitcoins, around 20 percent–currently worth around $140 billion–appear to be lost without a password. Many people gained the coins over a decade ago when the coins were worth nothing. Can you remember a password from 10 years ago?

Stefan Thomas, a German-born programmer living in San Francisco, has two guesses left to figure out a password that is worth over $220 million. The password will unlock a small hard drive, known as an IronKey, which contains the private keys to his digital wallet holding 7,000 Bitcoins. The problem is that Mr. Thomas years ago lost the paper where he wrote down the password for his IronKey, which gives users 10 guesses before it seizes up and encrypts its contents forever. He has since tried eight of his most commonly used password formulations–to no avail.

There are numerous pros and cons to a decentralized ledger–clearly losing your password without any help is a con. Why do you believe Bitcoins have value? Would you purchase Bitcoins? What are the pros and cons of using Bitcoins?

- ***Bitcoin***: A type of digital currency in which a record of transactions is maintained and new units of currency are generated by the computational solution of mathematical problems and which operates independently of a central bank.

Bitcoin is a new currency that was created in 2009 by an unknown person using the alias Satoshi Nakamoto. Blockchains were introduced in the same year by Satoshi Nakamoto. Bitcoin transactions are made with no intermediaries–meaning no banks–and Bitcoins are not tied to any country or subject to regulation! There are no transaction fees and no need to give your real name. Bitcoin was a system that was designed to run across a large network of machines–called Bitcoin miners–and anyone on Earth could operate one of these machines.

FIGURE 6.27

Centralized Ledger and Decentralized Distributed Ledger Examples

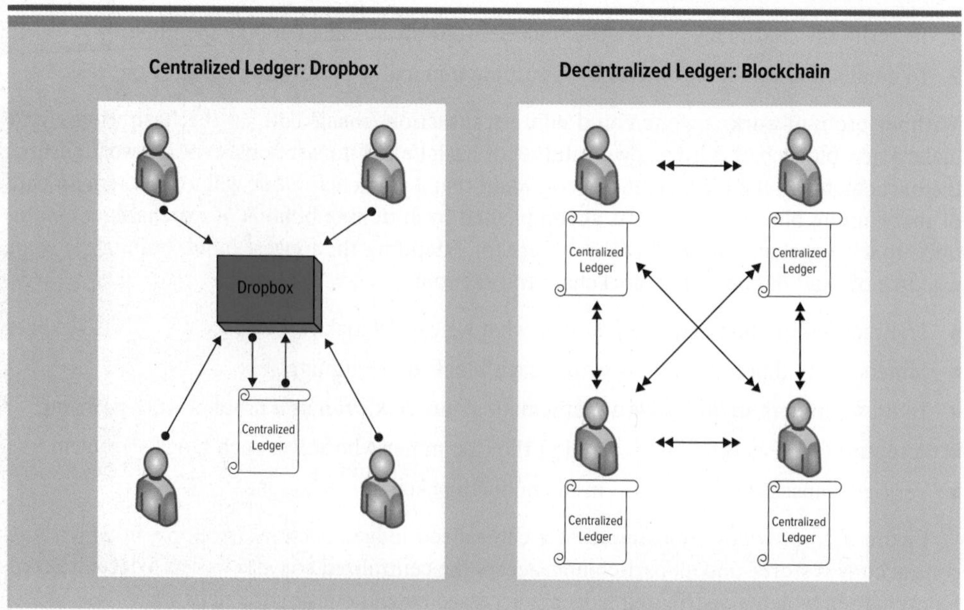

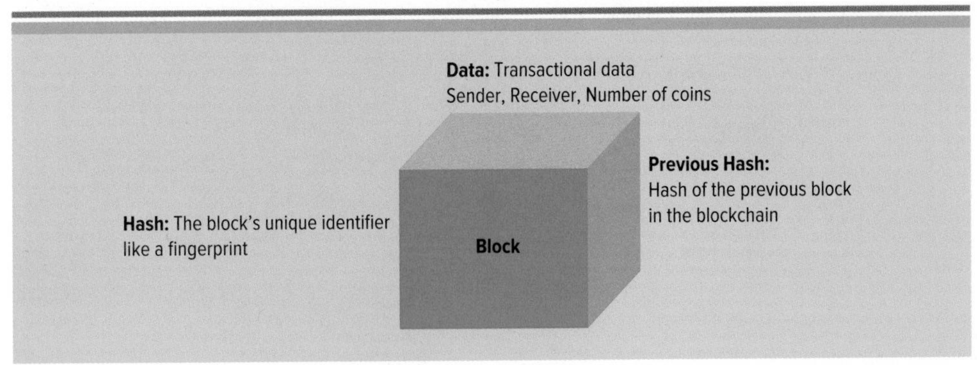

FIGURE 6.28

Block in a Blockchain

This distributed software seeded the new currency, creating a small number of Bitcoins. Basically, Bitcoins are just long digital addresses and balances, stored in an online ledger called a blockchain (see the earlier section "Blockchain: Distributed Computing"). But the system was also designed so that use of the currency would slowly expand and encourage people to operate Bitcoin miners to keep the system itself growing.

Bitcoins are stored in a digital wallet, a kind of virtual bank account that allows users to send or receive Bitcoins, pay for goods, or save their money. Although each Bitcoin transaction is recorded in a public log, names of buyers and sellers are never revealed–only their wallet IDs. Although that keeps Bitcoin users' transactions private, it also lets them buy or sell anything without easily tracing it back to them. That's why it has become the currency of choice for people buying drugs or engaging in other illicit activities online. No one knows what will become of Bitcoin. It is mostly unregulated, but that could change. Governments are concerned about taxation and their lack of control over the currency.

- ***Ethereum***: A decentralized, open-source blockchain with smart contract functionality. Ether is the native cryptocurrency of the platform. It is the second-largest cryptocurrency by market capitalization, after Bitcoin. Ethereum is the most actively used blockchain.
- ***Blocks***: Data structures containing a hash, previous hash, and data.
- ***Genesis block***: The first block created in a blockchain.
- ***Hash***: A function that converts an input of letters and numbers into an encrypted output of a fixed length (see Figure 6.28).

Hashes are the links in the blockchain. Each Bitcoin transaction contains a hash of the previous transaction. If transaction data is altered, then a computer can verify that the data is incorrect. Thus, the integrity and order of the transactions are protected. A hash is created using an algorithm and is essential to blockchain management. Each time a new transaction occurs, a new block is added to the blockchain containing the new data, a unique hash, and the hash of the previous block. Each transaction that is verified by the blockchain network is time-stamped and embedded into a "block" of data cryptographically secured by a hashing process that links to and incorporates the hash of the previous block and joins the chain as the next chronological update.

Computers use hashes to compare things. Imagine that you need to know if two images are exactly the same. One option is to write a program that examines each pixel and verifies that they match. This will take a tremendous about of time. Another option is to compute the hash of each image and compare the hashes. If they match, the images are identical. This can be done millions of times per second on an average computer.

The hashing process makes the chain "unbreakable"—it's impossible to manipulate or delete data after it has been validated and placed in the blockchain because if attempted, the subsequent blocks in the chain would reject the attempted modification (as their hashes would not be valid). In other words, if data is tampered with, the blockchain will break, and the reason could be readily identified. This characteristic is not found in traditional databases, in which data can be modified or deleted with ease.

The blockchain is essentially a ledger of facts at a specific point in time. For Bitcoin, those facts involve data about Bitcoin transfers between addresses. Figure 6.29 shows how the

FIGURE 6.29

Block in a Blockchain

checksum of transaction data is added as part of the header, which, in turn, is hashed into and becomes that entire block's checksum.

- ***Proof-of-stake***: A way to validate transactions and achieve a distributed consensus. It is still an algorithm, and the purpose is the same as the proof-of-work, but the process to reach the goal is quite different.

Unlike the proof-of-work, in which the algorithm rewards miners who solve mathematical problems with the goal of validating transactions and creating new blocks, with the proof-of-stake, the creator of a new block is chosen in a deterministic way, depending on its wealth, also defined as *stake*.

Blockchain Advantages

Three advantages of implementing blockchain technologies include:

1. **Immutability:** Blockchains offer huge advances in cryptography, creating a far more secure network than a traditional centralized database. In a traditional database, a rogue employee or a hacker can potentially change historical transactions because of his or her access levels to the data.
   - ***Immutable***: Simply means unchangeable.
   - ***Immutability***: The ability for a blockchain ledger to remain a permanent, indelible, and unalterable history of transactions.

   Immutability has the potential to transform the auditing process into a quick, efficient, and cost-effective procedure, and to bring more trust and integrity to the data that businesses use and share every day. It is considered a key benefit of blockchain technology.

   Traditional databases have Create, Read, Update, and Delete options. In a blockchain, only Create and Read options are allowed, making it impossible to update or delete any transactions. Each transaction is created once and kept forever, making the data in the blockchain continuously grow. However, with a blockchain implementation across data centers, one would need a large number of teams working together across data centers to modify historical data–which greatly reduces the possibility of data tampering. The more widespread the environments, the more difficult it is to tinker with data.
2. **Digital Trust:** The ledger is not stored in a single location nor managed by any particular company. The cryptographic linking between blocks ensures data unchangeability. It is public and easily verifiable because it is hosted by millions of computers simultaneously. Anyone can maintain a copy of it and verify its correctness. In other words, servers and clouds are replaced by a vast number of nodes run by volunteers across the globe. This provides resiliency and trust without a third party.
3. **Internet of Things Integration:** IoT devices linked wirelessly to a blockchain network are able to automatically update a distributed ledger of multiway transactions automatically and deliver data internally to other devices in the network or externally to operators entitled to access the data by previous agreement or on demand. To support paid, on-demand access, an IoT network needs a built-in payment system, which distributed ledger technology can natively support.

APPLY YOUR KNOWLEDGE

BUSINESS DRIVEN INNOVATION

Would You Pay $69 Million for Digital Art?

Michael Joseph Winkelmann, known professionally as Beeple or Beeple Crap, is an American digital artist, graphic designer, and animator. From his home in Charleston, South Carolina, he creates a variety of digital artwork, including short films and Everydays (a graphic a day). Beeple uses various mediums in creating comical, phantasmagoric works that make political and social commentary while using pop culture figures as references.

The following are some example sales featuring this new type of art:

- In 2021, Christie's, a 225-year-old auction house that previously only sold physical art, auctioned an entirely digital piece by Beeple representing 5,000 days of Everydays. It sold for a record-setting $69,346,250.
- A $95,000 Banksy piece was recently burned and turned into an NFT (non-fungible token; see the section below for a description), which was sold for nearly $400,000.
- A cat meme recently sold for $600,000.
- Jack Dorsey, co-founder and CEO of Twitter, sold his first tweet ever (as an NFT) for over $2.9 million. The tweet, which says, "just setting up my twttr," was first posted by Dorsey on March 21, 2006.

Blockchain-based smart contracts can provide the necessary coordination between IoT-connected smart devices, as well as the IoT interfaces with the external world. Imagine an IoT scenario in which a car lock operates only if the car has been paid for according to the terms in the smart contract.

Non-Fungible Tokens (NFTs)

A ***non-fungible token (NFT)*** is a digital signature backed by blockchain technology that proves ownership of something. Unlike Bitcoins, which are all identical by design, NFTs are unique. To some degree, what NFTs offer for sale is the idea of scarcity. It's possible to buy a token that represents art in the physical world, but NFTs also back digital assets such as an image or a tweet. Much of the current market for NFTs is centered around collectibles, such as digital artwork, sports cards, and rarities. Like physical money, cryptocurrencies are fungible (i.e., they can be traded or exchanged), one for another. For example, one Bitcoin is always equal in value to another Bitcoin. NFTs can be used to represent items such as photos, videos, audio, and other types of digital files. Cryptographic assets on blockchain have unique identification codes and metadata that distinguish them from each other. Unlike cryptocurrencies, they cannot be traded or exchanged at equivalency. This differs from fungible tokens such as cryptocurrencies, which are identical to each other and, therefore, can be used as a medium for commercial transactions.

NFTs shift the crypto paradigm by making each token unique and irreplaceable, thereby making it impossible for one non-fungible token to equal another. They are digital representations of assets and have been likened to digital passports because each token contains a unique, non-transferable identity to distinguish it from other tokens. They are also extensible, meaning you can combine one NFT with another to "breed" a third, unique NFT.

Just like Bitcoin, NFTs also contain ownership details for easy identification and transfer between token holders. Owners can also add metadata or attributes pertaining to the asset in NFTs. For example, tokens representing coffee beans can be classified as fair trade. Or artists can sign their digital artwork with their own signature in the metadata.

In a group, discuss the value of an NFT. Would you pay millions of dollars for a Tweet? How will NFTs disrupt the art world moving forward?

LEARNING OUTCOME REVIEW

Learning Outcome 6.1: Explain the four primary traits that determine the value of data.

Information is data converted into a meaningful and useful context. Information can tell an organization how its current operations are performing and help it estimate and strategize about how future operations might perform. It is important to understand the different levels, formats, and granularities of data, along with the four primary traits that help determine the value of data, which include (1) data type: transactional and analytical; (2) data timeliness; (3) data quality; and (4) data governance.

Learning Outcome 6.2: Describe a database, a database management system, and the relational database model.

A database maintains data about various types of objects (inventory), events (transactions), people (employees), and places (warehouses). A database management system (DBMS) creates, reads, updates, and deletes data in a database while controlling access and security. A DBMS provides methodologies for creating, updating, storing, and retrieving data in a database. In addition, a DBMS provides facilities for controlling data access and security, allowing data sharing, and enforcing data integrity. The relational database model allows users to create, read, update, and delete data in a relational database.

Learning Outcome 6.3: Identify the business advantages of a relational database.

Many business managers are familiar with Excel and other spreadsheet programs they can use to store business data. Although spreadsheets are excellent for supporting some data analysis, they offer limited functionality in terms of security, accessibility, and flexibility and can rarely scale to support business growth. From a business perspective, relational databases offer many advantages over using a text document or a spreadsheet, including increased flexibility, increased scalability and performance, reduced data redundancy, increased data integrity (quality), and increased data security.

Learning Outcome 6.4: Identify the advantages of using business intelligence to support managerial decision making.

Many organizations today find it next to impossible to understand their own strengths and weaknesses, let alone their biggest competitors', due to enormous volumes of organizational data being inaccessible to all but the MIS department. Organizational data includes far more than simple structured data elements in a database; the set of data also includes unstructured data such as voice mail, customer phone calls, text messages, and video clips, along with numerous new forms of data, such as tweets from Twitter. Managers today find themselves in the position of being data rich and information poor, and they need to implement business intelligence systems to solve this challenge.

Learning Outcome 6.5: Describe the roles and purposes of data warehouses and data marts in an organization.

A data warehouse is a logical collection of data, gathered from many different operational databases, that supports business analysis and decision making. The primary value of a data warehouse is to combine data, more specifically, strategic data, throughout an organization into a single repository in such a way that the people who need that data can make decisions and undertake business analysis.

Learning Outcome 6.6: Explain blockchain and its advantages over a centralized relational database.

A blockchain is a type of distributed ledger consisting of blocks of data that maintain a permanent and tamper-proof record of transactional data. Distributed ledgers allow many different parties around the world to access and verify the same data. Blockchains are a form of distributed computing in which a decentralized database is managed by computers belonging to a network. Each of the computers in the distributed network maintains a copy of the ledger to prevent a single point of failure, and all copies are updated and validated simultaneously. Because data is shared and continually reconciled by thousands or even millions of computers, it is almost impossible to corrupt a blockchain.

KEY TERMS

REVIEW QUESTIONS

1. Why does a business need to be concerned with the quality of its data?
2. Why would a company care about the timeliness of its data?
3. What are the five characteristics common to high-quality data?
4. What are the four primary traits that help determine the value of data?

5. What is the difference between an entity and an attribute?
6. What is a data warehouse and why would a business want to implement one?
7. How does ETL help transfer data in and out of the data warehouse?
8. What is the purpose of data cleansing (or scrubbing)?
9. What are the causes of dirty data?
10. What is business intelligence, and how can it help a company achieve success?
11. Why would a business be data rich but information poor?
12. What is the relationship between a database and a blockchain?

CLOSING CASE ONE

Big Data, Big Business, Big Opportunities

Imagine working 10 years to become the lead marketing executive at a large retail organization only to find that your competitor is invading your market share by 20 percent each year. You quickly decide to launch several online marketing promotions while improving your products but find your efforts are fruitless as your competitor continues to steal your customers, destroying your profits while raising its own.

As you begin to analyze your competitor's business strategy, you find that while you were focused on sales reports, product inventory analysis, and other traditional marketing efforts, your competitor was making a massive investment in upgrading all of its management information systems. This included systems capable of collecting, storing, and analyzing data from every store, product, and sales representative in the market. In fact, your competitor now knows more about your products and sales cycles than you do. The new systems collect data not only throughout your competitor's company but also from a group of suppliers, retailers, and distributors around the globe. These new systems provide your competitor with the ability to adjust prices instantly based on daily customer traffic patterns, reorder automatically from every entity in the supply chains, and even move items within a store or between stores for maximum selling efficiencies.

Your competitor has won, and not because it had a higher-quality product or better sales and marketing strategies, but because it identified the value of management information systems coupled with the ability to instantly access big data within and beyond the organization. You quickly realize that your competitor's agility simply cannot be mimicked, offering it a huge competitive advantage. You sigh as you realize your company is in big trouble because it did not understand the dynamics of the big data age.

We are all familiar with the information age and the improvements made to organizations around the world as they are able to better manage employees, track sales data, and analyze customer purchasing patterns. However, this scenario is an example of the game-changing impact of big data, the massive amounts of data being collected by humans and machines over the last few years. Companies are now capturing hundreds of terabytes of data on everything from operations and finances to weather patterns and stock market trends. Sensors are now embedded in everything from products and machines to store floors, collecting real-time data on operations and customers. Radical customization, continuous experimentation, and information-driven business models are the new trademarks of competition as organizations analyze massive volumes of data. Data volumes are exploding, and more data has been created in the past 2 years than in the entire previous history of the human race. Here are the top 20 facts every manager should know about big data, according to *Forbes* magazine.[3]

- Data is growing faster than ever before. In 2021, 2 megabytes of new information is created every second for every human being on the planet.
- Every second we create new data. For example, we perform 40,000 search queries every second (on Google alone), which totals 3.3 billion searches per day, or 1.2 trillion searches per year.
- In 2021, over 2.8 billion people used Facebook each day.
- Facebook users send, on average, 31.25 million messages and view 2.77 million videos every minute.
- Every minute, up to 300 hours of video are uploaded to YouTube alone.
- 3 billion smart phones are shipped yearly—all packed with sensors capable of collecting all kinds of data, not to mention the data the users create themselves.
- Distributed computing (performing computing tasks using a network of computers in the cloud) is real. Google uses it every day to involve about 1,000 computers in answering a single search query, which takes no more than a second to complete.

Questions

1. List the reasons a business would want to display information in a graphical or visual format.
2. Explain how issues with low-quality data will impact big data.
3. Explain how a marketing department could use data visualization tools to help with the release of a new product.
4. Categorize the five common characteristics of high-quality data and rank them in order of importance for big data.
5. Develop a list of some possible entities and attributes located in a marketing database.
6. Assess how a business could use a few of the data analysis techniques to understand how the business is operating.

CLOSING CASE TWO

Changing the Way You Think about Data

Since the beginning of humankind, we have been using pictures and images to communicate, moving from cave drawings to hieroglyphics to the Internet. Today, it is easier than ever to paint a picture worth 100,000 words, thanks to technological advances. The primary advantages are databases and data warehouses that capture enormous amounts of data. Informing means accessing large amounts of data from different management information systems. Any article or advertisement that uses visual images can significantly improve the number of views a message generates. This can be a true competitive advantage in the digital age.

Good data alone does not make a good data story. Data storytelling is only effective when it provides value, whether it teaches people something new, gives them a new perspective, or inspires them to take action. Data visualization can help reveal trends, patterns, and exceptions. It can empower businesses to make more informed, longer-term decisions, as well as communicate with

FIGURE 6.30

Oil Spill Infographic

Source: National Oceanic and Atmospheric Administration (NOAA)

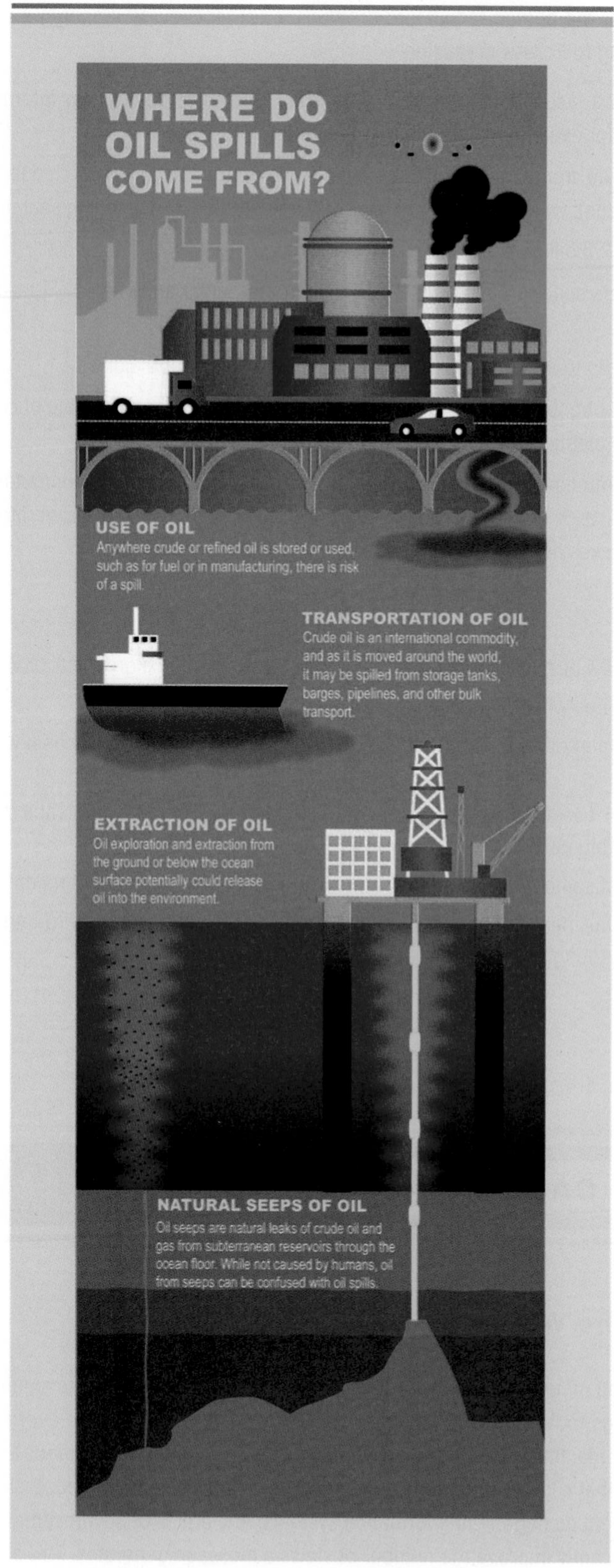

FIGURE 6.31

Oil Spill Response Infographic

Source: National Oceanic and Atmospheric Administration (NOAA)

customers and prospects more effectively. The way you deliver that story determines whether that message is communicated. Your narrative should guide readers through the data story, provide context about it, and help them synthesize it as effectively as possible.

Questions

Remember that your data story must provide visual representation of any data that can help make the data more interesting. In a group, review the examples (see Figure 6.30, 6.31, 6.32) and answer the following:

1. Does the visualization tell the whole story? Are there any questions you cannot answer just by reviewing the visualization?
2. Are there any data elements that should be removed or added to the visualization to make it more interesting?
3. Rank the visualization in order of best data story (1) to worst data story (3). What criteria did you use to rank the visualizations?
4. Find an example of a data story on the Internet and share it with your peers. Be sure to highlight the pros and cons of the data story.

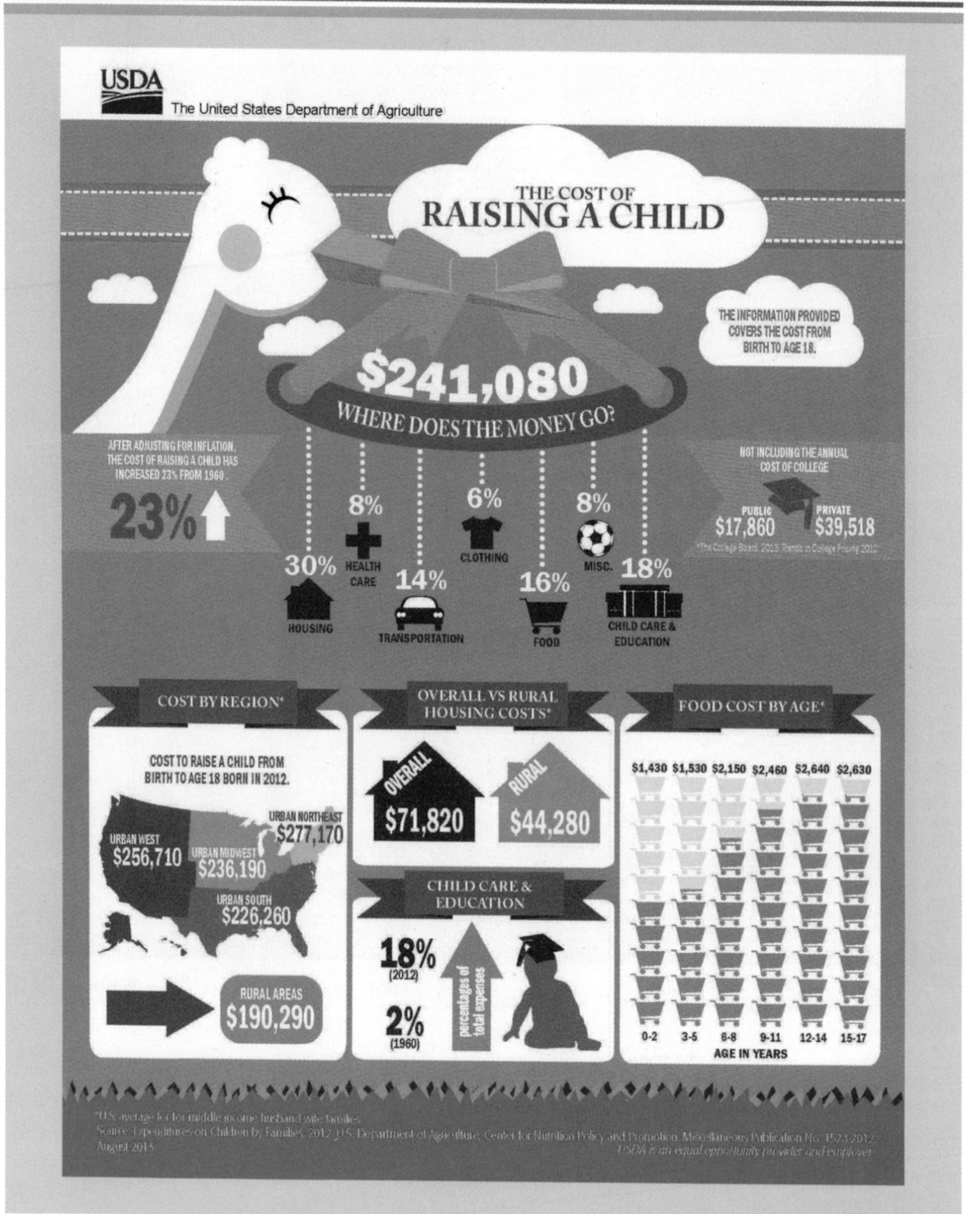

FIGURE 6.32

Child Expense Infographic

Source: United States Department of Agriculture

MAKING BUSINESS DECISIONS

1. **Improving Data Quality**

   HangUps Corporation designs and distributes closet organization structures. The company operates five different systems: order entry, sales, inventory management, shipping, and billing. The company has severe data quality issues, including missing, inaccurate, redundant, and incomplete data. The company wants to implement a data warehouse containing data from the five different systems to help maintain a single customer view, drive business decisions, and perform multidimensional analysis. Identify how the organization can improve its data quality when it begins designing and building its data warehouse.

2. **Data Timeliness**

   Data timeliness is a major consideration for all organizations. Organizations need to decide the frequency of backups and the frequency of updates to a data warehouse. In a team, describe the timeliness requirements for backups and updates to a data warehouse for:

- Weather tracking systems
- Car dealership inventories
- Vehicle tire sales forecasts
- Interest rates
- Restaurant inventories
- Grocery store inventories

3. That Is Not My Mother in the Casket

Information—you simply can't put a value on having the right (or the cost of having the wrong) information. Just look at the mistake made at the Crib Point cemetery in Victoria, Australia, when they were burying Mrs. Ryan, an 85-year-old woman with almost 70 children, grandchildren, and great-grandchildren attending her funeral. The bereaved family of Mrs. Ryan was shocked to lift the lid of her coffin during the funeral to discover another woman lying in her clothes and jewelry. Where was the body of Mrs. Ryan? Mrs. Ryan had been buried earlier that day in the other woman's clothes, jewelry, and plot. What type of data blunder could possibly occur to allow someone to be buried in the wrong clothes, coffin, and plot? What could the cemetery do to ensure its customers are buried in the correct places? Why is the quality of data important to any business? What issues can occur when a business uses low-quality data to make decisions?

4. Track Your Life

With wearable technology, you can track your entire life along with all of your physical activity, caloric burn, and sleep patterns. You can track your driving patterns, toothbrushing habits, and even laundry status. The question now becomes: How do you track all of your trackers?

A new company called Exist incorporates tracking devices with weather data, music choices, Netflix favorites, and Twitter activity all in one digital dashboard. Exist wants to understand every area of your life and provide correlation data between such things as your personal productivity and mood. As the different types of data expand, so will the breadth of correlations Exist can point out. For instance, do you tweet more when you are working at home? If so, does this increase productivity? Exist wants to track all of your trackers and analyze the data to help you become more efficient and more effective.

Create a digital dashboard for tracking your life. Choose four areas you want to track and determine three ways you would measure each area. For example, if you track eating habits, you might want to measure calories and place unacceptable levels in red and acceptable levels in green. Once completed, determine whether you can find any correlations among the areas in your life.

5. Free Data!

The U.S. Bureau of Labor Statistics states that its role is as the "principal fact-finding agency for the federal government in the broad field of labor economics and statistics." And the data that the bureau provides via its website is available to anyone, free. This can represent a treasure trove of business intelligence and data mining for those who take advantage of this resource.

Visit the website www.bls.gov. What type of data does the site provide? What data do you find most useful? What sort of data concerning employment and wages is available? How is this data categorized? How would this type of information be helpful to a business manager? What type of demographic data is available? How could this benefit a new start-up business?

6. Sorry, I Didn't Mean to Post Your Social Security Number on the Internet

Programming 101 teaches all students that security is the crucial part of any system. You must secure your data! It appears that some people working for the state of Oklahoma forgot this important lesson when tens of thousands of Oklahoma residents had their sensitive data—including numbers—posted on the Internet for the general public to access. You have probably heard this type of report before, but have you heard that the error went unnoticed for 3 years? A programmer reported the problem, explaining how he could easily change the page his browser was pointing to and grab the entire database for the state of Oklahoma. Also, because of the programming, malicious users could easily tamper with the database by changing data or adding fictitious data. If you are still thinking that isn't such a big deal, it gets worse. The website also posted the Sexual and Violent Offender Registry. Yes, the Department of Corrections employee data was also available for the general public to review.

In a group, discuss the following:

- Why is it important to secure data?
- What can happen if someone accesses your customer database?
- What could happen if someone changes the data in your customer database and adds fictitious data?
- Who should be held responsible for the state of Oklahoma data breach?
- What are the business risks associated with database security?

7. **Butterfly Effects**

The butterfly effect, an idea from chaos theory in mathematics, refers to the way a minor event—such as the movement of a butterfly's wing—can have a major impact on a complex system such as the weather. Dirty data can have the same impact on a business as the butterfly effect. Organizations depend on the movement and sharing of data throughout the organization, so the impact of data quality errors is costly and far-reaching. Such data issues often begin with a tiny mistake in one part of the organization, but the butterfly effect can produce disastrous results, making its way through MIS systems to the data warehouse and other enterprise systems. When dirty data or low-quality data enters organizational systems, a tiny error such as a spelling mistake can lead to revenue loss, process inefficiency, and failure to comply with industry and government regulations. Explain how the following errors can affect an organization:

- A cascading spelling mistake
- Inaccurate customer records
- Incomplete purchasing history
- Inaccurate mailing address
- Duplicate customer numbers for different customers

8. **Excel or Access?**

Excel is a great tool with which to perform business analytics. Your friend John Cross owns a successful publishing company specializing in do-it-yourself books. John started the business 10 years ago and has slowly grown it to 50 employees and $1 million in sales. John has been using Excel to run the majority of his business, tracking book orders, production orders, shipping orders, and billing. John even uses Excel to track employee payroll and vacation dates. To date, Excel has done the job, but as the company continues to grow, the tool is becoming inadequate.

You believe John could benefit from moving from Excel to Access. John is skeptical of the change because Excel has done the job up to now and his employees are comfortable with the current processes and technology. John has asked you to prepare a presentation explaining the limitations of Excel and the benefits of Access. In a group, prepare the presentation that will help convince John to make the switch.

9. **Predicting Netflix**

Netflix Inc., the largest online movie rental service, has more than 200 million subscribers and provides over 2.2 million minutes of content. That equates to almost four years of continuous watching. Data and information are so important to Netflix that it created The Netflix Prize, an open competition for anyone who could improve the data used in prediction ratings for films based on previous ratings. The winner would receive a $1 million prize.

The ability to search, analyze, and comprehend data is vital for any organization's success. It certainly was for Netflix—it was happy to pay anyone $1 million to improve the quality of its data.

In a group, explain how Netflix might use databases, data warehouses, and data marts to predict customer movie recommendations. What sources would they collect to determine their analysis algorithms? Here are a few characteristics you might want to analyze to get you started:

- Customer demographics
- Movie genre, rating, year, producer, and type
- Actor data
- Internet access
- Custom content

10. Twitter Buzz

Technology tools that can predict sales for the coming week, decide when to increase inventory, and determine when additional staff is required are extremely valuable. Twitter is not just for tweeting your whereabouts anymore. Twitter and other social media sites have become great tools for gathering business intelligence on customers, including what they like, dislike, need, and want. Twitter is easy to use, and businesses can track every single time a customer makes a statement about a particular product or service. Good businesses turn this valuable information into intelligence, spotting trends and patterns in customer opinion.

Do you agree that a business can use Twitter to gain business intelligence? How many companies do you think are aware of Twitter and exactly how they can use it to gain BI? How do you think Twitter uses a data warehouse? How do you think companies store Twitter data? How would a company use Twitter data in a data mart? How would a company use cubes to analyze Twitter data?

11. Two Trillion Rows Analyzed? No Problem!

eBay is the world's largest online marketplace, with 97 million global users selling anything to anyone at a yearly total of $62 billion—meaning more than $2,000 is exchanged every second. Of course, with this many sales, eBay is collecting the equivalent of the Library of Congress worth of data every three days, which must be analyzed to run the business successfully. Luckily, eBay discovered Tableau!

Tableau started at Stanford University when Chris Stolte, a computer scientist; Pat Hanrahan, an Academy Award–winning professor; and Christian Chabot, a savvy business leader, decided to solve the problem of helping ordinary people understand big data. The three created Tableau, which bridged two computer science disciplines: computer graphics and databases. No more need to write code or understand the relational database keys and categories; users simply drag and drop pictures of what they want to analyze. Tableau has become one of the most successful data visualization tools on the market, winning multiple awards. It has expanded internationally, won multiple awards, earned millions in revenue, and spawned a number of new inventions.

Tableau is revolutionizing business analytics, and this is only the beginning. Visit the Tableau website and become familiar with the tool by watching a few of the demos. Once you have a good understanding of the tool, create three questions eBay might be using Tableau to answer, including the analysis of its sales data to find patterns, business insights, and trends.

12. Different Dimensions

The focus of data warehousing is to extend the transformation of data into information. Data warehouses offer strategic level, external, integrated, and historical data so businesses can make projections, identify trends, and make key business decisions. The data warehouse collects and stores integrated sets of historical data from multiple operational systems and feeds them to one or more data marts. It may also provide end user access to support enterprisewide views of data.

You are currently working on a marketing team for a large corporation that sells jewelry around the world. Your boss has asked you to look at the following dimensions of data to determine which ones you want in your data mart for performing sales and market analysis (see Figure 6.33). As a team, categorize the different dimensions, ranking them from 1 to 5, with 1 indicating that the dimension offers the highest value and must be in your data mart, and 5 indicating that the dimension offers the lowest value and does not need to be in your data mart.

FIGURE 6.33

Data Warehouse Data

Dimension	Value (1–5)	Dimension	Value (1–5)
Product number		Season	
Store location		Promotion	
Customer net worth		Payment method	
Number of sales personnel		Commission policy	
Customer eating habits		Manufacturer	
Store hours		Traffic report	
Salesperson ID		Customer language	
Product style		Weather	
Order date		Customer gender	
Product quantity		Local tax data	
Ship date		Local cultural demographics	
Current interest rate		Stock market closing	
Product cost		Customer religious affiliation	
Customer political affiliation		Reason for purchase	
Local market analysis		Employee dress code policy	
Order time		Customer age	
Customer spending habits		Employee vacation policy	
Product price		Employee benefits	
Exchange rates		Current tariff data	
Product gross margin			

AYK APPLICATION PROJECTS

If you are looking for Access projects to incorporate into your class, try any of the following after reading this chapter.

Project Number	Project Name	Project Type	Plug-In	Focus Area	Project Level	Skill Set	Page Number
28	Daily Invoice	Access	T5, T6, T7, T8	Business Analysis	Introductory	Entities, Relationships, and Databases	AYK.15
29	Billing Data	Access	T5, T6, T7, T8	Business Intelligence	Introductory	Entities, Relationships, and Databases	AYK.17
30	Inventory Data	Access	T5, T6, T7, T8	SCM	Intermediate	Entities, Relationships, and Databases	AYK.18
31	Call Center	Access	T5, T6, T7, T8	CRM	Intermediate	Entities, Relationships, and Databases	AYK.19
32	Sales Pipeline	Access	T5, T6, T7, T8	Business Intelligence	Advanced	Entities, Relationships, and Databases	AYK.20
33	Online Classified Ads	Access	T5, T6, T7, T8	Ecommerce	Advanced	Entities, Relationships, and Databases	AYK.20

Design Element: © McGraw Hill Education

Networks: Mobile Business

7

CHAPTER

CHAPTER OUTLINE

SECTION 7.1

Connectivity: The Key to Communication in the Digital Age

- Understanding the Connected World
- Wireless Network Categories
- Protecting Wireless Networks

SECTION 7.2

Mobility: The Business Value of a Wireless World

- Mobile Enterprise Management
- Business Applications of Wireless Technologies

What's in IT for me?

The pace of technological change never ceases to amaze. Kindergarten classes are now learning PowerPoint, and many elementary school children have their own cell phones. What used to take hours to download over a dial-up modem connection can now transfer in a matter of seconds through an invisible, wireless network connection from a computer thousands of miles away. We are living in an increasingly wireless present and hurtling ever faster toward a wireless future. The tipping point of ubiquitous, wireless, handheld, mobile computing is approaching quickly.

As a business student, understanding network infrastructures and wireless technologies allows you to take advantage of mobile workforces. Understanding the benefits and challenges of mobility is a critical skill for business executives, regardless of whether you are a novice or a seasoned *Fortune* 500 employee. By learning about the various concepts discussed in this chapter, you will develop a better understanding of how business can leverage networking technologies to analyze network types, improve wireless and mobile business processes, and evaluate alternative networking options.

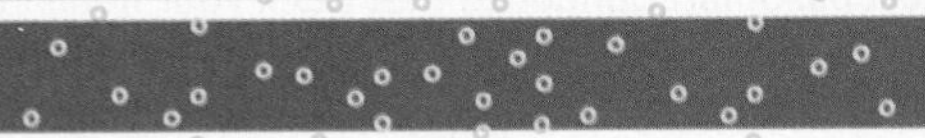

opening case study

gorodenkoff/Getty Images

Witthaya Prasongsin/Getty Images

PeopleImages/Getty Images

Why Do I Care about 5G?

I am sure you have all heard about 5G as the digital world advertises this new technology everywhere. But do you know why everyone is so excited about 5G? Let's take a high-level look at how 4G evolved and extrapolate how 5G will impact our lives. The first 4G cellphones appeared in the US in 2010. However, many of the 4G applications that changed our world did not appear until years later.

- 2010: Facetime (real-time video communications)
- 2010: Netflix Streaming (real-time mobile video)
- 2012: Snapchat (real-time tracking and communication)
- 2012: Instagram (mobile communication)
- 2012: Microsoft Xbox Live (real-time gaming)
- 2013: Uber (location-based ride sharing)

5G represents the fifth generation of mobile technology. It is a cellular network consisting of a system of cell sites divided by territory that sends encoded data through radio waves. Cell sites are connected via a wired or wireless backbone. 5G networks are smart and can connect thousands of IoT devices. The technical benefits of 5G include:

- **Low latency:** Small packets of data exchanged instantly.
- **Fast connection speeds:** Boost data transfer capacity by four times the current speeds by leveraging wider bandwidths and advanced antenna technologies.
- **Device connections:** Connect millions of IoT devices together.

The 5G applications that will once again redefine how we communicate, work, and live will be appearing over the next few years, and include the following:

- **Artificial intelligence:** Deliver data from devices to the central cloud to train or refine AI models.
- **Game streaming:** 5G gaming will not be tied down to devices with high computing power.
- **Machine learning:** Driverless cars interacting with each other.
- **Machine vision:** Smart security, including wireless cameras, will keep secure facilities safe with automatic recognition of potential security breaches or unauthorized visitors.
- **Smart cities:** Correlate traffic light data automatically and implement new patterns after an apartment complex nearby is opened.
- **Smart roads:** Everything on the road will be instantly communicating, helping to manage traffic and improve safety.
- **Virtual reality:** VR applications will explode onto the market as 5G offers the fast feedback and response times to provide a realistic experience. Remote physical therapy and checkups. Smart bandages that track your healing.[1]

section 7.1 | Connectivity: The Key to Communication in the Digital Age

LEARNING OUTCOMES

7.1 Understand wireless networks along with their benefits.

7.2 Describe the different wireless network categories.

7.3 Identify the security challenges of wireless networks.

UNDERSTANDING THE CONNECTED WORLD

LO 7.1: Understand wireless networks along with their benefits.

Networks range from small two-computer networks to the biggest network of all, the Internet. A network provides two principle benefits: the ability to communicate and the ability to share. Today's corporate digital networks include a combination of local area networks, wide area networks, and metropolitan area networks.

Networks connect our devices and ensure we can communicate with each other, our homes, and even our cars. Detailed information on the technical details of networking basics is included in Appendix B. This chapter will focus on the applications and business implications of wireless networks. For a brief review, the following lists the three primary types of networks.

- ***Local area network (LAN)***: Connects a group of computers in close proximity, such as in an office building, school, or home. LANs allow sharing of files, printers, games, and other resources. A LAN also often connects to other LANs and to wide area networks.
- ***Wide area network (WAN)***: Spans a large geographic area such as a state, province, or country. Perhaps the best example is the Internet. WANs are essential for carrying out the day-to-day activities of many companies and government organizations, allowing them to transmit and receive information among their employees, customers, suppliers, business partners, and other organizations across cities, regions, and countries and around the world. WANs often connect multiple smaller networks, such as local area networks or metropolitan area networks.
- ***Metropolitan area network (MAN)***: A large computer network usually spanning a city. Most colleges, universities, and large companies that span a campus use an infrastructure supported by a MAN (see Figure 7.1).

As far back as 1896, Italian inventor Guglielmo Marconi demonstrated a wireless telegraph, and in 1927, the first radiotelephone system began operating between the United States and Great Britain. Automobile-based mobile telephones were offered in 1947. In 1964, the first communications satellite, Telstar, was launched, and soon after, satellite-relayed telephone service and television broadcasts became available. Wireless networks have exploded since then, and newer technologies are now maturing that allow companies and home users alike to take advantage of both wired and wireless networks.

Before delving into a discussion of wireless networks, we should distinguish between *mobile* and *wireless,* terms that are often used synonymously but actually have different meanings.

- ***Mobile***: Means the technology can travel with the user. For instance, users can download software, email messages, and web pages onto a laptop or other mobile device for portable reading or reference.
- ***Mobile business*** (or ***mbusiness, mcommerce***): The ability to purchase goods and services through a wireless Internet-enabled device.
- ***Wireless***: Refers to any type of operation accomplished without the use of a hard-wired connection.

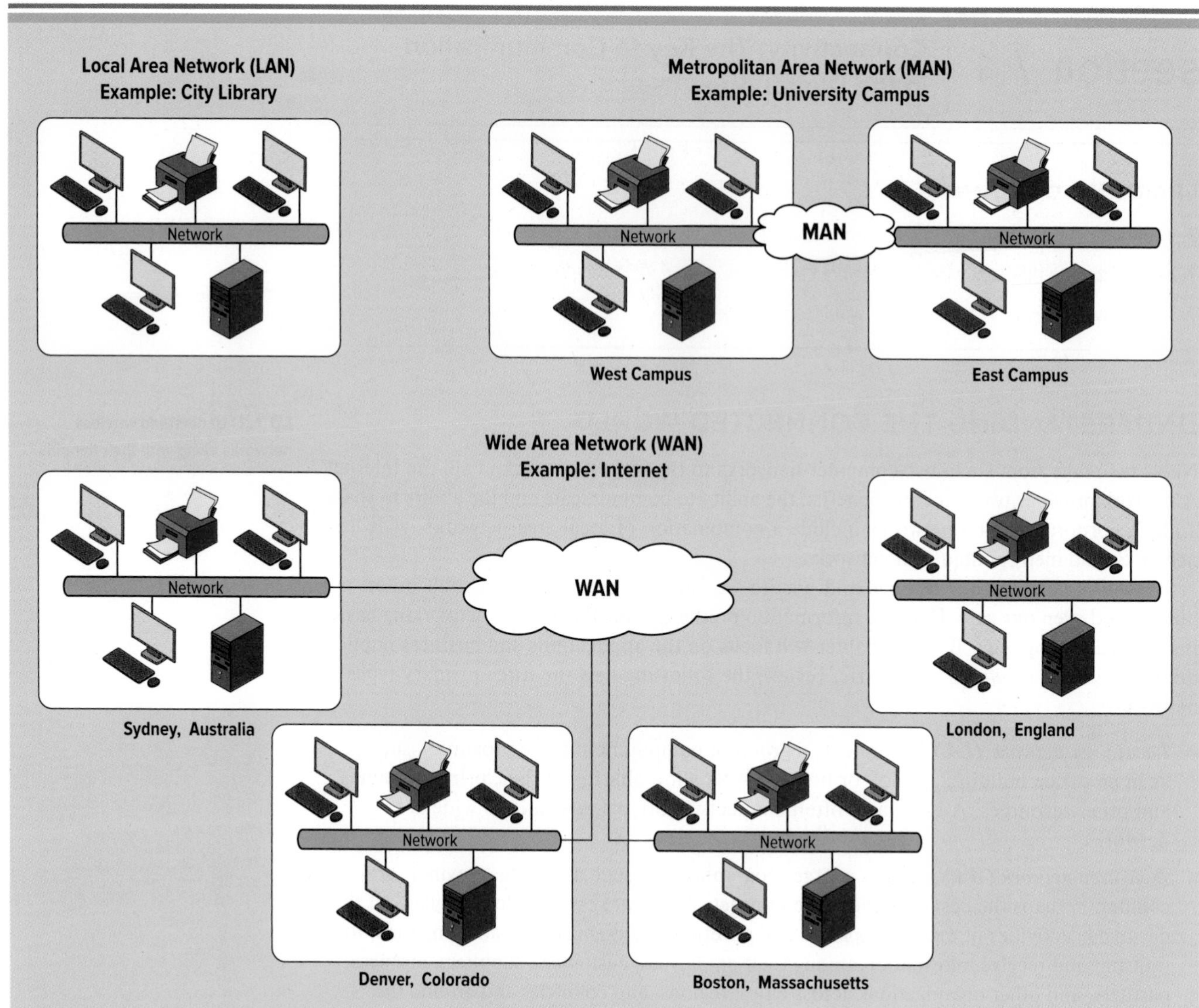

FIGURE 7.1

LAN, WAN, MAN

The emerging technology behind mbusiness is a mobile device equipped with a web-ready micro-browser that can perform the following services:

- Mobile entertainment–downloads for music, videos, games, voting, and ring tones, as well as text-based messaging services.
- Mobile sales/marketing–advertisements, campaigns, discounts, promotions, and coupons.
- Mobile banking–manage accounts, pay bills, receive alerts, and transfer funds.
- Mobile ticketing–purchase tickets for entertainment, transportation, and parking, including the ability to feed parking meters automatically.
- Mobile payments–pay for goods and services, including in-store purchases, home delivery, vending machines, taxis, gas, and so on.

There are many environments in which the network devices are wireless but not mobile, such as wireless home or office networks with stationary PCs and printers. Some forms of mobility do not require a wireless connection. For instance, a worker can use a wired laptop at home, shut down the laptop, drive to work, and attach the laptop to the company's wired network.

- ***Wireless fidelity (Wi-Fi)***: A means by which portable devices can connect wirelessly to a local area network, using access points that send and receive data via radio waves.

Wi-Fi allows computers, mobile devices, and other equipment (e.g., printers) to connect and exchange information with one another, creating a network. Wi-Fi has a maximum range of about 1,000 feet in open areas such as a city park, and 250 to 400 feet in closed areas such as an office building.

- ***Wi-Fi infrastructure***: Includes the inner workings of a Wi-Fi service or utility, including the signal transmitters, towers, or poles and additional equipment required to send out a Wi-Fi signal.

Most networks use a Wi-Fi infrastructure in which a wireless device, often a laptop, communicates through an access point or base station by means of, for instance, wireless fidelity.

Measuring Wireless Network Performance

Performance is the ultimate goal of any computer, computer system, or network. It is directly related to the network's speed of data transfer and capacity to handle transmission. A network that does not offer adequate performance simply will not get the job done for those who rely on it.

We measure network performance in terms of bandwidth.

- ***Bandwidth***: The maximum amount of data that can pass from one point to another in a unit of time.

Bandwidth is similar to water traveling through a hose. If the hose is large, water can flow through it quickly. Data differs from a hose in that it must travel great distances, and not all areas of the network have the same bandwidth. A network essentially has many hoses of unequal capacity connected together, which will restrict the flow of data when one is smaller than the others. Therefore, the speed of transmission of a network is determined by the speed of its smallest bandwidth.

- ***Bit*** (short for binary digit): The smallest element of data. It has a value of either 0 or 1.
- ***Bit rate*** (or ***data rate***): The number of bits transferred or received per unit of time.

Bandwidth is measured in terms of bit rate. Figure 7.2 represents bandwidth speeds in terms of bit rates. Bandwidth is typically given in bits per second (abbreviated as bps) and bytes per second (abbreviated as Bps). It is important to note that these two terms are not interchangeable.

Wireless Networks Benefits

Can you imagine operating in a world without networking capabilities or wireless technologies? How would you find your friends? How would you share your selfies? What would your life be like without streaming music services such as Spotify or streaming TV and movie services such as Netflix? The invention of technologies that allow us to use Wi-Fi and cellular to send and receive data to IoT devices has disrupted the world and changed how we communicate. Figure 7.3 highlights the benefits of wireless networks.

Bandwidth	Abbreviation	Bits per Second (bps)	Example
Kilobit	Kb	1 Kbps = 1,000 bps	Traditional modem = 56 Kbps
Megabit	Mb	1 Mbps = 1,000 Kbps	Traditional Ethernet = 10 Mbps Fast Ethernet = 100 Mbps
Gigabit	Gb	1 Gbps = 1,000 Mbps	Gigabit Ethernet = 1,000 Mbps

FIGURE 7.2

Bandwidth Speeds

FIGURE 7.3

Wireless Network Benefits

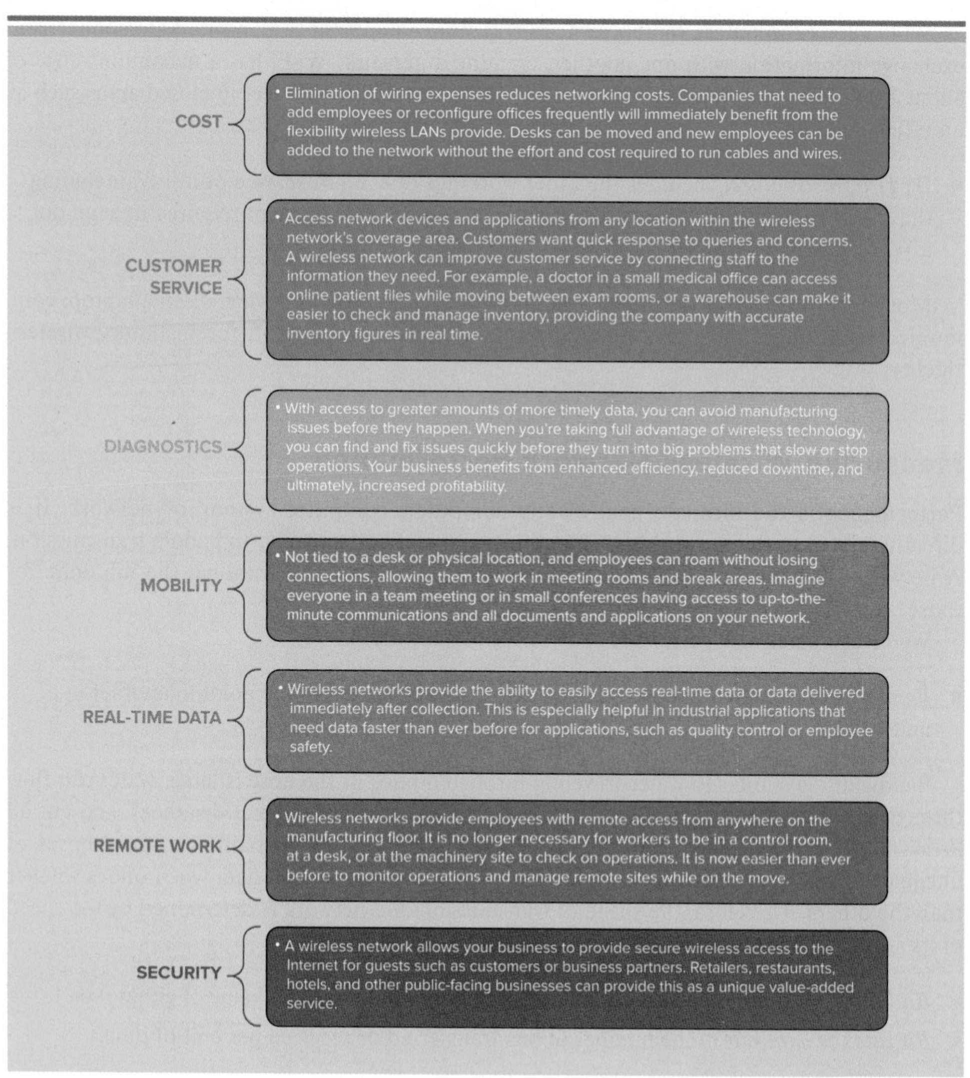

COST
• Elimination of wiring expenses reduces networking costs. Companies that need to add employees or reconfigure offices frequently will immediately benefit from the flexibility wireless LANs provide. Desks can be moved and new employees can be added to the network without the effort and cost required to run cables and wires.
CUSTOMER SERVICE
• Access network devices and applications from any location within the wireless network's coverage area. Customers want quick response to queries and concerns. A wireless network can improve customer service by connecting staff to the information they need. For example, a doctor in a small medical office can access online patient files while moving between exam rooms, or a warehouse can make it easier to check and manage inventory, providing the company with accurate inventory figures in real time.
DIAGNOSTICS
• With access to greater amounts of more timely data, you can avoid manufacturing issues before they happen. When you're taking full advantage of wireless technology, you can find and fix issues quickly before they turn into big problems that slow or stop operations. Your business benefits from enhanced efficiency, reduced downtime, and ultimately, increased profitability.
MOBILITY
• Not tied to a desk or physical location, and employees can roam without losing connections, allowing them to work in meeting rooms and break areas. Imagine everyone in a team meeting or in small conferences having access to up-to-the-minute communications and all documents and applications on your network.
REAL-TIME DATA
• Wireless networks provide the ability to easily access real-time data or data delivered immediately after collection. This is especially helpful in industrial applications that need data faster than ever before for applications, such as quality control or employee safety.
REMOTE WORK
• Wireless networks provide employees with remote access from anywhere on the manufacturing floor. It is no longer necessary for workers to be in a control room, at a desk, or at the machinery site to check on operations. It is now easier than ever before to monitor operations and manage remote sites while on the move.
SECURITY
• A wireless network allows your business to provide secure wireless access to the Internet for guests such as customers or business partners. Retailers, restaurants, hotels, and other public-facing businesses can provide this as a unique value-added service.

LO 7.2: Describe the different wireless network categories.

WIRELESS NETWORK CATEGORIES

In many networked environments today, users are both wireless and mobile. For example, a mobile user commuting to work on a train can maintain a cellular voice call while checking their email via a Wi-Fi network. Figure 7.4 displays the different categories of wireless networks.

Personal Area Networks

A ***personal area network (PAN)*** provides communication for devices owned by a single user that work over a short distance. PANs are used to transfer files, including email, calendar appointments, digital photos, and music. A PAN can provide communication between a wireless

FIGURE 7.4

Wireless Network Categories

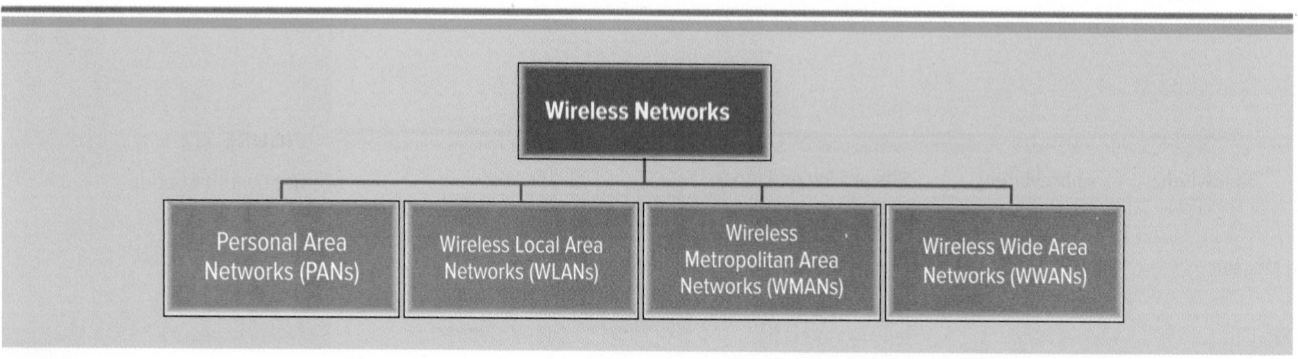

headset and a cell phone or between a computer and a wireless mouse or keyboard. Personal area networks generally cover a range of less than 10 meters (about 30 feet).

- ***Bluetooth***: A wireless PAN technology that transmits signals over short distances among cell phones, computers, and other devices.

The name is borrowed from Harald Bluetooth, a king in Denmark more than 1,000 years ago. Bluetooth eliminates the need for wires, docking stations, or cradles, as well as all the special attachments that typically accompany personal computing devices. Bluetooth operates at speeds up to 1 Mbps within a range of 33 feet or less. Devices that are Bluetooth-enabled communicate directly with each other in pairs, like a handshake. Up to eight can be paired simultaneously. And Bluetooth is not just for technology devices. An array of Bluetooth-equipped appliances, such as a television set, a stove, and a thermostat, can be controlled from a cell phone—all from a remote location.

Wireless LANs

A ***wireless LAN (WLAN)*** is a local area network that uses radio signals to transmit and receive data over distances of a few hundred feet. Think of a WLAN as your home Wi-Fi network that connects all of your smart devices. A few of the key terms associated with a WLAN include:

- ***Access point (AP)***: The computer or network device that serves as an interface between devices and the network. Each computer initially connects to the access point and then to other computers on the network. An access point sends data to the Internet over a wired broadband connection, as illustrated in Figure 7.5. An example might include the physical Internet cable connection coming into your home to your TV or router.
- ***Multiple-in/multiple-out (MIMO) technology***: Multiple transmitters and receivers, allowing them to send and receive greater amounts of data than traditional networking devices. MIMO systems can achieve significantly higher data rates than traditional channels and are a big driver of new technologies such as 5G.
- ***Wireless access point (WAP)***: Enables devices to connect to a wireless network to communicate with each other. An example might include connecting to a Wi-Fi network in a hotel or restaurant. In a Wi-Fi network, the user's laptop or other Wi-Fi-enabled device has a wireless adapter that translates data into a radio signal and transmits it to the wireless access point. The wireless access point, which consists of a transmitter with an antenna that is often built into the hardware, receives the signal and decodes it.

When receiving data, the wireless access point takes the information from the Internet, translates it into a radio signal, and sends it to the computer's wireless adapter. If too many people try to use the Wi-Fi network at one time, they can experience interference or dropped connections.

- ***Hotspots***: Designated locations where Wi-Fi access points are publicly available.

FIGURE 7.5
Wi-Fi Networks

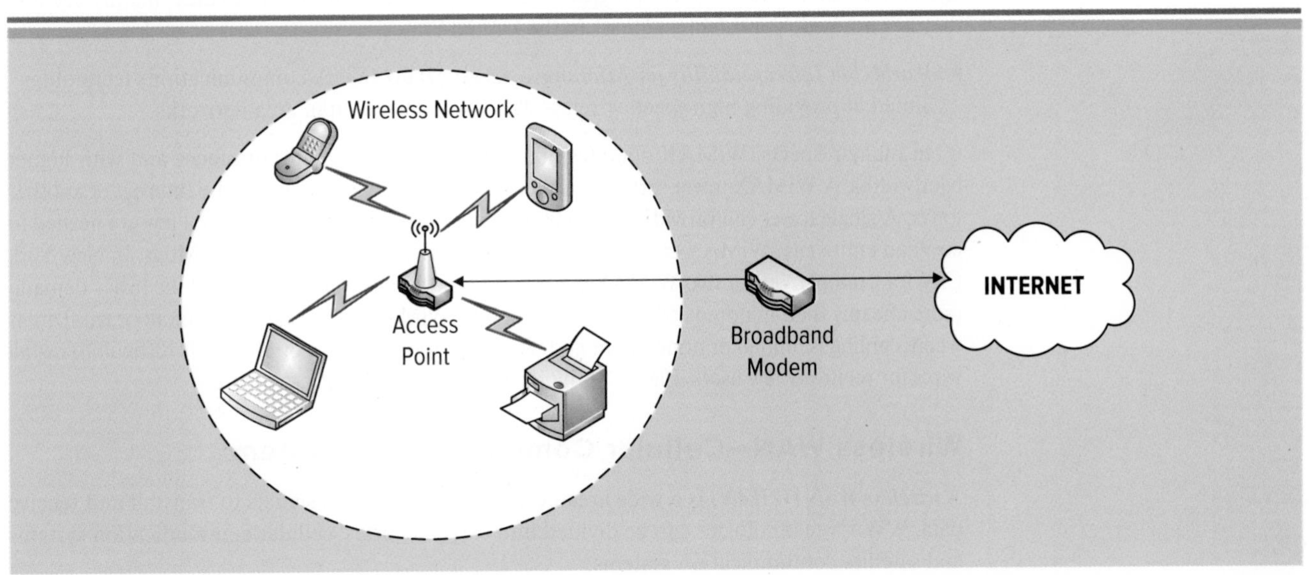

APPLY YOUR KNOWLEDGE

BUSINESS DRIVEN MIS

Sports Sensors

A sensor is a device that detects or measures a physical property such as heat, light, sound, or motion and records, indicates, or otherwise reacts to it in a particular way. With wireless apps and sensors, a number of new, high-tech tools for amateurs provide coach-quality feedback to athletes of all levels, including:

- **Tennis (Sony):** Sony recently created a tennis-tracking device and app that lets users collect the kind of game-play data that used to be available only to professionals.
- **Golf (Swingbyte):** The ultralight sensor clips to the club and monitors speed, acceleration, arc, and other statistics.
- **Hockey (Fwd Powershot):** This ultralight sensor fits into the handle end of the stick and measures swing speed, angle, and acceleration.
- **Basketball (94Fifty Smart Sensor):** Embedded in a standard ball, this sensor tracks shot speed, arc, and backspin, plus dribble speed and force.
- **Baseball (Zepp):** Stuck to the knob of the bat, the sensor tracks the speed and plane of a swing and the angle of impact.[2]

In a group, create a product that takes advantage of sensors, including what the sensor would measure and how it would deliver feedback to the user.

Areas around wireless access points where users can connect to the Internet are often called hotspots. Hotspots are found in places such as restaurants, airports, and hotels—locations where business professionals tend to gather. Hotspots are extremely valuable for those business professionals who travel extensively and need access to business applications. By positioning hotspots at strategic locations throughout a building, campus, or city, network administrators can keep Wi-Fi users continuously connected to a network or the Internet, no matter where they roam.

Wireless MANs

A ***wireless MAN (WMAN)*** is a metropolitan area network that uses radio signals to transmit and receive data. WMAN technologies have not been highly successful to date, mainly because they are not widely available, at least in the United States.

- ***Worldwide Interoperability for Microwave Access (WiMAX)***: A communications technology aimed at providing high-speed wireless data over metropolitan area networks.

In many respects, WiMAX operates like Wi-Fi, only over greater distances and with higher bandwidths. A WiMAX tower serves as an access point and can connect to the Internet or another tower. A single tower can provide up to 3,000 square miles of coverage, so only a few are needed to cover an entire city. WiMAX can support data communications at a rate of 70 Mbps. In New York City, for example, one or two WiMAX access points around the city might meet the heavy demand more cheaply than hundreds of Wi-Fi access points. WiMAX can also cover remote or rural areas where cabling is limited or nonexistent and where it is too expensive or physically difficult to install wires for relatively few users. Figure 7.6 illustrates the WiMAX infrastructure.

Wireless WAN—Cellular Communication System

A ***wireless WAN (WWAN)*** is a wide area network that uses radio signals to transmit and receive data. WWAN technologies can be divided into two categories: cellular communication systems and satellite communication systems.

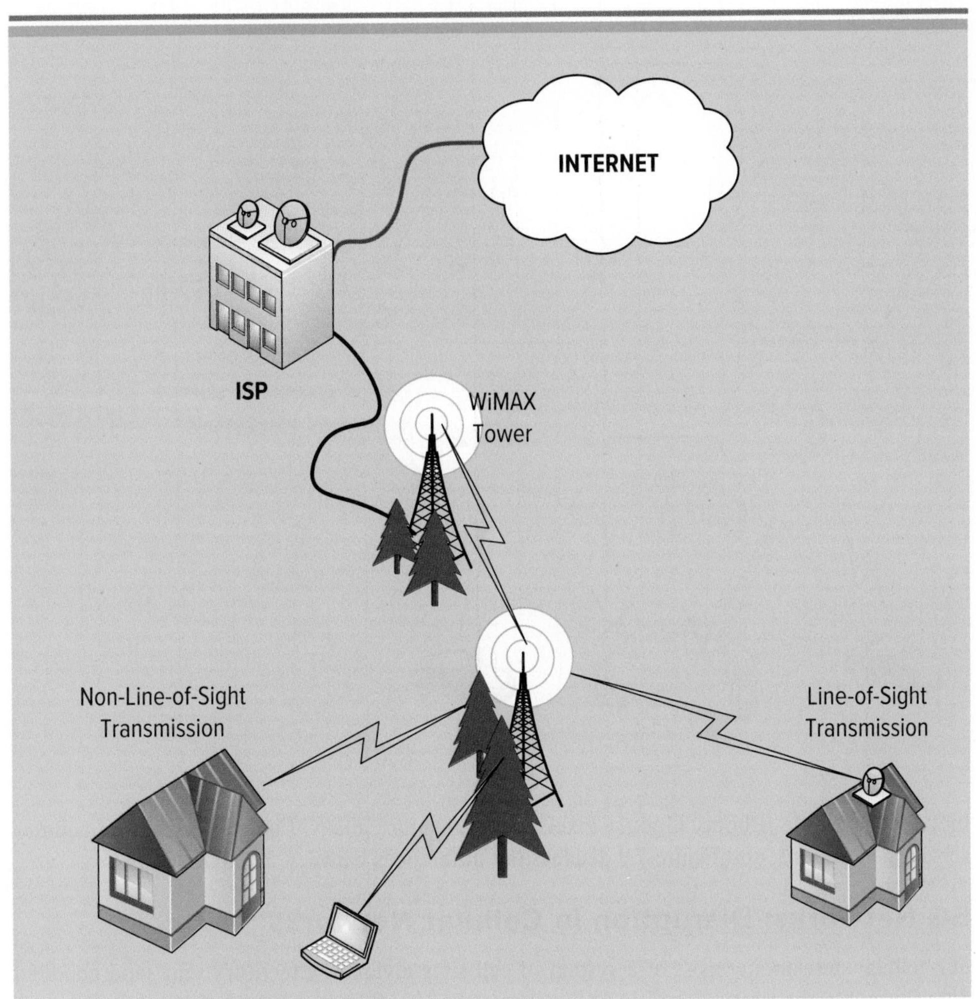

FIGURE 7.6

WiMAX Infrastructure

- ***Radio access network (RAN)***: A technology that connects individual devices to other parts of a network through radio connections.

The idea, pioneered decades ago, is that a handset or other item can be wirelessly connected to a backbone or core network that broadcasts the data. The radio access network gets the signal to and from the wireless access point, so it can travel with other traffic over networks built with a collective and deliberate purpose. It is a major part of modern telecommunications, with 3G and 4G network connections for mobile phones being examples of radio access networks.

Although mobile communications have been around for generations, including the walkie-talkies of the 1940s and mobile radiophones of the 1950s, it was not until 1983 that cellular telephony became available commercially. A cell phone is a device for voice and data, communicating wirelessly through a collection of stationary ground-based sites called base stations, each of which is linked to its nearest neighbor stations. Base station coverage areas are about 10 square miles and are called cells, as Figure 7.7 illustrates.

The first cell phone was demonstrated in 1973 by Motorola (it weighed almost 2 pounds), but it took 10 years for the technology to become commercially available. The Motorola DynaTAC, marketed in 1983, weighed 1 pound and cost about $4,000. Cellular technology has come a long way since then. Cell phones have morphed into smart phones.

- ***Smart phones***: Offer more advanced computing ability and connectivity than basic cell phones.

Smart phones allow for web browsing, emailing, listening to music, watching videos, computing, keeping track of contacts, sending text messages, and taking and sending photos. They

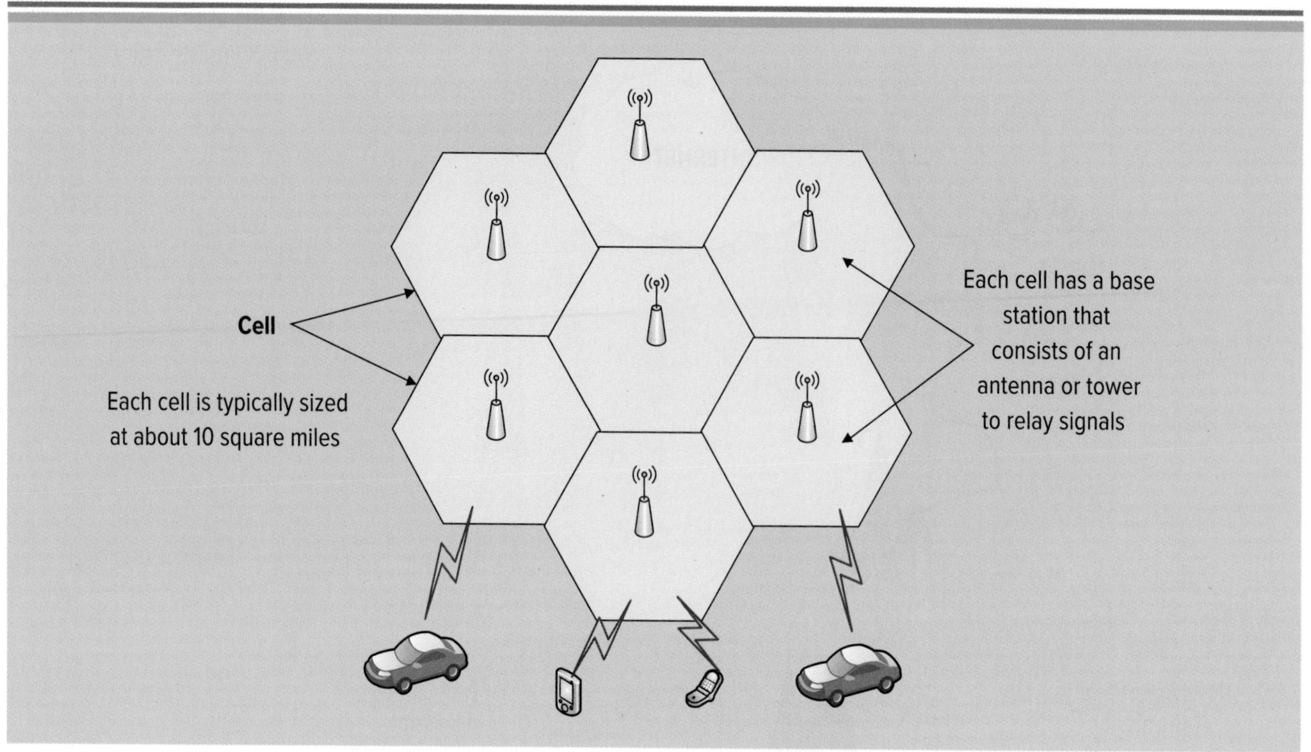
Cell
Each cell is typically sized at about 10 square miles
Each cell has a base station that consists of an antenna or tower to relay signals

FIGURE 7.7

Cell Phone Communication System Overview

include the Apple iPhone, Google Pixel, and Samsung Galaxy. Figure 7.8 lists the cellular service generations, and Figure 7.9 displays the differences between 3G, 4G, and 5G.

5G Networks: Disruption in Cellular Networks

5G cellular networks consist of a system of cell sites divided by territory that send encoded data through radio waves.

- *5G*: The fifth-generation wireless broadband technology that will greatly increase the speed and responsiveness of wireless networks.

Cell sites are connected via a wired or wireless backbone. 5G operates with a 5-Ghz signal and is set to offer record speeds 100× faster than 4G, our current connection. 5G will unleash a massive IoT ecosystem, allowing networks to connect billions of devices without sacrificing speed, latency, or cost. The technical benefits of 5G include:

- **Low latency:** Small packets of data will be exchanged instantly.
- **Fast connection speeds:** Will boost data transfer capacity by four times the current speeds by leveraging wider bandwidths and advanced antenna technologies.
- **Device connections:** Will connect millions of IoT devices together.[3]

FIGURE 7.8

Cell Phone Generations

	Wireless Communications	Speed
1G	—The original analog cell phone network	14.4 Kbps
2G	—Digital cell phone service	10 Kbps–144 Kbps
3G	—Broadband Internet services over cellular networks —Added MMSs (multimedia message services) or picture message services	144 Kbps–4 Mbps
4G	—High-speed access, anywhere, anytime, to anything digital—audio, video, text —Improved video transmissions	100 Mbps
5G	—Superior data communication rate —Expected to provide artificial intelligence capabilities on wearable devices	1.5 Gbps over a distance of 90 meters

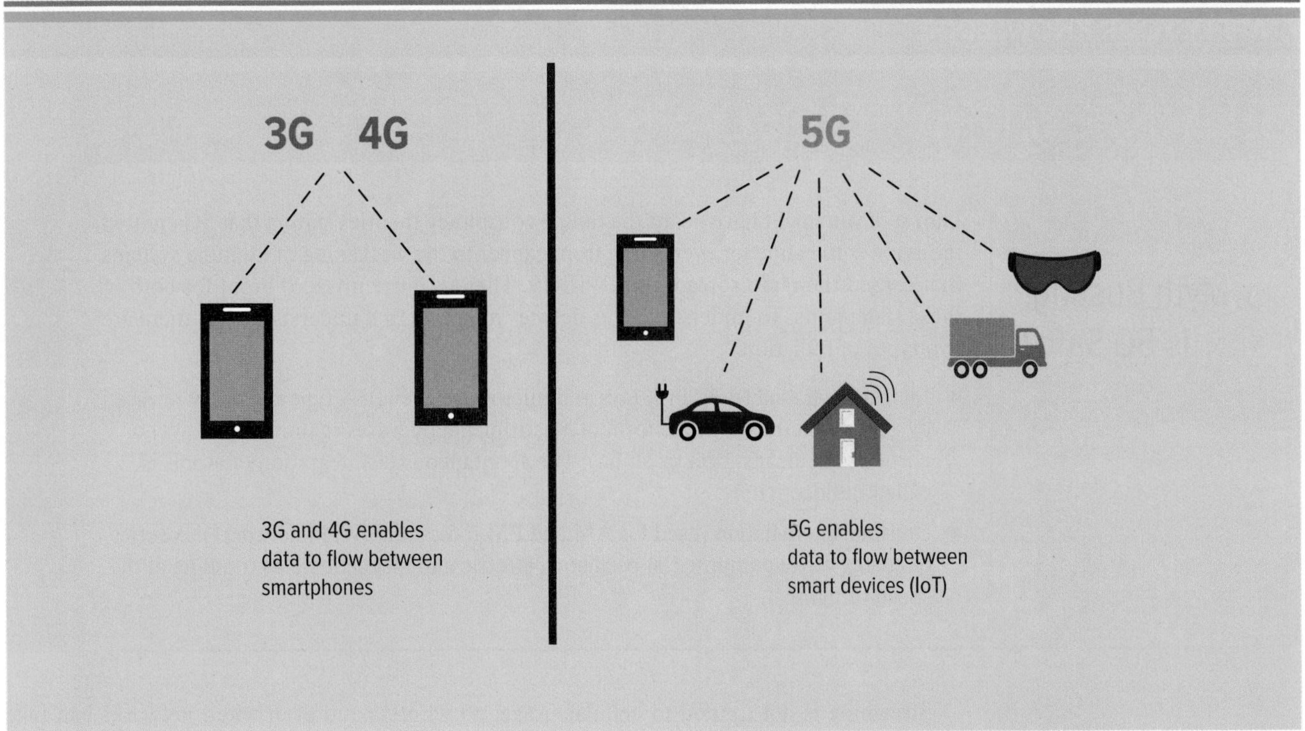
3G 4G
3G and 4G enables data to flow between smartphones
5G
5G enables data to flow between smart devices (IoT)

FIGURE 7.9

Comparison of 3G, 4G, and 5G Cellular Networks

The 5G applications that will once again redefine how we communicate, work, and live will be appearing over the next few years. They will include the following features:

- **Artificial intelligence:** Delivers data from devices to the central cloud to train or refine AI models.
- **Game streaming:** 5G gaming will not be tied down to devices with high computing power.
- **Machine learning:** Driverless cars will interact with each other.
- **Machine vision:** Smart security including wireless cameras will keep secure facilities safe with automatic recognition of potential security breaches or unauthorized visitors.
- **Smart cities:** Will correlate traffic light data automatically and implement new patterns after an apartment complex nearby is opened.
- **Smart roads:** Everything on the road will be instantly communicating, thus helping to manage traffic and improve safety.
- **Virtual reality:** VR applications will explode onto the market because 5G will offer the fast feedback and response times needed to provide a realistic experience. This will include remote physical therapy and checkups, and also smart bandages that track your healing.[4]

Currently, there is no scientific evidence supporting the notion that Wi-Fi radiation is dangerous, just as there is no evidence that radio waves used by walkie-talkies (that is, the radiation produced by walkie-talkies) are dangerous.

In a group, research and debate the following: Do you agree or disagree that 5G-emitted radiation is dangerous to your health?

One of the biggest benefits of a 5G network is its ability to stream gigabytes of real-time instantaneous data.

- ***Streaming*:** A method of sending audio and video files over the Internet in such a way that the user can view the file while it is being transferred.
- ***Streaming data*:** Data that is generated continuously by thousands of data sources, which typically send in the data records simultaneously, and in small sizes (order of kilobytes).

Streaming data includes a wide variety of data, such as log files generated by customers using mobile or web applications, ecommerce purchases, information from social networks, financial trading floors from connected devices, and data centers. Netflix is a great example of streaming videos.

APPLY YOUR KNOWLEDGE

BUSINESS DRIVEN DEBATE

Myth Busting: Is 5G Safe?

I am sure you might have heard the online conspiracy theories stating that 5G-emitted radiation is to blame for everything from cancer to the weakening of immune systems that caused the rapid spread of COVID-19. There is currently zero proof for both of these statements. To understand this debate, you must first understand that there are two types of radiation.

- **Ionizing radiation** (used in X-rays and microwave ovens): A type of energy released by atoms that travels in the form of electromagnetic waves (gamma or X-rays) or particles (neutrons, beta or alpha). The spontaneous disintegration of atoms is called radioactivity.
- **Non-ionizing radiation** (used for AM and FM radios, and Wi-Fi networks): A series of energy waves composed of oscillating electric and magnetic fields traveling at the speed of light.[5]

Streaming is not limited to cellular usage; all wireless and even wired networks can take advantage of this method. The most obvious advantage is speed, a direct benefit for mobile and wireless devices, because they are still not as fast as their wired counterparts. Until this point, all smart phones, though equipped with long-term evolution (LTE) or 4G broadband-based data transfer technology, could not support streaming video or broadband-based phone calls. For example, businesses can track changes in public sentiment on their brands and products by continuously analyzing social media streams, and respond in a timely fashion as the necessity arises. A few examples of streaming data include:

- A financial institution tracks changes in the stock market in real time, computes value-at-risk, and automatically rebalances portfolios based on stock price movements.
- A real estate website tracks a subset of data from consumers' mobile devices and makes real-time property recommendations of properties to visit based on their geolocation.
- A solar power company has to maintain power throughput for its customers, or pay penalties. It implemented a streaming data application that monitors all the panels in the field, and schedules service in real time, thereby minimizing the periods of low throughput from each panel and the associated penalty payouts.
- A media publisher streams billions of clickstream records from its online properties, aggregates and enriches the data with demographic information about users, and optimizes content placement on its site, delivering relevancy and better experience to its audience.
- An online gaming company collects streaming data about player-game interactions and feeds the data into its gaming platform. It then analyzes the data in real time and offers incentives and dynamic experiences to engage its players.
- Sensors in transportation vehicles, industrial equipment, and farm machinery send data to a streaming application. The application monitors performance, detects any potential defects in advance, and places a spare part order automatically, preventing equipment downtime.[6]

5G and Wi-Fi 6

Wi-Fi 6 will deliver an improved experience to address device and application needs in a range of consumer and enterprise environments.

- ***Wi-Fi 6***: The next generation of Wi-Fi expected to operate at 9.6 Gbps.

Wireless networking has made everyday life far simpler in numerous ways by providing the ability to work without wires and cables.

Wi-Fi 6 and 5G introduce the new era of wireless access. Their convergence enables organizations to do business anywhere while increasing productivity and offering the best user experience.

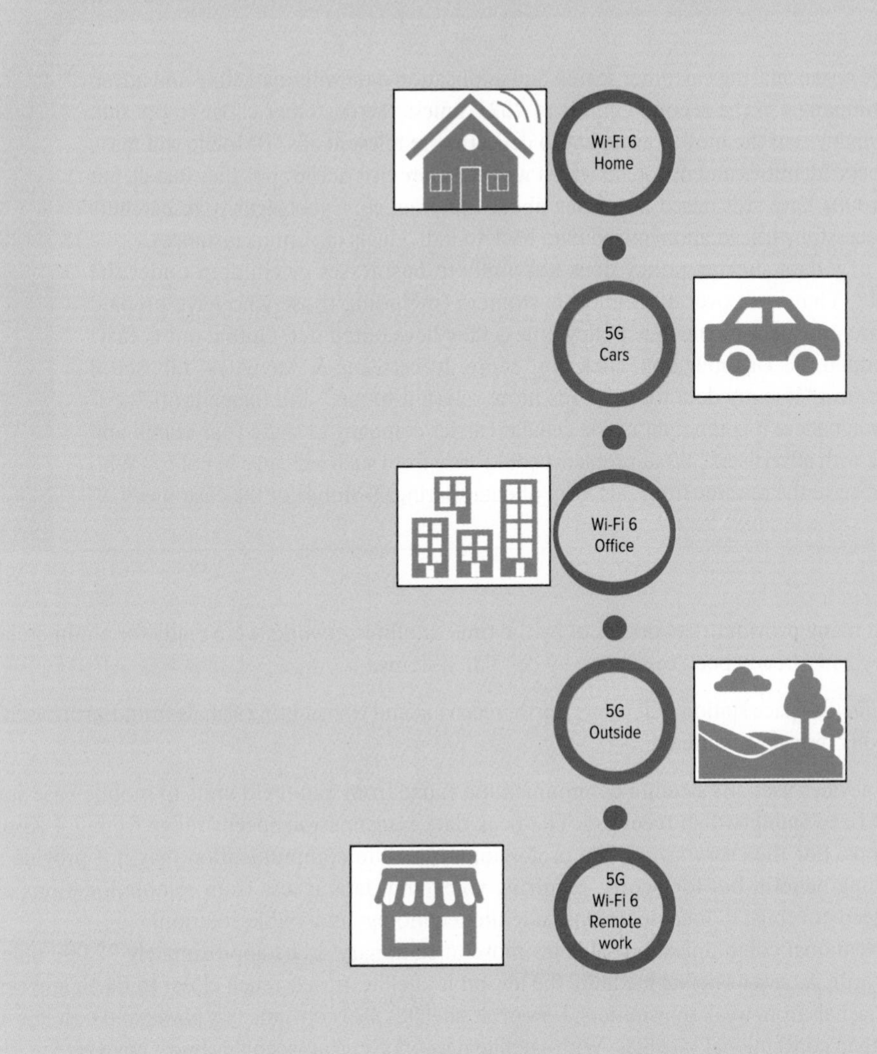

FIGURE 7.10

Use Cases for Wi-Fi 6 and 5G

- Wi-Fi 6 is the preferred choice for indoor networks offering improved speed, latency, and higher density of connected devices such as home networks, along with colleges, stadiums, and convention centers.
- 5G will be the designated choice for outdoor networks and early businesses. Examples include connected cars, drones, and smart cities (see Figure 7.10).

Both Wi-Fi 6 and 5G offer exciting opportunities to connect more mission-critical IoT devices reliably via wireless and they will handle upwards of 152,000 connected IoT devices per second by 2025. Wi-Fi 6 and 5G will also offer enhanced mobile broadband for an immersive experience via augmented and virtual reality. This will mean 12 times the increase in augmented reality and virtual reality traffic by 2024.[7]

Wireless WAN—Satellite Communication System

When satellite systems first came into consideration in the 1990s, the goal was to provide wireless voice and data coverage for the entire planet, without the need for mobile phones to roam

APPLY YOUR KNOWLEDGE

BUSINESS DRIVEN GLOBALIZATION

Sharing Mobile Data

T-Mobile began sharing customer search and application data with marketing and advertising companies in the second quarter of 2021, unless the customer chose to opt out. The company said the move was meant to deliver more relevant ads. T-Mobile will mask subscribers' identities and not share which websites they visit or the apps they install, but some groups have still raised a red flag about the practice. Cybersecurity researchers have successfully traced anonymized data back to individuals in various instances.

The new data sharing policy does not apply to businesses or children under the age of 18. That said, over 80 million customers (including those who have prepaid plans) are impacted by the new policy unless they have opted out. Opting out is easy: Simply open the T-Mobile app, click the "More, Advertising & Analytics" tab, scroll down to find "Use my data to make ads more relevant to me," and toggle it off.[8]

Do you believe it is the right of the cellular carrier company to share your search and app data with advertisers? What problems could arise from such a change in policy? Who should receive the revenue from this form of data sharing: T-Mobile or the customer?

between many provider networks. But by the time satellite networks were ready for commercial use, they had already been overtaken by cellular systems.

- ***Satellite***: A space station that orbits Earth, receiving and transmitting signals from Earth-based stations over a wide area.

The devices used for satellite communication range from handheld units to mobile base stations to fixed satellite dish receivers. The peak data transmission speeds range from 2.4 Kbps to 2 Mbps. For the everyday mobile professional, satellite communication may not provide a compelling benefit, but for people requiring voice and data access from remote locations or guaranteed coverage in local locations, satellite technology is a viable solution.

Conventional communication satellites move in stationary orbits approximately 22,000 miles above Earth. A newer satellite medium, the low-orbit satellite, travels much closer to Earth and can pick up signals from weak transmitters. Low-orbit satellites also consume less power and cost less to launch than conventional satellites. With satellite networks, businesspeople almost anywhere in the world have access to full communication capabilities, including voice, videoconferencing, and Internet access. Figure 7.11 briefly illustrates the satellite communication system.

FIGURE 7.11
Satellite Communication System

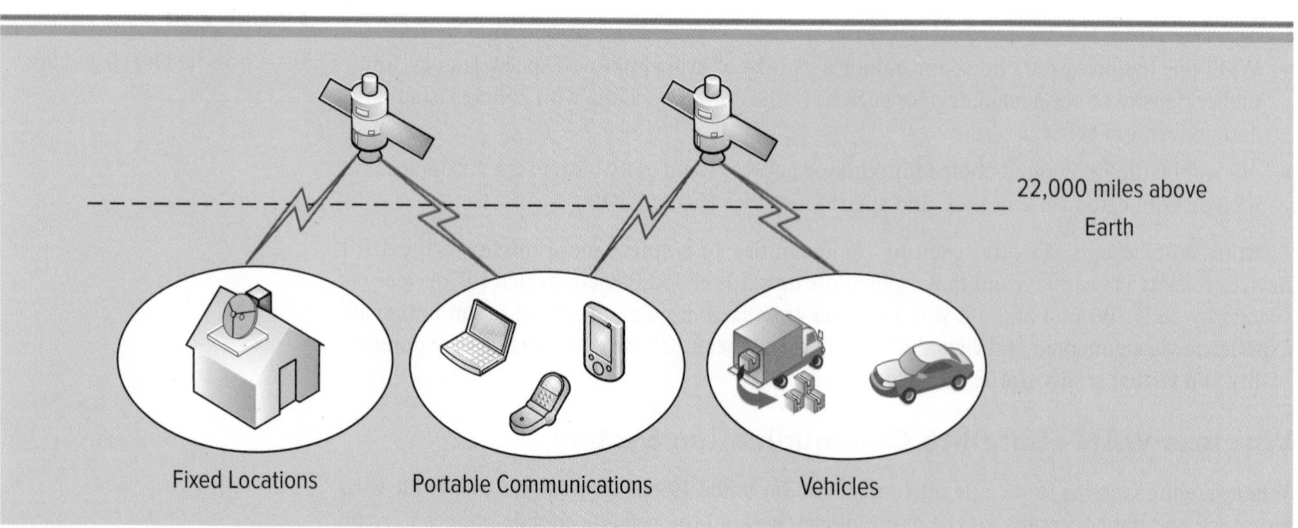

BUSINESS DRIVEN DISCUSSION

Virtual Reality (VR) and Augmented Reality (AU) Disrupting the Classroom

- **ImmerseMe:** Students choose between 9 different languages and from over 3,000 different scenarios. For example, students learn to order a baguette in Paris, buy a bento box in Tokyo, or try tapas at a Spanish restaurant.
- **Ocean Rift:** Students explore the vivid underwater world by swimming with various fish, dolphins, sharks, turtles, sea snakes, rays, manatees, sea lions, orcas, humpback whales, and even dinosaurs! A great app for a biology or natural sciences class.
- **Number Hunt:** Students embark on an adventure to find numbers and shoot them so they learn to add, multiply, divide, and subtract.
- **Google Earth:** With Google Earth VR, you can make a school trip out of every lesson! Stroll the streets of Tokyo, soar over Yosemite or the Grand Canyon, and visit famous monuments like the Colosseum in Rome.[9]

With the lockdowns associated with COVID-19, VR offered a great way to go on a field trip when it was impossible to do so in real life. Many free and educational VR apps are currently hitting the educational market. In a group, develop a VR app that you wish you had when you were in high school.

PROTECTING WIRELESS NETWORKS

LO 7.3: Identify the security challenges of wireless networks.

Network intrusions can occur if access codes or passwords are stored on a device that is lost or stolen. Two methods for encrypting network traffic on the web are secure sockets layer and secure hypertext transfer protocol.

1. ***Secure sockets layer (SSL)*** is a standard security technology for establishing an encrypted link between a web server and a browser, ensuring that all data passed between them remain private. Millions of websites use SSL to protect their online transactions with their customers. To create an SSL connection, a web server requires an ***SSL certificate,*** an electronic document that confirms the identity of a website or server and verifies that a public key belongs to a trustworthy individual or company. Typically, an SSL certificate will contain a domain name, the company name and address, and the expiration date of the certificate and other details. Verisign is the leading Internet certification authority that issues SSL certificates. When a browser connects to a secure site, it retrieves the site's SSL certificate, makes sure it has not expired, and confirms that a certification authority has issued it. If the certificate fails on any one of these validation measures, the browser will display a warning to the end user that the site is not secure. If a website is using SSL, a lock icon appears in the lower right-hand corner of the user's web browser.
2. ***Secure hypertext transfer protocol (SHTTP or HTTPS)*** is a combination of HTTP and SSL to provide encryption and secure identification of an Internet server. HTTPS protects against interception of communications, transferring credit card information safely and securely with special encryption techniques. When a user enters a web address using https://, the browser will encrypt the message. However, the server receiving the message must be configured to receive HTTPS messages. In summary, each company needs to create a network security policy that specifies aspects of data integrity availability and confidentiality or privacy, as well as accountability and authorization. With a variety of security methods, such as SSL and SHTTP, a company can protect its most important asset, its data.

Anytime a wireless network connects to a wired one, the wireless network can serve as a conduit for a hacker to gain entry into an otherwise secure wired network. This risk is especially high if the wireless network is not sufficiently secured in its own right. It is important to

APPLY YOUR KNOWLEDGE

BUSINESS DRIVEN ETHICS AND SECURITY

War Driving: Engineering or Privacy?

Wired connections can be intercepted physically only via wiretapping. Wireless connections have no such security. A wireless connection is by nature radiated in all directions, and unsecured connections are especially vulnerable to attack by hackers and cybercriminals.

Google engineers decided to use their Street View cars for war driving, which is the practice of driving streets and using equipment to locate LANs using Wi-Fi, such as wireless hotspots at coffee shops and home wireless networks. Google collected information about Wi-Fi networks (such as the MAC address, SSID, and strength of signal received from the wireless access point) and associated it with global positioning system (GPS) information. Google also added code to record all unencrypted packets–or what's known as payload data–within range of Google's Street View cars. But capturing payload data raises numerous privacy questions. The data captured by Google's Street View software could be highly sensitive.[10]

Google's recent controversy over war-driving Street View vehicles brings up core ethical issues regarding the wireless Internet. Google's defense claims that there is nothing wrong with collecting data from unsecured wireless networks because those networks by nature broadcast their activity for the world to see. Do you believe that is what you are agreeing to when you join an unsecured wireless network at a coffee shop or in a hotel? When you join an unsecured network, do you agree that your activity is public? Is this agreement implicit? If it were explicit, would you agree to it?

be aware that companies are opening back doors in their systems to a new type of network intrusion. It is vital for companies to use security network auditing on the wireless section of their networks. No matter how many firewalls are installed in the network, inappropriate wireless configurations can give hackers access to a corporate network without having to pass through a single firewall.

- ***War driving***: Deliberately searching for Wi-Fi signals while driving by in a vehicle.
- ***War chalking***: The practice of tagging pavement with codes displaying where Wi-Fi access is available.

War driving is a form of hacking into open Wi-Fi networks. Hackers equipped with an antenna connected to a laptop find signals and display the latitude and longitude of the signal strength and network name. Many individuals who participate in war driving simply map where Wi-Fi networks are available. Other individuals have a more malicious intent and use war driving to hack or break into these networks. War driving has been a controversial practice since its inception and has raised awareness about the importance of wireless network security.

The term *war chalking* was inspired by the use of chalk marks in old wartime days. During the 1930s and 1940s, homeless, wandering men used chalk marks to advise their colleagues of places that offered free food or places to wash up. Today, war chalking is actually creating a language for indicating free Internet access. It can be best described as marking a series of well-defined symbols on sidewalks, walls, pillars, and other structures to indicate nearby wireless access. Each symbol defines a specific wireless setting telling other users the kind of access available, the speed of the network, and if the network is secured. This practice enables users to go to those marked locations and use the symbols to figure out what the settings are to connect through a wireless connection to the Internet.

The primary problem with Wi-Fi networks is accessing a network that might not require authentication or not require a password. It is impossible to ascertain the security of the network or even verify and validate that it is truly the network and not an "Evil Twin." If you have ever stayed at a hotel, you know that everyone is given the password.

- *Actor*: An entity that is capable of participating in an action or a network.
- *Bad actor*: An entity that is participating with ill intentions.

Users have no way to determine whether a bad actor is on the network intercepting, reading, or modifying data. Also, the company whose network you are using has a right to monitor your connections, and depending on what acceptance you agreed to when requesting network access, they might be able to access your device and collect your data. This data could be the apps you have installed, location data, PII, etc. The same also applies for applications you install (Walmart Savings Catcher, Macy's App, Whole Foods App, etc.). These stores also have no legal obligation or responsibility to protect your device or data on their network. Ethical obligations and responsibilities are a different story and, as discussed, the lines between ethical behavior and legal behavior are frequently blurred.[11]

Public Wi-Fi networks are not much safer, if at all. While they may not have the same intentions as retail stores, there is no level of assurance or legal obligation for them to secure your device or data. Again, users have no way to determine whether bad actors can intercept and read and/or modify user data. You should question why this network exists, especially if the connection is free. You are probably the "product" via data mining or via advertising.

Before the emergence of the Internet, hackers generally had to be physically present within the office building to gain access to a wired network. The thousands, if not millions, of access points enabled by wireless networks now allow hackers to work from a distance. Several techniques can secure wireless networks from unauthorized access whether used separately or in combination. One method is authenticating Wi-Fi access points. Because Wi-Fi communications are broadcast, anyone within listening distance can intercept communications. Every time someone uses an unsecured website via a public Wi-Fi access point, his or her logon name and password are sent over the open airwaves with a high risk that someone might eavesdrop or capture login names, passwords, and credit card numbers. Two technologies securing Wi-Fi networks include:

- ***Wired equivalent privacy (WEP)***: An encryption algorithm designed to protect wireless transmission data. If you are using a Wi-Fi connection, WEP encrypts the data by using a key that converts the data to a nonhuman readable form. The purpose of WEP was to provide wireless networks with the equivalent level of security as wired networks. Unfortunately, the technology behind WEP has been demonstrated to be relatively insecure compared to newer protocols.
- ***Wi-Fi protected access (WPA)***: A wireless security protocol to protect Wi-Fi networks. It is an improvement on the original Wi-Fi security standard, WEP, and provides more sophisticated data encryption and user authentication. Anyone who wants to use an access point must know the WPA encryption key to access the Wi-Fi connection.

section 7.2 Mobility: The Business Value of a Wireless World

LEARNING OUTCOMES

7.4 Explain mobile enterprise management and its importance to a business.

7.5 Explain the three primary business applications of wireless technology.

MOBILE ENTERPRISE MANAGEMENT

LO 7.4: Explain mobile enterprise management and its importance to a business.

IT consumerization is the blending of personal and business use of technology devices and applications. Today's workforce grew up with the Internet, and its members do not differentiate between corporate and personal technology. Employees want to use the same technology they have at home in the office. This blending of personal and business technology is having a significant impact on corporate MIS departments, which traditionally choose all of the technology for the organization. Today, MIS departments must determine how to protect their networks and manage technology that they did not authorize or recommend. As pervasive computing, IT consumerization, and wireless networks are exploding over the globe, business managers are required to focus on how data moves not only throughout an organization but also around the globe.

Pervasive computing is the growing trend of embedding computer capabilities into everyday objects to make them effectively communicate and perform useful tasks in a way that minimizes the end user's need to interact with computers as computers. Examples of pervasive computing devices include Apple watch, Amazon Echo speaker, Fitbit, smart traffic lights, and self-driving cars. Pervasive computing devices are small, Internet-enabled devices and are always on or constantly available. The goal of pervasive computing is to make devices "smart," by collecting, processing, and sending data in real time, creating a network that can understand its surroundings and improve the human experience and quality of life. Your Apple watch can tell you how many calories you are burning, your current heart rate, and even your sleep patterns. It is always on and constantly collecting data to help you improve your life by monitoring your body.

The invention of pervasive computing drove the mobility era as employees began working whenever, wherever, and with whichever device they chose. However, this also created a serious problem as a high number of the corporate security breaches are the result of the loss or security breach of mobile devices. As a result, MIS managers need to find ways to securely manage these devices more than ever before, a difficult task given employees work remotely and use their own devices. A bring-your-own-device (BYOD) corporate culture is riddled with security risks and has blurred the lines between personal and professional communication devices. MIS managers must find ways to facilitate the use of personal devices while also keeping work and personal data both separate and secure. To mitigate these risks, businesses need to create enterprise mobility management strategies.

- ***Enterprise mobility management (EMM)*:** An enterprisewide security strategy to enforce corporate epolicies while enabling employee use of mobile devices such as smart phones and tablets.

EMM prevents unauthorized access to corporate applications and data on mobile devices. The goal of EMM is to customize a strategy for devices, applications, and information management among remote employees inside and outside the workplace. Figure 7.12 displays the common areas of an EMM.

Mobile Device Management

Mobile device management helps to enforce epolicies for maintaining the desired level of MIS control across platforms and geographic locations.

- ***Mobile device management (MDM)*:** A security strategy comprised of products and services that offer remote support for mobile devices, such as smart phones, laptops, and tablets.

FIGURE 7.12

Three Primary Areas of an Enterprise Mobility Management Strategy

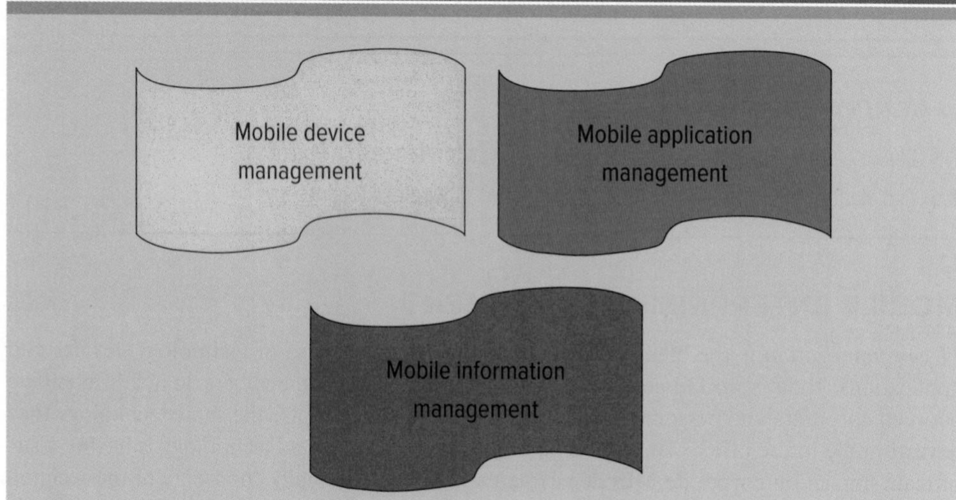

APPLY YOUR KNOWLEDGE

BUSINESS DRIVEN START-UP

Mobility as a Service Start-up

Would you sacrifice your privacy to save money? That is exactly what insurance companies are doing when they offer cheaper insurance rates in exchange for a tracking device. The tracking device plugs into the car's computer. It can see all the data the computer collects and grab whatever the insurance company has programmed it to find. It then wirelessly transmits that information to the insurance company, or a third-party company that it employs to analyze the data.

What data, you may ask? Well, whatever information your insurance company deems relevant to determining whether or not you're a good driver. This data is sent back to your insurance provider and, if it likes what it sees, it'll reduce your premiums or give you credits on your auto insurance. Most customers understand why an insurance company would want to see speed data (the faster you go, the more dangerous it is) and distance data (the more you drive, the more risk you incur).

Would you be willing to allow an insurance company to track your driving habits? What are the potential risks with sharing your driving data with an auto insurance company? Is it worth the privacy risk for saving a little money?

Just imagine your sales force is deployed all over the country or the world and you are attempting to ensure every network they use is safe and every device is protected. Most MIS departments implement MDM by requiring passcodes on corporate devices to ensure data encryption and, in the event of a lost device, that all data on the device can be deleted remotely. MDM tools can also enforce policies, track inventory, and perform real-time monitoring and reporting. An MIS department may use MDM to enforce basic security measures, such as the use of a device passcode.

The widespread proliferation of IT consumerization also means more personal consumer computing devices in the workplace using the corporate networks. How can an MIS department ensure the security of its wireless networks if employees are connecting personal devices that might not have the appropriate antivirus software? MDM policies must incorporate BYOD (bring your own device) strategies so it can deliver secure mobile solutions to its BYOD workforce. This can be a huge problem for some companies as their MDM policy could be too rigid for BYOD employees. Employees might wonder why photos of their children and dogs are erased if they lose their cell phone and the MDM policy states remote deletion of everything in the case of losing a device. They might also wonder why they need to have a corporate passcode on personal devices if they infrequently check corporate email on their personal smart phone.

An important feature of MDM is that it provides corporate network administrators with the ability to wipe corporate mobile applications from an end user's device remotely. Just imagine being on vacation in Spain and your cell phone and laptop are stolen. If you have corporate applications such as email on your smart phone, your company can access the device from the United States and delete your email application, ensuring the thief can't access corporate applications. Review Figure 7.13 for the three types of policies a company can implement to help with MDM.

Mobile Application Management

Mobile application management software assists with software delivery, licensing, and maintenance and can limit how sensitive applications can be shared among applications and help prevent corporate data leakage.

- ***Mobile application management (MAM)*:** A security strategy that administers and enforces corporate epolicies for applications on mobile devices.
- ***Mobile application development*:** The set of processes and procedures involved in writing software for use on wireless devices.

Mobile applications are often written specifically to take advantage of the unique features a particular mobile device offers. Figure 7.14 highlights the common characteristics of MAM.

FIGURE 7.13

MDM Device Policies

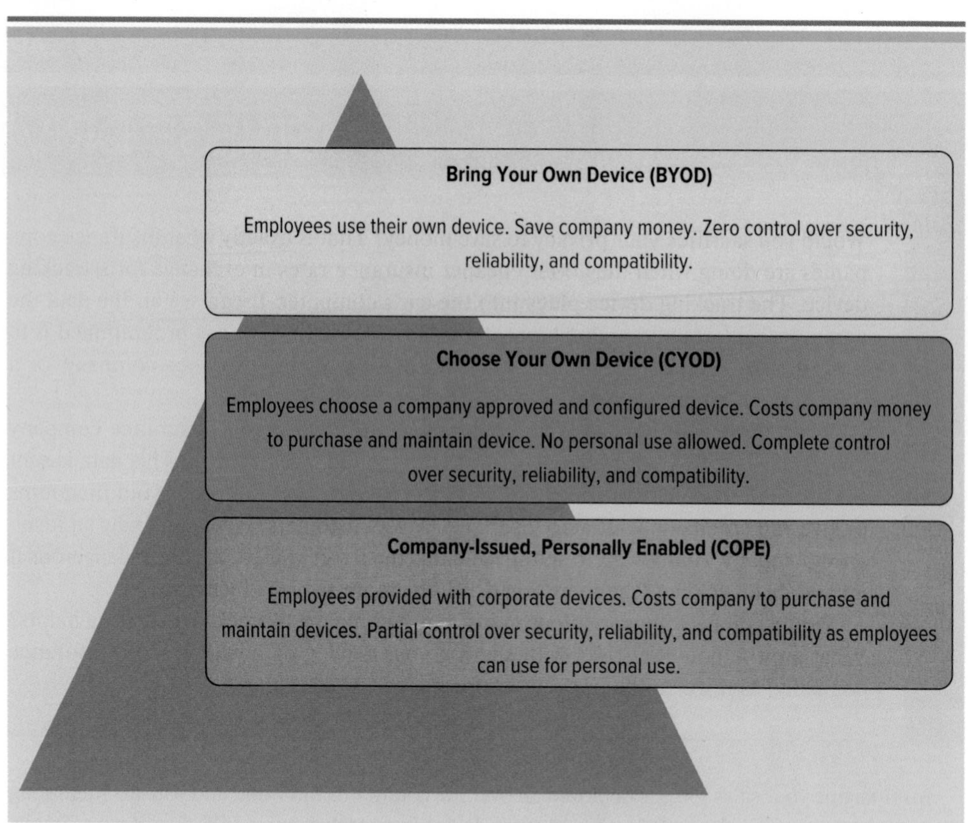

FIGURE 7.14

Mobile Application Management Characteristics

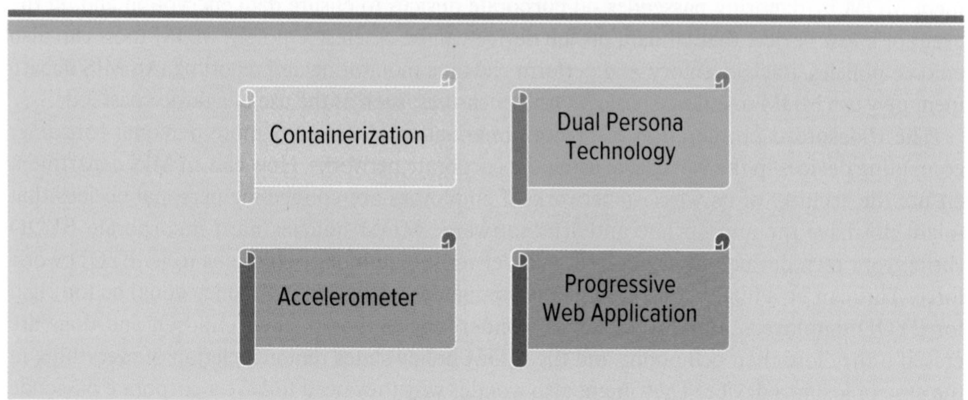

Features of MAM include:

- ***Containerization*** (application sandboxing): Isolates corporate applications from personal applications on a device. Data within this isolated area, known as a container, cannot leave, and apps within the container cannot interact with those on the outside.
- ***Dual persona technology*:** Creates two completely separate user interfaces on the same device, one for work and one for personal use. The two personas on the device are isolated and do not recognize each other. If a worker suddenly quits or loses a personal cell phone, the MIS department can delete the corporate applications and data from the user's cell phone without affecting the personal applications or data. Corporate policies can be implemented for the work persona, improving data security.
- ***Progressive web application (PWA)*:** A website that looks and behaves as if it is a mobile application but is just a normal website. PWAs are built to take advantage of all cellular devices without requiring the end user to visit an app store, make a purchase, and download software. Instead, a PWA can be accessed immediately through a browser, eliminating the need to develop the app for every possible device. Just like YouTube videos, PWA content is downloaded progressively, which provides the end user with a better user experience than a traditional website that uses responsive design.

- *Accelerometer*: A device that can measure the force of acceleration, whether caused by gravity or by movement. Accelerometers allow the user to understand the surroundings of an item and determine if an object is moving uphill or downhill, falling, flying, or lying still. For example, smart phones rotate their display between portrait and landscape mode depending on how the phone is tilted. A gaming app might be written to take advantage of the iPhone's accelerometer, or a mobile health app might be written to take advantage of a smart watch's temperature sensor.

In the early years of mobile apps, the only way to ensure an app had optimum performance on any given device was to develop the app specifically for a particular device. This meant that, at a very low level, new code had to be written specifically for each particular device's processor. Today, a majority of mobile application development efforts focus on building apps that can operate on any device, including Apple iPhones, Google Androids, and the Samsung Galaxy.

Mobile Information Management

The term *fast data* is often associated with business intelligence, and the goal is to quickly gather and mine structured and unstructured data so action can be taken.

- ***Fast data***: The application of big data analytics to smaller data sets in near real or real time in order to solve a problem or create business value.

As the flood of data from sensors, actuators, and machine-to-machine (M2M) communication in the Internet of Things (IoT) continues to grow, it has become more important than ever for organizations to identify what data is time-sensitive and should be acted upon right away and what data can sit in a data warehouse or data lake until there is a reason to mine it.

- ***Mobile information management (MIM)***: A security strategy that involves keeping sensitive data encrypted and allowing only approved applications to access or transmit it.

MIM limits the sharing of corporate data among applications and ensures a secure information management strategy for mobile workforces. Any MIM strategy has to start with encryption and password protection. Forgetting about the mobile devices or the applications, MIM concentrates on locking the information itself; that is what MIM actually does.

MIM strategies anticipate workforce mobility in company's data assets and allows the epolicies the capability of governing data not only within the company's own systems, but also when that data is mobile and moving outside the firewalls. MIM epolices allow the corporation to fully govern the data. This includes getting access to how digital assets are created, saved, accessed, modified, sent, received, stored, preserved, and scheduled for disposition. Imagine an app that knows the sharing of confidential internal planning documents with anybody outside of the company is against our epolicy so MIM turns off the sharing feature in any app using the data. At the same time, if you write down your workout routine, it will turn on sharing for any app using this customized workout planning document.

Data states are used by information security professionals to identify endpoints where data should be encrypted. In addition to encryption, some important ways that data in use is protected include user authentication at all stages, strong identity management, and well-maintained permissions for profiles within an organization (see Figure 7.15).

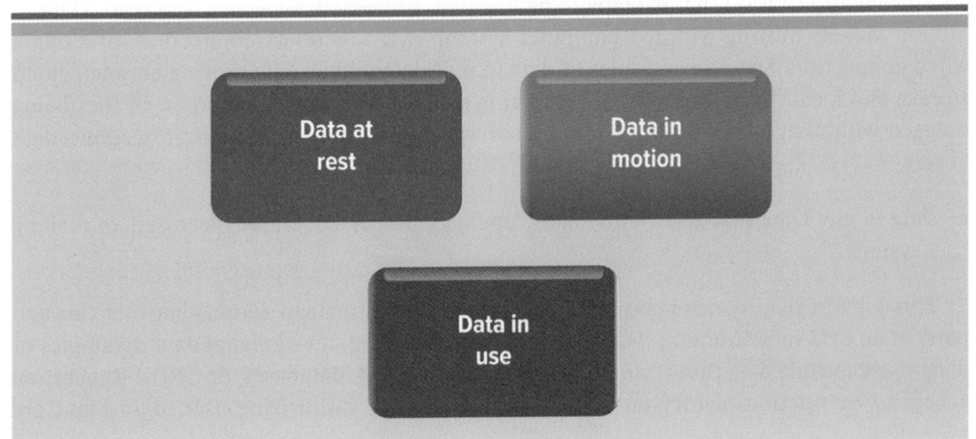

FIGURE 7.15

Mobile Information Management Characteristics

APPLY YOUR KNOWLEDGE

BUSINESS DRIVEN DISCUSSION

Should Airlines Allow Cell Phone Calls during Flights?

The Federal Communications Commission has proposed allowing passengers to use their mobile wireless devices, including cell phones, while flying above 10,000 feet. Cell phones on airplanes would not be using the traditional cellular networks because they are not designed to operate at 35,000 feet. Rather, calls would be batched and bounced down to the ground through a satellite or specialized air-to-ground cellular system, forcing airlines to charge much more per minute than standard carrier rates.

Supporters say that cell phone use does not interfere with aviation safety and that on foreign airlines where it is permitted, passengers' calls tend to be short and unobtrusive.[12]

Critics argue that allowing voice calls in flight would compromise flight attendants' ability to maintain order in an emergency, increase cabin noise and tension among passengers, and add unacceptable risk to aviation security. They also point out that a majority of the traveling public want the cell phone ban maintained. Do you agree or disagree with the use of cell phones on airlines?

Data at rest does not include data that is navigating a network or temporarily residing in computer memory to be read or updated.

- ***Data at rest***: Refers to all data in computer storage.

Data at rest can be archival or reference files that are changed rarely or never; data at rest can also be data that is subject to regular but not constant change. Examples include vital corporate files stored on the hard drive of an employee's notebook computer, files on an external backup medium, files on the servers of a storage area network, or files on the servers of an off-site backup service provider. Businesses, government agencies, and other institutions are concerned about the ever-present threat posed by hackers to data at rest. In order to keep data at rest from being accessed, stolen, or altered by unauthorized people, security measures such as data encryption and hierarchical password protection are commonly used. For some types of data, specific security measures are mandated by law.

- ***Data in motion*** (also known as transit or flight): A stream of data that is moving or being transported between locations within or between computer systems.

Data in motion can also be used to describe data that is within a computer's random access memory (RAM) that is ready to be updated, processed, accessed, and read. Data in motion may be moving within a computer system, over a wireless connection, or along a wired connection. Specific examples of data in motion could be data moving between cloud storage and local file storage, data transferring from one network to another, or files being dragged within an FTP site. Once the data arrives at its final destination, it becomes data at rest.

- ***Data in use***: Data that is currently being updated, processed, erased, accessed, or read by a system.

This type of data is not being passively stored, but is instead actively moving through parts of an MIS infrastructure. Data in use is one of three states of digital data. Examples of data in use include data that is stored or processed in RAM, databases, or CPUs. Requesting access to transaction history on a banking website and authorizing user login input are applications of data in use. Due to data in use being directly accessible by one or more users, data in this state is vulnerable to attacks and exploits. Additionally, security risks become greater as permissions and devices increase. Oftentimes, data in use could contain digital certificates, encryption keys, and intellectual property that make it crucial for businesses to monitor.

BUSINESS APPLICATIONS OF WIRELESS TECHNOLOGIES

LO 7.5: Explain the three primary business applications of wireless technology.

Only a small fraction of the world's population has access to the Internet, and some people who have had access in the past have lost it due to changes in their circumstances such as unemployment or poverty. Providing network access to those who want or need it helps to level the playing field and removes the digital divide.

- ***Digital divide***: A worldwide gap giving advantage to those with access to technology.

Organizations trying to bridge the divide include the Boston Digital Bridge Foundation, which concentrates on local schoolchildren and their parents, helping to make them knowledgeable about computers, programs, and the Internet. Other organizations provide inexpensive laptops and Internet access in low-income areas in developing countries.

Wireless technologies have also aided the creation of new applications. Some build upon and improve existing capabilities. UPS, for example, is combining several types of wireless network technologies from Bluetooth to WWANs and deploying scanners and wearable data-collection terminals to automate and standardize package management and tracking across all its delivery centers. Figure 7.16 displays the three business applications taking advantage of wireless technologies.

Radio-Frequency Identification (RFID)

Radio-frequency identification (RFID) uses electronic tags and labels to identify objects wirelessly over short distances. It holds the promise of replacing existing identification technologies such as the bar code. RFID wirelessly exchanges information between a tagged object and a reader/writer.

- ***RFID tag***: An electronic identification device that is made up of a chip and an antenna.
- ***RFID reader (RFID interrogator)***: A transmitter/receiver that reads the contents of RFID tags in the area.

An RFID system is composed of one or more RFID tags, one or more RFID readers, two or more antennas (one on the tag and one on each reader), RFID application software, and

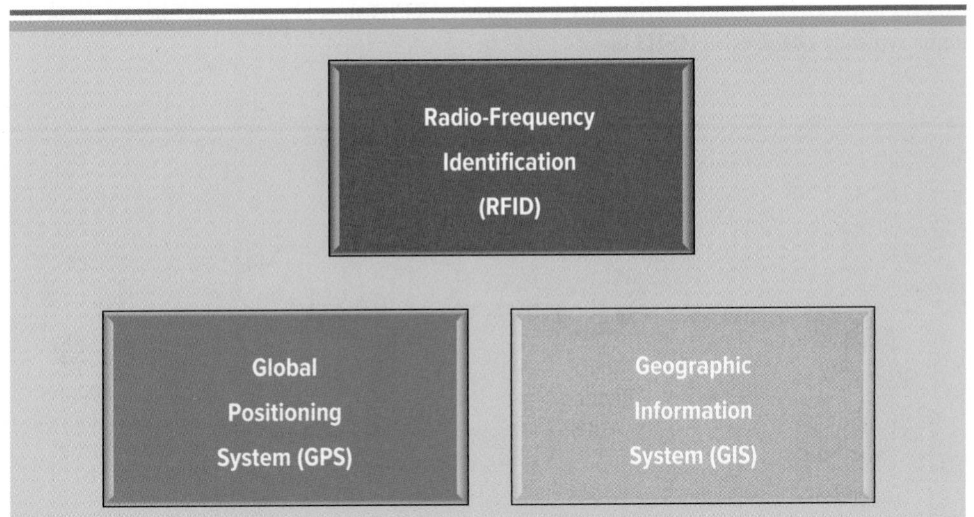

FIGURE 7.16
Wireless Business Applications

APPLY YOUR KNOWLEDGE

BUSINESS DRIVEN ANALYTICS

The Magic Mobility of Disney

The Walt Disney Company offers a MagicBand to all customers vising its parks. The MagicBand is a wristband with an RFID chip that transmits over 40 feet to track real-time information on customer locations throughout its park. The magic of this data is how Disney analyzes the data to help provide its customers with the ultimate service and convenience while in the park. Armed with customer and location data, park employees can personally greet customers at restaurants and rides, offer products and shows customers will favor, inform customers of wait times for rides, and even connect to their credit cards so there is no need to carry cash.

What security concerns would you have when using the MagicBand? What ethical concerns would you have knowing your personal and location data is being tracked and monitored in real time? What other businesses could benefit from using a device similar to Disney's MagicBand?

a computer system or server, as Figure 7.17 illustrates. Tags, often smaller than a grain of rice, can be applied to books or clothing items as part of an adhesive bar code label or included in items such as ID cards or packing labels. Readers can be stand-alone devices, such as for self-checkout in a grocery store; integrated with a mobile device for portable use; or built in as in printers. The reader sends a wireless request that is received by all tags in the area that have been programmed to listen to wireless signals. Tags receive the signal via their antennas and respond by transmitting their stored data. The tag can hold many types of data, including a product number, installation instructions, and history of activity (such as the date the item was shipped). The reader receives a signal from the tag using its antenna, interprets the information sent, and transfers the data to the associated computer system or server.

- ***Asset tracking*:** Occurs when a company places active or semi-passive RFID tags on expensive products or assets to gather data on the items' location with little or no manual intervention.

Asset tracking allows a company to focus on its supply chain, reduce theft, identify the last known user of assets, and automate maintenance routines. Active and semi-passive tags are useful for tracking high-value goods that need to be scanned over long ranges, such as railway cars on a track. The cost of active and semi-passive RFID tags is significant; hence, low-cost items typically use passive RFID tags.

FIGURE 7.17

Elements of an RFID system

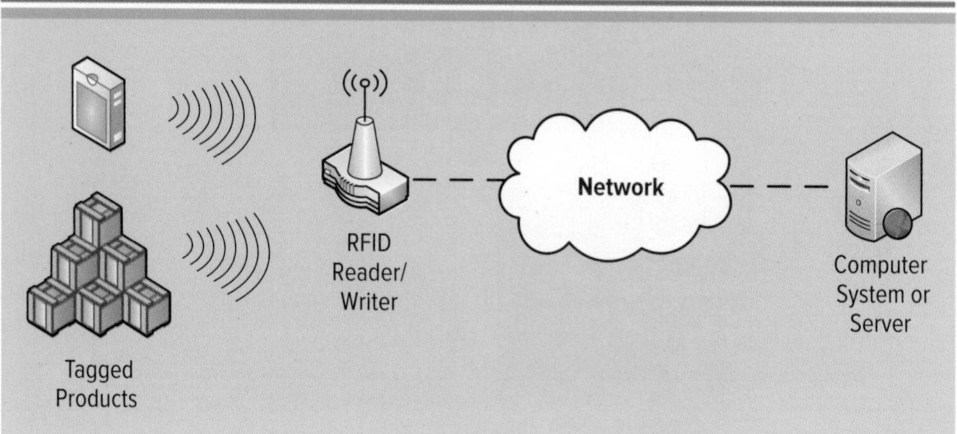

Global Positioning System (GPS)

A ***global positioning system (GPS)*** is a satellite-based navigation system providing extremely accurate position, time, and speed information. The U.S. Department of Defense developed the technology in the early 1970s and later made it available to the public. GPS uses 24 global satellites that orbit Earth, sending signals to a receiver that can communicate with three or four satellites at a time. A GPS receiver can be a separate unit connected to a mobile device using cable or wireless technology such as Bluetooth, or it can be included in devices such as mobile phones or vehicle navigation systems.

Automatic vehicle location (AVL) uses GPS tracking to track vehicles. AVL systems use a GPS receiver in the vehicle that links to a control center. Garmin is one of the more popular manufacturers of GPS tracking systems, offering vehicle tracking, phone and laptop integration, and hiker navigation for water and air.

The satellites broadcast signals constantly; the receiver measures the time it takes for the signals to reach it. This measurement, which uses the speed of the signal to determine the distance, is taken from three distinct satellites to provide precise location information. The time measurements depend on high-powered clocks on each satellite and must be precise because an error of one-thousandth of a second can result in a location variation of more than 200 miles. GPS can produce very accurate results, typically within 5 to 50 feet of the actual location (military versions have higher accuracy). GPS also provides latitude, longitude, and elevation information.

- ***Geocache***: A GPS technology adventure game that posts the longitude and latitude location for an item on the Internet for users to find. GPS users find the geocache and typically sign a guest book or take an item and leave an item for the next adventure players to find. Caches are often placed in locations that are interesting or challenging for people to discover.
- ***Geocoin***: A round coin-sized object that is uniquely numbered and hidden in geocache. Geocoins can also be shaped to match a theme such as the state of Colorado or a birthday party hat. Geocoins are often decorative or commemorative, making them collectible and highly valuable for technology adventures.

GPS applications are in every kind of company vehicle these days—from police cars to bulldozers, from dump trucks to mayoral limousines. Emergency response systems use GPS to track each of their vehicles and so dispatch those closest to the scene of an accident. If a vehicle is missing, its GPS locator can help locate it.

- ***Estimated time of arrival (ETA)***: The time of day of an expected arrival at a certain destination. It is typically used for navigation applications.
- ***Estimated time en route (ETE)***: The time remaining before reaching a destination using the present speed. It is typically used for navigation applications.

Geographic Information System (GIS)

GPS provides the foundation for geographic information systems.

- ***Geographic information system (GIS)***: Stores, views, and analyzes geographic data, creating multidimensional charts or maps. For example, GISs are monitoring global warming by measuring the speed of glaciers melting in Canada, Greenland, and Antarctica.
- ***Cartography***: The science and art of making an illustrated map or chart. GIS allows users to interpret, analyze, and visualize data in different ways that reveal patterns and trends in the form of reports, charts, and maps.
- ***GIS map automation***: Links business assets to a centralized system where they can be tracked and monitored over time.
- ***Spatial data (geospatial data or geographic information)***: Identifies the geographic location of features and boundaries on Earth, such as natural or constructed features, oceans, and more. Spatial data can be mapped and is stored as coordinates and topology. A GIS accesses, manipulates, and analyzes spatial data.
- ***Geocoding***: A coding process that assigns a digital map feature to an attribute that serves as a unique ID (tract number, node number) or classification (soil type, zoning category). GIS professionals are certified in geocoding practices to ensure that industry standards are met when classifying spatial data.

FIGURE 7.18

GIS Uses

Graphical Information System Uses	
Finding what is nearby	Given a specific location, the GIS finds sources within a defined radius. These might be entertainment venues, medical facilities, restaurants, or gas stations. Users can also use GIS to locate vendors that sell a specific item they want and get the results as a map of the surrounding area or an address.
Routing information	Once users have an idea where they want to go, GIS can provide directions to get there using either a map or step-by-step instructions. Routing information can be especially helpful when combined with search services.
Sending information alerts	Users may want to be notified when information relevant to them becomes available near their location. A commuter might want to know that a section of the highway has traffic congestion, or a shopper might want to be notified when a favorite store is having a sale on a certain item.
Mapping densities	GIS can map population and event densities based on a standard area unit, such as square miles, making it easy to see distributions and concentrations. Police can map crime incidents to determine where additional patrolling is required, and stores can map customer orders to identify ideal delivery routes.
Mapping quantities	Users can map quantities to find out where the most or least of a feature may be. For example, someone interested in opening a specialty coffee shop can determine how many others are already in the area, and city planners can determine where to build more parks

Companies that deal in transportation combine GISs with database and GPS technology. Airlines and shipping companies can plot routes with up-to-the-second information about the location of all their transport vehicles. Hospitals can locate their medical staff with GIS and sensors that pick up transmissions from ID badges. Automobiles have GPSs linked to GIS maps that display the car's location and driving directions on a dashboard screen. GM offers the OnStar system, which sends a continuous stream of information to the OnStar center about the car's exact location.

Some mobile phone providers combine GPS and GIS capabilities so they can locate users within a geographic area about the size of a tennis court to assist emergency services such as 911. Farmers can use GIS to map and analyze fields, telling them where to apply the proper amounts of seed, fertilizer, and herbicides.

A GIS can find the closest gas station or bank or determine the best way to get to a particular location. But it is also good at finding patterns, such as finding the most feasible location to hold a conference according to where the majority of a company's customers live and work. GIS can present this information in a visually effective way (see Figure 7.18).

A GIS can provide information and insight to both mobile users and people at fixed locations. Google Earth combines satellite imagery, geographic data, and Google's search capabilities to create a virtual globe that users can download to a computer or mobile device. Not only does this provide useful business benefits, but it also allows for many educational opportunities. Instead of just talking about the Grand Canyon, an instructor can use Google Earth to view that region.

GPS and GIS both use ***location-based services (LBSs)***, applications that use location information to provide a service. LBS is designed to give mobile users instant access to personalized local content and range from 911 applications to buddy finders ("Let me know when my friend is within 1,000 feet") to games (treasure hunts) to location-based advertising ("Visit the Starbucks on the corner and get $1.00 off a latte"). Many LBS applications complement GPS and GIS, such as:

- Emergency services
- Field service management
- Find-it services
- Mapping
- Navigation
- Tracking assets

BUSINESS DRIVEN INNOVATION

Snapping a Theftie

Has your smart phone ever been stolen? If so, you are not alone. Of course, every good entrepreneur can spot an opportunity, and a new antitheft app is one step ahead of criminals who are targeting smart phones.

Lookout is among the latest additions to the growing antitheft industry, and the app features some smart ways of helping you get one step ahead of thieves. A smart phone's front-facing camera is often regarded as merely a portal to endless selfie photographs. But Lookout puts the camera to good use by capturing a photo of you—or of any would-be thief—when someone inputs your phone's password incorrectly three times. That photo, or theftie, is instantly emailed to the phone's owner, along with the device's approximate location. The antitheft app is free to download, but this handy photo feature is not available on iPhones due to Apple restrictions and comes with an annual charge of $30.

Lookout's team has been adding new features to the app's alerts, based on the methods thieves use to steal phones undetected. The app also will send emails to its owner if anyone attempts to remove the phone's SIM card, enables airplane mode, or turns off the device. From that point, the owner can choose to lock or wipe the phone remotely.[13]

Do you agree that antitheft apps are smart business? Are any ethical issues involved in taking thefties? How would you feel if company security policy required you to install Lookout on your cell phone? If you could add a new feature to Lookout, how would it work and what would it do to deter smart phone theft?

- Traffic information
- Vehicle location
- Weather information
- Wireless advertising

Just as Facebook and Twitter helped fuel the Web 2.0 revolution, new mobile applications are bringing attention to LBS. Each application is a mobile phone service that helps social media users find their friends' location. Facebook and Twitter have added location-based services to complement their applications.

LEARNING OUTCOME REVIEW

Learning Outcome 7.1: Understand wireless networks along with their benefits.

Before networks, transferring data between computers was time-consuming and labor-intensive. People had to copy data physically from machine to machine using a disk. Networks offer many advantages for a business, including:

- Sharing resources
- Providing opportunities
- Reducing travel

Networks have created a diverse yet globally connected world. By eliminating time and distance, networks make it possible to communicate in ways not previously imaginable. Even though networks provide many business advantages, they also create increased challenges in (1) security and (2) social, ethical, and political issues.

Learning Outcome 7.2: Describe the different wireless network categories.

There are four types of wireless networks: PAN, WLAN, WMAN, and WWAN. A PAN provides communication over a short distance and is intended for use with devices owned and operated by a single user. A WLAN is a local area network that uses radio signals to transmit and receive data over distances of a few hundred feet. A WMAN is a metropolitan area network that uses radio signals to transmit and receive data, and a WWAN is a wide area network that uses radio signals to transmit and receive data.

Learning Outcome 7.3: Identify the security challenges of wireless networks.

Data theft and network intrusions can occur if access codes, passwords, or devices are not managed properly on and off corporate networks. Lost or stolen devices are big risks for a corporation's sensitive data.

Learning Outcome 7.4: Explain mobile enterprise management and its importance to a business.

Enterprise mobility management (EMM) is an enterprisewide security strategy to enforce corporate epolicies while enabling employee use of mobile devices such as smart phones and tablets. EMM prevents unauthorized access to corporate applications and data on mobile devices. The goal of EMM is to customize a strategy for devices, applications, and information management among remote employees inside and outside the workplace.

Learning Outcome 7.5: Explain the three primary business applications of wireless technology.

Mobile and wireless business applications and services are using satellite technologies. These technologies are GPS, GIS, and LBS. GPS is a satellite-based navigation system providing extremely accurate position, time, and speed information. GIS is location information that can be shown on a map. LBSs are applications that use location information to provide a service that both GPS and GIS use.

KEY TERMS

Accelerometer 287
Access point (AP) 273
Actor 283
Asset tracking 290
Automatic vehicle location (AVL) 291
Bad actor 283
Bandwidth 271
Bit 271
Bit rate (or data rate) 271
Bluetooth 273
Cartography 291
Containerization 286
Data at rest 288
Data in motion 288
Data in use 288
Digital divide 289
Dual persona technology 286
Enterprise mobility management (EMM) 284
Estimated time en route (ETE) 291
Estimated time of arrival (ETA) 291
Fast data 287
5G 276
Geocache 291
Geocoding 291
Geocoin 291
Geographic information system (GIS) 291
GIS map automation 291
Global positioning system (GPS) 291
Hotspot 273
IT consumerization 283
Local area network (LAN) 269
Location-based service (LBS) 292
Metropolitan area network (MAN) 269
Mobile 269
Mobile application development 285
Mobile application management (MAM) 285
Mobile business (or mbusiness, mcommerce) 269
Mobile device management (MDM) 284
Mobile information management (MIM) 287
Multiple-in/multiple-out (MIMO) technology 273
Personal area network (PAN) 272
Pervasive computing 284
Progressive web application (PWA) 286
Radio access network (RAN) 275
Radio-frequency identification (RFID) 289
RFID reader (RFID interrogator) 289
RFID tag 289
Satellite 280

REVIEW QUESTIONS

1. What is the difference between mobility and wireless?
2. What are the advantages of mobile business?
3. Why would a manager be concerned with bandwidth? How is bandwidth measured?
4. How does Wi-Fi work?
5. How has streaming data changed business?
6. What is the difference between war driving and war chalking?
7. What is the difference between WEP and WPA?
8. What are the three primary areas of enterprise mobility management?
9. What are the three MDM policies?
10. How does containerization support mobile application management?
11. How does an accelerometer support mobile application development?
12. What are the three different states of data?
13. What is RFID and how does it help track a product?
14. What are the three primary business applications of wireless technology?
15. How are businesses using wireless technology to build competitive advantages?

CLOSING CASE ONE

Liberating Drivers and Riders: Uber

In 2009, Uber, a technology start-up based in San Francisco, introduced a new way for passengers to book a ride: by hailing a nearby car using their smart phone, and then using their smart phone to track the vehicle until it arrives at their location. Once the ride is over, Uber pays the driver using the credit card that the customer has loaded into their Uber app. It is a simple and effective process.

Uber empowers its drivers to pick up nearby passengers and liberates riders to hail a cab whenever they want from wherever they want. Uber's customers praise the reliability, speed of the service, and ease of use when hailing a ride. Uber operates in 270 cities around the world.

Uber and other start-ups, such as Lyft, are disrupting the taxi industry and making booking a taxi one more thing consumers can do using their smart phone. These companies are well-funded by Silicon Valley venture capital. Uber, for example, has raised $307 million from supporters, including Google Ventures and Jeff Bezos, the founder of Amazon. These start-ups are making consumers question whether they need to own a car, especially in metropolitan cities where parking can be a challenge.

Uber's CEO believed the taxi industry was ready for disruption but needed new technology to truly do so. These new cab companies are battling each other, city regulators, entrenched taxi interests, and critics who claim they are succeeding only because they are violating laws meant to protect public safety. Uber has been blocked from operating in several markets by regulators who want to protect the interests of consumers and/or the entrenched incumbents.

Traditional taxi drivers often complain that they are no longer summoned to pick up riders in wealthier neighborhoods because of Uber and other similar companies. In Boston and Chicago, taxi operators even sued their cities for allowing unregulated companies, such as Uber, to devalue million-dollar operating permits. In Paris, upset taxi drivers shut down highway exits to the main airports and gridlocked city traffic.

Critics accuse Uber of risking the lives of their passengers by employing untested drivers. The director of the San Francisco Cab Drivers Association stated his personal mission would be to make it very difficult for Uber to operate. However, the Uber CEO believes that Uber liberates drivers and riders.

Questions

1. How did Uber take advantage of mobile technologies to create a disruptive business model?
2. As 5G enters the market, can you think of any new services Uber can offer its customers?
3. Lyft is a fast follower to Uber. Would you want to be CEO of Uber or Lyft? Why or why not?
4. How will driverless cars impact Uber's business model?

CLOSING CASE TWO

Spotify: Music as a Mobile Service

Daniel Ek spotted a business opportunity in the music industry when he was convinced that if you give away music for free and make it easy and pleasant for people to listen, they will become regular listeners. Ek wanted to disrupt the digital-download music business by replacing the iPod with on-demand music via mobile phones. As a habit formed, these users would almost magically be willing to pay for what they had been getting for free. Ek's Spotify start-up operates on this premise: The more you play, the more you'll pay. This counterintuitive idea continues to form the basis of Spotify's business model, even as it has confounded music labels and artists.

Since 2008, when Spotify launched, it has remained the global music leader using the cloud to stream music, popularizing the idea of music as a service rather than goods that consumers own. With 100 million paying subscribers, Spotify currently remains the top cloud music provider, although Apple and Google are approaching fast in the rearview mirror.

Apple, which dominated the digital-download music business with iTunes during the 2000s, launched its music subscription service in 2015. Analysts predicted it would pass Spotify in subscribers within a year, thanks to the power of the iPhone user base and Echo smart speakers. Amazon Prime Music Unlimited customers are signing up in droves to Amazon's cloud music service.

Google already has the globe's most popular digital music listening device in YouTube, and in an effort to make more money from it, the company recently introduced a Spotify-like YouTube Music subscription.[14]

Questions

1. How is Spotify taking advantage of mobile devices?
2. How is Spotify a music-as-a-service business?
3. Why should Spotify care about mobile device management?
4. Why should Spotify care about mobile application management?
5. Without wireless technologies and mobile devices, would Spotify be successful? Why or why not?

MAKING BUSINESS DECISIONS

1. Cars Hacked

Who would have thought that a car could be hacked? But that is exactly what happened in Austin, Texas. About a hundred cars were broken into, not by the usual method of either picking the lock or smashing a window but instead through a Wi-Fi connection. A local dealership, where all the cars were purchased, had installed a Wi-Fi-enabled black box under the dashboard that could disable the car and set off the horn if the owner did not make payments. However, in this case, the car owners were not in arrears but, rather, the victims of a recently laid-off employee at the dealership who was seeking revenge by using the web-based system to disable the cars one by one. After someone at the dealership figured out the cars had been hacked, the password that allowed authorization to the black boxes was quickly changed.

Is the black box a good idea? Do you consider this an ethical business practice? If you had bought a car with a black box, would you have it removed? How many customers do you think will consider buying another car from that dealership?

2. Google Collected Public Wi-Fi Data . . . by Mistake

Google has admitted to collecting data sent over unsecured Wi-Fi networks mistakenly, using its Street View cars. Google photographs homes from public streets, using a fleet of company cars. Google said it was trying to gather information about the location, strength, and configuration of Wi-Fi networks so it could improve the accuracy of location-based services such as Google Maps and driving directions. However, in the process, the cars were also collecting snippets of emails and other Internet activity from unprotected wireless networks in the homes. Google blamed this on a programming error, temporarily halted the Street View data collection, and announced it would stop collecting all Wi-Fi data. Do you believe this was a mistake by Google? If home users do not protect their wireless networks, what is to stop a neighbor from collecting the same information? Who is really at fault here?

3. Securing Your Home Wireless Network

Wireless networks are so ubiquitous and inexpensive that anyone can easily build one with less than $100 worth of equipment. However, wireless networks are exactly that—wireless: They do not stop at walls. Living in an apartment, dorm, or house means your neighbors can access your network.

It is one thing to let neighbors borrow sugar or a cup of coffee, but problems occur when you allow them to borrow your wireless network. There are several good reasons for not sharing a home wireless network, including:

- Slowing of Internet performance.
- Potential for others to view files on your computers and spread dangerous software such as viruses.
- Possibility for others to monitor the websites you visit, read your email and instant messages as they travel across the network, and copy your user names and passwords.
- Availability for others to send spam or perform illegal activities with your Internet connection.

Securing a home wireless network makes it difficult for uninvited guests to connect through your wireless network. Create a document detailing how you can secure a home wireless network.

4. Weather Bots

Warren Jackson designed a GPS-equipped robot when he was a graduate student at the University of Pennsylvania. The robot was created to bring weather balloons back down to Earth, allowing them to land in a predetermined location. The National Weather Service collects most of its information using weather balloons that carry a device to measure items such as air pressure, wind, and humidity. When the balloon reaches about 100,000 feet and the air pressure causes it to pop, the device falls and lands a substantial distance from its launch point. The weather service and researchers sometimes look for the $200 device, but of the 80,000 sent up annually, they write off many as lost.

Jackson's idea was so inventive that Penn's Weiss Tech House—a university organization that encourages students to innovate and bring their ideas to market—awarded Jackson and some fellow graduate engineering students first prize in its third annual PennVention Contest. Jackson won $5,000 and access to expert advice on prototyping, legal matters, and branding.

GPS and GIS can be used in all sorts of devices, in many industries, for multiple purposes. If you want to compete and win first prize in the PennVention next year, create a product using a GPS or GIS that is not currently on the market today that you can present at the next PennVention.

5. Free Wi-Fi in Africa

Covering Africa with free and low-cost Wi-Fi may not seem like a smart thing, but that is exactly what Paul English, the cofounder of travel search engine Kayak.com, plans to do. English has created a hybrid nonprofit/for-profit company, JoinAfrica, to explore the creation of two tiers of Wi-Fi access in Africa. The first tier will be free and offer basic email service (from Gmail, Yahoo!, etc.) and web browsing (Wikipedia, BBC, etc.). The second tier will be fee-based and offer additional capabilities, including audio, video, and high-quality images.

Although many countries in Africa struggle to have proper drinking water or even efficient electrical power, English and the JoinAfrica initiative believe having access to the Internet is just as important. JoinAfrica will work with for-profit telecommunication companies in Africa to first branch out with existing connections in villages, providing residents with the first-tier services, and residents can pay money to upgrade to the second tier. More bandwidth-intensive services such as streaming video and pornography will be throttled to ensure a basic level of service for all as the networks grow.

- List 10 ways wireless access could hurt remote villages in Africa.
- What other infrastructure requirements will JoinAfrica need to implement to ensure the project's success?
- How will changes in technology over the next decade affect the JoinAfrica project?
- What types of security and ethical issues will JoinAfrica face?
- If you were given $1 million, would you invest it in JoinAfrica?

6. Ding-A-Ling Took My $400!

A satellite television customer requested that her service be disconnected due to poor reception. Soon after disconnecting the service, the customer noticed a direct bank withdrawal for a $430 early-termination fee from the satellite provider. To make matters worse, the unplanned charge caused hundreds of dollars in overdraft charges. To top it all off, a customer service representative apparently named Ding-A-Ling called the customer to see if she would consider reconnecting the service.

Never give any company your checking account number or direct access to your bank account. If you want to establish a good relationship with a company, give it your credit card number. When a relationship with a supplier turns sour, the last thing you want is for that company to have direct access to your checking account.

Do you think what the satellite provider did was ethical? What could the customer do when disconnecting her service to avoid this type of issue? Can credit card companies enter your bank account and take out as much money as you owe at any time they want? Why is it important to never give a supplier direct access to your business checking account?

7. 911 McNuggets

Cellular technologies have changed the way we do business, and it is hard to imagine life without them. There are many wonderful advantages of using wireless technologies in business, but there are also some serious disadvantages, such as the ability to make a bad decision faster.

A woman in Florida called 911 three times after McDonald's employees told her they were out of Chicken McNuggets. The woman stated that this is an emergency and if she had known they didn't have any McNuggets, then she would not have given them any money. The woman said McDonald's offered her a McDouble but she didn't want one. The woman was cited on a charge of misuse of 911.

It is so easy to pick up the phone from anywhere, at any time, and make a bad call. How many times do you see people making calls on their cell phones from inappropriate locations? If this woman had to wait in line to use a pay phone, do you think it would have given her time to calm down and rethink her decision? With technology and the ability to communicate at our fingertips, do you agree it is easier than ever to make a bad decision? What can you do to ensure you think before you communicate?

8. Wireless Networks and Streetlights

Researchers at Harvard University and BBN Technologies are designing CitySense, a wireless network attached to streetlights that can report real-time data across the entire city of Cambridge, Massachusetts. The CitySense network mounts each node on a municipal streetlight, where it draws power from city electricity. Each node includes a Wi-Fi interface, weather sensors, and download and uploading data capabilities.

You are responsible for deploying a CitySense network around your city. What goals would you have for the system besides monitoring urban weather and pollution? What other benefits could a CitySense network provide? How could local businesses and citizens benefit from the network? What legal and ethical concerns should you understand before deploying the network? What can you do to protect your network and your city from these issues?

9. Teddy The Guardian

Two London-based entrepreneurs are building an Internet of huggable things for sick children to make any hospital visit more like a trip to Disneyland. Teddy The Guardian captures heart rate, temperatures, and blood-oxygen levels when a child grabs it by the paw to give it a cuddle. All measurements are sent wirelessly to nurses' and parents' mobile devices. The cute, cuddly teddy bear is packed full of sensors designed to track children's vital signs and help quickly find out potential issues. Teddy The Guardian takes from 5 to 7 seconds to record measurements and is programmed to run five times per hour. Future versions of Teddy The Guardian will be interactive, using machine learning to find out the child's favorite song or bedtime story and then play the related content for a more soothing hospital visit. Big pharmaceutical companies in the United States have already placed over $500,000 in orders and plan to donate the bears to hospitals and clinics.

This is clearly a brilliant idea, and soon we will see Teddy The Guardian in many local hospitals and clinics. Can you identify any additional markets on which Teddy The Guardian should focus? Can you think of any ethical issues related to huggable things? Can you think of any security issues related to huggable things?

10. Wi-Fi for Fishes

Not too long ago, the Seattle Aquarium decided it needed to take a deep dive into its network infrastructure and deploy wireless across its facilities. Now, a year and a half in, the aquarium has found Wi-Fi to be a tool that not only lets it serve visitors in unique ways but enriches the exchanges possible between staff members and the community, says Pam Lamon, the aquarium's web and social media coordinator. For instance, there are long stretches when Umi, the aquarium's 40-pound giant Pacific octopus, doesn't move at all. Now, staff members armed with tablets can roam around the exhibit showing visitors videos of Umi feeding while they field questions.

Wireless even lets the aquarium interact with people who can't visit in person. For instance, during a recent Google+ Hangouts on Air, a young boy from an East Coast school asked an aquarium diver how many fish were swimming in the tank with her. The diver, wearing a wet suit and a face mask with a microphone and speaker, began pointing out fish. "One, two, three, four, five, six, seven," she counted off, before giving up and telling him there were 500, give or take a few. "It's a little bit hard to know for sure because they just don't hold still while we count them," she joked.

The Seattle Aquarium is far from alone among businesses and organizations that are tapping into wireless to expand or improve services. As wireless has morphed from a pleasant perk to a necessity for employees and clients across industries, many businesses are finding they can no longer make do without wireless or with limited Wi-Fi services. Today, not only is there incentive to find better solutions, but companies also have access to more sophisticated equipment to help them pinpoint network problems. From next-generation access points to cloud-based management systems, wireless tools can provide expanded capabilities, are easy to manage, and are available in a range of prices.

In a group, choose a business in your area that could benefit from wireless technology, like the Seattle Aquarium, and create a plan detailing the additional services it could offer its customers.

11. Pokémon Go for Playgrounds

John Hanke, the CEO of Pokémon Go developer Niantic, posted a video of himself testing out the Augmented Reality Playground function in the game. Its goal is to get kids moving and have fun. With its technology embedded in some 4,000 playgrounds worldwide, Pokémon Go gets sedentary kids to move by creating augmented reality mobile games that encourage physical play, such as an enhanced hide-and-seek. The applications are designed for children to be active 80 percent of the time.

Can you think of another way to get kids moving using wireless technologies? How can Pokémon Go be used to help children exercise beyond a playground? How could a gym incorporate the same technology for adults?

12. Where Would You GoPro?

Just imagine a beautiful white-tailed eagle soaring high above the French Alps. Well, you can soar right along with this beautiful creature, getting a true bird's-eye view from the streaming wireless video sent from a GoPro camera attached to its back. The incredible footage went viral, and now everybody from new fathers to Olympic athletes is sharing their GoPro footage. Wil Tidman, who runs GoPro's 40-person production team, stated, "We want to show the cameras' diverse uses and give the users the ability to edit and share videos online." Currently, the company is averaging three GoPro-hashtagged videos uploaded to YouTube per minute.

Who's Shooting All That Action Footage?

- People with dramatic jobs, from soldiers to oil riggers, use GoPro in their work, and Tidman's team scours the web for potential hits. He found footage of a firefighter rescuing a cat from a burning building, and the resulting YouTube post got 18 million views.
- GoPro equipped the Rolling Stones with 40 cameras for their 2013 tour. Tidman's team also helps indies, some of whose clips have earned them a degree of fame, which is proof of a GoPro bump.

In a group, choose one of your favorite products or services and create a marketing strategy using GoPro.

AYK APPLICATION PROJECTS

If you are looking for Excel projects to incorporate into your class, try any of the following after reading this chapter.

Project Number	Project Name	Project Type	Plug-In	Focus Area	Project Level	Skill Set	Page Number
9	Security Analysis	Excel	T3	Filtering Data	Intermediate	Conditional Formatting, Autofilter, Subtotal	AYK.6
10	Gathering Data	Excel	T3	Data Analysis	Intermediate	Conditional Formatting	AYK.6
11	Scanner System	Excel	T2	Strategic Analysis	Intermediate	Formulas	AYK.7
12	Competitive Pricing	Excel	T2	Profit Maximization	Intermediate	Formulas	AYK.7
13	Adequate Acquisitions	Excel	T2	Break Even Analysis	Intermediate	Formulas	AYK.7
15	Assessing the Value of Information	Excel	T3	Data Analysis	Intermediate	PivotTable	AYK.8
16	Growth, Trends, and Forecasts	Excel	T2, T3	Data Forecasting	Advanced	Average, Trend, Growth	AYK.9
18	Formatting Grades	Excel	T3	Data Analysis	Advanced	If, LookUp	AYK.11
22	Turnover Rates	Excel	T3	Data Mining	Advanced	PivotTable	AYK.13
23	Vital Information	Excel	T3	Data Mining	Advanced	PivotTable	AYK.13
24	Breaking Even	Excel	T4	Business Analysis	Advanced	Goal Seek	AYK.14
25	Profit Scenario	Excel	T4	Sales Analysis	Advanced	Scenario Manager	AYK.14

Design Element: © McGraw Hill Education

module 3

Enterprise MIS

ORGANIZATIONS USE VARIOUS types of information systems to help run their daily operations. These primarily transactional systems concentrate on the management and flow of low-level data items for basic business processes such as purchasing and order delivery. The data are often rolled up and summarized into higher-level decision support systems to help firms understand what is happening in their organizations and how best to respond. To achieve seamless and efficient handling of data and informed decision making, organizations must ensure that their enterprise systems are tightly integrated, providing an end-to-end view of operations.

This module introduces various types of enterprise information systems and their role in helping firms reach their strategic goals, including supply chain management, customer relationship management, and enterprise resource planning. Organizations that can correlate and summarize enterprisewide information are prepared to meet their strategic business goals and outperform their competitors.

This module then dives into how enterprise systems can be built to support global businesses, the challenges in that process, and how well things turn out if systems are built according to good design principles, sound management practices, and flexibility to support ever-changing business needs. Making this happen requires not only extensive planning, but also well-honed people skills.

Module 3: Enterprise MIS

Enterprise Applications: Business Communications

8

CHAPTER

CHAPTER OUTLINE

SECTION 8.1
Supply Chain Management

- Building a Connected Corporation through Integrations
- Supply Chain Management
- Technologies Reinventing the Supply Chain

SECTION 8.2
Customer Relationship Management and Enterprise Resource Planning

- Customer Relationship Management
- Organizational and Analytical CRM
- Enterprise Resource Planning
- Organizational Integration with ERP

What's in IT for me?

This chapter introduces high-profile strategic initiatives an organization can undertake to help it gain competitive advantages and business efficiencies—supply chain management, customer relationship management, and enterprise resource planning. At the simplest level, organizations implement enterprise systems to gain efficiency in business processes, effectiveness in supply chains, and an overall understanding of customer needs and behaviors. Successful organizations recognize the competitive advantage of maintaining healthy relationships with employees, customers, suppliers, and partners. Doing so has a direct and positive effect on revenue and greatly adds to a company's profitability.

You, as a business student, must understand the critical relationship your business will have with its employees, customers, suppliers, and partners. You must also understand how to analyze your organizational data to ensure you are not just meeting but exceeding expectations. Enterprises are technologically empowered as never before to reach their goals of integrating, analyzing, and making intelligent business decisions.

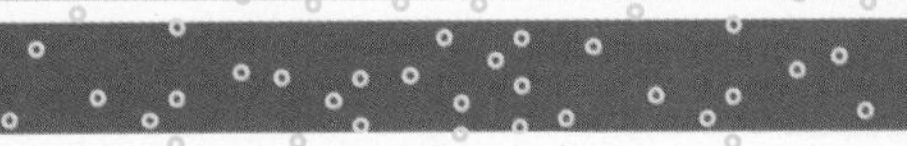

opening case study

Glowimages/Getty Images

UpperCut Images/Glow Images

Blend Images/Superstock

Blockchain Disrupting the Supply Chain

As an incorruptible digital ledger, blockchain could effectively store records for every product. It would add to its record every time a product changed hands, storing data such as who purchased it and for how much. Imagine a permanent history for every single product that would follow it from when it was made to when it was packed, shipped, displayed, and sold. For example, as goods move from one place to another or one part of a company to another, companies are interested in using blockchains to keep track of how goods are moving, along with all of the data attributes of the shipping process such as weather, temperature, vendor, supplier, etc.

Blockchain technology helps provide traceability across the supply chain. The technology also allows manufacturers, shippers, and customers to aggregate data, analyze trends, and perform predictive monitoring.

The advantages to this are pretty obvious. Analysts could identify new ways to reduce delays and remove human error, saving both time and resources. The data could also be shared throughout the company, enabling different departments to work more closely together toward a common goal. It could fundamentally change the way you work.

Blockchain can help supply chain management in a variety of ways, from recording the transfer of assets to tracking receipts, purchase orders, and other associated paperwork. It could also store other identifying data such as whether packages need to be handled with care or whether fresh produce is organic or not. A few examples of blockchain disrupting the supply chain include:

- **Shipping Goods:** One shipment of refrigerated goods from East Africa to Europe can pass through roughly 30 people and organizations, causing more than 200 interactions. Blockchain technology can help ensure provenance, providing traceability across the supply chain. This can thwart counterfeiters and ensure safety.
- **Providing Traceability:** Cross-contamination and the spread of foodborne illness, as well as unnecessary waste and the economic burden of recalls, are made worse by lack of data and traceability. It can take weeks—sometimes months—to identify the source of contamination or the point at which a product became contaminated. Blockchain can reduce the time it takes to pinpoint and eradicate the source of foodborne illness, reports Coin Desk. Blockchain technology enables companies to trace a contaminated product to its source quickly and ensure safe removal from store shelves and restaurants, according to IBM.

- **Eliminating Fraud and Counterfeit Products:** Blockchain's transparency may also help reduce fraud in pharmaceuticals. That's huge: The global counterfeit drug market size is around $200 billion. Blockchain's immutability provides a basis for traceability of drugs from manufacturer to end consumer, identifying where the supply chain breaks down. In addition to cutting losses, there is the potential to improve consumer safety and prevent some of the estimated 1 million deaths annually from counterfeit medicine.[1]

section 8.1 | Supply Chain Management

LEARNING OUTCOMES

8.1 Explain integrations and the role they play in connecting a corporation.

8.2 Describe supply chain management along with its impact on business.

8.3 Identify the three technologies that are reinventing the supply chain.

LO 8.1: Explain integrations and the role they play in connecting a corporation.

BUILDING A CONNECTED CORPORATION THROUGH INTEGRATIONS

Until the 1990s, each department in the United Kingdom's Ministry of Defense and Army headquarters had its own information system, and each system had its own database. Sharing information was difficult, requiring employees to input the same information manually into different systems multiple times. Often, management could not even compile the information it needed to answer questions, solve problems, and make decisions.

To combat this challenge, the ministry integrated its systems, or built connections among its many databases. These connections are integrations.

- ***Integrations***: Allow separate systems to communicate directly with each other, eliminating the need for manual entry into multiple systems.

Building integrations allows information sharing across databases along with dramatic increases in quality. The army can now generate reports detailing its state of readiness and other essential intelligence, tasks that were nearly impossible before the integrations. There are two primary types of integration:

- ***Application integration***: The integration of a company's existing management information systems.
- ***Data integration***: The integration of data from multiple sources, which provides a unified view of all data.

Regardless if you are integrating applications or data, two common methods are used for integrating databases. The first is to create forward and backward integrations that link processes (and their underlying databases) in the value chain.

- ***Forward integration***: Sends information entered into a given system automatically to all downstream systems and processes.
- ***Backward integration***: Sends information entered into a given system automatically to all upstream systems and processes.

Figure 8.1 demonstrates how this method works across the systems or processes of sales, order entry, order fulfillment, and billing. In the order entry system, for example, an employee can update the customer's information. Via the integrations, that information is sent upstream to the sales system and downstream to the order fulfillment and billing systems. Ideally, an organization wants to build both forward and backward integrations, which provide the flexibility to create, update, and delete information in any of the systems. However, backward integrations are expensive and difficult to build and maintain, causing most organizations to invest in forward integrations only.

The second integration method builds a common data repository for a particular type of information.

- ***Common data repository***: Allows every department of a company to store and retrieve information in real time, allowing information to be more reliable and accessible.

A common data repository can be a place where multiple databases or files are located for distribution over a network, or a repository can be a location that is directly accessible to the

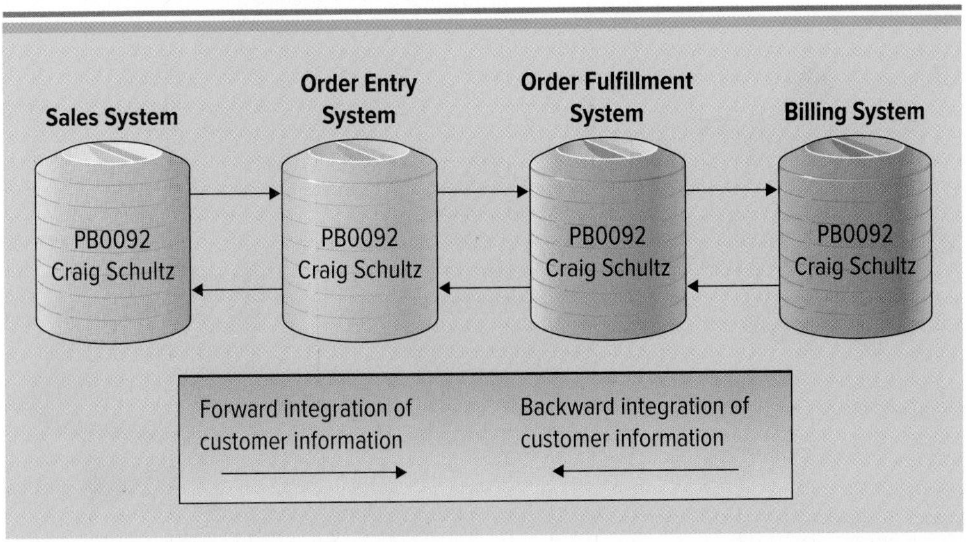

Sales System
Order Entry System
Order Fulfillment System
Billing System
PB0092 Craig Schultz
Forward integration of customer information
Backward integration of customer information

FIGURE 8.1

A Forward and Backward Customer Information Integration Example

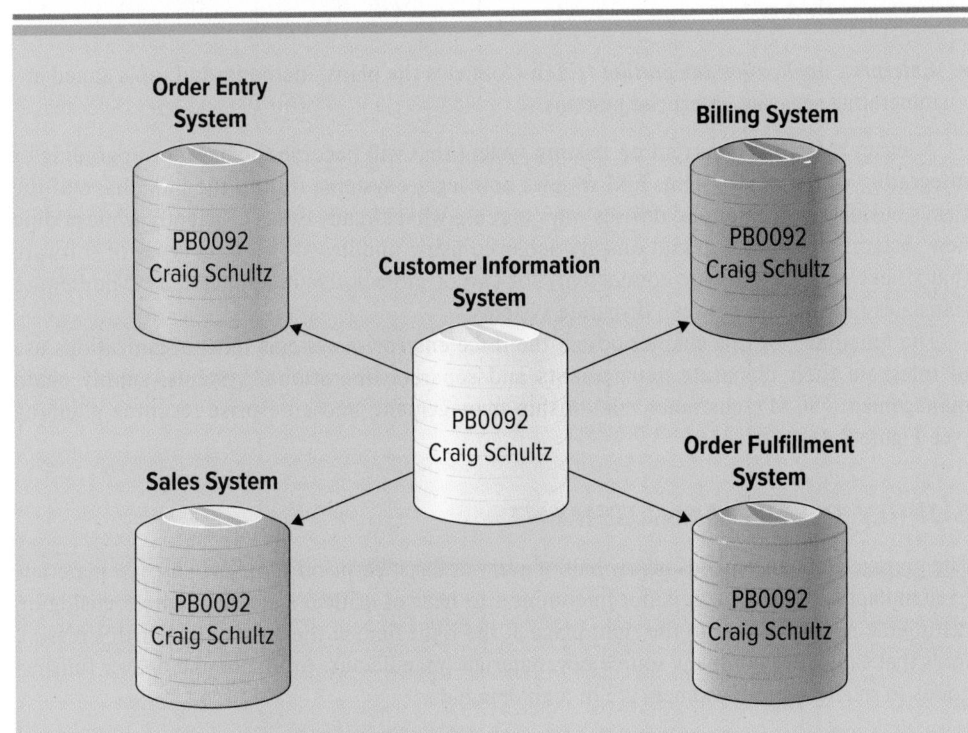

FIGURE 8.2

Integrating Customer Information among Databases

user without having to travel across a network. Figure 8.2 provides an example of customer information integrated using this method across four systems in an organization. Users can create, update, and delete customer information only in the central customer database. As users perform these tasks, integrations automatically send the new and/or updated customer information to the other systems. The other systems limit users to read-only access of the customer information stored in them. Neither integration method entirely eliminates information redundancy, but both do ensure information consistency among multiple systems.

Integration Tools

Enterprise systems provide enterprisewide support and data access for a firm's operations and business processes. These systems can manage customer information across the enterprise, letting you view everything your customer has experienced from sales to support. Enterprise systems are often available as a generic, but highly customizable, group of programs for business functions such as accounting, manufacturing, and marketing. Generally, the development tools for customization are complex programming tools that require specialist capabilities.

FIGURE 8.3

The Three Primary Enterprise Systems

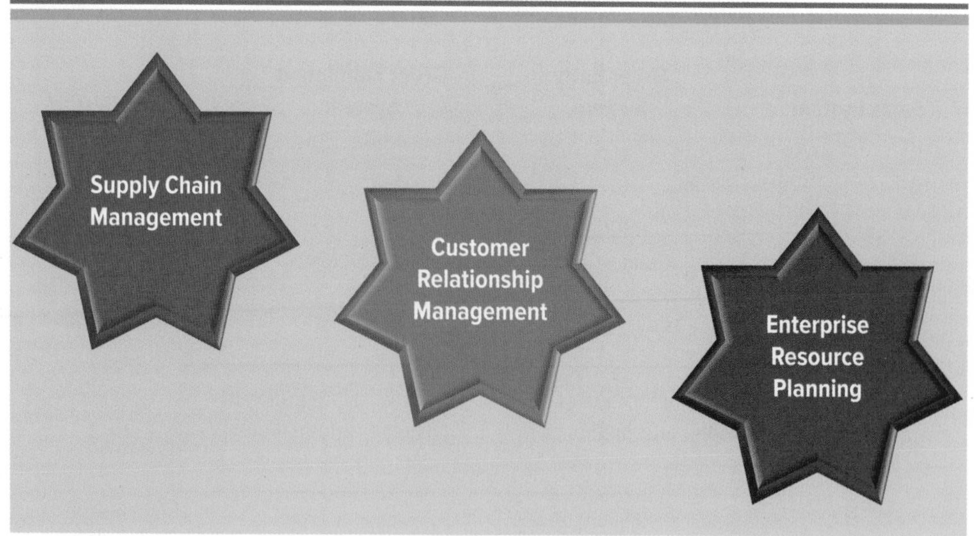

- ***Enterprise application integration (EAI)*:** Connects the plans, methods, and tools aimed at integrating separate enterprise systems.

A legacy system is a current or existing system that will become the base for upgrading or integrating with a new system. EAI reviews how legacy systems fit into the new shape of the firm's business processes and devises ways to reuse what already exists efficiently while adding new systems and data. Integrations are achieved using middleware–several types of software that sit between and provide connectivity for two or more software applications. Middleware translates information between disparate systems.

The remainder of this chapter covers the three enterprise systems most organizations use to integrate their disparate departments and separate operational systems: supply chain management (SCM), customer relationship management, and enterprise resource planning (see Figure 8.3).

LO 8.2: Describe supply chain management along with its impact on business.

SUPPLY CHAIN MANAGEMENT

The average company spends nearly half of every dollar it earns on suppliers and raw materials to manufacture products. It is not uncommon to hear of critical success factors focusing on getting the right products to the right place at the right time at the right cost. For this reason, tools that can help a company source raw materials, manufacture products, and deliver finished goods to retailers and customers are in high demand.

- ***Supply chain*:** Consists of all parties involved, directly or indirectly, in obtaining raw materials or a product.

Figure 8.4 highlights the five basic supply chain activities a company undertakes to manufacture and distribute products. To automate and enable sophisticated decision making in these critical areas, companies are turning to systems that provide demand forecasting, inventory control, and information flows between suppliers and customers.

- ***Supply chain management (SCM)*:** The management of information flows between and among activities in a supply chain to maximize total supply chain effectiveness and corporate profitability.

In the past, manufacturing efforts focused primarily on quality improvement efforts within the company; today these efforts reach across the entire supply chain, including customers, customers' customers, suppliers, and suppliers' suppliers. Today's supply chain is an intricate network of business partners linked through communication channels and relationships. Supply chain management systems manage and enhance these relationships with the primary goal of creating a fast, efficient, and low-cost network of business relationships that take products

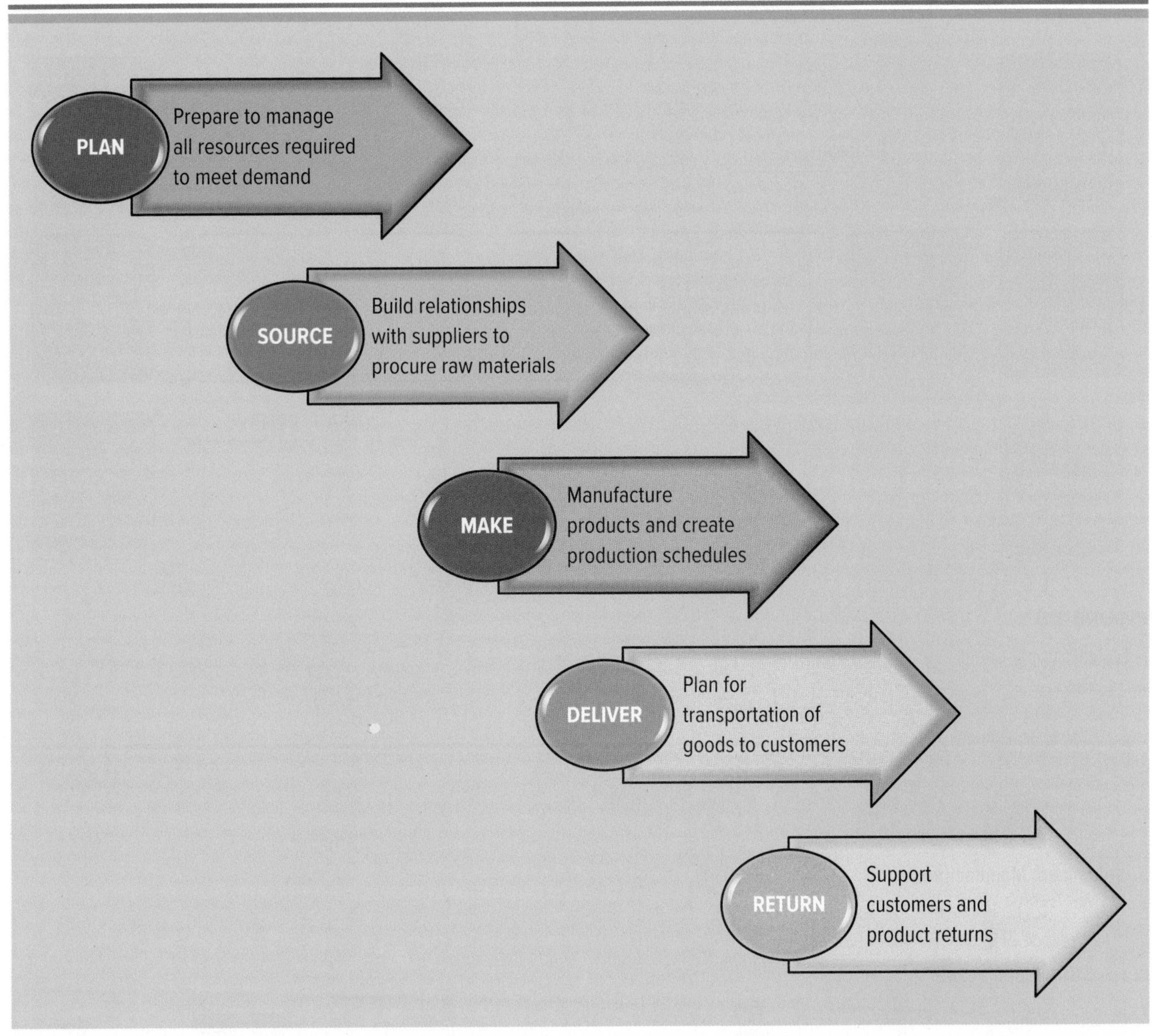

FIGURE 8.4

The Five Basic Supply Chain Activities

from concept to market. SCM systems create the integrations or tight process and information linkages between all participants in the supply chain. Supply chain management performs three main business processes (see Figure 8.5):

- Materials flow from suppliers and their upstream suppliers at all levels.
- Materials are transformed into semifinished and finished products–the organization's own production processes.
- Products are distributed to customers and their downstream customers at all levels.[2]

Consider a customer purchasing a mountain bike from a dealer. Dozens of steps are required to complete this transaction from beginning to end. The customer places an order with the dealer. The dealer purchases the bike from the manufacturer. The manufacturer purchases the raw materials required to make the bike such as aluminum, rubber tires, brakes, accessories, and packaging from different suppliers. The raw materials are stored in the manufacturer's warehouse until a production order requires the bike to be built, at which time the finished product is sent to the dealer or, in some cases, directly to the customer. The supply chain for a bike manufacturer includes all processes and people required to fulfill the customer's order (see Figure 8.6).

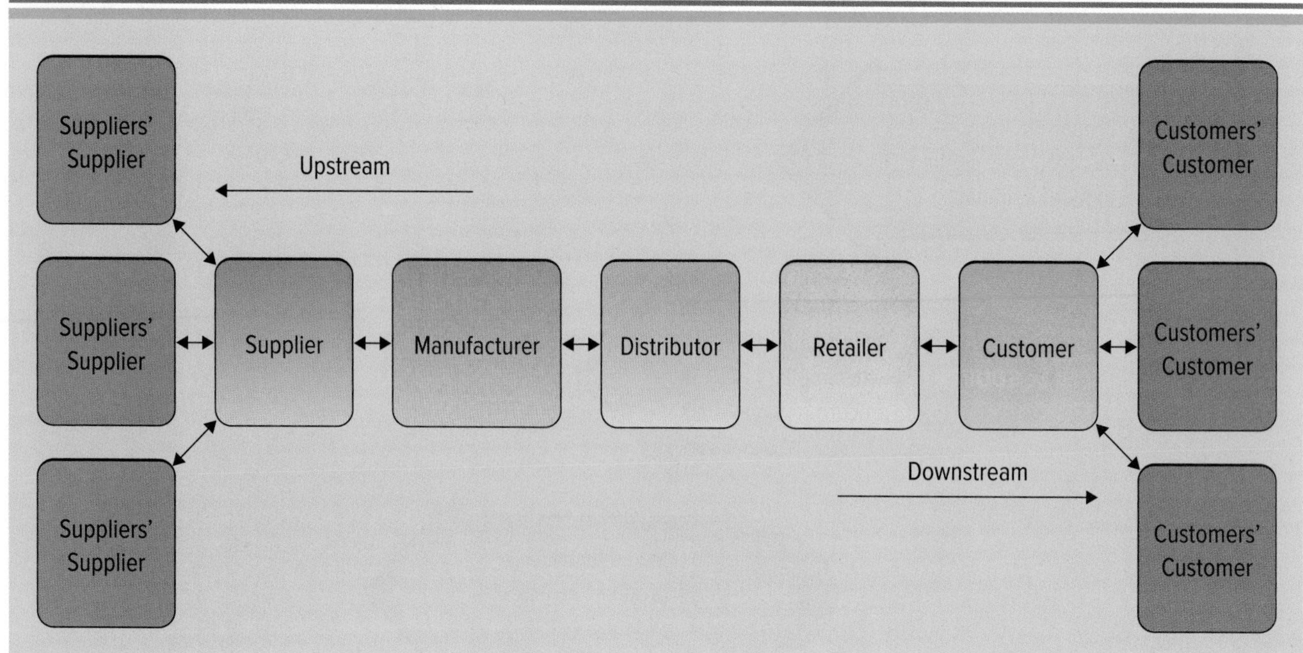

FIGURE 8.5

A Typical Supply Chain

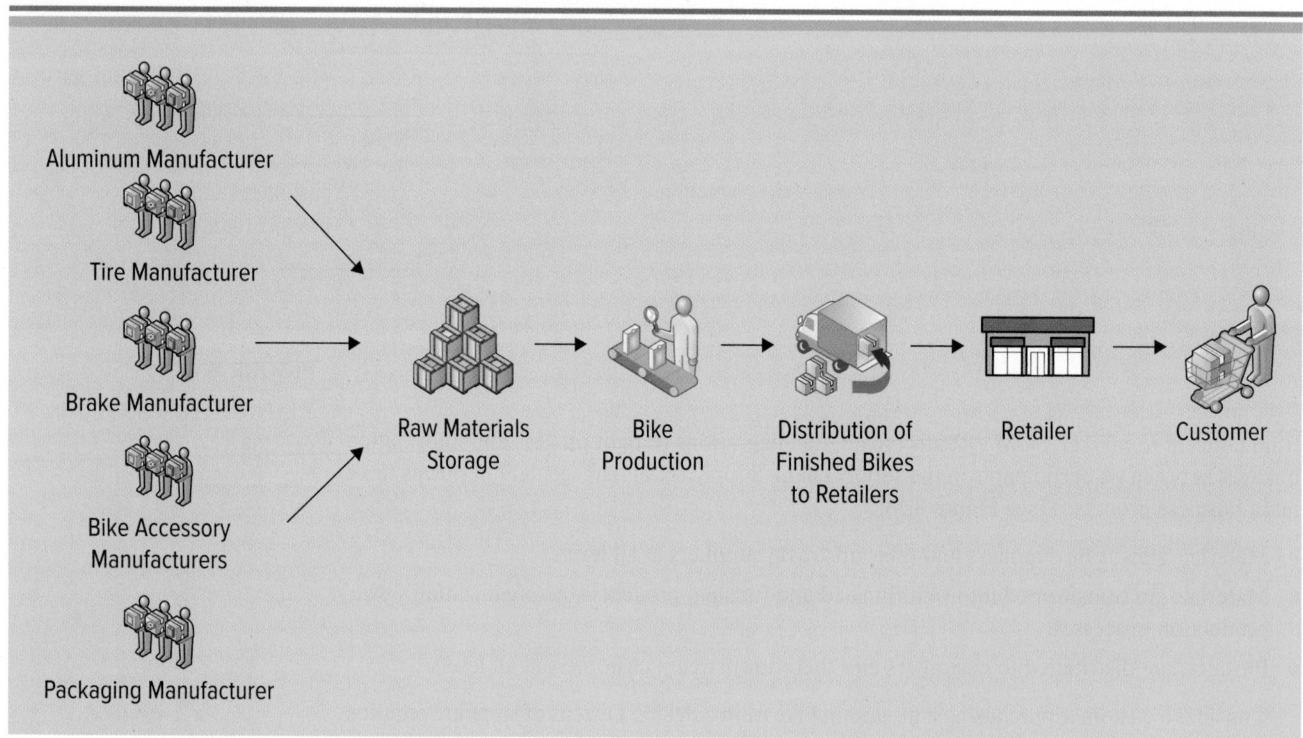

FIGURE 8.6

Supply Chain for a Bike Manufacturer

Walmart and Procter & Gamble (P&G) have implemented a successful SCM system that links Walmart's distribution centers directly to P&G's manufacturing centers (see Figure 8.7). The customer generates order information by purchasing a product from Walmart. Walmart supplies the order information to its warehouse or distributor. The warehouse or distributor transfers the order information to P&G, which provides pricing and availability information to the store and replenishes the product to the distributor. Payment is transferred electronically.

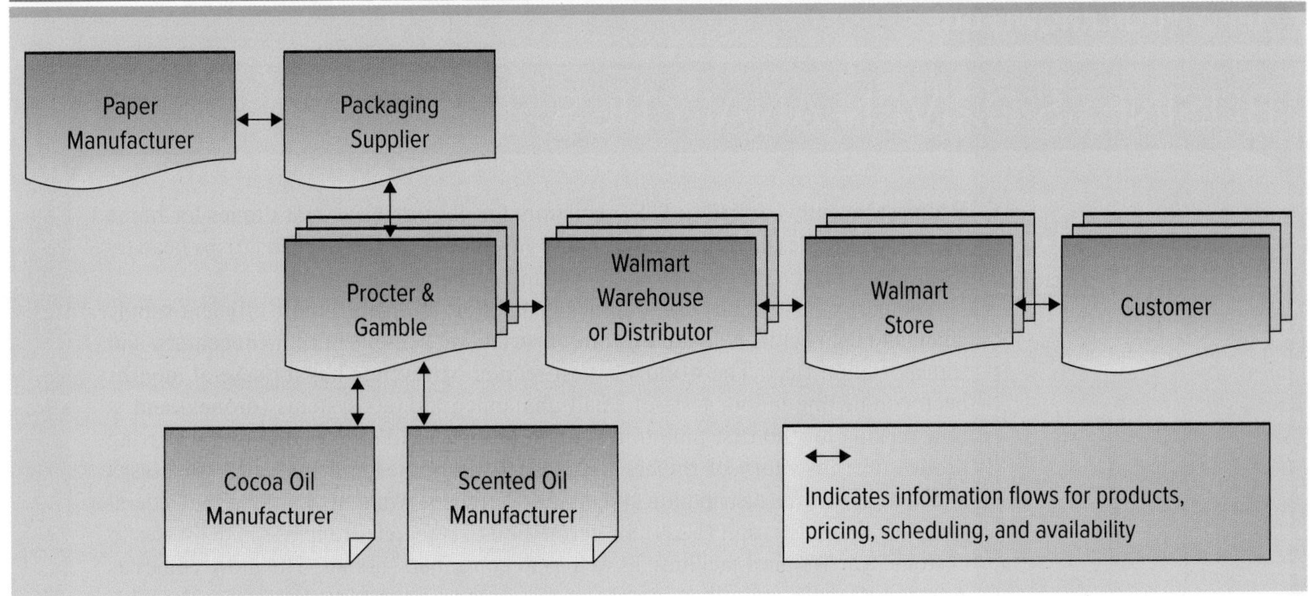

FIGURE 8.7

Supply Chain for a Product Purchased from Walmart

Effective and efficient supply chain management systems can enable an organization to have these impacts on Porter's Five Forces Model:[3]

- Decrease the power of its buyers.
- Increase its supplier power.
- Increase buyers' switching costs to reduce the threat of substitute products or services.
- Create entry barriers to reduce the threat of new entrants.
- Increase efficiencies while seeking a competitive advantage through cost leadership (see Figure 8.8).

Supply chain management systems can increase profitability across an organization. For example, a manufacturing plant manager might focus on keeping the inventory of Product A as low as possible, which will directly reduce the manufacturing costs and make the plant manager look great. However, the plant manager and the business might not realize that these savings are causing increased costs in other areas, such as having to pay more to procure raw materials for immediate production needs or increasing costs due to expedited shipping services. Only an end-to-end view or an integrated supply chain would uncover these issues, allowing a firm to adjust business strategies to increase profitability across the enterprise. A few of the common supply chain management metrics include:

- **Back order:** An unfilled customer order for a product that is out of stock.
- **Inventory cycle time:** The time it takes to manufacture a product and deliver it to the retailer.

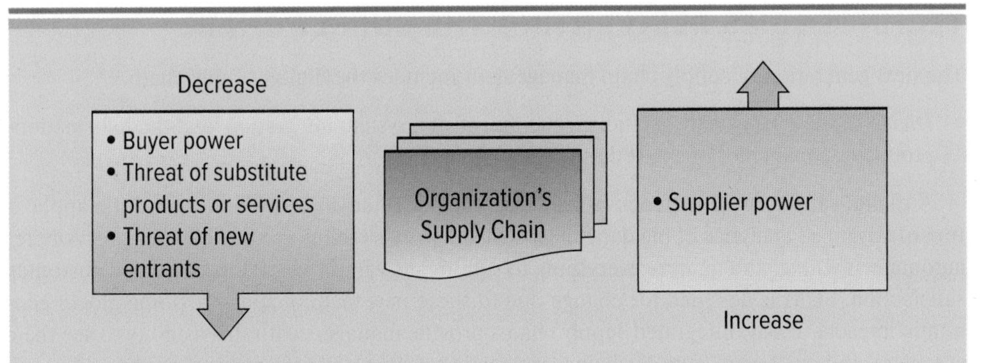

FIGURE 8.8

Effective and Efficient Supply Chain Management's Effect on Porter's Five Forces

APPLY YOUR KNOWLEDGE

BUSINESS DRIVEN ANALYTICS

Drone Races

Walmart recently applied to U.S. regulators for permission to test drones for home delivery, curbside pickup, and warehouse inventories, a sign it plans to go head-to-head with Amazon in using drones to fill and deliver online orders.

Walmart wants to start using drones in an effort to create a more efficient supply chain and connect its network of stores, distribution centers, fulfillment centers, and transportation fleet. The world's largest retailer by revenue has for several months been conducting indoor tests of small unmanned aircraft systems (drones) and is now seeking for the first time to test the machines outdoors. In addition to having drones take inventory of trailers outside its warehouses and perform other tasks aimed at making its distribution system more efficient, Walmart is asking the Federal Aviation Administration (FAA) for permission to research drone use in deliveries to customers at Walmart facilities, as well as to consumers' homes. The move comes as Amazon, Google, and other companies test drones in the expectation that the FAA will soon establish rules for their widespread commercial use.[4]

In a group, brainstorm three additional ways Walmart can use drones to create efficiencies in its supply chain. Choose another industry, such as fashion, food service, or sports, and identity three ways the industry can use drones to change its supply chain.

- **Customer order cycle time:** The agreed-upon time between the purchase of a product and the delivery of the product.
- **Inventory turnover:** The frequency of inventory replacement.

The supply chain is only as strong as its weakest link. Companies use supply chain management metrics to measure the performance of supply chains to identify weak links quickly. A good example of inventory issues that occur when a company does not have a clear vision of its entire supply chain or the right metrics is the bullwhip effect.

- ***Bullwhip effect*:** Occurs when distorted product-demand information ripples from one partner to the next throughout the supply chain.

The misinformation regarding a slight rise in demand for a product could cause different members in the supply chain to stockpile inventory. These changes ripple throughout the supply chain, magnifying the issue and creating excess inventory and costs for all. For example, if a car dealership is having a hard time moving a particular brand of car, it might offer significant discounts to try to move the inventory. Without this critical information, the car manufacturer might see a rise in demand for this particular brand of car and increase production orders, not realizing that the dealerships are actually challenged with selling the inventory.

LO 8.3: Identify the three technologies that are reinventing the supply chain.

TECHNOLOGIES REINVENTING THE SUPPLY CHAIN

The next generation of supply chain management includes the digital supply chain.

- ***Digital supply chain*:** Fully capitalize on connectivity, system integration, and the information-producing capabilities of smart devices.

A digital supply chain includes IoT devices, the use of advanced robotics, and the application of advanced analytics of big data: place sensors in everything, create networks everywhere, automate anything, and analyze everything to significantly improve performance and customer satisfaction. SCM is destined for change due to these new technologies providing global economic impacts. Today, integrated supply chains provide managers with the visibility to see their suppliers' and customers' supply chains, ensuring that supply always meets demand

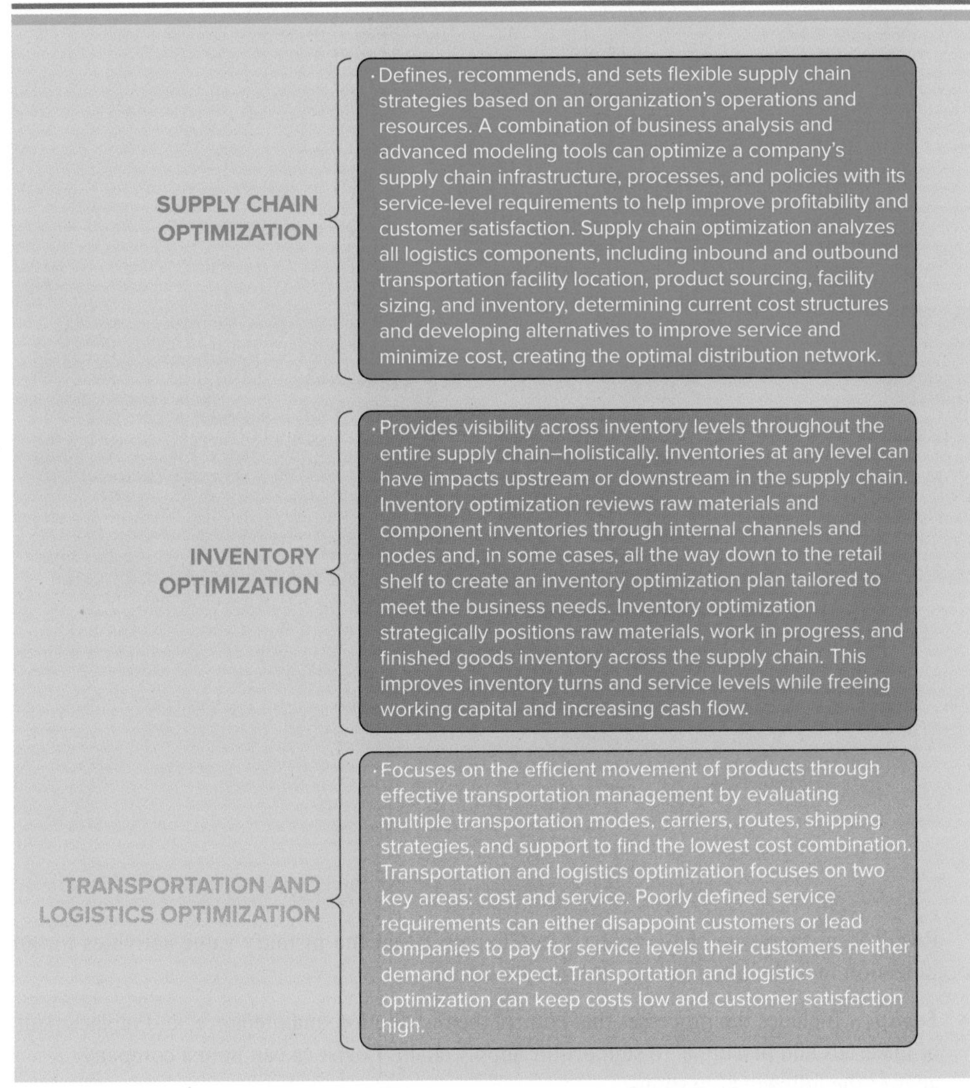

SUPPLY CHAIN OPTIMIZATION
· Defines, recommends, and sets flexible supply chain strategies based on an organization's operations and resources. A combination of business analysis and advanced modeling tools can optimize a company's supply chain infrastructure, processes, and policies with its service-level requirements to help improve profitability and customer satisfaction. Supply chain optimization analyzes all logistics components, including inbound and outbound transportation facility location, product sourcing, facility sizing, and inventory, determining current cost structures and developing alternatives to improve service and minimize cost, creating the optimal distribution network.
INVENTORY OPTIMIZATION
· Provides visibility across inventory levels throughout the entire supply chain–holistically. Inventories at any level can have impacts upstream or downstream in the supply chain. Inventory optimization reviews raw materials and component inventories through internal channels and nodes and, in some cases, all the way down to the retail shelf to create an inventory optimization plan tailored to meet the business needs. Inventory optimization strategically positions raw materials, work in progress, and finished goods inventory across the supply chain. This improves inventory turns and service levels while freeing working capital and increasing cash flow.
TRANSPORTATION AND LOGISTICS OPTIMIZATION
· Focuses on the efficient movement of products through effective transportation management by evaluating multiple transportation modes, carriers, routes, shipping strategies, and support to find the lowest cost combination. Transportation and logistics optimization focuses on two key areas: cost and service. Poorly defined service requirements can either disappoint customers or lead companies to pay for service levels their customers neither demand nor expect. Transportation and logistics optimization can keep costs low and customer satisfaction high.

FIGURE 8.9

SCM Optimization Models

Figure 8.9 displays the three different optimization models analyzing supply chains.

Optimizing the supply chain is a critical business process for any successful organization. Just think of the complexity of Walmart's supply chain and the billions of products being sent around the world, guaranteeing every shelf is fully stocked. The three components of supply chain management on which companies focus to find efficiencies include procurement, logistics, and materials management (see Figure 8.10).

Without the right inputs, the company simply can't create cost-effective outputs. For example, if McDonald's could not procure potatoes or had to purchase potatoes at an outrageous price, it would be unable to create and sell its famous French fries. In fact, procuring the right-sized potatoes to produce their famous long French fries is challenging in some countries where locally grown potatoes are too small.

- ***Procurement***: The purchasing of goods and services to meet the needs of the supply chain.

The procurement process is a key supply chain strategy because the capability to purchase input materials at the right price is directly correlated to the company's ability to operate. Procurement can help a company answer the following questions:

- What quantity of raw materials should we purchase to minimize spoilage?
- How can we guarantee that our raw materials meet production needs?
- At what price can we purchase materials to guarantee profitability?
- Can purchasing all products from a single vendor provide additional discounts?

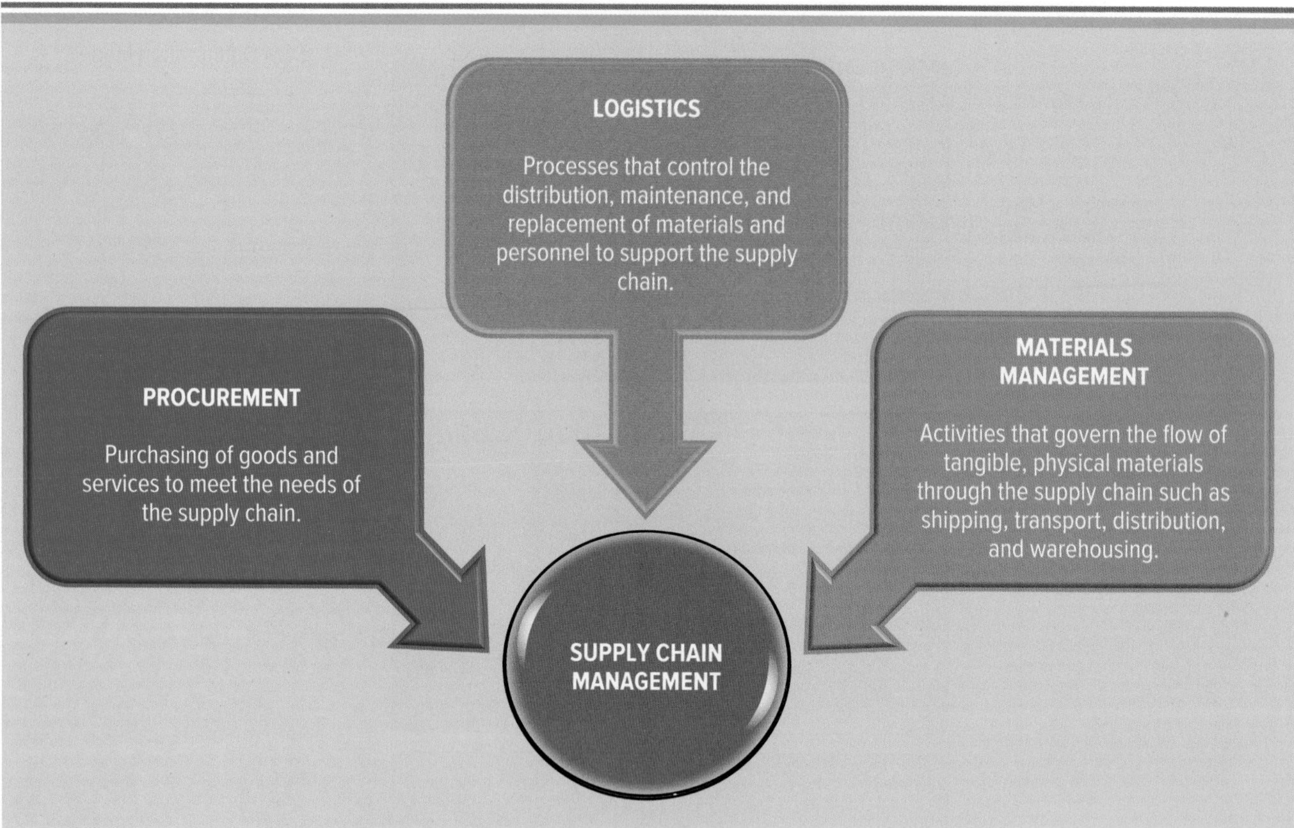

FIGURE 8.10

The Three Business Areas of Supply Chain Management

Recall from the value chain analysis in Chapter 1 that the primary value activities for an organization include inbound and outbound logistics.

- ***Logistics***: Includes the processes that control the distribution, maintenance, and replacement of materials and personnel to support the supply chain. Logistics can help a company answer the following questions:
  - What is the quickest way to deliver products to our customers?
  - What is the optimal way to place items in the warehouse for picking and packing?
  - What is the optimal path to an item in the warehouse?
  - What path should the vehicles follow when delivering the goods?
  - What areas or regions are the trucks covering?
- ***Inbound logistics***: Acquires raw materials and resources and distributes them to manufacturing as required.
- ***Outbound logistics***: Distributes goods and services to customers.

Logistics controls processes inside a company (warehouse logistics) and outside a company (transport logistics) and focuses on the physical execution part of the supply chain. Logistics includes the increasingly complex management of processes, information, and communication to take a product from cradle to grave.

- ***Cradle to grave***: Provides logistics support throughout the entire system or life of the product.

Materials management focuses on the quality and quantity of materials, as well as on how to plan, acquire, use, and dispose of these materials.

- ***Materials management***: Includes activities that govern the flow of tangible, physical materials through the supply chain, such as shipping, transport, distribution, and warehousing.

It can include the handling of liquids, fuel, produce, plants, and a number of other potentially hazardous items. Materials management focuses on handling all materials safely,

BUSINESS DRIVEN GLOBALIZATION

3D Printing for Poverty

Thirty-three-year-old Kodjo Afate Grikou wanted to help his community in West Africa print necessities they can't source locally, such as utensils for cooking. The structure of the 3D printer he had in mind uses very little in terms of new parts because it is mostly made up of ewaste and scrap metal. Before building this printer, he set up his project on the European social funding website ulule. The project received more than $10,000, despite the printer costing only $1,000, mostly through purchasing new parts that he couldn't find locally. Grikou hopes that his innovation will inspire teenagers and young people in his community to attend school and gain an education so they can make further life-changing developments that will benefit not only their lives but those of others around them.[5]

In a group, brainstorm ways 3D printing can help rural communities fight poverty.

efficiently, and in compliance with regulatory requirements and disposal requirements. Materials management can help a company answer the following concerns:

- What are our current inventory levels?
- What items are running low in the warehouse?
- What items are at risk of spoiling in the warehouse?
- How do we dispose of spoiled items?
- What laws need to be followed for storing hazardous materials?
- Which items must be refrigerated when being stored and transported?
- What are the requirements to store or transport fragile items?

As with all other areas of business, disruptive technologies are continuously being deployed to help businesses find competitive advantages in each component of the supply chain, as outlined in Figure 8.11.

3D Printing Supports Procurement

The process of ***3D printing*** (additive manufacturing) builds—layer by layer in an additive process—a three-dimensional solid object from a digital model. 3D printing is made possible by using a manufacturing technique called additive process. An additive process builds layer upon layer to create a 3D object. A computer controls the process, turning the printer into a type of robot that can create medical implants, shoes, auto parts, toys, cars, houses, and just about anything. In 2015, researchers at Wake Forest University in North Carolina developed a 3D printer, known as the Bone Printer, that can print human organs, tissues, and bones. It uses materials called hydrogels—water-based solutions containing human cells. While this technology is still new, the Bone Printer will theoretically allow doctors to 3D print transplants for their patients, eliminating the need for organ donors.

The additive manufacturing process of 3D printing is profoundly different from traditional manufacturing processes. Many sources are stating that 3D printing has the potential to be vastly more disruptive to business than the Internet. That is a bold statement! The reason people are betting on 3D printing to disrupt business is that it brings production closer to users, thus eliminating steps in the supply chain similar to disintermediation by the Internet. Three-dimensional printing also promotes mass customization, small production batches, and reduction in inventory.

Traditionally, the costs associated with 3D printing made it accessible only to large corporations. Now, with inexpensive printers, scanners, and applications, the technology is accessible to small and midsized businesses and home users. With the advances in 3D printing, the need to procure materials will become far easier because businesses can simply print the parts and

FIGURE 8.11

Disruptive Business Technologies

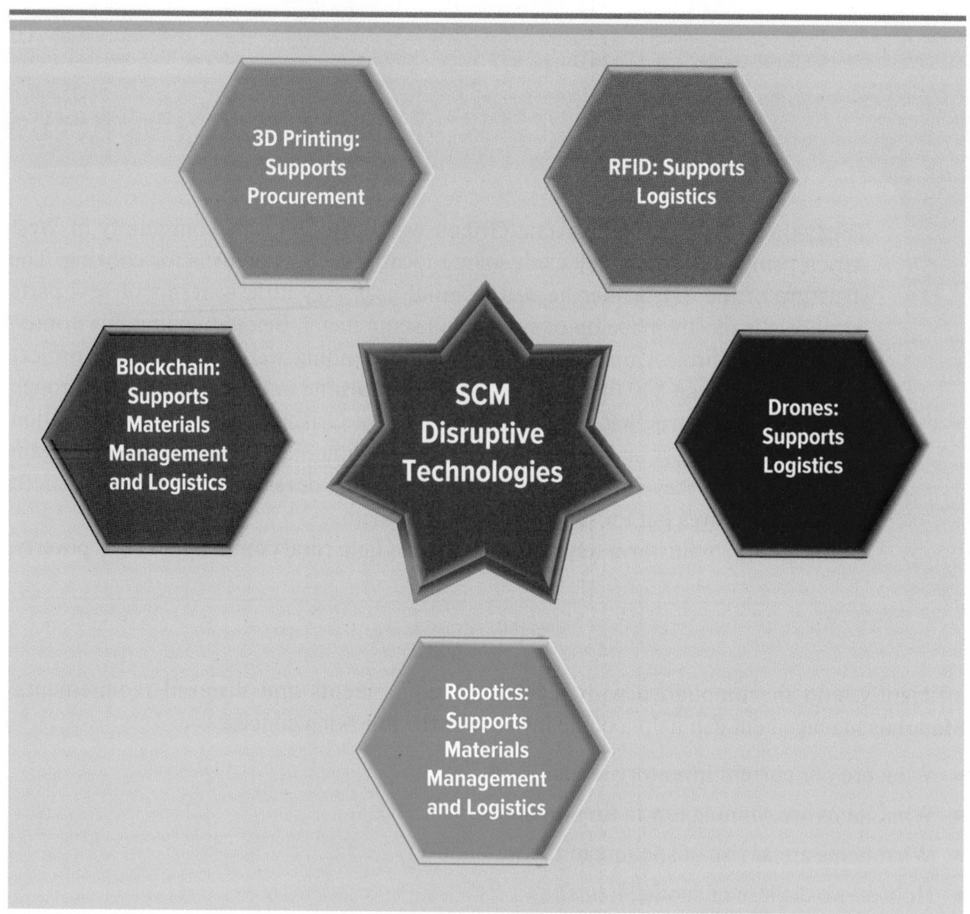

components required for the production process. There is no doubt about it: 3D printing will affect the production process and supply chains and cause business disruption.[6]

To print a 3D product, users create a digital model that is sliced into thin cross-sections called layers. During the printing process, the 3D printer starts at the bottom of the design and adds successive layers of material to complete the project. The two primary methods used in 3D printing include:

1. ***Computer-aided design (CAD)***: Software used by architects, engineers, drafters, artists, and others to create precision drawings or technical illustrations. CAD software can be used to create two-dimensional (2-D) drawings or three-dimensional (3-D) models. Depending on your software, your CAD file may be as simple as a raster image showing a picture you want to cut with a laser, or as complex as a 3-D model with multiple materials and parameters for assembly.
2. ***Computer-aided manufacturing (CAM)***: Uses software and machinery to facilitate and automate manufacturing processes. CAM is often used in tandem with computer-aided design. CAM software figures out the exact sequence of movements, cuts, and other operations required to produce the shape contained in your CAD file. CAM can also implement advanced productivity tools such as simulation and optimization. In addition to materials requirements, modern CAM systems include real-time controls and robotics.

For example, a user creates a design with a CAD application and then manufactures the product by using CAM systems. Before 3D printers existed, creating a prototype was time-consuming and expensive, requiring skilled workers and specific machinery. Instead of sending modeling instructions to a production company, advances in 3D printing allow users to create prototypes and products on demand from their desks. Shipping required parts from around the world could become obsolete because the spare parts can now be 3D printed on demand.

In the future, expect to see 4D printing transforming the supply chain.

- ***4D printing***: Additive manufacturing that prints objects capable of transformation and self-assembly.

When using 3D printing, a product is printed and then manually assembled. With the invention of 4D printing, a product will be printed and then be capable of changing form or self-assembling with minimal human interaction. The business benefits of 4D printing will include assemble-at-home products that will greatly reduce transportation costs. This could have a major impact on how businesses large and small operate and interact on a global scale in the future.

- ***Maker movement***: A cultural trend that places value on an individual's ability to be a creator of things, as well as a consumer of things.
- ***Makerspace***: Community centers that provide technology, manufacturing equipment, and educational opportunities to the public that would otherwise be inaccessible or unaffordable.

In this culture, individuals who create things are called "makers." The movement is growing rapidly and is expected to be economically disruptive; as ordinary people become more self-sufficient, they will be able to make their own products instead of procuring brand-name products from retail stores. Makers come from all walks of life, with diverse skill sets and interests. What they have in common is creativity, an interest in design, and access to tools and raw materials that make production possible.

RFID Supports Logistics

A television commercial shows a man in a uniform quietly moving through a family home. The man replaces the empty cereal box with a full one just before a hungry child opens the cabinet; he then opens a new sack of dog food as the hungry bulldog eyes him warily; and finally, he hands a full bottle of shampoo to the man in the shower whose bottle had just run out. The next wave in supply chain management will be home-based supply chain fulfillment. Walgreens is differentiating itself from other national chains by marketing itself as the family's just-in-time supplier. Consumers today are becoming incredibly comfortable with the idea of going online to purchase products when they want, how they want, and at the price they want. Walgreens is developing custom websites for each household that allow families to order electronically and then at their convenience go to the store to pick up their goods at a special self-service counter or the drive-through window. Walgreens is making a promise that goes beyond low prices and customer service and extends right into the home.

- ***Radio-frequency identification (RFID)***: Uses electronic tags and labels to identify objects wirelessly over short distances.

It holds the promise of replacing existing identification technologies such as the bar code. RFID tags are evolving, too, and the advances will provide more granular information to enterprise software. RFID tags are commonly used in a supply chain to store information about products. MIS systems can read the tags automatically and then process them. Therefore, the logic goes, why not use them for smart contracts in logistics? The possible setup could be as follows: RFID tags for cartons or pallets store information on delivery location and date. Logistics partners run applications to look for these tags and bid for a delivery contract. The partner offering optimal price and service gets the business. A smart contract then tracks status and final delivery performance. Figures 8.12 and 8.13 display how an RFID system works in the supply chain.

Of course, RFID can also be used in conjunction with blockchain technology. Food and pharmaceutical products often have specialized storage needs. Moreover, enterprises see the value in sharing warehouses and distribution centers instead of each one paying for its own. Sensors on sensitive products can record temperature, humidity, vibration, and other environmental conditions. These readings can then be stored on a blockchain. They are permanent and tamper-proof. If a storage condition deviates from what is agreed upon, each member of the blockchain will see it. A smart contract can trigger a response to correct the situation. For instance, depending on the size of the deviation, the action may be to adjust the storage. However, it could also extend to changing "use-by" dates, declaring products unfit, or applying penalties.

Drones Support Logistics

Domino's Pizza used a drone to deliver pizza in a video marketing campaign. Dutch engineer Alec Momont invented a drone that can deliver a defibrillator to heart attack patients. Agriculture drones allow farmers to quickly scout for fertile fields, mapping images of soil nutrients, moisture, and crop health. These advancements not only save time and money, but also prove invaluable for water conservation and low-cost food productivity.

FIGURE 8.12
RFID Components

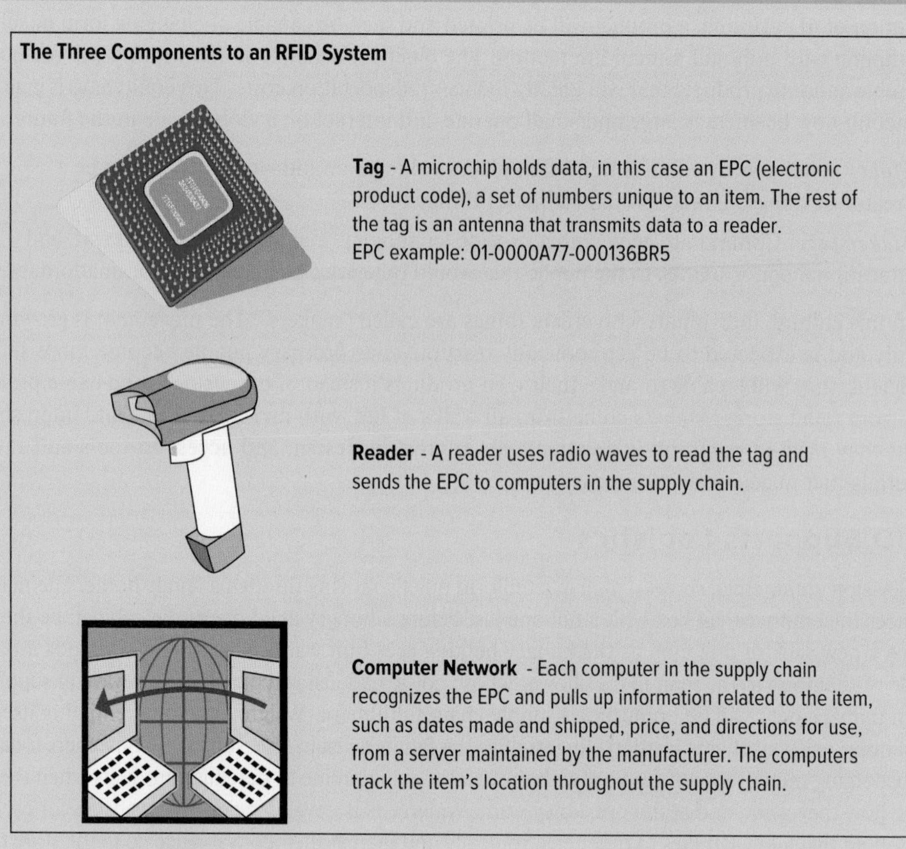

The Three Components to an RFID System
Tag - A microchip holds data, in this case an EPC (electronic product code), a set of numbers unique to an item. The rest of the tag is an antenna that transmits data to a reader.
EPC example: 01-0000A77-000136BR5
Reader - A reader uses radio waves to read the tag and sends the EPC to computers in the supply chain.
Computer Network - Each computer in the supply chain recognizes the EPC and pulls up information related to the item, such as dates made and shipped, price, and directions for use, from a server maintained by the manufacturer. The computers track the item's location throughout the supply chain.

FIGURE 8.13
RFID in the Supply Chain

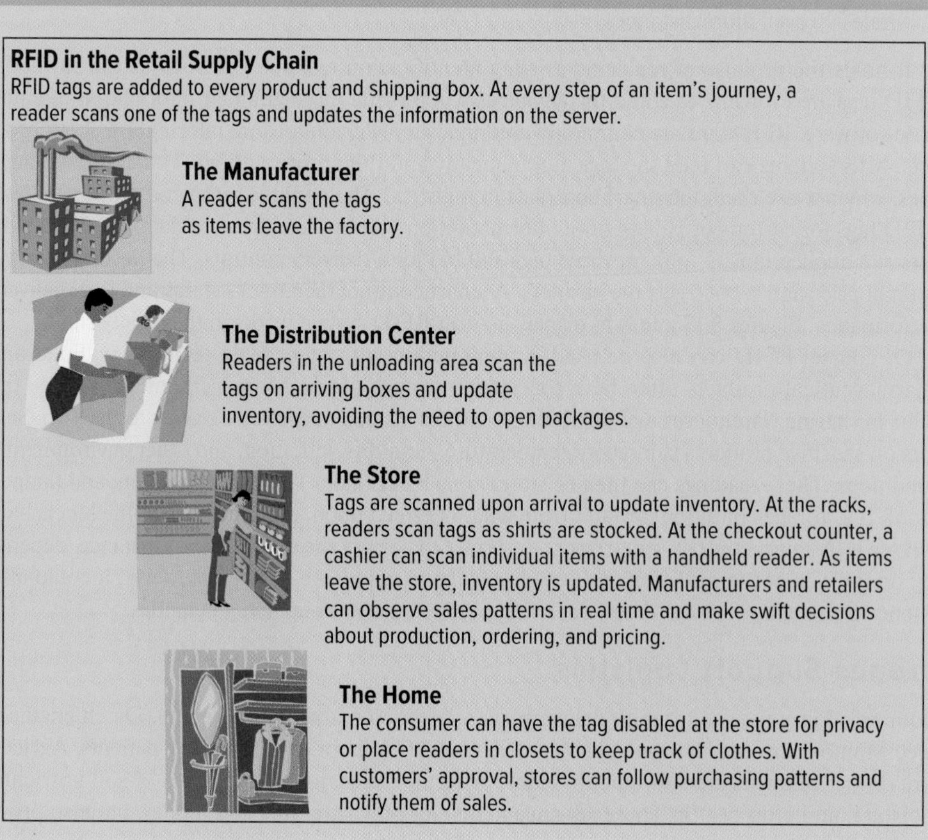

RFID in the Retail Supply Chain
RFID tags are added to every product and shipping box. At every step of an item's journey, a reader scans one of the tags and updates the information on the server.
The Manufacturer
A reader scans the tags as items leave the factory.
The Distribution Center
Readers in the unloading area scan the tags on arriving boxes and update inventory, avoiding the need to open packages.
The Store
Tags are scanned upon arrival to update inventory. At the racks, readers scan tags as shirts are stocked. At the checkout counter, a cashier can scan individual items with a handheld reader. As items leave the store, inventory is updated. Manufacturers and retailers can observe sales patterns in real time and make swift decisions about production, ordering, and pricing.
The Home
The consumer can have the tag disabled at the store for privacy or place readers in closets to keep track of clothes. With customers' approval, stores can follow purchasing patterns and notify them of sales.

FIGURE 8.14

iAmazon Drone Delivering a Package

undefined/Getty Images

- ***Drone***: An unmanned aircraft that can fly autonomously, or without a human.

Drones are primarily used by the military for surveillance or equipped with missiles for precision strikes. Nonmilitary uses for drones include fighting forest fires, law enforcement, traffic control, film-making, and scientific research. Drones operate with three primary capabilities:

- **Sensors:** Drones are able to collect a wealth of information about the world via an array of sensors. Depending on the model, these can include cameras, radar, infrared imaging, lasers, and more.
- **Navigation:** The drone commander sends instructions to the drone through an antenna on the remote, which sends radio waves into space. A GPS satellite captures the radio waves and bounces the instructions to the drone, which is fitted with a receiver antenna.
- **Stabilization:** Drones come in all shapes and sizes and use a horizontal stabilizer with a propeller on the end to stabilize flight. The entire drone body is made of strong yet lightweight materials. Military drones draw power from an engine or solar power, but consumer drones run on batteries.[7]

Amazon.com is piloting drone aircraft for package deliveries. Amazon is now working on small drones that could someday deliver customers' packages in half an hour or less (Figure 8.14). UPS and FedEx have also been experimenting with their own versions of flying parcel carriers. Drones are already here and use GPS to help coordinate the logistics of package delivery. The problems with drones include FAA approval and the advanced ability to detect and avoid objects. GPS coordinates can easily enable the drone to find the appropriate package delivery location, but objects not included in the GPS, such as cars, dogs, and children, will need to be detected and avoided.

Robotics Supports Materials Management

The term *robot* was coined by Czech playwright Karl Capek in his play *R.U.R.* (*Rossum's Universal Robots*), which opened in Prague in 1921. *Robota* is the Czech word for "forced labor."

- ***Robotics***: Focuses on creating artificial intelligence devices that can move and react to sensory input.

The term *robotics* was introduced by writer Isaac Asimov. In his science fiction book *I, Robot,* published in 1950, he presented three laws of robotics:

1. A robot may not injure a human being, or, through inaction, allow a human being to come to harm.
2. A robot must obey the orders given it by human beings except where such orders would conflict with the First Law.
3. A robot must protect its own existence as long as such protection does not conflict with the First or Second Law.[8]

FIGURE 8.15

Kiva Robot

Beth Hall/Bloomberg via Getty Images

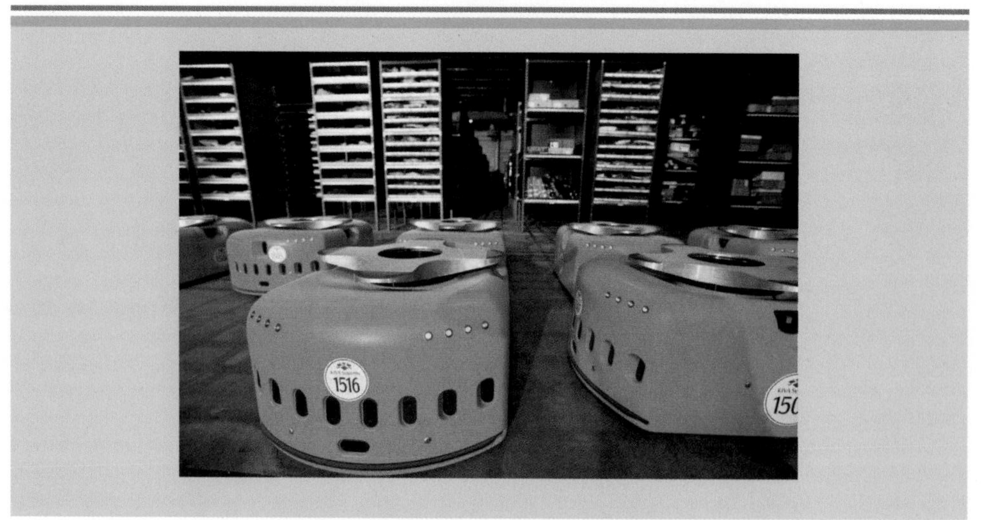

You can find robots in factories performing high-precision tasks, in homes vacuuming the floor and the pool, and in dangerous situations such as cleaning toxic wastes or defusing bombs. Amazon alone has more than 10,000 robots in its warehouses, picking, packing, and managing materials to fulfill customer orders (Figure 8.15).

The robots are made by Kiva Systems, a company Amazon bought for $775 million. Kiva pitches its robots–which can cost between a few million dollars and as much as roughly $20 million–as simplifying and reducing costs via materials management. The robots are tied into a complex grid that optimizes item placement in the warehouse and allows the robots to pick the inventory items and bring them to the workers for packing. Watching an order fulfillment center equipped with Kiva robots is amazing; the operators stand still while the products come to them. Inventory pods store the products that are carried and transferred by a small army of little orange robots, eliminating the need for traditional systems such as conveyors and sorters. Though assessing the costs and benefits of robots versus human labor can be difficult, Kiva boasts that a packer working with its robots can fulfill three to four times as many orders per hour. Zappos, Staples, and Amazon are just a few of the companies taking advantage of the latest innovation in warehouse management by replacing traditional order fulfillment technologies such as conveyor belts with Kiva's little orange robots.[9]

- ***Raspberry Pi***: A low cost, credit card-sized computer that plugs into a computer monitor or TV and uses a standard keyboard and mouse.

Raspberry Pi is a capable little device that enables people of all ages to explore computing and to learn how to program in languages such as Scratch and Python. It is capable of doing everything you would expect a desktop computer to do, from browsing the Internet and playing high-definition video, to making spreadsheets, doing word processing, and playing games.

What's more, Raspberry Pi has the ability to interact with the outside world and has been used in a wide array of digital maker projects, from music machines and parent detectors to weather stations and tweeting birdhouses with infrared cameras. We want to see Raspberry Pi being used by kids all over the world, so they can learn to program and understand how computers work.

For robotics enthusiasts everywhere, the invention of cheap, power-efficient microcontrollers like Raspberry Pi is a true blessing. With a microcontroller and some basic coding skills, an individual can make anything from a blinking LED flashlight to Twitter-enabled kitchen appliances. The following are the features included with a microcontroller:

- **Read and write:** Most microcontrollers marketed to hobbyists feature rewriteable and erasable memory, but not all. Make sure your choice is best suited to your project.
- **Expansion:** If your project is a complex one, you might choose a microcontroller with lots of memory and/or expansion ports for external memory.
- **Ease of use:** If you are a new hobbyist or experienced, you can pick a microcontroller that has a large board with widely spaced pins for easy manipulation and that employs a familiar programming language.[10]

BUSINESS DRIVEN ETHICS AND SECURITY

Can I Print a Weapon?

On May 6, 2013, Defense Distributed, an online open source sharing company, made files for the world's first 3D printable gun available to the public. The U.S. Department of Defense demanded that the files be removed two days later, but not before they had been downloaded more than 100,000 times.

Just think of cars, knives, guns, and computers: They are all used to break the law, and nobody would be allowed to produce them if they were held responsible for how people used them. Do you agree that if you make a tool and sell it to someone who goes on to break the law, you should be held responsible? Do you agree that 3D printers will be used to infringe on copyright, trademark, and patent protections? If so, should 3D printers be illegal?

Blockchain Revamping the Supply Chain

The SCM industry is a prime target for advanced applications of blockchain technology able to reduce costs and inefficiencies. In fact, the sector represents billions of dollars in enterprise revenue but is fraught with losses and inefficiencies resulting from risk, fraud, and manual paperwork delays. Global supply chains are open to the risk of counterfeiting with unscrupulous operators failing to report, or wrongly reporting, the exact provenance of their products, their subcontractors, or the details of their quality-control processes. Quality control in the supply chain is critical for industries such as food, pharmaceuticals, cosmetics, and even toys from which infants might ingest toxic materials.

As an incorruptible digital ledger, blockchain could effectively store records for every product. It would add to its record every time a product changed hands, storing data such as who purchased it and for how much. Imagine a permanent history for every single product that would follow it from when it was made to when it was packed, shipped, displayed, and sold. Still, private blockchains can achieve only so much, and most of the value from blockchain technology comes from the fact that it can tie together different ledgers and data points to provide one centralized bank of information.

Deploying blockchain technology to the supply chain industry boasts the same productivity increase that is comparable to the change from handwritten paperwork to electronic databases. Paperless trade will digitize and automate paperwork.

- ***Supply chain visibility***: The ability to view all areas up and down the supply chain in real time.

A shipping information pipeline will provide end-to-end supply chain visibility and enable everyone involved in managing a supply chain to securely and seamlessly exchange information in real time.

- ***Electronic data interchange (EDI)***: A standard format for the electronic exchange of information between supply chain participants.

Blockchain infrastructures can save the global shipping industry billions of dollars a year by replacing the current EDI- and paper-based system, which can leave containers in receiving yards for weeks. The advantages include identifying new ways to reduce delays and remove human error, saving both time and resources. Blockchain can record the transfer of assets, as well as track receipts, purchase orders, and other associated paperwork. It could also store other identifying data such as whether packages need to be handled with care or whether fresh produce is organic or not. The data could also be shared throughout the company, enabling different departments to work more closely together toward a common goal. It could fundamentally change the way you work. Figure 8.16 displays the benefits of blockchain for the supply chain.

FIGURE 8.16

Blockchain and Supply Chain Benefits

FRAUD AND COUNTERFEITS	• Blockchain fights fraud and other issues with its immutable record and trust people can have in it. If anything changes in a document, it's immediately apparent to all.
IMMUTABILITY	• No entity can tamper with an entry in the distributed ledger. It is not possible to erase a Bitcoin transaction. Only a new transaction can reverse the effect of a previous one. Similarly, with blockchain, it would not be possible to falsify a supply chain payment transaction or the records of inventory, warehousing conditions, delivery times and dates, and so on.
INTEROPERABILITY	• Blockchain data has far greater interoperability. Companies can easily share information with manufacturers, deliverers, suppliers, and vendors. This increased transparency can help to reduce delays and disputes, and it can also prevent shipments from getting stuck in the middle of nowhere. It is difficult to lose something when it is being tracked in real time.
PROVENANCE	• The entities in the chain know where each asset originated. They also know who owned it before and at what time. For Bitcoin, the asset is money. For a supply chain, assets can be anything from iron ore and wheat to cash, machines, and copyrights.
RECALLS	• IBM offered this scenario: What happens if a part has a flaw that requires a recall? The status quo is deeply inefficient. Blockchain provides an alternative. Contingencies could be codified into smart contracts. So, for instance, if the supplier discovers a fault, the provisions of the contract are triggered, and stakeholders are immediately notified once a permanent record of the flaw is recorded on the blockchain.
SCALABILITY	• Blockchain offers an almost unlimited database that can be accessed from multiple touch points around the world.
SECURITY	• Blockchain provides a higher standard of security and the ability to be customized to feed more specialized applications. Businesses can even create private blockchains to keep data internal and to share it only with those who are explicitly given permission. Private or "permissioned" blockchains can be created within a company's four walls or between trusted partners and centrally administered while retaining control over who has access to information on the network.
SMART CONTRACTS	• Supply chains are complicated. It takes days to make a payment between a manufacturer and a supplier, or a customer and a vendor. Contractual agreements require the services of lawyers and bankers, each of which adds extra cost and delay. Products and parts are often hard to trace back to suppliers, making defects challenging to eliminate.
TRACEABILITY	• Blockchain technology can help provide traceability across the supply chain. The technology also allows manufacturers, shippers, and customers to aggregate data, analyze trends, and perform predictive monitoring. Global retailer Walmart uses blockchain to track sales of pork in China. Its system lets the company see where each piece of meat comes from, each processing and storage step in the supply chain, and the products' sell-by date. In the event of a product recall, the company can also see which batches are affected and who bought them.

In-depth transformation of supply chains will not happen overnight. However, supply chains can already start using blockchain in some areas of their operations. Smart contracts can help eliminate costly delays and waste generated by manual handling of paperwork. From there, new doors may open to faster, more intelligent, and more secure processes throughout the entire supply chain.

section 8.2 | Customer Relationship Management and Enterprise Resource Planning

LEARNING OUTCOMES

8.4 Explain operational and analytical customer relationship management.

8.5 Identify the core and extended areas of enterprise resource planning.

8.6 Discuss the current technologies organizations are integrating in enterprise resource planning systems.

CUSTOMER RELATIONSHIP MANAGEMENT

LO 8.4: Explain operational and analytical customer relationship management.

Today, most competitors are simply a mouse click away. This intense marketplace has forced organizations to switch from being sales focused to being customer focused.

- ***Customer relationship management (CRM)***: Involves managing all aspects of a customer's relationship with an organization to increase customer loyalty and retention and an organization's profitability.

CRM allows an organization to gain insights into customers' shopping and buying behaviors in order to develop and implement enterprisewide strategies. The key players in CRM initiatives are outlined in Figure 8.17. CRM strategic goals include:

- **Find new profitable customers:** CRM can highlight that the most profitable market segment consists of women between 35 and 45 years old who drive SUVs and live within 30 miles of the city limits. The firm could then find a way to locate these customers for mailings and other opportunities.
- **Exceed current customer expectations:** CRM helps a firm move past the typical "Dear Mr. Smith" greeting by personalizing communications. For example, if the firm knows the customer's favorite brand and size of shoe, it can notify the customer that a pair of size 12 Nike cross trainers is available for him to try on the next time he visits the store.
- **Eliminate competition:** CRM can determine sales trends, enabling the company to provide customers with special deals and outsmarting its competition. A sports store might identify its best customers for outdoor apparel and invite them to a private sale right before the competition runs its sale.

The complicated piece of the CRM puzzle is identifying customers and the many communication channels they use to contact companies, including call centers, web access, email, sales representatives, and cell phones. CRM systems track every communication between the customer and the organization and provide access to cohesive customer information for all business areas from accounting to order fulfillment. Understanding all customer communications allows the organization to communicate effectively with each customer. It gives the organization a detailed understanding of each customer's products and services record regardless of the customer's preferred communication channel. For example, a customer service representative can easily view detailed account information and history through a CRM system when providing information to a customer such as expected delivery dates, complementary product information, and customer payment and billing information.

A single customer may access an organization multiple times through many different channels (see Figure 8.18). CRM systems can help to collect all of the points of customer contact, along with sales and financial information, to provide a complete view of each customer (see Figure 8.19.)

FIGURE 8.17

Customer Relationship Management Key Players

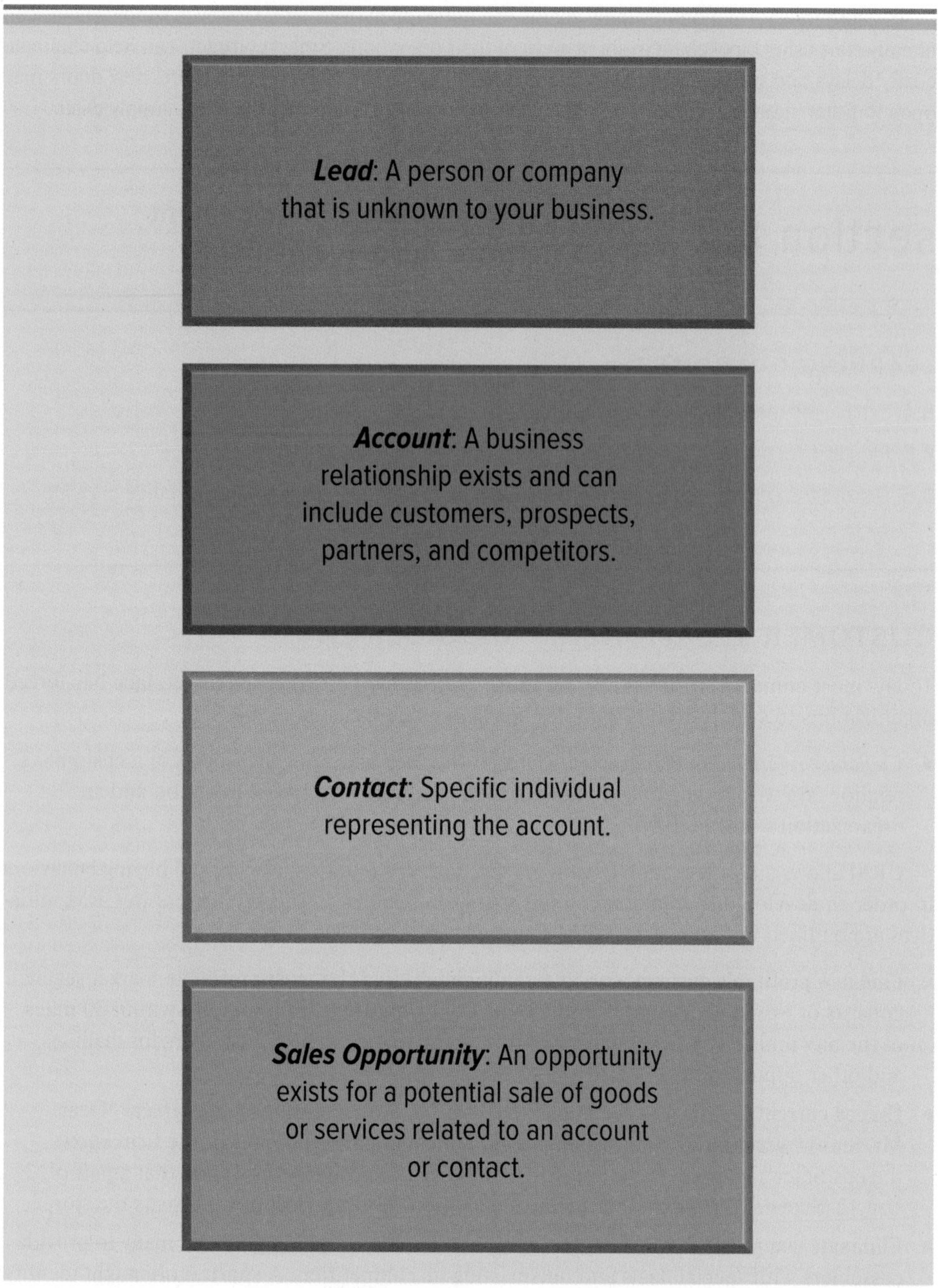

Lead: A person or company that is unknown to your business.
Account: A business relationship exists and can include customers, prospects, partners, and competitors.
Contact: Specific individual representing the account.
Sales Opportunity: An opportunity exists for a potential sale of goods or services related to an account or contact.

Companies that understand individual customer needs are best positioned to achieve success. Of course, building successful customer relationships is not a new business practice; however, implementing CRM systems allows a company to operate more efficiently and effectively in the area of supporting customer needs. CRM moves far beyond technology by identifying customer needs and designing specific marketing campaigns tailored to each. This enables a firm to treat customers as individuals, gaining important insights into their buying preferences and shopping behaviors. Firms that treat their customers well reap the rewards and generally see higher profits and highly loyal customers.

Identifying the most valuable customers allows a firm to ensure that these customers receive the highest levels of customer service and are offered the first opportunity to purchase new products.

- ***Customer analytics***: Involves gathering, classifying, comparing, and studying customer data to identify buying trends, at-risk customers, and potential future opportunities.
- ***Sales analytics***: Involves gathering, classifying, comparing, and studying company sales data to analyze product cycles, sales pipelines, and competitive intelligence.

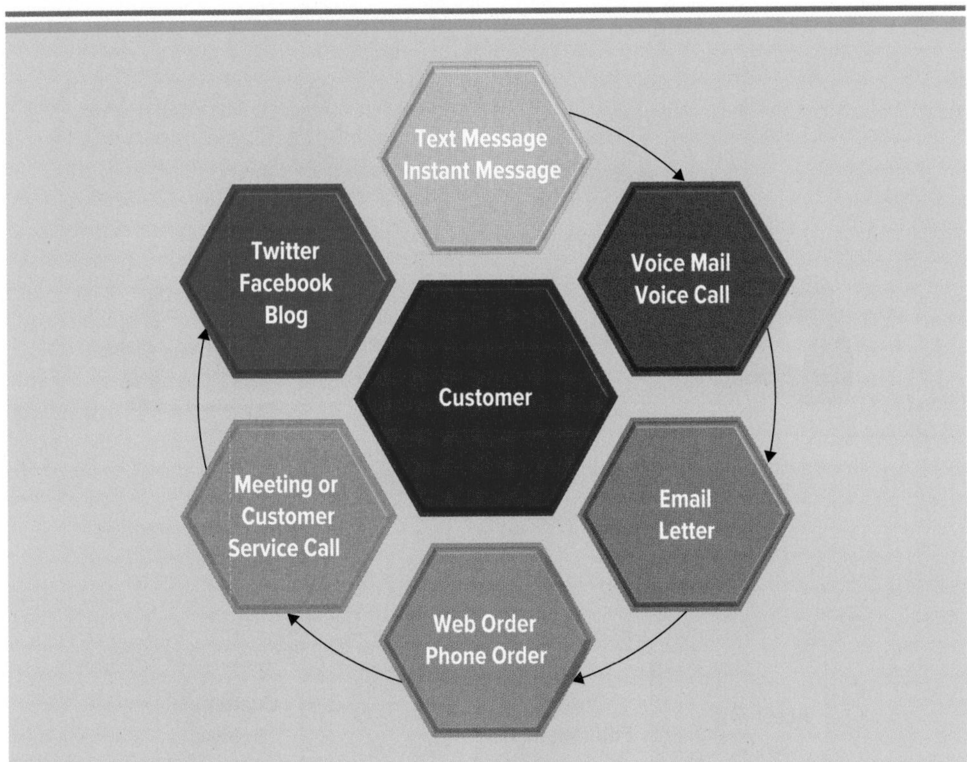

FIGURE 8.18

Customer Contact Points

- ***Uplift modeling***: A form of predictive analytics for marketing campaigns that attempts to identify target markets or people who could be convinced to buy products. The "uplift" refers to the increased sales that can follow after this form of CRM analysis.

Software with advanced analytics capabilities helps you attract and retain loyal and profitable customers and gives you the insight you need to increase revenues, customer satisfaction, and customer loyalty. CRM analytics can help a company identify their most valuable customers for uplift modeling by using the RFM formula–recency, frequency, and monetary value. In other words, an organization must track:

- How *recently* a customer purchased items.
- How *frequently* a customer purchases items.
- The *monetary value* of each customer purchase.

After gathering this initial CRM information, the firm can analyze it to identify patterns and create marketing campaigns and sales promotions for different customer segments. For example, if a customer buys only at the height of the season, the firm should send a special offer during the off-season. If a certain customer segment purchases shoes but never accessories, the firm can offer discounted accessories with the purchase of a new pair of shoes. If the firm determines that its top 20 percent of customers are responsible for 80 percent of the revenue, it can focus on ensuring that these customers are always satisfied and receive the highest levels of customer service.

Evolution of CRM

There are three phases in the evolution of CRM:

1. Reporting: ***CRM reporting technologies*** help organizations identify their customers across other applications.
2. Analyzing: ***CRM analysis technologies*** help organizations segment their customers into categories such as best and worst customers.
3. Predicting: ***CRM predicting technologies*** help organizations predict customer behavior, such as which customers are at risk of leaving. Figure 8.20 highlights a few of the important questions an organization can answer in these areas by using CRM technologies.

FIGURE 8.19

Customer Relationship Management Overview

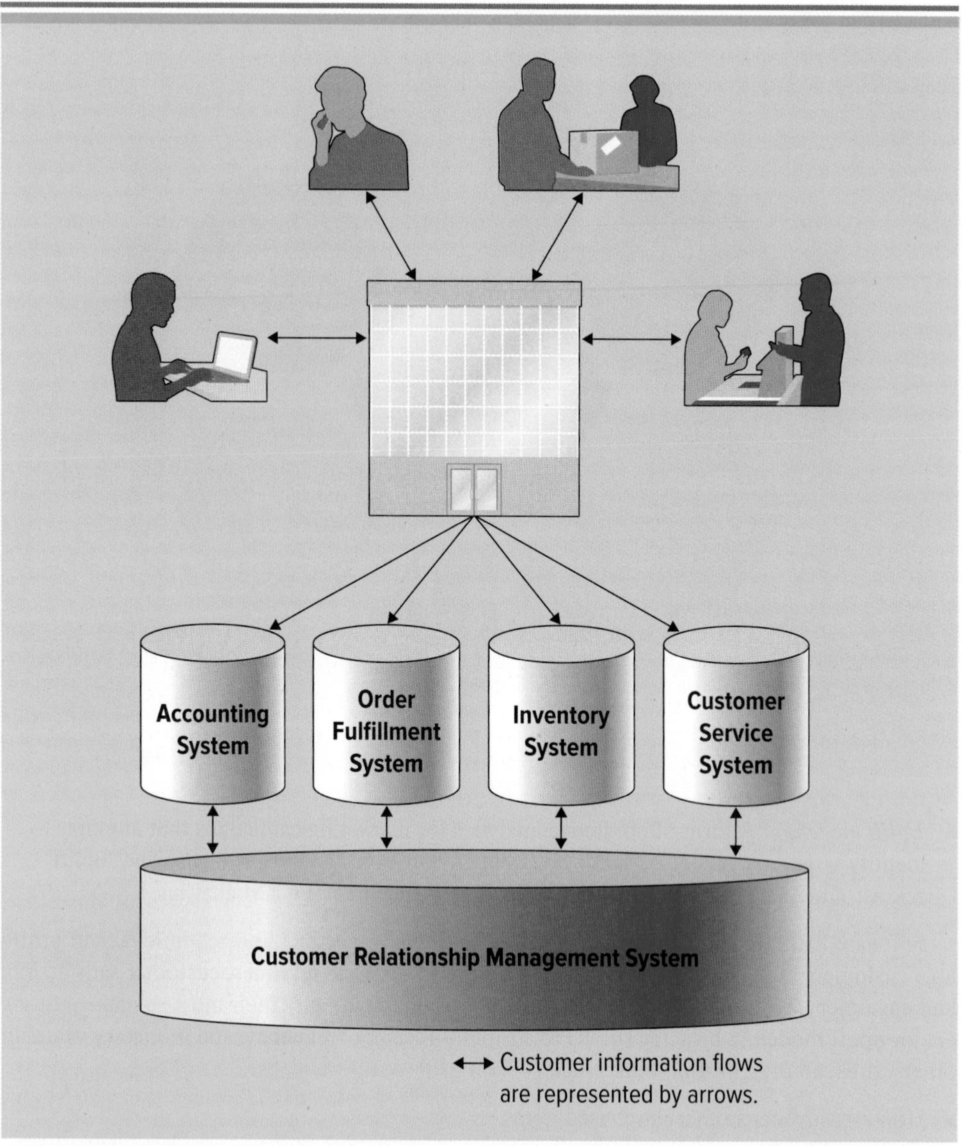

FIGURE 8.20

Evolution of CRM

REPORTING Customer Identification: Asking What Happened	**ANALYZING** Customer Segmentation: Asking Why It Happened	**PREDICTING** Customer Prediction: Asking What Will Happen
• What is the total revenue by customer? • How many units did we make? • What were total sales by product? • How many customers do we have? • What are the current inventory levels?	• Why did sales not meet forecasts? • Why was production so low? • Why did we not sell as many units as previous years? • Who are our customers? • Why was revenue so high? • Why are inventory levels low?	• What customers are at risk of leaving? • Which products will our customers buy? • Who are the best customers for a marketing campaign? • How do we reach our customers? • What will sales be this year? • How much inventory do we need to preorder?

BUSINESS DRIVEN DEBATE

AI Is My Co-worker

No worries! That answer is from a chatbot, an artificial intelligence (AI) program that simulates interactive human conversation by using key precalculated user phrases and auditory or text-based signals. Here are a few common replies from chatbots:

Your co-worker wants to reschedule a meeting? Chatbot answer: Sure thing! At a new time? That works! If you have opted into Gmail's Smart Replies, these exchanges should look familiar. Gmail's Smart Compose is Smart Reply's show-off cousin. It actually completes phrases for you as you are typing an email, and it is uncannily good at predicting what you intend to say next.

Microsoft is also integrating AI into its suite of productivity tools. Word now knows when you are making a to-do list and tracks those items as to-do items. PowerPoint uses computer vision and machine learning to color-match your slides with the hues in imported photos. And Excel allows you to snap a photo of a data table and import it directly and have a fully edited table.[11]

Explain the importance of customer service for customer relationship management. Do you agree that a company can improve customer service by using AI? What do chats and emails look like when we are all exchanging the same AI-created messages? If AI creates documents, will all our documents start looking the same? Or do you believe by allowing AI to handle the mundane tasks, people will have more time to be creative?

The Power of the Customer

A standard rule of business states that the customer is always right. Although most businesses use this as their motto, they do not actually mean it. Ebusiness firms, however, must adhere to this rule as the power of the customer grows exponentially in the information age. Various websites and videos on YouTube reveal the power of the individual consumer (see Figure 8.21). A decade ago if you had a complaint against a company, you could make a phone call or write a letter. Now you can contact hundreds or thousands of people around the globe and voice your complaint or anger with a company or product. You—the customer—can now take your power directly to millions of people, and companies have to listen.

Measuring CRM Success

Using CRM metrics to track and monitor performance is a best practice for many companies. Figure 8.22 displays a few common CRM metrics a manager can use to track the success of the system. Just remember that you only want to track between five and seven of the hundreds of CRM metrics available.

OPERATIONAL AND ANALYTICAL CRM

The two primary components of a CRM strategy are operational CRM and analytical CRM.

- ***Operational CRM***: Supports traditional transactional processing for day-to-day front-office operations or systems that deal directly with the customers.
- ***Analytical CRM***: Supports back-office operations and strategic analysis and includes all systems that do not deal directly with the customers.

Figure 8.23 provides an overview of the two. Figure 8.24 shows the different technologies marketing, sales, and customer service departments can use to perform operational CRM.

FIGURE 8.21

The Power of the Customer

(Top): www.dontbuydodgechrysler vehicles.com;
(bottom): www.jetbluehostage.com

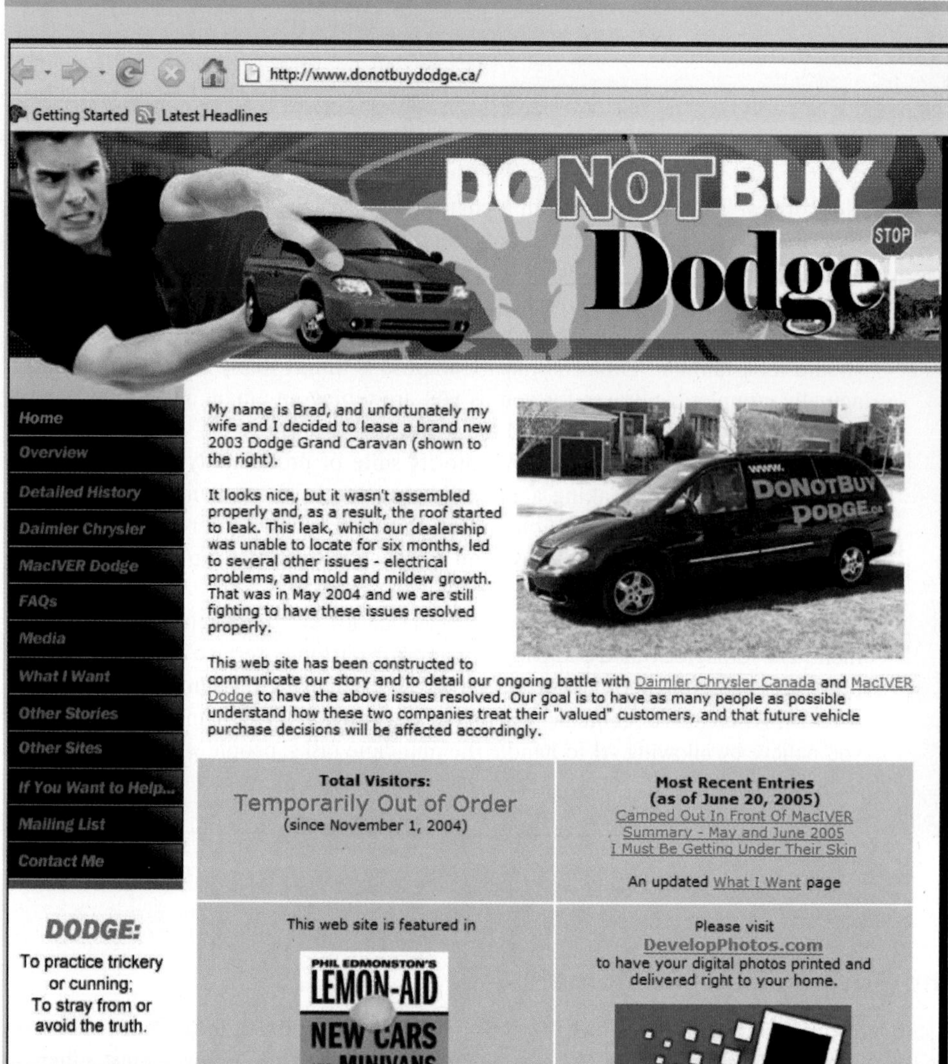

Sales Metrics	Customer Service Metrics	Marketing Metrics
Number of prospective customers	Cases closed same day	Number of marketing campaigns
Number of new customers	Number of cases handled by agent	New customer retention rates
Number of retained customers	Number of service calls	Number of responses by marketing campaign
Number of open leads	Average number of service requests by type	Number of purchases by marketing campaign
Number of sales calls	Average time to resolution	Revenue generated by marketing campaign
Number of sales calls per lead	Average number of service calls per day	Cost per interaction by marketing campaign
Amount of new revenue	Percentage compliance with service-level agreement	Number of new customers acquired by marketing campaign
Amount of recurring revenue	Percentage of service renewals	Customer retention rate
Number of proposals given	Customer satisfaction level	Number of new leads by product

FIGURE 8.22

CRM Metrics

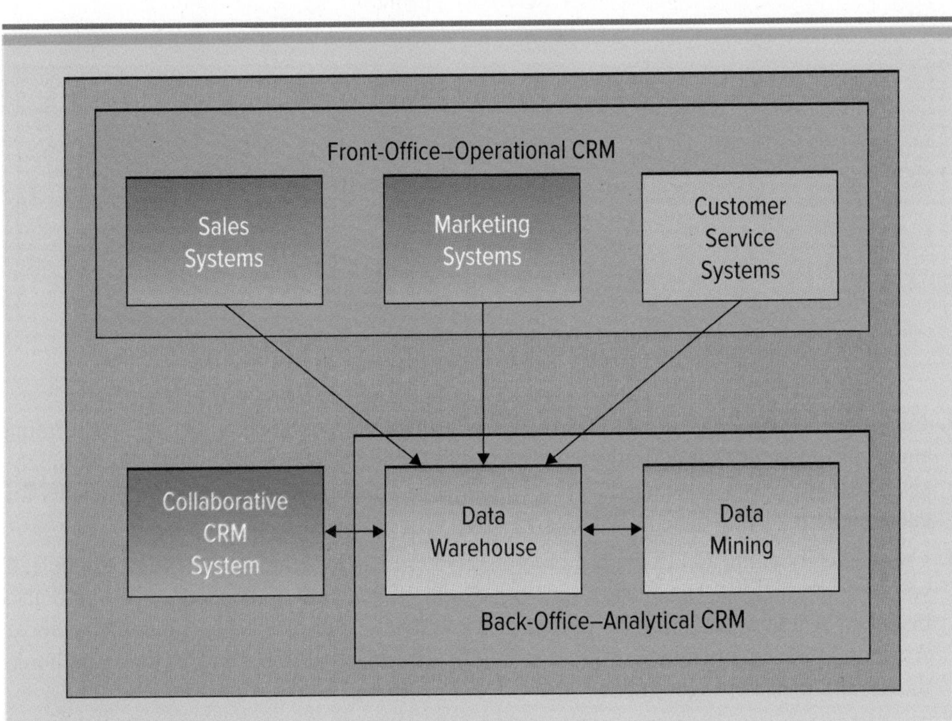

FIGURE 8.23

Operational CRM and Analytical CRM

Marketing and Operational CRM

Companies are no longer trying to sell one product to as many customers as possible; instead, they are trying to sell one customer as many products as possible. Marketing departments switch to this new way of doing business by using CRM technologies that allow them to gather and analyze customer information to tailor successful marketing campaigns. In fact, a marketing campaign's success is directly proportional to the organization's ability to gather and analyze the right customer information. The four primary operational CRM technologies a marketing department can implement to increase customer satisfaction are:

1. ***List generators***: Compile customer information from a variety of sources and segment it for different marketing campaigns. These sources include website visits, questionnaires, surveys, marketing mailers, and so on. After being compiled, the customer list can be filtered based on criteria such as household income, gender, education level, political affiliation, age, or other factors. List generators provide the marketing department with valuable information on the type of customer it must target to find success for a marketing campaign.

FIGURE 8.24

Operational CRM Technologies

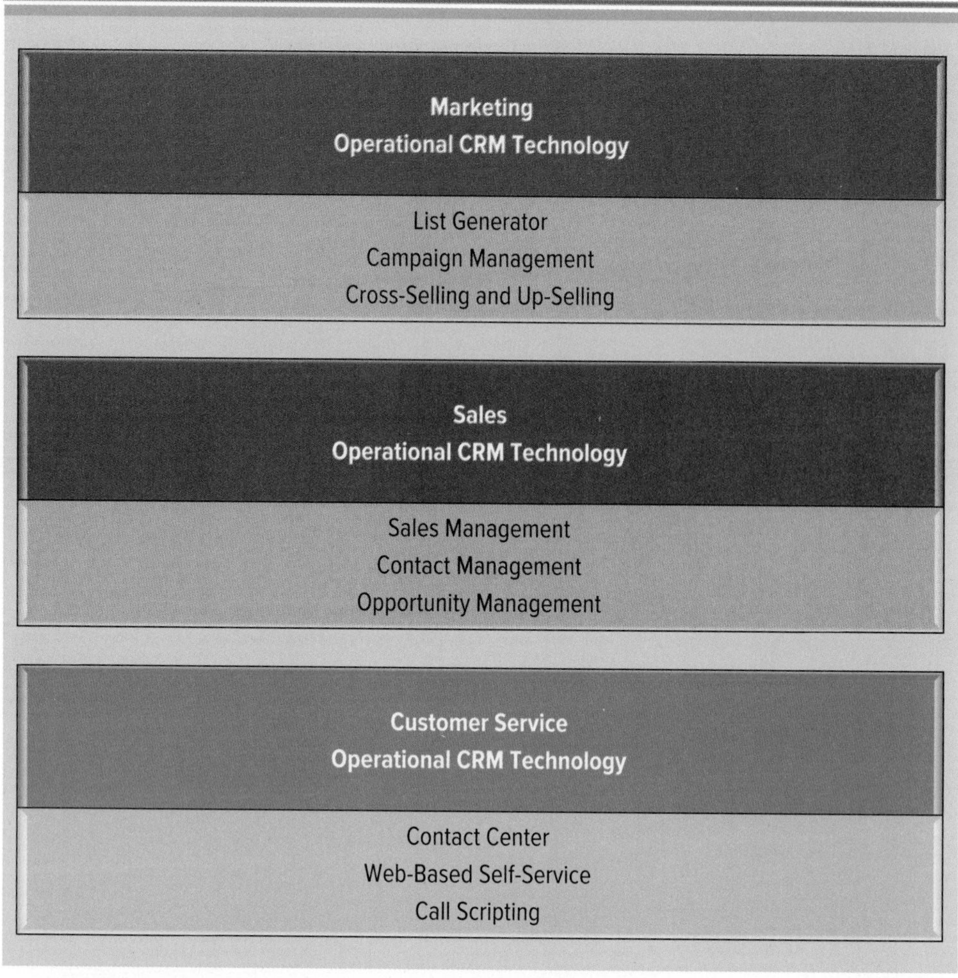

2. ***Campaign management systems***: Guide users through marketing campaigns by performing such tasks as campaign definition, planning, scheduling, segmentation, and success analysis. These advanced systems can even calculate the profitability and track the results for each marketing campaign.
3. ***Cross-selling***: Selling additional products or services to an existing customer. For example, if you were to purchase Tim Burton's movie *Alice in Wonderland* on Amazon, you would also be asked whether you want to purchase the movie's soundtrack or the original book. Amazon is taking advantage of cross-selling by offering customers goods across its book, movie, and music product lines.
4. ***Up-selling***: Increasing the value of the sale. McDonald's performs up-selling by asking customers whether they would like to supersize their meals for an extra cost. CRM systems offer marketing departments all kinds of information about customers and products, which can help identify up-selling and cross-selling opportunities to increase revenues.

Sales and Operational CRM

Sales departments were the first to begin developing CRM systems. They had two primary motivations to track customer sales information electronically. First, sales representatives were struggling with the overwhelming amount of customer account information they were required to maintain and track. Second, managers found themselves hindered because much of their vital customer and sales information remained in the heads of their sales representatives, even if the sales representative left the company. Finding a way to track customer information became a critical success factor for many sales departments.

- ***Customer service and support (CSS)***: A part of operational CRM that automates service requests, complaints, product returns, and information requests.

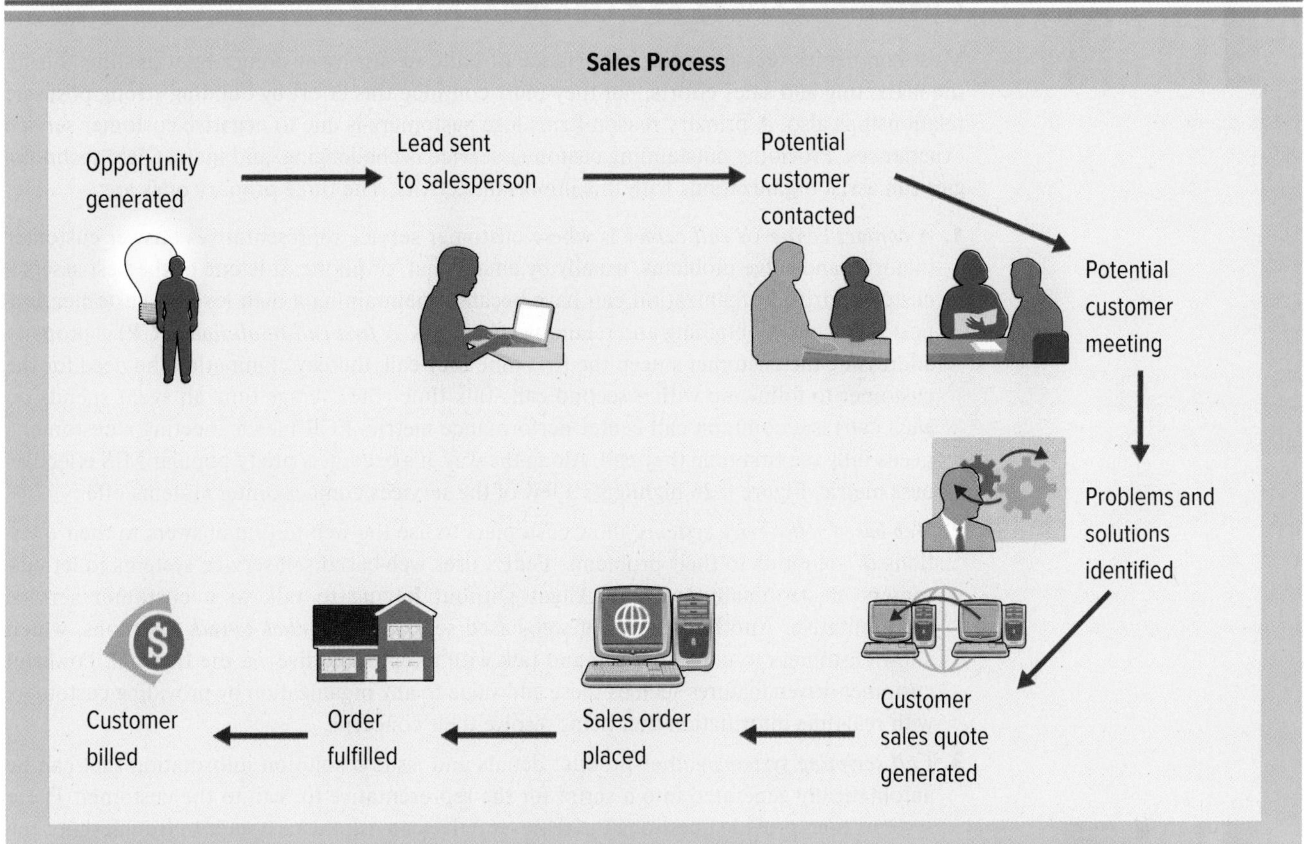

FIGURE 8.25
A Typical Sales Process

Figure 8.25 depicts the typical sales process, which begins with an opportunity and ends with billing the customer for the sale. Leads and potential customers are the lifeblood of all sales organizations, whether they sell computers, clothing, consulting, or cars. How leads are handled can make the difference between revenue growth and decline.

Sales force automation (SFA) automatically tracks all the steps in the sales process. SFA products focus on increasing customer satisfaction, building customer relationships, and improving product sales. The three primary operational CRM technologies a sales department can adopt are:

1. ***Sales management CRM systems*** automate each phase of the sales process, helping individual sales representatives coordinate and organize all their accounts. Features include calendars, reminders for important tasks, multimedia presentations, and document generation. These systems can even provide an analysis of the sales cycle and calculate how each sales representative is performing during the sales process.
2. ***Contact management CRM system*** maintains customer contact information and identifies prospective customers for future sales, using tools such as organizational charts, detailed customer notes, and supplemental sales information. For example, a contact management system can take an incoming telephone number and automatically display the person's name along with a comprehensive history, including all communications with the company. This allows the sales representative to personalize the phone conversation and ask such things as, "How is your new laptop working, Sue?" or "How was your family vacation to Colorado?" The customer feels valued since the sales associate knows her name and even remembers details of their last conversation.
3. ***Opportunity management CRM systems*** target sales opportunities by finding new customers or companies for future sales. They determine potential customers and competitors and define selling efforts, including budgets and schedules. Advanced systems can even calculate the probability of a sale, which can save sales representatives significant time and money when qualifying new customers. The primary difference between contact management and opportunity management is that contact management deals with existing customers and opportunity management with new or potential customers.

Customer Service and Operational CRM

Most companies recognize the importance of building strong customer relationships during the marketing and sales efforts, but they must continue this effort by building strong post-sale relationships also. A primary reason firms lose customers is due to negative customer service experiences. Providing outstanding customer service is challenging, and many CRM technologies can assist organizations with this important activity. The three primary ones are:

1. A ***contact center*** or ***call center*** is where customer service representatives answer customer inquiries and solve problems, usually by email, chat, or phone. It is one of the best assets a customer-driven organization can have because maintaining a high level of customer support is critical to obtaining and retaining customers. A ***first call resolution (FCR)*** is properly addressing the customer's need the first time they call, thereby eliminating the need for the customer to follow up with a second call. Talk time (the average time an agent spends on each call) is a common call center performance metric. FCR means meeting a customer's needs fully the first time they call. Along the way, it's become a pretty popular MIS effectiveness metric. Figure 8.26 highlights a few of the services contact center systems offer.
2. ***Web-based self-service systems*** allow customers to use the web to find answers to their questions or solutions to their problems. FedEx uses web-based self-service systems to let customers electronically track packages without having to talk to a customer service representative. Another feature of web-based self-service is ***click-to-talk*** functions, which allow customers to click a button and talk with a representative via the Internet. Powerful customer-driven features such as these add value to any organization by providing customers with real-time information that helps resolve their concerns.
3. ***Call scripting systems*** gather product details and issue resolution information that can be automatically generated into a script for the representative to read to the customer. These systems even provide questions the representative can ask the customer to troubleshoot the problem and find a resolution. This feature not only helps reps answer difficult questions quickly but also presents a uniform response so customers don't receive different answers.

Analytical CRM

CRM analytics can generate demographic, behavioral, and psychographic insights so that you are aware of the customer's satisfaction with service, price changes, response to marketing offers, etc. Analytical CRM can answer questions such as: Do I know my customers' family and office members? Are they my customers as well? Is social media playing a role in influencing my customers' behaviors? Can I measure the advocacy influence of my loyal customers?

Analytical CRM tools can slice-and-dice vast amounts of information to create custom views of customers, products, and market segments, highlighting opportunities for cross-selling and up-selling.

- ***Customer segmentation***: Divides a market into categories that share similar attributes such as age, location, gender, habits, and so on. By segmenting customers into groups, it becomes easier to create targeted marketing and sales campaigns, ensuring you are not wasting resources marketing products to the wrong customers.

FIGURE 8.26

Contact Center Services

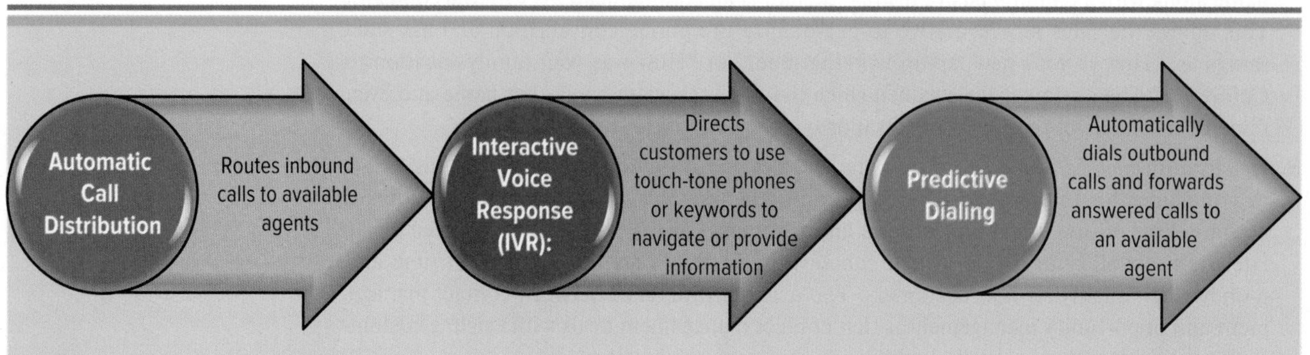

BUSINESS DRIVEN INNOVATION

Nice Emotions

New emotion-detection software called Perform, created by Nice Systems, helps firms improve customer service by identifying callers who are displeased or upset. Perform determines a baseline of emotion and can detect emotional issues during the first few seconds of a call; any variation from the baseline activates an alert. When an elderly person who was highly distressed over medical costs hung up during a phone call to the insurance company, Perform identified the customer's frustration and automatically emailed a supervisor. The supervisor was able to review a recording of the conversation and immediately called the customer back suggesting ways to lower the costs.[12]

How do you think emotion-detection software will affect customer relationships? What other departments or business processes could benefit from its use? Create a new product that uses emotion-detection software. What business problem would your product solve and who would be your primary customers?

Analytical CRM provides information about customers and products that was once impossible to locate, such as which type of marketing and sales campaign to launch and which customers to target and when. Unlike operational CRM, which automates call centers and sales forces with the aim of enhancing customer service, analytical CRM works by using business intelligence to identify patterns in product sales and customer behaviors. Analytical CRM provides priceless customer information, supports important business decisions, and plays a vital role in your organization's success.

- ***Customer profitability (CP)***: Measures the customer's worth over a specific period of time.
- ***Customer lifetime value (CLV)***: A metric that represents the total net profit a company makes from any given customer.

CLV is an important metric for determining how much money a company wants to spend on acquiring new customers and how much repeat business a company can expect from certain consumers. CLV is different from CP in that the metric for CLV predicts the future, whereas the metric for CP measures the past. If you look only at the sales record for a customer, you can incorrectly assume profitability of the relationship. A high-dollar client that is expensive to serve and manage may actually be unprofitable when all is said and tallied. Conversely, a customer that spends less with you but is profitable to serve can often be enticed to spend more without sacrificing your profit margin. Thus, a customer's past buying record does not tell you everything you need to know in determining overall profitability of the customer. Make sure you have an accurate calculation of actual customer value.

Two AI tools helping drive CLV include:

- ***Chatbot***: An artificial intelligence (AI) program that simulates interactive human conversation by using key pre-calculated user phrases and auditory or text-based signals. Chatbots are often used for basic customer service and marketing systems that frequent social networking hubs and instant messaging (IM) clients. They are also often included in operating systems as intelligent virtual assistants.
- ***Intelligent virtual agent***: An animated, humanlike graphical chatbot commonly displayed on website home pages and advertisement landing pages. Virtual agents are embedded with a predefined script and responses. Intelligent virtual agents are designed to provide customer services, product information, marketing, support, sales, order placing, reservations, or other custom services.

APPLY YOUR KNOWLEDGE

BUSINESS DRIVEN START-UP

Chatbot Sales

Over the last few years, we all have seen huge advancements in the field of data science. The standard statistical learning methods and neural networks have revolutionized our online and offline experiences. From chatting with AI bots to tracking pizza delivery, technology has changed everything. It is now common to leverage data to increase sales, target specific markets, and increase customer satisfaction.

Chatbots can even create and manage sales channels. Apart from being able to order stuff through a chatbot, don't you think it would be nice if the bot could manage the sales and marketing for you? Don't be confused; it's simple. I am sure we all have been in situations where we have been shopping online, have added things to our cart, but just did not proceed to the checkout. The bot, in this case, could send you an email reminder saying, "You've got an item in the cart." Not only that, it could give you compelling discounts that will have you reconsider buying the item.[13]

How would it be if you could do this in your business? How would it be if the bot could send a note to up-sell or down-sell a particular product? It could also do some redirect marketing.

LO 8.5: Identify the core and extended areas of enterprise resource planning.

ENTERPRISE RESOURCE PLANNING

Today's business leaders need significant amounts of information to be readily accessible, with real-time views into their businesses, so that decisions can be made when they need to be, without the added time of tracking data and generating reports.

- ***Enterprise resource planning (ERP)***: Integrates all departments and functions throughout an organization into a single MIS system (or integrated set of MIS systems) so employees can make decisions by viewing enterprisewide information about all business operations.

To truly understand the complexity of ERP systems, you must think about the many different functional business areas and their associated business processes, as well as cross-functional business processes such as supply chain management and customer relationship management and beyond. At its most basic level, ERP software integrates these various business functions into one complete system to streamline business processes and information across the entire organization. Essentially, ERP helps employees do their jobs more efficiently by breaking down barriers between business units.

Many organizations fail to maintain consistency across business operations. If a single department, such as sales, decides to implement a new system without considering the other departments, inconsistencies can occur throughout the company. Not all systems are built to talk to each other and share data, and if sales suddenly implements a new system that marketing and accounting cannot use or is inconsistent in the way it handles information, the company's operations become siloed. Figure 8.27 displays sample data from a sales database, and Figure 8.28 displays samples from an accounting database. Notice the differences in data formats, numbers, and identifiers. Correlating this data would be difficult, and the inconsistencies would cause numerous reporting errors from an enterprisewide perspective.

The two key components of an ERP system help to resolve these issues and include a common data repository and modular software design.

- ***Common data repository***: Allows every department of a company to store and retrieve information in real time, making information more reliable and accessible.
- ***Module software design***: Divides the system into a set of functional units (named modules) that can be used independently or combined with other modules for increased business flexibility.

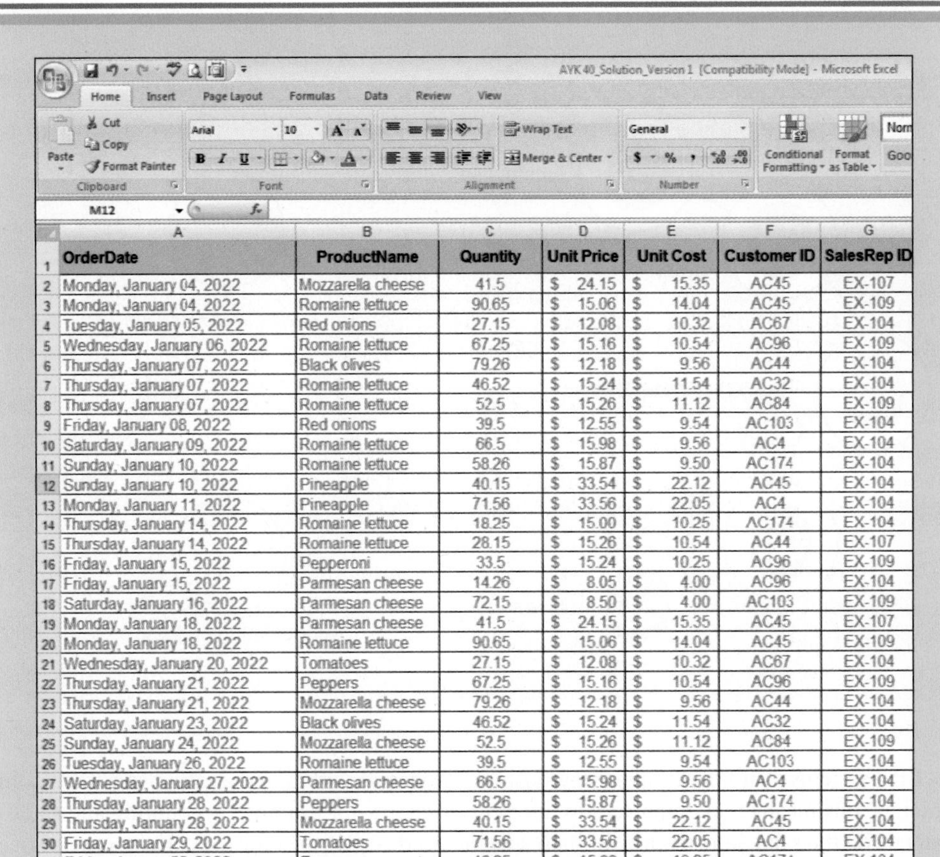

	OrderDate	ProductName	Quantity	Unit Price	Unit Cost	Customer ID	SalesRep ID
2	Monday, January 04, 2022	Mozzarella cheese	41.5	$ 24.15	$ 15.35	AC45	EX-107
3	Monday, January 04, 2022	Romaine lettuce	90.65	$ 15.06	$ 14.04	AC45	EX-109
4	Tuesday, January 05, 2022	Red onions	27.15	$ 12.08	$ 10.32	AC67	EX-104
5	Wednesday, January 06, 2022	Romaine lettuce	67.25	$ 15.16	$ 10.54	AC96	EX-109
6	Thursday, January 07, 2022	Black olives	79.26	$ 12.18	$ 9.56	AC44	EX-104
7	Thursday, January 07, 2022	Romaine lettuce	46.52	$ 15.24	$ 11.54	AC32	EX-104
8	Thursday, January 07, 2022	Romaine lettuce	52.5	$ 15.26	$ 11.12	AC84	EX-109
9	Friday, January 08, 2022	Red onions	39.5	$ 12.55	$ 9.54	AC103	EX-104
10	Saturday, January 09, 2022	Romaine lettuce	66.5	$ 15.98	$ 9.56	AC4	EX-104
11	Sunday, January 10, 2022	Romaine lettuce	58.26	$ 15.87	$ 9.50	AC174	EX-104
12	Sunday, January 10, 2022	Pineapple	40.15	$ 33.54	$ 22.12	AC45	EX-104
13	Monday, January 11, 2022	Pineapple	71.56	$ 33.56	$ 22.05	AC4	EX-104
14	Thursday, January 14, 2022	Romaine lettuce	18.25	$ 15.00	$ 10.25	AC174	EX-104
15	Thursday, January 14, 2022	Romaine lettuce	28.15	$ 15.26	$ 10.54	AC44	EX-107
16	Friday, January 15, 2022	Pepperoni	33.5	$ 15.24	$ 10.25	AC96	EX-109
17	Friday, January 15, 2022	Parmesan cheese	14.26	$ 8.05	$ 4.00	AC96	EX-104
18	Saturday, January 16, 2022	Parmesan cheese	72.15	$ 8.50	$ 4.00	AC103	EX-109
19	Monday, January 18, 2022	Parmesan cheese	41.5	$ 24.15	$ 15.35	AC45	EX-107
20	Monday, January 18, 2022	Romaine lettuce	90.65	$ 15.06	$ 14.04	AC45	EX-109
21	Wednesday, January 20, 2022	Tomatoes	27.15	$ 12.08	$ 10.32	AC67	EX-104
22	Thursday, January 21, 2022	Peppers	67.25	$ 15.16	$ 10.54	AC96	EX-109
23	Thursday, January 21, 2022	Mozzarella cheese	79.26	$ 12.18	$ 9.56	AC44	EX-104
24	Saturday, January 23, 2022	Black olives	46.52	$ 15.24	$ 11.54	AC32	EX-104
25	Sunday, January 24, 2022	Mozzarella cheese	52.5	$ 15.26	$ 11.12	AC84	EX-109
26	Tuesday, January 26, 2022	Romaine lettuce	39.5	$ 12.55	$ 9.54	AC103	EX-104
27	Wednesday, January 27, 2022	Parmesan cheese	66.5	$ 15.98	$ 9.56	AC4	EX-104
28	Thursday, January 28, 2022	Peppers	58.26	$ 15.87	$ 9.50	AC174	EX-104
29	Thursday, January 28, 2022	Mozzarella cheese	40.15	$ 33.54	$ 22.12	AC45	EX-104
30	Friday, January 29, 2022	Tomatoes	71.56	$ 33.56	$ 22.05	AC4	EX-104
31	Friday, January 29, 2022	Peppers	18.25	$ 15.00	$ 10.25	AC174	EX-104

FIGURE 8.27

Sales Information Sample

Microsoft Corporation

	OrderDate	ProductName	Quantity	Unit Price	Total Sales	Unit Cost	Total Cost	Profit	Customer	SalesRep
2	04-Jan-22	Mozzarella cheese	41	24	984	18	738	246	The Station	Debbie Fernandez
3	04-Jan-22	Romaine lettuce	90	15	1,350	14	1,260	90	The Station	Roberta Cross
4	05-Jan-22	Red onions	27	12	324	8	216	108	Bert's Bistro	Loraine Schultz
5	06-Jan-22	Romaine lettuce	67	15	1,005	14	938	67	Smoke House	Roberta Cross
6	07-Jan-22	Black olives	79	12	948	6	474	474	Flagstaff House	Loraine Schultz
7	07-Jan-22	Romaine lettuce	46	15	690	14	644	46	Two Bitts	Loraine Schultz
8	07-Jan-22	Romaine lettuce	52	15	780	14	728	52	Pierce Arrow	Roberta Cross
9	08-Jan-22	Red onions	39	12	468	8	312	156	Mamm'a Pasta Palace	Loraine Schultz
10	09-Jan-22	Romaine lettuce	66	15	990	14	924	66	The Dandelion	Loraine Schultz
11	10-Jan-22	Romaine lettuce	58	15	870	14	812	58	Carmens	Loraine Schultz
12	10-Jan-22	Pineapple	40	33	1,320	28	1,120	200	The Station	Loraine Schultz
13	11-Jan-22	Pineapple	71	33	2,343	28	1,988	355	The Dandelion	Loraine Schultz
14	14-Jan-22	Romaine lettuce	18	15	270	14	252	18	Carmens	Loraine Schultz
15	14-Jan-22	Romaine lettuce	28	15	420	14	392	28	Flagstaff House	Debbie Fernandez
16	15-Jan-22	Pepperoni	33	53	1,749	35	1,155	594	Smoke House	Roberta Cross
17	15-Jan-22	Parmesan cheese	14	8	112	4	56	56	Smoke House	Loraine Schultz
18	16-Jan-22	Parmesan cheese	72	8	576	4	288	288	Mamm'a Pasta Palace	Roberta Cross
19	18-Jan-22	Parmesan cheese	10	8	80	4	40	40	Mamm'a Pasta Palace	Loraine Schultz
20	18-Jan-22	Romaine lettuce	42	15	630	14	588	42	Smoke House	Roberta Cross
21	20-Jan-22	Tomatoes	48	9	432	7	336	96	Two Bitts	Loraine Schultz
22	21-Jan-22	Peppers	29	21	609	12	348	261	The Dandelion	Roberta Cross
23	21-Jan-22	Mozzarella cheese	10	24	240	18	180	60	Mamm'a Pasta Palace	Debbie Fernandez
24	23-Jan-22	Black olives	98	12	1,176	6	588	588	Two Bitts	Roberta Cross
25	24-Jan-22	Mozzarella cheese	45	24	1,080	18	810	270	Carmens	Loraine Schultz
26	26-Jan-22	Romaine lettuce	58	15	870	14	812	58	Two Bitts	Loraine Schultz
27	27-Jan-22	Parmesan cheese	66	8	528	4	264	264	Flagstaff House	Loraine Schultz
28	28-Jan-22	Peppers	85	21	1,785	12	1,020	765	Pierce Arrow	Loraine Schultz
29	28-Jan-22	Mozzarella cheese	12	24	288	18	216	72	The Dandelion	Debbie Fernandez
30	29-Jan-22	Tomatoes	40	9	360	7	280	80	Pierce Arrow	Roberta Cross

FIGURE 8.28

Accounting Information Sample

Microsoft Corporation

Module software design allows customers to mix and match modules so they purchase only the required modules. If a company wants to implement the system slowly, it can begin with just one module, such as accounting, and then incorporate additional modules, such as purchasing and scheduling.

FIGURE 8.29

Enterprise Resource Planning System Overview

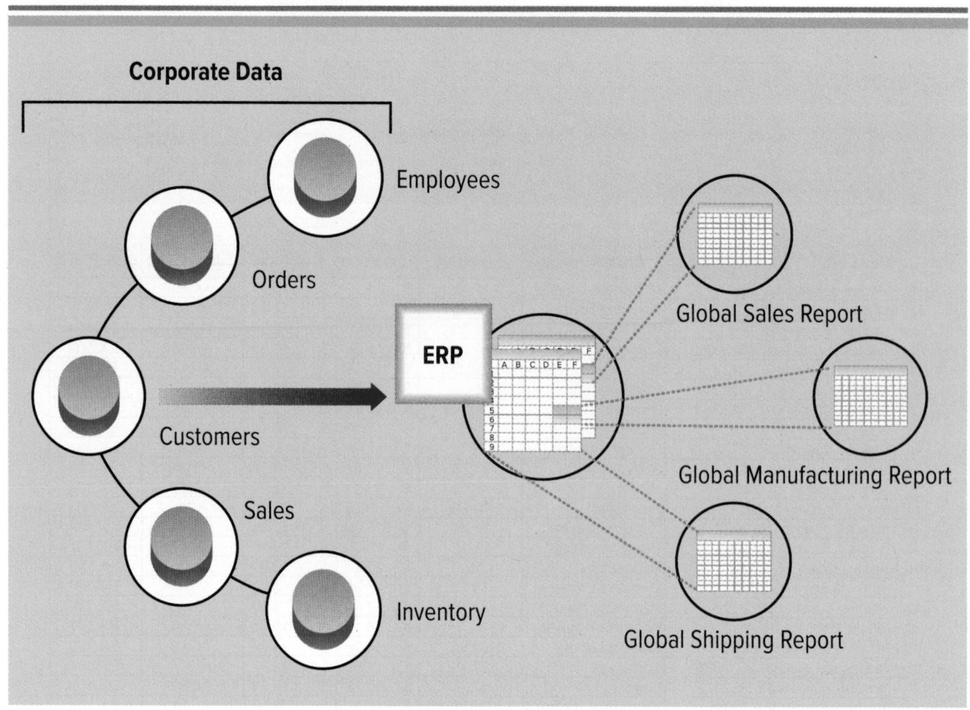

ERP systems share data supporting business processes within and across departments. In practice, this means that employees in different divisions–for example, accounting and sales–can rely on the same information for their specific needs. ERP software also offers some degree of synchronized reporting and automation. Instead of forcing employees to maintain separate databases and spreadsheets that have to be manually merged to generate reports, some ERP solutions allow staff to pull reports from one system. For instance, with sales orders automatically flowing into the financial system without any manual rekeying, the order management department can process orders more quickly and accurately, and the finance department can close the books faster. Other common ERP features include a portal or dashboard to enable employees to quickly understand the business's performance on key metrics.

Figure 8.29 shows how an ERP system consolidates and correlates data from across the enterprise and generates enterprisewide organizational reports. Original ERP implementations promised to capture all information onto one true "enterprise" system, with the ability to touch all the business processes within the organization. Unfortunately, ERP solutions have fallen short of these promises, and typical implementations have penetrated only 15 to 20 percent of the organization. The issue ERP intends to solve is that knowledge within a majority of organizations currently resides in silos that are maintained by a select few, without the ability to be shared across the organization, causing inconsistency across business operations.

The heart of an ERP system is a central database that collects information from and feeds information into all the ERP system's individual application components (called modules), supporting diverse business functions such as accounting, manufacturing, marketing, and human resources. When a user enters or updates information in one module, it is immediately and automatically updated throughout the entire system, as illustrated in Figure 8.30.

ERP automates business processes such as order fulfillment–taking an order from a customer, shipping the purchase, and then billing for it. With an ERP system, when a customer service representative takes an order from a customer, he or she has all the information necessary to complete the order (the customer's credit rating and order history, the company's inventory levels, and the delivery schedule). Everyone else in the company sees the same information and has access to the database that holds the customer's new order. When one department finishes with the order, it is automatically routed via the ERP system to the next department. To find out where the order is at any point, a user need only log in to the ERP system and track it down, as illustrated in Figure 8.31.

In most organizations, information has traditionally been isolated within specific departments, whether on an individual database, in a file cabinet, or on an employee's PC. ERP

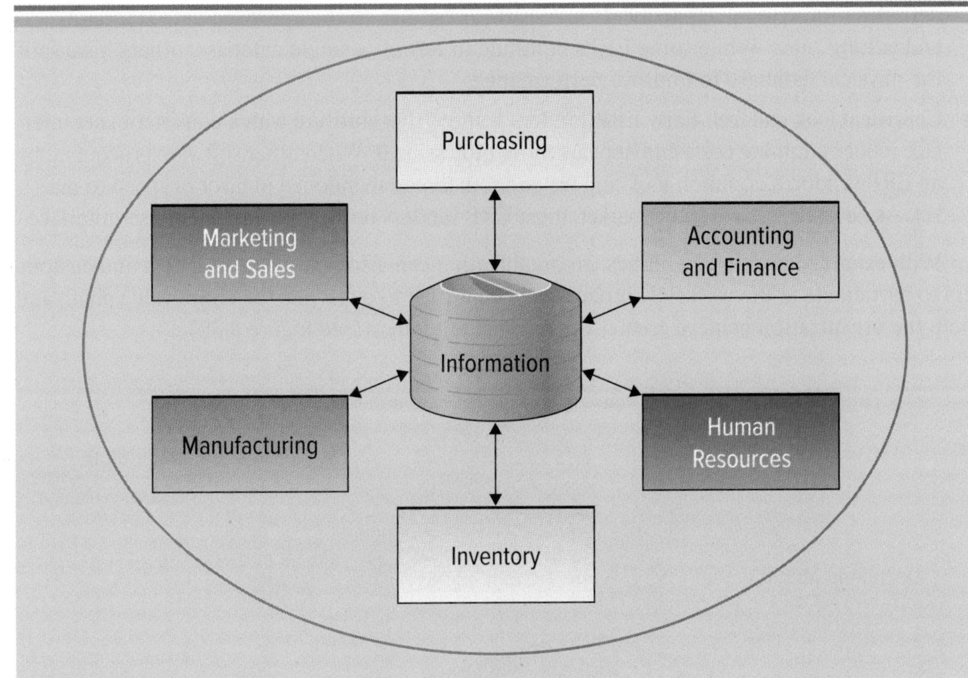

FIGURE 8.30

ERP Integration Data Flow

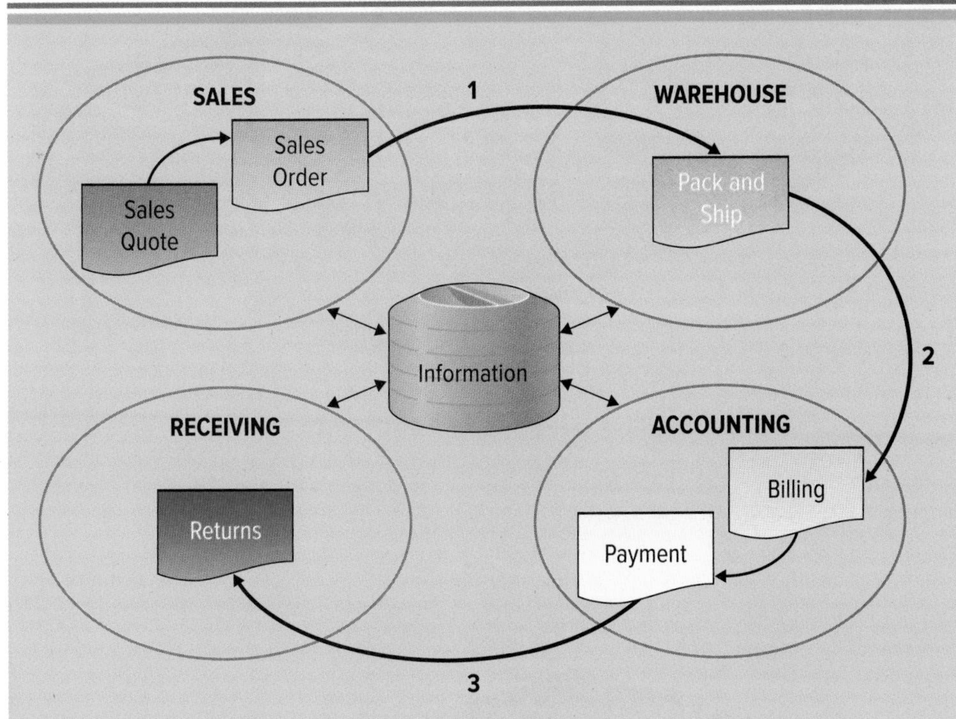

FIGURE 8.31

ERP Process Flow

enables employees across the organization to share information across a single, centralized database offering the following benefits:

- **Enterprisewide integration.** Business processes are integrated end-to-end across departments and business units. For example, a new order automatically initiates a credit check, queries product availability, and updates the distribution schedule. Once the order is shipped, the invoice is sent.
- **Real-time (or near real-time) operations.** Because the processes in the example above occur within a few seconds of order receipt, problems are identified quickly, giving the seller more time to correct the situation.
- **A common database.** A common database was one of the initial advantages of the ERP. It allowed data to be defined once for the enterprise with every department using the same

definition. Individual departments now had to conform to the approved data standards and editing rules. While some ERPs continue to rely on a single database, others have split the physical database to improve performance.

- **Consistent look and feel.** Early ERP vendors realized that software with a consistent user interface reduces training costs and appears more professional. When other software is acquired by an ERP vendor, a common look and feel are sometimes abandoned in favor of speed to market. As new releases enter the market, most ERP vendors restore the consistent user interface.

With extended portal capabilities, an organization can also involve its suppliers and customers to participate in the workflow process, allowing ERP to penetrate the entire value chain and help the organization achieve greater operational efficiency (see Figure 8.32).

FIGURE 8.32

The Organization before and after ERP

(top) Siloed Functional Areas before ERP (bottom) ERP with a Single Repository for Centralized Data

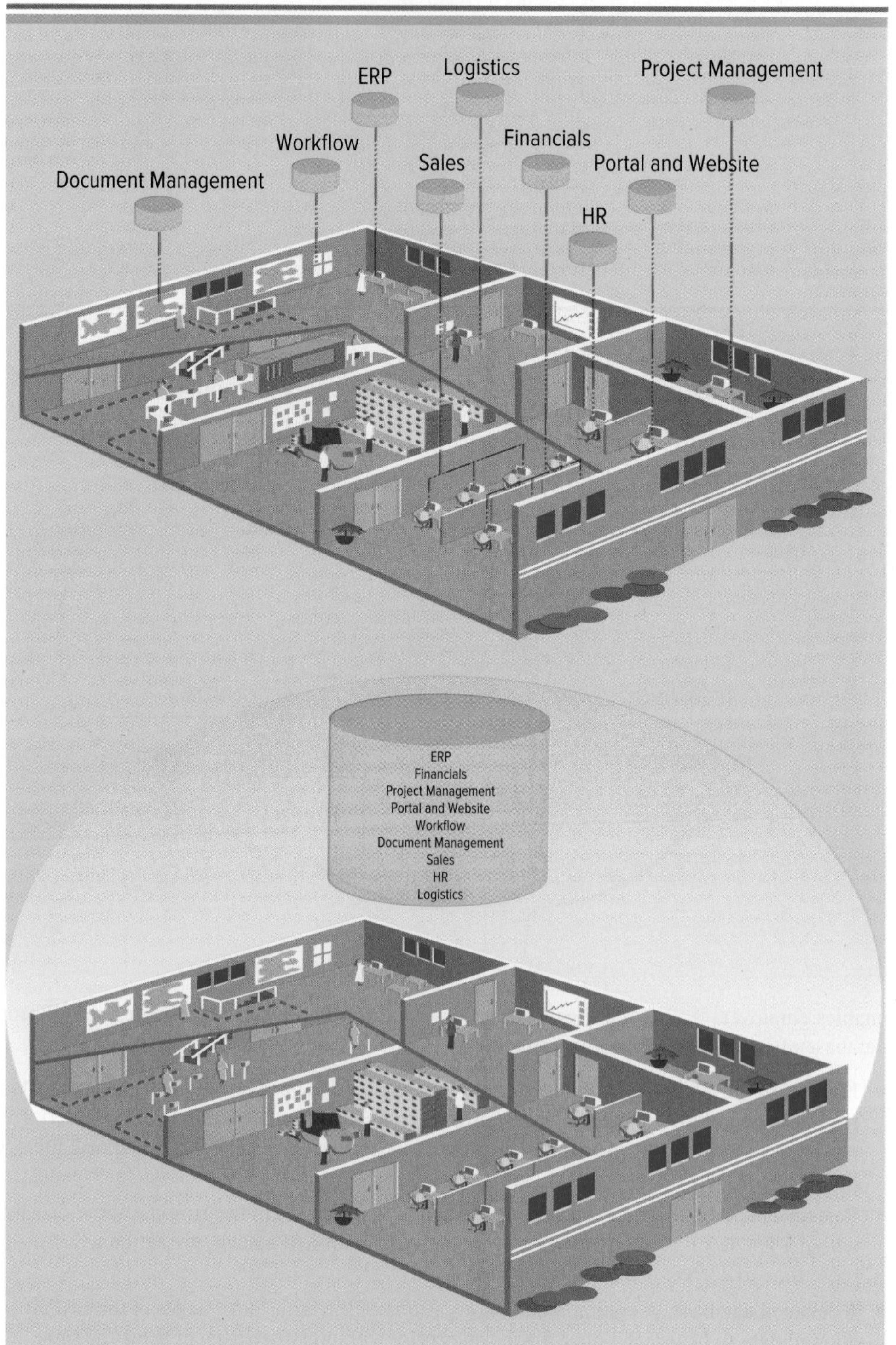

BUSINESS DRIVEN MIS

Classic Cars

Classic Cars Inc. operates high-end automotive dealerships that offer luxury cars along with luxury service. The company is proud of its extensive inventory, top-of-the-line mechanics, and especially its exceptional service, which includes operating a cappuccino bar at each dealership.

The company currently has 40 sales representatives at four locations. Each location maintains its own computer systems, and all sales representatives have their own contact management systems. This splintered approach to operations causes numerous problems in customer communication, pricing strategy, and inventory control, such as:

- A customer can get different quotes at different dealerships for the same car.
- Sales representatives frequently steal each other's customers and commissions.
- Sales representatives send their customers to other dealerships to see specific cars that turn out not to be on the lot.
- Marketing campaigns are typically generic and not designed to target specific customers.
- If a sales representative quits, all his or her customer information is lost.

You work for Customer One, a small consulting company that specializes in enterprisewide strategies. The owner of Classic Cars Inc. has hired you to help him formulate a strategy to put his company back on track. Develop a proposal detailing how an ERP system can alleviate the company's problems and create new sales opportunities.

The Evolution of ERP

Originally, ERP solutions were developed to deliver automation across multiple units of an organization, to help facilitate the manufacturing process and address issues such as raw materials, inventory, order entry, and distribution. However, ERP was unable to extend to other functional areas of the company such as sales, marketing, and shipping. It could not tie in any CRM capabilities that would allow organizations to capture customer-specific information, nor did it work with websites or portals used for customer service or order fulfillment. Call center or quality assurance staff could not tap into the ERP solution, nor could ERP handle document management, such as cataloging contracts and purchase orders.

ERP has grown over the years to become part of the extended enterprise. From its beginning as a tool for materials planning, it has extended to warehousing, distribution, and order entry. With its next evolution, ERP expands to the front office including CRM. Now administrative, sales, marketing, and human resources staff can share a tool that is truly enterprisewide. To compete on a functional level today, companies must adopt an enterprisewide approach to ERP that utilizes the Internet and connects to every facet of the value chain. Figure 8.33 shows how ERP has grown to accommodate the needs of the entire organization.

Applications such as SCM, CRM, and ERP are the backbone of ebusiness. Integration of these applications is the key to success for many companies. Integration allows the unlocking of information to make it available to any user, anywhere, anytime.

Most organizations today have no choice but to piece their SCM, CRM, and ERP applications together because no one vendor can respond to every organizational need; hence, customers purchase applications from multiple vendors. As a result, organizations face the challenge of integrating their systems. For example, a single organization might choose its CRM components from SalesForce.com, SCM components from SAP, and financial components and HR management components from Oracle. Figure 8.34 displays the general audience and purpose for each of these applications that have to be integrated.

FIGURE 8.33

The Evolution of ERP

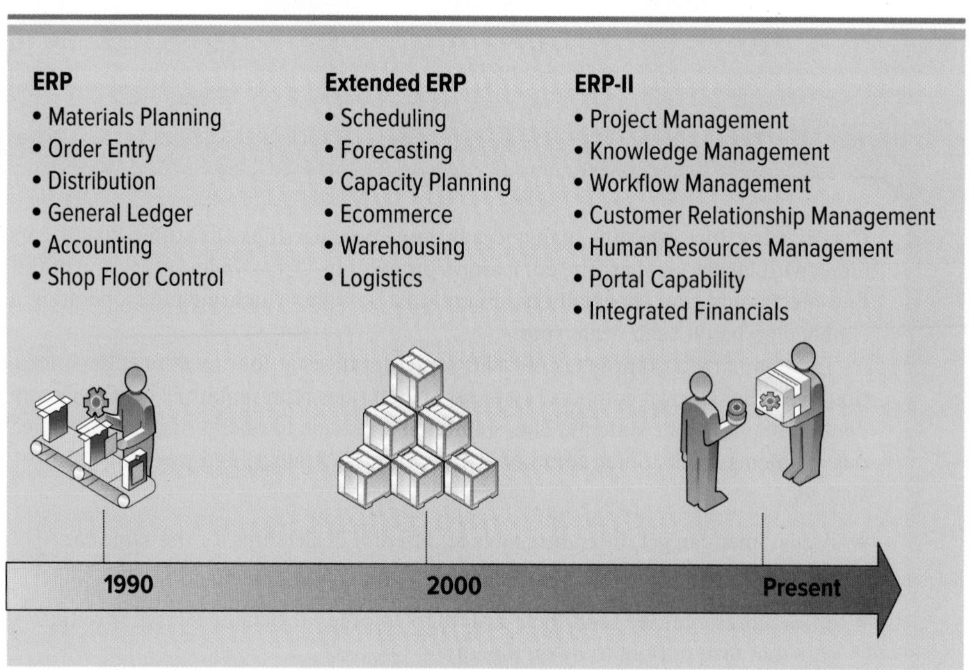

FIGURE 8.34

Primary Users and Business Benefits of Strategic Initiatives

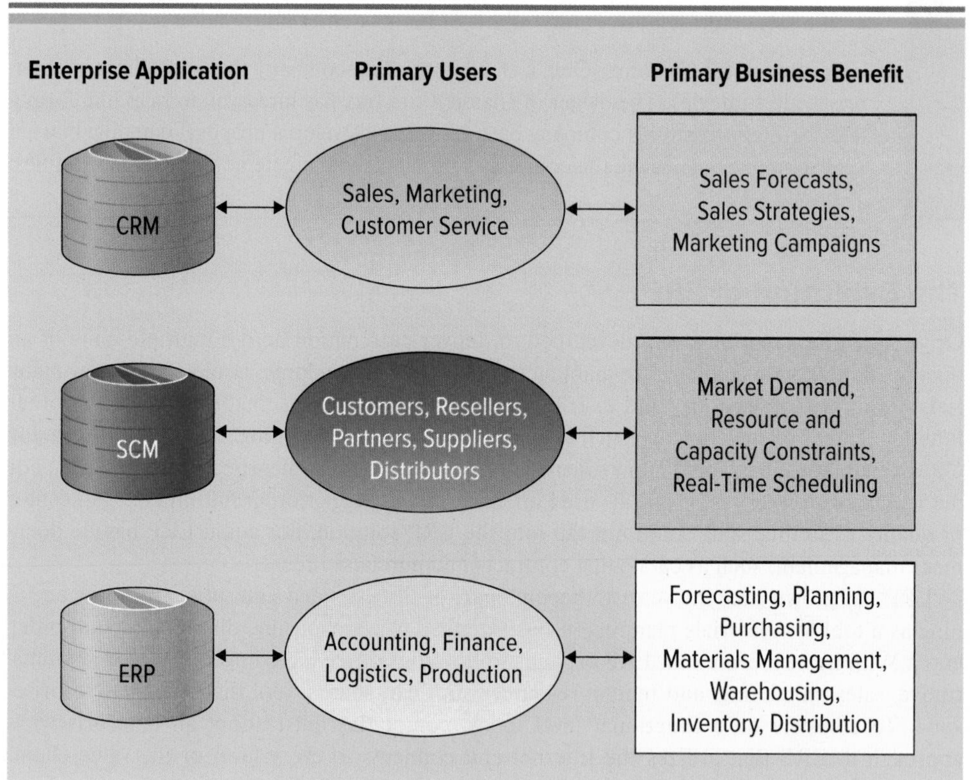

The current generation of ERP, ERP-II, is composed of two primary components–core and extended.

- ***Core ERP components***: The traditional components included in most ERP systems and that primarily focus on internal operations.
- ***Extended ERP components***: The extra components that meet organizational needs not covered by the core components and that primarily focus on external operations.

Figure 8.35 provides an example of an ERP system with its core and extended components.

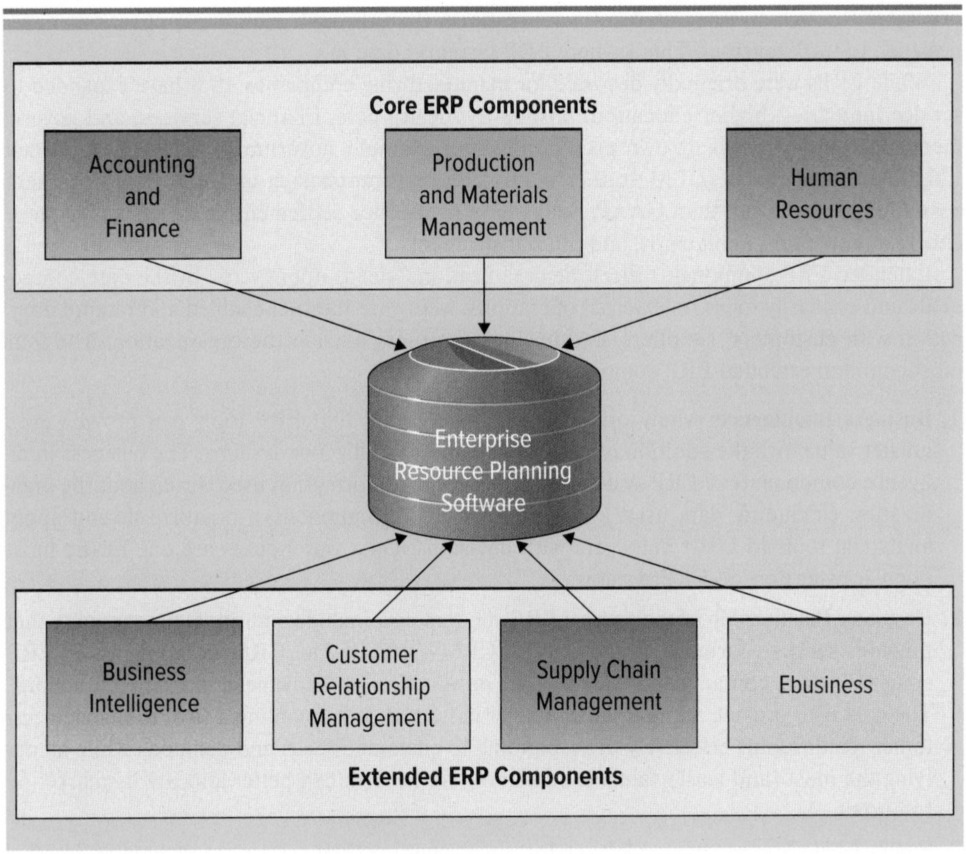

FIGURE 8.35

Core ERP Components and Extended ERP Components

Core ERP Components

The three most common core ERP components focusing on internal operations are:

1. ***Accounting and finance ERP components*** manage accounting data and financial processes within the enterprise with functions such as general ledger, accounts payable, accounts receivable, budgeting, and asset management. One of the most useful features of an ERP accounting/finance component is credit management. Most organizations manage their relationships with customers by setting credit limits, or limits on how much a customer can owe at any one time. ERP financial systems correlate customers' orders with their account balances to determine credit availability. They also perform all types of advanced profitability modeling techniques.
2. ***Production and materials management ERP components*** handle production planning and execution tasks such as demand forecasting, production scheduling, job cost accounting, and quality control. Demand forecasting helps determine production schedules and materials purchasing. A company that makes its own product prepares a detailed production schedule, and a company that buys products for resale develops a materials requirement plan.
3. ***Human resources ERP components*** track employee information, including payroll, benefits, compensation, and performance assessment, and ensure compliance with all laws. They even allow the organization to perform detailed employee analysis, such as identifying who is likely to leave the company unless additional compensation or benefits are provided and whether the most talented people are working in areas where they can have the greatest impact. Human resources components can also identify which employees are using which resources, such as online training and cellular services.

Extended ERP Components

Every organization manages people, purchases products and services, sells (or gives away) something, and accounts for money. The way each activity is handled will vary, but every enterprise performs these basic functions. In most cases, it is more effective to handle these processes through an integrated software platform than through multiple applications never designed to work together. That's where ERP systems come in.

While ERPs were originally designed for manufacturing companies, they have expanded to service industries, higher education, hospitality, health care, financial services, and government. Each industry has its own peculiarities. For example, government ERP uses Contract Lifecycle Management (CLM) rather than traditional purchasing and follows government accounting rules rather than GAAP. Banks have back-office settlement processes to reconcile checks, credit cards, debit cards, and other instruments.

Extended ERP components meet the organizational needs not covered by the core components and primarily focus on external operations. Many are Internet-enabled and require interaction with customers, suppliers, and business partners outside the organization. The four most common extended ERP components are:

1. **Business Intelligence:** Many organizations have found that ERP tools can provide even greater value with the addition of powerful business intelligence systems. The business intelligence components of ERP systems typically collect information used throughout the organization (including data used in many other ERP components), organize it, and apply analytical tools to assist managers with decisions. Data warehouses are one of the most popular extensions to ERP systems.
2. **Customer Relationship Management:** ERP vendors now include additional functionality that provides services formerly found only in CRM systems. The CRM components in ERP systems include contact centers, sales force automation, and advanced marketing functions. The goal is to provide an integrated view of customer data, enabling a firm to manage customer relationships effectively by responding to customer needs and demands while identifying the most (and least) valuable customers so the firm can better allocate its marketing resources.
3. **Supply Chain Management:** ERP vendors are expanding their systems to include SCM functions that manage the information flows between and among supply chain stages, maximizing total supply chain effectiveness and profitability. SCM components allow a firm to monitor and control all stages in the supply chain from the acquisition of raw materials to the receipt of finished goods by customers.
4. **Ebusiness:** The newest extended ERP components are the ebusiness components that allow companies to establish an Internet presence and fulfill online orders. A common mistake many businesses make is jumping into online business without properly integrating the entire organization on the ERP system. One large toy manufacturer announced less than a week before Christmas that it would be unable to fulfill any of its online orders. The company had all the toys in the warehouse, but it could not organize the basic order processing function to deliver the toys to consumers on time.

Measuring ERP Success

There is no guarantee of success for an ERP system. It is difficult to measure the success of an ERP system because one system can span an entire organization, including thousands of employees across the globe. ERPs focus on how a corporation operates internally, and optimizing these operations takes significant time and energy.

Two of the primary forces driving ERP failure include software customization and ERP costs.

- ***Software customization*:** Modifies existing software according to the business's or user's requirements.

Since ERP systems must fit business processes, many enterprises choose to customize their ERP systems to ensure that they meet business and user needs. Figure 8.36 displays the different forms of software customization a business will undertake to ensure the success of an ERP implementation. Heavy customization leads to complex code that must be continuously maintained and upgraded. It should be noted that customizing an ERP system is costly and complex and should only be done when there is a specific business advantage. According to Meta Group, it takes the average company 8 to 18 months to see any benefits from an ERP system. The primary risk for an ERP implementation includes the associated costs displayed in Figure 8.37.

Software Customization	
Business Processes or Workflows	Software can be customized to support the needs of business process workflows unique to each business or department.
Code Modifications	The most expensive customization occurs when application code is changed and should only be done if the code changes provide specific competitive advantages.
Integrations	Data integration is key for business process support that spans functional areas and legacy systems.
Reports, Documents, Forms	Customization to reports, documents, and forms can consist of simple layout or design changes or complex logic programming rules for specific business requirements.
User-Interface Changes	An ERP system can be customized to ensure that each user has the most efficient and effective view of the application.

FIGURE 8.36

Software Customization Examples

ERP Costs	
Software Costs	Purchasing the software, which can cost millions of dollars for a large enterprise
Consulting Fees	Hiring external experts to help implement the system correctly, which can cost millions of dollars
Process Rework	Redefining processes to ensure that the company is using the most efficient and effective processes
Customization	Customizing the software, if the software package does not meet all of the company's needs
Integration	Ensuring that all software products, including disparate systems not part of the ERP system, are working together or are integrated
Testing	Testing that all functionality works correctly, along with testing all integrations
Training	Training all new users and creating the training user manuals
Data Warehouse Integration and Data Conversions	Moving data from an old system into the new ERP system

FIGURE 8.37

ERP Costs

ORGANIZATIONAL INTEGRATION WITH ERP

LO 8.6: Discuss the current technologies organizations are integrating in enterprise resource planning systems.

The goal of ERP is to integrate all of the organizational systems into one fully functioning, high-performance system that is capable of meeting all business needs and user requirements. Traditional ERP systems were typically accessed from a computer on the customers' premises or office. Tomorrow's ERP systems will enhance the ability of organizations to apply context to decision making and adapt more easily to changing events. ERP systems in the future will focus on usability, ubiquity, accessibility, and mobility, drawing many advantages, including:

- Higher cost efficiencies
- Faster time to market
- Better-enabled mobile workforce
- Better leverage data to provide insights
- New product development

Of course, ERP of the future will have many challenges, including data management, source record management, and coordination of integrations and support activities. Figure 8.38 displays the three primary ERP implementation choices driving the next generation of business operations.

FIGURE 8.38

ERP Implementation Choices

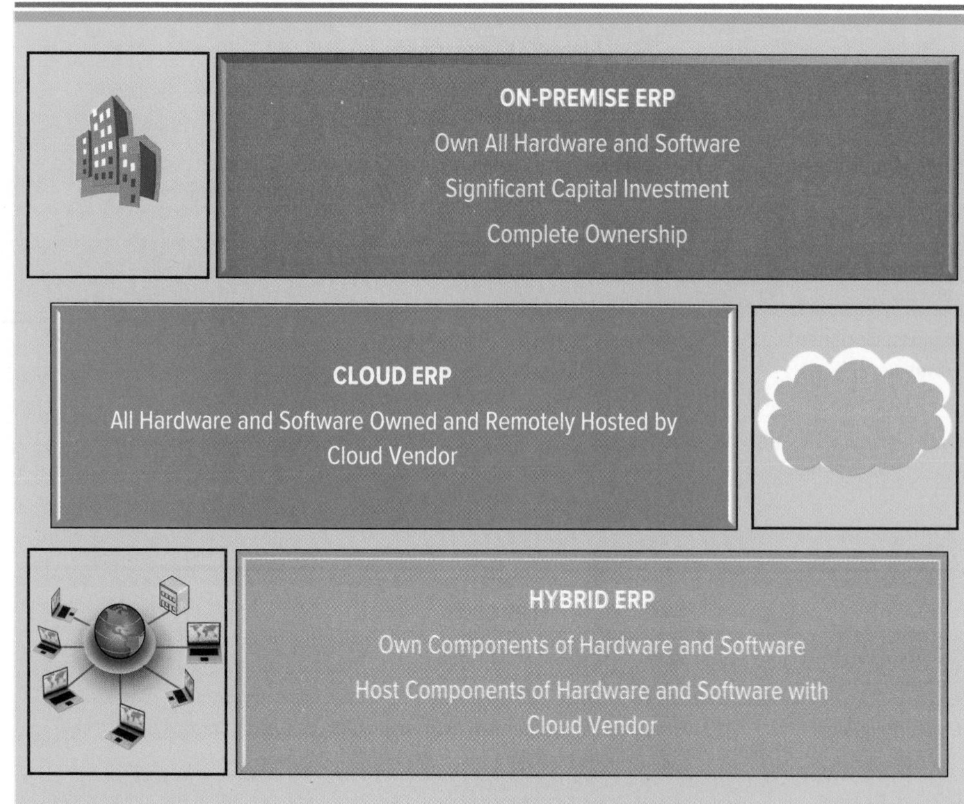

On-Premise ERP

Until a decade ago, virtually all ERP systems were installed on-premise.

- ***On-premise systems***: Include a server at a physical location using an internal network for internal access and firewalls for remote users' access.

Remote users had to access the ERP system through a firewall, which protected the system against unauthorized access. These systems are known as on-premise systems, and they are still in wide use today. The ERP, SCM, and CRM systems that run on-premise are referred to as legacy systems.

- ***Legacy system***: An old system that is fast approaching or beyond the end of its useful life within an organization.

Cloud ERP

The cloud has changed the legacy model of ERP implementation.

- According to the National Institute of Standards and Technology (NIST), ***cloud computing*** stores, manages, and processes data and applications over the Internet rather than on a personal computer or server.

Cloud computing offers new ways to store, access, process, and analyze information and connect people and resources from any location in the world where an Internet connection is available. As shown in Figure 8.39, users connect to the cloud from their personal computers or portable devices by using a client, such as a web browser. To these individual users, the cloud appears as their personal application, device, or document. It is like storing all of your software and documents in the cloud, and all you need is a device to access the cloud. No more hard drives, software, or processing power—that is all located in the cloud, transparent to the users. Users are not physically bound to a single computer or network; they can access their programs and documents from wherever they are, whenever they need to. Just think of having your hard drive located in the sky and being able to access your information and programs using any

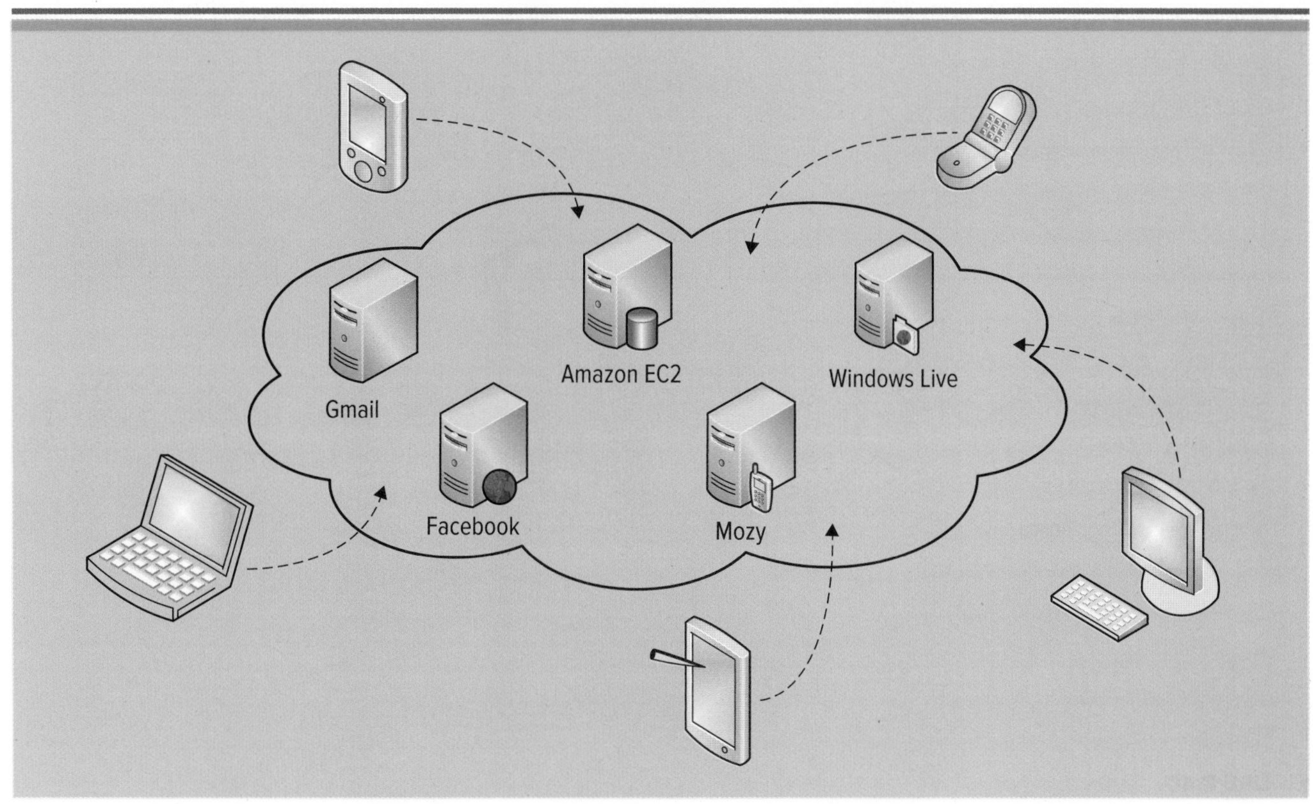

FIGURE 8.39

Cloud Computing Example

device from wherever you are. The best part is that even if your machine crashes, is lost, or is stolen, the information hosted in the cloud is safe and always available.

Software as a Service (SaaS) delivers applications over the cloud using a pay-per-use revenue model. Before its introduction, companies often spent huge amounts of money implementing and customizing specialized applications to satisfy their business requirements. Many of these applications were difficult to implement, expensive to maintain, and challenging to use. Usability was one of the biggest drivers for creating interest in and success for cloud computing service providers. SaaS ERP uses the cloud platform to enable organizations not only to unite around business processes but also to gather cloud data across supplier networks and supply chains to drive greater efficiency in manufacturing projects. The move to SaaS ERP is attracting many small and midsized businesses that simply cannot afford the costs associated with a traditional large ERP implementation.

SaaS offers a number of advantages; the most obvious is tremendous cost savings. The software is priced on a per-use basis with no up-front costs, so companies get the immediate benefit of reducing capital expenditures. They also get the added benefits of scalability and flexibility to test new software on a rental basis. Figure 8.40 displays the many advantages of SaaS implementations.

Cloud ERP has been slow to take off across business because many people were initially uncomfortable with placing sensitive data in the cloud. As the tremendous cost-saving advantages associated with cloud applications and SaaS become more apparent, the reservations against cloud ERP are dissipating.

Large organizations tend to have difficulty adjusting to cloud solutions simply because they want greater levels of control over their enterprise applications. Smaller, less complex organizations that lack sophisticated MIS departments are more likely to gravitate toward the cloud because it is easy for them to change business processes to fit the software. SaaS ERP can provide a company with the flexibility of on-premise software and the added benefits of a vendor maintaining and housing the applications off the premises. The biggest concerns for organizations interested in cloud ERP solutions are data security and potential vendor outages causing business downtime. Without an on-premise MIS department, the organization is truly at the mercy of the vendor during any system outage, and for critical organizational systems such as ERP, this could be an unacceptable risk.

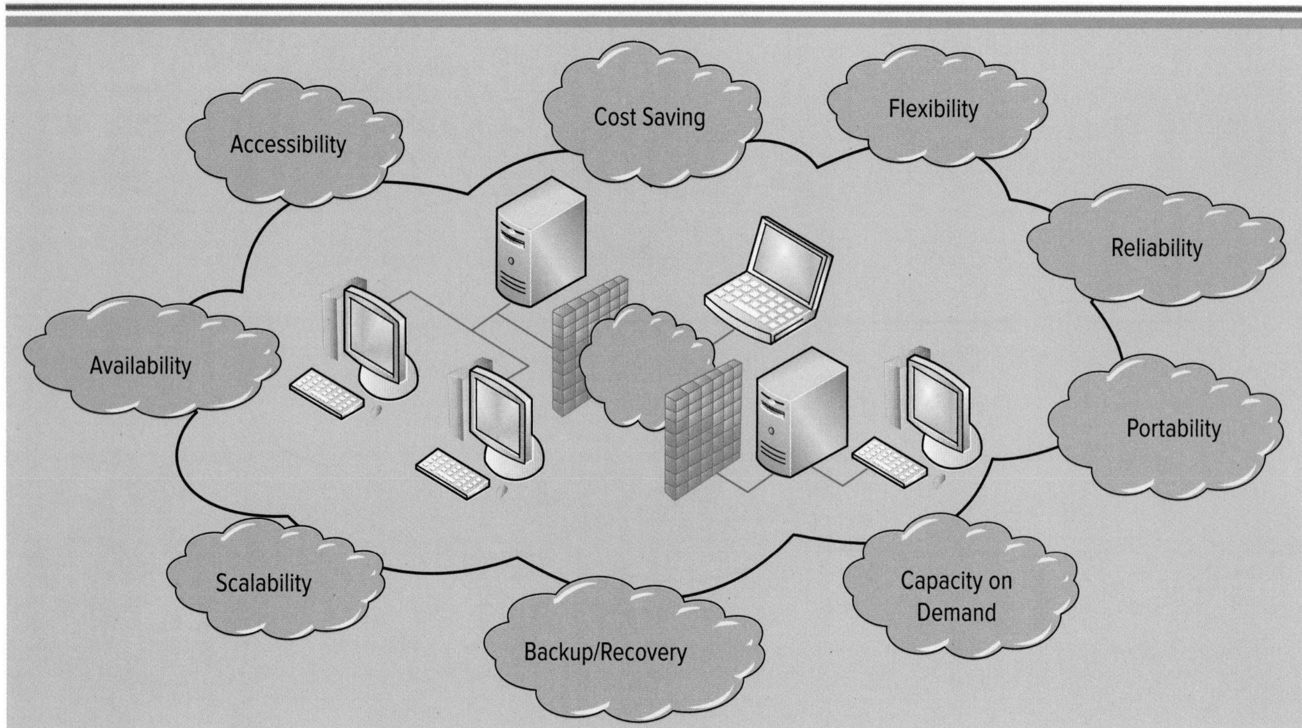

FIGURE 8.40

Advantages of SaaS Implementations

Hybrid ERP

It is conventional wisdom that a diversified stock portfolio is a very effective hedge against investment risk. For the same reason, companies that are not comfortable with the risk and/or loss of control associated with moving wholesale into ERP cloud computing but still want to explore this evolving infrastructure might find a hybrid ERP approach to be the perfect answer. By "hybrid ERP approach," we mean mostly on site but with some carefully selected hosted applications.

Building an all-encompassing ERP system traditionally ended in expensive failures. Nike, Kmart, and Hershey all lost over $100 million in failed ERP implementations. Based on the need to avoid expensive failures along with the emergence of cloud computing, enterprises can now adopt hybrid ERP architectures.

- ***Hybrid ERP***: Splits the ERP functions between an on-premise ERP system and one or more functions handled as Software as a Service in the cloud.

Typically, the on-premise legacy application operates at the corporate headquarters, whereas cloud-based specific applications support business needs such as mobility and web-based functionality. It is also becoming increasingly popular. In fact, many analysts are predicting that hybrid ERP will become a mainstay in the ERP market in the next few years.

Often a hybrid ERP system is implemented when the legacy system becomes very large and costly to customize, maintain, and upgrade or when mergers and acquisitions leave an organization with multiple ERP solutions that it is unable to consolidate to a single ERP system. Hybrid ERP architectures also support organizations with multiple operations based in multiple geographic locations. The following scenarios are common in organizations that use hybrid architectures of ERP:

- A business with a very specific local focus–single-site or multisite within a single country or region.
- A business with operations geared strongly toward a specific industry that doesn't feature strongly at corporate headquarters.
- A newly acquired operation with a mismatch of multiple outdated, unsupported ERPs.
- A small subsidiary with no formal ERP in place.

ERP Vendors by Tier		
	Enterprise Size	**ERP Vendor**
Tier I	Large Enterprise	■ SAP ■ Oracle ■ Microsoft
Tier II	Midsized Business	■ Infor ■ Lawson ■ Epicor ■ Sage
Tier III	Small Business	■ Exact Globe ■ Syspro ■ NetSuite ■ Consona

FIGURE 8.41

ERP Vendors by Tier

Managing the data across the enterprise is one of the biggest concerns for organizations deploying hybrid ERP architectures. It is critical for the business to have absolutely no duplication of effort between the two ERP systems. Consistency is required for any hybrid application to ensure that there is always a single source of information for accounting, financials, customer service, production, and other business areas. Hundreds of ERP vendors offer best-of-breed ERP applications or vertical market solutions to meet the unique requirements of specific industries such as manufacturing, distribution, retail, and others. Figure 8.41 displays an overview of ERP vendors by business size. Figure 8.42 displays the important factors driving the future of ERP.

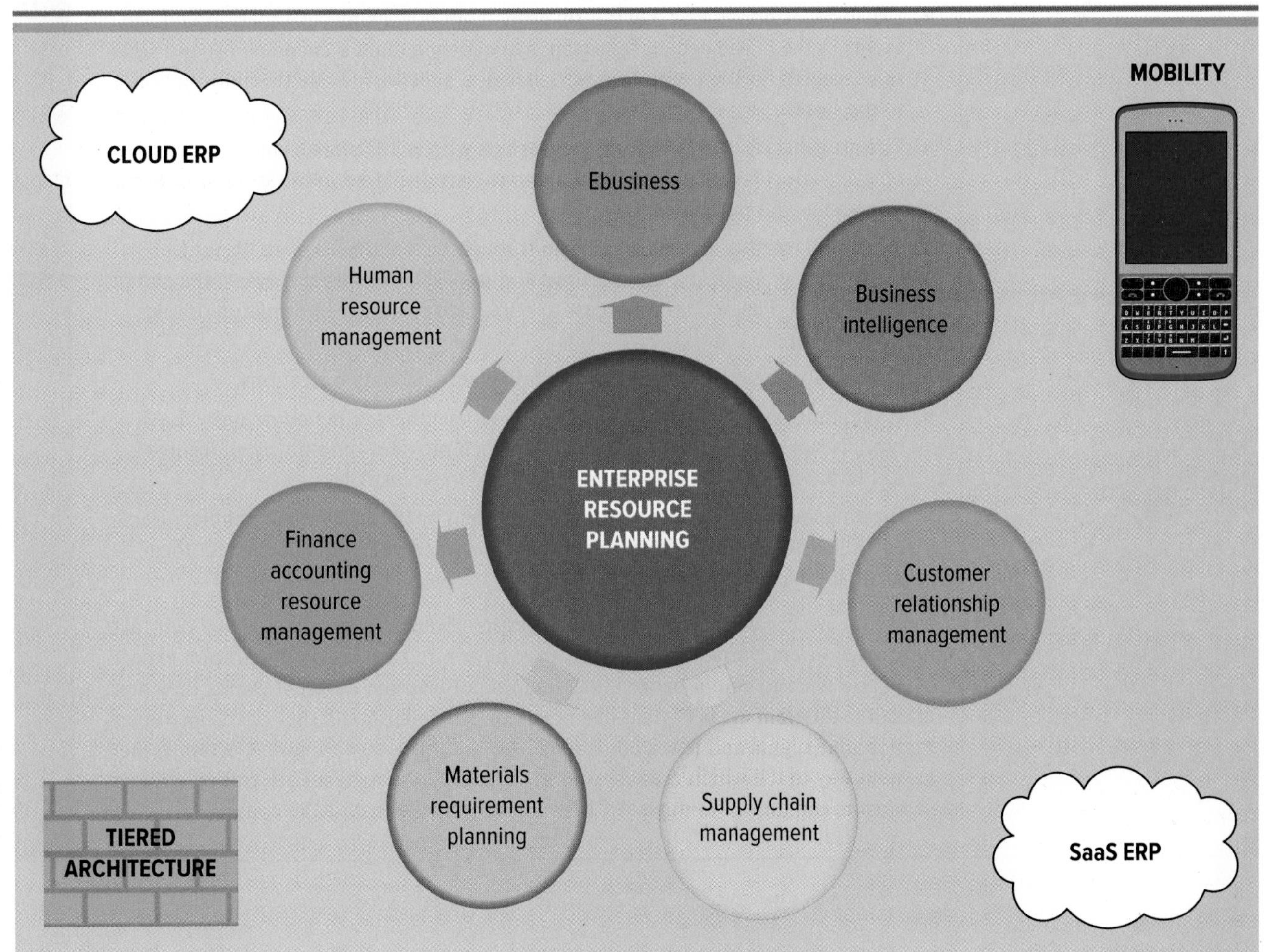

FIGURE 8.42

Organizational Integration of ERP

APPLY YOUR KNOWLEDGE

BUSINESS DRIVEN DISCUSSION

Bean Integration

At Flavors, a premium coffee shop, customers receive more than just a great cup of coffee. They also get exposure to music, art, literature, and town events. Flavors offers the following:

- Music center–information about all live music events occurring in the area and an open microphone two nights a week for local musicians.
- Art gallery–a space in the store filled with great pieces from local artists.
- Book clubs–a way for customers to meet to discuss current and classic literature.
- Coffee sampler–free tastings in which experts showcase coffees from around the world.
- Community calendar–weekly meetings to help customers find ways to become more involved in their community.
- Brewing courses–lessons in the finer details of the brewing, grinding, and blending using equipment for sale in Flavor stores, from the traditional press to a digital espresso machine. Also includes a troubleshooting guide developed by brewing specialists.

Flavors's sales are great and profits are soaring; however, operations need an overhaul. The following is a quick look at Flavors's current nonfood offerings.

- Flavors does not receive any information about how many customers attend live events in the music center. Musicians typically maintain a fan email list and CD sales records for the event; however, they don't always provide this information to the store.
- The art gallery is run by several local artists who pay Flavors a small commission on each sale. Flavors has no input about the art displayed in the store or information about who purchases it.
- Book club events are booked and run through the local bookstore, Pages Up, which runs a tab during the meetings and pays Flavors with a check at the end of each month. Flavors has no access to book club customer information or sales information.
- Coffee sampler events are run through Flavors's primary operations.
- Community event information is open to all members of the community. Each event is run by a separate organization, which provides monthly event feedback to Flavors in a variety of formats from Word to Access files.
- Brewing and machine resource courses are run by the equipment manufacturers, and all customer and sales information is provided to Flavors in a Word document at the end of each year.

Flavors's owners want to revamp the way the company operates so they can take advantage of enterprise systems, and they have hired you as an integration expert. They also want to gain a better understanding of how the different events they host affect the different areas of their business. For example, should they have more open-microphone nights and fewer book clubs? Or the other way around? Currently, they have no way to tell which events result in higher sales. Create an integration strategy so Flavors can take advantage of CRM, SCM, and ERP across the company.

LEARNING OUTCOME REVIEW

Learning Outcome 8.1: Explain integrations and the role they play in connecting a corporation.

Integrations allow separate systems to communicate directly with each other, eliminating the need for manual entry into multiple systems. Building integrations allows information sharing across databases, along with a dramatic increase in quality.

Learning Outcome 8.2: Describe supply chain management along with its impact on business.

A supply chain consists of all parties involved, directly or indirectly, in obtaining raw materials or a product. To automate and enable sophisticated decision making in these critical areas, companies are turning to systems that provide demand forecasting, inventory control, and information flows between suppliers and customers. Supply chain management (SCM) is the management of information flows between and among activities in a supply chain to maximize total supply chain effectiveness and corporate profitability. In the past, manufacturing efforts focused primarily on quality improvement efforts within the company. Today, these efforts reach across the entire supply chain, including customers, customers' customers, suppliers, and suppliers' suppliers. Today's supply chain is an intricate network of business partners linked through communication channels and relationships.

Improved visibility across the supply chain and increased profitability for the firm are the primary business benefits received when implementing supply chain management systems. Supply chain visibility is the ability to view all areas up and down the supply chain in real time. The primary challenges associated with supply chain management include costs and complexity. The next wave in supply chain management will be home-based supply chain fulfillment. No more running to the store to replace your products because your store will come to you as soon as you need a new product.

Learning Outcome 8.3: Identify the three technologies that are reinventing the supply chain.

The goal of ERP is to integrate all of the organizational systems into one fully functioning, high-performance system that is capable of meeting all business needs and user requirements. Of course, this goal is incredibly difficult to achieve because businesses and technologies experience rapid change, and ERP must support mobility, cloud, SaaS, and tiered architectures.

Learning Outcome 8.4: Explain operational and analytical customer relationship management.

Customer relationship management (CRM) is a means of managing all aspects of a customer's relationship with an organization to increase customer loyalty and retention and an organization's profitability. CRM allows an organization to gain insights into customers' shopping and buying behaviors. Every time a customer communicates with a company, the firm has the chance to build a trusting relationship with that particular customer.

Companies that understand individual customer needs are best positioned to achieve success. Building successful customer relationships is not a new business practice; however, implementing CRM systems allows a company to operate more efficiently and effectively in the area of supporting customer needs. CRM moves far beyond technology by identifying customer needs and designing specific marketing campaigns tailored to each.

The two primary components of a CRM strategy are operational CRM and analytical CRM. Operational CRM supports traditional transactional processing for day-to-day front-office operations or systems that deal directly with the customers. Analytical CRM supports back-office operations and strategic analysis and includes all systems that do not deal directly with the customers.

Learning Outcome 8.5: Identify the core and extended areas of enterprise resource planning.

Enterprise resource planning (ERP) integrates all departments and functions throughout an organization into a single IT system (or integrated set of IT systems) so employees can make decisions by viewing enterprisewide information about all business operations. The current generation of ERP, ERP-II, is composed of two primary components—core and extended. Core ERP components are the traditional components included in most ERP systems and primarily focus on internal operations. Extended ERP components are the extra components that meet organizational needs not covered by the core components and primarily focus on external operations.

Learning Outcome 8.6: Discuss the current technologies organizations are integrating in enterprise resource planning systems.

The goal of ERP is to integrate all of the organizational systems into one fully functioning, high-performance system that is capable of meeting all business needs and user requirements. Of course, this goal is incredibly difficult to achieve because businesses and technologies experience rapid change, and ERP must support mobility, cloud, SaaS, and tiered architectures.

KEY TERMS

Accounting and finance ERP component 341
Analytical CRM 327
Application integration 306
Backward integration 306
Bullwhip effect 312
Call scripting system 332
Campaign management system 330
Chatbot 333
Click-to-talk 332
Cloud computing 344
Common data repository 306, 334
Computer-aided design (CAD) 316
Computer-aided manufacturing (CAM) 316
Contact center or call center 332
Contact management CRM system 331
Core ERP component 340
Cradle to grave 314
CRM analysis technologies 325
CRM predicting technologies 325
CRM reporting technologies 325
Cross-selling 330
Customer analytics 324
Customer lifetime value (CLV) 333
Customer profitability (CP) 333
Customer relationship management (CRM) 323
Customer segmentation 332
Customer service and support (CSS) 330
Data integration 306
Digital supply chain 312
Drone 319
Electronic data interchange (EDI) 321
Enterprise application integration (EAI) 308
Enterprise resource planning (ERP) 334
Enterprise system 307
Extended ERP component 340
First call resolution (FCR) 332
Forward integration 306
4D printing 316
Human resources ERP component 341
Hybrid ERP 346
Inbound logistics 314
Integration 306
Intelligent virtual agent 333
Legacy system 344
List generator 329
Logistics 314
Maker movement 317
Makerspace 317
Materials management 314
Module software design 334
On-premise system 344
Operational CRM 327
Opportunity management CRM system 331
Outbound logistics 314
Procurement 313
Production and materials management ERP component 341
Radio-frequency identification (RFID) 317
Raspberry Pi 320
Robotics 319
Sales analytics 324
Sales force automation (SFA) 331
Sales management CRM system 331
Software customization 342
Supply chain 308
Supply chain management (SCM) 308
Supply chain visibility 321
3D printing 315
Uplift modeling 325
Up-selling 330
Web-based self-service system 332

REVIEW QUESTIONS

1. How do integrations connect a corporation?
2. What is the difference between forward and backward integrations?
3. What are the five primary activities in a supply chain?
4. What is the bullwhip effect and how can it affect a supply chain and a firm's profitability?
5. Why are customer relationships important to an organization? Do you agree that every business needs to focus on customers to survive in the information age?
6. What is the difference between operational and analytical CRM?
7. How can a sales department use CRM to improve operations?
8. How can a marketing department use CRM to improve operations?
9. What is an enterprise resource planning system?
10. What are the primary core and extended ERP components?

CLOSING CASE ONE

Dream It, Design It, 3D Print It

Can you imagine printing your drawing in 3D? Well, there is no need to imagine this because you can do it today for as little as $300. Just think of all the problems you can solve by having your own 3D printer. Did you recently lose the key to your car's roof rack? No worries, just download the specifications and print one. Did you forget your girlfriend's birthday? No worries, just download and customize a silver bracelet with her initials, and in less than 30 minutes you'll have the beautiful custom piece of jewelry on her wrist—without ever leaving your apartment.

Welcome to the wonderful world of 3D printing. For almost 30 years, 3D printing has been used by large manufacturing companies to create everything from custom parts to working prototypes. The medical industry uses 3D printing to create custom hearing aids, artificial limbs, and braces, and art designers and architects use 3D printers to create models and prototypes of statues and buildings. Traditionally, 3D printing was available only to large corporations and engineers who could code the intricate devices. Today, the first generation of consumer 3D printers is hitting the market at affordable prices with software easy enough for children to use.

The disruption occurring in the 3D printing world can, of course, be attributed to Moore's law as the technology has increased in capacity and processing power while decreasing in size and costs. Now you can purchase your own 3D printer for as little as $300 to $5,000; simply connect it to your Wi-Fi network and begin downloading files to create your own 3D objects. Current 3D printers offer a wide range of colors and materials, including plastics, metal, glass, and even chocolate. That's right—you can custom print your own valentine chocolates! The only barrier to 3D printing is that the software used to control the printer is still rather difficult for the average person to use, but you can expect that to change because software makers, such as Autodesk, are quickly releasing new, user-friendly applications. Autodesk just released 123D, a suite of free applications that enables ordinary people to design and customize objects on their PCs or even their iPads and then send them to a 3D printer.

3D printers work by first creating a digital computer-aided design (CAD) file, produced with a 3D modeling program or scanned into a 3D modeling program with a 3D scanner. To get from this digital file to instructions that the 3D printer understands, software then slices the design into hundreds or thousands of horizontal layers. Typically, the 3D printer uses either a fused deposition modeling printer, which applies the tiny layers of material, or a laser sintering process by which a laser fuses the material together. Names such as 3DSystems, Afinia, and MakerBot produce 3D printers for just a few thousand dollars for consumers and small businesses alike. Figure 8.43 represents a few of the best 3D-printed objects according to *PC Magazine* and *Wired*.[14]

FIGURE 8.43

3D Printed Objects

Acoustic guitar Why print a guitar? Well, a little-known fact is that the supplies of exotic woods are running considerably low, so manufacturers of instruments need to start researching for alternative materials. Scott Summit, cofounder of Bespoke Innovations, says that the good news is that there is no gold standard for guitars compared to other stringed instruments such as the violin, so they can be made of anything. In addition, guitarists prefer to have their own unique sound in addition to a customized guitar face, something that will be available with a truly original, 3D-printed guitar.
Bikinis The N12 is named after Nylon 12, the material in which the bikini was 3D printed by Continuum Fashion. Nylon 12 makes an ideal swimsuit material because it is innately waterproof. As well as being the first 3D-printed bikini, it is also the first bikini that actually becomes more comfortable when it gets wet.
Bionic ear To construct the ear, Princeton University researchers print the polymer gel onto an approximate ear shape and implant calf cells onto the matrix. The silver nanoparticles fuse to create an antenna, which picks up radio signals before being transferred to the cochlea, which translates the sound into brain signals. Despite all of this, researchers have yet to draw up plans to attach the ear to the human head.
Cars In 2010, Stratasys and Kor Ecologic teamed up to develop Urbee, the first car ever to have its entire body 3D printed by printing layers of material on top of each other until a finished product appeared.
Car parts for Jay Leno Comedian and car nut Jay Leno had a 1907 White Steamer with a badly damaged feedwater heater, a part that bolts onto the cylinders. Using a NextEngine 3D scanner and Dimension 3D printer, he was able to whip up a new one in 33 hours. "It's an amazingly versatile technology," Leno said on his website. "My EcoJet supercar needed air-conditioning ducts. We used plastic parts we designed, right out of the 3D copier. We didn't have to make these scoops out of aluminum—plastic is what they use in a real car. And the finished ones look like factory production pieces."
Chocolate heads Some people give roses, some people give 3D printed jewelry, and some people give their undying love. But in Japan, you can give your lover your chocolate head so they can bite into your brain as the ultimate expression of love.
Clothes Dutch designer Iris van Herpen was at Fashion Week in Paris, accompanied by MIT Media Lab's Neri Oxman, to showcase a dress that was fabricated using 3D printing technology. It was printed on an Objet Connex500 multimaterial 3D printer. Most 3D printers require creations to be printed using only one type of fabric or material, but the Connex500 allows mixing of different types of material.
Google Glasses Chinese entrepreneur Sunny Gao printed a fully functioning pair of Google Glasses at a hackathon event in Shanghai. Unfortunately, the 3D printed version of the glasses doesn't boast Wi-Fi or Bluetooth support, unlike the real thing—but they are identical in every other way.
Meat (yes, meat) U.S. start-up Modern Meadow believes it can make artificial raw meat using a 3D bioprinter, the BBC reported. Peter Thiel, one of Silicon Valley's most prominent venture capitalists, PayPal cofounder, and early Facebook investor, has just backed the company with $350,000. The team reportedly has a prototype, but it's "not ready for consumption."
Robotic prosthetic Easton LaChappelle, a 17-year-old high school student from Colorado, used free online resources for 3D printers to construct a fully functional prosthetic arm and hand. The high school student found inspiration from one of his past projects, which involved building a robotic hand made entirely of LEGOs when he was 14. His creation was able to open and close its fingers using two things: fishing line and servomotors.[15]

Questions

1. Explain 3D printing and how it is impacting business.
2. Explain CRM and how 3D printing could affect customer relations.
3. Explain SCM and how 3D printing could affect global supply chains.
4. Argue for or against the following statement: "3D printing will be more disruptive to business than the Internet."

CLOSING CASE TWO

Hootsuite

Hootsuite is an online social media management system that keeps track of and manages the myriad multiple networks, such as Facebook, Twitter, and Google+, and posts updates or replies directly about them. Hootsuite is like an online spy for your company—continually monitoring what people are saying about your brand across all platforms, from Facebook to Google+ to LinkedIn. And not only will it alert you to potential negative feedback, it will also help you with a crafted and creative instant response. With so many networks for businesses to manage, it is no surprise that social media management tools have become so popular and are relied upon by many companies today.

If you manage the updates for your business's social networks, it is highly likely that you will have heard of Hootsuite. Of course, there are a number of competitors to Hootsuite, including TweetDeck and SocialEngage, but Hootsuite continues to dominate this hypercompetitive market. Hootsuite offers the following services:

- **Analyze social media:** Social analytics is a strong feature of this impressive tool, allowing you to track and prove social ROI, measuring the impact of your social media campaigns through comprehensive reporting. With it, you can measure conversions by social channel and separate ROI between owned and paid media.
- **Respond and create social media:** Stay on message with preapproved content your teams can post, stored in your favorite cloud file service. Tagging, searching, and usage statistics make curating content a breeze.
- **Monitor social media:** Surveil the conversations that matter. Find and filter social conversations by keyword, hashtag, and location—in multiple languages—to hear what people are saying about your brand, competitors, and industry.
- **Schedule social media:** Keep your social presence active 24/7 by automatically scheduling hundreds of social media posts at once, across your social accounts. Save time and effort by uploading, editing, and scheduling hundreds of social media posts at one time in CSV format. Plan your content with ease. See your scheduled posts at a glance, streamline approvals, and collaborate with your team in real time using an interactive, media-rich planner.[16]

Questions

1. Why is social media critical to business success?
2. Why is monitoring, responding, creating, and analyzing social media content critical to any business?
3. What can you do if you find from Hootsuite that several customers are complaining about your product on Facebook?
4. What types of analytics will a business want to measure for analyzing its social media content?

MAKING BUSINESS DECISIONS

1. Customer Relationship Management Strategies

On average, it costs an organization six times more to sell to a new customer than to sell to an existing customer. As the co-owner of a medium-sized sports equipment distributor, you have recently been notified that sales for the past three months have decreased by an average of 20 percent. The reasons for the decline in sales are numerous, including a poor economy and some negative publicity your company received regarding a defective product line. In a group, explain how implementing a CRM system can help you understand and combat the decline in sales. Be sure to justify why a CRM system is important to your business and its future growth.

Also, search the Internet for at least one recent and authoritative article that compares or ranks customer relationship management systems. Select two packages from the list and compare their functions and features as described in the article(s) you found, as well as on each company's website. Find references in the literature where companies that are using each package have reported their experiences, both good and bad. Draw on any other comparisons you can find. Prepare a presentation for delivery in class on the strengths and weaknesses of each package, which one you favor, and why.

2. Driving Up Profits with Loyalty (or Driving Down?)

The Butterfly Café is located in downtown San Francisco and offers specialty coffees, teas, and organic fruits and vegetables. The café holds a number of events to attract customers, such as live music, poetry readings, book clubs, charity events, and local artists nights. A listing of all participants attending each event is tracked in the café's database.

The café uses the information for marketing campaigns and offers customers who attend multiple events additional discounts. A marketing database company, InTheKnow, has offered to pay the Butterfly Café a substantial amount of money for access to its customer database, which it will then sell to other local businesses. The owner of the Butterfly Café, Penny Dirks, has come to you for advice. She is not sure whether her customers would appreciate her selling their personal information and how it might affect her business. However, the amount of money InTheKnow is offering is enough to finance her much-needed new patio for the back of the café. InTheKnow has promised that the sale will be completely confidential. What should Dirks do?

3. Supporting Customers

Creative.com is an ebusiness that sells craft materials and supplies over the Internet. You have just started as the vice president of customer service, and you have a team of 45 customer service representatives. Currently, the only form of customer service is the toll-free number, and the company is receiving a tremendous number of calls regarding products, orders, and shipping information. The average wait time for a customer to speak to a customer service representative is 35 minutes. Orders are being canceled, and Creative.com is losing business due to its lack of customer service. Create a strategy to revamp the customer service center and get the company back on track.

4. Implementing an ERP System

Blue Dog Inc. is a leading manufacturer in the high-end sunglasses industry, reaching record revenue levels of more than $250 million last year. Blue Dog is currently deciding on the possibility of implementing an ERP system to help decrease production costs and increase inventory control. Many of the executives are nervous about making such a large investment in an ERP system due to its low success rates. As a senior manager at Blue Dog Inc., you have been asked to compile a list of the potential benefits and risks associated with implementing an ERP system, along with your recommendations for the steps the company can take to ensure a successful implementation. Be sure also to explain why ERP systems include CRM and SCM components and the advantages the company can gain by implementing all of the components for a connected corporation.

5. **Ruby Receptionists**

Great businesses are driven by exceptional customer experiences and interactions. Ruby is a company operating from Portland, Oregon, that has a team of smart and cheerful virtual receptionists you can hire to carry out all your customer interactions—remotely. Ruby aims to deliver the perfect mix of friendliness, charm, can-do attitude, and professionalism to all its clients' customer calls. Best of all, customers believe the Ruby receptionists are working right in your office, not in Portland, Oregon. Ruby promises to bring back the lost art of human interaction by delighting each and every customer who calls.

Explain the importance of customer service for customer relationship management. Do you agree that a company can improve customer service by hiring Ruby Receptionists? If you owned a small business, would you be comfortable hiring Ruby Receptionists?

6. **Buy One, Get One Groceries**

Grocery stores all over the United States use coupons as a way to compete for customers and keep customer loyalty high. Safeway produces coupons on demand based on the products currently in the customer's cart. Kroger analyzes customer loyalty data gathered over several years. Knowing most customers throw junk mail in the garbage, Kroger uses analytics to mine the customer loyalty program data to ensure the coupons are specific for each family, offering only items they have bought in the past. Kroger mails over 15 million coupons per quarter.

Safeway and Kroger are gathering data at different points in the supply chain. Safeway does not gather customer data and only analyzes what is currently in the customer's cart, giving coupons in real time to all daily customers. Kroger gathers customer data over several years and mails coupons based on historical data to loyalty customer cardholders only. What are the pros and cons of using these two different strategies to produce coupons? Given the choice, which method would you use and why?

7. **Great Stories**

When customers have an unpleasant customer experience, the company no longer has to worry about them telling a few friends and family; the company now has to worry about them telling everyone. Internet service providers are giving frustrated consumers another means of fighting back. Free or low-cost computer space for Internet websites is empowering consumers to tell not only their friends but also the world about the way they have been treated. A few examples of disgruntled customer stories from the Internet include:

- A bike-riding tourist requires stitches after being bitten on the leg by a dog. The tourism company is banned from renting bikes and in turn bars the tourist from taking any future tours.
- A customer leaving Best Buy refuses to show the receipt voluntarily to the guard at the door. The Best Buy employees try to seize the customer's cart and then decide to park a car behind the customer's vehicle.
- Enterprise Rent-A-Car operates a high-stress business, and frequently its customers find that the company did not honor reservations, did not have cars ready for reservations, rented cars with empty tanks of gas, and charged higher rates to corporate account holders.

The pervasive nature of the Internet is increasing customer power and changing business from product-focused to customer-focused. Explain the difference between product-focused business and customer-focused business and why CRM is more important than ever before.

8. **JetBlue on YouTube**

JetBlue took an unusual and interesting CRM approach by using YouTube to apologize to its customers. JetBlue's founder and former CEO, David Neeleman, apologized to customers via YouTube after a very bad week for the airline: 1,100 flights were canceled due to snowstorms, causing thousands of passengers to be stranded at airports around the country. Neeleman's unrehearsed, unrefined, and sincere YouTube apology made customers understand the issues and accept the company's apology.

You are the founder and CEO of GoodDog, a large pet food manufacturing company. Recently, at least 16 pet deaths have been tied to tainted pet food, fortunately not from your company.

A recall of potentially deadly pet food has dog and cat owners studying their animals for even the slightest hint of illness and swamping veterinarians nationwide with calls about symptoms. Considering JetBlue's example above, create a strategy for using YouTube as a vehicle to communicate with your customers as they fear for their pets' lives. Be sure to highlight the pros and cons of using YouTube as a customer communication vehicle. Are there any other new technologies you could use as a customer communication vehicle that would be more effective than YouTube? With all the new advances in technology and the many ways to reach customers, do you think using YouTube is a smart approach? What else could you do to help gain back customers' trust?

9. Searching Telephone Calls

Imagine being able to search a database of customer phone calls to find specific requests or to be able to sort through digital customer complaints to detect the exact moment when the interaction between the customer service representative and the customer went wrong. A new tool called Find It allows the sorting of digital voice records as easily as using Google to sift through documents. Find It is opening limitless business opportunities as organizations begin to understand how they can use this technology to help employees search voice mails or recorded calls for keywords and phrases.

You have recently started your own marketing firm, and you want to use the power of Find It to help your customers query all of their unique data records, including digital voice recordings. Now all you need is to prepare your marketing materials to send to potential customers. Create a marketing pitch you will deliver to customers detailing the business opportunities they could uncover if they purchase Find It. Your marketing pitch can be a one-page document, a catchy tune, a video, or a PowerPoint presentation.

10. Sharptooth Incorporated

Stephen Kern is the founder and CEO of Sharptooth, a small business that buys and sells comic strips to magazines and newspapers around the country. Some of Sharptooth's artists have made it big and are syndicated in hundreds of magazines and newspapers, whereas others are new to the industry. Kern started in the business as an artist and began contracting other artists when he realized he had a knack for promoting and marketing comic materials. His artistic background is great for spotting talented young artists, but not so great for running the business.

Kern recently began selling comics to new forms of media such as blogs, websites, and other online tools. He has hired you to build him a new system to track all online comic sales. You quickly notice that Kern has a separate system for each of his lines of business, including newspaper sources, magazine sources, billboard sources, and now online sources. You notice that each system works independently to perform its job of creating, updating, and maintaining sales information, but you are wondering how he operates his business as a whole. Create a list of issues Kern will encounter if he continues to run his business with four systems performing the same operations. What could happen to the business if he cannot correlate the details of each? Be sure to highlight at least 10 issues by which separate systems could cause problems.

11. Eating In

Having been employed by the same company for more than 20 years, Mary Lou Lively was shocked when she was suddenly terminated, along with about 900 of her co-workers. It took Lively a few weeks to recover from the shock, and then she finally began focusing her efforts on searching for a new job. Lively was sure her loyal employment history and strong skill set would land her a new job in no time; however, after several months of searching, she wasn't having any luck. With her emergency funds quickly being depleted, Lively knew she had to find a new job soon or she'd need to start selling her assets or cashing in her retirement savings.

The one positive aspect of having so much free time was that she could focus on her true passion: cooking. Mary Lou began making a little money by catering lunches and dinners for local businesses and neighbors. One day, she overheard a neighbor remark that she was hosting a large party and didn't have enough time to prepare the meal. Almost jokingly, Lively asked her how much she'd be willing to pay for a catered event. Soon Lively was catering for numerous neighbors and small businesses, and she knew she had to make a decision about whether she would go into business for herself or continue searching for other employment.

After a year in the catering business, Lively was earning a good living and building a stellar reputation. She began catering for all types of events, including weddings, and business was so good that she hired several employees to help grow her business. As Lively begins to plan her expansion, she has asked for your help in answering the following questions:

1. How important is customer loyalty for Lively's business? What can she do to ensure that her customers remain loyal? How could one disgruntled customer hurt business? What can she do to combat this challenge?
2. Research the business Yelp.com. What service does Yelp.com perform? Would a small business see Yelp.com as an opportunity or a threat? What are the pros and cons a customer should be aware of when using Yelp.com?
3. Lively's responsibilities include forecasting, inventory control, scheduling, and ensuring high-quality products. What types of forecasts should she require to run her business? What types of inventory should she want to track? What might happen if her inventory tracking tool was off by 50 percent? What types of schedules does Lively need to generate? What things might occur to disrupt schedules and cause her to reschedule? How can a supply chain management system help run the business?
4. Lively wants to create a business based on loyal customers and loyal employees. She offers her employees bonuses for new ideas, recipes, or business referrals. What risks is Lively encountering by offering these bonuses? One employee idea that she has implemented is turning out to be a competitive advantage for her business; however, the employee has quit and is now working for a competitor. Should Lively still pay the employee the bonus? What should she do to ensure that she is building strong employee relationships?
5. Lively overheard one of her customers talking about enterprise systems such as CRM, SCM, and ERP. However, she is sure they are available only to big companies that have lots of capital. Research the Internet and find examples of enterprise systems for small business. Do you think she should invest in these types of systems to run her business? Why or why not?

AYK APPLICATION PROJECTS

If you are looking for Excel projects to incorporate into your class, try any of the following after reading this chapter.

Project Number	Project Name	Project Type	Plug-In	Focus Area	Project Level	Skill Set	Page Number
9	Security Analysis	Excel	T3	Filtering Data	Intermediate	Conditional Formatting, Autofilter, Subtotal	AYK.6
10	Gathering Data	Excel	T3	Data Analysis	Intermediate	Conditional Formatting, PivotTable	AYK.6
11	Scanner System	Excel	T2	Strategic Analysis	Intermediate	Formulas	AYK.7
12	Competitive Pricing	Excel	T2	Profit Maximization	Intermediate	Formulas	AYK.7
13	Adequate Acquisitions	Excel	T2	Break-Even Analysis	Intermediate	Formulas	AYK.7
15	Assessing the Value of Information	Excel	T3	Data Analysis	Intermediate	PivotTable	AYK.8
16	Growth, Trends, and Forecasts	Excel	T2, T3	Data Forecasting	Advanced	Average, Trend, Growth	AYK.9
18	Formatting Grades	Excel	T3	Data Analysis	Advanced	If, LookUp	AYK.11
22	Turnover Rates	Excel	T3	Data Mining	Advanced	PivotTable	AYK.13
23	Vital Information	Excel	T3	Data Mining	Advanced	PivotTable	AYK.13
24	Breaking Even	Excel	T4	Business Analysis	Advanced	Goal Seek	AYK.14
25	Profit Scenario	Excel	T4	Sales Analysis	Advanced	Scenario Manager	AYK.14

Design Element: © McGraw Hill Education

CHAPTER 9 Systems Development and Project Management: Corporate Responsibility

CHAPTER OUTLINE

SECTION 9.1
Developing Enterprise Applications

- The Systems Development Life Cycle (SDLC)
- Software Development Methodology: The Waterfall
- Agile Software Development Methodologies

SECTION 9.2
Project Management

- Using Project Management to Deliver Successful Projects
- Primary Project Planning Diagrams
- Outsourcing Projects

What's in IT for me?

This chapter provides an overview of how organizations build information systems. As a business student, you need to understand this process because information systems are the underlying foundations of company operations. Your understanding of the principles of building information systems will make you a more valuable employee. You will be able to identify trouble spots early and make suggestions during the design process that will result in a better information systems project—one that satisfies both you and your business.

Building an information system is like constructing a house. You could sit back and let the developers do all the design work, construction, and testing, and hope the finished product will satisfy your needs. However, participating in the process helps guarantee that your needs are not only heard but also met. It is good business practice to have direct user input steering the development of the finished product. Your knowledge of the systems development process will allow you to participate and ensure you are building flexible enterprise architectures that support not only current business needs but also future ones.

Lentamart/Shutterstock

Ben Gabbe/Stringer/Getty Images

opening case study

Let My People Go Surfing: The Education of a Reluctant Businessman

In his book *Let My People Go Surfing,* Yvon Chouinard, founder of Patagonia, legendary climber, businessman, and environmentalist, shares his perspective on creating one of the most respected and environmentally responsible companies on earth. Chouinard explains how his business and environmental views have evolved over decades marked by global recession, intensifying environmental crisis, and threats to the natural world. Chouinard's beliefs are simple: Long-term success means accounting for the bottom line while doing the right thing by causing minimal harm to the planet, reducing carbon in the atmosphere, and restoring the soil that gives our planet life. Chouinard is a business hero bringing unprecedented success to Patagonia as it approaches $1 billion in sales, while continuing to challenge and simultaneously empower his employees. *Let My People Go Surfing* is a blueprint for creating all facets of responsible business, from analysis to design, and from development to implementation.

From his youth as the son of a French Canadian blacksmith to the thrilling, ambitious climbing expeditions that inspired his innovative designs for extreme sport's equipment, *Let My People Go Surfing* is the story of a man who brought doing good and having grand adventures into the heart of his company and employees—a difficult task for any individual.

Patagonia has begun investing heavily in regenerative agriculture, both to support practitioners on the cutting edge of this movement and to source food and natural fibers in ways that actually begin to reverse the damage humans have caused to our planet. As Chouinard writes, "All the work we do at Patagonia to be a more responsible company is for naught unless we can be part of the solution to this problem." Chouinard's philosophy has become embedded in the company's business model in the past decade—leading to plant-based wetsuits, a start-up food business, innovative standards to improve the lives of workers in Patagonia's global supply chain, and a venture fund designed to support like-minded young companies, among many other initiatives. Here are Chouinard's five words of wisdom:

1. I read every book on business, searching for a philosophy that would work for us. I was especially interested in books on Japanese or Scandinavian styles of management because I knew the American way of doing business offered only one of many possible routes.
2. Our philosophies aren't rules; they're guidelines. They're the keystone of our approach to any project, and although they are "set in stone," their applications to a situation isn't. In every long-lasting business, the methods of conducting business may constantly change, but the values, the culture, and the philosophies remain constant.

3. Who are businesses really responsible to? Their customers? Shareholders? Employees? We would argue that it's none of the above. Fundamentally, businesses are responsible to their resource base. Without a healthy environment, there are no shareholders, no employees, no customers, and no business.
4. Remember, work has to be fun. We value employees who live rich and rounded lives. We run a flexible workplace, and we have ever since we were a blacksmith shop that shut down whenever the waves were six feet, hot and glassy. Our policy has always allowed employees to work flexible hours, as long as the work gets done with no negative impacts on others. A serious surfer doesn't plan to go surfing next Tuesday at two o'clock. You go surfing when there are waves and the tide and wind are right.
5. People may be afraid of the term "activist" because they associate it with ecosabotage and violent protests, but I'm talking about normal citizens who want the government to live up to its obligations to protect our air, water, and all other natural resources. Activists have an infectious passion about the issues they support, whether they are mothers fighting to clean up toxic landfills that are killing their children or farmers trying to hold on to their fourth-generation family business threatened by urban sprawl. These are the people on the front lines, trying either to make the government obey its own laws or to recognize the need for a new law.[1]

section 9.1 | Developing Enterprise Applications

LEARNING OUTCOMES

9.1 Describe the seven phases of the systems development life cycle.

9.2 Summarize the different software development methodologies.

THE SYSTEMS DEVELOPMENT LIFE CYCLE (SDLC)

LO 9.1: Describe the seven phases of the systems development life cycle.

The multimillion-dollar Nike SCM system failure is legendary. As Nike CEO Philip Knight famously stated, "This is what we get for our $400 million?" Nike partnered with i2 to implement an SCM system that never came to fruition. i2 blamed the failed implementation on the fact that Nike failed to use the vendor's implementation methodology and templates. Nike blamed the failure on faulty software.[2]

It is difficult to get an organization to work if its systems do not work. In the information age, software success or failure can lead directly to business success or failure. Companies rely on software to drive business operations and ensure that work flows throughout the company. As more and more companies rely on software to operate, so do the business-related consequences of software successes and failures.

The potential advantages of successful software implementations provide firms with significant incentives to manage software development risks. However, an alarmingly high number of software development projects come in late or over budget, and successful projects tend to maintain fewer features and functions than originally specified. Understanding the basics of software development, or the systems development life cycle, will help organizations avoid potential software development pitfalls and ensure that software development efforts are successful. Before jumping into software development, it is important to understand a few key terms.

- ***Conversion***: The process of transferring information from a legacy system to a new system.
- ***Legacy system***: An old system that is fast approaching or beyond the end of its useful life within an organization.
- ***Off-the-shelf application software***: Supports general business processes and does not require any specific software customization to meet the organization's needs.
- ***Software customization***: Modifies software to meet specific user or business requirements.

The SDLC is the foundation for all systems development methods, and hundreds of activities are associated with each phase. These activities typically include determining budgets, gathering system requirements, and writing detailed user documentation.

- ***Systems development life cycle (SDLC)***: The overall process for developing information systems, from planning and analysis through implementation and maintenance.

The SDLC begins with a business need, proceeds to an assessment of the functions a system must have to satisfy the need, and ends when the benefits of the system no longer outweigh its maintenance costs. This is why it is referred to as a life cycle. The SDLC is composed of seven distinct phases: planning, analysis, design, development, testing, implementation, and maintenance (see Figure 9.1).

Phase 1: Planning

The ***planning phase*** establishes a high-level plan of the intended project and determines project goals. Planning is the first and most critical phase of any systems development effort, regardless of whether the effort is to develop a system that allows customers to order products online, determine the best logistical structure for warehouses around the world, or develop a strategic information alliance with another organization. Organizations must carefully plan the activities (and determine why they are necessary) to be successful.

FIGURE 9.1

The SDLC and Its Associated Activities

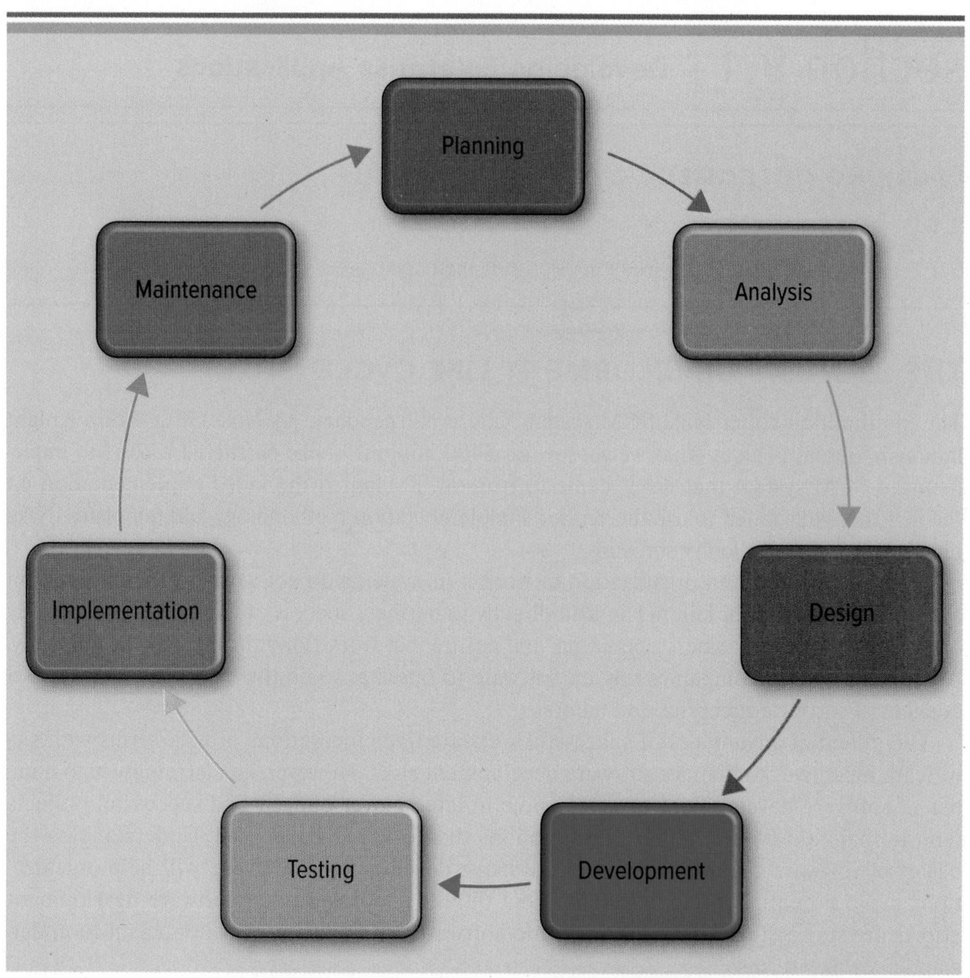

Phase	Associated Activity
Planning	■ Brainstorm issues and identify opportunities for the organization. ■ Prioritize and choose projects for development. ■ Set the project scope. ■ Develop the project plan.
Analysis	■ Gather the business requirement for the system. ■ Define any constraints associated with the system.
Design	■ Design the technical architecture required to support the system. ■ Design the system models.
Development	■ Build the technical architecture. ■ Build the database. ■ Build the applications.
Testing	■ Write the test conditions. ■ Perform system testing.
Implementation	■ Write detailed user documentation. ■ Provide training for the system users.
Maintenance	■ Build a help desk to support the system users. ■ Provide an environment to support system changes.

- ***Brainstorming***: A technique for generating ideas by encouraging participants to offer as many ideas as possible in a short period without any analysis until all the ideas have been exhausted. Many times, new business opportunities are found as the result of a brainstorming session.

APPLY YOUR KNOWLEDGE

BUSINESS DRIVEN START-UP

Meetings, Meetings, No More Meetings!

Bad meetings are the worst. If you have ever been stuck in a bad, ineffective meeting, you know what I am talking about. You arrive on time and the meeting starts 20 minutes late. Some person on the speaker phone can't seem to turn off the music playing on the mute button and a dog is barking in the background. One employee has his own agenda and attempts to hijack the meeting to focus on a different topic. We are in meeting hell. Here are a few tips to running an effective meeting:

- **Set the Agenda:** Start with a clear sense of purpose that every attendee agrees upon. The agenda is critical and sets a compass for the communication. If the meeting goes in a different direction, remind everyone of the agenda. Set time frames for each item and be sure to stick to the agenda.
- **Start and End on Time:** Time is valuable. Do not be late for your own meeting, and certainly do not be late for a co-worker's meeting. Just as important as starting on time is ending on time. A definitive end time will help ensure that the agenda is accomplished.
- **Make a "Parking Lot" Available for Off-Topic Items:** For items that need to be addressed but are not on the agenda, create a parking lot and delegate the item to a key decision maker.
- **End with an Action Plan:** Leave the last few minutes of every meeting to discuss the next steps. This discussion should include deciding who is responsible for what and what the deadlines are. Otherwise, all the time you spent on the meeting will be for naught.[3]

In a group, create a charter for your group meetings using the above list as a starter. Are there any other items you would add to the list, perhaps about distractions such as cell phones or side conversations? How can having meeting rules help foster more effective meetings? Do you foresee any issues with implementing a meeting charter for your own personal group meetings? If so, how would you combat such issues?

- ***Change agent***: A person or event that is the catalyst for implementing major changes for a system to meet business changes.

The Project Management Institute (PMI) develops procedures and concepts necessary to support the profession of project management (www.pmi.org). PMI defines the following key terms:

- ***Project***: A temporary activity a company undertakes to create a unique product, service, or result.
- ***Project management***: The application of knowledge, skills, tools, and techniques to project activities to meet project requirements.
- ***Project plan***: A formal, approved document that manages and controls the entire project.
- ***Project manager***: An individual who is an expert in project planning and management, defines and develops the project plan, and tracks the plan to ensure that the project is completed on time and on budget. The project manager is the person responsible for executing the entire project and defining the project scope that links the project to the organization's overall business goals.
- ***Project scope***: Describes the business need (the problem the project will solve) and the justification, requirements, and current boundaries for the project. Setting the project scope is critical because it defines what is and is not included in the project.

FIGURE 9.2

Methods for Gathering Business Requirements

Methods for Gathering Business Requirements
Conduct a joint application development (JAD) session where employees meet, sometimes for several days, to define or review the business requirements for the system.
Interview individuals to determine current operations and current issues.
Compile questionnaires to survey employees to discover issues.
Make observations to determine how current operations are performed.
Review business documents to discover reports, policies, and how information is used throughout the organization.

Phase 2: Analysis

In the ***analysis phase,*** the firm analyzes its end-user business requirements and refines project goals into defined functions and operations of the intended system.

- ***Business requirements***: The specific business requests that the system must meet to be successful. The analysis phase is critical because business requirements drive the entire systems development effort.

A sample business requirement might state, "The CRM system must track all customer inquiries by product, region, and sales representative." The business requirement will state what the system must accomplish to be considered successful. If a system does not meet the business requirements, it will be deemed a failed project. For this reason, the organization must spend as much time, energy, and resources as necessary to gather accurate and detailed business requirements. (Figure 9.2 displays ways to gather business requirements.)

Projects are typically dynamic in nature, and change should be expected and anticipated for successful project completion.

- ***Requirements management***: The process of managing changes to the business requirements throughout the project.
- ***Requirements definition document***: Prioritizes all of the business requirements by order of importance to the company.
- ***Sign-off***: The users' actual signatures, indicating they approve all of the business requirements.

Once a business analyst takes a detailed look at how an organization performs its work and its processes, the analyst can recommend ways to improve these processes to make them more efficient and effective.

- ***Process modeling***: Involves graphically representing the processes that capture, manipulate, store, and distribute information between a system and its environment.
- ***Data flow diagram (DFD)***: Illustrates the movement of information between external entities and the processes and data stores within the system (see Figure 9.3). Process models and data flow diagrams establish the specifications of the system.
- ***Computer-aided software engineering (CASE)***: Tools are software suites that automate systems analysis, design, and development. Process models and data flow diagrams can provide the basis for the automatic generation of the system if they are developed using a CASE tool.

Phase 3: Design

The ***design phase*** establishes descriptions of the desired features and operations of the system, including screen layouts, business rules, process diagrams, pseudocode, and other documentation. During the analysis phase, end users and MIS specialists work together to gather the detailed business requirements for the proposed project from a logical point of view. That is, during analysis, business requirements are documented without respect to technology or the technical infrastructure that will support the system. Moving into the design phase turns the project focus to the physical or technical point of view, defining the technical architecture that will support the system, including data models, screen designs, report layouts, and database models (see Figure 9.4).

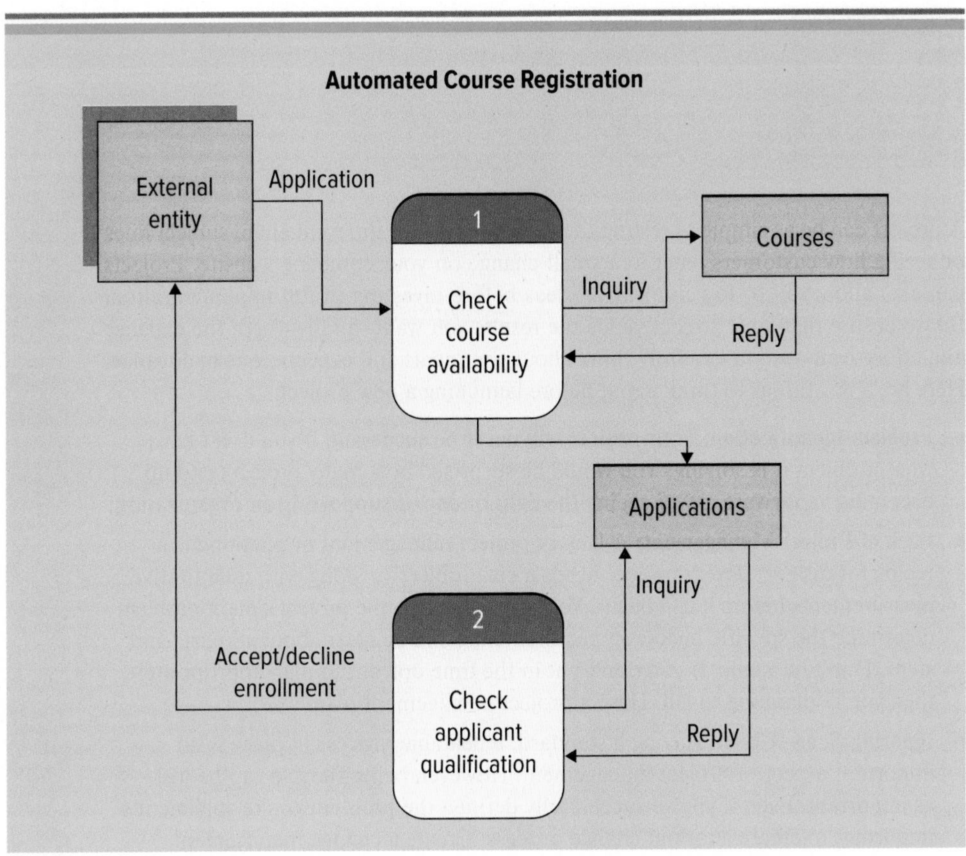

FIGURE 9.3

Sample Data Flow Diagram

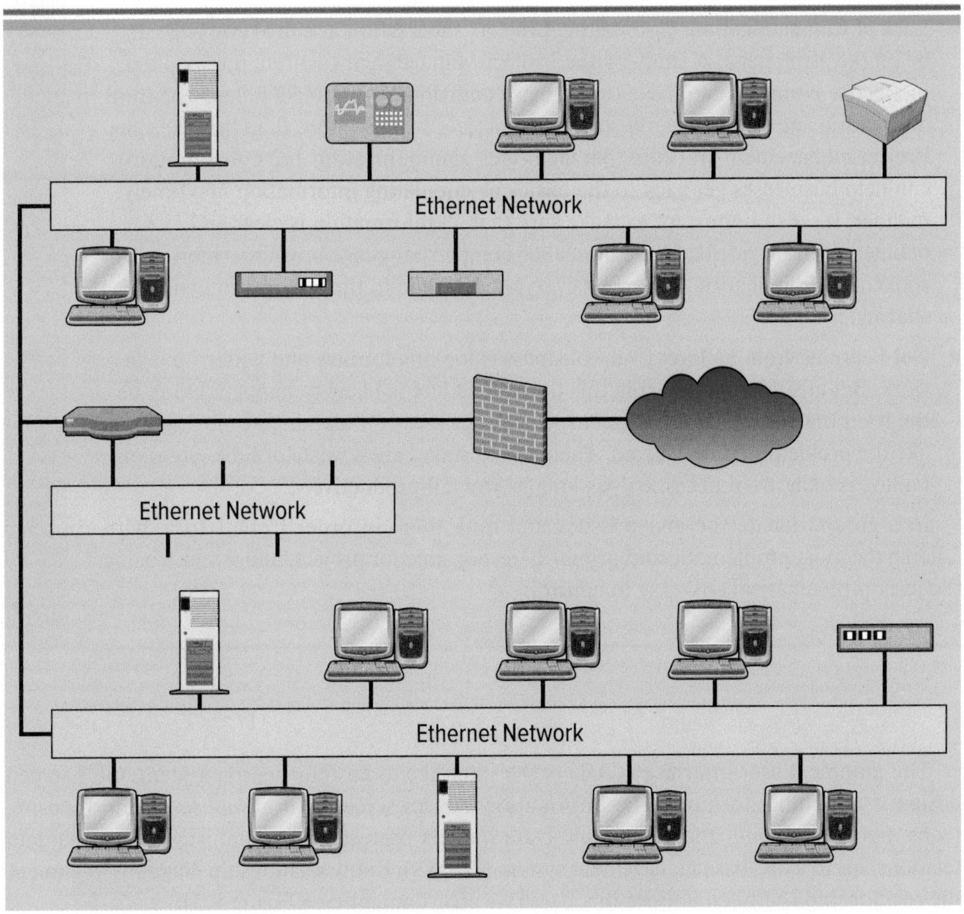

FIGURE 9.4

Sample Technical Architecture

APPLY YOUR KNOWLEDGE

BUSINESS DRIVEN DEBATE

Picking Great Projects

A project can be as simple as testing the response rate for different email subject lines or seeing how customers react to a small change on your company website. Projects can also allow you to test innovative ideas before investing in full implementation. But to ensure that your project yields the results you want–and is worth the expense and effort–you need to carefully think about your goals and expectations in advance. Here are a few things to think about before launching a new project:

- **Problem Identification:** Your project will never be successful if you don't know what problem it is solving. You would be surprised how many projects end up becoming vaporware, never seeing the light of day or supporting an organization.
- **Lack of Project Management:** A lack of project management or planning is a recipe for disaster. Every project needs a clear objective along with quantitative measurements before it can begin. You want to define the project's main problem, determine the specific necessary requirements, and be clear about all parts and steps. Don't be vague. If you don't put in the time upfront to plan appropriately, then you're planning to fail. Have a project management plan.
- **Ignoring Scope Creep:** Having a standard, repeatable process in place is an important aspect of project management. However, being flexible can be just as important. Even if you've successfully defined the problem you're solving, it's important to create a formal change process. Create a change management process in which new requirements are documented, reviewed, and approved. Examine why you need to change gears, reassess what new resources are needed, and communicate the updated goals so the entire team remains aligned.
- **Lack of Communication:** Completing projects successfully requires everyone to be on the same page. A study by the Project Management Institute revealed that ineffective communications is the primary contributor to project failure one-third of the time and had a negative impact on project success more than half the time. Project management software that facilitates communication and collaboration can help businesses get back to the basics by circulating information in a timely manner. It's also important to make sure that all information is clear and detailed. Refrain from using technical or complex language in your written or spoken communication. You want everyone to relate to the information you're sharing.
- **Not Learning from Failure:** Every business is looking for new and better ways to work. But at some point during this process, failure is likely to happen. Don't be the team that, when failure happens, you either focus on blaming or moving on like the problem never occurred. Then, the mistakes are a waste of time. Solution: Failing is okay, even necessary–as long as you fail productively.[4]

In a group, debate the above issues and rank them in order from 1 to 5, with 1 being the most problematic and primarily responsible for project failure and 5 being the least problematical and easy to control.

The graphical user interface (GUI) is the interface to an information system. GUI screen design is the ability to model the information system screens for an entire system by using icons, buttons, menus, and submenus. Data models represent a formal way to express data relationships to a database management system (DBMS). Entity relationship diagrams document the relationships between entities in a database environment (see Figure 9.5).

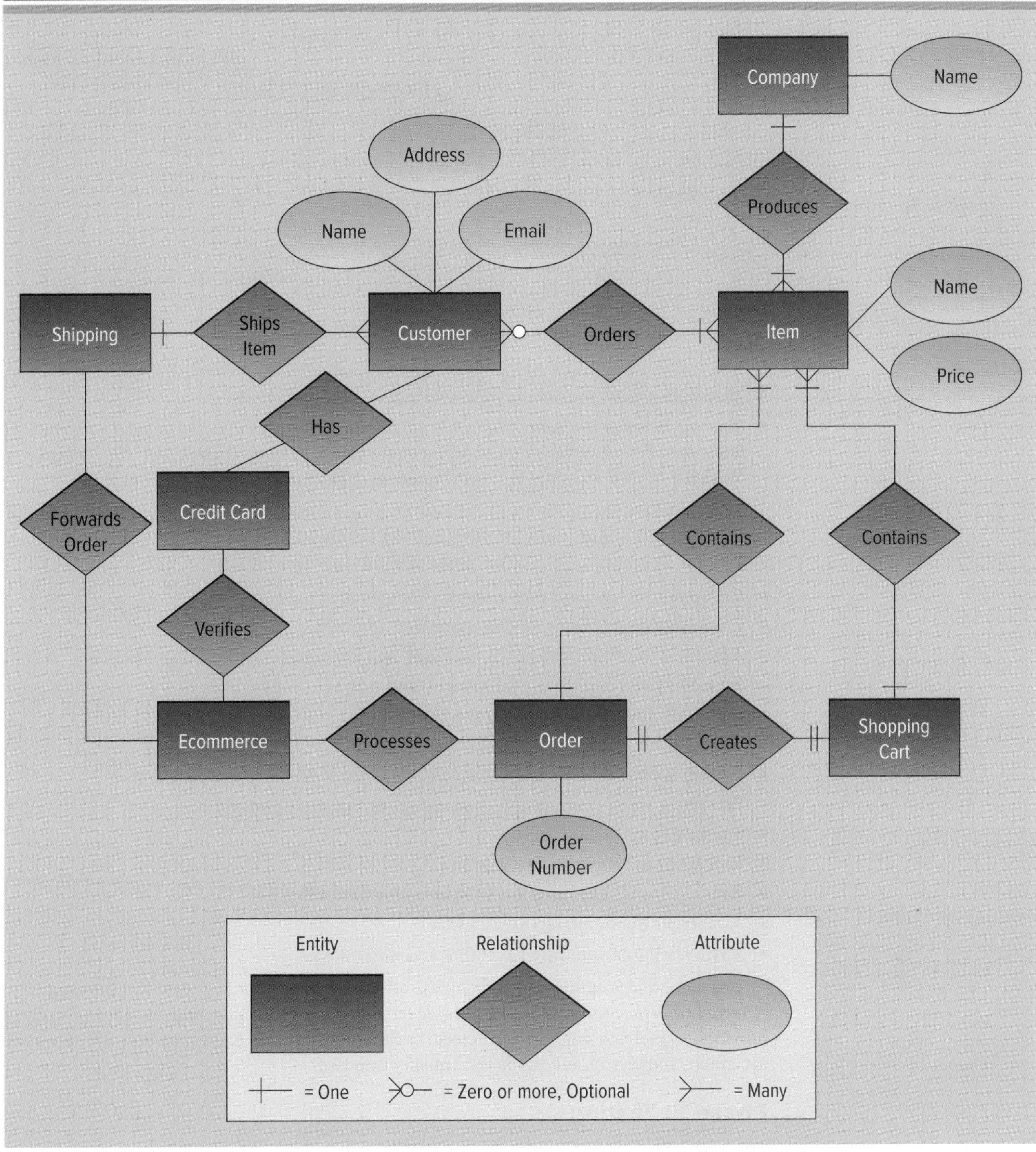

FIGURE 9.5

Sample Entity Relationship Diagram

Phase 4: Development

The ***development phase*** transforms all the detailed design documents from the design phase into the actual system. In this phase, the project transitions from preliminary designs to actual physical implementation. During development, the company purchases and implements the equipment necessary to support the architecture.

- ***Software engineering***: A disciplined approach for constructing information systems through the use of common methods, techniques, or tools.
- ***Programming language***: A unique set of keywords (words it understands) along with a special syntax for organizing program instructions that execute computer commands.

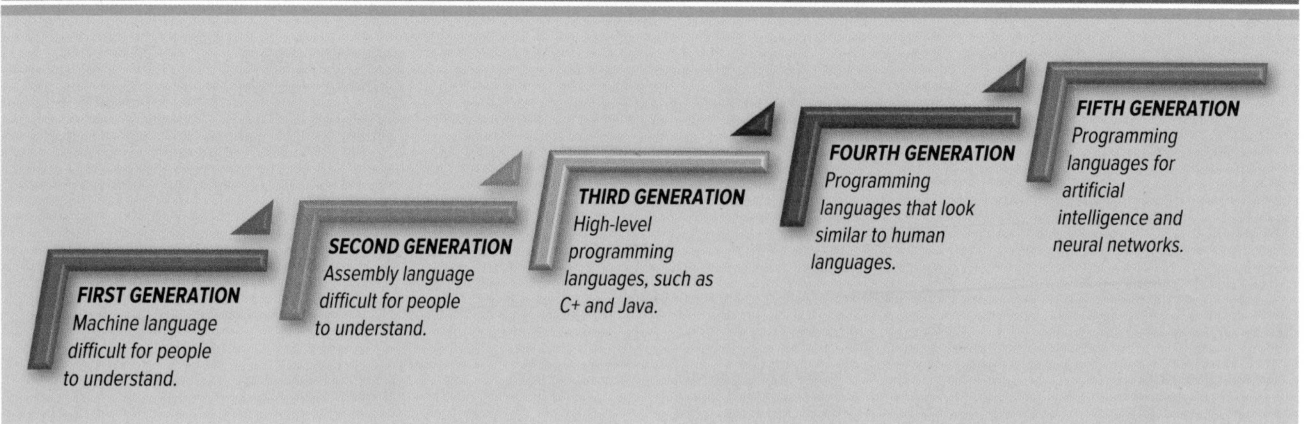

FIGURE 9.6

Overview of Programming Languages

- ***Coders***: People who write the programs that operate computers.
- ***Fourth-generation languages (4GLs)***: Programming languages that look similar to human languages. For example, a typical 4GL command might state, "FIND ALL RECORDS WHERE NAME IS 'SMITH'." Programming languages are displayed in Figure 9.6.

During development, the team defines the programming language it will use to build the system. There is a huge range of programming languages to choose from, and each one can be used for different purposes. The most common languages include:

- **C:** A powerful language used primarily for operating hardware.
- **C++:** Based on C using an object-oriented approach.
- **Ada:** Used to control spacecraft, satellites, and airplanes.
- **Java:** Works on computers, cell phones, and tablets.
- **MATLAB:** Ideal for mathematical computations.
- **PHP:** Creates interactive websites.
- **Python:** A text-based language that can be used to build computer programs.
- **Scratch:** A visual language that is ideal for learning programming.
- **Spark:** Streaming data analysis.
- **R:** Statistical computing and graphics.
- **Ruby:** Automatically turns lots of information into web pages.
- **JavaScript:** Builds interactive websites.
- **XML:** Used to manipulate Excel files and workbooks.

It is a good idea to perform a technical review when outsourcing technical development. A ***technical review (or peer review)*** is a meeting in which an independent team of experts provides an in-depth analysis of project results to ensure that team members did the work accurately, completely, and to the right quality standard.

Phase 5: Testing

The ***testing phase*** brings all the project pieces together into a special testing environment to eliminate errors and bugs and verify that the system meets all the business requirements defined in the analysis phase.

- ***Bugs***: Defects in the code of an information system.
- ***Test conditions***: Detail the steps the system must perform along with the expected result of each step (see Figure 9.7).

Testers execute test conditions and compare the expected results with the actual results to verify that the system functions correctly. Each time the actual result is different from the expected result, a bug is generated, and the system must be fixed in development. A typical systems development effort has hundreds or thousands of test conditions that must be verified against the business requirements to ensure that the system is operating as expected. Figure 9.8 displays the different types of tests typically included in a systems development effort.

Test Condition Number	Date Tested	Tested	Test Condition	Expected Result	Actual Result	Pass/ Fail
1	1/1/29	Ellie Durikins	Click system Start button.	Main menu appears.	Same as expected result	Pass
2	1/1/29	Ellie Durikins	Click Logon button in main menu.	Logon screen appears, asking for user name and password.	Same as expected result	Pass
3	1/1/29	Ellie Durikins	Type Emily Durikins in the user name field.	Ellie Durikins appears in the user name field.	Same as expected result	Pass
4	1/1/29	Ellie Durikins	Type X@$#7ABC!! in the password field.	X@$#7ABC!! appears in the password field.	Same as expected result	Pass
5	1/1/29	Ellie Durikins	Click OK button.	User logon request is sent to database, and user name and password are verified.	Same as expected result	Pass
6	1/1/29	Ellie Durikins	Click Start.	User name and password are accepted, and the system main menu appears.	Screen appears stating logon failed and user name and password were incorrect.	Fail

FIGURE 9.7

Sample Test Conditions

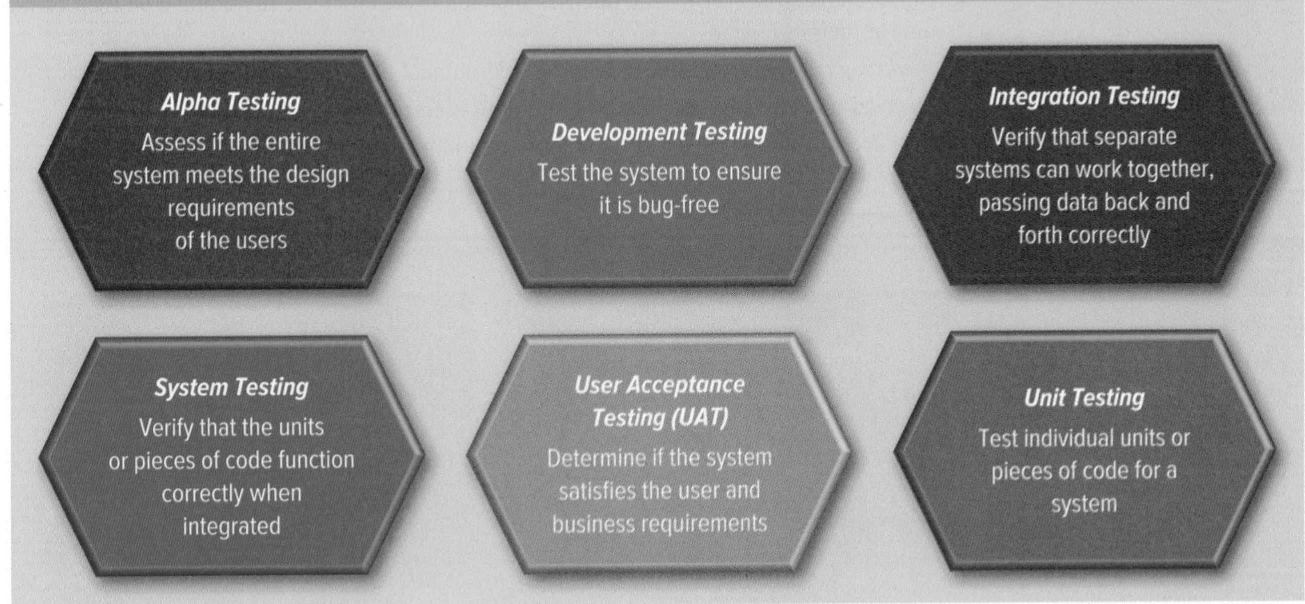

FIGURE 9.8

Different Forms of System Testing

Phase 6: Implementation

In the ***implementation phase,*** the organization places the system into production so users can begin to perform actual business operations with it. Figure 9.9 displays the different implementation methods an organization can choose to ensure success.

In this phase, the users are supported through different forms of training that take place either online or in a workshop.

APPLY YOUR KNOWLEDGE

BUSINESS DRIVEN ANALYTICS

Bugs Everywhere

Bug reports are an important part of software development. All bugs must be logged, fixed, and tested. There are three common types of bugs programmers look for when building a system.

- **Syntax error:** A mistake in the program's words or symbols.
- **Runtime error:** A mistake that causes the program to crash, such as dividing by 0 or adding together two strings.
- **Logic error:** A mistake that causes the output of the program to be wrong, such as adding instead of subtracting, using < instead of >, or using the wrong data in an equation.

Rank the three types of bugs by which one is the easiest to identify and which one is the most difficult to identify. What happens if metrics are not tracked on bug identification and bug fixes? What happens if a bug is not caught during development and goes live in production?

Imagine the following scenario: A tester creates a new bug report for a problem that was already identified as a bug; however, it is not detected as a duplicate. What happens to the project? This is a particularly common issue with large, complex system development efforts. How can you mitigate the problem of different users reporting the same bug or problem about the same system?

- ***Online training***: Runs over the Internet and employees complete the training on their own time at their own pace.
- ***Workshop training***: Held in a classroom environment and led by an instructor.
- ***Help desk***: A group of people who respond to users' questions.
- ***User documentation***: This is created for users to highlight how to use the system and troubleshoot issues or problems.

FIGURE 9.9

System Implementation Methods

Parallel Implementation Uses both the legacy system and new system until all users verify that the new system functions correctly	***Plunge Implementation*** Discards the legacy system and immediately migrates all users to the new system
Pilot Implementation Assigns a small group of people to use the new system until it is verified to work correctly; then the remaining users migrate to the new system	***Phased Implementation*** Installs the new system in phases (for example, by department) until it is verified to work correctly

Report	Examples
Internal report	Presents data that are distributed inside the organization and intended for employees within an organization. Internal reports typically support day-to-day operations monitoring that supports managerial decision making.
Detailed internal report	Presents information with little or no filtering or restrictions of the data.
Summary internal report	Organizes and categorizes data for managerial perusal. A report that summarizes total sales by product for each month is an example of a summary internal report. The data for a summary report is typically categorized and summarized to indicate trends and potential problems.
Exception report	Highlights situations occurring outside of the normal operating range for a condition or standard. These internal reports include only exceptions and might highlight accounts that are unpaid or delinquent or identify items that are low in stock.
Information system control report	Ensures the reliability of information, consisting of policies and their physical implementation, access restrictions, or record keeping of actions and transactions.
Information system audit report	Assesses a company's information system to determine necessary changes and to help ensure the information system's availability, confidentiality, and integrity.
Post-implementation report	Presents a formal report or audit of a project after it is up and running.

FIGURE 9.10

Examples of System Reports

Phase 7: Maintenance

Maintaining the system is the final sequential phase of any systems development effort. In the ***maintenance phase,*** the organization performs changes, corrections, additions, and upgrades to ensure that the system continues to meet business goals. This phase continues for the life of the system because the system must change as the business evolves and its needs change, which means conducting constant monitoring, supporting the new system with frequent minor changes (for example, new reports or information capturing), and reviewing the system to be sure it is moving the organization toward its strategic goals. During the maintenance phase, the system will generate reports to help users and MIS specialists ensure it is functioning correctly (see Figure 9.10).

- ***Corrective maintenance***: Makes system changes to repair design flaws, coding errors, or implementation issues.
- ***Preventive maintenance***: Makes system changes to reduce the chance of future system failure.

SOFTWARE DEVELOPMENT METHODOLOGY: THE WATERFALL

LO 9.2: Summarize the different software development methodologies.

Today, systems are so large and complex that teams of architects, analysts, developers, testers, and users must work together to create the millions of lines of custom-written code that drive enterprises. For this reason, developers have created a number of systems development life cycle methodologies.

- ***Methodology***: A set of policies, procedures, standards, processes, practices, tools, techniques, and tasks that people apply to technical and management challenges.

Firms use a methodology to manage the deployment of technology with work plans, requirements documents, and test plans, for instance. A formal methodology can include coding standards, code libraries, development practices, and much more.

The oldest and best known is the waterfall methodology.

- ***Waterfall methodology***: A sequence of phases in which the output of each phase becomes the input for the next (see Figure 9.11).

In the SDLC, this means the steps are performed one at a time, in order, from planning through implementation and maintenance. The traditional waterfall method no longer serves most of today's development efforts, however; it is inflexible and expensive, and it requires rigid adherence to the sequence of steps. Its success rate is only about 1 in 10. Figure 9.12 explains some issues related to the waterfall methodology.[5]

Today's business environment is fierce. The desire and need to outsmart and outplay competitors remain intense. Given this drive for success, leaders push internal development teams and

FIGURE 9.11

The Traditional Waterfall Methodology

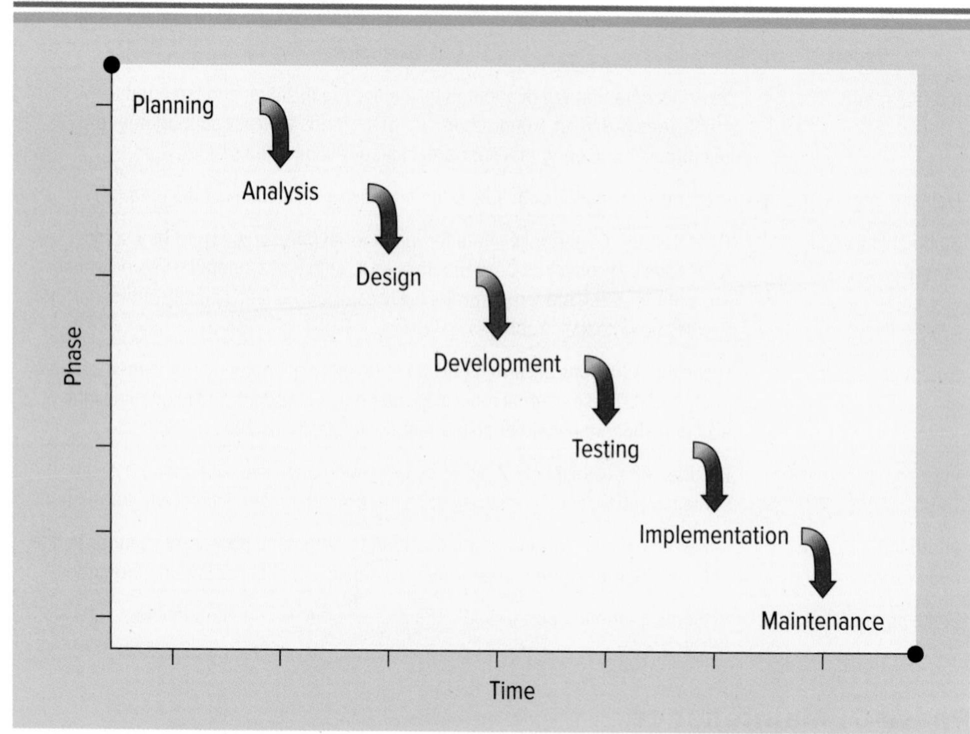

FIGURE 9.12

Disadvantages of the Waterfall Methodology

Issues Related to the Waterfall Methodology	
The business problem	Any flaws in accurately defining and articulating the business problem in terms of what the business users actually require flow onward to the next phase.
The plan	Managing costs, resources, and time constraints is difficult in the waterfall sequence. What happens to the schedule if a programmer quits? How will a schedule delay in a specific phase affect the total cost of the project? Unexpected contingencies may sabotage the plan.
The solution	The waterfall methodology is problematic in that it assumes users can specify all business requirements in advance. Defining the appropriate IT infrastructure that is flexible, scalable, and reliable is a challenge. The final IT infrastructure solution must meet not only current but also future needs in terms of time, cost, feasibility, and flexibility. Vision is inevitably limited at the head of the waterfall.

external vendors to deliver agreed-upon systems faster and cheaper so they can realize benefits as early as possible. Even so, systems remain large and complex. The traditional waterfall methodology no longer serves as an adequate systems development methodology in most cases. Because this development environment is the norm and not the exception anymore, development teams use a new breed of alternative development methods to achieve their business objectives.

- ***Prototyping***: A modern design approach by which the designers and system users use an iterative approach in building the system.

AGILE SOFTWARE DEVELOPMENT METHODOLOGIES

It is common knowledge that the smaller the project, the greater the success rate. The iterative development style is the ultimate in small projects.

- ***Iterative development***: Consists of a series of tiny projects. It has become the foundation of multiple agile methodologies. Figure 9.13 displays an iterative approach.

Agile methodology is just what it sounds like: fast and efficient, with lower costs and fewer features.

- ***Agile methodology***: Aims for customer satisfaction through early and continuous delivery of useful software components developed by an iterative process using the bare minimum requirements.

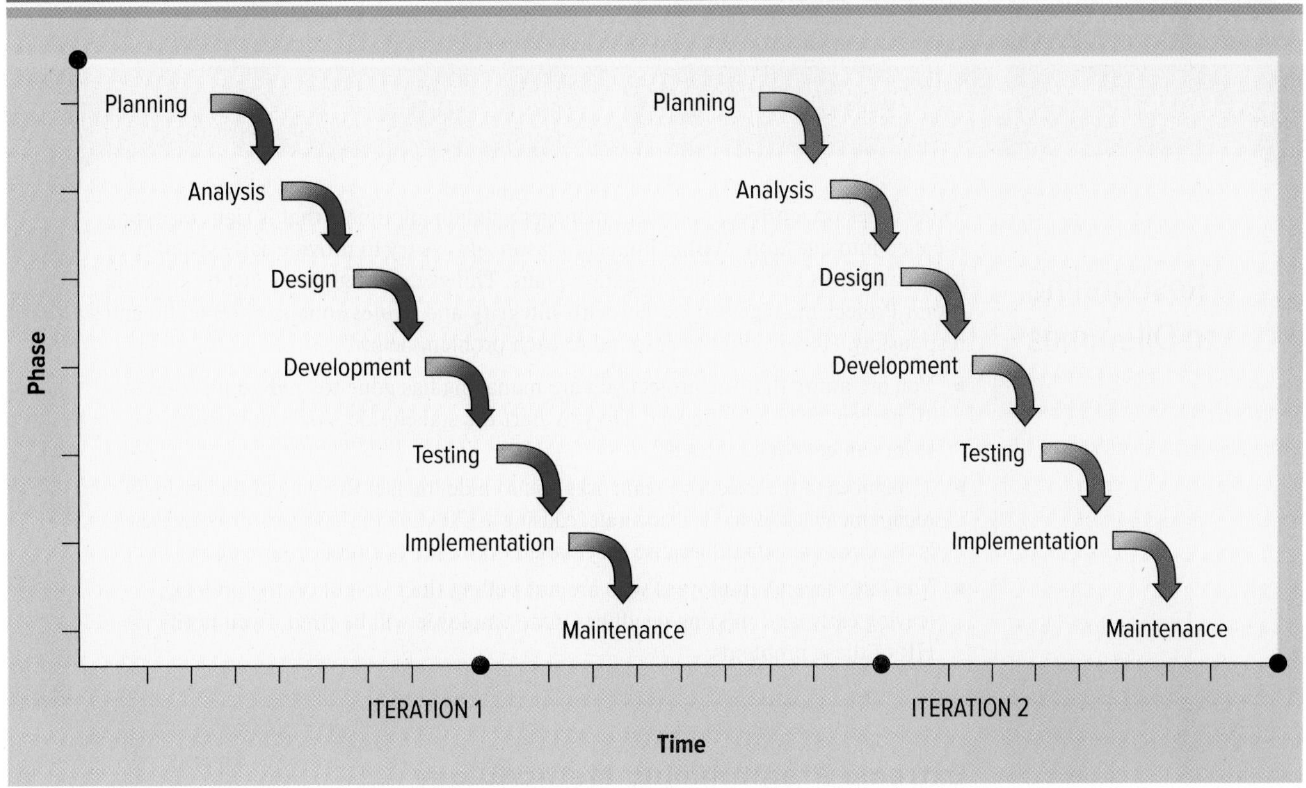

FIGURE 9.13

The Iterative Approach

Using agile methods helps refine feasibility and supports the process for getting rapid feedback as functionality is introduced. Developers can adjust as they move along and better clarify unclear requirements.[6]

One key to delivering a successful product or system is to deliver value to users as soon as possible—give them something they want and like early to create buy-in, generate enthusiasm, and, ultimately, reduce scope. Using agile methodologies helps maintain accountability and establish a barometer for the satisfaction of end users. It does no good to accomplish something on time and on budget if it does not satisfy the end user. The primary forms of agile methodologies include:

- Rapid prototyping or rapid application development methodology
- Extreme programming methodology
- Rational unified process (RUP) methodology
- Scrum methodology

It is important not to get hung up on the names of the methodologies—some are proprietary brand names; others are generally accepted names. It is more important to know how these alternative methodologies are used in today's business environment and the benefits they can deliver.

Rapid Application Development (RAD) Methodology

In response to the faster pace of business, rapid application development has become a popular route for accelerating systems development.

- ***Rapid application development (RAD) methodology*** (also called *rapid prototyping*): Emphasizes extensive user involvement in the rapid and evolutionary construction of working prototypes of a system, to accelerate the systems development process. Figure 9.14 displays the fundamentals of RAD.

FIGURE 9.14

Fundamentals of RAD

Fundamentals of RAD
Focus initially on creating a prototype that looks and acts like the desired system.
Actively involve system users in the analysis, design, and development phases.
Accelerate collecting the business requirements through an interactive and iterative construction approach.

APPLY YOUR KNOWLEDGE

BUSINESS DRIVEN ETHICS AND SECURITY

Responding to Dilemmas

Many times on a project, a project manager's judgment about what is right or wrong is called into question. Within limits of reason, always try to provide early visibility of issues and risks and provide mitigation plans. Things do not go away just by ignoring them. Project managers must act with integrity and professionalism, ethically and responsibly. How would you respond to each problem below?

- You are aware that the project you are managing has gone to "red" status due to a 10 percent schedule slippage. Do you alert the stakeholders or wait to see if the team can get back on track?
- A member of the executive team asks you to hide the fact that one of the business requirements collected is inaccurate, causing a $200,000 fix. The executive believes it is the customer's fault because they signed off on the business requirements.
- You have several employees who are not pulling their weight on the project, leaving early, and missing deadlines. One employee will be fired if you notify HR of these problems.

Extreme Programming Methodology

Extreme programming (XP) methodology, like other agile methods, breaks a project into four phases, and developers cannot continue to the next phase until the previous phase is complete. The delivery strategy supporting XP is that the quicker the feedback, the more improved the results. XP has four basic phases: planning, designing, coding, and testing. Planning can include user interviews, meetings, and small releases. During design, functionality is not added until it is required or needed. During coding, the developers work together soliciting continuous feedback from users, eliminating the communication gap that generally exists between developers and customers. During testing, the test requirements are generated before any code is developed. Extreme programming saves time and produces successful projects by continuously reviewing and revamping needed and unneeded requirements.[7]

Customer satisfaction is the primary reason XP finds success because developers quickly respond to changing business requirements, even late in the life cycle. XP encourages managers, customers, and developers to work together as a team to ensure the delivery of high-quality systems. XP is similar to a puzzle; there are many small pieces, and individually the pieces make no sense, but when they are pieced together, they can create a new system.

Rational Unified Process (RUP) Methodology

The ***rational unified process (RUP) methodology,*** owned by IBM, provides a framework for breaking down the development of software into four gates. Each gate consists of executable iterations of the software in development. A project stays in a gate waiting for the stakeholder's analysis, and then it either moves to the next gate or is canceled. The gates include:[8]

- **Gate one: inception.** This phase ensures that all stakeholders have a shared understanding of the proposed system and what it will do.
- **Gate two: elaboration.** This phase expands on the agreed-upon details of the system, including the ability to provide an architecture to support and build it.
- **Gate three: construction.** This phase includes building and developing the product.
- **Gate four: transition.** Primary questions answered in this phase address ownership of the system and training of key personnel.

Because RUP is an iterative methodology, the user can reject the product and force the developers to go back to gate one. RUP helps developers avoid reinventing the wheel and focuses on rapidly adding or removing reusable chunks of processes addressing common problems.

Scrum Methodology

Another agile methodology, ***scrum methodology,*** uses small teams to produce small pieces of software using a series of sprints, or 30-day intervals, to achieve an appointed goal. In rugby, a scrum is a team pack and everyone in the pack works together to move the ball down the field. In scrum methodology, each day ends or begins with a stand-up meeting to monitor and control the development effort.

section 9.2 | Project Management

LEARNING OUTCOMES

9.3 Explain project management and identify the primary reasons projects fail.

9.4 Identify the primary project planning diagrams.

9.5 Identify the three types of outsourcing.

USING PROJECT MANAGEMENT TO DELIVER SUCCESSFUL PROJECTS

LO 9.3: Explain project management and identify the primary reasons projects fail.

No one would think of building an office complex by turning loose 100 construction teams to build 100 rooms with no single blueprint or agreed-upon vision of the completed structure. Yet this is precisely the situation in which many large organizations find themselves when managing information technology projects. Organizations routinely overschedule their resources (human and otherwise), develop redundant projects, and damage profitability by investing in nonstrategic efforts that do not contribute to the organization's bottom line. Business leaders face a rapidly moving and unforgiving global marketplace that will force them to use every possible tool to sustain competitiveness; project management is one of those tools. For this reason, business personnel must anticipate being involved in some form of project management during their career. Figure 9.15 displays a few examples of the different types of projects organizations encounter.

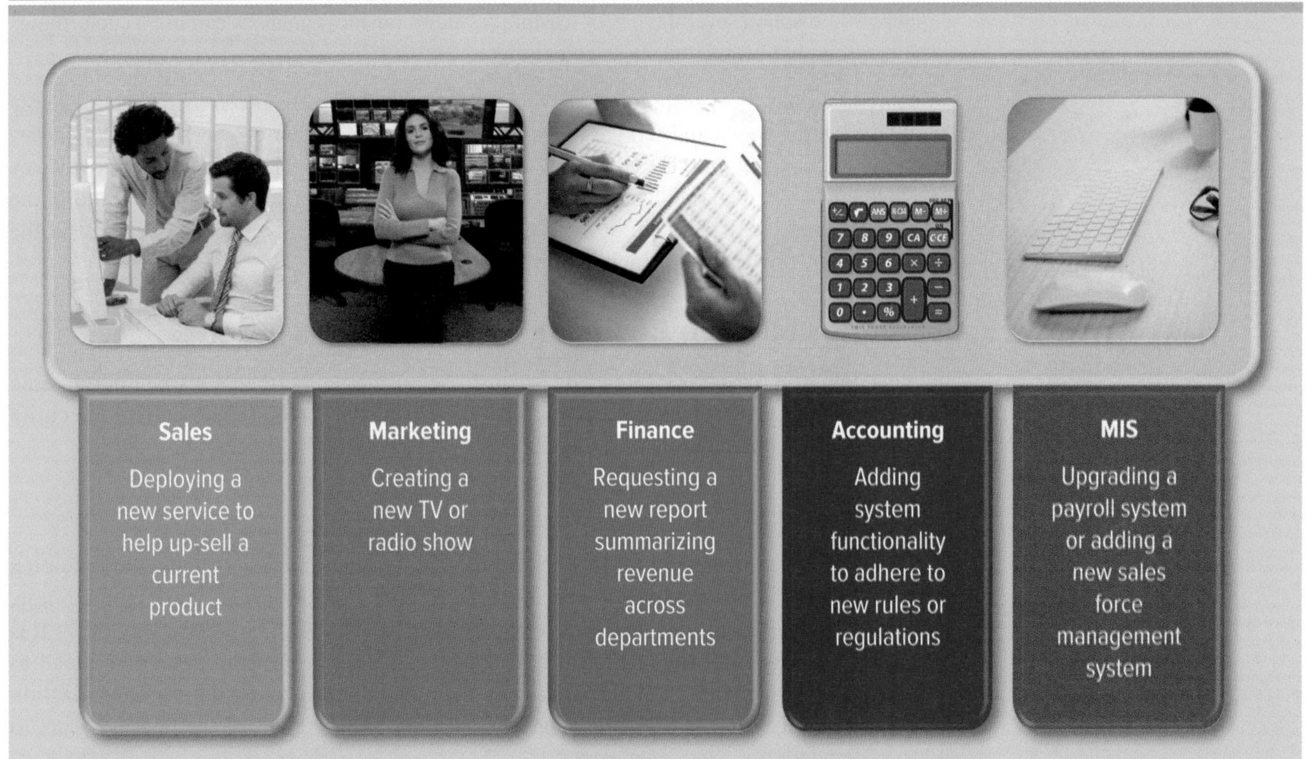

Sales
Deploying a new service to help up-sell a current product
Marketing
Creating a new TV or radio show
Finance
Requesting a new report summarizing revenue across departments
Accounting
Adding system functionality to adhere to new rules or regulations
MIS
Upgrading a payroll system or adding a new sales force management system

FIGURE 9.15

Types of Organizational Projects

Sources: (left): Wavebreakmedia Ltd/Getty Images; (left-middle): F64/Getty Images; (middle): PORTRAIT IMAGES ASIA BY NONWARIT/Shutterstock; (right-middle): McGraw Hill; (right): LightField Studios/Shutterstock

FIGURE 9.16

Examples of Tangible and Intangible Benefits

One of the most difficult decisions managers make is identifying the projects in which to invest time, energy, and resources. An organization must choose what it wants to do–justifying it, defining it, and listing expected results–and how to do it, including project budget, schedule, and analysis of project risks.

- ***Tangible benefits***: Easy to quantify and typically measured to determine the success or failure of a project.
- ***Intangible benefits***: Difficult to quantify or measure (see Figure 9.16 for examples).
- ***Feasibility***: The measure of the tangible and intangible benefits of an information system. Figure 9.17 displays several types of feasibility studies business analysts can use to determine the projects that best fit business goals.

Businesses today must respond quickly to a rapidly changing business environment by continually innovating goods and services. Effective project management provides a controlled way to respond to changing market conditions, to foster global communications, and to provide key metrics to enable managerial decision making. Developing projects within budget and on time is challenging, and with the help of solid project management skills, managers can avoid the primary reasons projects fail, which are displayed in Figure 9.18.

Unclear or Missing Business Requirements

The most common reason systems fail is because the business requirements are either missing or incorrectly gathered during the analysis phase. The business requirements drive the entire system. If they are not accurate or complete, the system will not be successful.

Skipped Phases

The first thing individuals tend to do when a project falls behind schedule is to start skipping phases in the SDLC. For example, if a project is three weeks behind in the development phase, the project manager might decide to cut testing from six weeks to three weeks. Obviously, it is impossible to perform all the testing in half the time. Failing to test the system will lead to unfound errors, and chances are high that the system will fail. It is critical for an organization to perform all phases in the SDLC during every project. Skipping any of the phases is sure to lead to system failure.

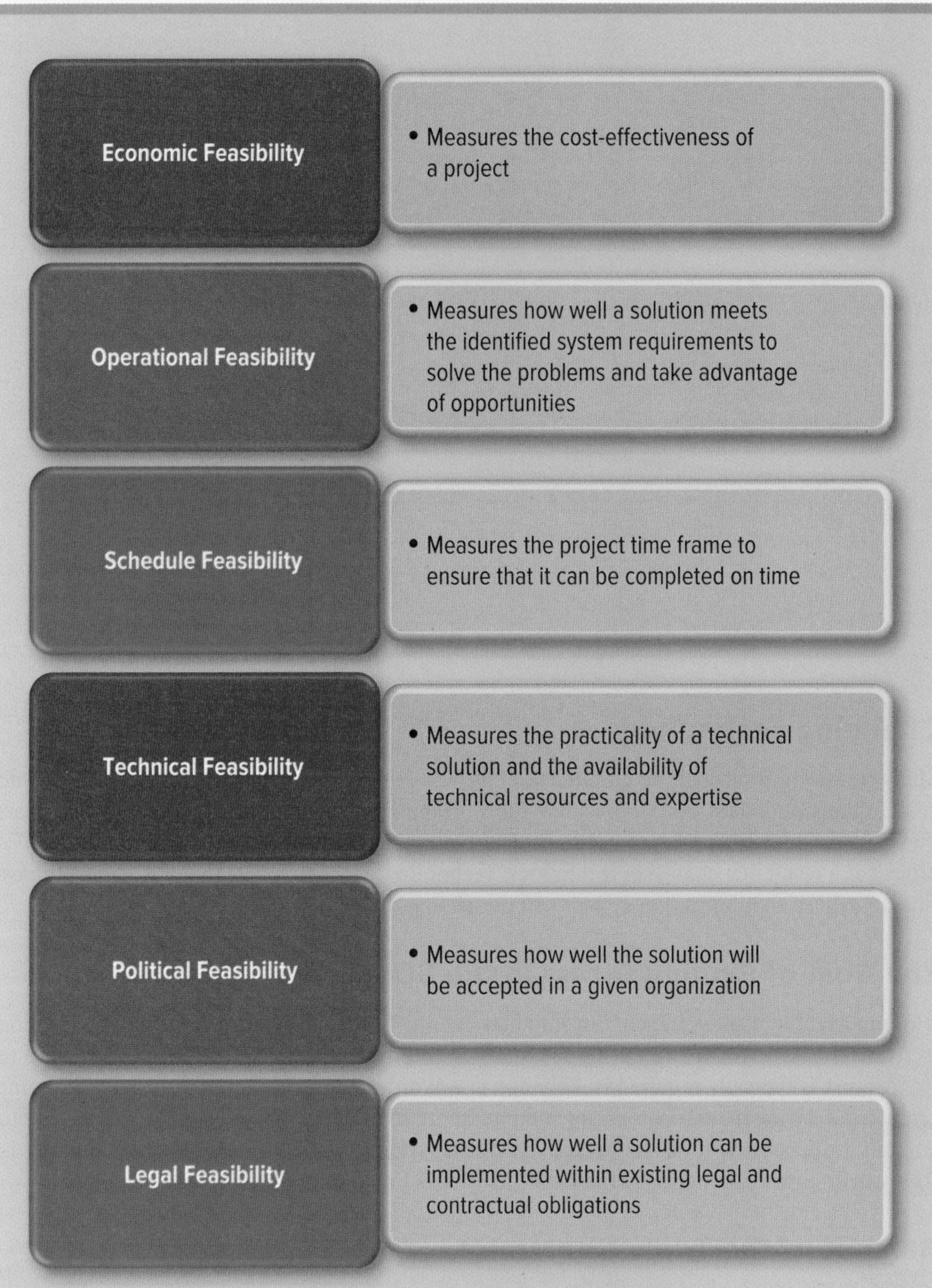

Economic Feasibility
• Measures the cost-effectiveness of a project
Operational Feasibility
• Measures how well a solution meets the identified system requirements to solve the problems and take advantage of opportunities
Schedule Feasibility
• Measures the project time frame to ensure that it can be completed on time
Technical Feasibility
• Measures the practicality of a technical solution and the availability of technical resources and expertise
Political Feasibility
• Measures how well the solution will be accepted in a given organization
Legal Feasibility
• Measures how well a solution can be implemented within existing legal and contractual obligations

FIGURE 9.17

Types of Feasibility Studies

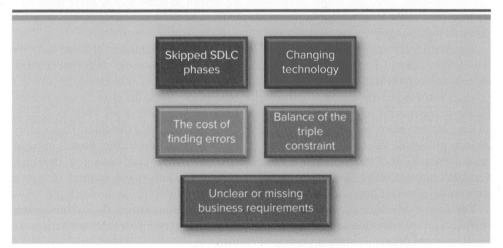

Skipped SDLC phases

Changing technology

The cost of finding errors

Balance of the triple constraint

Unclear or missing business requirements

FIGURE 9.18

Why Projects Fail

FIGURE 9.19

The Cost of Fixing Errors

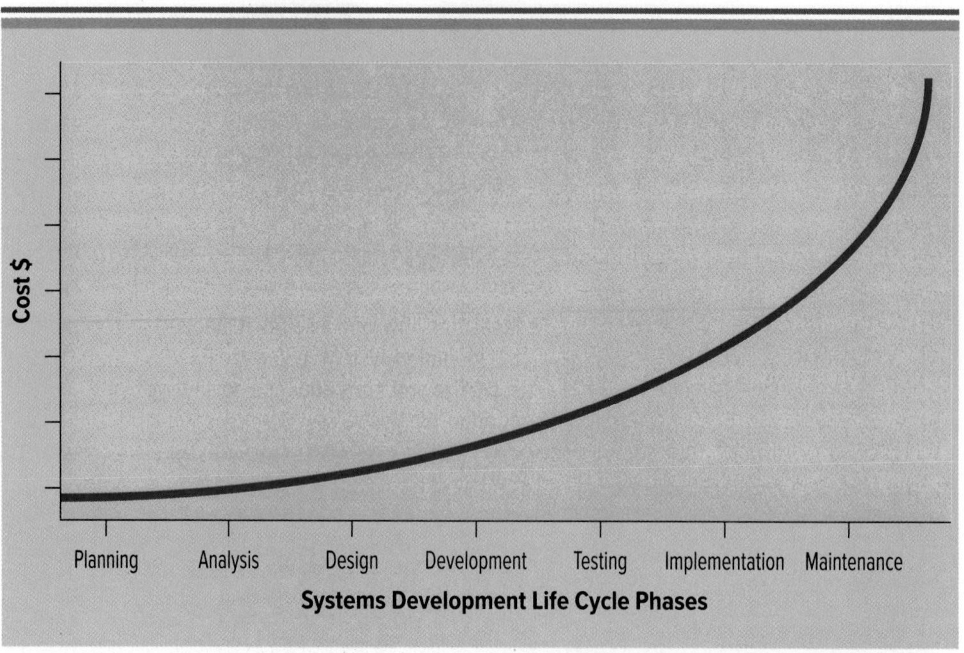

Changing Technology

Many real-world projects have hundreds of business requirements, take years to complete, and cost millions of dollars. As Moore's law states, technology changes at an incredibly fast pace; therefore, it is possible that an entire project plan will need to be revised in the middle of a project as a result of a change in technology. Technology changes so fast that it is almost impossible to deliver an information system without feeling the pain of updates.

The Cost of Finding Errors in the SDLC

It is important to discuss the relationship between the SDLC and the cost for the organization to fix errors. An error found during the analysis and design phase is relatively inexpensive to fix. All that is typically required is a change to a Word document. However, exactly the same error found during the testing or implementation phase will cost the organization an enormous amount to fix because it has to change the actual system. Figure 9.19 displays how the cost to fix an error grows exponentially the later the error is found in the SDLC.

Balance of the Triple Constraint

Figure 9.20 displays the relationships among the three primary and interdependent variables in any project–time, cost, and scope. All projects are limited in some way by these three constraints. The Project Management Institute calls the framework for evaluating these competing demands *the triple constraint.*

The relationship among these variables is such that if any one changes, at least one other is likely to be affected. For example, moving up a project's finish date could mean either increasing costs to hire more staff or decreasing the scope to eliminate features or functions. Increasing a project's scope to include additional customer requests could extend the project's time to completion or increase the project's cost–or both–to accommodate the changes. Project quality is affected by the project manager's ability to balance these competing demands. High-quality projects deliver the agreed-upon product or service on time and on budget. Project management is the science of making intelligent trade-offs between time, cost, and scope. Benjamin Franklin's timeless advice–*by failing to prepare, you prepare to fail*–applies to many of today's software development projects.

The Project Management Institute created the *Project Management Body of Knowledge (PMBOK)* for the education and certification of project managers. Figure 9.21 summarizes the key elements of project planning according to *PMBOK.*

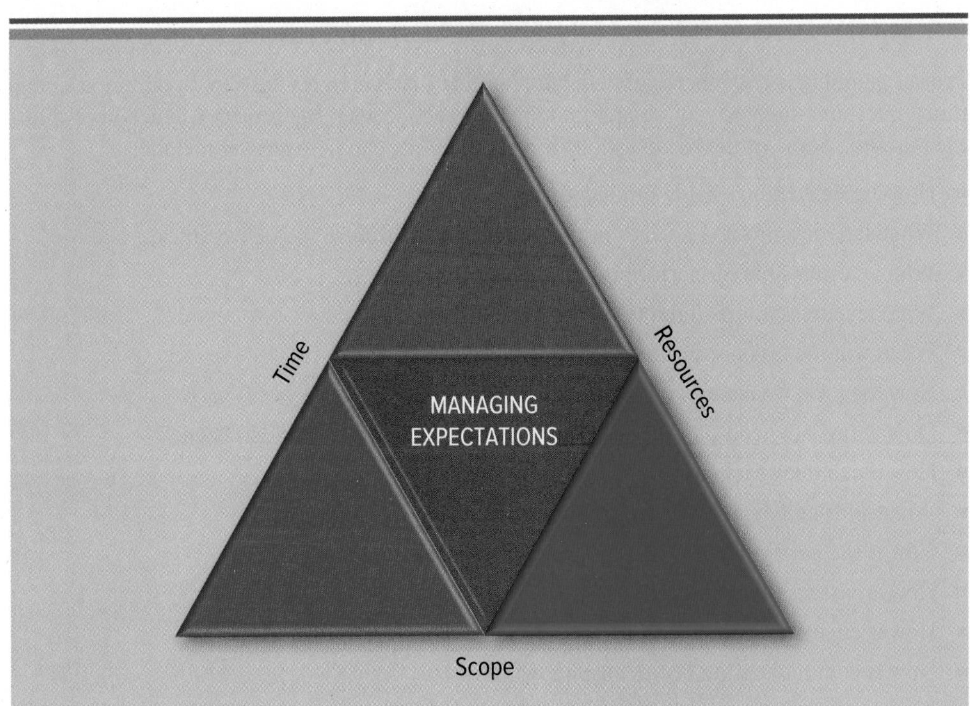

FIGURE 9.20

The Triple Constraint: Changing One Changes All

FIGURE 9.21

PMBOK Elements of Project Management

Tool	Description
Communication plan	Defines the how, what, when, and who regarding the flow of project information to stakeholders and is key for managing expectations.
Executive sponsor	The person or group who provides the financial resources for the project.
Project assumption	Factors considered to be true, real, or certain without proof or demonstration. Examples include hours in a workweek or time of year the work will be performed.
Project constraint	Specific factors that can limit options, including budget, delivery dates, available skilled resources, and organizational policies.
Project deliverable	Any measurable, tangible, verifiable outcome, result, or item that is produced to complete a project or part of a project. Examples of project deliverables include design documents, testing scripts, and requirements documents.
Project management office (PMO)	An internal department that oversees all organizational projects. This group must formalize and professionalize project management expertise and leadership. One of the primary initiatives of the PMO is to educate the organization on techniques and procedures necessary to run successful projects.
Project milestone	Represents key dates when a certain group of activities must be performed. For example, completing the planning phase might be a project milestone. If a project milestone is missed, then chances are the project is experiencing problems.
Project objectives	Quantifiable criteria that must be met for the project to be considered a success.
Project requirements document	Defines the specifications for product/output of the project and is key for managing expectations, controlling scope, and completing other planning efforts.
Project scope statement	Links the project to the organization's overall business goals. It describes the business need (the problem the project will solve) and the justification, requirements, and current boundaries for the project. It defines the work that must be completed to deliver the product with the specified features and functions, and it includes constraints, assumptions, and requirements—all components necessary for developing accurate cost estimates.
Project stakeholder	Individuals and organizations actively involved in the project or whose interests might be affected as a result of project execution or project completion.
Responsibility matrix	Defines all project roles and indicates what responsibilities are associated with each role.
Status report	Periodic reviews of actual performance versus expected performance.

LO 9.4: Identify the primary project planning diagrams.

PRIMARY PROJECT PLANNING DIAGRAMS

Project planning is the process of detailed planning that generates answers to common operational questions such as why we are doing this project or what the project will accomplish for the business. Some of the key questions project planning can help answer include:

- How are deliverables being produced?
- What activities or tasks need to be accomplished to produce the deliverables?
- Who is responsible for performing the tasks?
- What resources are required to perform the tasks?
- When will the tasks be performed?
- How long will it take to perform each task?
- Do any tasks depend on other tasks being completed before they can begin?
- How much does each task cost?
- What skills and experience are required to perform each task?
- How is the performance of the task being measured, including quality?
- How are issues being tracked?
- How is change being addressed?
- How is communication occurring and when?
- What risks are associated with each task?

The project objectives are among the most important areas to define because they are essentially the major elements of the project. When an organization achieves the project objectives, it has accomplished the major goals of the project and the project scope is satisfied. Project objectives must include metrics so that the project's success can be measured. The metrics can include cost, schedule, and quality metrics. Figure 9.22 lists the SMART criteria–useful reminders about how to ensure that the project has created understandable and measurable objectives. A ***project charter*** is a concise written description of the project's intended work. The

FIGURE 9.22

SMART Criteria for Successful Objective Creation

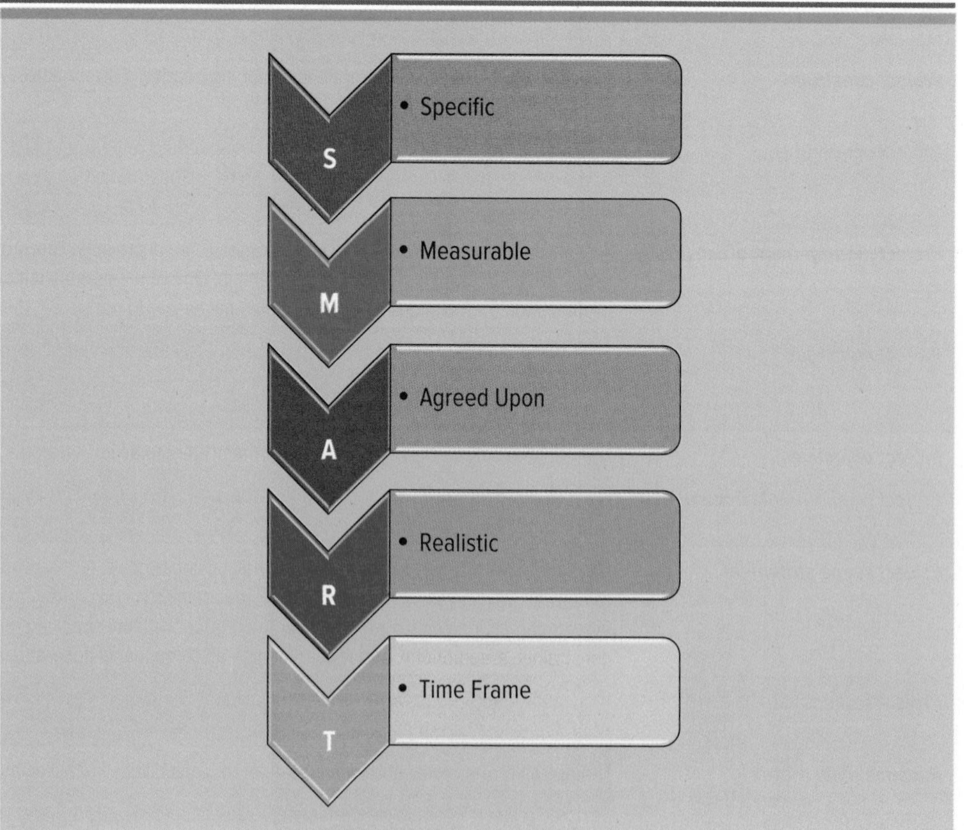

BUSINESS DRIVEN MIS

Time Management Applications

Time management is the key to success or failure. Wasting time is the absolute worst, and nobody likes to waste time. Creating a prioritized task list and planning the details of your project are key to successfully executing workflows. Here are a few tips to help you save time and stay on task as you begin working on projects.

- Schedule time to plan your projects and tasks each day, either in the evening or in the morning before you get to work. Do not wait until you get to work to schedule and prioritize your tasks.
- Schedule your most difficult tasks for the morning while you are still fresh and energized.
- Deadlines are essential; set them in eight-hour time frames. If someone else sets your deadlines, try setting your own deadline before the official deadline to ensure you have enough time to complete the task. For example, let's say it usually takes you three hours to complete a task. Set yourself a deadline of 90 minutes. You will be surprised that you usually complete the task within the deadline.
- Track everything you do for one week. Then perform an audit and determine where you underestimated or overestimated tasks to ensure better forecasting for your future.
- Top time management applications include Toggl, Rescue Time, Remember the Milk, FocusBooster, Toggl, Mind42, and MyLife Organized.

To empower your life and take back your time, research these applications and see if one can help you use your time more efficiently and effectively. Which one will you start using today and why? How much time do you think this application can help you regain? If you could create your own time tracking/project management application, what would it do and how would it work?

charter may contain the name of the sponsor, the project's benefits to the organization, a description of the objectives, the expected time frame, and a budget.

The project plan is a formal, approved document that manages and controls project execution. The project plan should include a description of the project scope, a list of activities, a schedule, time estimates, cost estimates, risk factors, resources, assignments, and responsibilities. In addition to these basic components, most project professionals also include contingency plans, review and communications strategies, and a ***kill switch***—a trigger that enables a project manager to close the project before completion.

A good project plan should include estimates for revenue and strategic necessities. It also should include measurement and reporting methods and details for how top leadership will engage in the project. It also informs stakeholders of the benefits of the project and justifies the investment, commitment, and risk of the project as it relates to the overall mission of the organization.

Managers need to monitor projects continuously to measure their success. If a project is failing, the manager must cancel the project and save the company any further project costs. Canceling a project is not necessarily a failure as much as it is successful resource management because it frees resources that can be used on other projects that are more valuable to the firm.

The most important part of the plan is communication. The project manager must communicate the plan to every member of the project team and to any key stakeholders and executives. The project plan must also include any project assumptions and be detailed enough to guide the execution of the project. A key to achieving project success is earning consensus and buy-in from all key stakeholders. By including key stakeholders in project plan development, the project manager allows them to have ownership of the plan. This often translates to greater commitment, which in turn results in enhanced motivation and productivity. The two primary diagrams most frequently used in project planning are PERT and Gantt charts.

- ***Dependency***: A logical relationship that exists between the project tasks, or between a project task and a milestone.
- ***PERT (Program Evaluation and Review Technique) chart***: A graphical network model that depicts a project's tasks and the relationships between them. PERT charts define dependency between project tasks before those tasks are scheduled.
- ***Critical path***: A critical path is the series of activities that determine the earliest time by which the project can be completed. In other words, it represents the longest path through the project and the maximum amount of time it will take you to finish.
- ***Critical path analysis***: A project diagramming method used to predict total project duration. This important tool will help ensure you complete your project on time and within your budget.
- ***Slack***: The amount of time an activity may be delayed without delaying a succeeding activity or the project finish date.
- ***Scope creep***: The tendency to permit changes that exceed a project's scope and may wreak havoc on the schedule, work quality, and budget.

The critical path has the least amount of slack. There are normally several tasks done in parallel on projects, and most projects have multiple paths they can take to complete the project. You are not finished with the project until you have finished all the tasks. The longest path or path containing the critical tasks is what is driving the completion date for the entire project. Figure 9.23 displays the critical path for the project.

A ***Gantt chart*** is a simple bar chart that lists project tasks vertically against the project's time frame, listed horizontally. A Gantt chart works well for representing the project schedule.

FIGURE 9.23

Critical Path Example

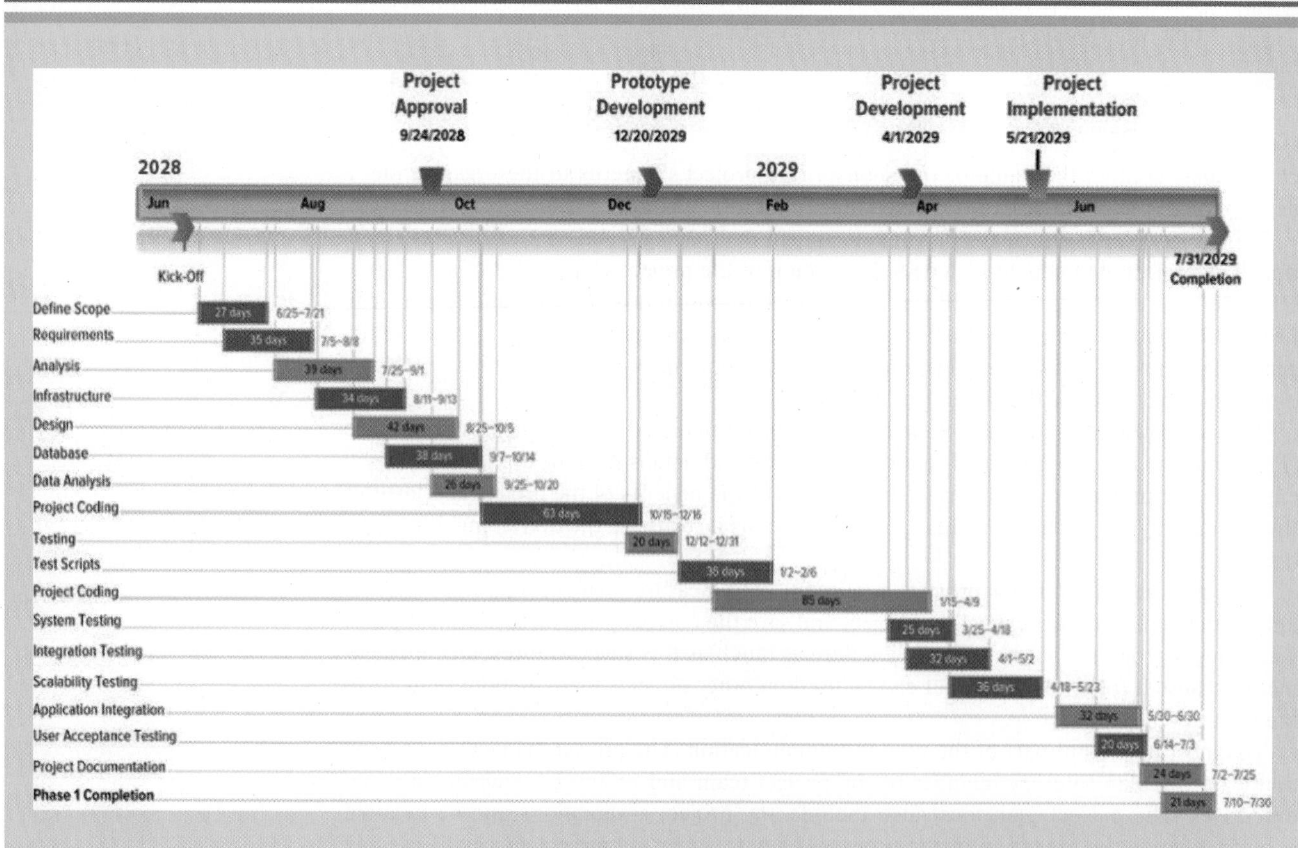

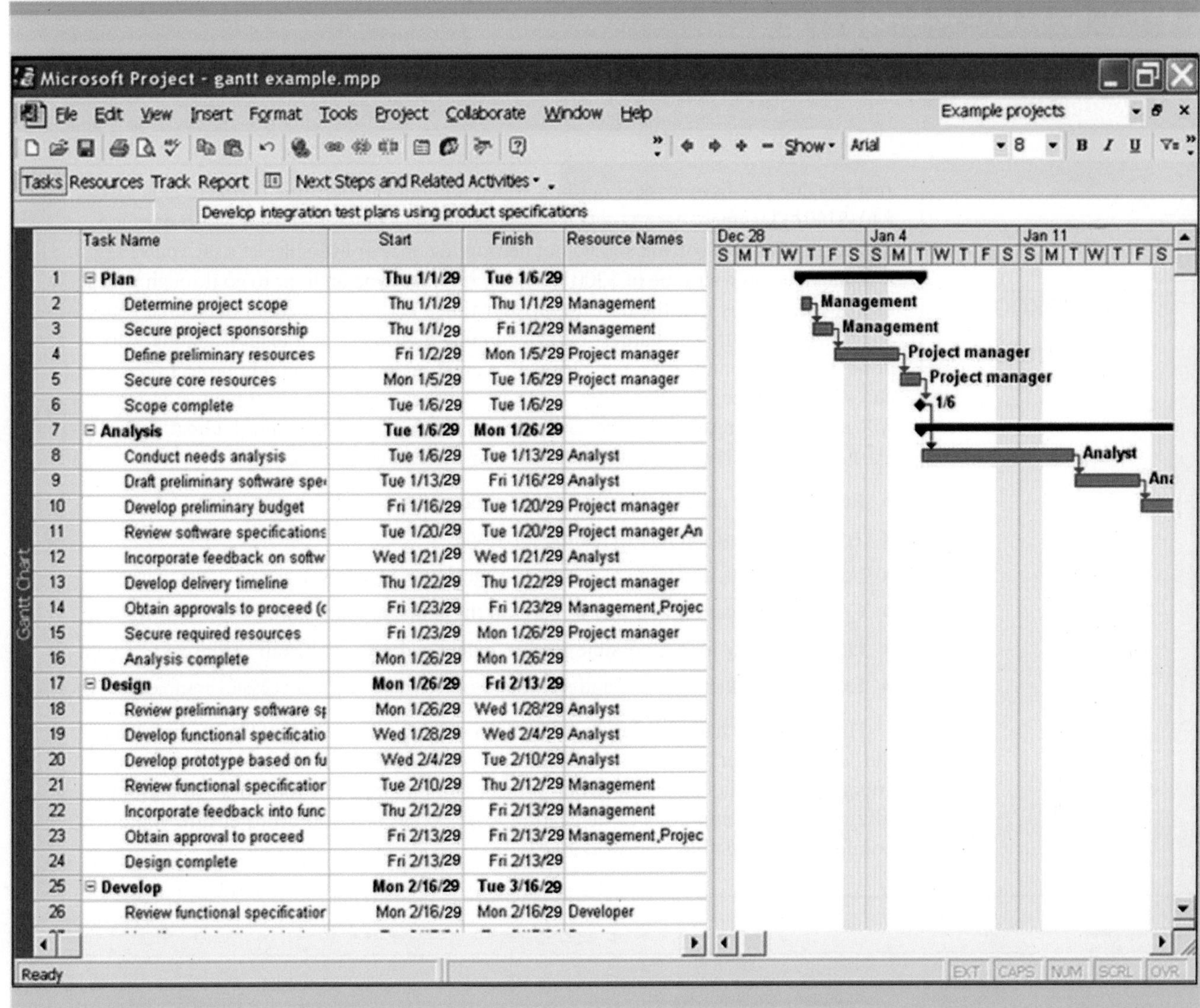

	Task Name	Start	Finish	Resource Names
1	**Plan**	**Thu 1/1/29**	**Tue 1/6/29**	
2	Determine project scope	Thu 1/1/29	Thu 1/1/29	Management
3	Secure project sponsorship	Thu 1/1/29	Fri 1/2/29	Management
4	Define preliminary resources	Fri 1/2/29	Mon 1/5/29	Project manager
5	Secure core resources	Mon 1/5/29	Tue 1/6/29	Project manager
6	Scope complete	Tue 1/6/29	Tue 1/6/29	
7	**Analysis**	**Tue 1/6/29**	**Mon 1/26/29**	
8	Conduct needs analysis	Tue 1/6/29	Tue 1/13/29	Analyst
9	Draft preliminary software spe	Tue 1/13/29	Fri 1/16/29	Analyst
10	Develop preliminary budget	Fri 1/16/29	Tue 1/20/29	Project manager
11	Review software specifications	Tue 1/20/29	Tue 1/20/29	Project manager,An
12	Incorporate feedback on softw	Wed 1/21/29	Wed 1/21/29	Analyst
13	Develop delivery timeline	Thu 1/22/29	Thu 1/22/29	Project manager
14	Obtain approvals to proceed (c	Fri 1/23/29	Fri 1/23/29	Management,Projec
15	Secure required resources	Fri 1/23/29	Mon 1/26/29	Project manager
16	Analysis complete	Mon 1/26/29	Mon 1/26/29	
17	**Design**	**Mon 1/26/29**	**Fri 2/13/29**	
18	Review preliminary software sp	Mon 1/26/29	Wed 1/28/29	Analyst
19	Develop functional specificatio	Wed 1/28/29	Wed 2/4/29	Analyst
20	Develop prototype based on fu	Wed 2/4/29	Tue 2/10/29	Analyst
21	Review functional specificatior	Tue 2/10/29	Thu 2/12/29	Management
22	Incorporate feedback into func	Thu 2/12/29	Fri 2/13/29	Management
23	Obtain approval to proceed	Fri 2/13/29	Fri 2/13/29	Management,Projec
24	Design complete	Fri 2/13/29	Fri 2/13/29	
25	**Develop**	**Mon 2/16/29**	**Tue 3/16/29**	
26	Review functional specificatior	Mon 2/16/29	Mon 2/16/29	Developer

FIGURE 9.24

Microsoft Project, a Gantt Chart Example

Microsoft Corporation

It also shows actual progress of tasks against the planned duration. Figure 9.24 displays a software development project using a Gantt chart.

Work Breakdown Structure

A ***work breakdown structure (WBS)*** is a plan that breaks down a project's goals into the many deliverables required to achieve it. WBS subdivides complex activities into their most manageable units and asks, "What will have to be done to accomplish X?" You continue to ask this question until you can't ask this question again. This is the point at which you know you have broken the work down into the smallest task. After assigning the tasks, the time and money required to complete those tasks are then estimated. The WBS defines the "what" of the project. Everything you need to accomplish in the project is displayed in a single, easy-to-understand chart. The purpose of this chart is to break down complex activities into smaller, more manageable tasks. Developing a work breakdown structure can ensure that you do not overlook a significant part of a complex activity or underestimate the time and money required to complete the work (see Figure 9.25). Following are a few reasons for creating a WBS in a project:

- Provides accurate and readable project organization.
- Allows for accurate assignment of responsibilities to the project team.
- Indicates the project milestones and control points.

APPLY YOUR KNOWLEDGE

BUSINESS DRIVEN INNOVATION

Work Breakdown Structures

Just imagine you have worked out how much an hour of your time is worth. Is it $10, $40, $150? Document each task you complete in a day and ask yourself which ones are not worth your time—or you should not be working on. For example, let's say you've set a dollar value on your time of $300 per hour. If it takes you an hour to go through your emails each day, is that the best use of your time? Perhaps you could outsource your email management. The hardest part of running a business or a team is getting work done. It always sounds easy, but even with a great project manager and project plan, it can still be challenging. Your best assets are your team: Hire the best people and you will gain the best results. But the hardest part is letting go of the control. Great leaders learn to delegate. Here are a few guidelines for delegating effectively:

- Recognize the capabilities of your team members.
- Trust your team's ability to get the job done.
- Focus on results, and let go of your need to get involved in how tasks are accomplished.
- Consider delegation as a way to develop the skills of your team.
- Delegate to the lowest possible level to make the best use of staff resources.
- Explain assignments clearly and provide resources needed for successful completion.[9]

Have you ever had to delegate to a co-worker or a fellow student? What problems did you encounter? Was the work done to your satisfaction? Have you ever found yourself as the student on the group project completing all of the work? In a group, discuss the pros and cons of delegating work. What can you do to ensure you are comfortable delegating your workload?

FIGURE 9.25

Sample Work Breakdown Structure

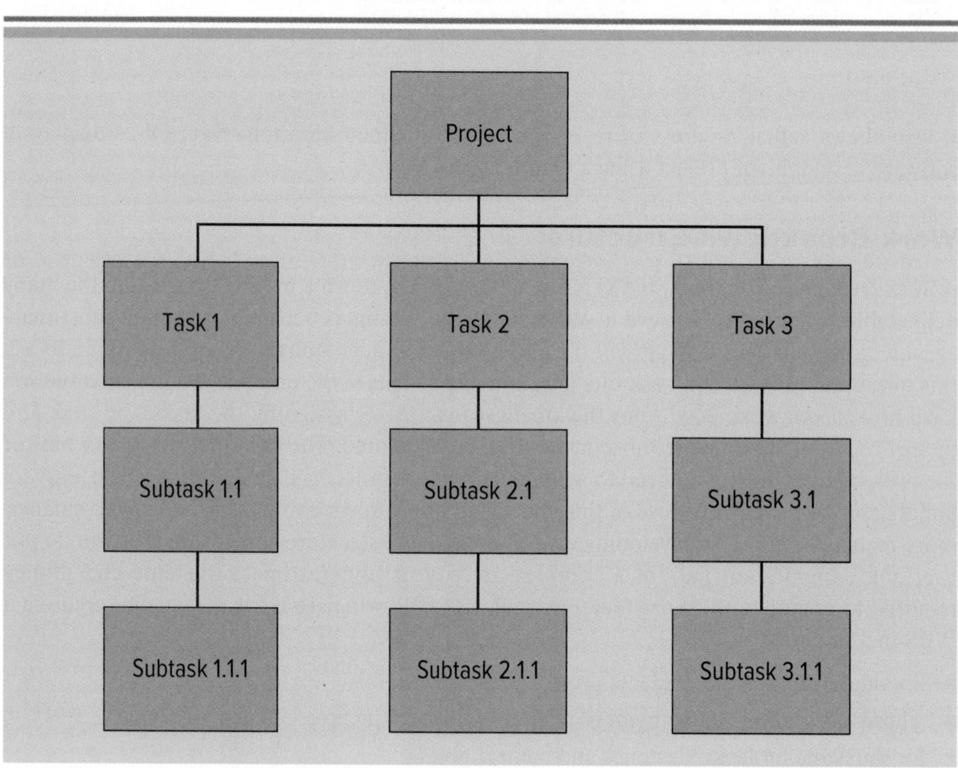

APPLY YOUR KNOWLEDGE

BUSINESS DRIVEN GLOBALIZATION

Global Work Breakdown Structures

The world is global, and I am positive that in your class right now there are students from around the world. Have you even contemplated how difficult it is to work on a global team? There are many challenges you may not have considered when it comes to global work. Just think of time zones for a team with participants from Europe, America, Asia, and India. Can you imagine the scheduling nightmare of setting up a meeting? Not to mention the language barriers and workflow issues. In a group, discuss the following list and identify three problems you might encounter in each area, along with potential solutions.

- Geographic boundaries
- Cultural differences
- Economic issues
- Technological differences

- Helps to estimate the cost, time, and risk.
- Illustrates the project scope, so the stakeholders can have a better understanding of the same.

OUTSOURCING PROJECTS

LO 9.5: Identify the three types of outsourcing.

In the high-speed global business environment, an organization needs to increase profits, grow market share, and reduce costs. Two basic options are available to organizations wishing to develop and maintain their information systems: in-sourcing or outsourcing.

- ***In-sourcing (in-house development)*:** Uses the professional expertise within an organization to develop and maintain its information technology systems. In-sourcing has been instrumental in creating a viable supply of MIS professionals and in creating a better quality workforce combining both technical and business skills.
- ***Outsourcing*:** An arrangement by which one organization provides a service or services for another organization that chooses not to perform them in-house.

In some cases, the entire MIS department is outsourced, including planning and business analysis, as well as the design, development, and maintenance of equipment and projects. Outsourcing can range from a large contract under which an organization such as IBM manages all MIS services for another company, to hiring contractors and temporary staff on an individual basis. Common reasons companies outsource include:

- **Core competencies.** Many companies have recently begun to consider outsourcing as a way to acquire best practices and the business process expertise of highly skilled technology resources for a low cost. Technology is advancing at such an accelerated rate that companies often lack the technical resources required to keep current.
- **Financial savings.** It is far cheaper to hire people in China and India than pay the required salaries for similar labor in the United States.
- **Rapid growth.** Firms must get their products to market quickly and still be able to react to market changes. By taking advantage of outsourcing, an organization can acquire the resources required to speed up operations or scale to new demand levels.
- **The Internet and globalization.** The pervasive nature of the Internet has made more people comfortable with outsourcing abroad as India, China, and the United States become virtual neighbors.

APPLY YOUR KNOWLEDGE

BUSINESS DRIVEN DISCUSSION

Death March

Edward Yourdon's book *Death March* describes the complete software developer's guide to surviving "mission impossible" projects. MIS projects are challenging, and project managers are expected to achieve the impossible by pulling off a successful project even when pitted against impossible challenges. In the book, Yourdon presents his project classification, as shown below. He measures projects based on the level of pain and the chances for success.

- **Mission Impossible Project:** This project has a great chance of success, and your hard work will pay off as you find happiness and joy in the work. For example, this is the type of project where you work all day and night for a year and become the project hero as you complete the mission impossible and reap a giant promotion as your reward.
- **Ugly Project:** This project has a high chance of success but is very painful and offers little happiness. For example, you work day and night to install a new accounting system, and although successful, you hate accounting and dislike the company and its products.
- **Kamikaze Project:** This is a project that has little chance of success, but you are so passionate about the content that you find great happiness working on the project. For example, you are asked to build a website to support a cancer foundation, a cause near to your heart, but the company is nonprofit and doesn't have any funds to help buy the software you need to get everything working. You patch the system together and implement many manual work-arounds just to keep the system functioning.
- **Suicide Project:** This project has no chance of success and offers you nothing but pain. This is the equivalent of your worst nightmare project. Word of caution: Avoid suicide projects![10]

Analyze your school and work projects and find a project that would fit in each box. What could you have done differently on your suicide project to ensure its success? What can you do to avoid being placed on a suicide project? Given the choice, which type of project would you choose to work on and why?

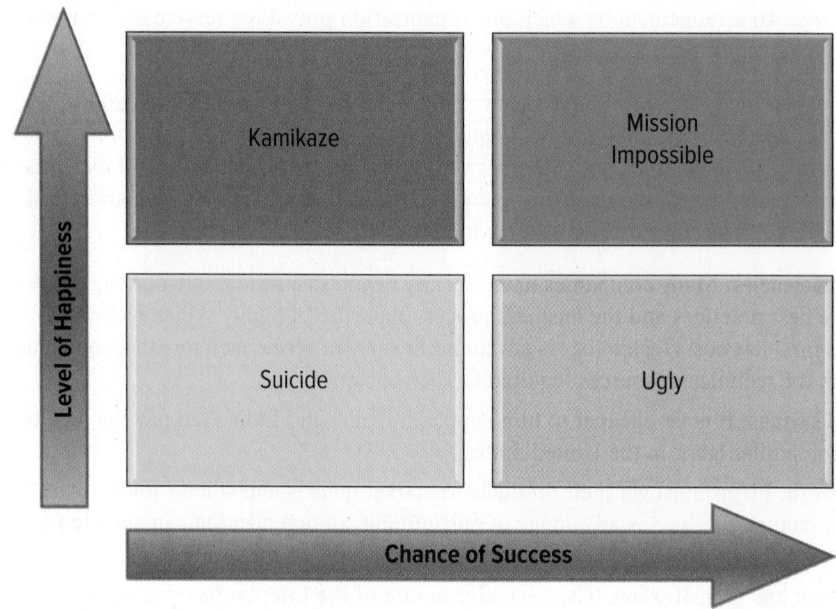

Source: Yourdon, Edward. *Death March*. 2nd edition, Prentice Hall, 2004.

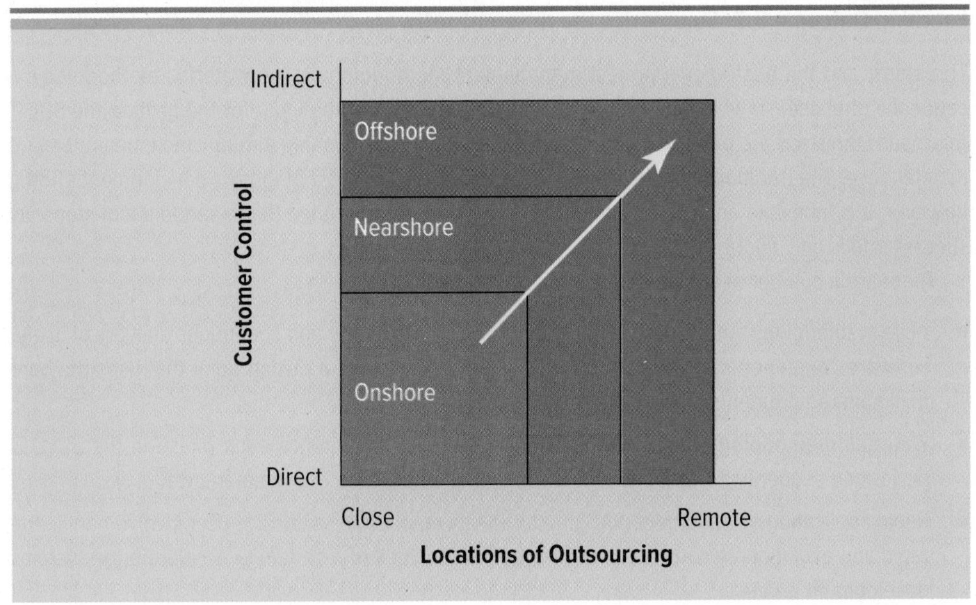

FIGURE 9.26

Outsourcing Models

Outsourcing MIS enables organizations to keep up with market and technology advances—with less strain on human and financial resources and more assurance that the MIS infrastructure will keep pace with evolving business priorities (see Figure 9.26). The three forms of outsourcing options available for a project are:

- ***Onshore outsourcing***: Engaging another company within the same country for services.
- ***Nearshore outsourcing***: Contracting an outsourcing arrangement with a company in a nearby country. Often, this country will share a border with the native country.
- ***Offshore outsourcing***: Using organizations from developing countries to write code and develop systems. In offshore outsourcing, the country is geographically far away.

LEARNING OUTCOME REVIEW

Learning Outcome 9.1: Describe the seven phases of the systems development life cycle.

The seven phases in the SDLC are:

- Planning—involves establishing a high-level plan of the intended project and determining project goals.
- Analysis—involves analyzing end-user business requirements and refining project goals into defined functions and operations of the intended system.
- Design—involves describing the desired features and operations of the system, including screen layouts, business rules, process diagrams, pseudocode, and other documentation.
- Development—involves transforming all the detailed design documents from the design phase into the actual system.
- Testing—involves bringing all the project pieces together into a special testing environment to test for errors, bugs, and interoperability and verifying that the system meets all the business requirements defined in the analysis phase.
- Implementation—involves placing the system into production so users can begin to perform actual business operations with the system.
- Maintenance—involves performing changes, corrections, additions, and upgrades to ensure that the system continues to meet the business goals.

Learning Outcome 9.2: Summarize the different software development methodologies.

The oldest and the best-known project management methodology is the waterfall methodology, a sequence of phases in which the output of each phase becomes the input for the next. In the SDLC, this means the steps are performed one at a time, in order, from planning through implementation and maintenance. The traditional waterfall method no longer serves most of today's development efforts, however; it is inflexible and expensive, and it requires rigid adherence to the sequence of steps. Its success rate is only about 1 in 10.

There are a number of software development methodologies:

- Agile methodology aims for customer satisfaction through early and continuous delivery of useful software components developed by an iterative process with a design point that uses the bare minimum requirements.
- Waterfall methodology follows an activity-based process in which each phase in the SDLC is performed sequentially from planning through implementation and maintenance.
- Rapid application development (RAD) methodology emphasizes extensive user involvement in the rapid and evolutionary construction of working prototypes of a system to accelerate the systems development process.
- Extreme programming (XP) methodology breaks a project into tiny phases, and developers cannot continue on to the next phase until the first phase is complete.
- Rational unified process (RUP) provides a framework for breaking down the development of software into four gates.
- Scrum uses small teams to produce small pieces of deliverable software by using sprints, or 30-day intervals, to achieve an appointed goal.

Learning Outcome 9.3: Explain project management and identify the primary reasons projects fail.

A project is a temporary or short-term endeavor undertaken to create a unique product, service, or result, such as developing a custom ecommerce site or merging databases. Project management is the application of knowledge, skills, tools, and techniques to project activities to meet project requirements. A project manager is an individual who is an expert in project planning and management, defines and develops the project plan, and tracks the plan to ensure that the project is completed on time and on budget. The primary reasons projects fail include unclear or missing business requirements, skipped phases, changing technology, the cost of finding errors in the SDLC, and imbalance of the triple constraints.

Learning Outcome 9.4: Identify the primary project planning diagrams.

A PERT (Program Evaluation and Review Technique) chart is a graphical network model that depicts a project's tasks and the relationships between those tasks. A dependency is a logical relationship that exists between the project tasks or between a project task and a milestone. A Gantt chart is a simple bar chart that depicts project tasks against a calendar. In a Gantt chart, tasks are listed vertically and the project's time frame is listed horizontally. A Gantt chart works well for representing the project schedule. It also shows the actual progress of tasks against the planned duration.

Learning Outcome 9.5: Identify the three types of outsourcing.

- Onshore outsourcing—engaging another company within the same country for services.
- Nearshore outsourcing—contracting an outsourcing arrangement with a company in a nearby country.
- Offshore outsourcing—using organizations from developing countries to write code and develop systems.

KEY TERMS

Agile methodology 372
Analysis phase 364
Brainstorming 362
Bugs 368
Business requirement 364
Change agent 363
Coders 368
Communication plan 379
Computer-aided software engineering (CASE) 364
Conversion 361
Corrective maintenance 371
Critical path 382
Critical path analysis 382
Data flow diagram (DFD) 364
Dependency 382
Design phase 364
Development phase 367
Executive sponsor 379
Extreme programming (XP) methodology 374
Feasibility 376
Fourth-generation languages (4GLs) 368
Gantt chart 382
Help desk 370
Implementation phase 369
In-sourcing (in-house development) 385
Intangible benefits 376
Iterative development 372
Kill switch 381
Legacy system 361
Maintenance phase 371
Methodology 371
Nearshore outsourcing 387
Offshore outsourcing 387
Off-the-shelf application software 361
Online training 370
Onshore outsourcing 387
Outsourcing 385
PERT (Program Evaluation and Review Technique) chart 382
Planning phase 361
Preventive maintenance 371
Process modeling 364
Programming language 367
Project 363
Project assumption 379
Project charter 380
Project constraint 379
Project deliverable 379
Project management 363
Project management office (PMO) 379
Project manager 363
Project milestone 379
Project objectives 379
Project plan 363
Project requirements document 379
Project scope 363
Project scope statement 379
Project stakeholder 379
Prototyping 372
Rapid application development (RAD) methodology (also called rapid prototyping) 373
Rational unified process (RUP) methodology 374
Requirements definition document 364
Requirements management 364
Responsibility matrix 379
Scope creep 382
Scrum methodology 375
Sign-off 364
Slack 382
Software customization 361
Software engineering 367
Status report 379
Systems development life cycle (SDLC) 361
Tangible benefits 376
Technical review (or peer review) 368
Test conditions 368
Testing phase 368
User documentation 370
Waterfall methodology 371
Work breakdown structure (WBS) 383
Workshop training 370

REVIEW QUESTIONS

1. What role does project management play in the systems development effort?
2. What role does the project manager play in determining a project's success?
3. Why would a project require an executive sponsor?
4. Which phase in the systems development life cycle is the most important?
5. If you had to skip a phase during the development of a system, which phase would it be and why?
6. Which phase in the systems development life cycle contains the most risk? Explain your answer.
7. Which project management methodology would you choose to run your software development project?
8. If you started on a new software development project and the project plan was using the waterfall methodology, would you remain on the project? What could you do to prepare your project better for success?
9. Explain the different types of feasibility studies a project manager can use to prioritize project importance.
10. Why should end users be involved in the systems development effort?

11. Why would a project manager use Gantt and PERT charts?

12. Why is gathering business requirements a challenge for most projects?

13. What are the different types of outsourcing available for a project?

14. What are the risks associated with outsourcing?

15. Explain the goals of the Project Management Institute and identify three key terms associated with *PMBOK*.

CLOSING CASE ONE

Gamer Delight

It is a dream come true when you can make an incredible salary doing what you love, and that is exactly what is happening in the gaming industry. To the gamer's delight, profitable careers can be found for people with design, development, and programming skills. Video programmers are finding success in technology companies, marketing corporations, advertising agencies, and video game development companies. In fact, video games are a $30 billion industry in the United States, especially as more people play games on their mobile phones, according to Reuters. Companies around the globe are paying application programmers, developers, and designers incredible salaries for their skills and capabilities.

Video Game Programmers

Video game programmers are software engineers who work on games for console or handheld video gaming systems. In addition to understanding computer languages and structures, they must also be familiar with the specific target systems on which their games will be played, as well as the development platforms used to create games

Video game programming experts specializing in networking or graphic engines are seeing starting salaries as high as $100,000. One of the great benefits of the video game industry is that it is hardly affected by recessions or bad economies. New college graduates without any industry experience are offered $60,000 annually.

Technical Directors

Technical directors for a game development company get high salaries even at the entry level. Those having the least experience are said to get an average of $60,000 every year, and that increases to more than $70,000 for individuals who have more than 3 years of know-how. The highest compensation for this particular job description is $195,500 annually.

Video Game Designers

Video game designers work with a team developing and designing video games. Game designers are an important part of a comprehensive team of designers and developers that coordinate the complex task of creating a new video game. Game designers have duties such as designing characters, levels, puzzles, art, and animation. They may also write code using various computer programming languages. Depending on their career duties, they may also be responsible for project management tasks and testing early versions of video games.

Video game designers also receive comparatively high compensation whether the knowledge comes from experience or formal education. The designer with fewer than 3 years of experience normally starts at $50,000 each year, which increases to $75,000 after the third year. Once the video game design expert earns more than 6 years of on-the-job experience, this can go up to $100,000 annually.

The creative director or lead designer earns up to $180,000 every year after getting substantial experience in the industry.

Video Game Producers

Video game producers supervise all aspects of creating a video game and are held liable for decisions from start to finish. These individuals coordinate the work of different departments involved and ensure that deadlines are met and the project remains within the budget. The minimum salary for producers is $62,000, while those with over 6 years of experience can earn up to $180,000 a year.

Video Game Artists and Animators

The artists and animators for video game development companies earn an average salary of $50,000 annually. Senior lead artists earn anywhere from $80,000 to $215,000 annually. Earning high income is quite easy in the video game industry if you have a good education, experience, determination, and creativity.[11]

Questions

1. What are the three interdependent variables shaping project management? Why are these variables important to a video game software development project?
2. If you were consulting a business that wanted to build a video game for a smart phone, which development methodology would you recommend and why?
3. Illustrate the triple constraints role when building a new game. Why is the cost of finding errors important to a business when developing and designing video games?
4. Which phase in the SDLC is the most critical when building a video game? Which phase in the SDLC is the least critical when building a video game?
5. What are the ethical and security issues associated with outsourcing the development of a video game?

CLOSING CASE TWO

Reducing Ambiguity in Business Requirements

The main reason projects fail is bad business requirements. Business requirements are considered bad because of ambiguity or insufficient involvement of end users during analysis and design.

A requirement is unambiguous if it has the same interpretation for all parties. Different interpretations by different participants will usually result in unmet expectations. Here is an example of an ambiguous requirement and an example of an unambiguous requirement:

Ambiguous requirement: The financial report must show profits in local and U.S. currencies.

Unambiguous requirement: The financial report must show profits in local and U.S. currencies, using the exchange rate printed in *The Wall Street Journal* for the last business day of the period being reported.

Ambiguity is impossible to prevent completely because it is introduced into requirements in natural ways. For example:

- Requirements can contain technical implications that are obvious to IT developers but not to customers.
- Requirements can contain business implications that are obvious to the customer but not to IT developers.

- Requirements may contain everyday words whose meanings are "obvious" to everyone, yet different for everyone.
- Requirements are reflections of detailed explanations that may have included multiple events, multiple perspectives, verbal rephrasing, emotion, iterative refinement, selective emphasis, and body language—none of which are captured in the written statements.

Tips for Reviewing Business Requirements

When reviewing business requirements, always look for the following words to help reduce ambiguity dramatically:

- *And* and *or* have well-defined meanings and ought to be completely unambiguous, yet they are often understood only informally and interpreted inconsistently. For example, consider the statement "The alarm must ring if button T is pressed and if button F is pressed." This statement may be intended to mean that to ring the alarm, both buttons must be pressed, or it may be intended to mean that either one can be pressed. A statement like this should never appear in a requirement because the potential for misinterpretation is too great. A preferable approach is to be very explicit. For example, "The alarm must ring if both buttons T and F are pressed simultaneously. The alarm should not ring in any other circumstance."
- *Always* might really mean "most of the time," in which case it should be made more explicit. For example, the statement "We always run reports A and B together" could be challenged with "In other words, there is never any circumstance in which you would run A without B and B without A?" If you build a system with an "always" requirement, you are actually building the system never to run report A without report B. If a user suddenly wants report B without report A, you will need to make significant system changes.
- *Never* might mean rarely, in which case it should be made more explicit. For example, the statement "We never run reports A and B in the same month" could be challenged with "So that means that if I see that A has been run, I can be absolutely certain that no one will want to run B." Again, if you build a system that supports a "never" requirement, the system users can never perform that requirement. For example, the system would never allow a user to run reports A and B in the same month, no matter what the circumstances.
- Boundary conditions are statements about the line between true and false and do and do not. These statements may or may not be meant to include end points. For example, "We want to use method X when there are up to 10 pages, but method Y otherwise." If you were building this system, would you include page 10 in method X or in method Y? The answer to this question will vary, causing an ambiguous business requirement.[12]

Questions

1. Why are ambiguous business requirements the leading cause of system development failures?
2. Why do the words *and* and *or* tend to lead to ambiguous requirements?
3. Research the web and determine other reasons for bad business requirements.
4. What is wrong with the following business requirement? "The system must support employee birthdays because every employee always has a birthday every year."

MAKING BUSINESS DECISIONS

1. Methods behind Methodologies

Signatures Inc. specializes in producing personalized products such as coffee mugs and pens with company logos. The company generates more than $40 million in annual revenues and has more than 300 employees. The company is in the middle of a large, multimillion-dollar SCM implementation, and it has just hired your project management outsourcing firm to take over the project management efforts.

On your first day, your team is told that the project is failing for the following reasons:

- The project is using the traditional waterfall methodology.
- The SDLC was not followed, and the developers decided to skip the testing phase.
- A project plan was developed during the analysis phase, but the old project manager never updated or followed the plan.

Determine what your first steps would be to get this project back on track.

2. Missing Phases in the Systems Development Life Cycle

Hello Inc. is a large concierge service for executives operating in Chicago, San Francisco, and New York. The company performs all kinds of services from dog walking to airport transportation. Your manager, Dan Martello, wants to skip the testing phase during the company's financial ERP implementation. He feels that because the system came from a vendor, it should work correctly. Draft a memo explaining the importance of following the SDLC and the ramifications to the business if the financial system is not tested.

3. Refusing to Sign Off

You are the primary client on a large extranet development project. After carefully reviewing the requirements definition document, you are positive there are missing, ambiguous, inaccurate, and unclear requirements. The project manager is pressuring you for your sign-off because he has already received sign-off from five of your co-workers. If you fail to sign off on the requirements, you will put the entire project at risk because the time frame is nonnegotiable. What would you do? Why?

4. Saving Failing Systems

Crik Candle Company manufactures low-end candles for restaurants. The company generates more than $40 million in annual revenues and has more than 300 employees. You are in the middle of a large, multimillion-dollar supply chain management implementation. Your project manager has just come to you with the information that the project might fail for the following reasons:

- Several business requirements were incorrect, and the scope has to be doubled.
- Three developers recently quit.
- The deadline has been moved up a month.

Develop a list of options that your company can follow to ensure that the project remains on schedule and within budget.

5. Explaining Project Management

Prime Time Inc. is a large consulting company that specializes in outsourcing people with project management capabilities and skills. You are in the middle of an interview for a job with Prime Time. The manager performing the interview asks you to explain why managing a project plan is critical to a project's success. The manager also wants you to explain scope creep and feature creep and your tactics for managing them on a project. Finally, the manager wants you to elaborate on your strategies for delivering successful projects and reducing risks. Create a document explaining your answers to these important questions.

6. Planning for the Unexpected

Unexpected situations happen all the time, and the more you plan for them, the better prepared you will be when developing software. Your employees will get into accidents, contract viruses and diseases, and experience other life issues. All of these scenarios lead to unplanned absenteeism, which can throw your project plan into a tailspin. What can happen to a project when a key employee suddenly quits or is forced to go on short-term disability? When reviewing all the different SDLC methodologies, which one offers the greatest flexibility for unplanned employee downtime? If you could choose when your employee was absent, which phase in the SDLC would be the safest for your project to still continue and achieve success? What can you do to ensure you are preparing for unplanned absenteeism on your project plan?

7. Scratch

Scratch is a visual programming language that is perfect for anyone learning to code. Scratch creates programs by connecting blocks of code by using a drag-and-drop GUI so users do not have to type programming languages. Users can simply select colored blocks of code that, when joined, create a script or a set of computer instructions that can make objects such as people and animals move and speak. Users can create interactive stories, games, and animations with the click of a button.

Scratch is a free project created by the Lifelong Kindergarten Group at the MIT Media Lab and currently has more than 8 million users. The goal of Scratch is to help young people learn to think creatively, reason systematically, and work collaboratively—essential skills for life in the 21st century.

In a group, visit the Scratch website at http://scratch.mit.edu/. What type of system development methodology is Scratch using? What skills can young people learn from creating Scratch programs?

8. Confusing Coffee

Business requirements are the detailed set of business requests that any new system must meet to be successful. A sample business requirement might state, "The system must track all customer sales by product, region, and sales representative." This requirement states what the system must do from the business perspective, giving no details or information about how the system will meet this requirement.

You have been hired to build an employee payroll system for a new coffee shop. Review the following business requirements and highlight any potential issues.

- All employees must have a unique employee ID.
- The system must track employee hours worked based on the employee's last name.
- Employees must be scheduled to work a minimum of eight hours per day.
- Employee payroll is calculated by multiplying the employee's hours worked by $7.25.
- Managers must be scheduled to work morning shifts.
- Employees cannot be scheduled to work more than eight hours per day.
- Servers cannot be scheduled to work morning, afternoon, or evening shifts.
- The system must allow managers to change and delete employees from the system.

9. Picking Projects

You are a project management contractor attempting to contract work at a large telecommunications company, Hex Incorporated. Your interview with Debbie Fernandez, the senior vice president of IT, went smoothly. The last thing she wants to see from you before she makes her final hiring decision is a prioritized list of the following projects. You are sure to land the job if Fernandez is satisfied with your prioritization.

Create a report prioritizing the following projects, and be sure to include the business justifications for your prioritization.

- Upgrade accounting system.
- Develop employee vacation tracking system.
- Enhance employee intranet.
- Cleanse and scrub data warehouse information.
- Performance-test all hardware to ensure 20 percent growth scalability.
- Implement changes to employee benefits system.
- Develop backup and recovery strategy.
- Implement supply chain management system.
- Upgrade customer relationship management system.
- Build executive information system for CEO.

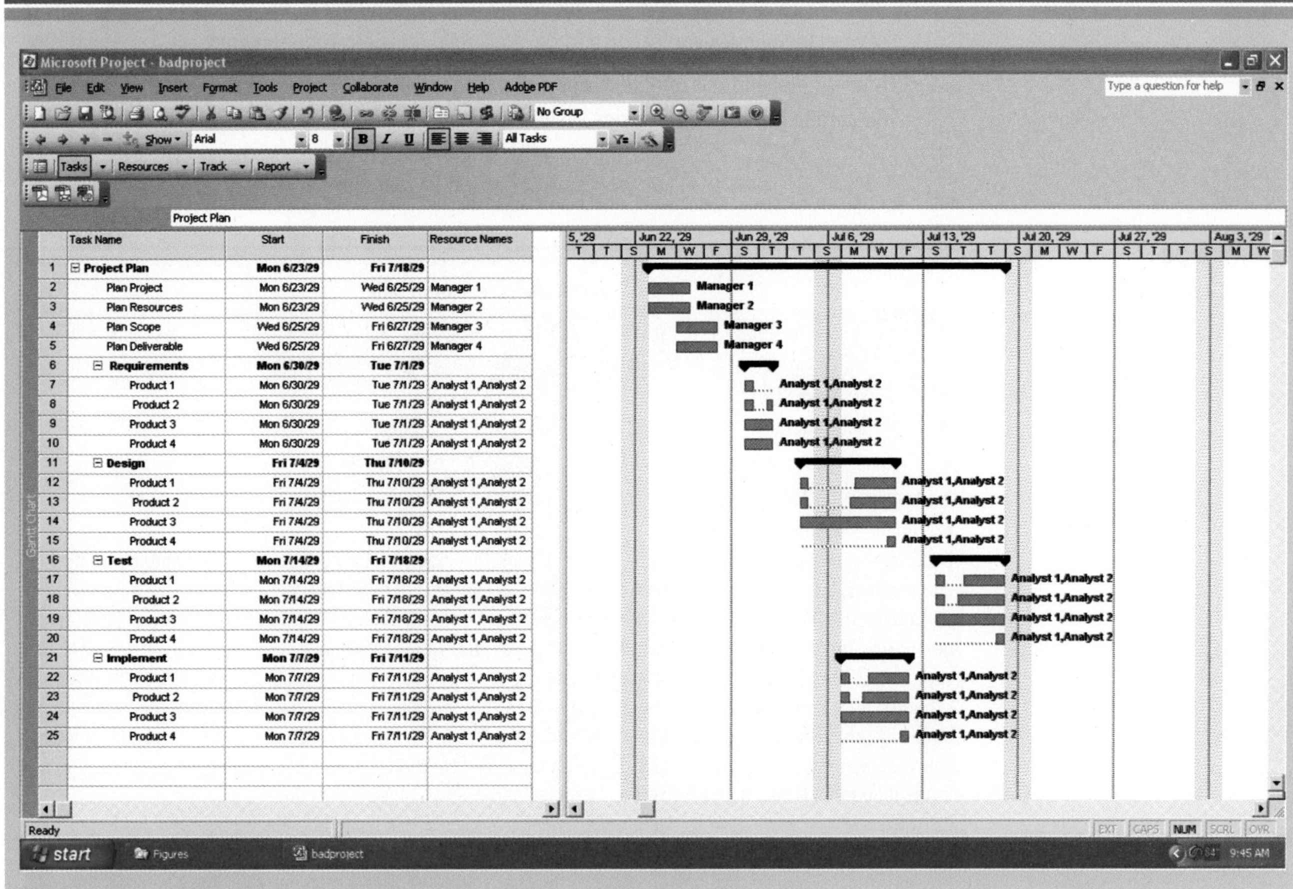

	Task Name	Start	Finish	Resource Names
1	Project Plan	Mon 6/23/29	Fri 7/18/29	
2	Plan Project	Mon 6/23/29	Wed 6/25/29	Manager 1
3	Plan Resources	Mon 6/23/29	Wed 6/25/29	Manager 2
4	Plan Scope	Wed 6/25/29	Fri 6/27/29	Manager 3
5	Plan Deliverable	Wed 6/25/29	Fri 6/27/29	Manager 4
6	Requirements	Mon 6/30/29	Tue 7/1/29	
7	Product 1	Mon 6/30/29	Tue 7/1/29	Analyst 1,Analyst 2
8	Product 2	Mon 6/30/29	Tue 7/1/29	Analyst 1,Analyst 2
9	Product 3	Mon 6/30/29	Tue 7/1/29	Analyst 1,Analyst 2
10	Product 4	Mon 6/30/29	Tue 7/1/29	Analyst 1,Analyst 2
11	Design	Fri 7/4/29	Thu 7/10/29	
12	Product 1	Fri 7/4/29	Thu 7/10/29	Analyst 1,Analyst 2
13	Product 2	Fri 7/4/29	Thu 7/10/29	Analyst 1,Analyst 2
14	Product 3	Fri 7/4/29	Thu 7/10/29	Analyst 1,Analyst 2
15	Product 4	Fri 7/4/29	Thu 7/10/29	Analyst 1,Analyst 2
16	Test	Mon 7/14/29	Fri 7/18/29	
17	Product 1	Mon 7/14/29	Fri 7/18/29	Analyst 1,Analyst 2
18	Product 2	Mon 7/14/29	Fri 7/18/29	Analyst 1,Analyst 2
19	Product 3	Mon 7/14/29	Fri 7/18/29	Analyst 1,Analyst 2
20	Product 4	Mon 7/14/29	Fri 7/18/29	Analyst 1,Analyst 2
21	Implement	Mon 7/7/29	Fri 7/11/29	
22	Product 1	Mon 7/7/29	Fri 7/11/29	Analyst 1,Analyst 2
23	Product 2	Mon 7/7/29	Fri 7/11/29	Analyst 1,Analyst 2
24	Product 3	Mon 7/7/29	Fri 7/11/29	Analyst 1,Analyst 2
25	Product 4	Mon 7/7/29	Fri 7/11/29	Analyst 1,Analyst 2

FIGURE 9.27

CRM Project Plan

Microsoft

10. Keeping Time

Time Keepers Inc. is a small firm that specializes in project management consulting. You are a senior project manager, and you have recently been assigned to the Tahiti Tanning Lotion account. The Tahiti Tanning Lotion company is currently experiencing a 10 percent success rate (90 percent failure rate) on all internal IT projects. Your first assignment is to analyze one of the current project plans being used to develop a new CRM system (see Figure 9.27).

Review the project plan and create a document listing the numerous errors in the plan. Be sure to provide suggestions on how to fix the errors.

11. GEM Athletic Center

First Information Corporation is a large consulting company that specializes in systems analysis and design. The company has more than 2,000 employees, and its first-quarter revenues reached $15 million. The company prides itself on maintaining an 85 percent success rate for all project implementations. The primary reason attributed to the unusually high project success rate is the company's ability to define accurate, complete, and high-quality business requirements.

The GEM Athletic Center located in Cleveland, Ohio, is interested in implementing a new payroll system. The current payroll process is manual and takes three employees two days each month to complete. The GEM Athletic Center does not have an IT department and is outsourcing the entire procurement, customization, and installation of the new payroll system to First Information Corporation.

You have been working for First Information for a little over one month. Your team has just been assigned the GEM Athletic Center project, and your first task is to define the initial business requirements for the development of the new payroll system.

a. Review the testimony of three current GEM Athletic Center accounting employees who detail the current payroll process, along with their wish list for the new system. Figure 9.28 presents the testimonies of Jim Poulos, Maggie Cleaver, and Anne Logan.

b. Review Closing Case Two, "Reducing Ambiguity in Business Requirements," and highlight several techniques you can use to develop solid business requirements.

c. After careful analysis, create a report detailing the business requirements for the new system. Be sure to list any assumptions, issues, or questions in your document.

FIGURE 9.28

Employee Testimonies

Jim Poulos, Director of Sales

Each week I have to review all of the new memberships sold in our club. Each of my seven sales representatives receives $50 from a new sale for the initiation fee. They also receive 10 percent of the type of membership sold. Membership types include:

- Adult, $450/month
- Youth, $300/month
- Family, $750/month
- Senior, $300/month

Each sales representative is also paid $4.50/hour and receives a 25 percent bonus for working overtime and holidays. If the sales representative sells over 200 percent of expected sales, they receive an additional 25 percent bonus on their commissions. If the membership is sold during a promotion, the commission rate decreases. The payroll department uses time sheets to track my sales representatives' hourly pay. I have to sign all time sheets once they are completed by the payroll department. I check my sales representatives' schedule to validate the times on the employee time sheets. I then have to submit a separate listing of each employee and their corresponding commissions for initiation fees and memberships sold. I track all of my sales representatives' vacation and sick time. If they are over their vacation or sick time, I have them sign a form stating that if they quit, they will pay back all negative vacation or sick time.

I would like a system that can automatically calculate commissions and be able to handle sales forecasting and "what if" analysis on my sales representatives' commission rates. I would like to be able to walk up to my sales representatives and tell them that if they sell four more family memberships and one adult, they will receive their bonus. I would also like to be able to design promotions for our best customers. These types of things would really help boost sales at our club.

Maggie Cleaver, Payroll Manager

The first thing I do each week is collect the time sheets. I review each time sheet to ensure that the employee punched in and out correctly. If the employee forgot to clock out, I contact that person's director to find the time that the employee should have clocked out. I then calculate all regular hours, overtime hours, and holiday hours and total these on the time sheet. I also track sick time and vacation time and total these on the time sheet. Once completed, I send the time sheet to the directors of each department for approval.

When I receive the signed time sheets back, I begin to calculate payments. First, I calculate regular pay, then overtime pay, and finally holiday pay. I then add in the sales representatives' commissions, which I receive from the director of sales. I then calculate payment amounts for aerobics instructors because they are paid by class, not by hour. I receive the aerobics class schedule from the fitness coordinator. I then total the entire pay and send a sheet with payment amounts to my co-worker Anne, who calculates taxes. I then calculate all sick time and vacation time and track this in a separate document. I then print labels that state each employee's name, department, and the pay period. I place the labels on a new time sheet, which is returned to the employee punch clock.

I would like a system that automatically tracks employee sick time and vacation time. I would also like a system that can automatically calculate regular pay, overtime pay, and holiday pay. I don't know if there is a system that can validate employee time sheets, but if there is, that would be great.

Anne Logan, Tax Manager

I receive the payment amounts from Maggie. I then calculate all city, state, and federal taxes. I also deduct health benefits and retirement plan benefits. I then cut the check to the employee and the corresponding checks for the taxes to the government. I manually calculate W2s and all quarterly taxes. I'm also responsible for correcting personal information such as a change of address. I'm also responsible for cutting checks if an incorrect amount was issued. I also track amounts owed by employees that have gone over their sick time or vacation time. I also generate checks for all salaried employees. The part of my job that takes the longest is correlating the total cash debit for all checks and the total amount calculated for all checks. It's amazing how many times these two figures do not match, which indicates that a check was written for the wrong amount.

I would like a system that determines taxes automatically, along with quarterly tax filing statements. I would also like a system that can perform audits.

AYK APPLICATION PROJECTS

If you are looking for Excel projects to incorporate into your class, try any of the following after reading this chapter.

Project Number	Project Name	Project Type	Plug-In	Focus Area	Project Level	Skill Set	Page Number
9	Security Analysis	Excel	T3	Filtering Data	Intermediate	Conditional Formatting, Autofilter, Subtotal	AYK.6
10	Gathering Data	Excel	T3	Data Analysis	Intermediate	Conditional Formatting, PivotTable	AYK.6
11	Scanner System	Excel	T2	Strategic Analysis	Intermediate	Formulas	AYK.7
12	Competitive Pricing	Excel	T2	Profit Maximization	Intermediate	Formulas	AYK.7
13	Adequate Acquisitions	Excel	T2	Break-Even Analysis	Intermediate	Formulas	AYK.7
15	Assessing the Value of Information	Excel	T3	Data Analysis	Intermediate	PivotTable	AYK.8
16	Growth, Trends, and Forecasts	Excel	T2, T3	Data Forecasting	Advanced	Average, Trend, Growth	AYK.9
18	Formatting Grades	Excel	T3	Data Analysis	Advanced	If, LookUp	AYK.11
22	Turnover Rates	Excel	T3	Data Mining	Advanced	PivotTable	AYK.13
23	Vital Information	Excel	T3	Data Mining	Advanced	PivotTable	AYK.13
24	Breaking Even	Excel	T4	Business Analysis	Advanced	Goal Seek	AYK.14
25	Profit Scenario	Excel	T4	Sales Analysis	Advanced	Scenario Manager	AYK.14

Design Element: © McGraw Hill Education

Hardware and Software Basics

LEARNING OUTCOMES

A.1 Describe the six major categories of hardware and provide an example of each.

A.2 Identify the different computer categories and explain their potential business uses.

A.3 Identify the two main types of software.

INTRODUCTION

LO A.1: Describe the six major categories of hardware and provide an example of each.

Managers need to determine what types of hardware and software will satisfy their current and future business needs, the right time to buy the equipment, and how to protect their investments. This does not imply that managers need to be experts in all areas of technology; however, building a basic understanding of hardware and software can help them make the right investment choices.

Information technology can be an important enabler of business success and innovation. Information technology can be composed of the Internet, a personal computer, a cell phone that can access the web, a personal digital assistant, or presentation software. All of these technologies help perform specific information processing tasks. There are two basic categories of information technology: hardware and software. ***Hardware*** consists of the physical devices associated with a computer system. ***Software*** is the set of instructions the hardware executes to carry out specific tasks. Software, such as Microsoft Excel, and various hardware devices, such as a keyboard and a monitor, interact to create a spreadsheet or a graph. This appendix covers the basics of computer hardware and software, including terminology, characteristics, and the associated managerial responsibilities for building a solid enterprise architecture.

HARDWARE BASICS

In many industries, exploiting computer hardware is key to gaining a competitive advantage. Frito-Lay gained a competitive advantage by using handheld devices to track the strategic placement and sale of items in convenience stores. Sales representatives could track sale price, competitor information, the number of items sold, and item location in the store, all from their handheld device.[1]

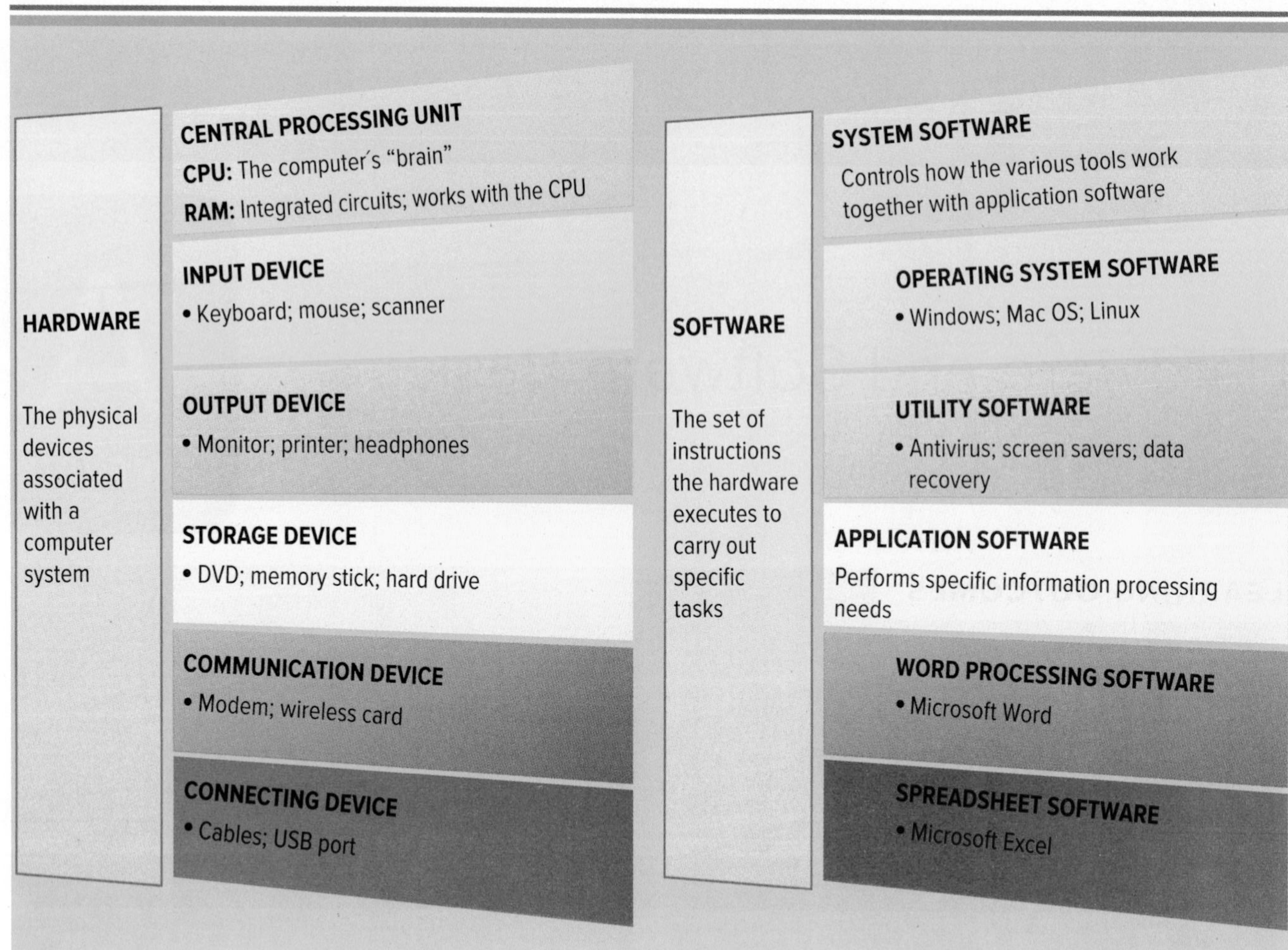

FIGURE A.1

Hardware and Software Overview

A ***computer*** is an electronic device operating under the control of instructions stored in its own memory that can accept, manipulate, and store data. Figure A.1 displays the two primary components of a computer–hardware and software. A computer system consists of six hardware components (see Figure A.2). Figure A.3 displays how these components work together to form a computer system.

Central Processing Unit

The dominant manufacturers of CPUs today include Intel (with its Celeron and Pentium lines for personal computers) and Advanced Micro Devices (AMD) (with its Athlon series).[2]

The ***central processing unit (CPU)*** (or ***microprocessor***) is the actual hardware that interprets and executes the program (software) instructions and coordinates how all the other hardware devices work together. The CPU is built on a small flake of silicon and can contain the equivalent of several million transistors. CPUs are unquestionably one of the 20th century's greatest technological advances.

A CPU contains two primary parts: control unit and arithmetic/logic unit. The ***control unit*** interprets software instructions and literally tells the other hardware devices what to do, based on the software instructions. The ***arithmetic-logic unit (ALU)*** performs all arithmetic operations (for example, addition and subtraction) and all logic operations (such as sorting and comparing numbers). The control unit and ALU perform different functions. The control unit obtains instructions from the software. It then interprets the instructions, decides which tasks other devices perform, and finally tells each device to perform the task. The ALU responds to the control unit and does whatever it dictates, performing either arithmetic or logic operations.

FIGURE A.2

Hardware Components of a Computer System

CPU	• The actual hardware that interprets and executes the program (software) instructions and coordinates how all the other hardware devices work together
Primary Storage	• The computer's main memory, which consists of the random access memory (RAM), the cache memory, and the read-only memory (ROM) that is directly accessible to the central processing unit (CPU)
Secondary Storage	• Equipment designed to store large volumes of data for long-term storage (diskette, CD, DVD, memory stick)
Input Devices	• Equipment used to capture information and commands (mouse, keyboard, scanner)
Output Devices	• Equipment used to see, hear, or otherwise accept the results of information processing requests (monitor, printer, microphone)
Communication Device	• Equipment used to send information and receive it from one location to another (modem, wireless card)

The number of CPU cycles per second determines how fast a CPU carries out the software instructions; more cycles per second mean faster processing, and faster CPUs cost more than their slower counterparts. CPU speed is usually quoted in megahertz and gigahertz. ***Megahertz (MHz)*** is the number of millions of CPU cycles per second. ***Gigahertz (GHz)*** is the number of billions of CPU cycles per second. Figure A.4 displays the factors that determine CPU speed.

Advances in CPU Design Chip makers are pressing more functionality into CPU technology. Most CPUs are ***complex instruction set computer (CISC) chips,*** which is a type of CPU that can recognize as many as 100 or more instructions, enough to carry out most computations directly. ***Reduced instruction set computer (RISC) chips*** limit the number of instructions the CPU can execute to increase processing speed. The idea of RISC is to reduce the instruction set to the bare minimum, emphasizing the instructions used most of the time and optimizing them for the fastest possible execution. An RISC processor runs faster than a CISC processor.

Primary Storage

Primary storage is the computer's main memory, which consists of the random access memory (RAM), cache memory, and read-only memory (ROM) that is directly accessible to the CPU.

Fuse/Getty Images

Stockbyte/Getty Images

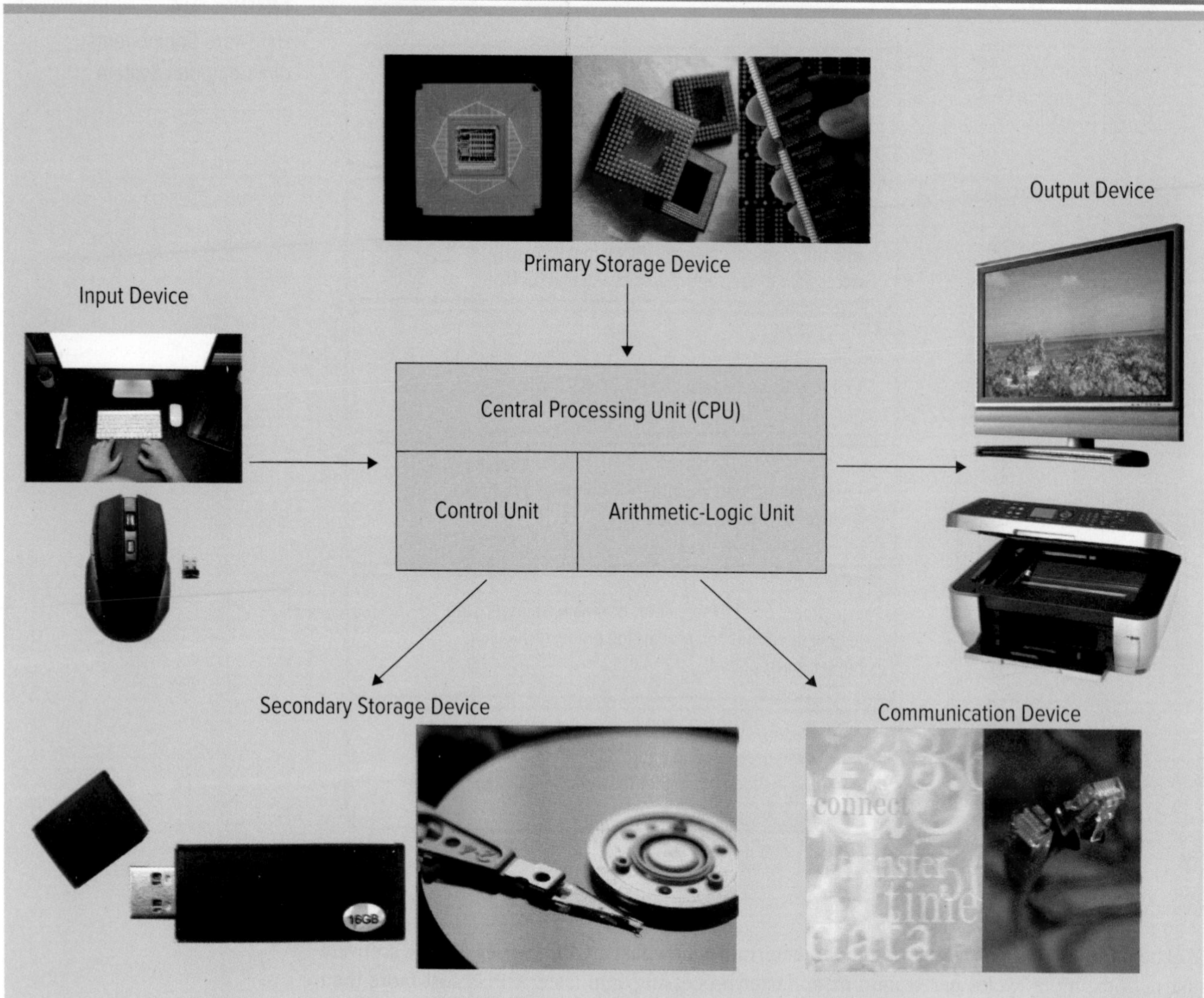

FIGURE A.3

How the Hardware Components Work Together

(clockwise from top left): Fuse/Getty Images; Stockbyte/Getty Images; Nick Rowe/Getty Images; Yasuhide Fumoto/Digital Vision/Getty Images; Stephen VanHorn/Alamy Stock Photo; Ingram/Media Bakery; Don Bishop/Photodisc/Getty Images; Daisuke Morita/Getty Images; Audrius Merfeldas/Shutterstock; rozbyshaka/Shutterstock; GaudiLab/Shutterstock

Random Access Memory ***Random access memory (RAM)*** is the computer's primary working memory, in which program instructions and data are stored so they can be accessed directly by the CPU via the processor's high-speed external data bus.

RAM is often called read/write memory. In RAM, the CPU can write and read data. Most programs set aside a portion of RAM as a temporary workspace for data so that one can modify (rewrite) as needed until the data are ready for printing or storage on secondary storage media, such as a hard drive or memory key. RAM does not retain its contents when the power

FIGURE A.4

Factors that Determine CPU Speed

CPU Speed Factors
Clock speed—the speed of the internal clock of a CPU that sets the pace at which operations proceed within the computer's internal processing circuitry.
Word length—number of bits (0s and 1s) that the CPU can process at any one time. Computers work in terms of bits and bytes using electrical pulses that have two states: on and off.
Bus width—the size of the internal electrical pathway along which signals are sent from one part of the computer to another. A wider bus can move more data, hence producing faster processing.
Chip line width—the distance between transistors on a chip. The shorter the chip line width, the faster the chip because more transistors can be placed on a chip and the data and instructions travel shorter distances during processing.

to the computer is switched off; hence, users should save their work frequently. When the computer is turned off, everything in RAM is wiped clean. ***Volatility*** refers to a device's ability to function with or without power. RAM is ***volatile,*** meaning it must have constant power to function; its contents are lost when the computer's electric supply fails.

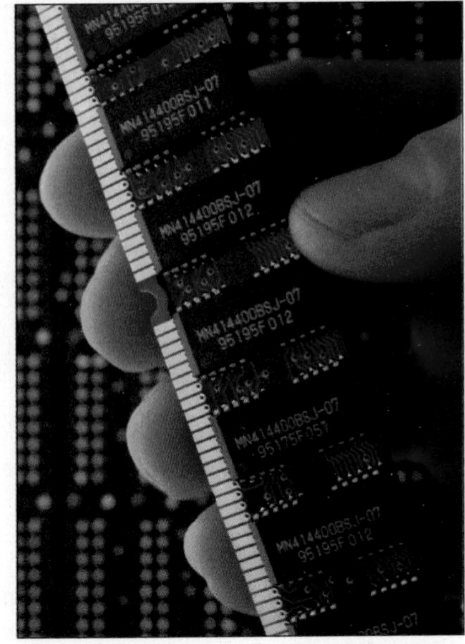

Nick Rowe/Getty Images

Cache Memory ***Cache memory*** is a small unit of ultra-fast memory that stores recently accessed or frequently accessed data so the CPU does not have to retrieve this data from slower memory circuits such as RAM. Cache memory that is built directly into the CPU's circuits is called primary cache. Cache memory contained on an external circuit is called secondary cache.

Read-Only Memory ***Read-only memory (ROM)*** is the portion of a computer's primary storage that does not lose its contents when one switches off the power. ROM is ***nonvolatile,*** meaning it does not require constant power to function. ROM contains essential system programs that neither the user nor the computer can erase. Because the computer's internal memory is blank during start-up, the computer cannot perform any functions unless given start-up instructions. These instructions are stored in ROM.

Flash memory is a special type of rewritable read-only memory (ROM) that is compact and portable. ***Memory cards*** contain high-capacity storage that holds data such as captured images, music, or text files. Memory cards are removable; when one is full, the user can insert an additional card. Subsequently, the data can be downloaded from the card to a computer. The card can then be erased and used again. Memory cards are typically used in digital devices such as cameras, cellular phones, and personal digital assistants (PDAs). ***Memory sticks*** provide nonvolatile memory for a range of portable devices, including computers, digital cameras, MP3 players, and PDAs.

Secondary Storage

Storage is a hot area in the business arena as organizations struggle to make sense of exploding volumes of data. ***Secondary storage*** consists of equipment designed to store large volumes of data for long-term storage. Secondary storage devices are nonvolatile and do not lose their contents when the computer is turned off. Some storage devices, such as a hard disk, offer easy update capabilities and a large storage capacity. Others, such as CD-ROMs, offer limited update capabilities but possess large storage capacities.

Storage capacity is expressed in bytes, with megabytes being the most common. A ***megabyte*** (***MB*** or ***M*** or ***Meg***) is roughly 1 million bytes. Therefore, a computer with 256 MB of RAM translates into the RAM being able to hold roughly 256 million characters of data and software instructions. A ***gigabyte (GB)*** is roughly 1 billion bytes. A ***terabyte (TB)*** is roughly 1 trillion bytes (refer to Figure A.5).[3]

A typical double-spaced page of pure text is roughly 2,000 characters. Therefore, a 40-GB (40 gigabytes or 40 billion characters) hard drive can hold approximately 20 million pages of text.

Common storage devices include:

- Magnetic medium
- Optical medium

Audrius Merfeldas/Shutterstock

Magnetic medium ***Magnetic medium*** is a secondary storage medium that uses magnetic techniques to store and retrieve data on disks or tapes coated with

FIGURE A.5

Binary Terms

Term	Size
Kilobyte (KB)	1,024 bytes
Megabyte (MB)	1,024 KB (1,048,576 bytes)
Gigabyte (GB)	1,024 MB (10^9 bytes)
Terabyte (TB)	1,024 GB (10^{12} bytes) 1 TB = Printing of 1 TB would require 50,000 trees to be made into paper and printed.
Petabyte (PB)	1,024 TB (10^{15} bytes) 200 PB = All production of digital magnetic tape in 1995
Exabyte (EB)	1,024 PB (10^{18} bytes) 2 EB = Total volume of information generated worldwide annually; 5 EB = All words ever spoken by human beings

magnetically sensitive materials. Like iron filings on a sheet of waxed paper, these materials are reoriented when a magnetic field passes over them. During write operations, the read/write heads emit a magnetic field that orients the magnetic materials on the disk or tape to represent encoded data. During read operations, the read/write heads sense the encoded data on the medium.

One of the first forms of magnetic medium developed was magnetic tape. ***Magnetic tape*** is an older secondary storage medium that uses a strip of thin plastic coated with a magnetically sensitive recording medium. The most popular type of magnetic medium is a hard drive. A ***hard drive*** is a secondary storage medium that uses several rigid disks coated with a magnetically sensitive material and housed together with the recording heads in a hermetically sealed mechanism. Hard drive performance is measured in terms of access time, seek time, rotational speed, and data transfer rate.

A ***solid state drive*** is an all-electronic storage device that is an alternative to a hard disk and is faster than a hard disk because there is zero latency (no read/write head to move). Instead of storing data magnetically like traditional hard drives, solid state drives store data using flash memory and have no moving parts so they do not need to "spin up" while in a sleep state and they don't need to move a drive head to different parts of the drive to access data. Therefore, solid state drives can access data faster than traditional hard drives and are far more rugged and reliable, offering greater protection in hostile environments.

Optical Medium Optical medium is a secondary storage medium for computers on which information is stored at extremely high density in the form of tiny pits. The presence or absence of pits is read by a tightly focused laser beam. Optical medium types include:

- **Compact disk-read-only memory (CD-ROM) drive**–an optical drive designed to read the data encoded on CD-ROMs and to transfer this data to a computer.
- **Compact disk-read-write (CD-RW) drive**–an optical drive that enables users to erase existing data and write new data repeatedly to a CD-RW.
- **Digital video disk (DVD)**–a CD-ROM format capable of storing up to a maximum of 17 GB of data, enough for a full-length feature movie.

Daisuke Morita/Getty Images

- **DVD-ROM drive**–a read-only drive designed to read the data encoded on a DVD and transfer the data to a computer.
- **Digital video disk-read/write (DVD-RW)**–a standard for DVD discs and player/recorder mechanisms that enables users to record in the DVD format.

CD-ROMs and DVDs offer an increasingly economical medium for storing data and programs. The overall trend in secondary storage is toward more direct-access methods, higher capacity with lower costs, and increased portability.

Input Devices

GaudiLab/Shutterstock

rozbyshaka/Shutterstock

An ***input device*** is equipment used to capture information and commands. A keyboard is used to type in information, and a mouse is used to point and click buttons and icons. A ***stylus*** is used as a pen-like device that taps the screen to enter commands. Numerous input devices are available in many environments, some of which have applications that are more suitable in a personal setting than a business setting. A keyboard, mouse, and scanner are the most common forms of input devices (see Figure A.6).

New forms of input devices allow people to exercise and play video games at the same time. The Kilowatt Sport from Powergrid Fitness lets people combine strength training with their favorite video games. Players can choose any PlayStation or Xbox game that uses a joystick to

FIGURE A.6

Input Devices

MANUAL INPUT DEVICES	
KEYBOARD	• Provides a set of alphabetic, numeric, punctuation, symbol, and control keys
MOUSE	• One or more control buttons housed in a palm-sized case and designed so that one can move it about on the table next to the keyboard
TOUCH PAD	• Form of a stationary mouse on which the movement of a finger causes the pointer on the screen to move; typically found below the space bar on laptops
TOUCH SCREEN	• Allows the use of a finger to point at and touch a monitor to execute commands
POINTING DEVICE	• Device used to navigate and select objects on a display screen
GAME CONTROLLER	• Device used for games to obtain better control screen action

AUTOMATED INPUT DEVICES	
IMAGE SCANNER	• Captures images, photos, graphics, and text that already exist on paper
BAR CODE SCANNER	• Captures information that exists in the form of vertical bars whose width and distance apart determine a number
BIOMETRIC SCANNER	• Captures human physical attributes such as a fingerprint or iris for security purposes
OPTICAL MARK READER	• Detects the presence or absence of a mark in a predetermined place (popular for multiple-choice exams)
OPTICAL CHARACTER READER	• Converts text into digital format for computer input
DIGITAL STILL CAMERA	• Digitally captures still images in varying resolutions
DIGITAL VIDEO CAMERA	• Digitally captures video
WEBCAM	• Digitally captures video and uploads it directly to the Internet
MICROPHONE	• Captures sounds such as a voice for voice-recognition software
POINT-OF-SALE (POS)	• Captures information at the point of a transaction, typically in a retail environment

run the elliptical trainer. After loading the game, participants stand on a platform while pushing and pulling a resistance rod in all directions to control what happens in the game. The varied movement targets muscle groups on the chest, arms, shoulders, abdomen, and back. The machine's display shows information such as pounds lifted and current resistance level, and players can use one-touch adjustment to vary the degree of difficulty.[4] ***Adaptive computer devices*** are input devices designed for special applications for use by people with different types of special needs. An example is a keyboard with tactile surfaces, which can be used by the visually impaired.

Another new input device is a stationary bicycle. A computer design team of graduate and undergraduate students at MIT built the Cyclescore, an integrated video game and bicycle. The MIT students tested current games on the market but found users would stop pedaling to concentrate on the game. To engage users, the team is designing games that interact with the experience of exercise itself; for example, monitoring heart rate and adjusting the difficulty of the game according to the user's bicycling capabilities. In one game, the player must pedal to make a hot-air balloon float over mountains while collecting coins and shooting at random targets.[5]

Output Devices

An ***output device*** is equipment used to see, hear, or otherwise accept the results of information processing requests. Among output devices, printers and monitors are the most common; however, speakers and plotters (special printers that draw output on a page) are widely used (see Figure A.7). In addition, output devices are responsible for converting computer-stored information into a form that can be understood.

FIGURE A.7

Output Devices

Yasuhide Fumoto/Digital Vision/Getty Images

Stephen VanHorn/Alamy Stock Photo

MONITORS	
CATHODE-RAY TUBE (CRT)	• A vacuum tube that uses an electron gun (cathode) to emit a beam of electrons that illuminates phosphors on a screen as the beam sweeps across the display repeatedly
LIQUID CRYSTAL DISPLAY (LCD)	• Low-powered displays used in laptop computers where rod-shaped crystal molecules change their orientation when an electrical current flows through them
LIGHT-EMITTING DIODE (LED)	• Tiny bulb used for backlight to improve the image on the screen
ORGANIC LIGHT-EMITTING DIODE (OLED)	• Displays use many layers of organic material emitting a visible light and therefore eliminating the need for backlighting

PRINTERS	
INK-JET PRINTER	• Printer that makes images by forcing ink droplets through nozzles
LASER PRINTER	• Printer that forms images using an electrostatic process, the same way a photocopier works
MULTIFUNCTION PRINTER	• Printer that can scan, copy, fax, and print all in one device
PLOTTER	• Printer that uses computer-directed pens for creating high-quality images, blueprints, schematics, etc.
3D PRINTER	• Printer that can produce solid, three-dimensional objects

A new output device based on sensor technology aims to translate American Sign Language (ASL) into speech, enabling the millions of people who use ASL to better communicate with those who do not know the rapid gesturing system. The AcceleGlove is a glove lined on the inside with sensors embedded in rings. The sensors, called accelerometers, measure acceleration and can categorize and translate finger and hand movements. Additional, interconnected attachments for the elbow and shoulder capture ASL signs that are made with full arm motion. When users wear the glove while signing ASL, algorithms in the glove's software translate the hand gestures into words. The translations can be relayed through speech synthesizers or read on a PDA-size computer screen. Inventor Jose L. Hernandez-Rebollar started with a single glove that could translate only the ASL alphabet. Now, the device employs two gloves that contain a 1,000-word vocabulary.[6]

Other new output devices are being developed every day. One British company, NeedAPresent, developed a vibrating USB massage ball that would plug into a computer's USB port to generate a warm massage for sore body parts during those long evenings spent coding software or writing papers. NeedAPresent also made a coffee cup warmer that would plug into the USB port.[7]

Ingram/Media Bakery

Communication Devices

A ***communication device*** is equipment used to send information and receive it from one location to another. A telephone modem connects a computer to a phone line to access another computer. The computer works in terms of digital signals, whereas a standard telephone line works with analog signals. Each digital signal represents a bit (either 0 or 1). The modem must convert the digital signals of a computer into analog signals so they can be sent across the telephone line. At the other end, another modem translates the analog signals into digital signals, which can then be used by the other computer. Figure A.8 displays the different types of modems.

FIGURE A.8

Comparing Modems

Carrier Technology	Description	Speed	Comments
Dial-up access	On-demand access using a modem and regular telephone line (POT).	2400 bps to 56 Kbps	■ Cheap but slow.
Cable	Special cable modem and cable line required.	512 Kbps to 20 Mbps	■ Must have existing cable access in area. ■ Bandwidth is shared.
DSL (digital subscriber line)	This technology uses the unused digital portion of a regular copper telephone line to transmit and receive information. A special modem and adapter card are required.	128 Kbps to 8 Mbps	■ Doesn't interfere with normal telephone use. ■ Bandwidth is dedicated. ■ Must be within 5 km (3.1 miles) of telephone company switch.
Wireless (LMCS)	Access is gained by connection to a high-speed cellular-like local multipoint communications system (LMCS) network via wireless transmitter/receiver.	30 Mbps or more	■ Can be used for high-speed data, broadcast TV, and wireless telephone service.
Satellite	Newer versions have two-way satellite access, removing the need for a phone line.	6 Mbps or more	■ Bandwidth is not shared. ■ Some connections require an existing Internet service account. ■ Setup fees can range from $500 to $1,000.

LO A.2: **Identify the different computer categories and explain their potential business uses.**

COMPUTER CATEGORIES

Supercomputers today can hit processing capabilities of well over 200 teraflops—the equivalent of everyone on Earth performing 35,000 calculations per second (see Figure A.9). For the past 20 years, federally funded supercomputing research has given birth to some of the computer industry's most significant technology breakthroughs, including:

- Clustering, which allows companies to chain together thousands of PCs to build mass-market systems.
- Parallel processing, which provides the ability to run two or more tasks simultaneously and is viewed as the chip industry's future.
- Mosaic browser, which morphed into Netscape and made the web a household name.

Federally funded supercomputers have also advanced some of the country's most dynamic industries, including advanced manufacturing, gene research in the life sciences, and real-time financial-market modeling.[8]

Computers come in different shapes, sizes, and colors. And they meet a variety of needs. An ***appliance*** is a computer dedicated to a single function, such as a calculator or computer game. An ***ebook*** is an electronic book that can be read on a computer or special reading device. Some are small enough to carry around; others are the size of a telephone booth. Size does not always correlate to power, speed, and price (see Figure A.10).

MIT's Media Lab is developing a laptop that it will sell for $100 each to government agencies around the world for distribution to millions of underprivileged schoolchildren. Using a simplified sales model and reengineering the device helped MIT reach the $100 price point. Almost half the price of a current laptop comprises marketing, sales, distribution, and profit. Of the remaining costs, the display panel and backlight account for roughly half, while the rest covers the operating system. The low-cost laptop will use a display system that costs less than $25, a 500 MHz processor from AMD, a wireless LAN connection, 1 GB of storage, and the Linux operating system. The machine will automatically connect with others. China and Brazil have already ordered 3 million and 1 million laptops, respectively. MIT's goal is to produce around 150 million laptops per year.[9]

LO A.3: **Identify the two main types of software.**

SOFTWARE BASICS

Hardware is only as good as the software that runs it. Over the years, the cost of hardware has decreased while the complexity and cost of software have increased. Some large software applications, such as customer relationship management systems, contain millions of lines of code, take years to develop, and cost millions of dollars. The two main types of software are system software and application software.

FIGURE A.9

Supercomputer

PhonlamaiPhoto/Getty Images

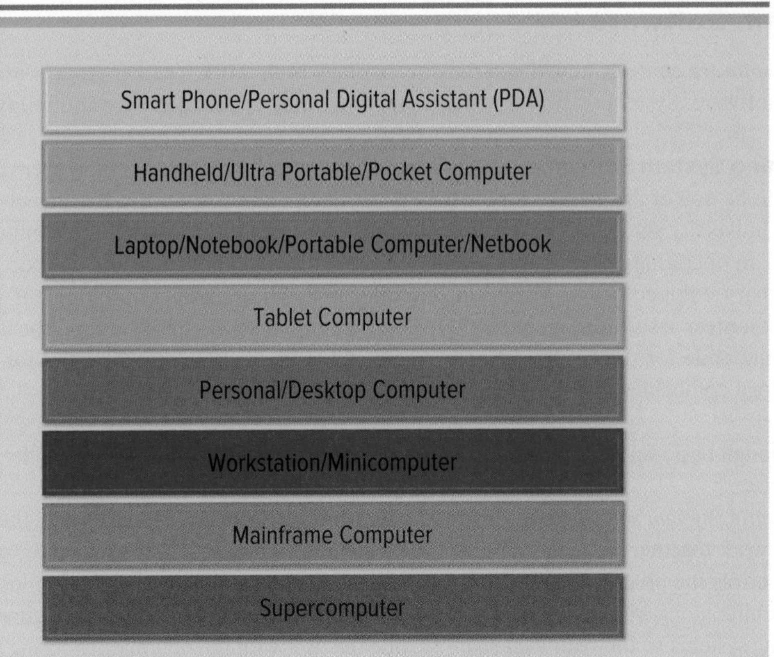

FIGURE A.10
Computer Categories

Computer Category	Description
Smart phone	A cellular telephone with a keypad that runs programs, music, photos, and email, and includes many features of a PDA.
Personal digital assistant (PDA)	A small, handheld computer that performs simple tasks such as taking notes, scheduling appointments, and maintaining an address book and a calendar. The PDA screen is touch-sensitive, allowing a user to write directly on the screen, capturing what is written.
Handheld (ultra portable, pocket) computer	Computer that is portable enough to fit in a purse or pocket and has its own power source or battery.
Laptop (portable, notebook) computer	Computer that is portable enough to fit on a lap or in a bag and has its own power source or battery. Laptops come equipped with all of the technology that a personal desktop computer has, yet weigh as little as 2 pounds.
Tablet computer	Computer with a flat screen that uses a mouse or fingertip for input instead of a keyboard. Similar to PDAs, tablet PCs use a writing pen or stylus to write notes on the screen and touch the screen to perform functions such as clicking a link while visiting a website.
Personal computer (microcomputer)	Computer that is operated by a single user who can customize the functions to match personal preferences.
Desktop computer	Computer that sits on, next to, or under a user's desk and is too large to carry around. The computer box is where the CPU, RAM, and storage devices are held with a monitor on top, or a vertical system box (called a tower) usually placed on the floor within a work area.
Workstation computer	Similar to a desktop but has more powerful mathematical and graphics processing capabilities and can perform more complicated tasks in less time. Typically used for software development, web development, engineering, and ebusiness tools.
Minicomputer (server)	Designed to meet the computing needs of several people simultaneously in a small to medium-sized business environment. A common type of minicomputer is a server and is used for managing internal company applications, networks, and websites.
Mainframe computer	Designed to meet the computing needs of hundreds of people in a large business environment. Mainframe computers are a step up in size, power, capability, and cost from minicomputers.
Supercomputer	The fastest, most powerful, and most expensive type of computer. Organizations such as NASA that are heavily involved in research and number crunching employ supercomputers because of the speed with which they can process information. Other large, customer-oriented businesses such as General Motors and AT&T employ supercomputers just to handle customer information and transaction processing.

System Software

System software controls how the various technology tools work together along with the application software. System software includes both operating system software and utility software.

Operating System Software Linus Torvalds, a Finnish programmer, may seem an unlikely choice to be one of the world's top managers. However, Linux, the software project he created while a university student, is now one of the most powerful influences on the computer world. Linux is an operating system built by volunteers and distributed for free and has become one of the primary competitors to Microsoft. Torvalds coordinates Linux development with a few dozen volunteer assistants and more than 1,000 programmers scattered around the globe. They contribute code for the kernel–or core piece–of Linux. He also sets the rules for dozens of technology companies that have lined up behind Linux, including IBM, Dell, Hewlett-Packard, and Intel.

Although basic versions of Linux are available for free, Linux is having a considerable financial impact.[10]

Operating system software controls the application software and manages how the hardware devices work together. When using Excel to create and print a graph, the operating system software controls the process, ensures that a printer is attached and has paper, and sends the graph to the printer along with instructions on how to print it. Some computers are configured with two operating systems so they can ***dual boot***–provide the user with the option of choosing the operating system when the computer is turned on. An ***embedded operating system*** is used in computer appliances and special-purpose applications, such as an automobile, ATM, or media player, that are used for a single purpose. An iPod has a single-purpose, embedded operating system.

Operating system software also supports a variety of useful features, one of which is multitasking. ***Multitasking*** allows more than one piece of software to be used at a time. Multitasking is used when creating a graph in Excel and simultaneously printing a word processing document. With multitasking, both pieces of application software are operating at the same time. There are different types of operating system software for personal environments and for organizational environments (see Figure A.11).

Utility Software ***Utility software*** provides additional functionality to the operating system. Utility software includes antivirus software, screen savers, and antispam software. Operating systems are customized by using the ***control panel,*** which is a Windows feature that provides options that set default values for the Windows operating system. For example, the ***system clock*** works like a wristwatch and uses a battery mounted on the motherboard to provide power when the computer is turned off. If the user moves to a different time zone, the system clock

FIGURE A.11

Operating System Software

Operating System Software	
Linux	An open source operating system that provides a rich environment for high-end workstations and network servers. Open source refers to any program whose source code is made available for use or modification as users or other developers see fit.
Mac OS X	The operating system of Macintosh computers.
Microsoft Windows	Generic name for the various operating systems in the Microsoft Windows family, including Microsoft Windows CE, Microsoft Windows, Microsoft Windows ME, Microsoft Windows XP, Microsoft Windows NT, and Microsoft Windows Server.
MS-DOS	The standard, single-user operating system of IBM and IBM-compatible computers, introduced in 1981. MS-DOS is a command-line operating system that requires the user to enter commands, arguments, and syntax.
UNIX	A 32-bit multitasking and multiuser operating system that originated at AT&T's Bell Laboratories and is now used on a wide variety of computers, from mainframes to PDAs.

Types of Utility Software	
Crash-proof	Helps save information if a computer crashes.
Disk image for data recovery	Relieves the burden of reinstalling applications if a hard drive crashes or becomes irretrievably corrupted.
Disk optimization	Organizes information on a hard disk in the most efficient way.
Encrypt data	Protects confidential information from unauthorized eyes.
File and data recovery	Retrieves accidental deletion of photos or documents.
Uninstaller	Can remove software that is no longer needed.

FIGURE A.12
Utility Software

can be adjusted in the control panel. ***Safe mode*** occurs if the system is failing and will load only the most essential parts of the operating system and will not run many of the background operating utilities. ***System restore*** enables a user to return to the previous operating system. Figure A.12 displays a few types of available utility software.

Application Software

Application software is used for specific information processing needs, including payroll, customer relationship management, project management, training, and many others. Application software is used to solve specific problems or perform specific tasks. From an organizational perspective, payroll software, collaborative software such as videoconferencing (within groupware), and inventory management software are all examples of application software (see Figure A.13). ***Personal information management (PIM) software*** handles contact information, appointments, task lists, and email. ***Course management software*** contains course information such as a syllabus and assignments and offers drop boxes for quizzes and homework, along with a grade book.

Distributing Application Software

After software has been deployed to its users, it is not uncommon to find bugs or additional errors that require fixing. ***Software updates (software patch)*** occur when the software vendor releases updates to software to fix problems or enhance features. A ***software upgrade*** occurs

Types of Application Software	
Browser	Enables the user to navigate the World Wide Web.
Communication	Turns a computer into a terminal for transmitting data to and receiving data from distant computers through the telephone system.
Data management	Provides the tools for data retrieval, modification, deletion, and insertion.
Desktop publishing	Transforms a computer into a desktop publishing workstation.
Email	Provides email services for computer users, including receiving mail, sending mail, and storing messages.
Groupware	Increases the cooperation and joint productivity of small groups of co-workers.
Presentation graphics	Creates and enhances charts and graphs so they are visually appealing and easily understood by an audience.
Programming	Possesses an artificial language consisting of a fixed vocabulary and a set of rules (called syntax) that programmers use to write computer programs.
Spreadsheet	Simulates an accountant's worksheet on-screen and lets users embed hidden formulas that perform calculations on the visible data.
Word processing	Transforms a computer into a tool for creating, editing, proofreading, formatting, and printing documents.

FIGURE A.13
Application Software

when the software vendor releases a new version of the software, making significant changes to the program. Application software can be distributed using one of the following methods:

- ***Single user license***–restricts the use of the software to one user at a time.
- ***Network user license***–enables anyone on the network to install and use the software.
- ***Site license***–enables any qualified users within the organization to install the software, regardless of whether the computer is on a network. Some employees might install the software on a home computer for working remotely.
- ***Application service provider license***–specialty software paid for on a license basis or per-use basis or usage-based licensing.

KEY TERMS

Adaptive computer device A.8
Appliance A.10
Application service provider license A.14
Application software A.13
Arithmetic-logic unit (ALU) A.2
Cache memory A.5
Central processing unit (CPU) (or microprocessor) A.2
Communication device A.9
Complex instruction set computer (CISC) chip A.3
Computer A.2
Control panel A.12
Control unit A.2
Course management software A.13
Dual boot A.12
Ebook A.10
Embedded operating system A.12
Flash memory A.5
Gigabyte (GB) A.5
Gigahertz (GHz) A.3
Hard drive A.6
Hardware A.1
Input device A.7
Magnetic medium A.5
Magnetic tape A.6
Megabyte (MB, M, or Meg) A.5
Megahertz (MHz) A.3
Memory card A.5
Memory stick A.5
Multitasking A.12
Network user license A.14
Nonvolatile A.5
Operating system software A.12
Output device A.8
Personal information management (PIM) software A.13
Primary storage A.3
Random access memory (RAM) A.4
Read-only memory (ROM) A.5
Reduced instruction set computer (RISC) chip A.3
Safe mode A.13
Secondary storage A.5
Single-user license A.14
Site license A.14
Software A.1
Software updates (software patch) A.13
Software upgrade A.13
Solid state drive A.6
Stylus A.7
System clock A.12
System restore A.13
System software A.12
Terabyte (TB) A.5
Utility software A.12
Volatile A.5
Volatility A.5

MAKING BUSINESS DECISIONS

1. A Computer

Dell is considered the fastest-growing company on Earth and specializes in computer customization. Connect to Dell's website at www.dell.com. Go to the portion of Dell's site that allows you to customize either a laptop or a desktop computer. First, choose an already-prepared system and note its price and capability in terms of CPU speed, RAM size, monitor quality, and storage capacity. Now, customize that system to increase CPU speed, add more RAM, increase monitor size and quality, and add more storage capacity. What is the difference in price between the two? Which system is more in your price range? Which system has the speed and capacity you need?

2. Small Business Computers

Many types of computers are available for small businesses. Use the Internet to find three vendors of laptops or notebooks that are good for small businesses. Find the most expensive and the least expensive that the vendor offers and create a table comparing the different computers based on the following:

- CPU
- Memory
- Hard drive
- Optical drive
- Operating system
- Utility software
- Application software
- Support plan

Determine which computer you would recommend for a small business looking for an inexpensive laptop. Determine which computer you would recommend for a small business looking for an expensive laptop.

Networks and Telecommunications

LEARNING OUTCOMES

B.1 Compare LANs, WANs, and MANs.

B.2 Compare the two types of network architectures.

B.3 Explain topology and the different types found in networks.

B.4 Describe protocols and the importance of TCP/IP.

B.5 Identify the different media types found in networks.

INTRODUCTION

LO B.1: Compare LANs, WANs, and MANs.

Change is everywhere in the information technology domain, but nowhere is change more evident and more dramatic than in the realm of networks and telecommunications. Most management information systems today rely on digital networks to communicate information in the form of data, graphics, video, and voice. Companies large and small from all over the world are using networks and the Internet to locate suppliers and buyers, to negotiate contracts with them, and to provide bigger, better, and faster services than ever before. ***Telecommunication systems*** enable the transmission of data over public or private networks. A ***network*** is a communications system created by linking two or more devices and establishing a standard methodology by which they can communicate. The world's largest and most widely used network is the Internet. The Internet is a global network of networks that uses universal standards to connect millions of networks around the world. Telecommunication systems and networks are traditionally complicated and historically inefficient. However, businesses can benefit from today's network infrastructures that provide reliable global reach to employees and customers.

NETWORK BASICS

Networks range from small two-computer networks to the biggest network of all, the Internet. A network provides two principal benefits: the ability to communicate and the ability to share.

Today's corporate digital networks include a combination of local area networks, wide area networks, and metropolitan area networks. A ***local area network (LAN)*** is designed to connect a group of computers in proximity to each other, such as in an office building, a school, or a home. A LAN is useful for sharing resources such as files, printers, games, or other applications. A LAN in turn often connects to other LANs and to the Internet or wide area networks. A ***wide area network (WAN)*** spans a large geographic area, such as a state, province, or country. WANs often connect multiple smaller networks, such as local area networks or metropolitan area networks. The world's most popular WAN is the Internet. A ***metropolitan area network (MAN)*** is a large computer network usually spanning a city. Figure B.1 highlights the three types of networks, and Figure B.2 illustrates each network type.

Direct data communication links between a company and its suppliers or customers, or both, have been successfully used to give the company a strategic advantage. The SABRE airline reservation system is a classic example of a strategic management information system that depends on communication provided through a network. SABRE Airline Solutions pioneered technological advances for the industry in areas such as revenue management, pricing, flight scheduling, cargo, flight operations, and crew scheduling. In addition, not only did SABRE help invent ecommerce for the travel industry, the company also holds claim to progressive solutions that defined–and continue to revolutionize–the travel and transportation marketplace.

A network typically includes four things (besides the computers themselves):

1. **Protocol**–a set of communication rules to make sure everyone speaks the same language.
2. **Network interface card (NIC)**–a card that plugs into the back (or side) of your computers and lets them send and receive messages from other computers.
3. **Cable**–the medium to connect all of the computers.
4. **Hub (switch or router)**–hardware to perform traffic control.

We will continue to define many of these terms and concepts in the sections that follow.

Networks are differentiated by the following:

- Architecture–peer-to-peer, client/server
- Topology–bus, star, ring, hybrid, wireless
- Protocols–Ethernet, transmission control protocol/Internet protocol (TCP/IP)
- Media–coaxial, twisted-pair, fiber-optic

FIGURE B.1
Network Types

Network Types	
Local area network (LAN)	Designed to connect a group of computers in proximity to each other, such as in an office building, a school, or a home. A LAN is useful for sharing resources such as files, printers, games, or other applications. A LAN in turn often connects to other LANs and to the Internet or wide area networks.
Wide area network (WAN)	Spans a large geographic area, such as a state, province, or country. WANs often connect multiple smaller networks, such as local area networks (LANs) or metropolitan area networks (MANs).
Metropolitan area network (MAN)	A large computer network usually spanning a city. Most colleges, universities, and large companies that span a campus use an infrastructure supported by a MAN.

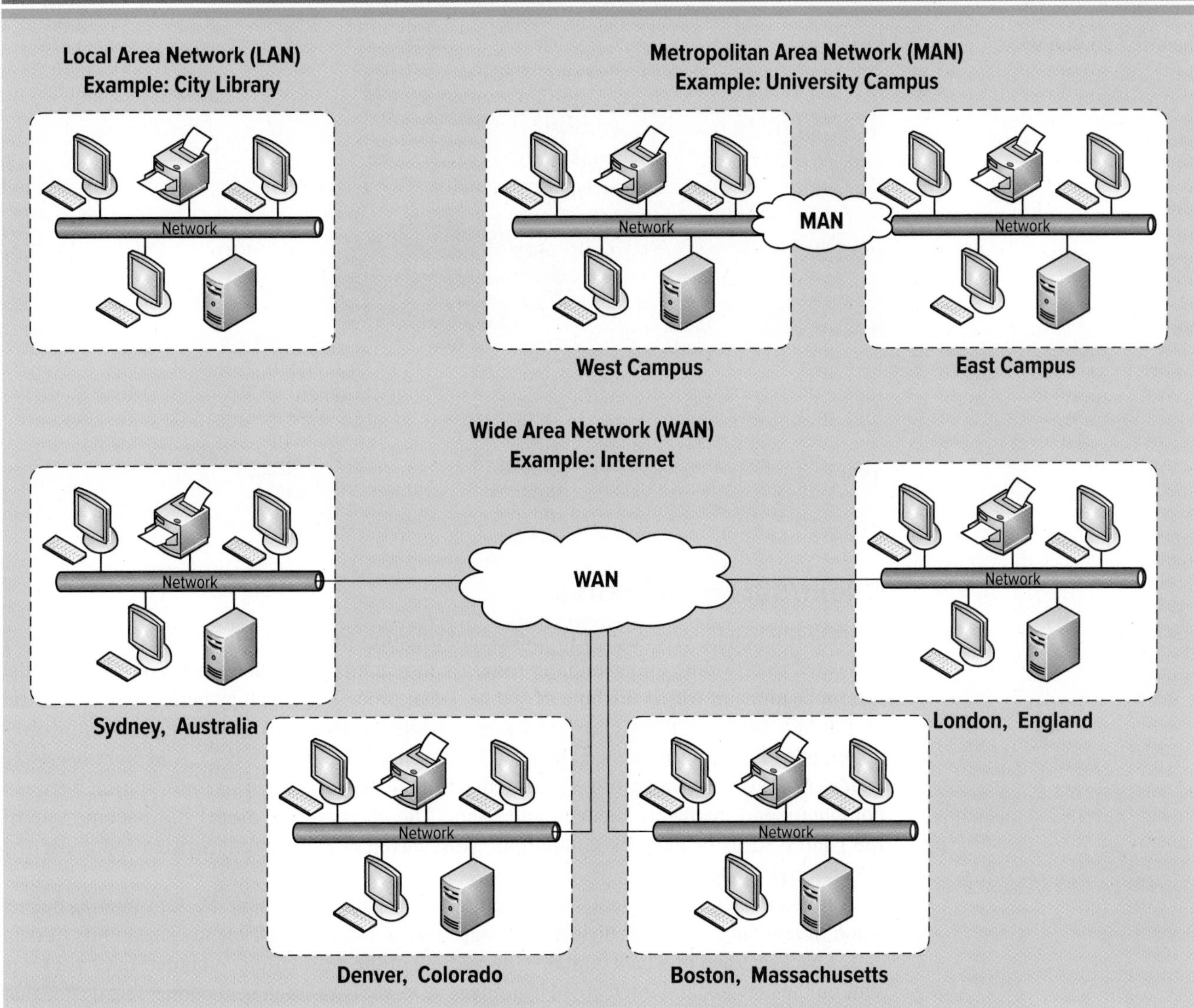

FIGURE B.2

LAN, WAN, and MAN

LO B.2: Compare the two types of network architectures.

ARCHITECTURE

The two primary types of network architectures are peer-to-peer networks and client/server networks.

Peer-to-Peer Networks

A ***peer-to-peer (P2P) network*** is a computer network that relies on the computing power and bandwidth of the participants in the network rather than a centralized server, as illustrated in Figure B.3. Each networked computer can allow other computers to access its files and use connected printers while it is in use as a workstation without the aid of a server.

Napster (now known as Rhapsody) may be the most widely known example of a P2P implementation, but it may also be one of the most narrowly focused because the Napster model takes advantage of only one of the many capabilities of P2P computing: file sharing. The technology has far broader capabilities, including sharing processing, memory, and storage and supporting collaboration among vast numbers of distributed computers, such as grid computing, described in Chapter 5. Peer-to-peer computing enables immediate interaction among people and computer systems.[1]

FIGURE B.3

Peer-to-Peer Networks

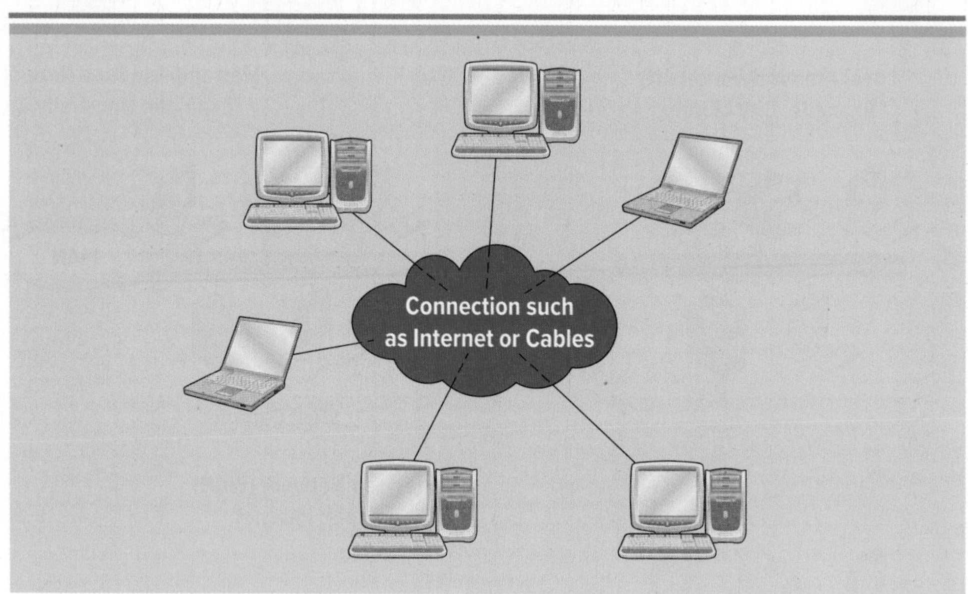

Client/Server Networks

A ***client*** is a computer designed to request information from a server. A ***server*** is a computer dedicated to providing information in response to requests. A ***client/server network*** is a model for applications in which the bulk of the back-end processing, such as performing a physical search of a database, takes place on a server, while the front-end processing, which involves communicating with the users, is handled by the clients (see Figure B.4). A ***network operating system (NOS)*** is the operating system that runs a network, steering information between computers and managing security and users. The client/server model has become one of the central ideas of network computing. Most business applications written today use the client/server model.

A fundamental part of client/server architecture is packet-switching. ***Packet-switching*** occurs when the sending computer divides a message into a number of efficiently sized units of data called packets, each of which contains the address of the destination computer. Each packet is sent on the network and intercepted by routers. A ***router*** is an intelligent connecting device that examines each packet of data it receives and then decides which way to send it onward toward its destination. The packets arrive at their intended destination, although some may have actually traveled by different physical paths, and the receiving computer assembles the packets and delivers the message to the appropriate application.

LO B.3: Explain topology and the different types found in networks.

TOPOLOGY

Networks are assembled according to certain rules. Cables, for example, have to be a certain length; each cable strand can support only a certain amount of network traffic. A ***network topology*** refers to the geometric arrangement of the actual physical organization of the computers (and other network devices) in a network. Topologies vary depending on cost and functionality. Figure B.5 highlights the five common topologies used in networks, and Figure B.6 displays each topology.

LO B.4: Describe protocols and the importance of TCP/IP.

PROTOCOLS

A ***protocol*** is a standard that specifies the format of data, as well as the rules to be followed during transmission. Simply put, for one computer (or computer program) to talk to another computer (or computer program), they must both be talking the same language, and this language is called a protocol.

A protocol is based on an agreed-upon and established standard. This way, all manufacturers of hardware and software that are using the protocol do so in a similar fashion to allow for

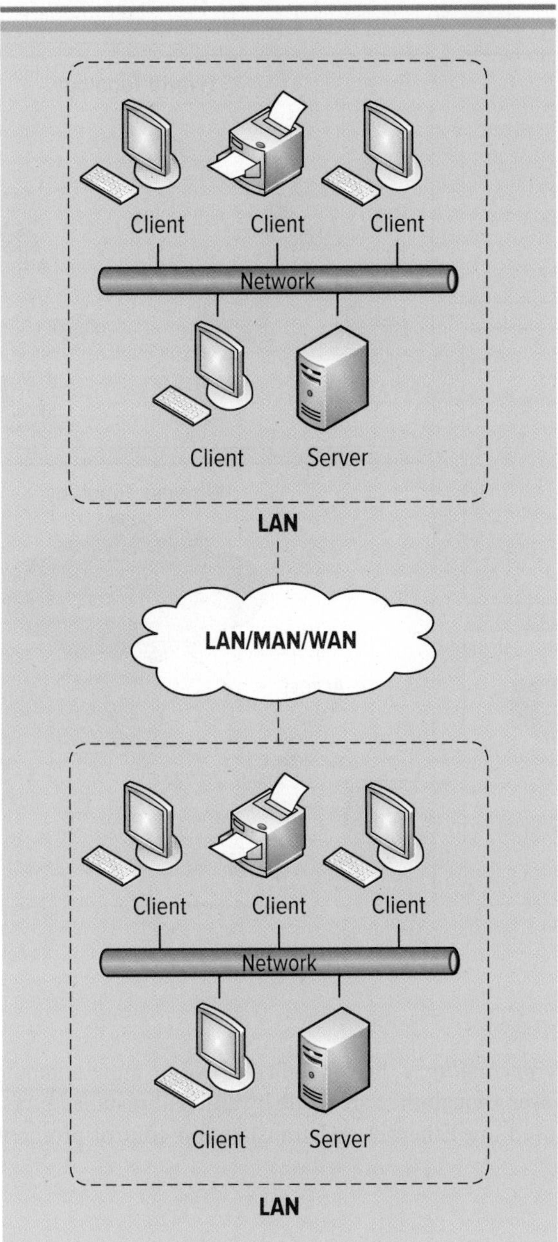

FIGURE B.4

Client/Server Network

FIGURE B.5

Five Network Topologies

Network Topologies	
Bus	All devices are connected to a central cable, called the bus or backbone. Bus networks are relatively inexpensive and easy to install for small networks.
Star	All devices are connected to a central device called a hub. Star networks are relatively easy to install and manage, but bottlenecks can occur because all data must pass through a hub.
Ring	All devices are connected to one another in the shape of a closed loop so that each device is connected directly to two other devices, one on either side of it. Ring topologies are relatively expensive and difficult to install, but they offer high speed and can span large distances.
Hybrid	Groups of star-configured workstations are connected to a linear bus backbone cable, combining the characteristics of the bus and star topologies.
Wireless	Devices are connected by signals between access points and wireless transmitters within a limited range.

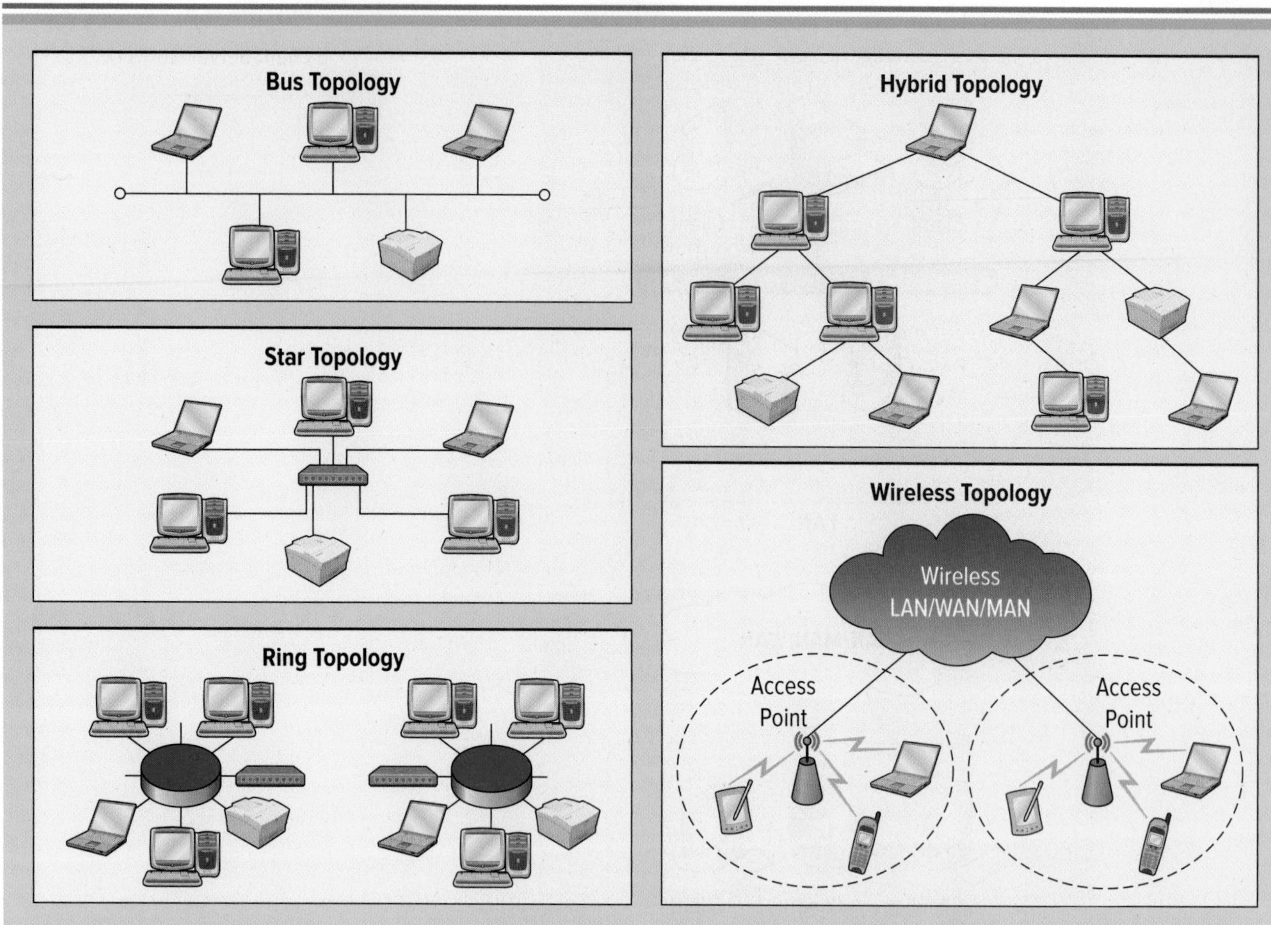

FIGURE B.6

Network Topologies

interoperability. ***Interoperability*** is the capability of two or more computer systems to share data and resources, even though they are made by different manufacturers. The most popular network protocols used are Ethernet and transmission control protocol/Internet protocol (TCP/IP).

Ethernet

Ethernet is a physical and data layer technology for LAN networking (see Figure B.7). Ethernet is the most widely installed LAN access method, originally developed by Xerox and then developed further by Xerox, Digital Equipment Corporation, and Intel. When it first began to be widely deployed in the 1980s, Ethernet supported a maximum theoretical data transfer rate of 10 megabits per second (Mbps). More recently, Fast Ethernet has extended traditional Ethernet technology to 100 Mbps peak, and Gigabit Ethernet technology extends performance up to 1,000 Mbps.

Ethernet is one of the most popular LAN technologies for the following reasons:

- It is easy to implement, manage, and maintain.
- It allows low-cost network implementations.
- It provides extensive flexibility for network installation.
- It guarantees interoperability of standards-compliant products, regardless of manufacturer.[2]

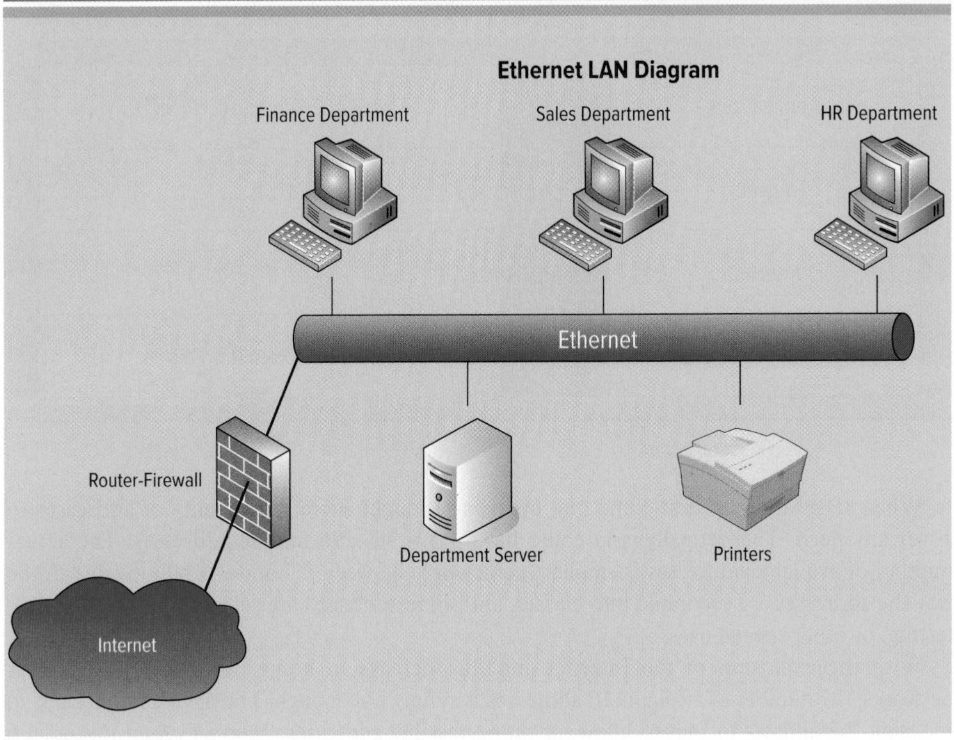

FIGURE B.7

Ethernet Protocols

Ethernet LAN Diagram

Finance Department

Sales Department

HR Department

Ethernet

Router-Firewall

Department Server

Printers

Internet

Transmission Control Protocol/Internet Protocol

The most common telecommunication protocol is transmission control protocol/Internet protocol (TCP/IP), which was originally developed by the Department of Defense to connect a system of computer networks that became known as the Internet. ***Transmission control protocol/Internet protocol (TCP/IP)*** provides the technical foundation for the public Internet, as well as for large numbers of private networks. The key achievement of TCP/IP is its flexibility with respect to lower-level protocols. TCP/IP uses a special transmission method that maximizes data transfer and automatically adjusts to slower devices and other delays encountered on a network. Although more than 100 protocols make up the entire TCP/IP protocol suite, the two most important of these are TCP and IP. **TCP** provides transport functions, ensuring, among other things, that the amount of data received is the same as the amount transmitted. **IP** provides the addressing and routing mechanism that acts as a postmaster. Figure B.8 displays TCP/IP's four-layer reference model:

- Application layer–serves as the window for users and application processes to access network services.
- Transport layer–handles end-to-end packet transportation.
- Internet layer–formats the data into packets, adds a header containing the packet sequence and the address of the receiving device, and specifies the services required from the network.
- Network interface layer–places data packets on the network for transmission.[3]

For a computer to communicate with other computers and web servers on the Internet, it must have a unique numeric IP address. IP provides the addressing and routing mechanism that acts as a postmaster. An IP address is a unique 32-bit number that identifies the location of a computer on a network. It works like a street address–as a way to find out exactly where to deliver information.

FIGURE B.8

TCP/IP Four-Layer Reference Model

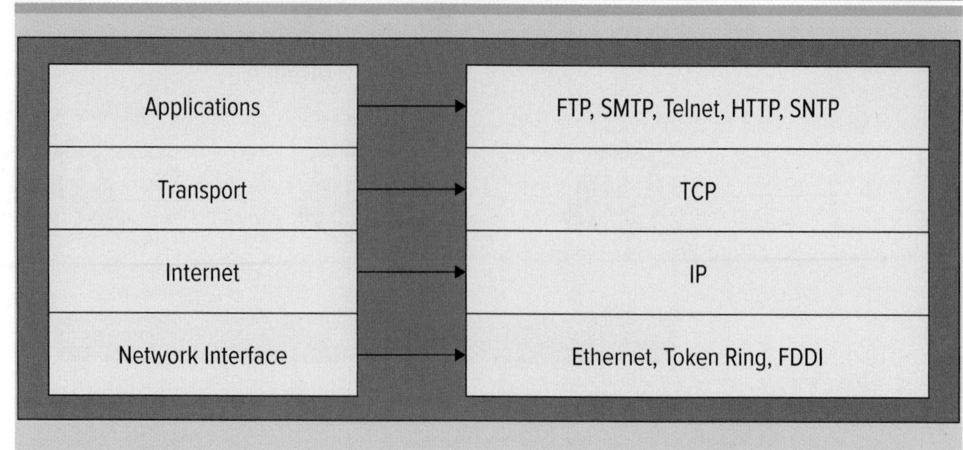

When IP addressing first came out, everyone thought there were plenty of addresses to cover any need. Theoretically, you could have 4,294,967,296 unique addresses. The actual number of available addresses is smaller (somewhere between 3.2 and 3.3 billion) due to the way the addresses are separated into classes, and some addresses are set aside for multicasting, testing, or other special uses.[4]

With the explosion of the Internet and the increase in home networks and business networks, the number of available IP addresses is simply not enough. The obvious solution is to redesign the address format to allow for more possible addresses. ***Internet protocol version 6 (IPv6)*** is the next-generation protocol designed to replace the current version Internet protocol, IP version 4 (IPv4). The main change IPv6 will bring is a much larger address space that allows greater flexibility in assigning addresses. IPv6 uses a 128-bit addressing scheme that produces 3.4×10^{38} addresses.[5]

The TCP/IP suite of applications includes five protocols–file transfer, simple mail transfer, telnet, hypertext transfer, and simple network management (see Figures B.9 and B.10).[6]

FIGURE B.9

TCP/IP Applications

TCP/IP Applications	
File Transfer Protocol (FTP)	Allows files containing text, programs, graphics, numerical data, and so on to be downloaded off or uploaded onto a network.
Simple Mail Transfer Protocol (SMTP)	TCP/IP's own messaging system for email.
Telnet Protocol	Provides terminal emulation that allows a personal computer or workstation to act as a terminal, or access device, for a server.
Hypertext Transfer Protocol (HTTP)	Allows web browsers and servers to send and receive web pages.
Simple Network Management Protocol (SNMP)	Allows networked nodes to be managed from a single point.

FIGURE B.10

TCP/IP Applications[7]

OSI Model
7. Application
6. Presentation
5. Session
4. Transport
3. Network
2. Data Link
1. Physical

MEDIA

LO B.5: Identify the different media types found in networks.

Network transmission media refers to the various types of media used to carry the signal between computers. When information is sent across the network, it is converted into electrical signals. These signals are generated as electromagnetic waves (analog signaling) or as a sequence of voltage pulses (digital signaling). To be sent from one location to another, a signal must travel along a physical path. The physical path used to carry a signal between a signal transmitter and a signal receiver is called the transmission medium. The two types of transmission media are wire (guided) and wireless (unguided).

Wire Media

Wire media are transmission material manufactured so that signals will be confined to a narrow path and will behave predictably. The three most commonly used types of guided media are (see Figure B.11):

- Twisted-pair cable
- Coaxial cable
- Fiber-optic cable

Twisted-Pair Cable ***Twisted-pair cable*** refers to a type of cable composed of four (or more) copper wires twisted around each other within a plastic sheath. The wires are twisted to reduce outside electrical interference. Twisted-pair cables come in shielded and unshielded varieties. Shielded cables have a metal shield encasing the wires that acts as a ground for electromagnetic interference. Unshielded twisted-pair (UTP) is the most popular and is generally the best option for LAN networks. The quality of UTP may vary from telephone-grade wire to high-speed cable. The cable has four pairs of wires inside the jacket. Each pair is twisted with a different number of twists per inch to help eliminate interference from adjacent pairs and other electrical devices. The connectors (called RF-45) on twisted-pair cables resemble large telephone connectors.[8]

Coaxial Cable ***Coaxial cable*** is cable that can carry a wide range of frequencies with low signal loss. It consists of a metallic shield with a single wire placed along the center of a shield and isolated from the shield by an insulator. Coaxial cable is similar to that used for cable television. This type of cable is referred to as coaxial because it contains one copper wire (or physical data channel) that carries the signal and is surrounded by another concentric physical channel consisting of a wire mesh. The outer channel serves as a ground for electrical interference. Because of this grounding feature, several coaxial cables can be placed within a single conduit or sheath without significant loss of data integrity.[9]

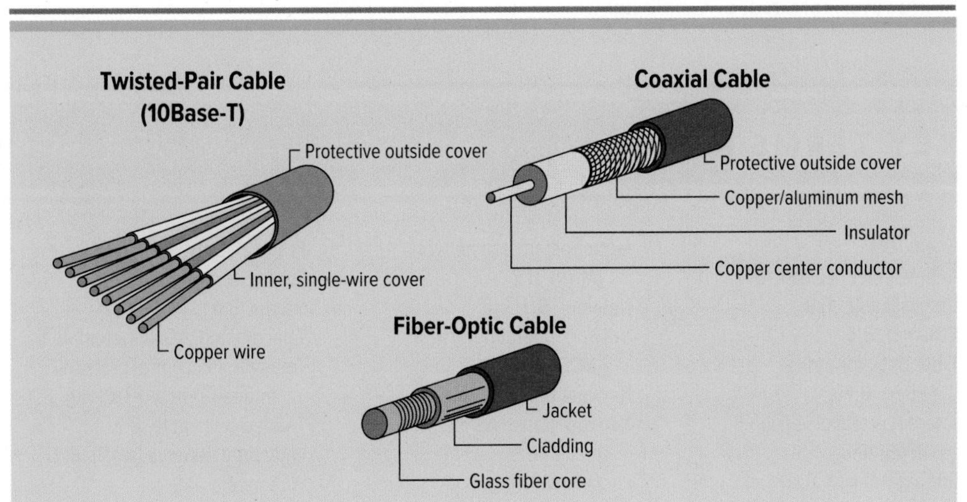

FIGURE B.11

Twisted-Pair, Coaxial, and Fiber-Optic Cable

FIGURE B.12

Communication Satellite Example

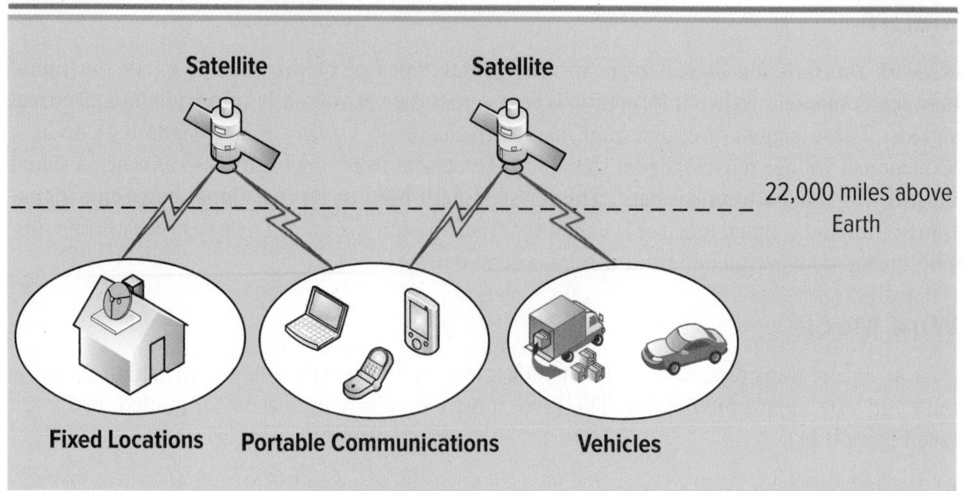

Fiber-Optic Cable ***Fiber optic*** (or ***optical fiber***) refers to the technology associated with the transmission of information as light impulses along a glass wire or fiber. Fiber-optic cable is the same type used by most telephone companies for long-distance service. Fiber-optic cable can transmit data over long distances with little loss in data integrity. In addition, because data are transferred as a pulse of light, fiber optical is not subject to interference. The light pulses travel through a glass wire or fiber encased in an insulating sheath.[10]

Fiber optic's increased maximum effective distance comes at a price. Optical fiber is more fragile than wire, difficult to split, and labor intensive to install. For these reasons, fiber optics is used primarily to transmit data over extended distances where the hardware required to relay the data signal on less expensive media would exceed the cost of fiber-optic installation. It is also used where large amounts of data need to be transmitted on a regular basis.

Wireless Media

Wireless media are natural parts of the Earth's environment that can be used as physical paths to carry electrical signals. The atmosphere and outer space are examples of wireless media that are commonly used to carry these signals. Today, technologies for wireless data transmission include microwave transmission, communication satellites (see Figure B.12), mobile phones, personal digital assistants (PDAs), personal computers (e.g., laptops), and mobile data networks.

Network signals are transmitted through all media as a type of waveform. When transmitted through wire and cable, the signal is an electrical waveform. When transmitted through fiber-optic cable, the signal is a light wave, either visible or infrared light. When transmitted through the Earth's atmosphere, the signal can take the form of waves in the radio spectrum, including microwaves, infrared, or visible light.

KEY TERMS

MAKING BUSINESS DECISIONS

1. Network Analysis

Global Manufacturing is considering a new technology application. The company wants to process orders in a central location and then assign production to different plants. Each plant will operate its own production scheduling and control system. Data on work in process and completed assemblies will be transmitted back to the central location that processes orders. At each plant, Global uses personal computers that perform routine tasks such as payroll and accounting. The production scheduling and control systems will be a package program running on a new computer dedicated to this application.

The MIS personnel at Global have retained you as a consultant to help with further analysis. What kind of network configuration seems most appropriate? How much bandwidth is needed? What data should be collected? Prepare a plan showing the information Global must develop to establish this network system. Should Global use a private network or can it accomplish its objectives through the Internet?

2. Secure Access

Organizations that have traditionally maintained private, closed systems have begun to look at the potential of the Internet as a ready-made network resource. The Internet is inexpensive and globally pervasive—every phone jack is a potential connection. However, the Internet lacks security. What obstacles must organizations overcome to allow secure network connections?

3. Telecommunications Options

Research the telecommunications options that currently exist for you to link to the Internet from where you live. Prepare a list of criteria on which to compare the different technologies, such as price (Is there tiered pricing depending on speed and amount you can download?), start-up cost (Do you need to buy a special modem, or is there an installation fee?), maximum data transfer rate, and so on. Compare your responses with several classmates and then develop a summary of all telecommunications options that you identified, including the criteria and your group comparison based on the criteria.

4. Frying Your Brains?

Radio waves, microwaves, and infrared all belong to the electromagnetic radiation spectrum. These terms reference ranges of radiation frequencies we use every day in our wireless networking environments. However, the very word *radiation* strikes fear in many people. Cell towers have sprouted from fields all along highways. Tall rooftops harbor many more cell stations in cities. Millions of cell phone users place microwave transmitters/receivers next to their heads each time they make a call. With all this radiation zapping around, should we be concerned? Research the Internet to find out what the World Health Organization has had to say about this.

5. Home Network Experience

If you maintain a home computer network (or have set one up in the past), create a document that describes the benefits the network provides, along with the difficulties you have experienced. Include in your document a network topology, a detailed description of the type of network you have, and the equipment you use. If you have no experience with home networking, interview someone who does and write up his or her comments. Compare this with several classmates and discuss the benefits and challenges.

Designing Databases

LEARNING OUTCOMES

C.1 Identify the relational database model's basic components.
C.2 Explain the importance of documenting entity-relationship diagrams.
C.3 Explain the need for an entity-relationship diagram in a database management system.

INTRODUCTION

LO C.1: Identify the relational database model's basic components.

Businesses rely on databases for accurate, up-to-date information. Without access to mission-critical data, most businesses are unable to perform their normal daily functions, much less create queries and reports that help make strategic decisions. For those decisions to be useful, the database must have data that is accurate, complete, consistent, timely, and unique. However, without a good underlying database design, decisions will be inaccurate and inconstant.

A ***database*** maintains information about various types of objects (inventory), events (transactions), people (employees), and places (warehouses). A ***database management system (DBMS)*** creates, reads, updates, and deletes data in a database while controlling access and security. A DBMS provides a way to create, update, delete, store, and retrieve data in the database.

Using a data model offers a method for designing a database correctly that will help in meeting the needs of the users in a DBMS environment.

THE RELATIONAL DATABASE MODEL

Numerous elements in a business environment need to store data, and those elements are related to one another in a variety of ways. In fact, a database must contain not only the data but also information about the relationships between those items of data. Designing a database properly is fundamental to establishing a solid foundation on which to base business decisions. This is done by using a ***data model,*** or the logical data structures that detail the relationships among data elements using graphics or pictures. A ***relational database model*** stores information in the form of logically related two-dimensional tables. Tables, or entities as they are formally referred to, will be discussed later.

In developing the relational database model to design a database, an entity-relationship diagram is used. An ***entity-relationship diagram (ERD)*** is a technique for documenting the entities and relationships in a database environment. Before describing the notation used for developing an ERD, it is important to understand what entities and attributes are.

Entities and Attributes

An ***entity*** stores information about a person, place, thing, transaction, or event. A customer is an entity, as are a product and an appointment. An ***attribute*** is the data elements associated with an entity. For example, consider Mega-Video, a physical and online retail store that sells movie DVDs. The company would need to store information about its customers (especially for online purchases) by creating an entity called *CUSTOMER* that contained many attributes such as *Customer Number, First Name, Last Name, Street, City, State, Zip Code, Phone Number,* and *Email* (refer to Figure C.1).

Type of Attributes

There are several types of attributes, including:

- **Simple versus composite.** A simple attribute cannot be broken down into smaller components. For example, a customer's first name and last name are simple. A composite attribute can be divided into smaller components, which represent more basic attributes that have their own meanings. A common example of a composite attribute is *Address* (see Figure C.2). *Address* can be broken down into a number of subparts, such as *Street, City, State, Zip Code.*
- **Single-valued versus multivalued.** When creating a relational database, the attributes in the data model must be single-valued. ***Single-valued attribute*** means having only a single value of each attribute of an entity. A person's age is an example of a single-valued attribute because a person cannot have more than one age. ***Multivalued attribute*** means having the potential to contain more than one value for an attribute. For example, an educational degree of a person is a multivalued attribute because a person can have more than one degree. An entity in a relational database cannot have multivalued attributes; those attributes must be handled by creating another entity to hold them. Therefore, in the example given previously, in designing the database, there would be two entities, one called *PERSON* (or something similar) and one called *DEGREE.* If a multivalued attribute has been identified, it typically is a clue that another entity is needed.

FIGURE C.1

Entities and Attributes Examples

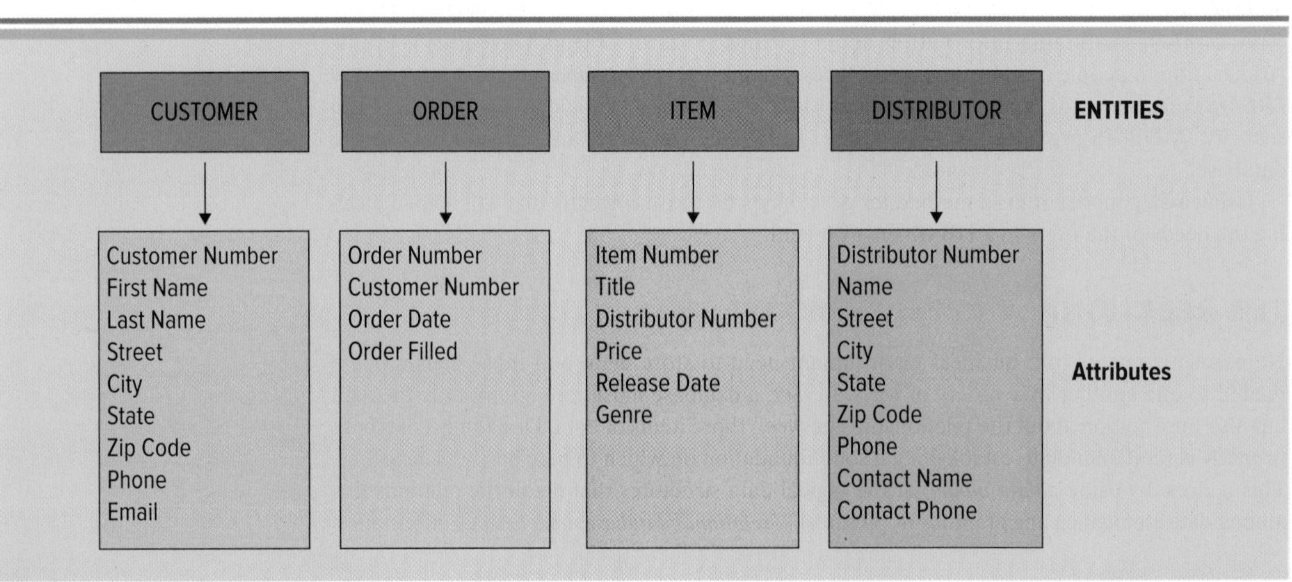

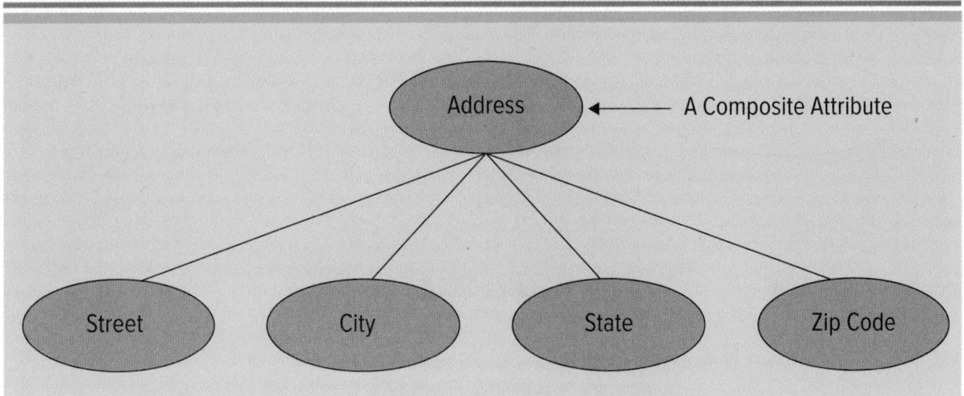

FIGURE C.2

Composite Attributes

- **Stored versus derived.** If an attribute can be calculated using the value of another attribute, it is called a derived attribute. The attribute that is used to derive the attribute is called a stored attribute. Derived attributes are not stored in the file but can be derived when needed from the stored attributes. One example of a derived and stored attribute is a person's age. If the database has a stored attribute such as the person's *Date of Birth,* then a derived attribute called *Age* can be created by subtracting the *Current Date* (this is retrieved from the DBMS) from the *Date of Birth* to get the age.
- **Null-valued.** Sometimes an attribute does not have an applicable value for an attribute. For these situations, the null-valued attribute is created. A ***null-valued attribute*** is assigned to an attribute when no other value applies or when a value is unknown. A person who does not have a mobile phone would have null stored for the value for the *Mobile Phone Number* attribute. Null can also be used when the attribute value is unknown, such as *Hair Color.* Every person has a hair color, but the information may be missing.

Business Rules

The "correct" design for a specific business depends on the business rules; what is correct for one organization may not be correct for another. A ***business rule*** is a statement that defines an aspect of a business. It is intended to convey the behavior and rules of a business. The following statements are examples of possible business rules for Mega-Video:

- A customer can purchase many DVDs.
- DVDs can be purchased by many customers.
- A DVD title can have many copies.

A typical business may have hundreds of business rules. Each business rule will have entities and sometimes even attributes in the statements. For instance, in the preceding example, *CUSTOMER* and *DVD* would be entities according to this business rule. Identifying the business rules will help to create a more accurate and complete database design. In addition, the business rules also assist with identifying relationships between entities. This is very useful in creating ERDs.

DOCUMENTING ENTITY-RELATIONSHIP DIAGRAMS

LO C.2: Explain the importance of documenting entity-relationship diagrams.

Once entities, attributes, and business rules have been identified, the ERD can be documented. The two most commonly used models of ERD documentation are Chen, named after the originator of entity-relationship modeling, Dr. Peter Chen, and information engineering, which grew out of work by James Martin and Clive Finkelstein. It does not matter which is used as long as everyone who is using the diagram understands the notation. For purposes of simplicity, only the Chen model will be described here.

The Chen model notation uses very specific symbols in representing entities and attributes. Rectangles represent entities. Each entity's name appears in the rectangle, is expressed in the singular, and is capitalized, as in *CUSTOMER.* Originally, attributes were not part of the Chen model; however, many database designers have extended it to include the attributes in ovals, as illustrated in Figure C.3.

FIGURE C.3

Chen Model with Attributes

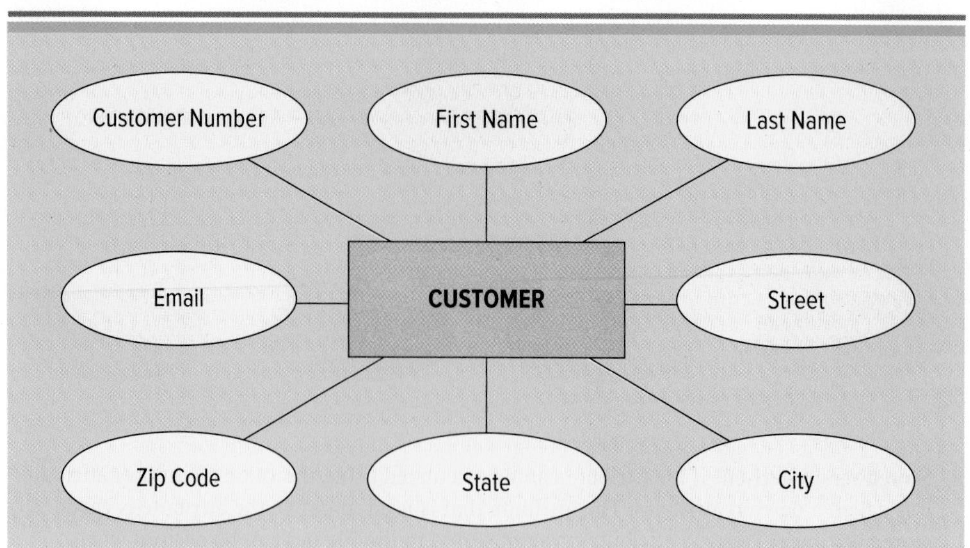

Basic Entity Relationships

One of the main reasons for creating an ERD is to identify and represent the relationships between entities. If the business rules for Mega-Video state that a customer can order many videos (in this case, an item), then a relationship needs to be created between *CUSTOMER, ORDER,* and *ITEM.* This is a purely conceptual representation of what the database will look like and is completely unrelated to the physical storage of the data. Again, what the ERD is doing is creating a model in which to design the database.

The Chen model uses diamonds for relationships and lines to connect relationships between entities. Figure C.4 displays the relationship between a Mega-Video *CUSTOMER* and *ORDER* using this notation. The word within the relationship gives some indication of the meaning of the relationship.

Once the basic entities and their attributes have been defined, the next task is to identify the relationships among those entities. There are three basic types of relationships: (1) one-to-one, (2) one-to-many, and (3) many-to-many.

One-to-One Relationship A ***one-to-one relationship (1:1)*** is between two entities in which an instance of one entity can be related to only one instance of a related entity. Consider Mega-Video, which has many stores with several employees and one manager. According to the company's business rules, the manager, who is an employee, can manage only one store. The relationship then becomes 1:1 between *EMPLOYEE* and *STORE.* Using the Chen model notation, as shown in Figure C.5, the relationships between the two instances can then be expressed as "An employee can manage one store and one store has one manager."

FIGURE C.4

Chen Method with Relationship

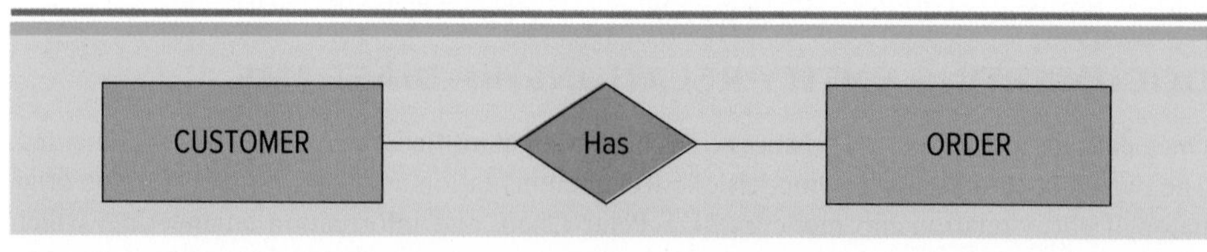

FIGURE C.5

A One-to-One Relationship

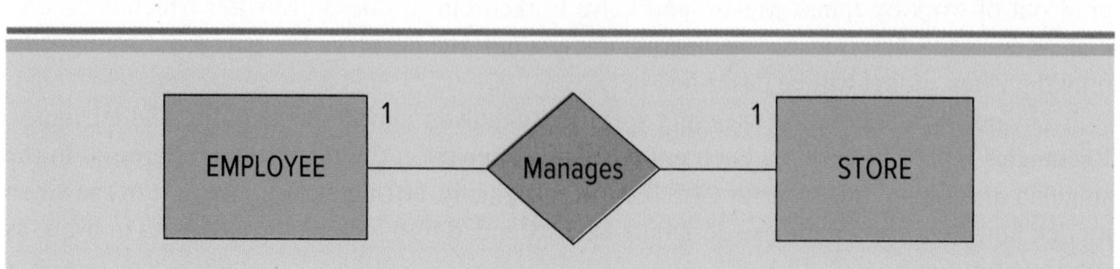

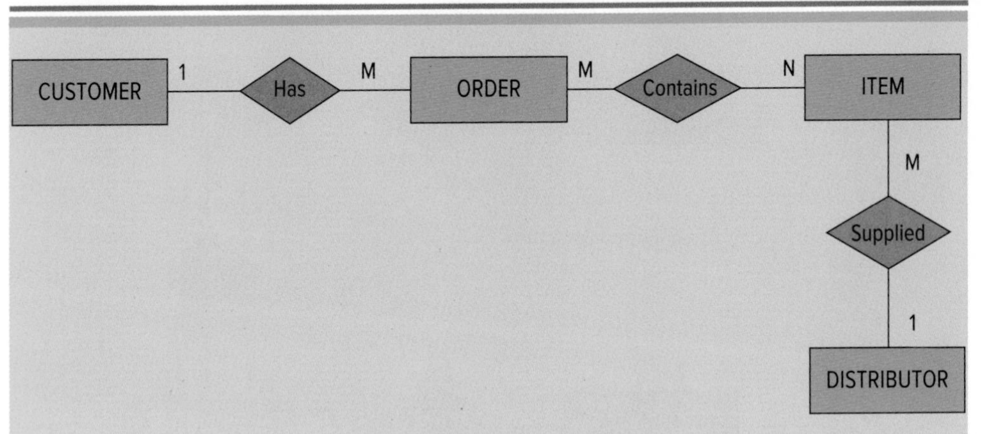

FIGURE C.6

A One-to-Many Relationship

The number "1" next to the *EMPLOYEE* and *STORE* entities indicates that only one *EMPLOYEE* manages one *STORE*.

One-to-Many Relationship Most relational databases are constructed from one-to-many relationships. A ***one-to-many relationship (1:M)*** is between two entities in which an instance of one entity can be related to many instances of a related entity. For example, Mega-Video receives many *ITEM*(s) from one *DISTRIBUTOR*, and each *DISTRIBUTOR* supplies many *ITEM*(s), as Figure C.6 illustrates. Similarly, a *CUSTOMER* can have many *ORDER*(s), but an *ORDER* has only one *CUSTOMER*. These are both examples of a one-to-many relationship. The "M" next to the *ORDER* entity indicates that a *CUSTOMER* can place one or more *ORDER*(s). That notation is also used with *ITEM* because an *ORDER* can contain one or more *ITEM*(s).

Many-to-Many Relationship Identifying and removing many-to-many relationships will help to create an accurate and consistent database. A ***many-to-many relationship (M:N)*** is between two entities in which an instance of one entity is related to many instances of another, and one instance of the other can be related to many instances of the first entity. There is a many-to-many relationship between a Mega-Video *ORDER* and *ITEM* (refer back to Figure C.6). An *ORDER* can contain many *ITEM*(s), and each *ITEM* can be on many *ORDER*(s). The letter "N" next to *ITEM* in Figure C.6 indicates the many-to-many relationship between *ORDER* and *ITEM*.

However, there are problems with many-to-many relationships. First, the relational data model was not designed to handle many-to-many relationships. This means they need to be replaced with a one-to-many relationship to be used in a relational DBMS. Second, many-to-many relationships will create redundancy in the data that is stored. This then has a negative impact on the accuracy and consistency that a database needs. To understand this problem better, consider the relationship between *ITEM* and *ORDER*. There is a many-to-many relationship between the *ORDER* and the *ITEM* because each *ORDER* can contain many *ITEM*(s) and, over time, each *ITEM* will be on many *ORDER*(s). Whenever a *CUSTOMER* places an *ORDER* for an *ITEM*, the number of *ITEM*(s) varies, depending on how many DVDs the *CUSTOMER* is buying. To break the many-to-many relationship, a composite entity is needed.

Entities that exist to represent the relationship between two other entities are known as ***composite entities***. The preceding example needs another entity that breaks up the many-to-many relationship between *ORDER* and *ITEM*. Figure C.7 displays the new relationship.

Creating a composite entity called *LINE ITEM* (think of it as a line item on an invoice slip) breaks up the many-to-many relationship between *ORDER* and *ITEM*, which then eliminates redundancy and other anomalies when deleting or updating information. Using the Chen model, composite entities are documented with a combination of a rectangle and a diamond.

Given the new ERD in Figure C.7, each *ORDER* can contain many *LINE ITEM*(s), but a *LINE ITEM* can belong to only one *ORDER*. As a result, the relationship between *ORDER* and *LINE ITEM* is one-to-many (one order has one or more line items), and the relationship between *LINE ITEM* and *ITEM* is one-to-many (one item can be in many line items). The composite

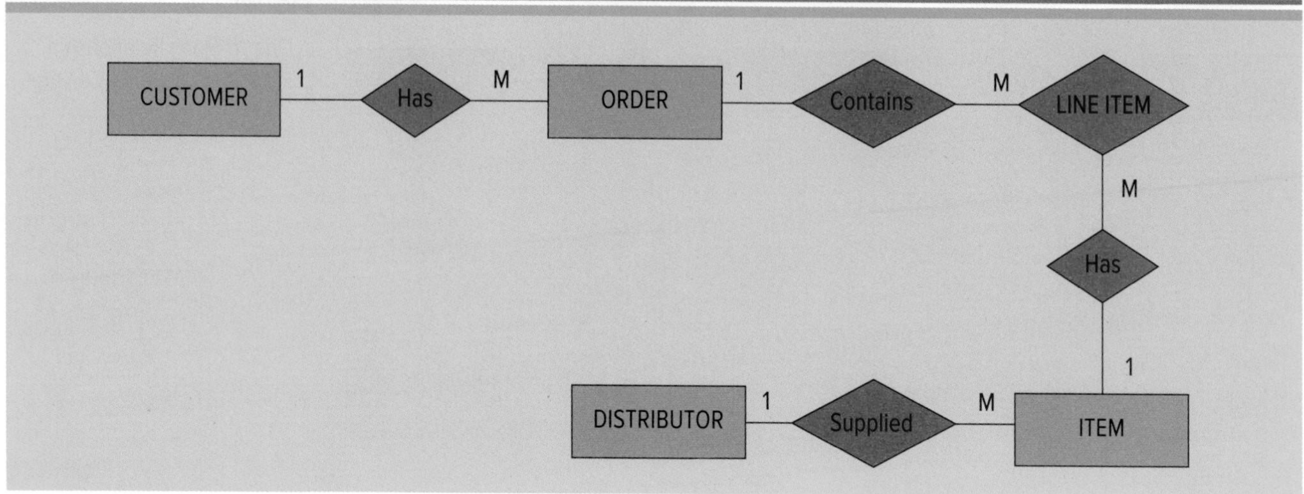

FIGURE C.7

A Composite Entity

entity has removed the original many-to-many relationship and turned it into two one-to-many relationships.

Relationship Cardinality

Cardinality expresses the specific number of instances in an entity. In the Chen model, the cardinality is indicated by placing numbers beside the entities in the format of (x, y). The first number in the cardinality represents the minimum value and the second number is for the maximum value.

Mega-Video can store data about a *CUSTOMER* in its database before the *CUSTOMER* places an *ORDER*. An instance of the *CUSTOMER* entity does not have to be related to any instance of the *ORDER* entity, meaning there is an optional cardinality.

However, the reverse is not true for the Mega-Video database; an *ORDER must* be related to a *CUSTOMER*. Without a *CUSTOMER*, an *ORDER* cannot exist. An instance of the *CUSTOMER* entity can be related to zero, one, or more *ORDER*(s) using the cardinality notation (0,N). An instance of the *ORDER* entity must be related to one and only one *CUSTOMER*, having a cardinality of (1,1). The relationship between an instance of *ORDER* and *CUSTOMER* is a mandatory relationship. Figure C.8 illustrates these cardinalities.

LO C.3: Explain the need for an entity-relationship diagram in a database management system.

RELATIONAL DATA MODEL AND THE DATABASE

Once the ERD is completed, it can be translated from a conceptual logical model into the formal data model required by the DBMS. The relational data model is the result of the work of Edgar (E. F.) Codd, a mathematician. During the 1960s, Dr. Codd was working with existing data models when he noticed that data relationships were very inefficient. Using his experience and knowledge in mathematics, he created the relational data model. Most databases, such as Access 2010 and SQL Server 2010, are based on the relational data model.

From Entities to Tables

In creating an ERD for the conceptual model, the focus was on identifying entities and attributes. For the logical relational data model, the attention is on tables and fields. Using the ERD, the entities become tables and attributes turn into fields. A ***table*** is composed of rows

FIGURE C.8

Example of Cardinalities

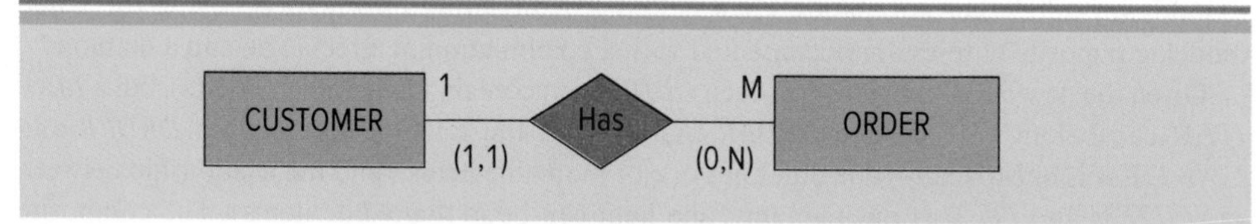

CUSTOMER			
Customer Number	First Name	Last Name	Phone Number
0001	Bill	Miller	777-777-7777
0505	Jane	Cook	444-444-4444
1111	Sam	Smith	555-555-5555
1212	John	Doe	666-666-6666

FIGURE C.9

A Sample Customer Table

and columns that represent an entity. A ***field*** is a characteristic of a table. A ***record*** is a collection of related data elements. The columns in the table definition represent the field, and a row is a record.

At first glance, a table along with the fields and records looks much like information in a spreadsheet, such as that displayed in Figure C.9 of a *CUSTOMER* table.

Fields Figure C.9 has four fields: *Customer Number, First Name, Last Name,* and *Phone Number.* Two or more tables within the same relational data model may have fields with the same names, but a single table must have unique field names. Using the relational data model notation, the table names are capitalized (e.g., *CUSTOMER*) and all columns are in title case (e.g., Customer Number), as in:

CUSTOMER (Customer Number, First Name, Last Name, Phone Number).

Records A record in a table has the following properties:

- A table cannot have multivalued attributes (as mentioned previously); therefore, only one value is allowed at the intersection of a field and record.
- Each record needs to be unique; there are no duplicate records in a table.
- A record must have an entity identifier, or ***primary key,*** which is a field (or group of fields), that uniquely identifies a given record in a table.

Primary Key A primary key makes it possible to identify every record uniquely in a table. The primary key is important to retrieve data accurately from the database.

Using a *Customer Number* as a primary key states that no two customers will ever have the same number. The primary key will be used to identify records associated with it. For example, if someone was searching the Mega-Video database for all the *ITEMS* that a *CUSTOMER* with a *Customer Number* of "112299" bought, that individual would retrieve only those records and not those associated with another customer.

Along with being unique, a primary key must not contain the value *null.* Recall that null is a special value meaning unknown; however, it is not the same as a field being blank or set to the value of zero. If one record has a null primary key, then the data structure is not in violation. But once a second null value for another record is introduced, the uniqueness of the primary key is lost. Therefore, nulls are forbidden when establishing primary keys.

The proper notation to use when documenting the primary key is to underline it, such as:

CUSTOMER (<u>Customer Number,</u> First Name, Last Name, Phone Number)

Logically Relating Tables

Once the primary key has been defined, tables can be logically related. Each table in Figure C.10 is directly analogous to the entities of the same name in the Mega-Video ERD presented in Figure C.8, excluding the *DISTRIBUTOR.* The *CUSTOMER* table is identified by a Customer Number, a randomly generated unique primary key. The *ORDER* table is identified by an Order Number, another arbitrary unique primary key assigned by Mega-Video. The table *ORDER LINE* tells the company which *ITEM*(s) are part of which *ORDER.* This table requires a concatenated primary key (that is to say, joining two fields that act as one primary key) because multiple *ITEM*(s) can appear on multiple *ORDER*(s). The selection of this primary key, however,

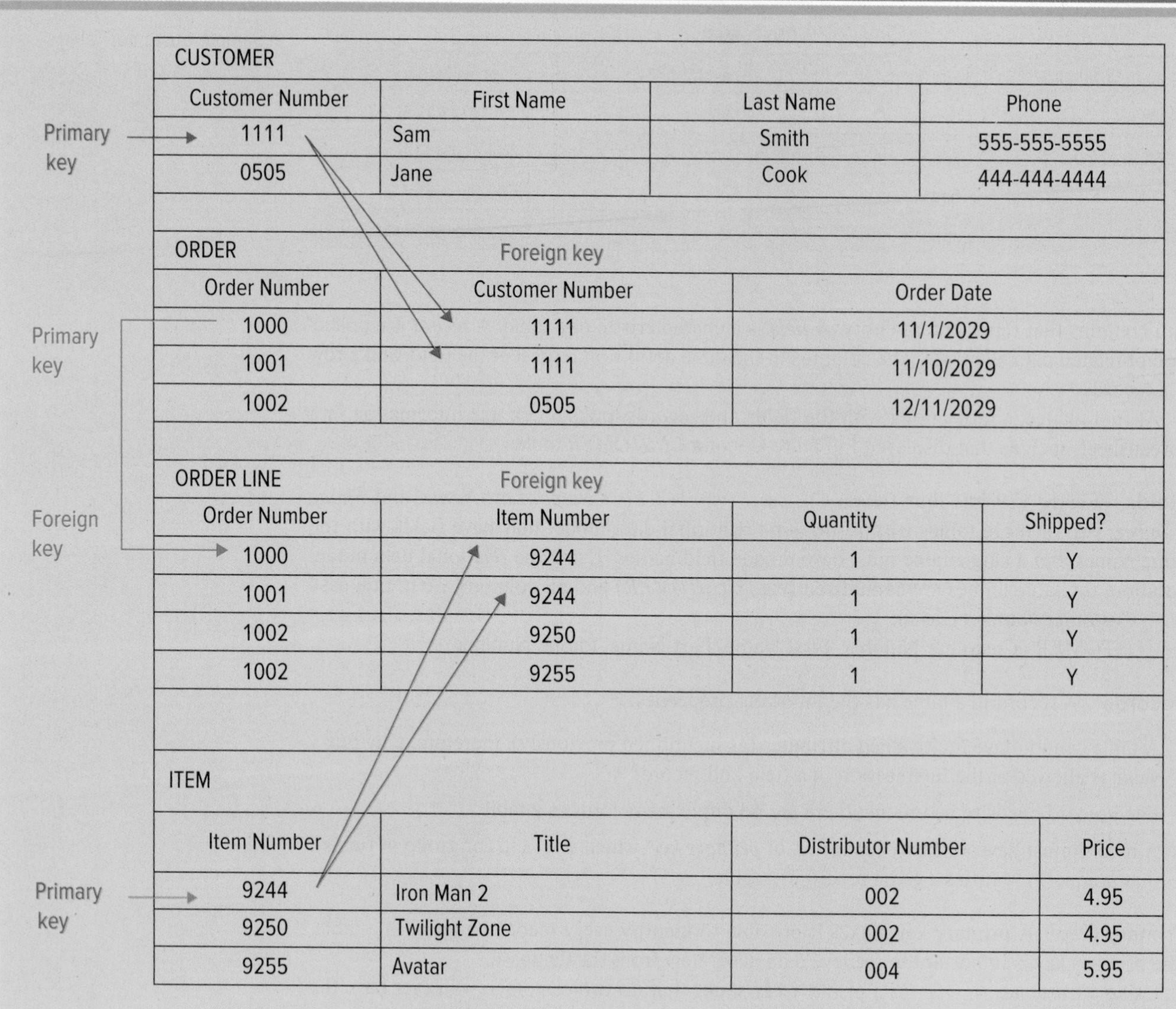

CUSTOMER

Customer Number	First Name	Last Name	Phone
1111	Sam	Smith	555-555-5555
0505	Jane	Cook	444-444-4444

ORDER

Order Number	Customer Number	Order Date
1000	1111	11/1/2029
1001	1111	11/10/2029
1002	0505	12/11/2029

ORDER LINE

Order Number	Item Number	Quantity	Shipped?
1000	9244	1	Y
1001	9244	1	Y
1002	9250	1	Y
1002	9255	1	Y

ITEM

Item Number	Title	Distributor Number	Price
9244	Iron Man 2	002	4.95
9250	Twilight Zone	002	4.95
9255	Avatar	004	5.95

FIGURE C.10

Logically Relating Tables

has more significance than simply identifying each record; it also represents a relationship among the *ORDER LINE,* the *ORDER*(s) on which they appear, and the *ITEM*(s) being ordered. The primary key for the *ITEM* table is identified by the *Item Number.*

The *Item Number* field in the *ORDER LINE* table is the same as the primary key in the *ITEM* table. This indicates a one-to-many relationship between the two tables. Similarly, there is also a one-to-many relationship between the *ORDER* and *ORDER LINE* tables because the *Order Number* column in the *ORDER LINE* table is the same as the primary key of the *ORDER* table.

When a table contains a field that is the same as the primary key of another table, it is called a foreign key. A ***foreign key*** is a primary key of one table that appears as an attribute in another table and acts to provide a logical relationship between the two tables. The matching of foreign keys to primary keys represents data relationships in a relational database.

Foreign keys may be a part of a concatenated primary key, as is the case in the *ORDER LINE* table in Figure C.10. By concatenating, or combining, both *Order Number* and *Item Number* in the *ORDER LINE* table as foreign keys, they then become primary keys. However, most foreign keys are not part of the table's primary key. Consider the relationship between Mega-Video's *CUSTOMER* and *ORDER* in Figure C.10. The *Customer Number* field in the *ORDER* table is a foreign key that matches the primary key of the *CUSTOMER* table. It represents the one-to-many relationship between *CUSTOMER* and *ORDER.* However, the *Customer Number* is not part of the primary key of the *ORDER* table; it is simply used to create a relationship between the two tables: *CUSTOMER* and *ORDER.*

A relational database uses the relationships indicated by matching data between primary and foreign keys. Assume that a Mega-Video employee wanted to see what *Titles* had been ordered with *Order Number* 1002. First, the database identifies the records in the *ORDER LINE* table that contain an *Order Number* of 1002. Then, it matches them to the *Item Number*(s) in the *ITEM* table. The results are those that match the records from each table.

KEY TERMS

Attributes C.2
Business rule C.3
Cardinality C.6
Composite entity C.5
Data model C.2
Database C.1
Database management system (DBMS) C.1
Entity C.2
Entity-relationship diagram (ERD) C.2
Field C.7
Foreign key C.8
Many-to-many relationship (M:N) C.5
Multivalued attribute C.2
Null-valued attribute C.3
One-to-many relationship (1:M) C.5
One-to-one relationship (1:1) C.4
Primary key C.7
Record C.7
Relational database model C.2
Single-valued attribute C.2
Table C.6

MAKING BUSINESS DECISIONS

1. SportTech Events

SportTech Events puts on athletic events for local high school athletes. The company needs a database designed to keep track of the sponsor for the event and where the event is located. Each event needs a description, date, and cost. Separate costs are negotiated for each event. The company would also like to have a list of potential sponsors that includes each sponsor's contact information, such as the name, phone number, and address.

Each event will have a single sponsor, but a particular sponsor may sponsor more than one event. Each location will need an ID, contact person, and phone number. A particular event will use only one location, but a location may be used for multiple events. SportTech asks you to create an ERD from the information described here.

2. Course and Student Schedules

Paul Bauer, the chair for the information technology (IT) department at the University of Denver, needs to create a database to keep track of all the courses the department offers. In addition to the course information, Bauer would like the database to include each instructor's basic contact information, such as ID number, name, office location, and phone number. Currently, the department has nine instructors (seven full-time faculty and two adjuncts). For each course, Bauer would like to keep track of the course ID, title, and number of credit hours. When courses are offered, the section of the course receives an ID number, and with that number, the department keeps track of which instructor is teaching the course. There is only one instructor per course.

Finally, Bauer needs to be able to keep track of the IT students and to know which courses each student has taken. The information he would like to know about each student includes ID number, name, and phone number. He also needs to know what grade the student receives in each course.

He has asked you to create an ERD from the information described here using the Chen model.

3. Foothills Athletics

Foothills Athletics is an athletic facility offering services in Highlands Ranch, Colorado. All property owners living in Highlands Ranch are members of the Highlands Ranch Community Association (HRCA), which has partnered with Foothills Athletics to provide recreation facilities for its residents. Foothills Athletics has been using a spreadsheet to keep track of its personnel, facilities, equipment, and the HRCA members. The spreadsheet has created many redundancies, along with several anomalies in adding, modifying, and deleting information. One of the HRCA members has suggested that the athletic facility should create a database to improve data collection that will also remove many of the difficulties the spreadsheet is creating.

Foothills Athletics primary business operations are based on the following:

- **Personnel:** Foothills Athletics has a number of employees, primarily fitness instructors and administrative personnel. Records are kept on each employee, detailing employee name, address, phone number, date of hire, position, and status as either a current or former employee. Employees are assigned a unique four-digit employee ID number when they are hired.
- **Members:** When joining Foothills Athletics, HRCA members are assigned a unique four-digit member ID number. This information, along with their name, address, phone number, gender, birth date, and date of membership are recorded. At the time of enrollment, each member decides on one of three available membership types, along with a fixed membership fee: Platinum ($400), Gold ($300), and Silver ($200). This is a one-time fee that establishes a lifetime membership.
- **Facilities and equipment:** Foothills Athletics has a variety of facilities and equipment choices. Each facility has a unique room number and a size limitation associated with it. Some of the rooms contain a variety of exercise equipment; all have a serial number that is used for inventory and maintenance purposes. In addition, for each piece of equipment, the purchase date and the date of its last maintenance are recorded. Each piece of equipment belongs to a specific equipment type, such as elliptical machine, and is assigned a unique three-digit identification number. The description, the manufacturer's model number, and the recommended maintenance interval for that model of equipment are also kept on file. Each equipment type is associated with a single manufacturer that is referenced by a unique two-digit manufacturer ID number.

You have been hired to assist Foothills Athletics in creating an ERD from the information described here using the Chen model.

4. Slopeside Ski Rentals

Vail Resort in Vail, Colorado, is internationally known as one of the best places in North America for skiing. Since 1973, Slopeside Ski Rentals has been a tradition in the area. At Slopeside Ski Rentals, customers will find the largest selection of skis, boots, snowboards, clothing, helmets, eyewear, and a variety of other accessories needed for the slopes.

You have been employed by the company for the past three winters. Recently, there has been a surge in business, and the owners need a more accurate way to manage the rental business. You have decided to create a database to help the owners keep track of the ski rentals, who the customers are, amount paid, and any damage to the skis when they are rented. The skis and snowboards vary in type, size, and bindings. When customers rent equipment, they are required to leave their driver's license number and to give a home address, phone number, and credit card number.

A few business rules you are aware of include:

- A customer can rent one or more skis or snowboards at one time.
- Skis and snowboards can be rented by many customers.
- A ski or snowboard need not be assigned to any customer.

Your job is to develop an ERD from the business rules mentioned here.

Emerging Trends and Technologies

LEARNING OUTCOMES

D.1 Identify the global trends that will have the greatest impact on future business.

D.2 Explain why businesses use trends to assess the future.

D.3 Identify the technologies that will have the greatest impact on future business.

INTRODUCTION

LO D.1: Identify the global trends that will have the greatest impact on future business.

Organizations anticipate, forecast, and assess future events using a variety of rational, scientific methods including:

- ***Trend analysis***: A trend is examined to identify its nature, causes, speed of development, and potential impacts.
- ***Trend monitoring***: Trends viewed as particularly important in a specific community, industry, or sector are carefully monitored, watched, and reported to key decision makers.
- ***Trend projection***: When numerical data are available, a trend can be plotted to display changes through time and into the future.
- ***Computer simulation***: Complex systems, such as the U.S. economy, can be modeled by means of mathematical equations, and different scenarios can be run against the model to conduct "what-if" analyses.
- ***Historical analysis***: Historical events are studied to anticipate the outcome of current developments.

Foresight is one of the secret ingredients of business success. Foresight, however, is increasingly in short supply because almost everything in our world is changing at a faster pace than ever before. Many organizations have little idea what type of future they should prepare for in this world of hyperchange. Figure D.1 displays the top reasons organizations should look to the future and study trends.

FIGURE D.1

Top Reasons to Study Trends

	Top Reasons to Study Trends	
1.	Generate ideas and identify opportunities	Find new ideas and innovations by studying trends and analyzing publications.
2.	Identify early warning signals	Scan the environment for potential threats and risks.
3.	Gain confidence	A solid foundation of awareness about trends can provide an organization with the confidence to take risks.
4.	Beat the competition	Seeing what is coming before others can give an organization the lead time it requires to establish a foothold in the new market.
5.	Understand a trend	Analyzing the details within a trend can help separate truly significant developments from rapidly appearing and disappearing fads.
6.	Balance strategic goals	Thinking about the future is an antidote to a "profit now, worry later" mentality that can lead to trouble in the long term.
7.	Understand the future of specific industries	Organizations must understand everything inside and outside their industry.
8.	Prepare for the future	Any organization that wants to compete in this hyperchanging world needs to make every effort to forecast the future.

LO D.2: Explain why businesses use trends to assess the future.

TRENDS SHAPING OUR FUTURE

According to the World Future Society, the following trends have the potential to change our world, our future, and our lives.

- The world's population will double in the next 40 years.
- People in developed countries are living longer.
- The growth in information industries is creating a knowledge-dependent global society.
- The global economy is becoming more integrated.
- The economy and society are dominated by technology.
- The pace of technological innovation is increasing.
- Time is becoming one of the world's most precious commodities.

The World's Population Will Double in the Next 40 Years

The countries that are expected to have the largest increases in population between 2000 and 2050 are:

- Palestinian Territory–217 percent increase
- Niger–205 percent increase
- Yemen–168 percent increase
- Angola–162 percent increase
- Democratic Republic of the Congo–161 percent increase
- Uganda–133 percent increase

In contrast, developed and industrialized countries are expected to see fertility rates decrease below population replacement levels, leading to significant declines in population (see Figure D.2).

Potential Business Impact

- Global agriculture will be required to supply as much food as has been produced during all of human history to meet human nutritional needs over the next 40 years.
- Developed nations will find that retirees will have to remain on the job to stay competitive and continue economic growth.
- Developed nations will begin to increase immigration limits.

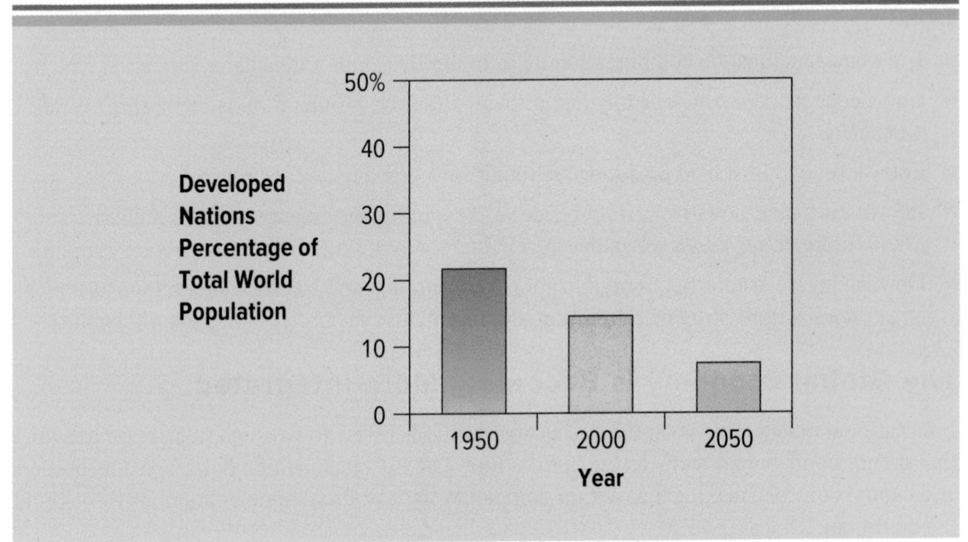

FIGURE D.2

Expected Population Decreases in Developed and Industrialized Nations

People in Developed Countries Are Living Longer

New pharmaceuticals and medical technologies are making it possible to prevent and cure diseases that would have been fatal to past generations. This is one reason each generation lives longer and remains healthier than the previous generation. On average, each generation in the United States lives 3 years longer than the previous one. An 80-year-old in 1950 could expect to live 6.5 years longer today. Many developed countries are now experiencing life expectancy over 75 years for males and over 80 years for females (see Figure D.3).

Potential Business Impact

- Global demand for products and services for older adults will grow quickly in the coming decades.
- The cost of health care is destined to skyrocket.
- Pharmaceutical companies will be pushed for advances in geriatric medicine.

The Growth in Information Industries Is Creating a Knowledge-Dependent Global Society

Estimates indicate that 90 percent of American management personnel are knowledge workers. Estimates for knowledge workers in Europe and Japan are not far behind. Soon, large organizations will be composed of specialists who rely on information from co-workers, customers, and suppliers to guide their actions. Employees will gain new power as they are provided with the authority to make decisions based on the information they acquire.

Rising Life Expectancy in Developed Countries

Country	Life Expectancy (Born 1950–1955)	Life Expectancy (Born 1995–2020)
United States	68.9	76.5
United Kingdom	69.2	77.2
Germany	67.5	77.3
France	66.5	78.1
Italy	66.0	78.2
Canada	69.1	78.5
Japan	63.9	80.5

FIGURE D.3

Rising Life Expectancy in Developed Countries

Potential Business Impact

- Top managers must be computer-literate to retain their jobs and achieve success.
- Knowledge workers are generally higher paid, and their proliferation is increasing overall prosperity.
- Entry-level and unskilled positions are requiring a growing level of education.
- Information now flows from front-office workers to higher management for analysis. Thus, in the future, fewer mid-level managers will be required, flattening the corporate pyramid.
- Downsizing, restructuring, reorganization, outsourcing, and layoffs will continue as typical large organizations struggle to reinvent and restructure themselves for greater flexibility.

The Global Economy Is Becoming More Integrated

International outsourcing is on the rise as organizations refuse to pay high salaries for activities that do not contribute directly to the bottom line. The European Union has relaxed its borders and capital controls, making it easier for companies to outsource support functions throughout the continent.

The Internet is one of the primary tools enabling our global economy. A big reason for the increase in Internet use is advancements in connectivity technology, all of which increase revenues for ebusinesses.

Potential Business Impact

- Demand for personnel in distant countries will increase the need for foreign-language training, employee incentives suited to other cultures, and many other aspects of performing business globally.
- The growth of ebusiness and the use of the Internet to shop globally for raw materials and supplies will reduce the cost of doing business.
- The Internet will continue to enable small companies to compete with worldwide giants with relatively little investment.
- Internet-based operations require sophisticated knowledge workers, and thus people with the right technical skills will be heavily recruited over the next 15 years.

The Economy and Society Are Dominated by Technology

Computers are becoming a part of our environment. Mundane commercial and service jobs, environmentally dangerous jobs, standard assembly jobs, and even the repair of inaccessible equipment such as space stations will be increasingly performed by robots. Artificial intelligence and expert systems will help most companies and government agencies assimilate data and solve problems beyond the range of today's computers, including energy prospecting, automotive diagnostics, insurance underwriting, and law enforcement.

Superconductors operating at economically viable temperatures are now in commercial use. Products eventually will include supercomputers the size of a 3-pound coffee can, electronic motors 75 percent smaller and lighter than those in use today, and power plants.

Potential Business Impact

- New technologies provide dozens of new opportunities to create businesses and jobs.
- Automation will continue to decrease the cost of products and services, making it possible to reduce prices while improving profits.
- The Internet is expected to push prices of most products to the commodity level.
- The demand for scientists, engineers, and technicians will continue to grow.

Pace of Technological Innovation Is Increasing

Technology is advancing at a phenomenal pace. Medical knowledge is doubling every 8 years. Half of what students learn in their freshman year of college about innovative technology is obsolete, revised, or taken for granted by their senior year. In fact, all of today's technical knowledge will represent only 1 percent of the knowledge that will be available in 2050.

Potential Business Impact

- The time to get products and services to market is being shortened by technology. Products must capture their market quickly before the competition can copy them. During the 1940s, the average time to get a product to market was 40 weeks. Today, a product's entire life cycle seldom lasts 40 weeks.
- Industries will face tighter competition based on new technologies. Those who adopt state-of-the-art technology first will prosper, while those who ignore it eventually will fail.

Time Is Becoming One of the World's Most Precious Commodities

In the United States, workers today spend around 10 percent more time on the job than they did a decade ago. European executives and nonunionized workers face the same trend. This high-pressure environment is increasing the need for any product or service that saves time or simplifies life.

Potential Business Impact

- Companies must take an active role in helping their employees balance their time at work with their family lives and need for leisure.
- Stress-related problems affecting employee morale and wellness will continue to grow.
- As time for shopping continues to evaporate, Internet and mail-order marketers will have a growing advantage over traditional stores.

TECHNOLOGIES SHAPING OUR FUTURE

LO D.3: Identify the technologies that will have the greatest impact on future business.

We sit at the center of an expanding set of devices, other people, information, and services that are fluidly and dynamically interconnected. This "digital mesh" surrounds the individual, and new, continuous, and ambient experiences will emerge to exploit it. In his session revealing Gartner's Top Strategic Technology Trends at Gartner/Symposium ITxpo 2015 in Orlando, David Cearley, vice president and Gartner Fellow, shared three categories for technology trends: the digital mesh, smart machines, and the new IT reality.

The Digital Mesh

Trend No. 1: The Device Mesh All devices such as cars, smart phones, appliances, and more are connecting people all over the globe, enabling them to access data, applications, social communities, governments, and businesses. As the mesh of these smart devices continues to evolve, Gartner expects connection models to expand, as well as greater cooperative interaction between devices. Recall that ***virtual reality*** is a computer-simulated environment that can be a representation of the real world or an imaginary world. ***Augmented reality*** is the viewing of the physical world with computer-generated layers of information added to it. Expect to see amazing developments in wearables and augmented reality—especially, virtual reality.

Trend No. 2: Ambient User Experience The ***ambient digital experience*** is a blend of the physical, virtual, and electronic environments, creating a real-time ambient environment that changes as the user moves from one place to another. All of our digital interactions can become synchronized into a continuous and ambient digital experience. Users will be able to interact with applications for extended periods of time. Organizations will need to consider their customers' behavior journeys to shift the focus on design from applications to the entire mesh of products and services involved in the user experience.

Trend No. 3: 3D Printing Materials ***3D printing*** builds—layer by layer in an additive process—a three-dimensional solid object from a digital model. To date, 3D printers are generally capable of printing only one type of material at a time. Expect the next generation of 3D printers to be able to mix multiple materials together in one build. Other advances for 3D printing include a wide range of materials such as advanced nickel alloys, carbon fiber, glass, conductive ink, electronics, and even pharmaceuticals and biological materials. ***Biological 3D printing*** includes the printing of skin and organs and is progressing from theory to reality; however, politicians and the public do not have a full understanding of the implications.

Smart Machines

Trend No. 4: Information of Everything The ***Internet of Things (IoT)*** is a world where interconnected Internet-enabled devices or "things" have the ability to collect and share data without human intervention. The ***Information of Everything (IoE)*** is a concept that extends the Internet of Things emphasis on machine-to-machine communications to describe a more complex system that also encompasses people and processes. IoE encompasses the huge surge of information produced by the digital mesh, including textual, audio, video, sensory, and contextual information, along with strategies and technologies to link data from all these disparate data sources. The digital mesh surrounds us, virtually producing unmeasurable amounts of information. Organizations must learn how to identify what information provides strategic value and how to access data from different sources, and explore how algorithms leverage the information of everything to fuel new business designs.

Trend No. 5: Advanced Machine Learning ***Machine learning*** is a type of artificial intelligence that enables computers to both understand concepts in the environment and also to learn. Machine learning focuses on the development of computer programs that can teach themselves to grow and change when exposed to new data and is responsible for making smart devices appear intelligent. For example, by analyzing vast databases of medical case histories, "learning" machines can reveal previously unknown insights in treatment effectiveness. This area is evolving quickly, and organizations must assess how they can apply these technologies to gain competitive advantage.

Trend No. 6: Autonomous Agents and Things In the future, people will move through a constant stream of information summoned at the touch of a finger. They will interact with life-size images, data, and text in homes and offices. The days of hunching over a computer will be gone. A ***virtual assistant (VA)*** will be a small program stored on a PC or portable device that monitors emails, faxes, messages, and phone calls. Virtual assistants will help individuals solve problems in the same way a real assistant would. In time, the VA will take over routine tasks such as writing a letter, retrieving a file, and making a phone call.

An ***autonomous agent*** is software that carries out some set of operations on behalf of a user or another program with some degree of independence or autonomy and employs some knowledge or representation of the user's goals or desires. Autonomous agent robotic salespeople will take on human appearances and have the ability to perform all tasks associated with a sales job. Robots, vehicles, virtual assistants, and smart advisers acting autonomously feed into the ambient user experience in which an autonomous agent becomes the main user interface. Instead of interacting with a tablet or a smart phone, users will talk directly to an autonomous application, which is really an intelligent agent.

The New IT Reality

Trend No. 7: Adaptive Security Architecture ***Real-time adaptive security*** is the network security model necessary to accommodate the emergence of multiple perimeters and moving parts on the network, and increasingly advanced threats targeting enterprises. The emerging "hacker industry," along with cyberwar and cyberterrorism, has significantly increased the threat surface for an organization. Technology leaders must increase their focus on detecting and responding to threats, as well as more traditional blocking and other measures to prevent attacks.

Trend No. 8: Advanced System Architecture ***Autonomic computing*** is a self-managing computing model named after, and patterned on, the human body's autonomic nervous system.

Autonomic computing is one of the building blocks of widespread computing, an anticipated future computing model in which small—even invisible—computers will be all around us, communicating through increasingly interconnected networks. The digital mesh and smart machines require autonomic computing architectures that function more like human brains that are particularly suited to be applied to deep learning and other pattern-matching algorithms. Autonomic architectures will allow distribution with less power into the tiniest IoT endpoints, such as homes, cars, wristwatches, and even human beings.[1]

KEY TERMS

MAKING BUSINESS DECISIONS

1. Identifying and Following Trends

Hot.com is a new business that specializes in helping companies identify and follow significant trends in their industries. You have recently been hired as a business analyst, and your first task is to highlight current trends in the ebusiness industry. Using the Internet and any other resources you have available, highlight five significant trends not discussed in this text. Prepare a PowerPoint presentation that lists the trends and discusses the potential business impacts for each trend.

2. NAO Robots

NAO (pronounced *now*) robots are about as cute as anything ever created, and boy, can they dance. A NAO robot is an autonomous, programmable, humanoid robot developed by Aldebaran Robotics, a French robotics company headquartered in Paris. NAO robots have been used for research and education purposes in numerous academic institutions worldwide. As of 2015, over 5,000 NAO units were in use in more than 50 countries. Visit the web to search for NAO robot videos and create a new product or service for a NAO robot.

3. Educational Robots

Robots have always grabbed the attention and imagination of kids (of all ages)! RobotLAB uses this attention to build core 21st-century skills such as programming and computational thinking. Using advanced robots, RobotLAB makes abstract math and computer science real by focusing lessons around complex problems that become intuitive through interaction and manipulation of the robots. Visit http://www.robotlab.com/ and review the many robots they are creating to help education. Create a new robot that could help you with your college experience.

4. Less Is More

Your organization is teetering on the edge of systems chaos. Your systems administrator is stressed beyond tolerance by too many systems, too many applications, too few resources, and too little time. The scope, frequency, and diversity of demand are causing greater risk than anyone dares to admit. Automating (and reducing the complexity of) the operating environment is critical for your business to survive. Research autonomic computing and write a report discussing how this technology can help an organization gain control over its systems.

5. Real-Time Adaptive Security

BusinessED specializes in creating new and innovative software for education in the business market. Danny Henningson, founder and president of BusinessED, is interested in developing educational products for elementary and high schools around the globe. Danny has hired you as the vice president of research and development and is excited to hear your ideas for new products. Your first assignment is to study the many threats and security issues facing public schools today and explain how real-time adaptive security measures could help BusinessED succeed.

6. Alternative Energy

With energy costs on the rise, many U.S. homes are turning to homegrown energy solutions. Your friend Cole Lazarus has decided to start a business offering such solutions. Cole would like your help developing his business. Begin by researching the Internet and find different ways you could design a home with its own energy sources. Create a document listing the different sources, along with the advantages and disadvantages of each source.

Connectivity: The Business Value of a Networked World

LEARNING OUTCOMES

E.1 Explain the five networking elements creating a connected world.

E.2 Identify the benefits and challenges of a connected world.

OVERVIEW OF A CONNECTED WORLD

LO E.1: Explain the five networking elements creating a connected world.

Computer networks are continuously operating all over the globe, supporting our 24/7/365 always on and always connected lifestyles. You are probably using several networks right now without even realizing it. You might be using a school's network to communicate with teachers, a cellular network to communicate with friends, and a cable network to watch TV or listen to the radio. Networks enable telecommunications or the exchange of information (voice, text, data, audio, video). The telecommunication industry has morphed from a government-regulated monopoly to a deregulated market in which many suppliers ferociously compete. Competing companies offer local and global telephony services, satellite service, mobile radio, cable television, cellular services, and Internet access (all of which are detailed in this appendix). Businesses everywhere are increasingly using networks to communicate and collaborate with customers, partners, suppliers, and employees. As a manager, you will face many communication alternatives, and the focus of this appendix is to provide you with an initial understanding of the different networking elements you will someday need to select (see Figure E.1).

Network Categories

The general idea of a network is to allow multiple devices to communicate at the highest achievable speeds and, most importantly, to reduce the cost of connecting. How a particular network achieves these goals depends in part on how it is physically constructed and connected. Networks are categorized based on geographic span: local area networks, wide area networks, and metropolitan area networks. Today's business networks include a combination of all three.

A ***local area network (LAN)*** connects a group of computers in close proximity, such as in an office building, school, or home. LANs allow sharing of files, printers, games, and other resources. A LAN also often connects to other LANs and to wide area networks. A ***wide area network (WAN)*** spans a large geographic area such as a state, province, or country. Perhaps the best example is the Internet. WANs are essential for carrying out the day-to-day activities of

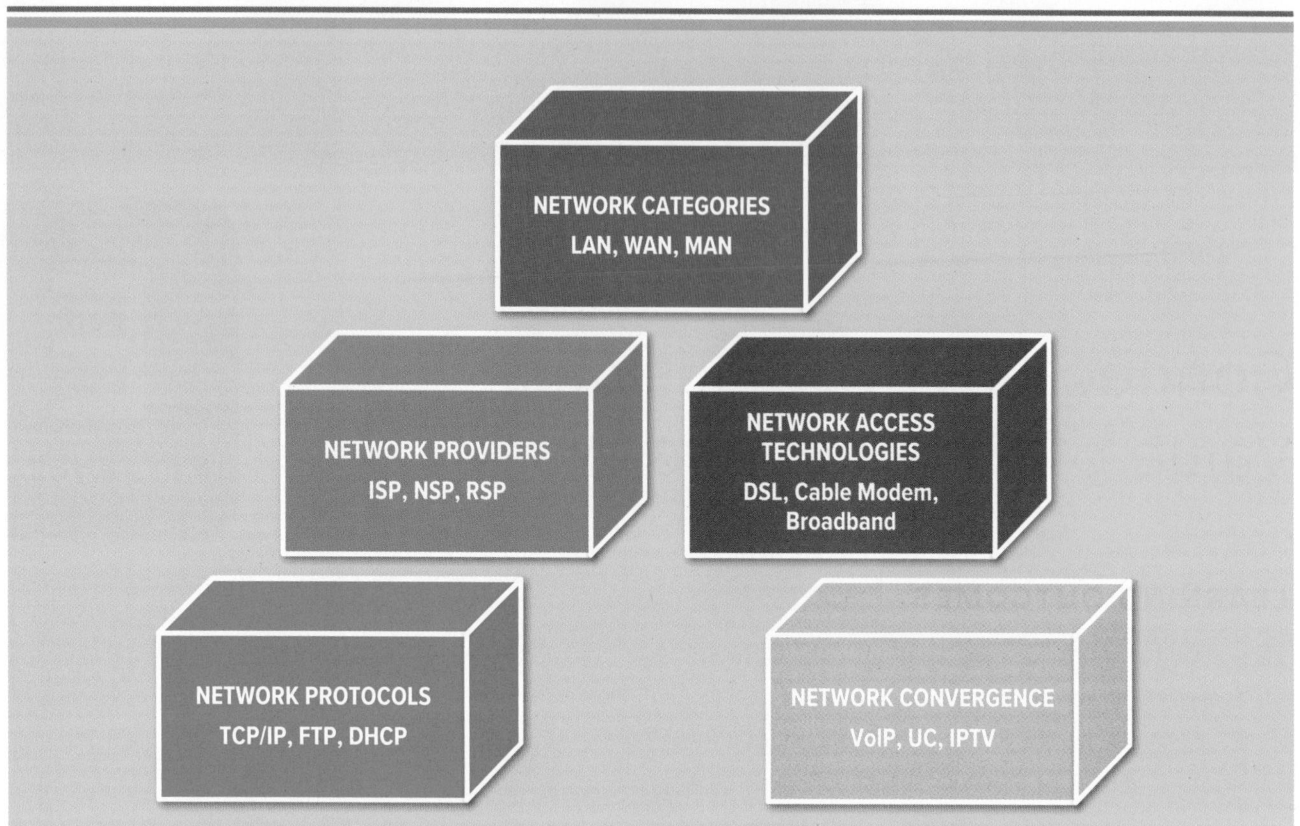

FIGURE E.1

Networking Elements Creating a Connected World

many companies and government organizations, allowing them to transmit and receive information among their employees, customers, suppliers, business partners, and other organizations across cities, regions, countries, and around the world. In networking, ***attenuation*** represents the loss of a network signal strength measured in decibels (dBs) and occurs because the transmissions gradually dissipate in strength over longer distances or because of radio interference or physical obstructions such as walls. A ***repeater*** receives and repeats a signal to reduce its attenuation and extend its range.

WANs often connect multiple smaller networks, such as local area networks or metropolitan area networks. A ***metropolitan area network (MAN)*** is a large computer network usually spanning a city. Most colleges, universities, and large companies that span a campus use an infrastructure supported by a MAN. Figure E.2 shows the relationships and a few differences among a LAN, WAN, and MAN. A cloud image often represents the Internet or some large network environment.

Although LANs, WANs, and MANs all provide users with an accessible and reliable network infrastructure, they differ in many dimensions; two of the most important are cost and performance. It is easy to establish a network between two computers in the same room or building but much more difficult if they are in different states or even countries. This means someone looking to build or support a WAN either pays more or gets less performance, or both. Ethernet is the most common connection type for wired networking and is available in speeds from 10 Mbps all the way up to 10,000 Mbps (10 Gb). The most common wire used for Ethernet networking is Cat5 (Category 5), and the connectors used are RJ45, slightly larger than the RJ11 connectors used by phones, but the same shape.

Network Providers

The largest and most important network, the Internet, has evolved into a global information superhighway. Think of it as a network made up of millions of smaller networks, each with the ability to operate independently of, or in harmony with, the others. Keeping the Internet operational is no simple task. No one owns or runs it, but it does have an organized network topology.

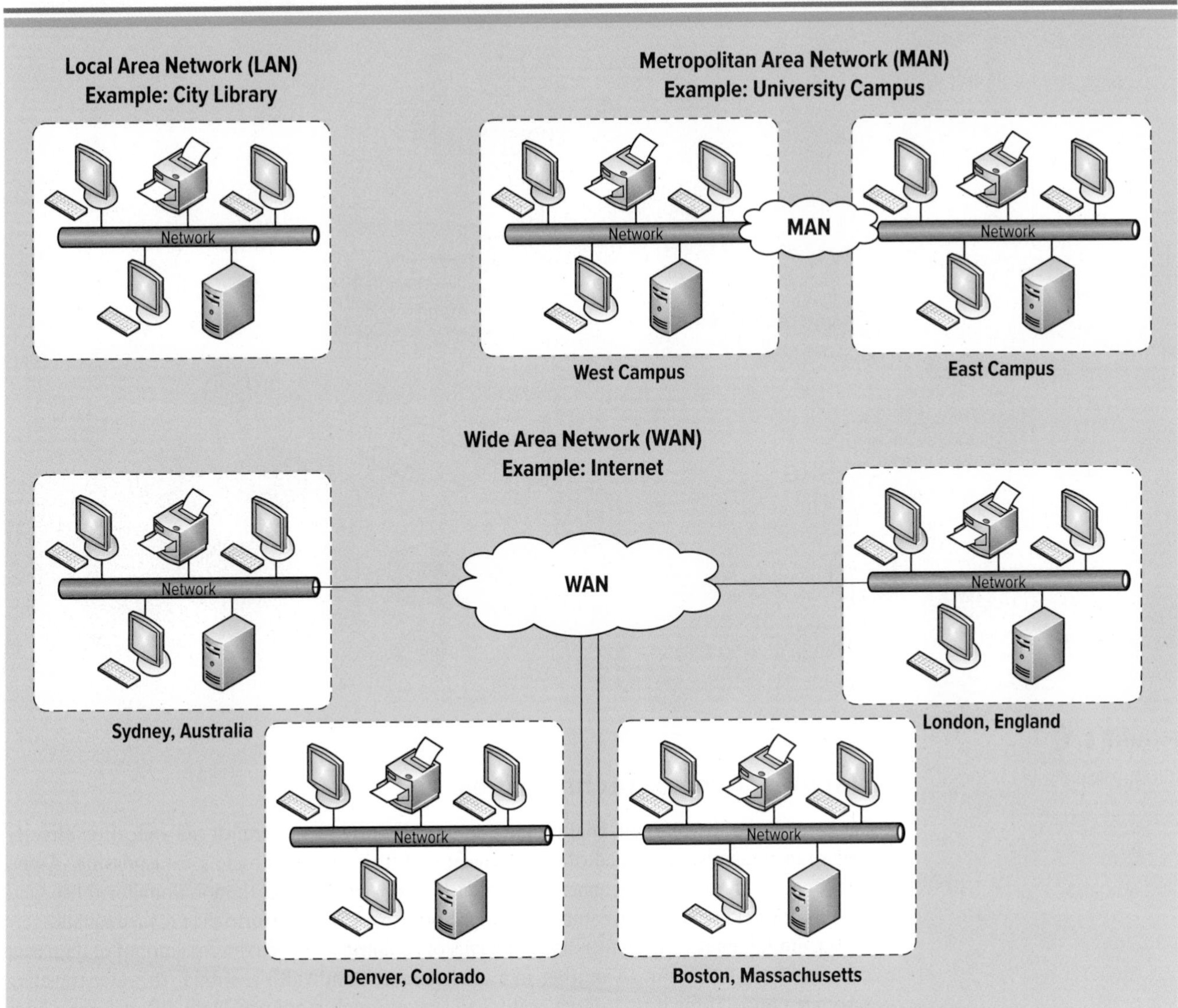

FIGURE E.2

Network Categories: LAN, WAN, and MAN

The Internet is a hierarchical structure linking different levels of service providers, whose millions of devices, LANs, WANs, and MANs supply all the interconnections. At the top of the hierarchy are ***national service providers (NSPs),*** private companies that own and maintain the worldwide backbone that supports the Internet. These include Sprint, Verizon, MCI (previously UUNet/WorldCom), AT&T, NTT, Level3, Century Link, and Cable & Wireless Worldwide. Network access points (NAPs) are traffic exchange points in the routing hierarchy of the Internet that connects NSPs. They typically have regional or national coverage and connect to only a few NSPs. Thus, to reach a large portion of the global Internet, a NAP needs to route traffic through one of the NSPs to which it is connected.

One step down in the hierarchy is the regional service provider. ***Regional service providers (RSPs)*** offer Internet service by connecting to NSPs, but they also can connect directly to each other. Another level down is an Internet service provider (ISP), which specializes in providing management, support, and maintenance to a network. ISPs vary services provided and available bandwidth rates. ISPs link to RSPs and, if they are geographically close, to other ISPs. Some also connect directly to NSPs, thereby sidestepping the hierarchy. Individuals and companies use local ISPs to connect to the Internet, and large companies tend to connect directly using an RSP. Major ISPs in the United States include AOL, AT&T, Comcast, EarthLink, and NetZero. The further up the hierarchy, the faster the connections and the greater the bandwidth. The backbone shown in Figure E.3 is greatly simplified, but it illustrates the concept that basic global interconnections are provided by the NSPs, RSPs, and ISPs.

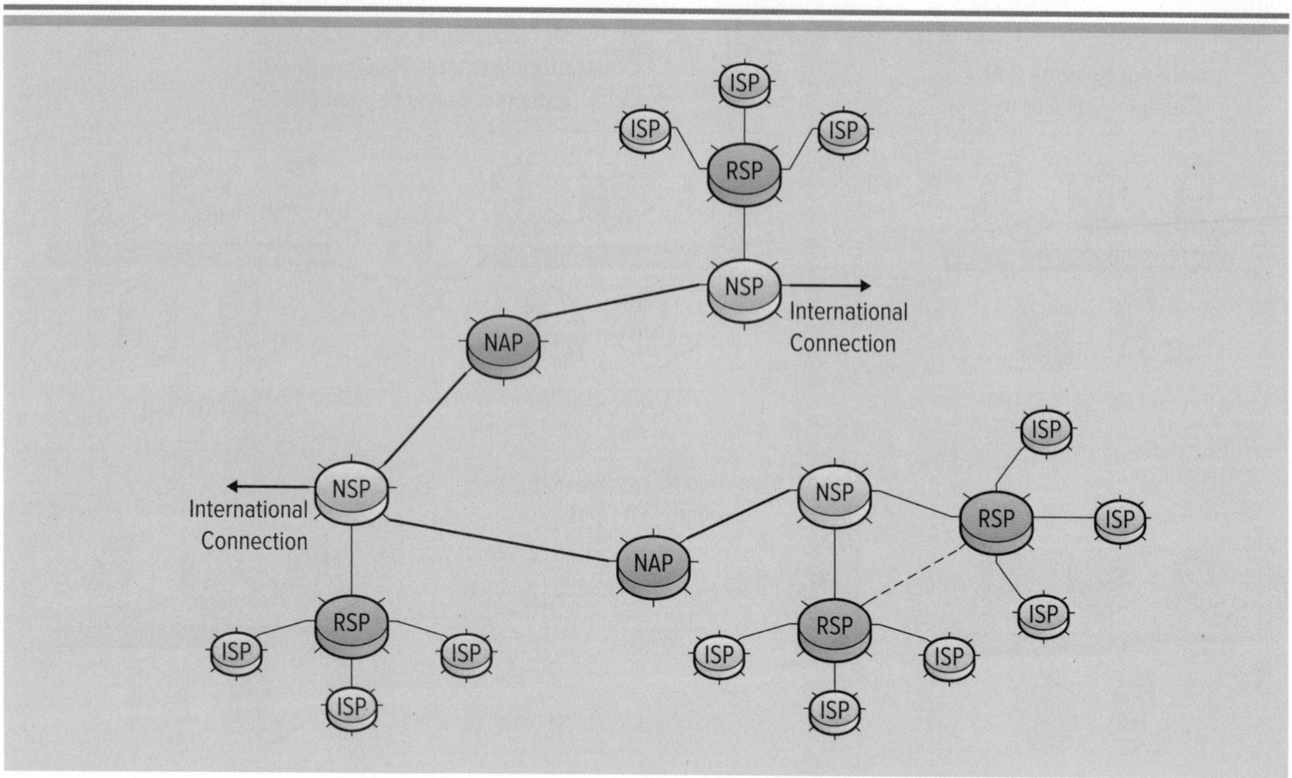

FIGURE E.3

Internet Topology

Network Access Technologies

Performance is the ultimate goal of any computer, computer system, or network. It is directly related to the network's speed of data transfer and its capacity to handle transmission. A network that does not offer adequate performance simply will not get the job done for those who rely on it. Luckily, networks can be upgraded and expanded if performance is inadequate.

We measure network performance in terms of ***bandwidth,*** the maximum amount of data that can pass from one point to another in a unit of time. Bandwidth is similar to water traveling through a hose. If the hose is large, water can flow through it quickly. Data differs from a hose in that it must travel great distances, especially on a WAN, and not all areas of the network have the same bandwidth. A network essentially has many hoses of unequal capacity connected together, which will restrict the flow of data when one is smaller than the others. Therefore, the speed of transmission of a network is determined by the speed of its smallest bandwidth.

A ***bit*** (short for binary digit) is the smallest element of data and has a value of either 0 or 1. Bandwidth is measured in terms of ***bit rate*** (or ***data rate***), the number of bits transferred or received per unit of time. Figure E.4 represents bandwidth speeds in terms of bit rates. Bandwidth is typically given in bits per second (abbreviated as bps) and bytes per second (abbreviated as Bps). It is important to note that these two terms are not interchangeable.

A ***modem*** is a device that enables a computer to transmit and receive data. A connection with a traditional telephone line and a modem, which most residential users had in the 1990s, is called dial-up access. Today, many users in underdeveloped countries and in rural areas in

FIGURE E.4

Bandwidth Speeds

Bandwidth	Abbreviation	Bits per Second (bps)	Example
Kilobit	Kbps	1 Kbps = 1,000 bps	Traditional modem = 56 Kbps
Megabit	Mbps	1 Mbps = 1,000 Kbps	Traditional Ethernet = 10 Mbps Fast Ethernet = 100 Mbps
Gigabit	Gbps	1 Gbps = 1,000 Mbps	Gigabit Ethernet = 1,000 Mbps

developed countries still use dial-up. It has two drawbacks. First, it is slow, providing a maximum rate of 56 Kbps. (At 56 Kbps, it takes eight minutes to download a three-minute song and more than a day to download a two-hour movie.) Second, dial-up modem access ties up the telephone line so the user cannot receive and make phone calls while online. The good news is this is not as big an issue as it once was because many people have cell phones and no longer require the telephone line for making phone calls.

Once the most common connection methods worldwide, dial-up is quickly being replaced by broadband. ***Broadband*** is a high-speed Internet connection that is always connected. "High-speed" in this case refers to any bandwidth greater than 2 Mbps. Not long ago, broadband speeds were available only at a premium price to support large companies' high-traffic networks. Today, inexpensive access is available for home use and small companies.

The two most prevalent types of broadband access are digital subscriber lines and high-speed Internet cable connections. ***Digital subscriber line (DSL)*** provides high-speed digital data transmission over standard telephone lines using broadband modem technology, allowing both Internet and telephone services to work over the same phone lines. Consumers typically obtain DSL Internet access from the same company that provides their wired local telephone access, such as AT&T or Century Link. Thus, a customer's telephone provider is also its ISP, and the telephone line carries both data and telephone signals using a DSL modem. DSL Internet services are used primarily in homes and small businesses.

DSL has two major advantages over dial-up. First, it can transmit and receive data much faster–in the 1 to 2 Mbps range for downloading and 128 Kbps to 1 Mbps for uploading. (Most high-speed connections are designed to download faster than they upload because most users download more–including viewing web pages–than they upload.) The second major advantage is that because they have an always-on connection to their ISP, users can simultaneously talk on the phone and access the Internet. DSL's disadvantages are that it works over a limited physical distance and remains unavailable in many areas where the local telephone infrastructure does not support DSL technology.

Whereas dial-up and DSL use local telephone infrastructure, ***high-speed Internet cable connections*** provide Internet access using a cable television company's infrastructure and a special cable modem. A ***cable modem (or broadband modem)*** is a type of digital modem used with high-speed cable Internet service. Cable modems connect a home computer (or network of home computers) to residential cable TV service; DSL modems connect to residential public telephone service. The ISP typically supplies the cable and DSL modems. Cisco Systems is one of the largest companies producing computer networking products and services, including the Linksys brand of networking components. Typically, broadband or high-speed Internet service has an average transfer rate 10 times faster than conventional dial-up service. ***Telecommuting (virtual workforce)*** allows users to work from remote locations, such as home or a hotel, using high-speed Internet to access business applications and data.

Unlike DSL, high-speed Internet cable is a shared service, which means everyone in a certain radius, such as a neighborhood, shares the available bandwidth. Therefore, if several users are simultaneously downloading a video file, the actual transfer rate for each will be significantly lower than if only one person were doing so. On average, the available bandwidth using cable can range from 512 Kbps to 50 Mbps for downloading and 786 Kbps for uploading.

Another alternative to DSL or high-speed Internet cable is dedicated communications lines leased from AT&T or another provider. The most common are T1 lines, a type of data connection able to transmit a digital signal at 1.544 Mpbs. Although this speed might not seem impressive and T1 lines are more expensive than DSL or cable, they offer far greater reliability because each is composed of 24 channels, creating 24 connections through one line. If a company has three plants that experience a high volume of data traffic, it might make sense to lease lines for reliability of service.

A company must match its needs with Internet access methods. If it always needs high bandwidth access to communicate with customers, partners, or suppliers, a T1 line may be the most cost-effective method. Figure E.5 provides an overview of the main methods for Internet access. The bandwidths in the figure represent average speeds; actual speeds vary, depending on the service provider and other factors, such as the type of cabling and speed of the computer.

FIGURE E.5

Types of Internet Access

Access Technology	Description	Bandwidth	Comments
Dial-up	On-demand access using a modem and regular telephone line	Up to 56 Kbps	Cheap but slow compared with other technologies
DSL	Always-on connection Special modem needed	Download: 1 Mbps to 2 Mbps Upload: 128 Kbps to 1 Mbps	Makes use of the existing local telephone infrastructure
Cable	Always-on connection Special cable modem and cable line required	Download: 512 Kbps to 50 Mbps Upload: 786 Kbps	A shared resource with other users in the area
T1	Leased lines for high bandwidth	1.544 Mbps	More expensive than dial-up, DSL, or cable

Broadband over power line (BPL) technology makes possible high-speed Internet access over ordinary residential electrical lines and offers an alternative to DSL or high-speed cable modems. BPL works by transmitting data over electrical lines using signaling frequencies higher than the electrical (or voice in the case of DSL) signals. BPL allows computer data to be sent back and forth across the network with no disruption to power output in the home. Many homeowners are surprised to learn that their electrical system can serve as a home network running speeds between 1 and 3 Mbps with full Internet access. Unfortunately, limitations such as interference and availability have affected BPL's popularity.

Network Protocols

A ***packet*** is a single unit of binary data routed through a network. Packets directly affect network performance and reliability by subdividing an electronic message into smaller, more manageable packets. ***Standard packet formats*** include a packet header, packet body containing the original message, and packet footer. The ***packet header*** lists the destination (for example, in IP packets the destination is the IP address) along with the length of the message data. The ***packet footer*** represents the end of the packet or transmission end. The packet header and packet footer contain error-checking information to ensure that the entire message is sent and received. The receiving device reassembles the individual packets into the original by stripping off the headers and footers and then piecing together the packets in the correct sequence. ***Traceroute*** is a utility application that monitors the network path of packet data sent to a remote computer. Traceroute programs send a series of test messages over the network (using the name or IP address) until the last message finally reaches its destination. When finished, traceroute displays the path from the initial computer to the destination computer. A ***proxy*** is software that prevents direct communication between a sending and receiving computer and is used to monitor packets for security reasons.

A ***protocol*** is a standard that specifies the format of data, as well as the rules to be followed during transmission. Computers using the same protocol can communicate easily, providing accessibility, scalability, and connectability between networks. ***File transfer protocol (FTP)*** is a simple network protocol that allows the transfer of files between two computers on the Internet. To transfer files with FTP, the FTP client program initiates a connection to a remote computer running FTP server software. After completing the connection, the client can choose to send and/or receive files electronically. Network access technologies use a standard Internet protocol called ***transmission control protocol/Internet protocol (TCP/IP),*** which provides the technical foundation for the public Internet, as well as for large numbers of private networks. One of the primary reasons for developing TCP/IP was to allow diverse or differing networks to connect and communicate with each other, essentially allowing LANs, WANs, and MANs to grow with each new connection. An ***IP address*** is a unique number that identifies where computers are located on the network. IP addresses appear in the form of xxx.xxx.xxx.xxx, though each grouping can be as short as a single digit.

FIGURE E.6

Example of TCP/IP

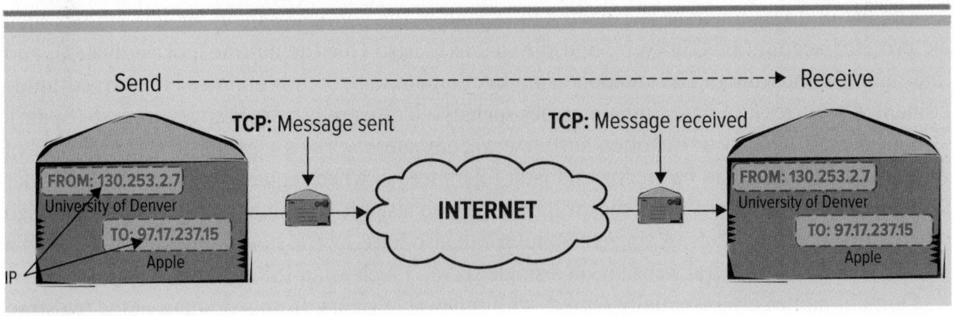

TCP (the TCP part of TCP/IP) verifies the correct delivery of data because data can become corrupt when traveling over a network. TCP ensures that the size of the data packet is the same throughout its transmission and can even retransmit data until delivered correctly. IP (the IP part of TCP/IP) verifies that the data is sent to the correct IP address, numbers represented by four strings of numbers ranging from 0 to 255 separated by periods. For example, the IP address of www.apple.com is 97.17.237.15.

Here is another way to understand TCP/IP. Consider a letter that needs to go from the University of Denver to Apple's headquarters in Cupertino, California. TCP makes sure the envelope is delivered and does not get lost along the way. IP acts as the sending and receiving labels, telling the letter carrier where to deliver the envelope and who it was from. The U.S. Postal Service mainly uses street addresses and zip codes to get letters to their destinations, which is really what IP does with its addressing method. Figure E.6 illustrates this example. However, unlike the Postal Service, which allows multiple people to share the same physical address, each device using an IP address to connect to the Internet must have a unique address or else it could not detect which individual device a request should be sent to.

One of the most valuable characteristics of TCP/IP is how scalable its protocols have proven to be as the Internet has grown from a small network with just a few machines to a huge internetwork with millions of devices. Although some changes have been required periodically to support this growth, the core of TCP/IP is the same as it was more than 25 years ago. ***Dynamic host configuration protocol (DHCP)*** allows dynamic IP address allocation so users do not need a preconfigured IP address to use the network. DHCP allows a computer to access and locate information about a computer on the server, enabling users to locate and renew their IP address. ISPs usually use DHCP to allow customers to join the Internet with minimum effort. DHCP assigns unique IP addresses to devices, then releases and renews these addresses as devices leave and return to the network.

If there is one flaw in TCP/IP, it is the complexity of IP addresses. This is why we use a ***domain name system (DNS)*** to convert IP addresses into *domains,* or identifying labels that use a variety of recognizable naming conventions. Therefore, instead of trying to remember 97.17.237.15, users can simply specify a domain name to access a computer or website, such as www.apple.com. Figure E.7 lists the most common Internet domains.

FIGURE E.7

Internet Domains

Domain Name	Use
.biz	Reserved for businesses
.com	Reserved for commercial organizations and businesses
.edu	Reserved for accredited postsecondary institutions
.gov	Reserved for U.S. government agencies
.info	Open to any person or entity but intended for information providers
.mil	Reserved for U.S. military
.net	Open to any person or entity
.org	Reserved for nonprofit organizations

The list of domain names is expected to expand in the coming years to include entities such as .pro (for accountants, lawyers, and physicians), .aero (for the air-transport industry), and .museum (for museums). The creation of an .xxx domain was recently approved for pornographic content. Countries also have domain names such as .au (Australia), .fr (France), and .sp (Spain).

Websites with heavy traffic often have several computers working together to share the load of requests. This offers load balancing and fault tolerance, so when requests are made to a popular site such as www.facebook.com, they will not overload a single computer and the site does not go down if one computer fails. A single computer can also have several host names; for instance, if a company is hosting several websites on a single server, much as an ISP works with hosting.

Domain names are essentially rented, with renewable rights, from a domain name registrar, such as godaddy.com. Some registrars only register domain names, whereas others provide hosting services for a fee. ICANN (Internet Corporation for Assigned Names and Numbers) is a nonprofit governance and standards organization that certifies all domain name registrars throughout the world. With the certification, each registrar is authorized to register domain names, such as .com, .edu, or .org.

Network Convergence

In part due to the explosive use of the Internet and connectivity of TCP/IP, there is a convergence of network devices, applications, and services. Consumers, companies, educational institutions, and government agencies extensively engage in texting, web surfing, videoconference applications, online gaming, and ebusiness. ***Network convergence*** is the efficient coexistence of telephone, video, and data communication within a single network, offering convenience and flexibility not possible with separate infrastructures. Almost any type of information can be converted into digital form and exchanged over a network. Network convergence then allows the weaving together of voice, data, and video. The benefits of network convergence allow for multiple services, multiple devices, but one network, one vendor, and one bill, as suggested by Figure E.8.

One of the challenges associated with network convergence is using the many tools efficiently and productively. Knowing which communication channel–PC, text message, videoconference–to use with each business participant can be a challenge. ***Unified communications (UC)*** is the integration of communication channels into a single service. UC integrates communication channels, allowing participants to communicate using the method that is most convenient for them. UC merges instant messaging, videoconferencing, email, voice mail, and voice over IP. This can decrease the communication costs for a business while enhancing the way individuals communicate and collaborate.

One area experiencing huge growth in network convergence is the use of the Internet for voice transmission. ***Voice over IP (VoIP)*** uses IP technology to transmit telephone calls. For the first time in more than 100 years, VoIP is providing an opportunity to bring about significant change in the way people communicate using the telephone. VoIP service providers–specialists as well as traditional telephone and cable companies and some ISPs–allow users to call anyone with a telephone number, whether local, long distance, cellular, or international.

FIGURE E.8

The Benefits of Network Convergence

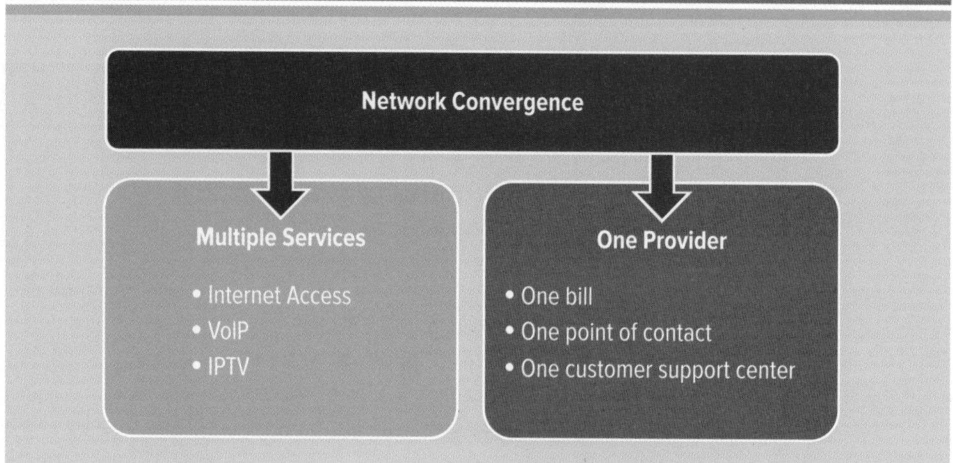

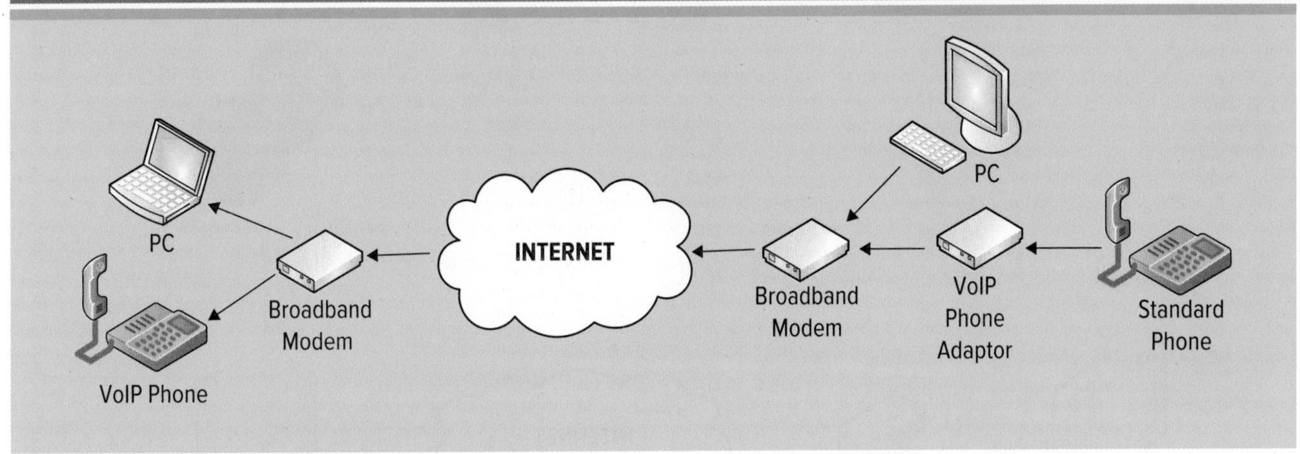

FIGURE E.9

VoIP Connectivity

Two ways to use VoIP for telephone calls are through a web interface that allows users to make calls from their computer and through a phone attached to a VoIP adapter that links directly to the Internet through a broadband modem. Figure E.9 illustrates these two ways, along with the use of VoIP-enabled phones, bypassing the need for an adapter.

VoIP services include fixed-price unlimited local and long-distance calling plans (at least within the United States and Canada), plus a range of interesting features, such as:

- The ability to have more than one phone number, including numbers with different area codes.
- Integration of email and voice mail so users can listen to their voice mail by using their computer.
- The ability to receive personal or business calls via computer, no matter where the user is physically located.

The biggest benefit of VoIP is its low cost. Because it relies on the Internet connection, however, service can be affected if the bandwidth is not appropriate or Internet access is not available.

Skype is a perfect example of IP applied to telephone use. Unlike typical VoIP systems that use a client and server infrastructure, Skype uses a peer-to-peer network. ***Peer-to-peer (P2P)*** is a computer network that relies on the computing power and bandwidth of the participants in the network rather than a centralized server. Skype's user directory is distributed among the users in its network, allowing scalability without a complex and expensive centralized infrastructure. Peer-to-peer networks became an overnight sensation years ago through a service called Napster that distributed digital music illegally. Skype has found a way to use this resource to provide value to its users.

As the popularity of VoIP grows, governments are becoming more interested in regulating it as they do traditional telephone services. In the United States, the Federal Communications Commission requires compliance among VoIP service providers comparable to those for traditional telephone providers such as support for local number portability, services for the disabled, and law enforcement for surveillance, along with regulatory and other fees.

An exciting and new convergence is occurring in the area of television with ***Internet Protocol TV (IPTV),*** which distributes digital video content using IP across the Internet and private IP networks. Comcast provides an example of a private IP network that also acts as a cable TV provider. Traditional television sends all program signals simultaneously to the television, allowing the user to select the program by selecting a channel. With IPTV, the user selects a channel and the service provider sends only that single program to the television. Like cable TV, IPTV uses a box that acts like a modem to send and receive the content (see Figure E.10). A few IPTV features include:

- **Support of multiple devices:** PCs and televisions can access IPTV services.
- **Interactivity with users:** Interactive applications and programs are supported by IPTV's two-way communication path.

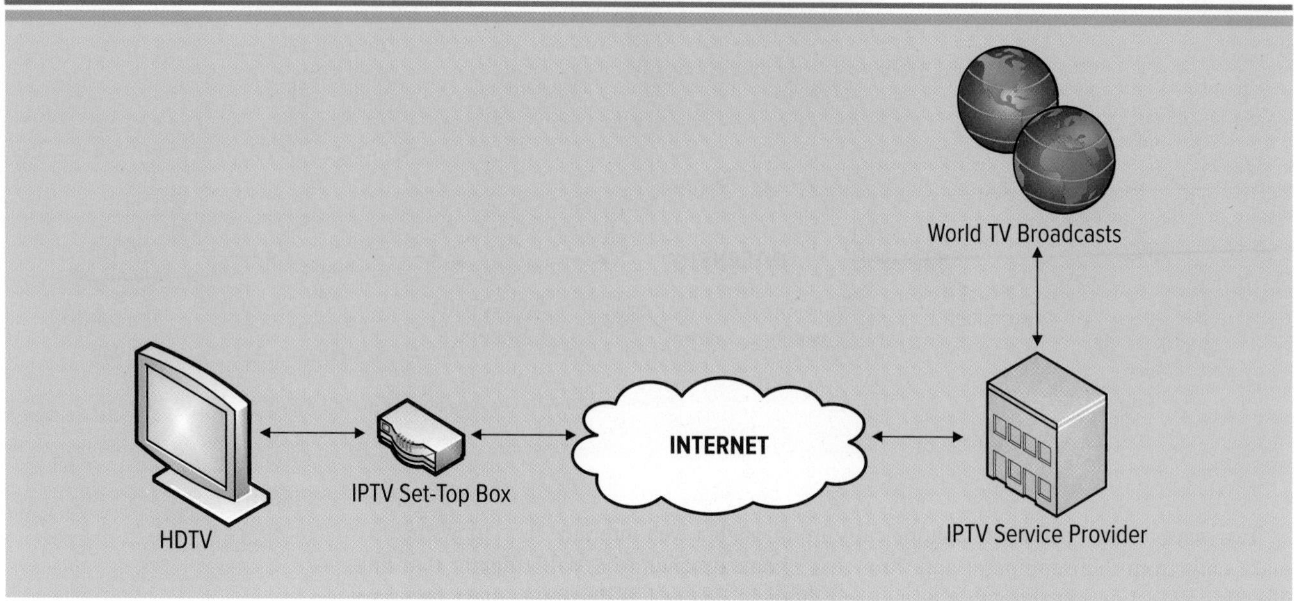

FIGURE E.10

IPTV Components

- **Low bandwidth:** IPTV conserves bandwidth because the provider sends only a single channel.
- **Personalization:** Users can choose not only what they want to watch but also when they want to watch it.

LO E.2: Identify the benefits and challenges of a connected world.

BENEFITS OF A CONNECTED WORLD

Before networks, transferring data between computers was time-consuming and labor-intensive. People had to copy data physically from machine to machine using a disk.

Resource sharing makes all applications, equipment (such as a high-volume printer), and data available to anyone on the network, without regard to the physical location of the resource or the user. Sharing physical resources also supports a sustainable MIS infrastructure, allowing companies to be agile, efficient, and responsible at the same time. Cloud computing and virtualization consolidate information as well as systems that enhance the use of shared resources. By using shared resources, cloud computing, and virtualization allow for collective computing power, storage, and software on demand.

Perhaps even more important than sharing physical resources is sharing data. Most companies, regardless of size, depend not just on their customer records, inventories, accounts receivable, financial statements, and tax information, but also on their ability to share these, especially with operations in remote locations. Networking with a LAN, WAN, or MAN allows employees to share data quickly and easily and to use applications such as databases and collaboration tools that rely on sharing. By sharing data, networks have made business processes more efficient. For example, as soon as an order is placed, anyone in the company who needs to view it—whether in marketing, purchasing, manufacturing, shipping, or billing—can do so.

Intranets and extranets let firms share their corporate information securely. An ***intranet*** is a restricted network that relies on Internet technologies to provide an Internet-like environment within the company for information sharing, communications, collaboration, web publishing, and the support of business processes, as suggested in Figure E.11. This network is protected by security measures such as passwords, encryption, and firewalls, and thus only authorized users can access it. Intranets provide a central location for all kinds of company-related information such as benefits, schedules, strategic directions, and employee directories.

An ***extranet*** is an extension of an intranet that is available only to authorized outsiders, such as customers, partners, and suppliers. Having a common area where these parties can share information with employees about, for instance, order and invoice processing can be a major

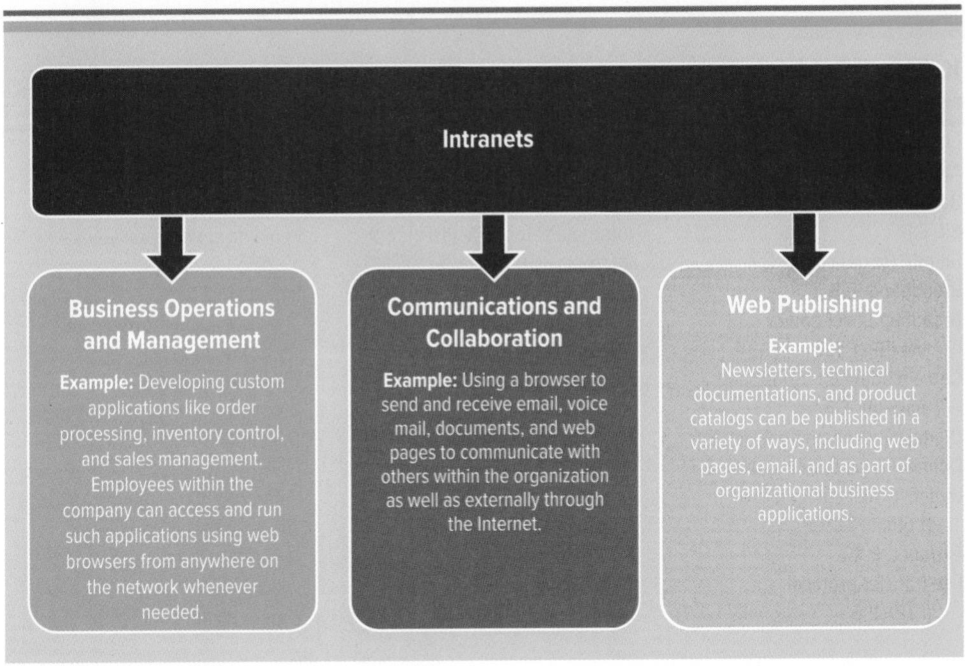

Intranets

Business Operations and Management

Example: Developing custom applications like order processing, inventory control, and sales management. Employees within the company can access and run such applications using web browsers from anywhere on the network whenever needed.

Communications and Collaboration

Example: Using a browser to send and receive email, voice mail, documents, and web pages to communicate with others within the organization as well as externally through the Internet.

Web Publishing

Example: Newsletters, technical documentations, and product catalogs can be published in a variety of ways, including web pages, email, and as part of organizational business applications.

FIGURE E.11

Intranet Uses

competitive advantage in product development, cost control, marketing, distribution, and supplier relations. Companies can establish direct private network links among themselves or create private, secure Internet access, in effect a private tunnel within the Internet, called a ***virtual private network (VPN)***. Figure E.12 illustrates using a VPN to connect to a corporate server.

Extranets enable customers, suppliers, consultants, subcontractors, business prospects, and others to access selected intranet websites and other company network resources that allow information sharing. Consultants and contractors can facilitate the design of new products or services. Suppliers can ensure that the raw materials necessary for the company to function are in stock and can be delivered in a timely fashion. Customers can access ordering and payment functions and check order status. The extranet links the company to the outside world in a way that improves its operations.

Extranets provide business value in several ways. First, by relying on web browsers, they make customer and supplier access to company resources easy and fast. Second, they enable a company to customize interactive web-enabled services for the intended audience to build and strengthen strategic relationships with customers and suppliers. Finally, extranets can allow and improve collaboration with customers and other business partners.

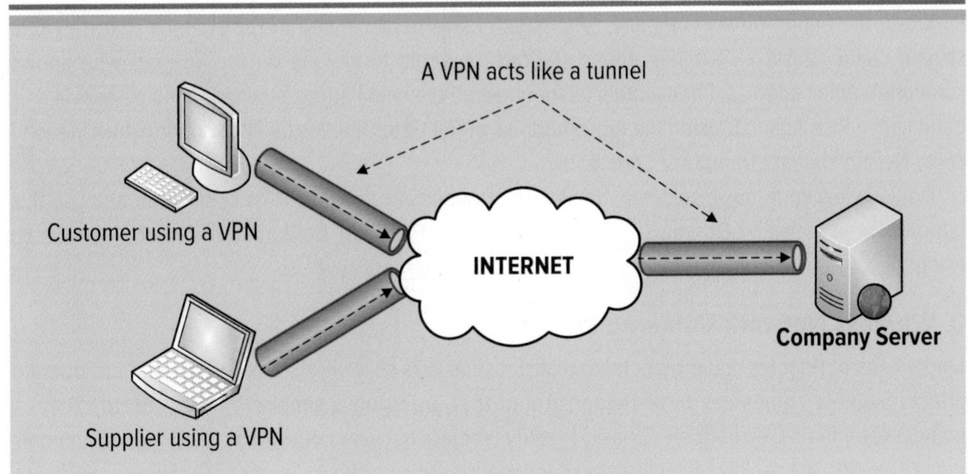

FIGURE E.12

Using a VPN

KEY TERMS

Attenuation E.2
Bandwidth E.4
Bit E.4
Bit rate (or data rate) E.4
Broadband E.5
Broadband over power line (BPL) E.6
Cable modem (or broadband modem) E.5
Digital subscriber line (DSL) E.5
Domain name system (DNS) E.7
Dynamic host configuration protocol (DHCP) E.7
Extranet E.10
File transfer protocol (FTP) E.6
High-speed Internet cable connection E.5
Internet Protocol TV (IPTV) E.9
Intranet E.10
IP address E.6
Local area network (LAN) E.1
Metropolitan area network (MAN) E.2
Modem E.4
National service provider (NSP) E.3
Network convergence E.8
Packet E.6
Packet footer E.6
Packet header E.6
Peer-to-peer (P2P) E.9
Protocol E.6
Proxy E.6
Regional service provider (RSP) E.3
Repeater E.2
Standard packet format E.6
Telecommuting (virtual workforce) E.5
Traceroute E.6
Transmission control protocol/Internet protocol (TCP/IP) E.6
Unified communications (UC) E.8
Virtual private network (VPN) E.11
Voice over IP (VoIP) E.8
Wide area network (WAN) E.1

MAKING BUSINESS DECISIONS

1. Building Nationwide Broadband

The Federal Communications Commission is proposing a nationwide broadband plan, a sweeping initiative to provide—among other things—100 megabit per second Internet access to 100 million people by 2020. The FCC also proposes to deliver 1 gigabit per second access to places such as schools, libraries, and government buildings. "The national broadband plan is a 21st-century roadmap to spur economic growth and investment, create jobs, educate our children, protect our citizens, and engage in our democracy,"[1] said FCC Chairman Julius Genachowski.

How will implementing nationwide broadband create technology jobs? Identify three new products or services you could create based on nationwide broadband. Will a nationwide broadband plan eliminate the digital divide in the United States?

2. Pandora Makes Users' Music Public

Pandora, the online music company, lets users create personalized music stations that they can stream online, but it also makes those stations viewable to anyone on the Internet who knows someone's email address. For example, someone with the email address sergey@google.com likes a band called Rise Against. Using the email address of Bill Gates implies he likes country music legend Willie Nelson and jazz trumpeter Chris Botti.

Do you view your music selection as private or public information? How could someone use this information unethically? Do you see this as a threat for Pandora? Do you think customers will stop using the service? What can Pandora do to ensure customer privacy?

3. Wireless Network Vulnerability

Empty cans of Pringles could be helping malicious hackers spot wireless networks that are open to attack. Security companies have demonstrated that, by using a simple Pringles can to create a homemade antenna, someone can easily identify wireless networks. Known as the PringlesCantenna, these networks are rapidly becoming popular because they are cheap (under $10) and easy to set up.

Wireless network security is a big concern of network managers. Because companies and home users have increasingly adopted wireless technology, security precautions need to be enforced. After all, the very nature of using wireless technology deliberately puts information on the airwaves, and anyone within range and equipped with an appropriate receiver (e.g., PringlesCantenna) can grab this information. This is why many wireless networks should apply authentication and encryption mechanisms to provide a trusted level of security.

Create a report based on Internet research that discusses the tips, techniques, and best practices to protect against this type of amateur hacking. Include a summary on the types of detection and prevention technology available, specifically the use of firewalls and built-in wireless security mechanisms.

4. Cars Hacked

Who would have thought that a car could be hacked? But that is exactly what happened in Austin, Texas. About a hundred cars were broken into, not by the usual method of either picking the lock or smashing a window but instead through a Wi-Fi connection. A local dealership, where all the cars were purchased, had installed a Wi-Fi-enabled black box under the dashboard that could disable the car and set off the horn if the owner did not make payments. However, in this case, the owners were not in arrears but, rather, they were the victims of a recently laid-off employee at the dealership who was seeking revenge by using the web-based system to disable the cars one by one. After someone at the dealership figured out the cars had been hacked, the password that allowed authorization to the black boxes was quickly changed.

Is the black box a good idea? Do you consider this an ethical business practice? If you had bought a car with a black box, would you have it removed? How many customers do you think will consider buying another car from that dealership?

Business Intelligence and Data Mining

LEARNING OUTCOMES

F.1 Compare tactical, operational, and strategic BI.

F.2 Explain how data mining can help improve the business process.

F.3 Describe the four categories of BI business benefits.

OPERATIONAL, TACTICAL, AND STRATEGIC BI

LO F.1 Compare tactical, operational, and strategic BI.

Claudia Imhoff, president of Intelligent Solutions, believes it is useful to divide the spectrum of data-mining analysis and business intelligence (BI) into three categories: operational, tactical, and strategic. Two trends are displayed when viewing the spectrum from operational through tactical to strategic. First, the analysis becomes increasingly complex and ad hoc. That is, it is less repetitive, it is less predictable, and it requires varying amounts and types of data. Second, both the risks and rewards of the analysis increase. That is, the often time-consuming, more strategic queries produce value less frequently, but, when they do, the value can be extraordinary. Figure F.1 illustrates the differences among operational, tactical, and strategic BI.

These three forms are not performed in isolation from each other. It is important to understand that they must work with each other, feeding results from strategic to tactical to promote better operational decision making. Figure F.2 demonstrates this synergy. In this example, strategic BI is used in the planning stages of a marketing campaign. The results of these analytics form the basis for the beginnings of a new campaign, targeting specific customers or demographics, for example. The daily analyses of the campaign are used by the more tactical form of BI to change the course of the campaign if its results are not tracking where expected.

For example, perhaps a different marketing message is needed, or the inventory levels are not sufficient to maintain the current sales pace, so the scope of marketing might be changed. These results are then fed into the operational BI for immediate actions–offering a different product, optimizing the sale price of the product, or changing the daily message sent to selected customer segments.

For this synergy to work, the three forms of BI must be tightly integrated with each other. Minimal time should be lost transporting the results from one technological environment to another. Seamlessness in terms of data and process flow is a must. TruServ, the parent company of True Value Hardware, has used BI software to improve the efficiency of its distribution

FIGURE F.1

Operational, Tactical and Strategic BI

	Operational BI	Tactical BI	Strategic BI
Business focus	Manage daily operations, integrate BI with operational systems	Conduct short-term analysis to achieve strategic goals	Achieve long-term organizational goals
Primary users	Managers, analysts, operational users	Executives, managers	Executives, managers
Time frame	Intraday	Day(s) to weeks to months	Months to years
Data	Real-time metrics	Historical metrics	Historical metrics

operations and reap a $50 million reduction in inventory costs. The marketing department uses BI to track sales promotion results, such as which promotions were most popular by store or region. Now that TruServ is building promotion histories into its databases, it can ensure all stores are fully stocked with adequate inventory. TruServ was able to achieve a positive return on investment in about 5 to 6 months.

Bi's Operational Value

A leading risk insurance company allows customers to access account information over the Internet. Previously, the company sent paper reports and diskettes to all of its customers. Any errors in the reports would take one to two months to correct because customers would first have to receive the report, catch the mistake, and then notify the company of the error. Now customers spot the errors in real time and notify the insurance company directly through an extranet, usually within a couple of days.

Richard Hackathorn of Bolder Technologies developed an interesting graph to demonstrate the value of operational BI. Figure F.3 shows the three latencies that impact the speed of decision making. These are data, analysis, and decision latencies.

FIGURE F.2

The Three Forms of BI Must Work toward a Common Goal

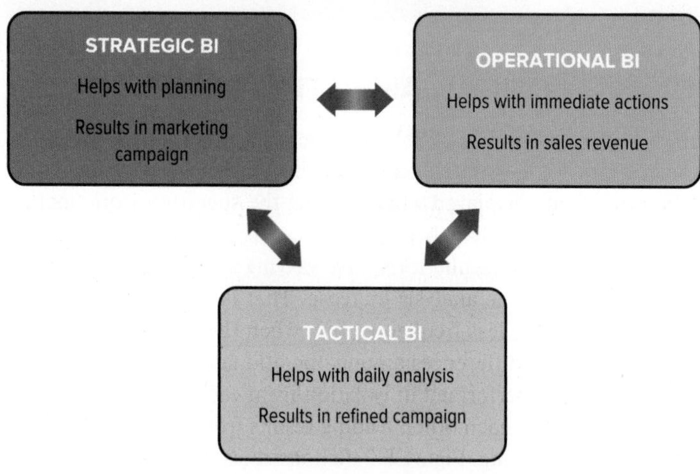

FIGURE F.3

The Latency between a Business Event and an Action Taken

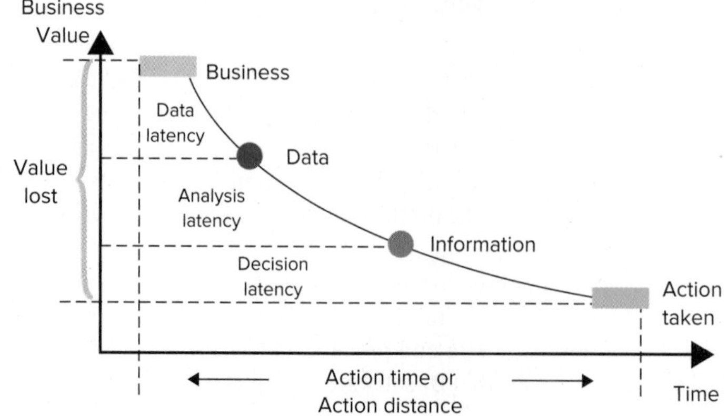

- ***Data latency*** is the time duration to make data ready for analysis (i.e., the time for extracting, transforming, and cleansing the data) and loading the data into the database. All this can take time depending on the state of the operational data to begin with.
- ***Analysis latency*** is the time from which data are made available to the time when analysis is complete. Its length depends on the time it takes a business to do analysis. Usually, we think of this as the time it takes a human to do the analysis, but this can be decreased by the use of automated analytics that have thresholds. When the thresholds are exceeded, alerts or alarms can be issued to appropriate personnel, or they can cause exception processes to be initiated with no human intervention needed.
- ***Decision latency*** is the time it takes a human to comprehend the analytic result and determine an appropriate action. This form of latency is very difficult to reduce. The ability to remove the decision-making process from the human and automate it will greatly reduce the overall decision latency. Many forward-thinking companies are doing just that. For example, rather than send a high-value customer a letter informing them of a bounced check (which takes days to get to the customer), an automated system can simply send an immediate email or voice message informing the customer of the problem.

The key is to shorten these latencies so that the time frame for opportunistic influences on customers, suppliers, and others is faster, more interactive, and better positioned. As mentioned above, the best time to influence customers is not after they have left the store or the website. It is while they are still in the store or still wandering around the website.

For example, a customer who is searching a website for travel deals is far more likely to be influenced by appropriate messaging actions then and there. Actions taken immediately, while customers are still at the site, might include:

- Offering customers an appropriate coupon for the trip they showed interest in while searching for cheap airfares.
- Giving customers information about their current purchase, such as the suggestion that visas are needed.
- Congratulating them on reaching a certain frequent-buyer level and giving them 10 percent off an item.

A website represents another great opportunity to influence a customer, if the interactions are appropriate and timely. For example:

- A banner could announce the next best product to offer right after the customer puts an item in their basket.
- The customer could receive an offer for a product they just removed from their shopping basket.
- Appropriate instructions for the use of a product could come up on the customer's screen, perhaps warning a parent that the product should not be used by children under age 3.

DATA MINING

LO F.2: Explain how data mining can help improve the business process.

With the onset of big data, organizations are collecting more data than ever. Historically, data were housed in functional systems that were not integrated, such as customer service, finance, and human resources. Today, companies can gather all of the functional data together by the petabyte, but finding a way to analyze the data is incredibly challenging

Reports piled on a manager's desk provide summaries of past business activities and stock market data. Unfortunately, these reports don't offer much insight into why these things are happening or what might happen over the next few months. Data mining to the rescue!

- ***Data mining***: The process of analyzing data to extract information not offered by the raw data alone.

Data mining can also begin at a summary information level (coarse granularity) and progress through increasing levels of detail (drilling down) or the reverse (drilling up). Companies use data mining techniques to compile a complete picture of their operations, all within a single view, allowing them to identify trends and improve forecasts. The three elements of data mining include:

1. **Data:** Foundation for data-directed decision making.
2. **Discovery:** Process of identifying new patterns, trends, and insights.
3. **Deployment:** Process of implementing discoveries to drive success.

One retailer discovered that loyalty program customers spent more over time, so it strategically invested in specific marketing campaigns focusing on these high spenders, thereby maximizing revenue and reducing marketing costs. One manufacturer discovered a sequence of events that preceded accidental releases of toxic chemicals, allowing the factory to remain operational while it prevented dangerous accidents. One insurance company discovered that one of its offices was able to process certain common claim types more quickly than others of comparable size. Armed with this valuable information, the company mimicked this office's best practices across its entire organization, improving customer service.

Data Mining Process Model

Data mining is a continuous process or cycle of activity in which you continually revisit the problems with new projects. This allows past models to be effectively reused to look for new opportunities in the present and future. Data mining allows users to recycle their work to become more effective and efficient on solving future problems. It is similar to creating a household budget and reusing the same basic budget year after year, even though expenses and income change. There are six primary phases in the data mining process, outlined in Figure F.4 and detailed in Figure F.5.

Data Mining Analysis Techniques

Data mining can determine relationships among such internal factors as price, product positioning, or staff skills, and external factors such as economic indicators, competition, and customer demographics. In addition, it can determine the impact on sales, customer satisfaction, and corporate profits, and drill down into summary information to view detailed transactional

FIGURE F.4

Data Mining Process Model Overview

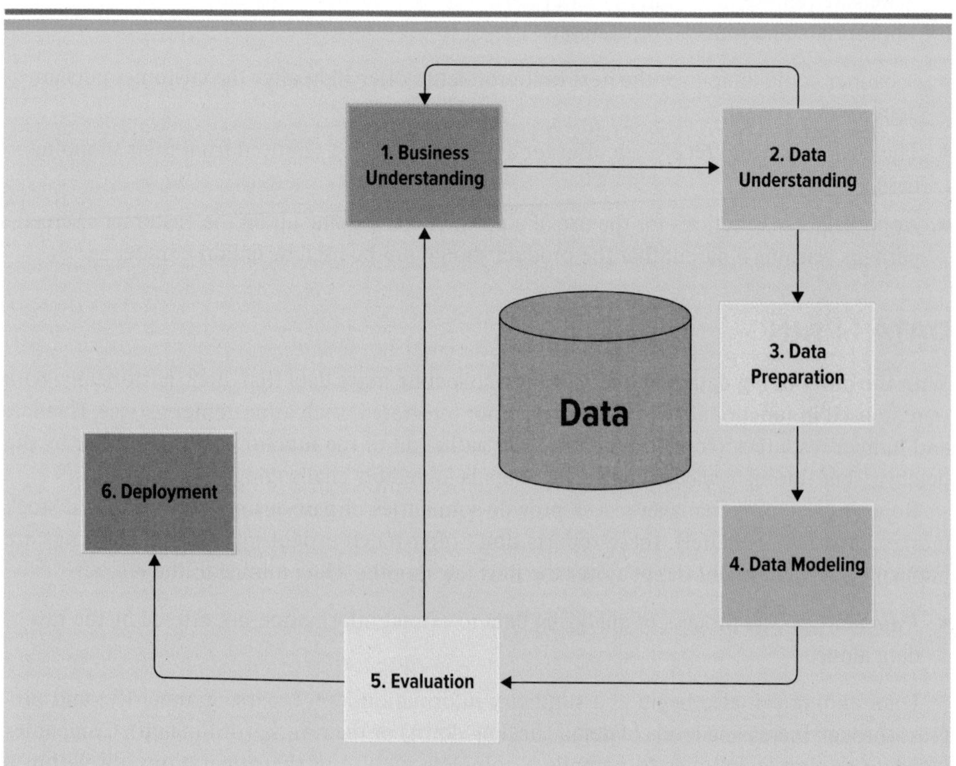

	Phase	Definition	Activities
1.	Business Understanding	Gain a clear understanding of the business problem that must be solved and how it impacts the company.	■ Identify business goals. ■ Assess the situation. ■ Define data mining goals. ■ Create a project plan.
2.	Data Understanding	Analyze all current data and identify any data quality issues.	■ Gather data. ■ Describe data. ■ Explore data. ■ Verify data quality.
3.	Data Preparation	Gather and organize the data in the correct formats and structures for analysis.	■ Select data. ■ Cleanse data. ■ Integrate data. ■ Format data.
4.	Data Modeling	Apply mathematical techniques to identify trends and patterns in the data.	■ Select the modeling technique. ■ Design tests. ■ Build models.
5.	Evaluation	Analyze the trends and patterns to assess the potential for solving the business problem.	■ Evaluate results. ■ Review the process. ■ Determine the next steps.
6.	Deployment	Deploy the discoveries to the organization for work in everyday business.	■ Plan the deployment. ■ Monitor the deployment. ■ Analyze the results. ■ Review the final reports.

FIGURE F.5

Data Mining Process Model Activities

data. With data mining, a retailer could use point-of-sale records of customer purchases to send targeted promotions based on an individual's purchase history. By mining demographic data from comment or warranty cards, the retailer could develop products and promotions to appeal to specific customer segments.

- ***Data profiling***: The process of collecting statistics and information about data in an existing source. Insights extracted from data profiling can determine how easy or difficult it will be to use existing data for other purposes, along with providing metrics on data quality.
- ***Data replication***: The process of sharing information to ensure consistency between multiple data sources.
- ***Recommendation engine***: A data mining algorithm that analyzes a customer's purchases and actions on a website and then uses the data to recommend complementary products.

Netflix uses a recommendation engine to analyze each customer's film-viewing habits to provide recommendations for other customers with Cinematch, its movie recommendation system. Using Cinematch, Netflix can present customers with a number of additional movies they might want to watch based on the customer's current preferences. Netflix's innovative use of data mining provides its competitive advantage in the movie rental industry. Figure F.6 displays the common data mining techniques used to perform advanced analytics such as Netflix's Cinematch.

Estimation Analysis An ***estimation analysis*** determines values for an unknown continuous variable behavior or estimated future value. Estimation models predict numeric outcomes based on historical data; for example, the percentage of high school students who will graduate based on student-teacher ratio or income levels. An estimate is similar to a guess and is one of the least expensive modeling techniques. Many organizations use estimation analysis to determine the overall costs of a project from start to completion or estimates on the profits from introducing a new product line.

FIGURE F.6

Data Mining Techniques

Estimation Analysis	***Affinity Grouping Analysis***
Determines values for an unknown continuous variable behavior or estimated future value.	Reveals the relationship between variables along with the nature and frequency of the relationships.
Cluster Analysis	***Classification Analysis***
A technique used to divide an information set into mutually exclusive groups such that the members of each group are as close together as possible to one another and the different groups are as far apart as possible.	The process of organizing data into categories or groups for its most effective and efficient use.

Affinity Grouping Analysis ***Affinity grouping analysis*** reveals the relationship between variables, along with the nature and frequency of the relationships. Many people refer to affinity grouping algorithms as association rule generators because they create rules to determine the likelihood of events occurring together at a particular time or following each other in a logical progression. Percentages usually reflect the patterns of these events; for example, "55 percent of the time, events A and B occurred together" or "80 percent of the time that items A and B occurred together, they were followed by item C within three days." One of the most common forms of association detection analysis is market basket analysis.

- ***Market basket analysis***: Evaluates such items as websites and checkout scanner information to detect customers' buying behavior and predict future behavior by identifying affinities among customers' choices of products and services (see Figure F.7).

FIGURE F.7

Market Basket Analysis Example

andresr/Getty Images

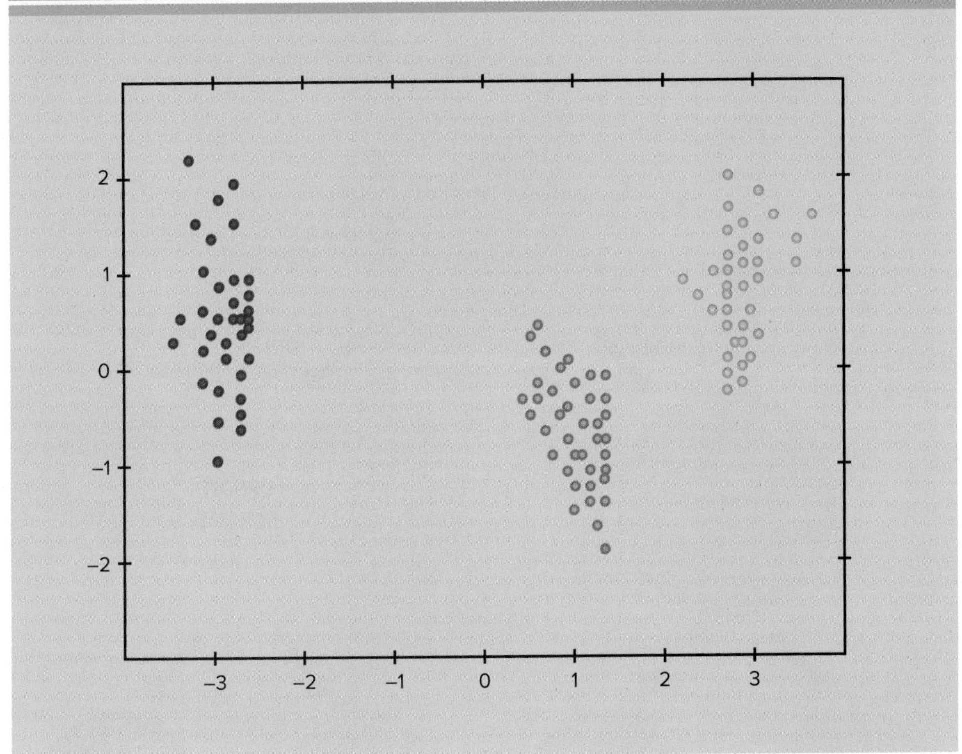

FIGURE F.8

Example of Cluster Analysis

Market basket analysis is frequently used to develop marketing campaigns for cross-selling products and services (especially in banking, insurance, and finance) and for inventory control, shelf-product placement, and other retail and marketing applications.

Cluster Analysis *Cluster analysis* is a technique used to divide an information set into mutually exclusive groups such that the members of each group are as close together as possible to one another and the different groups are as far apart as possible. Cluster analysis identifies similarities and differences among datasets, allowing similar datasets to be clustered together. A customer database includes attributes such as name and address, demographic information such as gender and age, and financial attributes such as income and revenue spent. A cluster analysis groups similar attributes together to discover segments or clusters and then examines the attributes and values that define the clusters or segments. Marketing managers can drive promotion strategies that target the specific group identified by the cluster analysis (see Figure F.8).

A great example of using cluster analysis in business is to create target-marketing strategies based on zip codes. Evaluating customer segments by zip code allows a business to assign a level of importance to each segment. Zip codes offer valuable insight into such things as income levels, demographics, lifestyles, and spending habits. With target marketing, a business can decrease its costs while increasing the success rate of the marketing campaign.

Classification Analysis *Classification analysis* is the process of organizing data into categories or groups for its most effective and efficient use; for example, groups of political affiliation and charity donors. The primary goal of a classification analysis is not to explore data to find interesting segments but to decide the best way to classify records. It is important to note that classification analysis is similar to cluster analysis because it segments data into distinct segments called classes; however, unlike cluster analysis, a classification analysis requires that all classes are defined before the analysis begins. For example, in a classification analysis, the analyst defines two classes: (1) a class for customers who defaulted on a loan and (2) a class for customers who did not default on a loan. Cluster analysis is exploratory analysis and classification analysis is much less exploratory and more grouping. (See Figure F.9.)

FIGURE F.9

Classification Analysis Example

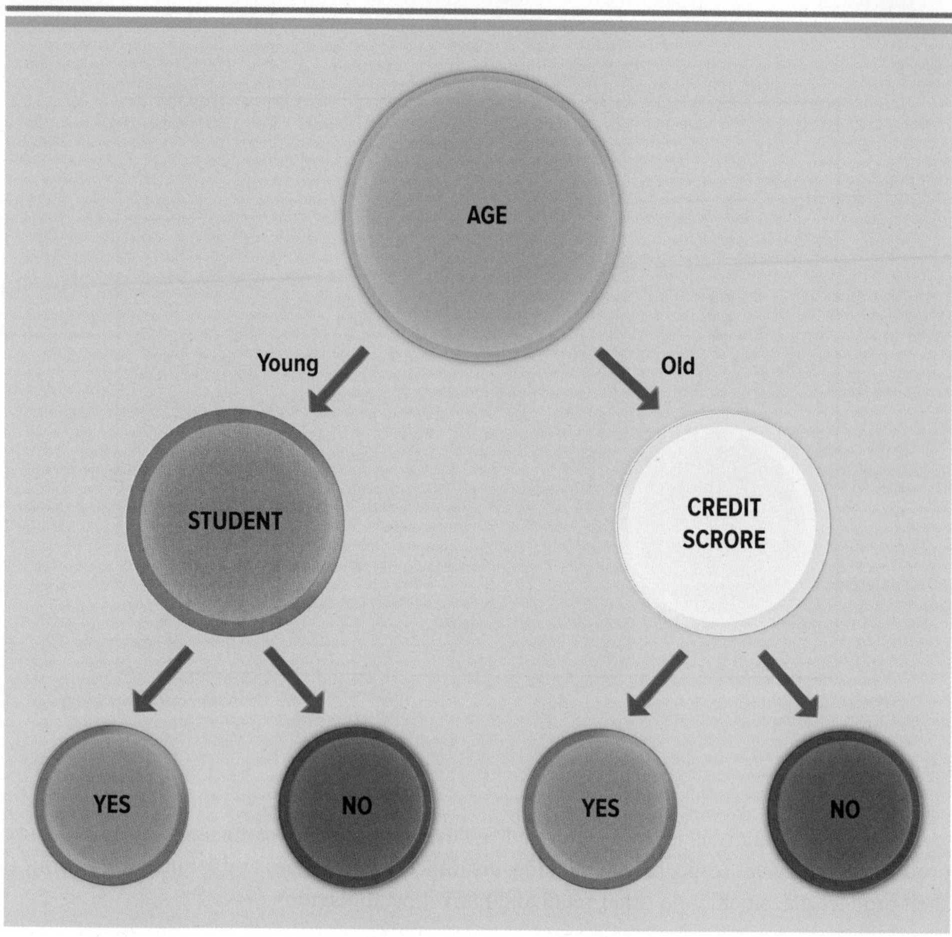

Data Mining Modeling Techniques for Predictions

To perform data mining, users need data mining tools.

- ***Data mining tools***: A variety of techniques to find patterns and relationships in large volumes of information that predict future behavior and guide decision making.

Data mining uncovers trends and patterns, which analysts use to build models that, when exposed to new information sets, perform a variety of information analysis functions. Data mining tools for data warehouses help users uncover business intelligence in their data. Data mining uncovers patterns and trends for business analysis such as:

- Analyzing customer buying patterns to predict future marketing and promotion campaigns.
- Building budgets and other financial information.
- Detecting fraud by identifying deceptive spending patterns.
- Finding the best customers who spend the most money.
- Keeping customers from leaving or migrating to competitors.
- Promoting and hiring employees to ensure success for both the company and the individual.

Figure F.10 displays the common DSS analysis techniques. What-if analysis, sensitivity analysis, and goal-seek are all forms of predictive analytics, and optimization analysis is a form of prescriptive analytics.

FIGURE F.10

Common DSS Analysis Techniques

WHAT-IF ANALYSIS

- ***What-if analysis*** checks the impact of a change in a variable or assumption on the model. For example, "What will happen to the supply chain if a hurricane in South Carolina reduces holding inventory from 30 percent to 10 percent?" A user would be able to observe and evaluate any changes that occurred to the values in the model, especially to a variable such as profits. Users repeat this analysis with different variables until they understand all the effects of various situations.

SENSITIVITY ANALYSIS

- ***Sensitivity analysis,*** a special case of what-if analysis, is the study of the impact on other variables when one variable is changed repeatedly. Sensitivity analysis is useful when users are uncertain about the assumptions made in estimating the value of certain key variables. For example, repeatedly changing revenue in small increments to determine its effects on other variables would help a manager understand the impact of various revenue levels on other decision factors.

GOAL-SEEKING ANALYSIS

- ***Goal-seeking analysis*** finds the inputs necessary to achieve a goal such as a desired level of output. It is the reverse of what-if and sensitivity analysis. Instead of observing how changes in a variable affect other variables, goal-seeking analysis sets a target value (a goal) for a variable and then repeatedly changes other variables until the target value is achieved. For example, goal-seeking analysis could determine how many customers must purchase a new product to increase gross profits to $5 million.

OPTIMIZATION ANALYSIS

- ***Optimization analysis***, an extension of goal-seeking analysis, finds the optimum value for a target variable by repeatedly changing other variables, subject to specified constraints. By changing revenue and cost variables in an optimization analysis, managers can calculate the highest potential profits. Constraints on revenue and cost variables can be taken into consideration, such as limits on the amount of raw materials the company can afford to purchase and limits on employees available to meet production needs.

Figure F.11 displays the three common data mining techniques for predictions.

- ***Prediction***: A statement about what will happen or might happen in the future; for example, predicting future sales or employee turnover.

Please note the primary difference between forecasts and predictions. All forecasts are predictions, but not all predictions are forecasts. For example, when you would use regression to explain the relationship between two variables, this is a prediction but not a forecast.

FIGURE F.11

Data Mining Modeling Techniques for Predictions

Model	Definition	Example
Optimization model	A statistical process that finds the way to make a design, system, or decision as effective as possible; for example, finding the values of controllable variables that determine maximal productivity or minimal waste.	■ Determine which products to produce given a limited number of ingredients. ■ Choose a combination of projects to maximize overall earnings.
Forecasting model	***Time-series information*** is time-stamped information collected at a particular frequency. Forecasts are predictions based on time-series information, allowing users to manipulate the time series for forecasting activities.	■ Web visits per hour. ■ Sales per month. ■ Customer service calls per day.
Regression model	A statistical process for estimating the relationships among variables. Regression models include many techniques for modeling and analyzing several variables when the focus is on the relationship between a dependent variable and one or more independent variables.	■ Predict the winners of a marathon based on gender, height, weight, hours of training. ■ Explain how the quantity of weekly sales of a popular brand of beer depend on its price at a small chain of supermarkets.

LO F.3 Describe the four categories of BI business benefits.

BUSINESS BENEFITS OF BI

When an organization embraces Agile BI, it generally embeds Agile software developers in the organization's business intelligence team.

- ***Agile BI***: An approach to business intelligence (BI) that incorporates Agile software development methodologies to accelerate and improve the outcomes of BI initiatives.

As with all Agile initiatives, BI projects are broken down into a series of smaller projects that are planned for, developed, tested, and rolled out on a continuous basis. This iterative development approach facilitates continuous improvement and helps an organization adapt more quickly to changing market conditions and organizational goals. Each iteration of an Agile BI project is planned and reviewed by both the software development team and the business owners who have requested work. This close collaboration between business and MIS results in better communication, clearly defined goals, and end results that more accurately meet expectations.

As with any Agile initiative, Agile BI tends to reduce total cost of change and promote a culture that values reflection, accepts change, and understands how to respond flexibly to shifts in organizational value. Because BI project iterations are released on a regular basis, changes to a business intelligence dashboard or data warehouse can be made functional in a matter of weeks or months, providing business users with the information they need to make data-driven decisions much faster than could be realized with a more traditional waterfall project approach.

Rapid innovations in systems and data-mining tools are putting operational, tactical, and strategic BI at the fingertips of executives, managers, and even customers. With the successful implementation of BI systems, an organization can expect to receive the following:

- **Single point of access to information for all users.** With a BI solution, organizations can unlock information held within their databases by giving authorized users a single point of access to data. Wherever the data reside, whether stored in operational systems, data warehouses, data marts, and/or enterprise applications, users can prepare reports and drill deep down into the information to understand what drives their business, without technical knowledge of the underlying data structures. The most successful BI applications allow users to do this with an easy-to-understand, nontechnical, graphical user interface.
- **BI across organizational departments.** There are many different uses for BI, and one of its greatest benefits is that it can be used at every step in the value chain. All departments across an organization from sales to operations to customer service can benefit from the value of BI. Volkswagen AG uses BI to track, understand, and manage data in every department–from finance, production, and development, to research, sales and marketing,

and purchasing. Users at all levels of the organization access supplier and customer reports relating to online requests and negotiations, vehicle launches, and vehicle capacity management and tracking.

- **Up-to-the-minute information for everyone.** The key to unlocking information is to give users the tools to quickly and easily find immediate answers to their questions. Some users will be satisfied with standard reports that are updated on a regular basis, such as current inventory reports, sales per channel, or customer status reports. However, the answers these reports yield can lead to new questions. Some users will want dynamic access to information. The information that a user finds in a report will trigger more questions, and these questions will not be answered in a prepackaged report. While users may spend 80 percent of their time accessing standard or personalized reports, for 20 percent of their tasks they need to obtain additional information not available in the original report. To address this need and to avoid frustration (and related report backlog for the IT team), a BI system should let users autonomously make ad-hoc requests for information from corporate data sources. For merchants of MasterCard International, access to BI offers the opportunity to monitor their businesses more closely on a day-to-day basis. Advertising agencies are able to use information from an extranet when developing campaigns for merchants. On the authorization side, a call center can pull up cardholder authorization transactions to cut down on fraud. MasterCard expects that, in the long term and as business partners increasingly demand access to system data, the system will support more than 20,000 external users.

Categories of BI Benefits

Management is no longer prepared to sink large sums of money into IT projects simply because they are the latest and greatest technology. Information technology has come of age, and it is expected to make a significant contribution to the bottom line.

When looking at how BI affects the bottom line, an organization should analyze not only the organization-wide business benefits, but also the various benefits it can expect to receive from a BI deployment. A practical way of breaking down these numerous benefits is to separate them into four main categories:

- Quantifiable benefits
- Indirectly quantifiable benefits
- Unpredictable benefits
- Intangible benefits

Quantifiable Benefits

Quantifiable benefits include working time saved in producing reports, selling information to suppliers, and so on. A few examples include:

- Moët et Chandon, the famous champagne producer, reduced its MIS costs from approximately 30 cents per bottle to 15 cents per bottle.
- A leading risk insurance company provides customers with self-service access to their information in the insurance company's database and no longer sends paper reports. This one benefit alone saves the organization $400,000 a year in printing and shipping costs. The total three-year ROI for this BI deployment was 249 percent.

Indirectly Quantifiable Benefits

Indirectly quantifiable benefits can be evaluated through indirect evidence–improved customer service means new business from the same customer, and differentiated service brings new customers. A few examples include:

- A customer of Owens & Minor cited extranet access to the data warehouse as the primary reason for giving the medical supplies distributor an additional $44 million in business.

- "When salespeople went out to visit TaylorMade's customers at golf pro shops and sporting goods retail chains, they didn't have up-to-date inventory reports. The sales reps would take orders for clubs, accessories, and clothing without confidence that the goods were available for delivery as promised," Tom Collard, vice president of information technology at TaylorMade, said. "The technology has helped TaylorMade not only reduce costs by eliminating the reporting backlog . . . it has eliminated a lot of wasted effort that resulted from booking orders that it couldn't fill."

Unpredictable Benefits

Unpredictable benefits are the result of discoveries made by creative users. A few examples include:

- Volkswagen's finance BI system allowed an interesting discovery that later resulted in significant new revenue. The customers of a particular model of the Audi product line had completely different behaviors than customers of other cars. Based on their socioeconomic profiles, they were thought to want long lease terms and fairly large up-front payments. Instead, the information revealed that Audi customers actually wanted shorter leases and to finance a large part of the purchase through the lease. Based on that insight, the company immediately introduced a program combining a shorter length of lease, larger up-front payments, and aggressive leasing rates, especially for that car model. The interest in the new program was immediate, resulting in over $2 million in new revenue.
- Peter Blundell, former knowledge strategy manager for British Airways, and various company executives had a suspicion that the carrier was suffering from a high degree of ticket fraud. To address this problem, Blundell and his team rolled out business intelligence. "Once we analyzed the data, we found that this ticket fraud was not an issue at all. What we had supposed was fraud was in fact either data quality issues or process problems," Blundell said. "What it did was give us so many unexpected opportunities in terms of understanding our business." Blundell estimated that the BI deployment has resulted in around $100 million in cost savings and new revenues for the airline.

Intangible Benefits

Intangible benefits include improved communication throughout the enterprise, improved job satisfaction of empowered users, and improved knowledge sharing. A few examples include:

- The corporate human resources (HR) department at ABN AMRO Bank uses BI to gain insight into its workforce by analyzing information on such items as gender, age, tenure, and compensation. Thanks to this sharing of intellectual capital, the HR department is in a better position to demonstrate its performance and contribution to the business successes of the corporation as a whole.
- Ben & Jerry's uses BI to track, understand, and manage information on the thousands of consumer responses it receives on its products and promotional activities. Through daily customer feedback analysis, Ben & Jerry's is able to identify trends and modify its marketing campaigns and products to suit consumer demand.

KEY TERMS

MAKING BUSINESS DECISIONS

1. Mining Physician Data

National Public Radio recently aired a story discussing how large pharmaceutical companies are mining physician data. Thousands of pharmaceutical drug company sales representatives visit doctors and try to entice them to prescribe their company's newest drugs. The pharmaceutical companies buy prescription information from pharmacies all over the country describing which drugs are prescribed by which doctors. There is no patient information in the data. The sales representatives receive this BI from their companies and can tailor their sales pitch based on what that particular doctor has been prescribing to patients. Many doctors do not even realize that the sales representatives have this information and know exactly which drugs each individual doctor prescribes. The drug companies love mining data, but critics contend it is an invasion of privacy and drives up the cost of health care. Maine has just become the third state to pass a measure limiting access to the data.

You are working for your state government and your boss has asked you to create an argument for or against pharmaceutical data mining of physician data in your state. A few questions to get you started:

- Do you agree that mining physician data should be illegal? Why or why not?
- As a patient, how do you feel about pharmaceutical companies mining your doctor's data?
- As an employee of one of the pharmaceutical companies, how do you feel about mining physician data?

AYK APPLICATION PROJECTS

Project Number	Project Name	Project Type	Plug-In	Focus Area	Project Level	Skill Set	Page Number
1	Financial Destiny	Excel	T2	Personal Budget	Introductory	Formulas	AYK.3
2	Cash Flow	Excel	T2	Cash Flow	Introductory	Formulas	AYK.3
3	Technology Budget	Excel	T1, T2	Hardware and Software	Introductory	Formulas	AYK.3
4	Tracking Donations	Excel	T2	Employee Relationships	Introductory	Formulas	AYK.3
5	Convert Currency	Excel	T2	Global Commerce	Introductory	Formulas	AYK.4
6	Cost Comparison	Excel	T2	Total Cost of Ownership	Introductory	Formulas	AYK.4
7	Time Management	Excel or Project	T12	Project Management	Introductory	Gantt Charts	AYK.5
8	Maximize Profit	Excel	T2, T4	Strategic Analysis	Intermediate	Formulas or Solver	AYK.5
9	Security Analysis	Excel	T3	Filtering Data	Intermediate	Conditional Formatting, Autofilter, Subtotal	AYK.6
10	Gathering Data	Excel	T3	Data Analysis	Intermediate	Conditional Formatting	AYK.6
11	Scanner System	Excel	T2	Strategic Analysis	Intermediate	Formulas	AYK.7
12	Competitive Pricing	Excel	T2	Profit Maximization	Intermediate	Formulas	AYK.7
13	Adequate Acquisitions	Excel	T2	Break-Even Analysis	Intermediate	Formulas	AYK.7
14	Customer Relations	Excel	T3	CRM	Intermediate	PivotTable	AYK.8
15	Assessing the Value of Information	Excel	T3	Data Analysis	Intermediate	PivotTable	AYK.8
16	Growth, Trends, and Forecasts	Excel	T2, T3	Data Forecasting	Advanced	Average, Trend, Growth	AYK.9
17	Shipping Costs	Excel	T4	SCM	Advanced	Solver	AYK.10
18	Formatting Grades	Excel	T3	Data Analysis	Advanced	If, LookUp	AYK.11

(continued)

Project Number	Project Name	Project Type	Plug-In	Focus Area	Project Level	Skill Set	Page Number
19	Moving Dilemma	Excel	T2, T3	SCM	Advanced	Absolute vs. Relative Values	AYK.11
20	Operational Efficiencies	Excel	T3	SCM	Advanced	PivotTable	AYK.12
21	Too Much Information	Excel	T3	CRM	Advanced	PivotTable	AYK.12
22	Turnover Rates	Excel	T3	Data Mining	Advanced	PivotTable	AYK.13
23	Vital Information	Excel	T3	Data Mining	Advanced	PivotTable	AYK.13
24	Breaking Even	Excel	T4	Business Analysis	Advanced	Goal Seek	AYK.14
25	Profit Scenario	Excel	T4	Sales Analysis	Advanced	Scenario Manager	AYK.14
26	Electronic Résumés	HTML	T9, T10, T11	Electronic Personal Marketing	Introductory	Structural Tags	AYK.14
27	Gathering Feedback	HTML	T9, T10, T11	Data Collection	Intermediate	Organization of Information	AYK.15
28	Daily Invoice	Access	T5, T6, T7, T8	Business Analysis	Introductory	Entities, Relationships, and Databases	AYK.15
29	Billing Data	Access	T5, T6, T7, T8	Business Intelligence	Introductory	Entities, Relationships, and Databases	AYK.17
30	Inventory Data	Access	T5, T6, T7, T8	SCM	Intermediate	Entities, Relationships, and Databases	AYK.18
31	Call Center	Access	T5, T6, T7, T8	CRM	Intermediate	Entities, Relationships, and Databases	AYK.19
32	Sales Pipeline	Access	T5, T6, T7, T8	Business Intelligence	Advanced	Entities, Relationships, and Databases	AYK.20
33	Online Classified Ads	Access	T5, T6, T7, T8	Ecommerce	Advanced	Entities, Relationships, and Databases	AYK.20

NOTE: Many of the Excel projects support multiple data files. Therefore, the naming convention you see in the text may not be the same as what you see in a data folder. As an example, in the text, we reference data files as AYK1_Data.xlsx; however, you may see a file named AYK1_Data_Version_1.xlsx or AYK1_Data_Version_2.xlsx.

Project 1:
Financial Destiny

You have been introduced to Microsoft Excel and are ready to begin using it to help track your monthly expenses and take charge of your financial destiny. The first step is to create a personal budget so you can see where you are spending money and whether you need to decrease your monthly expenses or increase your monthly income.

Create a template for a monthly budget of your income and expenditures, with some money set aside for savings (or you can use the data file, AYK1_Data.xlsx, we created). Create variations of this budget to show how much you could save if you cut back on certain expenses, found a roommate, or got a part-time job. Compare the costs of a meal plan to costs of groceries. Consider how much interest would be earned if you saved $100 a month or how much debt would be paid on student loans or credit card bills. To expand your dataset, make a fantasy budget for 10 years from now, when you might own a home, have student loan payments, and have a good salary.

Data file: AYK1_Data.xlsx

Project 2:
Cash Flow

Gears is a 5-year-old company that specializes in bike components. The company is having trouble paying for its monthly supplies and would like to perform a cash flow analysis so it can understand its financial position. Cash flow represents the money an investment produces after subtracting cash expenses from income. The statement of cash flows summarizes sources and uses of cash, indicates whether enough cash is available to carry on routine operations, and offers an analysis of all business transactions, reporting where the firm obtained its cash and how it chose to allocate the cash. The cash flow statement shows where money comes from, how the company will spend it, and when the company will require additional cash. Gears would like to project a cash flow statement for the next month.

Using the AYK2_Data.xlsx data file, complete the cash flow statement for Gears, using Excel. Be sure to create formulas so the company can simply input numbers in the future to determine cash flow.

Data file: AYK2_Data.xlsx

Project 3:
Technology Budget

Tally is a start-up website development company located in Seattle, Washington. The company currently has seven employees and is looking to hire six new employees in the next month.

You are in charge of purchasing for Tally. Your first task is to purchase computers for the new employees. Your budget is $250,000 to buy the best computer systems, with a scanner, three color printers, and business software. Use the web to research various products and calculate the costs of different systems, using Excel. Use a variety of Excel formulas as you analyze costs and compare prices. Use the AYK3_Data.xlsx data file as a template.

Data file: AYK3_Data.xlsx

Project 4:
Tracking Donations

Lazarus Consulting is a large computer consulting company in New York. Pete Lazarus, the CEO and founder, is well-known for his philanthropic efforts. Pete knows that most of his employees contribute to nonprofit organizations and wants to reward them for their efforts while encouraging others to contribute to charities. Pete began a program that matches 50 percent of each employee donation. The only stipulations are that the charity must be a nonprofit organization and the company will match only up to $2,000 per year per employee.

Open the AYK4_Data.xlsx data file and determine the following:

- What was the total donation amount per organization?
- What were the average donations per organization?

Data file: AYK4_Data.xlsx

Project 5:
Convert Currency

You have decided to spend the summer traveling abroad with your friends. Your trip will take you to France, England, Canada, Japan, and India. You want to use Excel to convert currencies as you travel around the world.

Locate one of the exchange rate calculators on the Internet (www.xe.com or www.x-rates.com). Find the exchange rates for each of the listed countries and create formulas in Excel to convert $100, $500, and $1,000. Use the AYK5_Data.xlsx data file as a template.

Data file: AYK5_Data.xls

Project 6:
Cost Comparison

You are thinking about purchasing a new computer because the machine you are using now is 4 years old, slow, and not always reliable, and does not support the latest operating system. Your needs for the new computer are simple: antivirus software, email, web browsing, word processing, spreadsheet, database, iTunes, and some lightweight graphical tools. Your concern is what the total cost of ownership will be for the next 3 years. You have to factor in a few added costs beyond just the initial purchase price for the computer itself, such as added hardware (this could include a new printer, docking station, or scanner), software (purchase of a new operating system), training (you're thinking about pursuing web training to get an internship next term), subsequent software upgrades, and maintenance.

- It is useful to think about costs over time—both direct as well as indirect costs. Part of the reason this distinction is important is that a decision should rest not on the nominal sum of the purchase but, rather, on the present value of the purchase.
- A dollar today is worth more than a dollar one year from now.
- The relevant discount rate (interest rate) is your marginal cost of capital corresponding to a level of risk equal with the purchase.
- Use the AYK6_Data.xlsx data file as a template.

Data file: AYK6_Data.xlsx

FIGURE AYK.1

Sample Layout of New Computer Spreadsheet

Microsoft Corporation

	A	B	C	D	E	F
1	COST OF NEW COMPUTER					
2	Discount Rate	1	0.9325	0.9109	0.7051	
3		Time 0	Year 1	Year 2	Year 3	Present Value Costs
4	Computer					
5	Software					
6	Additional Hardware					
7	Training					
8	Software Upgrades					
9	Maintenance					
10						
11	Total Costs					
12						

Project 7:

Time Management

You have just been hired as a business analyst by a new start-up company called Multi-Media. Multi-Media is an interactive agency that creates phased and affordable website marketing, providing its clients with real and measurable solutions that are supported by easy-to-use tools. Because the company is very new to the business arena, it needs help in creating a project management plan for developing its own website. The major tasks for the development team have been identified, but you need to create the timeline.

1. The task names, durations, and any prerequisites are:
   - Analyze and plan—two weeks. Cannot start anything else until done.
   - Create and organize content—four weeks. Can start to develop look and feel before this is done.
   - Develop the look and feel—four weeks. Start working on graphics and HTML at the same time.
   - Produce graphics and HTML documents—two weeks. Create working prototype after the first week.
   - Create a working prototype—two weeks. Give to test team when complete.
   - Test, test, test—four weeks.
   - Upload to a web server and test again—one week.
   - Maintain.
2. Using Microsoft Excel or Microsoft Project, create a Gantt chart using the information provided.

Project 8:

Maximize Profit

Books, Books, Books is a wholesale distributor of popular books. The business buys overstocked books and sells them for a discount of more than 50 percent to local area bookstores. The owner of the company, B. K. Kane, would like to determine the best approach to boxing books so he can make the largest profit possible. The local bookstores accept all shipments from Books, Books, Books because of B. K.'s incredibly low prices. B. K. can order as many overstocked books as he requires, and this week's options include:

Title	Weight	Cost	Sale Price
Harry Potter and the Deathly Hallows, J. K. Rowling	5 lb	$9	$17
The Children of Húrin, J. R. R. Tolkien	4 lb	$8	$13
The Time Traveler's Wife, Audrey Niffenegger	3.5 lb	$7	$11
The Dark River, John Twelve Hawks	3 lb	$6	$9
The Road, Cormac McCarthy	2.5 lb	$5	$7
Slaughterhouse-Five, Kurt Vonnegut	1 lb	$4	$5

When packing a single box, B. K. must adhere to the following:

- 20 books or fewer
- Books by three authors
- Between four and eight books from each author
- Weight equal to or less than 50 pounds

B. K. has come to you to help him determine which books he should order to maximize his profit based on this information. Using the AYK8_Data.xlsx data file, determine the optimal book order for a single box of books.

Data file: AYK8_Data.xlsx

Project 9:
Security Analysis

SecureWorks, Inc. is a small computer security contractor that provides computer security analysis, design, and software implementation for the U.S. government and commercial clients. SecureWorks competes for both private and U.S. government computer security contract work by submitting detailed bids outlining the work the company will perform if awarded the contracts. Because all of the work involves computer security, a highly sensitive area, almost all of SecureWorks tasks require access to classified material or company confidential documents. Consequently, all of the security engineers (simply known as "engineers" within the company) have U.S. government clearances of either secret or top secret. Some have even higher clearances for the 2 percent of SecureWorks work that involves so-called black-box security work. Most of the employees also hold clearances because they must handle classified documents.

Leslie Mamalis is SecureWorks's human resources (HR) manager. She maintains all employee records and is responsible for semiannual review reports, payroll processing, personnel records, recruiting data, employee training, and pension option information. At the heart of an HR system are personnel records. Personnel record maintenance includes activities such as maintaining employee records, tracking cost center data, recording and maintaining pension information, and absence and sick leave record keeping. Although most of this information resides in sophisticated database systems, Leslie maintains a basic employee worksheet for quick calculations and ad hoc report generation. Because SecureWorks is a small company, Leslie can take advantage of Excel's excellent list management capabilities to satisfy many of her personnel information management needs.

Leslie has asked you to assist with a number of functions (she has provided you with a copy of her trusted personnel data file, AYK9_Data.xlsx):

1. Copy the data worksheet to a new worksheet called Sort. Sort the employee list in ascending order by department, then by last name, then by first name.
2. Copy the data worksheet to a new worksheet called Autofilter. Using the Autofilter feature, create a custom filter that will display employees whose birth date is greater than or equal to 1/1/1965 and less than or equal to 12/31/1975.
3. Copy the data worksheet to a new worksheet called Subtotal. Using the subtotal feature, create a sum of the salary for each department.
4. Copy the data worksheet to a new worksheet called Formatting. Using the salary column, change the font color to red if the cell value is greater than or equal to 55000. You must use the conditional formatting feature to complete this step.

Data file: AYK9_Data.xlsx

Project 10:
Gathering Data

You have just accepted a new job offer from a firm that has offices in San Diego, Los Angeles, and San Francisco. You need to decide which location to move to. Because you have not visited any of these three cities and want to get in a lot of golf time, you determine that the main factor that will affect your decision is weather.

Go to www.weather.com and locate the box in which you can enter the city or zip code for which you want information. Enter San Diego, CA, and when the data appears, click the Averages and Records tab. Print this page and repeat this for Los Angeles and San Francisco. You will want to focus on the Monthly Average and Records section on the top of the page.

1. Create a spreadsheet to summarize the information you find.
2. Record the temperature and rainfall in columns and group the cities into four groups of rows labeled Average High, Average Low, Mean, and Average Precipitation.
3. Fill in the appropriate data for each city and month.
4. Because rain is your greatest concern, use conditional formatting to display the months with an average precipitation below 2.5 inches in blue and apply boldface.

5. You also want to be in the warmest weather possible while in California. Use conditional formatting to display the months with average high temperatures above 65 degrees in green and apply an italic font face.
6. Looking at the average high temperatures above 65 degrees and average precipitation below 2 inches, to which city do you think you should relocate? Explain your answer.

Project 11:

Scanner System

FunTown is a popular amusement park filled with roller coasters, games, and water features. Boasting 24 roller coasters, 10 of which exceed 200 feet and 70 miles per hour, and five water parks, the park's attendance remains steady throughout the season. Due to the park's popularity, it is not uncommon for entrance lines to exceed one hour on busy days. FunTown would like your help to find a solution to decrease park entrance lines.

FunTown would like to implement a handheld scanner system that can allow employees to walk around the front gates and accept credit card purchases and print tickets on the spot. The park anticipates an overall increase in sales of 4 percent per year with online ticketing, with an expense of 6 percent of total sales for the scanning equipment. FunTown has created a data file for you to use, AYK11_Data.xlsx, that compares scanning sales and traditional sales. You will need to create the necessary formulas to calculate all the assumptions, including:

- Tickets sold at the booth
- Tickets sold by the scanner
- Revenues generated by booth sales
- Revenues generated by scanner sales
- Scanner ticket expense
- Revenue with and without scanner sales
- Three-year row totals

Data file: AYK11_Data.xlsx

Project 12:

Competitive Pricing

Bill Schultz is thinking of starting a store that specializes in handmade cowboy boots. Bill is a longtime rancher in the town of Taos, New Mexico. Bill's reputation for honesty and integrity is well-known around town, and he is positive his new store will be highly successful.

Before opening his store, Bill is curious about how his profit, revenue, and variable costs will change depending on the amount he charges for his boots. Bill would like you to perform the work required for this analysis and has given you the AYK12_Data.xlsx data file. Here are a few things to consider while you perform your analysis:

- Current competitive prices for custom cowboy boots are between $225 and $275 a pair.
- Variable costs will be either $100 or $150 a pair, depending on the types of material Bill chooses to use.
- Fixed costs are $10,000 a month.

Data file: AYK12_Data.xlsx

Project 13:

Adequate Acquisitions

XMark.com is a major Internet company specializing in organic food. XMark.com is thinking of purchasing GoodGrow, another organic food Internet company. GoodGrow has current revenues of $100 million, with expenses of $150 million. Current projections indicate that GoodGrow's revenues are increasing at 35 percent per year and its expenses are increasing by 10 percent per year. XMark.com understands that projections can be erroneous, however; the company must determine the number of years before GoodGrow will return a profit.

You need to help XMark.com determine the number of years required to break even, using annual growth rates in revenue between 20 percent and 60 percent and annual expense growth rates between 10 percent and 30 percent. You have been provided with a template, AYK13_Data.xlsx, to assist with your analysis.

Data file: AYK13_Data.xlsx

Project 14:

Customer Relations

Schweizer Distribution specializes in distributing fresh produce to local restaurants in the Chicago area. The company currently sells 12 products through the efforts of three sales representatives to 10 restaurants. The company, like all small businesses, is always interested in finding ways to increase revenues and decrease expenses.

The company's founder, Bob Schweizer, has recently hired you as a business analyst. You have just graduated from college with a degree in marketing and a specialization in customer relationship management. Bob is eager to hear your thoughts and ideas on how to improve the business and help the company build strong lasting relationships with its customers.

Bob has provided you with last year's sales information in the AYK14_Data.xlsx data file. Help Bob analyze his distribution company by using a PivotTable to determine the following:

1. Who is Bob's best customer by total sales?
2. Who is Bob's worst customer by total sales?
3. Who is Bob's best customer by total profit?
4. Who is Bob's worst customer by total profit?
5. What is Bob's best-selling product by total sales?
6. What is Bob's worst-selling product by total sales?
7. What is Bob's best-selling product by total profit?
8. What is Bob's worst-selling product by total profit?
9. Who is Bob's best sales representative by total profit?
10. Who is Bob's worst sales representative by total profit?
11. What is the best sales representative's best-selling product (by total profit)?
12. Who is the best sales representative's best customer (by total profit)?
13. What is the best sales representative's worst-selling product (by total profit)?
14. Who is the best sales representative's worst customer (by total profit)?

Data file: AYK14_Data.xlsx

Project 15:

Assessing the Value of Information

Recently, Santa Fe, New Mexico, was named one of the safest places to live in the United States. Since then, housing development projects have been springing up all around Santa Fe. Six housing development projects are currently dominating the local market: Pinon Pine, Rancho Hondo, Creek Side, Vista Del Monte, Forest View, and Santa Fe South. These six projects each started with 100 homes, have sold all of them, and are currently developing phase two.

As one of the three partners and real estate agents of Affordable Homes Real Estate, you are responsible for analyzing the information concerning the past 600 home sales and choosing which development project to focus on for selling homes in phase two. Because your real estate firm is so small, you and your partners have decided that the firm should focus on selling homes in only one of the development projects.

From the New Mexico Real Estate Association, you have obtained a spreadsheet file that contains information concerning each of the sales for the first 600 homes. It contains the following fields:

Column	Name	Description
A	LOT #	The number assigned to a specific home within each project.
B	PROJECT #	A unique number assigned to each of the six housing development projects (see the following table).
C	ASK PRICE	The initial posted asking price for the home.
D	SELL PRICE	The actual price for which the home was sold.
E	LIST DATE	The date the home was listed for sale.
F	SALE DATE	The date on which the final contract closed and the home was sold.
G	SQ. FT.	The total square footage for the home.
H	# BATH	The number of bathrooms in the home.
I	# BDRMS	The number of bedrooms in the home.

The following numbers have been assigned to each of the housing development projects:

Project Number	Project Name
23	Pinon Pine
47	Rancho Hondo
61	Creek Side
78	Vista Del Monte
92	Forest View
97	Santa Fe South

It is your responsibility to analyze the sales list and prepare a report that details which housing development project your real estate firm should focus on. Your analysis should be from as many angles as possible.

1. You do not know how many other real estate firms will also be competing for sales in each of the housing development projects.
2. Phase two for each housing development project will develop homes similar in style, price, and square footage to their respective first phases.
3. As you consider the information provided to you, think in terms of what information is important and what information is not important. Be prepared to justify how you went about your analysis.
4. Upon completing your analysis, please provide concise, yet detailed and thorough documentation (in narrative, numeric, and graphic forms) that justifies your decision.

Data file: AYK15_Data.xlsx

Project 16:

Growth, Trends, and Forecasts

Founded in 2002, Analytics Software provides innovative search software, website accessibility testing software, and usability testing software. All serve as part of its desktop and enterprise content management solutions for government, corporate, educational, and consumer markets. The company's solutions are used by website publishers, digital media publishers, content managers, document managers, business users, consumers, software companies, and consulting services companies. Analytics Software solutions help organizations develop long-term strategies to achieve web content accessibility, enhance usability, and comply with U.S. and international accessibility and search standards.

You manage the customer service group for the company and have just received an email from CIO Sue Downs that the number of phone calls from customers having problems with one of your newer applications is on the increase. This company has a 10-year history of approximately 1 percent in turnover a year, and its focus had always been on customer service. With the informal motto of "Grow big, but stay small," it takes pride in 100 percent callbacks in customer care, knowing that its personal service was one thing that made it outstanding.

The rapid growth to six times its original customer-base size has forced the company to deal with difficult questions for the first time, such as, "How do we serve this many customers?"

One option might be for the company to outsource its customer service department. Before deciding to do that, Analytics Software needs to create a growth, trend, and forecast analysis for future predictions.

1. Create a weekly analysis from the data provided in AYK16_Data.xlsx.
2. The price of the products, the actual product type, and any warranty information are irrelevant.
3. Develop a growth, trend, and forecast analysis. You should use a three-day moving average; a shorter moving average might not display the trend well, and a much longer moving average would shorten the trend too much.
4. Upon completing your analysis, please provide concise yet detailed and thorough documentation (in narrative, numeric, and graphical forms) that justifies your recommendations.

Data file: AYK16_Data.xlsx

Project 17:
Shipping Costs

One of the main products of the Fairway Woods Company is custom-made golf clubs. The clubs are manufactured at three plants (Denver, Colorado; Phoenix, Arizona; and Dallas, Texas) and are then shipped by truck to five distribution warehouses in Sacramento, California; Salt Lake City, Utah; Chicago, Illinois; Albuquerque, New Mexico; and New York City, New York. Because shipping costs are a major expense, management has begun an analysis to determine ways to reduce them. For the upcoming golf season, the output from each manufacturing plant and how much each warehouse will require to satisfy its customers have been estimated.

The CIO from Fairway Woods Company has created a data file for you, AYK17_Data.xlsx, of the shipping costs from each manufacturing plant to each warehouse as a baseline analysis. Some business rules and requirements you should be aware of include:

- The problem presented involves the shipment of goods from three plants to five regional warehouses.
- Goods, which can be shipped from any plant to any warehouse, cost more to ship over long distances than over short distances.

1. Your goal is to minimize the costs of shipping goods from production plants to warehouses, thereby meeting the demand from each metropolitan area while not exceeding the supply available from each plant. To complete this project, it is recommended you use the Solver function in Excel to assist with the analysis.
2. Specifically, you want to focus on:
    - Minimal total shipping costs.
    - Total shipped being less than or equal to supply at a plant.
    - Total shipped to warehouses being greater than or equal to the warehouse demand.
    - Number to ship being greater than or equal to 0.

    Data file: AYK17_Data.xlsx

Project 18:

Formatting Grades

Professor Streterstein is a bit absentminded. His instructor's grade book is a mess, and he would like your help cleaning it up and making it easier to use. In Professor Streterstein's course, the maximum possible points a student can earn is 750. The following table displays the grade equivalent to total points for the course:

Total Points	Calculated Grade
675	A
635	A–
600	B
560	B–
535	C
490	C–
450	D
0	F

Help Professor Streterstein rework his grade book. Open the AYK18_Data.xlsx data file and perform the following:

1. Reformat the workbook so it is readable, understandable, and consistent. Replace column labels, format and align the headings, and add borders and shading as appropriate.
2. Add a column in the grade book for final grade next to the total points earned column.
3. Use the VLookup function to assess final grades automatically, based on the total points column.
4. Using the If function, format the workbook so each student's grade shows a pass or fail—P for pass, F for fail—based on the total points.

Data file: AYK18_Data.xlsx

Project 19:

Moving Dilemma

Pony Espresso is a small business that sells specialty coffee drinks at office buildings. Each morning and afternoon, Pony Espresso trucks arrive at offices' front entrances, and the office employees purchase various beverages such as Java du Jour and Café de Colombia. The business is profitable. Pony Espresso offices, however, are located north of town, where lease rates are less expensive, and the principal sales area is south of town. This means the trucks must drive across town four times each day.

The cost of transportation to and from the sales area plus the power demands of the trucks' coffee brewing equipment are a significant portion of variable costs. Pony Espresso could reduce the amount of driving, and, therefore the variable costs, if it moved the offices closer to the sales area.

Pony Espresso presently has fixed costs of $10,000 per month. The lease of a new office, closer to the sales area, would cost an additional $2,200 per month. This would increase the fixed costs to $12,200 per month.

Although the lease of new offices would increase the fixed costs, a careful estimate of the potential savings in gasoline and vehicle maintenance indicates that Pony Espresso could reduce the variable costs from $0.60 per unit to $0.35 per unit. Total sales are unlikely to increase as a result of the move, but the savings in variable costs should increase the annual profit.

Consider the information provided to you from the owner in the AYK19_Data.xlsx data file. Especially look at the change in the variability of the profit from month to month. From November through January, when it is much more difficult to lure office workers out into the cold to purchase coffee, Pony Espresso barely breaks even. In fact, in December, the business lost money.

1. Develop the cost analysis on the existing lease information using the monthly sales figures provided to you in the data file.
2. Develop the cost analysis from the new lease information provided.
3. Calculate the variability reflected in the month-to-month standard deviation of earnings for the current cost structure and the projected cost structure.
4. Do not consider any association with downsizing such as overhead—simply focus on the information provided to you.
5. You will need to calculate the EBIT (earnings before interest and taxes).

Data file: AYK19_Data.xlsx

Project 20:

Operational Efficiencies

Hoover Transportation, Inc. is a large distribution company located in Denver, Colorado. The company is seeking to gain operational efficiencies in its supply chain by reducing the number of transportation carriers it is using to outsource. Operational efficiencies for Hoover Transportation, Inc. suggest that reducing the number of carriers from the Denver distribution center to warehouses in the selected states will lead to reduced costs. Brian Hoover, the CEO of Hoover Transportation, requests the number of carriers transporting products from its Denver distribution center to wholesalers in Arizona, Arkansas, Iowa, Missouri, Montana, Oklahoma, Oregon, and Washington be reduced from the current five carriers to two carriers.

Carrier selection should be based on the assumptions that all environmental factors are equal and that historical cost trends will continue. Review the historical data from the past several years to determine your recommendation for the top two carriers that Hoover Transportation should continue to use.

1. Analyze the last 24 months of Hoover Transportation's carrier transactions found in the AYK20_Data.xlsx data file.
2. Create a report detailing your recommendation for the top two carriers with which Hoover Transportation should continue to do business. Be sure to use PivotTables and PivotCharts in your report. A few questions to get you started include:
   - What is the average cost per carrier?
   - What are the total shipping costs per state?
   - What are the total shipping weights per state?
   - What are the average shipping costs per pound?
   - What is the average cost per carrier?

Data file: AYK20_Data.xlsx

Project 21:

Too Much Information

You have just landed the job of vice president of operations for The Pitt Stop Restaurants, a national chain of full-service, casual-themed restaurants. During your first week on the job, Suzanne Graham, your boss and CEO of the company, has asked you to provide an analysis of how well the company's restaurants are performing. Specifically, she would like to know which units and regions are performing extremely well, which are performing moderately well, and which are underperforming. Her goal is to identify where to spend time and focus efforts to improve the overall health of the company.

Review the AYK21_Data.xlsx data file and determine how best to analyze and interpret the data. Create a formal presentation of your findings. A few things to consider include the following:

- Should underperforming restaurants be closed or sold?
- Should high-performing restaurants be expanded to accommodate more seats?

- Should the company spend more or less on advertising?
- In which markets should the advertising budget be adjusted?
- How is The Pitt Stop Restaurants performing compared to the competition?
- How are units of like size performing relative to each other?

Data file: AYK21_Data.xlsx

Project 22:

Turnover Rates

Employee turnover rates are at an all-time high at Gizmo Manufacturing's plants. The company is experiencing severe worker retention issues, which are leading to productivity and quality control problems. The majority of the company's workers perform a variety of tasks and are paid by the hour. The company currently tests potential applicants to ensure they have the skills necessary for the intense mental concentration and dexterity required to fill the positions. Because significant costs are associated with employee turnover, Gizmo Manufacturing wants to find a way to predict which applicants have the characteristics of being a short-term versus a long-term employee.

1. Review the information that Gizmo Manufacturing has collected from two of its data sources. The first data file, AYK22_Data_A.xlsx, contains information regarding employee wages. The second data file, AYK22_Data_B.xlsx, contains information regarding employee retention.
2. Using Excel analysis functions, determine the employee characteristics you would recommend Gizmo Manufacturing look for when hiring new personnel. It is highly recommended you use PivotTables as part of your analysis.
3. Prepare a report based on your findings (which should include several forms of graphical representation) for your recommendations.

Data files: AYK22_Data_A.xlsx and AYK22_Data_B.xlsx

Project 23:

Vital Information

Martin Resorts, Inc. owns and operates four spa and golf resorts in Colorado. The company has five traditional lines of business: (1) golf sales, (2) golf lessons, (3) restaurants, (4) retail and rentals, and (5) hotels. David Logan, director of marketing technology at Martin Resorts, Inc., and Donald Mayer, the lead strategic analyst for Martin Resorts, are soliciting your input for their CRM strategic initiative.

Martin Resorts's IT infrastructure is pieced together with various systems and applications. Currently, the company has a difficult time with CRM because its systems are not integrated. The company cannot determine vital information, such as which customers are golfing and staying at the hotel or which customers are staying at the hotel and not golfing.

For example, the three details showing that the customer Diego Titus (1) stayed four nights at a Martin Resorts–managed hotel, (2) golfed three days, and (3) took an all-day spa treatment the first day are discrete facts housed in separate systems. Martin Resorts hopes that by using data warehousing technology to integrate its data, the next time Diego reserves lodging for another trip, sales associates may ask him if he would like to book a spa treatment as well and even if he would like the same masseuse he had on his prior trip.

Martin Resorts is excited about the possibility of taking advantage of customer segmentation and CRM strategies to help increase its business.

The company wants to use CRM and data warehouse technologies to improve service and personalization at each customer touch point. Using a data warehousing tool, important customer information can be accessed from all of its systems daily, weekly, monthly, or once or twice per year. Analyze the sample data in AYK23_Data.xlsx for the following:

1. Currently, the quality of the data within the preceding disparate systems is low. Develop a report for David and Donald discussing the importance of high-quality information and how low-quality information can affect Martin Resorts's business.

2. Review the data that David and Donald are working with from the data warehouse in the AYK23_Data.xlsx data file.

   a. Give examples from the data showing the kind of information Martin Resorts might be able to use to gain a better understanding of its customers. Include the types of data quality issues the company can anticipate and the strategies it can use to help avoid such issues.

   b. Determine who Martin Resorts's best customers are and provide examples of the types of marketing campaigns the company should offer these valuable customers.

   c. Prepare a report that summarizes the benefits Martin Resorts can receive from using business intelligence to mine the data warehouse. Include a financial analysis of the costs and benefits.

   Data file: AYK23_Data.xlsx

Project 24:

Breaking Even

Mountain Cycle specializes in making custom mountain bikes. The company founder, P. J. Steffan, is having a hard time making the business profitable. Knowing that you have great business knowledge and solid financial sense, P. J. has come to you for advice.

P. J. would like you to determine how many bikes Mountain Cycle needs to sell per year to break even. Using Goal Seek in Excel, solve using the following:

- Fixed cost equals $65,000
- Variable cost equals $1,575
- Bike price equals $2,500

Project 25:

Profit Scenario

Murray Lutz owns a small shop, Lutz Motors, that sells and services vintage motorcycles. Murray is curious how his profit will be affected by his sales over the next year.

Murray would like your help creating best, worst, and most-likely scenarios for his motorcycle sales over the next year. Using Scenario Manager, help Murray analyze the information in the AYK25_Data .xlsx data file.

Data file: AYK25_Data.xlsx

Project 26:

Electronic Résumés

Résumés are the currency of the recruitment industry. They are the cornerstone of communication between candidates, recruiters, and employers. Technology is automating elements of the recruitment process, but a complete solution requires proper handling of the actual development of all the pieces and parts that comprise not just a résumé but also an erésumé. Electronic résumés, or erésumés, have moved into the mainstream of today's job market at lightning speed. Erésumés have stepped up the efficiency of job placement to such a point that you could get a call from a recruiter just hours after submitting your erésumé. With this kind of opportunity, you cannot afford to be left in the dark ages of using only a paper résumé.

In the text or HTML editor of your choice, write your erésumé as though you were putting it online and inviting prospective employers to see it. We recommend typing in all the text and then later adding the HTML tags (rather than trying to type in the tags as you go).

Use the following checklist to make sure you're covering the basics. You do not need to match it exactly; it just shows what can be done.

- Add structural tags.
- Add paragraphs and headings.
- Find an opportunity to include a list.

- Add inline styles.
- Play with the alignment of elements.
- Add appropriate font selection, font size, and color.

Project 27:
Gathering Feedback

Gathering feedback from a website's visitors can be a valuable way of assessing a site's success, and it can help build a customer or subscriber database. For example, a business could collect the addresses of people who are interested in receiving product samples, email newsletters, or notifications of special offers.

Adding form elements to a web page is simple; they are created using a set of HTML form tags that define menus, text fields, buttons, and so on. Form elements are generally used to collect information from a web page.

In the text or HTML editor of your choice, create a web page form that would collect information for a customer ordering a customized bicycle. Use proper web page design and HTML tools to understand the process and function of form elements. Be sure to pay attention to:

- Form layout and design.
- Visual elements, including labels, alignment, font selection, font size, color.
- Required versus nonrequired fields.
- Drop-down boxes, text fields, and radio buttons.

Project 28:
Daily Invoice

Foothills Animal Hospital is a full-service small animal veterinary hospital located in Morrison, Colorado, specializing in routine medical care, vaccinations, laboratory testing, and surgery. The hospital has experienced tremendous growth over the past six months due to customer referrals. Although Foothills Animal Hospital has typically kept its daily service records in a workbook format, it feels the need to expand its reporting capabilities to develop a relational database as a more functional structure.

Foothills Animal Hospital needs help developing a database, specifically to:

- Create a customer table—name, address, phone, and date of entrance.
- Create a pet table—pet name, type of animal, breed, gender, color, neutered/spayed, weight, and comments.
- Create a medications table—medication code, name of medication, and cost of medication.
- Create a visit table—details of treatments performed, medications dispensed, and date of the visit.
- Produce a daily invoice report.

Figure AYK.2 displays a sample daily invoice report that the Foothills Animal Hospital accountants have requested. Foothills Animal Hospital organizes its treatments using the codes displayed in Figure AYK.3. The entities and primary keys for the database have been identified in Figure AYK.4.

The following business rules have been identified:

1. A customer can have many pets but must have at least one.
2. A pet must be assigned to one and only one customer.
3. A pet can have one or more treatments per visit but must have at least one.
4. A pet can have one or more medications but need not have any.

Your job is to complete the following tasks:

1. Develop and describe the entity-relationship diagram.
2. Use normalization to ensure the correctness of the tables (relations).

3. Create the database by using a personal DBMS package (preferably Microsoft Access).
4. Use the data in Figure AYK.3 to populate your tables. Feel free to enter your own personal information.
5. Use the DBMS package to create the basic report in Figure AYK.2.

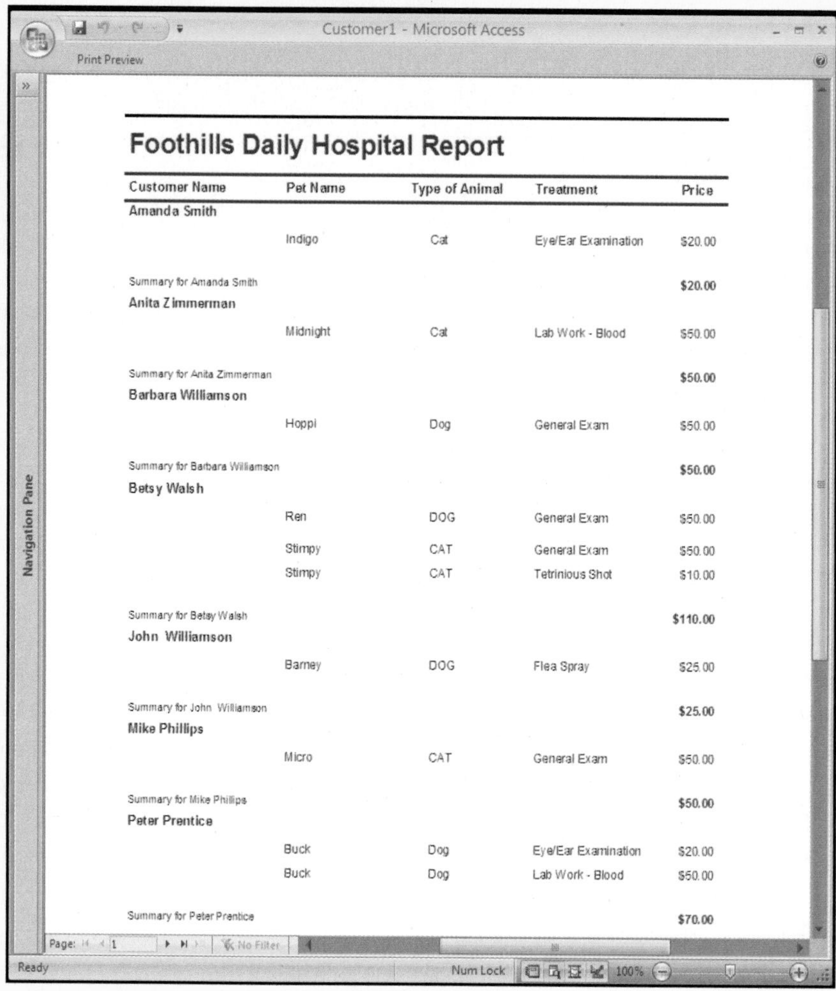

FIGURE AYK.2

Foothills Animal Hospital Daily Invoice Report

Microsoft Corporation

Treatment Code	Treatment	Price
0100	Tetrinious Shot	$10.00
0201	Rabonius Shot	$20.00
0300	General Exam	$50.00
0303	Eye/Ear Examination	$20.00
0400	Spay/Neuter	$225.00
0405	Reset Dislocation	$165.00
0406	Amputation of Limb	$450.00
0407	Wrap Affected Area	$15.00
0408	Cast Affected Area	$120.00
1000	Lab Work—Blood	$50.00
1003	Lab Work—Misc	$35.00
2003	Flea Spray	$25.00
9999	Other Not Listed	$10.00

FIGURE AYK.3

Treatment Codes, Treatments, and Price Descriptions

FIGURE AYK.4

Entity Names and Primary Keys, Foothills Animal Hospital

Entity	Primary Key
CUSTOMER	Customer Number
PET	Pet Number
VISIT	Visit Number
VISIT DETAIL	Visit Number and Line Number (a composite key)
TREATMENT	Treatment Code
MEDICATION	Medication Code

Project 29:

Billing Data

On-The-Level Construction Company is a Denver-based construction company that specializes in subcontracting the development of single-family homes. In business since 1998, On-The-Level Construction has maintained a talented pool of certified staff and independent consultants providing the flexibility and combined experience required to meet the needs of its nearly 300 completed projects in the Denver metropolitan area. The field of operation methods that On-The-Level Construction is responsible for includes structural development, heating and cooling, plumbing, and electricity.

The company charges its clients by billing the hours spent on each contract. The hourly billing rate depends on the employee's position according to the field of operations (as noted previously). Figure AYK.5 shows a basic report that On-The-Level Construction supervisors would like to see every week concerning what projects are being assigned, the overall assignment hours, and the charges for the assignment. On-The-Level Construction organizes its internal structure in four operations—Structure (500), Plumbing (501), Electrical (502), and Heating and Ventilation (503). Each of these operational departments can and should have many subcontractors who specialize in that area. On-The-Level Construction has decided to implement a relational database model to track project details according to project name, hours assigned, and charges per hour for each job description. Originally, On-The-Level Construction decided to let one of its employees handle the construction of the database. However, that employee has not had the time to implement the project completely. On-The-Level Construction has asked you to take over and complete the development of the database.

The entities and primary keys for the database have been identified in Figure AYK.6.

The following business rules have been identified:

1. A job can have many employees assigned but must have at least one.
2. An employee must be assigned to one and only one job number.
3. An employee can be assigned to work on one or more projects.
4. A project can be assigned to only one employee but need not be assigned to any employee.

Your job is to complete the following tasks:

1. Develop and describe the entity relationship diagram.
2. Use normalization to ensure the correctness of the tables (relations).
3. Create the database using a personal DBMS package (preferably Microsoft Access).
4. Use the DBMS package to create the basic report in Figure AYK.5.

ON-THE-LEVEL CONSTRUCTION PROJECT DETAIL

PROJECT NAME	ASSIGN DATE	EMPLOYEE LAST NAME	EMPLOYEE FIRST NAME	JOB DESCRIPTION	ASSIGN HOUR	CHARGE/HOUR
Chatfield						
	6/10/2029	Olenkoski	Glenn	Structure	2.1	$35.75
	6/10/2029	Sullivan	David	Electrical	1.2	$105.00
	6/10/2029	Ramora	Anne	Plumbing	2.6	$96.75
	6/11/2029	Frommer	Matt	Plumbing	1.4	$96.75
Summary of Assignment Hours and Charges					7.30	$588.08
Evergreen						
	6/10/2029	Sullivan	David	Electrical	1.8	$105.00
	6/10/2029	Jones	Anne	Heating and Ventalation	3.4	$84.50
	6/11/2029	Frommer	Matt	Plumbing	4.1	$96.75
	6/16/2029	Bavangi	Terry	Plumbing	4.1	$96.75
	6/16/2029	Newman	John	Electrical	1.7	$105.00
Summary of Assignment Hours and Charges					15.10	$1,448.15
Roxborough						
	6/10/2029	Washberg	Jeff	Plumbing	3.9	$96.75
	6/10/2029	Ramora	Anne	Plumbing	2.6	$96.75
	6/11/2029	Smithfield	William	Structure	2.4	$35.75
	6/11/2029	Bavangi	Terry	Plumbing	2.7	$96.75
	6/16/2029	Johnson	Peter	Electrical	5.2	$105.00
	6/16/2029	Joen	Denise	Plumbing	2.5	$96.75
Summary of Assignment Hours and Charges					19.30	$1,763.78

FIGURE AYK.5
On-The-Level-Construction Detail Report

Microsoft

Entity	Primary Key
PROJECT	Project Number
EMPLOYEE	Employee Number
JOB	Job Number
ASSIGNMENT	Assignment Number

FIGURE AYK.6

Entity Classes and Primary Keys for On-The-Level Construction

5. You may not be able to develop a report that looks exactly like the one in Figure AYK.5. However, your report should include the same information.
6. Complete personnel information is tracked by another database. For this application, include only the minimum: employee number, last name, and first name.
7. Information concerning all projects, employees, and jobs is not readily available. You should create information for several fictitious projects, employees, and jobs to include in your database.

Project 30:

Inventory Data

An independent retailer of mobile entertainment and wireless phones, iToys.com has built its business on offering the widest selection, expert advice, and outstanding customer service. However, iToys .com does not use a formal, consistent inventory tracking system. Periodically, an iToys.com employee visually checks to see what items are in stock. Although iToys.com does try to keep a certain level of each top seller in stock, the lack of a formal inventory tracking system has led to overstocking some items and understocking other items. On occasion, a customer will request a hot item, and it is only then that iToys.com realizes the item is out of stock. If an item is not available, iToys.com risks losing a customer to a competitor.

Lately, iToys.com has become concerned with its inventory management methods. The owner of iToys.com, Dan Connolly, wants to manage his inventory better. The company receives orders by mail, by telephone, or through its website. Regardless of how the orders are received, Dan needs a database to automate the inventory checking and ordering process.

Dan has provided you with a simplified version of the company's current system (an Excel workbook) for recording inventory and orders in an Excel spreadsheet data file, AYK30_Data.xlsx.

1. Develop an ERD diagram before you begin to create the database. You will need to use the information provided here, as well as the data given in the Excel workbook.
2. Create the database using a personal DBMS package (preferably Microsoft Access) that will track items (i.e., products), orders, order details, categories, suppliers, and shipping methods.
3. In addition to what is already mentioned, the database needs to track the inventory levels for each product, according to a reorder level and lead time.
4. At this time, Dan does not need to store information about the customer; he simply needs you to focus on the inventory structure.
5. Develop a query that will display the products that need to be ordered from their supplier. To complete this, you will want to compare a reorder level with how many units are in stock.
6. Develop several reports that display:
    a. Each product ordered by its supplier. The report should include the product name, quantity on hand, and reorder level.
    b. Each supplier ordered by shipping method.
    c. Each product that requires more than five days' lead time. (Hint: You will want to create a query for this first.)
    d. Each product ordered by category.
7. Here are some additional business rules to assist you in completing this task:
    a. An order must have at least one product but can contain more than one product.
    b. A product can have one or more orders but need not have any orders.
    c. A product must belong to one and only one category, but a category may contain many products.
    d. A product can only be stocked by one supplier, but a supplier can provide more than one product.
    e. A supplier will use one type of shipping method, but shipping methods can be used by more than one supplier.

    Data file: AYK30_Data.xlsx

Project 31:

Call Center

A manufacturing company, Teleworks, has been a market leader in the wireless telephone business for the past 10 years. Other firms have imitated its product with some degree of success, but Teleworks occupies a dominant position in the marketplace because it has a first-mover advantage with a quality product.

Recently, Teleworks began selling a new, enhanced wireless phone. This new phone does not replace its current product but offers additional features, greater durability, and better performance for a somewhat higher price. Offering this enhanced phone has established a new revenue stream for the company.

Many sales executives at Teleworks seem to subscribe to the-more-you-have, the-more-you-want theory of managing customer data. That is, they believe they can never accumulate too much information about their customers and that they can do their jobs more effectively by collecting infinite numbers of customer details. Having a firm grasp on a wide range of customer-focused details—specifically, reports summarizing call center information—can be critical in enabling your company to manage a customer relationship management (CRM) solution successfully that creates a positive impact.

To continue to provide excellent customer support, and in anticipation of increased calls due to the release of its new product, Teleworks needs a database it can use to record, track, and query call center information. Teleworks CIO Ken Davisson has hired you to develop this database.

1. Teleworks has provided you with a data file, AYK31_Data.xlsx; its current approach for recording cell center information is a spreadsheet file.
2. Develop an ERD diagram before you begin to create the database.
3. Create the database using a personal DBMS package (preferably Microsoft Access) that will allow data analysts to enter call center data according to the type of issue and the customer, assign each call to a consultant, and prioritize the call.
4. Develop a query that will display all issues that are open.
5. Develop a screen form to browse all issues.
6. Develop several reports that display:
    a. All closed issues.
    b. Each issue in detail ordered by issue ID.
    c. Each issue in detail ordered by consultant.
    d. Each issue in detail ordered by category.
    e. Each issue in detail ordered by status.
7. Here are some additional business rules to assist you in completing this task:
    a. An issue must have at least one customer.
    b. A customer can have more than one issue.
    c. Each issue must be assigned to one consultant.
    d. Each consultant can be assigned to more than one issue.
    e. An issue can only belong to one category.
    f. An issue must be assigned only one status code.
    g. An issue must be assigned a priority code.
8. Priorities are assigned accordingly:

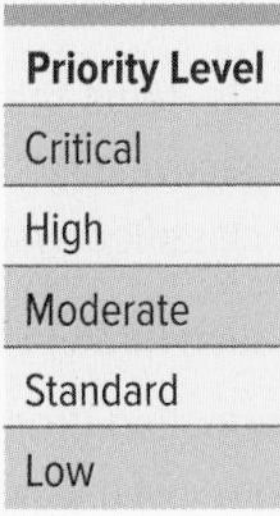

Priority Level
Critical
High
Moderate
Standard
Low

9. Status is recorded as either open or closed.
10. The categories of each issue need to be recorded as:

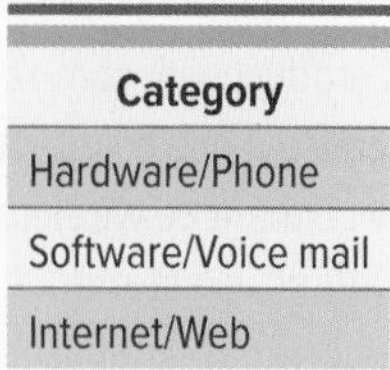

Category
Hardware/Phone
Software/Voice mail
Internet/Web

Data file: AYK31_Data.xlsx

Project 32:
Sales Pipeline

Sales drive any organization. This is true for every for-profit business, irrespective of size or industry type. If customers are not buying your goods or services, you run the risk of not having a business. This is when tough decisions have to be made, such as whether to slash budgets, lay off staff, or seek additional financing.

Unfortunately, you do not wield ultimate power over your customers' buying habits. Although you can attempt to influence buying behavior through strategic marketing, smart businesses remain one step ahead by collecting and analyzing historical and current customer information from a range of internal and external sources to forecast future sales. In other words, managing the sales pipeline is an essential ingredient of business success.

You have recently been hired by RealTime Solutions, a new company that collects information to understand, manage, and predict specific sales cycles (including the supply chain and lead times) in the automobile business. Having an accurate forecast of future sales will allow the company to increase or decrease the production cycle as required and manage personnel levels, inventory, and cash flow.

Using a personal DBMS package (preferably Microsoft Access), create a sales pipeline database that will:

1. Track opportunities from employees to customers.
   - Opportunities should have a ranking, category, source of opportunity, open date, closed date, description.
2. Create a form for inputting customer, employee, and opportunity data.
3. Create a few reports that display:
   - All open opportunities, including relevant customer and employee information.
   - Closed opportunities, including relevant customer and employee information.
   - All customers.
4. Create your own data to test the integrity of the relationships. Use approximately 10 records per table.

Project 33:
Online Classified Ads

With the emergence of the Internet as a worldwide standard for communicating information, *The Morrison Post,* a medium-sized community newspaper in central Colorado, is creating an electronic version of its paper-based classified ads.

Advertisers can place a small ad that lists items they wish to sell and provide a means (e.g., telephone number and email) by which prospective buyers can contact them.

The nature of a sale via the newspaper's classified system goes as follows:

- During the course of the sale, the information flows in different directions at different stages.
- First, there is a downstream flow of information (from seller to buyer): the listing in print in the newspaper. (Thus, the classified ad listing is just a way of bringing a buyer and seller together.)

- When a potential purchaser's interest has been raised, that interest must be relayed upstream, usually by telephone or by email.
- Finally, a meeting should result that uses face-to-face negotiation to finalize the sale if the sale can be agreed on.

By placing the entire system on the Internet, the upstream and downstream communications are accomplished using a web browser. The sale becomes more of an auction because many potential buyers, all with equal status, can bid for the same item, so it is fairer for all purchasers and gets a better deal for the seller.

Any user who is trying to buy an item can:

- View items for sale.
- Bid on an item he or she wishes to purchase.

Any user who is trying to sell an item can:

- Place a new item for sale.
- Browse a list of the items that he or she is trying to sell, and examine the bids that have been made on each of those items.
- Accept a bid on an item that he or she is selling.

Your job is to complete the following:

1. Develop and describe the entity-relationship diagram for the database that will support the listed activities.
2. Use normalization to ensure the correctness of the tables.
3. Create the database by using a personal DBMS package.
4. Use Figure AYK.7 as a baseline for your database design.

Data file: AYK33_Data.xlsx

FIGURE AYK.7

Source: *The Morrison Post*

The Morrison Post Classified Section
New User Registration

In order to bid on existing "for-sale" items, or sell your own items, you need to register first. Once you have done that, you will have full access to the system.

EMail Address:
First Name:
Last Name:
Address:
City:
State:
Postal Code:
Country:
Password:
Verify Password:

Submit Reset

3D printing (additive manufacturing) A process that builds—layer by layer in an additive process—a three-dimensional solid object from a digital model.

4D printing Additive manufacturing that prints objects capable of transformation and self-assembly.

5G The fifth-generation wireless broadband technology based on the 802.11ac standard engineered to greatly increase the speed and responsiveness of wireless networks.

A

accelerometer A device that can measure the force of acceleration, whether caused by gravity or by movement.

acceptable use policy (AUP) A policy that a user must agree to follow to be provided access to corporate email, information systems, and the Internet.

access point (AP) The computer or network device that serves as an interface between devices and the network.

accessibility Refers to the varying levels that define what a user can access, view, or perform when operating a system.

accounting and finance ERP component Manages accounting data and financial processes within the enterprise with functions such as general ledger, accounts payable, accounts receivable, budgeting, and asset management.

actor An entity that is capable of participating in an action or a network.

adaptive computer devices Input devices designed for special applications for use by people with different types of special needs.

administrator access Unrestricted access to the entire system.

adware Software that, while purporting to serve some useful function and often fulfilling that function, also allows Internet advertisers to display advertisements without the consent of the computer user.

AdWords Keywords that advertisers choose to pay for and appear as sponsored links on the Google results pages.

affiliate program Allows a business to generate commissions or referral fees when a customer visiting its website clicks a link to another merchant's website.

affinity bias A tendency to connect with, hire, and promote those with similar interests, experiences, or backgrounds.

affinity grouping analysis Reveals the relationship between variables along with the nature and frequency of the relationships.

agile BI An approach to business intelligence (BI) that incorporates agile software development methodologies to accelerate and improve the outcomes of BI initiatives.

agile methodology Aims for customer satisfaction through early and continuous delivery of useful software components developed by an iterative process using the bare minimum requirements.

agile MIS infrastructure Includes the hardware, software, and telecommunications equipment that, when combined, provide the underlying foundation to support the organization's goals.

algorithm Mathematical formula placed in software that performs an analysis on a dataset.

ambient digital experience A blend of the physical, virtual, and electronic environments creating a real-time ambient environment that changes as the user moves from one place to another.

analysis latency The time from which data are made available to the time when analysis is complete.

analysis paralysis Occurs when the user goes into an emotional state of overanalyzing (or overthinking) a situation so that a decision or action is never taken, in effect paralyzing the outcome.

analysis phase The firm analyzes its end-user business requirements and refines project goals into defined functions and operations of the intended system.

analytical CRM Supports back-office operations and strategic analysis and includes all systems that do not deal directly with the customers.

analytical information Encompasses all organizational information, and its primary purpose is to support the performance of managerial analysis or semistructured decisions.

analytics The science of fact-based decision making.

anti-spam policy Simply states that email users will not send unsolicited emails (or spam).

antivirus software Scans and searches hard drives to prevent, detect, and remove known viruses, adware, and spyware.

appliance A computer dedicated to a single function, such as a calculator or computer game.

application integration The integration of a company's existing management information systems with each other.

application service provider license Specialty software paid for on a license basis or per-use basis or usage-based licensing.

application software Used for specific information processing needs, including payroll, customer relationship management, project management, training, and many others.

arithmetic-logic unit (ALU) Performs all arithmetic operations (for example, addition and subtraction) and all logic operations (such as sorting and comparing numbers).

artificial intelligence (AI) Simulates human thinking and behavior such as the ability to reason and learn.

As-Is process model Represents the current state of the operation that has been mapped, without any specific improvements or changes to existing processes.

asset tracking Occurs when a company places active or semipassive RFID tags on expensive products or assets to gather data on the items' location with little or no manual intervention.

astroturfing The practice of artificially stimulating online conversation and positive reviews about a product, service, or brand.

asynchronous communication Communication such as email in which the message and the response do not occur at the same time.

attenuation Represents the loss of a network signal strength measured in decibels (dBs) and occurs because the transmissions gradually dissipate in strength over longer distances or because of radio interference or physical obstructions such as walls.

attributes The data elements associated with an entity.

augmented reality View of the physical world with computer-generated layers of information added to it.

authentication A method for confirming users' identities.

authorization The process of providing a user with permission, including access levels and abilities such as file access, hours of access, and amount of allocated storage space.

automatic vehicle location (AVL) Uses GPS tracking to track vehicles.

automation Involves computerizing manual tasks, making them more efficient and effective and dramatically lowering operational costs.

autonomic computing A self-managing computing model named after, and patterned on, the human body's autonomic nervous system.

autonomous agent Software that carries out some set of operations on behalf of a user or another program with some degree of independence or autonomy and employs some knowledge or representation of the user's goals or desires.

autonomous robotics A robot capable of making its own decisions and performing an action accordingly.

availability Refers to the time frames when the system is operational.

B

backup An exact copy of a system's information.

backward integration Sends information entered into a given system automatically to all upstream systems and processes.

bad actor An entity that is participating with ill intentions.

bandwidth The maximum amount of data that can pass from one point to another in a unit of time.

bar chart A chart or graph that presents grouped data with rectangular bars with lengths proportional to the values that they represent.

benchmark Baseline values the system seeks to attain.

benchmarking A process of continuously measuring system results, comparing those results to optimal system performance (benchmark values), and identifying steps and procedures to improve system performance.

best practices The most successful solutions or problem-solving methods that have been developed by a specific organization or industry.

bias A disproportionate weight in favor of or against an idea or thing, usually in a way that is closed-minded, prejudicial, or unfair.

big data A collection of large, complex datasets, which cannot be analyzed using traditional database methods and tools.

Big Data as a Service (BDaaS) Offers a cloud-based big data service to help organizations analyze massive amounts of data to solve business dilemmas.

biological 3D printing Includes the printing of skin and organs and is progressing from theory to reality; however, politicians and the public do not have a full understanding of the implications.

biometrics The identification of a user based on a physical characteristic, such as a fingerprint, iris, face, voice, or handwriting.

bit The smallest element of data. It has a value of either 0 or 1.

bit rate (or data rate) The number of bits transferred or received per unit of time.

Bitcoin A type of digital currency in which a record of transactions is maintained and new units of currency are generated by the computational solution of mathematical problems, and which operates independently of a central bank.

black box algorithm A decision-making process that cannot be easily understood or explained by the computer or the researcher.

black-hat hacker Breaks into other people's computer systems and may just look around or may steal and destroy information.

blockchain A type of distributed ledger, consisting of blocks of data that maintain a permanent and tamper-proof record of transactional data.

blocks Data structure containing a hash, previous hash, and data.

blog, or web log An online journal that allows users to post their own comments, graphics, and video.

Bluetooth Wireless PAN technology that transmits signals over short distances between cell phones, computers, and other devices.

botnets Malware that causes a collection of connected devices to be controlled by a hacker.

bottleneck Occurs when resources reach full capacity and cannot handle any additional demands; it limits throughput and impedes operations.

brainstorming A technique for generating ideas by encouraging participants to offer as many ideas as possible in a short period of time without any analysis until all the ideas have been exhausted.

bring your own device (BYOD) Policy allowing employees to use their personal mobile devices and computers to access enterprise data and applications.

broadband A high-speed Internet connection that is always connected.

broadband over power line (BPL) Technology that makes possible high-speed Internet access over ordinary residential electrical lines and offers an alternative to DSL or high-speed cable modems.

bug bounty program A crowdsourcing initiative that rewards individuals for discovering and reporting software bugs.

bugs Defects in the code of an information system.

bullwhip effect Occurs when distorted product-demand information ripples from one partner to the next throughout the supply chain.

business analytics The scientific process of transforming data into insight for making better decisions.

business continuity planning (BCP) Details how a company recovers and restores critical business operations and systems after a disaster or extended disruption.

business impact analysis A process that identifies all critical business functions and the effect that a specific disaster may have on them.

business intelligence (BI) Information collected from multiple sources such as suppliers, customers, competitors, partners, and industries that analyze patterns, trends, and relationships for strategic decision making.

business intelligence dashboards Track corporate metrics such as critical success factors and key performance indicators and include advanced capabilities such as interactive controls, allowing users to manipulate data for analysis.

business model A plan that details how a company creates, delivers, and generates revenues.

business process Standardized set of activities that accomplish a specific task.

business process improvement Attempts to understand and measure the current process and make performance improvements accordingly.

business process model A graphical description of a process, showing the sequence of process tasks, which is developed for a specific purpose and from a selected viewpoint.

Business Process Model and Notation (BPMN) A graphical notation that depicts the steps in a business process.

business process modeling (or mapping) The activity of creating a detailed flowchart or process map of a work process that shows its inputs, tasks, and activities in a structured sequence.

business process patent A patent that protects a specific set of procedures for conducting a particular business activity.

business process reengineering (BPR) The analysis and redesign of workflow within and between enterprises.

business requirement The specific business requests the system must meet to be successful.

business rule Defines how a company performs a certain aspect of its business and typically results in either a yes/no or true/false answer.

business strategy A leadership plan that achieves a specific set of goals or objectives.

business unit A segment of a company (such as accounting, production, marketing) representing a specific business function.

business-critical integrity constraint Enforces business rules vital to an organization's success and often requires more insight and knowledge than relational integrity constraints.

business-facing processes Invisible to the external customer but essential to the effective management of the business; they include goal setting, day-to-day planning, giving performance feedback and rewards, and allocating resources.

business-to-business (B2B) Applies to businesses buying from and selling to each other over the Internet.

business-to-consumer (B2C) Applies to any business that sells its products or services directly to consumers online.

buyer power One of Porter's five forces; measures the ability of buyers to directly affect the price they are willing to pay for an item.

C

cable modem (or broadband modem) A type of digital modem used with high-speed cable Internet service.

cache memory A small unit of ultra-fast memory that is used to store recently accessed or frequently accessed data so that the CPU does not have to retrieve this data from slower memory circuits such as RAM.

call scripting system Gathers product details and issue resolution information that can be automatically generated into a script for the representative to read to the customer.

campaign management system Guides users through marketing campaigns by performing such tasks as campaign definition, planning, scheduling, segmentation, and success analysis.

capacity Represents the maximum throughput a system can deliver; for example, the capacity of a hard drive represents the size or volume.

capacity planning Determines future environmental infrastructure requirements to ensure high-quality system performance.

carbon emissions Includes the carbon dioxide and carbon monoxide in the atmosphere produced by business processes and systems.

cardinality Expresses the specific number of instances in an entity.

cartography The science and art of making an illustrated map or chart.

central processing unit (CPU) (or microprocessor) The actual hardware that interprets and executes the program (software) instructions and coordinates how all the other hardware devices work together.

certificate authority A trusted third party, such as VeriSign, that validates user identities by means of digital certificates.

change agent A person or event that is the catalyst for implementing major changes for a system to meet business changes.

chatbot An artificial intelligence (AI) program that simulates interactive human conversation by using key precalculated user phrases and auditory or text-based signals.

chief automation officer Determines if a person or business process can be replaced by a robot or software.

chief data officer (CDO) Responsible for determining the types of information the enterprise will capture, retain, analyze, and share.

chief information officer (CIO) Responsible for (1) overseeing all uses of MIS and (2) ensuring that MIS strategically aligns with business goals and objectives.

chief intellectual property officer Manages and defends intellectual property, copyrights, and patents.

chief knowledge officer (CKO) Responsible for collecting, maintaining, and distributing company knowledge.

chief privacy officer (CPO) Responsible for ensuring the ethical and legal use of information within a company.

chief security officer (CSO) Responsible for ensuring the security of MIS systems and developing strategies and MIS safeguards against attacks from hackers and viruses.

chief sustainability officer Oversees the corporation's "environmental" programs such as helping adapt to climate change and reduce carbon emissions.

chief technology officer (CTO) Responsible for ensuring the speed, accuracy, availability, and reliability for an organization's information technology.

chief user experience officer Creates the optimal relationship between user and technology.

Child Online Protection Act (COPA) A law that protects minors from accessing inappropriate material on the Internet.

classification analysis The process of organizing data into categories or groups for its most effective and efficient use.

clean computing Refers to the environmentally responsible use, manufacture, and disposal of technology products and computer equipment.

click-fraud The practice of artificially inflating traffic statistics for online advertisements.

clickstream The exact path a visitor takes through a website including the pattern of a consumer's navigation.

clickstream analytics The process of collecting, analyzing, and reporting aggregate data about which pages a website visitor visits—and in what order.

click-thru A count of the number of people who visit one site and click an advertisement that takes them to the site of the advertiser.

click-to-talk Allows customers to click a button and talk with a representative via the Internet.

client A computer designed to request information from a server.

client/server network A model for applications in which the bulk of the back-end processing, such as performing a physical search of a database, takes place on a server, whereas the front-end processing, which involves communicating with the users, is handled by the clients.

closed source Any proprietary software licensed under exclusive legal right of the copyright holder.

cloud computing Stores, manages, and processes data and applications over the Internet rather than on a personal computer or server.

cluster analysis A technique used to divide an information set into mutually exclusive groups such that the members of each group are as close together as possible to one another and the different groups are as far apart as possible.

coaxial cable Cable that can carry a wide range of frequencies with low signal loss.

coders Coders are the people who write the programs that operate computers.

cold site A separate facility that does not have any computer equipment but is a place where employees can move after a disaster.

collaboration system A set of tools that support the work of teams or groups by facilitating the sharing and flow of information.

collective intelligence Collaborating and tapping into the core knowledge of all employees, partners, and customers.

common data repository Allows every department of a company to store and retrieve information in real time, allowing information to be more reliable and accessible.

communication device Equipment used to send information and receive it from one location to another.

communication plan Defines the how, what, when, and who regarding the flow of project information to stakeholders and is key for managing expectations.

community cloud Serves a specific community with common business models, security requirements, and compliance considerations.

comparative analysis Can compare two or more datasets to identify patterns and trends.

competitive advantage A feature of a product or service on which customers place a greater value than on similar offerings from competitors.

competitive click-fraud A computer crime in which a competitor or disgruntled employee increases a company's search advertising costs by repeatedly clicking the advertiser's link.

competitive intelligence The process of gathering information about the competitive environment, including competitors' plans, activities, and products, to improve a company's ability to succeed.

competitive monitoring Occurs when a company keeps tabs of its competitors' activities on the web using software that automatically tracks all competitor website activities such as discounts and new products.

complex instruction set computer (CISC) chip Type of CPU that can recognize as many as 100 or more instructions, enough to carry out most computations directly.

composite entity Entity that exists to represent the relationship between two other entities.

computer An electronic device operating under the control of instructions stored in its own memory that can accept, manipulate, and store data.

computer simulation Complex systems, such as the U.S. economy, can be modeled by means of mathematical equations, and different scenarios can be run against the model to conduct "what-if" analysis.

computer-aided design (CAD) Software used by architects, engineers, drafters, artists, and others to create precision drawings or technical illustrations.

computer-aided manufacturing (CAM) Uses software and machinery to facilitate and automate manufacturing processes.

computer-aided software engineering (CASE) Software tools that provide automated support for the development of the system.

confirmation bias Actively looking for evidence that backs up preconceived ideas about someone.

conformity bias Acting similarly, or conforming to those around you, regardless of your own views.

consumer-to-business (C2B) Applies to any consumer who sells a product or service to a business on the Internet.

consumer-to-consumer (C2C) Applies to customers offering goods and services to each other on the Internet.

contact center or call center Where customer service representatives answer customer inquiries and solve problems, usually by email, chat, or phone.

contact management CRM system Maintains customer contact information and identifies prospective customers for future sales, using tools such as organizational charts, detailed customer notes, and supplemental sales information.

containerization Isolates corporate applications from personal applications on a device.

content filtering Occurs when organizations use software that filters content, such as emails, to prevent the accidental or malicious transmission of unauthorized information.

content management system (CMS) Helps companies manage the creation, storage, editing, and publication of their website content.

control panel A Windows feature that provides a group of options that sets default values for the Windows operating system.

control unit Interprets software instructions and literally tells the other hardware devices what to do, based on the software instructions.

conversion The process of transferring information from a legacy system to a new system.

cookie A small file deposited on a hard drive by a website, containing information about customers and their browsing activities.

core ERP components The traditional components that are included in most ERP systems and primarily focus on internal operations.

core processes Business processes, such as manufacturing goods, selling products, and providing service, that make up the primary activities in a value chain.

corporate social responsibility Companies' acknowledged responsibility to society.

corrective maintenance Makes system changes to repair design flaws, coding errors, or implementation issues.

countermeasure An action, process, device, or system that can prevent, or mitigate, the effects of and threats to a computer, server, or network.

course management software Contains course information such as a syllabus and assignments and offers drop boxes for quizzes and homework, along with a grade book.

cracker A hacker with criminal intent.

cradle to grave Provides logistics support throughout the entire system or life of the product.

critical path The series of activities that determine the earliest time by which the project can be completed.

critical path analysis A project diagramming method used to predict total project duration.

critical success factors (CSFs) Crucial steps companies perform to achieve their goals and objectives and implement their strategies.

CRM analysis technologies Help organizations segment their customers into categories such as best and worst customers.

CRM predicting technologies Help organizations predict customer behavior, such as which customers are at risk of leaving.

CRM reporting technologies Help organizations identify their customers across other applications.

cross-selling Selling additional products or services to an existing customer.

crowdfunding Sources capital for a project by raising many small amounts from a large number of individuals, typically via the Internet.

crowdsourcing Refers to the wisdom of the crowd.

cryptography The science that studies encryption, which is the hiding of messages so that only the sender and receiver can read them.

customer analytics Involves gathering, classifying, comparing, and studying customer data to identify buying trends, at-risk customers, and potential future opportunities.

customer lifetime value (CLV) A metric that represents the total net profit a company makes from any given customer.

customer profitability (CP) Measures the customer's worth over a specific period of time.

customer relationship management (CRM) A means of managing all aspects of a customer's relationship with an organization to increase customer loyalty and retention and an organization's profitability.

customer segmentation Divides a market into categories that share similar attributes such as age, location, gender, habits, and so on.

customer service and support (CSS) A part of operational CRM that automates service requests, complaints, product returns, and information requests.

customer-facing process Results in a product or service that is received by an organization's external customer.

cyberattack Malicious attempts to access or damage a computer system.

cyberbullying Threats, negative remarks, or defamatory comments transmitted via the Internet or posted on a website.

cyberespionage Includes governments that are after some form of information about other governments.

cybersecurity Involves prevention, detection, and response to cyberattacks that can have wide-ranging effects on the individual, organizations, community, and at the national level.

Cybersecurity and Infrastructure Security Agency (CISA) Builds the national capacity to defend against cyberattacks and works with the federal government to provide cybersecurity tools, incident response services, and assessment capabilities to safeguard the ".gov" networks that support the essential operations of partner departments and agencies.

cyberterrorism The use of computer and networking technologies against persons or property to intimidate or coerce governments, individuals, or any segment of society to attain political, religious, or ideological goals.

cyberterrorists Seek to cause harm to people or to destroy critical systems or information and use the Internet as a weapon of mass destruction.

cybervandalism The electronic defacement of an existing website.

cybervigilantes Include individuals that seek notoriety or want to make a social or political point such as WikiLeaks.

cyberwar An organized attempt by a country's military to disrupt or destroy information and communication systems of another country.

cyborg anthropologist An individual who studies the interaction between humans and technology, observing how technology can shape humans' lives.

D

dark web The portion of the Internet that is intentionally hidden from search engines, uses masked IP addresses, and is accessible only with a special web browser; part of the deep web.

data Raw facts that describe the characteristics of an event or object.

data aggregation The collection of data from various sources for the purpose of data processing.

data analyst Collects, queries, and consumes organizational data to uncover patterns and provide insights for strategic business decision making.

data artist A business analytics specialist who uses visual tools to help people understand complex data.

Data as a Service (DaaS) Facilitates the accessibility of business-critical data in a timely, secure, and affordable manner.

data at rest Refers to all data in computer storage.

data augmentation Occurs when adding additional training examples by transforming existing examples.

data center A facility used to house management information systems and associated components, such as telecommunications and storage systems.

data cleansing or scrubbing A process that weeds out and fixes or discards inconsistent, incorrect, or incomplete data.

data cube The common term for the representation of multidimensional information.

data democratization The ability for information in a digital format to be accessible to the average end user.

data dictionary Compiles all of the metadata about the data elements in the data model.

data element (or data field) The smallest or basic unit of data.

data flow diagram (DFD) Illustrates the movement of information between external entities and the processes and data stores within the system.

data governance Refers to the overall management of the availability, usability, integrity, and security of company data.

data granularity The extent of detail within the data (fine and detailed or coarse and abstract).

data in motion A stream of data that is moving or being transported between locations within or between computer systems.

data in use Data that is currently being updated, processed, erased, accessed, or read by a system.

data inconsistency Occurs when the same data element has different values.

data integration The integration of data from multiple sources, which provides a unified view of all data.

data integrity A measure of the quality of data.

data integrity issue Occurs when a system produces incorrect, inconsistent, or duplicate data.

data lake A storage repository that holds a vast amount of raw data in its original format until the business needs it.

data latency The time duration to make data ready for analysis (i.e., the time for extracting, transforming, and cleansing the data) and loading the data into the database.

data mart Contains a subset of data warehouse data.

data mining The process of analyzing data to extract information not offered by the raw data alone.

data mining tool Uses a variety of techniques to find patterns and relationships in large volumes of information that predict future behavior and guide decision making.

data model Logical data structure that details the relationships among data elements using graphics or pictures.

data point An individual item on a graph or a chart.

data profiling The process of collecting statistics and information about data in an existing source.

data quality audit Determines the accuracy and completeness of its data.

data redundancy The duplication of data, or the storage of the same data in multiple places.

data replication The process of sharing information to ensure consistency between multiple data sources.

data scientist Extracts knowledge from data by performing statistical analysis, data mining, and advanced analytics on big data to identify trends, market changes, and other relevant information.

data scraping The process of extracting large amounts of data from a website and saving it to a spreadsheet or computer.

data silo Occurs when one business unit is unable to freely communicate with other business units, making it difficult or impossible for organizations to work cross-functionally.

data steward Responsible for ensuring the policies and procedures are implemented across the organization and acts as a liaison between the MIS department and the business.

data stewardship The management and oversight of an organization's data assets to help provide business users with high-quality data that is easily accessible in a consistent manner.

data visualization Describes technologies that allow users to "see" or visualize data to transform information into a business perspective.

data visualization tools Move beyond Excel graphs and charts into sophisticated analysis techniques such as pie charts, controls, instruments, maps, time-series graphs, etc.

data warehouse A logical collection of data, gathered from many operational databases, that supports business analysis activities and decision-making tasks.

database Maintains information about various types of objects (inventory), events (transactions), people (employees), and places (warehouses).

database management system (DBMS) Creates, reads, updates, and deletes data in a database while controlling access and security.

dataset An organized collection of data.

decision latency The time it takes a human to comprehend the analytic result and determine an appropriate action.

decision support system (DSS) Model information using OLAP, which provides assistance in evaluating and choosing among different courses of action.

decrypt Decodes information and is the opposite of encrypt.

deep learning A process that employs specialized algorithms to model and study complex datasets; the method is also used to establish relationships among data and datasets.

deep web The large part of the Internet that is inaccessible to conventional search engines.

dependency A logical relationship that exists between the project tasks or between a project task and a milestone.

descriptive analytics Analytical techniques that describe past performance and history.

design phase Establishes descriptions of the desired features and operations of the system including screen layouts, business rules, process diagrams, pseudocode, and other documentation.

destructive agents Malicious agents designed by spammers and other Internet attackers to farm email addresses off websites or deposit spyware on machines.

development phase Transforms all the detailed design documents from the design phase into the actual system.

diagnostic analytics Examines data or content to answer the question, "Why did it happen?"

digital certificate A data file that identifies individuals or organizations online and is comparable to a digital signature.

digital Darwinism Implies that organizations that cannot adapt to the new demands placed on them for surviving in the information age are doomed to extinction.

digital dashboard Tracks KPIs and CSFs by compiling information from multiple sources and tailoring it to meet user needs.

digital divide A worldwide gap giving advantage to those with access to technology.

digital subscriber line (DSL) Provides high-speed digital data transmission over standard telephone lines using broadband modem technology, allowing both Internet and telephone services to work over the same phone lines.

digital supply chain Fully capitalize on connectivity, system integration, and the information-producing capabilities of smart devices.

digital trust Measure of consumer, partner, and employee confidence in an organization's ability to protect and secure data and the privacy of individuals.

digital value chain Digitizes work across primary and supporting activities.

digitization The automation of existing manual and paper-based processes and workflows to a digital format.

direct-to-consumer (DTC) An ebusiness model where companies build, market, sell, and ship their products themselves, without relying on traditional stores or intermediaries.

dirty data Erroneous or flawed data.

Disaster Recovery as a Service (DRaaS) Offers backup services that use cloud resources to protect applications and data from disruption caused by disaster.

disaster recovery cost curve Charts (1) the cost to the company of the unavailability of information and technology and (2) the cost to the company of recovering from a disaster over time.

disaster recovery plan A detailed process for recovering information or a system in the event of a catastrophic disaster.

disinformation Refers to false information that is presented as fact with an intent to deceive and mislead.

disintermediation Occurs when a business sells direct to the customer online and cuts out the intermediary.

disruptive technology A new way of doing things that initially does not meet the needs of existing customers.

distributed computing Processes and manages algorithms across many machines in a computing environment.

domain name system (DNS) Converts IP address into domains, or identifying labels that use a variety of recognizable naming conventions.

dot-com The original term for a company operating on the Internet.

downtime Refers to a period of time when a system is unavailable.

drive-by hacking A computer attack by which an attacker accesses a wireless computer network, intercepts data, uses network services, and/or sends attack instructions without entering the office or organization that owns the network.

drone An unmanned aircraft that can fly autonomously, or without a human. Amazon.com is piloting drone aircraft for package deliveries.

dual boot Provides the user with the option of choosing the operating system when the computer is turned on.

dual persona technology Creates two completely separate user interfaces on the same device, one for work and one for personal use.

dumpster diving Looking through people's trash; another way hackers obtain information.

dynamic host configuration protocol (DHCP) Allows dynamic IP address allocation so users do not need a preconfigured IP address to use the network.

dynamic process A continuously changing process used to provide business solutions to ever-changing business operations.

dynamic report A report that changes automatically during creation.

dynamic scaling Means that the MIS infrastructure can be automatically scaled up or down based on needed requirements.

E

ebook An electronic book that can be read on a computer or special reading device.

ebusiness Includes ecommerce along with all activities related to internal and external business operations such as servicing customer accounts, collaborating with partners, and exchanging real-time information.

ebusiness model A plan that details how a company creates, delivers, and generates revenues on the Internet.

ecommerce The buying and selling of goods and services over the Internet.

ediscovery (or electronic discovery) Refers to the ability of a company to identify, search, gather, seize, or export digital information in responding to a litigation, audit, investigation, or information inquiry.

effectiveness MIS metrics Measure the impact MIS has on business processes and activities, including customer satisfaction and customer conversion rates.

efficiency MIS metrics Measure the performance of MIS itself, such as throughput, transaction speed, and system availability.

electronic data interchange (EDI) A standard format for the electronic exchange of information between supply chain participants.

email privacy policy Details the extent to which email messages may be read by others.

embedded operating system Used for a single purpose in computer appliances and special-purpose applications, such as an automobile, ATM, or media player.

emergency A sudden, unexpected event requiring immediate action due to potential threats to health and safety, the environment, or property.

emergency notification service An infrastructure built for notifying people in the event of an emergency.

emergency preparedness Ensures that a company is ready to respond to an emergency in an organized, timely, and effective manner.

employee monitoring policy States explicitly how, when, and where the company monitors its employees.

encryption Scrambles information into an alternative form that requires a key or password to decrypt.

energy consumption The amount of energy consumed by business processes and systems.

enterprise application integration (EAI) Connects the plans, methods, and tools aimed at integrating separate enterprise systems.

enterprise architect A person grounded in technology, fluent in business, and able to provide the important bridge between MIS and the business.

enterprise mobility management (EMM) An enterprisewide security strategy to enforce corporate epolicies while enabling employee use of mobile devices such as smart phones and tablets.

enterprise resource planning (ERP) Integrates all departments and functions throughout an organization into a single MIS system (or integrated set of MIS systems) so employees can make decisions by viewing enterprisewide information about all business operations.

enterprise system Provides enterprisewide support and data access for a firm's operations and business processes.

entity Stores information about a person, place, thing, transaction, or event.

entity-relationship diagram (ERD) A technique for documenting the entities and relationships in a database environment.

entry barrier A feature of a product or service that customers have come to expect and which entering competitors must offer to survive.

epolicies Policies and procedures that address information management, along with the ethical use of computers and the Internet in the business environment.

estimated time en route (ETE) The time remaining before reaching a destination using the present speed; typically used for navigation applications.

estimated time of arrival (ETA) The time of day of an expected arrival at a certain destination; typically used for navigation applications.

estimation analysis Determines values for an unknown continuous variable behavior or estimated future value.

Ethereum A decentralized, open-source blockchain with smart contract functionality.

ethernet A physical and data layer technology for LAN networking.

ethical computer use policy Contains general principles to guide computer user behavior.

ethics The principles and standards that guide our behavior toward other people.

ewaste Refers to discarded, obsolete, or broken electronic devices.

executive information system (EIS) A specialized DSS that supports senior-level executives and unstructured, long-term, nonroutine decisions requiring judgment, evaluation, and insight.

executive sponsor The person or group who provides the financial resources for the project.

expert system Computerized advisory programs that imitate the reasoning processes of experts in solving difficult problems.

explicit knowledge Consists of anything that can be documented, archived, and codified, often with the help of MIS.

extended ERP components The extra components that meet organizational needs not covered by the core components and primarily focus on external operations.

extraction, transformation, and loading (ETL) A process that extracts data from internal and external databases, transforms it using a common set of enterprise definitions, and loads it into a data warehouse.

extranet An extension of an intranet that is only available to authorized outsiders, such as customers, partners, and suppliers.

extreme programming (XP) methodology Breaks a project into four phases, and developers cannot continue to the next phase until the previous phase is complete.

F

fact The confirmation or validation of an event or object.

failback Occurs when the primary machine recovers and resumes operations, taking over from the secondary server.

failover A specific type of fault tolerance, occurs when a redundant storage server offers an exact replica of the real-time data, and if the primary server crashes, the users are automatically directed to the secondary server or backup server.

fair information practices (FIPs) A general term for a set of standards governing the collection and use of personal data and addressing issues of privacy and accuracy.

fake news Refers to false stories that appear to be news, spread on the Internet or using other media, usually created to influence political views or as a joke.

fast data The application of big data analytics to smaller datasets in near real or real time in order to solve a problem or create business value.

fault tolerance A general concept that a system has the ability to respond to unexpected failures or system crashes as the backup system immediately and automatically takes over with no loss of service.

feasibility The measure of the tangible and intangible benefits of an information system.

feedback Information that returns to its original transmitter (input, transform, or output) and modifies the transmitter's actions.

fiber optic (or optical fiber) Refers to the technology associated with the transmission of information as light impulses along a glass wire or fiber.

field A characteristic of a table.

file transfer protocol (FTP) A simple network protocol that allows the transfer of files between two computers on the Internet.

firewall Hardware and/or software that guard a private network by analyzing incoming and outgoing information for the correct markings.

first call resolution (FCR) Properly addressing the customer's need the first time they call, thereby eliminating the need for customers to follow up with a second call.

first-mover advantage An advantage that occurs when a company can significantly increase its market share by being first to market with a competitive advantage.

flash memory A special type of rewritable read-only memory (ROM) that is compact and portable.

folksonomy Similar to taxonomy except that crowdsourcing determines the tags or keyword-based classification system.

forecasting model Predictions based on time-series information allowing users to manipulate the time series for forecasting activities.

foreign key A primary key of one table that appears as an attribute in another table and acts to provide a logical relationship between the two tables.

forward integration Sends information entered in a given system automatically to all downstream systems and processes.

fourth-generation languages (4GLs) Programming languages that look similar to human languages.

fuzzy logic A mathematical method of handling imprecise or subjective information.

G

Gantt chart A simple bar chart that lists project tasks vertically against the project's time frame, listed horizontally.

General Data Protection Regulation (GDPR) A legal framework that sets guidelines for the collection and processing of personal information of individuals within the European Union (EU).

genesis block The first block created in the blockchain.

genetic algorithm An artificial intelligence system that mimics the evolutionary, survival-of-the-fittest process to generate increasingly better solutions to a problem.

geocache A GPS technology adventure game that posts on the Internet the longitude and latitude location of an item for users to find.

geocoding A coding process in spatial databases that assigns a digital map feature an attribute that serves as a unique ID (tract number, node number) or classification (soil type, zoning category).

geocoin A round coin-sized object that is uniquely numbered and hidden in geocache.

geographic information system (GIS) Stores, views, and analyzes geographic data, creating multidimensional charts or maps.

gigabyte (GB) Roughly 1 billion bytes.

gigahertz (GHz) The number of billions of CPU cycles per second.

GIS map automation Links business assets to a centralized system where they can be tracked and monitored over time.

global positioning system (GPS) A satellite-based navigation system providing extremely accurate position, time, and speed information.

goods Material items or products that customers will buy to satisfy a want or need. Clothing, groceries, cell phones, and cars are all examples of goods that people buy to fulfill their needs.

granularity Refers to the level of detail in the model or the decision-making process.

green personal computer (green PC) A computer built using environmentally friendly materials and designed to save energy.

grid computing A collection of computers, often geographically dispersed, that are coordinated to solve a common problem.

H

hackers Experts in technology who use their knowledge to break into computers and computer networks, either for profit or motivated by the challenge.

hactivists Have philosophical and political reasons for breaking into systems and will often deface the website as a protest.

hard drive A secondary storage medium that uses several rigid disks coated with a magnetically sensitive material and housed together with the recording heads in a hermetically sealed mechanism.

hardware Consists of the physical devices associated with a computer system.

hash A function that converts an input of letters and numbers into an encrypted output of a fixed length.

hashtag A keyword or phrase used to identify a topic and preceded by a hash or pound sign (#).

heat map A two-dimensional representation of data in which values are represented by colors.

help desk A group of people who respond to users' questions.

high availability Occurs when a system is continuously operational at all times.

high-speed Internet cable connection Provides Internet access by using a cable television company's infrastructure and a special cable modem.

HIPAA Security Rule Ensures national standards for securing patient data that is stored or transferred electronically.

histogram A graphical display of data using bars of different heights.

historical analysis Historical events are studied to anticipate the outcome of current developments.

hitbots Create the illusion that a large number of potential customers are clicking the advertiser's links, when in fact there is no likelihood that any of the clicks will lead to profit for the advertiser.

horizontal privilege escalation Attackers grant themselves the same access levels they already have but assume the identity of another user.

hot site A separate and fully equipped facility where the company can move immediately after a disaster and resume business.

hotspot Designated location where Wi-Fi access points are publicly available.

human resources ERP component Tracks employee information, including payroll, benefits, compensation, and performance assessment and ensures compliance with all laws.

human-generated data Data that humans, in interaction with computers, generate.

human-generated unstructured data Includes text messages, social media data, and emails.

hybrid cloud Includes two or more private, public, or community clouds, but each cloud remains separate and is only linked by technology that enables data and application portability.

hybrid ERP Splits the ERP functions between an on-premises ERP system and one or more functions handled as Software as a Service (SaaS) in the cloud.

I

identity management A broad administrative area that deals with identifying individuals in a system (such as a country, a network, or an enterprise) and controlling their access to resources within that system by associating user rights and restrictions with the established identity.

identity theft Forging someone's identity for the purpose of fraud.

immutability The ability for a blockchain ledger to remain a permanent, indelible, and unalterable history of transactions.

immutable Unchangeable.

implementation phase When the organization places the system into production so users can begin to perform actual business operations with it.

inbound logistics Acquires raw materials and resources and distributes them to manufacturing as required.

incident Unplanned interruption of a service.

incident management The process responsible for managing how incidents are identified and corrected.

incident record Contains all of the details of an incident.

infographic (information graphic) A representation of information in a graphical format designed to make the data easily understandable at a glance.

information Data converted into a meaningful and useful context.

information age The present time, during which infinite quantities of facts are widely available to anyone who can use a computer.

information MIS infrastructure Identifies where and how important information, such as customer records, is maintained and secured.

Information of Everything (IoE) A concept that extends the Internet of Things (IoT) emphasis on machine-to-machine communications to describe a more complex system that also encompasses people and processes.

information privacy policy Contains general principles regarding information privacy.

information reach Measures the number of people a firm can communicate with all over the world.

information richness Refers to the depth and breadth of details contained in a piece of textual, graphical, audio, or video information.

information security A broad term encompassing the protection of information from accidental or intentional misuse by persons inside or outside an organization.

information security plan Details how an organization will implement the information security policies.

information security policies Identify the rules required to maintain information security, such as requiring users to log off before leaving for lunch or meetings, never sharing passwords with anyone, and changing passwords every 30 days.

Infrastructure as a Service (IaaS) The delivery of computer hardware capability, including the use of servers, networking, and storage, as a service.

input device Equipment used to capture information and commands.

insiders Legitimate users who purposely or accidentally misuse their access to the environment and cause some kind of business-affecting incident.

in-sourcing (in-house development) Uses the professional expertise within an organization to develop and maintain its information technology systems.

instant messaging (sometimes called IM or IMing) A service that enables instant or real-time communication between people.

intangible benefits Difficult to quantify or measure.

integration Allows separate systems to communicate directly with each other, eliminating the need for manual entry into multiple systems.

integrity constraint Rules that help ensure the quality of data.

intelligent virtual agent An animated, humanlike graphical chatbot commonly displayed on website home pages and advertisement landing pages.

interactivity Measures advertising effectiveness by counting visitor interactions with the target ad, including time spent viewing the ad, number of pages viewed, and number of repeat visits to the advertisement.

intermediaries Agents, software, or businesses that provide a trading infrastructure to bring buyers and sellers together.

Internet A massive network that connects computers all over the world and allows them to communicate with one another.

Internet censorship Government attempts to control Internet traffic, thus preventing some material from being viewed by a country's citizens.

Internet of Things (IoT) A world in which interconnected, Internet-enabled devices or things can collect and share data without human intervention.

Internet Protocol TV (IPTV) Distributes digital video content by using IP across the Internet and private IP networks.

Internet protocol version 6 (IPv6) The next-generation protocol, designed to replace the current version Internet protocol, IP version 4 (IPv4).

Internet service provider (ISP) A company that provides access to the Internet for a monthly fee.

Internet use policy Contains general principles to guide the proper use of the Internet.

interoperability The capability of two or more computer systems to share data and resources, even though they are made by different manufacturers.

intranet A restricted network that relies on Internet technologies to provide an Internet-like environment within the company for information sharing, communications, collaboration, web publishing, and the support of business processes.

intrusion detection software (IDS) Features full-time monitoring tools that search for patterns in network traffic to identify intruders.

IP address A unique number that identifies where computers are located on the network.

IT consumerization The blending of personal and business use of technology devices and applications.

iterative development Consists of a series of tiny projects.

K

key performance indicators (KPIs) Quantifiable metrics a company uses to evaluate progress toward critical success factors.

keyword A word used in a performing a search.

kill switch A trigger that enables a project manager to close the project before completion.

knowledge Skills, experience, and expertise coupled with information and intelligence that create a person's intellectual resources.

knowledge assets The human, structural, and recorded resources available to the organization.

knowledge facilitator A person who helps harness the wealth of knowledge in the organization.

knowledge management (KM) Involves capturing, classifying, evaluating, retrieving, and sharing information assets in a way that provides context for effective decisions and actions.

knowledge management system (KMS) Supports the capture, organization, and dissemination of knowledge (i.e., know-how) throughout an organization.

knowledge workers Individuals valued for their ability to interpret and analyze information.

L

ledger Records classified and summarized transactional data.

legacy system An old system that is fast approaching or beyond the end of its useful life within an organization.

list generator Compiles customer information from a variety of sources and segments it for different marketing campaigns.

local area network (LAN) Connects a group of computers in proximity, such as in an office building, school, or home.

location-based service (LBS) An application that uses location information to provide a service.

logical view of data Shows how individual users logically access data to meet their own particular business needs.

logistics Includes the processes that control the distribution, maintenance, and replacement of materials and personnel to support the supply chain.

long tail Referring to the tail of a typical sales curve.

loyalty program A program to reward customers based on spending.

M

machine learning A type of artificial intelligence that enables computers to both understand concepts in the environment and also learn.

machine vision The ability of a computer to "see" by digitizing an image, processing the data it contains, and taking some kind of action.

machine vision resolution The extent to which a machine can differentiate between objects.

machine vision sensitivity The ability of a machine to see in dim light, or to detect weak impulses at invisible wavelengths.

machine-generated data Created by a machine without human intervention.

machine-generated unstructured data Includes satellite images, scientific atmosphere data, and radar data.

machine-to-machine (M2M) Devices that connect directly to other devices.

magnetic medium A secondary storage medium that uses magnetic techniques to store and retrieve data on disks or tapes coated with magnetically sensitive materials.

magnetic tape An older secondary storage medium that uses a strip of thin plastic coated with a magnetically sensitive recording medium.

mail bomb Sends a massive amount of email to a specific person or system that can cause that user's server to stop functioning.

maintainability (or flexibility) Refers to how quickly a system can transform to support environmental changes.

maintenance phase When the organization performs changes, corrections, additions, and upgrades to ensure that the system continues to meet its business goals.

maker movement A cultural trend that places value on an individual's ability to be a creator of things, as well as a consumer of things.

makerspace A community center that provides technology, manufacturing equipment, and educational opportunities to the public that would otherwise be inaccessible or unaffordable.

malware Software that is intended to damage or disable computers and computer systems.

management information system (MIS) A business function, such as accounting and human resources, that moves information about people, products, and processes across the company to facilitate decision making and problem solving.

managerial business process Semidynamic, semiroutine, monthly business processes such as resource allocation, sales strategy, or manufacturing process improvements.

managerial decisions Concern how the organization should achieve the goals and objectives set by its strategy. They are usually the responsibility of mid-level management.

managerial level Employees are continuously evaluating company operations to hone the firm's abilities to identify, adapt to, and leverage change.

many-to-many relationship (M:N) Between two entities in which an instance of one entity is related to many instances of another, and one instance of the other can be related to many instances of the first entity.

market basket analysis Evaluates such items as websites and checkout scanner information to detect customers' buying behavior and predict future behavior by identifying affinities among customers' choices of products and services.

market share The proportion of the market that a firm captures.

mass customization The ability of an organization to tailor its products or services to the customers' specifications.

master data management (MDM) The practice of gathering data and ensuring that it is uniform, accurate, consistent, and complete, including such entities as customers, suppliers, products, sales, employees, and other critical entities that are commonly integrated across organizational systems.

materials management Includes activities that govern the flow of tangible, physical materials through the supply chain such as shipping, transport, distribution, and warehousing.

measurement bias Occurs when there is a problem with the data collected skewing the data in one direction.

megabyte (MB, M, or Meg) Roughly 1 million bytes.

megahertz (MHz) The number of millions of CPU cycles per second.

memory cards Contain high-capacity storage that holds data such as captured images, music, or text files.

memory sticks Provide nonvolatile memory for a range of portable devices including computers, digital cameras, MP3 players, and PDAs.

metadata Details about data.

Metcalfe's law States that the value of a telecommunications network is proportional to the square of the number of connected users of the system.

methodology A set of policies, procedures, standards, processes, practices, tools, techniques, and tasks that people apply to technical and management challenges.

metrics Measurements that evaluate results to determine whether a project is meeting its goals.

metropolitan area network (MAN) A large computer network usually spanning a city.

microblogging The practice of sending brief posts (140 to 200 characters) to a personal blog, either publicly or to a private group of subscribers who can read the posts as IMs or as text messages.

MIS infrastructure Includes the plans for how a firm will build, deploy, use, and share its data, processes, and MIS assets.

MIS skills gap The difference between existing MIS workplace knowledge and the knowledge required to fulfill the business goals and strategies.

misinformation Refers to false information that is presented as fact without an intent to deceive.

mobile Means the technology can travel with the user; for instance, users can download software, email messages, and web pages onto a laptop or other mobile device for portable reading or reference.

mobile application development The set of processes and procedures involved in writing software for wireless devices.

mobile application management (MAM) Administers and enforces corporate epolicies for mobile applications on corporate and personal mobile devices.

mobile business (or mbusiness, mcommerce) The ability to purchase goods and services through a wireless Internet-enabled device.

mobile device management (MDM) A security strategy comprised of products and services that offer remote support for mobile devices, such as smart phones, laptops, and tablets.

mobile information management (MIM) A security strategy that involves keeping sensitive data encrypted and allowing only approved applications to access or transmit it.

model A simplified representation or abstraction of reality.

modem A device that enables a computer to transmit and receive data.

module software design Divides the system into a set of functional units (named modules) that can be used independently or combined with other modules for increased business flexibility.

Moore's law Refers to the computer chip performance per dollar doubling every 18 months.

multifactor authentication Requires more than two means of authentication such as what the user knows (password), what the user has (security token), and what the user is (biometric verification).

multiple-in/multiple-out (MIMO) technology Multiple transmitters and receivers allow sending and receiving greater amounts of data than traditional networking devices.

multitasking Allows more than one piece of software to be used at a time.

multi-tenancy A single instance of a system serves multiple customers.

multivalued attribute Having the potential to contain more than one value for an attribute.

N

name bias The tendency to prefer certain types of names.

national service providers (NSPs) Private companies that own and maintain the worldwide backbone that supports the Internet.

native advertising Online marketing concept in which the advertiser attempts to gain attention by providing content in the context of the user's experience in terms of its content, format, style, or placement.

nearshore outsourcing Contracting an outsourcing arrangement with a company in a nearby country.

net neutrality Ensures that everyone has equal access to the Internet.

network A communications system created by linking two or more devices and establishing a standard methodology in which they can communicate.

network behavior analysis Gathers an organization's computer network traffic patterns to identify unusual or suspicious operations.

network convergence The efficient coexistence of telephone, video, and data communication within a single network, offering convenience and flexibility not possible with separate infrastructures.

network effect Describes how products in a network increase in value to users as the number of users increases.

network operating system (NOS) Operating system that runs a network, steering information between computers and managing security and users.

network topology Refers to the geometric arrangement of the actual physical organization of the computers (and other network devices) in a network.

network transmission media Refers to the various types of media used to carry the signal between computers.

network user license Enables anyone on the network to install and use the software.

network virtualization Combines networks by splitting the available bandwidth into independent channels that can be assigned in real time to a specific device.

neural network A category of AI that attempts to emulate the way the human brain works.

noisy neighbor Refers to a multi-tenancy co-tenant that monopolizes bandwidth, servers, CPUs, and other resources that cause network performance issues.

non-fungible token (NFT) A unit of data stored on a digital ledger, called a blockchain, that certifies a digital asset to be unique and therefore not interchangeable.

nonrepudiation A contractual stipulation to ensure that ebusiness participants do not deny (repudiate) their online actions.

nonsensitive PII Information transmitted without encryption and includes information collected from public records, phone books, corporate directories, websites, etc.

nonvolatile Does not require constant power to function.

null-valued attribute Assigned to an attribute when no other value applies or when a value is unknown.

O

offshore outsourcing Using organizations from developing countries to write code and develop systems.

off-the-shelf application software Supports general business processes and does not require any specific software customization to meet the organization's needs.

one-to-many relationship (1:M) A relationship between two entities in which an instance of one entity can be related to many instances of a related entity.

one-to-one relationship (1:1) A relationship between two entities in which an instance of one entity can be related to only one instance of a related entity.

online analytical processing (OLAP) The manipulation of information to create business intelligence in support of strategic decision making.

online training Runs over the Internet or on a CD or DVD, and employees complete the training on their own time at their own pace.

online transaction processing (OLTP) The capture of transaction and event information by using technology to (1) process the information according to defined business rules, (2) store the information, and (3) update existing information to reflect the new information.

on-premise system Includes a server at a physical location using an internal network for internal access and firewalls for remote users' access.

onshore outsourcing Engaging another company within the same country for services.

open source Refers to any software whose source code is made available free for any third party to review and modify.

open system Consists of nonproprietary hardware and software based on publicly known standards that allow third parties to create add-on products to plug into or interoperate with the system.

operating system software Controls the application software and manages how the hardware devices work together.

operational business process Static, routine, daily business processes such as stocking inventory, checking out customers, or daily opening/closing processes.

operational CRM Supports traditional transactional processing for day-to-day front-office operations or systems that deal directly with the customers.

operational decisions Affect how the firm is run from day to day; they are the domain of operations managers, who are the closest to the customer.

operational level Employees develop, control, and maintain core business activities required to run the day-to-day operations.

opportunity management CRM system Targets sales opportunities by finding new customers or companies for future sales.

opt in Receiving emails by choosing to allow permissions to incoming emails.

opt out Customer specifically chooses to deny permission to incoming emails.

optimization model A statistical process that finds the way to make a design, system, or decision as effective as possible, for example, finding the values of controllable variables that determine maximal productivity or minimal waste.

organic search The unpaid entries in a search engine results page that were derived based on their contents' relevance to the keyword query.

outbound logistics Distributes goods and services to customers.

output device Equipment used to see, hear, or otherwise accept the results of information processing requests.

outsourcing An arrangement by which one organization provides a service or services for another organization that chooses not to perform them in-house.

overfitting Occurs when a machine learning model matches the training data so closely that the model fails to make correct predictions on new data.

P

packet A single unit of binary data routed through a network.

packet footer Represents the end of the packet or transmission end.

packet header Lists the destination (for example, in IP packets the destination is the IP address) along with the length of the message data.

packet-switching Occurs when the sending computer divides a message into a number of efficiently sized units of data called packets, each of which contains the address of the destination computer.

paid search Links a company paid to have displayed based on your keywords.

paradigm shift Occurs when a new radical form of business enters the market that reshapes the way companies and organizations behave.

peer-to-peer (P2P) network A computer network that relies on the computing power and bandwidth of the participants in the network rather than on a centralized server.

performance Measures how quickly a system performs a process or transaction.

personal area network (PAN) Provides communication over a short distance that is intended for use with devices that are owned and operated by a single user.

personal information management (PIM) software Software that handles contact information, appointments, task lists, and email.

personalization Occurs when a company knows enough about a customer's likes and dislikes that it can fashion offers more likely to appeal to that person, say by tailoring its website to individuals or groups based on profile information, demographics, or prior transactions.

personally identifiable information (PII) Any data that could potentially identify a specific individual.

PERT (Program Evaluation and Review Technique) chart A graphical network model that depicts a project's tasks and the relationships between them.

pervasive computing The growing trend of embedding computer capabilities into everyday objects to make them effectively communicate and perform useful tasks in a way that minimizes the end user's need to interact with computers as computers.

pharming Reroutes requests for legitimate websites to false websites.

pharming attack Uses a zombie farm, often by an organized crime association, to launch a massive phishing attack.

phishing A technique to gain personal information for the purpose of identity theft, usually by means of fraudulent emails that look as though they came from legitimate sources.

phishing expedition A masquerading attack that combines spam with spoofing.

physical security Tangible protection such as alarms, guards, fireproof doors, fences, and vaults.

physical view of data The physical storage of data on a storage device.

pie chart A type of graph in which a circle is divided into sectors that each represents a proportion of the whole.

planning phase Establishes a high-level plan of the intended project and determines project goals.

Platform as a Service (PaaS) Supports the deployment of entire systems, including hardware, networking, and applications, using a pay-per-use revenue model.

podcasting Converts an audio broadcast to a digital music player.

portability Refers to the ability of an application to operate on different devices or software platforms, such as different operating systems.

Porter's Five Forces Model A model for analyzing the competitive forces within the environment in which a company operates to assess the potential for profitability in an industry.

Porter's three generic strategies Generic business strategies that are neither organization nor industry specific and can be applied to any business, product, or service.

prediction A statement about what will happen or might happen in the future; for example, predicting future sales or employee turnover.

predictive analytics Analytical techniques that extract information from data and use it to predict future trends and identify behavioral patterns.

prejudice bias A result of training data that is influenced by cultural or other stereotypes.

prescriptive analytics Analytical techniques that create models indicating the best decision to make or course of action to take.

pretexting A form of social engineering in which one individual lies to obtain confidential data about another individual.

preventive maintenance Makes system changes to reduce the chance of future system failure.

primary key A field (or group of fields) that uniquely identifies a given record in a table.

primary storage Computer's main memory, which consists of the random access memory (RAM), cache memory, and read-only memory (ROM) that is directly accessible to the CPU.

primary value activities Found at the bottom of the value chain, these include business processes that acquire raw materials and manufacture, deliver, market, sell, and provide after-sales services.

private cloud Serves only one customer or organization and can be located on the customer's premises or off the customer's premises.

privilege escalation A network intrusion attack that takes advantage of programming errors or design flaws to grant the attacker elevated access to the network and its associated data and applications.

process modeling Graphical representation of the processes that capture, manipulate, store, and distribute information between a system and its environment.

procurement The purchase of goods and services to meet the needs of the supply chain.

product differentiation An advantage that occurs when a company develops unique differences in its products with the intent to influence demand.

production The process by which a business processes raw materials and or converts them into a finished product for its goods or services.

production and materials management ERP component Handles production planning and execution tasks such as demand forecasting, production scheduling, job cost accounting, and quality control.

productivity The rate at which goods and services are produced based on total output given total inputs.

programming language A unique set of keywords (words that it understands) along with a special syntax for organizing program instructions that execute computer commands.

progressive web application (PWA) A website that looks and behaves as if it is a mobile application.

project Temporary activity a company undertakes to create a unique product, service, or result.

project assumption Factors considered to be true, real, or certain without proof or demonstration.

project charter A concise written description of the project's intended work.

project constraint Specific factors that can limit options, including budget, delivery dates, available skilled resources, and organizational policies.

project deliverable Any measurable, tangible, verifiable outcome, result, or item that is produced to complete a project or part of a project.

project management The application of knowledge, skills, tools, and techniques to project activities to meet project requirements.

project management office (PMO) An internal department that oversees all organizational projects.

project manager An individual who is an expert in project planning and management, defines and develops the project plan, and tracks the plan to ensure that the project is completed on time and on budget.

project milestones Represent key dates when a certain group of activities must be performed.

project objectives Quantifiable criteria that must be met for the project to be considered a success.

project plan A formal, approved document that manages and controls project execution.

project requirements document Defines the specifications for product/output of the project and is key for managing expectations, controlling scope, and completing other planning efforts.

project scope Describes the business needs and the justification, requirements, and current boundaries for the project.

project scope statement Links the project to the organization's overall business goals.

project stakeholder Individuals and organizations actively involved in the project or whose interests might be affected as a result of project execution or project completion.

proof-of-stake A way to validate transactions and achieve a distributed consensus.

proof-of-work A requirement to define an expensive computer calculation, also called mining, that needs to be performed in order to create a new group of trustless transactions (blocks) on the distributed ledger or blockchain.

protocol A standard that specifies the format of data, as well as the rules to be followed during transmission.

prototyping A modern design approach by which the designers and system users use an iterative approach to building the system.

proxy Software that prevents direct communication between a sending and a receiving computer and is used to monitor packets for security reasons.

public cloud Promotes massive, global, industrywide applications offered to the general public.

public key encryption (PKE) Uses two keys: a public key that everyone can have and a private key for only the recipient.

Q

query-by-example (QBE) tool Helps users graphically design the answer to a question against a database.

R

radio access network (RAN) A technology that connects individual devices to other parts of a network through radio connections.

radio-frequency identification (RFID) Uses electronic tags and labels to identify objects wirelessly over short distances.

random access memory (RAM) The computer's primary working memory, in which program instructions and data are stored so that they can be accessed directly by the CPU via the processor's high-speed external data bus.

ransomware A form of malicious software that infects your computer and asks for money.

rapid application development (RAD) methodology (also called rapid prototyping) Emphasizes extensive user involvement in the rapid and evolutionary construction of working prototypes of a system to accelerate the systems development process.

Raspberry Pi A low-cost, credit card–sized computer that plugs into a computer monitor or TV, and uses a standard keyboard and mouse.

rational unified process (RUP) methodology Provides a framework for breaking down the development of software into four gates.

raw data Data that has not been processed for use.

read-only memory (ROM) The portion of a computer's primary storage that does not lose its contents when one switches off the power.

real-time adaptive security The network security model necessary to accommodate the emergence of multiple perimeters and moving parts on the network, and increasingly advanced threats targeting enterprises.

real-time communication Occurs when a system updates information at the same rate it receives it.

real-time data Immediate, up-to-date data.

real-time system Provides real-time data in response to requests.

recommendation engine A data mining algorithm that analyzes a customer's purchases and actions on a website and then uses the data to recommend complementary products.

record A collection of related data elements.

recovery The ability to get a system up and running in the event of a system crash or failure that includes restoring the information backup.

reduced instruction set computer (RISC) chip Limits the number of instructions the CPU can execute to increase processing speed.

redundancy Occurs when a task or activity is unnecessarily repeated.

regional service providers (RSPs) Offer Internet service by connecting to NSPs, but they also can connect directly to each other.

regression model A statistical process for estimating the relationships among variables.

reinforcement learning The training of machine learning models to make a sequence of decisions.

relational database management system Allows users to create, read, update, and delete data in a relational database.

relational database model Stores information in the form of logically related two-dimensional tables.

relational integrity constraint Rules that enforce basic and fundamental information-based constraints.

reliability (or accuracy) Ensures that a system is functioning correctly and providing accurate information.

repeater Receives and repeats a signal to reduce its attenuation and extend its range.

report A document containing data organized in a table, matrix, or graphical format allowing users to easily comprehend and understand information.

reputation system Where buyers post feedback on sellers.

requirements definition document Prioritizes all of the business requirements by order of importance to the company.

requirements management The process of managing changes to the business requirements throughout the project.

responsibility matrix Defines all project roles and indicates what responsibilities are associated with each role.

return on investment (ROI) Indicates the earning power of a project.

RFID reader (RFID interrogator) A transmitter/receiver that reads the contents of RFID tags in the area.

RFID tag An electronic identification device that is made up of a chip and antenna.

rivalry among existing competitors One of Porter's five forces; high when competition is fierce in a market and low when competitors are more complacent.

robotic process automation (RPA) The use of software with artificial intelligence (AI) and machine learning capabilities to handle high-volume, repeatable tasks that previously required a human to perform.

robotics Focuses on creating artificial intelligence devices that can move and react to sensory input.

router An intelligent connecting device that examines each packet of data it receives and then decides which way to send it toward its destination.

Rule 41 The part of the U.S. Federal Rules of Criminal Procedure that covers the search and seizure of physical and digital evidence.

S

safe mode Occurs if the system is failing and will load only the most essential parts of the operating system and will not run many of the background operating utilities.

sales analytics Involves gathering, classifying, comparing, and studying company sales data to analyze product cycles, sales pipelines, and competitive intelligence.

sales force automation (SFA) Automatically tracks all the steps in the sales process.

sales management CRM system Automates each phase of the sales process, helping individual sales representatives coordinate and organize all their accounts.

sample bias A problem with using incorrect training data to train the machine.

satellite A space station that orbits Earth receiving and transmitting signals from Earth-based stations over a wide area.

scalability Describes how well a system can scale up or adapt to the increased demands of growth.

scareware A type of malware designed to trick victims into giving up personal information to purchase or download useless and potentially dangerous software.

scope creep The tendency to permit changes that exceed a project's scope and may wreak havoc on the schedule, work quality, and budget.

script kiddies or script bunnies Find hacking code on the Internet and click-and-point their way into systems to cause damage or spread viruses.

scrum methodology Uses small teams to produce small pieces of software using a series of sprints, or 30-day intervals, to achieve an appointed goal.

search engine Website software that finds other pages based on keyword matching.

search engine optimization (SEO) Combines art along with science to determine how to make URLs more attractive to search engines, resulting in higher search engine ranking.

search engine ranking Evaluates variables that search engines use to determine where a URL appears on the list of search results.

secondary storage Consists of equipment designed to store large volumes of data for long-term storage.

secure hypertext transfer protocol (SHTTP or HTTPS) A combination of HTTP and SSL to provide encryption and secure identification of an Internet server.

secure sockets layer (SSL) A standard security technology for establishing an encrypted link between a web server and a browser, ensuring that all data passed between them remains private.

Security as a Service (SaaS) Involves applications such as antivirus software delivered over the Internet with constant virus definition updates that are not reliant on user compliance.

selfie A self-photograph placed on a social media website.

semantic web A component of Web 3.0 that describes things in a way that computers can understand.

semistructured decision Occurs in situations in which a few established processes help to evaluate potential solutions, but not enough to lead to a definite recommended decision.

sensitive PII Information transmitted with encryption and, when disclosed, results in a breach of an individual's privacy and can potentially cause the individual harm.

server A computer dedicated to providing information in response to requests.

server virtualization Combines the physical resources, such as servers, processors, and operating systems, from the applications.

serviceability How quickly a third party or vendor can change a system to ensure that it meets user needs and the terms of any contracts, including agreed levels of reliability, maintainability, or availability.

services Tasks that customers will buy to satisfy a want or need.

showrooming Occurs when a customer browses at a physical store and then decides to purchase the product online for a reduced cost.

sign-off Users' actual signatures, indicating they approve all of the business requirements.

single-factor authentication The traditional security process that requires a user name and password.

single-tenancy Each customer or tenant must purchase and maintain an individual system.

single-user license Restricts the use of the software to one user at a time.

single-valued attribute Having only a single value of each attribute of an entity.

site license Enables any qualified users within the organization to install the software, regardless of whether the computer is on a network. Some employees might install the software on a home computer for working remotely.

slack The amount of time an activity may be delayed without delaying a succeeding activity or the project finish date.

smart card A device about the size of a credit card containing embedded technologies that can store information and small amounts of software to perform some limited processing.

smart grid Delivers electricity using two-way digital technology.

smart phone Offers more advanced computing ability and connectivity than a basic cell phone.

snackable content Website content that is designed to be easy for readers to consume and to share.

snapshot A view of data at a particular moment in time.

social engineering Hackers use their social skills to trick people into revealing access credentials or other valuable information.

social media Refers to websites that rely on user participation and user-contributed content.

social media manager A person within the organization who is trusted to monitor, contribute, filter, and guide the social media presence of a company, individual, product, or brand.

social media monitoring The process of monitoring and responding to what is being said about a company, individual, product, or brand.

social media policy Outlines the corporate guidelines or principles governing employee online communications.

social network An application that connects people by matching profile information.

social networking The practice of expanding your business and/or social contacts by constructing a personal network.

social networking analysis (SNA) Maps group contacts identifying who knows each other and who works together.

social tagging Describes the collaborative activity of marking shared online content with keywords or tags as a way to organize it for future navigation, filtering, or searching.

sock puppet marketing The use of a false identity to artificially stimulate demand for a product, brand, or service.

software The set of instructions the hardware executes to carry out specific tasks.

Software as a Service (SaaS) Delivers applications over the cloud using a pay-per-use revenue model.

software customization Modifies software to meet specific user or business requirements.

software engineering A disciplined approach for constructing information systems through the use of common methods, techniques, or tools.

software updates (software patch) Occurs when the software vendor releases updates to software to fix problems or enhance features.

software upgrade Occurs when the software vendor releases a new version of the software, making significant changes to the program.

solid state drive An all-electronic storage device that is an alternative to a hard disk and is faster than a hard disk because there is zero latency (no read/write head to move).

source code Contains instructions written by a programmer specifying the actions to be performed by computer software.

source data Identifies the primary location where data is collected.

source document The original transaction record.

spam Unsolicited email.

sparkline A small embedded line graph that illustrates a single trend.

spatial data (geospatial data or geographic information) Identifies the geographic location of features and boundaries on Earth, such as natural or constructed features, oceans, and more.

spear phishing A phishing expedition in which the emails are carefully designed to target a particular person or organization.

spyware A special class of adware that collects data about the user and transmits it over the Internet without the user's knowledge or permission.

SSL certificate An electronic document that confirms the identity of a website or server and verifies that a public key belongs to a trustworthy individual or company.

stakeholder A person or group that has an interest or concern in an organization.

standard packet format Includes a packet header, packet body containing the original message, and packet footer.

static process Process that uses a systematic approach in an attempt to improve business effectiveness and efficiency continuously.

static report A report created once based on data that does not change.

status report Periodic review of actual performance versus expected performance.

stickiness Measures the amount of time visitors spend on a website or application.

storage virtualization Combines multiple network storage devices so they appear to be a single storage device.

strategic business process Dynamic, nonroutine, long-term business process such as financial planning, expansion strategies, and stakeholder interactions.

strategic decisions Involve higher-level issues concerned with the overall direction of the organization; these decisions define the organization's overall goals and aspirations for the future.

strategic level Managers develop overall business strategies, goals, and objectives as part of the company's strategic plan.

streaming A method of sending audio and video files over the Internet in such a way that the user can view the file while it is being transferred.

streaming data Data that is generated continuously by thousands of data sources, which typically send in the data records simultaneously, and in small sizes (order of kilobytes).

streamlining Improves business process efficiencies, simplifying or eliminating unnecessary steps.

structured data Data that has a defined length, type, and format and includes numbers, dates, or strings such as Customer Address.

structured decision Involves situations in which established processes offer potential solutions.

structured query language (SQL) Users write lines of code to answer questions against a database.

stylus A penlike device used to tap the screen to enter commands.

supplier power One of Porter's five forces; measures the suppliers' ability to influence the prices they charge for supplies (including materials, labor, and services).

supply chain All parties involved, directly or indirectly, in obtaining raw materials or a product.

supply chain management (SCM) The management of information flows between and among activities in a supply chain to maximize total supply chain effectiveness and corporate profitability.

supply chain visibility The ability to view all areas up and down the supply chain in real time.

support value activities Found along the top of the value chain and includes business processes, such as firm infrastructure, human resource management, technology development, and procurement, that support the primary value activities.

sustainable, or green, MIS Describes the production, management, use, and disposal of technology in a way that minimizes damage to the environment.

sustainable MIS disposal Refers to the safe disposal of MIS assets at the end of their life cycle.

sustainable MIS infrastructure Identifies ways that a company can grow in terms of computing resources while simultaneously becoming less dependent on hardware and energy consumption.

sustaining technology Produces an improved product customers are eager to buy, such as a faster car or larger hard drive.

swim lane Layout arranges the steps of a business process into a set of rows depicting the various elements.

switching costs Costs that make customers reluctant to switch to another product or service.

SWOT analysis Evaluates an organization's ***s***trengths, ***w***eaknesses, ***o***pportunities, and ***t***hreats to identify significant influences that work for or against business strategies.

synchronous communication Communications that occur at the same time such as IM or chat.

system A collection of parts that link to achieve a common purpose.

system clock Works like a wristwatch and uses a battery mounted on the motherboard to provide power when the computer is turned off.

system restore Enables a user to return to the previous operating system.

system software Controls how the various technology tools work together along with the application software.

system virtualization The ability to present the resources of a single computer as if it is a collection of separate computers ("virtual machines"), each with its own virtual CPUs, network interfaces, storage, and operating system.

systems development life cycle (SDLC) The overall process for developing information systems, from planning and analysis through implementation and maintenance.

systems thinking A way of monitoring the entire system by viewing multiple inputs being processed or transformed to produce outputs while continuously gathering feedback on each part.

T

table Composed of rows and columns that represent an entity.

tacit knowledge The knowledge contained in people's heads.

tag Specific keyword or phrase incorporated into website content for means of classification or taxonomy.

tangible benefits Easy to quantify and typically measured to determine the success or failure of a project.

taxonomy The scientific classification of organisms into groups based on similarities of structure or origin.

technical review (or peer review) A meeting where an independent team of experts provides an in-depth analysis of project results to ensure that team members did the work accurately, completely, and to the right quality standard.

technology failure Occurs when the ability of a company to operate is impaired because of a hardware, software, or data outage.

technology recovery strategies Focus specifically on prioritizing the order for restoring hardware, software, and data across the organization that best meets business recovery requirements.

teergrubing Anti-spamming approach by which the receiving computer launches a return attack against the spammer, sending email messages back to the computer that originated the suspected spam.

telecommunication system Enables the transmission of data over public or private networks.

telecommuting (virtual workforce) Allows users to work from remote locations such as a home or hotel, using high-speed Internet to access business applications and data.

terabyte (TB) Roughly 1 trillion bytes.

test condition Details the steps the system must perform along with the expected result of each step.

testing phase Brings all the project pieces together into a special testing environment to eliminate errors and bugs and verify that the system meets all the business requirements defined in the analysis phase.

the right to be forgotten Allows individuals to request to have all content that violates their privacy removed.

threat An act or object that poses a danger to assets.

threat of new entrants One of Porter's five forces; high when it is easy for new competitors to enter a market and low when there are significant entry barriers to joining a market.

threat of substitute products or services One of Porter's five forces; high when there are many alternatives to a product or service and low when there are few alternatives from which to choose.

time bomb Computer virus that waits for a specific date before executing instructions.

time-series chart A graphical representation showing change of a variable over time.

time-series information Time-stamped information collected at a particular frequency.

To-Be process model Shows the results of applying change improvement opportunities to the current (As-Is) process model.

tokens Small electronic devices that change user passwords automatically.

traceroute A utility application that monitors the network path of packet data sent to a remote computer.

transaction processing system (TPS) The basic business system that serves the operational level (analysts) and assists in making structured decisions.

transactional information Encompasses all of the information contained within a single business process or unit of work, and its primary purpose is to support the performance of daily operational or structured decisions.

transmission control protocol/Internet protocol (TCP/IP) Provides the technical foundation for the public Internet, as well as for large numbers of private networks.

trend analysis A trend is examined to identify its nature, causes, speed of development, and potential impacts.

trend monitoring Trends viewed as particularly important in a specific community, industry, or sector are carefully monitored, watched, and reported to key decision makers.

trend projection When numerical data are available, a trend can be plotted to display changes through time and into the future.

troll farms A groups of hundreds of people whose job is to infiltrate message boards and comments sections in order to advance Russian national aims or seed discord and disharmony.

twisted-pair cable Refers to a type of cable composed of four (or more) copper wires twisted around each other within a plastic sheath.

two-factor authentication Requires the user to provide two means of authentication: what the user knows (password) and what the user has (security token).

typosquatting A problem that occurs when someone registers purposely misspelled variations of well-known domain names.

U

unavailable When a system is not operating or cannot be used.

underfitting Occurs when a machine learning model has poor predictive abilities because it did not learn the complexity in the training data.

unified communications (UC) The integration of communication channels into a single service.

universal resource locator (URL) The address of a file or resource on the web such as www.apple.com.

unstructured data Data that is not defined, does not follow a specified format, and is typically free-form text such as emails, Twitter tweets, and text messages.

unstructured decision Occurs when no procedures or rules exist to guide decision makers toward the correct choice.

upcycle Reuses or refurbishes ewaste and creates a new product.

uplift modeling A form of predictive analytics for marketing campaigns that attempts to identify target markets or people who could be convinced to buy products.

up-selling Increasing the value of the sale.

usability The degree to which a system is efficient, easy to learn, and satisfying to use.

user documentation Highlights how to use the system and how to troubleshoot issues or problems.

user-contributed content (also referred to as user-generated content) Content created and updated by many users for many users.

utility computing Offers a pay-per-use revenue model similar to a metered service such as gas or electricity.

utility software Provides additional functionality to the operating system.

V

value chain analysis Views a firm as a series of business processes that each adds value to the product or service.

value-added The term used to describe the difference between the cost of inputs and the value of price of outputs.

variable A data characteristic that stands for a value that changes or varies over time.

variance bias A mathematical property of an algorithm.

vertical privilege escalation Attackers grant themselves a higher access level such as administrator, allowing the attacker to perform illegal actions such as running unauthorized code or deleting data.

video chat An online face-to-face, visual communication performed with other Internet users by using a webcam and dedicated software.

viral marketing A technique that induces websites or users to pass on a marketing message to other websites or users, creating exponential growth in the message's visibility and effect.

virtual assistant (VA) A small program stored on a PC or portable device that monitors emails, faxes, messages, and phone calls.

virtual private network (VPN) Companies can establish direct private network links among themselves or create private, secure Internet access, in effect a private tunnel within the Internet.

virtual reality A computer-simulated environment that can be a simulation of the real world or an imaginary world.

virtualization Creates multiple virtual machines on a single computing device.

virus Software written with malicious intent to cause annoyance or damage.

vishing (voice phishing) A phone scam that attempts to defraud people by asking them to call a bogus telephone number to confirm their account information.

visualization Produces graphical displays of patterns and complex relationships in large amounts of data.

Voice over IP (VoIP) Uses IP technology to transmit telephone calls.

voiceprint A set of measurable characteristics of a human voice that uniquely identifies an individual.

volatile Must have constant power to function; contents are lost when the computer's electric supply fails.

volatility Refers to a device's ability to function with or without power.

vulnerability A system weakness that can be exploited by a threat; for example, a password that is never changed or a system left on while an employee goes to lunch.

W

war chalking The practice of tagging pavement with codes displaying where Wi-Fi access is available.

war driving Deliberately searching for Wi-Fi signals from a vehicle.

warm site A separate facility with computer equipment that requires installation and configuration.

waterfall methodology A sequence of phases in which the output of each phase becomes the input for the next.

Web 1.0 (or Business 1.0) Refers to the World Wide Web during its first few years of operation between 1991 and 2003.

Web 2.0 (or Business 2.0) The next generation of Internet use—a more mature, distinctive communications platform characterized by new qualities such as collaboration and sharing, and being free.

web accessibility Means that people with disabilities—including visual, auditory, physical, speech, cognitive, and neurological disabilities—can use the web.

web accessibility initiative (WAI) Brings together people from industry, disability organizations, government, and research labs from around the world to develop guidelines and resources to help make the web accessible to people with disabilities, including auditory, cognitive, neurological, physical, speech, and visual disabilities.

web-based self-service system Allows customers to use the web to find answers to their questions or solutions to their problems.

website ebusiness analytics Uses clickstream data to determine the effectiveness of the site as a channel-to-market.

website name stealing The theft of a website's name that occurs when someone, posing as a site's administrator, changes the ownership of the domain name assigned to the website to another website owner.

website traffic analytics Uses clickstream data to determine the efficiency of the site for the users and operates at the server level.

white-hat hackers Work at the request of the system owners to find system vulnerabilities and plug the holes.

wide area network (WAN) Spans a large geographic area such as a state, province, or country.

Wi-Fi 6 The next generation of Wi-Fi; expected to operate at 9.6 Gbps.

Wi-Fi infrastructure Includes the inner workings of a Wi-Fi service or utility, including the signal transmitters, towers, or poles, along with additional equipment required to send a Wi-Fi signal.

Wi-Fi protected access (WPA) A wireless security protocol to protect Wi-Fi networks.

wiki A type of collaborative web page that allows users to add, remove, and change content, which can be easily organized and reorganized as required.

wire media Transmission material manufactured so that signals will be confined to a narrow path and will behave predictably.

wired equivalent privacy (WEP) An encryption algorithm designed to protect wireless transmission data.

wireless Refers to any type of operation accomplished without the use of a hard-wired connection.

wireless access point (WAP) Enables devices to connect to a wireless network to communicate with each other.

wireless fidelity (Wi-Fi) A means by which portable devices can connect wirelessly to a local area network, using access points that send and receive data via radio waves.

wireless LAN (WLAN) A local area network that uses radio signals to transmit and receive data over distances of a few hundred feet.

wireless MAN (WMAN) A metropolitan area network that uses radio signals to transmit and receive data.

wireless media Natural parts of Earth's environment that can be used as physical paths to carry electrical signals.

wireless WAN (WWAN) A wide area network that uses radio signals to transmit and receive data.

work breakdown structure (WBS) A plan that breaks down a project's goals into the many deliverables required to achieve it.

workflow Includes the tasks, activities, and responsibilities required to execute each step in a business process.

workplace MIS monitoring Tracks people's activities by such measures as number of keystrokes, error rate, and number of transactions processed.

workshop training Held in a classroom environment and led by an instructor.

Worldwide Interoperability for Microwave Access (WiMAX) A communications technology aimed at providing high-speed wireless data over metropolitan area networks.

worm Malware computer program that spreads itself not only from file to file but also from computer to computer.

Z

zombie A program that secretly takes over another computer for the purpose of launching attacks on other computers.

zombie farm A group of computers on which a hacker has planted zombie programs.

Chapter 1

1. https://www.mckinsey.com/, accessed 10/24/20.
2. Interesting Facts, *www.interestingfacts.org.*
3. https://www.ibm.com/ibm/history/ibm100/us/en/icons/ibm603/breakthroughs/, accessed 11/14/20.
4. https://www.forbes.com/sites/kashmirhill/2012/02/16/how-target-figured-out-a-teen-girl-was-pregnant-before-her-father-did/?sh=54526c766686, accessed 09/13/2019.
5. https://hbr.org/2019/08/are-your-companys-strengths-really-weaknesses, accessed 10/13/2019.
6. Porter, Michael E., "The Five Competitive Forces That Shape Strategy," The Harvard Business Review Book Series, *Harvard Business Review,* January 2008; Porter, Michael E., "Competitive Strategy: Techniques for Analyzing Industries and Competitors," *Harvard Business Review,* January 2002; Porter, Michael E., "On Competition," The Harvard Business Review Book Series. Boston: Harvard Business School Publishing, 1985; Harvard Institute for Strategy and Competitiveness, http://www.isc.hbs.edu/.
7. Porter, Michael E., "The Five Competitive Forces That Shape Strategy," The Harvard Business Review Book Series, *Harvard Business Review,* January 2008; Porter, Michael E., "Competitive Strategy: Techniques for Analyzing Industries and Competitors," *Harvard Business Review,* January 2002; Porter, Michael E., "On Competition," The Harvard Business Review Book Series. Boston: Harvard Business School Publishing, 1985; Harvard Institute for Strategy and Competitiveness, http://www.isc.hbs.edu/.
8. Porter, Michael E., "The Five Competitive Forces That Shape Strategy," The Harvard Business Review Book Series, *Harvard Business Review,* January 2008; Porter, Michael E., "Competitive Strategy: Techniques for Analyzing Industries and Competitors," *Harvard Business Review,* January 2002; Porter, Michael E., "On Competition," The Harvard Business Review Book Series. Boston: Harvard Business School Publishing, 1985; Harvard Institute for Strategy and Competitiveness, http://www.isc.hbs.edu/.
9. Porter, Michael E., "The Five Competitive Forces That Shape Strategy," The Harvard Business Review Book Series, *Harvard Business Review,* January 2008; Porter, Michael E., "Competitive Strategy: Techniques for Analyzing Industries and Competitors," *Harvard Business Review,* January 2002; Porter, Michael E., "On Competition," The Harvard Business Review Book Series. Boston: Harvard Business School Publishing, 1985; Harvard Institute for Strategy and Competitiveness, http://www.isc.hbs.edu/.
10. Porter, Michael E., "The Five Competitive Forces That Shape Strategy," The Harvard Business Review Book Series, *Harvard Business Review,* January 2008; Porter, Michael E., "Competitive Strategy: Techniques for Analyzing Industries and Competitors," *Harvard Business Review,* January 2002; Porter, Michael E., "On Competition," The Harvard Business Review Book Series. Boston: Harvard Business School Publishing, 1985; Harvard Institute for Strategy and Competitiveness, http://www.isc.hbs.edu/.
11. Porter, Michael E., "The Five Competitive Forces That Shape Strategy," The Harvard Business Review Book Series, *Harvard Business Review,* January 2008; Porter, Michael E., "Competitive Strategy: Techniques for Analyzing Industries and Competitors," *Harvard Business Review,* January 2002; Porter, Michael E., "On Competition," The Harvard Business Review Book Series. Boston: Harvard Business School Publishing, 1985; Harvard Institute for Strategy and Competitiveness, http://www.isc.hbs.edu/.
12. Porter, Michael E., "The Five Competitive Forces That Shape Strategy," The Harvard Business Review Book Series, Harvard *Business Review,* January 2008; Porter, Michael E., "Competitive Strategy: Techniques for Analyzing Industries and Competitors," *Harvard Business Review,* January 2002; Porter, Michael E., "On Competition," The Harvard Business Review Book Series. Boston: Harvard Business School Publishing, 1985; Harvard Institute for Strategy and Competitiveness, http://www.isc.hbs.edu/.
13. Porter, Michael E., "The Five Competitive Forces That Shape Strategy," The Harvard Business Review Book Series, *Harvard Business Review,* January 2008; Porter, Michael E., "Competitive Strategy: Techniques for Analyzing Industries and Competitors," *Harvard Business Review,* January 2002; Porter, Michael E., "On Competition," The Harvard Business Review Book Series. Boston: Harvard Business School Publishing, 1985; Harvard Institute for Strategy and Competitiveness, http://www.isc.hbs.edu/.
14. "Harvard Business Review on Managing the Value Chain," *Harvard Business School Press,* January 2000.
15. "Harvard Business Review on Managing the Value Chain," *Harvard Business School Press,* January 2000.
16. www.weforum.org/about/the-fourth-industrial-revolution-by-klaus-schwab, accessed January 2019.
17. "Internet of Things Applications across Industries," Intel, http://www.intel.com; Chui, Michael; Löffler, Markus; and Roberts, Roger, "The Internet of Things," *Mckinsey Quarterly,* March 2010, http://www.mckinsey.com; Ferber, Stefan, "How the Internet of Things Changes Everything," *Harvard Business Review,* May 2013.
18. Thompson, Clive, "Do You Speak Statistics?" *Wired,* May 2010, p. 35.
19. Seidell, Streeter, "10 Best Things We'll Say to Our Grandkids," *Wired,* September 21, 2009, www.wired.com/culture/culturereviews/magazine/17-10/st_best#ixzz0s65fFq1t.

Chapter 2

1. https://www.bbc.com/news/business-48842750, accessed 10/12/2020.
2. https://www.forbes.com/sites/kevinkruse/2016/03/07/80-20-rule/?sh=3bbea4cf3814, accessed 08/22/2019.
3. Blanchard, Ken, "Effectiveness vs. Efficiency," *Wachovia Small Business*, www.wachovia.com.
4. "What Is Systems Thinking," *SearchCIO.com*, http://searchcio.techtarget.com/.
5. https://www.hawking.org.uk/biography, accessed 09/09/2019.
6. https://www.ibm.com/analytics/machine-learning, accessed 09/12/2019.
7. https://www.ibm.com/analytics/machine-learning, accessed 09/12/2019.
8. https://www.ibm.com/analytics/machine-learning, accessed 09/12/2019.
9. https://executive-education-online.mit.edu/presentations/lp/mit-artificial-intelligence-online-short-course/, accessed 09/12/2019.

10. https://executive-education-online.mit.edu/presentations/lp/mit-artificial-intelligence-online-short-course/, accessed 09/12/2019.
11. https://www.sas.com/en_us/insights/analytics/deep-learning.html, accessed 09/14/2019.
12. https://blogs.sas.com/content/hiddeninsights/2018/01/29/ai-ml-ar-vr-acronyms-changing-world/, accessed 09/14/2019.
13. "Business Process Reengineering Six Sigma," iSixSigma, www.isixsigma.com/me/bpr/; Hammer, Michael, *Beyond Reengineering: How the Process-Centered Organization Is Changing Our Work and Our Lives.* New York: HarperCollins Publishers, 1996; Chang, Richard, *Process Reengineering in Action: A Practical Guide to Achieving Breakthrough Results,* Quality Improvement Series. San Francisco: Pfeiffer, 1996.
14. "Object Management Group Business Process Model and Notation," *BPMN*, www.bpmn.org.
15. "Object Management Group Business Process Model and Notation," *BPMN*, www.bpmn.org.
16. www.ibm.com/Watson, accessed January 2019.
17. https://www.cio.com/article/3236451/what-is-rpa-robotic-process-automation-explained.html, accessed 10/12/2020.
18. Harrington, H. James, *Business Process Improvement Workbook: Documentation, Analysis, Design, and Management of Business Process Improvement.* New York: McGraw-Hill, 1997; Hammer, Michael, *Beyond Reengineering: How the Process-Centered Organization Is Changing Our Work and Our Lives*. New York: HarperCollins Publishers, 1996; Hammer, Michael, and Champy, James, *Reengineering the Corporation: A Manifesto for Business Revolution.* New York: HarperCollins Publishers, 1993.
19. www.nytimes.com/2018/03/08/business/alexa-laugh-amazon-echo.html, accessed January 2019.
20. www.wired.com/story/erik-rynjolfsson-robots-steal-boring-parts-of-your-job/, accessed January 2019.

Chapter 3

1. https://www.entrepreneur.com/article/203472, accessed 2/13/2021.
2. Adam Lashinsky, "Kodak's Developing Situation," *Fortune,* January 20, 2003, p. 176.
3. Clayton Christensen, *The Innovator's Dilemma* (Boston: Harvard Business School, 1997).
4. Clayton Christensen, *The Innovator's Dilemma* (Boston: Harvard Business School, 1997).
5. Internet World Statistics, www.internetworldstats.com, January 20, 2010.
6. Selyukh, Alina, and David Ingram, "U.S. Appeals Court Strikes Down FCC Net Neutrality Rules," Reuters, February 2014, www.reuters.com.
7. info.cern.ch, accessed March 1, 2005. (site now discontinued)
8. www.duckduckgo.com, accessed 05/03/2020.
9. The Complete Web 2.0 Directory, "*All about Casino Hold Em.'*" www.go2web20.net; "Web 2.0 . . . for CIOs," *CIO Magazine*, www.cio.com/article/16807; www.emarketer.com.
10. https://hbr.org/2018/03/thriving-in-the-gig-economy, accessed 04/03/2019.
11. O'Reilly, Tim, "What Is Web 2.0: Design Patterns and Business Models for the Next Generation of Software," *O'Reilly*, www.oreillynet.com; "Web 2.0 . . . for CIOs," *CIO Magazine*, www.cio.com/article/16807.
12. O'Reilly, Tim, "What Is Web 2.0: Design Patterns and Business Models for the Next Generation of Software," *O'Reilly*, www.oreillynet.com; "Web 2.0 . . . for CIOs," *CIO Magazine*, www.cio.com/article/16807.
13. https://hbr.org/2020/03/reinventing-the-direct-to-consumer-business-model, accessed 02/03/2021.
14. https://www.businessinsider.com/major-us-tech-companies-blocked-from-operating-in-china-2019-5, accessed 10/2019.
15. Google Images, http://www.google.com/images.
16. Daniel Nations, "What Is Social Bookmarking and Why Do It?" About.com; Web Trends, http://webtrends.about.com/od/socialbookmarking101/p/aboutsocialtags.htm, accessed April 5, 2010.
17. Gary Matuszak, "Enterprise 2.0: Fad or Future," KPMG International, www.kpmg.com/Global/en/. . ./Enterprise. . ./Enterprise-2-Fador-Future.pdf, accessed April 10, 2010.
18. Rachel Metz, "Changing at the Push of a Button," *Wired,* September 27, 2004.
19. http://www.businessinsider.com/heres-how-retailers-can-reduce-shopping-cart-abandonment-and-recoup-billions-of-dollars-in-lost-sales-2014-4#ixzz38OdzCraQ.
20. https://www.technologyreview.com/2020/06/12/1002838/avi-schiffmann-17-year-old-guide-building-pandemic-protest-tracker, accessed 07/12/2020.
21. www.inc.com/magazine/201805/tom-foster/direct-consumer-brands-middleman-warby-parker.html, accessed January 2019.

Chapter 4

1. https://www.forbes.com/sites/kateoflahertyuk/2021/04/06/facebook-data-breach-heres-what-to-do-now, accessed April 2021.
2. Schrage, Michael, "Build the Business Case," *CIO Magazine*, March 15, 2003, http://www.cio.com.
3. https://www.federalrulesofcivilprocedure.org/frcp/title-vi-trials/rule-41-dismissal-of-actions/, accessed May 2017
4. Peter S. Green, "Take the Data Pledge," *Bloomberg Businessweek*, April 23, 2009.
5. https://www.wellsfargo.com/privacy-security/fraud/bank-scams/index, accessed March 2021.
6. https://www2.deloitte.com/us/en/insights/industry/public-sector/chief-data-officer-government-playbook/managing-data-ethics.html, February 2019.
7. https://gdpr-info.eu/, May 2019.
8. https://www.reuters.com/article/us-google-privacy-france/france-fines-google-57-million-for-european-privacy-rule-breach-idUSKCN1PF208.
9. https://www.wired.com/story/zeynep-tufekci-facts-fake-news-verification/, accessed June 2019.
10. Andy McCue, "Bank Boss Quits after Porn Found on PC," *Bloomberg Businessweek*, www.businessweek.com, accessed June 2004.
11. https://www.bbc.com/worklife/article/20191219-workplace-bullying-is-more-harmful-than-we-realised, June 2020.
12. AMA Research, "Workplace Monitoring and Surveillance," *AMA*, www.amanet.org; "2005 CSI/FBI Computer Crime and Security," *FBI*, https://www.fbi.gov.
13. https://www.cisa.gov/, accessed June 2020.
14. "Survey," *GoCSI*, www.gocsi.com.
15. https://www.wired.com/story/worst-hacks-2020-surreal-pandemic-year/, February 2021.
16. Thomas Claburn, "Web 2.0. Internet Too Dangerous for Normal People," *InformationWeek*, April 1, 2009, http://www.informationweek.com/news/internet/web2.0/showArticle.jhtml?articleID5216402352&queryText5web%202.0%20security%20concerns. (site now discontinued)
17. Paige Baltzan, email received May 21, 2010.

18. https://support.google.com/googlenest/answer/9231739?hl=en, accessed March 2021.
19. Brandon, John, "Five Ways Hackers Can Get Your Business," *Inc.*, December 2013, http://www.inc.com.
20. www.nytimes.com/2018/03/19/technology/facebook-cambridgeanalytica-explained.html, accessed January 2019.
21. Armen Keteyian, "Digital Photocopier Loaded with Secrets," CBSnews.com, April 15, 2010, http://www.cbsnews.com/stories/2010/04/19/eveningnews/main6412439.shtml.

Chapter 5

1. www.un.org/development/desa/disabilities/envision2030.html, accessed February 2019.
2. www.cnbc.com/2018/07/27/lanzatech-turns-carbon-waste-into-ethanol-to-one-day-power-planes-cars.html, accessed February 2019.
3. TechTarget.com, http://events.techtarget.com/html/topic-disaster_recovery.html, accessed May 2014.
4. U.S. Geological Service, "The Great 1906 San Francisco Earthquake," http://earthquake.usgs.gov/regional/nca/1906/18april/index.php, accessed July 14, 2010.
5. TechTarget.com. http://events.techtarget.com/html/topic-disaster_recovery.html, accessed May 2014.
6. www.inc.com/sonya-mann/aws-startups-conflict.html, accessed March 2019.
7. "Moore's Law," www.intel.com/technology/mooreslaw, accessed April 2, 2010; Electronics TakeBack Coalition, "Facts and Figures on E-Waste and Recycling," www.electronicstakeback.com, accessed April 3, 2010; U.S. Environmental Protection Agency, "EPA Report to Congress on Server and Data Center Energy Efficiency," www.energystar.gov/ia/partners/prod_development/downloads/EPA_Report_Exec_Summary_Final.pdf, accessed January 23, 2008.
8. "Moore's Law," www.intel.com/technology/mooreslaw, accessed April 2, 2010; Electronics TakeBack Coalition, "Facts and Figures on E-Waste and Recycling," www.electronicstakeback.com, accessed April 3, 2010; U.S. Environmental Protection Agency, "EPA Report to Congress on Server and Data Center Energy Efficiency," www.energystar.gov/ia/partners/prod_development/downloads/EPA_Report_Exec_Summary_Final.pdf, accessed January 23, 2008.
9. www.nature.org/greenliving/carboncalculator/, accessed May 2014.
10. "Switch on the Benefits of Grid Computing," http://h20338.www2.hp.com/enterprise/downloads/7_Benefits%20of%20grid%20computing.pdf, accessed April 2, 2010; "Talking to the Grid," www.technologyreview.com/energy/23706/, accessed April 3, 2010; "Tech Update: What's All the Smart Grid Buzz About?" www.fieldtechnologiesonline.com/download.mvc/Whats-All-The-Smart-Grid-Buzz-About-0001, accessed April 3, 2010.
11. "Switch on the Benefits of Grid Computing," http://h20338.www2.hp.com/enterprise/downloads/7_Benefits%20of%20grid%20computing.pdf, accessed April 2, 2010; "Talking to the Grid," www.technologyreview.com/energy/23706/, accessed April 3, 2010; "Tech Update: What's All the Smart Grid Buzz About?" www.fieldtechnologiesonline.com/download.mvc/Whats-All-The-Smart-Grid-Buzz-About-0001, accessed April 3, 2010.
12. "Switch on the Benefits of Grid Computing," http://h20338.www2.hp.com/enterprise/downloads/7_Benefits%20of%20grid%20computing.pdf, accessed April 2, 2010; "Talking to the Grid," www.technologyreview.com/energy/23706/, accessed April 3, 2010; "Tech Update: What's All the Smart Grid Buzz About?" www.fieldtechnologiesonline.com/download.mvc/Whats-All-The-Smart-Grid-Buzz-About-0001, accessed April 3, 2010.
13. Rich Miller, "Google Data Center FAQ," Data Center Knowledge, www.datacenterknowledge.com/archives/2008/03/27/google-data-center-faq/, accessed April 1, 2010.
14. http://www.livescience.com/41967-world-e-waste-to-grow-33-percent-2017.html; http://www.entrepreneur.com/article/226675, accessed March 2014.
15. McKendrick, Joe, "20 Most Popular Cloud-Based Apps Downloaded into Enterprises," *Forbes*, March 2013, http://www.forbes.com/fdc/welcome_mjx.shtml.
16. www.peloton.com, accessed February 2019.
17. www.mooreslaw.org/, accessed February 2019.
18. "Moore's Law," www.intel.com/technology/mooreslaw, accessed April 2, 2010; Electronics TakeBack Coalition, "Facts and Figures on E-Waste and Recycling," www.electronicstakeback.com, accessed April 3, 2010; U.S. Environmental Protection Agency, "EPA Report to Congress on Server and Data Center Energy Efficiency," www.energystar.gov/ia/partners/prod_development/downloads/EPA_Report_Exec_Summary_Final.pdf, accessed January 23, 2008.
19. Goodwill Industries International, "Dell and Goodwill Expand Free Recycling Program to Include Microsoft Product," April 21, 2010, http://www.goodwill.org/press-releases/dell-goodwill-expand-free-consumer-recycling-program-to-include-microsoft-products/, accessed June 3, 2010.
20. One Laptop Per Child, http://laptop.org/en/, accessed June 5, 2010.
21. "VMware—History of Virtualization," www.virtualizationworks.com/Virtualization-History.asp, accessed January 23, 2008.
22. Rich Miller, "Google Data Center FAQ," www.datacenterknowledge.com/archives/2008/03/27/google-data-center-faq/, accessed April 1, 2010.

Chapter 6

1. https://www.forbes.com/sites/gilpress/2013/05/28/a-very-short-history-of-data-science/?sh=17f1a41a55cf, accessed February 2021.
2. Kiling, "OLAP Gains Fans among Data-Hungry Firms," *ComputerWorld,* January 8, 2011, p. 4.
3. "The Complete Beginners Guide to Big Data in 2017," *Forbes*, https://www.forbes.com/sites/bernardmarr/2017/03/14/the-complete-beginners-guide-to-big-data-in-2017/#568cdf847365, accessed January 2017.

Chapter 7

1. https://www.pcmag.com/news/what-is-5g, accessed February 2021.
2. https://www.fastcompany.com/90458891/the-next-big-thing-in-sports-clothes-that-give-you-perfect-form, accessed March 2020.
3. https://www.forbes.com/sites/danielnewman/2018/08/14/5-emerging-technologies-that-5g-positively-disrupt/?sh=531641e366b6, accessed February 2020.
4. https://www.forbes.com/sites/danielnewman/2018/08/14/5-emerging-technologies-that-5g-positively-disrupt/?sh=531641e366b6, accessed February 2020.
5. https://www.bbc.com/news/world-europe-48616174, accessed February 2021.
6. aws.amazon.com/streaming-data/, accessed March 2019.
7. https://www.cisco.com/c/m/en_us/solutions/enterprise-networks/802-11ax-solution/nb-06-5-things-WiFi6-5G-infograph-cte-en.html, accessed February 2021.
8. https://www.wsj.com/articles/t-mobile-to-step-up-ad-targeting-of-cellphone-customers-11615285803, accessed January 2021.

9. https://www.digitaltrends.com/virtual-reality/best-virtual-reality-apps/, accessed April 2021.
10. https://www.oreilly.com/library/view/absolute-beginners-guide, accessed February 2019.
11. https://www.lifewire.com/intro-to-wi-fi-network-security-818349, accessed March 2019.
12. www.techopedia.com, accessed January 15, 2018.
13. https://www.lifewire.com/how-to-booby-trap-your-smartphone-to-prevent-theft-2487394, accessed February 2017.
14. www.spotify.com, accessed February 2019.

Chapter 8

1. https://openledger.info/insights/blockchain-in-the-supply-chain-use-cases-examples/, accessed January 2019.
2. http://www.isc.hbs.edu/strategy/business-strategy/pages/the-five-forces.aspx.
3. James P. Womack, Daniel Jones, and Daniel Roos, *The Machine That Changed the World.* New York: Harper Perennial, 1991.
4. Aouad, Ayoub, "Walmart Has Filed for 97 Drone Patents—Nearly Double the Amount of Amazon's," *Business Insider.* www.businessinsider.com, January 2019.
5. Ungerleider, Neal, "This African Inventor Created a $100 3-D Printer from E-Waste," *Fast Company*, www.fastcompany.com, accessed March 2017.
6. "The Future of 3D Printing and Manufacturing," *Forbes,* January 2014, https://www.forbes.com/sites/rakeshsharma/2014/01/15/1255/?sh=25af6c9e26a9.
7. www.dronezon.com, accessed March 2019.
8. Mervyn Rothstein, "Isaac Asimov, Whose Thoughts and Books Traveled the Universe, Is Dead at 72," *The New York Times.* http://www.nytimes.com/books/97/03/23/lifetimes/asi-v-obit.html.
9. https://www.therobotreport.com/news/filling-the-void-left-by-kiva-systems-acquisition-by-amazon, accessed April 10, 2010.
10. www.raspberrypi.org, accessed March 2019.
11. Mulani, Narendra, "Onboarding Your New Co-worker—AI," https://www.cio.com/article/3270947/onboarding-your-new-co-worker-ai.html.
12. "Nice Emotions," http://www.nice.com/smartcenter-suite, accessed March 10, 2010. (site now discontinued)
13. Schlicht, Matt, "The Complete Beginner's Guide to Chatbots," https://chatbotsmagazine.com/the-complete-beginner-s-guide-to-chatbots-8280b7b906ca.
14. Marker Media, "MAKE: Ultimate Guide to 3D Printing," *Make Magazine,* May 2017.
15. Helen Foley, "15 of the Best 3D Printed Products," *The Next Web,* November 2017, http://thenextweb.com/dd/2013/11/06/15-best-3d-printed-items-year/.
16. www.hootsuite.com, accessed June 2020.

Chapter 9

1. Yvon Chouinard, *Let My People Go Surfing: The Education of a Reluctant Businessman*, Penguin Books; September 5, 2006.
2. "Overcoming Software Development Problems," www.samspublishing.com, accessed October 2005. (site now discontinued)
3. Jay, Antony, "How to Run a Meeting," https://hbr.org/1976/03/how-to-run-a-meeting, accessed January 2019.
4. Romanelli, Mark, "Picking and Right-Sizing a Project," www.projecttimes.com, accessed March 2019.
5. "Project Management," *CIO Magazine*, June 1, 2006; "The Project Manager in the IT Industry," www.si2.com, accessed December 15, 2003; Jim Johnson, *My Life Is Failure*. Boston: Standish Group International, 2006, p. 46; Gary McGraw, "Making Essential Software Work," *Software Quality Management*, April 2003, www.sqmmagazine.com, accessed November 14, 2003.
6. Agile Alliance Manifesto, www.agile.com, accessed November 1, 2013.
7. "Software Costs," *CIO Magazine*, www.cio.com, accessed December 5, 2013.
8. IBM Rational Unified Process, http://www-01.ibm.com/software/awdtools/rup/, accessed January 2013.
9. https://www.workbreakdownstructure.com/, accessed March 2019.
10. Edward Yourdon, *Death March: The Complete Software Developer's Guide to Surviving "Mission Impossible" Projects*. Upper Saddle River, NJ: Prentice Hall PTR, 1999.
11. Jason W. Bay, "Video Game Programmer Salary for 2016," Game Industry Career Guide, http://www.gameindustrycareerguide.com/, accessed April 15, 2016.
12. "Overcoming Software Development Problems," www.samspublishing.com, accessed October 2015.

Appendix A

1. "Electronic Breaking Points," *PC World*, August 2005.
2. Tom Davenport, "Playing Catch-Up," *CIO Magazine*, May 1, 2001.
3. Hector Ruiz, "Advanced Micro Devices," *BusinessWeek*, January 10, 2005.
4. www.powergridfitness.com, accessed October 2005.
5. Denise Brehm, "Sloan Students Pedal Exercise," www.mit.edu, accessed May 5, 2003.
6. Margaret Locher, "Hands That Speak," *CIO Magazine*, June 1, 2005.
7. www.needapresent.com, accessed October 2005.
8. Aaron Ricadela, "Seismic Shift," *InformationWeek*, March 14, 2005.
9. www.mit.com, accessed October 2005.
10. "The Linux Counter," http://counter.li.org, accessed October 2005.

Appendix B

1. Andy Patrizio, "Peer-to-Peer Goes beyond Napster," *Wired,* February 14, 2001, http://www.wired.com/science/discoveries/news/2001/02/41768, accessed January 2009.
2. Intel in Communications, "10 Gigabit Ethernet Technology Overview," http://www.intel.com/network/connectivity/resources/doc_library/white_papers/pro10gbe_lr_sa_wp.pdf, accessed January 2009.
3. Cisco, "TCP/IP Overview," http://www.cisco.com/en/US/tech/tk365/technologies_white_paper09186a008014f8a9.shtml, accessed January 2009.
4. Cisco, "TCP/IP Overview," http://www.cisco.com/en/US/tech/tk365/technologies_white_paper09186a008014f8a9.shtml, accessed January 2009.
5. "IPv6," www.ipv6.org, accessed January 2009.
6. Cisco, "TCP/IP Overview," http://www.cisco.com/en/US/tech/tk365/technologies_white_paper09186a008014f8a9.shtml, accessed January 2009.
7. Cisco, "TCP/IP Overview," http://www.cisco.com/en/US/tech/tk365/technologies_white_paper09186a008014f8a9.shtml, accessed January 2009.

8. Cisco, “Network Media Types,” http://www.ciscopress.com/articles/article.asp?p=31276&seqNum=5, accessed January 2009.
9. Cisco, “Network Media Types,” http://www.ciscopress.com/articles/article.asp?p=31276&seqNum=5, accessed January 2009.
10. Cisco, “Network Media Types,” http://www.ciscopress.com/articles/article.asp?p=31276&seqNum=5, accessed January 2009.

Appendix D

1. https://www.forbes.com/sites/bernardmarr/2017/03/14/the-complete-beginners-guide-to-big-data-in-2017/#568cdf847365, accessed January 2017.

Appendix E

1. Federal Communications Commission.

INDEX

C

D

E

F

G

H

I

J

K

L

M

N

O

P

Q

R

S

X

Y

Z

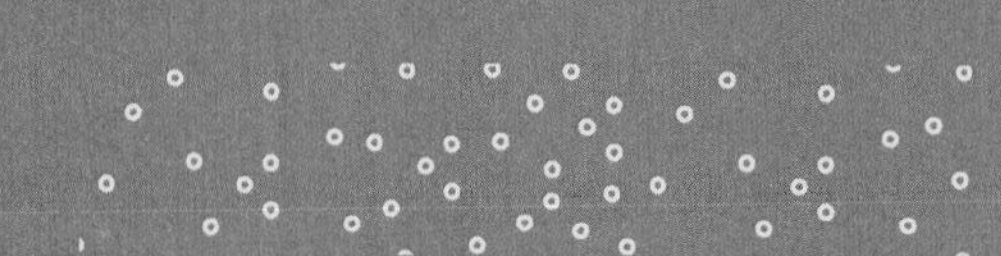